THE NEW
SCHAFF-HERZOG
ENCYCLOPEDIA

OF

RELIGIOUS KNOWLEDGE

Editor-in-Chief

SAMUEL MACAULEY JACKSON, D.D., LL.D.

Editor-in-Chief
of
Supplementary Volumes

LEFFERTS A. LOETSCHER, Ph.D., D.D.
ASSOCIATE PROFESSOR OF CHURCH HISTORY
PRINCETON THEOLOGICAL SEMINARY

BAKER BOOK HOUSE
GRAND RAPIDS, MICHIGAN

THE NEW

SCHAFF-HERZOG ENCYCLOPEDIA

OF

RELIGIOUS KNOWLEDGE

EDITED BY

SAMUEL MACAULEY JACKSON, D.D., LL.D.

(Editor-in-Chief)

WITH THE SOLE ASSISTANCE, AFTER VOLUME VI., OF

GEORGE WILLIAM GILMORE, M.A.

(Associate Editor)

AND THE FOLLOWING DEPARTMENT EDITORS

CLARENCE AUGUSTINE BECKWITH, D.D.
(Department of Systematic Theology)

JAMES FREDERIC McCURDY, PH.D., LL.D.
(Department of the Old Testament)

HENRY KING CARROLL, LL.D.
(Department of Minor Denominations)

HENRY SYLVESTER NASH, D.D.
(Department of the New Testament)

JAMES FRANCIS DRISCOLL, D.D.
(Department of Liturgics and Religious Orders)

ALBERT HENRY NEWMAN, D.D., LL.D.
(Department of Church History)

FRANK HORACE VIZETELLY, LL.D., F.S.A.
(Department of Pronunciation and Typography)

VOLUME XI

SON OF MAN — TREMELLIUS

BAKER BOOK HOUSE
GRAND RAPIDS, MICHIGAN

Reprinted 1977 by
Baker Book House

ISBN: 0-8010-7947-0

Printed in the United States of America

EDITORS

SAMUEL MACAULEY JACKSON, D.D., LL.D.
(Editor-in-Chief.)
Professor of Church History, New York University.

GEORGE WILLIAM GILMORE, M.A.
(Associate Editor.)
New York,
Formerly Professor of Biblical History and Lecturer on Comparative Religion,
Bangor Theological Seminary.

DEPARTMENT EDITORS, VOLUME XI

CLARENCE AUGUSTINE BECKWITH, D.D.,
(*Department of Systematic Theology.*)
Professor of Systematic Theology, Chicago Theological Seminary.

HENRY KING CARROLL, LL.D.,
(*Department of Minor Denominations.*)
Secretary of Executive Committee of the Western Section for the Fourth Ecumenical Methodist Conference.

JAMES FRANCIS DRISCOLL, D.D.,
(*Department of Liturgics and Religious Orders.*)
Rector of St. Gabriel's, New Rochelle, N. Y.

JAMES FREDERICK McCURDY, Ph.D., LL.D.,
(*Department of the Old Testament.*)
Professor of Oriental Languages, University College, Toronto.

HENRY SYLVESTER NASH, D.D.,
(*Department of the New Testament.*)
Professor of the Literature and Interpretation of the New Testament, Episcopal Theological School, Cambridge, Mass.

ALBERT HENRY NEWMAN, D.D., LL.D.,
(*Department of Church History.*)
Professor of Church History, Southwestern Baptist Theological Seminary, Fort Worth, Tex.

FRANK HORACE VIZETELLY, LL.D., F.S.A.,
(*Department of Pronunciation and Typography.*)
Managing Editor of the Standard Dictionary, etc.,
New York City.

CONTRIBUTORS AND COLLABORATORS, VOLUME XI

JUSTIN EDWARDS ABBOTT, D.D.,
Missionary in Bombay, India.

HANS ACHELIS, Ph.D., Th.D.,
Professor of Church History, University of Halle.

WILLIAM HENRY ALLISON, Ph.D.,
Dean of the Faculty and Professor of Ecclesiastical History, Theological Seminary, Colgate University, Hamilton, N. Y.

FRANK DE GRAFF ALTMAN, D.D.,
Former President of the Lutheran Western Theological Seminary, Atchison, Kan.

BRAYMAN WILLIAM ANTHONY, D.D., LL.D.,
President of Adrian College, Adrian, Mich.

GUSTAF EMANUEL HILDEBRAND AULEN, Th.Lic.,
Docent in the University of Upsala, Sweden.

HENRY AMANTIUS AYRINHAC, S.S., D.D., LL.D.,
President of St. Patrick's Seminary, Menlo Park, Cal.

JOHN WALTER BEARDSLEE, D.D., LL.D.,
President of Western Theological Seminary, Holland, Mich.

HERMANN GECRG JULIUS BECK,
Consistorial Councilor and First Preacher, Bayreuth.

CLARENCE AUGUSTINE BECKWITH, D.D.,
Professor of Systematic Theology, Chicago Theological Seminary.

WILLIS JUDSON BEECHER, D.D.,
Former Professor of Hebrew Language and Literature, Auburn Theological Seminary, Auburn, N. Y.

GEORG BEER, Ph.D., Th.Lic.,
Professor of Old Testament Exegesis, University of Heidelberg.

JOHANNES BELSHEIM (†),
Late Pastor Emeritus in Christiania.

KARL BENRATH, Ph.D., Th.D.,
Professor of Church History, University of Königsberg.

IMMANUEL GUSTAV ADOLF BENZINGER, Ph.D., Th.Lic.,
German Orientalist and Vice-Consul for Holland in Jerusalem.

CARL BERTHEAU (†), Th.D.,
Late Pastor of St. Michael's, Hamburg.

THOMAS JAMES GARLAND, B.D.,
Secretary of the Divinity School of the Protestant Episcopal Church in Philadelphia.

OWEN HAMILTON GATES, Ph.D.,
Librarian, Andover Theological Seminary, Andover, Mass.

GEORGE WILLIAM GILMORE, M.A.,
Former Professor of Biblical History and Lecturer on Comparative Religion, Bangor Theological Seminary, Bangor, Me.

FRANZ GOERRES, Ph.D.,
Assistant Librarian, University of Bonn.

WILHELM GOETZ (†), Ph.D.,
Late Honorary Professor of Geography, Technical High School, and Professor, Military Academy, Munich

JUAN ORTS GONZALEZ, D.D.,
Richmond, Va.

JAMES ISAAC GOOD, D.D.,
Professor of Reformed Church History and Liturgics, Central Theological Seminary, Dayton, Ohio.

THOMAS WAKEFIELD GOODSPEED, D.D.,
Registrar, University of Chicago.

FRANK GRETHER, D.D.,
Professor of Exegetical Theology, Mission House, Plymouth, Wis.

GEORG GRUETZMACHER, Ph.D., Th.Lic.,
Extraordinary Professor of Church History, University of Heidelberg.

RICHARD HEINRICH GRUETZMACHER, Th.D.,
Professor of Systematic Theology, University of Rostock.

EUGÈNE GUÉNIN,
Chief of the Staff of Stenographers, Senate of France.

ALMON GUNNISON, D.D., LL.D.,
President of St. Lawrence University, Canton, N. Y.

HERMANN GUTHE, Ph.D., Th.D.,
Extraordinary Professor of Old Testament Exegesis, University of Leipsic.

WILHELM HADORN, Th.Lic.,
Pastor in Bern and Lecturer on New Testament Exegesis, University of Bern.

ALFRED MARTIN HAGGARD, M.A.,
Dean of the Bible College, Drake University, Des Moines, Iowa.

ARTHUR CRAWSHAY ALLISTON HALL, D.D., LL.D.,
Protestant Episcopal Bishop of Vermont.

JULIUS HAMBERGER (†), Ph.D., Th.D.,
Late Professor of Theology, University of Munich.

FREDERICK WILLIAM HAMILTON, D.D., LL.D.,
President of Tufts College, Mass.

ADOLF HARNACK, M.D., Ph.D., Th.D., Dr.Jur.,
General Director of the Royal Library, Berlin.

JAMES RENDEL HARRIS, Litt.D., LL.D.,
Director of Studies at the Friends' Settlement, Woodbrooke, near Birmingham, England.

SAMUEL HART, D.D., D.C.L.,
Dean of Berkeley Divinity School, Middletown, Conn.

ALBERT HAUCK, Ph.D., Th.D., Dr.Jur.,
Professor of Church History, University of Leipsic, Editor-in-chief of the Hauck-Herzog *Realencyklopädie.*

JOHANNES HAUSSLEITER, Ph.D., Th.D.,
Professor of the New Testament, University of Greifswald.

CHARLES GIRVEN HECKERT, D.D.,
President of Hamma Divinity School, Springfield, Ohio.

MAX HEINZE (†), Ph.D., Th.D.,
Late Professor of Philosophy, University of Leipsic.

CHARLES ROBERT HEMPHILL, D.D., LL.D.,
President of the Presbyterian Theological Seminary of Kentucky, Louisville, Ky.

ERNST HENKE (†), Ph.D., Th.D.,
Late Professor of Theology, University of Marburg.

HEINRICH HERMELINK, Ph.D., Th.Lic.,
Privat-docent in Church History, University of Leipsic.

ALFRED HILLER, D.D.,
Senior Professor of Theology, Hartwick Seminary, near Cooperstown, N. Y.

GEORGE HODGES, D.D., D.C.L.,
Dean of the Episcopal Theological School, Cambridge, Mass.

HEINRICH FRIEDRICH MAX HOFFMANN, Ph.D., Th.Lic.,
Privat-docent in Church History, University of Leipsic.

RUDOLF HUGO HOFMANN, Ph.D., Th.D.,
Professor of Homiletics and Liturgics, University of Leipsic.

HJALMER FREDRIK HOLMQUIST, Th.D.,
Professor of Church History, University of Lund, Sweden.

EDMUND LYMAN HOOD, Ph.D.,
President of Atlanta Theological Seminary, Atlanta, Ga.

FRANKLIN EVANS HOSKINS, D.D.,
Missionary at Beirut, Syria.

GEORGE RICE HOVEY, D.D.,
President of Virginia Union University, Richmond, Va.

HENRY EYSTER JACOBS, D.D., LL.D., S.T.D.,
Dean of the Lutheran Theological Seminary, Mount Airy, Philadelphia, Pa.

JOSEPH JACOBS, Litt.D.,
Professor of English Literature and Rhetoric, Jewish Theological Seminary of America, New York.

HENRY HARRIS JESSUP (†), D.D.,
Late Missionary at Beirut, Syria.

EDMUND TALMA JILLSON, B.A.,
Kansas City Baptist Theological Seminary.

ARTHUR NEWTON JOHNSON, M.A.,
Home Secretary of the London Missionary Society.

GUSTAV ADOLF JUELICHER, Ph.D.,
Professor of Church History and New Testament Exegesis, University of Marburg.

MARTIN KAEHLER, Th.D.,
Professor of Dogmatics and New Testament Exegesis, University of Halle.

FERDINAND FRIEDRICH WILHELM KATTENBUSCH, Ph.D., Th.D.,
Professor of Dogmatics, University of Halle.

EMIL FRIEDRICH KAUTZSCH (†),
Ph.D., Th.D.,
Late Professor of Old Testament Exegesis, University of Halle.

PETER GUSTAV KAWERAU, Ph.D.,
Th.D.,
Supreme Consistorial Councilor, Provost of St. Peter's, Berlin, and Honorary Professor, University of Berlin.

JAMES ANDERSON KELSO, Ph.D., D.D.,
President of Western Theological Seminary, Pittsburg, Pa.

OTTO KIRN (†), Ph.D., Th.D.,
Late Professor of Dogmatics, University of Leipsic.

RUDOLF KITTEL, Ph.D., Th.D.,
Professor of Old Testament Exegesis, University of Leipsic.

RUDOLF KOEGEL (†), Ph.D., Th.D.,
Late Court Preacher, Berlin.

FRIEDRICH EDUARD KOENIG,
Ph.D., Th.D.,
Professor of Old Testament Exegesis, University of Bonn.

HEINRICH ADOLF KOESTLIN (†),
Ph.D., Th.D.,
Late Privy Councilor in Cannstadt, formerly Professor of Theology, University of Giessen.

KAUFMANN KOHLER, Ph.D.,
President of Hebrew Union College, Cincinnati, Ohio.

THEODOR FRIEDRICH HERMANN
KOLDE, Ph.D., Th.D.,
Professor of Church History, University of Erlangen.

OTTO EDWARD KRIEGE, D.D.,
President of the German Theological Seminary, Central Wesleyan College, Warrenton, Mo.

HERMANN GUSTAV EDUARD KRUEGER,
Ph.D., Th.D.,
Professor of Church History, University of Giessen.

EUGEN LACHENMANN,
City Pastor in Leonberg, Württemberg.

WARREN HALL LANDON, D.D.,
President of San Francisco Theological Seminary, San Anselmo, Cal.

WILLIAM HENRY LARRABEE, LL.D.,
Plainfield, N. J.

GEORGE THATCHER LASCELLE,
Secretary to the Dean of Nashotah House, Nashotah, Wis.

WILHELM JOHANNES LEIPOLDT,
Ph.D., Th.D.,
Professor of New Testament Exegesis, University of Kiel.

LUDWIG LEMME, Th.D.,
Professor of Systematic Theology, University of Heidelberg.

EDUARD LEMPP, Ph.D.,
Chief Inspector of the Royal Orphan Asylum, Stuttgart.

JAMES OTIS LINCOLN, M.A.,
Secretary and Librarian of the Church Divinity School of the Pacific, San Mateo, Cal.

CONRAD EMIL LINDBERG, D.D., LL.D.,
Vice-president and Professor of Theology, Augustana Theological Seminary, Rock Island, Ill.

GERHARD LOESCHCKE, Th.Lic.,
Privat-docent in Church History, University of Bonn.

FRIEDRICH ARMIN LOOFS, Ph.D., Th.D.,
Professor of Church History, University of Halle.

WILHELM PHILIPP FRIEDRICH
FERDINAND LOTZ, Ph.D., Th.D.,
Professor of Old Testament Exegesis, University of Erlangen.

FRANK ARTHUR McELWAIN, B.D.,
Warden, Seabury Divinity School, Faribault, Minn.

JOHN KNOX McLEAN, D.D.,
President of Pacific Theological Seminary, Berkeley, Cal.

WILLIAM MARCELLUS McPHEETERS,
D.D., LL.D.,
Chairman of the Faculty, Columbia Theological Seminary, Columbia, S. C.

FRANKLIN PIERCE MANHART, D.D.,
Dean of the School of Theology and Vice-president of Susquehanna University, Selingsgrove, Pa.

ERNEST CHRISTIAN MARGRANDER.
D.C.,
Chancellor to the Orthodox Catholic Archbishop of America.

ALBERT BRAIMERD MARSHALL, D.D.,
President of the Presbyterian Theological Seminary, Omaha, Neb.

AYLMER MAUDE,
Author and Lecturer, Great Baddow, Chelmsford, England.

PAUL MEDER,
Pastor in Gr. Urleben near Tennstedt.

FRIEDRICH MEYER, Th.D.,
Secretary of the Ecclesiastical Council, Zurich, Switzerland.

PHILIPP MEYER, Th.D.,
Supreme Consistorial Councilor, Hanover.

GEROLD MEYER VON KNONAU,
Ph.D., Th.D.,
Professor of History, University of Zurich.

KONRAD CHRISTIAN ERNST
MICHELSEN,
Secretary of the Nordfriesischer Verein für Heimatkunde und Heimatliebe, Klanxbüll in Sleswick.

CARL THEODOR MIRBT, Th.D.,
Professor of Church History, University of Marburg.

WALTER WILLIAM MOORE, D.D., LL.D.,
President of Union Theological Seminary, Richmond, Va.

WILLIAM GALLOGLY MOOREHEAD,
D.D., LL.D.,
President of Xenia Theological Seminary, Xenia, Ohio.

ROBERT SWAIN MORISON, S.T.B.,
Librarian Emeritus, Divinity School of Harvard University, Cambridge, Mass.

EDWARD DAFYDD MORRIS, D.D., LL.D.,
Former Professor of Theology, Lane Theological Seminary, Cincinnati, Ohio.

WILLIAM CHARLES MORRO,
B.D., Ph.D.,
Dean of the Faculty, College of the Bible, Lexington, Ky.

ERNST FRIEDRICH KARL MUELLER,
Th.D.,
Professor of Reformed Theology, University of Erlangen.

EDGAR YOUNG MULLINS, D.D., LL.D.,
President of the Southern Baptist Theological Seminary, Louisville, Ky.

HENRY SYLVESTER NASH, D.D.,
Professor of the Literature and Interpretation of the New Testament, Episcopal Theological School, Cambridge, Mass.

HEINRICH FRIEDRICH WILHELM NELLE, Th.D.,
Superintendent in Hamm, Westphalia.

CHRISTOF EBERHARD NESTLE, Ph.D., Th.D.,
Professor in the Theological Seminary, Maulbronn, Württemberg.

ALBERT HENRY NEWMAN, D.D., LL.D.,
Professor of Church History, Southwestern Baptist Theological Seminary, Fort Worth, Texas.

JOSEPH FORT NEWTON, M.A., Th.M.,
Professor of English, University of Iowa.

THEODOR JULIUS NEY, Th.D.,
Supreme Consistorial Councilor, Speyer, Bavaria.

FREDERIK KRISTIAN NIELSEN (†), D.D.,
Late Bishop of Aarhus, Denmark.

DAVID NYVALL,
President of Walden College, McPherson, Kan.

GUSTAV FRIEDRICH VON OEHLER (†), D.D.,
Late Professor of Old Testament Theology, Tübingen.

CONRAD VON ORELLI, Ph.D., Th.D.,
Professor of Old Testament Exegesis and History of Religion, University of Basel.

CHRISTIAN VON PALMER (†), Th.D.,
Late Professor of Theology, Tübingen.

CARL PFENDER,
Pastor of St. Paul's Evangelical Lutheran Church, Paris.

LEANDER LYCURGUS PICKETT,
Field Secretary of Asbury College, Wilmore, Ky.

FRANZ AUGUST OTTO PIEPER, D.D.,
President of Concordia Seminary, St. Louis, Mo.

MARIE POUTZ,
Fellow of the Theosophical Society, Norfolk, Va.

WALDO SELDEN PRATT, Mus.D.,
Professor of Music and Hymnology, Hartford Theological Seminary, Hartford, Conn.

ERWIN FRIEDRICH WILHELM FERDINAND PREUSCHEN, Ph.D., Th.D.,
Pastor at Hirschhorn-on-the-Neckar, Germany.

HARRY HEFFNER PRICE, M.A., B.D.,
President of Westminster College of Theology, Tehuacana, Texas.

RALPH EARL PRIME, D.C.L., LL.D.,
Attorney, Yonkers, N. Y.

TRAUGOTT OTTO RADLACH,
Pastor at Gatersleben, Prussian Saxony.

HERMANN RAHLENBECK,
Pastor in Cologne.

DELAVAN BLOODGOOD REED, D.D.,
Professor of New Testament Language and Literature and of Ecclesiastical History, Hillsdale Baptist Seminary, Hillsdale, Mich.

RICHARD CLARK REED, D.D., LL.D.,
Professor of Church History, Presbyterian Theological Seminary, Columbia, S. C.

GERHARD REICHEL, Th.Lic.,
Instructor in the Theological Seminary at Gnadenfeld, Prussia.

JOHN BALLARD RENDALL, D.D.,
President of Lincoln University, Pa.

EDWIN WILBUR RICE, D.D.,
Editor, American Sunday-School Union, Philadelphia, Pa.

GEORGE WARREN RICHARDS, D.D.,
Professor of Church History, Theological Seminary of the Reformed Church, Lancaster, Pa.

ROBERT WILLIAM ROGERS, M.A., Ph.D., LL.D.,
Professor of Hebrew and Old Testament Exegesis, Drew Theological Seminary, Madison, New Jersey.

HENRY KALLOCH ROWE, Ph.D.,
Assistant Professor of Church History, Newton Theological Institution, Newton Center, Mass.

WILLIAM OTIS RUSTON, D.D., LL.D.,
Dean of the Faculty, Dubuque German College and Seminary, Dubuque, Ia.

CARL VICTOR RYSSEL (†), Ph.D., Th.D.,
Late Professor of Theology, University of Zurich.

PHILIPP HEINRICH WILHELM THEODOR SCHAEFER, Th.D.,
Head of the Deaconess Institute, Altona.

DAVID SCHLEY SCHAFF, D.D.,
Professor of Church History, Western Theological Seminary, Pittsburg, Pennsylvania.

PHILIP SCHAFF (†), D.D., LL.D.,
Late Professor of Church History, Union Theological Seminary, New York.

JOHN SCHALLER,
President of the Lutheran Theological Seminary, Wauwatosa, Wis.

GEORGE HENRY SCHODDE, Ph.D., D.D.,
Secretary of the Faculty, Capital University, Columbus, O.

MAXIMILIAN VICTOR SCHULTZE, Th.D.,
Professor of Church History and Christian Archeology, University of Greifswald.

JOHANN KARL EDUARD SCHWARZ (†), Th.D.,
Late Professor of Theology, University of Jena.

WILLIAM NATHANIEL SCHWARZE, Ph.D.,
Resident Professor, Moravian College and Theological Seminary, Bethlehem, Pa.

PAUL SCHWEIZER, Ph.D.,
Professor of History, University of Zurich.

JOHN PRESTON SEARLE, D.D.,
President of the Theological Seminary of the Reformed Church, New Brunswick, N. J.

REINHOLD SEEBERG, Ph.D., Th.D.,
Professor of Systematic Theology, University of Berlin.

EMIL SEHLING, Dr.Jur.,
Professor of Ecclesiastical and Commercial Law, University of Erlangen.

FRANK SEWALL, S.T.D.,
President of the Swedenborg Scientific Association, Washington, D. C.

WILLIAM GREENOUGH THAYER SHEDD (†), D.D., LL.D.,
Late Professor of Systematic Theology, Union Theological Seminary, New York.

FRIEDRICH ANTON EMIL SIEFFERT, Ph.D., Th.D.,
Professor of New Testament Exegesis, University of Bonn.

ERNEST GOTTLIEB SIHLER, Ph.D.,
Professor of Latin, New York University.

EDUARD SIMONS, Th.D.,
Extraordinary Professor of Practical Theology, University of Berlin.

JOHN ALDEN SINGMASTER, D.D.,
President of the Lutheran Theological Seminary, Gettysburg, Pa.

FRANKLIN CHESTER SOUTHWORTH, D.D.,
President and Dean of the Faculty, Meadville Theological School, Meadville, Pa.

ERNST STAEHELIN, Ph.D.,
Pastor in Basel.

ADOLF VON STAEHELIN (†), Th.D.,
Late Bavarian Royal Councilor.

ANTHONY ANASTASIOU STAMOULI,
Formerly Member of the Editorial Staff of *Atlantis*, New York City.

K. F. STEIGER (†),
Late Pastor in Eglishof.

GEORGE BLACK STEWART, D.D., LL.D.,
President of Auburn Theological Seminary, Auburn, N. Y.

HERMANN LEBERECHT STRACK, Ph.D., Th.D.,
Honorary Professor of Old Testament Exegesis and Semitic Languages, University of Berlin.

ULRICH STUTZ, Dr.Jur.,
Professor of Ecclesiastical Law, University of Bonn.

GEORGE SVERDRUP, Jr., M.A.,
President of Augsburg Seminary, Minneapolis, Minn.

JUDSON SWIFT, D.D.,
General Secretary of the American Tract Society, New York.

MILTON SPENSER TERRY, D.D., LL.D.,
Professor of Christian Doctrine, Garrett Biblical Institute, Evanston, Ill.

FRIEDRICH TEUTSCH (†), Th.D.,
Late Consistorial Councilor, Hermannstadt, Hungary.

FRIEDRICH AUGUST THEODOR THOLUCK (†), Th.D.,
Late Professor of Theology, University of Halle.

JAMES WESTFALL THOMPSON, A.B.,
Associate Professor of History, University of Chicago.

FRIEDRICH WILHELM THUEMMEL, Th.D.,
Professor of Homiletics and Catechetics, University of Jena.

WILBUR FISK TILLET, D.D., LL.D.,
Dean of the Theological Faculty, Vanderbilt University, Nashville, Tenn.

FRANCIS EDWARD TOURSCHER, O.S.A., D.D.,
Regent of Studies, Monastery of St. Thomas, Villanova, Pa.

PAUL TSCHACKERT (|), Ph.D., Th.D.,
Late Professor of Church History, University of Göttingen.

FENNELL PARRISH TURNER, B.A.,
General Secretary of the Student Volunteer Movement for Foreign Missions, New York.

JOHANN GERHARD WILHELM UHLHORN (†), Th.D.,
Late Abbot of Lokkum, Germany.

MONROE VAYHINGER, D.D.,
President of Taylor University, Upland, Indiana.

HENRY CLAY VEDDER, D.D.,
Professor of Church History, Crozer Theological Seminary, Chester, Pa.

SIETSE DOUWES VAN VEEN, Th.D.,
Professor of Church History and Christian Archeology, University of Utrecht.

JOHN VIENOT, Th.D.,
Professor of Church History, Independent School of Divinity, Paris.

ROBERT ERNEST VINSON, D.D., LL.D.,
President of Austin Presbyterian Theological Seminary, Austin, Texas.

EDWARD HARMON VIRGIN, B.A.,
Librarian, General Theological Seminary, New York City.

ANDREW GEORGE VOIGT, D.D.,
Dean of Lutheran Theological Seminary, Columbia, S. C.

JULIUS AUGUST WAGENMANN (†), Th.D.,
Late Consistorial Councilor, Göttingen.

WILLISTON WALKER, Ph.D., D.D.,
Professor of Ecclesiastical History, Yale University, New Haven, Conn.

CARL GIDEON WALLENIUS, B.A.,
President of Swedish Theological Seminary, Evanston, Ill.

SAMUEL ALFRED WALLIS, D.D.,
Secretary of the Faculty of the Protestant Episcopal Theological Seminary in Virginia, near Alexandria, Va.

WILLIAM FAIRFIELD WARREN, S.T.D., LL.D.,
Dean of the School of Theology, Boston University.

HENRY JACOB WEBER, Ph.D., D.D.,
Professor of Theology and Church History, German Theological School, Bloomfield, N. J.

REVERE FRANKLIN WEIDNER, S.T.D., D.D., LL.D.,
President of the Chicago Lutheran Theological Seminary.

LOUIS WESSEL,
Professor of Theology, Concordia College, Springfield, Ill.

CARL MARCUS WESWIG, B.D.,
Professor of Church History and Homiletics, Seminary of the United Norwegian Lutheran Church, St. Anthony Park, Minn.

EDWARD ELIHU WHITFIELD, M.A.,
Retired Public Schoolmaster, London.

FRIEDRICH LUDWIG LEONHARD WIEGAND, Ph.D., Th.D.,
Professor of Church History, University of Greifswald.

EARL MORSE WILBUR, D.D.,
Dean of the Pacific Unitarian School for the Ministry, Berkeley, Cal.

DAVID BURT WILLSON, D.D.,
Professor of Biblical Literature, Reformed Presbyterian Seminary, Pittsburg, Pa.

PAUL WOLFF (†),
Late Pastor at Friedersdorf, Brandenburg, and Editor of the *Evangelische Kirchenzeitung*.

WILLIAM LORING WORCESTER, B.A.,
President of New Church Theological School, Cambridge, Mass.

KARL AUGUST WUENSCHE, Ph.D., Th.D.,
Retired Professor, Dresden.

RUDOLF ZEHNPFUND, Ph.D.,
Pastor in Oranienbaum, Germany.

THEOBALD ZIEGLER, Ph.D.,
Professor of Philosophy and Pedagogy, University of Strasburg.

OTTO ZOECKLER (†), Ph.D., Th.D.,
Late Professor of Church History and Apologetics, University of Greifswald.

BIBLIOGRAPHICAL APPENDIX—VOLS. I—XI

The following list of books is supplementary to the bibliographies given at the end of the articles contained in vols. I.–XI., and brings the literature down to June 20, 1911. In this list each title entry is printed in capital letters. It is to be noted that, throughout the work, in the articles as a rule only first editions are given. In the bibliographies the aim is to give either the best or the latest edition, and in case the book is published both in America and in some other country, the American place of issue is usually given the preference.

ABBOTT, L.: *The Problem of Human Destiny, as Conditioned by Free Will. Discussion*, Boston, 1911.

AFRICA: G. B. A. Gerdener, *Studies in the Evangelisation of South Africa*, London, 1911.
A. R. Tucker, *Eighteen Years in Uganda and East Africa*, New York, 1911.

ALBERTUS MAGNUS: *Albertus Magnus, Being the approved, verified, sympathetic and natural Egyptian Secrets, white and black Art for Man and Beast*, by that celebrated occult Student, new and revised ed., ed. L. W. de Laurence, Chicago, 1910.

ANTICHRIST: H. Preuss, *Die Vorstellungen vom Antichrist im spätern Mittelalter, bei Luther und in der konfessionellen Polemik*, Leipsic, 1906.

APOLOGETICS: W. H. Carslaw, *The Early Christian Apologists*, London, 1911.
W. Clert, *Prolegomena der Geschichtsphilosophie. Studie zur Grundlage der Apologetik*, Leipsic, 1911.
A. E. Garnie, *Christian Life and Belief. A Description and Defence of the Gospel*, London, 1911.
D. Macfadyen, *Truth in Religion. Studies in the Nature of Christian Certainty*, London, 1911.
C. H. Robinson, *Studies in the Character of Christ: an Argument for the Truth of Christianity*, New York, 1911.

ARCHEOLOGY, BIBLICAL: See below, JEREMIAS, A.

ARCHITECTURE: G. H. West, *Gothic Architecture in England and France*, London, 1911.

ATHANASIAN CREED: R. O. P. Taylor, *The Athanasian Creed in the Twentieth Century*, Edinburgh and New York, 1911.

ATONEMENT: S. H. Langdon, in *Expository Times*, April, 1911, pp. 320–325, and C. F. Burney in the same, pp. 325–327 (important).

AUGUSTINE: H. Scholz, *Glaube und Unglaube in der Weltgeschichte. Ein Kommentar zu Augustins De civitate Dei*, Leipsic, 1911.

BABYLONIA: A. Poebel, *Die sumerischen Personnamen zur Zeit der Dynastie von Larsam und der ersten Dynastie von Babylonien*, Breslau, 1910.

BABYLONIA: C. Frank, *Studien zur babylonischen Religion*, vol. i., Strasburg, 1911.
J. Krauss, *Die Götternamen in den babylonischen Siegelcylinderlegenden*, Leipsic, 1911.
S. Langdon, *A Sumerian Grammar and Chrestomathy, with a Vocabulary of the Principal Roots in Sumerian and a List of the most Important Syllabic and Vowel Transcriptions*, New York, 1911.

BAMBERG: J. Looshorn, *Die Geschichte des Bisthums Bamberg. Nach den Quellen bearbeitet*, vol. viii., *Das Bisthum Bamberg von 1729–1808*, fasc. 2, *Von 1747–1808*, Bamberg, 1910.

BAPTISM: D. E. Dortch, *Bible Lights on Baptism*, Tullahoma, 1911.

BAPTISTS: W. J. McGlothlin, *Baptist Confessions of Faith*, Philadelphia, 1911.

BEISSEL, S.: *Geschichte der Verehrung Marias*, vol. ii., Freiburg, 1910.

BELGIUM: D. C. Boulger, *Belgium of the Belgians*, New York, 1911.

BENEDICTION: A. Franz, *Die kirchlichen Benediktionen im Mittelalter*, 2 vols., Freiburg, 1909.

BENNETT, W. H.: *The Moabite Stone*, Edinburgh, 1911.

BIBLE SOCIETIES: W. Canton, *History of the British and Foreign Bible Society*, London, 1911.

BIBLE TEXT: *The Four Gospels from the Codex Veronensis, with Introduction descriptive of the MS.* by E. S. Buchanan. *Old Latin Biblical Texts* (no. 6), London, 1911.

BIBLE VERSIONS: J. Brown, *The History of the English Bible*, London, 1911.
Coptic Version of the New Testament in the Southern Dialect, otherwise called Sahidic and Thebaic, with critical Apparatus, with literal English Translation, Register of Fragments and Estimate of the Version, 3 vols, London, 1911.
W. Muir, *Our Grand Old Bible. Being the Story of the Authorized Version of the English Bible told for the Tercentenary Celebration*, New York, 1911.
J. D. Payne, *The English Bible. An Historical Survey, from the Dawn of English History, to the Present Day*, London, 1911.

BIBLE VERSIONS: *Records of the English Bible. The Documents relating to the Translation and Publication of the Bible in English, 1526–1611*, ed. with an introduction by A. W. Pollard, London and New York, 1911.
The Hexaplar Psalter. Being the Book of Psalms in Six English Versions, ed. W. A. Wright, Cambridge, 1911.

BIBLICAL CRITICISM: C. W. Emmet, *The Eschatological Question in the Gospels, and Other Studies in Recent New Testament Criticism*, Edinburgh, 1911.
A. Freitag, *Zerstört die historisch-kritische Theologie den Wert der neutestamentlichen Schriften als Geschichtsquellen?* Giessen, 1911.
E. A. Hutton, *An Atlas of Textual Criticism. Being an Attempt to show the Mutual Relationship of the Authorities for the Text of the New Testament up to about 1000 A.D.*, London, 1911.

BIBLICAL INTRODUCTION: J. Moffatt, *An Introduction to the Literature of the New Testament*, London and New York, 1911.

BIBLICAL THEOLOGY: M. Wohlrab, *Das neutestamentliche Christentum, auf psychologischer Grundlage dargestellt*, Dresden, 1910, 1911.
M. Slavic, *Des Ephesier- und Kolosserbriefes Lehre über die Person Christi und sein Heilswerk*, Vienna, 1911.
F. G. Smith, *Evolution of Christianity; or, Origin, Nature, and Development of the Religion of the Bible*, Anderson, Ind., 1911.
Also see below, ROBINSON.

BONAVENTURA: L. Costelloe, *Saint Bonaventure, the Seraphic Doctor*, London and New York, 1911.

BROWNE, SIR THOMAS: W. Schonack, *Sir Thomas Brownes Religio Medici* [in German]. *Ein verschollenes Denkmal des englischen Theismus*, Tübingen, 1911.

BUDDHISM: T. W. Rhys Davids, *Sacred Books of the Buddhists, Translated by various Oriental Scholars. Dialogues of the Buddha. Part II. Translated by T. W. and C. A. F. Rhys-Davids*, London, 1911.
G. A. Esengrini, *Le visioni del Bouddha*, Turin, 1911.
W. W. Hicks, *The Sanctuary*, Boston, 1911.

BULGARIA: W. Ruland, *Geschichte der Bulgaren*, Berlin, 1911.

CHEYNE, T. K.: *The Two Religions of Israel. With a Re-examination of the Prophetic Narratives and Utterances*, London, 1910, New York, 1911.

CHINA: W. E. Griffis, *China's Story in Myth, Legend, Art and Annals*, Boston, 1910.
A. E. Moule, *Half a Century in China. Recollections and Observations*, London, 1911.
Lin Shao-Yang, *A Chinese Appeal to Christendom concerning Christian Missions*, New York, 1911.

CHRISTIAN SOCIALISM: T. Fallot, *Christianisme social*, Paris, 1910.

CHRISTOLOGY: H. B. Swete, *The Ascended Christ: a Study in the earliest Christian Teaching*, London and New York, 1910.
W. J. Simpson, *The Resurrection and Modern Thought*, London, 1911.
K. Thieme, *Von der Gottheit Christi. Gegen den religiösen Rückschritt in Grützmachers Dreieinigkeitslehre*, Giessen, 1911.

CHURCH HISTORY: See above, BIBLICAL THEOLOGY, Wohlrab.
T. S. Holmes, *The Origin and Development of the Christian Church in Gaul during the First Six Centuries of the Christian Era*, London, 1911.

COMENIUS: J. Kvacala, *Analecta Comeniana*, Berlin, 1910.

COMMON PRAYER, BOOK OF: W. H. Frere, *Some Principles of Liturgical Reform. A Contribution towards the Revision of the Book of Common Prayer*, London, 1911.

COMPARATIVE RELIGION: M. Brückner, *Der sterbende und auferstehende Gottheiland in den orientalischen Religionen und ihr Verhältnis zum Christentum*, Tübingen, 1908.
W. W. Fowler, *The Religious Experience of the Roman People from the Earliest Times to the Age of Augustus*, London, 1911.
J. G. Fraser, *The Magic Art and the Evolution of Kings*, 2 vols., London, 1911 (a part of the 3d ed. of *The Golden Bough*).
Also see below, LOISY.

DAVIES, T. W.: See below, MAGIC.

DECIUS: P. M. Meyer, *Die Libelli aus der decianischen Christenverfolgung*, Berlin, 1910.

DISEASES AND THE HEALING ART, HEBREW: J. Preuss, *Biblisch-talmudische Medizin. Beiträge zur Geschichte der Heilkunde und der Kultur überhaupt*, Berlin, 1911.

DIVORCE: H. Ringrose, *Marriage and Divorce Laws of the World*, London, 1911.

DOCTRINE, HISTORY OF: J. P. Kirsch, *The Doctrine of the Communion of Saints in the Ancient Church*, St. Louis, 1911.

DOGMA, DOGMATICS: L. Labauche, *Leçons de théologie dogmatique. Dogmatique spéciale*, vol. i., Paris, 1910.

DREAMS: H. Ellis, *The World of Dreams*, London, 1911.

DUHM, B. L.: *The Ever-coming Kingdom of God: a Dissertation on religious Progress*, New York, 1911.

EGYPT: V. Ermoni, *La Religion de l'Égypte ancienne*, Paris, 1911.

ELAGABALUS: J. S. Hay, *The Amazing Emperor Heliogabalus*, London, 1911.

ENGLAND, CHURCH OF: *Visitation Articles and Injunctions of the Period of the Reformation*, ed. W. H. Frere, 3 vols., London, 1910.
G. A. Cobbold, *This Church of England*, London, 1911.
J. E. C. Welldon, *The Religious Aspects of Disestablishment and Disendowment*, London, 1911.

EPICUREANISM: A. E. Taylor, *Epicurus*, London, 1911.

ETHICS: S. W. Davis, *Origin and Evolution of Ethics*, Los Angeles, Cal., 1910.

EXEGESIS: D. Künstlinger, *Altjüdische Bibeldeutung*, Berlin, 1911.

FAITH: A. Chandler, *Faith and Experience: an Analysis of the Factors of Religious Knowledge*, London, 1911.

FEASTS AND FESTIVALS: F. Bünger, *Geschichte der Neujahrsfeier in der Kirche*, Göttingen, 1911.

FRANCE: D. Lortsch, *Histoire de la Bible en France*, Geneva, 1910.
Also see CHURCH HISTORY, Holmes.

FRANCIS, SAINT, OF ASSISI: H. Grimley, *Saint Francis and his Friends: rendered into English from Franciscan Chronicles*, Cambridge and New York, 1908.
N. Tamassia, *Saint Francis of Assisi and His Legend*, London, 1911.

GEORGE, SAINT: *Saint George for England. The Life, Legends and Lore of our Glorious Patron*. Compiled by H. O. F., 2d ed., London, 1911.

GERHARD, J.: Add to the bibliography: R. Hupfeld, *Die Ethik Joh. Gerhards*, Berlin, 1908.

GERMANY: F. Uhlhorn, *Geschichte der deutsch-lutherischen Kirche*, 2 vols., Leipsic, 1911.

GOD: J. R. Illingworth, *Divine Transcendence, and its Reflection in Religious Authority: an Essay*, London, 1911.
Also see below, POHLE, J.

GOSPEL AND GOSPELS: G. Fulliquet, *Sources des évangiles*, Paris, 1910, Geneva, 1911.
G. Friedlander, *The Jewish Sources of the Sermon on the Mount*, London, 1911.
E. Mangenot, *Les Évangiles synoptiques. Conférences apologétiques*, Paris, 1911.
Studies in the Synoptic Problem, by Members of the University of Oxford, ed. W. Sanday, New York, 1911.
Also see below, HARNACK; LOISY; LUKE.

GREGORY VII.: Add to sources: *A Selection of the Letters of Hildebrand, Pope Gregory VII. . . . by G. Finch*, London, 1853.

HABAKKUK: G. G. N. Stonehouse, *Introduction, Translation, and Notes on the Hebrew Text of the Book of Habakkuk*, London, 1911.

HAMMURABI AND HIS CODE: E. Wohlfromm, *Untersuchungen zur Syntax des Codex Hammurabis*, Königsberg, 1910.

HARNACK, A.: *Neue Untersuchungen zur Apostelgeschichte und zur Abfassungszeit der synoptischen Evangelien*, Leipsic, 1911.

HEBREW LANGUAGE: C. E. Hesselgrave, *The Hebrew Personification of Wisdom: its Origin, Development and Influence*, New York, 1911.

HEGEL: J. O. Knott, *Seekers after Soul*, Boston, 1911 (the seekers considered are: Job, Plato, Kant, Hegel, and Browning).

HELLENISTIC GREEK: L. Radermacher, *Neutestamentliche Grammatik*, Tübingen, 1911.

HEXATEUCH: J. S. Griffiths, *The Problem of Deuteronomy*, London, 1911.
F. P. Ramsay, *An Interpretation of Genesis*, Washington, D. C., 1911.

HITTITES: A. Gleye, *Hittitische Studien*, part 1, Leipsic, 1910.

HOLLAND: *Gedenkstukken der algemeene Geschiedenis van Nederland van 1795 tot 1840*, vol. v., ed. H. T. Colenbrander, The Hague, 1910.
Acta der particuliere Synoden van Zuid-Holland, vol. iii., *1646–56*, ed. W. P. C. Knuttel, The Hague, 1910.

HULSEAN LECTURES: E. A. Edghill, *The Revelation of the Son of God: some Questions and Considerations arising out of a Study of Second Century Christianity. Being the Hulsean Lectures for 1910–11*, London and New York, 1911.

IDEALISM: C. Dunan, *Les Deux Idéalismes*, Paris, 1910.
P. Natorp, *Philosophie. Ihr Problem und ihre Probleme. Einführung in den kritischen Idealismus*, Göttingen, 1911.
A. Wernicke, *Die Begründung des deutschen Idealismus durch Immanuel Kant. Ein Beitrag zum Verständnisse des gemeinsamen Wirkens von Goethe und Schiller*, Brunswick, 1911.

IGNATIUS OF LOYOLA: D. Angeli, *Sant' Ignazio de Loyola nella vita e nell'arte*, Lanciano, 1910.

IMMORTALITY: F. Blades, *Is the Life of Man eternal?* New York, 1911.
G. L. Dickinson, *Religion and Immortality*, Boston, 1911.

INDIA: T. C. Hodson, *The Naga Tribes of Manipur*, New York, 1911.

INNERE MISSION: J. F. Ohl, *The Inner Mission: a Handbook for Christian Workers*, Philadelphia, 1911.

ISAIAH: C. D. Ginsburg, *Isaias. Diligenter revisus juxta Massorah atque editiones principes cum variis lectionibus e mss. atque antiquis versionibus collectis*, London, 1909.
R. H. Kennett, *The Composition of the Book of Isaiah in the Light of History and Archeology*, London, 1911; idem, *The Servant of the Lord*, New York, 1911.
G. W. Wade, *The Book of the Prophet Isaiah. With Introduction and Notes*, London, 1911.

ISRAEL, HISTORY OF: R. Lescynsky, *Die Juden in Arabien zur Zeit Muhammeds*, Berlin, 1910.
M. Gemoll, *Grundsteine zur Geschichte Israels. Alttestamentliche Studien*, Leipsic, 1911.
C. F. Lehman-Haupt, *Israel. Seine Entwicklung im Rahmen der Weltgeschichte*, Tübingen, 1911.
M. Löhr, *Israëls Kulturentwickelung*, Strasburg, 1911.

JAMES, W.: E. Boutroux, *William James*, Paris, 1911.

JEREMIAS, A.: *The Old Testament in the Light of the Ancient East: Manual of Biblical Archæology*, 2 vols., London, 1911.

JESUITS: C. Coppens, *Who are the Jesuits?* St. Louis, 1911.

JESUS CHRIST: K. Dunkmann, *Der historische Jesus, der mythologische Christus und Jesus der Christ*, Leipsic, 1910.
P. Jensen, *Hat der Jesus der Evangelien wirklich gelebt?* Frankfort, 1910.
A. Drews, *Die Christusmythe*, part 2, *Die Zeugnisse für die Geschichtlichkeit Jesu*, Jena, 1911.
W. A. Grist, *The Historic Christ in the Faith of To-day*, London, 1911.
G. Jahn, *Ueber die Person Jesu und über die Entstehung des Christentums und den Wert desselben für moderne Gebildete, mit einer Kritik der Evangelien und der neuesten Schriften über Jesu*, Leyden, 1911.

JESUS CHRIST, MONOGRAM OF: F. J. Dölger, Ιχθύς *Das Fischsymbol in frühchristlicher Zeit*, vol. i., Rome, 1910.

JEWS, MISSIONS TO THE: A. L. Williams, *A Manual of Christian Evidences for Jewish People*, Cambridge, 1911.

JOB: See above, HEGEL.

JOHN THE APOSTLE: J. Chapman, *John the Presbyter and the Fourth Gospel*, London, 1910.
　　J. T. Dean, *Visions and Revelations. Discourses on the Apocalypse*, London, 1911.
　　A. Merx, *Das Evangelium des Johannes nach der syrischen im Sinaikloster gefundenen Palimpsisthandschrift erläutert*, Berlin, 1911.

JOHN, SAINT, ORDER OF: J. Delaville le Rouix, *Mélanges sur l'ordre de S. Jean de Jérusalem*, Paris, 1910.

KANT: See above, HEGEL.

KINGDOM OF GOD: See above, DUHM.

KOREA: M. C. Fenwick, *The Church of Christ in Corea*, New York, 1911.

LAMAISM: A. Cunningham, *Ladak*, London, 1854.
　　A. H. Francke, *History of Western Tibet*, London, 1907.

LOISY, A.: *À propos d'histoire des religions*, Paris, 1911; idem, *Jésus et la tradition évangélique*, ib. 1911.

LOLLARDS: J. Gairdner, *Lollardy and the Reformation in England*, vol. iii., London, 1911.

LORD'S SUPPER: F. Graebke, *Die Konstruktion der Abendmahlslehre Luthers in ihrer Entwicklung dargestellt*, Leipsic, 1908.

LUKE: H. Koch, *Die Abfassungszeit des lukanischen Geschichtswerkes. Eine historisch-kritische und exegetische Untersuchung*, Leipsic, 1911.
Also see above, HARNACK.

LUTHER: L. P. Winter, *A Life of Martin Luther, the Great Reformer of the 16th Century*, Nashville, 1911.

LUTHERANS: *The Book of Concord; or, the Symbolical Books of the Evangelical Lutheran Church; transl. from the original Languages, with Analyses and exhaustive Index; ed. by H. Eyster Jacobs*, Philadelphia, 1911.
　　L. B. Wolf, *Missionary Heroes of the Lutheran Church*, Philadelphia, 1911.

MCGIFFERT, A. C.: *Protestant Thought before Kant*, New York, 1911.

MAGIC: T. W. Davies, " *Magic* " *Black and White* (2d ed. of *Magic, Divination, and Demonology Among the Hebrews and Their Neighbours*, London, 1897), Chicago, 1910.
　　T. de Cauzons, *La Magie et la sorcellerie en France*, vol. iii., *La Sorcellerie de la Réforme à la Révolution. Les Couvents possédés. La Franc-Maçonnerie. Le Magnétisme animal*, Paris, 1911.

MARK: M. J. Lagrange, *Évangile selon saint Marc*, Paris, 1911 (translation and commentary).

MARRIAGE: See above, DIVORCE.

MARTINEAU, J.: *Prayers in the Congregation and in College*, London, 1911.

MARY, MOTHER OF JESUS CHRIST: See above, BEISSEL.

MENNONITES: D. Philipz, *Enchiridion; or Hand Book of the Christian Doctrine and Religion, composed (by the Grace of God) from the Holy Scriptures for the Benefit of all Lovers of the Truth*, Elkhart, Ind., 1910.

MESSIAH: E. A. Gordon, *Messiah: the Ancestral Hope of the Ages*, London, 1911.
　　E. F. Scott, *The Kingdom and the Messiah*, Edinburgh, 1911.

METHODISTS: J. R. Gregory, *A History of Methodism, chiefly for the Use of Students*, 2 vols., London, 1911.

MIRACLES: J. M. Thompson, *Miracles in the New Testament*, New York, 1911.

MISSIONS: J. M. Buckley, *Theory and Practice of Foreign Missions*, New York, 1911.
　　S. M. Zwemer, *The Unoccupied Mission Fields of Africa and Asia*, London and New York, 1911.
Also see above, LUTHERANS.

MITHRA, MITHRAISM: T. Kluge, *Der Mithrakult. Seine Anfänge, Entwicklungsgeschichte und seine Denkmäler*, Leipsic, 1911.

MOABITE STONE: See above, BENNETT.

MOBERLY, G.: Miss C. A. E. Moberly, *Dulce Domum: George Moberly, his Family and Friends*, London, 1911.

MODERNISM: *The Priest: a Tale of Modernism in New England. By the Author of " Letters to His Holiness, Pope Pius X,"* Boston, 1911.

MOFFATT, J.: See above, BIBLICAL INTRODUCTION.

MOHAMMED: D. B. Macdonald, *Aspects of Islam*, New York, 1911.
　　E. Montet, *De l'état présent et de l'avenir de l'Islam*, Paris, 1911.

MORMONS: C. A. Shook, *The True Origin of Mormon Polygamy*, Mendota, Ill., 1911.

MORRISON, R.: J. F. Goucher, *Growth of the Missionary Concept*, chaps. i.-ii., New York, 1911.

MYSTICISM: E. Underhill, *Mysticism: a Study in the Nature and Development of Man's Spiritual Consciousness*, London, 1911.

NIETZSCHE, F.: A. R. Orage, *Friedrich Nietzsche, the Dionysian Spirit of the Age*, Chicago, 1911.

NON-CONFORMISTS: G. L. Turner, *Original Records of Early Nonconformity under Persecution and Indulgence*, London, 1911.

NON-JURORS: H. Broxap, *A Biography of Thomas Deacon, the Manchester Non-Juror*, London, 1911.

OCCAM, WILLIAM OF: F. Kropatscheck, *Occam und Luther*, Gütersloh, 1900.

OSWALD, SAINT: A. C. Champneys, *Saint Oswald*, London, 1911.

PALESTINE: Kate B. Scheuerman, *The Holy Land as seen through Bible Eyes. Being a Record of a Journey through Syria, Palestine and Europe in the Years 1908–09*, Seattle, 1910.
　　L. L. Henson, *Researches in Palestine*, Boston, 1911.
　　E. Huntington, *Palestine and Its Transformation*, London and Boston, 1911.

PATON, J. G.: A. K. Langridge and F. H. L. Paton, *John G. Paton: Later Years and Farewell. A Sequel to John G. Paton, an Autobiography*, 2d ed., New York, 1911.

PAUL THE APOSTLE: R. Bultmann, *Der Stil der paulinischen Predigt und die kynisch-stoische Diatribe*, Göttingen, 1910.
　　J. R. Cohu, *St. Paul in the Light of Modern Research*, New York and London, 1911.
　　J. Weiss, *Der 1. Korintherbrief*, Göttingen, 1910.
　　T. W. Drury, *The Prison-Ministry of St. Paul*, London, 1911.
　　C. H. Dudley, *St. Paul's Friendships and his Friends*, Boston, 1911.
　　A. Robertson and A. Plummer, *A Critical and Exegetical Commentary on the First Epistle of St. Paul to the Corinthians*, London, 1911.

PEACE MOVEMENTS: H. M. Chittenden, *War or Peace: a Present Duty and a Future Hope,* Chicago, 1911.

PHARISEES AND SADDUCEES: W. Caspari, *Die Pharisäer bis an die Schwelle des Neuen Testaments,* Gross Lichterfelde, 1909.

PLATONISM. See above, HEGEL.

POHLE, J.: *Dogmatic Theology,* vol. i., *God,* St. Louis, 1911.

POPE, PAPACY: Add to bibliography: H. Grisar, *Geschichte Roms und der Päpste im Mittelalter,* Freiburg, 1898 sqq. (to be in 6 vols.), Eng. transl., *History of Rome and the Popes in the Middle Ages,* vol. i., London, 1911.

PRAGMATISM: L. B. Macdonald, *Life in the Making: an Approach to Religion through the Method of Modern Pragmatism,* Boston, 1911.

PROPHECY: O. Procksch, *Die kleinen prophetischen Schriften vor dem Exil,* Stuttgart, 1910.
Mary A. Taylor, *The Historic Meaning of Prophecy,* Cincinnati, 1911.
H. Wace, *Prophecy: Jewish and Christian,* London and Milwaukee, 1911.

PROTESTANT EPISCOPALIANS: *Constitution and Canons for the Government of the Protestant Episcopal Church in the United States of America Adopted in General Conventions, 1789–1910,* New York, 1910.

PSEUDEPIGRAPHA: J. Viteau, *Les Psaumes de Salomon,* Paris, 1910 (with introduction, Greek text, translation, and notes).

RED CROSS SOCIETY: H. Rundle, *With the Red Cross in the Franco-German War, A. D., 1870–71. Some Reminiscences,* London, 1911.

REFORMATION: *Documents Illustrative of the Continental Reformation,* ed. B. J. Kidd, London, 1911.

RELIGION: J. M. Hodgson, *Religion: the Quest of the Ideal,* Edinburgh, 1911.

RELIGION, PHILOSOPHY OF: J. J. Gourd, *Philosophie de la religion,* Paris, 1910.

REVELATION: G. A. Cooke, *The Progress of Revelation,* New York, 1911.

REVIVALS: T. B. Kilpatrick, *New Testament Evangelism,* New York, 1911.

REWARD: V. Kirchner, *Der " Lohn" in der alten Philosophie, im bürgerlichen Recht, besonders im Neuen Testament,* Gütersloh, 1908.

ROBINSON, J. A.: *The Advent Hope in St. Paul's Epistles,* New York, 1911.

ROSCELINUS: F. Picavet, *Roscelin, philosophe et théologien, d'après la légende et d'après l'histoire. Sa place dans l'histoire générale et comparée des philosophies médiévales,* Paris, 1911.

ROUSSEAU: G. Valette, *Jean Jacques Rousseau Genevois,* Paris, 1910.

RUSSIA: M. Tamarati, *L'Église géorgienne des origines jusqu'à nos jours,* London, 1910.

SAINTS: *Hagiographica orientalis. Bibliographie des textes hagiographiques publiés en arabe, en armenien, en ethiopien, en copte et en syriaque,* Brussels, 1910.
Vitæ sanctorum Danorum, ed. M. C. Gertz, part 2, Copenhagen, 1910.

SALVATION ARMY: A. M. Nicol, *General Booth and The Salvation Army,* London, 1911.

SANDAY, W.: See GOSPEL AND GOSPELS.

SCHOPENHAUER: T. Ruyssen, *Schopenhauer,* Paris, 1911.

SCOTLAND: G. Anderson, *The Scottish Pastor,* Edinburgh, 1911.

SCOTLAND: J. Dowden, *The Medieval Church in Scotland: its Constitution, Organization and Law,* New York, 1911.

SEVEN SLEEPERS OF EPHESUS: P. M. Huber, *Die Wanderlegende von den sieben Schläfern,* Leipsic, 1910.

SIAM: Mrs. L. Milne, *Shans at Home,* London, 1910 (contains 2 chapters on Shan history and literature by W. W. Cochrane).

SIN: M. L. Burton, *The Problem of Evil,* Chicago, 1910.

SINAI: M. J. Rendall, *Sinai in Spring,* London, 1911.

SOCIALISM: C. Noel, *Socialism in Church History,* Milwaukee, 1911.

SORCERY: V. J. Mansikka, *Ueber russische Zauberformeln mit Berücksichtigung der Blut- und Verrenkungssegen,* Helsingfors, 1910.

SOTERIOLOGY: E. Krebs, *Der Logos als Heiland im ersten Jahrhundert. Ein religions- und dogmengeschichtlicher Beitrag zur Erlösungslehre,* Freiburg, 1911.

SOULE, J.: H. M. Du Bose, *Life of Joshua Soule,* Nashville, 1911.

SOUTH SEA ISLANDS: W. Churchill, *The Polynesian Wanderings. Tracks of the Migration deduced from an Examination of the Proto-Samoan Content of the Efaté and other Languages Of Melanesia,* Washington, D. C., 1911.

SPAIN: G. H. B. Ward, *The Truth about Spain,* New York, 1911.

SPEAKING WITH TONGUES: E. Lombard, *De la glossolalie chez les premiers chrétiens et des phénomènes similaires,* Paris, 1911.
E. Mosiman, *Das Zungenreden,* Tübingen, 1911.

SPIERA, F.: Add to bibliography: P. Schaf, *Die Sünde wider den heiligen Geist . . . nebst einen . . . Anhange über das Lebensende des Francesco Spiera,* Halle, 1841.

STOICISM: V. Arnold, *Roman Stoicism,* Cambridge, 1911.

SUNDAY-SCHOOLS: A. H. McKinney, *Practical Pedagogy in the Sunday School,* New York and London, 1911.

SYMBOLISM: F. E. Hulme, *The History, Principles, and Practice of Symbolism in Christian Art,* 6th ed., London, 1911.

TALMUD: Add to bibliography: The most important parts of the Mishnah are edited from MSS., translated and explained by H. L. Strack as follows, all at Leipsic: Yoma, 1904; Abhodha Zara, 1909; Sanhedrin Makkoth, 1911; Pesahim, 1911; Berakhoth and the three Babhoth will appear 1912–13. Add also: H. L. Strack, *Jesus, die Häretiker und die Christen nach den ältesten jüdischen Angaben,* Leipsic, 1910.

TERTULLIAN: R. Heinze, *Tertullians Apologeticum,* Leipsic, 1911.

THEISM: G. Wobbermin, *Monismus und Monotheismus,* Tübingen, 1911.

THEODORET: *Kirchengeschichte,* ed. L. Parmentier for the Prussian Academy, Leipsic, 1911.

THOMAS AQUINAS: P. Conway, *Saint Thomas Aquinas of the Order of Preachers, 1225–74,* London, 1911.

TIME, BIBLICAL RECKONING OF: F. Westberg, *Zur neutestamentlichen Chronologie und Golgothas Ortlage,* Leipsic, 1911.

TRANSFIGURATION: E. Curling, *The Transfiguration. With other Sermons,* London, 1911.

BIOGRAPHICAL ADDENDA

ADLER, H. N.: d. in London July 18, 1911.

ATTERBURY, W. W.: d. at Bennington, Vt., Aug. 6, 1911.

BERNARD, J. H.: Chosen bishop of Ossory, 1911.

CURTIS, E. L.: d. near Rockland, Me., Aug. 26, 1911.

DARGAN E. C.: Elected professor of homiletics in the Southwestern Baptist Theological Seminary, Fort Worth, Tex., 1911.

DEVINS, J. B.: d. in Brooklyn, N. Y., Aug. 26, 1911.

DUNNING, A. E.: Retired from the editorial staff of *The Congregationalist*, 1911.

EWALD, H. A. P.: d. at Erlangen, Germany, May 27, 1911.

HUGHES, T. P.: d. at King's Park, Long Island, Aug. 8, 1911.

INGE, W. R.: Became dean of St. Paul's, London, 1911.

KIRN, O.: d. at Leipsic Aug. 18, 1911.

KNIGHT, G. T.: d. at Medford, Mass., Sept. 10, 1911.

MORAN, P. F.: d. at Sydney, New South Wales, Aug. 16, 1911.

MORGAN, G. C.: Becomes president of Cheshunt College, Cambridge, in 1911, without resigning his pastoral work.

PAGET, F.: d. in London, England, Aug. 2, 1911.

PARTRIDGE, S. C.: Enthroned bishop of Kansas City June 27, 1911.

PIERSON, A. T.: d. in Brooklyn, N. Y., June 2, 1911.

POWER, F. D.: d. at Washington, D. C., June 14, 1911.

REVEL, A.: d. at Florence, Italy, Nov. 22, 1888 (see vol. x., p. 3).

ROBSON, G.: d. at Edinburgh Aug. 2, 1911.

SIMONS, W. E.: Succeeded Achelis as professor of practical theology at Marburg, 1911.

STRONG, A. H.: Resigned presidency of Rochester Theological Seminary to take effect in 1912.

ADDENDA ET CORRIGENDA

Vol. i., p. 173, col. 2, line 23 from bottom: Read "Ohio" for "Ill."; p. 350, col. 2, line 2: Read "T. J. Crawford" for "T. G. Crawford"; p. 352, col. 1, line 37: Read "Trumbull" for "Trumbell."

Vol. ii., p. 68, col. 1, lines 44 and 47: Read "Greek Testament" for "Bible."

Vol. v., p. 162, col. 1, line 46: Read "Schultz Johnson" for "Schultz, Johnson."

Vol. vi., p. 19, col. 1, line 45: Read "Foster" for "Forster," and line 19 from bottom read "C. Elliott" for "E. Elliott"; p. 124, col. 2, line 16: Read "C. J. Ball" for "C. F. Ball"; p. 208, col. 1, line 25: Read "H. R. Reynolds" for "R. H. Reynolds"; p. 225, line 4 from bottom: Read "1893" for "1894"; p. 227, col. 1, line 13: Read "Thomson" for "Thompson"; p. 254, col. 1, last line: Read "410" for "140"; p. 267, col. 1, line 26: Read "*Albert*" for "*Robert*"; p. 345, col. 2, line 4 from bottom: Read "homiletics" for "polemics," and line 3 from bottom: Add "but did not accept"; p. 346, col. 1, line 28 from bottom: Read "Sparks" for "Spark"; p. 486, col. 2, line 13: Read "Cassel's" for "Cassels'."

Vol. vii., p. 378, col. 1, line 5: Read "Birks" for "Binks."

Vol. viii., p. 3, col. 1, line 4: Read "passed" for "based"; p. 143, col. 2, signature: Read "Odhner" for "Odlmer."

Vol x., p. 110, col. 1, line 40: Read "Chamier" for "Chanier"; p. 111, col. 2, line 18: Read "G. R." for "G. B."; p. 131, col. 1, line 29: Read "Felix" for "Filix"; p. 188, col. 1, line 22: Read "M. Bristol" for "T. Bristol"; p. 302, col. 1, line 19 from bottom: Read "Balmes" for "Balme"; p. 370, col. 1, line 21 from bottom: Read "1887–88" for "1899"; p. 401, col. 2, line 16: Read "W. R. Greg" for "R. W. Gregg"; p. 402, col. 1, line 28 from bottom: Read "New York" for "London."

Vol. xi., p. 19, col. 2, signature: Read "G. E." for "D."; p. 130, col. 2, line 17 from bottom: Read "*mosaische*" for "*mosäische*."

LIST OF ABBREVIATIONS

Abbreviations in common use or self-evident are not included here. For additional information concerning the works listed, see vol. i., pp. viii.–xx., and the appropriate articles in the body of the work.

ADB .... *Allgemeine deutsche Biographie*, Leipsic, 1875 sqq., vol. 53, 1907

Adv .... *adversus*, " against "

AJP........... *American Journal of Philology*, Baltimore, 1880 sqq.

AJT .... *American Journal of Theology*, Chicago, 1897 sqq.

AKR........... *Archiv für katholisches Kirchenrecht*, Innsbruck, 1857–61, Mainz, 1872 sqq.

ALKG........ *Archiv für Litteratur- und Kirchengeschichte des Mittelalters*, Freiburg, 1885 sqq.

Am........... American

AMA........... *Abhandlungen der Münchener Akademie*, Munich, 1763 sqq.

ANF........... *Ante-Nicene Fathers*, American edition by A. Cleveland Coxe, 8 vols. and index, Buffalo, 1887; vol. ix., ed. Allan Menzies, New York, 1897

Apoc........... Apocrypha, apocryphal

Apol........... *Apologia, Apology*

Arab........... Arabic

Aram........... Aramaic

art........... article

Art. Schmal ... Schmalkald Articles

ASB........... *Acta sanctorum*, ed. J. Bolland and others, Antwerp, 1643 sqq.

ASM........... *Acta sanctorum ordinis S. Benedicti*, ed. J. Mabillon, 9 vols., Paris, 1668–1701

Assyr........... Assyrian

A. T........... *Altes Testament*, " Old Testament "

Augs. Con...... Augsburg Confession

A. V........... Authorized Version (of the English Bible)

Baldwin, *Dictionary* .... J. M. Baldwin, *Dictionary of Philosophy and Psychology*, 3 vols. in 4, New York, 1901–05

Bardenhewer, *Geschichte* .... O. Bardenhewer, *Geschichte der altkirchlichen Litteratur*, 2 vols., Freiburg, 1902

Bardenhewer, *Patrologie* .... O. Bardenhewer, *Patrologie*, 2d ed., Freiburg, 1901

Bayle, *Dictionary* .. *The Dictionary Historical and Critical of Mr. Peter Bayle*, 2d ed., 5 vols., London, 1734–38

Benzinger, *Archäologie* ... I. Benzinger, *Hebräische Archäologie*, 2d ed., Freiburg, 1907

Bingham, *Origines* .... J. Bingham, *Origines ecclesiasticæ*, 10 vols., London, 1708–22; new ed., Oxford, 1855

Bouquet, *Recueil* M. Bouquet, *Recueil des historiens des Gaules et de la France*, continued by various hands, 23 vols., Paris, 1738–76

Bower, *Popes* ... Archibald Bower, *History of the Popes . . . to 1758*, continued by S. H. Cox, 3 vols., Philadelphia, 1845–47

BQR........... *Baptist Quarterly Review*, Philadelphia, 1867 sqq.

BRG........... See Jaffé

Cant........... Canticles, Song of Solomon

cap........... *caput*, " chapter "

Ceillier, *Auteurs sacrés* .... R. Ceillier, *Histoire des auteurs sacrés et ecclésiastiques*, 16 vols. in 17, Paris, 1858–69

Chron........... *Chronicon*, " Chronicle "

I Chron........... I Chronicles

II Chron .... II Chronicles

CIG........... *Corpus inscriptionum Græcarum*, Berlin, 1825 sqq.

CIL........... *Corpus inscriptionum Latinarum*, Berlin, 1863 sqq.

CIS........... *Corpus inscriptionum Semiticarum*, Paris, 1881 sqq.

cod........... codex

cod. Theod....... *codex Theodosianus*

Col........... Epistle to the Colossians

col., cols........ column, columns

Conf........... *Confessiones*, " Confessions "

I Cor........... First Epistle to the Corinthians

II Cor........... Second Epistle to the Corinthians

COT........... See Schrader

CQR...... *The Church Quarterly Review*, London, 1875 sqq.

CR........... *Corpus reformatorum*, begun at Halle, 1834, vol. lxxxix., Berlin and Leipsic, 1905 sqq.

Creighton, *Papacy* ..... M. Creighton, *A History of the Papacy from the Great Schism to the Sack of Rome*, new ed., 6 vols., New York and London, 1897

CSCO........... *Corpus scriptorum Christianorum orientalium*, ed. J. B. Chabot, I. Guidi, and others, Paris and Leipsic, 1903 sqq.

CSEL........... *Corpus scriptorum ecclesiasticorum Latinorum*, Vienna, 1867 sqq.

CSHB........... *Corpus scriptorum historiæ Byzantinæ*, 49 vols., Bonn, 1828–78

Currier, *Religious Orders* ...... C. W. Currier, *History of Religious Orders*, New York, 1896

D........... Deuteronomist

Dan........... Daniel

DB........... J. Hastings, *Dictionary of the Bible*, 4 vols. and extra vol., Edinburgh and New York, 1898–1904

DCA........... W. Smith and S. Cheetham, *Dictionary of Christian Antiquities*, 2 vols., London, 1875–80

DCB........... W. Smith and H. Wace, *Dictionary of Christian Biography*, 4 vols., Boston, 1877–87

DCG........... J. Hastings, J. A. Selbie, and J. C. Lambert, *A Dictionary of Christ and the Gospels*, 2 vols., Edinburgh and New York, 1906–1908

Deut........... Deuteronomy

De vir. ill........ *De viris illustribus*

DGQ........... See Wattenbach

DNB........... L. Stephen and S. Lee, *Dictionary of National Biography*, 63 vols. and supplement 3 vols., London, 1885–1901

Driver, *Introduction* ..... S. R. Driver, *Introduction to the Literature of the Old Testament*, 10th ed., New York, 1910

E........... Elohist

EB........... T. K. Cheyne and J. S. Black, *Encyclopædia Biblica*, 4 vols., London and New York, 1899–1903

Eccl........... *Ecclesia*, " Church "; *ecclesiasticus*, " ecclesiastical "

Eccles........... Ecclesiastes

Ecclus........... Ecclesiasticus

ed........... edition; *edidit*, " edited by "

Eph........... Epistle to the Ephesians

Epist........... *Epistola, Epistolæ*, " Epistle," " Epistles "

Ersch and Gruber, *Encyklopädie* .. J. S. Ersch and J. G. Gruber, *Allgemeine Encyklopädie der Wissenschaften und Künste*, Leipsic, 1818 sqq.

E. V........... English versions (of the Bible)

Ex........... Exodus

Ezek........... Ezekiel

fasc........... fasciculus

Fr........... French

Friedrich, *KD*.. J. Friedrich, *Kirchengeschichte Deutschlands*, 2 vols., Bamberg, 1867–69

Gal........... Epistle to the Galatians

Gams, *Series episcoporum* .. P. B. Gams, *Series episcoporum ecclesiæ Catholicæ*, Regensburg, 1873, and supplement, 1886

Gee and Hardy, *Documents* ... H. Gee and W. J. Hardy, *Documents Illustrative of English Church History*, London, 1896

Germ .... German

GGA........... *Göttingische Gelehrte Anzeigen*, Göttingen, 1824 sqq.

Gibbon, *Decline and Fall*..... E. Gibbon, *History of the Decline and Fall of the Roman Empire*, ed. J. B. Bury, 7 vols., London, 1896–1900

Gk........... Greek

Gross, *Sources*.. C. Gross, *The Sources and Literature of English History . . . to 1485*, London, 1900

Hab........... Habakkuk

Haddan and Stubbs, *Councils* .... A. W. Haddan and W. Stubbs, *Councils and Ecclesiastical Documents Relating to Great Britain and Ireland*, 3 vols., Oxford, 1869–78

Hær............	Refers to patristic works on heresies or heretics, Tertullian's *De præscriptione*, the *Pros haireseis* of Irenæus, the *Panarion* of Epiphanius, etc.
Hag	Haggai
Harduin, *Concilia*........	J. Harduin, *Conciliorum collectio regia maxima*, 12 vols., Paris, 1715
Harnack, *Dogma*	A. Harnack, *History of Dogma . . . from the 3d German edition*, 7 vols., Boston, 1895–1900
Harnack, *Litteratur*.....	A. Harnack, *Geschichte der altchristlichen Litteratur bis Eusebius*, 2 vols. in 3, Leipsic, 1893–1904
Hauck, *KD* ...	A. Hauck, *Kirchengeschichte Deutschlands*, vol. i., Leipsic, 1904; vol. ii, 1900; vol. iii., 1906; vol. iv., 1903
Hauck-Herzog, *RE*.........	*Realencyklopädie für protestantische Theologie und Kirche*, founded by J. J. Herzog, 3d ed. by A. Hauck, Leipsic, 1896–1909
Heb..........	Epistle to the Hebrews
Hebr..........	Hebrew
Hefele, *Conciliengeschichte*....	C. J. von Hefele, *Conciliengeschichte*, continued by J. Hergenröther, vols. i.–vi, viii.–ix., Freiburg, 1883–93
Heimbucher, *Orden und Kongregationen.*..	M. Heimbucher, *Die Orden und Kongregationen der katholischen Kirche*, 2d ed. 3 vols., Paderborn, 1907
Helyot, *Ordres monastiques*...	P. Helyot, *Histoire des ordres monastiques, religieux et militaires*, 8 vols., Paris, 1714–19; new ed., 1839–42
Henderson, *Documents*	E. F. Henderson, *Select Historical Documents of the Middle Ages*, London, 1892
Hist...........	History, *histoire, historia*
Hist. eccl.......	*Historia ecclesiastica, ecclesiæ*, "Church History"
Hom...........	*Homilia, homiliai*, "homily, homilies"
Hos...........	Hosea
Isa...........	Isaiah
Ital...........	Italian
J............	Jahvist (Yahwist)
JA...........	*Journal Asiatique*, Paris, 1822 sqq.
Jacobus, *Dictionary*....	*A Standard Bible Dictionary*, ed. M. W. Jacobus, . . . E. E. Nourse, . . . and A. C. Zenos, New York and London, 1909
Jaffé, *BRG*....	P. Jaffé, *Bibliotheca rerum Germanicarum*, 6 vols., Berlin, 1864–73
Jaffé, *Regesta*...	P. Jaffé, *Regesta pontificum Romanorum . . . ad annum 1198*, Berlin, 1851; 2d ed., Leipsic, 1881–88
JAOS.........	*Journal of the American Oriental Society*, New Haven, 1849 sqq.
JBL..........	*Journal of Biblical Literature and Exegesis*, first appeared as *Journal of the Society of Biblical Literature and Exegesis*, Middletown, 1882–88, then Boston, 1890 sqq.
JE...........	*The Jewish Encyclopedia*, 12 vols., New York, 1901–06
JE...........	The combined narrative of the Jahvist (Yahwist) and Elohist
Jer...........	Jeremiah
Josephus, *Ant*..	Flavius Josephus, "Antiquities of the Jews"
Josephus, *Apion*.	Flavius Josephus, "Against Apion"
Josephus, *Life*..	Life of Flavius Josephus
Josephus, *War*..	Flavius Josephus, "The Jewish War"
Josh	Joshua
JPT	*Jahrbücher für protestantische Theologie*, Leipsic, 1875 sqq.
JQR	*The Jewish Quarterly Review*, London, 1888 sqq.
JRAS.........	*Journal of the Royal Asiatic Society*, London, 1834 sqq.
JTS	*Journal of Theological Studies*, London, 1899 sqq.
Julian, *Hymnology* ...	J. Julian, *A Dictionary of Hymnology*, revised edition, London, 1907
KAT	See Schrader
KB...........	See Schrader
KD	See Friedrich, Hauck, Rettberg
KL...........	*Wetzer und Welte's Kirchenlexikon*, 2d ed., by J. Hergenröther and F. Kaulen, 12 vols., Freiburg, 1882–1903
Krüger, *History*	G. Krüger, *History of Early Christian Literature in the First Three Centuries*, New York, 1897
Krumbacher, *Geschichte*....	K. Krumbacher, *Geschichte der byzantinischen Litteratur*, 2d ed., Munich, 1897
Labbe, *Concilia*	P. Labbe, *Sacrorum conciliorum nova et amplissima collectio*, 31 vols., Florence and Venice, 1759–98
Lam	Lamentations
Lanigan, *Eccl. Hist*	J. Lanigan, *Ecclesiastical History of Ireland to the 13th Century*, 4 vols., Dublin, 1829
Lat...........	Latin, Latinized

Leg	*Leges, Legum*
Lev	Leviticus
Lichtenberger, *ESR*	F. Lichtenberger, *Encyclopédie des sciences religieuses*, 13 vols., Paris, 1877–1882
Lorenz, *DGQ* ..	O. Lorenz, *Deutschlands Geschichtsquellen im Mittelalter*, 3d ed., Berlin, 1887
LXX	The Septuagint
I Macc	I Maccabees
II Macc	II Maccabees
Mai, *Nova collectio*	A. Mai, *Scriptorum veterum nova collectio*, 10 vols., Rome, 1825–38
Mal...........	Malachi
Mann, *Popes* ...	R. C. Mann, *Lives of the Popes in the Early Middle Ages*, London, 1902 sqq.
Mansi, *Concilia*.	G. D. Mansi, *Sanctorum conciliorum collectio nova*, 31 vols., Florence and Venice, 1728
Matt...........	Matthew
MGH	*Monumenta Germaniæ historica*, ed. G. H. Pertz and others, Hanover and Berlin, 1826 sqq. The following abbreviations are used for the sections and subsections of this work: *Ant., Antiquitates*, "Antiquities"; *Auct. ant., Auctores antiquissimi*, "Oldest Writers"; *Chron. min., Chronica minora*, "Lesser Chronicles"; *Dip., Diplomata*, "Diplomas, Documents"; *Epist., Epistolæ*, "Letters"; *Gest. pont. Rom., Gesta pontificum Romanorum*, "Deeds of the Popes of Rome"; *Leg., Leges*, "Laws"; *Lib. de lite, Libelli de lite inter regnum et sacerdotium sæculorum xi. et xii. conscripti*, "Books concerning the Strife between the Civil and Ecclesiastical Authorities in the Eleventh and Twelfth Centuries"; *Nec., Necrologia Germaniæ*, "Necrology of Germany"; *Poet. Lat. ævi Car., Poetæ Latini ævi Carolini*, "Latin Poets of the Caroline Time"; *Poet. Lat. med. ævi, Poetæ Latini medii ævi*, "Latin Poets of the Middle Ages"; *Script., Scriptores*, "Writers"; *Script. rer. Germ., Scriptores rerum Germanicarum*, "Writers on German Subjects"; *Script. rer. Langob., Scriptores rerum Langobardicarum et Italicarum*, "Writers on Lombard and Italian Subjects"; *Script. rer. Merov., Scriptores rerum Merovingicarum*, "Writers on Merovingian Subjects"
Mic............	Micah
Milman, *Latin Christianity* ..	H. H. Milman, *History of Latin Christianity, Including that of the Popes to . . . Nicholas V.*, 8 vols., London, 1860–61
Mirbt, *Quellen*..	C. Mirbt, *Quellen zur Geschichte des Papsttums und des römischen Katholicismus*, Tübingen, 1901
MPG..........	J. P. Migne, *Patrologiæ cursus completus, series Græca*, 162 vols., Paris, 1857–66
MPL..........	J. P. Migne, *Patrologiæ cursus completus, series Latinæ*, 221 vols., Paris, 1844–64
MS., MSS.......	Manuscript, Manuscripts
Muratori, *Scriptores*.......	L. A. Muratori, *Rerum Italicarum scriptores*, 28 vols., 1723–51
NA	*Neues Archiv der Gesellschaft für ältere deutsche Geschichtskunde*, Hanover, 1876 sqq.
Nah	Nahum
n.d.	no date of publication
Neander, *Christian Church*..	A. Neander, *General History of the Christian Religion and Church*, 6 vols., and index, Boston, 1872–81
Neh	Nehemiah
Niceron, *Mémoires*.......	R. P. Niceron, *Mémoires pour servir à l'histoire des hommes illustrés . . .* , 43 vols., Paris, 1729–45
Nielsen, *Papacy*.	F. K. Nielsen, *History of the Papacy in the Nineteenth Century*, 2 vols., New York, 1906
Nippold, *Papacy*.	F. Nippold, *The Papacy in the Nineteenth Century*, New York, 1900
NKZ	*Neue kirchliche Zeitschrift*, Leipsic, 1890 sqq.
Nowack, *Archäologie*........	W. Nowack, *Lehrbuch der hebräischen Archäologie*, 2 vols., Freiburg, 1894
n.p.	no place of publication
NPNF........	*The Nicene and Post-Nicene Fathers*, 1st series, 14 vols., New York, 1887–92; 2d series, 14 vols., New York, 1890–1900
N. T.	New Testament, *Novum Testamentum, Nouveau Testament, Neues Testament*
Num............	Numbers
Ob............	Obadiah

O. S. B......... *Ordo sancti Benedicti*, "Order of St. Benedict"
O. T............. Old Testament
OTJC......... See Smith
P............. Priestly document
Pastor, *Popes*... L. Pastor, *The History of the Popes from the Close of the Middle Ages*, 8 vols., London, 1891–1908
PEA......... *Patres ecclesiæ Anglicanæ*, ed. J. A. Giles, 34 vols., London, 1838–46
PEF......... Palestine Exploration Fund
I Pet............. First Epistle of Peter
II Pet............. Second Epistle of Peter
Platina, *Popes*... B. Platina, *Lives of the Popes from ... Gregory VII. to ... Paul II.*, 2 vols., London, n.d.
Pliny, *Hist. nat.*... Pliny, *Historia naturalis*
Potthast, *Wegweiser.* A. Potthast, *Bibliotheca historica medii ævi. Wegweiser durch die Geschichtswerke*, Berlin, 1896
Prov......... Proverbs
Ps......... Psalms
PSBA......... *Proceedings of the Society of Biblical Archeology*, London, 1880 sqq.
q.v., qq.v......... *quod (quæ) vide*, "which see"
Ranke, *Popes*... L. von Ranke, *History of the Popes*, 3 vols., London, 1906
RDM......... *Revue des deux mondes*, Paris, 1831 sqq.
RE............. See Hauck-Herzog
Reich, *Documents*... E. Reich, *Select Documents Illustrating Mediæval and Modern History*, London, 1905
REJ............. *Revue des études juives*, Paris, 1880 sqq.
Rettberg, *KD*... F. W. Rettberg, *Kirchengeschichte Deutschlands*, 2 vols., Göttingen, 1846–48
Rev......... Book of Revelation
RHR......... *Revue de l'histoire des religions*, Paris, 1880 sqq.
Richardson, *Encyclopaedia*... E. C. Richardson, *Alphabetical Subject Index and Index Encyclopaedia to Periodical Articles on Religion, 1890–99*, New York, 1907
Richter, *Kirchenrecht*... A. L. Richter, *Lehrbuch des katholischen und evangelischen Kirchenrechts*, 8th ed. by W. Kahl, Leipsic, 1886
Robinson, *Researches*, and *Later Researches*... E. Robinson, *Biblical Researches in Palestine*, Boston, 1841, and *Later Biblical Researches in Palestine*, 3d ed. of the whole, 3 vols., 1867
Robinson, *European History*... J. H. Robinson, *Readings in European History*, 2 vols., Boston, 1904–06
Robinson and Beard, *Modern Europe*... J. H. Robinson, and C. A. Beard, *Development of Modern Europe*, 2 vols., Boston, 1907
Rom............. Epistle to the Romans
RTP............. *Revue de théologie et de philosophie*, Lausanne, 1873
R. V............. Revised Version (of the English Bible)
sæc.............. *sæculum*, "century"
I Sam............. I Samuel
II Sam............. II Samuel
SBA......... *Sitzungsberichte der Berliner Akademie*, Berlin, 1882 sqq.
SBE......... F. Max Müller and others, *The Sacred Books of the East*, Oxford, 1879 sqq., vol. xlviii., 1904
SBOT......... *Sacred Books of the Old Testament* ("Rainbow Bible"), Leipsic, London, and Baltimore, 1894 sqq.
Schaff, *Christian Church*... P. Schaff, *History of the Christian Church*, vols. i.–iv., vi., vii., New York, 1882–92, vol. v., 2 parts, by D. S. Schaff, 1907–10
Schaff, *Creeds*... P. Schaff, *The Creeds of Christendom*, 3 vols., New York, 1877–84
Schrader, *COT*... E. Schrader, *Cuneiform Inscriptions and the Old Testament*, 2 vols., London, 1885–88
Schrader, *KAT*... E. Schrader, *Die Keilinschriften und das Alte Testament*, 2 vols., Berlin, 1902–03
Schrader, *KB*... E. Schrader, *Keilinschriftliche Bibliothek*, 6 vols., Berlin, 1889–1901
Schürer, *Geschichte*... E. Schürer, *Geschichte des jüdischen Volkes im Zeitalter Jesu Christi*, 4th ed., 3 vols., Leipsic, 1902 sqq.; Eng. transl., 5 vols., New York, 1891
Script.......... *Scriptores*, "writers"
Scrivener, *Introduction*... F. H. A. Scrivener, *Introduction to New Testament Criticism*, 4th ed., London, 1894
Sent.......... *Sententiæ*, "Sentences"
S. J......... *Societas Jesu*, "Society of Jesus"
SMA......... *Sitzungsberichte der Münchener Akademie*, Munich, 1860 sqq.
Smith, *Kinship*... W. R. Smith, *Kinship and Marriage in Early Arabia*, London, 1903

Smith, *OTJC*... W. R. Smith, *The Old Testament in the Jewish Church*, London, 1892
Smith, *Prophets*... W. R. Smith, *Prophets of Israel ... to the Eighth Century*, London, 1895
Smith, *Rel. of Sem.*... W. R. Smith, *Religion of the Semites*, London, 1894
S. P. C. K...... Society for the Promotion of Christian Knowledge
S. P. G......... Society for the Propagation of the Gospel in Foreign Parts
sqq......... and following
Strom......... *Stromata*, "Miscellanies"
s.v......... *sub voce*, or *sub verbo*
Swete, *Introduction*... H. B. Swete, *Introduction to the Old Testament in Greek*, London, 1900
Syr......... Syriac
Thatcher and McNeal, *Source Book*... O. J. Thatcher and E. H. McNeal, *A Source Book for Mediæval History*, New York, 1905
I Thess......... First Epistle to the Thessalonians
II Thess......... Second Epistle to the Thessalonians
ThT......... *Theologische Tijdschrift*, Amsterdam and Leyden, 1867 sqq.
Tillemont, *Mémoires*... L. S. le Nain de Tillemont, *Mémoires ... ecclésiastiques des six premiers siècles*, 16 vols., Paris, 1693–1712
I Tim............. First Epistle to Timothy
II Tim............. Second Epistle to Timothy
TJB......... *Theologischer Jähresbericht*, Leipsic, 1882–1887, Freiburg, 1888, Brunswick, 1889–1897, Berlin, 1898 sqq.
Tob......... Tobit
TQ......... *Theologische Quartalschrift*, Tübingen, 1819 sqq.
TS......... J. A. Robinson, *Texts and Studies*, Cambridge, 1891 sqq.
TSBA......... *Transactions of the Society of Biblical Archæology*, London, 1872 sqq.
TSK......... *Theologische Studien und Kritiken*, Hamburg, 1826 sqq.
TU......... *Texte und Untersuchungen zur Geschichte der altchristlichen Litteratur*, ed. O. von Gebhardt and A. Harnack, Leipsic, 1882 sqq.
Ugolini, *Thesaurus*... B. Ugolinus, *Thesaurus antiquitatum sacrarum*, 34 vols., Venice, 1744–69
V. T.......... *Vetus Testamentum*, *Vieux Testament*, "Old Testament"
Wattenbach, *DGQ*... W. Wattenbach, *Deutschlands Geschichtsquellen*, 5th ed., 2 vols., Berlin, 1885; 6th ed., 1893–94; 7th ed., 1904 sqq.
Wellhausen, *Heidentum*... J. Wellhausen, *Reste arabischen Heidentums*, Berlin, 1887
Wellhausen, *Prolegomena*... J. Wellhausen, *Prolegomena zur Geschichte Israels*, 6th ed., Berlin, 1905, Eng. transl. Edinburgh, 1885
ZA......... *Zeitschrift für Assyriologie*, Leipsic, 1886–88, Berlin, 1889 sqq.
Zahn, *Einleitung*... T. Zahn, *Einleitung in das Neue Testament*, 3d ed., Leipsic, 1907; Eng. transl., *Introduction to the New Testament*, 3 vols., Edinburgh, 1909
Zahn, *Kanon*... T. Zahn, *Geschichte des neutestamentlichen Kanons*, 2 vols., Leipsic, 1888–92
ZATW......... *Zeitschrift für die alttestamentliche Wissenschaft*, Giessen, 1881 sqq.
ZDAL......... *Zeitschrift für deutsches Alterthum und deutsche Literatur*, Berlin, 1876 sqq.
ZDMG......... *Zeitschrift der deutschen morgenländischen Gesellschaft*, Leipsic, 1847 sqq.
ZDP......... *Zeitschrift für deutsche Philologie*, Halle, 1869 sqq.
ZDPV......... *Zeitschrift des deutschen Palästina-Vereins*, Leipsic, 1878 sqq.
Zech......... Zechariah
Zeph......... Zephaniah
ZHT......... *Zeitschrift für die historische Theologie*, published successively at Leipsic, Hamburg, and Gotha, 1832–75
ZKG......... *Zeitschrift für Kirchengeschichte*, Gotha, 1876 sqq.
ZKR......... *Zeitschrift für Kirchenrecht*, Berlin, Tübingen, Freiburg, 1861 sqq.
ZKT......... *Zeitschrift für katholische Theologie*, Innsbruck, 1877 sqq.
ZKW......... *Zeitschrift für kirchliche Wissenschaft und kirchliches Leben*, Leipsic, 1880–89
ZNTW......... *Zeitschrift für die neutestamentliche Wissenschaft*, Giessen, 1900 sqq.
ZPK......... *Zeitschrift für Protestantismus und Kirche*, Erlangen, 1838–76
ZWT......... *Zeitschrift für wissenschaftliche Theologie*, Jena, 1858–60, Halle, 1861–67, Leipsic, 1868 sqq.

SYSTEM OF TRANSLITERATION

The following system of transliteration has been used for Hebrew:

א = ' or omitted at the beginning of a word.	ז = z	ע = '
	ח = ḥ	פ = p
ב = b	ט = ṭ	פ = ph or p
ב = bh or b	י = y	צ = ẓ
ג = g	כ = k	ק = ḳ
ג = gh or g	כ = kh or k	ר = r
ד = d	ל = l	שׂ = s
ד = dh or d	מ = m	שׁ = sh
ה = h	נ = n	ת = t
ו = w	ס = s	ת = th or t

The vowels are transcribed by a, e, i, o, u, without attempt to indicate quantity or quality. Arabic and other Semitic languages are transliterated according to the same system as Hebrew. Greek is written with Roman characters, the common equivalents being used.

KEY TO PRONUNCIATION

When the pronunciation is self-evident the titles are not respelled; when by mere division and accentuation it can be shown sufficiently clearly the titles have been divided into syllables, and the accented syllables indicated.

a	as in sof*a*	e	as in n*o*t	iu	as in d*u*ration
ā	" " *arm*	ŏ	" " n*o*r	c = k	" " *cat*
a	" " *at*	u	" " f*u*ll[2]	ch	" " *church*
ā	" " *fare*	ū	" " r*u*le	cw = qu	as in *queen*
e	" " *pen*[1]	υ	" " b*u*t	dh (*th*)	" " *the*
ê	" " *fate*	ʊ	" " b*u*rn	f	" " *fancy*
i	" " *tin*	ai	" " p*i*ne	g (hard)	" " *go*
î	" " *machine*	au	" " *out*	н	" " *loch* (Scotch)
o	" " *obey*	ei	" " *oil*	hw (*wh*)	" " *why*
ō	" " *no*	iū	" " *few*	j	" " *jaw*

---

[1] In accented syllables only; in unaccented syllables it approximates the sound of e in over. The letter ṇ, with a dot beneath it, indicates the sound of n as in ink. Nasal n (as in French words) is rendered n.

[2] In German and French names ü approximates the sound of u in dune.

THE NEW SCHAFF-HERZOG

ENCYCLOPEDIA OF RELIGIOUS KNOWLEDGE

SON OF MAN: An expression occurring in the four Gospels as referring to Jesus no less than eighty-one times, elsewhere in the New Testament in this sense only once (Acts vii. 56). In addition to these instances, it is found in Dan. vii. 13 and Enoch xxxvii.–lxxi (cf. Job xxv. 6; Ps. viii. 4; Num. xxiii. 19; Ezek. ii. 1 et passim; Rev. xiv. 14). In the Gospels this title is associated with Jesus in three relations: his earthly life (Mark ii. 10; Luke xix. 10), his sufferings (Mark viii. 31), and his second advent (Matt. xxv. 31, xxvi. 64). The obscurity which veils the origin of the term whether traced to the book of Enoch, or to Daniel, or to both, as well as the various and contrasting uses of it, has given rise to wide diversity of interpretations. Among these are: (1) he was man and nothing human was foreign to him (F. C. Baur, *ZWT*, 1860, pp. 274 sqq.); (2) he is the heavenly ideal man (W. Beyschlag, *Die Christologie des Neuen Testaments*, pp. 9 sqq., Berlin, 1866); (3) he is head of the race in which type and ideal are realized (V. H. Stanton, *Jewish and Christian Messiah*, p. 246, New York, 1886); (4) it indicates a Messiah to whom suffering and sympathy are natural, destined to glory through suffering (A. B. Bruce, *Kingdom of God*, p. 176, New York, 1889); (5) it calls attention first of all to the lowliness of his appearance (H. H. Wendt, *Die Lehre Jesu*, p. 440, Göttingen, 1890; Eng. transl., *Teaching of Jesus*, ii. 139, Edinburgh, 1892); (6) as man, his glory lies through suffering, as the servant of Yahweh (V. Bartlett, *Expositor*, Dec., 1892, pp. 427–443), or as in the book of Daniel (R. H. Charles, *Book of Enoch*, Appendix B, Oxford, 1893); (7) a contrast is set up between his lowliness and his greatness (G. Dalman, *Die Worte Jesu*, Leipsic, 1898; Eng. transl., *The Words of Jesus*, pp. 255 sqq., Edinburgh, 1902); (8) it contains a veiled designation of messiahship (G. B. Stevens, *Theology of the New Testament*, p. 53, New York, 1899; cf. Otto Holtzmann, *Life of Jesus*, p. 168, London, 1904); (9) it signifies Jesus' human nature, i.e., "man" in general (N. Schmidt, *Prophet of Nazareth*, p. 120, New York, 1905). The expression "son of man" means that the kingdom of God, although originating in a supersensible world (Dan. vii. 13–14), is established among men by one who is exempted from no position or lot which belongs essentially to his fellow-men in the purpose of God. If by virtue of inner ethical unity with the Father Jesus has become aware of his unique vocation as Messiah, yet he will interpret this consciousness by a term which, instead of dissolving the tie between him and other men, only discloses the deeper identity of ideal aim which belongs to him and them alike.   C. A. BECKWITH.

BIBLIOGRAPHY: The subject is discussed in the principal treatises in the life of Jesus Christ, e.g., Keim, and Weiss; of course in the commentaries on Daniel and on the Gospels, some of which contain excursuses on the subject; in the works on messianic prophecy (see under MESSIAH, MESSIANISM); in the commentaries on Enoch (see under PSEUDEPIGRAPHA); and in the discussions of Biblical theology, especially H. J. Holtzmann's, i. 246–264, Freiburg, 1896. Consult further: C. H. Weisse, *Die Evangelienfrage*, pp. 22 sqq., Leipsic, 1856; F. C. Baur, in *ZWT*, 1860, pp. 277 sqq.; T. Colani, *Jesus Christ et les croyances messianiques*, pp. 74 sqq., Strasburg, 1864; W. C. Van Manen, in *ThT*, 1890, p. 544, 1894, pp. 177 sqq.; H. H. Wendt, *Die Lehre Jesu*, pp. 441 sqq., Göttingen, 1890; W. Baldensperger, *Selbstbewusstsein Jesu*, pp. 169 sqq., Strasburg, 1892; R. H. Charles, *Book of Enoch*, pp. 312–317, Oxford, 1893; J. Wellhausen, *Israelitische und jüdische Geschichte*, pp. 346 sqq., Berlin, 1895; idem, *Skizzen und Vorarbeiten*, vi. 187 sqq., ib. 1899; H. Lietzmann, *Der Menschensohn*, Tübingen, 1896; idem, in *Theologische Arbeiten aus dem rheinischen Predigerverein*, 1898, part 2, pp. 1–14; N. Schmidt, *JBL*, 1896, pp. 36–53; A. Réville, *Jesus de Nazareth*, ii. 190 sqq., Paris, 1897; G. Dalman, *Die Worte Jesu*, pp. 191 sqq., Leipsic, 1898, Eng. transl., *The Words of Jesus*, Edinburgh, 1902; Schmiedel, in *Protestantische Monatshefte*, 1898, pp. 252–267, 291–308, 1901, pp. 333 sqq.; J. F. H. Gunkel, in *ZWT*, 1899, pp. 581 sqq.; P. Fiebig, *Der Menschensohn*, Tübingen, 1901; J. Drummond, in *JTS*, Apr. and July, 1901; G. B. Stevens, *Teaching of Jesus*, pp. 91 sqq., New York, 1901; W. Bousset, *Jesus*, New York, 1906; F. Bard, *Der Sohn des Menschen. Eine Untersuchung über Begriff und Inhalt und Absicht solcher Jesubezeichnung*, Wismar, 1908; E. A. Abbott, *The Message of the Son of Man*, New York, 1909; *DB*, iv. 579–589; *EB*, iv. 4705–40; *DCG*, ii. 659–665.

SONER, ERNST. See SOCINUS, FAUSTUS, SOCINIANS, I., § 3.

SONG OF SOLOMON
(SONG OF SONGS, CANTICLES).

The Song of Solomon (Song of Songs, Canticles) is the book which follows Ecclesiastes in the arrangement of the English Bible. The title in Hebrew, "Song of Songs which is Solomon's," conveys the idea that it is the noblest of songs, the author of which is Solomon. It is clearly a love song, but whether to be understood of earthly or spiritual love is the question. Its date is long after Solomon's time. Since the time of Herder its unity has been denied by many, and it has been regarded as a collection of love songs. But commentators agree on the principal Dramatic characters as being King Solomon, his beloved (a peasant maiden), and the daughters [i.e., female residents] of Jerusalem. Peculiarities of speech abound from beginning to end. And there are characteristic expressions which repeat themselves with slight variations throughout (cf. ii. 7, iii. 5, viii. 4, and v. 8; iii. 6, vi. 10, and viii. 5; ii. 17, iv. 6, and viiii. 14; ii. 6, and viiii. 3; i. 2 and iv. 10; ii. 5 and v. 8). Many parts are parallels (cf. ii. 8 sqq., iii. 1 sqq., and v. 2 sqq.). In view of the many unmistakable interrelationships and indications of unity which bind the poem together (cf. i. 6 with viii. 12), it may be regarded as proved that the parts of the poem are well welded together. But since different voices are heard in the song and since the scenes change, the piece can not be taken as purely lyric; it is dramatic poetry, examples of which are found also in the Psalms (ii. and xxiv.). But it is necessary for the understanding of the whole to mark off the scenes, to determine the *dramatis personæ*, and to apportion the text among them although the text contains no express directions for doing this. Near to King Solomon stands a celebrated beauty who in vi. 13 is called the Shulamite (from the village of Shulam, modern Sulam, formerly Shunem; cf. I Kings i. 3), a maiden from the country characterized by a noble grace and unaffected humility. According to the older view not only is this one honored by the king, but his enraptured preference is prized and his affection tenderly returned; the newer and till recently dominant conception was that she affirms her love for a third person and over against the homage of the king sets the praise of a simple shepherd of her native heath until finally the king yields the field and fidelity conquers. Into the mouth of this rival of Solomon's certain parts are put, or at least the maiden speaks them as though they were the words which he would speak were he present. It is evident how differently the poem will be construed whether the viewpoint is that of a pouring-out of confession of love by two united spirits or the contest of two rivals in which the simple shepherd gains the victory over the king.

The last view is held by so weighty authorities that it is in the main points to be followed. According to Ewald and others the following story is gained from indications in the poem.

2. Narrative of the Drama. In one of his journeys to the north of his kingdom the king had come to the neighborhood of Shulam when some in his train found in a nut-garden (vi. 11–12) an attractive maiden in a condition of delighted ecstasy. Although somewhat hardly treated by her own people and put to guard a vineyard near, she displays so rare a grace that the king desires her for his harem. With this encounter the first scene begins (i. 1 sqq.), in which she states that she has given her heart to a shepherd of her own home to whom she will be true in spite of all the allurements of the king and of his surroundings.

1. The Interpretation; Dramatic Theory.

The conflict intensifies in the course of the poem as the suit of the king becomes more eager and pressing. While he praises her, she answers with the eulogies of her beloved. In this elevated state of feeling she hopes to see him and to hear his voice (ii. 8 sqq., iii. 5, cf. viii. 4); in her dreams she seeks him in the streets of Jerusalem until she finds him. The contest reaches its climax when Solomon makes her the offer of his throne. As his queen in due right he carries her to his capital, but even this fails of its purpose, since her vision returns to her beloved. The king then makes a final attempt to win her by the influence of magical words (vi. 4 sqq.). But as her longing for home becomes still more irresistible he renounces her and dismisses her in peace to her own possessions. In the last act she arrives home with her friends where the bonds of love are sealed. The moral of the piece is in vii. 6; love is unconquerable, inextinguishable, unpurchasable. True love wins the victory.

It can not be denied that this hypothesis is very attractive and avoids many difficulties, putting as it does at the close a moral which is drawn from an incident portrayed in dramatic colors, but perhaps not altogether fictitious, in the life of the splendor-loving king. The moral verity harmoniously expressed at the close becomes not unworthy of the higher tone of the canonical books generally, even though allegory have almost nothing to do with the poem. The firmly-true betrothed may as well have her memorial in the Scriptures as the virtuous wife. Still on a closer examination this understanding of the poem is not altogether unassailable. Decidedly against it is the following circumstance: iii. 6 to v. 1 describes precisely the royal wedding-day, ending in the royal bridegroom's gratification in the assured obtaining of all his desires. If this wedding, according to the conception of the rivalry of the shepherd, must become tragic, while not once in this passage does the required impotence of love appear, through the last words of the Shulamite (iv. 16) the whole finely conceived theory of the unwillingness of the shepherd-betrothed to yield to the king falls apart. In this section, where the relations of love find their most concrete form, the sponsors for the shepherd theory find no support. Decisive appears vii. 11 sqq., where the Shulamite, in words impossible to misunderstand, promises herself, her person (her own vineyard), fully and wholly to Solomon, but only a moderate reward to her guardians, her brothers, in which she refers to the general custom followed by Solomon.

Other reflections against the shepherd hypothesis have only recently been appreciated. The hypothesis set forth by Herder and others of an unconnected anthology of marriage songs has been accepted, for example by Budde and others who find in Wetzstein's communications about the celebration of marriage in modern Syria the solution of the puzzle. The latter published in Bastian's *Zeitschrift für Ethnologie,* 1873, an article on the " Syrian Threshing Floor " in which the threshing-floor in the " king's week " comes in for discussion. The primitive threshing-

3. Objections to this Theory.

4. Syrian Marriage-week Theory.

implement, consisting of two plain planks bent outward, is used in the marriage week to make the throne upon which bride and groom take their seat of honor, as they play for the week the part of king and queen, watching the games produced in their honor and listening to the songs sung in competition. Among these songs is always one which commends the beauty of bride and groom, for the composition of which they summon the best poet obtainable. An especial part is the sword-dance song which the bride sings on the evening before the wedding (while with a sword she keeps at a distance the groom), the singing of which gives the company an occasion to extol her charms; on the second day the praise of the wedded queen is sung with more of reserve. On this interpretation it follows that the poem has to do with a marriage among peasants in town or country in which the bridegroom plays the part of king. Just so the Shulamite appears only once, is so called with reference to Abigail of Shunem, the most beautiful woman in Israel, and is herself the most beautiful of women. The sword dance of the bride, and particularly the song in praise of the betrothed, is discerned in vii. 2 sqq., though it should stand at the beginning of the poem; the more moderate song to the wedded bride is seen in iv. 1–6, that to the spouse in chap. v. The entire poem is a collection of songs which have no other bond than that they sing of wedded love; moreover, they are not arranged in the order in which they are employed. Budde discovers not less than twenty-three such songs or fragments, while Siegfried discovers only ten.

But not even with this explanation has the last word been spoken. That the unity of the whole is strongly evident was remarked at the first. The form is throughout delicate and refined and leaves the productions of the threshing-floor poet far in the rear. With this delicacy is contrasted the simple rusticity of scene in many of the parts. The contrast between the court dames and the shepherdess appears in chap. i. Different is the fact that the Shulamite extols her beloved as white and ruddy (v. 10; cf. 14), which, according to Lam. iv. 7, describes his noble rank while she herself, according to i. 5–6, can not disavow the evidences of her country origin. She nowhere appears as queen, a position which is demanded on the Budde hypothesis. That the Wetzstein data of the marriage-week usages and songs are very serviceable in the explanation of the Song, Franz Delitzsch long ago perceived. He saw in vii. 2 sqq. the description of the dancer (but of the sword there is here no word); while the Hebrew marriage festival continued seven days, varied performances of a festal character found place without necessitating a very complete unity, such as the playing of the maiden lover, her search on all sides, and her finding of happy companionship. Budde's remark may also be noticed, to the effect that the Song is a text-book of the Palestinian-Israelitic wedding ceremony. But this text-book is not a collection of shepherd- and peasant-songs, though the most beautiful popular songs are found therein; it is an art-poem, perhaps composed for the celebration of some definite mar-

5. Objections to this Theory.

riage, the composer of which represented the groom as Solomon and the bride as the Shulamite. The union of these two were, according to our hypothesis, set forth, as Delitzsch and Zöckler rightly perceived. So she loves in him not the king, nor does she require sensual pleasure nor riches; she seeks only to find in him real companionship as though he were her brother and friend and of the rank of shepherd as she is herself. Such love is strong as death and unpurchasable. If the rural environment is looked on rather as poetic adornment than as trustworthy narrative, let iv. 8 have its weight and one need not have recourse to Budde's theory of a gloss.

How the Song is to be understood the last act teaches. It is the love of a bride with its longings and hopes, its search and discovery, its disillusioning and surprises, the pure love which as a divine spark suffers nothing impure and through its might overcomes all earthly obstacles, set forth here in rare completeness in the two noblest exemplars the author could find. This object is in itself not unworthy of the Bible, all the more that the opposition to a simply sensual or sham affection works out in the poem. Were there not something lofty and mysterious in the love of a bride for her husband, it could not elsewhere be used as the picture of the holiest relations. The value of the canonical Song of Songs becomes noticeable first when one remarks the singular worth of the king whom it mentions. Solomon was to the consciousness of his times like David the anointed of the Lord, the Messiah, who stood to the people for the invisible King of kings. If now such a king, in the way the poet describes as he follows some tradition, seeking a purer and holier love than he found in the capital, determined to elevate a simple daughter of the people to the highest honor, the while she offered him wifely love in complete purity, such a marriage would be like that of the Messiah sung in Ps. xlv., an achievement in the visible kingdom of God, which would find itself repeated the oftener among posterity the more they learned from the prophets.

Without difficulty the notion might spring up that Solomon was himself the author of this poem which deals with himself. Anew in favor of this has been adduced the imagery of the Song, built up out of the plant-world, the geographical relations with the whole Solomonic kingdom from Lebanon to Engedi, the connection with Ps. lxxii., attributed to Solomon, the poet of 1,005 songs (I Kings v. 12). But the person pictured in the poem with the brilliancy of Solomon is evidently a matter of poetic interest in one who is removed from the poet in time. The vocabulary of the poem is individual, the little piece having between fifty and sixty *hapaxlegomena;* if it is pre-exilic, it must belong to the north. Grätz has found little sympathy with his idea that the poem displays a knowledge of Greek custom and is dependent upon the Idyls of Theocritus. Oettli argues for a pre-exilic date, König and Strack place it about 500 B.C. Under the shepherd hypothesis the piece would have been lost; into the Judaic canon this anti-Solomonic tendency-writing could not have come nor Solomonic authorship been attributed to it. Also on the threshing-

6. Authorship and Date.

floor hypothesis the lofty designation of the Song and the allegorical interpretation are hard to explain. How comes it that the scribes did not recognize this song which on the hypothesis was sung at every Palestinian wedding, and that the playing at being king was so grossly misunderstood, a custom which has lasted until modern times? On the explanation given here the Song has higher claims on regard, and the time of its composition is entirely a subordinate question.　　　　　(C. VON ORELLI.)

BIBLIOGRAPHY: On matters of introduction consult the works named in and under BIBLICAL INTRODUCTION, especially Driver, pp. 436–453; J. G. Herder, *Lieder der Liebe, die ältesten und schönsten aus dem Morgenlande*, Leipsic, 1778; E. Cunitz, *Hist. critique de l'interpretation du cantique des cantiques*, Strasburg, 1834; A. L. Newton, *The Song of Solomon Compared with other Parts of Scripture*, New York, 1867; E. Renan, *Le Cantique des cantiques, . . . avec une étude sur le plan, l'âge et le caractère du poème*, 4th ed., Paris, 1879; S. Salfeld, *Das Hohe Lied Salomons bei den jüdischen Erklärer des Mittelalters*, Berlin, 1879; G. Bickell, *Carmina Veteris Testamenti*, Innsbruck, 1882; J. G. Stickel, *Das Hohelied in seiner Einheit und dramatischen Gliederung*, Berlin, 1888; R. Martineau, in *American Journal of Philology*, 1892, pp. 307–328; W. Riedel, *Die Auslegung des Hohen Lieds in der jüdischen Gemeinde und der griechischen Kirche*, Leipsic, 1898; *DB*, iv. 589–597; *EB*, i. 681–695; *JE*, xi. 466–467.

Commentaries are: H. Ewald, Göttingen, 1826; J. C. Döpke, Leipsic, 1829; B. Hirzel, Zurich, 1840; E. J. Magnus, Halle, 1842; F. Böttcher, Leipsic, 1850; F. Delitzsch, Leipsic, 1851; H. A. Hahn, Breslau, 1852; G. Burrowes, Philadelphia, 1853; E. W. Hengstenberg, Berlin, 1853; J. Gill, London, 1854; F. Hitzig, Leipsic, 1855; C. D. Ginsburg, London, 1857; L. Withington, Boston, 1861; J. F. Thrupp, London, 1862; R. F. Littledale, London, 1869; A. M. Stuart, Philadelphia, 1869; H. Cowles, New York, 1870; H. Grätz, Vienna, 1871; F. C. Cook, in *Bible Commentary*, London, 1874; O. Zöckler, in Lange's Commentary, New York, 1875; B. Schäfer, Münster, 1876; T. Gessner, Quakenbrück, 1881; S. J. Kämpf, 3d ed., Prague, 1884; P. Schegg, Munich, 1885; W. C. Daland, Leonardsville, N. Y., 1888; J. G. Stickel, Berlin, 1888; W. E. Griffis, *The Lily among Thorns*, Boston, 1889; S. Oettli, Nordlingen, 1889; Le Hir, Paris, 1890; D. Castelli, Florence, 1892; M. Rainsford, London, 1892; R. A. Redford, in *Pulpit Commentary*, New York, 1893; J. W. Rothstein, Halle, 1893; M. S. Terry, Cincinnati, 1893; C. Bruston, 2d ed., Paris, 1894; E. Réveillaud, Paris, 1895; K. Budde, Freiburg, 1898; C. Siegfried, Göttingen, 1898; P. Baarts, Nuremberg, 1901; A. Harper, in *Cambridge Bible*, Cambridge, 1902; V. Zapletal, Freiburg, 1907; G. C. Martin, in *Century Bible*, London, 1908; P. Haupt, Leipsic, 1908; J. Hontheim, Freiburg, 1908; P. Joüon, Paris, 1909.

SONG OF SONGS. See SONG OF SOLOMON.

SOPHRONIUS, so-frō′nĭ-ŭs: The name of two men of note in the early Church.

1. A contemporary of Jerome, whom the latter describes (*De vir. ill.*, cxxxiv., *NPNF*, 2 ser., iii. 384) as " a man of superlative learning " who wrote while a lad a *Laudes Bethlehem*, and later a book on " The Overthrow of Serapis " (i.e., the destruction of the Serapeum in Alexandria in 392). But perhaps his best title to distinction in Jerome's eyes was his translation into Greek of certain works by the latter, viz., *De virginitate*, *Vita Hilarion*, and of Jerome's rendering of the Psalter and the Prophets. The translation of the *Vita* was published by A. Papadopulos-Kerameus in *Analekta Hierosolymitikes strachuologias*, v. 82–136 (St. Petersburg, 1898). Recently Sophronius has been held to be the author of the Greek translation of Jerome's *De vir. ill.*, this upon the authority of Erasmus, for which further authority fails. The translation in question be-

longs perhaps to the period between the sixth or seventh and the ninth century.

2. The sophist and patriarch of Jerusalem; b. at Damascus; d. in 638, his day in the Greek Church being March 11. He tells at the close of his panegyric of St. Cyrus and St. John of his origin at Damascus of parents known as Plynthas and Myro. He was a monk. His birth year has been guessed as 550, in which case he must have been eighty or eighty-five when he became patriarch—not impossible, indeed, but unlikely, considering his activity. His learning must have been noteworthy, his title of " sophist " referring to his lectures on rhetoric. He was in Egypt in 579, but was not then a monk, entering the cloister on his return in 580, making that his home for thirty years, though leaving it for journeys through Palestine in company with John Moschus. During the lifetime of the Patriarch Eulogius (d. 607) the two friends visited Alexandria again, coming into close relations with Eulogius and with his successor, Johannes Eleemon (q.v.). There Sophronius was attacked with a disease of the eyes, the cure of which he attributed to the saints Cyrus and John. During the stay there, lasting ten years, news came of the capture of Jerusalem by the Persians in 614, which led Sophronius to compose an ode of lamentation. Soon after the friends went to Rome, where Moschus wrote the *Pratum spirituale*, which he dedicated to his companion. There Moschus died, and Sophronius carried his body back to Palestine probably in 619 (not 634), after which he reentered the monastery. In 633 he was again in Alexandria to treat with the Patriarch Cyrus against union with the Apollinarians (see MONOTHELITES); failing in his mission there he went to Constantinople, where he fared no better; in 634 he was made patriarch of Jerusalem, a reward for his activities against monothelitism and monergism. In his inaugural, he dealt with the doctrinal contest, and called attention to the danger from the Saracens. He lived to see the assault on Jerusalem and fell into the hands of Omar, probably at the beginning of 638, and soon after died, probably an exceedingly aged man.

The uncertainty whether Sophronius the sophist and Sophronius the patriarch are the same person appears also in considering his writings, though they furnish strong arguments for the identity, especially in the rhythmic law of the double dactylic close which appears in the writings. Yet this was a common practise and the argument is not conclusive. So the Anacreontic odes appear to belong to the sophist, and one from the time of the patriarchate is not yet known. Of the prose works may be named such hagiographic writings as (1) the *Laudes in SS. Cyrum et Johannem* (*MPG*, lxxxvii. 3, cols. 3379–3676), the saints to whom Sophronius attributed relief from the trouble with his eyes; it falls into two parts, the encomium and a narrative of seventy miracles by the saints, and was written before 615. (2) The life of Johannes Eleemon, probably a joint composition of Sophronius and Moschus, completed by the former after the death of the latter; it is no longer extant, but probably Simeon Metaphrastes copied it in the first chapters of his *Vita*. (3) *Vita Mariæ Ægyptiæ* (*MPG*, ut sup., cols. 3697–3726) is attributed to him on account of a notice in the Munich manuscript, but John of Damascus does not name the author and its authorship is disputed also on internal grounds. (4) *Acta martyrii Anastasiæ Persiæ* is ascribed in a Florentine manuscript to George of Pisidia and printed in his works (*MPG*, xcii. 1680–1829), but by Usener is attributed to Sophronius on the basis of the Berlin manuscript Phill. 1458. (5) According to Papadopulos-Kerameus (*Hierosolymitikē Bibliothēkē*, iv. 162–163, St. Petersburg, 1899) a life of the Four Evangelists is to be ascribed to Sophronius. (6) The *Pratum Spirituale* of Moschus was possibly revised or edited by Sophronius, to whom tradition ascribed it. In *MPG* (ut sup.), cols. 3201–3364, appear eight (or nine) orations, to which A. Papadopulos-Kerameus (in *Analecta*, ut sup., v. 151–168) adds a tenth. Of dogmatic works may be noted the *Epistola synodica* (*MPG*, ut sup., cols. 3147–3200), two fragments on confession of sins and the baptism of the apostles (cols. 3365–72) and one on a decision of Basil of Cæsarea (cols. 4011–12); and possibly a collection of about 600 sayings of the Fathers; a " Dogmatic Discourse on Faith " (cf. Papadopulos-Kerameus, *Bibliothēkē*, ii. 403, ut sup.). The prayer still recited on Epiphany in the Greek Church (*MPG*, ut sup., 4001–04) is carried back to Sophronius.

In the history of Greek church poetry the Anacreontic odes ascribed to Sophronius are very celebrated; many critics, indeed, compare them with the products of the golden age of Greek literature. With this valuation Krumbacher totally disagrees, but his harshly unfavorable decision (*Geschichte*, p. 672) is not well supported. Many of the poems have a warm, appealing, and personal note, together with a certain independence in the choice of poetic figures. Twenty-two odes are to be found in *MPG* (ut sup., cols. 3725–3838), and some of them appear in various reprints and anthologies. The first thirteen arose in the period of his first stay in the monastery, the rest either during his wanderings or during his second monastic period. Sophronius also wrote occasional poems.

The foregoing discussion assumes the identity of Sophronius the patriarch and Sophronius the sophist. This identity has been disputed. The problems are better settled by assuming the identity than by assuming two personalities, and tradition supports this, especially as represented by John of Damascus (*MPG*, xciv. 1280, 1316, 1336) and Johannes Zonaras (" Life of Sophronius," in Papadopulos-Kerameus, *Analecta*, ut sup., v. 137–151). A final decision must be awaited until a final critical edition of the works appears. (G. KRÜGER.)

BIBLIOGRAPHY: On 1: G. Wentzel, in *TU*, xiii. 3 (1895); O. von Gebhardt, in *TU*, xiv. 1 (1896); M. Schanz, *Geschichte der römischen Litteratur*, iv. 407–408, 448–449, Munich, 1904; *DCB*, iv. 718; Ceillier, *Auteurs sacrés*, vi. 278–279, vii. 553, 595; *KL*, xi. 519–520.
On 2 consult: John of Damascus, *MPG*, xciv. 1280, 1316, 1336; Photius, in *MPG*, ciii. 668; Eustathius, in Mansi, *Concilia*, xiii. 60; Krumbacher, *Geschichte*, pp. 188 sqq. et passim; Fabricius-Harles, *Bibliotheca Græca*, ix. 162–169, Hamburg, 1804; A. Mai, *Spicilegium Romanum*, iii., pp. v.–xx.,10 vols., Rome, 1839–44; E. Bouvy, *Poètes et mélodes*, pp. 169–182, 195 sqq., Nîmes, 1886 (on the literary characteristics); H. Usener, *Religionsgeschichtliche Untersuchungen*, i. 326–330, Bonn, 1889; H. Gelzer, in *Historische Zeitschrift*, lxi (1889), 4; idem, *Leontios' von Neapolis Leben des heiligen Johannes des Barmherzigen*, pp. 117–120, Freiburg, 1893; W. Meyer, *Der akzentuierte Satzschluss in der griechischen Prosa vom 4. bis zum 16. Jahrhundert*, Göttingen, 1891; Johannes Zonaras, *Vita Sophronii*, in A. Papadopulos-Kerameus, *Analecta*, v. 137–151, St. Petersburg, 1898; S. Vailhé, in *Revue de l'orient chrétien*, vii (1902), 360–385, viii (1903), 32–69, 356–387 (gives list of earlier literature); *DCB*, iv. 719–721; *KL*, xi. 516–519.

SORBONNE, sor'ben: A school at Paris, founded in 1254 by Robert de Sorbon (1201–70), canon of Notre Dame and confessor and counselor of Louis IX., for poor theological students, and later dominating not only the theological faculty, but also the entire University of Paris. Primarily designed for those who were unable to pay the high prices demanded for board and lodging, and to instruct those who were not in sympathy with the scholastic subtleties propounded in the other schools, as well as with the added design of having the teachers reside in the same house as their pupils, the Sorbonne was established in the Rue Coupe-Gorge, opposite the baths of the Emperor Julian. Robert himself made a small endowment for his foundation, which later received many augmentations, although he earnestly desired that the institution might never become rich. The members of the Sorbonne were not bound by monastic rules, and its regulations, formulated by Robert after eighteen years of testing, remained almost unchanged until the Revolution. According to these regulations, published at Paris in 1740 under the title *Disciplina Sorbonæ domus*, there were three classes of members of the Sorbonne: *socii* (" fellows "), who were not bound to residence within its precincts; *hospites* (" guests "), chiefly priests living in the house; and *beneficiarii* (" beneficiaries"), who were either poor French aspirants for the ministry receiving free maintenance while preparing for the priesthood, or well-to-do foreign students who, on payment, might reside there for several months. The *socii* and *hospites* formed the majority. The latter were admitted only after a rigid examination in character and theology, and no one could become a *socius* unless he had been a *hospes* for several years, the new *socius* likewise pledging himself in the chapel of the Sorbonne to obey all the regulations and never to enter a monastic order. The *hospites* and *socii*, both those who enjoyed free residence and those who paid (the charge originally being three sous weekly, later increased to six), ate at the same table and had the same rights, the house providing bread and wine, although other food had to be purchased. When a *hospes* received his licentiate in theology, he gave place to another. No one was permitted to remain longer than ten years, although the title of *socius Sorbonæ* was inalienable. The officers were elected by the members, the term being for one year, except in the case of the president (*provisor*), who had control of discipline. The prior kept the keys and directed the studies and examinations, the librarian had charge of the books, and the censor drew up the reports of the council. There was also a standing committee, composed of the oldest *socii* elected from each " nation " (cf.

Foundation and Organization.

UNIVERSITIES) which supervised the moral conditions of the Sorbonne, as well as a finance committee and a committee to supervise the clergy. The *socii* met in general assembly four times annually.

Robert de Sorbon sought not only to furnish shelter for poor clerks, but also to provide thorough theological instruction for them, the mornings being devoted to Old-Testament exegesis and the afternoons to the interpretation of the New Testament. For two centuries the teachers were chosen from
the former *socii* or *hospites*, nor was it
Courses of until 1532 that a legacy rendered pos-
Study. sible the foundation of a paid lecture-
ship. Between 1577 and 1625 six other chairs were established, and later still teachers were drawn from other colleges of the university, while as early as 1270 Robert de Sorbon, recognizing that students of divinity should first have a good literary and philosophical training, established, as an annex to the Sorbonne, the Collège de Calvi for this purpose. In the Sorbonne itself the course was threefold: reading and interpretation of the Bible and of the maxims of the Church Fathers, disputations, and preaching. The exegetical exercises were held twice daily, each student being required to write a summary of the main points presented; the disputations, upon some theme previously announced, took place between two students each Sunday, a *socius* being the presiding officer; but preaching seems to have received little attention. A most important part of the Sorbonne was its library, founded by Robert and enriched with manuscripts by Guiard d'Abbeville, while in 1469 the prior of the Sorbonne, acting in harmony with the rector of the university, established the first printing-press in France, whence the Bible of 1478 was issued.

The Sorbonne furnished the leaders of the University of Paris who, in the fifteenth century, demanded the reform of the Church by a general council; but in the following century the institution
became hostile to the new spirit, cen-
History. suring the writings of Erasmus and
Faber Stapulensis, and condemning the works of Luther and Melanchthon. In the seventeenth century it was the leader of Roman Catholicism in France, and such prelates as Richelieu, Mazarin, De Retz, and De Noailles considered it a distinction to be elected *provisor* of the Sorbonne. Richelieu in particular manifested affection for the institution, taking one of its *hospites* for his confessor, completely rebuilding it, and desiring to be buried in its chapel. A century later the Sorbonne defended the new spirit of the times, but in 1791 the Convention decreed the suppression of the " priests of the Sorbonne," although the 160 *socii* were unmolested, and even Revolutionary vandalism spared the chapel with its tomb of Richelieu. When, after the concordat, Napoleon organized the University of France (1808), he established at the Sorbonne a faculty of Roman Catholic theology, to which the Bourbons added the faculties of letters and sciences, the whole organization bearing the name of Sorbonne. Since, however, Leo XIII. refused the institution canonical recognition, it became useless for the education of the higher clergy, and it was accordingly suppressed by the Chamber

of Deputies in 1885. Since that year the Sorbonne has been entirely rebuilt (1889), and by reorganization it now forms part of the University of Paris.
(G. BONET-MAURY.)

BIBLIOGRAPHY: C. E. Bulæus, *Hist. Universitatis Parisensis*, 6 vols., Paris, 1665–73, *Continuation* (by C. Jourdain), ib. 1862–64; T. I. Duvernet, *Hist. de la Sorbonne*, Paris, 1790; A. Morellet, *Mémoires*, 2d ed., Paris, 1822; C. Jourdain, *Index chartarum pertinentium ad hist. Universitatis Parisensis*, Paris, 1862; A. Franklin, *La Sorbonne, Ses origines et sa bibliothèque*, 2d ed., Paris, 1875; M. Jadart, *Robert de Sorbon*, Reims, 1880; H. Denifle, *Documents relatifs à la fondation et aux premiers temps de l'université*, Paris, 1883; G. Bonet-Maury, in *Vie chrétienne*, Nîmes, 1884; E. Méric, *La Sorbonne et son fondateur*, Reims, 1888; O. Gréard, *Nos adieux à la vieille Sorbonne*, Paris, 1893; P. Féret, *La Faculté de théologie de Paris*, 8 vols., Paris, 1894–1905; H. Rashdall, *The Universities of Europe in the Middle Ages*, 2 vols., Oxford, 1895; H. Calhiat, *Les Grandes Figures chrétiennes de la Sorbonne au xix. siècle*, Paris, 1896; L. Delisle, in *Journal des savants*, Paris, 1898; Claudin, in *Bulletin des bibliophiles*, 1898; P. Alary, *L'Imprimerie au xvi. siècle, Étienne Dolet et ses luttes contre la Sorbonne*, Paris, 1898; G. Compayré, *Abelard and the Origin and Early Hist. of Universities*, pp. 156, 205, 300, New York, 1899; H. P. Nénot, *Monographie de la nouvelle Sorbonne*, Paris, 1903; Schaff, *Christian Church*, v. 1, p. 572.

SORCERY AND SOOTHSAYING.

Description and Extent (§ 1).
Among Primitive Races (§ 2).
Among Civilized Peoples (§ 3).
Among Hebrews (§ 4).
In the Christian Church (§ 5).

By sorcery as viewed by Christians is meant an employment of demonic power in the service of men, and it is therefore regarded as a gross sin against God because the Christian should trust in God alone.
Christian conceptions thus square with
1. Descrip- those of the Old and the New Testa-
tion and ment. Among polytheistic religions the
Extent. phases of sorcery are many and varied, and a definition sufficiently comprehensive is difficult to give. Its operations neither depend upon competent physical experiences nor do they rest upon ethical mediation; it is arbitrary meddling of men with supernatural or at least secret powers. As a rule sorcery deals with spirits—personal powers of the unseen world, whence is the connection with religion. The sorcerer works through word, look, gesture, and varied operations such as the tying of knots, the giving of drinks and concoctions, behind which a profounder meaning and connection lie hidden. One precondition for the rise of belief in sorcery is the existence of a realm of unexplained and inexplicable phenomena; the larger this is, the more room there is for sorcery, so that the latter reigns in the lowest culture. Moreover, there must be a trust in man's ability to accomplish such works in unison with higher powers. Animism and polydemonism are the native homes of sorcery, monotheism and ethics make against it. The relation to religion depends upon the conception of religion; some regard sorcery as an evidence of religion and a tendency of religious life, others as a conscious alienation from deity. Some members of the anthropological school regard it as the first stage in religious development, deriving prayer from sorcery or avertive exercises. The lowest races show, however, a sense of dependence upon the unseen; their attitude is not one of command entirely. Sorcery

is a later phenomenon in development, is allied to Magic (q.v.), is found alongside of religion, but in it religion itself is not to be found. Indeed, sorcery tends to drown out religion or to drive it into the background; the more meager religion is, the more luxuriant are the parasitic growths of sorcery. Yet it is a fact that the sorcerer or Shaman (q.v.) often seeks power through a loftily conceived divinity regarded as good, aiming to subject lower and ill-disposed spirits. Magic is sorcery technically developed. Among races of the lower order there is often a science of secrets to which only the consecrated are admitted. Sorcery also has relations with Divination (q.v.), and the professions of sorcerer and diviner are often plied by the same person, who claims to have insight into the unseen and to be able to control more or less the course of events.

Among primitive peoples, then, sorcery is especially at home. Ignorance of nature leads to the belief in the possibility of supernatural operations in the sphere of man. The sorcerer covers himself with a veil of secrecy, speaks in dark figures, performs acts that are outré, thus giving **2. Among** the impression of secret power and in- **Primitive** scrutable doings. The results expected **Races.** from the exercise of these activities cover the field of man's needs and desires; moreover, evil spirits are warded off or conciliated, the cooperation of good spirits is gained. There are sorcerers and counter-sorcerers; the dangerous exerciser of these powers must be mastered by a more powerful one. The method is not to subject oneself to the will of God, as in true religion, but magic works as a concurrent with religion, and is thus irreligious and irrational. It is regarded in two ways—as a serious crime, when it produces damage; and as a high art when it averts injury and brings a blessing. To the user it seems not at all wrong to injure an enemy by sorcery, though it is a crime to use it against a friend or blood brother. Among the vicious means of sorcery, as regarded by the most varied peoples, is the evil eye, which is believed by many to be able to affect with illness and death those on whom it is cast, while the possessors are supposed, as in Africa, to meet in the desert to counsel how they shall effect their purposes. So the suspicion regarding vampires as the cause of death and illness is a concomitant of sorcery. From this " illegitimate " use of these means is distinguished a " legitimate " method, which takes especially the form of protecting from evil powers and the increase of the natural good of man in life—well-being, fruitfulness, and possessions—having the ability to ward off evil spirits. Charms and potions are employed, which, however, require for their proper use the advice of the expert. In pestilences and epidemics the counsel of these experts is needed to define the causes, and in case of guilt to determine the blame. Thus a connection is made with soothsaying and the deliverance of oracles, while the Ordeal (q.v.) is under the guardianship of this branch in the preparation of potions. Through these means the sorcerers in some regions, as in Africa, wield enormous power and influence, especially as sickness is regarded as the work of demons, whose work must be undone through the counter-sorcerer or the medi-

cine man. One of the means employed by this class is the word of power, which binds to or looses from evil, and this word only the sorcerer knows and can turn to a hundred uses. The formula is usually an unintelligible or irrational expression, the names of divine and demonic powers being included and their assistance invoked. At times the effigy of the person to whom evil is to be done is treated as the person himself is expected to suffer [after the manner of sympathetic magic; see COMPARATIVE RELIGION, VI., 1, a, § 5; other methods of using magic are described in that place]. The formula used has often a similarity to prayer, but it is utterly without ethical relations and has in mind the arbitrary will of the sorcerer, not submission to deity. A similar difference exists between prophecy and soothsaying; prophecy depends upon the will of God, soothsaying contemplates man's self-chosen purposes and employs not inspiration but certain means of attaining its ends, such as the Lot (q.v.), the interpretation of various natural phenomena, and the like, a set of rules being formulated to this purpose. The spirits of the dead are also evoked. See also DREAM.

Sorcery appears also as a custom of the civilized peoples of antiquity, and shows a great tenacity of persistence even in connection with a grade of culture with which it is not in harmony. In course of time sorcery becomes a complicated art, and its **3. Among** bonds are dissolved only by the ad- **Civilized** vance of thought, as when magic in **Peoples.** illness gives way to medicine, astrology to astronomy, and the like, though superstitious practises persist with real advance in knowledge (see SUPERSTITION). There seems to remain a feeling that external and corporeal affairs are governed by the unseen, and irrational elements and practises abide, even in partial connection with religion. This is especially true of peoples like the Chinese, among whom a certain stage of civilization has been reached with a resulting stagnation. The religion of early people had magical elements and therein showed their heathen character. The relation to deity is not purely religious, but is influenced by external factors. Thus, in Babylonia (q.v.) while such literature as the " penitential psalms " shows high ethical consciousness and a realization of sin and of repentance, the usages reveal magic practises, burning of spices, and the like. So in Egypt (q.v.), the " Book of the Dead " contains a chapter dealing with purity of heart and conscience as the essential condition of happiness after death, yet the most of the book is taken up with directions of magical character directing the soul in its course. Similarly Zoroastrianism (see ZOROASTER, ZOROASTRIANISM) is full of ethical truths, yet magical conceptions abound and Ahura Mazda comes to earth to act as priest of sorcery. Similar facts meet one in India. As among primitive peoples, so among the more advanced exists the idea of an illegitimate sorcery, which is a crime. Thus the Twelve Tables of the Roman law contained enactments against these practises, as did the Cornelian law against assassins and poisoners; the possession of books on magic was a crime [cf. for a strong passage the sixth satire of Juvenal].

Apuleius stood trial for witchcraft about 150 A.D., and Constantinian and Justinian legislation dealt with it.

The Hebrew religion took strong ground against sorcery from the beginning, though residuary traces from the former heathenism or reintroduction from surrounding sources occurred and had **4. Among** to be combated. The Hebrew word **Hebrews.** *keseph*, which forms the basis of the common terms for sorcery, etc., in Hebrew has its Assyrian cognate, and its occurrence in the feminine indicates that women were the chief practisers of the art. Death was the penalty for the crime (Lev. xx. 27; I Sam. xxviii. 9, cf. xv. 23), it being a sin which ranks with idolatry. Passages like Isa. ii. 6 show the reimportation of the practise from the East and from Philistia; but the prophets inveigh against the degradation of the worship of Yahweh into a spirit cult. The height of prophetic religion was not maintained among the people, especially under Assyrian influence sorcery resumed an unwonted sway; and after monotheism had come to its own, magical remainders and superstition furnished a background of demonic powers among which the imagination worked. Especially was belief in demons rife in the postexilic period, though their place was that of subjection, not of equality with God, and did not affect the doctrine of his unity; the name of God was invoked as an avertive power. Yet this very fact was employed magically, the name of God and of the archangels, particularly the tetragrammaton, being used both orally and written and regarded as a powerful charm. So people fell into sorcery almost unconsciously, these means being used as a sort of holy magic to oppose the unholy magic of other kinds of sorcery. The Talmud treats often of the sorcerers referred to in the Old Testament, interpreting their names generally arbitrarily; its general spirit is that of condemnation; though the methods of sorcery were to be studied, the better to combat them. Some of the great rabbis received instruction in the art, while men generally accepted sorcery as a fact; still the true Israelite was regarded as so under the protection of God that the art was powerless against him. The Cabala (q.v.) contributed to the degradation of religion from this source, as is so often the case with mystic Superstition (q.v.). The Haggada and Midrashic references to the superstition of the people are numerous, and around the person of Solomon stories gathered with reference to his mastery of the demons, whose help in building, e.g., he compelled. These legends were taken over by Islam, where the same general position with regard to sorcery obtained as in Judaism. Mohammedan missionaries often sell sentences from the Koran as amulets, and indeed the entire book serves such a purpose to those who can not read it, being regarded as an avertive of evil and a means to insure good fortune.

Christianity from its beginning has been no less uncompromisingly opposed to sorcery than Judaism; it has regarded these practises as a turning away from God and as dealing with ungodly powers. Jesus was himself suspected of using sorcery (Mark iii. 22; Luke xi. 15, etc.), to which aspersion he replied by showing that this would be dividing the kingdom of evil against itself. The exorcists of Ephesus used the name of Jesus in their **5. In the** work. The episode of Simon (Acts **Christian** viii. 9 sqq.) is instructive, while no **Church.** less illustrative of the common estimation is the episode of Elymas in Cyprus (Acts xiii.), who received the rebuke of Paul and severe punishment. A center of heathen sorcery at that time was Ephesus, where amulets with an ambiguous inscription and a representation of Diana were sold, and one of the triumphs of Christianity was the burning of costly books dealing with the art (Acts xix. 19). Distinction was made then between the wonder-working of the apostles and ordinary magic (II Cor. xii. 12), though that might be misunderstood as simple magic (Acts v. 15, xix. 12) and the real connection lost, the conception passing to the shadow and the napkins, etc., from the persons of the apostles. So on the confines of Christianity belief in magic showed itself in the materializing of the means of grace after heathen-magical methods of thought, in the magical use of " the word of power " and like ceremonies. Of course, a more spiritual and more nearly religious conception inheres in Christian surroundings, the divine powers being supposed to work under ethical conditions. The Christian ritual and cultus were affected by the magical remains which inhered in the life of the peoples converted to this faith or which came in through contact with heathen peoples, though such ideas were always attacked by the Church. In the early Church, Gnosticism was a breeding-point for these conceptions and practises. In the Middle Ages the belief in witches had its rise in the old German faith in spirits. Even those who combated the effects of this heathen heritage showed themselves under the spell of surviving superstitions, and the inquisitors manifested more of gruesome zeal than of wisdom in their measures. These errors were due, however, rather to the condition of the natural, mental, and juristic sciences than to theology. New forms constantly arise, an example of which is Spiritism (q.v.), in which direct opposition to Biblical commands is discernible. Another example of this same class of novelties is the so-called crystal-gazing, while the various phenomena of spiritualism, hypnotism, somnambulism, and the like illustrate the older sorcery in its connection with soothsaying (see MAGIC). Hardly less dangerous are the phenomena of suggestion, even in its relation to the medical profession, though it is brought into connection with the Bible and prayer. These illustrations show that danger of lapse into sorcery is not altogether a thing of the past. See SUPERSTITION.

(C. VON ORELLI.)

BIBLIOGRAPHY: Much of the literature under COMPARATIVE RELIGION; MAGIC; SHAMANISM; SUPERSTITION; and WITCHCRAFT will be found pertinent. Consult further: W. Mannhart, *Zauberglaube und Geheimwissen im Spiegel der Jahrhunderte*, Leipsic, 1890; J. Diesenbach, *Besessenheit, Zauberei und Hexenfabeln*, Frankfort, 1893; F. Delacroix, *Les Procès de sorcellerie au xviii. siècle*, Paris, 1894; J. Regnault, *La Sorcellerie*, Paris, 1897; T. Witton Davies, *Magic, Divination, and Demonology among the Hebrews and their Neighbours*, Edinburgh, 1898; E. Pauls, *Zauberwesen und Hexenwahn am Niederrhein*, Düsseldorf, 1898; I. Bertrand, *La Sorcellerie*, Paris, 1899; E. Gilbert,

Les Plantes magiques et la sorcellerie, Moulins, 1899; J. N. Sepp, Orient und Occident: Kapitel über der Nachseite der Natur Zauberwerk und Hexenwesen in alter und neuer Zeit, Berlin, 1903; E. Crawley, The Tree of Life, pp. 50, 79, 253–254, London, 1905; L. R. Farnell, Evolution of Religion, London, 1905; H. A. Junod, The Theory of Witchcraft amongst South African Natives, Cape Town, 1907; A. Abt, Die Apologie des Apulejus von Madaura und die antike Zauberei, Giessen, 1908; A. Bertholet, Religionsgeschichtliches Lesebuch, pp. 150 sqq., Tübingen, 1908; W. Caland, Altindische Zauberei. Darstellung der altindischen Wünschopfer, Amsterdam, 1908; K. Frank, Babylonische Beschwörungsreliefs, Leipsic, 1908; J. E. Harrison, Prolegomena to the Study of Greek Religion, 2d ed., Cambridge, 1908 (contains much on avertive procedure); T. Schermann, Griechische Zauberpapyri und das Gemeinde- und Dankgebet im I. Klemensbriefe, Leipsic, 1909; I. King, The Development of Religion. A Study in Anthropology and Social Psychology, New York, 1910.

SORTES APOSTOLORUM or SANCTORUM (Lat., " Lots of the apostles " or " saints "): A means of foretelling the future by opening the Bible at random, the passage on which the eye first lights being taken as an admonition of the deity in regard to the problem prompting such means of divination. The term is probably derived from the Vulgate of Acts i. 26 and Col. i. 12, and the usage is widespread, pagan Rome thus consulting Vergil, Islam the Koran, and China the sayings of Confucius. While rejecting divination with pagan writings, the Christians employed the Bible for this purpose (cf. Augustine's account of his conversion, Confessiones, VIII., xii. 29–30, Eng. transl. in NPNF, 1 ser., i. 127–128), despite the disapproval of Church Fathers (cf. Augustine, Epist., lv. 37, Eng. transl. in NPNF, 1 ser., i. 315; Jerome on Jonah i.). It became especially prevalent in the days of Gregory of Tours (Hist. Francorum, iv. 16, v. 14, 49), although it was forbidden by the synods of Vannes (465), Agde (506), Orléans (511), and Auxerre (between 570 and 590), as well as by Gregory the Great (Epist., ix. 204, xi. 33). The Carolingian legislation against the sortes apostolorum (cf. MGH, Leg., sectio iii., part 1, p. 64) was reenforced, partly on the basis of Lev. xix. 26, by the prohibitions of the Church, yet the system had official sanction in determining the character of bishops elect (cf. e.g., William of Malmesbury, Gesta pontificum Anglorum, i. 214, 219, etc.). Greek monks made a similar use of " The Sayings of the Fathers " while the humanists returned to Vergil.

There were a number of minor ways of consulting the sortes apostolorum, and in the later Middle Ages lot-books circulated throughout Christendom. In more recent times Pietism especially affected divination by the Bible; and it is still practised in many places. (Cf. also DIVINATION, III.; LOTS, HEBREW USE OF.)   (E. VON DOBSCHÜTZ.)

BIBLIOGRAPHY: Besides the literature under DIVINATION, consult. H. Winnefeld, Sortes Sangallenses, Bonn, 1887; P. Cassel, Weihnachten; Ursprünge, Bräuche, und Aberglauben, Berlin, 1862; F. Rocquain, Les Sorts des saints ou des apôtres, pp. 457 sqq., Paris, 1880; R. Heim, Incantamenta magica Græca-Latina, Leipsic, 1893; J. R. Harris, in American Journal of Philology, ix. 58; idem, in Journal of Theological Studies, ii. 1, pp. 7–8; idem, The Annotators of Codex Bezæ, pp. 45 sqq., London, 1901.

SOTER, sō'ter: Pope c. 166–174. According to Hegesippus (in Eusebius, Hist. eccl., IV., xxii.) and Irenæus (Hær., III., iii. 3) Soter was successor of Anicetus, but the papal lists make him follow Pius. Eusebius (Hist. eccl., IV., xix.) makes his episco-

pate reach from the ninth to the seventeenth year of Marcus Aurelius; the " Liberian Catalogue " gives him a pontificate of nine years, three months, and two days; Lipsius assigns as his dates 166 (167)–174 (175). A fragment of a letter from the Corinthian Dionysius (in Eusebius, Hist. eccl., IV., xxiii.) makes Soter revive an old custom and send a hortatory letter to the Corinthians which Harnack identifies with the so-called II Clement. A late tradition makes Soter one of the earliest writing opponents of Montanism.   (A. HAUCK.)

BIBLIOGRAPHY: Liber pontificalis, ed. Mommsen in MGH, Gest. pont. Rom., i (1898), 16; Jaffé, Regesta, i. 9; R. A. Lipsius, Chronologie der römischen Bischöfe, p. 86, Kiel, 1869; J. Langen, Geschichte der römischen Kirche, i. 152 sqq.; T. Zahn, in Forschungen zur Geschichte des neutestamentlichen Kanons, v. 51 sqq., Leipsic, 1892; Harnack, Litteratur, i. 589, ii. 1, pp. 440 sqq.; idem, in TU, xiii (1895), 48–49; Bower, Popes, i. 14; Platina, Popes, i. 31–32; DCB, iv. 721–722.

SOTERIOLOGY.

Soteriology is that branch of Christian theology which treats of the work of the Savior; it is the doctrine of salvation, so far as such salvation has been wrought out by the second person in the Trinity. It is to be carefully distinguished from Christology (q.v.), which treats solely of the person of the Redeemer—his incarnation, his divinity, and his humanity, and the combination of these two elements in his single and perfect personality. Yet it should be borne in mind always, that any adequate conception of his soteriological work must be based on right views, antecedently obtained and established, respecting the Christ as he is in himself—the appointed and qualified savior of men. Soteriology does not include the concurrent work of the Son of God in other spheres, such as creation, or providence, or moral administration. Nor does it include those aspects of salvation which involve, on the one side, the elective purpose and love of the Father, or, on the other, the interior ministry of the Spirit in the application of saving grace. While the Son is concerned with the Father in the original plan of redemption and in the selection of those in whom that plan becomes effectual (see PREDESTINATION), his specific work lies rather in the execution of that plan, and in the actual securing of redemption to all who believe. While, again, the Son is concerned with the Holy Spirit in the conviction of sinners, and in bringing them, through regeneration and sanctification, into the full enjoyment of the salvation provided (see HOLY SPIRIT), his primary work is rather the provision itself on which, as a divine foundation, this subsequent work of spiritual restoration must be based. The Father creates, preserves, governs, plans, elects, as introductory; the Spirit enlightens, educates, sanctifies, and completes the saving process in the individual soul; the Son, acting as intermediate, represents, reveals, instructs, atones for sin, placates law, and lays a foundation

1. Definition.

in justice, whereby, under an economy of grace, every one who believes in him, the Father and the Spirit concurring, may be saved.

The most general conception of this specific work of the Son of God is expressed in the term mediation (see MEDIATOR). His peculiar mission is to interpose, in the temper of grace and **2. Relation** for the purpose of both forensic and **to Media-** spiritual reconciliation, between man **tion.** as a sinner, and the Deity against whom man has offended, with whom he is morally at variance. As a mediator, the Son of God, who was also the Son of Man (qq.v.), was amply qualified, both by inherent endowment and through official appointment; and in his work of mediation, he is actually successful in removing alienation, in restoring the lost harmony between God and the sinner, and in securing to man a complete and blessed and eternal at-one-ment with his heavenly Father. This generic work of mediation is generally described by Calvinistic theologians under the three specific forms indicated in the terms prophet, priest, and king (see JESUS CHRIST, THREEFOLD OFFICE OF). It has been questioned whether this distribution is in all respects desirable; whether, by the division of the one work into these three parts or offices, our sense of the essential unity of that work is not impaired; and whether the underlying idea of mediation is not weakened by such multiplicity of particular functions and relations (J. J. van Oosterzee, *Christian Dogmatics*, § cviii., New York, 1874). Is this central idea adequately expressed in these three forms? Do they contain neither more nor less than the underlying conception? And, where the distribution is made, are these three offices always kept in their proportionate place, and severally invested with their proper dignity and value in the one mediatorial work? Whatever answer may be given to these questions on exegetical or speculative grounds, there is no adequate reason for rejecting an analytic presentation which has gained such definite expression in current evangelical creeds (Heidelberg Catechism, Ans. 31; Westminister Confession, chap. viii.) and has been so extensively adopted as a regulative guide in modern theology.

Studying soteriology in this triple aspect, there appears first the prophetic function of the Savior, as including that entire revelation of saving truth which he, as the divine Logos, came **3. Relation** among men to make. All religious, **to Christ's** and especially all inspired, teachers **Prophetical** who were prior to him as revealers of **Work.** sacred doctrine or duty, were only messengers to prepare the way before him; and all who followed after had it as their mission simply to elucidate and expand what he taught. Christ was the one perfect Logos, in virtue both of his eternal relationship within the Trinity (see TRINITY) and of his specific appointment as the Word of the Godhead to man. In him resided all the qualifications requisite to the complete fulfilment of this prophetical work, and from him came in highest form, and with most commanding power, all the truth which man needs to know in order to his salvation. This prophetical function may be subdivided into direct and indirect—direct teaching through the formal enunciation of saving truths, and indirect teaching through the superadded power of example and personality. Christ, as teacher and prophet, becomes an enduring pattern also. In himself, as well as in his message, was light; and the light was the life of men. It may be queried, whether, in consequence of the strong inclination of Evangelical Protestantism to exalt the priestly work of our Lord as central, this prophetical mission has not been relatively too much ignored, and, more specifically, whether the Biblical view of him as the true norm and example of our humanity has not been surrendered too much to the uses of those who altogether reject his priestly character and mission.

Concerning this priestly function, it is needless to repeat what has been said elsewhere (see ATONEMENT; CALVINISM, § 5; JESUS CHRIST, THREEFOLD OFFICE OF; PRIEST, PRIESTHOOD; SACRIFICE). The essential fact in the case is the voluntary and vicarious surrender of himself by our Lord as a sacrifice before God for sinners, on account of their sin, and in order to expiate sin, and to secure the reconciliation and restoration of man as sinful to God. As a sacrifice, Christ was inherently and judicially perfect, a lamb without blemish and without spot; as a priest, he was in every way qualified for the sacrificial work in which he was thus engaged; and his administration of the priestly office was voluntary, official, and acceptable. In him both the Aaronic priesthood and the peculiar priesthood of Melchisedec were singularly blended. He was, in his own person, the absolute culmination of the priestly as well as the prophetic order and idea. As priest and as sacrifice he was perfect.

That this vicarious intervention and offering of himself in behalf of sinners and for sin was an essential part of the mediatorial work of the Savior, is too clearly revealed in Scripture to be **4. Relation** questioned by any who receive its tes- **to the** timony in the case as conclusive. The **Atonement.** exigencies of that moral government against which the sinner had rebelled, the requisitions of justice as an eternal principle in the Deity, and the needs of the soul itself in order to its spiritual recovery, alike required—as the Bible in multiplied ways asserts—such a sacrifice of himself, even unto death, on the part of the Redeemer. Without this, mediation would have been both inadmissible and ineffectual (see SATISFACTION. For differing views on the nature and the extent of the atonement see ATONEMENT). Whatever may be the views of believers as to either the nature or the extent and scope of this sacrificial work of Christ, all are agreed in regarding the fact itself as both unquestionable and vital. That the Lord suffered as well as taught, and that he suffered on account of sin and in order to save men from it, and that through his suffering men are actually saved from both the condemnation and the power of evil, and that this salvation is immediate and certain, and will be complete at last—these are the great facts of grace which lie at the basis of the Evangelical system, and which constitute the foundation of all Evangelical hope.

Justification (q.v.) is the divine act of pardoning

sin, and accepting sinners as if they were righteous, on the ground generically of all that Christ has done

5. Relation to Justification. in the *munus triplex* of mediation, and specifically on the ground of what he has suffered as well as done in our behalf as our great high priest and sacrifice. To accept the sinner as if he were righteous, and to adopt him (see ADOPTION) into the family of God, and make him an heir of spiritual privileges and blessings, without requiring from him repentance, and return to loyalty, as conditions, and with no provision for his deliverance from the legal penalties incurred by his sin, would be an unworthy transaction. The only adequate warrant for such acceptance and adoption must be found, not in any worthiness inherent in the nature of man or any merit seen in his life, nor even in his faith and repentance viewed as concomitants or consequences, but in the mediatorial, and especially in the sacrificial, work of Christ.

The kingly office of the Savior is a necessary element in his broad work of mediation. He is king because he has been prophet and priest; he is also

6. Relation to Christ's Kingly Office. king inherently, as divine. His kingdom commences in the believing heart, and is essentially spiritual: it is an authority exercised in love, and for the purpose of salvation. His church, as composed of those who have thus submitted to him personally, is his gracious empire; and over that empire he is the supreme head, everywhere and always. This kingdom was founded by him before his earthly advent; it has been extended through many lands and centuries by his grace and power; it will continue to increase, through the agency of the forces now incorporated in it, until it has filled the earth. The notion, that, as a kingdom of love, it will ere long be supplanted by a kingdom of power, in which Christ will visibly appear as an earthly monarch, subduing his enemies by irresistible strength, and exalting his saints with him to a species of temporal domination (see MILLENNIUM, MILLENARIANISM), is at variance with the truth. Beyond this earthly empire of the Lord as already defined, may be discerned his princely exaltation even now, at the right hand of the Father, to be advocate and intercessor for his people. This advocacy and intercession are to continue until all who are his are finally brought together with him into what is literally the kingdom of heaven.

Returning from this survey of the specific functions or offices of Christ to the underlying idea of

7. Summary. mediation, in one view may be comprehended the full doctrine of salvation as wrought out by him in behalf of man. There is indeed a subjective soteriology, which includes especially the work wrought within the soul of man by the Savior through his spirit, and which is expressed in the terms regeneration and sanctification. But objective soteriology, which is here under consideration, is summed up rather in the triple phrase of Aquinas—*Christus legislator, sacerdos, rex.* To the Protestant mind it is pictured forth essentially in the term justification, which, equally with regeneration and sanctification, shows wherein the divine salvation consists.   E. D. MORRIS.

BIBLIOGRAPHY: The place of the topic in systematic theology is discussed in G. R. Crooks and J. F. Hurst, *Theological Encyclopædia and Methodology*, pp. 455–457, New York, 1894; and in A. Cave, *Introduction to Theology*, consult Index under "Salvation, Doctrine of," Edinburgh, 1896. The subject hardly needs a separate bibliography, being a topic treated in practically all works on systematic theology (see DOGMA, DOGMATICS; e.g., Shedd, ii. 353–587, iii. 400–470; Hodge, ii. 455–608), which usually provide abundant references to literature. Moreover, relevant literature is noted under the articles to which reference is made in the text, especially under ATONEMENT, and SATISFACTION.

SOTO, sō'tō, DOMINGO DE: Spanish Dominican; b. at Segovia (45 m. n.w. of Madrid) 1494; d. at Salamanca Nov. 15, 1560. Educated, after a youth of poverty which obliged him to begin as a sacristan in the village of Ochando, at Alcala and Paris, he became, in 1520, professor of philosophy at the former university, gaining a reputation as an opponent of nominalism. At this same period he also began his commentaries on Aristotle's "Dialectics" (Salamanca, 1544), "Physics" (1545), and "Categories" (Venice, 1583), as well as the preparation of his own *Summulæ* (Salamanca, 152?, abridged ed., 1539 and often). Determining to embrace the monastic life, he entered the Dominican order at Burgos in 1524, being professed in the following year and taking the name Domingo instead of his baptismal Francisco. He now taught philosophy and theology at Burgos until 1532, when he returned to Salamanca as professor of scholastic philosophy. He was an important figure at the Council of Trent, where he maintained that the Roman Catholic Church did not teach assurance of grace, likewise defending Thomistic teachings regarding the doctrines of original sin, justification, predestination, good works, etc., these controversies also bearing fruit in his *De natura et gratia libri tres* (Venice, 1547) and *Apologia . . . de certitudine gratiæ* (1547). When, in 1547, the council was transferred to Bologna, de Soto returned to the court of Charles V., who made him his confessor, and in 1549 appointed him to the bishopric of Segovia. Not only was the latter honor declined, but in 1550 de Soto resigned his post of confessor and retired to the monastery at Salamanca, where he became prior. About this time he wrote his anti-Protestant *Commentarii in epistolam Pauli ad Romanos* (Antwerp, 1550), and he also sought to allay the controversy between Sepulveda and Las Casas regarding the treatment of the American aborigines. In 1552 he resumed teaching at Salamanca, but in 1556 he returned to his monastery and was again chosen prior. His chief works, besides those already mentioned, were *De ratione tegendi et detegendi secretum* (Salamanca, 1551); *De justitia et jure libri septem* (1556); *In quartum librum Sententiarum commentaria, sive de sacramentis* (2 vols., 1557–60); and the still unedited *De ratione promulgandi Evangelium* and *In primam partem Sancti Thomæ et in utramque secundam commentarii.*   (O. ZÖCKLER†.)

BIBLIOGRAPHY: N. Antraius, *Bibliotheca Hispaniæ*, i. 255–258, Rome, 1672; J. Quétif and J. Échard, *Scriptores ordinis prædicatorum*, ii. 171 sqq., Paris, 1721; N. Paulus, *D. Soto und die Beichte in Nürnberg*, in *Der Katholik*, 1899, i. 282–288; G. Hoffmann, *Die Lehre von der Fides implicita innerhalb der katholischen Kirche*, pp. 227–230, Leipsic, 1903; *KL*, xi. 530–531.

SOTO, PETRUS DE: Spanish Dominican; b. at Cordova about 1500; d. at Trent Apr. 20, 1563. He entered the Dominican order at Salamanca in 1518 and quickly attained a reputation as a rigid and learned Thomist. Charles V. made him his confessor, but his order appointed him vicar for the Netherlands, and later he became professor of theology at the newly founded seminary of Dillingen, where he wrote his catechetical *Institutiones Christianæ* (Augsburg, 1548), *Methodus confessionis, sive doctrinæ pietatisque Christianæ epitome* (Dillingen, 1553), *Compendium doctrinæ Catholicæ* (Antwerp, 1556), and *Tractatus de institutione sacerdotum qui sub episcopis animarum curam gerunt, sive manuale clericorum* (Dillingen, 1558), the latter his chief work. His *Assertio Catholicæ fidei circa articulos confessionis* (Antwerp, 1552) involved him in a controversy with Johann Brenz (q.v.), thus occasioning his *Defensio Catholicæ confessionis et scholiorum circa confessionem* (1557). De Soto later accompanied Philip II. to England, where Mary appointed him professor of theology at Oxford, but on the queen's death in 1558 he returned to Dillingen. In 1561 Pius IV. summoned him to Trent, where he bravely defended the sacramental nature of the priesthood and episcopal rights, but died before the council adjourned.   (O. ZÖCKLER†.)

BIBLIOGRAPHY: J. Quétif and J. Échard, *Scriptores ordinis prædicatorum*, ii. 183 sqq., Paris, 1721; *KL*, xi. 531–532.

SOUL AND SPIRIT, BIBLICAL CONCEPTIONS OF.

"Spirit"—in classical Greek, *pneuma*, like the Hebr. *ruah*—denotes not merely the breath as symbol of life but also life itself in distinction from *sōma*. The soul (Goth. *saiwala*, Hebr. *nephesh*, Gk. *psychē*, Lat. *anima*) signifies in general the life as it animates the individual material organism which is the medium of its action. Both spirit and soul are applied to man (Job x. 12; Ps. xxxii. 2; Ezek. xxxvii. 8; cf. with Gen. xlvi. 15, Ex. i. 5), and also to animals (Eccl. iii. 19 sqq.; Gen. vi. 17, vii. 15, 22; Ps. civ. 30; Gen. i. 20, 30; Job. xii. 10; Rev. viii. 9). The animal *nephesh* is identical with the animal body. "Spirit" indicates that the creature originates in and is bound to God (Ps. civ. 29; Job. xxxiv. 14 sqq.; Ezek. xxxvii. 5, 9, 10; Rev. xi. 11). The Old but not the New Testament speaks of the *nephesh* of God (Lev. xxvi. 11; Judges x. 16; Isa. xlii. 1). Soul and spirit are sometimes used synonymously (cf. Gen. xlv. 27 with Ps. cxix. 175; I Sam. xxx. 12 with I Kings xvii. 21, 22; Ps. cxlvi. 4 with Gen. xxxv. 18). The Septuagint never translates *nephesh* by *pneuma*, *ruah* very rarely by *psychē* (cf. Gen. xli. 8; Ex. xxxv. 21). *Sōma* and *pneuma* (cf. I Cor. vii. 34) are opposed to each other as are *sarx* and *pneuma;* not *sarx* but *sōma* is opposed to *psychē*, hence *sarx* and *pneuma*, *sōma* and *psychē* are the proper opposites; *pneuma* and *psychē* are interrelated as are *sarx* and *sōma*. Soul and spirit

1. Biblical Terms.

are not seldom sharply distinguished—not merely in point of view (Wendt). (1) Dying is a giving up of the *pneuma* and of the *psychē*, but it is never said that the spirit, but only that the soul, dies or is killed (Judges xvi. 16; Matt. x. 28; Mark xiv. 34). (2) *Pneuma* and *psychē* are often used interchangeably with reference to sensation and impulse, knowledge and self-consciousness (Matt. xi. 29; I Cor. xvi. 18; Luke i. 46, 47), but only the soul is the subject of willing and desire, inclination and aversion (Deut. xii. 20; I Sam. ii. 16; Job xxiii. 13; Prov. xxi. 10; Isa. xxvi. 8; Micah vii. 1), and of redemption (Isa. xxxviii. 17; Matt. xvi. 26; cf., however, I Cor. v. 5; I Pet. iv. 6). Consciousness, perception, and willing are indeed ordinarily referred to the heart, but when the emphasis is to be laid on the hidden state to which these feelings belong, soul and spirit are used (see HEART, BIBLICAL USAGE). (3) The dead are designated as spirits (Luke xxiv. 37, 39; Acts xxiii. 8–9; Heb. xii. 23; I Pet. iii. 19; cf. however, Rev. vi. 9). (4) Most important of all, *nephesh* and *psychē* refer to the individual, the subject of life, while *ruah* and *pneuma* are never used of the subject as individual.

As an independent subject, *pneuma* is always something other than the human spirit. The distinction depends on the original difference in terms: spirit is the condition, soul the manifestation, of life. Whatever belongs to the spirit belongs to the soul also, but not everything that belongs to the soul belongs to the spirit. It does not suffice to speak of the inner being of man, now as spirit, now as soul; one must regard the spirit as the principle of the soul, the divine principle of life, included in but not identical with the individual. Spirit may be distinguished but not separated from the soul. Body and spirit are not two poles between which is the soul. Since the soul includes the spirit as part of itself, it may be called spirit. The soul may sin and die, but the spirit, as a divine principle having its source in God, can neither sin nor die. The human soul is indeed bound to corporeality, yet it survives death because it possesses the Spirit of God as its immanent principle of life. The loss of the body caused by death will in those who share in the consummation give place to a redeemed corporeality (I Cor. xv. 42 sqq.; Rev. vi. 9). The occasion for a distinction between soul and spirit lies in the religious consciousness of the difference between the actual man and his divine destination (cf. Plato's distinction between a rational and an irrational, a mortal and an immortal division (E. Zeller, *Plato and the Older Academy*, pp. 413 sqq., London, 1888). To understand this one has but to see the meaning of the spirit for man, and the relation of the human spirit to the Spirit of God. The Spirit of God is indeed wherever life is, but man possesses this in a unique degree (Gen. i. 26–27, ii. 19–20; cf. Eccles. iii. 19–21), since he alone is conscious of dependence upon God. And it is the Spirit of God in him—the principle of his true life—which gives him his special relation to other creatures and to God and provides the foundation for his consciousness and will.

Here then arises the question whether the Spirit

2. Distinction Between Soul and Spirit.

of God is an immanence of God (cf. John xiv. 23; Rom. viii. 9 sqq.; J. C. K. Hofmann, *Weissagung und Erfüllung*, i. 17 sqq., Nördlingen, 1841), or a created spirit (cf. Job xxxii. 8, xxxiii.

3. Pauline Doctrine. 4). According to the New Testament, the Holy Spirit which dwells in believers is always distinguished from the spirit of the believer (cf. Rom. viii. 16). Two views of the Pauline psychology are: (1) That Paul knows no *pneuma* of the natural man (Holsten, Weiss, Holtzmann); (2) that he knows such a *pneuma*, but not as divine or related to God (Lüdermann, Pfleiderer). The Scriptures, however, leave the question of the relation of the human spirit to the Spirit of God unanswered. Holsten's view rests on a dualistic conception of the opposition of the flesh and spirit (see Flesh), as the opposition of the finite and infinite, where spirit is identical with the infinite. But the Pauline doctrine of *pneuma* is that of a divine principle of life, related to the human spirit. Lüdermann and Pfleiderer abandon Holsten's position and recognize a Pauline *pneuma tou anthrōpou*, but their theory is neither clearer nor more acceptable. Lüdermann conceives of the *pneuma* as a substantial subject for the *nous*, not to be interchanged with the *psychē;* no substance is, however, supposable which is not identical with some human power. Pfleiderer admits that Paul knows of a *pneuma* alongside of the *sarx* (*Paulinismus*, 3d ed., p. 215). He appears to regard the *pneuma* as the general divine spirit of life—the Old Testament *nephesh*, identical with the *psychē*. But when he conceives it as the indifferent substratum both of the *nous* and of the *sarx*, without relation to God, he is at odds with the apostle. According to Weiss, God recognizes no *pneuma* which belongs to man by nature, for he always thinks of the *psychē* as in immediate unity with the *sarx*, hence the *psychē* can not be the bearer of a bodily life independent of the higher spiritual life. H. J. Holtzmann (*Lehrbuch der neutestmaentlichen Theologie*, ii. 15 sqq., Leipsic, 1897) maintains that according to Paul there is no natural *pneuma* in man; if Paul appears to teach the contrary, this is due to use of popular instead of exact language. It may, however, be declared that Paul knew of a *pneuma tou anthrōpou*, that the *pneuma hagion* never takes the place of our spirit, or fills in a cleft caused by sin. The *psychikos* of Jude 19 is not in contradiction to the human *pneuma*, but to the Holy Spirit of redemption (cf. Rom. viii. 9, 11, 14, 16; I Cor. ii. 3–4). Regeneration, due to the " outpouring of the Spirit " (Isa. xliv. 3–4; Joel ii. 28–29; John iii. 5–6; Titus iii. 6), is the self-appropriation of God's grace through the Holy Spirit in relation to our spirits. Moreover, the Spirit assures our spirit that we are children of God.

The spirit of man is God's Spirit—spirit of God's Spirit—only so far as it is of like nature with this; it is not then strictly created " out of nothing," nor an emanation, nor an *inclusa in corpore Spiritus divini, ut ita dicam, particula* (Oehler), yet this last is nearest the truth. The Spirit of God entering the human organism begets the soul which therefore bears and propagates the

4. Spirit, Divine and Human.

imperishable because divine power of life. The connection of the human spirit, which is thus the ground of the human soul, with the Spirit of God is one of essential fellowship of spirit with spirit. The distinction between soul and spirit is the peculiar characteristic of the Biblical idea of the nature of man. The Scriptures do indeed contain trichotomy (not that of Plato, however), resting on the experience of sin and salvation (I Thess. v. 23; Heb. iv. 12), but this does not exclude a decisive dichotomy, as I Pet. ii. 11 where the soul or spirit is regarded simply with reference to its spiritual destination as the bearer of the divine principle of life (cf. Phil. i. 27).

On the basis of the foregoing discussion one finds a solution of various debated questions. First, as to creationism and traducianism. If the soul bears

5. Origin of Soul and Spirit. the spirit, not as an indwelling of the Spirit of God, but as spirit of God's Spirit, and is so connected with corporeality that this can only become the body of the soul, then the transmission of the bodily life is at the same time the transmission of the soul, and with the soul the spirit. Life is from life, soul from soul. There is thus no room for a creative act in which spirit originates (cf. Ps. cxxxix. 13, 7; Isa. lvii. 16; Zech. xii. 1; Job xxxiii. 4), all life is from the Spirit of God (Ps. civ. 30; Acts xvii. 28). Traducianism and not generationism is right. The preference of Scholasticism and Roman Catholic theology for creationism depends on their theory of sin, especially original sin and sensuousness; on the other hand, Lutheranism, on account of its deeper knowledge of sin, especially of original sin, declared for traducianism. Although this view is without explicit Scriptural proof, yet it is recommended by the doctrine of the world, by the relation of God to the world and to creative potencies, as well as by the conception of soul and spirit (cf. F. H. R. Frank, *System der christlichen Wahrheit*, i. 382 sqq., Erlangen, 1878).

The task of man lies in willing and determining his soul in accordance with the inner divine principle of life. He has, however, through sin turned

6. Consequences of Sin. from his spiritual divine destination, so that now his own will strives against the impulse of the spirit, and the latter makes itself felt only in the conscience. The divine nature appears only as a demand, a law awaking the consciousness to the sense of its inner discord (cf. Rom. ii. 15) between the divine principle of life and the *nous tēs sarkos* (see Flesh). The side of man's nature turned from God and to the world apart from God gets the upper hand and he becomes flesh—*sarkikos* and *sarkinos*, i.e., *kata sarka*, and *sarx*. Thus the soul, in spite of its immanent spirit, becomes sinful, and the entire life of the spirit suffers. Hence the divided ego, pictured by the apostle in Rom. vii., the halfhearted man, constantly wavering between God and himself, is a divided soul (Jas. i. 8, iv. 8; cf. Matt. xxvi. 41). So far as the divine principle of life is not renewed by the Holy Spirit, the sinner is *psychikos* in opposition to *pneumatikos*. As a consequence of sin he no longer controls his life, but has become a victim of *phthora*, i.e., of death as the opposition of eternal life. In the loss of his corporeal-

ity his soul suffers; but since it bears the Spirit of
God, it can not die; in this connection of death and
immortality lies the sharpest conceivable torment
(see HADES; IMMORTALITY). Had the natural and
just consequences of sin followed directly upon the
first sin, history would have ended where it began
and the creative thought of God would have been
annulled. But now the redemptive purpose has
become the principle of conservation, and the patience of God has postponed the judgment and the
end, in order that man may once more by trustful
acceptance of the promise share a renewing of his
spirit (Jer. xxxi. 31 sqq.; John vii. 39; Acts i. 4–5;
Rom. viii. 4). Yet the changed condition of his
life caused by sin has not ceased. A constitution is
transmitted which renders sin a natural necessity
without its ceasing to be sin and subjecting to those
conditions which are involved in a wrong relation
to God and our divine destination. *Psychikos* designates man not simply as *sarkikos* or *harmatōlos*
as interchangeable with these (cf. I Cor. iii. 1), but
according to his natural condition and because he
is at present *sarkinos* and *hamartōlos*, he does not
share the divine principle of life.

The true knowledge of the relation of the soul and
the spirit is of great significance in relation to the
person of Christ. The preexistence and incarnation of Christ do not imply the union of two persons in him, but the subject of the
7. Bearing incarnation is identical with the man
on Person- Jesus, and accordingly the spirit of the
ality of Son of God is the personal principle in
Jesus. him. But this does not justify Apollinaris' conception of a divine principle
of life, with body and soul as the human aspect of
Christ, resting on the distinction between spirit,
soul, and body. On the contrary, the Spirit of God,
as this belonged to the eternal Son, was the principle of growth of the God-man in the womb of the
Virgin; the child of the mother along with his life
from her received his human soul. The soul is the
bearer of the spirit, hence Jesus is man according to
spirit, soul, and body—human spirit, human soul,
and human body, and yet divine-human; in the
soul of Christ God's Spirit and man's spirit are so
united that there is no duality of personal life. There
would be no person of Christ without the incarnation. He who is eternal God has in spirit, soul, and
body become perfectly member of our race. But one
must hold that this fact is not dependent on our
capacity to think it, and the limits of its conceiva-
bility are not the limits of its truth, or of the necessary expressions of faith. See HEART, BIBLICAL
USAGE. C. A. BECKWITH.

BIBLIOGRAPHY: F. Delitzsch, *Biblical Psychology*, Edinburgh, 1867; J. T. Beck, *Outlines of Biblical Psychology*,
ib. 1877; H. H. Wendt, *Die Begriffe Fleisch und Geist im
biblischen Sprachgebrauch*, Gotha, 1878; C. I. Ives, *The
Bible Doctrine of the Soul*, Philadelphia, 1878; E. White,
Life in Christ, London, 1878; C. M. Mead, *The Soul Here
and Hereafter*, Boston, 1879; J. B. Heard, *Tripartite Nature of Man*, Edinburgh, 1882; B. Weiss, *Biblical Theology of the N. T.*, 2 vols., ib. 1882; W. P. Dickson, *St. Paul's
Use of the Terms Flesh and Spirit*, Glasgow, 1883; G. F.
Oehler, *Theology of the O. T.*, New York, 1883; A. West-
phal, *Chair et esprit*, Toulouse, 1885; E. Wörner, *Biblische
Anthropologie*, pp. 77 sqq., Stuttgart, 1887; H. Schultz,
Theology of the O. T., London, 1892; J. Laidlaw, *Bible
Doctrine of Man*, Edinburgh, 1895; W. Beyschlag, *The-
ology of the N. T.*, 2 vols., ib. 1896; O. Pfleiderer, *Paulinis-
mus*, pp. 60 sqq., Leipsic, 1890, Eng. transl., London, 1897;
T. Simon, *Die Psychologie des Apostels Paulus*, Göttingen,
1897; F. E. Brightman, in *JTS*, ii (1900), 273 sqq.; W. H.
Schoemaker, in *JBL*, xxiii (1894), 13 sqq.; E. W. Win-
stanley, *Spirit in the New Testament*, London, 1908; P.
Torge, *Seelenglaube und Unsterblichkeitshoffnung im Alten
Testament*, Leipsic, 1909; *DB*, ii. 14–15, iv. 163–169; *EB*,
ii. 1534–36, iv. 4751–54; *DCG*, ii. 668–670, 671–673.
For the archeology and symbolism of the subject in
early art the reader should consult F. Cabrol, *Dictionnaire
d'archéologie chrétienne et de liturgie*, i. 1470 sqq.'(fasc. v.),
Paris, 1904 (exceedingly rich, and with a wealth of
literature).

SOULE, sūl, JOSHUA: Methodist Episcopal
South; b. at Bristol, Me., Aug. 1, 1781; d. at Nashville, Tenn., Mar. 6, 1867. He was converted 1797,
licensed to preach 1798, and admitted into the New
England Conference, 1799; was presiding elder,
with the exception of one year, 1804–16, when he
was appointed book-agent in New York. He was
the author of the plan for a delegated general conference of the church, which was accepted at Baltimore in 1808; and was editor of the *Methodist
Magazine*, 1816–19. He preached in New York
1820–22, and in Baltimore, 1822–24; was elected
bishop, 1824; and at the division of the church in
1844, he adhered to the Methodist Episcopal Church
South, and thereupon moved to Nashville, Tenn.
He was a presiding officer of great executive ability,
and in the graver and more important councils of
the church had no superior for discreet judgment,
and prudence in counsel. As a preacher he was slow
and deliberate, but always sound in doctrine, strong
in argument, and vigorous in style. He was a man
of remarkable strength, both of character and of
intellect.

BIBLIOGRAPHY: The subject is treated in the works on the
Methodist Episcopal Church North and South under
METHODISTS, such as those of A. Stevens, C. Elliott, N.
Bangs, G. Alexander, and J. M. Buckley (for bibliograph-
ical data see vii. 356 of this work).

SOULS, SLEEP OF. See INTERMEDIATE STATE.

SOUTER, sau'ter, ALEXANDER: Scotch-English
Presbyterian layman; b. at Perth, Scotland, Aug.
14, 1873. He was educated at the University of
Aberdeen (M.A., 1893) and Gonville and Caius College, Cambridge (B.A., 1896). From 1897 to 1903
he was assistant in humanity and lecturer in Latin
and in classical paleography in the University of
Aberdeen, and since 1903 has been Yates professor
of New-Testament Greek and exegesis in Mansfield
College, Oxford. He was an examiner in the University of London in 1906 and in the University of
Aberdeen in 1906–10, and a representative of the
Joint Board of the Scottish Universities for 1906–
1907. He has edited R. Ogilvie's *Horæ Latinæ* (London, 1901) and the twenty-eighth book of Livy (in
collaboration with G. Middleton; Edinburgh, 1902),
and has written *De codicibus manuscriptis Augus-
tini quæ feruntur Quæstionum Veteris et Novi Testamenti* (Vienna, 1905) and *A Study of Ambrosiaster*
(Cambridge, 1905).

SOUTH SEA ISLANDS, MISSIONS IN THE: Under this term are included the various groups of
islands lying between the continent of America
on the east and Australia, the East Indies, and
the Philippines on the west, and south of 20°

north latitude, with the exception of Fiji and the Hawaiian Islands, to which separate articles are devoted.

Austral or Tubuai Islands: A small group extending from about 149° to 151° 50′ west longitude in about 22° south latitude, under French control, with a steadily decreasing population (1,400 in 1880, 1,000 in 1900). The principal islands are Rurutu, Tubuai, and Rapa Iti. A terrible epidemic having appeared in Rurutu in 1821, two of the chiefs resolved to sail to a happier land. One of them, Auura, after long exposure reached the Society Islands and eventually landed at Raiatea, where he met the Rev. John Williams (q.v.) of the London Missionary Society. In three months he and his companions had learned to read and went back to Rurutu accompanied by some Christians from Raiatea. These were the first of a large company of South Sea Islanders who have been foreign missionaries. The idols were soon given up, and Christianity was firmly established. John Williams visited some of the islands in 1823. In 1887 two of the members of the native church in Rurutu volunteered for mission work in New Guinea. As the islands passed to French rule the Paris Missionary Society took over the work in 1890, and now has 8 stations, 10 native pastors, 477 church-members, and 624 scholars.

Bismarck Archipelago: A large group lying north of eastern New Guinea, in 145°–155° east longitude, and about 6° south latitude, part of which was formerly known as the New Britain Archipelago, since 1884 under the German flag. The native population (1906) is about 188,000 with 299 non-native colored, and 463 whites. The principal islands are Neu Pommern, Neu Mecklenburg, Neu Lauenburg, Neu Hannover, Admiralty, Anchorite, Commerson, and Hermit. The Methodist Missionary Society of Australasia under Rev. George Brown, with teachers from Fiji and Samoa, began work in 1875 in New Britain and New Ireland—now Neu Pommern and Neu Mecklenburg. It has 186 churches, 18 preaching-stations, 8 missionaries, 5 missionary sisters, 7 native ministers, 12 catechists, 168 native teachers, 249 class leaders, 4,608 church-members, one college, named after Rev. George Brown, 6 training-institutions with 169 students, 189 Sunday-schools with 5,481 scholars, 196 day schools with 5,463 scholars, and 21,017 hearers. In Neu Pommern the Roman Catholics number 15,045, with 24 mission priests, 37 lay brothers, 28 sisters, 82 native catechists, 75 head- and sub-stations, 85 schools, 4,123 scholars, and 479 children in 13 orphan asylums.

Caroline Islands: Lying north of the Bismarck Archipelago, these islands cover about 140°–163° east longitude, in north latitude 5°–10°. Since 1899 they have been in possession of Germany by purchase from Spain. The native population is about 55,000, with about 140 whites. The Spanish discoveries in these seas in 1686 were followed by a series of religious expeditions. The American Board of Commissioners for Foreign Missions began work on Kusaie and Ponape under Revs. B. G. Snow and Luther Halsey Gulick (q.v.) in 1852, and with valuable help from the Hawaiian Evangelical Association the work prospered. In 1857

the Rev. Hiram Bingham (q.v.) of the American Board arrived, and work was soon begun in the Marshall and Gilbert Islands (see below). In 1865 the mission was extended to the Truk Archipelago. The Protestant missionaries were expelled by the Spanish government in 1887, but returned in 1900, and before long there were 135 native workers, 57 outstations, 99 schools, 2 printing-houses, 2 dispensaries and 5,500 communicants. The American Board is handing over its work in the Caroline Islands to the Liebenzeller Mission, and has now only five missionaries in these islands. The Roman Catholic mission was established in 1887, and now has 1,880 adherents, 12 priests, 12 lay brothers, 6 sisters, 18 head- and sub-stations, 7 schools, and 200 scholars.

Cook or Hervey Islands: These islands, belonging to Great Britain, lie between 157° and 170° west longitude and about 20° south latitude. The principal islands are Rarotonga, Mangaia, Aitutaki, and Atiu (Vatiu). The group was annexed to New Zealand in 1901. In 1821 Papeiha and Vahopata, Christians connected with the London Missionary Society from Raiatea in the Society Islands, landed in Aitutaki where Christianity was soon accepted. Papeiha passed on to Mangaia, but it was not till 1825 that the mission was established there. Papeiha was also the apostle of Rarotonga, which was discovered by the Rev. John Williams in 1821, who frequently visited the island between 1823 and 1834. When he landed the people were ignorant of Christian worship, when he left he did not know of a house in the island where family prayer was not offered morning and evening. Over 500 men and women have passed through the Training Institution begun in 1839, many of whom have gone to evangelize other islands. The London Missionary Society now has 3 missionaries, 21 ordained natives, 23 day schools with 1,283 scholars and 22 Sunday-schools with 1,152 scholars, and 4,885 adherents. The Roman Catholics arrived in 1894, and now have 6 priests and six sisters and about 100 converts. The Seventh Day Adventists began work in 1890, and have one missionary and 50 adherents.

Ellice Islands: These islands, under British control, are situated 176°–180° east longitude and 5° to 11° south latitude. The area is about fifteen square miles, and the population about 2,400. The principal islands are Sophia, Ellice, Nukufetan, and Vaitupu. In 1861 Elikana and other Christians from Manihiki in the Penrhyn Group were carried by stress of weather some 1,200 miles to Nakulælæ in the Ellice Islands. Elikana, who was a deacon, began preaching Christianity. Rev. Archibald Wright Murray, of the London Missionary Society, from Samoa visited the islands and settled Samoan teachers there in 1865. Some years previously a knowledge of the true God had been brought by a man named Stuart, who was the master of a trading-vessel from Sydney. The group is now worked with the Tokelau Islands as part of the Samoan mission. In the two groups there are 13 ordained natives, 1,488 church-members, 2,411 adherents, 13 day schools with 1,428 scholars, and 13 Sunday-schools with 1,543 scholars.

Gilbert Islands: These islands, belonging to Great

Britain and consisting of atolls, lie on both sides of the equator between 172° and 177° east longitude. They have an area of 166 square miles and a population of about 30,000 natives and 100 whites. The principal islands are Tarawa, Apamana, Aranaka, Tamana, Marakei, and Nonouti. After a brief visit in 1855 the American Board of Commissioners for Foreign Missions began work in 1857 under the Rev. Hiram Bingham, with the help of Hawaiian teachers, and he after seven years' labor retired because of ill-health to Honolulu, where he devoted himself to literary labor for the Gilbert Islanders, and took charge of a Gilbert Island colony. The American Board now works in the nine northern islands, two southern islands, and Ocean Island. There are training-institutions at Kusaie in the Carolines, and in Ocean Island. Three missionaries work for the group, and much progress is made. The London Missionary Society began work in 1870 and for thirty years the islands were served by native teachers from Samoa. In 1900 a resident missionary was placed in the island of Beru. The London Missionary Society now has 2 missionaries with 5 stations in the Southern Islands, 13 ordained natives, 19 preachers, 576 church-members, 5,281 adherents, 28 Sunday-schools with 1,568 scholars, 29 day schools with 1,462 scholars, and a training-institution. The Roman Catholics started work in 1892, and there are 12,965 Roman Catholics, 1,800 catechumens, 19 priests, 13 lay brothers, 20 sisters, 87 catechists, 15 head- and sub-stations, 98 schools, and 3,310 scholars.

Loyalty Islands: This French group, consisting of the three large islands of Uvea, Lifu, and Maré, and a number of very small ones, lies in 166°–168° east longitude and about 20°–22° south latitude. They have an area of about 800 square miles and a population of over 15,000. The Rev. Archibald Wright Murray of the London Missionary Society, from Samoa, visited Maré in 1841, and found that a Christian from Tonga had been working there for seven years. Two teachers from Samoa were settled in Maré and the work prospered. In 1854 two missionaries began their residence there. In 1841 Pao from Rarotonga began his apostolic service. The Rev. Samuel Macfarlane arrived in 1859. Two years later a training-institution was started. Native Christians from Maré carried the Gospel to Uvea in 1856. The London Missionary Society has now one missionary in Lifu, and in Lifu and Uvea there are 37 ordained natives, 101 preachers, 37 Sunday-schools with 2,243 scholars, 2,348 church-members, and 6,173 adherents. The Paris Missionary Society has one missionary in Maré. The Roman Catholics came in 1864, but were not firmly established till 1875.

Marianne or Ladrone Islands: The Ladrone group, bought from Spain by Germany in 1899 (with the exception of Guam, which is held by the United States), consists of about twenty islands in 142°–148° east longitude and 13°–21° north latitude, with a population of about 2,700 natives. Guam has an area of about 200 square miles and a population of 11,490, of whom 331 are foreigners. The Jesuits settled in these islands in 1667. In 1907 the mission became an apostolic prefecture, and now has 12,216

adherents and 6 priests. The American Board of Commissioners for Foreign Missions opened a station in Guam in 1900, and is represented by one married missionary and 50 church-members.

Marquesas Islands: These islands, under the French flag, are closely grouped on both sides of 140° west longitude and in 9°–11° south latitude. They have an area of about 480 square miles and a population of about 4,000. The largest islands are Nukahiva and Hivaoa. In 1797 William Pascoe Crook of the London Missionary Society landed from the ship " Duff " and stayed two years. Other abortive attempts were made by the same society in 1826, 1829, and 1834, and by the American Board of Commissioners for Foreign Missions in 1833. In 1853 a Marquesan chief whose daughter had married a Hawaiian asked for missionaries from Hawaii, and in response Kanwealoha and others went. There are now 600 Christians under the care of Hawaiian teachers. The Paris Missionary Society has 5 stations, one missionary, and 2 native pastors. The Roman Catholics number 2,800 with 8 priests, 7 lay brothers, 12 sisters, and 29 head- and sub-stations.

Marshall Islands: This group, belonging to Germany and situated northeast of the Carolines (ut sup.) in about 161°–171° east longitude and 4°–13° north latitude, has an area of about 1,400 square miles and an estimated population of about 10,000. The principal islands are Majeru, Jaluit, Mulgrave, Ralick, and Mentschikoff. The American Board of Commissioners for Foreign Missions paid these islands a brief visit in 1855, and opened a mission in 1857 under Dr. G. Pierson and Rev. E. T. Douane with the help of Hawaiian native teachers. In 1880 the headquarters were removed to Kusaie in the Caroline Islands, and a training-college was opened there. Some Gilbert Islanders trained at Kusaie opened work in Nauru or Pleasant Island, where the Pacific Phosphate Co. employs about 1,500 Marshall and other islanders. In 1899 a resident missionary was placed there, and substantial progress ensued. The American Board has now 4 missionaries for the group, two residing at Kusaie, 20 churches, 83 places of worship, 3,371 church-members, 4,163 Christian Endeavorers, 87 schools, and 1,417 scholars. The Roman Catholic mission has 7 priests, 8 lay brothers, 15 sisters, 4 head- and sub-stations, 6 schools, 170 scholars, 323 Roman Catholics, and 523 catechumens.

New Caledonia: This island is united under French control with the Loyalty Islands (ut sup.) and the Isle of Pines. It is a long, narrow island lying northwest and southeast in 164°–166° east longitude and 20°–23° south latitude. Its area is 7,650 square miles, and the native population of the group is about 28,000; the white and other population, including convicts, numbers about 26,000. The London Missionary Society settled native teachers from Samoa in the Isle of Pines and New Caledonia in 1840. Four years later three of them were murdered in the Isle of Pines, and the rest were removed in 1845. The French, who took possession in 1853, would not allow the mission to be recommenced in 1861 and subsequently, but some native evangelists from Uvea in the Loyalty Islands have worked there occasionally. New Caledonia is now a French penal colony, with over 7,000 convicts. The Roman

Catholics began work in 1847, and have a bishop, 49 priests, 33 lay brothers, 109 sisters, 32 head- and sub-stations, 59 churches, 45 schools, 1,933 scholars, and 32,500 adherents. The Paris Missionary Society maintains two missionaries.

Dutch New Guinea: The part of the island of New Guinea (lying north of Australia) belonging to Holland extends from the western coast to 171° east longitude; the area is 151,789 square miles, and the population'is estimated to be 200,000. The first missionaries to New Guinea were C. W. Ottow and J. G. Geissler who were sent to Dutch New Guinea by Pastor Gossner of Berlin in 1855. The Utrecht Missionary Society, which sent missionaries thither in 1862, has now 4 missionaries, 1,200 Christians, 3,000 attendants at worship, 30 native helpers, and many schools. There are 1,200 Roman Catholics, 210 catechumens, 7 priests, 8 lay brothers, 5 sisters, 4 stations, 13 schools, and 404 scholars.

British New Guinea or Papua: To the British belong, under the name of the Territory of Papua (since 1906), the southeastern part of New Guinea from 171° east longitude eastwards and the islands between 141° and 155° east longitude and 8° and 12° south latitude. The area is about 90,540 square miles, with a population estimated at half a million natives with about 1,200 others. The London Missionary Society began work in 1871 under the Revs. Archibald Wright Murray and Samuel McFarlane, with teachers from Maré and Lifu. They settled at first in the Torres Straits Islands and established a training-institution in Murray Island; in 1872 some teachers were settled on the mainland. The Rev. William George Lawes, from Nive, arrived 1874, and the Rev. James Chalmers from Rarotonga in 1877. Chalmers, with Rev. Oliver Tomkins, was killed and eaten by cannibals at Goaribari in 1901, Native teachers from the South Seas have rendered conspicuous service, especially Tepeso of Maré, in the Loyalty Islands, and Ruatoka of Mangaia, in the Cook Islands. The training-institution is now at Vatorata. There are now 15 head stations, 188 out-stations and schools, 38 Sunday-schools with 1,900 scholars, 15 missionaries, 2,514 church-members in New Guinea and the Torres Straits Islands, 188 South Sea and Papuan native teachers, and 14,000 adherents. The society's sphere extends over 1,000 miles of coast line from the Dutch frontier to Milne Bay. The Methodist Missionary Society of Australasia began work in 1891 under the Rev. George Brown, with South Sea teachers. Its sphere is from Milne Bay to Cape Vogel. It has 62 churches, 209 other preaching-places, 10 missionaries, 120 native teachers, 127 class leaders, 1,497 church-members, 2,150 catechumens, 4 training-institutions, 83 Sunday-schools with 4,166 scholars, 77 day schools with 3,995 scholars, and 22,065 attendants at worship. The Anglican Mission connected with the Australian Board of Missions, whose sphere is from Cape Vogel to Mitre Rock, began work in 1891 under the Rev. A. A. Maclaren. It now has a bishop, 8 clergy, 5 laymen, 10 ladies, 30 South Sea teachers, 16 Papuan teachers and evangelists, 540 members, 432 catechumens. The Roman Catholics, with headquarters at Yule Island, number 4,597, with 25 priests, 20 lay brothers, 37 sisters, 15

catechists, 29 stations, 28 schools, and 1,596 scholars.

German New Guinea (Kaiser Wilhelm's Land): The northeastern section of New Guinea, together with some adjacent islands, has been in German possession since 1884. The area is estimated at 70,000 square miles, and the native population at 110,000, with 184 whites and 207 others (mostly Chinese). The Neuendettelsau Mission began work in 1886. It has 13 stations, 45 churches, 2,180 church-members, 1,414 communicants, 1,359 catechumens, 3,395 adherents, 35 missionaries and assistants, 18 native preachers, and 25 schools. The Rhenish Missionary Society began work in 1887. It has 4 stations, 12 missionaries, 3 native teachers, 94 baptized natives, 75 communicants, and 7 schools with 296 scholars. The Roman Catholics number 1,000 with 24 priests, 20 assistants, 29 sisters, 10 stations, and 10 schools with 495 scholars.

New Hebrides: A group of islands in 166°–171° east longitude and 15°–21° south latitude, under the joint supervision and protectorate of France and Great Britain. The population is estimated at 80,000. The principal islands are Espiritu Santo, Mallicolo, Aurora, Pentecost, Tanna, Sandwich, and Efate or Vate. The mission history of the New Hebrides falls into three periods: (1) From 1839 to 1848, when it was under the care of the London Missionary Society. (2) From 1848 to 1864, when the Presbyterian missionaries from Nova Scotia and Scotland had charge, assisted by the Marine Service of the London Missionary Society. (3) From 1864 onward, when the Presbyterian churches of Australasia undertook the responsible control.

The Rev. John Williams (q.v.) of the London Missionary Society left Samoa in 1839 with a party of Samoan teachers for the New Hebrides. He placed three of them at Tanna and proceeded to Erromanga, where with James Harris, who was on a visit from Sydney, he was murdered and eaten by cannibals. Visits to various islands in the group were soon afterward paid by the Revs. Thomas Heath and Archibald Wright Murray from the same mission, and teachers were settled. In 1842 the Rev. George Turner and Henry Nesbit of the same mission made a few months' stay in Tanna, but had to withdraw through the hostility of the natives. Three years later native teachers from Samoa and Rarotonga were settled in Tanna. In the early days of the New Hebrides Mission, Christian teachers from other islands did splendid service, of whom at least 100 came from the London Missionary Society's training-institutions. During the second period, native agents from the same institutions were placed at nine or ten of the islands. In 1848 the Rev. John Geddie was sent out by the Presbyterians of Nova Scotia and settled in Aneiteum. Four years later he was joined there by the Rev. John Inglis of the Reformed Presbyterian Church of Scotland. Geddie retired in 1872. The following memorial is put up in his memory:—
" When he landed here in 1848 there were no Christians, when he left in 1872 there were no heathen." In 1854 another futile attempt was made on Tanna, but in 1858 Rev. John G. Paton (q.v.) with two other missionaries from Scotland settled there. Now after more than sixty years' toil there are three

well-established mission stations in Tanna with scores of out-stations and some thousands of converts. Paton spent afterwards fifteen years at Aniwa. In 1857 the Rev. George N. Gordon, a Presbyterian from Nova Scotia, settled on Erromanga. Three years later he was killed there with his wife, and some twelve years later his brother, James D. Gordon, was also murdered there. In 1864 the Australian Presbyterians took the responsible control of this mission, now called the New Hebrides Mission. It works in the southern islands of the group, and is supported by the Presbyterian Church in Canada, New Zealand, Australia, and Scotland, with the help of the special John G. Paton Mission Fund. It has now 27 missionaries, 5 hospitals, 300 native teachers, 20,000 professing Christians, and 20,000 other adherents. The work in the northern Hebrides is carried on by the Melanesian Mission. When George Augustus Selwyn (q.v.) was consecrated bishop of New Zealand in 1841, it was suggested that he should carry on a mission among the Melanesian Islands. From 1847 to 1849 he made many missionary voyages among these islands. In 1850 that part of the island world was adopted at a meeting of bishops of Australasia as their special sphere under the Australian Board of Missions. The Rev. John Coleridge Patteson (q.v.) joined the mission in 1855 and was consecrated bishop of Melanesia in 1861; he made many missionary voyages and established teachers in many islands. He was murdered in 1871 at Nakupu in the Solomon Islands (see below). The work was effectively carried on by Rev. H. Codrington and George Sarawia, the native deacon. In 1877 Rev. John Richard Selwyn was made bishop and carried on the work successfully. The headquarters are now in Norfolk Island. The language of Mota in the Banks Islands has been made the lingua franca of the mission, and every scholar is trained in it at Norfolk Island also, and teaches it on his return home. The work is carried on in three of the north islands of the New Hebrides, and also in the Banks Islands and Torres Islands, with 9 clergy, 344 teachers, 1,181 communicants, and 2,202 hearers. It has a hospital and training-school in Norfolk Island, with central schools in several of the groups.

Samoa: The Samoan group, extending over approximately 167°–174° west longitude and 13°–16° south latitude, is (since 1900) partitioned between the United States and Germany, the latter possessing all west of longitude 171°. The largest islands under German rule are Upolu, Manono, Apolinia, and Savaii; and under American, Tutuila and Manua, in the former is the commodious harbor of Pago Pago. The Rev. John Williams visited the islands of this group in 1830, and found that a mission had been started by some Christians from the Marquesas Islands, who after drifting about for three months had been carried to Manua. The first resident white missionary settled in 1836, the printing-press was established in 1839, the Manua Training Institution was founded in 1844. Under the Revs. George Turner and Charles Hardie, a central school for girls at Papauta was opened in 1891. There are now 11 missionaries, 174 ordained natives, 326 preachers, about 200 churches, 8,861

church-members, 232 Sunday-schools with 9,263 scholars, 211 day schools with 7,975 scholars, and 24,912 adherents. The Wesleyan Missionary Society began work in 1835, and that mission is now under the charge of the Methodist Missionary Society of Australasia. It has 47 churches, 29 preaching-stations, 3 missionaries, 5 native ministers, 35 catechists, 96 teachers, 487 class leaders, 255 local preachers, 76 Sunday-schools with 1,783 scholars, and about the same number of day schools and scholars, 2,683 church-members, and 6,778 attendants at public worship. The Roman Catholics began work in 1845, and have a bishop, 22 priests, 12 lay brothers, 13 sisters, 15 stations, 25 schools, and 6,315 adherents. The Mormon Mission has 17 elders and 303 adherents. The Seventh Day Adventists arrived in 1890, and have 2 missionaries, 10 adherents, and one school.

Santa Cruz: This group, under British control, lies north of the New Hebrides between 165° and 170° east longitude and 8°–12° south latitude; is sometimes reckoned with the New Hebrides. The largest islands are Santa Cruz, Tupua, and Vanikoro. Alvaro de Mendana of Peru made a disastrous attempt in 1567 to found a colony in the island which he named Santa Cruz. After his death his widow returned home with the colonists. In 1856 the Rev. John Coleridge Patteson (q.v.) visited the island, but did not land till 1862. Two years later he spent two days in the island, but the mission boat was attacked by the natives and two Norfolk Islanders named Edwin Nobbs and Fisher Young lost their more lives. In the next year or two Patteson paid more visits, but was not able to make much advance. In 1871 he attempted to land at Nukapu, one of the islands in the group, and entered a native canoe and went ashore. He was soon killed. Joseph Atkin and Stephen, a native of Bauro, died from wounds they had received. Bishop John Richard Selwyn visited Santa Cruz three years later, and had some of the natives educated at Norfolk Island, the headquarters of the Melanesian Mission. The work is now well established throughout the islands of the group under that mission, with 22 native teachers, 11 schools, 77 baptized, 16 communicants, 4 catechumens, and 221 hearers.

The Society Islands or **Tahiti Archipelago:** This group, under French rule, extends over 148°–155° west longitude and 15°–18° south latitude. It is sometimes made to include the Austral Isles (see above). The principal island is Tahiti, with an area of 600 square miles, while Moorea has an area of about 50 square miles. The total population is about 15,000. Missions were begun by the London Missionary Society, whose ship " The Duff " under the command of Captain James Wilson reached Tahiti in 1797 with 30 missionaries. Severe hardships were endured and the missionary band was soon much reduced in numbers. The first Christian church in the Pacific was dedicated here in 1800, and the long night of toil ended in 1811, when the conversion of King Pomare and the burning of idols in several islands ushered in a brighter day, a printing-press was established in 1817, and a Tahitian Missionary Society started in the following year. The Rev. John Williams arrived in 1817, and for fifteen years made Raiatea his home. A complete Bible was published in 1839, chiefly through the labors of Rev. Henry Nott, one of the first missionaries, who rendered forty-eight years of valuable service. In 1836 two French Roman Catholic priests who attempted to settle in Tahiti were expelled by the queen, but shortly afterwards the Roman Catholics were established in the island by the French government. The Paris Missionary Society has 18 stations, 5 missionaries, 11 European teachers, 27 native pastors, 4,615 church-members, 253 catechumens, 1,794 scholars. There are 7,008 Roman Catholics, 23 mission priests, 10 lay brothers, 24 sisters, 80 catechists, 85 stations, and 14 schools with 207 scholars. The Seventh Day Adventists arrived in 1892, and have 7 missionaries, 73 adherents, and one school with 30 scholars.

Niue or Savage Island: See Vol. xii., supplement.

The Solomon Islands: These islands lie in 155°–163° east longitude and 5°–11° south latitude. The large eastern island Bougainville and some smaller islands and islets belong to Germany; the western islands have since 1899 been in possession of Great Britain, and these include the important islands of Choiseul, Mahaga, Guadalcanar, Malayta, and Christoval; area 8,357 square miles, population about 150,000. The Roman Catholic missions were begun in the South Solomon Islands by the Marist Fathers in 1845 under Bishop Epalle, who with three priests was killed and eaten by cannibals on Ysabel Island. In 1895 a mission was begun in the North Solomon Islands. There are now in both groups 390 Roman Catholics, a bishop, a rector, 20 priests, 12 stations, 1,180 catechumens, and 12 schools with 357 scholars. The congregation of The Sacred Heart has also 12 priests at Issoudun. The Melanesian Mission began work in the Solomon Islands in 1857 under Bishop G. A. Selwyn and Rev. John Coleridge Patteson. It now has stations and schools on most of the group, with 11 clergy, 393 teachers, 151 schools, 8,026 baptized, 1,822 communicants, 1,163 catechumens, and 2,377 hearers. The Methodist Missionary Society of Australasia commenced work in 1902 under Rev. George Brown. It now has 27 churches, 13 preaching-stations, 4 missionaries, 2 missionary sisters, 127 class leaders, 68 church-members, 12 South Sea teachers, 6 Sunday-schools with 1,050 scholars, 15 day schools with 857 scholars, and 8,800 hearers. The South Sea Evangelical Mission began work in these islands in 1904. It has on four of the islands 11 missionaries, 4 stations, and 45 out-stations with native teachers, 1 boarding-school with 100 scholars; about 430 islanders have been baptized.

Tonga or Friendly Islands: The Tonga Islands lie south of the Samoan group and east of the Fijian, in 173°–177° west longitude and 15°–23° 30′ south latitude; area 390 square miles, population 22,000. Since 1899 they have been under British protection. Mission work was begun in 1797 by the London Missionary Society, whose ship " The Duff " settled ten missionaries there. Three of them, Daniel Bowell, Samuel Gaulton, and Samuel Harper, were killed by natives and the mission was abandoned without success in 1800. The Wesleyan

Methodist Missionary Society reopened the work in 1822 under the Rev. W. M. Lawry, but he left in the following year so that the Wesleyan Methodist Mission practically dates from 1826 when the Rev. John Thomas landed. In the mean time some native missionaries, sent from Tahiti, in the Society Islands, to open a station in Fiji, were detained through stress of weather in Tongatabu. Other workers were soon sent from Tahiti, and the adherence of a chief and 400 people was gained, and a church was built. After the Rev. John Thomas, who was the evangelist of Tonga, the Rev. Stephen Rabone and Thomas Adams and others consolidated the work. A most remarkable feature of the past thirty years has been the Tubou College, founded by Dr. Egan Moulton, where a number of young men have been trained for New Guinea and other mission fields. The whole group has been Christianized, and Tonga has taken its place among the civilized nations. In 1885 the Rev. Sidney Baker, who was afterwards premier, caused a disruption by founding the Tonga Free Church, which, though not connected with any conference, has remained loyal to Methodist doctrine and polity. It has 15,000 adherents. The original Wesleyan Church claims about 5,000, and there is a prospect of reunion in the near future. The Roman Catholics have a bishop, 22 priests, and 14 stations. The Seventh Day Adventists, who arrived in 1890, have 4 missionaries, 12 adherents, 2 schools with 69 scholars.

ARTHUR N. JOHNSON.

BIBLIOGRAPHY: Consult the literature under the articles on the workers to which reference is made in the text, the *Reports* of the various societies operating in these islands, and the literature on the missionary societies given in vii. 417 of this work. Also the following selected from a large range of books: *A Missionary Voyage to the Southern Pacific Ocean, 1796–98, in the Ship " Duff,"* London, 1799; W. Ellis, *Polynesian Researches,* ib. 1829; J. Williams, *A Narrative of Missionary Enterprises in the South Sea Islands,* late eds., ib. 1866, Philadelphia, 1889; W. Hoffmann, *Sieg des Kreuzes auf Tahiti,* Basel, 1844; M. Duby, *Hist. de la distraction des missions évangiles à Taiti en 1844,* Paris, 1845; G. A. Lundie, *Missionary Life in Samoa, 1840–41,* Edinburgh, 1845; H. Weginer, *Geschichte der christlichen Kirche auf dem Gesellschafts-Archipel,* Berlin, 1845; H. Melville, *Typee; or, Marquesas Island. Polynesian Life,* New York, 1846; E. Michelis, *Die Völker der Südsee und die Geschichte der protestantischen und katholischen Missionen unter derselben,* Münster, 1847; H. T. Cheever, *Island World of the Pacific,* New York, 1851; W. F. Besser, *Der Missionär und sein Lohn, oder die Früchte des Evangeliums in der Süd-See,* Halle, 1852; Abbé Verguet, *Hist. de la première mission catholique . . . de Mélanesie,* Paris, 1854; Sarah S. Farmer, *Tonga and the Friendly Islands; with a Sketch of their Mission History,* London, 1855; *Tahiti and its Missionaries,* ib. 1858; G. Cuzent, *Iles de la Société.* Tahiti, Paris, 1860; T. West, *Ten Years in South Central Polynesia; Reminiscences of a Mission to the Friendly Islands and their Dependencies,* London, 1865; G. Pritchard, *Missionary's Reward: Gospel in the Pacific,* ib. 1866; C. F. Angus, *Polynesia,* ib. 1867; S. Macfarlane, *Story of the Lifu Mission,* ib. 1873; idem, *Among the Cannibals of New Guinea,* ib. 1888; Mrs. H. S. Thompson, *Ponape,* Philadelphia, 1874; A. W. Murray, *Missions in Western Polynesia,* London, 1862; idem, *Forty Years' Mission Work in Polynesia and New Guinea,* ib. 1876; idem, *Martyrs of Polynesia,* ib. 1885; A. Fornander, *An Account of the Polynesian Race,* 3 vols., ib. 1878–85; P. A. Lesson, *Les Polynésiens, leur origine, leur migrations, leur langage,* Paris, 1880; R. Steele, *The New Hebrides and Christian Missions,* London, 1880; Mrs. M. V. Dahlgren, *South Sea Sketches,* Boston, 1881; R. W. Logan, *The Work of God in Micronesia, 1853–83,* ib. 1884; J. Mbulu; *Joel Bulu; native Minister in the South*

Seas, London, 1884; W. W. Gill, Jottings from the Pacific, ib. 1885; idem, From Darkness to Light in Polynesia, ib. 1894; G. S. Rowe, A Pioneer. J. Thomas, Missionary to the Friendly Isles, ib. 1885; A. Williamson, Missionary Heroes in the Pacific, Edinburgh, 1885; E. E. Crosby, Persecutions in Tonga, 1886, London, 1886; H. Bingham, Story of the Morning Star, Boston, 1886; A. Buzacot, Mission Life in the Pacific, London, 1886; J. Inglis, In the New Hebrides, ib. 1887; A. Penny, Ten Years in Melanesia, ib. 1887; J. Chalmers, Pioneer Life in New Guinea, ib. 1888, new ed., 1895; idem, Work and Adventure in New Guinea, ib. 1902; J. B. F. Pompallier, Early History of the Catholic Church in Oceania, Auckland, 1888; R. H. Codrington, Melanesian Studies in Anthropology and Folklore, London, 1891; A. Monfat, Dix années en Melanésia, Lyon, 1891; O. Michelsen, Cannibals won for Christ, London, 1893; The New Hebrides South Sea Islands. Quarterly Jottings of the J. G. Paton Mission Fund, Woodford, 1893; G. Cousins, Story of the South Seas, London, 1894; idem, From Island to Island in the South Seas, ib. 1894; J. M. Alexander, The Islands of the Pacific, New York, 1895; C. S. Horne, Story of the London Missionary Society, 1795–1895, London, 1895; Père Margaret, Mgr. Batallion et les missions de l'Océanie centrale, 2 vols., Lyon, 1895; A. E. Keeling, What he did for Convicts and Cannibals. Life and Work of S. Leigh, London, 1896; H. H. Montgomery, The Light of Melanesia. Record of thirty-five Years Mission Work in the South Seas, ib. 1896; A. C. P. Watt, Twenty-five Years' Mission Life on Tanna, New Hebrides, Paisley, 1896; J. King, Christianity and Polynesia, Sydney, 1899; idem, W. G. Lawes of Savage Island and New Guinea, London, 1909; R. Lovett, Hist. of the London Missionary Society, 1795–1895, vol. i., ib. 1899; idem, Tamate: Life of James Chalmers, ib. 1902; E. Nijland, J. Williams, de Apostel van Polynesië, Nijkerk, 1899; E. S. Armstrong, History of the Melanesian Mission, London, 1900; R. W. Thompson, My Trip in the " John Williams " to the South Sea Islands, ib. 1900; J. Watsford, Glorious Gospel Triumphs as seen in my Life and Work in Australasia, ib. 1900; P. Delord, Société des missions évangeliques. Voyage d'enquête en Nouvelle-Calédonie, Paris, 1901; F. Awdry, In the Isles of the Sea: the Story of fifty Years in Melanesia, London, 1902; C. Lennox, J. Chalmers of New Guinea, ib. 1902; H. A. Robertson, Erromanga, the Martyr Isle, ib. 1902; F. H. L. Paton, Lomai of Lenakei: a Hero of the New Hebrides, ib. 1903; H. H. Montgomery, The Light of Melanesia, ib. 1904; R. Parkinson, 30 Jahre in der Südsee. Land und Leute, Sitten und Gebräuche im Bismarckarchipel und . . . Salomoinseln, Stuttgart, 1907; G. Brown, Autobiography, London, 1908; idem, Melanesians and Polynesians: their Life Histories described and compared, London, 1910; H. A. Krose, Katholische Missionstatistik, Freiburg, 1908; H. N. Allen, The Islands of the Pacific; from the old to the new. A Collection of Sketches missionary and diplomatic, New York and Chicago, 1908; F. W. Christian, Eastern Pacific Lands; Tahiti and the Marquesas Islands, London, 1910; J. C. Lambert, Missionary Heroes in Oceania, Philadelphia, 1910; P. G. Peekel, Religion und Zauberei auf dem mittleren Neu Mecklenburg, Bismarckarchipel, Südsee, Münster, 1910; C. G. Seligmann, The Melanesians of British New Guinea, Cambridge, 1910; W. D. Westervelt, Legends of Ma-ui, a Demigod of Polynesia, and of his Mother Hina, Honolulu, 1910.

SOUTH, ROBERT: Church of England prelate and preacher of first rank ; b. at Hackney, London, Sept. 4, 1634; d. in London July 8, 1716. His father was a wealthy London merchant, who afforded his son every advantage for a thorough education. His preparatory studies were pursued in the Westminster School, where he became a king's scholar, under the famous master, Dr. Richard Busby. In 1651 he was admitted as a student of Christ Church, Oxford (B.A., 1655; M.A., 1657, also 1659 at Cambridge; B.D., and D.D., 1663; and D.D., at Cambridge, 1664). During this year he composed a Latin poem congratulating Oliver Cromwell on the peace which he had concluded between England and Holland. South was ordained in 1658 by one of the bishops who had been deprived of his bishopric during the protectorate. In 1660, the year of the restoration of the monarchy, he was elected orator to the University of Oxford, and preached before the royal commission a sermon entitled the Scribe Instructed, which immediately placed him in the front rank of English preachers. He delivered the university oration when Clarendon was installed chancellor of Oxford—a discourse which so impressed Clarendon that he appointed him his domestic chaplain. This led to his installation, in 1663, as the prebendary of St. Peter's, Westminster. In the same year he took the degree of doctor in divinity; and in 1670 he was made a canon of Christ Church, Oxford. In 1678, he was presented to the rectory of Islip in Oxfordshire, the revenue of which, some £200, he applied, half to the payment of his curate, and half to educating and apprenticing the poorer children of the parish. He soon became one of the king's chaplains, and preached a sermon before Charles II., marked by invective against Cromwell, and, what is not very common with South, violation of good taste. This recommended him to the monarch, who suggested his appointment to the next vacant bishopric. But South declined all such offers. While he was a strenuous defender of the English church, he was a determined enemy of the Roman Catholics. The concealed popery of Charles and the open popery of James met with determined opposition from South. His stiff loyalty led him to refuse to sign the invitation, drawn up by the archbishop of Canterbury and bishops, to the prince of Orange to assume the throne; but subsequently, when James had formally abdicated, and the crown was settled upon William and Mary, South gave in his allegiance to the new government. While he did not seek the honors of the Establishment, he was the determined enemy of dissent, and preached against it. He opposed the Act of Toleration (see LIBERTY, RELIGIOUS). When an attempt was made, through a royal commission, to unite the Dissenters with the Established Church, by modifying the liturgy, South entreated them to part with none of its ceremonial. In 1693, due to his Animadversions upon Dr. Sherlock's Book, entitled: A Vindication of the Holy . . . Trinity (London, 1693; cf., Tritheism Charged upon Dr. Sherlock's New Notion of the Trinity, 1695), he had a controversy with William Sherlock, a fellow churchman, and dean of St. Paul's, who, in his construction of the doctrine of the Trinity, fell into tritheism. South advocated the Nicene view. The last part of his life was clouded with sickness and debility which laid him aside from the active duties of his calling.

South's distinction is that of a preacher, and he is second to none in any language. No one has combined and blended logic and rhetoric in more perfect proportions. He argues closely and rigorously; but the argument never interferes with the fluency and impetuosity of the discourse; even such subjects as predestination and the Trinity are made popular and interesting by his powerful grasp and handling, and all this is heightened by his remarkable style. The closeness and intimacy of the connection between thought and word is hardly excelled by Shakespeare.

South was a Calvinist at a time when the drift of the High-church episcopacy, which he favored, set strongly toward Arminianism. Though anti-Puritan, and bitterly so, in regard to polity, both civil and ecclesiastical, he was a Puritan in theology. John Owen was not a higher predestinarian than he, and Richard Baxter was a lower one. It must have been from an intense conviction of the truth of this type of doctrine, that South, in the face of all his prejudices and of his ecclesiastical and courtly connections, defended it with might and main. For this reason, the great anti-Puritan has continued to have warm admirers among Puritans and Non-conformists.

There have been many editions of his *Sermons* (best ed., 12 vols., London, 1704–44, with a memoir of his life and writings in vol. xii., 1717; reissued, ed. W. G. T. Shedd, 5 vols., Boston, 1866–71).

W. G. T. Shedd†.

Bibliography: The standard memoir is that in the *Sermons*, ut sup. Consult further John Barber's funeral oration, *The Character of the Rev. and Learned Dr. Robert South*, London, 1716; A. à Wood, *Athenæ Oxionenses*, ed. P. Bliss, iv. 631–632, and *Fasti*, ii. 158, 182, 200, 276, 281, 334, 4 vols., London, 1813–20; W. C. Lake, *South the Rhetorician*, in J. E. Kempe, *Classic Preachers of the English Church*, 2 series, London, 1877–78; W. H. Hutton, *The English Church (1625–1714)*, pp. 268, 298, London, 1903; *DNB*, liii. 275–277.

SOUTHCOTT, sauth′cet, **JOANNA, AND THE SOUTHCOTTIANS:** The founder of a short-lived English sect (b. at Gittisham, 14 m. n.e. of Exmouth, Devonshire, Apr., 1750; d. at London Dec. 27, 1814) and her followers. Interpreting the text Rev. xii. 1 sqq. as signifying the speedy advent of the Messiah, she declared herself to be the bride of the Lamb, and, although sixty-four years old, announced that she was about to give birth to the future Messiah, this belief being caused probably by tympanites. She required her followers to keep the Jewish laws regarding clean and unclean meat and the observance of the Sabbath. A magnificent cradle was made to receive the future prince, or "second Shiloh," and both Joanna and her adherents waited patiently for her delivery. She died, however, of the disease named above; but her tracts, some sixty in number, and her works, of which the most important were *The Strange Effects of Faith, with Remarkable Prophecies . . . of Things which are to come* (2 parts, Exeter, 1801–02; contains autobiographical material); *A Dispute between the Woman and the Power of Darkness* (London, 1802); *Divine and Spiritual Communications* (1803); *Warning to the Whole World from the Sealed Prophecies of Joanna Southcott* (2 parts, 1803); *The Second Book of Visions* (1803); *Copies and Parts of Copies of Letters and Communications, written from Joanna Southcott* (1804); *Second Book of the Sealed Prophecies* (1805); *A Caution and Instruction to the Sealed* (1807); *The True Explanation of the Bible* (7 parts, 1804–10); and *The Book of Wonders* (5 parts, 1813–1814), were still eagerly read by her followers, who did not abandon hope of the predicted Messiah. The gradually dwindling sect assembled for a time in London to hear the words of the prophetess Elisabeth Peacock, and later met in the house of her son, in Trafalgar Street, but it is unlikely that it survived the year 1880.   (O. Zöckler†.)

Bibliography: A considerable literature, belonging to the period of her life and a very few years after her death, is indicated in the *British Museum Catalogue*, s.v. The sources are her own writings, which contain, in fragmentary form, considerable biographical detail. Consult: *The Life and Death of Joanna Southcott*, London, 1815; (J. Fairburn), *The Life of Joanna Southcott, the Prophetess*, ib. 1814; *Memoirs of the Life and Mission of Joanna Southcott*, ib. 1814; *The Life and Prophecies of Joanna Southcott*, ib. 1815; J. H. Blunt, *Dictionary of Sects, Heresies,. . . .*, pp. 568–570, Philadelphia, 1874; *DNB*, liii. 277–279; Alice Seymour, *The Express, Containing the Life and Divine Writings of Joanna Southcott*, London, 1909.

SOUTHGATE, HORATIO: Protestant Episcopal missionary bishop; b. in Portland, Me., July 5, 1812; d. in Astoria, L. I., Apr. 12, 1894. He was graduated from Bowdoin College, Brunswick, Me., 1832, and from Andover Theological Seminary, 1835, and was ordained deacon the same year; was engaged, under appointment by the Protestant Episcopal Church, in investigating the state of Mohammedanism in Turkey and Persia, 1836–38; ordained priest, 1839; missionary in Constantinople, as delegate to the oriental churches, 1840–44; Episcopalian missionary bishop for the dominions and dependencies of the Sultan of Turkey, Oct. 26, 1844–49; was rector of St. Luke's Church, Portland, Me., 1851–52; of the Church of the Advent, Boston, Mass., 1852–1858; and of Zion Church, New York City, 1859–1872; and then took up his residence at Ravenswood, L. I. He is the author of *Narrative of a Tour through Armenia, Kurdistan, Persia, and Mesopotamia* (2 vols., New York, 1840); *Narrative of a Visit to the Syrian (Jacobite) Church of Mesopotamia* (1844); *A Treatise on the Antiquity, Doctrine, Ministry, and Worship of the Anglican Church* (in Greek; Constantinople, 1849); *Parochial Sermons* (New York, 1860); and *The Cross above the Crescent, a Romance of Constantinople* (Philadelphia, 1877).

Bibliography: W. S. Perry, *The Episcopate in America*, p. 103, New York, 1895.

SOUTHWORTH, FRANKLIN CHESTER: Unitarian; b. at North Collins, N. Y., Oct. 15, 1863. He received his education at Harvard University (B.A., 1887; M.A., 1892; S.T.B., 1892); was a teacher in secondary schools, 1887–89; served the Unitarian church at Duluth, Minn., 1892–97, and the Third Unitarian Church, Chicago, 1897–99; was secretary of the Western Unitarian Conference, 1899–1902; and became president of the Meadville Theological School, dean of the faculty, and professor of practical theology in 1902.

SOWER, sō′er, **CHRISTOPHER (CHRISTOPH SAUR):** American printer and publisher; Laasphe (18 m. w.n.w. of Marburg), Germany, 1693; d. at Germantown, Pa., Sept. 25, 1758. He studied at the University of Halle; in 1724 he emigrated to America and settled as a farmer in Lancaster county, Pa., but removed to Germantown in 1731 and practised medicine there. In 1738 he acquired, largely from philanthropic motives, a printing-press at Germantown, and began the publication of a German almanac, which was continued by his descendants for sixty years. In 1739 he issued the first number of the *Hoch-Deutsch pensylvanische Geschichts-Schreiber*, a religious and secular journal that exerted a large influence upon the Germans of

Pennsylvania. In 1743 he brought out a large quarto edition of Luther's translation of the Bible. This was the first Bible in a European language printed in America. The type was brought from Frankfort. Thereafter he issued many other works, both in German and English. In the German books the German form of his name is used. In connection with his printing business he established a paper-mill, a small ink factory, and a type-foundry, the first in America. Sower wrote *Ein abgenöthigter Bericht* (Germantown, 1739; Eng. transl. in *The Pennsylvania Magazine*, xii. 78–96, Philadelphia, 1888), pertaining to his quarrel with Conrad Beissel, founder of Ephrata (see COMMUNISM, II., 5); and *Verschiedene christliche Wahrheiten* (1748), an answer to Franklin's *Plain Truth* (Philadelphia, 1747).

SOZOMEN, sez'ō-men, **SALAMANIUS HERMIAS:** Church historian; b. at Bethelia, a town near Gaza, Palestine, c. 400. He came of a Christian family, his grandfather having been converted to Christianity, together with his household, through a miracle

Life. reputed to have been wrought by Saint Hilarion (q.v.) by casting out a demon from a neighbor Alaphrion. These were the beginnings of Christianity in the place, and Alaphrion is said to have built churches and cloisters, while the grandfather of Sozomen was celebrated as an exegete. Under Julian, on account of his faith, he was forced to seek safety in flight (*Hist. eccl.*, V., xv.). Sozomen seems to have been brought up in the circle of Alaphrion and acknowledges a debt of gratitude to the monastic order (I., i. 19). He appears familiar with the region around Gaza, and mentions having seen Bishop Zeno of Majuma, the sea-port of Gaza (VII., xxviii. 6). It is probable that he visited Jerusalem (II., xxvi. 3). Later he adopted the vocation of advocate, in which capacity he was active in Constantinople at the time he composed his history.

Sozomen wrote two works on church history; the first (cf. *Hist. eccl.*, I., i. 12), which has entirely disappeared, comprised in twelve books the history of the Church from the ascension to Licinius. Euse-

Two Works; Editions. bius, the Clementine Homilies, Hegesippus, and Sextus Julius Africanus were used in this history. The second and longer work was a continuation of the first, and was dedicated to Emperor Theodosius the Younger (editio princeps by R. Stephens, Paris, 1544, on the basis of Codex Regius, 1444). The text was first placed on a firm foundation by Valesius (Cambridge, 1720), who used, besides the text of Stephens, a Codex Fucetianus (now at Paris, 1445), "Readings" of Savilius, and the indirect traditions of Theodorus Lector and of Cassiodorus-Epiphanius. Reading reprinted the text of Valesius adding collations of a *Codex Castellani episc.* and a "Codex Jones." Hussey's posthumous edition (largely prepared for the press by John Barrow, who wrote the preface) is important, since in it the archetype of the Codex Regius, the Codex Baroccianus 142, is collated for the first time. But this manuscript was written by various hands and at various times and therefore is not equally authoritative in all its parts. [The ed. by R. Hus-

sey, Oxford, 1860, ought to be mentioned.] The "Church History" of Sozomen has not been preserved in its entirety, as is shown by the fact that IX., xvi. 4 promises matter which is not forthcoming. How much of the history is wanting can be estimated from the preface, where it is said that the work was to extend to the seventeenth consulate of Theodosius, that is, to 439 A.D., while the extant history ends about 425, so about half a book may be wanting. Güldenpenning supposed that Sozomen himself suppressed the end of his work because in it he mentioned the Empress Eudocia, who later fell into disgrace through her supposed adultery. But this assumption can scarcely be correct, since Nicephorus and Theodorus Lector appear to have read the end of Sozomen's work.

From what has been said, the history must have been written between 439 and 450, the latter the year of the death of Theodosius. Sozomen certainly

Sources of the "Church History." wrote after Socrates (cf. Socrates, *Hist. eccl.*, I., xxxviii. 9 with Sozomen, *Hist. eccl.*, II., xxx. 6–7). The literary relationship of these writers appears everywhere. Valesius asserted that Sozomen read Socrates, and Hussey and Güldenpenning have proved this. For example, Socrates, in I., x., relates an anecdote which he had heard, and says that neither Eusebius nor any other author reports it, yet this anecdote is found in Sozomen, I., xxii., the similarity of diction showing that the text of Socrates was the source. Doubts have been expressed as to the truth of Sozomen's claim in his preface that he used in his history reports of the councils, imperial letters, and other documents; but closer investigation shows this to be correct. He also seems to have consulted the laws (cf. XVI., i. 3, regarding the installation of patriarchs over the five dioceses of the Eastern Empire, where he cites more correctly than does Socrates). The ecclesiastical records used by Sozomen are principally taken from Sabinus, to whom he continually refers. In this way he uses records of the synods from that of Tyre (335) to that of Antioch in Caria (367). As an example, in II., xxvii. 14, he treats of the council of Jerusalem and says: "When they had done this they wrote to the emperor and to the church of Alexandria and to the bishops and clergy in Egypt, the Thebaïd and Lybia." Socrates speaks of the letter to the emperor and to the Alexandrians, but he knows nothing of the other letters. Sozomen appears also to have consulted the *Historia Athanasii* and also the works of Athanasius; for he completes the statements of Socrates from the *Apologia contra Arianos*, lix. sqq., and copies Athanasius' *Adv. episcopos Ægypti*, xviii.–xix. He also consulted the writings of Eusebius and Rufinus. The *Vita Constantini* of Eusebius is expressly cited in the description of the vision of Constantine, Rufinus is frequently used, and especially instructive in this respect is a comparison of Sozomen, II., xvii. 6 sqq. with Socrates, I., xv. and Rufinus X., xiv. For the anecdote regarding the childhood of Athanasius, Rufinus is the original; Socrates expressly states that he follows Rufinus, while Sozomen knows Socrates' version, but is not satisfied with it and follows Rufinus more closely. Of secular historians Sozomen probably used only Olympiodorus. A comparison with Zosimus, who also made use of this writer, seems to show that the whole ninth book of Sozomen, excepting the reflections of the author, is nothing more than an abridged extract from Olympiodorus. Oral tradition is occasionally utilized, also the *Vita Antonii* of Athanasius, lists of Persian martyrs (II., xiv. 5), *logoi* of Eustathius of Antioch (II., xix. 7), the letter of Cyril of Jerusalem to Constantius concerning the miraculous vision of the cross (IV., v. 4), letters of Julian (V., iii. 4), and other sources.

The spirit and interest of Sozomen's history is clearly apparent; he follows the thread of the narrative of Socrates but seeks to improve upon and to excel his original by elegance of diction, and by

Character of the History.

the use of excellent sources of which he makes skilful use. Generally he follows his authorities closely, sometimes almost literally; when they differ, he occasionally gives the various versions. The historical exposition is altogether impersonal; Sozomen assumes (III., xv.) that the task of history is to assemble facts without adding anything to them, hence he indulges in little criticism and usually adopts the views of his sources. This he does to such an extent that he has been charged with Arianism and Novatianism. In reality, in accord with his legal training, he has no opinion in theological questions; at the same time he was thoroughly pious and a great admirer of monasticism. The attempt of Sozomen to compose a better church history than that of Socrates was only partially successful. He frequently offers additional material but rarely improves upon his prototype. The errors into which Socrates fell in his treatment of the Eastern Church, and especially touching the first phase of the Arian controversy, are quietly copied by Sozomen. But as to the Western Church he was better informed and has made several important corrections. Still, those who would use his work should seek to disengage his citations from the context, and endeavor to reach his original sources. (G. LOESCHCKE.)

BIBLIOGRAPHY: The most convenient Eng. transl. is in *NPNF*, 2 ser., vol. ii., where useful prolegomena are to be found. The editions named in the text are usually accompanied by a *Vita*. Consult: Fabricius-Harles, *Bibliotheca Græca*, vii. 427 sqq., Hamburg, 1801; F. A. Holzhausen, *De fontibus quibus Socrates, Sozomenus . . . usi sunt*, Göttingen, 1825; Nolte, in *TQS*, 1861, pp. 417 sqq.; J. Rosenstein, in *Forschungen zur deutschen Geschichte*, i. 167–204, Göttingen, 1862; A. Güldenpenning and I. Ifland, *Der Kaiser Theodosius der Grosse*, pp. 21 sqq., Halle, 1878; C. de Boor, in *ŽKG*, vi (1883–84), 478–494; A. Güldenpenning, *Die Kirchengeschichte des Theodoret von Kyrrhos*, pp. 12 sqq., Halle, 1889; P. Batiffol, in *Byzantinische Zeitschrift*, vii (1898), 265–284, x (1901), 128 sqq.; Bardenhewer, *Patrologie*, p. 333, Eng. transl., St. Louis, 1908; J. Bidez, *La Tradition manuscrite de Sozomène et la tripartite de Theodore le lecteur*, in *TU*, xxxii. 2b (1908); Ceillier, *Auteurs sacrés*, viii. 525–34, xi. 102–103, 220; *DCB*, iv. 722–723; *KL*, xi. 534–536; and the literature named under Socrates (the church historian).

SPAETH, spêt, **PHILLIP FRIEDRICH ADOLF THEODOR:** Lutheran; b. at Esslingen (7 m. s.e. of Stuttgart), Württemberg, Oct. 29, 1839; d. in Philadelphia June 26, 1910. He was educated at the University of Tübingen, where he completed his studies in 1861, and, after being a tutor in the family of the Duke of Argyle in 1863, was pastor of St. Michael's and Zion's Lutheran Church, Philadelphia (1864–67). After 1867 he was pastor of St. Johannis' German Lutheran Church in the same city, and professor in the Lutheran Theological Seminary, Philadelphia, after 1873. From 1880 to 1888 he was president of the General Council of the Evangelical Lutheran Church in North America. He edited the General Council's German Sunday-school book in 1875 and the same body's German church book in 1877, as well as the magazine *Jugendsfreund* in 1877, being also joint editor of the Ministerium of Pennsylvania's Documentary History (Philadelphia, 1898). His independent works include *Evangelien des Kirchenjahres* (Philadelphia, 1870); *Brotsamen von des Herrn Tische* (1871); *General Council of the Evangelical Lutheran Church in North America* (1885); *Liederlust* (Allentown, Pa., 1886); *Saatkörner* (Philadelphia, 1893); *Dr. Wilhelm Julius Mann, ein deutsch-amerikanischer Theologe* (Reading, Pa., 1895); *Biography of Dr. Charles Porterfield Krauth* (vol. i., New York, 1898); *Annotations on the Gospel according to St. John* (1896). His " Order of Lutheran Worship " has been translated into English by H. D. Spaeth (Burlington, Ia., 1906).

SPAIN: A kingdom occupying the greater part of the most westerly peninsula in southwestern Europe; area (including the Canary Islands and the Balearic Isles) 196,173 square miles; population (1900) 18,618,086. The inhabitants nearly all belong to the Roman Catholic, which is the State Church. The constitution of 1875 declares (art. 11, § 2) that no one shall be molested on account of his religious opinion or in the exercise of his worship, provided the due observance of Christian morals is maintained; but declares again (§ 3) with apparent contradiction that ceremonies and public evidences other than of the state religion shall not be tolerated. By the term " public evidences " was implied not only the building of churches whose object is distinctly recognizable from without by such marks as portals, towers, or inscriptions, but also the singing of sacred music. On this account, for instance, the Evangelical Germans at Barcelona had to dispense with a tower in building a modest house of worship in 1903. This spirit of intolerance is explained by the fixed public estimate placed upon the unity of the Roman Catholic faith, which is a result of the early age of Christianity in Spain. After the rapid progress of Christianity from the first till the third century there followed a period of much stress; first through the Arian Visigoths and other Germanic races, but far more through the plundering and lawless violence of the Moorish conquerors. Yet the Church maintained at least three archbishoprics out of six, and twenty-nine bishoprics. But the religious ardor was especially revived and tenaciously developed in the persistent and bitter wars for the expulsion of the Mohammedans.

An invigorating reinforcement was constituted by the four orders of knights, which originated for the restoration of the sovereignty of the Roman

Catholic faith in Spain. Hand in hand with this was the work of the new monastic orders, especially the Dominicans, who spread rapidly and gained in influence from 1215, obtaining in 1233 the administration of the Inquisition (q.v.), introduced in 1215. This institution attained a more definite organization in Spain than elsewhere. By agreement in 1483, the king was authorized to nominate to the pope the grand inquisitor, and the court of first instance of this institution was subordinated to the royal supreme court. The Inquisition operated first against the spiritual remnants of Moorish Islam; then against those of the Jews after the act of expulsion in the sixteenth century; and, finally, after a brief restraint, against the incoming Evangelical movement. The *autos da fé* of such as were accused of heresy and executions by garroting occurred frequently, and at not a few places; for not only had a number of Evangelical congregations organized themselves, but also very resolute martyrs died for the cause. By the close of the century, the Roman Catholic Church had been completely reestablished, not without bloodshed. Such ecclesiastical disturbances as arose until after 1850 consisted in the occasional opposition of kings and governments to the popes' excessive claims of independence and the power of the Jesuits: for example, the king's acquisition, from 1757, of the right to nominate bishops; the expulsion of the Jesuits, in 1767; retrenchments on ecclesiastical property, from 1789, after the number of the clergy had been fixed in 1768 at 149,800 in a given population of 9,307,000 souls. In 1808, under Napoleon's king, Joseph, many larger cloisters were abolished; and in 1835, the smaller ones were likewise closed. In 1859, the Church relinquished all its real possessions, and these were afterward awarded to the separate congregations. In the way of compensation, the State guaranteed the maintenance of public worship and the clergy; and the pope obtained the right to nominate a spiritual dignitary in every diocese.

By the concordat of 1881, the hierarchical apportionment of the country provided seven metropolitan districts and thirty-eight bishoprics as follows: Burgos, with six suffragans; Santiago de Compostella, with five; Granada, with five; Saragossa, with seven; Toledo, with four (including Madrid); Valencia, with five; and Valladolid, with six episcopal sees. In addition, the abbot who has jurisdiction over the provinces of the orders of knighthood, who has residence at Ciudad Real, has episcopal rank. There are 2,200 parishes divided into two classes. A new Evangelical movement arose in Spain in 1855 through the Spaniard Francisco de Paula Ruet (q.v.), who, returning from Italy, where the Waldensian preaching was being eagerly received, published the Evangelical faith in Barcelona. The cause was further promoted by a man of spiritual force, Matamoros. However, imprisonment and exile were used against the movement until after the end of Bourbon rule in 1868. From that time, and after the return of the Bourbons in 1874, not a little has been done through the efforts of Evangelical associations and circles in Great Britain, Switzerland, and the German states

of the Rhine toward creating an Evangelical fellowship composed of native Spanish. Most successful was the Rhenish Pastor Fliedner, in Madrid. There is, however, no Spanish Evangelical Church as such, but there are four separate ones. What is known as the Iglesia España Reformatoria was organized by the Anglican Spanish Church Aid Society; and is, accordingly, High-church in its order and worship. It comprises eleven congregations and is directed by a bishop. The Methodists and the Baptists, together with the Plymouth Brethren, have a smaller scattering of congregations and members. The strongest Protestant body is the Iglesia Evangelica España, as founded by Fliedner and continued by one of his sons. This has twenty-one distinct congregations, and thirty-six preaching-stations. The supreme government is vested in an annual synod. The total number of Spanish Protestants is estimated at 13,000 to 14,000. Also the Germans have two Evangelical congregations in Spain; one in Madrid, and a stronger one in Barcelona, with two associate congregations. There are a great many weekly church periodicals and other tracts in circulation, furnished from England, Scotland, North America, and Germany for the support of Spanish Protestantism. See the following article.

W. Götz.

BIBLIOGRAPHY: On the general and Roman Catholic history of Spain consult: D. J. Saenz d'Aguirre, *Collectio maxima conciliorum omnium Spaniæ*, 2d ed., 6 vols., Rome, 1753; H. Florez, *España sagrada* (with continuations), 51 vols., Madrid, 1754–1879; F. W. Lembke, *Geschichte von Spanien* (continued by Schäfer and Schirrmacher), 6 vols., Hamburg, 1831–93; P. B. Gams, *Die Kirchengeschichte von Spanien*, 5 vols., Regensburg, 1862–79; P. Rousselot, *Les Mystiques espagnols*, 2d ed., Paris, 1869; G. Diercks, *Das moderne Geistesleben Spaniens*. Leipsic, 1883; idem, *Das moderne Spanien*, Berlin, 1908; P. Förster, *Der Einfluss der Inquisition auf das geistige Leben der Spanier*, Berlin, 1890; O. Werner, *Orbis terrarum catholicus*, pp. 38–49, Freiburg, 1890; H. C. Lea, *Chapters from the Religious Hist. of Spain connected with the Inquisition*, Philadelphia, 1890; idem, *History of the Inquisition of Spain*, 4 vols., New York, 1906–07; F. Meyrick, *The Church in Spain*, London, 1892; M. R. Burke, *Hist. of Spain*, 2 vols., London, 1900; M. A. S. Hume, *The Spanish People*, London, 1901; A. Astrian, *Historia de la Compañia de Jésus en la asistencia de España*, Madrid, 1902 sqq.; W. Webster, *Gleanings in Church Hist. in Spain and France*, London, 1903; H. Leclercq, *L'Espagne chrétienne*, Paris, 1906; C. Rudy, *The Cathedrals of Northern Spain. Their History and their Architecture, together with much of Interest concerning their Bishops, Rulers, etc.*, London, 1906; K. Häbler, *Geschichte Spaniens unter den Habsburgern*, vol. i., Gotha, 1907; M. Andujar, *Spain of To-day from Within*, New York, 1909; W. W. Collins, *Cathedral Cities of Spain*, ib. 1909; H. Giessen, *Die christlich-arabische Literatur der Mozaraber*, Leipsic, 1909; C. C. Perkins, *Builders of Spain*, 2 vols., London, 1909; R. Tyler, *Spain: Study of her Life and Arts*, New York, 1909; *KL*, xi. 539–551.

On Protestantism in this country consult the literature under the following articles, and: *The Spanish Reformed Church. The Declaration set forth by the Central Consistory . . . with some Account of the Members and their Meetings at Gibraltar, . . . 1868*, London, 1868; J. A. Wylie, *Daybreak in Spain; its new Reformation*, London, 1870; F. G. J. Grape, *Spanien und das Evangelium*, Halle, 1896; H. E. Noyes, *Church Reform in Spain. A Short History of the Reformed Episcopal Churches of Spain and Portugal*, London, 1897; E. Schäfer, *Beiträge zur Geschichte des spanischen Protestantismus und der Inquisition im 16. Jahrhundert*, 3 vols., Gütersloh, 1902; G. Borrow, *The Bible in Spain*, late ed., London, 1908; F. E. and H. A. Clark, *The Gospel in Latin Lands*, pp. 125–159, New York, 1909; G. H. B. Ward, *The Truth about Spain*, London, 1911.

SPAIN, EVANGELICAL WORK IN.

I. The Reformation in Spain: At the close of the Middle Ages the type of Christianity prevailing in Spain was more militant, more independent, more
Evangelical, that is, more nearly Prot-
1. The estant, than that to be found in any
Early other nation of Christendom. More
Movement. militant, because the 700 years' war
which the Christians of Spain had waged with the Mohammedans had given strength and tenacity to their religious sentiments; more independent, because the unbroken spirit of the Spanish rulers and people had secured the interposition of the secular authority to combat the deteriorating influence of the Roman Curia upon the local church; more Evangelical, because twenty years before Luther nailed his theses to the church door at Wittenberg the Spanish church had felt the purifying and regenerating influence of a reformation largely Protestant in spirit and aims. This reform was the outcome of a plan conceived by Queen Isabella, upon the union of the peninsular states to form the Spanish kingdom in 1492. Its execution was accomplished under the leadership of Francisco Ximenes de Cisneros (see XIMENES DE CISNEROS), a Franciscan monk and confessor to the queen. The concordat of 1482 had given the Spanish crown the right of visitation and of nomination to benefices. Cisneros was permitted to use these powers to restore the strictest monastic discipline in the convents, and to purge the secular clergy of those abuses which were common to the time. Having improved the morals of the Spanish clergy he set himself to overcome their ignorance and lack of culture. The reading and study of the Bible were made a special feature in their training, something previously unknown; new schools of theology were established, with courses in Bible exegesis; and a band of scholars was collected at Alcala in 1502, who undertook at the expense of Cisneros the preparation of the celebrated Complutensian Polyglot (see BIBLES, POLYGLOT, I.). About the same time he was instrumental in the establishment of universities at Alcala, Seville, and Toledo, where the study of the classics was fostered and a large sympathy was shown with the labors of Erasmus and the Humanists. Unlike Luther, Cisneros made no direct attack on the abuses or authority of the papacy, yet when he encountered the opposition of the pope, in dealing with the abuses of the local church, he assumed an attitude of virtual independence, and was protected in it by the Spanish rulers. The immediate influences of this movement were largely confined to the clergy, but it gradually wrought a distinct change in the religious life of the whole nation and developed in Spain a unique type of Roman Catholicism. In its essential features it represents a partial and limited development of the Protestant thesis, and, with its Humanistic and Evangelical tendencies, it was fitted to serve as the natural forerunner of a truly Protestant Reformation. At the same time, catching up as it did the religious zeal and initiative of the Spanish people and fusing them into a relatively pure and intelligent form of Catholicism, it forged the very weapon that was destined to give the death stroke to Evangelical Christianity on Spanish soil, and trained the leaders who were to rally the forces of Roman Catholicism in the sixteenth century for the long and bitter struggle against Protestant principles throughout Western Christendom.

The advancement of the Spanish monarch to the imperial throne in 1520, as Charles V., opened a wide channel for the introduction of Lutheran and Reformed teachings into Spain. At first,
2. Protes- Luther's doctrines were generally re-
tant ceived among the educated classes with
Movement. interest and favor, and their spread
was helped for a time by the liberal tendencies prevailing among the Spanish hierarchy, as well as by the temporizing policy of Charles V. in dealing with Luther and the Protestant princes of Germany. With respect to Charles' attitude, it was even asserted by the confessor of the emperor, who himself favored the Protestants, that Charles secretly sympathized with the movement and that he hoped to use Luther as a lever for forcing upon the German church a Reformation after the Spanish model. Subsequently a gradual reaction against reform among the Spanish clergy and a change in the policy of Charles made Protestantism a proscribed religion in Spain, narrowed the circle of its adherents to the more earnest and daring spirits, and, after the Diet of Augsburg in 1530, subjected the Protestants to a persecution constantly growing in severity. The principal features marking its growth were its almost exclusive confinement to the privileged and educated classes; the lack of organization, except small congregations at Seville and Valladolid; the large numbers from the Roman Catholic clergy and theologians who embraced it; and especially the large numbers of persons among its converts, illustrious either for their rank or learning. Notable among them are the following: Alphonso Valdes, secretary of Charles V.; Alphonso de Bernaldez, chaplain to the emperor, who suffered condemnation in 1537; Bartalome Carranza y Miranda, archbishop of Toledo, who was condemned for holding Protestant views; Roderigo de Valera, who laid the foundations of the church in Seville and was condemned by the Inquisition in 1541; Juan Gil, otherwise known as Doctor Egidius, a famous preacher of Seville who was nominated in 1550 to the bishopric of Tortosa, but before his installation was condemned for heresy; Don Carlos de Seso, a distinguished nobleman who did much for the Protestant cause throughout Spain; Jayme Enzinas and his brother Francesco de Enzinas (qq.v.), two young men of noble birth who were converted while students abroad, the former of whom suffered martyrdom in Rome in 1546, and the latter translated the first Spanish ver-

sion of the New Testament and had it printed at Antwerp in 1543 for distribution in Spain. Besides, many convents of monks and nuns, especially those in the neighborhood of Seville and Valladolid, were largely leavened with the Protestant heresy. In spite of this impetus, Protestantism was effectually suppressed in Spain after a brief career of scarcely half a century. The chief repressive agency was the Inquisition, which assumed in Spain, as the joint instrument of civil and religious absolutism, its sternest form, and made use of the most drastic and arbitrary methods. But it is to be remarked that the Protestant forces in Spain were paralyzed and finally overcome, not so much by the violent persecution at home as by the unfavorable impression made upon the Spanish people by the actions of Protestants abroad. The uprising of the German peasants in 1524 in behalf of social reform caused great alarm among the privileged classes in Spain and greatly prejudiced them against the introduction of doctrines which seemed to foment revolution elsewhere. Greater antagonism was aroused by the alliance of the Protestant princes of Germany with the king of France, Francis I., the bitter enemy of Spain, and later was increased by the revolt of the Protestants in the Netherlands against Spanish rule, so that after a time Protestants came to be looked upon not only as heretics but as traitors and rebels, and it became increasingly difficult for any loyal Spaniard to embrace Protestantism. Prior to the abdication of Charles V. in 1546 the activities of the Inquisition against Protestants were somewhat restricted, and though Philip II. on his accession gave it a free hand, the work of extermination was not begun in deep earnest until 1557. The first " auto da fé " was celebrated at Valladolid in 1559, and thereafter the work of executing Protestant victims in the principal cities of Spain was conducted under the joint auspices of Church and State, combining the features of a religious festival and a popular holiday. In 1559 it is estimated that there were 1,000 Protestants in each of the cities, Seville and Valladolid, and a relatively large number in other sections of Spain. By the year 1570 Protestantism in Spain was cut off, root and branch, practically all of its converts having suffered either banishment or martyrdom, and for the three centuries that followed the blood of its martyrs was as seed in barren soil.

II. Anticlerical Movements: If it was fanatical patriotism allied with ecclesiasticism that crushed the Protestant movement in Spain in the sixteenth century, it has been an enlightened **1. Political** patriotism arrayed against ecclesiasticism that has afforded a shield for the **Opposition.** Evangelical forces in Spain in modern times. The radical and revolutionary philosophy of the French skeptics of the eighteenth century early found an easy, though a restricted, ground in Spain. Under its tuition many Spaniards saw their country fastened on by a parasitic tribe of nearly 140,000 priests, nuns, and sacristans, and they welcomed the Voltairean estimate of their worth. The cataclysm of the French Revolution did still more to disseminate the seeds of popular freedom, and before the downfall of Napoleon, liberalism was fully

born in Spain and prepared to enter, as in other Latin countries, into the long war against absolutism and clericalism. The first decisive step was taken in 1812, during the exile of King Ferdinand VII. The Spanish cortes, assembled for the first time in many years, was largely composed of lawyers and literary men, and though they swore to tolerate no faith but Roman Catholicism in the land, they abolished the Inquisition, curtailed the power of the clergy, and framed a constitution. The restoration of Ferdinand in 1814 resulted in the overturning of their work and a violent persecution in the vain attempt to exterminate the Liberal party. From the death of Ferdinand, in 1833, until 1873 occurred a series of heated revolutionary conflicts between the liberal and conservative elements, with alternating victories, but with the anti-clerical cause steadily gaining ground. In 1851, by the concordat established with the pope (see CONCORDATS AND DELIMITING BULLS, VII.), the monastic orders were limited to three. In 1854 the Liberals, being then in power, after granting compensation, sold the church lands. In 1858 and again in 1868 religious liberty and freedom of worship were proclaimed, but this meant only freedom to attack the Church of Rome, and full religious tolerance was by no means established. In 1873 the cortes proclaimed a republic, but this was overthrown by the army and Alphonso XII. was seated on the throne. From that time onward the monarchy has continued, and political questions have usually been settled by an appeal to the electorate, rather than to force. Politics among the leaders has largely degenerated into a scramble for the spoils of office, accompanied by more or less compromise with the church party, but there has come to Spain in these years, through the spread of liberal principles, an increasing measure of civil and religious liberty. The most significant event for Protestantism of late years was the returning to power, in the election of 1910, of Premier José Canalejas and his party, upon a platform pledging, among other reforms, absolute freedom of worship, civil supervision of conventual establishments, and the laicization of schools and colleges. The significance of this may be seen when it is understood that, previous to 1910, the Protestant denominations and missions were prohibited from displaying any insignia of worship or of propagating their doctrines publicly; and that, according to a recent count, the number of monks and nuns and other ecclesiastical officials in Spain totalled 154,517, receiving about eight million dollars yearly directly from the national treasury, besides various exemptions and privileges. The first step in the execution of this program brought about a break with Rome, the papal nuncio was recalled, and at the close of the year he had not returned to the Spanish court.

Another phase of this anticlerical movement is the constantly diminishing respect shown by layman and ecclesiastic for ecclesiastical **2. Dissent** authority even in the sphere of religion. **and** This tendency is noticeable in the independent spirit animating the several **Unbelief.** orders in their relation to each other and to the local clergy. Indeed, so loose has grown the bond between them and so bitter has become the antagonism that the assertion is more than justified that the ecclesiastical unity existing within the Roman Catholic Church in Spain is scarcely more real than that existing between the principal Evangelical denominations of Protestant countries. Again, this spirit has manifested itself within the ranks of the secular clergy in their protests against the tyranny and abuses of their superiors in the hierarchy, and they have usually been supported in their contentions by the common people. The most striking instance of this occurred in a movement originating in Sept., 1898, and led by an eminent Spanish priest, Seguismundo Pey Ordiex. This brilliant priest was born in Vich, in the north of Spain, educated in the University of Salamanca, and was for many years a parish priest in Mallorca and Barcelona. The despotism of the bishops became so offensive that he began to combat them in a weekly newspaper which he published and called *El Urbion*. This paper being suppressed by the bishop of Mallorca, Pey Ordiex went to Barcelona and founded a second paper, and, when this was suppressed, still a third, *El Cosmopolita*, which was condemned by the church in Nov., 1900. The rupture finally came because of the refusal of Pey Ordiex to obey an arbitrary order of the bishop of Barcelona, whereupon he was publicly suspended by the bishop, and forbidden to enter a church. He began to speak to the people in the open air, in theaters, and in public halls, attacking clericalism and preaching the Gospel. He at once became the popular idol and quickly gathered a great company of followers estimated at 100,000 or more. Among the number were at least 1,000 of the most zealous priests and friars in the various provinces of Spain. The movement was not properly organized, and, after two years, when the enthusiasm had somewhat abated, Pey Ordiex fell into a trap skilfully laid by the Jesuits and was compromised in the eyes of his followers; his influence was destroyed, and the movement collapsed, but it had demonstrated the readiness of many people and priests to respond to a stirring appeal against ecclesiastical abuses in behalf of freedom and purity in religion. Still another manifestation of this spirit has been the gradual, silent revolt of the great body of intelligent laymen against the asserted authority of the Roman Catholic Church. This drift has been in progress for more than a century and it has moved apace with the spread of culture and republican principles. Joseph M'Cabe (*Decay of the Church of Rome*, p. 88, London, 1909), writing in 1909, says: " Of the four or five million adult males in the country [Spain], only about one million are Roman Catholics, and these are for the most part illiterate." A distinguished visitor to Spain in 1910, speaking of the men of intelligence, says: " There are tens of thousands in the country whose only use for the Church is at marriage, christening, and burial services." And this must be the feeling that oppresses the visitor to Spain when he sees the few scattered worshipers in the magnificent cathedrals in the cities, and hears the contemptuous and jesting manner in which the average intelligent Spaniard refers to the liaisons of the priests, the worship of saints and images, the miracles wrought by relics, the pretentious ceremonies of the

church, or the solemn assumptions of the Roman pontiff.

III. Evangelical Activities: The memorable revolution of Sept., 1868, and the proclamation of liberty of conscience and worship by the new " provisional government " threw Spain open for the first time to all kinds of Evangelical work. The opportunity was speedily improved by the entrance of missionaries, representing various Protestant denominations of Great Britain, Ireland, the United States, Germany, Holland, Switzerland, and Sweden. In 1910 Protestant missions were conducted in forty-four large cities, with out-stations in 149 villages and towns; the total number of buildings regularly employed for Protestant worship being 116. The following societies were at work: (1) **Iglesia Española Reformada,** or the Reformed Church of Spain. This church is the outgrowth of an independent movement initiated and conducted exclusively by native Spaniards, but fostered and supported by the Spanish and Portuguese Church Aid Society, organized in 1867 among English and Irish Episcopalians. Under its auspices The Church of the Redeemer was organized in Madrid in 1869, and subsequently ten other churches were founded and united to constitute The Reformed Church of Spain, under the leadership of Bishop Juan Bautista Cabrera, formerly a Roman Catholic friar who was consecrated to his office by the archbishop of Dublin, in 1887. The number of congregations has increased to more than a score, the most important of which are found at Madrid, Valladolid, Salamanca, Villaescusa, Monistrol, San Vicente, Malaga, and Seville. Schools are conducted at each of these places and at numerous others. (2) **The American Board of Commissioners for Foreign Missions** opened its first mission in Spain at Santander in 1871, in charge of Rev. William H. Gulick, a Congregational minister, and his wife, Alice Gordon Gulick. At Santander Mrs. Gulick first established her celebrated school for girls. Later, in 1881, it was moved to San Sebastian, and after the Spanish-American War it was moved to Madrid and established in commodious quarters under the name of the " International Institute for Girls." An offshoot of this same school is the International College, now under the charge of the (Congregational) Woman's Board of Missions of the United States. In these schools many girls have been fitted to become Protestant teachers, or the wives of Protestant workers throughout Spain. The first church was organized in Santander in 1876 with seventeen members. Subsequently churches and day schools were established at San Sebastian and other points with a central station at Madrid. In 1899 these churches, seven in number, of the Congregational polity, were united with twelve of the Presbyterian order which had been founded by the several Presbyterian societies named below. This is an organic union with a ministry of twenty-three ordained pastors and five evangelists, and is called The Spanish Evangelical Church. (3) **The United Free Church of Scotland,** through the agency of the Spanish Evangelization Society (founded in Edinburgh in 1885), has established missions and schools in Seville,

Cadiz, Huelva, Granada, and various other places. (4) **The Irish Presbyterian Church** has opened missions and schools in Cordova and Puerta Santa Maria; and conducts a theological school in the latter place which has done not a little in training evangelists and pastors. (5) **The Dutch Presbyterians** are reported to have stations at Malaga, Almeria, and Cartagena. (6) **The Reformed Churches of Lausanne, and Geneva,** Switzerland, sustain missions at Barcelona, Reus, Tarragona, and Pontevedra. (7) **The English Wesleyan Methodists** undertook their first mission in Spain in 1816 from Gibraltar. This was soon abandoned because of the Roman Catholic opposition. Other efforts were made from 1830 to 1840, with Cadiz as a center, but were also abandoned. The mission was revived in 1869, at Barcelona, and a growing work has been conducted in that vicinity and in the Balearic Isles, just off the coast. The work at Barcelona has prospered greatly of late years under the leadership of Rev. Franklyn G. Smith. (8) **The German Lutherans** have an important work in Madrid, with several stations in the province, and a publication house which has done much to supply the country with evangelical literature. In Madrid also is located, in a fine building, the celebrated Lutheran " College of the Future " (Colegio de Porvenir). (9) **The American Baptist Missionary Union** has a station at Barcelona, with several preaching-points in the province. (10) **The Swedish Baptists** support one missionary in Valencia who has charge of several small churches. (11) **The Plymouth Brethren** (q.v.) have chapels and schools in La Coruña, Marin, San Tomé, Vigo, Figueras, Barcelona, Madrid, and various other places throughout the kingdom. (12) **The Christian Endeavor Societies** have been organized in connection with the Protestant churches throughout Spain and, to quote the words of a Protestant missionary on the field, " No other agency yet operating in Spain has [so vitally] produced the spirit of Christian fellowship and [so] helped toward vital union in Evangelical work as the Christian Endeavor." The number of societies is forty-eight, with a total membership of 1,549. Conventions are frequently held in the principal cities and practically all the Protestant communions are represented.

In 1910, statistics show that primary schools were conducted by Protestants in fifty-one of the principal cities and towns of Spain, with 167 teachers and 6,462 pupils. Secondary schools were conducted in the larger Evangelical centers such **2. Schools** as Alicante, Huelva, Rio Tinto, Madrid, **and Other** Santander, and Seville. The higher **Agencies.** institutions of learning were the " Presbyterian Theological Institute," at Puerta Santa Maria, the " International College," and the " International Institute for Girls," both at Madrid, and at Barcelona " The College of the Future." Two Protestant hospitals are located in Madrid, one in Barcelona, and a medical dispensary in Figueras. The Protestants have two orphanages in Madrid, and one at Escorial. The principal Evangelical periodicals are *La Luz, Amigo de la Infancia,* and *Esfuerzo Christiano,* all published at Madrid; *El Evangelista,* at Barcelona; *El Heraldo,* at Figuer-

as; *El Correo,* at Valencia, with others making eleven in all, most of which are issued monthly. The British and Foreign Bible Society, which entered Spain in 1868, has a central depository in Madrid and supports several colporteurs. Three other Protestant depositories and publishing-houses in Madrid, two in Barcelona, and one in Figueras, issue devotional, controversial, and educational literature at a low price. All of these agencies have been useful in the spread of Protestant culture and Evangelical Christianity throughout Spain.

The great hindrance to the propagation of Evangelical Christianity in Spain in modern times is the existing ecclesiastical corporation, with the ignorance, intolerance, and irreligion which it has fostered among the people. The strongest ally of the Protestant forces is the **3. Summary of Conditions.** new national spirit which has gradually emerged in the course of a century and has come in large measure to dominate Spanish thought and feeling, especially since the loss of colonial possessions has centered the interests of the nation on internal enterprises.

It is not surprising that the transition from the medieval to the modern point of view in the national consciousness of the Spanish people has been accompanied by a general drift toward skepticism. To them the Roman Church has appeared as the opponent of progress in every sphere, religious, social, intellectual. Therefore they say, "away with the Church"; and as Rome has consistently claimed to be the only representative of Christianity, the only true religion, they say " religion is Romanism, and we will have none of it." At the same time it could hardly be expected that they should assume other than an indifferent, or even hostile, attitude toward Protestantism. Their knowledge of Protestantism has come exclusively from their priests, who have presented to the people only caricatures of the Reformers and of Protestantism and have filled the minds of the people with prejudice and contempt for any enterprise promoted by Protestants. More than this, the Roman Catholic Church, by its emphasis on forms, ceremonies, and non-essentials, and by its failure to give the people the Bible or adequate instruction in the fundamental principles of morality, has perverted the conscience and corrupted the morals of the great mass of the people to such an extent that there can be little to appeal to them in the high moral teachings of Evangelical Christianity; and this is notoriously true of the entire Roman Catholic body, notwithstanding the fact that within it there are now thousands of sincere and faithful Christians, especially in the convents.

If the Protestant propaganda is to meet successfully the present crisis in Spain, the Protestant leaders by taking a stronger grasp on the agencies already in use and those which lie ready at hand, and by a sympathetic approach, and **4. Opportunities.** specific adaptation of their methods to the Spanish point of view, must speedily strive to attract the attention and win the respect of all classes. The opposition of the ecclesiastical corporation can best be offset by an intelligent and earnest effort to reach the individuals within the ranks of the clergy, to invite them to enter the Protestant ranks, and to provide means for their support and training until they can be fitted for active work. A converted Spanish friar, one who has the right to know, asserts that there are thousands of the purest and most zealous priests and friars in Spain, who are dissatisfied with their own religious status and inexpressibly grieved at the pitiable moral conditions which prevail among their brethren throughout Spain, and these would gladly welcome Protestantism, if their minds could be disabused of prejudice and they could be convinced that it was purer than Romanism. This is a point of strategic importance, which has hitherto been almost entirely overlooked by Protestants. The ignorance of the great mass of the people can be overcome only through the public schools, and Protestants should not only prosecute with all vigor the work of their own schools but should show their sympathy in every way with the cause of liberal education. To meet the intolerance and prejudice of the people the Protestant forces must become more aggressive. Through the secular press and on the platform they must challenge the assertions of Rome and show themselves willing and able to defend the doctrines and history of Protestantism before the bar of reason, and must show that Protestantism is at least entitled to the consideration of intelligent men. It must be demonstrated that Christianity is not necessarily compromised by the history and vicious practises of the Roman Catholic Church, and that true Christianity is not inconsistent with human freedom and progress in any sphere, scientific, social, or religious. In other words, they must provoke both the Romanists and infidels to public discussion of the issues involved, and must project the Protestant enterprise generally upon such a plane as will appeal to the intelligence, the imagination, and the patriotism of the Spanish people. This was the method of Luther and the Reformers, and it is justified by its fruits. To meet the irreligion of the people the surest method, both of attack and defense, is to give them the Bible. This must be accompanied by an aggressive evangelism that will restore vital religion and quicken the conscience of all classes; while everywhere Protestant leaders must insist upon such standards of morality among the converts as will commend the teachings of Protestantism to the whole people and put to shame the licentious abuses tolerated under the present religious régime.　　　　JUAN ORTS GONZALEZ.

The following is the text of an address (copied from *Evangelical Christendom*, Nov.–Dec., 1910, p. 130), signed on behalf of the British organization of the Evangelical Alliance by the president, chairman, treasurer, and general secretary, which was forwarded to Señor Canalejas, the president of the council of ministers, for transmission to H. M. the king of Spain:—

TO HIS MAJESTY DON ALFONSO XIII., KING OF SPAIN.

Sir,—On behalf of the Council and Members of the Evangelical Alliance (British Organization), representing Evangelical Christians of various Churches throughout the British Empire, we humbly address to Your Majesty this expression of our heartfelt gratitude for the publication of the Royal Order of June 6th, 1910, which interprets in its natural sense Article XI. of the Spanish Constitution, and grants to Spanish Evangelicals the toleration which the framers of the Constitution desired to give them.

We are convinced that this wise step has secured for Spain the good-will of all progressive peoples.

We rejoice with all friends of Religious Liberty that those who are unable to accept the State religion are permitted to worship God in accordance with their conscience, free from the disabilities which compelled them to conceal their existence as members of the Evangelical Churches, and subjected them to many inconveniences.

We earnestly trust that this enlightened policy will be continued until Spanish Evangelicals enjoy the Religious Liberty extended to Roman Catholics by Protestant nations.

BIBLIOGRAPHY: Besides the literature under the following article, consult: H. Dalton, *Die evangelische Bewegung in Spanien*, Wiesbaden, 1872; W. Pressel, *Das Evangelium in Spanien*, Freienwald, 1877; F. E. and H. A. Clark, *The Gospel in Latin Lands*, New York, 1909; J. M'Cabe, *The Decay of the Church of Rome*, ib. 1909.

SPAIN, SIXTEENTH-CENTURY REFORMATION MOVEMENTS IN: The Evangelical movement in Spain was preceded by, and partly simultaneous with, the movements of the mystics and Humanists. The mystics, called *alumbrados*, " enlightened," followed Pietism, and showed a certain independent attitude toward the external precepts of the Church. Francesco de Ossuna, 1527, in part three of his *Abencedario* (Toledo, 1527), laid stress on the worthlessness of all good works, and on " faith alone." The Humanism of Erasmus found an enthusiastic admirer in Alfonso de Valdés (q.v.), the imperial secretary. His brother Juan (q.v.) labored in behalf of the principle of justification by faith within the Roman Church, particularly in Italy, before attempts at reconciliation with the Protestants had been given up. Great persecution was encountered by the brothers Jaime and Francesco de Enzinas (q.v.) of Old Castile, from the now aroused Church. Francesco de San Roman, sent to Bremen, 1541, attended an Evangelical church service and was deeply stirred by the sermon of Jacobus Probst. He read Evangelical literature and drew up a Spanish catechism. Upon his return to Antwerp, he was seized and imprisoned for eight months. At Louvain Enzinas discouraged him from preaching because of his meager training and experience, but, borne away by his zeal, he went to Regensburg, where the emperor was presiding over the diet. Here his importunities caused his arrest and at the departure of the emperor, July 29, 1541, he was taken to Italy and Spain in chains and at Mallorca delivered to the Spanish Inquisition. He was brought to Valladolid, and, refusing to recant, was burned in 1542. Francesco de Enzinas, after going to Wittenberg and translating the Greek New Testament into Spanish, was imprisoned in 1543, but escaped two years later. His brother Jaime translated a catechism into Spanish, but in 1545 was arrested in Rome and died at the stake, 1547. Juan Diaz of Cuenca, the native town of the brothers Valdés, studied theology at Paris for thirteen years, and was made a convert by Jaime Enzinas. After sojourning several months at Geneva with Calvin, 1545, and assisting Butzer at the colloquy at Regensburg, he retired to Neuburg-on-the-Danube and published his brief *Summa* (1546). At the instigation of his brother Alfonso, attached to the papal court at Rome, he was treacherously assassinated Mar. 27, 1546.

The first Evangelical groups as nuclei of a congregation were formed at Seville. Juan Perez de Pineda, prior of the church of Osma, and secretary of the imperial embassy at Rome, 1547, was there impressed by the papal abuses. After his return to Andalusia he became director of the Colegio de doctrina at Seville, and made an effort to promote true piety. Threatened by the Inquisition, he emigrated in the fifties to Geneva. In the mean time, Rodrigo de Valera, a layman, who by diligent study of the Latin Bible had been led to depart from the Roman doctrine and who had preached his new faith in the streets, influenced Juan Egidio, who worked in unison with Constantino Ponce de la Fuente, from 1533 powerful preacher at the cathedral. The latter issued *Confessio hominis peccatoris* published in the *Serinium antiquarum* of Dr. Gerdes (Groningen, 1749-65) and *Summa*, in *Españoles Reformados* (Madrid, 1847). Egidio, suspended by the Inquisition (1552) from preaching and lecturing for ten years, retracted, but died in repentance at Seville, 1556. In 1555 seven men and women from Seville fled to Geneva, and likewise twelve monks from the Isidore monastery at Seville. Perez who had been at Frankfort, 1556-58, secured permission at Geneva to be preacher of a Spanish congregation. He had published a Spanish translation of the New Testament (Geneva, 1556); *Sumario breve de doctrina Christiana* (1556); the Commentary by Juan de Valdés on Romans (q.v.; 1557), and on I Corinthians (1557). In 1557 some of his publications were brought to Seville. Their discovery led to the arrest of a great number of people who were suspected of heresy; others fled from the country. Constantino was placed under arrest. Similarly there arose an Evangelical movement in the capital, Valladolid, and vicinity, on the initiative of Carlos de Seso, of Verona, who in Italy had become acquainted with the doctrine of the Reformation. He cautiously gathered adherents, particularly the family of Cazalla, among them the court preacher Augustin de Cazalla. In 1558 the Inquisition interfered and May 21, 1559, there took place in Valladolid an *auto da fé* of Protestants. Cazalla retracted but was burned alive; a brother and sister were garroted; a brother and sister condemned to imprisonment; and the exhumed remains of the mother were burned. The only one who refused to retract was the advocate Antonio de Herrezuelo, who suffered a heroic death. In Aug., 1559, Carranza, archbishop of Toledo, was arrested; after an imprisonment of seventeen years he was condemned to abjure heresy. On Sept. 24, 1559, an *auto da fé* took place in Seville. A house in which Evangelicals had frequently held meetings was torn down. The king attended a second *auto da fé* in Valladolid, Oct., 1559, and took an oath that he would assist and favor the Inquisition. Carlos de Seso was burned; also Juan Sanchez the sacristan of another brother of Augustin Cazalla, who in turn was garroted. In Seville, Dec. 22, 1560, Julian

Hernandez, a lay brother of the Isidore cloister, and others were sent to the stake. The remains of Egidio and Constantino, who had died in prison, and the effigy of Pineda were consigned to the flames. Several *autos da fé* followed in 1562 with a number of victims including Garcia Arias, called Maestro Blanco, who had kindled evangelism in the monastery. With these *autos*, but barely mentioned, the Evangelical movement in Spain was practically smothered. The rest of the acts of the Inquisition pertain to resident French, Dutch, and English traders and seamen, apart from any national movement. A group of French Protestants were thus executed at Toledo, 1565.

From the group of fugitive monks of San Isidro originated the *Artes Inquisitionis* (Heidelberg, 1567), under the pseudonym Reinaldus Gonsalvius Montanus, the reliability of which was evidently made uncertain by the author's hatred of his tormentors, and his southern temperament. Of the other fugitive monks of San Isidro Antonio del Corro arrived at Geneva, 1557; he soon went to Lausanne to study at the academy. Theodor Beza (q.v.) honored him with his friendship. In 1559 Corro with the recommendation of Calvin returned to southern France in order to be nearer to his countrymen. In 1563, he, together with his convent friend Cassiodoro de Reyna and Valera (*ut sup.*) printed the Spanish New Testament in one of the castles of the Queen of Navarre. Corro was proscribed at Toulouse, but escaped by flight. In Bergerac, where Reyna visited him, he was forbidden to preach because he was a foreigner. Juan Perez de Pineda met the same fate in Blois. All these fugitives from Seville were sheltered in Montargis by Renée of France (q.v.). In 1566 Corro followed a call as preacher to Antwerp. For the queen regent, however, a Spaniard as Evangelical preacher was objectionable. William of Orange desired that the Evangelicals of the Netherlands should declare for the Augsburg Confession in order to assure imperial aid. The Evangelical preachers were banished from the Netherlands, however, and Alva's régime began. In the mean time Corro had gone to England. At London his known friendship with Reyna, who had gone there from Geneva, 1559, and taken charge of the Spanish congregation and left England because of unfounded charges, barred Corro from the French congregation. He served the Italian, but was denied the communion and deprived of the pulpit by the bishop. He united with the Anglican Church, and under the auspices of the legal corporation of the Knights Templars in London delivered Latin theological lectures. He became religious teacher in three institutes of the University of Oxford, 1597; was theological censor of Christ Church College, 1581-85; received a prebend of St. Paul's, London, 1582; and died, 1591, at London. He transformed the Epistle to the Romans into a dialogue between the apostle and a Roman (London, 1574). His Latin paraphrase of Ecclesiastes (1579) has been printed several times. Highly esteemed as a theologian by the Arminians, he denied predestinate reprobation and is said to have opposed the interference of the State against heretics. When Cassiodoro de Reyna left England in 1565 he settled with his family at Frankfort-on-the-Main, where he made his living in the silk trade and worked on his translation of the Bible (Basel, 1568–69), which is the first complete Spanish Bible translated from the original languages. Frankfort conferred on him citizenship. In 1578 he became French pastor of the adherents of the Augsburg Confession at Antwerp. In 1585 he returned to Frankfort, and became, 1594, preacher of the Netherland colony of the Lutheran persuasion. Cipriano de Valera (*ut sup.*) fled with his friends from San Isidro to Geneva and in 1562 was burned in effigy like Reyna and Corro. He studied at Cambridge (B.A., 1560; M.A., 1563); was fellow of Magdalen College; and, 1566, was connected with Oxford. He published *Los dos Tratados del Papa i de la Misa* (1588); *Tratado para confirmar los pobres Cantivos de Berberia* (1594); a new edition of the Spanish catechism of Geneva of 1559 (1596); *El Testamento Nuevo* of C. de Reyna (1596; 1870); *Institucion de la Religion Christiana* (1597), a translation of J. Calvin's Institutes; and *La Biblia* of C. de Reyna (Antwerp, 1602 sqq.; 1869). Pedro Galés, a young Catalonian, was arrested about 1559 at Rome because he had asserted that it was unnecessary to confess to a priest and to abstain from meat on certain days, and was compelled to abjure. He studied at Bologna and Paris, and became professor at Geneva, 1582. Afterward he went to southern France and taught in several places until a Calvinistic pastoral conference found him unsound in doctrine. On the way to Bordeaux, with wife and children, he was captured by members of the holy league and in 1593 surrendered to Spain. In the prison of the Inquisition at Saragossa he declared that the doctrine of the Roman church was frequently in contradiction with that of Christ and the Apostles. His second trial was completed after his death, and his remains were dug up and burned, Apr. 17, 1595. Melchior Roman of Aragon entered the order of the Jacobins. In the province of Toulouse he was appointed Procureur Provincial and sent to Rome; subsequently he became provincial vicar and confessor of the Dames du Chapellet d'Agen. The sight of a victim burned at the stake made a deep impression upon him, and he entered the Reformed church at Bergerac in 1600.

(THEODOR SCHÄFER.)

BIBLIOGRAPHY: T. McCrie, *Hist. of the Progress and Suppression of the Reformation in Spain*, Edinburgh, 1829 and 1856; A. de Castro, *Hist. of Religious Intolerance in Spain*, London, 1853; *Mémoires de Francisco de Enzinas*, 2 vols., Brussels, 1862–63; H. Dalton, *Die evangelische Bewegung in Spanien*, Wiesbaden, 1872; E. Boehmer, *Spanish Reformers of Two Centuries*, London, 1874–83; M. Droin, *Hist. de la réformation en Espagne*, 2 vols., Lausanne, 1880; M. Menendez y Pelayo, *Hist. de los heterodoxos Españoles*, 3 vols., Madrid, 1881; J. Lassalle, *La Réforme en Espagne au xvi. siècle*, Paris, 1883; J. Stoughton, *The Spanish Reformers*, London, 1883; C. A. Wilkens, *Geschichte des spanischen Protestantismus*, Gütersloh, 1888, Eng. transl., *Spanish Protestants in the 16th Century*, London, 1897; M. F. van Lennep *De Hervorming in Spanje in de zestiende eeuw*, Haarlem, 1901; E. Schäfer, *Beiträge zur Geschichte der spanischen Protestantismus . . . im 16. Jahrhundert*, 3 vols., Gütersloh, 1902; idem, *Sevilla und Valladolid, die evangelischen Gemeinden Spaniens im Reformationsalter*, Halle, 1903.

SPALATIN, spä-lä-tîn′, **GEORG:** German Reformer; b. at Spalt (21 m. s.w. of Nuremberg) Jan. 17, 1484; d. at Altenburg (26 m. s. of Leipsic) Jan. 16, 1545. His family name was Burkhardt, which he changed to Spalatin—from his birthplace—after a frequent custom of the humanists. He was educated at the universities of Erfurt (1498–99, 1505) and Wittenberg (1502–03), early coming into contact with humanistic circles. In 1505 he began to teach in the monastery of Georgenthal, and in 1508 was ordained to the priesthood. In the following year he was appointed tutor to the prince who later became Elector John Frederick, although here, as at the monastery, his innovating tendencies rendered his position uncomfortable. In 1511 he was for a time one of the guardians of the princes Otto and Ernest of Brunswick-Lüneburg, although without severing his connection with the court of their uncle, Elector Frederick the Wise, who, in the following year, appointed him his own librarian—a most congenial post. Spalatin gradually became the elector's most trusted confidant and a power at court, but though he was a priest, he had taken orders merely to escape the trials of a poverty-stricken humanist and poet. His association with Luther, whom he seems first to have met at Wittenberg, changed his life, and even before he broke with the ancient faith, he found in the Wittenberg theologian his most acceptable adviser. It was Spalatin, moreover, who won the elector to sympathy with Luther, even while endeavoring to restrain the more impetuous Augustinian from the course into which he was plunging, and it is to Spalatin that the vacillating tactics of Luther during the earlier years of the Reformation are to be traced.

In 1518 Spalatin accompanied the elector to the diet of Augsburg, and conducted negotiations with Cajetan and Miltitz, and he was likewise present at the election and coronation of Charles V. as well as at the Diet of Worms, while during Luther's concealment at the Wartburg he provided means for him to correspond with Wittenberg. Despite the difficulty of his position with the elector, who still remained faithful to the Roman Catholic Church, Spalatin constantly sought to win him over to the views of Luther, who demanded the abolition of the ritual maintained in the seminary at Wittenberg. After the death of Frederick the Wise, Spalatin still remained in the service of the court, although he was now able to take up permanent residence in Altenburg, where he had received a canonry in 1511, and where he also assumed the position of preacher vacated by the departure of Wenceslaus Link (q.v.). On Aug. 13, 1525, he delivered his first sermon, but his demand for a change of conditions in the Altenburg seminary led to bitter controversy, complicated by his speedy marriage, which led to his deprivation, although by the aid of secular law he reinstated himself and gradually carried out his proposed reformation. In 1526 he accompanied Elector John to the Diet of Speyer, where he took a prominent part in formulating instructions for the permanent embassy to the emperor determined upon by the diet. He was also employed repeatedly in visitations. In 1530 he attended the Diet of Augsburg, later accompanying the elector to the election of Ferdinand at Cologne. In 1532 he attended the Diet of Schweinfurth; in 1535 he went with Elector John Frederick when the latter visited Vienna to do homage; and he was a leading figure in such important matters as the peace of Cadan (1534) and the formulation of the Schmalkald Articles. Throughout his life he was deeply interested in the University of Wittenberg, of which he had been appointed a visitor as early as 1518, and which he regularly visited two or three times each year. In 1536 he sought to be relieved of his many duties, and from this time on he became more and more melancholy, although he remained active until the last.

Spalatin was a prolific writer, although some of his works still remain unpublished. His only really original contributions, however, are historical studies, especially on Saxon and contemporary themes, these including his *Chronicon et annales* (ed. J. B. Mencke, *Scriptores rerum Germanicarum*, ii. 590 sqq., Leipsic, 1728–30) and his biography of Frederick the Wise (ed. C. G. Neudecker and L. Preller, *Georg Spalatins historischer Nachlass und Briefe aus den Originalhandschriften*, Jena, 1851). A still more valuable source for the history of the Reformation period is afforded by his voluminous correspondence, of which only a small portion has appeared in print, although almost all the archives of Germany contain specimens, the library at Weimar being especially rich in this respect. (T. Kolde.)

Bibliography: C. Schlegel, *Hist. vitæ G. Spalatini*, Jena, 1693; J. Wagner, *G. Spalatin und die Reformation der Kirchen und Schulen in Altenburg*, Altenburg, 1830; E. Engelhardt, *G. Spalatins Leben*, Leipsic, 1863; A. Seelheim, *G. Spalatin als sächsischer Historiograph*, Halle, 1876; G. Berbig, *Spalatin und sein Verhältnis zu Martin Luther*, Halle, 1906; and works on the life of Luther and the Reformation in Germany.

SPALDING, spōl'ding, FRANKLIN SPENCER: Protestant Episcopal missionary bishop of Salt Lake; b. at Erie, Pa., Mar. 13, 1865. He was educated at Princeton (A.B., 1877) and at the General Theological Seminary (graduated, 1891), after having taught in the Princeton Preparatory School in 1887–88. He was ordered deacon in 1891 and ordained priest in the following year, being minister of All Saints', Denver, Col., during this time, and from 1892 to 1896 was principal of Jarvis Hall Military Academy in the same city. He was then rector of St. Paul's, Erie, Pa. (1896–1904), and in 1904 was consecrated missionary bishop of Salt Lake, his diocese comprising all Utah, the eastern half of Nevada, the western half of Colorado, and part of a county of Wyoming.

SPALDING, JOHANN JOACHIM: German Lutheran; b. at Tribsees (24 m. s.w. of Greifswald) Nov. 1, 1714; d. at Berlin May 22, 1804. After studying at the University of Rostock (1731–33), he was for several years private tutor, private secretary, etc., also finding considerable time for writing. In 1748 he published at Greifswald the work which first brought him distinction, the *Gedanken über die Bestimmung des Menschen*, in which he earnestly combated the increasing materialism of his time. A year later he was chosen pastor of Lassahn, where, though too radical for his congregation, he found opportunity for studying and translating standard works of English deism and antideism. In 1757 Spalding was called to Barth as first preacher and provost, and here he wrote, against Pietism, his second great work, *Gedanken über den*

Wert der Gefühle im Christentum (Leipsic, 1761; Eng. transl., *Thoughts on the Value of Feelings in Religion*, London, 1827). In 1764 he was called to Berlin as provost, supreme consistorial councilor, and first preacher at the Marienkirche and St. Nicholas'. Here for more than twenty years he enjoyed the highest reputation as a pulpit orator, his sermons being collected in a number of volumes. It was at this time also that he published the work which exposed him to much attack, the *Ueber die Nutzbarkeit des Predigtamts und deren Beförderung* (1st ed. anonymously, Berlin, 1772), in which he advocated the preaching of ethical sermons only, to the complete ignoring of dogmatic problems. The true motive of this position was the desire to retain only what he deemed essential, to oppose the shallow infidelity proceeding from France and England, and to reconcile Christianity with the spirit of the times. This same attitude led Spalding to write his *Vertraute Briefe, die Religion betreffend* (1st ed. anonymously, Breslau, 1784), which have a distinct interest in that they give a vivid picture of the shallowness and religious indifference then prevailing in the higher circles of society.

In 1786 the situation was abruptly changed by the accession of Frederick William II., and feeling himself put at a decided disadvantage, Spalding secured the acceptance of his resignation in 1788. He then retired to private life, and now wrote his last work, *Religion, eine Angelegenheit des Menschen* (1st ed. anonymously, Berlin, 1797), while after his death his autobiographical *Lebensbeschreibung von ihm selbst* was edited by his son, G. L. Spalding (Halle, 1805). He was neither a great theologian nor a great philosopher; he was essentially a popularizer who sought to bring the divine truths of Christianity close to the hearts and wills of rational men, though himself far from being an adherent of the Enlightenment, Rationalism, or Deism (q.v.).

(J. A. Wagenmann†.)

Bibliography: The chief source is the *Lebensbeschreibung von ihm selbst*, ed. his son, G. L. Spalding, Halle, 1905. Consult further: J. M. Schröckh, *Christliche Kirchengeschichte seit der Reformation*, viii. 138 sqq., Leipsic, 1808; F. K. G. Hirsching, *Historisch-litterarisches Handbuch berühmter Personen*, xii. 1, pp. 298 sqq., ib. 1808; K. G. Sack, in *TSK*, 1864, part 4; G. W. Frank, *Geschichte der protestantischen Theologie*, iii. 93 sqq., Leipsic, 1875.

SPALDING, JOHN LANCASTER: Roman Catholic bishop of Peoria, Ill., nephew of the following; b. at Lebanon, Ky., June 2, 1840. He was educated at Mount St. Mary's College, Emmitsburg, Md., at the University of Louvain, Belgium, and in Rome, where he was ordained priest in 1863. After an additional year of study, he returned to the United States. In 1865 he was secretary to the bishop of Louisville, Ky., and in 1869 built, and was rector of, St. Augustine's (colored) Church at Louisville, while in 1871 he was chancellor of the diocese of Louisville. From 1872–77 he was curate of St. Michael's, New York City, and in the latter year was consecrated bishop of the newly created diocese of Peoria, which office he resigned in 1908. He is the author of *Life of Archbishop Spalding of Baltimore* (New York, 1872); *Essays and Reviews* (1877); *Religious Mission of the Irish People* (1880); *Lectures and Discourses* (1882); *Education and the*

Higher Life (Chicago, 1890); *Things of the Mind* (1894); *Means and Ends of Education* (1895); *Songs, chiefly from the German* (1895); *Thoughts and Theories of Life and Education* (1897); *Opportunity and other Essays* (1900); *Aphorisms and Reflections* (1901); *God and the Soul* (New York, 1901); *Religion, Agnosticism and Education* (Chicago, 1902); *Socialism and Labor* (1902); *Glimpses of Truth* (1903); *The Spalding Year Book* (1905); *Religion and Art, and Other Essays* (1905).

SPALDING, MARTIN JOHN: Roman Catholic; b. near Lebanon, Ky., May 23, 1810; d. at Baltimore, Md., Feb. 7, 1872. He was graduated from St. Mary's College, Lebanon, Ky., 1826; studied theology in St. Joseph's Seminary, Bardstown, 1826–30; completed his course in the Propaganda College in Rome, where he was ordained priest Aug. 13, 1834; was pastor of the cathedral at Bardstown, Ky., 1834–1838, 1841–48; president of St. Joseph's Theological Seminary, Bardstown, 1838–40; pastor of St. Peter's Church, Lexington, Ky., 1840–41; coadjutor bishop of Louisville, Ky., 1848–50; bishop 1850–54; archbishop of Baltimore from 1864 till his death. He founded *The Catholic Advocate*, Louisville, in 1835, and was connected with it until 1858; *The Louisville Guardian* in 1858; was main promoter of the Catholic Publication Society and *Catholic World*, both New York City. While coadjutor bishop, he established a colony of Trappist monks at Gethsemane, near Bardstown, Ky., and a house of Magdalens in connection with the Convent of the Good Shepherd, and while bishop of Louisville he built a magnificent cathedral in that city. In 1857 he founded the American College in Louvain. Spalding was the author of *D'Aubigne's History of the Great Reformation in Germany and Switzerland Reviewed* (Baltimore, 1844; subsequently enlarged and reissued as *History of the Protestant Reformation in Germany and Switzerland ; and in England, Ireland, Scotland, the Netherlands, France, and Northern Europe*, 2 vols., Louisville, 1860); *Sketches of the Early Catholic Missions in Kentucky, 1787–1827: . . . Compiled from authentic Sources, with the Assistance of . . . S. T. Badin* (1844); *Lectures on the General Evidences of Catholicity* (1847); *Life, Times, and Character of the Right Rev. B. J. Flaget* (Louisville, 1852); *Miscellanea: comprising Reviews, Lectures, and Essays on Historical, Theological, and Miscellaneous Subjects* (1855); and edited, with introduction and notes, Abbé J. E. Darras' *General History of the Catholic Church* (4 vols., New York, 1865–66).

BIBLIOGRAPHY: J. L. Spalding, *Life of Archbishop Spalding of Baltimore*, New York, 1872; T. O'Gorman, in *American Church History Series*, ix. passim, ib. 1895.

SPANGENBERG, späng'en-berн, **AUGUST GOTT-LIEB:** Bishop of the Unity of the Brethren; b. at Klettenberg (34 m. e. of Göttingen) July 15, 1704; d. at Herrnhut Sept. 18, 1792. In 1717 he entered the cloister school of Ilfeld and in 1722 the University of Jena. Here he became amanuensis of Johannes Franciscus Buddeus (q.v.), whose house was a center of Pietism, through whose influence his entire life was transformed, and he resolved to study theology. In 1725 his development underwent a new change as he was attracted by a circle of mystical separatists and afterward by Gichtelianism (see

GICHTEL, JOHANN GEORG), but after the death of Johann Otto Glüsing, the leader of the Gichtelians, in 1727, and his first contact with the Herrnhuters, he regained the simple faith of the Bible and the Church. In the summer of 1728 Zinzendorf sojourned at Jena advocating his movement, and soon gathered a circle of Pietistic students, among whom Spangenberg took a leading position. In 1729 Spangenberg took his master's degree and delivered philological and philosophical lectures, but his whole heart was with the movement of Zinzendorf, with whom his relations became most intimate, especially after a visit to Herrnhut (Apr. 21–28, 1730). He continually took part in the affairs of the community, and Zinzendorf at various times claimed him as collaborator. In spring, 1732, however, Spangenberg accepted a call to Halle as adjunct in the theological faculty and assistant in the orphans' home, but did not sever his connection with Herrnhut. By his attempts to connect himself with a circle of Pietistic citizens of separatistic tendencies, he became involved in a conflict with his superiors. Early in 1733 he was called before a series of conferences of officers of the orphans' home, it being considered a duty of the teachers to conform with the principles and practise of the church. Spangenberg was finally deposed and left the city on Apr. 4, 1733. With his dismissal the rupture between the movement of Zinzendorf and the Halle movement became complete.

Spangenberg then formally joined the Brethren. Immediately after his dismissal from Halle Zinzendorf made him his assistant and entrusted him with various diplomatic missions in connection with his plans of colonization. Spangenberg brought colonists to Copenhagen and made the contracts in 1733, superintended the beginnings of the colony on the Savannah river (1735), and finally turned to Pennsylvania in order to care for the Schwenckfeldians (1736–39) who had emigrated under the protection of the Moravian Brethren. The time from 1739 to 1744 Spangenberg spent in his native country. During this stay in his native country he had opportunities to show his talent for organization. He organized the Brethren in England and founded in London an auxiliary society for mission work, the Society for the Furtherance of the Gospel among the Heathen (1741). But his best work was achieved in America. In 1744 the synod of Marienborn appointed him bishop and entrusted to him the supervision of the work in America. Here two settlements of the Brethren were founded in Bethlehem and Nazareth, large areas of land were purchased, in New York and Philadelphia congregations were formed, while preaching-stations and school-houses were scattered all over the country. The financial difficulties which arose were solved by Spangenberg through the peculiar organization at Bethlehem, the so-called " common economy," according to which all work was done in the interest of the whole community, which in its turn provided for the needs of individuals. Spangenberg returned in 1749 to Europe, but in 1751 he resumed his work in America and founded a second great complex of colonies in North Carolina. In 1762 he again left America and made his permanent abode in Germany.

He became member of the provisional board of directors formed after the death of Zinzendorf (1760), and until his death took a leading position among the Brethren, one of his services being his assistance in formulating their system of doctrine. It is chiefly owing to Spangenberg that the Congregation of Brethren was saved from developing into sectarianism and that it maintained friendly relations with the Evangelical church. Among his literary works were *Deklaration über die zeither gegen uns ausgegangenen Beschuldigungen* . . . (Leipsic and Görlitz, 1751); *Darlegung richtiger Antworten auf mehr als 300 Beschuldigungen gegen den ordinarium fratrum* . . . (1751); *Apologetische Schlussschrift* . . . (2 parts, 1752); *Leben des Herrn Nicolaus Ludwig Grafen und Herrn von Zinzendorf* . . . (8 parts, 1772–1775; Eng. transl., *The Life of N. L., Count Zinzendorf*, London, 1838); *Idea fidei fratrum oder kurzer Begriff der christlichen Lehre in den evangelischen Brüdergemeinen* (Barby, 1779; Eng. transl., *Exposition of Christian Doctrine*, London, 1784). Spangenberg was also a writer of hymns, ten of which went into the denominational hymn-book of 1778. Some of these have been rendered into English, among them " The Church of Christ that he hath hallowed here," by Miss Winkworth.   (G. REICHEL.)

BIBLIOGRAPHY: Spangenberg left in manuscript three accounts of his life, of which the first has not been published, the second and third appeared in *Archiv für neueste Kirchengeschichte*, i. 40 sqq., ii. 429–487, and *Nachrichten aus der Brüdergemeinde*, 1872, pp. 135–180. Letters of his are published in *Der Brüderbote*, 1872, pp. 9 sqq., 241 sqq., 1874, pp. 10 sqq., 1876, pp. 309 sqq.; and in J. Bernoulli's *Sammlung kurzer Reisebeschreibung*, xvi (1784), 195 sqq., is found a sketch of him by a contemporary, Jänichen. Sketches or lives have been written by J. Loretz, in *Lausitzische Monatsschrift*, 1793, i. 336–358, ii. 13–31, 75–89; J. Risler, Barby, 1794; K. F. Ledderhose, Heidelberg, 1846; C. J. Nitzsch, in *Evangelisches Jahrbuch*, 1855, pp. 197 sqq.; G. C. Knapp, ed. O. Frick, Halle, 1884; and (best of all) by G. Reichel, Tübingen, 1906.

SPANGENBERG, CYRIAKUS: Son of Johann Spangenberg; b. at Nordhausen (105 m. w. of Leipsic) June 7, 1528; d. at Strasburg Feb. 10, 1604. He began study at the University of Wittenberg in 1542; took his master's degree in 1550, and in the same year the counts of Mansfeld made him preacher at the Church of St. Andrew in Eisleben. Afterward he became town and court preacher in Mansfeld, and in 1559, after the death of Michael Coelius, general dean of the county and assessor of the Eisleben consistory. He was a zealous champion of pure Lutheranism, combating the school of Melanchthon. The theologians of Mansfeld became the stanchest partizans of Flacius. The three counts, Volrad, Karl, and Hans Ernst, were in ecclesiastical affairs under the influence of Spangenberg, whose authority grew wherever anti-Philippine Lutheranism appeared. The severe invectives of Hieronymus Menzel, general superintendent of Mansfeld, and of Spangenberg induced Elector August in 1567 to cite them to Dresden to vindicate themselves, but as Counts Volrad and Christoph protested against such summons as an intrenchment of their rights, the two theologians refused to go. Spangenberg had offended the theologians of Electoral Saxony especially by seven sermons *De prædestinatione* (Erfurt, 1567), in

which he taught the *servum arbitrium* in the sense of the older Reformed theology. In Mansfeld there developed also the tragedy of the controversy on hereditary sin which had a fatal influence upon the future life of Spangenberg. As early as 1560 Flacius had used against Strigel the expression that hereditary sin is the substance of man. Spangenberg came to the defense of Flacius after the issuance of Johann Wigand's treatise, *Von der Erbsünde*, with its blunt condemnation of Flacius, with the final result that in 1575 Spangenberg and his adherents were excommunicated and Spangenberg himself was forced to flee into the district of Sangerhausen where he occupied himself with the composition of historical works and of polemical treatises. In 1578 he, together with his protector, Count Volrad, was expelled from Sangerhausen and went to Strasburg; but in 1581 he was appointed preacher at Schlitzsee-on-the-Fulda in Hesse, where he was allowed to remain until 1590. During this quiet time he concluded his large works of history, but in 1591 he was deprived of office though he was allowed to live in Vacha-on-the-Werra. About 1595 Count Ernst of Mansfeld, the nephew of Count Volrad, brought about Spangenberg's return to Strasburg, where he spent the rest of his life.

Spangenberg left an immense number of writings, in many respects faithfully following the lines of his father's literary activity. He furnished practical commentaries on Thessalonians (1557), the pastoral epistles (1559 sqq.), Corinthians (1559 sqq.); and compiled tables on the Pentateuch (1563) and other historical books of the Old Testament (1567). He also continued the hymnological work of his father, *Christliches Gesangbüchlein, Von den fürnembsten Festen* (137 songs, among them some of his own, 1568); *Cithara Lutheri*, a series of sermons on the hymns of Luther (1569, reprinted Berlin, 1855); *Der ganze Psalter . . . gesangsweise und 114 schöne geistreiche Lieder . . . der lieben Patriarchen* (1582). Among his sermons special mention may be made of *Theander Lutherus* (1589), a cycle of twenty-one sermons on Luther. His polemical writings refer chiefly to the controversy on original sin, on synergism, and on the Lord's Supper. In German literature he has a place as composer of spiritual comedies (1589–90). But his chief services were in the sphere of history, his most prominent works being *Chronicon Corinthiacum* (1562); *Mansfeldische Chronica* (Eisleben 1572); *Historia Manicheorum* (Ursel, 1578); *Sächssische Chronica* (Frankfort, 1580); *Quernfurtische Chronica* (Erfurt, 1590); *Adels Spiegel* (Schmalkald, 1591–94); *Hennebergische Chronica* (Strasburg, 1599); *Bonifacius oder deutsche Kirchen-Historie von 714–755* (1603), and others.

(G. KAWERAU.)

BIBLIOGRAPHY: The principal collection of Spangenberg's letters is by H. Rembe, 2 parts, Dresden, 1887–88, others are printed in J. Fecht, *Historiæ ecclesiasticæ sæculi XVI.*, supplement, Frankfort, 1684, and in *Mansfelder Blätter*, xxii. 155 sqq. On his life consult: M. Adam, *Vitæ Germanorum theologorum*, pp. 731 sqq., Frankfort, 1653; J. Fecht, ut sup., Apparatus, pp. 107 sqq.; J. G. Leuckfeld, *Hist. Spangenbergensis*, Quedlinburg. 1712 (the best); H. Rembe, in the reprint of Spangenberg's *Formularbüchlein*, Dresden, 1887; W. Hotz, in *Beiträge zur hessischen Kirchengeschichte*, iii. 205 sqq.; J. J. I. von Döllinger, *Die Reformation*, ii. 270 sqq., Regensburg, 1848;

J. W. Preger, *M. Flacius Illyricus und seine Zeit*, vol. ii., Erlangen, 1861; A. G. Meyer, *Der Flacianismus in der Grafschaft Mansfeld*, Halle, 1873; *ADB*, xxxv. 37 sqq.

SPANGENBERG, JOHANN: German theologian; b. at Hardegsen (10 m. n.n.w. of Göttingen) Mar. 29, 1484; d. at Eisleben (43 m. s. of Magdeburg) June 13, 1550. He was educated at Göttingen and Einbeck; in 1508 he entered the University of Erfurt (B.A., 1511). Afterward Count Botho of Stolberg called him as rector to the Latin School in Stolberg; about 1520 he became also preacher at the Church of St. Martin. He accepted the teaching of Luther and was soon known and esteemed as a prominent preacher of the Gospel. In 1524 the council of Nordhausen appointed him preacher of the Church of St. Blasius where during an activity of twenty-two years he established the Evangelical doctrine, and after the disturbances of the Peasants' War carried out a new church order in a conservative spirit. Spangenberg rendered especially valuable services for the advancement of higher education in Nordhausen. As the cathedral and municipal schools had perished in the storms of the Peasants' War, Spangenberg opened a private school in his own house until the council at his request in 1525 established a new Latin school in the Dominican monastery, for which Spangenberg wrote text-books. In 1546, at his last visit to Eisleben, Luther proposed Spangenberg to the counts of Mansfeld as general inspector of all churches and schools in the county, and in this new position Spangenberg remained until his death. Of his numerous writings mention may be made of *Prosodia in usum juventutis Northusanæ* (Augsburg, 1535); *Quæstiones musicæ in usum scholæ Northusianæ* (Nuremberg, 1536); *Evangelia dominicalia in versiculos versa* (1539); *Artificiosæ memoriæ libellus, in usum studiosorum collectus* (Wittenberg, 1539); *Computus ecclesiasticus* (1539); *Margarita theologica* (1540; Eng. transl., *The Sũ of Divinitie*, London, 1548); *Gross Katechismus . . . Lutheri . . . in Fragstücke verfasset* (1541); *Ein new Trostbüchlin für die Krancken, Und vom christlichen Ritter* (1541–1542); *Alt und neue geistliche Lieder und Lob-Geseng von der Geburt Christi . . . für die junge Christen* (1543); *Psalterium carmine Elegiaco redditum* (1544); *Cantiones ecclesiasticæ latinæ simul ac synceriores quædam præculæ . . . Kirchengesänge deutsch durchs gantze Jar . . .* (1545); *Des ehelichen Ordens Spiegel und Regel* (1545); *Kommentar zur Apostelgeschichte* (Frankfort, 1546); *Explicationes evangeliorum et epistolarum, quæ dominicis diebus more usitato proponi in ecclesia populo solent, in tabulos . . . redactæ* (Basil, 1564), edited by his son Cyriakus (q.v.).   (G. KAWERAU.)

BIBLIOGRAPHY: H. Menzel, *Epicedion in memoriam Johannis Spangenberg*, Wittenberg, 1551; idem, *Narratio historica de statu ecclesiæ in comitatu Mansfeldensi*, reproduced in *Zeitschrift des Harzvereins*, xvi (1883), 86 sqq.; M. Adam, *Vitæ Germanorum theologorum*, p. 98, Frankfort, 1653; J. G. Leuckfeld, *Verbesserte historische Nachricht von dem Leben und Schriften Johann Spangenbergs*, Quedlinburg, 1720; E. G. Förstemann, *Mittheilungen zu einer Geschichte der Schulen in Nordhausen*, pp. 22 sqq., Nordhausen, 1824, G. H. Klippel, *Deutsche Lebens- und Charakterbilder* i. 1 sqq., Bremen, 1853; K. Krumhaar, *Die Graffschaft Mansfeld im Reformationszeitalter*, pp. 345 sqq., Eisleben, 1855, T. Perschmann, *Die Reformation in Nordhausen*, pp. 19 sqq., Halle, 1881.

SPANHEIM, spān'haim, **EZECHIEL, BARON:** Eldest son of Friedrich Spanheim the Elder; b. at Geneva Dec. 7, 1629; d. at London Nov. 7, 1710. After 1642 he studied philology and theology at Leyden, and in 1650 returned to Geneva. In 1656 he became tutor of Karl Ludwig, elector of the Palatinate, when studies in political science led him into a diplomatic career for which he showed great aptitude. By order of the elector he went in 1661 to Rome to investigate the intrigues of the Roman Catholic electors against his sovereign. After his return in 1665 the elector employed him as ambassador at different courts, finally in England where after 1679 he was charged also with the affairs of the elector of Brandenburg. In 1680 he entered the service of electoral Brandenburg as minister of state. As ambassador of the great elector he spent nine years at the court of Paris, and subsequently devoted some years to studies in Berlin, but after the Peace of Ryswyk in 1697 he returned as ambassador to France where he remained until 1702. In 1702 he finally went as first Prussian ambassador to England. His principal works are *Disputationes de usu et præstantia numismatum antiquorum* (Rome, 1664; best edition, 2 vols., London and Amsterdam, 1706–17) and *Orbis Romanus* (London, 1704; Halle, 1728). He also edited with Petavius the *Opera* of Cyril of Alexandria and of the Emperor Julian (Leipsic, 1696).   (S. D. VAN VEEN.)

BIBLIOGRAPHY: A sketch of Spanheim's life by I. Verburg is prefixed to the Amsterdam ed. of the *Disputationes*, ut sup.

SPANHEIM, FRIEDRICH, THE ELDER: Calvinistic professor at the University of Leyden; b. at Amberg (35 m. e. of Nuremberg) Jan. 1, 1600; d. at Leyden May 14, 1649. He entered in 1614 the university of Heidelberg where he studied philology and philosophy, and in 1619 removed to Geneva to study theology. In 1621 he became tutor in the house of Jean de Bonne, Baron de Vitrolle, governor of Embrun in Dauphiné, and after three years he visited Switzerland (Geneva), and France (Paris), and England, returning to Geneva in 1626 and becoming professor of philosophy; in 1631 he went over to the theological faculty, and was rector of the academy 1633–37. In 1642 he removed to Leyden as professor of theology. In Holland Spanheim became one of the most decided defenders of the Calvinistic doctrine of predestination against Amyraut. He published anonymously, *Le Soldat suedois* (1634), a history of the Thirty Years' War until 1631; *Le Mercure suisse* (1634); *Commentaire historique de la vie et de la mort de . . . Christofle Vicomte de Dohna* (1639). His principal theological works are: *Dubia evangelica* (3 vols., Geneva, 1631–39; Eng. transl., *Englands Warning by Germanies Woe*, London, 1646); *Disputatio de gratia universali* (3 vols., Leyden, 1644–48); *Epistola ad Buchananum super controversiis . . . in ecclesiis Anglicanis* (Leyden, 1645). Against the Anabaptists he wrote *Variæ disputationes anti-Anabaptisticæ* (1643) and *Diatribe historica de origine, progressu, sectis et nominibus anabaptistarum* (1645).   (S. D. VAN VEEN.)

BIBLIOGRAPHY: A. Heidan, *Oratio funebris in obitum . . . F. Spanhemii*, Leyden, 1649; Bayle, *Dictionary*, v. 193–195, Niceron, *Mémoires*, xxix. 35, J. Senebier, *Hist. lit-*

téraire de Genève, ii. 191 sqq., Geneva, 1786; Lichtenberger, *ESR*, xi. 656.

SPANHEIM, FRIEDRICH, THE YOUNGER: Son of Friedrich the Elder; b. in Geneva May 1, 1632; d. at Leyden May 18, 1701. He studied at Leyden (M.A., 1648), continuing his studies in theology after the death of his father, and in 1655 accepted a call to assist in reorganizing the University of Heidelberg, having previously received his doctorate at Leyden, whither he went as professor of theology in 1670, giving instruction after the next year in church history, becoming librarian in 1674, being four times rector, and in 1684 becoming professor primarius.

The results of his literary activity, which was great, were collected in his *Opera* (3 vols., Leyden, 1701–03). They included works in history, exegesis, and dogmatics, to which must be added a certain polemic activity against Arminians, Cartesians, Cocceians, and Jesuits. In this last respect important is his *De novissimis circa res sacras in Belgio dissidiis epistola* (Leyden, 1677). His theology was conservative, and he opposed the "*novatores.*" His commentary on Job is regarded as of high value. He issued also a *Brevis Introductio ad historiam utriusque Testamenti* (1694), and a large number of sermons. [The list of his writings takes up two pages in the *British Museum Catalogue*.]

(S. D. VAN VEEN.)

BIBLIOGRAPHY: The funeral oration by J. Triglandius was published at Leyden, 1701, and was included in vol. ii. of Spanheim's *Opera*, ut sup. Sketches of his life are given in their alphabetical place in Niceron, *Mémoires*, xxix. 11–26 and in Chauffepié's *Nouveau Dictionnaire*, Amsterdam, 1750–56.

SPARROW, WILLIAM: Protestant-Episcopalian; b. at Charlestown, Mass., Mar. 12, 1801; d. at Alexandria, Va., Jan. 17, 1874. His parents returning to Ireland in 1805, he attended a boarding-school in the Vale of Avoca; returned to America, 1817; was a student at Columbia College, New York, 1819–21; professor of Latin and Greek at Miami University, 1824–25; ordained in 1826; colaborer with Bishop Chase in founding Kenyon College; eleven years Milnor professor at Gambier; and professor of systematic divinity and Christian evidences in the Theological Seminary of Virginia, 1840–74. During the civil war (1861–64) he carried on the work of the seminary in the interior of Virginia. At its close his unique relations to both sections enabled him to exert important influence in restoring the Protestant Episcopal Church in Virginia to its former ecclesiastical relations.

Sparrow was recognized as the ablest theologian and the most original thinker of the evangelical school in the Protestant Episcopal Church. He bowed with unquestioning faith to the supremacy of Scripture, yet welcomed modern criticism as an ally; all his thinking proceeded on the conviction of the ultimate harmony of revelation and science. An earnest Evangelical and a zealous Protestant, he was usually classed as Arminian in theology; yet he abhorred the narrowness of theological systems, and led his pupils to independent thought and rational inquiry. He was an earnest Episcopalian, but put doctrine before order; hence he felt himself at one with Protestant Christendom, and rejoiced in the Evangelical Alliance as an expression of Protestant unity. Although he sympathized with the difficulties of Bishop George David Cummins (q.v.), he deprecated his secession, and remained firm in his adherence to the church. Perhaps no man of his time in America did more to check the spread of the tractarian theology. He was an earnest antagonist of the dogma of a tactual apostolical succession, holding it to be essentially unscriptural and anti-Protestant. To his great intellectual powers he added the influence of exalted piety, a character of great modesty and humility, and a life of simplicity and self-denial. His life-long feebleness of health unhappily prevented his entering the field of authorship; but a number of his occasional sermons and addresses were published. In collaboration with J. Johns he wrote *Memoir of Rev. W. Meade* (Richmond, 1867); and, independently, *Select Discourses* (New York, 1877).

BIBLIOGRAPHY: C. Walker, *Life and Correspondence of William Sparrow*, Philadelphia, 1876.

SPEAKING WITH TONGUES.

Basal New-Testament Passages (§ 1).
Manifestations in the Early Church (§ 2).
Old-Testament and Ethnic Parallels (§ 3).
The New-Testament Phenomena (§ 4).
Meaning of Glossa (§ 5).

Of the early Christian phenomenon called " speaking with tongues " (Gk. *glossolalia*) I Cor. xii.–xiv. gives a fairly comprehensible picture. It is represented as an activity of the Spirit of God coming upon man and constraining him to external expressions directed to God but not understood by others (xii. 10–11, xiv. 2), during which the soul life is passive and the understanding in abeyance (xiv. 14–15); the condition is that of Ecstasy (q.v.), the utterances are words or sounds of prayer or praise, but are not clear in meaning (xiv. 5, 13–16), and give the impression to the hearer of being mysteries or insane expressions (xiv. 2, 23), and need, at any rate, to be interpreted, though an unbeliever might see in the phenomenon a divine sign (xiv. 21–22). Three sets of illustrations used by Paul serve to make this clear: in the use of pipe and harp distinct and separate notes are necessary to give meaning, a definite set of sounds of the trumpet is required to give the signal to battle, and knowledge of a strange tongue is needed in order to interpret it (xiv. 7–11). This phenomenon seems to include sighs, groanings, shoutings, cries, and utterances either of disconnected words (such as Abba, hosanna, hallelujah, maranatha) or of connected speech of a jubilating sort which impresses the observer as ecstatic prayer or psalmodic praise. Other passages in the New Testament refer to the practise. So the ungenuine Mark xvi. 17, as well as Acts x. 46, xix. 6, refers to something like that in I Cor. xii.–xiv. But Acts ii. 1–13, referring to the events at Pentecost, needs to be distinguished, though the phenomena mentioned in verses 4 and 13 range themselves with those of I Cor. xiv. 21, 23. But the intention of the writer in Acts is not to describe ecstatic speech, it is rather to describe a miracle of tongues. The noise resulting, happening at the festival of weeks, drew a large concourse,

1. Basal New-Testament Passages.

and in verses 9–11 are named nations representatives of which each heard in his own tongue the disciples make known the wonders of God. While only four varieties of speech are necessarily involved, the implication is that these Galileans were enabled to speak the Gospel in the languages of the world. But the problem here presented is difficult. How could men of different nationality hear, each of them, all the disciples speaking his mother tongue? and it is not suggested that certain disciples addressed groups. Indeed, this appears to be within the region of legend. Moreover, it would not be strange for the Jew of verse 9 to hear a Galilean speak his mother tongue; the conjectures of Tertullian, Jerome, and of modern men that some other word is to be read for " Judea " does not help in view of the text, and the conclusion is that the story of the miracle is a late intrusion. The speech of Peter in verses 17–18 implies a prophetic inspiration, but says nothing of strange tongues. The enlargement which is to be seen here can be traced to Judaistic sources, as in the belief that the law of Sinai was not to be restricted to the Hebrews but to be given to the nations in a miracle like that of Pentecost (cf. Philo, *De septenario*, and *De decalogo*, §§ 9, 11). Such a conception as this, embodied in the work of the Alexandrian Jew, could easily become the basis of an insertion like that in Acts ii. This conception is the more easily understood in that the character of Luke's representation is to make Christianity universalistic.

Related phenomena appear elsewhere. In I Cor. xii. 1–3 Paul evidently means by the *pneumatikoi* especially those in ecstasy; in verses 4–11 he shows that the working of the Spirit is varied, and in xiv. 37–39 the *pneumatikoi* may be those who speak with tongues. He also places here the prophets who were endowed with the Spirit alongside those speaking with tongues; with verse 39 should be

2. Manifes- compared I Thess. v. 19–20. Paul had **tations in** not had occasion to warn at Thessalon-**the Early** ica against ecstatic and related phe-**Church.** nomena (cf. II Thess. ii. 2). Gal. iv. 6 and Rom. viii. 15–16, 26–27 are to be brought into this relation, in which the crying (Gk. *krazon*) of the Spirit and its testimony are distinguished from that of man's spirit. It is God's spirit which speaks within us, and when we know not how to pray, the Spirit makes intercession with unutterable groanings (Rom. viii. 26), and this God understands (verse 27). The apostle himself has had experience of this speaking with tongues (I Cor. xiv. 18; cf. II Cor. xii. 1, in which he describes ecstasy, and note verse 4, which is to be placed with I Cor. ii. 9). Somewhat unrelated to this species of ecstasy are the phenomena of Rev. i. 10, iv. 2, xvii. 3, xxi. 10, which deal with apocalyptic vision. Justin Martyr relates that in his own times spiritual gifts were active in the Church (*Trypho*, lxxxii., lxxxviii., Eng. transl., *ANF*, i. 240, 243–244) though it is not certain that speaking with tongues is here intended; in chap. xxxix. he speaks of seven kinds of gifts, and this seems to combine Isa. xi. 2 and I Cor. xii. 7–10, though speaking with tongues is again not mentioned. The " Address to the Greeks," chap. x., hardly comes into account here, since the Greek doctrine of inspiration is here under discussion.

In the *Acta Perpetuæ et Felicitatis*, viii., the Spirit overpowers Perpetua and constrains her to utterance of a name of which she had not thought. The description of the outbreak of Montanism in Eusebius, *Hist. eccl.*, V., xvi. 7 sqq. (*NPNF*, 2 ser., i. 231) does not exclude speaking with tongues, though the concern here is not with unmeaning and unintelligible speech but with prophetic utterance, and not only Montanus but two women had the seizures. Epiphanius (*Hær.*, xlviii. 4) makes Montanus describe his experience as a taking-out of his own heart by the Lord and the implanting of a new one. Tertullian (*Adv. Marcionem*, V., viii., Eng. transl. *ANF*, iii. 445–446) seems to include, among his demands of Marcion, that the latter explain what seems to be a claim to *glossolalia*, and the same thing is probably meant when in his *De resurrectione carnis* there is a kind of utterance mentioned which no one can know without interpretation. A weighty witness for the continuance of this gift is presented by Irenæus (*Hær.*, V., vi. 1), who speaks of " many brethren in the Church who . . . through the Spirit speak all kinds of languages " (*ANF*, i. 531), and he evidently refers to the phenomena noted by Paul. Yet it can not be decided whether Irenæus meant speech in foreign languages like that of Pentecost or a phenomenon like that of Corinthians. But that some such phenomena were in his mind is clear, with a probable reference to I Cor. xiv. Chrysostom appears at a loss to describe the facts, which are no longer manifested in his times. In a book that is half Jewish and half Christian, the Testament of Job, is a description of the ecstatic speech of the daughters of Job, one of whom used the method of one class of angels; and this implies the conception of a foreign tongue. Yet the phenomenon is not altogether common, and it can not have been important in the apostolic Church; later manifestations of which church history knows, such as those of the Irvingites, must be explained as repristinations of the events of Pentecost and early Christianity.

Conditions similar to those outlined in the foregoing are indicated in the Old Testament, where the influence either of the Spirit of God or of an evil spirit is represented as producing exalted, enthusiastic, ecstatic speech or action. To the examples noted under Ecstasy (q.v.) may be

3. Old-Tes- added the seventy elders of Num. xi. **tament and** 24–30, and the illustrations furnished **Ethnic** by Jer. xxiii. 32, xxix. 26. Having a **Parallels.** connection with these phenomena is the condition of the prophet when having his vision; the consciousness however permits the prophet to give a clear and connected account of what he sees and an interpreter is not needed, and nothing is said in this relation of ecstatic speech. But the things seen in the visions appear to the prophet to be psychological realities. The Greek-Roman world furnishes many evident parallels. The Greek oracles were mediated through priests or priestesses who uttered what the divinity suggested to them while their consciousness was in complete abeyance. Another characteristic of the giving of oracles is the obscurity or unintelligibility of the oracle, which ever needs explication. So

Plutarch (*De pythiæ oraculis*) brings out the complete passivity of the pythia, Heraclitus (*Sermo*, lxxix.) notes the necessity of elucidation of the oracle, Dio Chrysostom (*Oratio*, x.) remarks upon the use of rather uncommon, poetic, strange, and circumlocutory expressions. Very illustrative for this class of phenomena is the description which Plato gives in the *Timæus* of the mantis or prophet. He says that the inspired and true seer's art is not practised under full consciousness, but that the vision comes when the understanding is under constraint, or in sleep, sickness, or ecstasy, and what he sees or says under such circumstances is to be interpreted by one who has his reason. The last is the gift of the prophet. This representation is analogous to that of Paul, except that the latter does not make the prophet interpret the utterances, but speaks of an interpreter of the same. In post-Homeric times the cult of the Dionysiac orgies made their entrance into the Greek world. According to this, music, the whirling dance, and means of intoxication had power to make men "full of deity," to produce a condition in which the normal state was left behind and the inspired perceived what was external to himself and to sense. The soul was supposed to leave the body, hence the word "ecstasy," a being out of oneself, while other expressions used were "to rave" and "to be in the divinity," the latter expressing the thought that in its absence from the body the soul was united with deity, and so the deity spoke in and from the person in that condition. At such times the ecstatic person had no consciousness of his own. It was to this quality that Philo attributed the prophet's power (*De spec. leg.*, IV., viii.), while Plato regarded true poetry as the result of divine inspiration through the poet's being *entheoi* —"in the divinity." Out of the Dionysiac rites, then, developed a species of prophesying which through ecstasy put itself into connection with the divine and spirit world and so foretold the future. Cicero (*Pro Sexto*, x.) joins prophesying and madness, and in *De divinatione*, I., lxvii., asserts that it was not Cassandra who spoke, but the divinity inclosed in the human body. A prophetess officiated in a Thracian temple of Dionysus as did the pythia in Delphi. And this same frenzy spread into Italy (Livy, XXXIX., viii. sqq.). Origen (*Contra Celsum*, VII., ix., Eng. transl. in *ANF*, iv. 614) quotes Celsus to the effect that both in and outside the sanctuaries people exhibited ecstatic phenomena and uttered unknown, unintelligible speech. In modern times, such demonstrations are not entirely unknown, as in the case of the dervishes (see DERVISH).

Consideration of these examples enables one to arrive at a decision regarding the New-Testament speaking with tongues. It is significant in this connection that the two places, Jerusalem and Corinth, where the phenomenon in question appeared recall the Old-Testament phenomena and the practise in the Greek world. Accord-

4. The New-Testament Phenomena. ing to the opening verses of I Cor. xii. it appears that the Corinthians had asked Paul how one could recognize the working of the Spirit of God. They had learned that the demonstrations of demons were like the operations of the Christian charismata,

but they had no means of discriminating. Paul then recalls for them that they had had experience of the power of demons, but that now they were ruled by the Spirit of God; no one so ruled could call Jesus accursed, nor could one call Jesus Lord except in the Holy Spirit (I Cor. xii. 2–3). Paul then made the distinction rest upon the content of spiritual qualification (I Cor. xiv.). While the physiological basis of the phenomena was the same in the two classes, Paul saw a distinct difference; the Corinthians were in danger of putting undue stress upon this one gift, perhaps because it was connected with memories of their old life; but as a matter of fact it was of value solely to the one who experienced it unless it were interpreted to others. Hence Paul would regulate its employment; it was to be used only when an interpreter was present, and not by more than two or three at a time even then, that no confusion might result. Indeed, prophecy was a far more desirable gift than speaking with tongues. A slightly different condition is that of Pentecost, where the events resemble the ecstasy of the Old Testament and of the Greeks; but a new force is at work in that it makes them rejoicingly speak of the wonderful works of God, and have new knowledge, inner illumination, and firmness in propagating the news of the Gospel.

In considering the meaning of *glossa*, "tongue," in the various combinations in which it appears in referring to the phenomena in question, it may be said that this word is used in general to designate the organ of speech, to denote a method

5. Meaning of Glossa. of speech (in which it has various significations), and also speech itself. But in the passages in the New Testament under discussion it is best to take *glossa* in the metaphorical sense as a technical term denoting a strange and unwonted form of words. With this meaning it occurs not only in the literary monuments but as employed by the common people especially in referring to phenomena which seemed supernatural or unordinary, like the utterances of the pythia, of poets, or of the muses. This could then easily be taken over by Christianity to express something different from "teaching" and from prophecy, something which impressed one as being of the nature of secrets or as inspired. No insuperable difficulties inhere in this meaning. The most important arises from the fact that the term seems to have been used in Jerusalem before it was in Corinth, and could not have derived directly from the Greek world. The explanation may be offered, however, that in IV Macc. x. 21, and often in the Psalms (e.g., Ps. cxxvi. 2) the tongue is used to mean the instrument of the praise of God. The Jews also thought of the tongue as the unconditioned instrument of God and of his Spirit, and from this "to speak with tongues" could easily come to mean an ecstatic and jubilant method of speech in praise of God. So that if *glossa* means "tongue," "to speak with other tongues" or "with new tongues" would be analogous to the expression in I Cor. xiii. 1, "Though I speak with the tongues of men and of angels." On Greek soil *glossa* was employed to express an unusual, poetic, or unintelligible method of expression. Whether Paul as a Hellenist gave the expression the peculiar cast it has in I Corinthians or whether he borrowed it, it is equally explicable from the basis here afforded.

(P. Feine.)

Bibliography: The literature of especial worth is that contained in the commentaries on Acts and I Corinthians, many of which contain excursuses on the phenomena of Pentecost, with which may be employed the discussions in the works on the history of the Apostolic Age—e.g., McGiffert, pp. 50–51, 308, 521–522, 526; in the works on general church history, e.g., Schaff, Christian Church, i. 230–243; and in works on the life of the Apostle Paul, e.g., Conybeare and Howson, vol. i., chap. xiii. Consult further: F. Bleek, in TSK, 1829, pp. 3–79, 1830, pp. 45–64; F. C. Baur, in Tübinger Zeitschrift für Theologie, 1830, pp. 78–133; idem, in TSK, 1838, pp. 618–702; M. Schneckenburger, Beiträge zur Einleitung in das N. T., Stuttgart, 1832; D. Schultz, Die Geistergaben der ersten Christen, Breslau, 1836; Wieseler, in TSK, 1848, pp. 703–772; C. Bohm, Reden mit Zungen und Weissagen, Berlin, 1848; A. Hilgenfeld, Die Glossolalie in der alten Kirche, Leipsic, 1850; E. Rossteuscher, Gabe der Sprachen im apostolischen Zeitalter, Marburg, 1850; A. Maier, Die Glossolalie, Freiburg, 1855; W. A. Van Hengel, De Gave der Talen, Leyden, 1864; J. Gloël, Der heilige Geist in der Heilsverkündigung des Paulus, pp. 337–346, Halle, 1888; C. Weizsäcker, Das apostolische Zeitalter, pp. 589 sqq., 2d ed., Freiburg, 1892, Eng. transl., 2 vols., London, 1894–95; M. Beverslius, De heilige Geist en zijne Werkingen volgens het . . . N. Verbond, Utrecht, 1896; A. Wright, Some N. T. Problems, pp. 277–302, London, 1898; H. Gunkel, Die Wirkungen des heiligen Geistes, pp. 18–20, 2d ed., Göttingen, 1899; H. Weinel, Die Wirkungen des Geistes und der Geister, pp. 71–100, Freiburg, 1899; D. Walker, The Gift of Tongues and Other Essays, London, 1906 (conservative in tone); C. Lombard, De la glossolalie chez les premiers Chrétiens et des phénomènes similaires, Lausanne, 1910; DBT, iv. 793–796; EB, iv. 4761–76.

SPECHT, speHt, THOMAS: German Roman Catholic; b. at Türkheim (25 m. s.s.ẘ of Augsburg), Bavaria, Jan. 29, 1847. He was educated at the Lyceum of Dillingen and at the University of Munich (D.D., 1875). He was ordained to the priesthood in 1873; was curate at St. Ulrich's, Augsburg (1875–81); and professor of religion and Hebrew at the gymnasium at Neuburg, Bavaria, until 1887. Since 1887 he has been professor of apologetics and dogmatics at the lyceum of Dillingen, and librarian since 1902. He has been an episcopal spiritual counselor since 1901. He has written Die Wirkungen des eucharistischen Opfers (Augsburg, 1876); Die Lehre von der Einheit der Kirche nach dem heiligen Augustin (Neuburg, 1885); Die Lehre von der Kirche nach dem heiligen Augustin (Paderborn, 1892); Geschichte der ehemaligen Universität Dillingen (Freiburg, 1902); Geschichte des königlichen Lyceums Dillingen (Regensburg, 1904); and Lehrbuch der Dogmatik (vol. i., 1907).

SPEE, spê, FRIEDRICH VON: German Roman Catholic religious poet; b. at Kaiserswerth (27 m. n.n.w. of Cologne) Feb. 25, 1591; d. at Treves Aug. 7, 1635. In 1610 he entered the Society of Jesus, and after ordination to the priesthood became, in 1621, professor of grammar, philosophy, and ethics in the Jesuit college at Cologne. Four years later he was sent to Paderborn as cathedral preacher, and in 1627 became parish priest in Würzburg. In the following year he was transferred to Lower Saxony, where he distinguished himself as a successful leader of the Roman Catholic Counter-Reformation, especially at Peine in the diocese of Hildesheim. While at Würzburg, Von Spee was required to perform the last

offices of religion for some 200 persons executed for witchcraft, although he believed them all to be innocent, later assailing the entire system of trial for witchcraft in his Cautio criminalis, seu de processibus contra sagas (Rinteln, 1631), the first edition of which appeared anonymously. For several months he was seriously ill at Hildesheim, apparently in consequence of a Protestant attempt to assassinate him, and for a time he lived at the little village of Falkenhagen, but in 1632 he was again teaching moral theology at Cologne, inspiring the Medulla theologiæ moralis of Hermann Busenbaum (q.v.). Subsequently he was parish priest at Treves, where his devotion to the sick and wounded during the siege and after the capture of the city by the imperial and Spanish troops in 1635 exposed him to a contagious fever of which he died.

It is, however, as a religious poet that Von Spee is now best known, both his Trutz Nachtigall, oder geistlichs-poetisch Lust-Waldlein (Cologne, 1649) and his Güldenes Tugendbuch (1649) having passed through repeated editions, the latest of the Trutz Nachtigall, including the poems of the Güldenes Tugendbuch, being that of A. Weinrich (Freiburg, 1908), and of the Tugendbuch that of F. Hattler (1894). Two of his hymns have been translated into English: " Bei stiller Nacht, zur ersten Wache " as " Within a garden's bound "; and " Der trübe Winter ist vorbei " as " The gloomy winter now is o'er."

(O. Zöckler†.)

Bibliography: Lives have been written by J. B. Diel, 2d ed., by B. Duhr, Freiburg, 1901; H. Cardauns, Frankfort, 1884; I. Gebhardt, Hildesheim, 1893; R. Müller, in Historisch-politische Blätter, cxxiv (1900), 785 sqq., cxxv (1901), 430 sqq.; in ADB, xxxv. 92 sqq.; and KL, xi. 575 sqq.; cf. T. Ebner, F. Spee und die Hexenprozesse seiner Zeit, Hamburg, 1900.

SPEER, ROBERT ELLIOTT: Presbyterian layman; b. at Huntingdon, Pa., Sept. 10, 1867. He was educated at Princeton College (A.B., 1899) and also studied for a year at Princeton Theological Seminary. He was secretary of the Student Volunteer Movement for Foreign Missions in 1889–90 and instructor in English Bible in Princeton College in 1890–91. Since 1891 he has been secretary of the Presbyterian Board of Foreign Missions. In 1896–1897 he made a tour of the Christian missions in the orient, visiting Persia, India, China, Japan, and Korea. In theology he is Evangelical, and has written Studies in the Gospel of Luke (New York, 1892); Studies in the Book of Acts (1892); The Man Christ Jesus (1896); Missions and Politics in Asia (1898); A Memorial of a True Life (1898); Remember Jesus Christ (1899); The Man Paul (1900); Presbyterian Foreign Missions (Philadelphia, 1901); Christ and Life (New York, 1901); Principles of Jesus applied to some Questions of To-Day (1902); Missionary Principles and Practice (1902); A Young Man's Questions (1903); A Memorial of Horace Tracy Pitkin (1903); Missions and Modern History (2 vols., 1904); Young Men who Overcame (1905); Marks of a Man; Essentials of Christian Character (1907); Master of the Heart (1908); Memorial of Alice Jackson (1908); Paul the All Round Man (1909); Servants of the King (1909); Second Coming of Christ (1910); and Christianity and the Nations (1910).

SPELLMEYER, HENRY: Methodist Episcopal bishop; b. in New York City Nov. 25, 1847. He was educated at New York University (A.B., 1866) and Union Theological Seminary (graduated, 1869). For thirty-five years he held various pastorates of his denomination in and around Newark, N. J., and in 1904 was elected bishop.

SPENCE, JAMES: Synod of United Original Seceders; b. at Evie (20 m. e. of Kirkwall), Orkney Islands, May 22, 1845. He was educated at the University of Aberdeen, and in theology in the Original Secession Hall, Glasgow, and New College, Edinburgh; became minister of the Original Secession church at Auchinleck, Ayrshire, 1870, and so remains. In 1876 he was appointed professor of systematic theology in the divinity hall of his communion in Glasgow, and was transferred to his present chair of Biblical criticism, 1895.

SPENCE-JONES, HENRY DONALD MAURICE: Church of England; b. at London Jan. 14, 1836. He was educated at Corpus Christi, Cambridge (B.A., 1864), and was ordered deacon in 1865 and ordained priest in the following year. He was professor of English literature and lecturer in Hebrew at St. David's College, Lampeter, Wales (1865–70); rector of St. Mary-de-Crypt with All Saints and St. Owen, Gloucester (1870–77); and principal of Gloucester Theological College (1875–77); vicar and rural dean of St. Pancras, London (1877–86), and since 1886 has been dean of Gloucester of which he had been honorary canon since 1875. He was select preacher at Cambridge in 1883, 1887, 1901, and 1905, and at Oxford in 1892 and 1903. In 1906 he was elected professor of ancient history in the Royal Academy. In theology he is a moderate evangelical. He has contributed the volumes on I Samuel and the Pastoral Epistles to Bishop Ellicott's Commentary (2 vols., London, 1880–84), and on Acts (in collaboration with J. S. Howson) to Schaff's *Popular Commentary on the New Testament* (New York, 1880). He also edited *The Pulpit Commentary* (48 vols., London, 1880–97) in collaboration with J. S. Exell, to which he himself contributed the section on Luke (2 vols., 1889), and edited and translated the *Didache* (1885). As independent works he has written *Dreamland and History: The Story of the Norman Dukes* (London, 1891); *Cloister Life in the Days of Cœur de Lion* (1892); *Gloucester Cathedral* (1897); *The Church of England* (4 vols., 1897–98); *The White Robe of Churches of the Eleventh Century; Pages from the Story of Gloucester Cathedral* (1900); *The History of the English Church* (1900); *Life and Work of the Redeemer* (1901); *Early Christianity and Paganism: A History, A.D. 64–320* (1902); *The Golden Age of the Church: Studies in the Fourth Century* (1906); and *The Early Christians in Rome* (1910).

SPENCER, HERBERT: Philosopher; b. in Derby, England, Apr. 27, 1820; d. in Brighton Dec. 8, 1903. He was a son of William George and Harriet Holmes Spencer. His father was a schoolmaster and private teacher. His early education was unacademic, partly at home, partly under an uncle. After trials at engineering (1837–46), and journalism (an economist newspaper, 1848–53), he became

contributor to various reviews. He was an early convert to the doctrine of development already formulated by Lamarck. In 1855, four years before the appearance of Darwin's *Origin of Species,* he published *Principles of Psychology,* based on the principles of evolution. Evolution is defined as a continuous change from indefinite, incoherent homogeneity to definite, coherent heterogeneity of structure and function, through successive differentiations and integrations. By a law of the persistence of force, the entire universe, inorganic, organic, and superorganic, becomes both more specialized and complex and at the same time more organic and unified. Three laws are appealed to: homogeneity tends to heterogeneity; heterogeneity tends to integration and equilibrium; the equilibrium reached is unstable and tends to dissolution. In his enlarged *Principles of Psychology* (London, 1870–72) he treats consciousness from a genetic point of view as analogous to developing biological organisms. Certain tendencies of mental reaction are traced to racial heredity and hence the explanation of what appear to be innate or intuitive ideas. Society is an organism and social institutions are the product of development with two opposing tendencies—the State and the individual; with the individual lies the initiative, only he must be prevented from aggressive self-assertion (*Principles of Sociology,* 1877). In the field of ethics development is also the rule. The moral sense is traced to the experience of the race; conscience originates in social customs, either permissive or restrictive; the moral life is an equilibrium between the claims of altruism and egoism. Pleasure is indeed the summum bonum, but it must be defined by such an ideal adjustment to environment that moral conduct will be seen to be a perfectly natural functioning; this, however, is a condition only possible in a future and final stage of social development when the sense of duty shall wholly disappear (*Data of Ethics,* 1879; *Justice,* ib. 1891). His attitude toward ultimate reality is twofold: intellectually, a modified agnosticism; religiously, a feeling of mystery and awe. Agnosticism springs from the irreconcilable contradictions in our assertions concerning the Absolute, and is partly resolved by the necessary affirmations of an " Infinite and Eternal Energy, from Which all things proceed." Even if religions have a history, they are reducible to a sense of awe which is awakened by the ultimate mystery of the universe (cf. *First Principles,* 1862, rev. ed., 1867). The chief significance of Spencer is found in two directions: first, his explanation of consciousness and all human institutions by reference to a law of functional development; secondly, while he has been denounced as a materialist, yet many parts of his writings are charged with postulates and implications which require only further elucidation to disclose their essential theism. His relations with America, which he visited and where he had a large circle of readers, were from the first reciprocally cordial.   C. A. BECKWITH.

BIBLIOGRAPHY. Spencer's *System of Synthetic Philosophy* appeared in 10 vols., London, 1860–97, 15 vols., ib. and New York, 1900, new uniform ed. of his *Works,* 18 vols., New York, 1910. For his life consult: H. Spencer, *An Autobiography,* 2 vols., London and New York, 1904;

D. Duncan, *Life and Letters of Herbert Spencer*, ib. 1908 (the authorized biography); S. H. Mellone, *Leaders of Religious Thought in the Nineteenth Century*, London, 1902; *Home Life with Herbert Spencer*, ib. 1906.

On his philosophy consult: G. S. Morris, *British Thought and Thinkers*, pp. 337–388, ib. 1870; W. B. Green, *The Facts of Consciousness and the Philosophy of Herbert Spencer*, New York, 1871; B. P. Bowne, *The Philosophy of Herbert Spencer*, ib. 1874; J. L. Porter, *Science and Revelation*, Belfast, 1874; R. Watts, *An Examination of H. Spencer's Biological Hypothesis*, ib. 1875; C. Wright, *Philosophical Discussions*, pp. 43–96, New York, 1877; E. Blanc, *Les Nouvelles Bases de la morale d'après M. Herbert Spencer*, Lyons, 1881; T. R. Birks, *Modern Physical Fatalism and the Doctrine of Evolution, including an Examination of Mr. H. Spencer's 'First Principles,'* 2d ed., London, 1882; W. H. Rolph, *Biologische Probleme zugleich als Versuch einer rationellen Ethik*, Leipsic, 1882; C. E. Beeby, *The Woes of the Gospel*, London, 1884; T. Fairman, *Herbert Spencer on Socialism*, ib. 1884; J. Iverach, *The Philosophy of Herbert Spencer Examined*, ib. 1884; W. Arthur, *Religion without God, and God without Religion*, part 2, ib. 1885; P. S. Bridel, *Les Bases de morale évolutioniste d'après H. Spencer*, Paris, 1886; K. Gaquoin, *Die Grundlage der spencer'schen Philosophie*, Berlin, 1888; A. Roder, *Der Weg zum Glück. Auf Grund einer Darstellung der Entwickelungslehre H. Spencers*, Leipsic, 1888; J. Watson, *Gospels of Yesterday: Drummond, Spencer*, Glasgow, 1888; C. Laurens, *L'Évolution et M. Herbert Spencer*, Lyons, 1889; D. G. Thompson, *Herbert Spencer*, New York, 1889; E. Grosse, *Herbert Spencer's Lehre von dem Unerkennbaren*, Leipsic, 1890; B. F. Underwood, *Herbert Spencer's Synthetic Philosophy*, New York, 1891; E. A. E. Shirreff, *Moral Training: Froebel and Herbert Spencer*, London, 1892; A. Weismann, *Das Keimplasma*, Jena, 1892, Eng. transl., *Germ Plasm*, London, 1893; K. Busse, *Herbert Spencer's Philosophie der Geschichte*, Leipsic, 1894; W. H. Hudson, *Introduction to the Philosophy of Herbert Spencer*, New York, 1894; E. de Roberty, *Auguste Comte et Herbert Spencer*, Paris, 1894; J. M. Bösch, *Die entwicklungstheoretische Idee sozialer Gerechtigkeit*, Zurich, 1896; G. Vidari, *Rosmini e Spencer*, Milan, 1897; G. Allievo, *La Psicologia di Herbert Spencer*, Turin, 1898; F. H. Collins, *An Epitome of the 'Synthetic Philosophy,'* 4th ed., London, 1899; J. Dubois, *Spencer et le principe de la morale*, Paris, 1899; J. Ward, *Naturalism and Agnosticism*, London, 1899; H. Macpherson, *Spencer and Spencerism*, New York, 1900; J. Royce, *Herbert Spencer*, ib. 1904; C. W. Saleeby, *Evolution, the Master Key*, ib. 1906 (entertaining, candid, lucid); J. A. Thomson, *Herbert Spencer*, London and New York, 1906; W. P. Steenkamp, *Het Agnosticisme van Herbert Spencer*, Amsterdam, 1910.

SPENCER, JOHN: English theologian and Hebraist; b. at Bocton (near Blean, 3 m. n.w. of Canterbury), Kent, baptized Oct. 31, 1630; d. at Ely May 27, 1693. He was educated at Corpus Christi College, Cambridge (B.A., 1648; M.A., 1652; B.D., 1659; D.D., 1665), and then served the parishes of St. Giles and St. Benedict in Cambridge; had the care of Landbeach in Cambridgeshire (1667–83); became prebendary at the cathedral of Ely (1671); archdeacon of Sudbury (1677); and dean of Ely in the same year. In 1667 he was chosen master of Corpus Christi College, Cambridge. Not without justice has he been called the founder of the science of comparative religion, tracing as he did the relations between Hebrew and other Semitic religions. In his first treatise, *Dissertatio de Urim et Thummim* (Cambridge, 1669), he derived these emblems from the Egyptians. This treatise prepared the way for his chief work, *De legibus Hebræorum ritualibus et earum rationibus libri tres* (1685; in four books, Tübingen, 1732). Here he investigated the origins of the Mosaic ritual and arrived at the conclusion that the Mosaic religion was not wholly based upon

revelation, but was to a certain extent derived from existing customs. Spencer's views were severely attacked by men like Hermann Witsius, John Edwards, and others. Spencer replied with a carefully revised edition of his work to which was appended a fourth book, which appeared only after his death, in 1727, edited by Leonhard Chappelow. Besides these works, Spencer published *A Discourse concerning Prodigies* (London, 1663; 2d ed., 1665, with an appendix, *Treatise concerning Vulgar Prophecies*). His chief work is still regarded as the most important work on the religious antiquities of the Hebrews.

BIBLIOGRAPHY: *DNB*, liii. 359–360 (where may be found references to scattering notices); a life by C. M. Pfaff was prefixed to book iv. of the Tübingen edition of the *De legibus*.

SPENER, PHILIPP JAKOB. See PIETISM, I.

SPENGLER, speng′ler, **LAZARUS:** Town clerk of Nuremberg and zealous adherent of Luther; b. at Nuremberg Mar. 13, 1479; d. there Sept. 7, 1534. In 1494 he entered the University of Leipsic, but on his father's death, two years later, was obliged to terminate his studies. He then entered the Nuremberg chancery, becoming first town clerk in 1507 and a member of the council in 1516. A decided admirer of Staupitz, and publicly accused of "being a disciple or follower of Luther," Spengler wrote, late in 1519, his *Schutzred und christliche Antwort eines ehrbaren Liebhabers christlicher Wahrheit*, in which he boldly defended Luther's teachings. The work, which ran through five editions within a year, exposed its author to much hostility, especially on the part of Johann Eck, and Spengler was included in the bull of excommunication against Luther. In compliance with the desire of his superiors, and in the interest of Nuremberg, Spengler yielded externally, though only that he might gradually lead the council and city to his own position, his attitude being strengthened by his observations during his attendance, as delegate of the Nuremberg council, at the Diet of Worms in 1521. His name is intimately connected with the beginning and gradual development of the Reformation in Nuremberg. At his suggestion the Irish monastery of St. Ægidius was transformed into a Protestant gymnasium; he proposed the church visitation of 1528 in the territories of Nuremberg and Brandenburg; the formulation of the Nuremberg-Brandenburg church order was largely due to him; and it was in great part his reluctance to make war upon the emperor that prevented Nuremberg and Brandenburg from joining the Schmalkald League. He also maintained continual correspondence with Wittenberg, especially with Luther, with whom he sided against Butzer in the Eucharistic controversy, exactly as he had opposed the compliant position of Melanchthon at Augsburg in 1530. Besides the *Schutzred* already mentioned, Spengler wrote *Schrift-Ermanung und Undterweysung zu einem tugenhaften Wandel* (1520); *Ein tröstliche Christenliche anweisung vnd artzney in allen widerwertigkeiten* (Nuremberg, 1521); *Ein kurtzer Begriff wie sich ein warhaffter Christ in allem seinem wesen und wandel, gegen got vnd seinen nechsten halten soll* (1525); *Trost in Cleinmutigkeit der heiligen Evangelii sachen belangend* (1529); *Christliche Trostschrift* *samt dem 54. Psalm ausgelegt* (1529); *Eyn kurtzer ausszug auss den Bepstlichen Rechten, der Decret vnd Decretalen* (1530), and a number of minor works. He is also supposed to have been the author of the anonymous *Hauptartikel, durch welche gemeine Christenheit bisher verführt worden, darneben auch Grund und Anzeigen eines ganzen rechten christlichen Wesens* (1522). Spengler wrote two hymns, one of which, " Durch Adams Fall ist ganz verderbt," was translated by Bishop Miles Coverdale in 1539, and in other versions is still used by the Moravians, also appearing in the *Evangelical Lutheran Hymnal* published at Columbus, O., in 1880. (T. KOLDE.)

BIBLIOGRAPHY: U. G. Haussdorf, *Lebensbeschreibung eines christlichen Politici, . . . Lazari Spenglers*, Nuremberg, 1740; M. M. Mayer, *Spengleriana*, ib. 1830; F. Roth, *Die Einführung der Reformation in Nürnberg*, Würzburg, 1885; P. Drews, *W. Pirkheimers Stellung zur Reformation*, Leipsic, 1887; G. Ludewig, *Die Politik Nürnbergs im Zeitalter der Reformation*, Göttingen, 1893; P. Kalkoff, *Pirkheimers und Spenglers Lösung vom Banne, 1521*, Breslau, 1896; H. Westermeyer, in *Beiträge zur bayerischen Kirchengeschichte*, vol. ii., Erlangen, 1896; cf. idem, *Der brandenburgisch-nürnbergische Kirchenordnung*, ib. 1894; K. Schornbaum, *Zur Politik des Markgrafen Georg von Brandenburg*, Munich, 1906; Julian, *Hymnology*, p. 1072.

SPERATUS, sper-ā'tus, **PAUL:** Reformer of Prussia and one of the oldest Protestant hymn-writers; b. at Rötlen (a village near Ellwangen, 45 m. e.n.e. of Stuttgart) probably Dec. 13, 1484; d. at Marienwerder (45 m. s.s.e. of Danzig) Aug. 12, 1551. He studied in Paris and Italy, and probably at Freiburg and Vienna. About 1506 he was ordained to the priesthood and was later ennobled as a papal and imperial palsgrave. As a priest he was stationed at Salzburg in 1514, became cathedral preacher there in 1516, removed to Dinkelsbühl in 1520, and in July of the same year became cathedral preacher in Würzburg. His Lutheran sympathies, complicated by his marriage and his debts, forced him to flee on Nov. 21, 1521, to Salzburg, only to be speedily expelled. He then accepted a call to Ofen, in Hungary, but his denunciation of monastic vows in a sermon preached by him in St. Stephen's, Vienna (Jan. 12, 1522; printed at Königsberg in 1524 as *Sermon vom hohen Gelübde der Taufe*), led the theological faculty of Vienna to excommunicate him on Jan. 20, 1522. This precluded a position at Ofen, but before long he found a place at Iglau, where, in 1523, he was imprisoned by the bishop of Olmütz and condemned to death, escaping this fate only by the intervention of influential friends on condition that he would leave Moravia. He then went, by way of Prague, to Wittenberg, where he assisted Luther in the preparation of the first Protestant hymnal (1524). In 1524, on the recommendation of Luther, he was called to Königsberg by Albert of Prussia (q.v.). There he was court chaplain until 1529, and from 1530 until his death was Protestant bishop of Pomerania, with his residence at Marienwerder. It was largely through his efforts that East Prussia was thoroughly Lutheranized, and its religious conditions completely reorganized. In all this he was aided by Johannes Briessmann and Johann Poliander (qq.v.); and with George of Polentz (q.v.), bishop of Samland, Ehrhard of Queiss, bishop of Pomerania, and Councilor Adrian of Waiblingen he conducted the first and most important church visi-

tation in the duchy of Prussia (1526), also taking a prominent part in the second visitation of 1528. In Jan., 1530, Speratus succeeded Ehrhard of Queiss as bishop of Pomerania, where, despite the greatest financial difficulties, he displayed marvellous ability in the Protestantizing of Prussia. He seems to have inspired the division of Prussia into three district synods and one national synod, and from 1531 to 1535 he made every effort to suppress the Schwenck-feldian movement (see SCHWENCKFELD VON OSSIG, CASPAR, SCHWENCKFELDIANS), his task being made still more difficult by Albert's harboring of Dutch Protestant (though non-Lutheran) refugees. The Münster outrages, however, led the duke to require unity of doctrine in Prussia in the spirit of the Lutheran church order of 1525 (the *Artikel der Ceremonien und anderer Kirchenordnung*, in the preparation of which Speratus himself seems to have had a share).

Speratus stood ready in 1537 to attend the proposed ecumenical council at Mantua on condition that free expression of opinion be allowed and the Bible be taken as the basis of all decrees, at the same time maintaining the right of resistance to the forcible suppression of religious opinions. In 1549 he was arbiter in the dispute between the Melanchthonian Lauterwald and the Osiandrian Funck, and though he died too soon to become a prominent figure in the Osiandrian controversy, after it had been allayed the life-work of Speratus became fully effective, influencing the Church in East Prussia until the rise of Kantian rationalism. Besides translating some of Luther's works from Latin into German and assisting in the preparation of the *Etlich Gesang . . . alles aus Grund göttlicher Schrift* (Königsberg, 1527), he wrote *Wie man trotzen soll aufs Kreuz, wider alle Welt zu stehen bei dem Evangelio* (Wittenberg, 1524); the lost *Epistola ad Batavos vagantes;* and probably the *Episcoporum Prussiæ Pomezaniensis atque Sambiensis constitutiones synodales evangelicæ* (manuscript in the archives at Königsberg). The greater portion of his dogmatic writings and of his correspondence is edited by P. Tschackert in his *Urkundenbuch zur Reformationsgeschichte des Herzogthums Preussen* (3 vols., Leipsic, 1890). Of the five hymns of Speratus two have been translated into English: " Es ist das Heil uns kommen her " as " To us salvation now is come"; and " In Gott gelaub ich, dass er hat aus nicht " as " In God I trust, for so I must " (by Miles Coverdale, who also made a version of the former hymn, "Now is our health come from above ").

(PAUL TSCHACKERT.)

BIBLIOGRAPHY: As sources use should be made of his works as given in the text, and of his *Briefwechsel*, in P. Tschackert, *Urkundenbuch zur Reformationsgeschichte des Herzogthums Preussen*, 3 vols., Leipsic, 1890. Consult further: C. J. Cosack, *Paulus Speratus, Leben und Lieder*, Brunswick, 1861; P. Tschackert, *Paul Speratus von Rötlen*, Halle, 1891; T. Kolde, in *Beiträge zur bayerischen Kirchengeschichte*, vol. vi., part 2, Erlangen, 1899; B. Schumacher, *Niederländische Ansiedlungen im Herzogtum Preussen zur Zeit Herzog Albrechts*, Leipsic, 1903; J. Zeller, *Paulus Speratus, seine Herkunft, sein Studiengang, und seine Thätigkeit bis 1522*, Stuttgart, 1907; Julian, *Hymnology*, pp. 1073–74.

SPEYER, spai'er or spair, **BISHOPRIC OF:** A German diocese first specifically mentioned in 614 although Christianity may have been implanted in the region during the Roman period. It later became part of the archdiocese of Mainz, the larger portion of the see being on the right bank of the Rhine, and the smaller portion on the left bank. The northern and southern limits respectively were Altrip and Lauterburg, while in the east the diocese extended to the present Württemberg circle of Jagst, and in the west to the vicinity of Pirmasenz.

(A. Hauck.)

For a long time after the rise of Lutheranism the diocese of Speyer, although almost invariably administered by faithful and able prelates, was exposed to many vicissitudes. In 1546 the deanery of Weissenburg was incorporated in the diocese, but a few years later the troops of Margrave Albert of Brandenburg-Culmbach plundered and desecrated the cathedral. The majority of the old monasteries came into the possession of adherents of the new faith, although sturdy resistance was made to Protestantism both in its religious and its political aspects. In 1621 Ernest of Mansfeld again sacked Speyer, and in 1632 the victorious advance of Gustavus Adolphus led the bishop to make alliance with the French. This union, even though aided by Swedish neutrality, could not protect the diocese against the horrors of the Thirty-Years' War, and for ten years (1635–45) the bishop was a prisoner at Vienna. The years following were devoted to the restoration of the almost ruined diocese, but the War of the Palatinate and of the Orléans and Spanish successions brought new distress upon Speyer, while occasional conflicts between city and diocese still further complicated the situation. The wars of the Polish and Austrian successions also worked to the disadvantage of the see. In 1801 that portion of the diocese to the left of the Rhine, which had been permanently occupied by the French, was divided between the sees of Mainz and Strasburg, while the district to the right of the river was later shared by Freiburg and Rottenburg. In 1817 the Bavarian concordat created a new diocese of Speyer, which is identical in limits with the Bavarian Rhenish Palatinate and forms part of the archdiocese of Bamberg.

Bibliography: *Annales Spirenses*, ed. G. H. Pertz, in *MGH, Script.*, xvii (1861), 80–85; *Fontes rerum Germanicarum*, ed. J. F. Böhmer and A. Huber, iv. 315–355, Stuttgart, 1868; F. X. Remling, *Urkundliche Geschichte der ehemaligen Abteien und Klöster im jetzigen Rheinbayern*, 2 vols., Neustadt, 1836; idem, *Das Reformationswerk in der Pfalz*, Mannheim, 1846; idem, *Geschichte der Bischöfe zu Speyer*, 2 vols., Mainz, 1852–54; idem, *Urkundenbuch zur Geschichte der Bischöfe zu Speyer*, 2 vols. ib. 1852–53; idem, *Der Speyerer Dom*, ib. 1861; idem, *Die Rheinpfalz in der Revolution 1792–98*, 2 vols., Speyer, 1865; idem, *Neuere Geschichte der Bischöfe zu Speyer*, ib. 1867; W. Molitor, *Die Immunität des Domes zu Speyer*, ib. 1859; *Urkunden zur Geschichte der Stadt Speyer*, ed. A. Hilgard, Strasburg, 1885; N. Meyer-Schwartau, *Der Dom zu Speyer*, Berlin, 1893; J. Zimmern, *Der Kaiserdom zu Speyer*, Ludwigshafen, 1897; *Urkunden zur pfalzischen Kirchengeschichte im Mittelalter*, ed. F. X. Glasschröder, Munich, 1903; *KL*, xi. 589–614. For list of the bishops consult Gams, *Series episcoporum*, pp. 313–315; and Hauck-Herzog, *RE*, xviii. 589.

SPEYER, DIETS OF.

I. Diet of 1526: When Archduke Ferdinand opened the imperial diet in Speyer June 15, 1526, the political situation was unfavorable to the friends of the Reformation. Through the peace of Madrid, Jan. 14, 1526, the Emperor Charles V. had gained a free hand, and could hope to enforce within the German empire the provisions of the edict of Worms. The South German Roman Catholic princes had formed a compact alliance at Regensburg in July, 1524; the North German princes, at Dessau on June 26. So when, early in 1526, Duke Henry of Brunswick reached Spain, to entreat the emperor's support in behalf of the ancient faith, Charles joyfully acceded to the appeal. On Mar. 23, 1526, he announced that he expected to start for Rome in June, then to proceed to Germany to put an end to Lutheranism.

1. The Political Situation.

Accordingly, the imperial instructions to the estates at Speyer demanded no more than advisement over the ways and means whereby the ordinances of the Church might be administered as usual. But although the chiefs of the Evangelical party, Elector John of Saxony and Landgrave Philip of Hesse, had not yet arrived, the two princely colleges, on June 30, demanded some action in the matter of terminating abuses. The cities declared the execution of the edict of Worms to be impossible. At the same time they demanded that such practises as opposed the word of God be abolished. On July 4, this memorial of the cities was communicated to the princely colleges, and it was accepted unaltered. At this juncture, each of the three tribunals, electoral, princely, municipal, elected a separate committee, whose office was to decide between abuses to be abolished and the good practises to be retained. The anti-Roman temper of the major part of the German nation again came openly to the front, and powerful reenforcement was received by the arrival in Speyer of Landgrave Philip on July 12, and of Elector John on July 20. By an agreement subscribed at Torgau May 2, approved by other Evangelical princes on June 12, the leaders pledged themselves to open confession of the Evangelical truth. The committee for the princes endorsed the marriage of priests and the cup for the laity as articles worthy of resolute endeavor, but the municipal committee proposed to leave to a free vote with every estate of the realm how it would deal with ceremonial affairs until convention of the council. Subsequently, on July 30, a " great committee " was appointed for further consideration of the whole matter; but on Aug. 3, Archduke Ferdi-

2. Demands of the Estates.

nand appeared with the abrupt and summary notification that an imperial collateral advice of Mar. 23 prohibited all that procedure, and called simply for the execution of the edict of Worms. Most of the estates heard this communication with aversion. Finally the princely colleges agreed to inform the imperial commissioners that, in the question of religious belief, each estate would " so abide and behave that it might render loyal account before God, his imperial majesty, and the kingdom."

A memorial tendered on Aug. 4 by the cities to the estates called attention to the alteration in the political situation since the debated instructions had been decreed. The emperor, being now **3. Changed** at war with the pope, must admit the **Political** practical inexpediency of the mandate **Situation;** of Worms. Since a council could not **Embassy** convene at short notice, it was advised **to the** that they report by despatches and en- **Emperor.** voys to the emperor concerning the present state of affairs, and beseech him to suspend the edict of Worms, and to approve the national assembly that had been forbidden by the emperor. So early as Aug. 5, the estates concurred in the cities' proposal, and the instructions to be despatched with the envoys were concluded Aug. 21. The envoys were to remind the emperor that while some of the imperial estates were still of the former faith and practise, others adhered to a different ecclesiastical teaching, which in their estimation was also Christian; therefore let both parties hold their own way in behalf of the Christian truth. The emperor was entreated to come to Germany as soon as practicable, so that counsel might be devised through his presence. Furthermore, he was asked to bring it about that within a year and a half a " common free council " should be set afoot on German soil, or, at all events, a free national assembly. He was also asked to set at rest the matter of the edict of Worms. This proposition was adopted in the diet Aug. 27, and accepted by the imperial commissioners. The friends of the Reformation had cause to be content with the result of the diet. While the proviso which gave to the diet its lasting historical significance brought about no permanent peace, it was designed to aid in tiding over the momentary embarrassment by a truce that deferred the ultimate decision. But inasmuch as the regulation of the religious issue never came to pass, and as neither the council nor the national assembly, nor even the proposed embassy to the emperor, was realized, the embassy being expressly forbidden by the emperor, on May 27, 1527, the Evangelical estates of the realm held themselves to be justified by the diet's ruling to continue and complete the reforms already begun in their jurisdictions. In this way the resolutions of Speyer came to be the legal foundation for the Evangelical party's further innovations in religion. But since the Roman Catholic estates, in their suppression of the Gospel, could also appeal to the ruling of Speyer, the religious division of the German nation dates effectively from this diet.

II. Diet of 1529: The political situation had become still more threatening for the Evangelical estates when a second imperial diet convened at Speyer in 1529. Charles V., just then on the point of concluding peace with the pope, was resolved to make an end of Lutheranism in the **1. The** empire. At the opening of the diet on **Emperor's** Mar. 15, the imperial address to the **Position.** estates expressed in the bluntest terms the emperor's disfavor on account of the " pernicious errors " abroad in Germany, seeing they had even caused tumult and riot. The emperor would connive no longer at these disorders; the council, which the pope, too, would now gladly promote, was to be convoked as soon as possible. Till then the emperor forbade, under penalty of the ban of the empire, that any one be coerced or enticed into unrighteous belief. From the former ruling of Speyer, there had ensued " great mischief and misunderstanding over against our holy faith "; wherefore the emperor did now repeal the same, and commanded the regulation prescribed in his manifesto.

In the diet, this time, the Roman Catholic party had vastly the majority. Among the eighteen members of the " great committee " that was appointed on Mar. 18 for drafting the diet's **2. Roman** enactments, only three were Evangel- **Catholic** ical. Hence the Roman Catholics **Preponder-** carried their motions, notwithstanding **ance.** the Evangelical members' resistance. No later than Mar. 22, the committee resolved to lay before the diet the repeal of the preceding decree of Speyer. The committee's memorial was communicated to the estates on Apr. 3, and accepted by the princes Apr. 6 and 7. But when the Evangelical princes declared that they would not be forced from the former decree of Speyer, the motion was returned to the committee for modification, with the proviso, however, that the " substance " thereof should remain unchanged. The memorial, so unpalatable to the Evangelical party, was left practically unaltered, and was referred to the princely estates on Apr. 10, and adopted on Apr. 12, although Elector John at once made it publicly known that he would protest against it. Shortly afterward, it was delivered to the cities for final passage. When the municipal envoys were summoned one by one to pronounce whether they accepted the decree, twenty-one cities yielded their assent on Apr. 12 and 13; others answered evasively. All the rest, however, besides the still protesting cities of Frankfort, Hall in Swabia, Goslar, and Nordhausen, had the courage to refuse compliance. On Apr. 12, the Evangelical princes caused a writ of grievance to be read aloud, wherein they offered searching arguments for their declension of the majority resolution, and begged for its alteration. But the estates answered merely (on Apr. 13) that they had delivered their decree, together with the grievance, to the imperial commissioners. The estates being then assembled in solemn convocation on Apr. 19, the commissioners, through King Ferdinand, announced that in the name of the emperor they adopted the resolution of the estates. Touching the grievance of the Evangelical estates, they remarked that they had taken cognizance thereof, and left the same to stand or fall by its own weight, and they trusted that the estates concerned would not refuse the ruling by majority duly decreed.

Thus the situation of the Evangelical estates had come to be serious. In the imperial diet, they stood completely isolated. Yet the Evangelical leaders held firm and unanimous, even though the opposition attempted to effect their separation by utilizing the dissension between Luther and

3. Withdrawal of the Evangelicals. Zwingli. The magistrates of Evangelical cities, especially of Nuremberg and Strasburg, contributed not a little, by their animating instructions, to the result that their advocates in Speyer maintained their courageous determination. After the imperial commissioners' ultimatum, Elector John, Margrave George, Landgrave Philip, and Prince Wolfgang of Anhalt, as also the chancellor of Dukes Ernst and Franz of Lüneburg, who had not yet reached Speyer, returned to the audience chamber, whence they had withdrawn for a brief consultation, and protested orally against the decree. stating also that they would take no part in any subsequent proceedings of the imperial diet. And when Jacob Sturm announced that the Evangelical cities adhered to the protestation, they filed in the records of the diet a writ of protest, which meanwhile had been hastily drawn up by the Saxon chancellor, wherein they declared that they were not bound, without their assent, to vacate the former unanimously resolved decree, and that they protested against the majority ruling as null and void. For the drafting of a second, more explicitly detailed writ of protestation, they commissioned the chancellor of Brandenburg, George Vogler, who now prepared with the utmost expedition a draft, which is still extant in the district archives of Bamberg, in sixteen folio pages. This document meeting with the approbation of the Evangelical princes, a clean copy thereof was despatched to King Ferdinand on Apr. 20. At first, indeed, he accepted the same, but afterward he returned it with disapproval. At the last moment, Duke Henry of Brunswick and Margrave Philip of Baden made an attempt at mediation that found ready response with the Evangelical princes, but was rejected by Ferdinand. The decree was signed on April 22; and the diet, wherein the Evangelical princes no longer took part, was closed. The protesting delegates announced, however, that they meant to conduct themselves peaceably and friendly toward all estates.

For security against hostile attacks, Elector John and Landgrave Philip, on April 22, had an "understanding" with Nuremberg, Strasburg, and Ulm, as

4. The "Protest." to which more particular terms were to be defined in June, at a diet in Rotach. On Apr. 25, the formal act of protestation was vested with legal finality by an attested instrument of appeal, wherein all antecedent records were duly cited and reviewed. In this connection, the counselors of Elector John of Saxony, Margrave George of Brandenburg, Dukes Ernst and Franz of Lüneburg, Landgrave Philip of Hesse, and of Prince Wolfgang of Anhalt, protested by every form of law against the decree; and at the same time appealed to the emperor, the council, the national assembly, indeed to every impartial Christian judge. The delegations of the fourteen cities made simultaneous declaration of their adherence to this appeal. The Evangelical princes departed from Speyer on Apr. 25 and straightway arranged for the publication of the protestation. This was effected by the landgrave on May 5, and by the elector on May 12. A deputation, whose members were determined at Nuremberg on May 26, was to convey the appeal to the emperor. These envoys did also set out in July, but not till Sept. 12, at Piacenza, could they deliver their message to the emperor. On Oct. 12, he then assured them that he expected the protesting estates to obey the decree, since otherwise he must proceed against them with severe measures. Lastly he had the envoys arrested, nor were they released until Oct. 30.

It was from the protest at Speyer that the adherents of the Reformation obtained the designation of "Protestants" (see PROTESTANTISM), and this act received a worthy memorial in the commemorative "Church of the Protestation," erected by means of gifts from all Evangelical countries, and solemnly dedicated on Aug. 31, 1904.

The "protest" from which thus "Protestants" derived their name has been charged by Roman Catholics with being a protest against tolerance as expressed with reference to the edict of Worms by the diet. But the edict bound those who maintained it to deny to Luther and his adherents all rights, even of food and shelter, and

5. Roman Catholic Charges. permitted their spoliation and persecution; the diet's terms required the execution of these commands. The directions of the diet further did not admit the legitimacy of the Reformation where it was already deeply rooted, and forbade further progress; had the Evangelical party signed this, they would by that fact have admitted the Reformation to be at fault. The diet further attempted to prohibit preaching against the Roman Catholic doctrine of the sacrament of the Lord's Supper, even where the Lutheran position was held by the majority; since it also required that the mass be not abolished in Evangelical jurisdictions, even the Evangelical clergy would have been compelled to read mass, and this involved practically the prohibition of the Evangelical celebration of the Lord's Supper. The charge which has most behind it as stated by Roman Catholics is that of intolerance by Evangelicals, in that the masses had proceeded to the length of riot in their opposition to Roman Catholic observances and institutions. The medieval theories were in this respect still in practise. On the other hand, the Roman Catholic position was no better, but explicitly involved the extinction of Protestant religion and practises. But the "protest" embodied a clear and concrete presentation of the principles of Protestantism, and was a courageous statement in the face of an adverse majority.

III. Diet of 1542: The purpose of this third imperial diet of Speyer, opened by King Ferdinand on Feb. 9, 1542, was to afford him aid against the Turks, who were closely pressing Austria. The Protestant estates declared themselves ready to attend on condition that the religious peace of Nuremberg (see NUREMBERG, RELIGIOUS PEACE OF), whose provisions had been renewed at Regensburg in 1541, be maintained intact. It was not until Apr. 11, and after protracted negotiations, that a ruling was devised by which the desired aid was granted, and the status of peace, as at Regensburg, was extended for five years. By the terms of a bond to the Protestant estates, executed by Ferdinand's order the day before, the Regensburg " declaration " was also to remain in force during the same period. The Roman Catholic estates did not recognize this arrangement, but accepted a proffer tendered by the papal legate Morone, for convening a council on Aug. 15, at Trent. The Evangelical estates made written protest against the place selected.

IV. Diet of 1544: At the brilliant fourth imperial diet of Speyer, opened on Feb. 20, 1544, by Charles V. in person, the emperor especially labored to obtain the support of the empire in his war with France. The Protestant estates again made their consent depend upon the condition that the Regensburg " declaration " be renewed; and they demanded that this proviso be embodied in the diet's ruling, a point which the Roman Catholic estates refused. After months of prolonged negotiations, it was finally resolved, on May 27, to defer the drafting of the proper provisions to the emperor. In this connection the Roman Catholic estates announced that they must needs endure what the emperor might resolve. The ruling of the imperial diet, as then sealed on June 10, yielded essential concessions to the Protestants. On occasion of a new imperial diet, in the ensuing autumn or winter, when the emperor hoped again to be present, they would arrange on what footing they should stand in the disputed articles of religion, until the council. The proceedings were to be outlined in advance, according to projects of reform that were to be furnished by the emperor and the estates. Meanwhile the public peace should be observed; whereas the decree of Augsburg and the trials pending before the supreme court for the cause of religion should be suspended. The clergy, endowments, cloisters, schools, and hospitals, irrespective of religious confession, were to continue in the enjoyment of the incomes to their credit in 1541. The supreme court itself was to be supplied anew with devout and learned judges, without regard to religious affiliations. The Roman Catholic estates were far from satisfied with this measure, while the pope formally protested against it in a brief of Aug. 24. But indeed, even the Protestants, whom the emperor at this diet had treated with more favor than ever before, could not feel altogether content with the actual result. The emperor's concessions were merely provisional, and were equivocally worded; nor did the Roman Catholic estates deem themselves bound thereby. Then again, the aid of the empire, that had been granted the emperor, not only so strengthened his material power that he was able to advance victoriously into France and force to his will the peace of Crespy (Sept. 14, 1544), but freed his hand, by the same stroke, for contingent action against the Protestants. For that matter, the evidence that Charles had not changed his mind in relation to the Reformation, but had fully harbored the intention of opposing it with force if occasion required, came clearly to light in the outbreak of the Schmalkald war, a few years later.   JULIUS NEY.

BIBLIOGRAPHY: The subject is treated more or less fully in the works on the history of the Reformation, and the treatments of the life of Luther generally deal with it. Also to be noted is the literature under PHILIP OF HESSE; F. B. von Bucholtz, *Geschichte der Regierung Ferdinand des Ersten*, vols. i.–ii., Vienna, 1831; G. Egelhaaf, *Deutsche Geschichte im Zeitalter der Reformation*, Berlin, 1885. On the diet of 1526 consult: W. Friedensburg, *Zur Vorgeschichte des torgauischen Bundnisses*, Marburg, 1884; idem, *Der Reichstag zu Speier 1526*, Berlin, 1887; G. Kawerau, *Johann Agricola*, pp. 90 sqq., Berlin, 1881; J. Ney, *Der Reichstag zu Speier 1526*, Hamburg, 1889; idem, in *ZKG*, viii. 300 sqq., ix. 137 sqq., xii. 334 sqq., 593 sqq.; A. Kluckhohn, *Der Reichstag zu Speier 1526*, in *Historische Zeitschrift*, lvi. 193 sqq.; J. Janssen, *Hist. of the German People*, v. 59 sqq., St. Louis, 1903; *Cambridge Modern History*, ii. 196, New York, 1904; Ranke, *Popes*, i. 79–80; Hefele, *Conciliengeschichte*, ix. 454 sqq.; T. Brieger, *Der Speierer Reichstag von 1526 und die religiöse Frage der Zeit*, Leipsic, 1910.

On the diet of 1529 consult: J. J. Müller, *Historie von den evangelischen Stände-Protestation zu Speyer*, Jena, 1705; J. A. H. Tittmann, *Die Protestation der evangelischen Stände auf dem Reichstage zu Speier . . . 1529*, Leipsic, 1829; A. Jung, *Geschichte des Reichstags zu Speyer*, Strasburg, 1830; J. Ney, *Geschichte des Reichstags zu Speier . . . 1529*, Halle, 1880; idem, *Die Protestation der evangelischen Stände zu Speier . . . 1529*, Halle, 1890; E. Heuser, *Die Protestation von Speier*, Neustadt, 1904; idem, *Die Appellation und Protestation der evangelischen Stände zu Speier 1529*, Leipsic, 1906; J. Janssen, *Hist. of the German People*, v. 188 sqq., St. Louis, 1903; *Cambridge Modern History*, ii. 203–204, 206, 330, New York, 1904; Hefele, *Conciliengeschichte*, ix. 568 sqq.

On the diets of 1542 and 1544 consult: The work of Bucholtz, ut sup.; also Janssen, ut sup., pp. 164–172, 247 sqq.; A. de Boor, *Beiträge zur Geschichte des Speierer Reichstags . . . 1544*, Strasburg, 1878; *Cambridge Modern History*, ut sup., pp. 77, 244, 661.

SPIEKER, spî′ker or spai′ker, **GEORGE FREDERICK:** Lutheran; b. at Elk Ridge Landing, Md., Nov. 17, 1844. He was educated at Baltimore City College and in the Lutheran theological seminaries of Gettysburg and Philadelphia, being graduated from the latter in 1867. He was acting professor of German in Pennsylvania College (1864–66); professor at the Keystone Normal School, Kutztown, Pa. (1867–68); professor of Hebrew at Muhlenberg College (1887–94); and since 1894 professor of church history, Old-Testament theology, and introduction in the Lutheran Theological Seminary at Philadelphia. He was pastor of the Lutheran Church at Kutztown (1867–83), and occupied a pulpit of the same denomination at Allentown, Pa. (1883–94). He is associate editor of the *Lutheran Church Review*, and has written *Commentary on II Corinthians* (New York, 1897), besides translating L. Hutter's *Compend of Lutheran Theology* (Philadelphia, 1868) and K. A. Wildenhahn's *Martin Luther* (in collaboration with H. E. Jacobs; 1883).

SPIERA, spî-ê′ra, **FRANCESCO:** Italian jurist; b. at Cittadella (13 m. n. of Padua), Italy, 1502; d. there Dec. 27, 1548. Interest in Spiera is due to the fact that the Protestants of the sixteenth century used his case as an example of the dreadful consequences of the sin against the Holy Ghost, since he discerned Evangelical truth, but denied and abjured it for external reasons. Spiera had won an esteemed position in his native town; and a well bestowed house, in which ten children grew up, appeared to insure his happiness. Besides the Scriptures, there fell into his hands various Evangelical

writings, such as " The Benefit of Christ's Death,"
" Doctrine Old and New," and " Summary of
Sacred Scripture," which instilled in him doubt as to
the Roman Catholic teachings on purgatory, veneration of the saints, etc. With others he was ar-
raigned before the inquisition at Venice; and his trial
came off between May 24 and June 20, 1548. The
minutes of the trial are still extant in the archives
at Venice, and are reprinted in Comba's *Francesco Spiera* (1872). On the latter day in St. Mark's
Spiera made solemn abjuration of his " errors," and
subscribed the abjuration, which he then repeated
on the following Sunday in Cittadella, after mass
in the cathedral. On returning home, so he related
it himself, " the Spirit," or the voice of his conscience, began to reproach him for having denied
the truth. Amid grounds of comfort that either he
or his friends advanced, and a state of despair that
grew more and more hopeless, there began a terrible struggle within himself, which soon so affected
even his sturdy physique that it gave occasion for
conveying him to Padua to be treated by the most
celebrated physicians. The treatment was vain, and
the conflict, which Vergerio and others witnessed,
ended in his death, shortly after his return to his
home. That Spiera laid violent hands on himself
is later invention.　　　　　　　　K. BENRATH.

BIBLIOGRAPHY: C. S. Curio, *F. Spieræ . . . historia*, Geneva,
1550 [?] (contains accounts by Curio, M. Gribaldus, H.
Scotus and S. Gelvus, with preface by Calvin and apology by Vergerius); P. P. Vergerio, *La Historia di M.
Franc. Spiera . . .*, [Tübingen], 1551, reprinted Florence,
1883; N. Bacon, *Relation of the Fearefull Estate of Francis
Spira*, London, 1638, very numerous editions, latest ap-
parently Manchester, 1845; F. Laurence, *Hist. de François
Spira*, Leyden, 1645; E. Comba, *F. Spiera, Episodio della
reforma religiosa in Italia*, Rome, 1872; C. Rönneke,
Francesco Spiera, Hamburg, 1874; K. Benrath, *Geschichte
der Reformation in Venedig*, pp. 35–36, Halle, 1887; W.
Sommerfelt, *F. Spira, ein Unglücklicher*, Leipsic, 1896;
Cambridge Modern History, ii. 394–395, New York, 1904.

SPIFAME, JACQUES PAUL: French Calvinist;
b. at Paris 1502; executed at Geneva Mar. 23 (or
25), 1566. He was at first a Roman Catholic and,
having studied law, became a parliamentary counselor and later a counselor of state. He then suddenly took orders and was made canon, as well as
chancellor of the University of Paris, etc., besides
accompanying the cardinal of Lorraine to the Council of Trent as his vicar-general. In 1548 he was
consecrated bishop of Nevers, but eleven years
later resigned his see in favor of his nephew and retired to Geneva, where he soon professed open allegiance to Protestantism. This step was clearly
due in great measure to his adulterous relations
with Catharine de Gasperne, whom he had induced
to abandon her husband, and with whom he lived
after the latter's death. To legitimate the two
children of this union, Spifame pretended to reveal
the state of affairs to the council and consistory of
Geneva, alleging that his orders had prevented him
from marrying the woman, and that he had been
forced to leave Paris because of his fear of persecution. The union was declared legitimate on July 27,
1559, and Beza and Calvin readily accepted him as
pastor, so that in the following year he became minister at Issoudun. Other congregations soon desired
his services, among them his old city of Nevers, but

though Calvin urged him to accept this post, Spifame was next found in Bourges and Paris. With
the outbreak of the first religious war he became a
still more important figure, particularly at the
princes' diet at Frankfort (Apr.-Nov., 1562), where
he was the envoy of Condé. While returning to
France, he came into the midst of military operations, and until the concluding of the Treaty of
Amboise (Mar. 19, 1563) was civil governor of
Lyons. He then went back to Geneva, where he had
meanwhile been elected to the Council of Sixty, and
in Jan., 1564, he accepted the invitation of Jeanne
d'Albret, queen of Navarre, to visit Pau to arrange her affairs. Here he committed the astounding indiscretion of declaring that her son,
Henry IV., was the offspring of adultery, and in
Apr., 1565, he returned to Geneva. Suspicions now
began to cluster around him; he was supposed to
be intriguing with France, either to become bishop
of Toul or to be made controller of finances; his
nephew, who knew the true story of his relations
with Catharine de Gasperne, declared his two
children incapable of inheriting; and he was formally charged with insulting the queen of Navarre.
On Mar. 11, 1566, he was imprisoned, especially as
there were rumors that he had forged papers at-
testing a common-law union with Catharine de
Gasperne in 1539 while her husband was still alive.
Investigation proved the falsity of his documents,
and though he pleaded that his adultery was out-
lawed and denied all other charges brought against
him, his acts of forgery were deemed by the council
to be sufficient reason to condemn him to be beheaded.　　　　　　　　　(EUGEN LACHENMANN.)

BIBLIOGRAPHY: The account of the trial and confession of
Spifame was printed at Geneva, 1566. Consult further:
T. Beza, *Hist. ecclésiastique des églises reformées . . . de
France*, ii. 156 sqq., Geneva, 1580, new ed. by J. W. Baum
and A. E. Cunitz, 3 vols., Paris, 1883–88, also ed. P.
Vesson, 2 vols., Toulouse, 1882–83; Calvin, *Opera*, vols.
xviii.–xxi. passim; J. Spon, *Hist. de Genève*, vol. ii., Geneva,
1730; J. Senébier, *Hist. littéraire de Genève*, i. 384–385,
ib. 1786; E. and É. Haag, *La France protestante*, ix. 309
sqq., Paris, 1859; *Bulletin de la société de l'hist. du protestantisme français*, ix. 276–277, xii. 483, xlviii. 228 sqq.;
Lichtenberger, *ESR*, xi. 674.

SPINA, spî'na, ALFONSO DE: Spanish anti-
Jewish and anti-Mohammedan apologist of the
fifteenth century; d. at Orense (115 m. s.w. of Leon),
Galicia, 1469. Entering the Franciscan order, he
became rector of the University of Salamanca, and
in 1466 was consecrated bishop of Orense. He is
generally, and probably justly, held to be the author
of the anonymous *Fortalitium fidei contra Judæos,
Saracenos aliosque Christianæ fidei inimicos* (n.p.,
1487 and often), which, according to its preface,
was written by a Franciscan teacher at Valladolid
in 1458. The work is in four books: the first proving the messiahship of Jesus from the fulfilment of
prophecy; the second dealing with heretics and their
manifold punishments; the third attacking the Jews;
and the fourth polemizing against the Mohammedans, with an interesting, though one-sided, account of the struggles between the Christians and
the Saracens.　　　　　　　　　(O. ZÖCKLER†.)

BIBLIOGRAPHY: J. A. Fabricius, *Delectus argumentorum et
syllabus scriptorum . . .*, pp. 575–576, Hamburg, 1725;
R. Simon, *Bibliothèque critique*, iii. 316–322, Paris, 1708;

J. M. Schröckh, *Christliche Kirchengeschichte*, xxx. 573–574, Leipsic, 1802; I. M. Jost, *Geschichte des Judenthums und seiner Sekten*, iii. 96, ib. 1859, H. Graetz, *Geschichte der Juden*, viii. 228–229, ib. 1890, Eng. transl., 5 vols., Philadelphia, 1891–98; *JE*, xi. 510.

SPINOLA, spî-nō′lä, **CRISTOVAL ROJAS DE:** Spanish Roman Catholic advocate of union; b. near Roermond (27 m. n.e. of Maestricht), Holland, 1626; d. at Vienna Mar. 12, 1695. He was educated at Cologne and at an early age entered the order of the Observantine Franciscans. He taught philosophy and scholastic theology at Cologne, and rose to be general of his order. In 1661 he was called from Madrid to Vienna to become confessor of Maria Theresa, wife of Leopold I., and in 1668 was consecrated titular bishop of Tina, while in 1685 he was made bishop of Wiener-Neustadt. Thoroughly versed in diplomacy and irenic in temperament, he labored unceasingly to reconcile Protestantism with the Roman Catholic Church, willing to make certain concessions for the furtherance of a plan which lukewarm Protestantism and notable conversions from its bickerings rendered plausible. In 1671, after gaining the approval of the papal nuncio at Vienna, Spinola began negotiations with German Lutheran and Reformed princes and theologians, but in nearly every case his advances were met with profound distrust. His most favorable reception was in Brunswick and Lüneburg, and especially in Hanover, where he had the sympathy of the converted duke, John Frederick, as well as of Gerhard Walter Molanus and Gottfried Wilhelm von Leibnitz (qq.v.). The first conference, in 1676, amounted to little, but in 1683 Spinola made verbally a number of concessions, such as communion under both kinds, marriage of the clergy, continued possession of secularized estates of the Church, the suspension of the decrees of the Council of Trent, and remission of formal adjuration, the sole requirement being recognition of the supremacy of the pope. At a conference over which Molanus presided the plan proposed by Spinola was practically adopted, but when the proceedings became generally known, they aroused the anger of Protestants, while Roman Catholics regarded them as futile. Nevertheless, Molanus and Leibnitz remained in correspondence with Spinola, and in 1691 the plan was submitted to Bossuet, who bluntly rejected the entire affair, demanding unconditional submission to the authority of the Church and the Council of Trent, although he was unable finally to break off negotiations until 1694. Meanwhile Spinola had entered into communication with the Hungarian Protestants, having received, in 1691, an imperial appointment as commissioner general for the promotion of religious union in Austria. Here again his hopes were ill-founded, and although a conference was expected to be held in 1693, it never took place. After the death of Spinola a few attempts at Roman Catholic and Protestant union were made by his successor, Graf of Buchheim, and by Leibnitz, only to prove equally abortive. (Paul Tschackert.)

Bibliography: J. D. Gruber, *Commercii epistolici Leibnitiani*, i. 411 sqq., Hanover, 1722; J. Schmidt, in *Grenzboten*, 1860, nos. 44–45; J. X. Kiesl, *Der Friedensplan des Leibniz zur Wiedereinigung der getrennten christlichen Kirchen*, Paderborn, 1904; *KL*, xi. 620–625.

SPINOZA, spî-nō′zä, **BARUCH (BENEDICT DE):** Philosopher; b. at Amsterdam Nov. 24, 1632; d. at The Hague Feb. 21, 1677. His parents were Jews who had been driven from Portugal by religious persecution. He devoted himself to the study of the Bible and the Talmud; was instructed in Latin by Franz van der Ende, a celebrated physician of naturalistic sympathies; and, turning to free philosophical speculations, was excommunicated by the synagogue. Employing himself with the study of the Cartesian philosophy and the development of his own, he dwelt near Amsterdam, 1656–60 or 61; at Rhynsburg near Leyden until 1664; at Voorburg near The Hague until 1670; and at The Hague from 1670 until his death, supporting himself by grinding lenses. In 1673 he declined a call to the professorship of philosophy at the University of Heidelberg, so as not to restrict his liberty of thought. His works written at the Hague, 1660–77, were, *Reni Descartes principiorum philosophiæ* (2 parts, Amsterdam, 1663); *Tractatus theologico-politicus* (Hamburg, 1670); and, most important of all, *Ethica ordine geometrico demonstrata*, which, together with *Tractatus politicus*, *Tractatus de intellectus emendatione*, and *Epistolæ*, was published in *Opera posthuma* (Amsterdam, 1677). His *De Deo homine, ejusque felicitate* was not known before it appeared in a Dutch translation (Halle, 1852).

For the basis of his method Spinoza depended on René Descartes (q.v.) and for his point of view in part upon the influence of Giordano Bruno (q.v.). Aiming to arrive at mathematical certainty, he proceeds by a method of exact demonstration, analogous to the geometry of Euclid, with series of definitions, axioms, propositions, and proofs. His fundamental notion is that of substance, which he defines as " that which is in itself and is conceived by itself, i.e., the conception of which does not need the conception of any other thing in order to be formed." There is but one substance, which is absolute and infinite, and is God. Nothing can be predicated of it, because " all determination is negation." It can be comprehended only by attributes which belong only to the mind. Having neither intellect nor will, it cannot have an ultimate end in view, but is the immanent cause of all things. There being nothing to constrain it, it is absolutely free, acting from an inner self-determination or necessity. This substance has two fundamental attributes cognizable by man; namely, thought and extension, although an infinite number of attributes is possible. There is no extended substance as separate from thinking substance. An attribute is "that which the mind perceives as constituting the essence of substance." Movement, intellect, and will, on the whole, are infinite modes or affections of substance; all individual things are finite and changing modes. A " mode is that which is in something else, through the aid of which also it is conceived." Modes of the attribute of extension are physical objects; modes of thought are ideas. There is no causal nexus between the attribute and modes of extension on the one hand, and the attribute and modes of thought on the other, inasmuch as they belong to the same substance; although in either attribute there are chains of cause and effect, and between the two series there is a complete parallelism (*ordo idearum idem est ac ordo rerum*). Finite things including individuals being only modes, God is no individual. Likewise succession in time or duration holds among existences or modes; but essence or substance is non-temporal, and God is eternal.

Man as an individual, being a mode, first sees things in relation to himself discretely, or the world of things as *natura naturata*. He thus has inadequate ideas by *opinio* or *imaginatio*. *Ratio* affords adequate ideas of the common agreements of things. Intuition is the full perception *sub specie æternitatis* of God as infinite substance in immanent causation, or *natura naturans*. The criterion of truth is truth itself; for the human mind in so far as it has a true idea is a part of the infinite divine intellect. Volition is a form of assent to, or dissent from, the idea, and is identical with it; just as will is identical with intellect. Man as a mode, being conditioned by the multiplicity of things about him, is in a state of constraint, having inadequate ideas (in the form of duration) of the complex self as affected, of the things affecting him, and of the affections or passions thus produced. This is commonly illustrated by the fact that the same thing appears differently to different men from different points of view. But man is active when he has adequate ideas, or when anything follows from his essence or nature clearly understood: he is passive when he has inadequate ideas. Desire or conscious appetite as an affection is the assertion of man's essence toward this greater freedom. The agreeable transition to a higher degree of perfection is the occasion of the passion of joy; the opposite is the occasion of sadness. Joy accompanied by the idea of its external cause is the passion of love; sadness so accompanied is hate. Impotence to prevail over one's passions is bondage, or the opposite of freedom. Evil, which is relative, is impediment. To get rid of a passion, i.e., an affection or a state of suffering, is to have a clear idea of it. This means to know all things as necessary. He who has such a knowledge of self and passions rejoices, and the idea of the external cause of such supreme joy involves the love of God, just as adversely the knowledge of all things as necessary involves the knowledge of God as immanent cause. This is what Spinoza calls the intellectual love to God conceived under the form of eternity. As God has only adequate ideas and is not subject to progressive perfection and passions, he cannot be affected by love or hate. In God, so far as he may be explained by the essence of man conceived " under the form of eternity," the loving subject and the object loved are one and the same; the intellectual love of God denotes absolute acquiescence in the divine in the law of his nature. The intellectual love of the mind to God is a part of that love, based upon the intellect which is part of the infinite divine intellect and therefore immortal, i.e., non-temporal. Virtue, which is the power to produce that which is according to one's essence, or nature, is not the reward of happiness but its own reward.

In the *Theologico-politicus* Spinoza argues for religious freedom so long as the interest of the State in good works is satisfied. He maintains that theology and philosophy have nothing in common, and

repudiates the authority demanded by the former over the latter on the ground that theology deals with the anthropomorphic attributes and relations of God and philosophy with clear notions. In daring and imagination and fidelity to method, Spinoza ranks as one of the greatest philosophers. The practical lessons which his system taught, those of necessity and stoical resignation, were best illustrated in his own life. Undermined by consumption, harassed by persecutors, and burdened by overwork, he was a model of patience and sweet kindliness. See PANTHEISM, § 4.

BIBLIOGRAPHY: The chief editions of the *Opera* are by H. E. G. Paulus, 2 vols., Jena, 1802–03, C. H. Bruder, 3 vols., Leipsic, 1843–46, J. van Vloten and J. P. Land, 2 vols., The Hague, 1883, and 3 vols., 1895–96; Eng. transl. of the chief works by R. H. M. Elwes, 2 vols., London, 1883–84; Fr. transl., by É. Saisset, 2 vols., Paris, 1842, 2d ed., 1861; by J. G. Prat, Paris, 1863, and by C. Appuhn, Paris, 1907 sqq. Further details respecting partial eds. and issues of separate works are given in the *British Museum Catalogue*, s.v., and in Baldwin, *Dictionary*, iii. 1, pp. 488–489 (followed by a very full general bibliography). Special works translated into English are *Tractatus theologico-politicus* (by R. Willis), London, 1689, reissues, 1737, and another, 1862, 1868; the *Ethica*, by W. H. White, London, 1813, 2d ed. by A. H. Stirling, ib. 1894, by R. H. M. Elwes, ib. 1884, by H. Smith, Cincinnati, 1866, and selections by G. S. Fullerton, New York, 1892, 2d ed., 1894; *Tractatus de intellectus emendatione* by W. H. White, London, 1895; *Principles of Descartes' Philosophy*, London, 1907; and *Short Treatment on God, Man and his Well-Being*; transl. and ed., *with an Introduction and Commentary and a Life of Spinoza*, by A. Wolf, New York, 1910.

As sources for a life consult *Der Briefwechsel des Spinosa im Urtexte*, ed. H. Ginsberg, Leipsic, 1876; *Die Briefe mehrer Gelehrten an Benedict von Spinoza und dessen Antworten*, ed. J. H. von Kirchmann, Berlin, 1871; and *Lettres inédites en français*, translated and annotated by J. G. Prat, Paris, 1884, 2d ed., 1885. Consult further: F. Pollock, *Spinoza, his Life and Philosophy*, 2d ed., London, 1899; M. Saverien, *Hist. des philosophes modernes*, Paris, 1760; A. Saintes, *Hist. de la vie et des ouvrages de B. Spinoza*, ib. 1842; C. von Orelli, *Spinoza's Leben und Lehre*, 2d ed., Aarau, 1850; J. B. Lehmann, *Spinoza: sein Lebensbild und seine Philosophie*, Würzburg, 1864; K. Fischer, *Baruch Spinoza's Leben und Charakter*, Heidelberg, 1865, 4th ed., 1898; S. S. Coronel, *Bar. d'Espinoza in de lijst van zyn tijd*, Zalt-Bommel, 1871; J. van Vloten, *Baruch d'Espinoza, zijn leven en schriften*, 2d ed., Schliedam, 1871; J. E. Linter, *Spinoza*, London, 1873; H. J. Betz, *Levenschechts van Baruch de Spinoza*, The Hague, 1876; H. Ginsberg, *Leben und Charakterbild B. Spinozas*, Leipsic, 1876; J. Martineau, *A Study of Spinoza*, London, 1882; W. Bolin, *Spinoza*, Berlin, 1894; J. Freudenthal, *Die Lebensgeschichte Spinozas*, Leipsic, 1899; P. L. Couchoud, *Benoît de Spinoza*, Paris, 1902; J. Freudenthal, *Das Leben Spinozas*, Stuttgart, 1904; S. von Dunin-Borowski, *Der junge De Spinoza. Leben und Werdegang im Lichte der Weltphilosophie*, Münster, 1910.

On the philosophy of Spinoza consult: C. Schaarschmidt, *Descartes und Spinoza; urkundlich Darstellung der Philosophie Beider*, Bonn, 1850; B. Auerbach, *Spinoza; ein Denkerleben*, Mannheim, 1855; E. Saisset, *Précurseurs et disciples de Descartes*, pp. 185–352, Paris, 1863; F. W. Barth, *Einige Gedanken über Atheismus und über die Meinungen des Spinoza*, Brandenburg, 1868; P. W. Schmidt, *Spinoza und Schleiermacher*, Berlin, 1868; M. Brasch, *B. v. Spinoza's System der Philosophie mit einer Biographie Spinozas*, ib. 1870; J. A. Froude, *Short Studies on Great Subjects*, London, 1873; R. Albert, *Spinoza's Lehre über die Existenz einer Substanz*, Dresden, 1875; G. Busolt, *Die Grundzüge der Erkenntnis-Theorie und Metaphysik Spinozas*, Berlin, 1875; M. Arnold, *Essays in Criticism*, pp. 237–362, 3d ed., New York, 1876; H. J. Betz, *Spinoza en de vrijheid*, The Hague. 1877; T. Camerer, *Die Lehre Spinozas*, Stuttgart, 1877; M. Dessauer, *Der Socrates der Neuzeit und sein Gedankenschatz*, Cöthen, 1877; R. Flint, *Anti-theistic Theories*, pp. 353–375, notes 547–552, Edinburgh and London, 1879; J. Martineau,

A Study of Spinoza, 2d ed., London, 1883; A. B. Moss, *Bruno and Spinoza*, London, 1885; A. Baltzer, *Spinoza's Entwicklungsgang insbesondere nach seinen Briefen geschildert*, Kiel, 1888; J. Caird, *Spinoza*, Edinburgh and London, 1888, new ed., 1901; J. Stern, *Die Philosophie Spinozas*, Stuttgart, 1890; R. Worms, *La Morale de Spinoza*, Paris, 1802; G. J. Bolland, *Spinoza*, ib. 1899; E. Ferrière, *La Doctrine de Spinoza*, ib. 1899; S. Rappaport, *Spinoza und Schopenhauer*, Berlin, 1899; R. Wahle, *Kurze Erklärung der Ethik von Spinoza*, Vienna, 1899; J. Zulawski, *Das Problem der Causalität bei Spinoza*, Bern, 1899; J. D. Bierens de Hann, *Levensleer naar de beginselen van Spinoza*, The Hague, 1900; J. H. von Kirchmann, *Erläuterungen zu Benedict von Spinozas Ethik*, Leipsic, 1900; H. H. Joachim, *A Study of the Ethics of Spinoza*, Oxford, 1901; B. Auerbach, *Spinoza*, Stuttgart, 1903; R. A. Duff, *Spinoza's Political and Ethical Philosophy*, Glasgow, 1903; J. Iverach, *Descartes, Spinoza, the New Philosophy*, Edinburgh, 1904; E. E. Powell, *Spinoza and Religion*, Chicago, 1906; W. Prümers, *Spinozas Religionsbegriff*, Halle, 1906; J. A. Picton, *Spinoza, a Handbook to the Ethics*, London and New York, 1906; A. Wenzel, *Die Weltanschauung Spinozas*, Leipsic, 1907; F. Erhardt, *Die Philosophie des Spinoza im Lichte der Kritik*, ib. 1908; J. Stern, *Die Philosophie Spinozas*, 3d ed., Stuttgart, 1908; K. Fischer, *Geschichte der neueren Philosophie*, vol. ii., 5th ed., Heidelberg, 1909.

SPIRES. See SPEYER.

SPIRIT OF GOD, BIBLICAL VIEW OF: According to the final Old-Testament presentation, the Spirit of God is the divine power which proceeds from God in creation and preservation in nature and in human historical life, especially in Israel. This power of God is active at the precise point where energy is manifested, i.e., the Spirit of God is the immediate cause of all kinds of change; it comes and goes, it is given or withdrawn wholly according to the divine will. Special attention is directed to unusual forms of human action which are attributed to this Spirit—heroism, genius, prophetic utterance, singular personal consecration, in a word, all rare individual physical and religious phenomena. In their suddenness, strangeness, involuntariness, irresistibleness, and in their results they seem to reveal a more than human power. Religious psychology had not yet distinguished the form from the ultimate source of these experiences. The obverse of this conception appears in the belief in the influence and possession of men by evil spirits, and later by Satan as the prince of demons. For the history of this belief one would need to trace the development of the notion of the power of discarnate good and evil spirits over men in its varied stages of unfolding from animism through polytheism up to ethical monotheism (see COMPARATIVE RELIGION, VI.). The conception of the good Spirit of God influencing men differs from the Greek and other national ideas of divine possession, (1) in the concentration of the entire divine activity in one personal source, and (2) in the aim to which the activity is directed —furtherance of the theocratic ideals. Distinctive redemptive functions are rarely attributed to the Spirit of God in the Old Testament.

The New Testament has no elaborated doctrine of the Spirit of God. There is material for the personal and trinitarian aspect of the Spirit, but the time was not ripe for the theological construction of the Constantinopolitan Creed (q.v.). On the other hand, many allusions imply that the Spirit is an influence or a form of the action of God or of Christ (see HOLY SPIRIT, I.). In the New Testament, how-

ever, one discovers several lines of development in the idea of the Spirit. (1) The tendency to hypostatize the divine power of action appears already in the Old Testament (cf. Isa. xliv. 3, xlviii. 16, lxi. 1; Gen. i. 2; Ps. li. 11), and is part of that movement of thought which was accelerated by Aryan influences, in which God becomes metaphysically elevated above the world, while his withdrawal and isolation are compensated for by the introduction of intermediary beings and forces by which his will was effected. Moreover, before the close of the apostolic age the Spirit has begun to be differentiated from the Father and the Son. (2) Whereas in the entire Old Testament and in many portions of the New Testament the Spirit is conceived of as transcendent, intermittent, and frequently miraculous in action, yet side by side with this earlier and common notion, in the later writings of Paul and John —not in the Synoptics—the Spirit is presented as an immanent and abiding personal power. For this change no other occasion need be sought than that which springs from the permanent necessities of Christian experience—a continuous inner redemptive influence by which the follower of Christ is quickened and empowered for every good work. (3) This idea of the immanence of the Spirit of God completes itself in the removal of the divine activity from the region of nature whether of the physical world or of the human soul, and in the entire reference of it to the ethical and spiritual life.

C. A. BECKWITH.

BIBLIOGRAPHY: The reader should consult the works on Biblical theology given in the article on that subject, especially the works of H. Schultz, Duff, and Bennett on the Old Testament, and of Beyschlag, Holtzmann, Adeney, Stevens, and Gould on the New; the subject is treated also, more or less fully, in the literature given under HOLY SPIRIT (q.v.). Consult further: C. A. Beckwith, *Realities of Christian Theology*, pp. 277–286, Boston, 1906; H. H. Wendt, *Die Begriffe Fleisch und Geist im biblischen Sprachgebrauch*, Gotha, 1878; H. Gunkel, *Die Wirkungen des heiligen Geistes nach der . . . Anschauung der apostolischen Zeit und der Lehre des Paulus*, Göttingen, 1888; K. von Lechler, *Die biblische Lehre vom heiligen Geiste*, Leipsic, 1899; I. W. Wood, *The Spirit of God in Biblical Literature*, New York, 1904. Further discussions will be found in the various works on systematic theology (see DOGMA, DOGMATICS).

SPIRITUAL CONTENTMENT: The harmony of personal feeling with outer conditions; self-satisfaction being the harmony of personal feeling with inward conditions. Contentment presupposes that the means for the satisfaction of the necessities of life are inadequate (Prov. xvii. 1), and signifies a willingness not to suffer the inner equanimity to be disturbed by the scantiness of outward means (Phil. iv. 11–12; I Tim. vi. 6). While such contentment may be natural, and conditioned by climate, social order, racial instinct, or national circumstances, it may also be acquired as a cultured religious and ethical state of life, and as such it is a requirement of Christian religiousness (Matt. vi. 25–34; I Tim. vi. 8; Heb. xiii. 5). Discontent is unworthy of the Christian, who must remember that, though all is his (I Cor. iii. 21–22), he can not lose his soul to the world since he belongs to Christ. Religiously it is the inner result of the piety produced by the theistic contemplation of God, which obtains quietude and peace of soul through its conviction of the divine governance both of the individual (Ps. cxvi. 6) and of the universe. Yet such satisfaction is active, finding room for ends and aims, the desire of improvement, and the joyous taking up of tasks. There is a wide difference between the satisfaction based on natural instinct and temperament and that founded on religious ethical self-culture, even though temperamental predispositions are of the utmost importance in the ethical world. Dissatisfaction is aroused by instincts, desires, and passions; is stimulated by sensibility and the imagination; and may be awakened by the exercise of the will and by ideals; but receives few stimuli from the understanding, and almost none from the reason.

Christianity does not teach satisfaction with all public conditions. It demands dissatisfaction with all that is evil, corrupt, morbid, and disorderly; and requires that this disapproval be not merely a matter of opinions and words, but that it enlist the reforming activity within the confines of vocation. Self-satisfaction, in both the Pharisaic and the Stoic sense, is opposed to Christian teaching, which rejects the moral self-complacency of the natural man (Luke xviii. 11 sqq.), because it is an insuperable barrier to repentance (Luke v. 30–32) and to the kingdom of heaven (Matt. v. 3–6). The power that is possessed in the kingdom of God is not one's own strength (I Cor. iv. 7), but the divine gift of grace (I Cor. xv. 10), so that there is no place for self-glorification (I Cor. i. 31). The highest Christian capability is proportionate to the most humble sense of personal incapability (II Cor. iii. 5, xii. 8–10). Persistent Christian dissatisfaction with oneself, therefore, does not denote a peaceful disquietude, but the sense of indispensable and limitless dependence on divine grace, which in Christ does not impair strength, but sets it free (Phil. iii. 12 sqq., iv. 13).   (L. LEMME.)

SPIRITUALISM, SPIRITUALISTS: Terms applied to the belief in the actuality of intercourse between the living and the spirits of the dead and to those who hold this belief. Such a belief has been existent in practically all stages of culture (see DIVINATION; MAGIC), and in the
Early   Roman Empire manifestations similar
Phenomena. to those common to modern " Spiritualism " were reported. To those who hold to the belief in modern times, who have formed what in some respects corresponds to a denomination, the name " Spiritualists " has been given. Many of these accept, for instance, the statement that the writings of Swedenborg (q.v.) were the result of communications from spirits; while the declarations of Andrew Jackson Davis (b. 1826) are treated as part of the evidences for the alleged fact. His *Principles of Nature, her divine Revelations, and a Voice to Mankind* (New York, 1847) is said to have run through fifty editions. Since the middle of the nineteenth century Spiritualism has gained in the United States a large following. The rise of this movement goes back to 1848, the year of the " Rochester knockings," though the Shakers (see COMMUNISM, II., § 10) claim that similar phenomena in their communities in 1837–44 had resulted in valuable communications from Ann Lee. The

" Rochester knockings " were first heard in the family of John D. Fox of Hydeville, near Rochester, N. Y., always in the presence of his daughters Margaret and Kate, and continued after the removal of the family to Rochester, communications being made by rappings after an established code. These and more violent demonstrations were given near Stratford, Conn., always, it was claimed, without visible human agency. The phenomena grew still more varied and even violent in character as the area enlarged, including table-tipping, playing on musical instruments, levitation of various objects and even of the medium, appearance of objects in the atmosphere, spirit writing, and materialization. Mediumship became a lucrative profession, and the returns offered temptations to fraud which were not resisted, while the frauds were often exposed. But interest became extended and believers many. As early as 1855 adherents were reckoned at nearly 2,000,000 in the United States (*North American Review*, Apr., 1855), while over a dozen periodicals were devoted to the interests of the cult. The movement was introduced into England through Mrs. Hayden in 1852, while the Davenport brothers intensified the impression already made by the phenomena which they exhibited there in 1864. Dr. Henry Slade was also distinguished by the character of the exhibitions which he gave. In Germany spiritistic writing was introduced by Baron Ludwig von Guldenstubbe (d. 1873) in 1856, who received in twelve years more than 2,000 communications in twenty different languages, but the substance of these was trivial and even jejune.

A new stage was begun with the advent of the mediums Daniel Douglas Home, William Stainton Moses, and Mrs. Leonora Piper, and with the investigations undertaken by men of science of international reputation. Home was a
Later   Scotchman by birth, but lived for some
Stage. years in America in the house of an aunt, where the manifestations were begun in the form of violent movements of the furniture. He visited England, where Mr. (now Sir) William Crookes accepted the materializations, which Home then showed, as probably genuine. Home's travels extended to Italy, Russia, and France, but his work was discredited by the results of a suit at law which obligated him to return £65,-000 to the heirs of a rich widow. Moses (b. 1840; studied at Bedford and Exeter College, Oxford, B.A., 1863; d. in London 1892) became convinced of the truths of Spiritualism, became a medium against his own predilections, exhibited remarkable trance phenomena, and also automatic writing which was claimed to evince the personality of spirits of persons long dead. But he resented investigation by scientists as casting suspicion upon his honesty and sincerity. The general trend of the later phenomena has been outside of materialistic happenings and in the direction of communications of information supposedly beyond the sphere of personal knowledge of the mediums. Such communications, covering a number of years, were preserved by Moses and appeared in his *Spirit Identity* (London, 1879) and *Spirit Teachings* (1893). Similarly, the exhibitions of Mrs. Piper are apart from the physical and con-

sist of communications of varied character. She first became a medium in 1885, and soon after came under the observation of Professor William James of Harvard and of Dr. Richard Hodgson, secretary of the American branch of the Society for Psychical Research. The various sets of phenomena, an outline merely of which is given above, aroused scientific interest, and have been under consideration by various learned or scientific bodies. One of the year 1884 from the University of Pennsylvania achieved little because of inability to come to an understanding with the mediums. In 1882 the Society for Psychical Research was formed in England for the accumulation and investigation of data upon this and related subjects. Parts of the results of the work of this organization are presented and reviewed by F. W. H. Myers in his *Human Personality and its Survival of Bodily Death* (London, 1903), while the whole range of alleged spiritistic phenomena is reviewed by F. Podmore in *Modern Spiritualism* (London, 1902). The general trend of opinion among scientists, when considering phenomena of the sort under consideration, from which the element or possibility of fraud has been eliminated, is that the manifestations are not those of spirits, but are to be referred to powers of the human mind which are beginning to be the objects of systematic study, such as the " subliminal consciousness " and various other phenomena, many of these coming in the domain of abnormal psychology. One of the characteristics of most of the " communications," the inherent unimportance, has thus received explanation. The way is probably being prepared for a scientific explanation of other kinds of manifestation, which have been supposed to show the interference of spirits, by profounder and patient study of the lower regions of psychology. The exposure of those " mediums " who resorted to fraud and the formulation of tests by which to assure the reality of the manifestations presented have reduced the field to be covered, while they have also greatly diminished the number of adherents of spiritualism.

The belief in the actuality of communication between discarnate spirits and the living drew together in various places those of like mind, and led in the course of time to the formation of bodies corresponding to congregations and
Organized churches in other Christian denomina-
Form. tions, and utimately to the formation of a national organization, through which a statement of belief and platform of practises have been issued. Thus determined, the belief of Spiritualists involves the actuality of communications, as stated above; they reject the doctrine of the Trinity and of the deity of Christ, and also that of the supreme authority of the Scriptures; they hold to the existence of an infinite intelligence expressed by the physical and spiritual phenomena of nature, a correct understanding of which and a following of which in life constitute the true religion; the continued conscious existence of the spirit after death is a postulate, and with this goes belief in progress as the universal law of nature. All legislation respecting the observance of Sunday as a holy day is opposed by the National Spiritualists' Association, as also all attempts to unite Church and State,

sectarian instruction in the public schools, the granting of special favors to the clergy, and the appointment of paid chaplains in the public service; the organization favors equal taxation of all secular and ecclesiastical property, an educational qualification for all voters, and the elimination of sex as a criterion of availability for civil office and the suffrage. The Association has offices in Washington, D. C., holds annual conventions (nineteenth held in Wichita, Kan., 1911), maintains a free library at Washington, employs salaried missionaries, an editor at large, arranges for lectures and camp-meetings, carries on correspondence with organizations in other lands, and has at Whitewater, Wis., the Morris Pratt Institute with a two-years' course of instruction. It reports twenty-two state associations, 437 active local societies with 216 others meeting irregularly, 32 camp-meeting associations, 120 churches and temples with a valuation of $2,000,000; 75,000 avowed adherents with a constituency of nearly 2,000,000; 370 ordained ministers, and 1,500 public mediums.   W. H. Larrabee.

Bibliography: J. W. Edmonds and G. T. Dexter, *Spiritualism*, New York, 1854–55; E. W. Capron, *Modern Spiritualism; its Facts*, Boston, 1855; R. Ware, *Experimental Investigations of the Spirit Manifestations*, New York, 1856; R. D. Owen, *Footfalls on the Boundary of Another World*, Philadelphia, 1859; idem, *The Debatable Land between this World and the Next*, New York, 1872; W. Howitt, *The Hist. of the Supernatural in All Ages and Nations*, London, 1863; A. De Morgan, *From Matter to Spirit*, ib. 1863; H. Tuttle, *Philosophy of Spiritual Existence and of the Spirit World*, 2d ed., Boston, 1864; idem, *Arcana of Nature*, new ed., London, 1908; W. McDonald, *Spiritualism Identical with Ancient Sorcery, New Testament Demonology and Modern Witchcraft*, New York, 1866; E. Sargent, *Planchette, or the Despair of Science*, Boston, 1869; H. S. Olcott, *People from the Other World; wonderful Doings of the " Eddy Brothers,"* Hartford, n. d.; E. W. Cox, *Spiritualism Answered by Science*, London, 1872; M. Hull, *Contrast: Evangelism and Spiritualism compared*, Boston, 1874; J. M. Peebles, *Seers of the Ages; ancient, medieval, and modern Spiritualism*, 6th ed., Boston, 1874; idem, *Spiritualism Defined and Defended*, ib. 1875; F. G. Lee, *The Other World*, London, 1875; idem, *Sights and Shadows; Examples of the Supernatural*, ib. 1894; A. Mahan, *Phenomena of Spiritualism scientifically Explained and Exposed*, New York, 1876; W. B. Carpenter, *Mesmerism, Spiritualism . . . historically and scientifically Considered*, London, 1877; D. D. Home, *Lights and Shadows of Spiritualism*, ib. 1878; T. B. Hall, *Modern Spiritualism*, Boston, 1883; J. W. Truesdell, *Bottom Facts concerning Spiritualism*, New York, 1883; J. Chester, *Earthly Watchers at the Heavenly Gates; the false and true Spiritualism*, Philadelphia, 1886; E. Gurney and F. W. Meyers, *Phantasms of the Living*, 2 vols., London, 1887; F. Johnson, *The New Psychic Studies in their Relation to Christian Thought*, New York, 1887; J. C. Street, *The Hidden Way across the Threshold*, Boston, 1887; Sir W. Crookes, *Researches in the Phenomena of Spiritualism*, London, 1891; A. R. Wallace, *Miracles and Modern Spiritualism*, new ed., London, 1895; J. Jastrow, *Fact and Fable in Psychology*, Boston, 1901 (adverse to spiritualistic claims); F. Podmore, *Modern Spiritualism*, 2 vols., London, 1902 (history of the movement in England and America); idem, *The Newer Spiritualism*, ib., 1910; E. W. Cook and F. Podmore, *Spiritualism; is Communication with the Spirit World an accomplished Fact?* ib, 1903 (gives both sides of the argument); F. W. H. Myers, *Human Personality and its Survival of Bodily Death*, ib. 1903 (important); E. T. Bennett, *Physical Phenomena popularly Classed under the Head of Spiritualism*, ib. 1906; J. H. Hyslop, *Borderland of Psychical Research*, Boston, 1906; idem, *Enigmas of Psychical Research*, ib. 1906; J. G. Raupert, *Modern Spiritism*, London, 1904 (critical examination of the alleged phenomena); idem, *The Dangers of Spiritualism*, ib. 1906; D. P. Abbott, *Behind the Scenes with Mediums*, Chicago, 1907; C. Flammarion, *Mysterious*

Psychic Forces, Boston, 1907; C. M. Lane, *The Theory of Spiritualism*, St. Louis, 1907; W. N. Wilson, *Theocosmia: the Spirit World explored*, London, 1907; W. F. Barrett, *On the Threshold of a New World of Thought. An Examination of the Phenomena of Spiritualism*, ib. 1908; H. Carrington, *The Psychical Phenomena of Spiritualism, Fraudulent and Genuine*, ib. 1908; G. Delaune, *Evidence for a Future Life*, ib. 1908; J. Robertson, *Spiritualism: the open Door to the unseen Universe*, ib. 1908; C. Lombroso, *After Death—What?* ib. 1909; Sir Oliver Lodge, *The Survival of Man*, ib. 1910; Amy Eliza Tanner, *Studies in Spiritism*, New York, 1910 (a thoroughgoing review of the recent phenomena of Spiritism, with decidedly adverse decision); T. Flournoy, *Esprits et médiums*, Paris, 1911; the literature under PSYCHICAL RESEARCH AND THE FUTURE LIFE.

SPIRITUALS. See FRANCIS OF ASSISI, III., § 4–5; OLIVI, PIERRE.

SPITTA, spit′ä, **FRIEDRICH ADOLF WILHELM:** German Protestant, son of Karl Johann Philipp Spitta (q.v.); b. at Wittingen (35 m. n.e. of Brunswick), Hanover, Jan. 10, 1852. He was educated at the universities of Göttingen and Erlangen (1871–75); was teacher in the high school at Hanover (1876–77); inspector of the Tholuck Seminary at Halle (1877–79); assistant pastor at Bonn (1879–81), and pastor at Ober-Kassel, near Bonn (1881–87); privat-docent for Evangelical theology at the University of Bonn (1880–87); and went to Strasburg as professor of New-Testament exegesis and practical theology, as well as university preacher (1887). Besides editing the *Monatsschrift für Gottesdienst und kirchliche Kunst* since 1896, he has written:

Der Brief des Julius Africanus an Aristides (Halle, 1877); *Die liturgische Andacht am Luther-Jubiläum* (1883); *Der Knabe Jesus, eine biblische Geschichte und ihre apokryphischen Entstellungen* (1883); *Luther und die evangelische Gottesdienst* (1884); *Der zweite Brief des Petrus und der Brief des Judas* (1885); *Die Passionen nach den vier Evangelisten von Heinrich Schütz* (Leipsic, 1886); *Heinrich Schütz, sein Leben und seine Kunst* (Hildburgh, 1886); *Predigten* (3 vols., Bonn and Strasburg, 1886–99); *Drei kirchliche Festspiele für Weinachten, Ostern und Pfingsten* (Strasburg, 1889); *Die Offenbarung des Johannes untersucht* (Halle, 1889); *Christi Predigt an die Geister der Unterwelt* (Göttingen, 1890); *Zur Reform des evangelischen Kultus* (1891); *Die Apostelgeschichte, ihre Quellen und deren geschichtlicher Wert* (Halle, 1891); *Zur Geschichte und Literatur des Urchristentums* (3 vols., Göttingen, 1893–1907); *Der Entwurf der preussischen Agende* (1893); *Verteidigung des preussischen Agendenentwurfes* (1894); *Das Gesangbuch für die evangelischen Gemeinden von Elsass-Lothringen kritisch beleuchtet* (Strasburg, 1894); *Gottesdienst und Kunst* (1895); *Ludwig Schöberleins musica sacra für Kirchenchöre* (Göttingen, 1895); *Der Brief des Jakobus untersucht* (1896), *J. Zwicks Gebete und Lieder für die Jugend* (1901); *Untersuchungen über den Brief des Paulus an die Römer* (1901); *Musik und Kunstpflege auf dem Land* (Berlin, 1902); *Das Magnificat ein Psalm der Maria und nicht der Elisabeth* (Tübingen, 1902); *Die Kelchbewegung in Deutschland und die Reform der Abendmahlsfeier* (Göttingen, 1904); *Die Konstanzer Liederdichter* (Hamburg, 1904); " *Ein feste Burg ist unser Gott*," die Lieder Luthers in ihrer Bedeutung für das evangelische Kirchenlied (Göttingen, 1905); *Streitfragen der Geschichte Jesu* (1907); *Das Testament Hiobs und das Neue Testament* (1907); *Jesus und die Heidenmission* (Giessen, 1909); *Das Johannes-Evangelium als Quelle der Geschichte Jesu* (Göttingen, 1910); and *Beiträge zur Frage nach der geistlichen Dichtung des Herzogs Albrecht von Preussen* (Königsberg, 1910).

SPITTA, KARL JOHANN PHILLIPP: German Lutheran hymn-writer; b. at Hanover Aug. 1 (or July 31), 1801; d. at Burgdorf (13 m. s. of Celle) Sept. 28, 1859. He was educated at the University of Göttingen (1821–24), though he there devoted more attention to poetry and music than to theol-

ogy, as is shown by his anonymous *Sangbüchlein der Liebe für Handwerksleute* (Göttingen, 1824). In 1824 he became a private tutor at Lüne, near Lüneburg, where true religion was for the first time roused within him, and during his residence here the greater and better portion of his hymns were composed. From 1828 to 1830 he was curate at Sudwalde, and from 1830 to 1837 was military and prison chaplain at Hameln, where, despite rationalistic opposition, he succeeded in reviving religious life and in gaining the esteem of both ecclesiastical and military authorities. In 1837–47 Spitta was pastor at Wechold, near Hoya, where he again succeeded in reviving interest in religion, as he also did while stationed as superintendent at Wittingen (1847–53). At Peine, on the other hand, where he was pastor in 1853–59, religious life was too dead for him to achieve any great results. In 1859 he went as superintendent to Burgdorf, but died suddenly within the year.

The attitude of Spitta was distinctly one of devout Lutheran orthodoxy, filled with deep religious conviction, but absolutely free from sectarianism and fanaticism. At the same time his fidelity to Luther's teachings rendered it impossible for him to accept calls to the unionistic congregations of Barmen (1844) and Elberfeld (1846). He published anonymously two volumes of *Biblische Andachten* (Halle, 1836–39), but his chief fame was attained by the phenomenal success of his *Psalter und Harfe* (2 ser., Pirna and Leipsic, 1833–43, and in innumerable editions since, e.g., Gotha, 1890, Halle, 1901; Eng. transl., by R. Massie, " Lyra Domestica," 2 ser., London, 1860–64, and in part by Lady E. A. Durand, " Imitations from the German of Spitta and Tersteegen," 1873). [A large number of his hymns have been rendered into English; cf. Julian, *Hymnology*, pp. 1075–80.] After his death a further collection of his hymns was published under the title *Nachgelassene geistliche Lieder* (Leipsic, 1861), and later still his *Lieder aus der Jugendzeit* appeared (ed. Peters, 1898).　　　　(WILHELM NELLE.)

BIBLIOGRAPHY: The one biography is by K. K. Münkel, Leipsic, 1861, 2d ed., with notes by O. Mejer, 1892, with which should be compared the biographical sketch in L. Spitta's ed. of the *Psalter und Harfe*, pp. i.–cxxxvi., Gotha, 1890. Consult further: E. E. Koch, *Geschichte des Kirchenliedes*, vii. 232 sqq., Stuttgart, 1872; S. W. Duffield, *English Hymns*, pp. 239–241, 149, 426, New York, 1886; W. Nelle, *Philipp Spitta, ein Gedenkbüchlein*, Berlin, 1901; idem, *Geschichte des deutschen evangelischen Kirchenlieds*, 2d ed., Hamburg, 1909; and Julian, *Hymnology*, pp. 1075–80.

SPITTLER, spit′ler, **CHRISTIAN FRIEDRICH:** German Lutheran layman distinguished for his services in behalf of missions; b. at Wimsheim (a village of Württemberg near Leonberg, 8 m. w.n.w. of Stuttgart) Apr. 12, 1782; d. at Basel Dec. 8, 1867. After a brief trial of the revenue and administrative service (1796–1800), he was called, in 1801, to Basel as assistant in the Christentumsgesellschaft (see CHRISTENTUMSGESELLSCHAFT, DIE DEUTSCHE), where he kept the books and conducted the correspondence both of this society and of the Bible and tract society which it soon established. In 1807 all secretarial work was placed in his hands, and in the following year he received the official appointment to this position, which he retained for the remainder of his life. In 1812 he founded a publishing-house at Basel, and in 1834 a lending library, but in 1841 he limited his establishment to Bibles, tracts, and the publication of the literature of the Christentumsgesellschaft. He was by no means a clear or systematic thinker, and his work was characterized by a lack of fixed plan which was reflected by the premature and impracticable nature of many of his projects, yet nearly all the activities, institutions, and undertakings of the Innere Mission had in him their pioneer. The diversity of his philanthropic interests was marvelous. During the war of 1812–13 he labored in behalf of all in distress, regardless of nationality, station, and creed, and in the war of 1866 he made provision for the distribution of Bibles and the care of the sick; while during the Greek War of Independence he established a society for the moral and religious betterment of the Greeks and a short-lived institution for the training of a number of Greek slaves whom he ransomed, even as he provided an English school for the children of the English workmen engaged in tunneling the Hauenstein. In 1812 he established a home for poor students of theology, and in 1830 an institution for distributing Bibles to poor children; in 1833 he changed the Greek institution already mentioned into an asylum for deaf-mutes which still flourishes at Riehen near Basel; and he was also instrumental in the founding of several other philanthropic institutions. The development of the deaconess system, like Jewish missions, found an enthusiastic advocate in him, and to him was ultimately due the establishment of the seminary for teachers of ragged schools at Beuggen.

Spittler is particularly noteworthy for his effort to carry Protestantism into Roman Catholic districts and unchurched Protestant regions, by means of peasants, artizans, and other laymen, who should travel from place to place and in their wanderings spread the tenets of the faith. He soon realized that a certain degree of training and organization was necessary for such missionaries, but after a number of abortive attempts (including the establishment of colonies of such laymen about a day's journey apart, and the training of quasi-missionaries for Palestine), he was compelled by the missionary society at Basel to restrict his activities to the Innere Mission and the education of missionaries to work among the German emigrants to the United States. Real progress now began, and in 1854 Spittler's " Chrischona " founded some small communities in Säckingen and Rheinfelden, while a number of missionaries were even trained for the foreign field. The long-cherished plan of sending missionaries from the " Chrischona " to Abyssinia also seemed on the eve of realization when the war between England and Abyssinia (1866–68) put an abrupt end to all such plans. While, however, the foreign missionary field of the " Chrischona " was practically annihilated at the time of Spittler's death, his Innere Mission work was most successful, and has been most prosperously carried on to the present day. (WILHELM BORNEMANN.)

BIBLIOGRAPHY: The one complete biography is by J. Kober, Basel, 1887, since the more ambitious *C. F. Spittler im Rahmen seiner Zeit*, Basel, 1876, begun by Spittler's adopted daughter, reached only the end of vol. i., coming down to 1812. Consult further: T. Jäger, *Jakob Ludwig Jäger, ein Lebensbild*, Basel, 1898; W. Hadorn, *Geschichte des Pietismus in den schweizerischen reformirten Kirchen*, pp. 493–504, Constance, 1901.

SPITTLER, LUDWIG TIMOTHEUS: German Protestant church historian; b. at Stuttgart Nov. 11, 1752; d. there Mar. 14, 1810. He early developed a marked interest in history, and the main subjects of his study at Tübingen (1771–75) were philosophy and church history. His publications while lecturer at Tübingen (1777–79) included his *Kritische Untersuchung des sechzigsten Laodicäischen Canons* (Bremen, 1777) and the anonymous *Geschichte des kanonischen Rechts bis auf die Zeiten des falschen Isidors* (Halle, 1778), the latter winning him an appointment as professor of church history and the history of dogma at Göttingen in 1779. Here his lectures developed into his *Grundriss der Geschichte der christlichen Kirche* (Göttingen, 1782), a work long much admired, being both somewhat popular in tone and decidedly rationalistic. To church history Spittler also contributed, among other works, his *De usu textus Alexandrini apud Josephum* (Göttingen, 1779); *Geschichte des Kelchs im Abendmahl* (Lemgo, 1780); and *Von der ehemaligen Zinsbarkeit der nordischen Reiche an den römischen Stuhl* (Hanover, 1797), as well as his *Vorlesungen über die Geschichte des Kirchenrechts*, and *Ueber die Geschichte des Mönchtums* (both in his *Sämmtliche Werke*, x.); *Vorlesungen über die Geschichte des Papsttums* (ed. H. E. G. Paulus, Heidelberg, 1826); *Geschichte der Kreuzzüge* (ed. C. Müller, Hamburg, 1827); and *Geschichte der Hierarchie von Gregor VII. bis auf die Zeiten der Reformation* (ed. C. Müller, 1828).

In 1782 Spittler began to lecture on general history, and in 1784 he ceased all courses on church history, so that his writings were henceforth practically restricted to secular history, political economy, and statistics. He was one of the most popular and influential of the Göttingen professors, although his political attitude caused the king to regard him with little favor. In 1797 he accepted the invitation of Duke Frederick Eugene of Württemberg to return to his native city as a privy councilor, but the sudden death of his patron was almost fatal to his plans, and though he was created a baron in 1806, and made minister of state, curator of the University of Tübingen, etc., his real influence was scanty, nor could his new honors compensate for the days at Göttingen. The *Sämmtliche Werke* of Spittler were edited in fifteen volumes by K. Wächter (Stuttgart, 1827–37; the vols. of chief interest for the theologian are i.–ii. and viii.–x.).

(N. BONWETSCH.)

BIBLIOGRAPHY: G. J. Planck, *Ueber Spittler als Historiker*, Göttingen, 1811; K. L. von Woltmann, *Werke*, xii. 311 sqq., Berlin, 1821; A. H. L. Heeren, *Historische Werke*, vi. 515 sqq., 15 vols., Göttingen, 1821–26; D. F. Strauss, *Kleine Schriften*, pp. 68 sqq., Leipsic, 1862; G. Waitz, *Göttingen Professoren*, pp. 245 sqq., Gotha, 1872; F. X. von Wegele, *Geschichte der deutschen Historiographie*, pp. 872 sqq., Munich, 1885; *ADB*, xxxv. 212 sqq.

SPOILS, RIGHT OF (*Jus spolii*): The claim of the Church, the clergy, or secular rulers to a share in the estates of deceased ecclesiastics. The Church persistently adhered to the Roman law until late in the Middle Ages, but made an excep-

The Claim of the Church. tion in regard to the laws of property, which in the Roman code had been developed with a rigid consistency. When, at least in later times, burial was refused to laymen who had bequeathed nothing to the Church (cf. E. Friedberg, *De finium inter ecclesiam et civitatem regundorum judicio*, p. 187, Leipsic, 1861), it is not strange that the Church considered itself heir of the clergy and as mother assumed the heritage of her own children, the priests. According to the older church laws the right of ecclesiastics to dispose of their possessions was not restricted; but bishops were early required to make a will, and they were subject to penalty if they did not devise in favor of the Church or of blood-relations. Theodosius II. (408–450) awarded to the Church all possessions of ecclesiastics which had not been disposed of by will. In course of time the obligation to make a will was extended from the bishops to all holders of benefices. But strong obstacles continually met the desire of the Church to become sole heir of clerical possessions. Ecclesiastics disregarded church ordinances and seized the possessions of deceased colleagues. Various councils and synods condemned the right of spoils and prescribed severe punishments, but without avail. Ecclesiastics at times did not wait for the death of a brother, and the right of spoils was extended even to the estate of the pope. To do away with these abuses, Charlemagne appointed *œcbnomi* for the administration of church possessions, but without success. A capitulary of Charles the Bold issued in 844 seems to have been more successful.

The laity also tried to obtain a share in the estates of deceased churchmen. As long as the clergy lived according to Roman law, their right to dispose of their property by will was acknowledged by the

Claims of Secular Rulers. State; but when they were subjected to the law of the country, they could make their wills only under the same restrictions as laymen. If they left no will, their property did not go to their relatives or to the Church, but the manorlords, later the church-patrons, claimed it; and after Frederick I., the German kings claimed the estates of the bishops. It is true, Frederick I. threatened with severe punishment all those who tried to curtail the liberty of ecclesiastics in making a will, but neither he nor his successors regarded their own laws and promises. Even after the emperors had renounced the right of spoils, it was maintained by the German princes. Conditions were not different in England, Scotland, Sicily, and France. The right of spoils was practised in France especially. The Church there complained that the rulers delayed to fill episcopal seats in order to enjoy their revenues so much the longer. Gradually the same abuse started anew within the Church itself. Abbots claimed the possessions of priors and regulars; bishops claimed the estates of their canons, priests, and other clergy, even the estate of whole churches; priors and chapters the estate of bishops; and all this in spite of the continued prohibitions of councils and

popes. The liberty of making wills, which had been granted by the State to ecclesiastics, was now restricted anew by the bishops. And even after it had been granted again, there still remained of the right of spoils the *Ferto* (fourth of a mark), which the clergy had to leave to the bishop and this was customary in some German states as late as the nineteenth century (cf. E. Friedberg, *Kirchenrecht*, p. 562, Leipsic, 1903).

Even the popes, who had so zealously opposed the robbery of churches, claimed the right for which they had envied the bishops. In France the kings shared with the pope the spoil of churches and eccle-

The Claim of the Popes. siastics. It was in vain that the University of Paris denounced such abuses. The leaders of the protesting party were thrown into prison, and fear and terror led others to keep silence. But when the consequences of these abuses clearly showed themselves, when bishops were regarded as the worst debtors since their estates offered no security to creditors, Charles VI. ordered, in 1385, the abolishment of the papal right of spoils for monasteries and bishoprics. After a few years, however, the Council of Constance was forced to oppose the same abuses, also in vain; but in France at least the reintroduction of the right of spoils failed, owing to the rigid opposition of the French kings. In 1643 Louis XI. repeated the ordinances of Charles VI. and emphasized his edict by threats of severe punishment. But even the resistance of secular princes, which found the willing support of the Church, did not induce the popes to deprive the apostolic treasury of the lucrative spoils. As late as 1560 Pius IV. forbade all ecclesiastics to make a will without the permission of the apostolic seat, and did not hesitate to declare future donations invalid, while Pius V. (1567) and Gregory XIII. (1577) reasserted the old claims. It is true, however, that these were the last phenomena on a large scale of an abuse that had been practised for centuries by laymen and ecclesiastics with equal rapacity, which abuse in Italy even yet has not been abolished.

(E. Friedberg†.)

Bibliography: L. Thomassin, *Vetus et nova ecclesiæ disciplinæ*, III., ii., chaps. 51–57; *Zeitschrift für Philosophie und katholische Theologie*, parts 23–25; S. Sugenheim, *Staatsleben des Klerus im Mittelalter*, i. 267 sqq., Berlin, 1839; A. Friedberg, *De finium inter ecclesiam et civitatem regundorum judicio*, pp. 220 sqq., Leipsic, 1861; E. Friedberg, *Lehrbuch des . . . Kirchenrechts*, § 179, Leipsic, 1903 (useful for references to late literature); *KL*, xi. 657–661.

SPONDANUS, spon-dā′nus, **HENRICUS (HENRI DE SPONDE):** French Roman Catholic convert, church historian and bishop of Pamiers; b. at Mauléon (25 m. s.w. of Pau), Gascony, Jan. 6, 1568; d. at Toulouse May 18, 1643. He was brought up in the Reformed faith and studied at the College at Orthez and the Academy of Geneva. He practised law at Tours and won such distinction that Henry IV. appointed him *maître des requêtes* for Navarre. On Sept. 21, 1595, he renounced the Reformed tenets, and through the influence of Cardinal Jacques Davy du Perron (q.v.) he obtained a canonry. In 1600 he went to Rome, where he became a close friend of Cæsar Baronius (q.v.), whose

Annales he continued to 1622, and was there ordained priest on Mar. 7, 1606. Spondanus remained at Rome until 1626, when Louis XIII. nominated him bishop of Pamiers, in which capacity he manifested the utmost diligence in the extirpation of heresy. In 1639 failing health obliged him to resign his see, and, after devoting himself to literary labors at Paris, he finally retired to Toulouse. His writings were as follows: *Défence de la déclaration du sieur de Sponde par Henry de Sponde son frère contre les cavillations des ministres Bonnet et Souis* (Bordeaux, 1597); *Les Cimitières sacrez* (1598; Lat. ed., much enlarged, Paris, 1638); *Annales ecclesiastici Cardinalis Baronii in epitomen redacti* (Paris, 1612); *Annales sacri a mundi creatione ad ejusdem redemptionem* (1637); and *Annalium Baronii continuatio ab anno 1127 ad annum 1622* (1639).

(EUGEN LACHENMANN.)

BIBLIOGRAPHY: There is a biography by P. Frizon prefixed to the *Annalium Baronii continuatio*, ut sup. Consult also: E. and É. Haag, *La France protestante*, ix. 316, Paris, 1859; Lichtenberger, *ESR*, xi. 693–694.

SPORTS, BOOK OF: A royal proclamation drawn up by Bishop Morton for James I., issued by that king in 1618; republished by Charles I., under the direction of Laud, in the ninth year of his reign. Its object was to encourage those people who had attended divine service to spend the remainder of Sunday after evening prayers in such " lawful recreation " as dancing, archery, leaping, vaulting, May games, Whitsun ales, Morris dances, and setting of May-poles. The proclamation was aimed at the Puritans, and Charles required it to be read in every parish church. The majority of the Puritan ministers refused to obey, and some were in consequence suspended. See PURITANS, PURITANISM, § 13.

BIBLIOGRAPHY: D. Wilkins, *Concilia Magnæ Britanniæ*, iv. 483, London, 1737; W. Benham, *Dictionary of Religion*, pp. 989–990, ib. 1887; W. H. Hutton, *The English Church (1625–1714)*, pp. 107–108, ib. 1903.

SPOTTISWOOD, spot′is-wud **(SPOTTISWOODE, SPOTISWOOD, SPOTSWOOD), JOHN:** Archbishop of Glasgow; b. at Mid-Calder (12 m. s.w. of Edinburgh) 1565; d. in London Nov. 26, 1639. He studied at Glasgow University (M.A., 1581); succeeded his father as pastor at Calder, in 1583, when only eighteen; in 1601 accompanied the duke of Lennox as chaplain in his embassy to France, and in 1603 went with James VI. to England; in 1603 was made archbishop of Glasgow, and in 1605 privy-councilor for Scotland; was transferred to St. Andrews in 1615, so that he became primate and metropolitan; on June 18, 1633, crowned Charles I. at Holyrood; and in 1635 was made chancellor of Scotland. He was at first opposed to the introduction of the liturgy into the Church of Scotland, but, seeing that it was inevitable, he resolved to further the royal wishes, and personally led the movement. Owing to the opposition offered he tried to modify the policy of the king, but in 1638 the covenant was signed, and he was forced to remove to Newcastle for his safety, and in 1639 went to London, where he died. He wrote *The History of the Church of Scotland (203–1625)* (London, 1655; best ed., 3 vols., with life of the author, Edinburgh, 1847–51).

BIBLIOGRAPHY: A life of the author was prefixed to the original ed. of *The History*, and another (by M. Russell) to the Edinburgh ed., ut sup. Consult further: J. F. S. Gordon, *Scotichronicon*, i. 360–616, Glasgow, 1867; *DNB*, liii. 412–415; and the literature on the Church of Scotland given under PRESBYTERIANS.

SPRAGUE, sprêg, **WILLIAM BUELL:** American Presbyterian, pulpit orator, and biographer; b. in Andover, Conn., Oct. 16, 1795; d. at Flushing, N. Y., May 7, 1876. He was graduated from Yale College in 1815 (A.M., 1819); was private tutor for about a year; was graduated from Princeton Theological Seminary, 1819; and was immediately ordained pastor of the Congregational Church in West Springfield, Mass., as a colleague of Joseph Lathrop; on the death of Lathrop, Sprague was left sole pastor, 1820–29; was pastor of the Second Presbyterian Church of Albany, 1829–69; he then removed to Flushing, N. Y., where he died.

Sprague attained very high eminence as a preacher and speaker, and was besides a voluminous author. More than 150 of his sermons and occasional discourses were published by request. He published more than a dozen other separate works, among which may be mentioned *Letters from Europe in 1828* (New York, 1828); *Lectures on Revivals of Religion; with an introductory Essay by L. Woods* (1832); *Life of Rev. Dr. E. D. Griffin* (1838); *The Life of Timothy Dwight* (1844); *Aids to Early Religion* (1847); *Words to a Young Man's Conscience* (1848); *Visits to European Celebrities* (1855); *Memoirs of . . . J. McDowell, D.D., and . . . W. McDowell* (1864); *Life of Jedidiah Morse, D.D.* (1874).

The great literary work of his life was the *Annals of the American Pulpit: Notices of American Clergymen to 1855* (vols. i.–ii., Trinitarian Congregationalists, iii.–iv., Presbyterians, v., Episcopalians, vi., Baptists, vii., Methodists, viii., Unitarians, ix., Lutherans, Reformed, Associate, Associate Reformed, and Reformed Presbyterians; 9 vols., 1858–61). The manuscript of the tenth and concluding volume was completed for publication before his death; it included Quakers, German Reformed, Moravians, Cumberland Presbyterians, Freewill Baptists, Swedenborgians, and Universalists.

SPRECHER, sprek′er, **SAMUEL:** Lutheran (General Synod); b. near Hagerstown, Md., Dec. 28, 1810; d. at San Diego, Cal., Jan. 10, 1896. He studied at Pennsylvania College and Theological Seminary, Gettysburg, Pa., 1830–36; was pastor at Harrisburg, Pa., Martinsburg, Va., and Chambersburg, Pa., 1836–49; president of Wittenberg College, Springfield, O., 1849–74; and from 1874 was professor of systematic theology there. He was the author of *Groundwork of a System of Evangelical Lutheran Theology* (Philadelphia, 1879).

BIBLIOGRAPHY: P. G. Bell, *Portraiture of the Life of Samuel Sprecher*, Philadelphia, 1907.

SPRENG, SAMUEL PETER: Evangelical Association; b. in Clinton Township, O., Feb. 11, 1853. He was educated at Northwestern College, Naperville, Ill. (A.B. 1875), and, after holding various pastorates in his denomination and being presiding elder from 1875 to 1887, was elected, in the latter year, editor of *The Evangelical Messenger*, the official organ of the Evangelical Association, a position which he still retains. He was likewise president of the Missionary Society of the Evangelical Association in 1894–95 and secretary of the same body in 1904–07, and a member of the committee to revise the discipline of his denomination in 1895–99, while he has also been book editor since 1887, and president of the Young People's Alliance of the Evangelical Association since 1895. In theology he is " an Arminian of the Evangelical type," and has written *Rays of Light on the Highway to Success* (Cleveland, O., 1885); *Life and Labors of Bishop John Seybert* (1888); *History of the Evangelical Association* (New York, 1894); and *The Sinner and his Saviour: or, The Way of Salvation made Plain* (Cleveland, 1906).

SPRING, GARDINER: American Presbyterian; b. at Newburyport, Mass., Feb. 24, 1785; d. in New York Aug. 18, 1873. He was graduated from Yale College, 1805; taught in Bermuda, 1805–07; was admitted to the bar, 1808; abandoned law for theology, and studied at Andover Theological Seminary, 1809–10; was ordained pastor of the Brick (Presbyterian) Church, Aug. 8, 1810, and held the position till his death. The first four years of his ministry were years of steady, quiet growth, but from 1814 to 1834 there were frequent revivals. He took part in the formation of the American Bible Society (1816), American Tract Society (1825), and American Home Missionary Society (1826). His congregation first met in Beekman Street, but in 1856 removed to Fifth Avenue and Thirty-sixth Street. After 1861 he had a colleague. His ministry was remarkable both for length and power. His principal publications were *Essays on the Distinguishing Traits of Christian Character* (New York, 1813); *Memoirs of the Rev. S. J. Mills, Late Missionary to the Southwestern Section of the United States* (1820); *An Appeal to the Citizens of New York, on Behalf of the Christian Sabbath* (1823); *The Attraction of the Cross; designed to illustrate the leading Truths, Obligations, and Hopes of Christianity* (1846); *The Bible not of Man; or, the Argument for the divine Origin of the sacred Scriptures, drawn from the Scriptures themselves* (1847); *First Things. A Series of Lectures on the great Facts and moral Lessons first revealed to Mankind* (2d ed., 2 vols., 1851); *The First Woman* (1852); *Pulpit Ministrations; or, Sabbath Readings. A Series of Discourses on Christian Doctrine and Duty* (1864); *Personal Reminiscences of the Life and Times of Gardiner Spring* (2 vols., 1866); and occasional sermons and collections of sermons.

BIBLIOGRAPHY: Besides his *Personal Reminiscences*, ut sup., consult the *Memorial Discourse* of J. O. Murray, New York, [1873]; and S. Knapp, *Hist. of the Brick Presbyterian Church, N. Y.*, New York, 1909.

SPRING, SAMUEL: American theologian; b. at Northbridge, Mass., Feb. 27, 1746; d. at Newburyport, Mass., Mar. 4, 1819. He graduated at Princeton College in 1771; studied theology under John Witherspoon, Joseph Bellamy, Samuel Hopkins, and Stephen West (qq.v.). In 1775 he became a chaplain in the continental army, joining a volunteer corps under Benedict Arnold, with which

he marched to Quebec. He was ordained to the ministry Aug. 6, 1777, and became pastor of the Second Congregational Church at Newburyport, Mass., which he served for over forty-one years. He was one of those who gave a powerful impulse to the cause of theological education, culminating in the founding of Andover Theological Seminary. He also assisted in the organization of the Massachusetts Historical Society and the American Board of Commissioners of Foreign Missions. He was an editor of *The Massachusetts Missionary Magazine*. His most memorable theological treatises are: *Dialogue on the Nature of Duty* (1784); and *Moral Disquisitions and Strictures on the Rev. David Tappan's Lectures* (2d ed., 1815).

BIBLIOGRAPHY: W. B. Sprague, *Annals of the American Pulpit*, ii. 85–89, New York, 1859; W. Walker in *American Church History Series*, iii. 323, 332, 349–351, ib. 1894; idem, *Ten New England Leaders*, passim, ib. 1901; A. E. Dunning, *Congregationalists in America*, pp. 286–288, ib. 1894.

SPRINZL, sprin′zl, **JOSEF:** Roman Catholic; b. at Linz (100 m. w. of Vienna), Austria, Mar. 9, 1839; d. at Prague Nov. 8, 1898. He studied in the priests' seminary at Linz, 1857–61; was ordained priest, 1861; studied in the priests' institute at Vienna, 1861–64; became professor of theology in the Linz Seminary, 1864; professor of dogmatics at Salzburg University, 1875; ordinary professor of the same at Prague, 1881; spiritual councilor to the bishop of Linz Feb. 23, 1873, and of the prince-bishop of Salzburg Jan. 28, 1880. He published *Die altkatholische Bewegung im Lichte des katholischen Glaubens* (Linz, 1872); *Handbuch der Fundamentaltheologie* (Vienna, 1876); *Die Theologie der apostolischen Väter* (1880); *Compendium summarium theologiæ dogmaticæ in usum prælectionum academicarum concinnatum* (1882).

SPROULL, sproul, **THOMAS:** Reformed Presbyterian (Old School); b. near Freeport, Pa., Sept. 15, 1803; d. in Pittsburg, Pa., Mar. 20, 1892. He was graduated from the Western University of Pennsylvania, Pittsburg, 1829; was pastor of the Reformed Presbyterian Congregation of Allegheny and Pittsburg, 1834–68; professor in Reformed Presbyterian Western Theological Seminary, 1838–1840; in the united Eastern and Western Seminaries, 1840–45; again from 1856; and professor emeritus from 1875. He edited *The Reformed Presbyterian*, 1855–62, and *The Reformed Presbyterian and Covenanter*, 1862–74, both published in Pittsburg, Pa. Besides sermons, he wrote *Prelections on Theology* (Pittsburg, 1882).

SPURGEON, spur′jun, **CHARLES HADDON:** English Baptist; b. at Kelvedon (40 m. n.e. of London), Essex, June 19, 1834; d. at Mentone (13 m. n.e. of Nice), France, Jan. 31, 1892. His father and grandfather had been Independent ministers. From the age of seven to fifteen he was educated in a school at Colchester; he spent a few months in an agricultural college at Maidstone in 1842; and in 1849 became usher in a school at Newmarket, kept by a Baptist. As a youth he was subject to inner restlessness and conflict and dated his conversion from Dec. 6, 1850, at the chapel of the Primitive Methodists in Colchester, on which occasion he was deeply stirred and greatly relieved by a sermon preached by a layman on Isa. xlv. 22. However, the study of the Scriptures brought further misgivings and he was not content until he was immersed. This took place in the Lark at Isleham May 3, 1851, and he then united with the Baptist communion. In 1851 he became usher in a school at Cambridge, and entered the lay preachers' association in connection with the Baptist church meeting in St. Andrews Street, Cambridge. Forced by circumstance he preached unprepared his first sermon in a cottage at Teversham near Cambridge, at the age of sixteen. His gifts were recognized at once and his fame spread. He preached in chapels, cottages, or in the open air in as many as thirteen stations in the villages surrounding Cambridge, and this after his school duties for the day were past. In 1852 he became pastor of the small Baptist church at Waterbeach, and in 1854, after preaching three months on probation, he was called to the pastorate of the New Park Street Church, Southwark, London. Only 100 persons attended his first service; but before the end of the year the chapel had to be enlarged, and he preached in Exeter Hall during the alterations. When the enlarged chapel was opened it proved at once too small, and a great tabernacle was projected. Meanwhile, in 1856, Spurgeon preached at the Surrey Gardens music-hall to congregations which numbered 10,000 people; and at twenty-two he was the most popular preacher of his day. In 1861 the Metropolitan Temple, seating 6,000, was opened and there he ministered until his death, retaining his popularity and power as a preacher to the end.

Beside preaching, other enterprises made their demand upon his energy. In 1855 he accepted his first student for the ministry; soon a class assembled in his house every week for instruction in theology, pastoral duties, and other practical matters. This work was assigned mainly to a tutor. Out of it grew the Pastors' College, located first in his house; under the Tabernacle, 1861–74; and, after 1874, in the New College buildings. The local mission work of these students in the slums formed the nuclei of new Sunday-schools and churches, a circle of which banded around the central church. Its internal needs were provided by a number of auxiliary associations. Spurgeon was president of a society for the dissemination of Bibles and tracts employing the service of ninety colporteurs. The Stockwell Orphanage was incorporated in 1867 with an endowment of £20,000 given by Mrs. Hillyard. It grew to a group of twelve houses and accommodated 500 children.

The figure of Spurgeon was a composite one. Methodist by conversion, Baptist by profession, he was fundamentally Calvinistic by descent and is sometimes called " the last of the Puritans." He was minded to carry his obduracy even to the extent of disunion among the churches. In 1864 he invited a controversy with the Evangelical party in the Church of England by a powerful sermon, Baptismal Regeneration, a doctrine which he opposed; 300,000 copies were sold, and numerous pamphlets written in reply, the most important was by a Bap-

tist, B. W. Noel, Evangelical Clergy Defended (1864), in which Spurgeon was censured for introducing needless divisions among men of like faith. He, however, ended by withdrawing from the Evangelical Alliance. He also watched with misgivings the growth among Baptists of what seemed to him indifference to orthodoxy, deploring that not enough stress was laid on Christ's divine nature. He opposed what he called the " down-grade " movement of Biblical criticism; and, not being able to win the Baptist Union to his view, he withdrew in 1887, remaining independent until the end of his life, although still a stanch Baptist. Personally unambitious and unselfish, industrious in his exacting parish service and incessant Biblical study, human in sympathy and sane on social questions, democratic in temperament, he was ever zealous in the gospel of grace and redemption, and fearless in denouncing evil and upholding what he deemed true and right. As a preacher his early success was due to the sensation of his youth, his spontaneous humor, the fervor of his appeals to the conscience, but mostly to his natural gift of oratory. With a clear sympathetic voice and easy gesture, he knew how most effectively to present his appeal for salvation, projected from a shrewd comment on contemporary life and sustained upon his characteristic expository treatment of Scripture derived from the old Puritan divines. He was in later life a great sufferer from gout, and frequently was obliged to leave his pulpit.

The results of Spurgeon's literary labors had an enormous circulation. He conducted The Sword and the Trowel, a monthly church magazine; and published more than 1,900 sermons, including, from 1855, a sermon every week, contained in The Metropolitan Tabernacle Pulpit, continued after his death (49 vols., London, 1856–1904). Other works were, The Saint and his Savior (London, 1857); Morning by Morning; or Daily Readings for the Family or the Closet (1866); Evening by Evening (1868); John Ploughman's Talk (1869); and John Ploughman's Pictures (1880). Famous also is Our Own Hymn Book, with paraphrases of Psalms (1866). His most important work was The Treasury of David, an exposition of the book of Psalms (7 vols., 1870–1885). In view of his own lack of higher training, he was dependent in Biblical work upon the research of his assistants for scientifical material and on the Puritan divines for method and point of view; and his commentaries are practical and homiletical rather than scientific. Shortly before his death he completed The Gospel of the Kingdom, a popular exposition of Matthew (1893).

BIBLIOGRAPHY. Besides Spurgeon's Autobiography, Compiled from his Diary, Letters, Records, by his Wife and his Secretary, 4 vols., London, 1897–1900, there are biographies by: G. H. Pike, new ed., London, 1887, R. H. Conwell, Philadelphia, 1892; J. D. Fulton, Chicago, 1892; G. C. Lorimer, Boston, 1892; R. Shindler, From the Usher's Desk to the Tabernacle Pulpit, New York, 1892, H. L. Wayland, Philadelphia, 1892. J. J. Ellis, new ed., London, 1902; C. Ray, ib. 1903, cf. the same author's A Marvelous Ministry, ib. 1905. Consult further J. Fernandez, Nonconformity in Southwark, London, 1882; W. Williams, Personal Reminiscences of Charles Haddon Spurgeon, New York, 1895; W. M. Higgs, The Spurgeon Family, London, 1906.

SPURGEON, THOMAS: English Baptist; b. in London Sept. 20, 1856. After studying at the Pastor's College of the Metropolitan Tabernacle, London, as well as in South Kensington, he visited Australia and Tasmania in 1877 and again in 1879, and from 1881 to 1889 was pastor of a Baptist church in Auckland, New Zealand. He was then an evangelist of the New Zealand Baptist Union until 1893, when he succeeded his father, Charles Haddon Spurgeon (q.v.), as minister of the Metropolitan Tabernacle. He resigned this position in 1908, in consequence of ill-health, and has since been president of Pastor's College and of Stockwell Orphanage, London. Besides a volume of poems, *Scarlet Threads and Bits of Blue* (London, 1892), he has published several collections of sermons: *The Gospel of the Grace of God* (1884), *Down to the Sea* (1895), *Light and Love* (1897), *God Save the King* (1902), and *My Gospel* (1902).

SRAWLEY, srô'lî, JAMES HERBERT: Church of England; b. at Handsworth, Birmingham, Dec. 13, 1868. He received his education at King Edward VI.'s School, Birmingham, and Gonville and Gaius College, Cambridge (B.A., 1891; M.A., 1895; B.D., 1903; D.D., 1907); was made deacon, 1893, and priest, 1894; was curate of St. Matthew's, Walsall, Sheffield, 1893–95; vice-principal of Lichfield Theological College, 1895–97; lecturer in theology at Selwyn College, Cambridge, since 1897, and tutor since 1907, being also curate of St. Mary the Less, Cambridge, 1898–1906, examining chaplain to the bishop of Lichfield since 1905, and general secretary of the Central Society for Sacred Study. He has published *The Epistles of St. Ignatius, Translated with Introduction and Notes* (2 vols., London, 1900); and *The Catechetical Oration of St. Gregory of Nyssa* (Cambridge, 1903).

STABAT MATER. See JACOPONE DA TODI.

STACKHOUSE, THOMAS: Church of England; b. at Witton-le-Wear (10 m. s.w. of Durham), England, 1677; d. at Beenham (8 m. w.s.w. of Reading) Oct. 11, 1752. He studied at St. John's College, Cambridge; was head master of Hexham grammar-school, 1701–04; ordained priest in London, 1704, becoming curate of Shepperton in Middlesex; was minister of the English Church in Amsterdam from 1713; curate of Finchley, 1731; and in 1733 was relieved from extreme distress by an appointment to the vicarage of Beenham. He is remembered for his *New History of the Holy Bible, from the Beginning of the World to the Establishment of Christianity* (2 vols., London, 1737; best ed., 6 vols., Edinburgh, 1767); he was also the author of *Memoires of the Life, Character, Conduct and Writings of Dr. Francis Atterbury, Late Bishop of Rochester, from his Birth to his Banishment* (2d ed., London, 1727); *A Complete Body of Divinity . . . Extracted from the Best Ancient and Modern Writers* (1729; best ed. 1755); *A Defence of the Christian Religion from the Several Objections of Modern Antiscripturists; wherein the literal Sense of the Prophecies contained in the Old Testament, and of the Miracles recorded in the New, is explained and vindicated, in which is included the whole State of the Controversy between Mr. Woolston*

and his Adversaries (2d ed., 1733); *A New . . . Exposition of the Apostles' Creed* (1747); *The Life of our Lord and Saviour Jesus Christ. With the Lives of the Apostles and Evangelists* (1754).

BIBLIOGRAPHY: J. Nichols, *Literary Anecdotes of the 18th Century*, ii. 393–399, 9 vols., London, 1812–15; *DNB*, liii. 442–443.

STADE, shtä'de, BERNHARD: German Protestant; b. at Arnstadt (20 m. s.w. of Weimar) May 11, 1848; d. at Giessen Dec. 7, 1906. He was educated at the universities of Leipsic (1867–69; Ph.D., 1871) and Berlin (1869–70), and in 1871 became assistant in the library of the former institution, where he was also privat-docent in 1873–75; professor of Old-Testament exegesis at the University of Giessen (1875–1906), and rector in 1882–83, and 1896–97; after 1894 he was overseer of the theological students at Giessen. In addition to his work as editor of the *Zeitschrift für alttestamentliche Wissenschaft*, which he founded in 1881, he wrote *Ueber den Ursprung der mehrlautigen Tatwörter der Ge'ezsprache* (Leipsic, 1871); *De Isaiæ vaticiniis Æthiopicis* (1873); *Ueber die alttestamentlichen Vorstellungen vom Zustande nach dem Tode* (1877); *Lehrbuch der hebräischen Sprache*, vol. i. (1879); *De populo Javan parergon* (Giessen, 1880); *Ueber die Lage der evangelischen Kirche Deutschlands* (1883); *Geschichte des Volkes Israel* (2 vols., the second half of the second volume in collaboration with O. Holtzmann; Berlin, 1887–88); *Hebräisches Handwörterbuch zum Alten Testament* (in collaboration with C. Siegfried; Leipsic, 1893); *Die Reorganisation der theologischen Fakultät zu Giessen* (Giessen, 1894); *Ausgewählte akademische Reden und Abhandlungen* (1899); *The Books of Kings* in *The Polychrome Bible* (in collaboration with F. Schwally; New York, 1904); *Biblische Theologie des Alten Testaments*, vol. i. (Tübingen, 1905); and *Einst und jetzt, Rückblicke und Ausblicke* (Giessen, 1905).

STAEHELIN, shtê'e-lin, JOHANN JAKOB: Swiss theologian; b. at Basel May 6, 1797; d. at Langenbruck (15 m. s.e. of Basel) Aug. 27, 1875. His entire active life was passed as docent or professor in the University of Basel. He came under the pietistic influences of the Württemberg school, and devoted himself as a scholar to Semitic studies. His literary activity began in 1827 with a dissertation which discussed the Blessing of Jacob. In Pentateuchal criticism he issued *Kritische Untersuchungen über die Genesis* (Basel, 1830), in which he advocated the application to Bible study of historical linguistic work and the comparison of Biblical literature with other oriental writings. This was followed by *Kritische Untersuchungen über den Pentateuch, Josua, Richter, Samuel, und Könige* (Berlin, 1843), in which he anticipated in certain respects the results of more recent critics. The last work of this character was *Das Leben Davids* (Basel, 1866), an interesting account of the different phases of David's career. A second series of Stähelin's writings is concerned with the Hebrew prophets, for example, *Die messianische Weissagungen* (Berlin, 1847), in which he cast some light on the relations of these prophetical texts to the New Testament; and his *Die Propheten des Alten Testaments* (1867).

For many years Stähelin devoted his attention to the Psalms, the results of which he printed mainly in *ZDMG*. His chief work, however, is *Spezielle Einleitung in die kanonischen Bücher des A. T.s* (Elberfeld, 1862), though his presentation of the subject lacked form and attraction, and this interfered with the popularity and usefulness of his work. Moreover, he had an insufficient sense of proportion; the material points are often thrust in the background in favor of philological observation. Yet the value of his contributions to the critical and religious investigation of the Old Testament can not be questioned. (E. STÄHELIN.)

STAEHELIN, RUDOLF: Swiss Protestant theologian; b. at Basel Sept. 22, 1841; d. there Mar. 13, 1900. He studied at the gymnasium of his native city, also at the university there and at Lausanne, Berlin, and Tübingen. He undertook pastoral duties at Stein-on-the-Rhine in 1866, and the next year at Arlesheim. Sickness compelled a rest from duties in 1871, which he took in Sicily, and this resulted in his *Reisebriefe aus Italien* (Basel, 1903). Upon his return he settled in his native city as a private teacher in the theological faculty and was soon after appointed to the chair of church history, becoming regular professor in 1875. After declining a call to succeed Harnack at Marburg, he was seized by a disease of the eyes, which threatened to stop his work on the biography of Zwingli, but by the help of his wife and of friends he was able to bring out the two volumes, *Huldreich Zwingli* (1895–97). The rest of Stähelin's works are in part preparatory studies for this chief production, partly studies out of the history of Humanism and of the Reformation, some of which appeared in various serial or university publications.

In a period of theological and ecclesiastical change Stähelin kept aloof from all extremes, and maintained as a moderate the respect and admiration of all by his sincerity, nobility of manner, and regard for the feelings of others. (O. KIRN.)

BIBLIOGRAPHY: K. Stockmeyer, *R. Stähelin*, Basel, 1901; idem, in A. Bettelheim's *Biographisches Jahrbuch*, v (1903).

STAEHLIN, shtê′lin, ADOLF VON: German ecclesiastical administrator; b. at Schmahingen in the deaconry of Nördlingen (60 m. e. of Stuttgart) Oct. 27, 1823; d. at Munich May 4, 1897. He entered the University of Erlangen in 1840, and later spent two years in the Seminary at Munich. He was assistant pastor at Windsbach and other places until, in 1856, he was placed as pastor at Tauberscheckenbach, whence he went to Rothenburg in 1860, and to Nördlingen in 1864, where he became first pastor, and also a leader in the matter of reform of the schools, writing on this his first production, *Zur Schulreform* (Nördlingen, 1865). In 1866 he was called to Ansbach as consistorial councilor, and during his activity there of thirteen years wrote among other things, *Das landesherrliche Kirchenregiment und sein Zusammenhang mit Volkskirchentum* (Leipsic, 1871). In 1879 he was called to the upper council of Munich, and in 1883 to the head of the government of the church in Bavaria, which brought him into relations with the civil power as councilor. In all these relations soberness in action and wise thoughtfulness distinguished his actions. (T. KOLDE.)

BIBLIOGRAPHY: T. Kolde, *Adolf von Stählin*, Erlangen, 1897; O. Stählin, *Oberkonsistorialpräsident D. Adolf von Stählin*, Munich, 1898.

STAERK, WILLY OTTO ALEXANDER: Old-Testament scholar; b. at Berlin Dec. 15, 1866. He received his education at the universities of Berlin and Marburg, 1887–92; was engaged in various places in the teaching office, 1894–1903; became privat-docent for Old Testament at Jena, 1905, extraordinary professor, 1908, and ordinary professor, 1909. He has issued *Das Deuteronomium, sein Inhalt und seine literarische Form* (Leipsic, 1894); *Studien zur Religion und Sprachgeschichte des alten Testament* (2 vols., Berlin, 1899); *Ueber den Ursprung der Grallegende* (Tübingen, 1903); *Die Entstehung des alten Testament* (Leipsic, 1905); *Sünde und Gnade nach der Vorstellung des alten Judentums, besonders der Dichter der sogenannten Busspsalmen* (Tübingen, 1905); *Neutestamentliche Zeitgeschichte* (2 parts, Leipsic, 1907); an edition of *Jesaias Dichtungen* (1907); *Die jüdisch-aramäischen Papyri von Assuan, sprachlich und sachlich erklärt* (Bonn, 1907); an edition of Amos, Nahum, and Habakkuk (Leipsic, 1908); *Das assyrische Weltreich im Urteil der Propheten* (Göttingen, 1908); and *Aramäische Urkunden zur Geschichte des Judentums im VI. und V. Jahrhundert vor Christum* (Bonn, 1908).

STAEUDLIN, KARL FRIEDRICH: German theologian; b. at Stuttgart July 25, 1761; d. at Göttingen July 5, 1826. He studied philosophy and theology, particularly exegesis and oriental languages, at Tübingen, 1779–84; and was professor of theology at Göttingen, 1790–1826. He lectured in almost all the departments of scientific theology. He published, *Geschichte und Geist des Skepticismus* (2 vols., Leipsic, 1794); *Grundriss der Tugend- und Religionslehre* (Göttingen, 1798–1800); *Philosophische und biblische Moral* (1805); and *Neues Lehrbuch der Moral für Theologen* (1815). In these works he passed from a speculative and critical to a more empirical and authoritative point of view. He was the first to attempt a history of ethics, 1794–1812 and later. His *Geschichte der Sittenlehre Jesu* (4 vols., 1799–1822) he did not complete. He confined himself later to the preparation of *Geschichte der christlichen Moral seit dem Wiederaufleben der Wissenschaften* (1808). In addition appeared, *Geschichte der philosophischen, hebräischen und christlichen Moral* (Hanover, 1806); and *Geschichte der Moralphilosophie* (1823). In church history he left *Universalgeschichte der christlichen Kirche* (Hanover, 1806); *Geschichte der theologischen Wissenschaften* (2 vols., Göttingen, 1810–11); *Geschichte des Rationalismus und Supranaturalismus* (1826); and *Geschichte und Litteratur der Kirchengeschichte* (Hanover, 1827). (J. A. WAGENMANN†.)

BIBLIOGRAPHY: The chief source is the *Selbstbiographie*, ed. J. T. Hemsen, Göttingen, 1826. Consult further G. W. Frank, *Geschichte der protestantischen Theologie*, iii. 292 sqq., Leipsic, 1875; *ADB*, xxxv. 516 sqq.

STAFF or CROZIER. See VESTMENTS AND INSIGNIA, ECCLESIASTICAL.

STAFFORTIAN BOOK: The name of a confession of Baden-Durlach in the seventeenth century. After the religious peace of Augsburg, the Margrave Karl II. introduced in 1556 the Lutheran church order. After his death in 1577, the guardians of the three sons subscribed to the Book of Concord (q.v.); but when they had attained to the government in 1584, the eldest, Ernst Friedrich, who received as his share the lower part including the cities of Durlach and Pforzheim, manifested his dissatisfaction with the Lutheran confession, and introduced Calvinistic theologians at the school at Durlach, and attempted to introduce by force the Reformed faith in his dominion. A printing-press was established at the castle at Staffort, 1599, and the Staffortian Book was issued. In the shorter edition, covered by pp. 359–555 of the larger, only the articles are treated on which the adherents of the Augsburg Confession (q.v.) differed. Caution is prescribed against the new Semipelagians who accept foreseen faith as the cause of election. Reprobation is very guardedly touched upon. Earnest protest is raised against the doctrine of ubiquity and the confusion of natures. Appeal is made to the Augsburg Confession and Apology in behalf of a doctrine of the sacrament that does not coerce faith out of its proper position. Regeneration is represented as the redemptive gift of baptism, and spiritual sustenance of the " essential body and blood of Christ, together with all his treasures and merits," is claimed for believers only. The larger edition, *Christliches Bedencken und erhebliche wolfundierte Motiven,* attempts (pp. 1–358) a criticism of the text of the Formula of Concord (q.v.). The effort to enforce it raised a stubborn conflict. At Pforzheim the recalcitrant clergy were dismissed; for weeks there were no pastors; and the new Calvinistic preachers met with organized civic resistance. Ernst Friedrich prepared to move against the city by force of arms, when his death (1604) ended the strife. His successor returned to Lutheranism.   (E. F. KARL MÜLLER.)

BIBLIOGRAPHY: C. A. Salig, *Vollständige Historie der augsburgischen Confession,* pp. 748 sqq., Halle, 1730; J. C. Sachs, *Einleitung in die Geschichte der Markgravschaft . . . Baden,* iv. 252 sqq., Carlsruhe, 1770; K. F. Vierordt, *Geschichte der evangelischen Kirche in dem Grossherzogthum Baden,* ii. 29 sqq., ib. 1856; E. F. K. Müller, *Die Bekenntnisschriften der reformierten Kirche,* Leipsic, 1903.

STAHL, shtāl, FRIEDRICH JULIUS: German ecclesiastical jurist and statesman; b. at Munich Jan. 16, 1802; d. at Brückenau (50 m. e.n.e. of Frankfort-on-the-Main) Aug. 10, 1861. He was of Jewish parentage, but embraced Christianity in his seventeenth year. He studied jurisprudence at Würzburg, Heidelberg, and Erlangen; and was professor at Erlangen, 1832; at Würzburg, 1832; and at Berlin, 1840. In Berlin he gathered crowded audiences, not only of juridical students, but of men of all ranks; as when, in 1850, he lectured on *Die gegenwärtige Parteien in Staat und Kirche* (Berlin, 1863). He also held the highest positions in the state government of the Church, and took an active part in Prussian politics. His brilliant parliamentary talent soon made him one of the most prominent leaders of the conservative party, both in political and ecclesiastical affairs. His ideas are clearly de-

fined in *Die Philosophie des Rechts* (vol. i., *Geschichte der Rechtsphilosophie,* Heidelberg, 1830, vol. ii., *Rechts- und Staatslehre,* 1833; rev. ed., 1847). Of the fundamental problems of human life, he considered two solutions as possible, both philosophically and juridically,—one on the basis of pantheism, and one on the basis of faith in a personal God who has revealed himself to man; one giving the absolute power to the mass of the people, the majority, and one organizing the State after the idea of the highest personality, as a sphere of ethical action. What lay between those two extremes he despised as destitute of character. But his own choice he expressed in " No majority, but authority ! " In *Die Kirchenverfassung nach Lehre und Recht der Protestanten* (Erlangen, 1840), he aimed at a restoration of the old Protestant doctrine of church constitution. He held that the three systems, episcopal, territorial, and collegial, represented different views of the nature of church government, and were the outgrowths of the prevailing sentiment of three epochs of development; respectively, the orthodox, the Pietistic, and the rationalistic. Stahl advocated the Episcopal order. In his *Die lutherische Kirche und die Union* (1860) he opposed a formal union of the two Protestant churches. Among his other works are *Der christliche Staat und sein Verhältniss zu Deismus und Judenthum* (Berlin, 1847); and *Der Protestantismus als politisches Princip* (1856).   (RUDOLPH KÖGEL†.)

BIBLIOGRAPHY: P. A. S. van L. Brouwer, *Stahl redivivus,* The Hague, 1862; Pernice, Savigny, *Stahl,* Berlin, 1862 (biographies).

STAHR, stär, JOHN SUMMERS: Reformed (German); b. at Applebachsville, Pa., Dec. 2, 1841. He was educated at Franklin and Marshall College (A.B., 1867), with which he has been connected ever since, being tutor in German and history (1867–1868), assistant professor of the same subjects (1868–1871), professor of natural science and chemistry (1871–89), acting president (1889–90), and president (since 1890). After studying theology privately, he was ordained to the German Reformed ministry in 1872 and assisted Benjamin Bausman, later supplying the pulpit of the First Reformed Church, Reading, Pa. He has been a member of the International Sunday-school Lesson Committee since 1890, and has also been a consulting member of the editorial staff of the *Standard Dictionary,* a member of the eighth Council of the Alliance of Reformed Churches held at Liverpool in 1904, and president of the Eastern Synod of the Reformed Church. In theology he is a progressive conservative, " holding to the fundamental verities of the Christian faith and doctrine in the sense that our apprehension of them is advancing with the progress of human experience and scholarship." He has been an editor of *The Reformed Church Review* since 1905, and translated J. Grob's *Life of Zwingli* (New York, 1883).

STALKER, JAMES: United Free Church of Scotland; b. at Crieff (17 m. w. of Perth), Perthshire, Feb. 21, 1848. He was educated at the University of Edinburgh (M.A., 1869), New College, Edinburgh (1870–74), and the universities of Berlin (1872) and Halle (1873). He held pastorates at St. Brycedale's,

Kirkcaldy (1874–87), and St. Matthew's, Glasgow (1887–1902), and since 1902 has been professor of church history in the United Free Church College, Aberdeen. He was Lyman Beecher lecturer on preaching at Yale in 1891, Cunningham lecturer in New College, Edinburgh, in 1899, and in 1901 was Gay lecturer in Louisville Baptist Seminary and also lectured at Richmond Presbyterian Seminary. In theology he " rests his faith on the threefold foundation of Scripture, tradition, and personal experience, with emphasis on the third." He has written *The Life of Jesus Christ* (Edinburgh, 1879); *The New Song: Sermons for Children* (1883); *The Life of St. Paul* (1884); *Imago Christi* (London, 1889); *The Preacher and his Models* (1891); *The Four Men* (1892); *The Trial and Death of Jesus* (1894); *The Two Saint Johns* (1895); *The Christology of Jesus* (1899); *The Seven Deadly Sins* (1901); *The Seven Cardinal Virtues* (1902); *John Knox, his Ideas and Ideals* (1904); *The Atonement* (1908); *The Ethic of Jesus according to the Synoptic Gospels* (London, 1909).

STALL, SYLVANUS: Lutheran; b. at Elizaville, N. Y., Oct. 18, 1847. He was educated at Pennsylvania College, Gettysburg, Pa. (A.B., 1872), after which he studied theology there and at Union Theological Seminary for two years. He held pastorates in his denomination at Cobleskill, N. Y. (1874–77), Martin's Creek, Pa. (1877–80), Lancaster, Pa. (1880–88), and Baltimore, Md. (1888–1901). In 1901 he retired from the active ministry to become the head of his newly established Vir Publishing Company, Philadelphia. He edited *Stall's Lutheran Year Book and Historical Quarterly* (1884–1888), while from 1890 to 1901 he was associate editor of *The Lutheran Observer*. He has prepared *Pastor's Pocket Record* (Albany, N. Y., 1875); *Minister's Handbook to Lutheran Hymns in the Book of Worship* (Philadelphia, 1879); *How to pay Church Debts* (New York, 1880); *Methods of Church Work, Religious, Social, and Financial* (1887); *Five Minute Object Sermons* (1894); *Talks to the King's Children* (1896); *Bible Selections for Daily Devotion* (1896); *What a Young Boy ought to Know* (Philadelphia, 1897); *What a Young Man ought to Know* (1897); *What a Young Husband ought to Know* (1899); *What a Man of Forty-five ought to Know* (1901); *Faces toward the Light* (1903); *The Social Peril* (1905); and *Parental Honesty* (1905).

STANCARI, stän-cä′rî **(STANCARO), FRANCESCO:** Unitarian; b. at Mantua, Italy, in 1501; d. at Stobnitz, Poland, Nov. 12, 1574. He entered a religious order, and evidently underwent a systematic training in theology, since his method, for instance, in his first theological work, *De trinitate*, is scholastic in type. Stancari appeared prominently first in 1543, when he lived in Chiavenna; at Basel, in 1546, he issued a Hebrew grammar. In course of the shifting life that was especially common with Italian fugitives, he was later found at Cracow, whence, after seizure as a heretic, he escaped to Königsberg, there to teach in the high school. But becoming involved in strife with Osiander, only three months elapsed before he requested his dismission. Afterward, at Frankfort-on-the-

Oder, he continued the controversy in his *Apologia contra Osiandrum,* and the elector of Brandenburg intervened, while Melanchthon, in 1553, published a *Responsio de controversiis Stancari* (*CR,* xxiii. 87). He then went to Poland, Hungary, and Transylvania, but returned to Pinczow in 1558. He there associated with such men as Lismanini and Blandrata (q.v.); and contended for the proposition that Christ is a mediator with God only in his human nature. The dispute reached beyond the borders of Poland; Calvin answered in a " Response " of the Genevan Church (*Tractatus theologici,* p. 682); while in a further message (*Epistolæ et responsa,* p. 290) Zurichers made answer, also through Josias Simler's *Responsio ad maledicum Fr. Stancari libellum* (1563). Both new and old material on the subject has been compiled by Wotschke in letters and other documents, in *Briefwechsel der Schweizer mit den Polen* (*Archiv für Reformations-Geschichte,* Ergänzungsband iii., 1908). In several of these documents, Lismanini protests against the theology of Stancari, which was combated in Poland as being Nestorian. Yet it had significance in the history of dogma, as in opposing it the attempts of the Lutheran theologians to carry the point of their *Communicatio idiomatum* (q.v.) gained special consequence. Wigand (*De Stancarismo,* 1585) and Schlüsselburg (*Catalogus hæreticorum*) were opponents of Stancari.

K. BENRATH.

BIBLIOGRAPHY: Sources are: The letters of Calvin, in his *Opera* in *CR;* S. Orzechowski, *Roxolani Chimæra: sive de Stancari funesta regno Poloniæ secta,* Cologne, 1563; *Orichoviana,* ed. J. Korzeniowski, pp. 722 sqq., Cracow, 1891 (contains six letters by Stancari). Consult further: Bayle, *Dictionary,* v. 226–233 (quotes extensively from sources); S. Lubienski, *Historia reformationis Polonicæ,* Freistadt, 1685; C. Hartknoch, *Preussische Kirchen-Historia,* i. 330 sqq., Frankfort, 1686; G. J. Planck, *Geschichte . . . unseres protestantischen Lehrbegriffs,* iv. 449 sqq., 6 vols., Leipsic, 1781–1800; H. Dalton, *Johannes a Lasco,* Gotha, 1881; and Wotschke, in *Altpreussische Monatsschrift,* 1909.

STANDING FISHES BIBLE. See BIBLE VERSIONS, B, IV., § 9.

STANFORD, CHARLES: English Baptist; b. at Northampton (45 m. w. of Cambridge), England, Mar. 9, 1823; d. in London Mar. 18, 1886. He commenced preaching, 1839; entered the Baptist College at Bristol, 1841; became minister at Loughborough, 1845; Deniges, 1847; co-pastor in London of the Denmark-place Church, Camberwell, 1858, and was sole pastor from 1861 till his death. He was the author of *Central Truths* (London, 1860); *Joseph Alleine: his Companions and Times;* a Memorial of " Black Bartholomew," 1662 (1861); *Instrumental Strength; Thoughts for Students and Pastors* (1862); *Home and Church* (1871); *Homilies on Christian Work* (1879); *Voices from Calvary; a Course of Homilies* (1881); *From Calvary to Olivet. Being a Sequel to " Voices from Calvary"* (1884); *The Alternatives of Faith and Unbelief* (1885); *The Evening of Our Lord's Ministry, being Preludes to " Voices from Calvary." A Course of Homilies* (1886); together with a collection of sermons, and many smaller works.

BIBLIOGRAPHY: *Charles Stanford, Memories and Letters,* ed. his wife, London, 1889; *Baptist Handbook,* 1887, pp. 120–122; *DNB,* liii. 478–479.

STANGE, CARL: German Protestant; b. in Hamburg Mar. 3, 1870. He was educated at the universities of Halle and Göttingen (1888–92) and at Leipsic (1893–94), became privat-docent at Halle in 1895, extraordinary professor of systematic theology in the University of Königsberg in 1903, and professor of the same at Greifswald in 1904. He has written *Die christliche Ethik in ihrem Verhältnis zur modernen Ethik* (Göttingen, 1892); *Die systematischen Prinzipien in der Theologie des Johann Musäus* (Halle, 1897); *Das Dogma und seine Beurteilung in der neueren Dogmengeschichte* (Berlin, 1898); *Einleitung in die Ethik* (2 vols., Leipsic, 1901–02); *Der Gedankengang der Kritik der reinen Vernunft* (1902); *Luthers älteste ethische Disputationen* (1904); *Heilsbedeutung des Gesetzes* (1904); *Was ist schriftgemäss?* (1904); *Theologische Aufsätze* (1905); and *Das Frömmigkeitsideal der modernen Theologie* (1907).

STANISLAUS, stăn′is-lōs: The name of two saints.
1. Bishop of Cracow, and patron-saint of Poland; b. near Cracow (210 m. n.e. of Vienna) July 26, 1030; d. there May 8, 1079. After studying canonical law at Gnesen and Paris he entered the clerical profession at Cracow. He was a stern ascetic, distributed his patrimony amongst the poor, and boldly denounced the cruelty and licentiousness of Boleslas II., king of Poland, whom he finally excommunicated. In revenge, the king murdered Stanislaus while he was celebrating mass near Cracow. Miracles are ascribed to the bishop before and after his death. In 1253 Innocent IV. canonized him. Many altars and churches were built to his memory in Poland. His day is May 7.
2. Jesuit; b. at Kostcou (50 m. e. of Breslau, Germany), Poland, Oct. 20, 1550; d. in Rome Aug. 15, 1568. In his fourteenth year he went to Vienna where he was an object of admiration because of his exemplary life and his remarkable progress in studies; he had there a vision of two angels and the Virgin Mary, who urged him to become a Jesuit; after seeking admission to the order at Vienna, which was refused on account of his father's aversion to the step, he finally went to Rome, where he was admitted Oct. 28, 1567. He predicted the day of his death, and on account of his severe ascetic practises was beatified by Clement X., 1670, and canonized by Benedict XIII., 1726. His day is Nov. 13.

BIBLIOGRAPHY: On 1: The *Vita* by Johannes Longinus (Dlugosch) with other matter and commentary is in *ASB*, May, ii. 198–280. Other accounts and details are in *MGH, Script.*, xxix (1892), 504–517. A *Carmen Sapphicum in vitam gloriossissimi martyris Stanislai*, by P. Callimachus, was printed at Cracow in 1511. Consult further: R. Roepell, *Geschichte Polens*, i. 100 sqq., Hamburg, 1840; H. Zeissberg, *Die polnische Geschichtsschreibung des Mittelalters*, pp. 71, 82–90, 266–268, Leipsic, 1873. On 2: The *Vita* by Urbano Ubaldini is given in *Analecta Bollandiana*, ix (1890), 360–378, xi (1892), 416–467, with abundant literature.

STANLEY, ARTHUR PENRHYN: Church of England; b. at Alderley Rectory (32 m. e.s.e. of Liverpool) in Cheshire, Dec. 13, 1815; d. at London July 18, 1881. He was the grandson of Thomas Stanley, sixth baron of Alderley Park, and the son of Edward Stanley, bishop of Norwich. At Rugby (1829–34) he became attached by an ideal friendship to Thomas Arnold (q.v.), attended by an admiration and affection which served to shape the motives and activities of all his life. He entered Baliol College, Oxford, 1834; became a fellow of University College, 1838; and was ordained, 1839. In 1840–41, he made the first of many journeys abroad, his interest in foreign lands being entirely historical, while he was indifferent to scenery. He became college tutor at Oxford, 1843–51; and select preacher there, 1846–47. These discourses, *Sermons on the Apostolic Age* (Oxford, 1847), marked a crisis in his career, at a point of transition between the old and the new at Oxford. They showed a divergence from the views of both ecclesiastical parties; acknowledged obligations to Arnold and German theology, and demanded free inquiry in the matter of Biblical study. Stanley was appointed secretary of the Oxford University Commission, 1850, the report of which was mainly his work; and canon of Canterbury, 1851. A journey to the Holy Land and Egypt in 1852 resulted in the publication of *Sinai and Palestine* (London, 1856). *Memorials of Canterbury* (1855) exhibits the development of his taste for ecclesiastical landmarks, and illustrates his gifts for dramatic, pictorial narrative. He was professor of ecclesiastical history at Oxford, 1856–64, to which was attached a canonry of Christ Church, in which he was installed, 1858. At the same time he was appointed examining chaplain to Archibald Campbell Tait (q.v.), then bishop of London. To this period belong *Three Introductory Lectures on the Study of Ecclesiastical History* (Oxford, 1857); *Lectures on the History of the Eastern Church* (London, 1861); and *Lectures on the History of the Jewish Church* (3 vols., 1863–76).

Through the lecture-room, pulpit, and in social life he exercised a remarkable influence over the young men at the university, but he was not an intellectual leader among his elder colleagues. He eschewed party spirit, and his sense of justice and championship of freedom led him to defend J. W. Colenso, although regretting his work (*The Pentateuch*, London, 1862 sqq.); and, likewise, in the controversy caused by the *Essays and Reviews* (1860), while disapproving of some of the essays, he pleaded against the unfairness of indiscriminate censure. His courage to battle against inert ecclesiasticism and his moderately stated consideration of all sides of a problem, secured him, as champion of liberal ideas, a growing support from men of the press, science, and society as a whole.

In 1864 he was installed dean of Westminster, a position which he made conspicuous until his death. A year before, he was married to Lady Augusta Bruce, daughter of the fifth earl of Elgin and friend of the queen, and his married life was remarkably filled with happiness, so that when his wife died in 1876, he was deeply affected and did not long survive her. In 1862 he accompanied the Prince of Wales to the East. These events issued in unrivalled opportunities, so that by the further extension of political, literary, scientific, and ecclesiastical connections, facilitated by his characteristic *savoir-faire* and his brilliant social relations, he obtained that extraordinary influence which, for more than a decade, made him one of the most prominent figures in the English capital. Westminster Abbey afforded the material embodiment of his catholic ideal of a national church, reconciling under the spell of its vast and silent historical perspective every variety of creed and promotive activity. He endeared its historical memories and lessons to the people by the work *Memorials of Westminster Abbey* (London, 1868); enhanced the attractiveness of its worship for throngs representing all classes, placing his pulpit at the disposal of clergymen of every shade of opinion and of laymen, and admitting even Unitarians to the communion. At certain hours he conducted parties through the aisles of the sacred edifice, communicating his rich treasures of information as well as his enthusiasm. He wove the charm of his personality about the high and the low, gathering even the poor, sick, and disconsolate from the most wretched quarters of the city in the garden festivals of the deanery.

On account of the character of his personal influence the leadership of the Broad-church party devolved upon him unsought. He published addresses and brochures on the most important religious and social questions of the day; showed his interest in the Old Catholics (1872); favored a movement for the reunion of the Anglican and Oriental Churches; and used his influence for the return of the dissenters into the State Church. In his Biblical and historical methods Stanley was the grateful pupil of Arnold, to whom he erected a glorious monument of loyalty, *The Life and Correspondence of Thomas Arnold* (London, 1844), a work that assured him his position at Oxford and in the world of letters. His friends admit that his Biblical work was neither profound nor exact; but he won the soul of the people as the interpreter of the great rector of Rugby. In the depreciation of dogma, however, he opposed Arnold, and he was also governed thereby in his ecclesiastical principle. The Church, being rational, may not close her doors to any member of the nation, and must represent all views and aspirations of the nation. His time he regarded as a period of transition. The first task of the modern theologian, as he conceived it, is the study of the Bible for the sake of its content. The Biblical scholar must subordinate all the immaterial, temporal, and secondary to the essential and supernatural elements. He represented as a churchman a broad catholic tolerance, emphasizing the character of the formulæ of the Anglican Church assumed to be universal and mediating. He was enthusiastic in the recognition of the truth that binds all Christian bodies. He advocated the union of Church and State more and more positively. This he understood to subsist (1) in the recognition and promotion of religious faith in the community on the part of the State, and (2) the subjection of religion thus formulated to the control and conduct of the Church at large by the authority of law. With such views he was at variance with both of the great church parties. From the evangelicals he was estranged by his contempt of dogma, by his views on Biblical criticism, inspiration, justification, and the punishments of hell, and by his toleration of ideas well-nigh Roman Catholic. From the High-churchmen he differed on fundamental principles, disagreeing essentially even where there was formal accord on outward doctrine and practise.

The extravagances of ritual, such as vestments, incense, and the posture of head and hands, he treated with amused contempt. By the combination of a pious interpretation with an honest truth-searching criticism, Stanley was the sagacious and inspiring advance combatant of a new order of Biblical and historical study. He visited the United States in 1878, and, as a result, there was published *Addresses and Sermons Delivered in the United States and Canada* (New York, 1879). Other works are a commentary on the epistles to the Corinthians (2 vols., London, 1855); *Questions of Church and State* (1870); *Lectures on the History of the Church of Scotland* (1872); *Addresses Delivered at St. Andrews* (1877); and *Christian Institutions* (1881; new ed., 1906).

BIBLIOGRAPHY: The indispensable works are: R. E. Prothero, *Life and Correspondence of Dean Stanley*, 2 vols., London, 1893, new ed., 1909; idem, *Letters and Verses of Dean Stanley*, ib. 1895; G. W. E. Russell, *Anglican Church Portraits*, Edinburgh, 1876; G. G. Bradley, *Recollections of A. P. Stanley*, London and New York, 1882; A. J. C. Hare, *Biographical Sketches*, London, 1895; F. Locker-Lampson, *My Confidences*, ib. 1896; E. Abbott and L. Campbell, *Benjamin Jowett*, 3 vols., ib. 1897–99; Julia Wedgwood, *Nineteenth Century Teachers*, ib. 1909; *DNB*, liv. 44–48.

STANTON, VINCENT HENRY: Church of England; b. at Victoria, Hong-Kong, June 1, 1846. He was educated at Trinity College, Cambridge (B.A., 1870; M.A., 1873), and was ordered deacon in 1872 and ordained priest in 1874. Since 1872 he has been fellow of his college, of which he was junior dean (1874–76), senior dean (1876–84), and tutor (1884–89), and divinity lecturer (1882–89). Since 1889 he has been Ely professor of divinity in Cambridge University and canon of Ely. He was university extension lecturer in 1873, select preacher at Cambridge in 1874–78 and at Oxford in 1896–98, Hulsean lecturer in 1879, Cambridge Whitehall preacher in 1880–82, and examining chaplain to the bishop of Ely from 1875 to 1905. He has written *The Jewish and the Christian Messiah* (London, 1887); *The Place of Authority in Matters of Religious Belief* (1891); and *The Gospels as Historical Documents*, parts 1 and 2 (Cambridge, 1903–09).

STAPFER, shtap'fer: The name of a distinguished family of Bernese theologians.

1. Johann Friedrich Stapfer: The best-known of the elder generation; b. at Brugg (17 m. n.w. of Zurich) 1708; d. at Diessbach (a village near Thun, 16 m. s.s.e. of Bern) 1775. After studying at Bern and Marburg and traveling in Holland, he was military chaplain in 1738–40 and private tutor at Diessbach in 1740–50, while from the latter year until his death he was pastor at Diessbach, declining no less than four calls to Marburg. His first great work was his *Institutiones theologicæ polemicæ universæ* (5 vols., Zurich, 1743–47), followed by his *Grundlegung zur wahren Religion* (12 vols., 1746–53). The latter work, which was mainly dogmatic in character (the *Institutiones* being largely symbolic), was supplemented by the much inferior *Sittenlehre* (6 vols., 1757–66) and was abridged by the author in two volumes (1754). His theological position was one of orthodox rationalism of the mild Reformed type.

2. Johannes Stapfer: Brother of the preceding; b. at Brugg 1719; d. at Bern 1801. He was pastor of Aarburg, and in 1756 he was appointed professor of dogmatic theology at Bern, where he was professor of didactic theology from 1776 until his retirement from active life in 1796. He was a popular preacher, and his sermons were collected in seven volumes (Bern, 1762–1806). He collaborated in the revision of the Bern *Psalmenbuch* and wrote *Theologia analytica* (Bern, 1763), a systematic presentation of the chief tenets of faith.

3. Daniel Stapfer: Brother of the preceding. After being pastor at Murten, he was called, in 1766, to the cathedral in Bern, and attained the reputation of being one of the best pulpit orators of his time.

4. Philipp Albert Stapfer: Elder son of the preceding and the most distinguished of the family; b. at Bern Sept. 23, 1766; d. at Paris Mar. 27, 1840. He was educated at Bern and Göttingen, and then visited London and Paris, being in the latter city during the early part of the French Revolution. Returning to Bern, he was appointed, in 1791, deputy professor to Johannes Stapfer (see above), likewise being a teacher of languages at the academy. On his uncle's resignation in 1796 he was made his successor. The events connected with the overthrow of the old Swiss Confederation, however, entirely changed the course of Stapfer's life, who, being in sympathy with the new government, was sent on an embassy to Paris, in 1798. While there, he was appointed by the Helvetic Directory minister of sciences, arts, buildings, bridges, and streets, a position which he accepted after some hesitation. Here he rendered valuable service in stemming the tide of irreligion then prevalent in Switzerland, and accomplished still more tangible results in the organization of schools and charities. In 1800–03 he was ambassador to Paris, but on the fall of the Helvetic Republic in the latter year he retired to private life. In 1806 he removed to France, where the remainder of his life, except for less and less frequent visits to Switzerland, was passed, his residence at first being Belair, near Paris, and later Talcy, near Mer. During these latter years he worked quietly but effectually in behalf of French Protestantism, upon which, while himself becoming steadily more orthodox, he brought to bear the influence of German theology; nor should his labors in all philanthropic causes be forgotten. Among his works mention may be made of his *De philosophia Socratis* (Bern, 1786); *Einige Bemerkungen über den Zustand der Religion und ihrer Diener in Helvetien* (1800); and *Mélanges philosophiques, littéraires, historiques et religieux* (2 vols., Paris, 1844; contains a biography by Vinet).

5. Friedrich Stapfer: Younger brother of the preceding; d. at Meikirch (a village near Aarberg, 12½ m. n.w. of Bern) 1840. In the early years of the Helvetic Republic he was assistant to his brother at the University of Bern, where he was appointed professor of didactic theology in 1801. Being unsuccessful as a teacher, he became, in 1805, pastor at Diessbach, near Thun, but in 1818 was recalled to Bern as professor of Biblical studies. On the victory of the Liberals and the reorganization of the

university in 1833 he again resigned, spending the remainder of his life as pastor at Meikirch.

(W. Hadorn.)

Bibliography: C. Meusel, *Kirchliches Handlexikon*, part 55, pp. 391–392, Leipsic, n.d.; H. J. Leu, *Allgemeines Helvetisches . . . Lexicon*, xvii. 513 sqq., supplement v. 605 sqq., 20 vols., Zurich, 1747–65; *ADB*, xxxv. 450 sqq.; R. Luginbühl, *Ph. Alb. Stapfer*, Basel, 1887. Luginbühl ed. in *Quellen der schweizerischen Geschichte*, xi.–xii. and in *Archiv des historischen Verein*, Bern, vol. xiii., the correspondence of Philipp Albert Stapfer.

STAPFER, EDMOND LOUIS: French Protestant; b. at Paris Sept. 7, 1844; d. at Paris Dec. 13, 1908. He was educated at the Lycée Bonaparte, Paris, and the theological faculty of Montauban (1864–68), and also studied at the universities of Tübingen and Halle (1869–70). He was pastor of the Reformed church in Tours (1870–76); was maitre de conference in the Protestant theological faculty at Paris (1877–90); professor of New-Testament exegesis in the same faculty (1890–1906) of which he was dean (1901–06). In addition to making a French translation of the New Testament (Paris, 1889), he wrote *Jésus de Nazareth et le développement de sa pensée par lui même* (1872); *Les Idées religieuses en Palestine au temps de Jésus-Christ* (1876); *Le Palestine au temps de Jésus-Christ* (1884; Eng. transl. by A. H. Holmden, *Palestine in the Time of Christ*, London, 1886); *Le Château de Laley* (1888); *Jésus-Christ, sa personne, son autorité* (3 vols., 1895–98; Eng. transl. by Mrs. L. S. Houghton, 3 vols., New York, 1896–98); *La Mort et la resurrection de Jésus-Christ* (1898); a volume of sermons (1904); and *De l'état actuel du protestantisme en France* (Paris, 1908).

STAPHYLUS, shtὰ-fai′lus, **FRIEDRICH:** Lutheran theologian, subsequently Roman Catholic polemist; b. at Osnabrück (70 m. w. of Hanover) Aug. 27, 1512; d. at Munich Mar. 5, 1564. He studied at the University of Cracow, and later at Padua. About 1533 he returned to Danzig, but in 1536 went to Wittenberg where he remained about ten years. In 1541, at the recommendation of Melanchthon, he became private tutor of Count Ludwig of Eberstein and Neugarten. In 1545 he accepted a call from Duke Albrecht of Prussia to the newly founded university of Königsberg. In the very beginning he involved himself in a controversy with Gulielmus Gnapheus (Fullonius, q.v.), who as a teacher and lecturer of the university was accused by Staphylus of leaning toward Anabaptist views; by continual attacks Staphylus finally drove Gnapheus away. After the resignation of Georg Sabinus (Aug., 1547), Staphylus became rector of the university, but as such did not justify the hopes of the duke and of his friends at Wittenberg; in 1548 he gave up his theological lectures and served the duke as councilor. In the controversy with Osiander he still represented the Lutheran position, but the general instability caused by continual dogmatic dissensions induced him to adhere more closely to the dogmatic consensus of the Roman Catholic Church and in this way he gradually arrived at an un-Evangelical conception of tradition which after his removal to Danzig in Aug., 1551, led him to oppose the Protestant norm of the perspicuity of Scripture and to advocate the authentic interpretation of the Church. The decisive step was taken by him at Breslau, whither he had gone from Danzig, where, during a severe illness toward the end of 1552, he received the Lord's Supper after the Roman rite and confirmed his rehabilitation as a Roman Catholic by confession. He then removed to Neisse, the seat of Bishop Promnitz, in whose service he erected a school and was active in other directions. Hand in hand with Canisius, he aided in the restoration of Roman Catholicism in Austria and Bavaria. Being elected superintendent of the University of Ingolstadt toward the end of 1560, he undertook a reformation of that demoralized institution. He hailed the idea of a general council, but thought that it should be preceded by negotiations between the emperor and the Protestants in order to win their consent. A great advantage, according to him, could be derived from the inner discord of the Protestants. In 1562 Emperor Ferdinand requested Staphylus to extract from the opinions of different theologians a definite statement of what in the name of the emperor should be presented to the council as a program of reform. It appeared as *Consultatio imperatoris Ferdinandi I. iussu instituta de artic. ref. in Conc. Trident. prop.* Staphylus published also: *Synodus sanctorum patrum antiquorum contra nova dogmata Andreæ Osiandri* (Nuremberg, 1553); *Theologiæ Martini Lutheri trimembris epitome* (1558); *Scriptum colloquentium August. Conf. . . . cum oppositis annotationibus* (1558); *Historia et apologia . . . de dissolutione colloquii nuper Wormatiæ instituti* (Nisæ, 1558). In these polemical works against the Protestants he criticized especially the idolatry of Luther and opposed to Protestant subjectivism the objective norms of tradition and the consensus of the Church. His last work was, *Vom letzten und grossen Abfall, so vor der Zukunft des Antichrist geschehen soll* (Ingolstadt, 1565). By *Abfall,* " apostasy," he meant Lutheranism.

(P. Tschackert.)

Bibliography: His *Opera* were digested into a single volume, Ingolstadt, 1613, and selections are in G. T. Strobel, *Miscellaneen literarischen Inhalts*, i. 219 sqq., ii. 225 sqq., 6 vols., Nuremberg, 1778–82, and in J. G. Schellhorn, *Amœnitates historiæ ecclesiasticæ et literariæ*, i. 611 sqq., ii. 564 sqq., 2 vols., Erfurt, 1737–40, as well as in the same author's *Ergötzlichkeiten*, ii. 136 sqq., 337 sqq., 469 sqq., Ulm, 1763. Sources are the sketch by his son in the *Opera*, ut sup.; that by Strobel, *Miscellaneen*, ut sup., i. 3–4; C. Hartknoch, *Preussischen Kirchen-Historia*, pp. 295 sqq., Frankfort, 1686. Consult further: C. A. Salig, *Vollständige Historie der augsburgischen Konfession*, ii. 902 sqq., 3 vols., Halle, 1730–35; M. Töppen, *Die Gründung der Universität zu Königsberg*, passim, Königsberg, 1844; W. Möller, *Andreas Osiander*, 309 sqq., et passim, Elberfeld, 1870; P. Tschackert, *Urkundenbuch zur Reformations-Geschichte des Herzogtums Preussen*, i. 294 sqq., and vol. iii., Leipsic, 1890; *ADB*, xxxv. 457 sqq.

STARBUCK, EDWIN DILLER: Writer on the psychology of religion; b. at Bridgeport, Ind., Feb. 20, 1866. He received his education at Indiana University (B.A., 1890), Harvard University (M.A., 1895), and Clark University (Ph.D., 1897); was professor of mathematics in Vincennes University, Ind., 1891–93; assistant professor of education in Leland Stanford Jr. University, Cal., 1897–1903; professor of education in Earlham College, Ind., 1904–06; and of philosophy in the State University of Iowa since 1906. His interest for theology lies in his contributions to the psychology of religion, among which may be noted: *Psychology of Religion* (London and New York, 1899; Germ. transl., Leipsic, 1909); a series of studies on " The Child Mind and Child Religion " in *The Biblical World*, Jan., 1907–08; and on, "Reinforcement to the Pulpit from Modern Psychology " in *The Homiletic Review*, 1907–09. His theological position is that of monistic idealism.

STARCK, shtärk, **JOHANN FRIEDRICH:** German author; b. at Hildesheim (18 m. s.e. of Hanover) Oct. 10, 1680; d. at Frankfort-on-the-Main July 17, 1756. While at the University of Giessen he was greatly influenced by the hours of devotion. After being preacher at the home of the poor and orphans at Frankfort, he became deacon of the German church at Geneva, 1709–11; pastor at Sachsenhausen 1715, and at Frankfort, 1723; and member of the consistory 1742. Starck represented a mild, practical Pietism after the model of Spener, and his career of thirty years at Frankfort was marked by private meetings for devotion after the Sunday afternoon services, interest in maintaining the sacred observance of the Sabbath, the seeking of souls, and personal charity. He exerted a far-reaching influence by his numerous devotional writings. His principal work, which made his a household name in all Evangelical Germany, is *Tägliches Handbuch in guten und bösen Tagen* (4 parts, Frankfort, 1727; 6 parts, 1731; latest ed., 1907; Eng. transl., *Daily Handbook*, Philadelphia, no date). The work is composed of long prayers, introduced by a brief instruction based on a passage of Scripture to induce a devout attitude on the subject of the petition. The prayer is followed by a hymn written by Starck. Some of his sermons were published as *Sonn- und Festtags-Andachten über die Evangelien* (Reutlingen, 1854); the same *über die Episteln* (Stuttgart, 1845; Nuremberg, 1881). He was the author also of *Güldnes Schatzkästlein* (Frankfort, 1857).

(Hermann Beck.)

Bibliography: The current editions of the *Handbuch* contain a sketch. The fundamental source is the account furnished by himself in E. F. Neubauer's *Nachrichten von den jetztlebenden Theologen*, ii. 884–898, Züllichau, 1764. Consult further: J. M. H. Döring, *Die gelehrten Theologen Deutschlands*, iv. 307–311, Neustadt, 1835; E. E. Koch, *Geschichte des Kirchenlieds und Kirchengesanges*, iv. 543–549, Stuttgart, 1876; C. Grosse, *Die alten Tröster*, pp. 335–370, Hermannsburg, 1900.

STARKE, shtär'ke, **CHRISTOPH:** German exegete; b. at Freienwalde (33 m. n.e. of Berlin) Mar. 21, 1684; d. at Driesen (64 m. n.e. of Frankfort) Dec. 12, 1744. He studied at Halle, coming under the influence of Spener and Breithaupt (qq.v.); became pastor and teacher at Nennhausen near Rathenow, 1709; first preacher and military chaplain at Driesen, in 1737, where the rest of his life was passed. He wrote in German a well-known theological-homiletical commentary upon the Bible under the Latin title *Synopsis Bibliothecæ exegeticæ in V. et N. Testamentum* (9 vols., Leipsic, 1733–41). The parts on the Psalms, the writings attributed to Solomon, and the major prophets were contributed by his son, Johann Georg. See Bibles, Annotated, I., § 5.

STARS.

I. In the Old Testament: In the general mention of stars in the Bible nothing unusual appears. Men speak of their innumerability (Gen. xv. 5), brilliancy (Dan. xii. 3), lordship (Wisdom vii. 29), and height above the earth (Isa. xiv. 13); stars also figure in dream (Gen. xxxvii. 9) and prophecy (Num. xxiv. 17). Of a scientific knowledge of the stars there are no traces in the Old Testament, though Wisdom vii. 19 attributes to Solomon knowledge of the position of the stars during the course of the year; nevertheless close observation of the heavens by the Hebrews is to be assumed, especially in connection with the seasons and agriculture by way of observing the days when certain constellations either disappeared or appeared in connection with the sun. Of course the Hebrews observed the changing course of the planets, though this does not receive specific mention; Jude 13 probably refers to comets. Two planets receive specific mention, Saturn (see REMPHAN) and Venus. The latter appears in II Peter i. 19 as the announcer of the coming day, Christ appears Rev. xxii. 16 as " the bright and morning star," and receives (Rev. ii. 28) the morning star (i.e., its brilliancy) as the prize of victory, while the high priest, Simon, is compared with the morning star (Ecclus. l. 6). Venus is the symbol of a brilliant humanity (Isa. xiv. 12), where the Hebrew *helel* (or *helal*) is probably the morning star. Indeed it may also mean the moon, since its derivation from the verb *halal*, " to give light," might give rise to designation of either, but the waning moon only is visible in the morning.

1. General Conceptions in the Old Testament.

Fixed stars appear to be mentioned in Amos v. 8 (the Pleiades); Isa. xiii. 10, where the English " constellations " adequately represents the Hebrew " Orions "; Job ix. 9, the Bear or Arcturus, Orion, the Pleiades, and " the chambers of the south "; Job xxxviii. 31–32, the Pleiades, Orion, the signs of the Zodiac, and Arcturus or the Bear. Two pairs of Hebrew words occur, *kesil* and *kimah*, of which the first probably is Orion and the second the Pleiades; to this as the meaning of *kesil* the Septuagint testifies, as well as the Syriac and the Targum. The Hebrews saw in the constellation of Orion a human form, a giant chained to the heavens, and post-Biblical tradition called him Nimrod. The Septuagint also testifies to the Pleiades as the rendering of *kimah*. Bar Ali (Gesenius, *Thesaurus*, p. 665) confirms this, though he points out other meanings for the word and many Syrians understood by it Arcturus. The Talmud's use shows that *kimah* is not to be understood of a single star (cf. Job xxxviii. 31), and the conception seems frequent that the Pleiades were bound together by bonds, and were spoken of as a rosette or a nosegay, while the Talmud (in *Berachoth* 58b) speaks of the Pleiades as of 100 stars. Stern has supposed that *kimah* is Sirius, i.e., that the stars of Job ix. 9 are all in the same declination of the heavens. In that case, since *kesil* is surely Orion, the other names in the passage designate Sirius, the Hyades, and the Pleiades. Hoffmann, who in general agrees with Stern, then makes the " sweet influences " (Job xxxviii. 31) refer to the overflow of the Nile, preceded by the early rising of Sirius. But this must be rejected as impossible; no Hebrew could have understood " canst thou bind the refreshings of Sirius? " This and like interpretations are shattered on the imperative conclusion that *kimah* must mean a group of stars. The Arabic equivalent of this word means " heaps "; the Assyrian cognate *kimtu* is used for " family." Many, with the Syriac version, find mention of Orion and the Pleiades in Job xv. 27b, but this must be rejected. In Job ix. 9 and xxxviii. 32 there is mention of a constellation —Hebrew *'ash* or *'ayish*, Syriac *'iyutha*, Septuagint *Hesperos*, Vulgate *Vesper*—which is definitely identified either as the Hyades or as the chief star therein, Aldebaran, and this is confirmed by the Talmud (*Berachoth*, 58b), although the latter would also lead to an identification with Aries. The identification of this with the Great Bear, attempted by some, has practically no support. The " chambers of the south " of Job ix. 9 is probably to be explained by the many bright stars in Argo, the Cross, and the Centaur visible on the southern horizon in the regal period of Hebrew history, out of which, however, definite figures had not been made. The Hebrew *mazzaroth* of Job xxxviii. 32 is probably a scribal error for the *mazzaloth* of II Kings xxiii. 5, though it may represent a different pronunciation of the same word. It is of Assyrian origin, and denotes " position," i.e., of astral deities, and then the deities themselves. The passage in Job is best explained by thinking of the zodiacal constellations, that in Kings by the planets in general; the rendering " Hyades " offered by Stern and Hoffmann does not recommend itself, nor does the Syriac rendering " Great Bear."

2. Fixed Stars: Constellations.

The Hebrews had no clear notion of the nature of the stars; in Gen. i. 16 they are called " lights " set by God in the heavens, only in poetic literature do they appear as living beings. But that to them was ascribed a causal relation in connection with the course of nature as they arose or set may be plausibly suspected. It was a fast assumption that God was their creator (Gen. i. 14–18; Ps. viii. 3–4), that he appointed for them their rigidly appointed courses (Jer. xxxi. 35), and that they are in subjection to him (Isa. xl. 26). Expressions like that in the last-cited passage to the effect that God calls them by name do not imply that they were conceived as living beings, while Job xxxviii. 7 is only a literary figure, as is that in Judges v. 20; Isa. xxiv. 21, " the host of the high ones," has nothing to do with the stars, as there is no connection immediately between verses 22 and 23 (see SABAOTH). Prophetic declarations of par-

3. Significance of Stars for Hebrews.

ticipation of the heavenly bodies in the events of great world crises is also poetic diction or expressions which deal with fateful appearances in the heavens (e.g., Joel ii. 10). With the significance of the constellations men did not so concern themselves that there resulted a science of the stars in Israel; the references in the Old Testament to an art or science of this sort imply such among the Babylonians, however (Isa. xlvii. 13; Dan. v. 11), though in the last passage Daniel appears as leader among readers of the stars, and this shows that among the Jews of the author's times some had taken up a profession which they plied till the Middle Ages. This art of astrology flourished in Babylon, Egypt, Rome, during the Middle Ages in Christian circles, and especially among the Arabs. It was denounced by Cicero, Tacitus, and the Christian Fathers, yet flourished not only among the ignorant but even among the better informed. An event in the heavens contemporary with some mundane happening was related to the latter as cause, in the general ignorance of the course of nature. Hence astrology was by pious people not regarded as opposed to true faith in God, while it was considered also that the signs read in the heavens were given by God himself and so astrology was discriminated from Sorcery (q.v.).

The star of the Magi (Matt. ii.) was probably a conjunction, in the sign of the fish, of Jupiter and Saturn in the year of Rome 747, a coincidence which Abarbanel states was regarded by Jewish astrologers as an indication of the Messiah. Cal-
4. Hebrew culations of the appearance of definite
Star- constellations for certain countries
Worship. were made by the Babylonians. In an
assumed significance of the stars is one root of star-worship, though the two developed very differently. Even in Babylonia there was great difference between the mythological and the astrological significance of the stars. But star-worship is an old heirloom of the Semites, found among all branches. Especially was this developed in Babylonia, where the entire pantheon had relation to the stars; and this suggests that the Sumerian religion, adopted by the Semites, was largely astral, though perhaps the Semites had already developed it. It does not follow that with the Semites star-worship was the original form of their religion; even the Babylonians, whose deities were so closely related with the stars, knew that the gods and the stars were different beings. Nothing proves that the Yahweh religion of Israel had anything to do with worship of the stars. The Astarte and Baal worship apart, star-worship comes in during the late regal period. The cults which Amos denounced were idolatries of his period, not Mosaic in derivation. Before him there is no trace of this worship in Israel, and to this refer such passages as II Kings xxi. 3, 5, and the prohibition of Deut. iv. 19, xvii. 2–3. In Judah Manasseh probably introduced the cult, and Josiah attempted to destroy it (II Kings xxiii. 4–5) though it arose again (Jer. vii. 18, xix. 13).
(W. Lotz.)

II. **Star-Deities:** Actual adoration of the stars as such is not so easily established as common opinion would lead one to suppose, though that it took place

is hardly open to question. The basis of this cult was primarily the animistic conception of stars as
living beings due to the fact of their ap-
1. General parent motion, combined later with the
Aspects of assumption that they influenced the af-
Star- fairs of earth. Thus Cicero (*De natura*
Worship. *deorum*) testifies to the existence of
a belief in the divinity of the constellations. The accounts in classical mythology and poetry of the origin of constellations and stars, such as the story of the Pleiades or of Cassiopeia, are not to be mistaken for worship; they are merely the exercise of a rude philosophy attempting to account for origins or of the pleasing fancy of the poetic imagination. The comparative insignificance of star-worship is easily accounted for by the vast number of the stars, which made individualization (one of the first steps to worship) difficult except in the case of the planets which, by their motion, seemed to emphasize their several degrees of importance, and of a few fixed stars whose superior brilliance marked them out or whose position made them remarkable, such as Sirius and the North Star.

What closely resembled star-worship and perhaps involved it existed in Babylonia. Indeed the ideograph for star is the sign of deity thrice repeated (cf. P. Jensen, *Kosmologie der Babylonier*, pp. 43–
44, Strasburg, 1890). In the Marduk
2. In Baby- cycle of myths that deity is said to have
lonia. set the courses of the planets and to
have assigned guardianship of them to certain deities (cf. translation of part of a tablet accessible in *DB*, i. 191). Thus he himself assumed as his charge Jupiter, gave Venus to Ishtar (Ishtar was also associated with Sirius), Saturn to Ninib, Mars to Nergal, and Mercury to Nebo. These deities, possibly as representative of the planets, are characteristically pictured as riding on certain animals, some of them mythological, and in this form received homage (such a representation is easily accessible in A. Jeremias, *Das alte Testament im Lichte des alten Orients*, fig. 5, p. 11, Leipsic, 1906). This order of assignment was not universal in Babylonia, since both Nergal and Kaiwan are known to have been associated with Saturn, and Ninib and Nergal with Mars, while a deity Gud-bir had Jupiter. Marduk, Ninib, and Nergal, with Shamash, are in another relation regarded as representing the sun and controlling it at critical points of its diurnal and annual motions. Similarly, and perhaps consequently, Jupiter, Mars, Mercury, and Saturn took the same prominence in their nightly places as the sun in its corresponding positions, and were compared with that body in its relative importance. The Pleiades (*Sibitti*, "the Seven") were worshiped in Babylonia, and the name occurs in incantation texts as that of a group of demons (Schrader, *KAT*, pp. 413, 459), possibly represented in Canaan by Beersheba; in this case the word is wrongly etymologized as "well of swearing" (Gen. xxi. 30, xxxi. 33). The sun, moon, and Venus were thought of as in control of the zodiacal signs, and so of all the influences that effect on the earth increase and decay, light and darkness, cold and heat, life and death.

In Egypt star-worship was, in historical times,

not that of the star itself but of the divinity conceived as animating it. That this is a developed conception is at once evident, and points to the earlier belief in the life and divinity of the heavenly body itself. The fact of

3. In Egypt. a certain type of star-worship is established by the figuring of the deities of Jupiter, Saturn, Mercury, Mars, and Venus as mounted on their boats (this fixes their divine character, as it is the Egyptian method of representing the journeyings of the gods and corresponds to the Babylonian method referred to above, where deities are riding various animals), and making their progress under the guidance of Orion and Sirius (E. Lefébure, *Les Hypogees royaux de Thebes*, part 4, plate xxxvi., Paris, 1886). So there was a Sothis or Isis-Sothis, the deity of Sirius or the Dog Star. But the notice of such divinities is rare, and invocation of them is not frequent.

In China among the objects of imperial worship at the capital are the Pleiades, the five planets, and the constellations, as well as the starry

4. China and Japan. heavens as a whole. The high ceremonies of this worship take place at the winter solstice at the Temple of Heaven situated in the southern part of the Chinese city of Peking. There are tablets to the souls of these bodies, as well as to the sun and the moon, which last are included in the worship. In the common or popular religion these bodies have either a far less prominent place or none at all, though certain heavenly bodies which superstition connects with wind and rain receive special attention. These bodies are supposed to be the agents of the Yin and the Yang, the male and female elements of the universe. The star-cult in Japan, so far as early testimony (the *Nihongi*) is concerned, is confined to the star-deity Amatsu mike hoshi (" dread star of heaven ") or Ame no Kagase wo (" scarecrow male of heaven "), a malignant god who was vanquished in the cosmic battle between forces malign and benign (for control of man), and to Vega and the North Star, whose worship came from China (W. G. Aston, *Shinto*, p. 142, London and New York, 1905). The worship of the malign deity was probably avertive. Similarly in India the worship of Saturn is that of a malignant and dreaded deity, who is propitiated by sacrifice.

The indications of star-worship among primitive peoples are elusive and unsatisfactory, and the most that can be said with certainty is that much of the material is rather that of folk-lore and mythology than of ritual. Yet it may be noted, for example, that the Berbers offer worship to Venus, the Pleiades, Orion, the Great Bear, and the Little Bear. For some details of folk-lore, cf. J. G. Frazer, *Golden Bough*, ii. 19 sqq. (London, 1900).

GEO. W. GILMORE.

BIBLIOGRAPHY: J. G. Rohde, *Versuch über das Alter des Tierkreises und den Ursprung der Sternbilder*, Breslau, 1809; M. A. Stern, in *Zeitschrift für Wissenschaft und Leben des Judentums*, iii (1864–65), 258–276; E. von Bunsen, *Einheit der Religion*, Berlin, 1870; idem, *Die Plejaden und der Tierkreis*, ib. 1879; G. Hoffmann, in *ZATW*, iii (1883), 107–110; C. Ploix, *La Nature des dieux*, Paris, 1888; P. Jensen, *Kosmologie der Babylonier*, Strasburg, 1890; R. H. Allen, *Star-Names and Their Meanings*, New York, 1899; R. Brown, *Researches into the Origin of the Primitive Constellations of the Greeks, Phœnicians, and Babylonians*, 2 vols., London, 1900; C. Thomson, *Reports of the Magicians and Astrologers of Nineveh and Babylon*, London, 1900; F. Hommel, *Der Gestirndienst der alten Araber und die altisraelitische Ueberlieferung*, Munich, 1901; L. Frobenius, *Das Zeitalter des Sonnengottes*, vol. i., Berlin, 1904; G. Schiaparelli, *Astronomy in the Old Testament*, chaps. iii.–v., London, 1905; A. Jeremias, *Das alte Testament im Lichte des alten Orients*, 2d ed., Leipsic, 1906; idem, *Das Alter der babylonischen Astronomie*, Leipsic, 1908; F. Wilke, *Die astralmythologische Weltanschauung und das Alte Testament*, Lichterfelde, 1907; H. Grimme, *Das israelitische Pfingstfest und der Plejadenkult*, Paderborn, 1907; Schrader, *KAT*, pp. 620 sqq.; Smith, *Semites*, passim; Benzinger, *Archäologie*, pp. 159, 165–166, 186, 391, et passim; *DB*, i. 191–194, iv. 613; *EB*, iii. 3354–57, iv. 4779–86; *JE*, xi. 527–528. For details of worship in separate countries recourse must be had to the literature under the articles on Arabia, Assyria, Babylonia, China, India, and the like, and to some extent to that under COMPARATIVE RELIGION.

STATION: A word having several significations in liturgical and historical theology.

1. Stations as Fasts: Fasting was a practise of the early Christians derived from Judaism, which observed Monday and Thursday (cf. Luke xvii. 12). With the early Christians these days were superseded by Wednesday and Friday. In the time of Hermas (III., v. 1) these fasts were already known as " stations," being compared with the sentry duty of soldiers (cf. Paul's frequent use of military metaphors and similes; Tertullian, " On fasting," xiv.; " On prayer," xix.; Eng. transl., *ANF*, iv. 112, iii. 687). At first optional and not a precept, the observance of stations became obligatory in the pontificate of Innocent I. (402–417). " The two stational days were also marked by meetings for worship. But these were held in different manners in different localities. In some places the liturgy, properly so called, was used; that is, the Eucharist was celebrated. This was the custom in Africa at the time of Tertullian, and at Jerusalem toward the end of the fourth century. In the Church of Alexandria, on the other hand, the station did not include the liturgy " (L. Duchesne, *Christian Worship: its Origin and Evolution*, p. 230, London, 1904). Duchesne thinks that the usage at Rome was like that of Alexandria as described by Socrates (*Hist eccl.*, V., xxii.; Eng. transl. in *NPNF*, 2 ser.; ii. 130–134). It is certain that the mysteries were not celebrated on Fridays either at Alexandria or at Rome. Nothing is known of the Wednesday service, and it was abandoned in the West, a fact which scandalized the Greek Church and became one of its grievances against the Latin Church.

The observance of stations is clearly indicated in the Gregorian Sacramentary. "The place of the station is always expressly indicated, unless the name of the saint alone is sufficient to designate the Church at which the festival was held. For instance, it was not deemed necessary to say where the station was on the days of St. Marcellus, St. Agnes, St. Sylvester, etc. But for the days of Lent, for the festival of the Holy Innocents, and for that of St. Felix of Nola, the Church is indicated. There are sometimes even two indications, when the station is preceded by a general procession. In that case the Church is denoted from which the procession starts, and that also wherein Mass is celebrated. Similar indications are given when there are several stations on the same day, or several stopping-places in a procession, as, for instance, at the festival of Christmas, on the day of the Greater Litany, and at Vespers in Easter Week" (Duchesne, *ut sup.*, pp. 122–123). Liturgical stations for Monday and Thursday were instituted later, but the early Church, with the exception of Wednesday and Friday, recognized no other station except Maundy Thursday. Saturday is sometimes erroneously called a station day, but the service for that day is really the Easter Vigil anticipated.

2. Stations of the Cross: This practise, familiar to every one who enters the Roman Catholic Church, is of modern origin. It is said that Alvar of Cordova (q.v.), upon returning from Palestine, caused various oratories to be constructed in the Convent of St. Dominic, forming " stations " where the chief incidents of the passion were portrayed. The idea was no doubt suggested by a reminiscence of the crusades, during which period indulgence was granted those who in person visited the Holy Sepulcher. The Franciscans, who were the ecclesiastical custodians of the holy places in Jerusalem, borrowed the idea and developed it into the " Road of the Cross " (*Via crucis*) with fourteen distinct stations. The practise obtained but slowly in the church. It was not until late in the seventeenth century that the stations were officially recognized by the popes—Innocent XI., 1686; Innocent XII., 1694; Benedict XIII., 1726; Clement XII., 1731. Each of the fourteen stations recalls some particular incident of the passion, but not all of them are to be found recorded in the New Testament, for example that which has to do with St. Veronica. Each station is marked by a cross which alone secures indulgence; pictures are not necessary, though they are commonly found. The fourteen stations are as follows: (1) The judgment of Pilate; (2) the taking of the cross; (3) Christ's first fall; (4) Christ's meeting with his mother; (5) The bearing of the cross by Simon of Cyrene; (6) the wiping of Christ's face with a handkerchief by St. Veronica; (7) Christ's second fall; (8) Christ's word to the women of Jerusalem, " Weep not for me "; (9) Christ's third fall; (10) Christ stripped of his garments; (11) the crucifixion; (12) Christ's death; (13) the descent from the cross; (14) the burial. An unauthorized innovation sometimes added is a fifteenth, the discovery of the true cross by St. Helena (see CROSS, INVENTION OF THE).

The stations may be within or without the church edifice. The privilege of instituting them pertains to the Franciscan Order. Bishops not belonging to this order and even simple priests, when duly authorized, may, however, establish stations of the cross within churches, but not without.

3. In French Usage: In France, until the recent dissolution of the concordat of 1801, the word " station " had a particular application. The fifteenth article of the Articles Organiques, of eighteenth Germinal, year X (1801), provided that " Solemn preachings, called sermons, and those known under the name of Stations, at Advent and Carême shall not be made save by such priests as have received special authorization of the Bishop."

JAMES WESTFALL THOMPSON.

BIBLIOGRAPHY: L. Thomassin, *Traité historique et dogmatique sur divers ponts de la discipline de l'église*, part ii., chap. 15, Paris, 1682–83; Bingham, *Origines*, XIII., ix. 2, XXI., iii.; Duchesne, ut sup.; H. Liemke, *Quadragesimal-Fasten der Kirche*, Paderborn, 1854; H. Thurston, *The Stations of the Cross, their Hist. and Purpose*, London, 1906; *DCA*, ii. 1928–29.

STATISTICS, ECCLESIASTICAL: A numerical representation of the progress and state of the Church within given periods by the collation and classification of religious data. For a long time [in Germany] the church registers furnished the principal material for all statistics, and hence it is that theologians have taken a prominent part in the development of this science. But perceiving that private studies in this respect are not sufficient, in more recent times the authorities of State and Church engage in the periodical publication of official tables, thus making possible more accurate and complete statistics. In the German Empire the quinquennial census includes also ecclesiastical data. The state church authorities make a tabulated report of their districts annually, and these are collated by a statistical committee under the German Evangelical auspices. These results are supplemented by those of societies and private labors, and official experts in empire, states, and cities, by improved methods, carry them to further results and conclusions and combine them with those pertaining to other vital interests. Statistical year-books appear also in most countries. The International Statistical Institute of London assembles every two years a special congress for the mutual promotion of statistical labors. The statistics of missions provides a comparative survey at the time being of Christianity and the non-Christian religions. Besides, denominational statistics has at the present time obtained a prominent place, not only in determining the relative losses and gains but also in the study of significant problems. Specially valuable are these methods for the unbiased tabulation of such items as theological growth and congregational offerings. An application to the concrete conditions and relations of the church life of the present has been made by P. Drews, *Evangelische Kirchenkunde*. This presents, among other results, the increase and decrease of communicants in the state churches, the ratio of baptisms to births, of sacred ceremonies to marriages, of burials to deaths, the number of members who vote for the governing board of the church, as well as conclusions from the numbers of those entering and leaving the churches.

(F. W. DIBELIUS.)

In the United States of America the decennial census now includes materials upon religious denominations, and under the general law regarding the census, dated May 23, 1850, in the censuses taken since that year the government has been approaching more nearly the idea of completeness. The publication of the special report on Religious Bodies, 1906, issued by the Department of Commerce and Labor, Bureau of the Census (2 vols., Washington, 1910) makes available to the general public the latest governmental tabulation of statistics, and affords a review almost exhaustive of all matters which are institutionally connected with religious life. Other data (annual) are furnished by the handbooks of the various denominations, in most cases these being the result of compilation by central officers or authorities in each religious body.

STAUFF, shtɑuf, **ARGULA VON (ARGULA VON GRUMBACH):** First authoress of the German Reformation; b. before 1490; d. at Zeilitzheim in Lower Franconia, 1554. She received an unusually good education; under Duke Albrecht of Bavaria (d. 1508) she became lady-in-waiting to Duchess Kunigunde, and probably while at court married Friedrich von Grumbach of Franconia. She early adopted the doctrine of Luther, with whom she was on terms of friendship after 1522, and became a zealous student of the Bible. Her first step in literary activity was induced by the condemnation of Arsacius Seehofer (q.v.). On Sept. 20, 1520, on the ground that no one else had protested against forcing Seehofer to deny the Gospel, she addressed to the rector and University of Ingolstadt a protest, which was printed and widely circulated. The religious edict of Bavaria of Mar. 5, 1522, against all Lutheranism did not change her attitude and she declared that " One must bow to authority, but concerning the Word of God neither pope, emperor, nor prince has the right to command." When she continued her literary activity, the authorities of the university would not deign to answer a woman, but requested the duke to punish her. Chancellor L. von Eck advised to depose her husband and to send her into exile. Her husband was deposed, but no further steps can be proved, while the medieval contempt of woman makes it probable that no further notice was taken of her. Although she soon ceased to write, she continued to take a lively interest in the Reformation and maintained her intercourse with the Reformers.

(T. KOLDE.)

BIBLIOGRAPHY: G. C. Rieger, *Leben der Argula von Grumbach,* Stuttgart, 1787; F. F. Lipowsky, *Argula von Grumbach,* Munich, 1801; H. A. Pistorius, *Frau Argula von Grumbach und ihr Kampf mit der Universität Ingolstadt,* Magdeburg, 1845; E. Engelhardt, *Argula von Grumbach, die bayerische Tabea,* Nuremberg, 1860; C. Prantl, in *AMA,* III. Klasse, vol. xvii.; S. Riezler, *Geschichte Bayerns,* iv. 86 sqq., Gotha, 1899; T. Kolde, in *Beiträge zur bayerischen Geschichte,* vol. xi., Erlangen, 1905.

STAUPITZ, shtɑu'pitz, **JOHANN VON:** Augustinian vicar-general and friend of Luther; d. at Salzburg (156 m. w.s.w. of Vienna) Dec. 28, 1524. He came of a noble family, but the earliest certain date in his life is that of his matriculation at Leipsic in 1485 as Johannes Stopitz de Mutterwitz, the last word of this entry appearing to give his birthplace, which may be Motterwitz near Leisnig (25 m. s.e. of Leipsic) or Moderwitz near Neustadt-on-the-Orla (24 m. s.e. of Weimar). A further notice in the university records of Leipsic mentions that Oct. 30, 1489, N. Stopitz, " Master of Arts of Cologne," was received into the faculty of arts; if this entry relates to the subject of this sketch, it implies a period of study at Cologne. In 1497 as master of arts and reader in theology he was received into the Augustinian monastery at Tübingen, where he became prior; on Oct. 29, 1498, baccalaureus biblicus, on Jan. 10, 1499, sententiarius, proceeding to licentiate and doctor in theology in 1510. His maiden essay, *Decisio questionis de ⁀udiencia misse in parochiali ec-*

clesia dominicis et festivis diebus, appeared at Tübingen Mar. 30, 1500, and in three subsequent issues there was appended a catechetical effort. By 1503 Staupitz was prior of the monastery at Munich, and openly advocated in addresses the positions taken in his first publication, in the direction of purification of monastic life, but was opposed by the Franciscan Kaspar Schatzgeyer. He was next called by Frederick the Wise to the direction of the newly founded University of Wittenberg, becoming first dean of the theological faculty; and in 1503 he was made vicar-general of the Augustine Observantist congregations in Germany. In the latter office his first care was the codification and publication of the constitution, printing it in 1504. One note in this constitution was the recommendation of Bible study. He was concerned also for the strengthening and spread of the order and for the care of the individual houses; to the rebuilding of the Wittenberg cloister he gave much attention, and received therein Martin Luther (1508), with whom he came into contact at Erfurt during one of his visitation journeys. Him Luther afterward praised as having led him into a knowledge of the grace of God, and it was Staupitz who incited Luther to aspire to the doctorate in theology.

Even after Staupitz settled in South Germany, he remained in essential concord with Wittenberg. An evidence of this is the letter of introduction given by Spalatin to Johann Lang addressed to Staupitz, in which the last-named was enthusiastically greeted as a friend of Conrad Mutian and of Reuchlin (cf. Gillert, *Der Briefwechsel des Conradus Mutianus,* i. 170, ii. 151, etc., Halle, 1890). Carlstadt opened his explanations of Augustine's *De spiritu et litera* (1519) with a preface (dated Nov. 18, 1517) in which he spoke of Staupitz as a " promoter of sincere theology and a distinguished preacher of the grace of Christ " (cf. H. Barge, *Andreas Bodenstein von Carlstadt,* i. 90 sqq., ii. 533 sqq., Leipsic, 1905). Staupitz was often engaged in long journeys of visitation to the religious houses of his order—like that of 1514, when he was in the Netherlands, and that of the summer of 1516 to the Lower Rhine and Belgium. When not on these tours of duty, he lived in Munich, Salzburg, and especially in Nuremberg, where he was in close touch with such men as Christoph Scheurl (q.v.), Hieronymus Holzschuher, Lazarus Spengler, Wilibald Pirkheimer (qq.v.), and Albrecht Dürer. Indeed, Staupitz was universally beloved. Erasmus said: " I indeed greatly admire Staupitz " (A. Horawitz, *Erasmiana,* ii. 597, Vienna, 1879).

Light is thrown upon the relations of Luther and Staupitz after 1518 by the researches of P. Kalkoff (*Forschungen zu Luthers römischem Prozess,* pp. 44 sqq., Rome, 1905). Following the direction of Leo X., in February of 1518 the promagister of the order, Gabriel Venetus, notified Staupitz that Luther had been denounced to the pope as a heretic and urged him to call Luther to account. Staupitz notified Luther of the bad impression his teaching was making; the latter on March 31 replied that the charge was unjustified and declined to alter his behavior. But Luther at Heidelberg set forth before associates of his order an explanation of his position

and promised to justify himself to the pope through
the vicar-general by a detailed exposition of his indulgence theses. Thereafter Staupitz was under
suspicion of the Curia as a follower of Luther.
Staupitz advised Luther to withdraw to a cloister
and so relieve his superiors, spiritual and temporal,
from the embarrassment he was causing them, and
later suggested a retirement to the University of
Paris. His dealing with Luther at this juncture
was not that merely of superior officer, but of friend
and like-minded thinker. He wished also to relieve
the order from the danger of sharing in Luther's
fortunes. On Aug. 20, 1520, Staupitz laid aside his
office as vicar-general.

The next activity of Staupitz came through a call
of the cardinal-bishop Matthäus Lang as court
preacher to Salzburg, but the pope required of him
a sworn statement of non-participation in Luther's
articles. Staupitz refused on the ground that he
would not take back what he had never advanced;
in this Luther with some right saw a half-lie. In
order totally to part Staupitz and Luther, Lang
made Staupitz abbot of the old wealthy Benedictine
abbey of St. Peter in Salzburg. Staupitz had now
become frightened because of the new attacks of
Luther in the matter of monastic vows and the marriage of priests, the abolishing of the mass, and the
exit of monks and nuns from the houses. In his
office as abbot he devoted himself to religious instruction and the service of souls with a singular
zeal. Two deliverances of Staupitz are of importance here. In one, of the year 1523 (printed in
C. Gärtner, *Salzburgische gelehrte Unterhandlungen*,
ii. 67–72, Salzburg, 1812), he mildly reproached
Stephan Agricola (q.v.) for opposing his subjective
opinion to the decisions of the Church. The second,
later in the same year, was sharper, and advanced
the propositions that heretics must be punished since
the sheep must be protected from the wolves, that
the adherents of Luther were by the pope's bulls
and the emperor's edicts placed in the position of
heretics, that a single proved point of heresy was
sufficient to convict, and that Agricola was guilty in
many points. On Dec. 28 Staupitz had a stroke of
apoplexy which brought him to his end.

Of his printed works the following may be named:
the *Decisio quæstionis*, ut sup.; *Von der Nachfolg-
ung des willigen Sterbens Christi* (Leipsic, 1515);
Libellus de executione œternœ prœdestinationis (ed.
Scheurl, Nuremberg, 1517); *Von der Liebe Gottes*
(Leipsic, 1518); and *Von dem heiligen christlichen
Glauben* (n.p., 1525). (O. CLEMEN.)

BIBLIOGRAPHY: The German writings of Staupitz were edited by J. K. F. Knaake, Potsdam, 1867. A life, using a
rich fund of new sources and antiquating earlier accounts
is T. Kolde's *Die deutsche Augustinerkongregation und Johann von Staupitz*, Gotha, 1879. For readers of English
the best consecutive account is in C. Ullmann, *Reformers
before the Reformation*, ii. 234–253. Further literature is
by L. Keller, *Die Reformation und die älteren Reformparteien in ihrem Zusammenhange dargestellt*, Leipsic, 1885;
idem, *Johann von Staupitz und die Anfänge der Reformation*, ib. 1888 (cf. T. Kolde in *ZKG*, vii., 1885, pp. 426
sqq.); A. Ritschl, *Die christliche Lehre von der Rechtfertigung und Versöhnung*, i. 124 sqq., 3d ed., Bonn, 1889,
Eng. transl. of earlier ed., *Critical Hist. of the Christian
Doctrine of Justification and Reconciliation*, Edinburgh,
1872; E. Favre, in *Libre Chrétien*, vi. 17–34. Valuable
periodical literature is indicated in Richardson, *Encyclopædia*, p. 1041; the reader is also directed to the litera-

ture under LUTHER, since the biographies of that Reformer
contain necessarily many references to the subject of this
sketch.

STAVE, stä've, ERIK ERIKSON: Swedish
Protestant; b. at Gustafs (a village of Dalarne)
June 10, 1857. He was educated at the University
of Upsala (1880–89), where he became privat-docent
for exegesis in 1889, and was substitute professor in
the same university for exegesis, dogmatics, and
moral theology (1892–99). In 1899 he was appointed associate professor of exegesis at Upsala,
and since the following year has been full professor
of the same subject. Since 1901 he has been editor
of the quarterly *Bibelforskaren*, and has written *Om
aposteln Pauli förhållande till Jesu historiskt lif och
lära* (Upsala, 1889); *Sjön Gennesaret och dess
närmaste omgifningar* (Stockholm, 1892); *Genom
Palestina, Minnen från en resa våren 1891* (1893);
Daniels bok översatt och i korthet förklarad (Upsala,
1894); *Ueber den Einfluss des Parsismus auf das
Judentum* (Haarlem, 1898); *Bilder från landtbe-
folkningens lif i Palestina* (Upsala, 1899); *Mat-
teus-evangeliet utlagdt för bibelläsare* (1900); *Bilder
från folkets lif i Palestina* (Stockholm, 1901); *Om
Gamla Testamentets messianska profetior* (Upsala,
1903); and *Bibliska föredrag för ungdom* (1904).

STEARNS, LEWIS FRENCH: American Congregationalist; b. at Newburyport, Mass., Mar.
10, 1847; d. at Bangor, Me., Feb. 9, 1892. He was
graduated from the College of New Jersey, Princeton,
N. J., 1867; studied at Princeton Theological Seminary, 1869–70; in the universities of Berlin and Leipsic, 1870–71; was graduated from Union Theological
Seminary, New York, 1871–72; was pastor of the
Presbyterian Church of Norwood, N. J., 1873–76;
professor of history and belles-lettres, Albion College,
Albion, Mich., 1876–79; from 1880 professor of systematic theology in the Bangor Theological Seminary. He was the author of *Evidence of Christian
Experience: Ely Lectures for 1890* (New York, 1890);
Henry Boynton Smith (1892); and the posthumous
*Present-day Theology; with biographical Sketch, by
G. L. Prentiss* (1893). Just before his death he declined on conscientious grounds a call to the chair
of systematic theology in Union Theological Seminary, New York. He was one of the most promising
of American theologians of his day.

STEARNS, OAKMAN SPRAGUE: American
Baptist; b. at Bath, Me., Oct. 20, 1817; d. in Newton Centre, Mass., Apr. 20, 1893. He was graduated
from Waterville College, Me., 1840, and from Newton Theological Institution, Mass., 1846; was instructor in Hebrew there, 1846–47; pastor at
Southbridge, Mass., 1847–54; Newark, N. J., 1854–
1855; Newton Centre, Mass., 1855–68; and from
1868 was professor of Biblical interpretation of the
Old Testament in Newton Theological Institution.
He translated Sartorius' *The Person and Work of
Christ* (Boston, 1848); was author of *A Syllabus of
the Messianic Passages in the Old Testament* (1884);
and *Introduction to the Books of the Old Testament;
with Analyses and Illustrative Literature* (1888).

STEBBINS, GEORGE COLES: Congregational
evangelist; b. at East Carlton, N. Y., Feb. 26, 1846.
He was educated at Albion Academy, Albion, N. Y.

(graduated, 1866), and after studying music in Rochester, Chicago, and Boston, was director of music in the First Baptist Church, Chicago (1870–1874). He then occupied a similar position at the Clarendon Street Baptist Church and Tremont Temple, Boston (1874–76), and was associated with D. L. Moody and I. D. Sankey in their evangelistic work (1876–99), touring Great Britain and the United States. He likewise spent a winter in India in evangelistic work with G. F. Pentecost, and in the same work has made other extensive tours in Egypt, Palestine, and Europe. Since 1880 he has been conductor of music at the Northfield Conferences, Northfield, Mass. Besides being one of the editors of *Gospel Hymns*, nos. 3–6, New York, 1877–91 (in collaboration with I. D. Sankey and J. McGranahan), and other popular collections of hymns, he has compiled *The Northfield Hymnal* (1904).

STECK, shtec, **RUDOLF:** Swiss Protestant; b. at Bern Jan. 18, 1842. He was educated at the universities of his native city, Jena, and Heidelberg, and, after being pastor at the Reformed Church in Dresden (1867–81), was appointed in 1881 to his present position of professor of New-Testament exegesis at Bern. In theology he belongs to the extreme critical school; he is a member of the Swiss Geschichtsforschende Gesellschaft. He has written *Galaterbrief, nach seiner Echtheit untersucht* (Berlin, 1888); *Die Piscatorbibel und ihre Einführung in Bern im Jahre 1684* (Bern, 1897); *Der Berner Jetzerprozess, 1507–1509* (1902); *Akten des Jetzerprozesses* (Basel, 1904; and *Die ersten Seiten der Bibel, Schöpfung, Paradies und Sündenfall, Sintflut* (Bern, 1909).

STEDINGERS, THE: Name of the inhabitants of the lowlands on both banks of the Weser near the North Sea; they were mostly Frisians who retired to these marshlands from the bishopric of Utrecht in the twelfth century. They acknowledged the territorial authority of the archbishops of Hamburg-Bremen, but actually lived in independence, withstanding the attacks of the counts of Oldenburg and of Archbishop Hartwig II. The struggle was resumed, however, with great energy by Gerhard II., one of the most prominent archbishops of Hamburg-Bremen in the thirteenth century. With the aid of his brother Hermann von der Lippe, he gathered an army in order to enforce his tithes and humiliate the peasants. On Christmas eve, 1229, in a decisive battle the peasants won a brilliant victory. In order to avenge the death of his brother and crush the Stedingers the archbishop sought the aid of the Church. He called a diocesan synod at Bremen in 1230, and charged them with heresy and contempt of the sacrament. By the bull of Pope Gregory IX. (1227–41) a crusade was preached against them, in order to carry the synodal judgment into effect. The bishops of Minden, Lübeck, and Ratzeburg, aided by the mendicant friars of North Germany, soon succeeded in gathering an army of crusaders; but the first crusade in the winter of 1232–33 failed. The Stedingers advanced to Bremen and found an important ally in Otto of Lüneburg, duke of the Guelphs. The wrath of the archbishop was only increased by these misadven-

tures. The pope now requested still other bishops, those of Paderborn, Hildesheim, Verden, Münster, and Osnabrück, to preach the crusade against the Stedingers. At his instigation also there was made a solemn compact between the archbishop and the council of Bremen (Mar., 1233) against them. In June, 1233, the second crusade was undertaken, and first against the East Stedingers. Hundreds of men under arms were slain, the captives burnt as heretics; the others, including wives and children, were reduced to submission by fire and sword, murder, spoliation, and rapine. The West Stedingers repulsed the hostile attacks, although their position became more and more desperate owing to the reduction of the East Stedingers, the failure of expected aid from Friesland to arrive, and the desertion of their ally. At the same time the number of the crusaders was increased by a fresh bull, advancing them the same indulgence and privileges as those extended to the crusaders to the Holy Land. Notwithstanding, the third crusade under the leadership of Count Burchard of Oldenburg ended with a defeat of the crusaders and the death of their leader at Treffen. The fanatical preaching of the crusade on the part of the Dominicans swept over all the low countries, and the revolting tales of heresy and superstitious horrors were exaggerated. The bull of Gregory authorizing mediation for peace came too late. The fanatic hosts of the counts of the broad lowlands, variously estimated from 10,000 to 40,000, assembled against the 2,000 Stedingers! The decisive battle took place Sunday, before Ascension Day, May 27, 1234, at Altenesch. The Stedingers were overwhelmed by numbers; few resorted to flight; most of them, including women, were slain in battle. A small remnant escaped to the Frisians, and others remained, in submission to the archbishop. The territory was divided between the archbishop and the count of Oldenburg. Six months after the battle the pope ordered a rededication of the churches and burial-places, and in 1235 the anathema upon the Stedingers was removed. In memory of the victory a special festival took place annually at Bremen, by order of the archbishop, on the Saturday before Ascension Day, until the beginning of the sixteenth century. On the six-hundredth anniversary of the battle, in 1834, there was dedicated a monument in honor of the heroic peasants.　　　　　　(A. Hauck.)

Bibliography: Sources for history are to be found in *MGH, Script.*, xvi (1859), 197–231, xxiii (1874), 83, 516, 265, xxv (1880), 504, and ib. *Deutsche Chroniken*, ii (1877), 236 sqq. The earlier accounts are superseded by H. A. Schumacher, *Die Stedinger*, Bremen, 1865. For comparison there may be consulted: F. W. Schirrmacher, *Kaiser Friedrich II.*, i. 227 sqq., Göttingen, 1859; E. Winkelmann, *Geschichte Kaiser Friedrichs II.*, ii. 437 sqq., Berlin, 1863; R. Usinger, *Deutsche-dänische Geschichte*, pp. 169 sqq., ib. 1863; G. Denio, *Geschichte des Erzbistums Bremen-Hamburg*, ii. 119 sqq., ib. 1877; J. Felten, *Gregor IX.*, p. 220, Freiburg, 1886; Hefele, *Conciliengeschichte*, v. 1018 sqq.

STEELE, ANNE: English hymn-writer; b. at Broughton (10 m. w.n.w. of Winchester), England, 1716; d. there Nov. 11, 1778. She was the daughter of a Baptist minister. Her personal sufferings are reflected in her verse, for she was always an invalid. Her *Poems on Subjects chiefly Devotional,* *by Theodosia* (2 vols., London, 1760) were reprinted, to which was added *A Third Volume Consisting of Miscellaneous Pieces in Verse and Prose* (Bristol, 1780), with a biographical preface by Dr. Caleb Evans; the profits in each case being devoted to benevolent uses. The whole were reissued at Boston, Mass., in two volumes, 1808, and again as *Hymns, Psalms, and Poems. By A. Steele. With Memoir by J. Sheppard* (London, 1863). Her hymns, to the number of sixty-five, were included in Ash and Evans's Collection, 1769, and were accordant with the best taste of that period, and remarkably adapted to public worship. Dr. Rippon (1787) used fifty-six of them, and Dobell (1806), forty-five. To probably a majority of the hymn-books published in England and America she is the largest contributor after Watts, Doddridge, and Charles Wesley. Although few of her hymns can be placed in the first rank of lyrical composition, they are full of genuine Christian feeling and are natural and pleasing. She had more elegance than force, and was less adapted to stand the test of time than her masculine rivals, though a fragment of her hymn, "Father, whate'er of earthly bliss," may last as long as anything of Watts or Doddridge.

BIBLIOGRAPHY: Besides the prefatorial memoirs noted in the text, consult the treatises on English Hymns given under HYMNOLOGY, particularly S. W. Duffield, pp. 536–538 et passim, and Julian, *Dictionary*, pp. 1089–90; also *DNB*, liv. 128–129.

STEELE, DANIEL: Methodist Episcopalian; b. at Windham, N. Y., Oct. 5, 1824. He was educated at Wesleyan University (A.B., 1848), where he was a tutor from 1848 to 1850. He then held pastorates of his denomination in various cities in Massachusetts until 1862, when he was appointed professor in Genesee College, Lima, N. Y., a position which he occupied until 1871. In 1872 he was elected first president of Syracuse University, while from 1884 to 1893, when he retired from active life, he was professor in the School of Theology of Boston University. He has written a *Commentary on Joshua* (New York, 1873); *Binney's Theological Compend Improved* (1874); *Love Enthroned* (1875); *Milestone Papers* (1878); *Commentary on Leviticus and Numbers* (1891); *Half Hours with St. Paul* (1895); *Defense of Christian Perfection* (1896); *Gospel of the Comforter* (Chicago, 1897); *Jesus Exultant* (1899); *A Substitute for Holiness, or Antinomianism Revived* (1899); and *Half Hours With St. John's Epistles* (1901).

STEELE, DAVID: Reformed Presbyterian; b. near Londonderry, Ireland, Oct. 20, 1827; d. at Philadelphia June 15, 1906. He was educated at Miami University, Miami, O. (A.B., 1857), where he was professor of Greek in 1858–59. He was licensed to preach in 1860 and ordained the following year (1861), after which he was pastor of the Fourth Reformed Presbyterian Church, Philadelphia, until his death. From 1863 to 1875 he was professor of Greek, Hebrew, and pastoral theology in the Theological Seminary of the Reformed Presbyterian Church, Philadelphia, and after 1875 was professor of doctrinal theology in the same institution, thus filling a pastorate of forty-five years in one church and occupying chairs in a single institution for forty-

three years. From 1867 to 1877 he edited *The Reformed Presbyterian Advocate*, and published several sermons and addresses, and a *History of the Reformed Presbyterian Church in North America* (in the *Journal* of the Presbyterian Historical Society, 1898).

STEENSTRA, stên'strä, **PETER HENRY:** Protestant Episcopalian; b. near Franeker, Friesland, Holland, Jan. 24, 1833; d. at Robbinston, Me., Apr. 27, 1911. He was educated at Shurtleff College, Upper Alton, Ill. (A.B., 1858), and entered the Baptist ministry, but became a Protestant Episcopalian in 1864 and was rector of Grace Church, Newton, Mass. In 1868 he was appointed professor of Hebrew and Old- and New-Testament exegesis in the Episcopal Divinity School, Cambridge, Mass., and was professor of Hebrew literature and interpretation of the Old Testament in the same institution, 1883–1907, when he became emeritus. Besides translating and editing Judges and Ruth in the American edition of Lange's *Commentary* (New York, 1872), he wrote *The Being of God as Unity and Trinity* (Boston, 1891).

STEIGER, stai'ger, **WILHELM:** Swiss theologian; b. at Flawil (15 m. w. of St. Gall), Switzerland, Feb. 9, 1809; d. at Geneva Jan. 9, 1836. He studied theology at Tübingen and Halle, where he opposed the rationalistic tendency. Returning to Switzerland in 1828, he was ordained at Aarau, and corresponded for the church periodical of E. W. Hengstenberg at Berlin, whither he repaired, 1829, as collaborator. In its columns appeared, anonymously, the noted brochure, *Bemerkungen über die hallesche Streitsache und die Frage ob die evangelischen Regierungen gegen den Rationalismus einzuschreiten haben* (Leipsic, 1830). This was followed by his first book, *Kritik des Rationalismus in Wegscheiders Dogmatik* (Berlin, 1830). In Biblical work he wrote an excellent commentary on I Peter (1832), and at the same time was called as professor of New-Testament exegesis to Geneva. There he began to publish with H. A. C. Haevernick (q.v.) a journal, *Mélanges de théologie réformée* (1833–34), and commenced his commentaries on the Pauline Epistles, but on account of his untimely death was able to finish only the first volume, on Colossians (Erlangen, 1835). (K. F. STEIGER†.)

STEIN, stain, **FRANZ JOSEPH VON:** German Roman Catholic; b. at Amorbach (33 m. s.e. of Darmstadt), Bavaria, Apr. 4, 1832. He was educated at the University of Würzburg (D.D., 1859), and was ordained to the priesthood in 1855. After being a curate at Hilders, Heidingsfeld, and Schweinfurt, he was instructor in religion at the gymnasium in Würzburg 1860–65, and was then appointed associate professor of moral theology at the university of the same city, where he was full professor of moral and pastoral theology in 1871–1878 and rector magnificus in 1875–76. In 1878 he was consecrated bishop of Würzburg, and in 1897 was enthroned archbishop of Munich and Freising. He has written *Historisch-kritische Darstellung der pathologischen Moralprinzipien* (Vienna, 1871) and *Studien über die Hesychasten des vierzehnten Jahrhunderts* (1874).

STEINBECK, stain'bec, **FRANZ ALBERT JO-
HANNES:** Lutheran; b. at Potsdam (17 m. s.w.
of Berlin) Aug. 6, 1873. He received his education
at the Kloster Gymnasium at Magdeburg, and at
the universities of Erlangen and Berlin; he was
then a private tutor at Rome and Potsdam; served
as inspector and next as assistant preacher at the
cathedral in Berlin; was pastor at Erfurt, 1903–08;
he then became extraordinary professor of practical
theology in the University of Greifswald. He has
published *Das Verhältnis von Theologie und Erkennt-
nis-Theorieen* (Leipsic, 1898); *Das göttliche Selbstbewusstsein Jesu nach dem Zeugnis der Synoptiker.
Eine Untersuchung zur Christologie* (1908); and
*Der Konfirmandenunterricht nach Stoffwahl, Charak-
ter und Aufbau* (1909).

STEINDORFF, stain'dörf, **GEORG:** Egyptologist; b. at Dessau Nov. 12, 1861. He was
educated at the universities of Berlin and Göttingen
(Ph.D., 1884), and was in Berlin from 1885 to 1893
as an assistant at the Royal Museum, being also
privat-docent for Egyptology at the university
in 1890–93. In 1893 he was called to Leipsic as
associate professor of the same subject, becoming
honorary professor in 1900 and being appointed
to his present position of full professor in 1904. He
has made extensive travels and excavations in
Egypt, and in 1904 delivered a course of lectures in
the United States under the auspices of the American Committee for Lectures on the History of Religions. Besides editing the German translation
of G. Maspero's *L'Archéologie égyptienne* (Leipsic,
1889); G. Eber's *Aegyptische Studien und Verwand-
tes* (Stuttgart, 1899); Baedeker's *Ægypten* (Leipsic,
1901); and *Urkunden des ägyptischen Altertums*
(1904 sqq.); he has written *Koptische Grammatik* (Berlin, 1894); *Grabfunde des mittleren Reichs
in den königlichen Museen zu Berlin* (2 vols., 1897–
1901); *Die Apokalypse des Elias, eine unbekannte
Apokalypse und Bruchstücke der Sophonias-Apoka-
lypse* (Leipsic, 1898); *Die Blüthezeit des Pharaonen-
reiches* (Bielefeld, 1900); *Durch die libysche Wüste
zur Amonsoase* (1905); and *The Religion of the
Ancient Egyptians* (New York, 1905). He is also
editor of the *Urkunden des ägyptischen Altertums*
(1904–08), and of the *Zeitschrift für ägyptische
Sprache und Altertumskunde* (in collaboration with
A. Erman).

STEINHOFER, stain'hō-fer, **MAXIMILIAN
FRIEDRICH CHRISTOPH:** German theologian;
b. at Owen (18 m. s.e. of Stuttgart) Jan. 16, 1706;
d. at Weinsberg (27 m. n. of Stuttgart) Feb. 11,
1761. After studying theology at Tübingen, he
visited Herrnhut and met Count Zinzendorf (q.v.),
who secured his appointment as court chaplain to
the count of Reuss at Ebersdorf. He entered with
his congregation the fellowship of the Unity of the
Brethren in 1746, but after two years retired from
it and returned to Württemberg, where he occupied
various pastoral fields. Steinhofer had a remarkably impressive and pious personality. He belonged to the Württemberg school of Biblical
theology. His aim was to enrich and deepen the
Christian knowledge of redemption, and his interpretation of Scripture was conveyed with a warm

pietistic spirit. His works are commentaries on
Hebrews (Schleiz, 1743 and 1746), Colossians (Frank-
fort, 1751), and I John (Tübingen, 1762); *Tägliche
Nahrung des Glaubens nach den wichtigsten Schrift-
stellen aus dem Leben Jesu in 83 Reden* (1764); re-
issued, with autobiography, Ludwigsburg, 1859);
*Evangelischer Glaubensgrund in Predigten für alle
Sonn-, Fest- und Feiertage* (1753); *Evangelischer
Glaubensgrund in der heilsamen Erkenntniss der
Leiden Jesu Christi* (Tübingen, 1759); *Christliche
Reden nach den Zeugnissen des Briefs Pauli an die
Römer* (1851); *Christologie* (Nuremberg, 1797);
and *Die Haushaltung des dreieinigen Gottes* (Tü-
bingen, 1761). (HERMANN BECK.)

BIBLIOGRAPHY: Besides the autobiography in the *Tägliche
Nahrung*, ut sup., consult: C. Grosse, *Die alten Tröster*, pp.
461–468, Hermannsburg, 1900; A. Knapp, *Altwürttem-
bergische Charaktere*, Stuttgart, 1870.

STEINHUBER, stain'hū-ber, **ANDREAS:** Jesuit
and cardinal; b. at Uttlau (15 m. s.w. of Passau),
Bavaria, Nov. 11, 1825; d. in Rome Oct. 15, 1907.
He studied first at Passau, then in the Collegia
Germanica in Rome (1845–54), fitting himself for
the priesthood. Having returned to Bavaria he
was a secular priest, and as such catechist to the
children of Duke Maximilian. In 1854 he entered
the Society of Jesus, taught philosophy, then
theology, in the University of Innsbruck, but from
1867 to 1880 was rector of the Collegia Germanica
in Rome. He then became consultant to the Propaganda and Inquisition. In 1894 Leo XIII. made
him a cardinal deacon, with the title St. Agatha in
Suburra; and called him to the prefecture of the
Index. He exerted great influence during the latter
part of the pontificate of Leo XIII. and under the
present pope. He was sternly opposed to the ideas
comprehended under Modernism (q.v.) and urged
the pope to issue his encyclical *Pascendi dominici
gregis* (Sept. 8, 1907) condemnatory of it. His
principal publication is *Geschichte des Collegium
Germanicum-Hungaricum in Rom* (2 vols., Freiburg,
1895).

STEINMEYER, stain'mai-er, **FRANZ KARL
LUDWIG:** German Evangelical theologian; b.
at Beeskow (43 m. s.e. of Berlin) Nov. 15, 1811;
d. at Berlin Feb. 5, 1900. In 1830 he entered the
University of Berlin where he came into close personal contact with Neander and was influenced by
Schleiermacher's preaching. In 1835 at the Seminar
at Wittenberg he was permanently won by Richard
Rothe (q.v.); he was assistant preacher in the same
institution, 1837–40; and in 1840 accepted a call
as preacher and teacher to the military academy in
Kulm; in 1843 he became preacher in Nowawes,
a colony of Bohemian weavers near Potsdam. In
1848 he established himself as privat-docent at the
University of Berlin, and in the following year became also first preacher of the Charité, the famous
hospital of Berlin. Here his extraordinary gifts of
preaching showed themselves for the first time, and a
select congregation gathered under his pulpit. In
1852 he was called as professor to Breslau where
he taught exegesis and dogmatics; in 1854 he accepted a call to Bonn as professor of practical
theology and preacher to the university, and in
1858 removed to Berlin as professor of the New

Testament and of practical theology and preacher to the university. Steinmeyer is important in the history of preaching. He is the representative of a strictly synthetic method which stands in closest connection with his ritualistic ideal. Starting from the idea of Schleiermacher, he regarded the sermon as that part of the divine service the function of which is to elevate the devotion of the worshiping congregation to adoration. Of his works may be mentioned: *Beiträge zum Schriftverständnis in Predigten* (4 vols., 2d ed., Berlin 1859–66); *Apologetische Beiträge* (4 vols., 1866–73); *Beiträge zur praktischen Theologie* (5 vols., 1874–79); *Beiträge zur Christologie* (3 parts, 1880–82); *Die Wundertaten des Herrn* (1884); *Die Parabeln des Herrn* (1884); *Die Rede des Herrn auf dem Berge* (1885); *Das hohepriesterliche Gebet* (1886); *Beiträge zum Verständnis des Johanneischen Evangeliums* (8 parts, 1886–93); *Studien über den Brief des Paulus an die Römer* (2 parts, 1894–95). After his death several collections of sermons and his lectures on homiletics appeared, ed. Reyländer (Leipsic, 1901).

(G. KAWERAU.)

BIBLIOGRAPHY: E. Haupt, in *Halte was du hast*, vol. xxiii.; L. Schultze, in *Evangelische Kirchenzeitung*, 1901, pp. 97 sqq., and in *Biographisches Jahrbuch*, v (1903), 345 sqq.; J. Bauer, in *Monatsschrift für die kirchliche Praxis*, 1903, pp. 405 sqq., 444 sqq.

STEITZ, staits, GEORG EDUARD: German theologian; b. at Frankfort-on-the-Main July 25, 1810; d. there Jan. 19, 1879. He studied at Tübingen, 1829–31, and at Bonn, 1831–33; taught in his native city, 1833–42; was pastor at Sachsenhausen and Frankfort, 1842–79, and member of the consistory from 1873. He wrote *Das römische Busssakrament* (Frankfort, 1854); and *Die Privatbeichte und Privatabsolution der lutherischen Kirche aus den Quellen des XVI. Jahrhunderts aus Luthers Schriften und den alten Kirchenordnungen dargestellt* (1854).

(H. DECHENT.)

BIBLIOGRAPHY: Jung und Dechent, *Zur Erinnerung an . . . Eduard Steitz. Zwei Reden*, Frankfort, 1879.

STELLHORN, FREDERICK WILLIAM: Lutheran; b. at Brüninghorstedt, Hanover, Germany, Oct. 2, 1841. He was educated at Concordia College, Fort Wayne, Ind. (A.B., 1862), and Concordia Seminary, St. Louis, Mo. (1865); was pastor at St. Louis, Mo. (1865–67), and in DeKalb County, Ind., until 1869. He has held professorships in Northwestern University, Watertown, Wis. (1869–74), and Concordia College (1874–81), and has been professor of theology and German in Capital University since 1881. In 1894 he was appointed president of the university and served until 1900, and since 1903 has been dean of the theological seminary attached to the same institution. In theology he is a very conservative Lutheran. He was editor of the *Lutherische Kirchenzeitung* (Columbus, O.), from 1881 to 1898, except for a very brief intermission, and has edited the *Theologische Zeitblätter* since 1882. He is the author of *Kurzgefasstes Wörterbuch zum griechischen Neuen Testament* (Leipsic, 1886); *A Brief Commentary on the Four Gospels for Study and Devotion* (Columbus, O., 1891); *Annotations on the Acts of the Apostles* (New York, 1896); *The Error of Modern Missouri* (Columbus, 1897); *Die Pastoralbriefe Pauli übersetzt und erklärt* (Gütersloh, 1899); and a commentary on Romans (1899).

STELZLE, stels′le, CHARLES: Presbyterian; b. in New York City June 4, 1869. He was educated in the public schools of his native city and at Moody Bible Institute, Chicago (1894–95), after having been for many years a machinist. He was then pastor of Hope Chapel, Minneapolis, Minn. (1895–1897), Hope Chapel, New York City (1897–99), and Markham Memorial Church, St. Louis, Mo. (1899–1903). Since 1903 he has been superintendent of the Presbyterian Department of Church and Labor, a division of the Home Mission Board. He organized the Labor Temple in New York City in 1910. He is also director of the department of Christian sociology in the Bible Teachers' Training School, New York City. He is widely known as a lecturer and has written *The Workingman and Social Problems* (New York, 1903); *Boys of the Street: How to Win Them* (1904); *Messages to Workingmen* (1906); *Christianity's Storm Centre: Study of the Modern City* (1907); *Letters from a Workingman* (1908); *Principles of Successful Church Advertising* (1909); and *The Church and Labor* (1910).

STENNETT, JOSEPH: English hymn-writer; b. at Abingdon (6 m. s. of Oxford), England, 1663; d. at Knaphill, near Hughenden (16 m. n.e. of Reading), July 11, 1713. He received an excellent education at the grammar-school of Wallingford; settled in London as a schoolmaster in 1685; and in 1690 he was ordained pastor of a Baptist congregation in Devonshire Square, London, which he served till his death. He was the author of *Advice to the Young: or, the Reasonableness and Advantages of an early Conversion to God Demonstrated* (London, 1695); *Hymns in Commemoration of the Sufferings of . . . Jesus Christ. Composed for the Celebration of His Holy Supper* (1697; 3rd ed., with thirteen more hymns, 1709); *A Version of Solomon's Song of Songs, together with the XLVth Psalm* (1700); *An Answer to Mr. D. Russen's Book Entitul'd, " Fundamentals without a Foundation, or, a true Picture of the Anabaptists "* . . . (1704); *Hymns Composed for the Celebration of the Holy Ordinance of Baptism* (1712); also there was published *The Works of Joseph Stennett . . . . To which is prefixed some Account of his Life* (4 vols., 1731–32). Stennett was the author of the hymn " Another six days' work is done," which in the original had fourteen stanzas.

BIBLIOGRAPHY: Besides the account in the *Works*, ut sup., consult: Walter Wilson, *Hist. and Antiquities of Dissenting Churches in London*, ii. 592 sqq., 4 vols., London, 1808–14; S. W. Duffield, *English Hymns*, pp. 35–36, New York, 1886; *DNB*, liv. 150; Julian, *Hymnology*, p. 1091

STENNETT, SAMUEL: English hymnist; b. in Exeter, England, 1727; d. in London Aug. 24, 1795. In 1748 he became assistant to his father as pastor of the Baptist Church in Little Wild Street, London, and in 1758 his successor, remaining with the church till his death. He was a fine scholar, held a very prominent position among the dissenting ministers of London, enjoyed the confidence of George III.

and had John Howard for a frequent hearer and an attached friend. Stennett's works are: *Discourses on Personal Religion* (2 vols., 1769; 4th ed., Edinburgh, 1891); *Remarks on the Christian Minister's Reasons for Administering Baptism by Sprinkling or Pouring of Water* (London, 1772); *An Answer to the Christian Minister's Reasons for Baptizing Infants* (1775); *Discourses on the Parable of the Sower* (1786). His works were collected as *The Works of S. Stennett . . . With some Account of his Life and Writings by W. Jones* (3 vols., 1824). His best hymns are " On Jordan's stormy banks I stand," " Majestic sweetness sits enthroned," " 'Tis finished! so the Saviour cried."

BIBLIOGRAPHY: Besides the *Life* in the *Works*, ut sup., consult: S. W. Duffield, *English Hymns*, pp. 443–444, New York, 1886; Julian, *Hymnology*, pp. 1091–92; *DNB*, liv. 150.

STENOGRAPHY AND CHURCH HISTORY.

Stenography in Trials of Christians (§ 1).
Collections for the Acta Martyrum (§ 2).
Use by the Church Fathers (§ 3).
Use in Church Councils (§ 4).
Medieval and Modern Disuse (§ 5).

Notarii or independent (non-official) stenographers were accustomed to take down the thrilling words spoken by the early Christians in the Roman catacombs or in their examination by the magistrates. Thus they performed a great service, for these words, circulating thereafter under cover of secrecy, were instrumental toward converting those who were not yet Christians, in reviving the courage of the faint, and were no less transporting to others who were hazarding their lives that they might publicly hear some expression of their adopted creeds. Thus it was that Christ's teachings became spread to the very ends of the Roman world. Nor was this the only service rendered by stenography to the new religion. For the Church owes to the shorthand art the preservation of the Acts of the Martyrs; both those records which have been preserved intact, under the form of legal examinations concluded by a verdict, and other proceedings which for want of being stenographed, or else having been distorted in sequel to the loss of the originals, have come down augmented by tradition, and adorned with miracles, in the shape of tales and legends.

The proconsular tribunals had their special recorders, in the guise of stenographers, who were known as *exceptores*, who belonged to the *officium*, and reproduced the debates which ran their course in their hearing. As officials these are **1. Sten-** to be distinguished from the notarii, **ography in** who had no such rank. The legal ex- **Trials of** aminations, once taken down by the **Christians.** aid of shorthand notes (in a form of syllabic abbreviation), were transcribed in full, handed over to the judge, and included in the brief of the case at issue. The judicial archives (*archivum proconsulis*) became the depository of these court reports, which formed the official collection of the public records (*acta publica*) to which there is frequent reference by various writers, including Eusebius, Cyprian, Apollonius, and Jerome. These acts are precious not only because they give the family names and Christian names of the ac-

cused, together with their qualities; for whether or not the judge was acquainted with the party appearing before him, he was first expected to take official cognizance of his identity; but because they furnish certain interesting particulars about the future martyr and the proconsul's state of mind. As an example use may be made here of the dialogue between Tatian Dulas and the Governor Maximus, his examiner. Dulas says: " My God is the true God. He became man, was crucified, laid in the sepulcher; he rose again the third day; he sits at the right hand of the Father." Answers the governor: " Wretch, thou seest plainly thou hast two gods." Dulas: " Thou errest in speaking of two gods; for I adore the Trinity." Governor: " Thou hast then three? " Dulas: " I confess and adore the Trinity. I believe in the Father, I confess the Son, and I adore the Holy Ghost." Astounded by these replies, to which he can ascribe no meaning, Maximus then says to the accused: " Try to explain to me how, believing in one only God, thou canst yet proclaim three? " The record from which this passage is taken is evidently authentic; such a series of questions and answers could hardly be invented. The Christians would then seek to obtain copies of the Acts of the martyrs, and had to pay dear for them to the people of the *officium*. " It being of moment," as is stated in the Acts of Tarachus, Probus, and Andronicus, " to collect the evidence bearing on our brethren's confession, we have obtained for 200 denarii, from one of the recorders named Sabastus, the right to copy the Acts." The reading of these copies kindled the courage and increased the number of the believers. Accordingly the Roman magistrates directed their attention to the matter, and measures were more than once taken to put an end to these secret communications. When Vincent of Saragossa was examined, it was forbidden to commit the debates or proceedings of the case to writing. In the history of the martyrdom of Victor the Moor, a pagan magistrate, who distrusted the venality of his agents, took pains to insure that the " Acts " of the trial should not be distributed, or circulated abroad. " Anolinus, the proconsul, even had all the exceptores apprehended who happened to be in the palace, to satisfy himself that they were concealing no note, no writing. These men swore by the gods and the emperor's weal that they would secrete nothing of the kind. All the papers were brought forward; whereupon Anolinus had them burned in his presence by the hands of the executioner. The emperor highly approved this measure " (L. P. and E. Guenin, *Hist. de la sténographie dans l'antiquité et au moyen âge*, Paris, 1908).

In the year 92, Clement, bishop of Rome (q.v.), ordered a compilation of the first Acts of the martyrs. In 237, Bishop Anterus (q.v.) continued the work of Clement. He made a careful research of the **2. Collec-** Acts of the martyrs among compila- **tions for** tions of the exceptores and the notarii; **the Acta** which he then deposited in the custody **Martyrum.** of the fourteen churches constituting Christian Rome. In a painting of the underground cemetery of St. Calixtus, Arrenghi reports having seen Bishop Anterus represented as being surrounded by notarii, who appear to be handing him rolls or volumes carried in baskets. Prosecuted by the Prefect Maximus, Anterus paid with his life for the zeal he had displayed in collecting the materials accumulated for two centuries past by the proconsul's exceptores. His successor Fabian (q.v.) pursued the work with a new ardor. The *Liber pontificalis* [ed. Mommsen in *MGH, Gest. pont. Rom.*, i (1898), 27] mentions that this pope reenforced the seven notarii with seven subdeacons who collected the Acts intact and referred them to the deacons. He suffered martyrdom in the time of Emperor Decius (q.v.). All the bishops of Rome, for that matter, have concerned themselves with compiling the Acts that were so precious to the Christians. In a letter to a bishop of Vienne, one of the second-century bishops advises the collection thereof with no less care than the bones of the victims they describe. The Acts of the saints, as ultimately compiled by the Bollandists, form fifty-six huge folios, which were published from 1659 to 1794 (see ACTA MARTYRUM; BOLLAND, JAN, BOLLANDISTS). When finally, after 300 years of struggle, the Christians witnessed Constantine adopting Christianity and abjuring the old gods whom his defeated rival had invoked in vain, the Church in triumph had then another part to play; from a persecuted Church there arose a dominating Church, and the great men placed at its head assured to it the supremacy over civil society and over the emperors themselves.

Christianity owed too much to the spoken word and its inseparable adjunct, stenography, not to continue employing these two very powerful elements of touching the masses with practical effect; and the notarii, whose function has been shown as it existed at the outset of the struggle between the Church and the Empire, still potently aided the Christian orators in spreading their **3. Use by** doctrine. In particular, the Fathers **the Church** of the Church had stenographers in **Fathers.** their service, and in the most varied conditions [cf. Jerome's chance remark in *Epist.*, cxvii., Eng. transl., *NPNF*, 2 ser., vi. 220: " my volubility has baffled the expedients of shorthand "]; while other notarii, freely practising their profession, took down the sermons of the Fathers in churches, and sold the copies to the wealthy among the faithful who were prevented by the condition of their health or other causes from coming to hear the sacred word. These great orators were not wont to elaborate their works at leisure; their discourses were nearly always improvised, being homilies pronounced in the church before the people; and later these discourses, being collected together by the notarii, became books. They thus belong to the history of Christian preaching, and exhibit its primitive model. A text selected from the Bible and commented upon, such is the origin of all the pulpit literature of Christianity; while the constant themes of these informal efforts were the contempt of riches, charity in all its forms, the fear of the Lord, the practise of household virtues (see PREACHING, HISTORY OF). The pagan rhetoricians both shunned and disdained improvising. They would have refused to speak at length, without long preparation, before emperors and the great of this world. On the contrary, among the Christian orators, the speaker would have blushed to prepare, to refine in advance, the phrases of a homily. A Father of the Church entered the pulpit with the Gospel or the Old Testament, read a verse therefrom, and spoke as his heart and his thought inspired him. The notarii, taking down his words, reproduced them and spread them abroad to the four winds of heaven. Moreover, where would the Christian orator have found time to elaborate and polish his discourses? The bishops had not only to speak, as rhetoricians might, but they were obliged to baptize, instruct, administer the Church, govern the same, contend for its interests against princes or magistrates, against other and opposing churches; they had the poor and captive to look after, and, in critical hours, to bear all the burden of persecutions. By this very activity, this affluence of speaking and action alike, these men carried the palm over the rhetoricians. While the latter, devoid of convictions, were shutting themselves up in their schools, and laboriously fashioning their periods, the often unpolished, but ever living, word of Christian priests was despoiling them of the world.

To stenography, then, and to it alone, is owing the enormous bulk of materials, of so much use for the history of the Church, and, consequently, for the history of society, which antiquity has bequeathed us in this department of preaching and spoken discourse. One may mention Tertullian (*Opera*, Paris, 1641), Cyprian (*Opera*, ed. Baluze, Paris, 1726), Athanasius, whose " Discourses against the Gentiles," " Letters to the Bishops," " Apology against the Arians," " Exposition of the Faith," " Life of St. Anthony," and other works, fill four folio volumes (Padua, 1778), Origen, the most prolific of either sacred or profane writers, who had with him seven notarii, writing incessantly under his dictation, besides the skilled young girls who assisted him as copyists. This was the Origen of whom Jerome could say in his letter to Paula, " Who has ever managed to read all that he has written? " (Letter xxix. of the Benedictine edition, no. xxxiii. in *MPL*, xxii., cf *ANF*, vi. 46); and in fact, even the slight portion of his works transmitted to modern times fills no less than fifteen octavo volumes (Würzburg, 1780-1794). One may adduce still further Ambrose, who dictated to his stenographers day and night; and the works of Basil, which are contained in three folio volumes (Paris, 1721–30); two folio volumes are to be credited to Gregory Nazianzen (Benedictine edition, Paris, 1768–1840); thirteen folios to John Chrysostom (Benedictine edition, Paris 1718-1738); five huge folios to Jerome (Benedictine edition, Paris, 1696–1706), the sole remains of the 6,000 " volumes " which this great orator is supposed to have dictated according to Isidore of Seville (the word volume in this connection is to be taken in the sense of its antique use, whereby, for instance, each book of the Æneid, or of the work of Homer, formed a volume). The writings of Jerome afford an interesting study from the professional standpoint. They discover an intensity of animation that strikes all who have read them. Everywhere is perceived the man of utterance whose soul is diffused through his words aglow

The style is incorrect; certain expressions appear strange; the form sometimes astonishes, yet all to no purpose; for, to counterbalance this, everything is alive with intense animation, and all because of "writer's cramp," which compelled dictation; but of this surely Jerome had no good reason to complain, if it hindered him from writing himself. The fact is, while he improvised and dictated, his thought, flowing from his lips, was taken down by the notarii and immediately " translated " to their notes, or from them; and yielded a work for immortality. As touching Augustine, eleven folio volumes (Benedictine edition, Paris, 1679–1700) are necessary for accommodating that part of his works which has been transmitted, so voluble was he.

Thus, not one author of antiquity, not Aristotle or even Cicero (though he, too, was indebted immensely to stenography), has left a bulk of documents to be compared with what is supplied by most of the Church Fathers; leaving out of account the appreciable qualification that what the years have spared constitutes but a very scanty portion of those full tides of eloquence once " taken down " by the stenographers on their waxen tablets. (On the tablets cf. the work of Guénin, ut sup., and *La Revue de sténographie française*, June, 1906.)

To the shorthand art, those who concern themselves with the history of the Church are still further indebted for documents of another class. The debates of most of the councils and synods, and, in particular, those of the Synod of **4. Use in** Carthage in the year 411 (on the **Church** synod of Carthage cf. L. P. and E. **Councils.** Guénin, ut sup.; L. P. Guénin, in the *Procès verbaux* of the 8th International Congress of Stenography at Brussels, 1905; and the *Revue de sténographie française*, May and September, 1906) were preserved by stenography. The synod of St. Basil, so called because in the basilica by that name near Reims, which convened on June 17, 991, and pronounced the deposition of Arnulf, archbishop of Reims, was one of the last, if not the last, whose proceedings were thus taken down. The stenographer, in this instance, was Gerbert, who became pope under the name of Sylvester II. (q.v.).

Along with the Latin language, the shorthand notes, or a system of syllabic writing once applied to Latin, become swamped in the medieval darkness (cf. E. Guénin, *Les Notes tironiennes et la sténographie syllabique latine*, Paris, 1909); nor does the shorthand art make its appearance again until a long while afterward, and then it was **5. Medie-** based upon wholly different principles. **val and** Neither, in modern times, in France **Modern** at least, does the Church account sten- **Disuse.** ography to be so much as a very useful aid,—not to say an indispensable adjunct. Among preachers, there are some who write their sermons and recite them; others, distrusting, doubtless, their oratorical talent and maybe, too, the skill of stenographers, try to avoid the reproduction of what they utter. So in 1851 there was a formal protest against such reports of their discourses made by such eminent preachers as Lacordaire and De Ravignan: " More than ever do we see the spread of enterprises aiming, as they directly announce, to publish verbatim issues of sermons, lectures, instructions, delivered in the churches of Paris by the most celebrated preachers; and this against the express wish of these preachers, against their incontestable rights, and to the prejudice of the dignity and liberty of the sacred Word. Consequently, the priests undersigned, who more than others have had to suffer from this lamentable industry, avow that not only are they averse to these reproductions, but that the same are generally inexact, marred, and even so deformed as to compromise, in outward opinion, the purity of their orthodoxy and, to that extent, the authority of their mission. They declare, besides, that there has even been abuse of their names under cover of attributing to them entire discourses which they had not delivered, but which were the work of others, or had been drawn from works already printed.

"Independently of this declaration, which they believe it their duty to render public at once, the priests undersigned reserve to themselves the right to bring lawful action against the authors of these counterfeits, and to have recourse to that ecclesiastical authority upon which devolves the punitive control of churches; with reference to the stoppage of these unworthy abuses."   E. GUÉNIN.

Considering the amount of writing which the ordinary preacher has to produce during the year it is remarkable that so few employ any of the numerous systems of short writing which are now published. Many of these are very easily acquired and well adapted to his purpose. Shorthand is more in use in Great Britain than in America, and still more so in Germany. In America shorthand is rarely practised by preachers, but not a few in cities dictate their correspondence and their sermons to professional stenographers. But in the eighteenth century the non-conformist clergy made extensive use of the systems which had been evolved from the primitive system called *Characterie*, invented by Timothy Bright, a clergyman of the Church of England, and published in 1588. The best known of the numerous writers of modifications of Bright's system is Philip Doddridge (q.v.), who not only himself wrote Rich's system (1699) but made its learning obligatory on all the students of his academy (C. Stanford, *Philip Doddridge*, p. 78, New York, 1881).

BIBLIOGRAPHY: J. Westby-Gibson, *The Bibliography of Shorthand*, London, 1887; F. Fauvel-Gouraud, *Practical Cosmophonography*, pp. 31 sqq., New York, 1850; R. Fischer, *Die Stenographie nach Geschichte, Wesen und Bedeutung*, Leipsic, 1860; M. Levy, *Hist. of Shorthand Writing*, London, 1862; T. Anderson, *Hist. of Shorthand*, London, 1882; I. Pitman, *Hist. of Shorthand*, London, 1884; H. Moser, *Allgemeine Geschichte der Stenographie*, vol. i., Leipsic, 1889; M. Gitlbauer, *Die drei Systeme der griechischen Tachygraphie*, Vienna, 1894; K. Faulmann, *Geschichte und Litteratur der Stenographie*, Vienna, 1895; J. W. Zeibig, *Geschichte und Literatur der Geschwindschreibkunst*, new ed., Dresden, 1899; A. Cappelli, *Lexicon abbreviaturarum quæ in lapidibus, codicibus et chartis præsertim medii-ævi occurrunt*, Milan, 1899, Germ. transl., Leipsic, 1901; F. W. G. Fort, " On Old Greek Tachygraphy," in *Journal of Hellenic Studies*, xxi (1901), 238–267 (provides very full bibliography); A. Meister, *Grundriss der Geschichtswissenschaft*, chap. x., Anhang 1, pp. 124–127, Leipsic, 1906 sqq.; idem, *Die Geheimschrift im Dienste der päpstlichen Kurie*, Paderborn, 1906; A. Mentz,

Geschichte und Systeme der griechischen Tachygraphie, Berlin, 1907.

STEPHAN; FOUNDER OF THE ORDER OF GRAMMONT. See GRAMMONT, ORDER OF.

STEPHAN, stef′ān, **MARTIN, STEPHANISTS:** Lutheran, and originator of the congregation which became the nucleus of the Lutheran Missouri Synod; b. at Stramberg (130 m. n.e. of Vienna), Moravia, Aug. 13, 1777; d. in Randolph County, Illinois, Feb. 21, 1846. He was of humble parentage, and became an apprentice to a weaver. In 1798 he went to Breslau, where he soon became intimate with pietistic circles, and entered the gymnasium. From 1804 to 1809 he studied theology at Halle and Leipsic in a narrow way, but not without energy; and in 1810 was called to a church in Haber, Bohemia, then was appointed pastor of the congregation of Bohemian exiles in Dresden. He was a Lutheran of the strictest type, and his success as a preacher and an organizer was extraordinary. Though he severed his connection with the Moravian Brethren, and though the revival movement he started bore a decidedly separatistic character, his congregation grew rapidly, and gifted and serious men became devoted to him. He maintained stations all through the valley of the Mulde, sent out young missionaries whom he had educated, and found followers even in Württemberg and Baden. The separatistic tendency, however, of his work, and perhaps, also, the very success of his labor, brought him into conflict with the regular clergy of Dresden; and certain peculiarities in his personal habits and in his arrangements finally brought him into collision with the police, and he was suspended from the ministry in 1837. In the spring of 1838 the congregation for which he originally had been appointed pastor formally brought accusation against him, and in the fall he secretly left the city for Bremen, where he was joined by no less than seven hundred followers; and at the head of this congregation, " the Stephanists," he sailed for America on Nov. 18. Though his early ministerial life had been brilliant and remarkable, uncommendable qualities now became apparent that cast a blemish upon his early success and character. Before the vessel arrived at New Orleans, he had himself elected bishop and made master of the emigration-fund; and at St. Louis, where the colony stopped for two months, he gave himself up to a life of pleasure. A tract of land was finally bought at Wittenberg, Perry County, Mo.; and in Apr., 1839, the larger portion of the congregation, and the bishop, removed thither. Hardly one month elapsed, however, before new accusations came from Dresden and, as the statements made were found to be correct, he was deprived of his dignity and excommunicated. But the congregation, after passing through various vicissitudes and troubles, prospered, and became the nucleus of the " Missouri " type of High-church Lutheranism, which adheres most closely to the symbolical books, and has its headquarters in the Concordia College at St. Louis (see LUTHERANS, III., 5, § 1). His writings embrace *Der Christliche Glaube* (a collection of sermons, Dresden, 1825); *Herzlicher Zuruf an alle evangelischen Christen* (1825); and *Gaben für unsere Zeit* (Nuremberg, 1834).

BIBLIOGRAPHY: Von Polenz, *Die öffentliche Meinung und der Pastor Stephan,* Dresden, 1840; Vehse, *Die Stephan'sche Auswanderung nach America,* ib. 1840; C. Hochstetter, *Geschichte der Missouri Synode,* ib. 1885; H. E. Jacobs, in *American Church History Series,* iv. 396 sqq., 405, New York, 1893. Scattering references will be found in much of the literature under LUTHERANS.

STEPHEN: Christian protomartyr, and the first named of the seven who, according to Acts vi. 5, were appointed to take care of the poor and to " serve tables " (see DEACON, I., §§ 1–2). That Stephen was a Hellenist is not expressly declared but is probable, since the trouble described would best be relieved were Hellenists chosen to the office, and Acts vi. 9 is thus best explained. Although service of the tables was the especial function of the seven (verse 2), teaching was not excluded (verse 9). The testimonies of the apostolic and postapostolic age show that while in early times both bishops and deacons received and distributed gifts for charity, the later diaconate grew out of the office to which Stephen was elected.

But the significance of Stephen does not lie in his connection with the seven. He is the first disciple whose teaching led to a conflict with Judaism: he is the Christian protomartyr. His death was the occasion of an outbreak of persecution which led to the spread of Christianity. The report given in Acts vi. 1–viii. 3 is generally received as essentially historical, though it contains difficulties. It is not a unit, the stoning and the charges being repeated (vii. 58–59, vi. 11, 13–14); for Stephen's speech either two sources or a source edited must be supposed. Was Stephen the victim of mob law or of legal procedure? In the first case the Romans had a case against the people; in the second case the sanction of the Roman procurator was required, of which Acts knows nothing. It has been sought to parallel the death of Stephen with that of Jesus, but the parallel fails in many particulars. The charge against Stephen (Acts vi. 13–14) is that he assailed the temple service and the law, saying that Jesus would destroy the Temple and alter Mosaic customs (Acts vi. 13–14). His speech sets forth that God's activity was not restricted to a definite place or time, that Israel had always striven against God's will, persecuted the prophets, disregarded God's law and had done with Jesus as their forefathers had with Jesus's forerunners. Had Stephen really assailed Jewish institutions, he would not have been entrusted with his office as things then were. Stephen's proposition had as basis Isa. lxvi. 1; note also Jesus's declaration in John iv. 20–24, and with Acts vi. 14 cf. Mark xiv. 58, xiii. 2. The teaching of Stephen links itself with that of Jesus in its inner meaning, as when Jesus assailed the externalizing of service (Mark vii. 6 sqq.) or called the generation adulterous (Matt. xvi. 4) or demanded a higher righteousness than that of the Pharisees (Matt. v. 20), while the Jews regarded the ideas of their time as identically Mosaic. This latter was the view of the Hellenistic Jews (Acts vi. 9, ix. 29, xxi. 27–28) illustrated by Philo's declaration (*Vita Mosis,* ii. 3). If Stephen took the view of Jesus, to the Hellenist the charge would seem correct, he would seem to be changing the customs left by Moses.

Since Schneckenburger the teaching of Stephen

and that of the letter of Barnabas have been regarded as related, seeming (wrongly) to point to postapostolic times. The epithet of " uncircumcised in heart and ears " goes back upon prophetic expression, though a spiritualizing of circumcision is excluded by Acts vii. 8. Moses' law is to Stephen " lively oracles " because Stephen saw in Moses the complete antetype of Jesus, who expressed the full content of what Hebrews had possessed since Moses. In Barnabas Judaism is mere externalism, which is opposed to Christianity as the free religion of the Spirit. The representation of Barnabas is totally different from that of Stephen, especially in the significance given to Moses. Similarly in Heb. iii. 5–6 the religion of the Old Testament is the incomplete antetype of that of the New, Moses being the servant, Christ the Son. While the representation of Stephen reminds also of Philo, no connection between Philo and Stephen is to be traced.

Acts pictures Stephen as the forerunner of Paul, and as such many still regard him, although it is true only in a limited sense. In Christianity Stephen saw the divine revelation of the Old Testament; Paul, a new religion in contrast with it. Stephen saw in the law the living divine word; Paul, a mediating instrument which could not give life (Gal. iii. 17–21). The mission to the Gentiles was not within Stephen's ken; for Paul this was the essence of his apostolic call. Yet the persecutors of Stephen rightly felt that there was in his stand danger to the exclusiveness and absoluteness of the revelation to Israel, and the persecuting zeal of the Pharisaic Saul had justification therein. It is notable that against Paul practically the same charge was brought as against Stephen (cf. Acts vi. 13 with xxi. 28). The Church early began to celebrate St. Stephen's day, in general on Dec. 26, though in some places on Jan. 7. The legends regarding him are collected in Tillemont, *Mémoires* (vol. ii., Paris, 1701).   (P. FEINE.)

BIBLIOGRAPHY: The literature on the Acts (given under Luke) in the shape of commentaries and introductions discusses the literary and other features of the narrative; while works on the Apostolic Age discuss the history. Consult: F. Nitzsch, in *TSK*, 1860, pp. 479–502; F. C. Baur, *Paulus*, i. 39–62, Tübingen, 1866; W. J. Conybeare and J. S. Howson, *Life, Times and Travels of St. Paul*, i. 66–77, New York, 1869; E. Zeller, *Contents and Origin of Acts*, i. 237–246, ii. 175–176, London, 1875; F. W. Farrar, *Life and Work of St. Paul*, chap. viii., 2 vols., London, 1879 and often; W. Schmidt, *Bericht der Apostelgeschichte über Stephanus* (Programm), 1882; A. Sabatier, *The Apostle Paul*, pp. 39–46, London, 1891; K. Schmidt, *Beweis des Glaubens*, 1892, pp. 69–86; J. Weiss, in *TSK*, 1893, pp. 489–501; C. von Weizsäcker, *The Apostolic Age*, i. 62–71, New York and London, 1894; A. Hilgenfeld, in *ZWT*, 1895, pp. 384–412; A. C. McGiffert, *Apostolic Age*, pp. 78–93, New York, 1897; W. M. Ramsay, *St. Paul the Traveller*, pp. 372–377, London, 1897; Kranichfeld, in *TSK*, 1900, pp. 541–562; B. W. Bacon, in *Biblical and Semitic Studies*, pp. 211–276, New Haven, 1902; O. Pfleiderer, *Das Urchristentum*, 3d ed., Berlin, 1902, Eng. transl., *Primitive Christianity*, New York, 1906; R. Schumacher, *Der Diakon Stephanus*, Münster, 1910; Soltau, in *ZNTW*, 1903, pp. 142–150; Tillemont, *Mémoires*, ii (1701), 1–23; *KL*, xi. 771–774; *DB*, iv. 613–615; *EB*, iv. 4787–97.

STEPHEN, stī'vn: The name of nine popes.

Stephen I.: Pope May 254–Aug. 257. He was intent upon the elevation of the position of the bishops in general and of his own position as bishop of Rome in particular. After certain Spanish bishops, Basilides of Emerita and Martialis of Legio and As-

turica, had been deposed as being *libellatici* (see LAPSI), a certain Sabinus was elected bishop of Emerita. But the deposed bishops appealed to Stephen, and he fell back upon the principle advanced by Calixtus that a bishop can not be deprived of office, and would not acknowledge their deposition. He does not seem to have carried his point, however, for the Spaniards asked the advice of African Christians who confirmed the Spaniards in their position. Stephen was involved in dispute also with Cyprian of Carthage (q.v.) on the question of the baptism of heretics. Cyprian argued against the pope that converted heretics should be rebaptized, which Stephen regarded as an offense against the tradition of the Roman church, which was based on Peter and Paul (see HERETIC BAPTISM, § 1). While Stephen did not claim the position of bishop over the whole church, whose decisions were to be obeyed everywhere, as the successor of Peter he claimed to act as the representative of the Roman tradition and required unconditional obedience to it.   (A. HAUCK.)

BIBLIOGRAPHY: Sources are: *Liber pontificalis*, ed. Mommsen in *MGH, Gest. pont. Rom.*, i (1898), 33; Cyprian, *Epist.*, lxvi., lxxi (lxviii., lxxii.; Eng. transl. in *ANF*, v. 367–369, 378–379); Eusebius, *Hist. eccl.*, VIII., ii. sqq., Eng. transl. in *NPNF*, 2 ser., i. 293 sqq.; Jaffé, *Regesta*, i. 20. Consult further: J. Ernst, *Papst Stephen I. und der Ketzertaufstreit*, Mainz, 1905; J. Langen, *Geschichte der römischen Kirche*, i. 313, Gotha, 1881; Harnack, *Litteratur*, i. 410, 425, 656, ii. 2, pp. 62, 348, 356 sqq. et passim; idem, *Dogma*, ii. 87 sqq., et passim; Bower, *Popes*, i. 30–34; Platina, *Popes*, i. 52–53; Milman, *Latin Christianity*, i. 88–90; *DCB*, iv. 727–730 (valuable); and the literature under HERETIC BAPTISM.

Stephen II.: Pope 752–757. The policy of Stephen was conditioned by the relation of Rome to the Lombards. After Gregory III. had sought in vain the aid of Charles Martel against Lombardic aggression, Pope Zacharias had both maintained peace with his dangerous neighbors and had gained the objects of the papal policy without foreign aid. But his death seemed to the Lombards the opportune moment to realize their steady aim, the incorporation under their rule of the remainders of Greek dominion in Italy (see PAPAL STATES). Stephen sent an embassy to King Aistulf in order to obtain the maintenance of peace, but Aistulf summarily rejected all overtures and seems to have doubted (possibly with reason) the pope's good faith. Stephen, therefore, in 753, after failing in obtaining help from Constantinople, sought the aid of the Franks. Pippin was inclined to grant the requests of the pope, seeing that he owed much of his power to the spiritual authority of Peter's successor. At a personal meeting with the pope in Jan., 754, after considerable negotiation through embassies, Pippin agreed to conquer the exarchate of Ravenna and to deliver to the pope these territories, and to force Aistulf to renounce claim to dominion over Rome. The pope himself spoke of placing the Roman church and the Roman people under the protection of the Frankish king.

Stephen remained during the winter in St. Denis, and Pippin began to fulfil his promises by sending an embassy to Aistulf requesting him to comply with the Roman demands, but in vain. At the Frankish assemblies of Bernaco (Braisne near Soissons or Berny-Rivière in Aisne) and Carisiacus (Quierzy

near Laon) in 754 the league between the king and
the pope was ratified by the nobles, and it was
decided to send an army against the Lombards.
The pope showed his gratitude by anointing on July
28, 754, in St. Denis Pippin and his two sons kings
and patricians of Rome and binding the Franks
under menace of ban and interdict never to elect a
king except from the house of Pippin. Before the
outbreak of the war Aistulf made an attempt to
separate Pippin from Stephen, and for this purpose
in the spring of 754 sent the monk Karlmann,
brother of Pippin, who since 747 had lived in Italy,
across the Alps to remind the king of the solidarity
of the Frankish and Lombardic interests. Karlmann met his brother in Quierzy, but he came too
late. Pippin put his brother into a monastery at
Vienne, where he soon afterward died. All en-
treaties of Pippin and Stephen by other embassies
to yield peacefully were disregarded by Aistulf, for
the incorporation of Rome and Ravenna was a vital
question for the Lombardic kingdom. Here the
sword had to decide and the decision favored the
Franks. In the autumn of 754 Aistulf was forced
to make peace; he promised indemnification to the
Roman church and the surrender of Ravenna and a
number of other cities between the mountains and
the Adriatic Sea. Stephen returned to Rome victorious; but the joy of victory was short-lived.
Aistulf broke his promises, and in the winter of
755-756 marched against Rome and besieged the
pope. In order to maintain the results of the first
war of the Lombards, Pippin had to undertake a
second campaign. He was again victorious; Aistulf
now surrendered Ravenna and twenty other cities to
Stephen with a deed of donation, while Rome came
to be regarded as a province of the Frankish kingdom. The death of Aistulf (Dec., 756) delivered
Stephen from apprehension; he lived to see the
enthronement of the Frankish protégé Desiderius
(Mar., 757), and died Apr. 27, 757.   (A. HAUCK.)

BIBLIOGRAPHY: Sources are: *Liber pontificalis*, ed. L.
Duchesne, i. 440, Paris, 1886; the continuation of Frede-
gar's *Chronicon*, ed. B. Krusch, in *MGH, Script. rer.
Merov.*, ii (1888), 168–193; Jaffé, *Regesta*, i. 271–272;
Acta regum et imperatorum Karolinorum, ed. T. Sickel,
ii. 380–381, Vienna, 1868; the *Epistolæ* in Bouquet, *Recueil*, vol. v.; the *Epistolæ et decreta*, in *MPL*, vol. lxxxix.
Consult further: A. von Reumont, *Geschichte der Stadt
Rom*, ii. 113 sqq., Berlin, 1867; R. Baxmann, *Die Politik
der Päpste*, i. 233 sqq., Elberfeld, 1868; P. Genelin, *Die
Schenkungsversprechen und die Schenkung Pippins*, Vienna,
1880; H. Thelen, *Die Lösung der Streitfrage über die Verhandlungen Pippins mit Stephan II.*, Oberhausen, 1881;
W. Martens, *Die römische Frage unter Pippin und Karl
dem Grossen*, pp. 6 sqq., Stuttgart, 1881; idem, *Neue Erör-
terungen zur römischen Frage*, ib. 1882; idem, *Beleuchtung
der neuesten Kontroversen*, Munich, 1898; Hirsch, *Die
Schenkungen Pippins und Karls des Grossen*, Berlin, 1882;
J. Langen, *Geschichte der römischen Kirche*, ii. 649 sqq.,
Bonn, 1885; K. Lamprecht, *Die römische Frage*, Leipsic,
1889; F. Gregorovius, *Hist. of the City of Rome*, ii. 272–
304, London, 1894; G. Schnürer, *Die Entstehung des
Kirchenstaats*, Cologne, 1894; T. Lindner, *Die sogenannten
Schenkungen Pippins . . .*, Stuttgart, 1896; J. A. Ket-
terer, *Karl der Grosse und die Kirche*, Munich, 1898; H.
Lilienfein, *Die Anschauungen von Staat und Kirche*, pp. 8
sqq., Heidelberg, 1902; Hauck, *KD*, ii. 17 sqq.; Bower,
Popes, ii. 90–108; Platina, *Popes*, i. 189–192; Milman,
Latin Christianity, ii. 417–424; *DCB*, iv. 730–735. The
literature under PAPAL STATES is of primary importance
here.

Stephen III.: Pope 768–772. He was a Sicilian

by birth; under Gregory III. he came to Rome
where he entered the monastery of St. Chrysogonus.
Pope Zacharias took him into his service and consecrated him presbyter of St. Cecilia; he had close
relations also with Stephen II. and especially with
Paul I. This explains his election by the opponents
of Constantine II., which signified the intention to
adhere to the Frankish alliance. The first care of
Stephen was the entire removal of his predecessor.
Therefore he asked Pippin and his sons to send some
bishops versed in Scripture and canon law to Rome,
so that Constantine might be condemned at a synod
in their presence. When the papal legate arrived
Pippin was already dead, but his two sons met the
desire of the new pope; the intended synod was held
Apr. 12–14, 769, in the Lateran basilica in the presence of twelve Frankish bishops. The most important work of the synod was not the deposition of
Constantine, but the regulations concerning election
of popes, which was put into the hands of the clergy,
the share of laymen being restricted to acclamation
after the election and to the signature of the protocol of election. The third matter discussed at the
synod referred to the veneration of images, which
was confirmed in opposition to the Greeks (see
IMAGES AND IMAGE WORSHIP, II., § 3).

Stephen appears but a tool of the party which
elected him, unable to stop the bloodshed of the
period. The difficulties of Stephen's position arose
from his relations with the Lombards. The Roman
leaders Christophorus and Sergius had overthrown
Constantine with the aid of the Lombards; but it
immediately appeared that their interests and
those of the Lombards were not identical. The two
party leaders now openly opposed the Lombards
and became the spokesmen of the demands of the
Church. But Stephen perceived that the Roman
and Lombardic powers were too unequal for him
to venture on a rupture, unless he could oppose
Desiderius with a superior ally. Thus he turned to
the Franks. Soon after the Lateran synod he addressed a letter to Charles and Carloman in which
he asked their assistance in his attempt to enforce
the still unsatisfied claims of St. Peter from King
Desiderius. But Stephen saw that his design had
little chance of being carried out. Since the death of
Pippin the government of the Frankish empire had
lacked unity, the relations between Charles and
Carloman being strained; moreover, since Charles
had married Desiderata, the daughter of the Lombard king, the Lombardic and Frankish relations had
improved and the policy of the Franks had changed.
In the winter of 770–771 the pope came to an agreement with Desiderius. Desiderius demanded the
overthrow of the leaders of the anti-Lombardic
party, while he himself made concessions toward
satisfying the Roman demands. Christophorus
and Sergius took up arms for their defense; but
their resistance was unavailing, and Stephen was
compelled to sacrifice to his foes the men to whom
he owed his position. In consequence of the overthrow of the leaders of the Frankish party in Rome
the guidance of the papal policy fell into the hands
of Lombard partizans. Desiderius broke his
promises; yet the pope was unable to extract any
advantage from the breach between Franks and

Lombards which occurred in 770. Stephen died Sept. 24, 772.   (A. HAUCK.)

BIBLIOGRAPHY: Sources are: *Liber pontificalis*, ed. L. Duchesne, i. 468, Paris, 1886; the *Epistolæ* in Bouquet, *Recueil*, vol. v., in *MPG*, vol. xcviii., and in J. Gretser, *Volumen epistolarum*, *Opera*, vol. vi., 17 vols., Regensburg, 1734–40; Einhard's *Vita Karoli Magni*, in *MGH*, *Script.*, ii (1829), 443–463; Jaffé, *Regesta*, i. 285. Consult further: A. von Reumont, *Geschichte der Stadt Rom*, ii. 121 sqq., Berlin, 1868; R. Baxmann, *Die Politik der Päpste*, i. 262 sqq., Elberfeld, 1868; S. Abel, *Jahrbücher des fränkischen Reiches unter Karl dem Grossen*, ed. B. Simson, pp. 61 sqq., Leipsic, 1888; H. Dopffel, *Kaisertum und Papstwechsel*, pp. 15 sqq., Freiburg, 1889; F. Gregorovius, *Hist. of the City of Rome*, ii. 327–343, London, 1894; L. Duchesne, in *Revue d'hist. et de littérature religieuses*, 1896, pp. 238 sqq.; J. A. Ketterer, *Karl der Grosse und die Kirche*, pp. 19 sqq., Munich, 1898; Hefele, *Conciliengeschichte*, iii. 433 sqq., Fr. transl., iii. 2, pp. 727 sqq., Eng. transl., v. 331 sqq.; Mansi, *Concilia*, v. 680 sqq.; Bower, *Popes*, ii. 114–125; Platina, *Popes*, i. 194–198; Milman, *Latin Christianity*, ii. 433–439; *DCB*, iv. 735–738; and the literature under CHARLEMAGNE.

Stephen IV.: Pope 816–817. He was a Roman and of noble birth. Like that of his predecessors, his policy involved agreement with the Franks; consequently after his election he induced the Romans to swear obedience to Louis the Pious, whom in Oct., 816, he crowned emperor at Reims. On this occasion the alliance between the pope and the Frankish rulers was renewed. In Nov. he returned to Italy and died Jan. 24, or 25, 817.

         (A. HAUCK.)

BIBLIOGRAPHY: Sources are: *Liber pontificalis*, ed. L. Duchesne, ii. 49, Paris, 1892; Jaffé, *Regesta*, i. 316; J. Gretser, *Volumen epistolarum*, in *Opera*, vol. vi., 17 vols., Regensburg, 1734–40; and the *Vitæ* of Louis the Pious, in *MGH*, *Script.*, ii (1829), 585 sqq. Consult further: R. Baxmann, *Die Politik der Päpste*, i. 328, Elberfeld, 1868; J. Langen, *Geschichte der römischen Kirche*, ii. 797, Bonn, 1885; B. Simson, *Jahrbücher des fränkischen Reiches*, i. 66, Leipsic, 1874; H. Dopffel, *Kaisertum und Papstwechsel*, i. 45, Freiburg, 1889; F. Gregorovius, *Hist. of the City of Rome*, iii. 33–45, London, 1895; Bower, *Popes*, ii. 192–193; Platina, *Popes*, i. 209–210; Milman, *Latin Christianity*, ii. 518–519; Mann, *Popes*, v. 111–121.

Stephen V.: Pope 885–891. This pope lived in a period of decline of the Roman bishopric. In the negotiations with Emperor Basil and his son Leo VI. concerning Photius he adhered to the Roman standpoint; not to him, however, but to Emperor Leo was it due that the decision of Rome was finally acknowledged. In the policy toward the newly founded Slavonic church he followed his predecessors, aiming on the one side to preserve the connection of that church with Rome, on the other side to concede to it only a small measure of independence. But in the relations to the occident he was powerless. The decline of the empire under Charles the Fat had an immediate influence upon the papacy and the Church. After the deposition of Charles in Nov., 887, began the period of the less powerful rulers, on whom the popes became more and more dependent. Stephen died on Sept. 14, 891, having previously crowned one of these kings, Guido of Spoleto, emperor, Feb. 21, 891.

         (A. HAUCK.)

BIBLIOGRAPHY: Sources are: *Liber pontificalis*, ed. L. Duchesne, ii. 191, Paris, 1892; fragments of documents, ed. P. Ewald, in *NA*, v. 399; Jaffé, *Regesta*, i. 427; J. M. Watterich, *Romanorum pontificum . . . vitæ*, i. 83, Leipsic, 1862; and the *Epistolæ* in Bouquet, *Recueil*, vol. ix.

Consult further: A. von Reumont, *Geschichte der Stadt Rom*, ii. 218 sqq., Berlin, 1868; R. Baxmann, *Die Politik der Päpste*, ii. 62 sqq., Elberfeld, 1869; E. Dümmler, *Geschichte des ostfränkischen Reiches*, iii. 248 sqq., Leipsic, 1888; H. Dopffel, *Kaisertum und Papstwechsel*, pp. 152–153, Freiburg, 1889; J. Langen, *Geschichte der römischen Kirche*, iii. 280 sqq., Bonn, 1892; F. Gregorovius, *Hist. of the City of Rome*, iii. 208–215, London, 1895; Bower, *Popes*, ii. 294–296; Platina, *Popes*, i. 235–236; Milman, *Latin Christianity*, iii. 105; Mann, *Popes*, vi. 367–402 et passim.

Stephen VI.: Pope 896–897. After the death of Formosus, who had crowned Arnulf emperor, the faction of Spoleto elected a pope of their own party, Stephen VI., the short pontificate of Boniface VI. alone intervening. Stephen's consecration took place probably in May, 896. He was one of the most violent opponents of Formosus. His short pontificate is disgraced by his unheard-of judgment upon Formosus after his death (see FORMOSUS). The horror aroused by this outrage led to a sudden uprising of the people (July, 897) on which occasion Stephen was murdered.   (A. HAUCK.)

BIBLIOGRAPHY: Sources are: *Liber pontificalis*, ed. L. Duchesne, ii., pp. xviii., 229, Paris, 1892; Jaffé, *Regesta*, i. 439; J. M. Watterich, *Pontificum Romanorum . . . vitæ*, i. 35 sqq., Leipsic, 1862; the *Epistolæ*, in Bouquet, *Recueil*, vol. ix.; and the *Epistolæ et privilegia* in *MPL*, vol. cxxix. Consult further: Mann, *Popes*, vii. 76 sqq.; E. Dümmler, *Auxilius und Vulgarius*, pp. 10 sqq., Leipsic, 1866; idem, *Geschichte des ostfränkischen Reiches*, iii. 426, ib. 1888; A. von Reumont, *Geschichte der Stadt Rom*, ii. 224, Berlin, 1868; R. Baxmann, *Die Politik der Päpste*, ii. 70, Elberfeld, 1869; H. Dopffel, *Kaisertum und Papstwechsel*, p. 157, Freiburg, 1889; J. Langen, *Geschichte der römischen Kirche*, iii. 303, Bonn, 1892; F. Gregorovius, *Hist. of the City of Rome*, iii. 225–229, London, 1895; Bower, *Popes*, ii. 300; Platina, *Popes*, i. 237–239; Milman, *Latin Christianity*, iii. 110–111.

Stephen VII.: Pope 929–931. His pontificate fell during the time when Theodora and Marozia ruled in Rome. The pope vanished so completely into the background beside his ambitious mistresses that information concerning him is very scanty.

         (A. HAUCK.)

BIBLIOGRAPHY: *Liber pontificalis*, ed. L. Duchesne, ii. 242, Paris, 1892; J. M. Watterich, *Pontificum Romanorum . . . vitæ*, i. 33, Leipsic, 1862; Jaffé, *Regesta*, i. 453; A. von Reumont, *Geschichte der Stadt Rom*, ii. 231, 1868; R. Baxmann, *Die Politik der Päpste*, ii. 90, Elberfeld, 1869; J. Langen, *Geschichte der römischen Kirche*, iii. 333, Bonn, 1892; F. Gregorovius, *Hist. of the City of Rome*, iii. 282, London, 1895; Bower, *Popes*, ii. 311; Platina, *Popes*, i. 247–248; Mann, *Popes*, viii. 189–190.

Stephen VIII.: Pope 939–942. His pontificate was coincident with the rule of Alberich, the son of Marozia, as prince and senator of the Romans in Rome; and his importance was small compared with that of the energetic Alberich, who regarded Rome as his property. But before foreign powers Stephen upheld the claims of the papacy, threatening France and Burgundy with the ban unless they acknowledged Louis d'Outremer as king, which they were forced to do.   (A. HAUCK.)

BIBLIOGRAPHY: *Liber pontificalis*, ed. L. Duchesne, ii. 244, Paris, 1892; Jaffé, *Regesta*, i. 457; J. M. Watterich, *Pontificum Romanorum . . . vitæ*, i. 34, Leipsic, 1862; A. von Reumont, *Geschichte der Stadt Rom*, ii. 233, Berlin, 1868; R. Baxmann, *Die Politik der Päpste*, ii. 93, Elberfeld, 1869; J. Langen, *Geschichte der römischen Kirche*, iii. 333, Bonn, 1892; F. Gregorovius, *Hist. of the City of Rome*, iii. 317, London, 1895; Mann, *Popes*, ix. 209, 212 sqq., 232; Bower, *Popes*, ii. 313–314; Platina, *Popes*, i. 249–250.

Stephen IX. (Frédéric of Lorraine): Pope 1057–1058. He was one of the three sons of Duke Gozelo of Lorraine. He was educated at Liége, and became archdeacon at the church of St. Lambert. Leo IX. induced him in 1049 to go to Rome, where he became cardinal deacon, and in 1051 chancellor and librarian; in 1054 he was a member of an embassy to Constantinople, returning after the death of Leo and retiring into the monastery of Monte Cassino (1055), the abbot of which he became two years later. In the same year (1057) Victor II. died, and Frédéric was elected in his place. Since the election occurred without understanding with the widow of Henry III., it implied an open violation of the imperial rights; at the same time it showed that the reform party considered it the right time to abolish imperial control over the papacy. If this was the aim, there could have been found no more suitable person than Frédéric for the papal chair, since his brother Duke Godfrey, as husband of Marchioness Beatrix of Tuscany, possessed the chief power in Italy. But an immediate rupture with the empire was avoided. The activity of Stephen was directed in the first place to the enforcement of the law of celibacy; but more important for the future was his attitude toward the Patarenes of Milan. By not merely tolerating, but even approving, revolutionary procedures, he formed the union between the papacy and the democrats of Upper Italy which was so successful for both parties. He died at Florence Mar. 29, 1058.

(A. HAUCK.)

BIBLIOGRAPHY: *Liber pontificalis*, ed. L. Duchesne, ii. 278, 334, 356, Paris, 1892; Jaffé, *Regesta*, i. 553 sqq.; J. M. Watterich, *Pontificum Romanorum . . . vitæ*, i. 188 sqq., Leipsic, 1862; A. von Reumont, *Geschichte der Stadt Rom*, ii. 351, Berlin, 1868; R. Baxmann, *Die Politik der Päpste*, ii. 262, Elberfeld, 1869; J. Wattendorff, *Papst Stephan IX.*, Paderborn, 1883; G. Meyer von Knonau, *Jahrbücher des deutschen Reiches unter Heinrich IV. und Heinrich V.*, i. 30 sqq., Leipsic, 1890; J. Langen, *Geschichte der römischen Kirche*, iii. 494, Bonn, 1892; F. Gregorovius, *Hist. of the City of Rome*, iv. 70–111, London, 1896; Mann, *Popes*, x. 381 sqq.; Bower, *Popes*, ii. 363–365; Platina, *Popes*, i. 276–277; Milman, *Latin Christianity*, iii. 279–294; Hauck, *KD*, iii. 669 sqq.; Hefele, *Conciliengeschichte*, iv. 791.

STEPHEN BAR ẒUDHAILE (ẒUD(H)AILI or SUDAILI): Syrian mystic of the sixth century. He lived for a time in Egypt as the pupil of one John the Egyptian, and later resided at Edessa and finally at Jerusalem. He was a contemporary of Jacob of Sarug (q.v.), who addressed a letter to him, while Philoxenus (q.v.) wrote certain priests of Edessa concerning him. He is said to have taught that the punishments of hell were finite, and that baptism and the Eucharist were superfluous. He receives a special anathema in the creed of Philoxenus and in the Jacobite ordination liturgy. According to Barhebræus, Stephen was the author of a work "On the Hidden Mysteries of God," which was ascribed to Hierotheus, a disciple of St. Paul (MSS. in the British Museum and Bibliothèque Nationale, and at Berlin; the British Museum MS., *cod. Rich.* 7189, is evidently the very one used by Barhebræus). The exact relation of the work to Dionysius the Areopagite (q.v.) is not yet entirely clear. It is held by A. Merx that not only the medieval mystics of the West, but also the Mohammedan

Sufis, derived their most fruitful concepts from the Syrian mystic, Stephen bar Ẓudhaile. E. NESTLE.

BIBLIOGRAPHY: Older literature and sources are: Abulfáraj (Barhebræus), *Hist. eccl.*, i. 221; J. S. Assemani, *Bibliotheca orientalis*, i. 303, ii. 30–33, 290; J. Abbeloos, *De vita et scriptis S. Jacobi Bathnarum Sarugi episcopi*, Louvain, 1867. Consult further: A. L. Frothingham, *On the Book of Hierotheus by a Syrian Mystic of the 5th Century*, in *Proceedings of the American Oriental Society*, 1884, pp. x.–xiii.; idem, *Stephen bar Sudaili, the Syrian Mystic and the Book of Hierotheus*, Leyden, 1886 (cf. Loofs in *Theologische Literaturzeitung*, 1884, pp. 554–555, and Bäthgen in the same, 1887, no. 10); V. Ryssel, *Das "Buch des Hierotheus,"* in *ZKG*, x (1887), 156–158; A. Merx, *Die Idee und Grundlegung einer allgemeinen Geschichte der Mystik*, Heidelberg, 1893; W. Wright, *A Short Hist. of Syriac Literature*, pp. 76–77, London, 1894; R. Duval, *La Littérature syriaque*, pp. 358–360, 438, Paris, 1899; C. Brockelmann, in *Litteratur des Ostens*, vii. 2 (1907), 28.

STEPHEN DE BORBONE (DE VELLAVILLA): Dominican author; b. at Belleville (24 m. n. of Lyons) c. 1190; d. at Lyons c. 1261. He studied at the cathedral school in Mâcon and at Paris. In 1223 he was in Lyons among the Dominicans whose first settlement he had witnessed in Paris. He was zealous in his attempt to convert heretics; in Vézelay (Yonne) he preached the crusade against the Albigenses; about 1235 he labored in the diocese of Valence in Dauphiné to convert the Waldenses (q.v.) and soon afterward was entrusted with the conduct of Inquisition against them. The last years of his life he devoted to the book which made him famous, *Tractatus de diversis materiis prædicabilibus, ordinatis et distinctis in septem partes secundum septem dona Spiritus Sancti*. It was primarily intended to be used in the preparation of sermons, and was a compilation of anecdotes, illustrations, incidents, and the like, taken in part from previous compilations, in part derived from contemporaneous events in his own official life. It is of historical value as a source of knowledge of the thirteenth century.

(FERDINAND COHRS.)

BIBLIOGRAPHY: J. Quétif and J. Echard, *Scriptores ordinis prædicatorum*, i. 174 sqq., Paris, 1719; *Hist. littéraire de la France*, xix. 27 sqq.; A. Lecoy de la Marche, *La Chaire française au moyen-âge*, pp. 106 sqq., ib. 1868; idem, *Anecdotes historiques, légendes et apologues, tirés du recueil inédit d'Étienne de Bourbon*, ib. 1877; B. Hauréau, in *Journal des savants*, 1881, pp. 591 sqq., 739 sqq.; K. Müller, *Die Waldenser und ihre einzelnen Gruppen*, Gotha, 1866; *KL*, xi. 766–767.

STEPHEN HARDING. See HARDING, STEPHEN.

STEPHEN OF TOURNAI: Canonist; b. at Orléans shortly before 1130; d. at Tournai in Sept., 1203. He received his first instruction in his native city, and entered the chapter of St. Evurtius of the Congregation at St. Victor. He must have been canon and cantor as early as 1152. He then received permission to complete his studies in Bologna, where he heard Bulgarus on civil law and Rufinus on canon law. In 1167 Stephen became abbot of St. Evurtius, and ten years later abbot of St. Geneviève in Paris, belonging to the Congregation of St. Victor. In 1192 he was elected bishop of Tournai. The work, completed about 1160, that made his name famous, was his *Summa* on the *Decretum Gratiani*. It had an important influence upon ecclesiastical jurisdiction and canon law in the Middle Ages. Stephen was a gifted and enthusiastic preacher,

though his sermons betray the exaggerated rhetoric
of his time. (FERDINAND COHRS.)

BIBLIOGRAPHY: A selection of the *Opera* was published by
C. du Molinet, Paris, 1679, whence, with a supplement, it
was reproduced in *MPL*, ccxi. 295–562. His "Letters"
were first published by J. B. Masson, Paris, 1611; their are
taken into the *MPL*, ut sup.; forty of them are in Bouquet,
Recueil, xix. 282–306; and a new ed. was issued by J.
Desilve, *Lettres d'Etienne de Tournai*, Valenciennes, 1893.
Consult: F. Maassen, *Beiträge zur Geschichte der juristischen
Litteratur des Mittelalters*, Vienna, 1857; J. F. von Schulte,
Geschichte der Quellen und Litteratur des kanonischen Rechts,
i. 133 sqq., Stuttgart, 1875; L. Bourgain, *La Chaire française au xii. siècle*, Paris, 1879; H. Denifle, *Chartularium
universitatis Parisiensis*, i. 12 et passim, Paris, 1889; *Archiv
für katholisches Kirchenrecht*, lxvi (1891), 460; *Deutsche
Zeitschrift für Kirchenrecht*, III., i (1892), 252 sqq.; *KL*, xi.
770–771.

STEPHENS, ESTIENNE, STEPHANUS: The
name of a distinguished Parisian family of printers,
which did most brilliant service in the interest of
literature, and by their publications promoted the
cause of the Reformation.

1. Henry, the first printer of this name, had an
establishment of his own in Paris from 1503 to 1520.
He was on friendly terms with some of the most
learned men of the day, Budé, Briçonnet, and Faber
Stapulensis (q.v.), and had among his proof-readers
Beatus Rhenanus. Among his publications were
Faber's editions of Aristotle, the *Psalterium quin-
cuplex*, and his commentary on the Pauline Epistles.
Henry left three sons, François, Robert, and Charles.
François published a number of works (1537–47)
which had no bearing upon theology. His few impressions, chiefly issues of the classics, were all in
Latin except *Psalterium* and a *Horæ Virginis* in
Greek. **Charles** studied medicine, wrote some works
on natural history, and gained an honorable position
both as scholar and as author. In 1551 he assumed
control of the Paris printing establishment, on
Robert's departure to Geneva, and printed a number of works till 1561, using the title "royal typographer" (*typographus regius*). One of his works that
long remained an authority was a *Dictionarium
Latino-Gallicum*, 1552. He published a number of
smaller editions of Hebrew texts and targums, which
were edited by J. Mercier.

2. Robert, the second son of Henry, and the
founder of the splendid reputation which the name
of Stephens still enjoys, was born in Paris, 1503,
and died in Geneva Sept. 7, 1559. He early became
acquainted with the ancient languages, and entered
the printing-establishment of Simon de Colines, who
married his mother upon his father's death. He
corrected the edition of the Latin New Testament of
1523. This work was the first occasion of the endless
charges and criminations of the clerical party,
especially the theological faculty of the Sorbonne,
against him. In 1524 he became proprietor of the
press of his father. In 1539 he adopted as his devices
an olive branch around which a serpent was twined,
and a man standing under an olive-tree, with grafts
from which wild branches were falling to the ground,
with the words of Rom. xi. 20, *Noli altum sapere,
sed time*, "Be not high-minded, but fear." The
latter was called the olive of the Stephens family.
In 1539 he received the distinguishing title of
"Printer in Greek to the king." But the official
recognition and the crown's approval to his under-

taking could not save him from the censure and
ceaseless opposition of the divines, and in 1550, to
escape the violence of his persecutors, he emigrated
to Geneva. With his title of "royal typographer"
Robert made the Paris establishment famous by his
numerous editions of grammatical works and other
school-books (among them many of Melanchthon's),
and of old authors, as Dio Cassius, Eusebius, Cicero,
Sallust, Cæsar, Justin. Many of these, especially
the Greek editions, were famous for their typographical elegance. In 1532 he published the remarkable *Thesaurus linguæ latinæ*, and twice he published the Hebrew Bible entire—in 1539–44, thirteen
parts, in four volumes, and 1544–46 in seventeen
parts. Both of these editions are rare. Of more
importance are his four editions of the Greek New
Testament, 1546, 1549, 1550, and 1551, the last in
Geneva. The first two are among the neatest Greek
texts known, and are called *O mirificam;* the third
is a splendid masterpiece of typographical skill, and
is known as the *Editio regia;* the edition of 1551 contains the Latin translation of Erasmus and the Vulgate, is not nearly as fine as the other three, and is
exceedingly rare. It was in this edition that the
versicular division of the New Testament was for the
first time introduced (see BIBLE-TEXT, II., 2, § 2,
III., § 3). A number of editions of the Vulgate also
appeared from his presses, of which the principal
are those of 1528, 1532, 1540 (one of the ornaments
of his press), and 1546. The text of the Vulgate
was in a wretched condition, and Stephens's editions,
especially that of 1545, containing a new translation
at the side of the Vulgate, was the subject of sharp
and acrimonious criticism from the clergy. On his
arrival at Geneva, he published a defense against the
attacks of the Sorbonne. He issued the French
Bible in 1553, and many of Calvin's writings; the
finest edition of the *Institutio* being that of 1553.
His fine edition of the Latin Bible with glosses
(1556) contained the translation of the Old Testament by Santes Pagninus, and the first edition of
Beza's translation of the New Testament.

Three of Robert's sons, Henry, Robert, and
François, became celebrated as printers. **François,**
the second (b. in 1540), printed on his own account
in Geneva from 1562–82, issuing a number of
editions of the Bible in Latin and French, and some
of Calvin's works. French writers identify him with
a printer by the name of Estienne in Normandy,
whither he is supposed to have emigrated in 1582.
Robert, the second (b. in 1530; d. in 1570), began
to print in Paris on his own account in 1556, and in
1563 received the title of *Typographus regius;* his
presses were busily employed in issuing civil documents. He held to the Roman Catholic faith and
thus won the support of Charles IX., and by 1563
appears to have fully reconstituted his father's establishment in Paris. His edition of the New Testament of 1568–69 a reprint of his father's first
edition, and equal to it in elegance of execution, is
now exceedingly rare.

3. Henry, the second, the eldest son of the great
Robert, and without doubt the most distinguished
member of the family, was born in Paris, 1528, and
died at Lyons March, 1598. He displayed in his
youth a genuine enthusiasm for Greek and Latin;

and his father took special pains with his education, and, as a part of his general training, he undertook in his nineteenth year a protracted journey to Italy, England, and Flanders, where he busied himself in collecting and collating manuscripts for his father's press. In 1554 he published at Paris his first independent work, the *Anacreon*. Then he went again to Italy, helping Aldus at Venice, discovered a copy of Diodorus Siculus at Rome, and returned to Geneva in 1555. In 1557 he seems to have had a printing-establishment of his own, and, in the spirit of modern times, advertised himself as the " Parisian printer " (*typographus parisiensis*). The following year he assumed the title, *illustris viri Huldrici Fuggeri typographus*, from his patron, Fugger of Augsburg. In 1559 Henry assumed charge of his father's presses, and distinguished himself as the publisher, and also as the editor and collator, of manuscripts. Athenagoras, Aristotle, Æschylus, appeared in 1557; Diodorus Siculus, 1559; Xenophon, 1561; Thucydides, 1564; Herodotus, 1566 and 1581. He improved old translations, or made new Latin translations, of many Greek authors. His most celebrated work, the *Thesaurus linguæ græcæ*, which has served up to the nineteenth century as the basis of Greek lexicography, appeared in 4 vols., 1572, with a supplement in 2 vols. Of the Greek editions of the New Testament that went forth from his presses, there deserve mention those of Beza, with his commentary, 1565, 1569, 1582, 1588–89, and the smaller editions of 1565, 1567, 1580. A triglot containing the Peshito appeared in 1569, of which some copies are in existence, bearing the date Lyons, 1571. In 1565 a large French Bible was printed. Henry's own editions of the Greek New Testament of 1576 and 1587 are noteworthy; the former containing the first scientific treatise on the language of the apostolic writers; the latter, a discussion of the ancient divisions of the text. In 1594 he published a concordance of the New Testament, the preparatory studies for which his father had made. Much earlier he translated Calvin's catechism into Greek, which was printed in 1554 in his father's printing-room.

Henry was married three times, and had fourteen children, of whom three survived him. His son **Paul** (b. 1567), of whose life little is known, assumed control of the presses. Two of Paul's sons were printers—Joseph at La Rochelle, and Antoine (d. 1674), who became " Printer to the king " in Paris in 1613. Fronton Le Duc's *Chrysostom*, and Jean Morin's Greek Bible (3 vols., 1628) were issued from Antoine's presses. His son Henry succeeded to the title of " Printer to the king " in 1649, and his work closed about 1659. He left no children, and was the last of the family who took active interest in editing and printing. The high standard that had been established by the early Stephens was maintained to the last, and the publications of the later publishers were mainly in the division of Greek and Roman classics.

BIBLIOGRAPHY. M. Maittaire, *Stephanorum historia, vitas ipsorum ac libros complectens*, London, 1709; idem, *Hist. typographorum aliquot Parisensium*, 2 vols., ib. 1717; A. A. Renouard, *Annales de l'imprimerie des Estienne, ou hist. de la famille des Estienne et de ses éditions*, 2 parts, Paris, 1837–38; G. A. Crapelet, *Robert Estienne . . . et le roi François I.*, Paris, 1839; L. J. Feugère, *Essai sur la vie et les ouvrages de H. Estienne*, Paris, 1853; E. Frommann, *Aufsätze zur Geschichte des Buchhandels im 16. Jahrhundert*, Jena, 1876; P. Schaff, *Companion to the Greek Testament and the English Version*, pp. 236–237, 536–539, New York, 1883; F. H. Reusch, *Index der verbotenen Bücher*, i. 152, 337, 416, ii. 166, et passim, Bonn, 1885; *Nouveaux documents sur les Estienne, imprimeurs parisiens, 1517–1665*, in *Mémoires* of the Paris Society of History, vol. xxii., Paris, 1895; G. H. Putnam, *Books and their Makers during the Middle Ages*, ii. 15–100, New York, 1897; idem, *Censorship of the Church of Rome*, i. 102, 228 sqq., 296, 238, 411, ib. 1907; P. Renouard, *Imprimeurs parisiens depuis 1470 jusqu'à la fin du XVI. siècle*, Paris, 1898; A. Claudin, *Hist. de l'imprimerie en France au xv. et xvi. siècle*, Paris, 1900; L. Radigeur, *Maîtres imprimeurs et ouvriers typographes, 1470–1903*, Paris, 1903.

STEPHENS, THOMAS: English Jesuit and missionary. See INDIA, I., 4, § 2.

STERCORANISTS: The name given (from *stercus*, " excrement ") in the Middle Ages to those who might possibly hold, as a theoretical position, that the body of Christ, received in the Lord's Supper, was masticated, digested, and finally excreted. It was first mentioned as a possible error and rejected by Radbertus Paschasius (*De corpore et sanguine Domini*, xx.) in reference to the pseudo-Clementine Epistle to James, but Radbertus did not assert that it was held by his opponents. Amalarius of Metz (q.v.) left the question open whether the body of Christ was eaten and digested in a natural way, but appealed to Matt. xv. 17. Rabanus appealed to the same passage. But after the doctrine of transubstantiation had been adopted, the question concerning the natural eating of the body of Christ no longer permitted discussion. The term " Stercoranist " seems to have been used first by Cardinal Frederic of Lorraine, later Pope Stephen IX., in his *Responsio sive contradictio adversus Nicetæ Pectorati libellum*, xxii., and thence came into quite common use. **(A. HAUCK.)**

BIBLIOGRAPHY: L. d'Achery, *Spicilegium*, iii. 330, Paris, 1723; C. M. Pfaff, *De stercoranistis medii ævi*, Tübingen, 1750; J. M. Schröckh, *Kirchengeschichte*, xxiii. 429 sqq., 35 vols., Leipsic, 1772–1803; J. Bach, *Dogmengeschichte des Mittelalters*, i. 185–186, Vienna, 1873; K. Werner, *Gerbert von Aurillac*, pp. 165–166, ib. 1878; J. Schwane, *Dogmengeschichte des Mittelalters*, p. 630, Freiburg, 1882; J. Schnitzer, *Berengar von Tours*, pp. 205 sqq., Stuttgart, 1892; R. Mönchemeier, *Amalar von Metz*, pp. 108 sqq., Münster, 1893; *KL*, xi. 782–783.

STERNE, LAURENCE: Church of England, clergyman, wit, and novelist; b. at Clonmel (46 m. n.e. of Cork), Ireland, Nov. 24, 1713; d. in London Mar. 18, 1768. He was the great grandson of Richard Sterne, archbishop of York, and his father was an officer in the army, whose death in 1731 left Laurence unprovided for. Young Sterne was a student at Halifax, but was unsystematic in his work; by his uncle he was sent to Jesus College, Cambridge (B.A., 1736; M.A., 1740), where physical weakness was indicated by a hemorrhage of the lungs before he finished his studies. He was ordained deacon in 1736 and ordained priest in 1738, this step being taken on the advice of his uncle, who had sent him to college; but his tastes and temperament were not such as really to qualify him for the ministry, the work of which was probably always irksome to him. He became vicar of Sutton-in-the Forest in Yorkshire, 1738; prebend of Givendale

in York cathedral, 1740–41; commissary of Picker-
ing and Pocklington in the same year; the next
year he married Elizabeth (Eliza) Lumley, who
was possessed of a small patrimony; in 1742–43
Sterne received in addition to his other charges the
living of Stillington; he also at this time attempted
to add to his income by farming. His first publication was a charity sermon (York, 1747). A second
commissaryship was awarded him in 1747, and a
claim by another upon his first office of this kind
led to Sterne's entrance on the field of satiric humor,
A Political Romance addressed to ——, *esq. of
York* (1769), often appearing later as *The History
of a Warm Watch Coat*. This line of work proved so
congenial that he continued it, and began to write
the work which marks his place in English literature, *Tristram Shandy*, the first two books of which
were published by himself (late in 1759) after the
work had been refused by a London publisher. The
work found instant success, a second edition was
arranged for by the publisher, and its continuance
was assured upon contract at the rate of a volume
a year. A volume of sermons was also put through
the press. In 1760 he became perpetual curate of
Coxwold, retaining his other charges of Sutton and
Stillington, which were served by curates. His
residence at Coxwold was broken by a visit to
France, where he was lionized, and by frequent
journeys to London on business connected with the
publication of the later volumes of *Tristram Shandy*,
of sermons, and of his *Sentimental Journey*. His
works were first collected in 7 vols., Dublin, 1779,
then in 10 vols., London, 1780; a late edition is by
G. Saintsbury, 6 vols., 1894.

BIBLIOGRAPHY: P. Fitzgerald, *Life of Laurence Sterne*, 2
vols., London, 1864, 2d ed. ib. 1896; W. M. Thackeray,
The English Humourists of the 18th Century, 2d ed., ib.
1853; P. S. Stapfer, *Laurence Sterne, sa personne et ses
œuvres*, Paris, 1870; E. Scherer, *Études critiques de littérature*, pp. 195–221, ib. 1876; H. D. Traill, *Life of Sterne*,
new ed., London, 1889; L. Stephen, *Hours in a Library*,
iii. 139–174, ib. 1892; J. Texte, *J.-J. Rousseau et les
origines du cosmopolitisme littéraire*, pp. 337–354, Paris,
1895; *DNB*, liv. 199–221.

STERNHOLD, THOMAS: One of the founders
of English psalmody; b. either at Southampton,
England, or on the Hayfield estate near Blakeney
(20 m. n. of Bristol, England), about 1500; d. Aug.
23, 1549. He studied at Oxford but did not take a
degree; was groom of the chambers to Henry VIII.
and Edward VI. He is said to have versified fifty-
one psalms, of which nineteen appeared in 1548,
and thirty-seven the next year, immediately after
his death (for other data, and developments after
Sternhold, see HYMNOLOGY, IX., § 2). The work
was continued by John Hopkins of the Woodend,
Aure, Gloucestershire (B.A., Oxford, 1544; said to
have held a living in Suffolk). *The Whole Booke of
Psalms Collected into English Metre* appeared 1562,
and was bound up with innumerable editions of the
Prayer Book; making for two centuries or more the
only or chief metrical provision of the Church of
England. Since 1700 or so, it has been called the
" Old Version," in distinction from its rival, Tate
and Brady. Of its contents about forty-one psalms
bear the initials of Sternhold (the only notable
sample of his skill being a few stanzas of Ps. xviii.),

and sixty-four, those of Hopkins. The rest are by
Thomas Norton, a lawyer who translated Calvin's
Institutes, and d. about 1600; William Whittingham,
b. at Chester, 1524; d. 1589; educated at Oxford;
married Calvin's sister, and was from 1563 dean of
Durham; and William Kethe, who was in exile with
Knox at Geneva, 1555, chaplain to the English
forces at Havre 1563, and afterward rector or vicar
of Okeford in Dorsetshire. Kethe is memorable as
the author of the only rendering now much used of
all these, " All people that on earth do dwell "
(Ps. c.), which has a venerable solidity and
quaintness.

BIBLIOGRAPHY: S. W. Duffield, *English Hymns*, pp. 525–
526, New York, 1886; N. Livingston, *The Scottish Metrical Psalter of A. D. 1635*, Edinburgh, 1864; Julian,
Hymnology, pp. 860–861, 863; *DNB*, liv. 223–224.

STERRY, PETER: Puritan; b. in Surrey; d.
in London Nov. 19, 1672. He was graduated from
Emmanuel's College, Cambridge (B.A., 1633; M.A.,
1637; fellow, 1636); was one of Cromwell's chaplains, one of the fourteen divines proposed by the
Lords in May, 1642, and sat as an Independent in
the Westminster Assembly almost from the first.
He was characterized as mystical and obscure, but
his doctrines of conversion and of religious life, of
Christian experience, duty, and hope were of the
usual Evangelical type. Among his works may be
mentioned *The Clouds in Which Christ Comes* (London, 1648); four Parliament sermons, *The Spirit's
Conviction of Sinne* (1645); *The Teachings of Christ
in the Soule* (1648); *The Coming forth of Christ in the
Power of his Death* (1650); *The Way of God with his
People in These Nations* (1657); *Englands De-
liverance from the Northern Presbytery, Compared
with its Deliverance from the Roman Papacy; or a
Thanksgiving Sermon on Jer. xvi. 14, 15* (1652);
Discourse on the Freedom of the Will (1675); *The
Rise, Race, and Royalty of the Kingdom of God in the
Soul of Man together with an Account of the State of a
Saint's Soul and Body in Death* (1683); *The Ap-
pearance of God to Man in the Gospel and Gospel
Change, to Which is Added an Explication of the
Trinity, and a Short Catechism* (1710).

BIBLIOGRAPHY: D. Neal, *Hist. of the Puritans*, ed. J. Toulmin, 5 vols., Bath, 1793–97; B. Brooke, *Lives of the Puritans*, iii. 347, London, 1813; A. à Wood, *Athenæ Oxonienses*, ed. P. Bliss, iii. 197, 912, 1170, 4 vols., ib. 1813–20;
D. Masson's *Life of Milton*, passim, 6 vols., ib. 1859–80;
DNB, liv. 224–225; and the literature under WESTMINSTER
STANDARDS.

STEUDEL, JOHANN CHRISTIAN FRIEDRICH:
German theologian; b. at Esslingen (8 m. s.e. of
Stuttgart) Oct. 25, 1779; d. at Tübingen Oct. 24,
1837. He was educated at Tübingen, 1797–1804;
was vicar at Oberesslingen 1802–06; tutor at
Tübingen, 1806–08; studied Arabic and Persian
at Paris, 1808–10; was deacon at Canstatt, 1810–
1812; after 1812 subdeacon and deacon at Tübing-
en and professor of theology, 1815–37. In 1822
he became morning preacher at the principal church
of the city and after 1826 senior of the faculty and
assessor of the seminary inspection. His lectures
at first were on the Old Testament, including later
oriental languages, and after 1826 dogma and apologetics. He founded in 1828 the *Zeitschrift für Theologie*. A rational supernaturalist, Steudel is usually

regarded as the last representative of the older Tübingen School (q.v.). With his writings he opposed Roman Catholic union in 1811–16, and the union of the two Protestant churches in 1822. He wrote *Ueber die Haltbarkeit des Glaubens an geschichtliche Offenbarung Gottes* (Stuttgart, 1814); *Glaubenslehre* (Tübingen, 1834); and *Theologie des Alten Testaments* (Berlin, 1840). He entered into a sharp controversy with D. F. Strauss upon the appearance of the latter's *Leben Jesu.*

(G. F. OEHLER†.)

BIBLIOGRAPHY: The memorial address by Dorner and the sketch of the life by Dettinger are in *Tübinger Zeitschrift für Theologie*, 1838, part 1. Consult further M. A. Landerer, *Neueste Dogmengeschichte*, pp. 170 sqq., Heilbronn, 1881.

STEUERNAGEL, stoi'er-nä"gel, **KARL:** German Protestant; b. at Hardegsen (10 m. n.n.w. of Göttingen) Feb. 17, 1869. He was educated at the University of Halle (1887–91) and at the theological seminary at Wittenberg, and became privat-docent for Old-Testament exegesis at Halle in 1895, and extraordinary professor in 1907. Besides editing the *Zeitschrift des deutschen Palästina-Vereins* since 1903, he has prepared the volumes on Deuteronomy (1898) and Joshua (1899) for W. Nowack's *Handkommentar zum Alten Testament*, to which he has also contributed *Allgemeine Einleitung in das Hexateuch* (1900), and has written *Der Rahmen des Deuteronomiums* (Halle, 1894); *Die Entstehung des deuteronomischen Gesetzes* (1896); *Die Einwanderung der israelitischen Stämme in Kanaan* (Berlin, 1901); *Hebräische Grammatik* (1903; 3d ed., 1909); and *Methodische Einleitung zum hebräischen Sprachunterricht* (1905).

STEVENS, ABEL: Historian of Methodism; b. in Philadelphia, Pa., Jan. 19, 1815; d. in San José, Cal., Sept. 12, 1897. He was educated at Wesleyan Academy, Wilbraham, Mass., and at Wesleyan University, Middletown, Conn.; he completed a course of study at the latter institution in 1834; joined the New England Conference in 1834; was appointed to churches in Boston, Mass., and Providence, R. I.; became editor of *Zion's Herald*, Boston, 1840; *The National Magazine*, New York, 1852; *The Christian Advocate*, New York, 1856; was joint editor, with Drs. McClintock and Crooks, of *The Methodist*, 1860–74; and pastor of churches in New York City and Mamaroneck, N. Y. On retiring from editorial life, he traveled extensively in the United States and then in Europe, where he settled finally at Geneva, Switzerland, taking charge of the American Union Church there, and became correspondent of American journals. In a series of works that remain the standard authority he reduced the history of Methodism to a connected narrative. He was the author of *Sketches and Incidents* (New York, 1843); *Memorials of the Introduction of Methodism into the Eastern States* (2 vols., 1848–1852); *Essay on Church Polity* (1847); *Essay on the Preaching Required by the Times* (1855); *Essay on The Great Reform in Systematic Beneficence* (1856); *The History of the Religious Movement of the Eighteenth Century, Called Methodism* (3 vols., 1858–61); *Life and Times of Nathan Bangs* (1863); *History of the Methodist Episcopal Church in the United States*

(4 vols., 1864–67); *The Centenary of American Methodism* (1865); *Women of Methodism: its three Foundresses, S. Wesley, the Countess of Huntingdon, and B. Heck; with Sketches of their female Associates* (1866); *Madame de Staël: Study of her Life and Times* (2 vols., 1881); *Character Sketches* (1882); *Christian Work and Consolation; the Problem of an effective and happy Life* (1882).

STEVENS, GEORGE BARKER: Congregationalist; b. at Spencer, N. Y., July 13, 1854; d. at New Haven, Conn., June 22, 1906. He was graduated from the University of Rochester, N. Y., 1877, and from Yale Divinity School, New Haven, Conn., 1880; became pastor of the First Congregational Church, Buffalo, N. Y., 1880; and of the First Presbyterian Church, Watertown, N. Y., 1883; studied in Germany, 1885–86; and was professor of New-Testament criticism and interpretation, Yale Divinity School, New Haven, Conn., 1886–95. He published *Pauline Theology; a Study of the Origin and Correlation of the doctrinal Teachings of the Apostle Paul* (New York, 1892); *Johannine Theology: Study of the Doctrinal Contents of the Gospel and Epistles of the Apostle John* (1894); *Doctrine and Life: Study of some of the principal Truths of the Christian Religion in their Relation to Christian Experience* (1895); *Theology of the New Testament* (1899); *Messages of Paul* (1900); *Messages of the Apostles* (1900); *Teaching of Jesus* (1901); and *Christian Doctrine of Salvation* (1905). He edited Chrysostom's " Homilies on Acts and Romans " in *NPNF* (1 ser., vol. xi., New York, 1889); and *A Short Exposition of the Epistle to the Galatians* (Hartford, Conn., 1890).

BIBLIOGRAPHY: W. Walker, *George Barker Stevens: an Address*, New Haven, 1906.

STEVENS, PETER FAYSSOUX: Reformed Episcopal bishop; b. near Tallahassee, Fla., June 22, 1830; d. at Charleston, S. C., Jan. 9, 1910. He was graduated from the South Carolina Military Academy, Charleston, S. C., in 1849, and was connected with this institution as professor of mathematics 1853–57 and of belles lettres 1857–59, and as superintendent 1859–61. After serving in the Confederate Army throughout the Civil War, he was ordained priest in the Protestant Episcopal Church, but in 1875 became connected with the Reformed Episcopalians, and four years later was appointed bishop of the special jurisdiction of the South, having special oversight of the colored churches of that region. In 1890–96 he was also professor of mathematics in Claflin University.

STEVENS, WILLIAM ARNOLD: Baptist; b. at Granville, O., Feb. 5, 1839; d. at Rochester, N. Y., Jan. 2, 1910. He was educated at Denison University, Granville (A.B., 1862), Rochester Theological Seminary (1865), and the universities of Harvard, Leipsic, and Berlin (1865–68). He was professor of Greek at Denison University (1868–77), and after 1877 was professor of New-Testament exegesis at Rochester Theological Seminary. He edited *Select Orations of Lysias* (Chicago, 1876); and wrote *Commentary on the Epistles to the Thessalonians* Philadelphia, 1887); *Outline Handbook of the Life of*

Christ (in collaboration with E. D. Burton; New York, 1892); *Harmony of the Gospels for Historical Study* (with the same collaborator, 1894); and *Life of the Apostle Paul* (Rochester, 1894).

STEVENS, WILLIAM BACON: Protestant Episcopal bishop of Pennsylvania; b. at Bath, Me., July 13, 1815; d. in Philadelphia, Pa., June 11, 1887. He attended Phillips Academy, Andover, Mass., but was obliged, through failure of health, to give up his studies; he then spent two years in travel, and on his return graduated from Dartmouth, Hanover, N. H. (M.D., 1837); he practised as a physician in Savannah, Ga., 1838–43; was ordained deacon 1843, and priest 1844; was historian of the State of Georgia, 1841; professor of belles-lettres and moral philosophy in the University of Georgia, Athens, Ga., 1844–48; became rector of St. Andrew's, Philadelphia, Pa., 1848; assistant bishop of Pennsylvania, 1862, and bishop 1865. He was in 1868 appointed by the presiding bishop to take charge of the American Episcopal churches on the continent of Europe, and held the position for six years. He edited with prefaces and notes the *Georgia Historical Collections* (vols. i. and ii., Savannah, 1841–42); and is the author of *A History of Georgia from its First Discovery by Europeans to the Adoption of the Present Constitution in 1798* (vol. i., New York, 1847; vol. ii., Philadelphia, 1859); *The Parables of the New Testament Practically Unfolded* (Philadelphia, 1855; memorial ed., 1887); *Consolation; the Bow in the Cloud* (1855); *Sunday at Home: Manual of Home Service* (1856); *The Lord's Day, its Obligations and Blessings* (1857); *The Past and Present of St. Andrew's Church, Philadelphia* (1858); *Sabbaths of our Lord* (1872); *Sermons* (New York, 1879); and many addresses, charges, essays, and occasional sermons.

BIBLIOGRAPHY: The memorial ed. of the *Parables* (ut sup.) contains a sketch of the life. Consult further W. S. Perry, *The Episcopate in America*, pp. 151–153, New York, 1895.

STEVENSON, JAMES HENRY: Methodist Episcopal, orientalist; b. at Peterborough, Ontario, Apr. 16, 1860. He was educated at McGill University (A.B., 1889) and at the Wesleyan Theological College at Montreal, Canada (graduated, 1891). He was a teacher in the public schools of Ontario (1879–1881); pastor in Islington, near Toronto (1890–91); and later spent three years (1896, 1899, 1902) in the British Museum copying Assyrian contract tablets, while during 1900 he was a student in Berlin. He has been professor of Hebrew at Vanderbilt University since 1892. Besides being associate editor, with H. C. Tolman, of the *Vanderbilt Oriental Series*, he has written *Herodotus and the Empires of the East* (with Tolman; New York, 1898); and *Babylonian and Assyrian Contracts, with Aramaic Reference-Notes* (1902).

STEVENSON, JOSEPH ROSS: Presbyterian; b. at Ligonier, Pa., Mar. 1, 1866. He was graduated from Washington and Jefferson College (1886) and McCormick Theological Seminary, Chicago, Ill. (1889). He studied for a year at the University of Berlin, then was pastor of the Broadway Presbyterian Church, Sedalia, Mo. (1890–94); became professor of church history in McCormick Theological

Seminary (1894); pastor of the Fifth Avenue Presbyterian Church, New York (1902–09); and of the Brown Memorial Church, Baltimore, since 1909.

STEVENSON, WILLIAM FLEMING: Irish Presbyterian pastor and organizer of mission work; b. in Strabane (65 m. w.n.w. of Belfast), Ireland, Sept. 20, 1832; d. at Rathgar, Dublin, Ireland, Sept. 16, 1886. He was of that Ulster Presbyterian stock which has given a special character to the northern province of Ireland. He was graduated from the University of Glasgow (M.A., 1851), and finished his theological studies in Scotland and Germany. Occasional passages in his writings show that while interested in the speculative and critical sides of German theology, it was the warm, spiritual, Christian life of Germany, as displayed in German hymns and missions, which attracted him most. In 1856 he was licensed to preach by the Presbytery of Strabane, became town missionary, and worked in the fever-stricken lanes of the poor part of Belfast. In 1860 he accepted the call of the newly organized Rathgar-road Presbyterian Church, situated in a suburb of Dublin. Stevenson was the first minister of this church, and it was his first and only regular charge. Literary work occupied much of his attention. His *Praying and Working* (London, 1862; new ed., 1886) is of interest to the student of social problems, as well as to the friends of missions. *Lives and Deeds worth Knowing* (New York, 1870), composed of collected articles, and published without authority, is not less interesting. *Hymns for Church and Home* (London, 1873) has a scholarly accuracy and thoroughness which make it very valuable to hymnologists.

In 1871 Stevenson was called to the work which, in some sense, was the most important of his life, becoming coadjutor with James Morgan, the convener of the Assembly's Foreign Mission; and in 1873 he became sole convener, while retaining the pastorate of his church. Successful as a preacher and a pastor, he seemed even better fitted for this new work, which he assumed with great diffidence, and in its interest he undertook extensive journeys. In 1881 he was unanimously chosen moderator of the General Assembly of the Presbyterian Church in Ireland. As a pulpit orator, Stevenson belonged to the first rank.

BIBLIOGRAPHY: His *Life and Letters* was issued by his wife, London, 1888, and a sketch is given also in the 1886 edition of *Praying and Working*, ut sup. Consult further *DNB*, liv. 257–258.

STEWARD. See METHODISTS, I., § 8.

STEWART, ALEXANDER: Church of Scotland; b. at Liverpool Jan. 27, 1847. He was educated at Queen's College, Liverpool (1862–64), United College (1864–68), and St. Mary's College, St. Andrews (1868–71), and at the universities of Heidelberg and Leipsic (1869–70). After being minister at Mains and Strathmartine, near Dundee, from 1873 to 1887, he was appointed professor of systematic theology at the University of Aberdeen in 1887, and principal and primarius professor of divinity at St. Mary's College, St. Andrews, New Brunswick, in 1894, which position he still holds. He was Croall lecturer in 1902. In theological position he is " a moderate broad churchman, averse to all extremes and laying stress upon the rational and ethical elements in religion while recognizing and allowing for the emotional and mystical elements," and holds " that forms of belief, organization, and worship are necessary, but that special forms may change and pass away with fuller light or changed circumstances." He has written *Handbook of Christian Evidences* (Edinburgh, 1892) and *Life of Christ* (London, 1905).

STEWART, DUGALD: Scotch philosopher; b. at Edinburgh, Nov. 22, 1753; d. there June 11, 1828. He was educated at Edinburgh University, 1765–69; and attended the lectures of Thomas Reid (q.v.) at Glasgow, 1771–72; began to teach mathematics at Edinburgh in 1772; succeeded his father as professor of the same, 1775–85; and was professor of moral philosophy, 1785–1820. From 1809 he lived in retirement at Kinneil House, Linlithgoshire, engaged in preparing the substance of his lectures for publication. Stewart was the representative and expounder of Reid's " philosophy of common sense " after the latter's death. He was greatly distinguished for elegance and eloquence, and his lectures were thronged not only by native students, but by many young men of position from England. Like Reid he made philosophy dependent on inductive psychology, making much of external perception as furnishing evidence of objective reality; but, though approximating pure empiricism, yet he strenuously opposed that school with intuitionism, representing intelligence as fundamental to the process of knowledge. He repudiated the ontological argument and was a thorough nominalist. His works were, *Elements of the Philosophy of the Human Mind* (3 vols., Edinburgh, 1792–1827); *Outlines of Moral Philosophy* (1793); and *Philosophy of the Active and Moral Powers of Man* (2 vols., 1828). *The Collected Works* are by Sir W. Hamilton, with biography by John Veitch (11 vols., 1854–60).

BIBLIOGRAPHY: Besides the biography by J. Veitch, in vol. x. of the *Works*, consult: F. Horner, in *Edinburgh Review*, vii (1805), 113–134; S. Parr, *Works*, vii. 542–553, London, 1828; M. Stewart (son of Dugald), *Life of Dugald Stewart*, in *Annual Biography and Obituary* for 1829, pp. 256–269; A. H. Everett, *Stewart's Moral Philosophy*, in *North American Review*, xxxi (1838), 213–267; H. Cockburn, *Memorials*, passim, Edinburgh, 1856; J. McCosh, *Scottish Philosophy*, New York, 1885; S. Leslie, *English Utilitarians*, i. 142–168, London, 1900; *DNB*, liv. 282–286.

STEWART, GEORGE BLACK: Presbyterian; b. at Columbus, O., Feb. 28, 1854. He studied at Princeton College (B.A., 1876; M.A., 1879) and at McCormick Theological Seminary and Auburn Theological Seminary (graduated 1879); was pastor of Calvary Church, Auburn, N. Y., 1878–84, and of the Market Square Church, Harrisburg, Pa., 1884–99; and became president of Auburn Theological Seminary and professor of practical theology, 1899. He has written *Study of the Life of Jesus* (Boston, 1907), and is the editor of the *Auburn Seminary Record*.

STEWART, JAMES: United Free Church of Scotland; b. in Edinburgh Feb. 14, 1831; d. at Lovedale (near the east border of Cape Colony, South Africa, 700 m. n.e. of Cape Town) Dec. 21,

1905. His early education was at the Edinburgh high school and at the Perth academy. His father had a farm in Perthshire and one day in his fifteenth year while James was plowing one of its fields the determination to be a foreign missionary was suddenly formed. With this mode of life in view after leaving the academy, he entered upon higher studies, first in Edinburgh University (1850–52), then in St. Andrews (1852–54), again in Edinburgh (1854–1855), and in the divinity hall of the Free Church there (1855–59). He did not go in for honors but for a wide culture. That he put in much of his time on botany comes out in the two elaborate and beautifully illustrated books which he published while an undergraduate: *A Series of Botanical Diagrams, Exhibiting the Structure, Physiology and Classification of Plants. With explanatory Notes* (London [1857]); and *Stewart's Botanical Chart, comprising a Tabular View of Structural and Physiological Botany* [1857]. Both were text-books in Scottish schools and colleges for many years. With the end of still better fitting himself for his chosen career he studied medicine in Edinburgh (1859–61 and 1865–66) and took his degree.

In 1857 David Livingstone visited Scotland and pleaded for men to enter the open door into Africa's heathen world. Stewart was one of those who responded to this appeal. In 1859 he formally offered himself to his church for this service, and, as he could not be sent at once, became an active preacher of the missionary cause among his own countrymen. In 1860 he became a probationer, but with no idea of settling. In 1861 he went to South Africa and met Livingstone, who cordially welcomed him. He went up the Zambesi and into Central Africa and returned to Scotland in 1864. In 1866 he married and went back to Africa, there to spend the rest of his life. In 1841 the Rev. William Govan had founded an institute at Lovedale, and in 1867 Stewart became his associate and in 1870 his successor. The place had been named for the Rev. John Love, D.D. (1757–1825), a Presbyterian divine who in 1795 founded the London Missionary Society and was its first secretary. Stewart believed that God had made the black man of the same blood as the white man and was accordingly susceptible to the same educational influences. This was a novel idea, but he succeeded in finding persons of means who enabled him to teach the blacks the professions, the arts and sciences, and industrial pursuits, including farming. He took black girls and trained them in similar fashion for teachers, nurses, housekeepers, wives, and mothers. He demonstrated on a great scale his theories, for under him the Lovedale Institute became one of the triumphs of missions. He won great fame by doing these things, and as " Stewart of Lovedale " was known the world over long before he died. He was indeed the first great industrial and educational missionary. But though to many his theories were the interesting thing, to him the missionary interest was dominant, and the thousands who came under his influence felt that dearer to him than anything else was his religion, and that he wanted his colored friends to know his Savior as the best acquisition they could make.

In 1873 he had the satisfaction of starting at Blythswood, named after Captain Blyth, magistrate of the Fingoes, a second Lovedale. In 1874 he made a tour in Scotland in the interest of both institutions, and also proposed the African mission now known as Livingstonia. In 1899 he was moderator of the general assembly of the Free Church of Scotland. In 1902 he delivered the Duff missionary lectures at Edinburgh. His life was too crowded with practical matters to allow him leisure for authorship of a general nature, but he produced these volumes which were in the line of his work: *Lovedale, Past and Present* (Edinburgh, 1884); *Lovedale Illustrated* (1894); *Livingstonia, its Origin* (1894); *Kafir Phrase Book and Vocabulary* (Lovedale, 1898); *Dawn in the Dark Continent, Africa and its Missions* (the Duff lectures; Edinburgh, 1903).

BIBLIOGRAPHY: J. Wells, *The Life of James Stewart*, London, 1908.

STEWART, ROBERT LAIRD: Presbyterian; b. at Murrysville, Pa., Aug. 11, 1840. He was graduated from Washington and Jefferson College (B.A., 1866; M.A., 1867) and from the Western Theological Seminary (1869); was pastor at Conneautville, Pa., 1869–73, and at Golden, Col., 1873–79; was also superintendent of schools, Jefferson County, Col., 1874–79; pastor of the Mahoning Church, Danville, Pa., 1880–90; and after 1890 professor of pastoral theology, Biblical archeology, and Christian evidences in the theological department of Lincoln University, and also dean of the faculty. He has written *The Place and Value of Pastoral Theology in the Curriculum of Theological Study* (1894); *The Land of Israel* (1899); *Memorable Places among the Holy Hills* (1903); and *Sheldon Jackson, Pathfinder and Prospector of the Missionary Vanguard in the Rocky Mountains and Alaska* (1908).

STEWART, WILLIAM: Church of Scotland; b. at Annan (14 m. s.e. of Dumfries), Dumfriesshire, Aug. 15, 1835. He was educated at the University of Glasgow (B.A., 1861; B.D., 1867), where he was examiner in mental philosophy (1867–70). He was minister of St. George's-in-the-Fields, Glasgow (1868–75); since 1873 has been professor of divinity and Biblical criticism in the university of the same city, and dean of the faculty of theology since 1895. He has written *The Plan of St. Luke's Gospel* (Glasgow, 1873).

STICHARION. See VESTMENTS AND INSIGNIA, ECCLESIASTICAL.

STICHOMETRY.

I. In General. The data of stichometry consist chiefly of subscriptions at the close of manuscripts, expressing the number of lines which are contained in the book that has been copied; of marginal annotations from point to point, expressing the extent of the previous text; or of quotations and allusions which are found in various writers, which indicate

1. Use of the Term. either the locality of some passage in a quoted work, or the compass of the whole or part of the works of a given author. For example, at the close of Isocrates, Busiris, in *Codex Urbinas*, there is, in the archaic character, the number 390; while on the margin of the same work, in the more recent character, there is on fol. 22ᵛ, 10 (§ 25), before τούτων αἴτιοι, the number 2 (B); and on 25ᵛ, 12 (§ 39), before γεγονότας ἢ τούς, the number 3 (Γ); and these numbers represent the second and third hundreds of lines measured on some exemplar, either actual or ideal; Diogenes Laërtius quotes a passage from Chrysippus, κατὰ τοὺς χιλίους στίχους; and Galen estimates the extent of a certain portion of the works of Hippocrates at 240 verses; τούτου τοῦ βιβλίου τὸ μὲν κατὰ τὸ ἐν γράμμα μέρος τὸ πρῶτον εἰς σμ' στίχους ἐξήκει (Galen, *In Hippokratem de natura hominis*, xv., p. 9). Full collections of such data may be found in F. W. Ritschl, *Opuscula philologica*, i. 74 sqq., Leipsic, 1866; and in T. Birt, *Das antike Buchwesen*, chap. iv., Berlin, 1882. Everything in these data suggests that the numeration has reference to standard lines or copies; and since the actual number of lines in the manuscripts never tallies with the stichometric record, and we are unable to point to any copies which do furnish an agreement, it is evident that there is somewhere a common unit of measurement upon which these subscriptions and quotations are based: in other words, the stichos must have an element of fixity in it, even if it be not absolutely fixed. It is important, therefore, to determine in what direction the meaning of stichos deflects from its normal indefinite sense of " line," " row," and " verse."

The term stichos is of itself extremely vague. It may be nothing more than row or line; as when the Septuagint uses it for the rows of stones in the

2. " Stichos " Equivalent to " Hexameter Line." high priest's breastplate; or, in a military sense, it may represent the number of men in a rank or file of soldiers, especially the latter; and so in other cases. But in literature it is easy to demonstrate that the stichos is deflected in meaning in the direction of a hexameter line. In the first place, such a unit is convenient for the comparison of prose-works with poetry; in the next place, actual instances of prose-passages are reduced to their equivalent verse-lengths; in the third place, the term is used of hexameter poetry, in distinction from any other; and, finally, any given work may be divided into hexameter rhythms and results compared with the transmitted numerical data. If these points be taken in order, it may be said that the prose-unit is more likely to be taken from poetry than that the unit of measurement for poetry is likely to be adopted from prose; for the line of poetry is already measured in a sensibly constant unit, and no reason exists for a change of that unit. The only question that would arise here is whether there may not be expected a variety of units of measurement; as, for instance, an iambic unit in distinction from a hexameter unit. It is sufficient to observe at this point, that such varieties of measurement, if they exist, are extremely rare. In regard to the actual reduction of a prose-passage to its equivalent verse-length, there is an important case in Galen (v. 655, ed. Kühn), where, having quoted a sentence from Hippocrates, he continues:

εἰς μὲν οὗτος ὁ λόγος ἐννέα καὶ τριάκοντα συλλαβῶν ὅπερ ἐστὶ δυοῖν καὶ ἡμίσεως ἐπῶν ἐξαμέτρων κτέ.

If Galen, according to this, then reckons thirty-nine syllables as being equivalent to two hexameters and a half, or, as he continues, eighty-two syllables to five hexameters, the hexameter can hardly be different from a sixteen-syllabled rhythm. The assumption is easy that stichometric measurement is made by preference in syllables of which sixteen go to the hexameter, or unit-verse. The number sixteen invites attention as being the number of syllables in the first line of the *Iliad*, and as being a square number, a peculiarity which always had a certain attractiveness for early calculators. That the term stichos deflects in the direction of hexameter verse as against any other line of poetry which might have been chosen for a proper unit of measurement, will appear from Montfaucon (*Bibl. Coislin.*, p. 597), where there is quoted from a tenth-century manuscript a catalogue of poets as writers by stichoi, and writers of iambics can only have resulted from a specialization of the meaning of the term stichos by constant use in a particular sense.

In the demonstration of the same point by actual measurement, the most important researches are those published by the late C. Graux (in *Revue de Philologie*, Apr., 1878), in which he demonstrated, by an actual estimation of the number **3. This** of letters in certain works, that the **Measure-** stichos represented not a clause, nor a **ment** number of words, but a fixed quantity **Confirmed.** of writing. The average number of letters to the verse he found to vary between narrow limits, generally thirty-four to thirty-eight letters; and an enumeration of the letters in fifty lines of the *Iliad* opened at random supplied him with an average of 37.7 letters to the verse. This very important identification of the stichos with the hexameter is the starting-point for a great many new critical investigations as to the integrity of transmitted texts, their early form, etc. Whether the unit of measurement is a certain number of syllables, or a certain number of letters, is not at first sight easy to decide. It is tolerably certain that the measured line is, as above stated, a space-line, and not a sense-line; but to discriminate between a letter-line and a syllable-line is a more delicate matter. If the former be adopted, the unit should probably be fixed at thirty-six letters, because this is the nearest symmetrical number to the average hexameter. There are very few instances, however, in which the actual letters of a line are found to be numbered; while the custom can readily be traced of limiting a line by the division of the syllables, in the earliest manuscripts. Moreover, there is the actual measurement in the passage quoted from Galen; and Pliny seems to allude to the custom of syllable-counting, when, in one of his epistles, he demands an equally long reply from

his correspondent, and threatens to count, not only the pages, but the verses on the page, and the syllables of each verse (*Ego non paginas tantum, sed versus etiam syllabasque numerabo;* Pliny, iv. 11). The preference must, therefore, be given to the syllable-line. It is comparatively easy to count the compass of a book in sixteen-syllable rhythms, but a toilsome process to estimate with equal accuracy the number of thirty-six-letter lines.

It is interesting to compare the relative sizes of the two line-units. M. Graux deduces 37.7 as the average hexameter in letters, and Diels (*Hermes*, vol. xvii.) makes the average of the first fifty lines in Homer to be 15.6 syllables. A verse **4. Partial** of sixteen syllables is then equivalent **Stichometry.** to about 1.074 verses of thirty-six letters each. In precisely the same way as M. Graux determined the average number of letters to the verse from the total stichometry, in the manuscripts of Herodotus, Demosthenes, Eusebius, Gregory of Nazianzus, etc., one may examine the partial stichometry. This has been done for Isocrates by Fuhr (*Rheinisches Museum*, xxxvii. 468); for the Plato manuscripts, by Schanz (*Hermes*, xvi. 309); and for the Demosthenes manuscripts, by W. v. Christ, in the able discussion entitled *Die Atticusausgabe des Demosthenes* (München, 1882). The partial stichometry is of the highest value for the study of texts; and in every case the data which it supplies are found to accord very closely with the fundamental statements above as to the paleographical meaning of the word stichos. There are traces of partial stichometry in the great Vatican manuscript of the Old and New Testaments (cf. E. Nestle, in *Correspondenz-Blatt für die Gelehrten und Realschulen Württembergs*, 1883; and J. R. Harris, *Stichometry*, pp. 59–64, London, 1893). The foregoing investigations received striking and unexpected confirmation through the discovery by Professor Mommsen in 1885 of a list of the canonical books of the Old and New Testaments and of the works of Cyprian in the Phillipps Library at Cheltenham. These lists were accompanied by stichometric annotations, to which the scribe attached the information that the index of verses in the city of Rome is not clearly given, and elsewhere, through greed of gain, they do not preserve it in full; but that he went through the books in detail, counting sixteen syllables to the line, according to the standard line of Vergil, and appended the number of verses. The importance of this statement is evident. There was not only a stichometry of the Vulgate and of the works of Cyprian by which the purchaser of books in Carthage or elsewhere could be protected against the rapacity of the bookseller, but the hexameter standard was clearly defined as the unit of measurement.

Some degree of confusion is introduced by the existence, apparently, in early times, of an alternative iambic verse of twelve syllables, **5. Cola and** as well as by the introduction of wri- **Commata.** ting by *cola* and *commata*. The latter of these points has been an especial ground of combat, in consequence of the countenance which the custom seemed to lend to the theory of sense-lines in opposition to space-lines. The explanation of the matter seems to be as follows: when the earlier uncial form of writing was deserted for one more convenient for purposes of reading and recitation, the text was broken up into short sentences, named, according to their lengths, *cola* and *commata;* and in some instances an attempt was made, not only to number these *cola,* so as to form a colometry similar to stichometry, and sharing the advantages which it offered for reference and book-measuring, but even to accommodate the arrangement of these *cola* so as to reproduce the original number of verses. Thus the rhetorician Castor (C. Walz, *Rhetōres Græci,* iii. 721, Stuttgart, 1834) discusses the pseudo-oration of Demosthenes against Philip as follows: τοῦτον τὸν λόγον στίξομεν κατὰ κῶλον καταντήσαντες εἰς τὴν ποσότητα τῶν κώλων κατὰ τὸν ἀριθμὸν τὸν ἐγκείμενον ἐν τοῖς ἀρχαίοις βιβλίοις, ὡς ἐμέτρησεν αὐτὸς ὁ Δημοσθένης τὸν ἴδιον λόγον. It seems also that this change of form took place first for those books which were publicly recited, or which had a semi-poetical structure; so that the oldest Bible manuscripts desert the continuous uncial writing in the Psalms, in Job, the Proverbs, Canticles, etc.; and St. Jerome proposed to imitate this peculiarly divided text in the prophets: " What is usually done in the cases of Demosthenes and Cicero, viz., that those writings which are in prose and not in verse are arranged in *cola* and *commata,* we also, looking to the convenience of the readers, distinguish a new interpretation by a new kind of writing " (preface to commentary on Isaiah).

II. New-Testament Stichometry: In turning to the New Testament, and particularly to the epistles, it will appear that the theory already advanced is completely confirmed, and that there is a very powerful critical implement for the restoration of early New-Testament texts in the tra-
1. Eutha- ditional data. As before, both total
lius. and partial stichometry exists. There is, however, a good deal of variation between the transmitted data, arising from various causes, such as variation in the text, variation in the unit employed in the measurement, difference in versions measured, and difference in the abbreviations employed. The greatest authority, however, for New-Testament stichometry, is found in the work of Euthalius (q.v.), ed. L. A. Zacagni, *Collectanea monumentorum veterum ecclesiæ Græcæ ac Latinæ* (Rome, 1698; *MGP,* lxxxv.). Euthalius was a deacon of the church of Alexandria, and afterward bishop of Sulci in Sardinia. (For modern discussions with reference to Euthalius, his history and ecclesiastical office, besides the literature under EUTHALIUS, consult Ehrhard, in *Centralblatt für Bibliothekswesen,* viii. 9, pp. 385–411; Von Dobschütz, in the same, x. 2, pp. 49–70. These discussions do not affect the problem of stichometry.) He has frequently but erroneously been credited with the introduction of stichometry to the New Testament, and these verses which he measured have been by many persons identified with the colonwriting previously described. There is very little ground for any such ideas; and it appears that the stichoi mentioned by Euthalius are hexameters of sixteen syllables, a very slight allowance being made for certain common abbreviations. The work of

Euthalius consisted in editing the Acts and Catholic Epistles, with a complete system of prologues, prefaces, and quotations: every book was divided into lections, and to every lection, as well as to the greater part of the prefaces, was appended its numerical extent. The verses were also marked on the margin from fifty to fifty. There is thus a mine of stichometric information sufficient to test any theory in the closest manner. Moreover, the work has this importance, that Euthalius professes to have measured his verses accurately, and to have employed the best manuscripts, viz., those preserved in the Pamphilian Library at Cæsarea. It is consequently permissible to set a high value on the measurements made, on the ground of antiquity as well as of accuracy.

It remains to test these results given by Euthalius for the lections of the Acts of the Apostles; and, no account being taken of the abbreviations which might have been found in the text, the
2. Eutha- text of the Acts in Westcott and Hort's
lius Tested. New Testament will be divided into sixteen-syllabled rhythms. If allowance were made for abbreviation, the results would have been somewhat less, as a syllable might be subtracted at every occurrence of the words θεὸς and χριστὸς, and two syllables for each occurrence of ἰησοῦς and κύριος, with perhaps a few other rarely recurring words, as πατήρ, οὐρανός. The data for Euthalius are taken from *Cod. Escorial,* ψ. iii. 6, as there are some errors in Zacagni's figures. Allowing for one or two obvious corruptions, such as the dropping of the figure ρ in lection 6, the agreement is very complete.

The lines of the following table are nearly hexameters, so that the table affords a picture of the arrangement of an early bicolumnar codex:

Lection.	Begins.	Cod. Esc.	Westcott and Hort.
1	1.1	40	40
2	1.15	30	30
3	2.1	109	111
4	3.1	136	143
5	4.32	100	121
6	6.1	88	190
7	8.1 (ἐγένετο)	92	94
8	9.1	75	77
9	9.23	216	210
10	11.27	283	272
11	15.1	193	201
12	17.1	164	164
13	19.1	239	242
14	21.15	293	307
15	24.27	168	160
16	27.1	198	192

Still more remarkable is the harmony between the measured text of Westcott and Hort and the Euthalian figures, when allowance is made for the abbreviations previously mentioned. In the following table the first column represents the stichometric number supplied by Euthalius and the best manuscripts; the second gives the result of the actual subdivision of the text of Westcott and Hort into sixteen-syllabled verses; and the third expresses the same result with the proper deduction made for four leading abbreviations.

The agreement between the first and third columns is very complete and decisive as a test of the hypothesis proposed with regard to the nature of the Euthalian stichoi.

James	237 or 242	240	237
I Peter	236 or 242	245	240
II Peter	154	162	158
I John	274	268	262
II John	30	31	30
III John	32	31	31
Jude	68	70	68
Romans	920	942	919
I Corinthians	870	897	874
II Corinthians	590	610	596
Galatians	293	304	296
Ephesians	312	325	314
Philippians	208	218	209
Colossians	208	215	209
I Thessalonians	193	202	194
II Thessalonians	106	112	106
Hebrews	703	714	705
I Timothy	230	239	234
II Timothy	172	177	170
Titus	97	98	97
Philemon	38	42	40

In the Gospels the data may be handled in a similar manner; but the difficulties arising from variety of text, etc., are great: moreover, many manuscripts transmit not only the number of verses, but also another number corresponding to the ῥήματα of the separate books. From a large group of cursive manuscripts the following numbers for the four Gospels appear:

	Matthew.	Mark.	Luke.	John.
ῥήματα	2,524	1,675	3,803	1,938
στίχοι	2,560	1,616	2,740	2,024

From this it appears that the number of ῥήματα is sometimes in excess, and sometimes in defect, of the number of verses. It is doubtful, moreover, whether the verses of the Gospels are measured by the same unit as is found employed in the Acts and Epistles. A fifteen-syllabled hexameter seems to agree best with the traditional figure. The Gospel of John, in the text of Westcott and Hort, is 2,025 abbreviated fifteen-syllabled hexameters, an almost absolute agreement with the result given above (2,024). The question as to the meaning of the ῥήματα subscribed side by side with the stichoi has caused not a little perplexity. It was pointed out by Harris (Stichometry, pp. 65–68) that the word ῥήματα was only a blundering retranslation of the Syriac pethgame, which may mean either " words " or " verses." Thus the reckoning of the ῥήματα is only a disguised form of the ancient stichometry which has come back again from an eastern version. If, for example, the ῥήματα as given above be compared with the pethgame as numbered in a Syriac manuscript on Mt. Sinai (Cod. Syr. Sin., 10), there results:

	Matthew	Mark.	Luke.	John.
ῥήματα	2,524	1,675	3,803	1,938
pethgame	2,522	1,675	3,083	1,737

It appears clearly that the two systems are the same, when once allowance is made for the obvious errors in Luke and John.   J. RENDEL HARRIS.

BIBLIOGRAPHY: J. R. Harris, Stichometry, Cambridge, 1893; idem, in AJP, nos. 12 (supplement), 14, 15; C. Tischendorf, Monumenta sacra inedita, nova collectio, i., p. xvii. sqq., Leipsic, 1855; F. Scrivener, in the prolegomena to his Codex Bezæ, London, 1867; Graux, in Revue de Philologie, Apr., 1878; W. Christ, Atticusausgabe des Demosthenes, Munich, 1882; W. Sanday, in Studia Biblica, iii (1891), 217–303; Turner, in the same, pp. 304–325; idem, in JTS, ii (1901), p. 236; E. Preuschen, Analecta, pp. 138 sqq., Freiburg, 1893; F. C. Burkitt, in JTS, ii (1901), 429; contributions in Rheinisches Museum as follows: in ii (1847), by Vömel; xxiv (1869), by Blass; xxxiv (1879), by Blass and by Wachsmuth; and xxxviii (1882), by Fuhr; and in Hermes as follows: xvi (1881), 309, by Schanz; xvii (1882), by Diels; and xxi (1885), 142–153, by Mommsen; and the works named in the text.

STIEFEL, stī'fel (STIFFEL, STEFEL), **ESAJAS:** Religious fanatic; b. at Langensalza (19 m. n.w. of Erfurt) between 1556 and 1564; d. at Erfurt (62 m. s.w. of Leipsic) Aug. 12, 1626. He traveled about selling dyer's-weed and salted fish, and when tired of this pursuit conducted a wine-shop in his native place; but in 1603 the city withdrew this privilege. The next year he separated from the church and kept his children away from church and school. This involved him in violent controversies with the clerical ministerium and the council, resulting in his imprisonment. In 1606 he abjured his errors and was released. He moved to Erfurt and soon after to Gispersleben. From there he issued a great number of tracts; for example, " The Different Explanation of the First Man before the Fall, of the Other after the Fall, and of the Third and Last Adam Born of God from Above." This tract was the one answered by Jakob Boehme (q.v.) with Stifelius I. These writings found willing readers at Langensalza, where Stiefel's nephew, Ezechiel Meth, was continuing his propaganda. Both were placed under arrest in 1613 and the next year were brought before the superior consistory at Dresden. They were compelled to make public retraction and pay the costs, and Stiefel had to meet, besides, a heavy fine. He next acquired property at Gispersleben, Kiliani, and Solomonsborn, where he assembled his sister's family with his own, and their religious adherents. Forbidden to hold meetings, 1614, he violated his oath, at which the Erfurt council attempted his correction, with apparent success. Shortly after, the council instigated a posse of farmers to seize him and a company engaged in a festival. All were released after promising under oath to abstain from meeting, and Stiefel was likewise bound not to proselyte. Not fulfilling this, he was banished, together with wife and child, from the city. His journey to Basel was a triumphal march. There he met with no success and returned, in spite of the prohibition, to Gispersleben, Christmas, 1616, where he and his kin were immediately cast into prison. After a little more than a year his wife, sister, and nephew were released; but his confinement continued until he recanted in 1619. He was granted the right of residence at Erfurt and opened a traffic in dyer's-weed; but resumed his religious efforts in 1621. He inveigled the Countess Erdmuth Juliane of Gleichen and Ohrdruf, whereupon the council was deliberating whether it should sentence him to death, when he fled into Thuringia. On Mar. 31,

RELIGIOUS ENCYCLOPEDIA

1624, he was sent back to Erfurt, and remained a prisoner at the hospital until he died. He is said to have repented of his errors.

Stiefel was a highly gifted man, well educated, and very familiar with the Latin and German Bible. The theological bickerings which then prevailed in the pulpits repelled him, and dry dogmatic dissertations turned him from the Church. He had been studying the writings of Thomas Münzer (q.v.) for a long time, whose fundamental ideas he adopted: the renunciation of infant baptism and the Lord's Supper, as taught by the Church, the control of the secular power, and the Scripture as a dead letter; and the advocation of dreams and visions and of the inner word of the Spirit. The community idea of Münzer he followed in practise.

(PAUL MEDER.)

BIBLIOGRAPHY: The one work of accessibility and value is P. Meder, Der Schwärmer Esajas Stiefel, in Jahresbericht des Erfurter Geschichts- und Altertumsvereins, 1898.

STIEFEL (STYFEL), MICHAEL: German Reformer and mathematician; b. at Esslingen (8 m. s.e. of Stuttgart) 1486 or 1487; d. at Jena Apr. 19, 1567. He entered the Augustine monastery of his native city, and in 1511 was consecrated priest. He first assumed an active part in the Reformation with the treatise, Von der Christfermigen rechtgegründten Leer Doctoris Martini Luthers (1522), being specially affected by reading the book of Revelation. He took refuge in May, 1522, with Hartmut of Cronberg; but upon the surrender of Cronberg Oct. 15, he fled to Wittenberg, and, Mar., 1523, became court preacher of Count Albrecht of Mansfeld. With great zeal he devoted himself to mathematical studies, setting up a strange cabalistic system by transforming letters into the so-called trigonal numbers 1, 3, 6, 10, 15, 21, thus disclosing secrets of the Bible. Luther, however, assured him of the futility of his practise, from which he desisted for awhile. Luther also sent him as preacher to Christoph Jörger of Tollet and Kreusbach, a nobleman in upper Austria. Compelled to flee from Austria in 1527, he found refuge in Luther's house, where he collected and transcribed the works and letters of Luther, until Sept., 1528, when he became pastor in Lochau. From 1532 he returned to his apocalyptical calculations and published Ein Rechenbüchlein Vom End Christi, Apocalypsis in Apocalypsim (Wittenberg, 1532). He unearthed the mysteries of the history of the Scripture, the Church, and the papacy, and calculated the date of the advent of Christ as eight a.m., Oct. 19, 1533. In consequence he was brought to Wittenberg by the officers of the elector, held in confinement for four weeks to await the elector's sentence and only the intercession of Luther and Melanchthon saved him from prison and secured his reinstatement in the parish of Holzdorf, 1534 or 1535. Holding himself aloof from prophecies, for fourteen years, he prosecuted genuine mathematical studies, resulting in Arithmetica integra (1543); and Deutsche Arithmetica (Nuremberg, 1545). He matriculated at Wittenberg, 1541, probably for the purpose of giving mathematical instruction to students. During the Schmalkald war Stiefel returned to his cabalistic play with numbers, was expelled from Holzdorf by the soldiers

of Spain, fled to Frankfort-on-the-Oder, and thence to Prussia, and was stationed at Memel, where he carried his calculations on Daniel into the pulpit. After a brief stay in Eichholz, near Königsberg, on account of antagonism to Andreas Osiander (q.v.) there, he returned to Saxony as pastor of Brück. At Eichholz he issued Ein sehr wunderbarliche Wortrechnung Sampt einer mercklichen Erklerung etlicher Zalen Danielis und der Offenbarung Sanct Johannis (1553), composed of a mass of strophes, the sentences of which afforded the apocalyptical numbers and disclosed their mysteries. His partizanship for Flacius against Melanchthon induced him to go from Electoral Saxony to the territory of the Ernestines. After 1559 he held mathematical lectures at the University of Jena. His German explanation of Revelation, which he represented as a prophecy of all history, finally reached the Thomas Library of Leipsic; for specimens, see H. Pipping's Arcana bibliothecæ Thomæ, pp. 70 sqq. (Leipsic, 1703).

(G. KAWERAU.)

BIBLIOGRAPHY: G. T. Strobel, Neue Beiträge, i. 1, pp. 5 sqq., Nuremberg, 1790; T. Keim, Reformationsblätter der Reichsstadt Esslingen, pp. 77 sqq., Esslingen, 1860; G. Bossert, Luther und Württemberg, pp. 7 sqq., Ludwigsburg, 1883; ADB, xxxvi. 208 sqq.; TSK, 1907, pp. 450 sqq.

STIER, sti'er, RUDOLF EWALD: German Biblical theologian; b. at Fraustadt (57 m. n.w. of Breslau) Mar. 17, 1800; d. at Eisleben (40 m. n.w. of Leipsic) Dec. 16, 1862. He entered the University of Berlin in 1815 to study law, but finding this subject ill suited to his poetic taste, he was registered as a theological student in 1816; but his romantic spirit led him to the pursuit of poesy, adopting Jean Paul as his ideal, and engaging in correspondence with him. In 1818 he went to the University of Halle and became president of the Halle Burschenschaft. In consequence of the decease of a young woman whom he loved and a change of life in that intense period of religious revival, he abandoned his literary adventure and took up the study of theology seriously at Berlin, 1819. From 1821 to 1823 he occupied a position in the seminary at Wittenberg, where he devoted himself to a comprehensive study of the Bible. In 1823 he took a position in the teachers' seminary at Karalene, and in the following year became teacher at the mission seminary at Basel; was pastor at Frankenleben, 1829–38; at Wichlinghausen, 1838–47; spent a season in literary retirement at Wittenberg, 1847–1850; was called by the consistory of Magdeburg to the office of superintendent at Schkeuditz, 1850; and was superintendent at Eisleben, 1859–62. During all these years Stier's main interest was in Biblical study in which J. von Meyer's annotated Bible was his basis and guide. Not satisfied with the Lutheran version he collaborated with Von Meyer in the production of his last edition of 1842, and in his own (Bielefeld, 1856) he made extensive alterations. His translation is specially valuable for the parallel passages given. His exegetical works are practical and devotional, here and there parenetic, and somewhat lacking in dogmatic relevance and pointedness. He was author of Siebzig ausgewählte Psalmen (Halle, 1834); and of commentaries on Ephesians (1846; popular ed., Berlin, 1859), on

Hebrews (2d ed., Brunswick, 1862), and on James (2d ed., Leipsic, 1860). His experience of the inner life, familiarity with ascetic literature, and a fresh and piquant interest, mark these as well as his widely distributed *Reden des Herrn* (2d ed., 5 vols., Leipsic, 1851–55; Eng. transl., *Words of the Lord Jesus*, 8 vols., Edinburgh, 1855–58, 4th American ed., New York, 1864), a commentary on the Gospels; and *Reden des Herrn vom Himmel her* (1859; Eng. transl., *Words of a Risen Savior*, Edinburgh, 1859), on the Acts and Revelation. He represented a doctrine of direct and organic inspiration, according to which the personality of the authors disappears entirely, and the Holy Spirit implies in one passage what he expresses in all others. This inspiration was not of the letter but of the Word. He upheld, however, the integrity of the canon, being influenced more by church tradition than by historical criticism, and is to be characterized as a dogmatic mystic. Mention should be made of the well-known and useful Polyglot Bible prepared together with K. G. W. Theile (4 vols., Bielefeld, 1846–55).   (F. A. Tholuck†.)

Bibliography: C. I. Nitzsch, *Rudolph Stier als Theologe*, Barmen, 1865; G. and F. Stier, *Ewald Rudolf Stier*, 2d ed. Wittenberg, 1871; J. P. Lacroix, *The Life of R. Stier*, New York, 1874; M. A. Landerer, *Neueste Dogmengeschichte*, p. 371, Heilbronn, 1881.

STIGEL, sti'gel (STIGELIUS), JOHANN: German humanist; b. at Frimar, near Gotha (77 m. s.w. of Leipsic), May 13, 1515; d. at Jena Feb. 11, 1562. Johann Stigel was a man who held a prominent position in the Wittenberg circle of Melanchthonian humanists, because of his extraordinary endowments. He entered the University of Wittenberg, 1531, where he first studied the ancient languages; and, later, medicine, physics, and astronomy; and soon became famous through his poems. By 1541 he was at Regensburg; and for a congratulatory poem to Charles V., *Germaniæ epistola gratulatoria* (1541), he received the imperial thanks and the title, *poëta laureatus*. In 1543 he received the *professura Terentiana* at the University of Wittenberg, and lectured on Terence, Hesiod, and Ovid. At the outbreak of the Schmalkald war he removed to Weimar, and, in 1547, to Jena, where he, with Victorinus Strigel, established a higher gymnasium, teaching rhetoric and poetics. This was the foundation of the new university, at the dedication of which, 1558, he delivered the oration. Difficult was his somewhat neutral position in the Philippist controversy (see Philippists), on account of his friendships in both camps, and just before the downfall of Flacius, 1561, it became almost intolerable. His poems indicate a pious and pure heart, and include elegies on Johann Friedrich, duke of Saxony, and Luther. Collections were published as *Poëmata* (in 9 books, Jena, 1566–72; 2 vols., 1577; 3 vols., 1600–01). A German hymn may be found in *Kirchenlied*, iv. 541 (Leipsic, 1862–77) by C. E. P. Wackernagel; and his Latin spiritual hymns (ib., i. 481–490). Besides, he was author of *Oratio de origine et usu sermonis* (1559); *Annotationes in Quintiliani institutionum librum x.*, in P. Melanchthon's *Annotationes in Quintilianum*, 1570; and *De anima commentarii, Melanchthonis explicatio* (Wittenberg, 1575).   (G. Kawerau.)

Bibliography: Among sources are his correspondence, in *CR*, vols. iii.–ix. Consult: K. Göttling, *Vita J. Stigelii Thuringi*, Jena, 1858; H. Fincelius, *Oratio de vita et obitu J. Stigelii*, ib. 1563; M. Adam, *Vitæ Germanorum philosophorum*, Heidelberg, 1615; *ADB*, xxxvi. 228 sqq.

STIGMATIZATION: The spontaneous formation of wounds on the persons of Christians similar to those received by Christ from the crown of thorns, crucifixion, and the spear. No reports of stigmatization date earlier than the thirteenth century, Francis of Assisi (q.v.) being the first who was affected with it, this taking place in 1224 at Mt. Alverna in the Apennines. Besides his, the Roman Catholic Church relates about eighty other cases, some of them exhibiting only a partial stigmatization; not all, however, are so strongly attested as that of Francis. Single cases of stigmatization have been observed even in recent times, attested both by men of repute and by many thousands who observed them. A case of this kind is that of Anna Katharina Emmerich (b. of pious peasants in 1774 near Coesfeld, 20 m. w. of Münster). From her youth she showed deep religious feelings and a rare modesty and humility. In 1803 she entered the convent of Agnetenberg, where she was affected with chronic illness. Soon after 1811 her body began to show complete stigmatization, which remained with her until 1819, when the scars were healed after prayer, though every Friday they assumed a red color and exuded blood. A similar case is that of Maria von Mörl (b. 1812 at Kaltern, 61 m. s. of Innsbruck, d. 1868), who showed stigmata in side, hands, and feet, witnessed by over 40,000 persons. The most recent instance is that of Louise Lateau of Bois d'Haine near Charleroi, 30 m. s. of Brussels (b. 1850; d. Aug. 25, 1883). Stigmatization may, therefore, be accepted as a fact, but its explanation is to be sought.

Roman Catholics regard stigmatization as a miracle, and Gregory IX., Alexander IV., and other popes have put themselves on record in the case of St. Francis. But the phenomenon may be explained in a natural way. The human soul possesses not only normal but what pass as abnormal powers. A work of art, for instance, owes its origin not merely to reason, but also to a subconscious instinct for creation. The same instinct appears in dream life, while unconscious powers direct the functions of the human organism. It is noteworthy that St. Francis and the other notable examples among the stigmatized suffered from morbid conditions from which an excess of psychic influence upon a morbidly inclined and weak body is intelligible. Protestants, therefore, while admitting stigmatization, do not attach to it the same value as Roman Catholics; on the other hand, it is admitted that stigmatization shows itself only in those who in glowing love have devoted themselves to the Savior.

(Julius Hamberger.†)

The phenomenon is one that is known outside religious circles. The exudation of blood through the skin is recognized by the medical profession and is described in many books on dermatology. There is, of course, no miracle in connection with the phenomenon.

Bibliography: The literature under Francis, Saint, of Assisi, especially the life (French and English) by P, Sabatier, to which is attached a critical study of stigmata, and that by F. E. Chavin de Malan, chaps. 14–15, Paris, 1845; A. Paleotti, *Historia admiranda de Jesu Christi stigmatibus*, ed. R. Gibbon, Antwerp, 1616; *Evangelische Kirchenzeitung*, 1835, pp. 180–201, 345–390; A. Tholuck, *Vermischte Schriften*, i. 97–133, Hamburg, 1839; the introduction to *Das bittere Leiden unseres Herrn Jesu Christi*, Munich, 1852; J. Ennemoser, *Der Magnetismus im Verhältnis zur Natur und zur Religion*, pp. 92–95, 131–142, Stuttgart, 1853; B. Johnen, *Louise Lateau. Kein Wunder, sondern Täuschung*, Leipsic, 1874; A. Rohling, *Louise Lateau*, Paderborn, 1874; Charbonnier de Batty, *Maladies et facultés diverses des mystiques*, Brussels, 1875; P. Majunke, *Louise Lateau*, Berlin, 1875; T. Schwann, *Mein Gutachten über die Versuche an Louise Lateau*, Cologne, 1875; Warlomont, *Louise Lateau, Rapport médical sur la stigmatisée de Bois d'Haine*, Brussels and Paris, 1875; *Die Stigmatisierten des 19. Jahrhunderts*, Regensburg, 1877; C. Berens, *Louise Lateau nach den neuesten Beobachtungen und Erscheinungen*, Paderborn, 1878; J. J. von Görres, *The Stigmata: a History of various Cases*, London, 1883 (a transl. of part of *Die christliche Mystik*, ii. 410–456, 494–510, 4 vols., Regensburg, 1836–42); P. Pansier, *Les Manifestations oculaires de l'hystérie*, Paris, 1892; A. Imbert-Goubeyre, *La Stigmatication, l'extase divine, et les miracles de Lourdes*, 2 vols., Paris, 1894; P. Janet, *The Mental State of Hystericals. A Study of Mental Stigmata*, New York, 1901.

STILES, EZRA: American Congregationalist; b. at North Haven, Conn., Dec. 15, 1727; d. in New Haven May 12, 1795. He was graduated from Yale College, 1746; was tutor there 1749–55; he studied theology but turned to law, and was admitted to the bar in 1753; practised law two years, but returned to the ministry in 1755; he was pastor in Newport, R. I., 1755–77; in 1777, when the place was occupied by the British, he removed to Portsmouth to become pastor of the North Church. In Sept., 1777, he was elected president of Yale College, where he was professor of ecclesiastical history till 1780, when he became professor of divinity. He was accounted in his day the most learned and accomplished divine of the United States. He published *An Account of the Settlement of Bristol, R. I.* (Providence, 1785); and *A History of Three of the Judges of King Charles I., Major General Whalley, Major General Goffe, and Colonel Dixwell, who . . . fled to America and were secreted . . . for near thirty Years. With an Account of Mr. T. Wale of Narragansett, supposed to have been one of the Judges* (Hartford, 1794). He left an unfinished *Church History of New England*, and more than forty volumes of manuscripts.

BIBLIOGRAPHY: Consult the *Life* by A. Holmes, Boston, 1798; that by J. L. Kingsley, in J. Sparks's *Library of American Biography*, 10 vols., ib. 1834–38; W. B. Sprague, *Annals of the American Pulpit*, i. 470–479, New York, 1859; W. Walker, *Ten New England Leaders*, passim, ib. 1901; and *The Literary Diary of Ezra Stiles*, ed. F. B. Dexter, 3 vols. New York, 1901.

STILLING, JOHANN HEINRICH JUNG-: German mystic and writer of devotional works; b. in the village of Grund (23 m. n.e. of Göttingen) Sept. 12, 1740; d. at Carlsruhe Apr. 2, 1817. His name was Johann Heinrich Jung, but in the last twenty years of his life he called himself Jung-Stilling because he had written his autobiography under the name of Stilling. He was the son of a poor tailor and school-teacher and grandson of a charcoal-burner. In his tenth year Stilling was entrusted to the rector of the Latin school at Hilchenbach, where he studied Latin, mathematics, and history, and

attracted the attention of Pastor Seelbach, who in 1755 made him school-teacher at Litzel, at the age of fifteen. Here he read Homer, and also the works of Boehme, but lost the favor of Seelbach by his intercourse with separatists. Stilling returned to his home and assisted his father, but after a short interval began to teach again in Dreisbach and Klefeld. In 1762 he went as journeyman tailor on his travels, ultimately reaching Solingen, where he found work and spiritual advancement in the communities influenced by Spener and Tersteegen. Then he became tutor in the house of a well-to-do merchant. After a short time spent with a tailor, he taught again in the family of a merchant named Flender who gave him leisure and the means to continue his studies, especially in ancient and modern languages. During this time he became acquainted with the Roman Catholic preacher Molitor in Attendorn who was very successful in curing diseases of the eye and taught him his methods. From 1770 to 1772 Stilling studied medicine in Strasburg, where he became acquainted with Herder and Goethe. He then settled as physician in Elberfeld. In 1778 he received a call to Kaiserslautern as professor in the school of political economy. After the removal of this school to Heidelberg in 1784 and its connection with the university, Stilling went to Heidelberg, and in 1787 to Marburg in the same capacity. But, in spite of his success as teacher and physician, he became dissatisfied with his calling, and gave up his position in Marburg (1803) to accept a call of Elector Karl Friedrich of Baden, who settled an annuity upon him so that he might devote himself entirely to his religious calling and propagate religion and practical Christianity through his correspondence and literary activity. He lived in Heidelberg as a witness of the living God and herald of Christ, 1803–06; the rest of his life he spent in Carlsruhe.

Stilling was a "patriarch of revivals" who, in the time of indifference and of the atrocities of the French revolution, showed thousands of people where salvation from moral degeneration could be found, and led them again to a profounder religious feeling. His books still have influence, being the products of immediate personal experience. Three works of Stilling have especially established his fame and importance: *Heinrich Stillings Jugend* (1777); *Heinrich Stillings Jünglingsjahre* (1778); and *Heinrich Stillings Wanderschaft* (1778). The first of these won Goethe's ardent admiration. Of his attempts in the domain of belles-lettres, only *Theobald oder die Schwärmer* (1784–85) survived, and even that because it contains contributions to the history of the Separatists. *Heinrich Stillings häusliches Leben* (1789) and *Heinrich Stillings Lehrjahre* (1804) are continuations of the story of his life mentioned above, but they lack the depth and originality of the first works. *Das Heimweh, Scenen aus dem Geisterreiche, Siegesgeschichte der christlichen Religion* and *Theorie der Geisterkunde*, works of a mystical nature, were soon forgotten, but Stilling showed the irresistible power of personally experienced faith in his periodical publication, *Der graue Mann* (1795–1816), and in *Der christliche Menschenfreund* (1803–1815); *Taschenbuch für Freunde des Christentums*

(1805–16); and *Biblische Erzählungen* (1808–16). The poems of Stilling were collected after his death and published by his grandson W. E. Schwarz (Frankfort, 1821); his *Sämtliche Schriften* appeared Stuttgart, 1835–39; and *Sämtliche Werke*, in the same place, 1841–44.　　　　　　(A. Freybe.)

Bibliography: There have appeared in Eng. transl., *Theory of Pneumatology*, London, 1834; *Heinrich Stilling*, 3 parts, London, 1835–36 (transl. of the *Jugend, Jünglingsjahre*, and *Wanderschaft*, ut sup.); *Autobiography*, 2 vols., ib. 1835, 2d ed., 1842, abridged, 1847; and *Interesting Tales*, ib. 1837. For Stilling's life his autobiographic writings, as indicated in the text, are of course authoritative. Among sketches of the life may be named that by A. G. Rudelbach, in *Christliche Biographie. Lebensbeschreibungen der Zeugen der christlichen Kirche*, i. 435–514, Leipsic, 1849–50; the anonymous *Lebensgeschichte*, 3d ed., Berlin, 1859; and *ADB*, xiv. 697–705. Consult further: Nessler, *Étude théologique sur Jung Stilling*, Strasburg, 1860; and Stilling's correspondence with his friends, Berlin, 1905.

STILLINGFLEET, EDWARD: Church of England bishop of Worcester; b. at Cranborne (22 m. w. of Southampton) Apr. 17, 1635; d. at Westminster Mar. 27, 1699. He was educated at St. John's College, Cambridge (B.A. and fellow, 1653; M.A., 1656; B.D., 1663; D.D., 1668). He then served as private tutor, and in 1657 became rector of Sutton. Just after the Restoration, he published his *Irenicum, a Weapon Salve for the Churches Wounds* (London, 1661), an attempt at a compromise between the established church and the Presbyterians. The following year appeared his *Origines Sacræ, or Rational Account of the Christian Faith as to the Truth and Divine Authority of the Scriptures*, in which he dwelt upon the knowledge, fidelity, and integrity of Moses, and the inspiration of the prophets, as inferred from the fulfilment of their prophecies, and extended the work in the line of a general apologetic. While in many points the work is superseded by later productions, it remains a storehouse of learning, and displays much logical ability and lawyerlike habits of thought. This volume was followed, in 1665, by *A Rational Account of the Grounds of the Protestant Religion*, a publication issued to meet the Jesuit account of the Laud-Fisher controversy. In 1665 he became rector of St. Andrew's, Holborn, and preacher at the Rolls Chapel; in 1667, prebend of Islington in St. Paul's, exchanged for Newington in 1672; royal chaplain in 1667–68; canon in Canterbury cathedral in 1669; archdeacon of London, 1677; dean of St. Paul's, 1678. *The Unreasonableness of Separation* (2 parts, 1681–82) gave unmistakable proof that he had abandoned the moderate opinions, and dropped the conciliatory temper, expressed in his *Irenicum*. This brought on him answers in the way of defense, written by Owen, Baxter, and other non-conformists; and he candidly acknowledged his mistake. His *Origines Britannicæ* (1685) was an investigation of the sources of British ecclesiastical history (standard ed., 2 vols., Oxford, 1842). In 1689 he became bishop of Worcester, and as such took part in the commission for revising the Book of Common Prayer. In 1695 a violent dispute went on among certain non-conformists respecting Antinomianism; and some of the disputants appealed to Stillingfleet as a sort of arbitrator, a circumstance which showed that by this

time he had recovered his reputation as a healer of strife. An active mind like his would meddle in all sorts of questions, and he could not refrain from taking part in the great doctrinal controversy of the age. *A Discourse in Vindication of the Doctrine of the Trinity* was published in 1697. Stillingfleet was a metaphysician, as well as a divine, and criticized Locke's *Essay on the Human Understanding* the same year, following that up soon afterward by a rejoinder to Locke's reply. Other works are *The Council of Trent Examin'd and Disprov'd* (1688); and *Sermons* (4 vols., 1696–1701). A collected edition of his works, with his life by Richard Bentley, was published (6 vols., London, 1709–10).

Bibliography: Besides the Life by Bentley in the *Works*, ut sup., consult: G. Burnet, *Hist. of his own Time*, 6 vols., Oxford, 1833; T. Baker, *Hist. of the College of St. John . . . Cambridge*, ed. J. E. B. Mayor, ii. 698–703, London, 1869; *DNB*, lix. 375–378.

STILLMAN, CHARLES ALBERT: Southern Presbyterian; b. in Charlestown, S. C., Mar. 14, 1819; d. at Tuscaloosa, Ala., Jan. 25, 1895. He received his education at Oglethorpe University, Midway, Ga. (B.A., 1841) and at the Theological Seminary at Columbia, S. C. (graduated, 1844); was licensed by Charleston presbytery in 1844; in the same year served as substitute pastor of the Second Presbyterian Church of Charleston for six months during the absence of the pastor; was ordained by the presbytery of Tuscaloosa, Ala., in 1845; was pastor at Eutaw, Ala., 1844–53; at Gainesville, Ala., 1853–70; and at Tuscaloosa, Ala., 1870 till his death. He was moderator of the general assembly in 1876.

He was on the editorial staff of *The Southern Presbyterian* for a number of years, while that paper was published in Columbia, S. C. To him, more than to any one else, was due the founding at Tuscaloosa, Ala., of an institution for the training of colored ministers. From the time of its founding in 1878 up to within a few months of his death, he was the superintendent of the institution and watched over it with fatherly care. When he resigned from the superintendency, the general assembly in recognition of his services named the school the Stillman Institute for Training Colored Ministers.

　　　　　　　　　　　　　　　R. C. Reed.

STIRLING TRACT ENTERPRISE. See Tract Societies, III., 3.

STOCK, EUGENE: Church of England layman; b. at Westminster Feb. 26, 1836. He received his education at private schools, and was in mercantile life till 1873, though he acted as honorary editor to the Church of England Sunday School Institute, 1867–75; he was in succession editor, editorial secretary, and general secretary of the Church Missionary Society, 1873–1906, and vice-president since 1906; member of the London diocesan conference since 1882, member of the house of laymen of the Canterbury ecclesiastical province since 1885, and diocesan reader for the diocese of London since 1891; and contributor to the American *Sunday School Journal*, 1873–81. He belongs to the Evangelical party in the Church of England. He has published: *Lessons on the Life of our Lord* (London, 1871, and often, 200,000 copies sold); *Lessons on the Acts of the Apostles* (1872); *Story of the Fuh-Kien Mission of the Church Missionary Society* (1877); *Steps to Truth* (1878, many editions, also translations into other languages); *Japan and the Japan Mission of the Church Missionary Society* (1880); *Lesson Studies in Genesis* (1885); *History of the Church Missionary Society* (3 vols., 1899); *One Hundred Years of the Church Missionary Society* (1899); *Short Handbook of Missions* (1904); *Notes on India for Missionary Students* (1905); *The Story of Church Missions* (1907); *Talks on St. Luke's Gospel* (1907); and *My Recollections* (1909).

STOCK, SIMON. See SIMON (SIMEON) STOCK, SAINT.

STOCKFLETH, stoc′flet, NILS JOACHIM CHRISTIAN VIBE: Norwegian missionary; b. at Fredriksstad Jan. 11, 1787; d. at Sandefjord (58 m. s.s.w. of Christiania) Apr. 26, 1866. By the death of his father, who was a preacher, in 1794, his mother was left in dire poverty with three children of whom Nils was the oldest. She afterward moved to Copenhagen in order to give the two oldest boys a legal education. Nils, however, had a strong inclination for theology. In 1805 the mother died; and the two boys, overcome by sickness, grief, and overwork, were brought into a hospital in great destitution. Nils received a lieutenancy in the army during the European war, and upon the conclusion of peace (1814) was honorably discharged with the rank of captain. He then returned and entered the Norwegian army. He became a tutor in the family of a rural preacher near Waldres in 1818, which led to a revival of his desire for the study of theology. He entered the University of Christiania in 1823, and was ordained a missionary to Finmark (northernmost Norway) in 1825; and in spite of his weak lungs and his paralyzed right arm, he, accompanied by his wife, went to Vadsö on the Arctic Ocean, the same year. Finmark has an area of 18,250 square miles and a scattered Finnish population of 21,000, either engaged in the fisheries or following with their reindeer a nomadic life inland. As the only other church district was without a pastor, Stockfleth's field included this wide extent. At the beginning of the eighteenth century, the Finns of this province were only nominally Christians, demoralized by the liquor traffic and the selfish spoliation of the Norwegians. The Gospel had been planted by the zealous teacher Isaac Olsen (1703–16) and by Thomas von Westen (q.v.), the "Apostle to the Finns." In order to serve the six churches Stockfleth was obliged to make long and perilous journeys, sometimes by boat, sometimes by sled, even as far as into the Russian empire. Finding the work undertaken beyond one man's strength, he determined to confine himself to the ministry of the Lapps, sharing with them their huts and fare, in order to master their speech and win their confidence. At one-fourth his former income he therefore assumed the Lebesby pastorate (1828). His work was an incessant itinerancy; he tarried usually about eight weeks in a district and stopped only briefly with the families scattered miles apart. More and more the conviction increased upon him of the inadequacy

of the literature for the Finns. With great exertion he had translated Erik Pontoppidan's explanation of the catechism, the New Testament, and the book of Genesis. These he consigned with others to the flames in 1830. He was more and more impressed with the necessity for the establishment of the Lappish literary language upon a new basis. In preparation for this work he spent the years 1831–33 in Christiania, Copenhagen, Stockholm, and Helsingfors, holding conferences with leading scholars. Having returned to Finmark in 1833, he invented a new phonic alphabet. In 1836 he journeyed to Christiania to publish his writings, and prepared two students in the Lappish language. The year 1837 he spent in Finland for a more thorough study of Finnish, and, upon his return to Christiania, published a primer and reader, Luther's Shorter Catechism, a translation of Matthew and Mark, and a Biblical history. This was done at the expense of the Storthing, which authorized also a complete translation of the Bible. Then he turned his attention again to the mountain Lapps (1840–1845, 1851–62), always intent upon the instruction of pastors for the people. The history of all his missionary expeditions he published in his *Dagbog over mine Missionsreiser i Finmarken* (Christiania, 1860), with an appendix giving an excerpt from the most important writings on Finnish history and language. An episode in the last period of his work was a wave of religious frenzy originating from the preaching of Lars Lewi Læstadius in a neighboring Swedish diocese. This movement threatened the public peace as well as public and private morals. Stockfleth hastened to the scene, and for six months waged battle against the morbid outbreak. Exhausted in strength, he retired in 1853, after having been pensioned; and spent the remaining years of his life (1853–66) at the baths of Sandefjord. His "Religious Letters" (1845) show a profound religious life. (J. BELSHEIM.)

BIBLIOGRAPHY: The principal source is his own *Dagbog*, ut sup. Sketches of his life are by J. Forschhammer, Copenhagen, 1867; and C. H. Kalkar, in F. Piper's *Evangelisches Kalendar*, 1867. Consult also H. Steffens, *Ueber die Lappen und Pastor Stockfleths Wirksamkeit unter diesen*, Berlin, 1842.

STOCKTON, THOMAS HEWLINGS: Methodist Protestant; b. at Mount Holly, N. J., June 4, 1808; d. in Philadelphia Oct. 9, 1868. Converted in the Methodist Episcopal Church, he joined the Methodist Protestant Church on its organization, and in 1829 was placed upon a circuit. He was stationed in Baltimore, 1830; was chaplain to the house of representatives, 1833–35 and 1859–61, and to the senate, 1862. He preached in Philadelphia, 1838–1847; in Cincinnati, 1847–50; as associate pastor in Baltimore, 1850–56; as sole pastor in Philadelphia, 1856–68. He was one of the most eloquent preachers of his day, and was an anti-slavery pioneer. He compiled a hymn-book for his denomination (1837), and published *Sermons for the People* (Pittsburg, 1854); *Poems, with Autobiographic and Other Notes* (Philadelphia, 1862); and *Book above All; or, the Bible the only sensible, infallible and divine Authority on Earth: Discourses* (1870).

BIBLIOGRAPHY: A. Clark, *Memory's Tribute to the Life, Character, and Work of the Rev. T. H. Stockton*, New York

1869; J. G. Wilson, *Life, Character and Death of Rev. T. H. Stockton*, Philadelphia, 1869.

STODDARD, CHARLES AUGUSTUS: Presbyterian; b. in Boston, Mass., May 28, 1833. He was educated at Williams College, Williamstown, Mass. (A.B., 1854), the University of Edinburgh and Free Church of Scotland Theological Seminary (1855–56), and at Union Theological Seminary (graduated, 1859), after which he was pastor of the Washington Heights Presbyterian Church, New York City, until 1883. In 1869 he was associate editor, in 1873 part owner, and from 1885 to 1902 editor-in-chief of *The Observer;* he has also been active in directing and promoting various philanthropic enterprises. He edited *The Centennial Celebration of Williams College* (Williamstown, Mass., 1894) and has written *Across Russia from the Baltic to the Danube* (New York, 1891); *Spanish Cities, with Glimpses of Gibraltar and Tangier* (1892); *Beyond the Rockies* (1894); *A Spring Journey in California* (1895); and *Cruising Among the Caribbees* (1895; new ed., 1903).

STODDARD, DAVID TAPPAN: Congregational missionary; b. at Northampton, Mass., Dec. 2, 1818; d. at Urumiah, Persia, Jan. 22, 1857. He studied at Round Hill Academy and Williams College; was graduated from Yale College, 1838, and from Andover Theological Seminary, 1841; sailed as missionary to the Nestorians, 1843, among whom he labored successfully. From 1848 to 1851 he was in America on a visit. He was particularly interested in the Nestorian youths whom he gathered in the seminary established in 1844 at Urumiah. His theological lectures, which embraced a complete course of doctrinal theology, he delivered in Syriac. His *Grammar of the Modern Syriac Language* was published in the *Journal of the American Oriental Society*, New Haven, Conn., 1855.

BIBLIOGRAPHY: J. P. Thompson, *Memoir of David Tappan Stoddard* New York, 1858.

STODDARD, SOLOMON: Congregationalist; b. in Boston, Mass., 1643; d. at Northampton, Mass., Feb. 11, 1729. He was graduated from Harvard College, 1662; was chaplain in Barbados for two years; preached at Northampton 1669–1729, when he was succeeded by his grandson, and colleague from 1727, Jonathan Edwards. From 1667 to 1674 he was first librarian at Cambridge. He is remembered for his theory that " the Lord's Supper is instituted to be a means of regeneration," and that persons may and ought to come to it, though they know themselves to be in a " natural condition." He wrote *The Safety of Appearing at the Day of Judgement, in the Righteousness of Christ* (Boston, 1687; 3d ed., 1742); *The Doctrine of Instituted Churches Explained and Proved from the Word of God* (Boston, 1700; a reply to Increase Mather's *The Order of the Gospel, Professed and Practised by the Churches of Christ in New England, Justified*, Boston and London, 1700); *An Appeal to the Learned, Being a Vindication of the Right of visible Saints to the Lord's Supper, though they be Destitute of a saving Work of God's Spirit on their Hearts; Against the Exceptions of Mr. Increase Mather* (1709); *A Guide to Christ, or the Way of Directing*

Souls that are under Conversion (1714); *An Answer to some Cases of Conscience* (1722).

BIBLIOGRAPHY: W. B. Sprague, *Annals of the American Pulpit*, i. 172–174, New York, 1859; W. Walker, *Creeds and Platforms of Congregationalism*, passim, ib. 1893; idem, in *American Church History Series*, iii. 180–182, 188, 251, 254, ib. 1894; idem, *Ten New England Leaders*, pp. 219, 227, 232, 245–247, ib. 1901; L. W. Bacon, *The Congregationalists*, pp. 81, 113, 117, 119, ib. 1904; F. H. Foster, *Genetic Hist. of New England Theology*, pp. 30, 32, 36–40, 51, Chicago, 1907.

STOECKER, stuk'er, ADOLF: German United Evangelical; b. at Halberstadt (31 m. s.w. of Magdeburg) Dec. 15, 1835; d. at Nuremberg Feb. 25, 1908. He was educated at the universities of Halle and Berlin (1854–57); was private tutor in Neustadt (1857–59) and in Kurland (1859–63); became pastor at Seggerda, near Halberstadt, where he remained until 1866, when he was called in a similar capacity to Hamersleben; from 1871 to 1874 he was military divisional pastor at Metz (1871–74); was court and cathedral preacher at Berlin (1874–91); in 1891 his political views caused his dismissal. In 1878 he became a member of the general synod of the Evangelical Church. Stöcker's chief fame is due to his foundation, in 1878, of the Christian socialist party, and to his sturdy advocacy of anti-Semitism, since he regarded Judaism as a danger both to Christianity and to the political strength of Germany.

Stoecker was elected as the avowed advocate of these views to the Prussian diet in 1879, retaining office until 1898, while from 1881 to 1893 he was likewise a member of the Reichstag, reelected in 1898. He served as president of the Christlich-Sozialer Verein, which, owing to the decline of the anti-Semitic movement in Germany, had diminished in prestige. In 1887 he founded the *Deutsche evangelische Kirchenzeitung*, which he edited after 1892. He wrote *Christlich-Sozial* (Bielefeld, 1884); *Eins ist Not, ein Jahrgang Volkspredigten über freie Texte* (Berlin, 1884); *O Land, höre des Herrn Wort, ein Jahrgang Volkspredigten über die Episteln* (1885); *Den Armen wird das Evangelium gepredigt* (1887); *Die sozialen und kirchlichen Notstände in grossen Städten* (Stuttgart, 1888); *Wandelt im Geist* (Berlin, 1888); *Die sonntägliche Predigt* (1889); *Salz der Erde* (1892); *Wach auf, evangelisches Volk* (1893); *Dreizehn Jahre Hofprediger und Politiker* (1895); *Gesammelte Schriften* (1896); *Verheissung und Erfüllung* (1896); *Das Evangelium eine Gotteskraft* (1900); *Beständig in der Apostel Lehre* (1901); and *Das Leben Jesu in täglichen Andachten* (1903).

STOESSEL, JOHANN: German theologian; b. at Kitzingen (10 m. s.e. of Würzburg) June 23, 1424; d. at Senftenberg (33 m. n.e. of Dresden) Mar. 18, 1576. After taking his degree at Wittenberg in 1549, he was called, as an anti-Philippist, to Weimar by Duke John Frederick as chaplain, and in this capacity he took part with Maximilian Mörlin, court chaplain at Coburg, in introducing the Reformation in the margravate of Baden-Durlach in 1556, vigorously opposing everything divergent from strict Lutheranism. In the same spirit he opposed Melanchthon at the colloquy of Worms in the following year. He was made superintendent at Heldburg, and in 1558 took part, with Mörlin and Simon Musaeus, in the preparation of the Weimar "Book of Confutation," which they defended against Victorinus Strigel and Pastor Hügel in a special *Apologie* in 1559. The next year Stössel and Mörlin accompanied John Frederick to Heidelberg, in the hope of keeping the duke's father-in-law, Elector Frederick the Pious, firm in Lutheranism. This proved impossible, however, and shortly after Stössel's return a change became apparent in his own attitude. In ensuing controversies between Lutheran and Calvinistic theologians both he and Mörlin assumed an intermediate position, and in this frame of mind became councilors of John Frederick, though at the Naumburg Diet of princes in 1561 they still worked on the side of Flacius. But when Stössel was appointed, first temporarily and then (Sept., 1561) definitely, superintendent in Jena, his mediating position became more pronounced, and with his limitation of the theological controversy of the Jena professors and the elevation of the Weimar consistory, at his instance, to the supreme church authority in Thuringia, with himself as its assessor, the breach between him and the Flacian party became complete, so that when Flacius and Wigand protested in writing against him, he lodged complaint against them at court.

The result of this controversy was the deposition of both his opponents and the rout of their whole party, while Stössel was appointed to a theological professorship and undertook the difficult task of mediating between the Flacian clergy and the synergistic Strigel. But his *Superdeclaratio*, composed to this end, caused fresh dissension and the dismissal of some forty recalcitrant pastors in 1562–1563, as well as a bitter literary controversy. Strigel, suspicious of Stössel, resigned from the faculty, and for a time Stössel was the sole theological professor at Jena, of which he was rector in 1563, 1565, and 1567. After the fall of John Frederick, his brother and successor, John William, recalled the exiled pastors in 1567, and they issued, against Stössel's *Superdeclaratio*, their own *Responsio exulum Thuringicorum*, compelling all who had subscribed to his work to resign. Through the influence of the Elector August he was appointed superintendent in Mühlhausen, whence he was transferred to Pirna, becoming ecclesiastical councilor and confessor to the elector. In May, 1570, at the colloquy of Zerbst, he sought recognition for the *Corpus doctrinæ Philippicum*. But his plea for the crypto-Calvinism of the Philippists doomed him, and in March he was confined to his house in Pirna, where he signed a declaration submitted to him by the elector. At the Diet of Torgau, however, his disrespectful utterances about high personages were brought to formal notice, in August he was removed to the fortress of Senftenberg, and in Jan., 1576, again underwent a formal trial.

Stössel's revulsion from the Flacians of Jena receives its explanation from their terrorism, but his change to crypto-Calvinism is more difficult to account for. Many of his contemporaries ascribed it to unworthy motives; and it is impossible to tell how far personal ambition was the cause, or how far the reason lies simply in the development of his views of theology and of the Church.

(G. Kawerau.)

Bibliography: H. Heppe, *Geschichte des Protestantismus*, vols. i.–ii., Marburg, 1852–53; A. Kluckhohn, *Friedrich der Fromme*, pp. 69 sqq., Nördlingen, 1879; R. Hofmann, *Geschichte der Kirche St. Marien in Pirna*, pp. 38 sqq., Pirna, 1890; *ADB*, xxxvi. 471 sqq.

STOICISM: One of the philosophic-ethical schools of ancient Greece and Rome. The founder of Stoicism was Zeno of Citium in Cyprus (d. in Athens c. 260 B.C.), originally a trader, who in middle life determined to reside permanently in Athens. Here, in the *Stoa poikile*, the colonnade adorned with frescoes of patriotic themes of Attic legends and history, he was wont to meet his followers, hence the name. The formal resolutions of the Attic government in his honor seem to attest the substantial consistency of his conduct and of his doctrine. Neither his direct successors, Cleanthes of Assos (d. about 220 B.C.), and Chrysippus the Cilician (d. about 207 B.C.), nor Panætius (d. 112 B.C.) and Posidonius (d. about 50 B.C.) can be here discussed. What is of interest is the attitude of the school toward religion and ethics.

Formally the Stoics were materialists. Even deity, divinity, God, was to them a substance, ether, the most delicate and all-pervasive element. In the periodic processes of cosmic making and unmaking, whether through fire or deluge, this alone is imperishable and eternal. Of this substance are the individual souls of men, but they are not immortal. "God," "universe," "the world," "fate," "providence," "Zeus," all these as well as "reason" are merely terms and names for one and the same thing (Diogenes Laertius, vii. 135). God is immanent in the world, dissolving it in cosmic periods into himself and creating it again out of himself. Intelligence and providence pervade and permeate the world. Past and future are infinite eternities, the present only is limited. Toward the physical personifications of the so-called religion of the Greeks, this school assumed an attitude which, when superficially considered, appeared to be conservative, but it was in effect destructive. They resorted to allegories and allegorical interpretation. This matter and method found its way into the schools of those who expounded Homer and Hesiod, and was reasserted later on by Cornutus in Rome, a contemporary of Claudius and Nero, as well as by Neoplatonists like Porphyry and Servius. How practise of sincere worship could abide with this allegorical dissolution of Hera, Athena, Zeus, and the rest it is hard to see; at the same time the scandalous elements of Homeric anthropomorphism were abolished, names, legends, and symbols being preserved.

The relation of man to himself, to God or the world, and to his fellow men, is best expressed in the axiomatic postulate that "man must live in consonance with nature"; here they differed profoundly from their chief adversaries, the Epicureans, as well as from the Greek contentment with mere physical felicity. They claimed that "nature," "God," "reason," direct man to seek the highest good in virtue, not in pleasure. This was the voice of that nature, that rational ideal of giving sovereignty to God in man, to that precept which will justify conduct before the universal reason, and thus make it by implication obligatory on all.* Thus the Stoics elevated Socrates to a dominating position. Between virtue and moral wrong there are no intermediate steps or gradations. Nor are there any degrees of difference or elevation within the category of virtue or of vice. Virtue, unless it appears in action, is of no value. What men mainly cherish, the boons of health, wealth, honor, power, pleasure, must not be the objects of action, for they are neither good nor bad in themselves, but are intermediate or indifferent (*adiaphora*).

Stoics thus took a distinctly spiritual ground, and a vigorous " contempt for the world " can not be denied to some members of the school. At the same time everything, at bottom, is centered in the subject, and suicide is commended as a termination of trouble or as preservation of freedom. Cato, the opponent of Cæsar, and afterward, under the emperors, Pætus Thrasea, Seneca (q.v.), Lucan, Cornutus, and his pupil the poet Persius, Helvidius Priscus, and Epictetus were notable adherents of this school, which really made great demands on its followers, and gained from the general body of their various contemporaries a large measure of respect, being by far the most virile form of thought which arose among the ancients. The Antonine emperors, whose creed Stoicism was, did much for the improvement of slavery, but Marcus also directed a persecution of the Christians. See NATURAL LAW.

E. G. SIHLER.

BIBLIOGRAPHY: Sources are Diogenes Laertius, book vii., Eng. transls. were published, London, 1688, 1696, and in *Bohn's Library*, 1853; Plutarch, from his *Opera*, best ed., ed. T. Doehner and others, 3 vols., Paris, 1846–55, may be named *De Stoicorum repugnantiis, De placitis philosophorum;* Cicero, *De natura deorum*, Eng. transl., London, 1896, *De finibus*, Eng. transl., ib. 1890; Epictetus, *Works* (Eng. transl.), new ed., Boston, 1891; idem, *Discourses*, 2 vols., London, 1897 (a fine ed., published by Humphreys), other translations are issued by Dent, London, 1899, and by Bell, ib. 1903; Marcus Aurelius, *Golden Book*, ed. W. H. D. Rouse, London, 1900 (another transl., 1906); idem, *Meditations*, Edinburgh, 1904 (a fine edition), London, 1905 (in *Standard Library*), with title *Marcus Aurelius to Himself*, transl. and introductions by G. H. Rendall, London and New York, 1901; idem, *Thoughts*, London, 1890, with introduction by J. L. Spalding, London and New York, 1900; Seneca, *Minor Dialogues*, London, 1886; idem, *Morals*, ib. 1888; idem, *On Benefits*, ib. 1887; idem, *Tranquillity of Mind and Providence*, New York, 1900.

The subject is discussed in the works on the history of philosophy by H. Ritter, 4 vols., Oxford, 1836–46; J. E. Erdmann, New York, 1893; H. Ritter and L. Preller 8th ed., by E. Wellmann, Gotha, 1898. Consult further: W. W. Capes, *Stoicism*, London, 1880; E. Zeller, *Stoics, Epicureans, and Sceptics*, London, 1880; D. Tiedemann, *System der stoischen Philosophie*, 3 vols., Leipsic, 1776; A. Grant, *The Ancient Stoics*, Oxford, 1858; M. Arnold, *Marcus Aurelius*, in his *Essays in Criticism*, series 1, London, 1865; F. May Holland, *Reign of the Stoics*, New York, 1879; G. P. Weygoldt, *Die Philosophie der Stoa nach ihrem Wesen und ihren Schicksalen*, Leipsic, 1883; T. Jordan, *Stoic Moralists in the First Two Centuries*, Dublin, 1884; H. de Stein, *Die Psychologie der Stoa*, 2 vols., Berlin, 1886–88; J. Favre, *La Morale stoïcienne*, Paris, 1888; C. H. Herford, *The Stoics as Teachers*, Cambridge, 1889; F. W. Farrar, *Seekers after God*, new ed., London and New York, 1891; A. C. Pearson. in his *Fragments of Zeno and Cleanthes*, Cambridge, 1891; T. W. Rolleston, *The Teaching of Epictetus*, London, 1891; J. B. Lightfoot, *St. Paul and Seneca*, in his *Dissertations on the Apostolic Age*, London, 1892; A. Schmekel, *Die Philosophie der mittleren Stoa*, Berlin, 1892; J. B. Brown, *Stoics and Saints*, Glasgow, 1893; A. Bonhöffer, *Epiktetos und die Stoa*, Stuttgart, 1890; idem, *Die Ethik des Stoikers Epiktet*, ib. 1894; A. W. Benn, *The Philosophy of Greece*, London, 1898; A. Dyroff, *Die Ethik der alten Stoa*, Berlin, 1898; T. Gomperz, *Greek Thinkers*, 3 vols., London, 1901–05; A. P. Ball, *Satire of Seneca on the Apotheosis of Claudius: a Study*, New York, 1902; C. H. S. Davis, *Greek and Roman Stoicism*, Boston, 1903; E. Renan, *Marcus Aurelius*, recent issue, London, 1903; E. A. Abbott, *Silanus the Christian*, London, 1906 (a historical novel, but valuable); L. Alston, *Stoic and Christian in the Second Century*, London, 1906; W. H. D. Rouse, *Words of the Ancient Wise*, London, 1906 (selections from Epictetus and Marcus Aurelius); W. L. Davidson, *The Stoic Creed*, Edinburgh, 1907; St. George Stock, *Stoicism* (in *Philosophies, Ancient and Modern*), Edinburgh, 1908, New York, 1909; T. Zielinski, *Cicero im Wandel der Jahrhunderte*, Leipsic, 1908; F. W. Bussell, *Marcus Aurelius and the Later Stoics*, Edinburgh, 1909; R. D. Hicks, *Stoic and Epicurean*, London and New York, 1910; E. V. Arnold, *Roman Stoicism*, London, 1911; and the literature under EPICTETUS, MARCUS AURELIUS ANTONINUS, and SENECA.

STOKES, GEORGE THOMAS: Irish ecclesiastical historian; b. at Athlone (70 m. w. of Dublin), Ireland, Dec. 28, 1843; d. in Dublin Mar. 24, 1898. He studied at Galway grammar-school and at Queens College, Galway; was graduated from Trinity College, Dublin (B.A., 1864; M.A., 1871; B.D., 1881; and D.D., 1886); was vicar of All Saints, Newtown Park, Dublin, 1868–98; became assistant to the regius professor of divinity, 1880, and professor of ecclesiastical history in the University of Dublin, 1883; librarian of St. Patrick's Library, Dublin, 1887; and prebend and canon of St. Andrew, 1893. He published *Ireland and the Celtic Church. A History of Ireland from St. Patrick to the English Conquest in 1172* (London, 1886); a commentary on the Acts, 2 vols., in *The Expositor's Bible* (1888); *Ireland and the Anglo-Norman Church. A History of Ireland and Irish Christianity from the Anglo-Norman Conquest to the Dawn of the Reformation* (1889); *Dudley Loftus: A Dublin Antiquary of the seventeenth Century* (Dublin, 1890); *The Island Monasteries of Wales and Ireland* (1891); *St. Fechin of Fone, and his Monastery* (1892); *Greek in Gaul and Western Europe down to A.D. 700. The Knowledge of Greek in Ireland between A.D. 500 and 900* . . . (1892); *Calendar of the Liber Niger Alani* (1893); and, in collaboration with C. H. H. Wright, *The Writings of St. Patrick;* . . . *a . . . Translation,* . . . *with Notes* (1887).

BIBLIOGRAPHY: *DNB*, Supplement iii. 361–362; *Athenæum*, Apr. 2, 1898.

STOLBERG, FRIEDRICH LEOPOLD, COUNT: German author and convert to the Roman Catholic faith; b. at Bramstedt (23 m. n. of Hamburg) Nov. 7, 1750; d. on the estate of Sondermühlen near Osnabrück (65 m. s.s.w. of Bremen) Dec. 5, 1819. After the removal of his family to Copenhagen, he was educated there, together with his brother Christian, two years older than himself. Klopstock, a friend of the family, exercised a deep influence upon the two boys. They studied at Halle in 1770–71, and at Göttingen in 1772–73. In Göttingen they became a part of the well-known " Hainbund,"

---

* ὅσα λόγος αἱρεῖ ποιεῖν (Diogenes Laertius, vii. 108) is essentially as sound as Kant's " categorical imperative."

which names a certain period of development in modern poetry. In 1775 the two brothers undertook a journey through Germany to Switzerland, making the acquaintance of prominent men, in Frankfort associating with Goethe, and at Geneva meeting Voltaire. In 1776 Friedrich Leopold was appointed ambassador at the Danish court by the prince-bishop of Lübeck and the duke of Oldenburg. The literary productions of Stolberg were at that time in the region of lyrical poetry. At the same time he occupied himself with the study of the Greeks, translating the Iliad, also some portions of Æschylus, and composing several dramas in the Greek form. In 1785 he was sent on a mission to St. Petersburg, where he met Klinger. In 1789 he was appointed Danish ambassador in Berlin, and in 1791 the prince-bishop of Lübeck appointed him president of the government in Eutin, but before he entered his new position, he traveled to Italy, and also visited Münster, where he met the Princess Galitzin, a devoted Roman Catholic. Münster at that time was the seat of a Catholicism in which Biblical Christianity predominated over Romanism. An interview with the pope later filled Stolberg with admiration. In 1793 he returned to Eutin and entered his new position, but remained in close contact with the circle of Münster while Voss, with whom he had hitherto been in close relations, seemed the representative of superficial rationalism. In 1793 Princess Galitzin returned his visit; in 1794 Stolberg visited in Münster, being powerfully attracted by Fürstenberg and the princess. The change in his opinions appears in a ·letter to F. H. Jacobi, written in February, 1794, in which he says: " I know and love the mysticism of a Plato, one of my first favorites . . . but the kind of revelation that was granted them remains as distinct from that of the Bible as the heaven is above the earth "; while later it was declared of him: " The miserable condition of Protestantism, that leads to deism, atheism, to a rationalism that eats and destroys all mystic roots like cancer, the philosophy of Kant, and the whole Enlightenment repelled him more and more." In 1798 he visited the Brethren in Herrnhut to see whether he could there find peace and rest. On June 1, 1800, Stolberg, together with his family, adopted the Roman Catholic faith in the chapel of Princess Galitzin. By this step he offended most deeply all Protestant North Germany, but especially his older circle of friends, Voss, Jacobi, Gleim, and others. After tendering his resignation to the duke, Stolberg retired into private life and settled near Münster, on the estate of Lütjenbeck. In 1811 he removed to the estate of Tatenhausen near Bielefeld, and in 1816 to Sondermühlen. Meanwhile he had published his lyrical poems, together with those of his brother Christian (Leipsic, 1779, new ed., 1821, and separately Vaterländische Gedichte, again combined with those of his brother, Hamburg, 1815). He was the author also of Zwo Schriften des heiligen Augustin von der wahren Religion und von den Sitten der katholischen Kirche (1803). But the work which filled almost the whole remainder of his life was his Geschichte der Religion Jesu Christi (15 vols., Hamburg, 1806-18). It extends only to the year 430, and was continued by

F. von Kerz (vols. xvi.–xlv., Mainz, 1825–46) and by J. N. Brischar (vols. xlvi.–li., 1849–53). The work shows a lack of critical discernment and system, and a hasty pen. He also published Leben Alfreds des Grossen (Münster, 1817), with an introduction on Anglo-Saxon history; and Ein Büchlein von der Liebe (1818; Eng. transl., A Little Book of the Love of God, London, 1849), a coherent representation of the Biblical doctrine of love. His Reise in Deutschland, der Schweiz, Italien und Sicilien (4 vols., Königsberg, 1794) was translated into English (2 vols., London, 1796–97).   (A. Freybe.)

Bibliography: Biographies· have been written by A. Nicolovius, Mainz, 1846; T. Menge, 2 vols., Gotha, 1862; J. Janssen, 3d ed., Freiburg, 1882; and K. Windel, 2d ed., Potsdam, 1896. Consult further: C. F. A. Schott, Voss und Stolberg, oder der Kampf des Zeitalters zwischen Licht und Verdunkelung, Stuttgart, 1820; W. von Bippen, Eutiner Skizzen. Zur Kultur- und Litteraturgeschichte des 18. Jahrhundert, Weimar, 1859; W. Herbst, Johannes H. Voss, vol. ii., Leipsic, 1874; also J. H. Hennes, F. L. Graf zu Stolberg und Herzog Peter Friedrich Ludwig von Oldenburg aus ihrem Briefwechsel, Mainz, 1870.

STOLE. See Vestments and Insignia, Ecclesiastical.

STOLE FEES, SURPLICE FEES: Name applied to fixed contributions to the clergy for certain official services rendered, paid by the person at whose behest such service is rendered. In a

History in the Roman Catholic Church. wider sense the term includes the fees of such lower clergy as cantors, organists, and sacristans. The term first appears in the later Middle Ages, and originated in the fact that the clergy in the Roman Catholic Church, then as now, was obligated to perform those offices clad in the stole. In the Eastern Church these fees are known by the corresponding term for stole, epitrachelium. In the Middle Ages there is mention of justitia, jura presbyteri, and jura parochialia, or the fee is designated according to the particular service performed, as baptisterium, nuptiæ, or sepultura. In the early Church, the bishops furnished the support of the clergy, but many voluntary gifts were made as evidences of gratitude, as well as for support. But, by authority of Matt. x. 8, the acceptance of a voluntary gift for the performance of a holy act was expressly forbidden. Nevertheless, the desire of the people to retain the good-will of the clergy and prove their own acknowledgment, on the one hand, and the cupidity of the latter, on the other, led not only to offensive practise among the ordinary clergy, but even the bishops came to accept gifts for such transactions as ordination, dedication of churches, and confirmation. Again and again it became necessary for the Church to forbid the practise, excepting, however, voluntary gifts to the support of the clergy (I Cor. ix. 11–14; Matt. x. 10), if not given specifically for services performed. This standpoint appears in the ecclesiastical enactments of the twelfth century. Meanwhile an influence among the lower churches and clergy operated to restrict the right of stole fees. This was the Germanic system of private temples. In the north, even in pagan times, the earl or private owner imposed upon those who frequented his temple a toll for the maintenance of the same and the support of his priest, as well as fees for specific services. The west and south Germans brought this custom with the system of private temples into the Church, and now the latter had to encounter as a system what before appeared only as more or less scattered abuses. The Church was a private enterprise of the landlord, who was not content with voluntary offerings and gifts, but demanded a fixed price for every important service by the priest, who was his private official. Naturally, this was extended to include baptism, marriage, penance, and unction; and, in combination with the other Germanic principle recognizing not free services but only those recompensed as efficacious, the system soon extended to the churches in the hands of the bishops and became universal. The stole fees were regarded as legal appurtenances of the churches, and were included in sales and investitures. In spite of earnest protest by legislation and through its representatives, the Church was not able to restrict this barter of religious offices, entrenched as it was behind the power and self-interest of the landlord and the legal order. In the end, when the danger of lay domination was, in principle at least, removed by the substitution of the right of Patronage (q.v.), the Church was not unwilling to assume this system of fees as resting upon custom, not without, inside of certain limits, a commending acquiescence in its origin. This took place in connection with the act on Simony (q.v.) of the Fourth Lateran Council under Innocent III. in 1215. Extortion for spiritual official services was forbidden, but where the payment of fees was according to established custom it was commended and sustained. To make this consistent with the prohibition of simony, such payments were not to be understood as specific recompense for the services, but simply as a tribute rendered in view of the obligation of clerical support and the recognition of parochial jurisdiction. It was also understood that the clergy were not to regard such fees as per contract, nor to direct their ministry accordingly; and for the poor the necessary services were to be gratis. In following times the acceptance of such contributions was made legitimate and it was only a step to sanctioning the right of the clerical to demand compensation, and also the legal obligation on his part to render the service. To this day the right to stole fees within " laudable custom " has retained the sanction of the Roman Catholic Church.

In the Evangelical church, some of the older regulations either wholly or partly abolished the stole-fees; as, for instance, for baptism and the communion. Generally, they have been permitted and remained customary in the Evangel-
History in ical church. Where, as in electoral
the Evan- Saxony, demand of them was forbid-
gelical den until the seventeenth century, the
Church. communion excepted, the practise of payments as free-will offerings persisted with reference to baptism and confession. Under the new régime of state government from the sixteenth century the states have assumed the control of, and, with the concurrence of the spiritual authorities, regulated, the system of stole fees. This standpoint has not been universally maintained, however, since the authorization of the

autonomy of the Roman Catholic Church in 1848. In fact, the right of the respective churches to fix and regulate fees for ecclesiastical transactions is inalienable; yet obligations involved are imposed upon the subjects of the State for the enforcement of which the State must lend its arm. Hence, the matter may not be wholly left in the hands of the Church, and the State is also entitled to the privilege of a normative cooperation. This rule prevails, for example, in Prussia; in Austria, on the other hand, alterations in the regulations are reserved by the State after the concurrence of the bishops. A state concurrence takes place where the Evangelical church possesses organized government and by the adaptation of presbyterial and synodal elements maintains a certain independence, and where the regulation of stole fees therefore devolves on the church boards in common with the parish organs. In principle, the obligation of paying stole fees pertains only to the members of the church of the officiating clergyman, which members alone are in a position to require the services. This is the present conception. But formerly, before the parity of the churches was established, the members of the merely tolerated bodies were forced to pay the fees to the pastor of the prevailing church, even where they were performed by pastors of their own confession.

Voices have been raised in the Roman Catholic Church for the abolition of stole fees, namely, in the Council of Trent, and spontaneously in the eighteenth and nineteenth centuries,
Efforts at though in vain against the practical
Abolition. difficulties involved. More earnestly was the practise felt to be improper in the Evangelical church (beginning with Spener) and its abolition was demanded. Until the last quarter of the last century this demand was met only in isolated instances. In 1818 Nassau, 1849 Oldenburg, and 1871 Brunswick abolished the fees in lieu of recompense from church funds or other sources. The introduction of the civil register and civil marriage by imperial statute (1875) provided for an indemnification of the clergy, and occasioned in a number of states the abolition of stole fees for baptisms, wedding ceremonies, and publishing of the bans, either in all churches or the Evangelical alone. Universal abolition was consummated in Prussia in 1890–1900. In Baden the redemption of the stole fees is assigned to the churches; elsewhere it is effected by state provisions. In Prussia the churches are reenforced, if the redemption taxes make an increase in the total expenses, by a state-church fund.

While the Old Catholics did not adopt the system at all, it is in full sway in the Eastern Church, as well as in the Roman Catholic
Modern Church. Those entitled to stole fees
Practise. in the latter are the parish priest, a clerical whose position is materially the same, or an assistant, either on formal assignment by the parish priest or through special title. Stole fees must be authorized by church statute or recognized custom. They usually occur in connection with baptisms, publishing of bans, marriages, the blessing and attendance upon the deceased, and the churching of women. It is excluded in respect

to the dispensation of the other sacraments, as the communion, extreme unction, and ordination, and frequently, penance. In individual dioceses the fees in connection with baptisms, penance, and the churching of women are dispensed with. The amount depends on the regulations or local custom. The earlier practise of proportioning the tax according to the rank of the person is discontinued, but instead there is introduced a grading according to the means of the applicant, that is, his civic assessment. The regulation of the stole-fee system is under the jurisdiction of the bishop, with the advice of the priests and his assistants. By a decree of 1896 this is conditioned by previous concurrences in provincial synods or bishops' conventions. Disputes, according to canon law, are subject to the ecclesiastical courts. In Prussia the state courts, by virtue of state control, may hear and adjudicate complaints. In Bavaria the administrative boards and administrative courts control disputes and enforce payments, and in Austria these, in addition, punish exorbitant charges by a fine and enforced restitution. From stole fees are to be excepted the stipends for masses, and fees for burial sites, pews, utensils, and candles. The legal administration of stole fees according to Evangelical church law is similar to the Roman Catholic. They must not be asked in advance, nor must the rites be suspended until payment has been made, and the necessary official services must be rendered to the poor. Those legally entitled are the official pastors, or, relatively, church treasuries, or those who administer the pastoral income. The whole amount is regulated by the church order or canonical precept with allowance for local observances. The levy and approval of the taxes belongs to the church governing boards. With the introduction of presbyterial and synodal provisions the initiative to alteration devolves upon the congregational organs. (U. STUTZ.)

BIBLIOGRAPHY: H. M. G. Grellmann, *Kurze Geschichte der Stolgebühren*, Göttingen, 1785; F. F. Fertsch, *Das Beichtgeld in der protestantischen Kirche*, Giessen, 1830; J. A. H. Tittmann, *Ueber die Fixierung der Stolgebühren*, Leipsic, 1831; P. Baldauf, *Die . . . Stolgebühren in den österreichischen Provinzen*, Graz, 1835; E. L. Hagen, *Die pfarramtlichen Besoldungen*, Neustadt, 1844; F. Koldewey, *Das Alter der Stolgebühren in der evang.-lutherischen Kirche des Herzogtums Braunschweig*, Brunswick, 1871; R. D. Urlin, *Legal Guide to the Clergy*, London, 1881; H. W. Cripps, *The Law Relating to the Church and Clergy*, ed. C. A. Cripps, London, 1886; J. H. Blunt, *Book of Church Law*, Revised by Sir W. G. F. Phillimore, London, 1888; G. Bossert, *Die Stolgebührenfrage in der evangelischen Landeskirche Württembergs*, Stuttgart, 1891; A. Luchaire, *Manuel des institutions françaises, période des Capétiens directs*, pp. 350–351, Paris, 1892; L. Benario, *Die Stolgebühren nach bayerischem Staatskirchenrecht*, Munich, 1894; V. Karl, *Grundzüge des bayerischen Stolrechtes*, Würzburg, 1894; U. Stutz, *Die Eigenkirche als Element des mittelalterlich-germanischen Kirchenrechts*, p. 27, Berlin, 1895; idem, *Geschichte des kirchlichen Benefizialwesens*, i. 1, pp. 93, 272, ib. 1895; J. Imbart de la Tour, *Les Paroisses rurales du iv. au xi. siècle*, Paris, 1900; C. Meurer, *Bayerisches Kirchenvermögensrecht*, ii. 299 sqq., Stuttgart, 1901; B. Kaltner, *Die neue Stolordnung für das Herzogtum Salzburg*, Brünn, 1904; G. Lüttgert, *Evangelisches Kirchenrecht in Rheinland und Westfalen*, pp. 553 sqq., Gütersloh, 1905; Milasch-Pessič, *Das Kirchenrecht der morgenländischen Kirche*, 2d ed., pp. 546–547, Mostar, 1905; A. Freisen, *Der . . . Pfarrzwang und seine Aufhebung in Oesterreich und den deutschen Bundesstaaten*, Paderborn, 1906; Hauck, *KD*, ii. 273, 717, iv. 21, 48.

STONE OF MESHA. See MOABITE STONE.

STONE, BARTON WARREN: Disciple of Christ; b. near Port Tobacco, Md., Dec. 24, 1772; d. at Hannibal, Mo., Nov. 9, 1844. He graduated from the academy at Guilford, N. C., in 1793; taught in Washington, Ga., and studied theology, then entered the Presbyterian ministry as a licentiate in 1796, being ordained as pastor of the churches at Caneridge and Concord, Ky., 1798; in 1801 he was led to renounce Calvinism, and with four other clergymen formed the Springfield Presbytery in 1803, though this was dissolved in 1804 and formed into the Christian Church (see CHRISTIANS, 2); he then turned for a time to farming and teaching, meanwhile preaching and founding churches in Ohio, Kentucky, and Tennessee; in 1826 he was editor of *The Christian Messenger;* in 1832 he assisted in a union of the churches known after him as "Stoneite" with the "Campbellite" churches in Kentucky (see DISCIPLES OF CHRIST, § 1); after removing to Jacksonville, Ill., in 1834, he continued to labor for the denomination until his death, both by preaching and editing. He wrote *Letters on the Atonement* (1805); *Address to the Christian Churches* (1805); and *Letters to Dr. James Blythe* (1822).

BIBLIOGRAPHY: B. B. Tyler, in *American Church History Series*, xii. 11, 13, 20, 22, 31, 32, New York, 1894, and in general the works on the early history of the denominations with which he was connected.

STONE, DARWELL: Church of England; b. at Rosset, Denbighshire (19 m. s. of Liverpool), Sept. 15, 1859. He received his education at Merton College, Oxford (B.A., 1882; M.A., 1885; B.D., 1909; D.D., 1909); was made deacon in 1883 and priest in 1885; was curate of Ashbourne, Derbyshire, 1883–84; vice-principal of Dorchester Missionary College, 1885–88, and principal, 1888–1903; librarian of Pusey Memorial Library, Oxford, 1903–1909, and principal of the same since 1909. He "accepts the principles of the Tractarian movement in the Church of England, and is a student of the history of doctrine and criticism." He has published: *Holy Baptism* (London, 1899; 4th ed., 1905); *Outlines of Christian Dogma* (1900; 4th ed., 1908); *Christ and Human Life* (1901); *Meditations for Use in Retreat* (1902); *The Church of England. An Appeal to Facts and Principles* (1903; in collaboration with W. C. E. Newbolt); *The Invocation of Saints* (1903); *The Discipline of Faith* (1904); *The Holy Communion* (1904); *The Christian Church* (1905); and *A History of the Doctrine of the Holy Eucharist* (2 vols., 1909).

STONING, HEBREW USE OF: The employment of stones as a weapon of offense is common to various stages of civilization. Cases may be cited from the heroic age of the Greeks (*Iliad*, iii. 57; Æschylus, *Agememnon*, 1608) or from their historical period (Thucydides, v. 60; Pausanius, VIII., v. 8), while the Roman mobs were not averse to the use of stones as weapons (Cicero, *Pro domo*, v.; Quintilian, *Declamatio*, XII., xii.). It was a custom also to throw stones toward the grave of a hated individual. It is not surprising to hear that in Persia Antiochus Epiphanes was reputed to have met his death by stoning (II Macc. i. 16), and that in Israel also stones were thus used (Ex. xvii. 4; I Sam. xxx. 6; Matt. xxi. 35, and many other places). The question is interesting—what is the source of stoning as a punishment imposed by the governing body? The practise of stoning by official direction is wider than has been supposed. While this does not appear in the code of Hammurabi (see HAMMURABI AND HIS CODE), Arabs are known to throw stones at the grave of a transgressor and at the place where a shameful deed has been committed; this method of execution was employed by Persians, Macedonians (Curtius, *De rebus gestis Alexandri*, VI., xi. 38), and Spaniards. The scholiast on Euripides, *Orestes*, 432, makes the death of Palamedes occur by stoning, and many other cases are reported (cf. O. Crusius, *Beiträge*, p. 20, Leipsic, 1886). There needs no special explanation of the use of this means of punishment—that it involves a certain roughness or low state of culture is not true. Thus Israel revealed in its earliest code of laws in several respects a nobler sense of humaneness than the code of Hammurabi, as is proved by its prescriptions regarding the care of animals (Ex. xx. 10) and the treatment of slaves and the poor (Ex. xxi. 2, 20, 26, etc.). Two reasons may be assigned for the custom of stoning among the Hebrews. The first was a notable and lively ethical consciousness which was evident throughout Jewish history with a certain earnestness in punishment of certain kinds of breaches of law. There was also apparent a definite effort to bring the liveliest realization to the largest number of people possible of the heinousness of certain transgressions by making part of the people executors of justice. Benzinger sees also in the participation of so many an effort to release themselves from guilt.

This punishment was decreed among the Hebrews, according to the Old Testament, in cases where the vitality of the nation was assailed, i.e., when its religious consciousness was offended; as when true prophecy was imitated by false prophecy (Deut. xiii. 6–11) or by soothsaying and sorcery (Lev. xx. 27), when Yahweh's oneness was assaulted by the practise of idolatry (Deut. xvii. 2 sqq.), when Yahweh's sanctuary was invaded by incompetent persons (Ex. xix. 12), in cases of blasphemy (I Kings xxi. 10), or desecration of the sabbath (Num. xv. 32–35), or when the ban was broken (Josh. vii. 25). In Hammurabi's code stealing from the temple was the one capital crime in this category. In addition to these religious offenses, the worst sins against morality were punished by stoning, such as extreme filial impiety (Deut. xxi. 18–21), cursing of parents (Lev. xx. 9), breach of betrothal vows (Deut. xxii. 20–24), adultery (Lev. xx. 10; cf. Ezek. xvi. 40, xxiii. 47), incest (Lev. xx. 11, 12, 14), pederasty (Lev. xx. 13), and unnatural crime (Lev. xx. 15, 16). The one case, of adultery, in which the law does not explicitly threaten stoning, while Ezekiel (ut sup.) shows that to be the method of punishment, suggests that other transgressions were also visited with stoning. Legal execution with the sword occurred, according to the Old Testament, when sentence was by the king and execution was by the military (II Sam. i. 15; I Kings ii. 25; II Kings x. 25). In the New Testament stoning is the punishment for blasphemy (Acts vi. 13, vii. 58)· and for adultery (John viii. 5). The Mishnah (Sanhedrin, vii. 4) regards as punishable by stoning the offenses enumerated above, which either by express direction or by assured deduction were in the Old Testament so indicated; but Sanhedrin xi. 1 indicates for adultery death by strangling, and in general the Talmud divides capital penalties according as they are executed by stoning, burning, the sword, or strangling.

Respecting the carrying-out of the sentence the Bible directs that it be done outside the dwelling-place of the community (Lev. xxiv. 14; I Kings xxi. 13; Acts vii. 58), and that the witnesses cast the first stone, to the end that witness-bearing be done with greater circumspection (Deut. xiii. 10, xvii. 7; John viii. 7; Acts vii. 58–59). The Talmud gives the following directions (Sanhedrin, vi.): As soon as judgment is pronounced, the condemned is to be led away to the place of execution, which is at a distance from the court of judgment; one person remains at the entrance of the court-house with a large cloth in his hand, while another, on horseback, is at a considerable distance away, yet within sight of the first; in case some one affirms that he has testimony for the condemned, the signal is given with the cloth, and the horseman rides at once to suspend execution; the condemned is brought back, and this may be done four or five times. Similarly execution may be suspended if the accused alleges that he has something vital to offer. In case he produces what is found essential, he goes free; otherwise he is led forth, while some one precedes him announcing: Such a one, son of so and so, is led forth to be stoned for such an offense; so and so are the witnesses; whoever has anything to produce in his favor, let him produce it. When the condemned is distant four ells from the place of execution, he is stripped almost nude. The place of stoning is the height of two men. One of the witnesses casts a stone, and if this does not kill the man, then another, and then, if death has not ensued, the people take up the task. Those so executed are afterward hanged (Rabbi Eliezer); others say that only blasphemers and idolaters are hanged; Eliezer directs that men and women both be hanged, other authorities, only men. The Jerusalem Gemara in the tract Sanhedrin gives the directions on folios 23–24, the Babylonian Gemara on folios 42–49. The latter affirms (folio 43a) that with reference to Prov. xxxi. 6 before the stoning noble women gave to the condemned wine with frankincense in it to produce stupefaction.   (E. KÖNIG.)

BIBLIOGRAPHY: For the practise among non-Israelitic peoples consult: W. Wachsmuth, *Hellenische Altertumskunde*, vol. ii., part 1, Beilage 3, Halle, 1829; K. F. Hermann, *Griechische Privataltertümer*, ed. K. B. Stark, 73, 5, Heidelberg, 1870; Pauly, *Realencyklopädie der klassischen Altertumswissenschaft*, ed. W. S. Teuffel, Stuttgart, 1870; F. Justi, *Geschichte des alten Persiens*, p. 62, Berlin, 1879; Haberland, in *Zeitschrift für Völkerpsychologie*, xii (1880), 289–309. For the practise among the Hebrews much of the literature under LAW, HEBREW, CIVIL AND CRIMINAL, is pertinent, and for purposes of comparison that under HAMMURABI AND HIS CODE. Consult further: F. S. Ring, *De lapidatione Hebræorum*, Frankfort, 1716; C. B. Michaelis, *De judiciis poenisque capitalibus in Scriptura sacra commemoratis*, Halle, 1749; H. B. Fassel, *Das mosaisch-*

rabbinische Strafgesetz und strafrechtliche Gerichts-Verfahren, Gross-Kanizsa, 1870; P. B. Benny, *Criminal Code of the Jews according to the Talmud Masseceth Synhedrin,* London, 1880; S. Mendelsohn, *The Criminal Jurisprudence of the Ancient Hebrews,* Baltimore, 1891; S. Mandl, *Der Bann,* pp. 22–23, Brünn, 1898; R. Hirzel, *Die Strafe der Steinigung,* in the *Abhandlungen* of the Royal Saxon Academy, Philosophical-historical class, xxvii. 7 (1909); Benzinger, *Archäologie,* p. 277; *DB,* i. 527; *EB,* iii. 2722; *JE,* iii. 554–558; and the commentaries on the passages cited in the text.

STORCH, NIKOLAUS. See ZWICKAU PROPHETS.

STORR, GOTTLOB CHRISTIAN: See TÜBINGEN SCHOOL, THE OLDER.

STORRS, RICHARD SALTER: Congregationalist; b. at Braintree, Mass., Aug. 21, 1821; d. in Brooklyn, N. Y., June 5, 1900. He was the grandson of Rev. Richard Salter Storrs (1763–1819) of Longmeadow, Mass., and the son of the Rev. Richard Salter Storrs (1787–1873) who was for sixty-three years the eminent pastor of the Congregational church of Braintree, Mass. He was prepared for college at Monson Academy and graduated at Amherst College in 1839. After two years spent partly in teaching and partly in the study of law in the office of Rufus Choate in Boston, he entered the Andover Theological Seminary from which he was graduated in 1845. He was immediately called to the Harvard Congregational Church at Brookline, Mass., but after a year of service there he accepted an urgent invitation to become the pastor of the Church of the Pilgrims, Brooklyn, N. Y., which had been organized two years before. He was installed Nov. 19, 1846. In spite of numerous calls to important churches in New York, Boston, and elsewhere, he remained in this position till his death, performing all its duties until 1899, when he was made pastor emeritus. In 1896 the fiftieth anniversary of his installation was celebrated not only by the church but by various organizations throughout the city and by a notable meeting of citizens in the Academy of Music. He was a preacher of great eloquence and power, an orator who was much in demand on important occasions, a recognized leader in the church, an eminent and influential citizen. He was one of the founders of *The Independent* and one of its editors, 1848–61; was for several years prominent as a lyceum lecturer; was president of the American Board of Commissioners for Foreign Missions 1887–98, a critical period in its history; was for many years a trustee of Amherst College and of various benevolent and missionary societies; was one of the founders of and for a long time president of the Long Island Historical Society and an incorporator and officer of the Brooklyn Institute of Arts and Sciences, rendering important services to both these institutions, besides serving for a time as park commissioner and as commissioner of the civil service; and was the orator of the day when the statue of Lincoln was unveiled, when the city of New York celebrated the centennial of the Declaration of Independence, July 4, 1876, when the first Brooklyn Bridge was opened to the public, at the semi-millennial celebration of the birth of John Wyclif in 1880, and on many other occasions. Two of his most remarkable orations, delivered several times in 1875 and 1876, on " The

Ottoman and the Muscovite " were spoken without notes and were never printed; several others were collected and published after his death in a volume entitled *Orations and Addresses* (Boston, 1901). In addition to these and to numerous occasional discourses his most important publications are: *The Constitution of the Human Soul* (New York 1857); *Preaching without Notes* (1875); *The Divine Origin of Christianity Indicated by its Historical Effects* (1884); *Bernard of Clairvaux* (1888); and *Addresses on Foreign Missions* (1899). E. B. COE.

BIBLIOGRAPHY: E. A. Park, *Richard S. Storrs: Memorial Address,* New York, 1900.

STORY-BIBLES. See BIBLES, HISTORICAL.

STORY, ROBERT HERBERT: Church of Scotland; b. at Roseneath (22 m. n.w. of Glasgow), Dunbartonshire, Jan. 28, 1835; d. at Glasgow Jan. 13, 1907. He was educated at the universities of Edinburgh (M.A., 1853) and Heidelberg (1853), and received his theological training at Edinburgh (1853–56) and St. Andrews (1856–57). He was minister at Roseneath (1860–87); professor of church history in Glasgow University (1887–98); from 1898 until his death he was principal and vice-chancellor of the university. In theology he belonged to the liberal school. Besides editing the *Scot Magazine,* he wrote *Memoir of the Life of Robert Story* (Cambridge, 1862); *Christ the Consoler* (Edinburgh, 1865); *Life and Remains of Robert Lee* (2 vols., London, 1870); *William Carstares: a Character and Career of the Revolutionary Epoch* (1874); *Creed and Conduct* (Glasgow, 1878); and *The Apostolic Ministry in the Scottish Church* (London, 1897). He likewise edited *The Church of Scotland, Past and Present* (5 vols., London, 1890–91). BIBLIOGRAPHY: *Memoir of R. H. Story, by his Daughters,* Glasgow, 1909.

STOSCH, JOHANN ERNST GEORG: German Protestant; b. at Bautzen (30 m. n.e. of Dresden) Sept. 2, 1851. He was educated at the universities of Leipsic and Erlangen (1871–74); became curate in Ispringen, 1874; pastor in Rosenthal, near Königstein, 1877, and at Helmstädt, 1880; missionary in India, 1888; pastor in Berlin (1892) and privat-docent for the science of missions in the University of Berlin, 1902; in 1907 he became pastor primarius at Neuwedell (Neumark). He has written: *Briefe über die Offenbarung St. Johannis* (1892); *Sankt Paulus der Apostel* (Leipsic, 1894); *Die Augenzeugen des Lebens Jesu* (Gütersloh, 1895); *Alttestamentliche Studien* (6 vols., 1896–1903; Eng. transl. of the first vol., *Die Entstehung der Genesis,* 1896, under the title " The Origin of Genesis," London, 1897); *Im fernen Indien, Eindrücke und Erfahrungen im Dienst der lutherischen Mission unter den Tamulen* (Berlin, 1896); *Der pastoral-theologischer Ertrag der Bergpredigt* (1898); *Zeitgedanken über die heilige Taufe* (1902); *Das Heidentum als religiöses Problem* (1903); *Für heilige Güter, Aphorismen zur geschichtlichen Rechtfertigung des alten Testaments* (Stuttgart, 1905); *Der innere Gang der Missionsgeschichte in Grundlinien* (Gütersloh, 1905); *Die Prophetie Israels in religionsgeschichtlicher Würdigung* (1907); *Die apostolischen Sendschreiben nach ihren Gedankengängen* (3 vols., 1908–10).

STOUGHTON, JOHN: Congregationalist; b. in Norwich, England, Nov. 18, 1807; d. at Ealing (8 m. w. of Charing Cross), London, Oct. 24, 1897. He studied at the Norwich grammar-school; was engaged in law till 1828, when he entered Highbury College, Islington; was pastor at Windsor 1833–43, and at Kensington 1843–74; professor of historical theology and homiletics in New College, St. John's Wood, London, 1872–84; and Congregational Union lecturer 1855. He edited *The Evangelical Magazine* for many years, and was author of the following works, many of which have passed through several editions: *Lectures on Tractarian Theology* (London, 1843); *Spiritual Heroes; or Sketches of the Puritans, their Character and Times* (1848); *P. Doddridge, his Life and Labours: a centenary Memorial* (1851); *Stars of the East: or Prophets and Apostles* (1854); *Ages of Christendom before the Reformation* (1857; the Congregational Union lectures for 1855); *The Pen, the Palm, and the Pulpit* (1858); *Church and State Two Hundred Years ago. A History of ecclesiastical Affairs in England from 1660–63* (1862); *Ecclesiastical History of England* (5 vols., 1867–74; from the Revolution to the Restoration); *Homes and Haunts of Luther . . . With . . . Illustrations* (1875); *Our English Bible: its Translations and Translators* (1878); *The Progress of Divine Revelation, or the Unfolding Purpose of Scripture* (1878); *Religion in England under Queen Anne and the Georges. 1702–1800* (2 vols., 1878; new ed., 6 vols., 1881); *Worthies of Science* (1879); *An Introduction to Historical Theology: Being a Sketch of doctrinal Progress from the Apostolic Era to the Reformation* (1880); *William Wilberforce* (1880); *Footprints of Italian Reformers* (1881); *William Penn, the Founder of Pennsylvania* (1882); *Congregationalism in the Court Suburb* (1883); *The Spanish Reformers, their Memories and Dwelling Places* (1883); *Howard the Philanthropist and his Friends* (1884); *Religion in England from 1800 to 1850* (1884); *Golden Legends of the Olden Time* (1885); *The Revolution of 1688 in its Bearings on Protestant Nonconformity* (1888); *Shades and Echoes of Old London* (1889); and *Lights and Shadows of Primitive Christendom* (1891; new ed., with title *Lights and Shadows of Church Life*, 1895).

BIBLIOGRAPHY: Besides the autobiographic *Recollections of a Long Life*, 2d ed., London, 1894, consult G. K. Lewis, *John Stoughton, D.D. A Short Record of a long Life*, ib. 1898.

STOW, BARON: Baptist; b. at Croydon, N. H., June 16, 1801; d. at Boston, Mass., Dec. 27, 1869. He was graduated from Columbian College, Georgetown, D. C., 1825; became pastor of the Baptist church in Portsmouth, N. H., 1827; of the Baldwin Place Baptist Church, Boston, 1832, and of the Rowe Street Church in the same city, 1848, retaining this connection till his retirement from active work in 1867. He was active and influential as a member of the executive committee of the American Missionary Union, and was noted as a pulpit orator. He assisted in compiling the *Psalmist* (Boston, 1849; a hymnal); and edited *Daily Manna for Christian Pilgrims* (1846; new ed., London, 1871), and *Missionary Enterprise* (1846; a volume of sermons on missions); and was besides the author of *Memoir*

of *Harriet Dow* (1832); *History of the Baptist Mission to India* (1835); *History of the Danish Mission to the Coast of Coromandel* (1837); *The Whole Family in Heaven and Earth* (1845); *Christian Brotherhood* (1859); and *First Things* (1859).

BIBLIOGRAPHY: J. C. Stockbridge, *Memoir of Rev. Baron Stow*, Providence, R. I., 1895; R. H. Neale, *The Pastor and Preacher: a Memorial of . . . B. Stow*, Boston, 1870.

STOWE, CALVIN ELLIS: Congregationalist; b. at Natick, Mass., Apr. 26, 1802; d. at Hartford, Conn., Aug. 22, 1886. He studied at the academy in Gorham, Me.; was graduated from Bowdoin College, Brunswick, Me., 1824, where he was librarian and instructor, 1824–25; was graduated from Andover Theological Seminary, Mass., 1828; was assistant teacher of sacred literature in Andover Seminary, as well as editor of the Boston *Recorder*, 1828–30; started his career as a university preacher, 1830; was professor of Latin and Greek in Dartmouth College, Hanover, N. H., 1831–33; of Biblical literature, Lane Theological Seminary, Cincinnati, O., 1833–50; of natural and revealed religion, Bowdoin College, 1850–52; and of sacred literature, Andover Theological Seminary, 1852–64. He made a tour of Europe in 1837, investigating the various systems of elementary instruction, the results of which were embodied in his *Report on Elementary Public Instruction in Europe* (Harrisburg, 1838). His wife was Harriet Beecher Stowe, author of *Uncle Tom's Cabin*. He translated Jahn's *History of the Hebrew Commonwealth* (Andover, 1828), and from the Latin Lowth's *Lectures on Hebrew Poetry* (1829), both with additions; and wrote *Introduction to the Criticism and Interpretation of the Bible* (vol. i., Cincinnati, 1835; vol. ii. not published); and *Origin and History of the Books of the Bible*. Pt. 1. *New Testament* (Hartford, 1867).

BIBLIOGRAPHY: Illustrative matter will be found in the life of Harriet Beecher Stowe by her son, C. E. Stowe, Boston, 1899; *The Life and Letters of Harriet Beecher Stowe by her Son and Grandson*, New York, 1911.

STOWELL, HUGH: Church of England, hymnist; b. at Douglas, Isle of Man, Dec. 3, 1799; d. at Pendleton (3 m. n.w. of Manchester), England, Oct. 5, 1865. He entered, in 1819, St. Edmund Hall, Oxford (B.A., 1822; M.A., 1826); became curate of Shepscombe, Gloucestershire, 1823, and a few months later of Trinity Church, Huddersfield, Yorkshire; in 1828, vicar of St. Stephen's, Salford, Lancashire, where he became first incumbent of Christ Church, Action Square, 1831; honorary canon of Chester Cathedral, 1845; chaplain to Lee, bishop of Manchester, 1851; and later rural dean of Eccles. He was popular and effective as a preacher. He edited *A Selection of Psalms and Hymns Suited to the Services of the Church of England* (Manchester, 1831); and wrote *The Pleasures of Religion, with other Poems* (London, 1832); *The Duty of England in Regard to the Traffic in Intoxicating Drinks* (Leeds, 1840?); *Tractarianism Tested by Holy Scripture and the Church of England, . . . Sermons* (2 vols., London, 1845), and other collections of sermons; and *A Model for Men of Business; or, Lectures on the Character of Nehemiah* (1854). He was also noted as the author of the hymn " From every stormy wind that blows," and numerous others published by his son in the 12th ed. of the *Selection of Psalms and Hymns* (1864).

BIBLIOGRAPHY: Rev. J. B. Marsden, *Memoirs of the Life and Labours of Rev. Hugh Stowell*, London, 1868; S. W. Duffield, *English Hymns*, pp. 156–157, New York, 1886; Julian, *Hymnology*, pp. 1096–97; *DNB*, lv. 7.

STRABO, WALAFRIED. See WALAFRIED STRABO.

STRACK, HERMANN LEBRECHT: German Protestant theologian; b. in Berlin May 6, 1848. He studied at the universities of Berlin and Leipsic (Ph.D., 1872; Th. Lic., 1877; Th.D., 1884), and, after teaching at the Kaiser Wilhelm Gymnasium in Berlin (1872–73) and working in the Imperial Library at St. Petersburg (1873–76), became extraordinary professor of theology at the University of Berlin in 1877, and honorary professor in 1910. While acknowledging the full right of critical investigation, he is "convinced that such investigation can be and ought to be combined with reverence for the Holy Scriptures and earnest Christian faith." That Christ died for us and rose again he regards as an irrefutable fact. He has made it one of the tasks of his life to promote Christianity among the Jews by combating Antisemitism and refuting misrepresentations regarding the Jews and their ritual practises. His literary activity has been extensive. His more important publications are, *Prolegomena critica in V. T. Hebraicum* (Leipsic, 1873); *Katalog der hebräischen Bibelhandschriften der kaiserlichen öffentlichen Bibliothek in St. Petersburg* (in collaboration with A. Harkavy, 1875); *Prophetarum posteriorum codex Babylonicus Petropolitanus* (1876), which was published at the expense of Alexander II. of Russia; *Abraham Firkowitsch und seine Entdeckungen* (1876); five Mishnah tracts: *Sprüche der Väter* (Carlsruhe, 1882; 3d ed., Leipsic, 1901), *Versöhnungstag* (Berlin, 1888; 2d ed., Leipsic, 1904), *Götzendienst* (Berlin, 1888; 2d ed., Leipsic, 1909), *Sabbath* (Berlin, 1890), *Sanhedrin-Makkoth* (1910); *Einleitung in das Alte Testament* (1883; 6th ed., Munich, 1906); *Einleitung in den Talmud* (Leipsic, 1887; 5th ed., 1911); *Das Blut im Glauben und Aberglauben der Menschheit* (Munich, 1891; 8th ed., 1900); *Grammatik des Biblisch-Aramäischen* (Leipsic, 1895; 4th ed., 1905); *Die Sprüche Jesus, des Sohnes Sirachs* (1903); *Das Wesen des Judentums* (1906); and *Jesus, die Häretiker und die Christen nach den ältesten jüdischen Angaben* (1910). In collaboration with O. Zöckler he edited the *Kurzgefasster Kommentar zu den heiligen Schriften* (Munich, 1886 sqq.), to which he has contributed the commentaries on Genesis, Exodus, Leviticus, Numbers, and Proverbs. He also edits the *Nathanael; Zeitschrift für die Arbeit der evangelischen Kirche an Israel* (Berlin, 1885 sqq.), the *Jahrbuch der evangelschen Judenmission* (Leipsic, 1906 sqq.), and the publications of the Institutum Judaicum, a Jewish missionary society in Berlin.

STRANGE, ROBERT: Protestant Episcopal bishop of East Carolina; b. at Wilmington, N. C., Dec. 6, 1857. He was graduated from the University of North Carolina in 1879, and from Berkeley Divinity School, Middletown, Conn., in 1883. He was ordered deacon in 1884 and ordained to the priesthood in 1885. He was a missionary to the negroes of southern Virginia during his diaconate, and was then rector of the Church of the Good Shepherd, Raleigh, N. C. (1885–87), St. James', Wilmington, N. C. (1887–1900), and St. Paul's, Richmond, Va. (1900–04). In 1904 he was consecrated bishop-coadjutor of East Carolina, and in 1905, on the death of Bishop Alfred A. Watson, succeeded him in the full administration of the diocese.

STRANGER: The translation in the English versions of the Hebrew *ger*, "a wanderer, traveler," and especially "an alien living in a foreign land." Originally all individual rights were based upon the blood-relationship which, according to the old Semitic view, bound the members of the tribe together (see COMPARATIVE RELIGION, VI., 1, b). A relationship corresponding to that of consanguinity could, however, be brought about artificially, and in this way aliens were often taken into the tribe. There was also the relationship corresponding to protectorship or guardianship; the fugitive or outlaw could place himself under the care of a family, and in this way acquire a degree of citizenship. Otherwise, the alien, merely passing through or residing temporarily in the territory of a tribe, enjoyed no rights except the hospitality usually accorded to strangers. This, however, is held sacred in the orient, and as a guest the stranger is safe in the tent even of his enemy. Accordingly, in Israel there was always a distinction made between the *ger*, the stranger who was under the protection of some family, and the *nokhri*, who was an alien and stood in no relation to the tribe and could claim no legal rights (Gen. xxxi. 15; Job xix. 15); and even the humane laws in Deuteronomy for the protection of the poor and needy leave the alien out of account (Deut. xv. 3, xxiii. 20). The *ger*, on the other hand, enjoyed legal protection in a comparatively high degree. He had the right of *connubium* (see FAMILY AND MARRIAGE RELATIONS, HEBREW); and the children of such a union were Israelites (I Chron. ii. 17). The *ger*, unless he was a Canaanite, had not the right of hereditary possession in real estate (Isa. xxii. 16; Ezek. xlvii. 22). Impartial treatment before the courts had been assured to him by the Book of the Covenant (Ex. xxii. 21, xxiii. 9).

Deuteronomy deprived the *ger* of the right of marriage (Deut. vii. 1 sqq., xxiii. 4); but it repeated the command to treat him humanely, to allow him to take part in festivities (Deut. x. 18, xiv. 29, xxiv. 14 sqq.), and to grant him justice before the courts (Deut. xxiv. 17, xxvii. 19). He is put on a level with Levites, widows, and orphans, and is recommended as an object of love, of which as a stranger he is doubly in need. But all this is made a matter of compassion, not of law; and the *ger's* legal status was inferior. This was true of the *nokhri* in a still higher degree (Deut. xiv. 21). The *ger* had to adopt, in a way, the religion of his protector; but anciently very little was required in this respect, and he might retain his *sacra* (Deut. v. 14, xvi. 11 sqq.; cf. I Kings ii. 7–8; Deut. xiv. 21).

In the matter of religion, the Priest-code was more exacting, in order that there might be no sin among the people of Israel. The *ger* was required to avoid everything that was unclean for Israelites (Lev. xvii. 8 sqq., xviii. 26, xx. 2; Num. xix. 10 sqq.), to observe the Sabbath, to fast on the Day of Atonement (Lev. xvi. 29), to avoid leavened bread at the Passover, and not to profane the name of Yahweh (Lev. xxiv. 16). Further, he was as responsible for any violations of the Law as were the Israelites (Num. xv. 14 sqq.). On the other hand, he was given equal rights before the courts instead of the bare right to appeal to the compassion of the judge (Lev. xxiv. 22; Num. xxxv. 15). By submitting to circumcision the *ger* became a full citizen (Gen. xxxiv. 15; Ex. xii. 48; Num. ix. 14). Otherwise he might not keep an Israelite as a slave, but had to treat a servant as a free wage-earner (Lev. xxv. 47 sqq.). The right of *connubium* was also denied him (Ezra ix. 1 sqq., x. 2 sqq.).

I. Benzinger.

Bibliography: A. Bertholet, *Die Stellung der Israeliten und Juden zu den Fremden*, Freiburg, 1896; M. Peisker, *Die Beziehung der Nichtisraeliten zu Jahve nach der Anschauung der altisraelitischen Quellenschriften*, Giessen, 1909; Benzinger, *Archäologie*, pp. 284–286, 293; *DB*, ii. 49–51, iv. 622–623; *EB*, iv. 4814–18.

STRASBURG, stras'bŭrg, **BISHOPRIC OF:** A German diocese first definitely mentioned in the sixth century, although both ancient remains and the testimony of Irenæus (*Hær.*, I., x. 2) prove that Christianity had entered upper Germany during the Roman period. The old diocese lay on both banks of the Rhine. On the left bank it practically coincided with the modern Lower Alsace, except that the southern boundary was somewhat further south, while in the north the district beyond the Hagenau forest belonged to Speyer and that beyond the Vosges to Metz. On the right bank the diocese extended from the mouth of the Elz beyond Baden-Baden, stretching inland to the Black Forest. (A. Hauck.)

Strasburg eagerly embraced the Reformation and became one of the strongholds of Protestantism, the adherents of the ancient faith being exposed to bitter persecution. Even some of the canons renounced the Roman Catholic faith, and from 1592 to 1604 there was internecine strife as to whether a Protestant or a Roman Catholic should be bishop of the diocese. Protestant supremacy in Strasburg was finally ended by the Peace of Westphalia, and the see then became part of France, although the bishop continued to rank as a prince of the Empire on account of his territories on the right bank of the Rhine. During the French Revolution Roman Catholicism, like every form of religion, suffered heavily, but by the concordat of 1801 the diocese was reorganized, becoming coterminous with Alsace. Hitherto forming part of the archdiocese of Metz, Strasburg was made a suffragan see of Besançon in 1822. Henceforth it remained unchanged until 1870, when Alsace became German territory, and since 1874 the diocese has been under the immediate jurisdiction of the pope.

Bibliography: J. D. Schopflin. *Alsatia illustrata*, 2 vols., Colmar, 1751; idem. *Alsatia . . . diplomatica*, 2 vols., Mannheim, 1772–75; P. A. Grandidier, *Hist. de l'église et des évêques de Strasbourg*, 2 vols., Strasburg, 1776–78; *Code historique et diplomatique de la ville Je Strassbourg,*

ib. 1843; *Urkunden und Akten der Stadt-Strassburg*, 10 vols., ib. 1879 sqq.; H. Müller, *Die Restauration des Katholicismus in Strassburg*, Halle, 1882; J. Fritz, *Das Territorium des Bisthums Strassburg um die Mitte des 14. Jahrhunderts*, Köthen, 1885; A. Erichson, *L'Église française de Strasbourg au 16. siècle*, Paris, 1886; A. Baum, *Magistrat und Reformation in Strassburg*, Strasburg, 1887; W. Horning, *Briefe von Strassburger Reformatoren, 1548–1554*, ib. 1887; *Kleine Strassburger Chronik, 1424–1615*, ib. 1889; A. Seyboth, *Strasbourg historique*, ib. 1894; *Die Bischöfe von Strassburg von 1592 bis 1890*, ib. 1897; A. Meister, *Der Strassburger Kapitelstreit 1538–92*, ib. 1899; W. Kothe, *Kirchliche Zustände Strassburgs in 14. Jahrhundert*, Freiburg, 1903; F. F. Leitschub, *Strassburg*, Leipsic, 1903; E. von Borries, *Geschichte der Stadt Strassburg*, Strasburg, 1905; *Regesten der Bischöfe von Strassburg*, Innsbruck, 1907 sqq.; Hauck, *KD*, 4 vols., passim; Gams, *Series episcoporum*, pp 315–316, supplement 76–77.

STRATON, NORMAN DUMENIL JOHN: Church of England, bishop of Sodor and Man; b. at Somershall (13 m. w. of Derby), Derbyshire, Nov. 4, 1840. He was educated at Trinity College, Cambridge (B.A., 1862), and was ordained priest in 1865. He was curate of Market Drayton 1865–66, vicar of Kirkby Wharfe, Yorkshire, 1866–75, and vicar and rural dean of Wakefield 1875–92. In 1892 he was consecrated bishop of Sodor and Man, of which he has also been dean since 1895. He was proctor in York Convocation for the archdeaconry of Craven, 1880–85; honorary canon of Ripon, 1883–88, and of Wakefield Cathedral, 1888–92; and archdeacon of Huddersfield in 1888–92. In theology he is an Evangelical Churchman, opposed to the ritualistic movement. He has written *Thoughts for Communicants* (London, 1905).

STRAUSS, straus, **DAVID FRIEDRICH:** German radical theologian; b. at Ludwigsburg (9 m. n. of Stuttgart) Jan. 27, 1808; d. there Feb. 8, 1874. Strauss was the son of a merchant. He attended the Latin school in his native **Early** town and in 1821 entered the seminary **Life.** at Blaubeuren, whence he passed in 1825 to the University of Tübingen, where he was a faithful and industrious student. His former teacher, Ferdinand Christian Baur (q.v.), formerly at Blaubeuren, but now at Tübingen, relieved what Strauss deemed the dulness of the university courses. During his student days Strauss was much taken with the teachings of Schleiermacher, Schelling, and Hegel, and graduated with high rank, having obtained a good theological and philosophical foundation.

Strauss acted as vicar for a while at a village near Ludwigsburg, and then journeyed to Berlin, 1831–1832, in order to study the Hegelian philosophy at its source. He also heard Schleiermacher, but was rather repelled by his lecture style. He read the manuscript of Schleiermacher's lectures on the life of Jesus, and resolved on returning to Tübingen where he received an appointment as repetent, with the privilege of lecturing at the university, of which he took advantage, giving courses on Hegel's logic, the history of modern philosophy, and Plato. He aroused great enthusiasm for the Hegelian philosophy among the students, and thought of entering the philosophical faculty, but, meeting with some opposition from the university authorities, he returned to his theological studies. His *Leben Jesu* (2 vols., Tübingen, 1835–36; Eng. transl., 3 vols.

London, 1846) was written at this period, in the short space of one year.

The impression of profound theological scholarship which the " Life of Jesus " makes on the reader

" Life of
Jesus."

is the more remarkable in view of the fact that it was the work of a young man of twenty-seven. There were at that time three parties to the controversy on the problem of the life of Jesus: supernaturalists, who accepted the New-Testament narratives and miracles; rationalists, who rejected the miracles; and radical rationalists, who rejected the Gospel narratives as fabrications, though this position was held practically alone by Paulus at Heidelberg. Strauss took an independent position. He began with the assumption that the Gospel narrative must be interpreted exactly like any other historical work. But although he rejected the miracles, he refused to attribute intentional fabrication to the Evangelists. To reconcile these two positions, he advanced his " mythical " theory. This conception he derived from Hegel's philosophy of religion. Philosophical ideas are preceded by mythical presentations which are comparatively inaccurate, but are true to the intellectual state of the myth-maker. But even though an idea be promulgated with full knowledge on the part of its author of its fictitious character, it may be called " myth " if it is accepted and passed on confidently by the multitude as being in harmony with their religious feelings and ideas. A certain remoteness in time is necessary to constitute a myth. Hence the Gospel of John could not have been written by an eye-witness, i.e., not by John the apostle. The synoptic Gospels do not claim to have been by eye-witnesses. Another Hegelian conception Strauss applied to the theory of the life and personality of Jesus. According to the supernaturalists, Jesus was a unique and perfect personality, and, as such, God's son. Strauss replies that the " idea " does not realize itself in this fashion—by pouring itself in all its completeness into one example; but rather, through a multitude of examples that mutually supplement one another. The true God-man, hence, is not an individual, but humanity as a species. The writers of the Gospels, he asserts, had before their eyes the Messianic prophecies of the Old Testament, and ascribed to Jesus words and deeds that should have been his according to the prophecies; in doing so, however, they often added original ideas and breathed a new soul into the old material. Strauss' work was throughout critical. In his opinion, the time had not yet come for a constructive picture.

His book caused so great a sensation that one may call the year of its appearance, 1835, a turning-point in modern theology. It brought squarely be-

Results
upon his
Career.

fore the Christian world the question: Who was Jesus, the founder of the Christian religion? Strauss had to bear almost alone the storm of attacks that followed. He was released from his repetentship and transferred to the lyceum at Ludwigsburg. This position he soon left and removed to Stuttgart, where he wrote his *Streitschriften zur Verteidigung meiner Schrift über das Leben Jesu und zur Characteristik der gegenwärtigen Theologie* (1837),

which is one of his most brilliant performances. His friends succeeded in getting him an appointment to the University of Zurich, but clerical opposition prevailed, and he was not permitted to enter upon his duties. He refused to resign voluntarily, but drew to the end of his days the pension of 1,000 francs that was granted him, a large portion of which he spent in charity.

His next most important work, *Die christliche Glaubenslehre in ihrer geschichtlichen Entwickelung und im Kampfe mit der modernen Wissenschaft* (2 vols., Tübingen, 1840–41), was begun while he was

Later
Life and
Works.

preparing to go to Zurich. It is more negative in character than the *Leben Jesu*, sharply polemical, and from a literary point of view superior to his first work. It bears clear traces of the author's sense of the injustice that had been done him. During the following twenty years Strauss wrote nothing on theology. His marriage to the opera-singer, Agnes Schebest, proved unhappy. For a short time he represented Ludwigsburg in the Württemberg Landtag. He published a volume of political speeches (1847) and biographies of Schubart (2 vols., Berlin, 1849), Christian Märklin (1850), Nikodemus Frischlin (Frankfort, 1855), Ulrich von Hutten (3 parts, Leipsic, 1858–60), and Hermann Samuel Reimarus (1862). Strauss returned to theology in 1860 with a translation of the conversations of Ulrich von Hutten, to which he prefixed a polemic against the Württemberg prelate, Mehring. He then set to work upon a new *Leben Jesu für das deutsche Volk* (1864). While the work was still in manuscript, though nearly completed, Renan's brilliant " Life of Jesus " appeared, and Strauss for a while thought of letting his own work go unpublished. But, on second thought, he concluded that his book might serve for the German people just as Renan's did for the French. The new work was an attempt at positive construction, but the author finally was obliged to admit that the data for such an attempt were insufficient: " It all still remains in a certain sense a tissue of hypotheses." He was unable to bridge the chasm between the Christ of faith and the Jesus of history. In the winter of 1869–70 Strauss delivered some lectures from which arose the masterly little work on Voltaire (1870). The outbreak of the Franco-Prussian war called forth two patriotic open letters to Ernest Renan that met with universal applause in Germany. In 1872 he again issued a popular version of a theme he had handled long before: *Der alte und der neue Glaube*. Artistically it was a masterpiece, according to Zeller on the same high plane as the work on Voltaire. It aroused, however, a storm of criticism and even of abuse for its skeptical views. To the question, " Are we still Christians?" the author answers bluntly, " No." To the question " Have we still religion? " he replies, " Yes or no," according to one's conception of religion; the old belief in a personal God and in immortality is gone; there remains the feeling of absolute dependence on the universe. The tone of the book in discussing the nature of the soul is materialistic. The author adopts the Darwinian theory and takes his stand frankly on the ground of natural science. His last illness followed soon after the publication of the book, while attack and criticism were still proceeding. A series of poems written on his death-bed, breathing pious resignation, show how truly in his own way he possessed religious feeling. In 1910 a sightly memorial was erected to him in his home town.

In the critical study of the life of Jesus, Strauss stands at the middle point. All previous investigations converge in him, and all later work, either in agreement or opposition, takes him as its point of departure. He accomplished his greatest feat at the beginning of his career. The remainder of his life was tragically incomplete. Even his bitterest enemies—with the single exception of Nietzsche—have admitted that he was a brilliant writer and a brave, truth-loving man. (T. ZIEGLER.)

BIBLIOGRAPHY: Strauss' Gesammelte Schriften, ed. E. Zeller, appeared in 12 vols., Bonn, 1876–78. On his life and works consult: E. Zeller, D. F. Strauss in seinem Leben und seinem Schriften geschildert, Bonn, 1874, Eng. transl., London, 1874; E. Mussard, Examen critique du système de Strauss, Genève, 1839; De Valenti, Hegel, Strauss und der Christenglaube, Basel, 1843; C. Albrecht, Epoche aus der Straussenzeit, Biel, 1863; J. Cairns, False Christs and the True, Edinburgh, 1864; C. E. Luthardt, Die modernen Darstellungen des Lebens Jesu, Leipsic, 1864; O. Bagge, Das Prinzip des Mythus im Dienst der christlichen Position, Leipsic, 1865; G. P. Fisher, Essays on the Supernatural Origin of Christianity, New York, 1866; H. Rogers, Reason and Faith, London, 1866; W. H. Scott, The Christ of the Apostle's Creed, New York, 1867; B. Bauer, Philo, Strauss und Renan und das Urchristenthum, Berlin, 1874; W. Lang, D. F. Strauss, Leipsic, 1874; J. de LeRoi, D. F. Strauss, Paris, 1875; H. Ulrici, Der Philosoph Strauss: Kritik seiner Schrift "Der alte und der neue Glaube," Halle, 1873, Eng. transl., Philadelphia, 1875; A. Hausrath, D. F. Strauss und die Theologie seiner Zeit, 2 vols., Heidelberg, 1876–78; C. Schlottmann, David Strauss als Romantiker des Heidenthums, Halle, 1878; H. Künkler, Zum Gedächtnis an David Friedrich Strauss, Wiesbaden, 1898; S. Eck, D. F. Strauss, Stuttgart, 1899; K. Harræus, D. F. Strauss, Leipsic, 1901; O. Gramzow, David Friedrich Strauss, Charlottenburg, 1904; K. Fischer, Ueber D. F. Strauss. Gesammelte Aufsätze mit Einleitung von H. Falkenheim, Heidelberg, 1908; H. Kard, Ein Vorkämpfer moderner Weltanschauung. Gedenkworte an David Friedrich Strauss (dazu ein Jugendbildnis), Zürich, 1908; A. Kohut, David Friedrich Strauss als Denker und Erzieher, Leipsic, 1908; T. Ziegler, David Friedrich Strauss, 2 vols., Strasburg, 1908; A. Lévy, David Frédéric Strauss. La Vie et l'œuvre, Paris, 1910.

STRAUSS, JAKOB: Reformer in Hall, Wertheim, and Eisenach; b. at Basel between 1480 and 1485; d. possibly in Baden probably in 1533. He received his early education in his native town, left there in 1495 and became teacher in Wertheim, Strasburg, probably in Horb also; in 1515 he went to Freiburg, where he took his bachelor's and doctor's degree, and was afterward Evangelical preacher in Berchtesgaden. In 1521 he went to Schwaz in the Tyrol, but was compelled to withdraw before the Franciscans under Michel von Bruneck and went to Hall, where he lectured to priests upon the Gospel of Matthew and preached in the churches and in the open air before vast crowds upon confession and the monastic life, attacking the hierarchy and demanding the administration of both elements in the sacrament. He was guarded by the citizens from attack, but was compelled to leave there in May, 1522, amid the bitter weeping of the people, to whom he sent on May 16 from Haslach Ein kurzer Unterricht von erdichteten Bruderschaften. He went

to Saxony and on Aug. 4 was in Kemberg, where a sermon preached in Hall was printed: Eine verstendige tröstlich Leer über das Wort S. Paulus: der Mensch soll sich selbs probieren, etc. In September he went on Luther's recommendation as preacher to Count Georg of Wertheim, but his domineering ways caused his dismissal the next month. He was at Weimar at Christmas, 1522, and at the beginning of 1523 at Eisenach as preacher, where he printed his document on the Weimar disputation and his Wunderbarlich Beichtbüchlein, abolished the mass, pictures in the churches, and the use of oil and the chrism in baptism, advocated the marriage of priests, and wrote Wider den simoneischen Tauff, und erkauften, ertichten Krysam and Fegefeuer und Opfer für die Toten. He replied also to those who slandered and accused him in a number of pamphlets. He assailed the burdens of taxation, church endowments, payment of interest. Luther, being appealed to, attempted to correct Strauss' mistaken zeal and to moderate it, and Melanchthon did the same in 1524. The result was a more temperate advocacy of his principle that the Mosaic law should be a basis for church law in a tract of 1524, though demanding the introduction of the jubilee year. In 1524 Duke Johann Friedrich charged Strauss with a visitation in Eisenach and neighboring parts, and this Strauss conducted imprudently, arbitrarily deposing and installing ministers. Disaffection arose among the peasants, which Strauss tried in vain to quell; after the rebellion Strauss was arrested and tried, submitted, and was discharged. His position in Eisenach was untenable. He was at Nuremberg in 1525, and later went to Hall in Swabia; he received a rebuke from Œcolampadius, whom he had challenged to a disputation. Meanwhile Strauss was made preacher in Baden-Baden, where he entered the sacramental controversy, and wrote against Zwingli. In 1527 he wrote again against Œcolampadius' Antisyngramma, who, however, did not deign to notice Strauss. Little is known of his career after that, though it is probable that in disappointment he reentered the Roman Catholic Church.

He was a restless, turbulent spirit, combining elements of the new and the old, proud of his erudition, yet unpractical, having a deep sympathy for the people, strong in his critical faculties but without constructive ability. G. BOSSERT.

BIBLIOGRAPHY: Ayn freuntlich gesprech zwyschen ainem Barfüsser Münch aus der Provynz Osterreych, der Observanz, und ainem Löffelmacher, cf. Zeitschrift der deutschen Philologie, xxxvii. 75 sqq.; F. A. Sinnacher, Beiträge zur Geschichte der bischöflichen Kirche von Säben und Brixen, vii. 1888 sqq., 314, 7 vols., Innsbruck, 1821 sqq.; G. T. Strobel, Miscellaneen, iii. 1–94, 6 parts, Nuremberg, 1778–82; C. A. Cornelius, Geschichte der münsterischen Aufruhrs, ii. 243 sqq., 246, Leipsic, 1860; Schmidt, Jakob Strauss, Programm des Realgymnasiums, Eisenach, 1865; G. Kawerau, Johann Agricola, pp. 51 sqq., Berlin, 1881; H. Neu, Geschichte der evangelischen Kirche in der Grafschaft Wertheim, Heidelberg, 1903. A number of references to further information are given in Hauck-Herzog, RE, xix. 92.

STRAWBRIDGE, ROBERT: Methodist Episcopal pioneer and lay preacher; b. at Drummer's Nave near Carrick-on-Shannon, Ireland; d. near Baltimore in 1781. He seems to have been a local preacher before his emigration to America, which took place between 1760 and 1765; he settled on Sam's Creek, Frederick Co., Md., and soon began to hold meetings and to preach in his own house, later building a log meeting-house, and the *Minutes* of 1773 record him as assisting Francis Asbury (q.v.); again he appears in 1775 as second preacher on Frederick circuit, but acting as with the full rights of an itinerant, including the administration of baptism and the Lord's Supper; in his ministrations he appears to have manifested an independent spirit, and to have determined on the exercise of full ministerial functions in spite of directions from the conference. In 1776 he moved to a farm, the full use of which was granted to him during his life; but he continued to preach, and, the Revolution causing many ministers from England to withdraw, he took charge of the churches at Sam's Creek and Bush Forest, Harford County, remaining as pastor until his death, but not recognizing the authority of conference.

Bibliography: J. B. Wakeley, *Lost Chapters Recovered from the Early Hist. of American Methodism*, New York, 1858; W. Hamilton, in *Methodist Quarterly Review*, July, 1856; N. Bangs, *Hist. of the Methodist Episcopal Church*, 4 vols., ib. 1860; W. B. Sprague, *Annals of the American Pulpit*, vii. 3–4, ib. 1861; J. M. Buckley, in *American Church History Series*, v. 113–116, 201, ib. 1896; and, in general, works on the early history of Methodism in America.

STREANE, ANNESLEY WILLIAM: Church of England; b. at Easternsnow Rectory, County Roscommon, Ireland, Apr. 8, 1844. He received his education at Trinity College, Dublin, and Emmanuel College, Cambridge (B.A., 1874; M.A., 1877; B.D., 1891; D.D., 1895); he was made deacon in 1875 and priest in 1876; has been fellow of Corpus Christi College, Cambridge, since 1875; was dean of the same 1877–83 and 1886–92, Hebrew lecturer there 1875–97 and from 1906 to the present; curate of St. Luke, Chesterton, Cambridge, 1883–85; senior proctor, University of Cambridge, 1891–92; and vicar of Grantchester, Cambridge, 1898–1904. In theology he is a moderate Anglican. Among his literary productions are to be noted *Prolegomena* (part vii.) *to Tregelles' Greek Testament, edited jointly with F. J. A. Hort* (Cambridge, 1879); *The Treatise Chagigah Translated from the Babylonian Talmud, with Introduction and Notes* (1891); *Jesus Christ in the Talmud* (1893); *The Double Text of Jeremiah* (1896); *The Age of the Maccabees* (1898); an edition of Ecclesiastes for the Churchman's Bible (London, 1899), of the Psalms for the Temple Bible (1902), and of Esther for the Cambridge Bible for Schools (1902). He has also translated Karl von Hase's *Handbuch der protestantischen Polemik* as *Handbook to the Controversy with Rome* (2 vols., 1906).

STRICKLER, GIVENS BROWN: Presbyterian; b. in Strickler's Springs, Va., Apr. 25, 1840. He was graduated from Washington College, Washington and Lee University (A.B., 1868), and Union Theological Seminary, Va. (1870). He was ordained to the ministry of his denomination, 1870; was pastor of Tinkling Spring Church, Augusta County, Va. (1870–83); of the Central Church, Atlanta, Ga. (1883–96); and was appointed professor of systematic theology in Union Theological Seminary, Richmond, Va., where he still remains. During the Civil

War he served in the "Stonewall Brigade" of the Confederate Army.

STRIGEL, strī′gel, **VICTORINUS:** German Melanchthonian theologian; b. at Kaufbeuren (36 m. s.s.w. of Augsburg) Dec. 26, 1524; d. at Heidelberg June 26, 1569. He studied at the University of Freiburg, 1538–42, and then at Wittenberg, where he attached himself to Melanchthon. After his promotion in 1544 he gave private instruction at Wittenberg. During the Schmalkald war he went to Magdeburg and then to Erfurt, where he lectured acceptably. He received a call to Jena, where he, together with Johann Stigel, opened the new Gymnasium academicum. He began with lectures on philosophy and history, subsequently also on the *Loci* of Melanchthon. He was, however, soon involved in the theological controversies of the time; his relations with Melanchthon and the sentiments and tendency of the theologians in Ernestine Saxony were destined to lead him into conflicts which destroyed the happiness of his life. Melanchthon tried in vain to induce him to accept a call to Augsburg. Matters assumed an especially critical condition after Flacius (q.v.) went to Jena in 1557. Strigel published a written statement to the effect that he did not approve the attitude of Flacius toward the Wittenberg theologians. The dominating influence of Flacius made itself felt immediately at the Colloquy of Worms (see Worms), where Strigel together with the other deputies of Thuringia, in accordance with the instructions of Flacius, was compelled to participate in the protest of the Gnesio-Lutherans and contributed to the lamentable outcome of the colloquy. When Flacius induced the duke to order the drawing-up of the Weimar Book of Confutation, Strigel, Schnepff, and Superintendent Hügel were entrusted with the task, but against their desires. In the ensuing discussions at Weimar Flacius and Strigel were involved in dispute, but the former gained his point, and Strigel returned to Jena in an embittered state of mind. The polemic was continued in their lectures; the duke tried to reconcile them, but in vain. At the beginning of 1559 there appeared the "Book of Confutation," sanctioned by Johann Friedrich and modeled in the spirit of Flacius. Hügel and Strigel refused to accept it, the latter because of the condemnation of the thesis that the rational will of man cooperates in conversion and regeneration; he rejected the doctrine of Flacius that the attitude of the will is purely passive, and that the Holy Spirit is given to those who reject him. After the refusal of Strigel to be silent, he, together with Hügel, was imprisoned on Mar. 27, 1559, but they were released on Sept. 5, at the intercession of the university, the most prominent Evangelical princes, and even the emperor; Strigel, however, was suspended from teaching. The duke finally conceded to the general desire that Flacius and Strigel should discuss the disputed points in a colloquy, which took place on Aug. 2, 1560, in the old castle at Weimar, in the presence of the duke, the court, and a large audience from all estates; but the only point discussed was the relation of human will to divine grace in the act of conversion. Strigel presented the synergism of his teacher Melanchthon, with a protest against the charge of Pelagianism. The initiative in conversion he conceded to the Word and the Spirit of God, but he asserted that the will cooperates. Against this view Flacius formulated the thesis so fatal for him at a later time, that original sin is the very substance of the natural man. After thirteen sessions, from Aug. 2 to Aug. 8, the disputation was broken off without result. Both parties were requested to remain silent until the matter was fully decided. As Flacius did not conform to this request, he, together with his closer associates, was dismissed Dec. 10, 1561.

Before rehabilitating Strigel, the duke asked Christoph of Württemberg to send two theologians to bring about an agreement. Jacob Andreä and Christoph Binder arrived for this purpose at Weimar in May, 1562. After an oral discussion a declaration was formulated which was signed by Strigel and approved by all present. It stated that the natural man is entirely incapable of doing good, but that he has preserved the capacity to be converted. The *Declaratio Victorini* (as it was called) only caused new dissension. But few signed it; most of the preachers, instigated by men like Hesshusen and Flacius, preached against it as being ambiguous, and refused their signature. Consequently about forty preachers were deposed and expelled. On May 24 Strigel was rehabilitated and resumed his lectures, but he felt the discomfort of his position so much that in autumn, 1562, he went to Leipsic, with the intention of never returning. He was appointed professor in Leipsic, and on May 1, 1563, began his lectures on theology and philosophy. Here his doctrine of synergism became still more evident than before; he taught that the human will must not be inactive in conversion, but must itself will obedience; faith is a gift of God, but is not given to those who resist it, but to those who listen and incline themselves; the innate image of God is not completely destroyed and extinguished. He lectured especially on dogmatics and ethics, but suddenly in Feb., 1567, his lecture hall was closed and he was prohibited from teaching because of the suspicion that he inclined toward Calvinism in the doctrine of the Lord's Supper. This suspicion was not without foundation. He went to Amberg in the Upper Palatinate where Frederic III. was on the point of abolishing Lutheranism and introducing Calvinism; here Strigel openly confessed the Reformed doctrine of the Lord's Supper. On Sept. 14, 1567, he entered a new position as professor of ethics in Heidelberg, but was soon called away by death.

Strigel always was and remained a true Melanchthonian. He distinguished himself by his efficient philosophical training, his dialectic cleverness, and his brilliant oratory. His extensive literary activity lay in the sphere of philology, philosophy, and history, and in Biblical, patristic, and systematic theology. He wrote commentaries on Psalms (1563, 1567), Isaiah (1566), Wisdom Literature (1565), Daniel (1565), Jeremiah (1566), the Pentateuch (1566), Joshua (1567), Samuel, Kings, Chronicles (1569), Ezra, Nehemiah, Esther, Ruth (1571), Job (1571), Ezekiel (1570), Minor Prophets (1570), Rev-

elation (1569–71); and the New Testament (1565–1583). Still more esteemed, though dependent on Melanchthon, were his dogmatic text-books, *Loci theologici, quibus loci communes . . . Philippi Melanchthonis illustrantur . . .* (ed. Pezel, 4 parts, Neustadt, 1581–84), the most important work of dogmatics of the school of Melanchthon in the narrower sense; *Hypomnemata in epitomen philosophiæ moralis Philippi Melanchthonis* (ed. Pezel, 1582); *Enchiridion theologicum* (1584); *Enchiridion locorum theologicorum* (Wittenberg, 1591).

(G. KAWERAU.)

BIBLIOGRAPHY: Sources are: *Disputatio de originali peccato et libero arbitrio inter M. Flacium Ill. et V. Strigelium . . . Vinariæ . . . 1560 . . . habita,* ed. S. Musæus, 1562 and 1563; *V. Strigelii epistolæ aliquot de negocio eucharistico,* Neustadt, 1584. Letters are in *Matthæi, Wesenbecii Papinianus,* Wittenberg, 1569; J. Voigt, *Briefwechsel der berühmtesten Gelehrten mit Herzog Albrecht,* pp. 575–604, Königsberg, 1841; H. L. J. Heppe, *Geschichte des deutschen Protestantismus,* vol. i., Beilage 6–8, Marburg, 1853; cf. G. Wolf, *Zur Geschichte der deutschen Protestantismen, 1555–59,* pp. 300 sqq., Berlin, 1888. Consult: H. Erdmann, *De Strigelianismo,* Jena, 1658 and 1675; J. C. Zeumer, *Vitæ professorum Jenensium,* pp. 16 sqq., 2 parts, Jena, 1703–06; H. Merz, *Hist. vitæ et controversiæ V. Strigelii,* Tübingen, 1732; G. J. Planck, *Geschichte des protestantischen Lehrbegriffs,* vol. iv., Leipsic, 1796; J. C. T. Otto, *De V. Strigelio liberioris mentis in ecclesiæ Lutherana vindice,* Jena, 1843; A. Beck, *Johann Friedrich der Mittlere,* vols. i.–ii., ib. 1843; J. J. I. von Döllinger, *Die Reformation,* ii. 237 sqq., 325 sqq., 3 vols., Regensburg, 1846–48; H. L. J. Heppe, ut sup., i. 157 sqq., 192 sqq., 298 sqq.; idem, *Dogmatik des deutschen Protestantismus im 16. Jahrhundert,* i. 163 sqq., Gotha, 1857; W. Preger, *Flacius,* vol. ii., Erlangen, 1861; J. Janssen, *Hist. of the German people,* vii. 145, 275, 355, x. 263, London, 1905–06; *ADB,* xxxvi. 590 sqq.

STRIGOLNIKI. See RUSSIA, I., § 2.

STROHSACKER, strō′sac″er, **HARTMANN:** Austrian Roman Catholic; b. at Mauternbach (a village near Krems, 88 m. n.w. of Vienna) July 6, 1870. He entered the Benedictine order in 1888, after completing his gymnasium education; studied at the Benedictine seminary at Göttweig (1889–93), and at the University of Innsbruck (1893–97; D.D., 1897); was professor of philosophy and dogmatics at the seminary of Göttweig (1897–99); and since 1899 has been professor of dogmatics at the Benedictine university, Rome.

STRONG, AUGUSTUS HOPKINS: Baptist; b. at Rochester, N. Y., Aug. 3, 1836. He was educated at Yale (A.B., 1857) and at Rochester Theological Seminary (graduated 1859), completing his education in Germany in 1859–60. He then held pastorates at the First Baptist Church, Haverhill, Mass. (1861–65), and at the First Baptist Church, Cleveland, O. (1865–72); became professor of systematic theology and president of Rochester Theological Seminary 1872); resigned presidency in 1912. He has written *Systematic Theology* (Rochester, 1886); *Philosophy and Religion* (New York, 1888); *The Great Poets and their Theology* (Philadelphia, 1897); *Christ in Creation and Ethical Monism* (1899); *Systematic Theology* (3 vols., 1907–09); and *Outlines of Systematic Theology* (1908).

STRONG, JAMES: Methodist layman; b. in New York Aug. 14, 1822; d. at Round Lake, N. Y., Aug. 7, 1894. He was graduated from Wesleyan University, Middletown, Conn., 1844; teacher of ancient languages in Troy Conference Academy, West Poultney, Vt., 1844–46; owing to failure in health he occupied himself in study and held various economic positions, 1846–57; was professor of Biblical literature, and acting president of Troy University, 1858–61; and professor of exegetical theology in Drew Theological Seminary, Madison, N. J., from 1868. He was a member of the Old Testament Company of revisers; and was the author of *Harmony and Exposition of the Gospels* (New York, 1852); *Harmony of the Gospels in the Greek of the Received Text* (1854); *Irenics: A Series of Essays showing the virtual Agreement between Science and the Bible* (New York, 1883); and edited Daniel (1876) and Esther (1877) in the American edition of Lange. His most important work was the editing, at first with Dr. McClintock for 3 vols., and afterward alone, of a *Cyclopædia of Biblical, Theological, and Ecclesiastical Literature* (10 vols., New York, 1867–81; with a supplement in 2 vols., 1885–87); the work was begun in 1853. He also published a literal translation of Ecclesiastes (1877).

BIBLIOGRAPHY: *Methodist Review*, lxxvi (1894), 783–788; J. W. Mendenhall, in *Old and New Testament Student*, xiv (1892), 71–76.

STRONG, JOSIAH: Congregationalist; b. at Naperville, Ill., Jan. 19, 1847. He was educated at Western Reserve College (A.B., 1869) and at Walnut Hills Seminary (now Lane Theological Seminary), Cincinnati, O. (graduated 1871). He was home missionary at Cheyenne, Wyo. (1871–1873); instructor in natural theology in Western Reserve College (1873–76); pastor at Sandusky, O. (1876–81); secretary of the Ohio Home Missionary Society (1881–84); pastor in Cincinnati (1884–86); secretary of the Evangelical Alliance (1886–98). Since 1898 he has been president of the American Institute of Social Service. Besides editing *Social Progress* from 1904 to 1907 he has written *Our Country* (New York, 1885); *The New Era* (1893); *The Twentieth Century City* (1898); *Religious Movements for Social Betterment* (1900); *Expansion* (1900), *The Times and Young Men* (1901); *The Next Great Awakening* (1902); *The Challenge of the City* (1908); *Studies in the Gospel of the Kingdom* (1910); and *My Religion in Everyday Life* (1910).

STRONG, NATHAN: Congregationalist: b. in Coventry, Conn., Oct. 16, 1748; d. in Hartford, Conn., Dec. 25, 1816. Having been graduated at Yale College in 1769, he pursued the study of law for a time; was tutor in Yale College in 1772–73; and, after a brief course of theological reading, was ordained pastor of the First Congregational Church in Hartford, Conn., Jan. 5, 1774, holding this pastorate nearly forty-two years, and making the church the strongest in the state. During the early part of his work, in the midst of the colonial troubles with Great Britain, he published many political papers which exerted a wide and deep influence. These and other discussions were characterized by a wit sometimes keenly sarcastic in character. During the last twenty years of his pastorate he became eminent as a revivalist, and was, in the best sense of the term, a pulpit orator. His knowledge of human nature was remarkable. This gave him an exceptional degree of authority among the churches, and a rare degree of skill in conducting revivals. He was an indefatigable student; but his learning was developed in his intellectual character, not in his references to books. He was also a pioneer in the cause of Christian missions, and has been regarded as the father of the Connecticut Missionary Society (1798), the oldest of the permanent missionary societies in the land. His most noted work was *The Doctrine of Eternal Misery Consistent with the Infinite Benevolence of God* (1796); he published also two volumes of *Sermons* (1798–1800); and was the projector and principal compiler of the *Hartford Collection of Hymns* (1799), to which he contributed several hymns, among them "Swell the anthem, raise the song."

BIBLIOGRAPHY: W. B. Sprague, *Annals of the American Pulpit*, ii. 34–41, New York, 1859; F. H. Foster, *New England Theology*, pp. 209–210, Chicago, 1907.

STRONG, THOMAS BANKS: Church of England; b. in London Oct. 24, 1861. He was educated at Christ Church College, Oxford (B.A., 1883), and was ordered deacon in 1885 and ordained priest in the following year. He was lecturer of his college (1884–1901), where he was also student (1888–1901); and has been dean since 1901. He was examining chaplain to the bishop of Durham 1889–1901; and has been examining chaplain to the bishop of London since 1905. He was Bampton lecturer in 1895, and has written *Manual of Theology* (London, 1892); *Christian Ethics* (Bampton lectures; 1896); *Doctrine of the Real Presence* (1899); *Historical Christianity* (1902); and *Authority in the Church* (1903).

STRYKER, MELANCHTHON WOOLSEY: Presbyterian; b. at Vernon, N. Y., Jan. 7, 1851. He was graduated from Hamilton College (A.B., 1872) and from Auburn Theological Seminary (1876). He held pastorates at Presbyterian churches at Auburn, N. Y. (1876–78), and Ithaca, N. Y. (1878–1883), at the Second Congregational Church, Holyoke, Mass. (1883–85), and the Fourth Presbyterian Church, Chicago, Ill. (1885–92), and since 1892 has been president of Hamilton College, Clinton, N. Y. He has written *The Song of Miriam* (Chicago, 1888); *Church Song* (hymnal; New York, 1889); *Dies Iræ, with Versions* (Chicago, 1893); *Hamilton, Lincoln, and Addresses* (Utica, N. Y., 1895); *Letter of James* (Boston, 1895); *Lattermath* (poems; Utica, 1896); *College Hymnal* (New York, 1897); *Well by the Gate* (sermons; Philadelphia, 1903); and *Baccalaureate Sermons to the Graduating Classes of Hamilton College 1893–1905* (Utica, 1905).

STRYPE, JOHN: Historiographer of the English Reformation; b. at Houndsditch Nov. 1, 1643; d. at Hackney Dec. 11, 1737. After passing through St. Paul's school, he entered Jesus College, Cambridge, 1662, from which he was transferred to Catherine Hall (B.A., 1665; M.A., 1669). He was made curate of Theydon Bois, Essex, and of Low Leyton, Essex, 1669. Archbishop Tenison conferred upon him the sinecure of West Tarring, Sussex, 1711, and he was lecturer of Hackney, 1689–1724. He published vol. ii. of *J. Lightfoot's Works* (London, 1684); *Memorials of . . . Thomas Cranmer, Archbishop of Canterbury. Wherein the History* of the Church and the Reformation of it during the Primacy of the said Archbishop . . . are greatly illustrated . . . In three Books, 2 parts (1694); Life of the Learned Sir Thomas Smith (Oxford, 1698); Historical Collections of the Life and Acts of . . . J. Aylmer, Lord Bishop of London in the Reign of Queen Elizabeth (London, 1701); The Life of the Learned Sir J. Cheke, Kt., . . . (1705); his most important work Annals of the Reformation and Establishment of Religion and . . . other Occurrences in the Church of England; during the first twelve Years of Queen Elizabeth's . . . Reign: . . . With an Appendix, 2 parts (1708–09; a 2d ed., more complete, 4 vols., 1725–31, Oxford, 1824); The History of the Life and Acts of . . . Edmund Grindal . . . Archbishop of . . . Canterbury, 2 parts (1710); The Life and Acts of Matthew Parker, . . . Archbishop of Canterbury, 2 parts (1711); The Life and Acts of John Whitgift . . . Archbishop of Canterbury, 2 parts (1718); Ecclesiastical Memorials Relating chiefly to Religion, and the Reformation of it, and the Emergencies of the Church of England under King Henry VIII., King Edward VI., and Queen Mary the First (3 vols., 1721). Strype was a diligent collector of materials, but lacked literary style and skill in methodical arrangement. The complete works of Strype were issued at Oxford, 1822-40, in 27 vols.

BIBLIOGRAPHY: S. K. Maitland, Remarks on the First Volume of Strype's Life of Archbishop Cranmer, London, 1848; DNB, lv. 67–69.

STUART, CHARLES MACAULAY: Methodist Episcopalian; b. at Glasgow, Scotland, Aug. 20, 1853. After completing his high-school studies in his native city, he left Scotland for the United States, and was educated at Kalamazoo College, Kalamazoo, Mich. (A.B., 1880), and at the Garrett Biblical Institute, Chicago. Entering the ministry of his denomination, he remained in its pastorate until 1885, when he was associate editor of the Michigan Christian Advocate for a year. From 1886 to 1896 he occupied a similar position on the Northwestern Christian Advocate, and since 1896 has been professor of sacred rhetoric in the Garrett Biblical Institute. Besides editing the Methodist Hymnal (New York, 1905), and The Books and their Message (1910), he has written Descriptive Text of Photogravures of the Holy Land (New York, 1890); Life and Selected Writings of Francis Dana Hemenway (in collaboration with C. F. Bradley and A. W. Patten; 1890); Gospel Singers and their Songs (in collaboration with F. D. Hemenway; 1891); Vision of Christ in the Poets (1896); and Story of the Masterpieces (1897).

STUART, CLARENCE ESME: Plymouth Brother; b. at Tempsford Hall, Sandy (8 m. e. of Bedford), England, 1828; d. at Reading 1903. He was grandson of William Stuart, Archbishop of Armagh; went from Eton to St. John's College, Cambridge, where he took his master's degree, after obtaining a Tyrwhitt university scholarship in Hebrew. About the year 1860 he entered the ranks of the Brethren at Reading, where he continued to reside until his death. He wrote on the sacrifices, the Church of God, textual criticism of the New Testament (he was of the Tregelles school), and criticized William Robertson Smith's Lectures on the Old Testament in the Jewish Church. In 1885 he put forth a pamphlet on Christian Standing and Condition, which aroused acrimonious discussion culminating in a division of the Brethren, not yet healed (see PLYMOUTH BRETHREN). This was followed by a series of papers on propitiation, in which Stuart insisted on the detailed fulfilment of the presentation of the Savior's blood, immediately after death, in the heavenly sanctuary; this doctrine also was obnoxious to old associates. There followed expositions of the Gospels and Acts, of the epistles to the Romans and the Hebrews, and of the Psalter. A pamphlet entitled The Critics: shall we follow them? did battle for traditional views of the Old Testament. Stuart adhered closely to belief in verbal inspiration. With independent judgment he held firmly the general body of doctrine, prophetic as well as ecclesiastical, characteristic of the Brethren.   E. E. WHITFIELD.

STUART, GEORGE HAY: Presbyterian layman; b. at Rose Hall, County Down, Ireland; d. at Chestnut Hill, Philadelphia, Pa., Apr. 11, 1890. He came to Philadelphia in 1861, went into business and accumulated wealth. He was for many years president of the Merchants' National Bank of Philadelphia. He acquired a national reputation as a philanthropist and Christian worker. During the Civil War he was president of the Christian Commission. Later he was president of the Philadelphia branch of the Evangelical Alliance, vice-president of the American Bible Society, of the American Tract Society, and of the National Temperance Society, and was prominently connected with many other religious and philanthropic associations.

BIBLIOGRAPHY: Life of George H. Stuart, written by himself, edited by R. E. Thompson, Philadelphia, 1890.

STUART, MOSES: American Hebraist; b. in Wilton, Conn., Mar. 26, 1780; d. at Andover, Mass., Jan. 4, 1852. He was graduated from Yale College with the highest honor (1799); taught school at North Fairfield and Danbury, Conn.; studied law and was admitted to the bar 1802, and the same year was called as tutor to Yale; pursued the study of theology with President Dwight, and was ordained pastor of the First Congregational Church, New Haven, Conn., 1806, showing remarkable talent as preacher and pastor; became professor of sacred literature in Andover Theological Seminary in 1810, retaining his place there until his retirement in 1848. His first literary work was a Hebrew grammar, which was circulated among the students in manuscript because it was not possible to print Hebrew in this country at that time; when it was finally printed (1813), he was compelled himself to set up part of the type for lack of compositors equipped for the task; later editions long remained the textbooks for American students. To Americans he brought the knowledge of what was being done for Biblical scholarship in Germany, and thus founded in America the scientific study of Biblical archeology and linguistics. For his services in this department he has been called " the father of American Biblical literature"; in the course of his labors he trained more than 1,500 ministers, 70 professors or presidents of colleges, more than 100 foreign missionaries, and about 30 translators of the Bible into foreign tongues.

His literary work was extensive. He translated Winer's *Greek Grammar of the New Testament* (1825); in collaboration with Professor Robinson), and Roediger's Gesenius' *Hebrew Grammar* (1846); prepared commentaries on Hebrews (2 vols., 1827–28), Romans (2 vols., 1832), Revelation (2 vols., 1845), Daniel (1850), Ecclesiastes (1851), and Proverbs (1852); and wrote, besides his *Hebrew Grammar, Letters to Rev. William E. Channing . . . on the Divinity of Christ* (1819); *Letters to Rev. Samuel Miller . . . on the Eternal Generation of the Son of God* (1822); *Hebrew Chrestomathy* (1829); *Elementary Principles of Interpretation, from the Latin of Ernesti* (1842); *Hints on the Prophecies* (1842); *Critical History and Defence of the Old Testament Canon* (1845); *Miscellanies; consisting of Letters and Sermons, on the Trinity, the Atonement, etc.* (1846); and *Exegetical Essays* (1867).

BIBLIOGRAPHY: The *Funeral Sermon*, by E. A. Park, was published, Andover, 1852. Consult further W. Adams, *Discourse on the Life and Services of Moses Stuart*, New York, 1852; W. B. Sprague, *Annals of the American Pulpit*, ii. 475–481, ib. 1859; W. Walker, in *American Church History Series*, iii. 341, 352–353, 355, ib. 1894; idem, *Ten New England Leaders*, pp. 372, 388, 398, 415–417, ib. 1901.

STUBBS, CHARLES WILLIAM: Church of England; b. at Liverpool Sept. 3 1845. He was educated at Sidney Sussex College, Cambridge (B.A., 1868), and was ordered deacon in 1868 and ordained priest in 1869. He was senior curate of St. Mary's, Sheffield (1868–71), vicar of Granborough, Bucks (1871–84), and of Stokenham, Devonshire (1884–88); rector of Wavertree, Liverpool (1888–94); dean of Ely (1894–1906); and bishop of Truro since 1906. He has been honorary fellow of his college since 1904, and was select preacher at Cambridge in 1881, 1894, 1896, and 1901, and at Oxford in 1883 and 1898–99, Lady Margaret preacher at Cambridge in 1896–97, select preacher at Harvard in 1900, and Hulsean lecturer in 1904–05. He has written, in addition to several volumes of poems, *Origin and Growth of Sentiments of International Morality* (London, 1869); *Village Politics: Addresses and Sermons on the Labour Question* (1878); *The Mythe of Life* (1880); *Christ and Democracy* (University sermons; 1883); *God's Englishmen: Sermons on the Prophets and Kings of England* (1887); *For Christ and City* (Liverpool sermons; 1890); *The Land and the Labourers* (1890); *Christ and Economics* (1893); *Christus Imperator* (1894); *A Creed for Christian Socialists, with Expositions* (1896); *Historical Memorials of Ely Cathedral* (1897); *Handbook to Ely Cathedral* (Ely, 1898); *Charles Kingsley and the Christian Social Movement* (London, 1898); *The Social Teachings of the Lord's Prayer* (University sermons; 1900); *Pro Patria!* (cathedral and university sermons; 1900); *In a Minster Garden: Colloquies of Ely* (1901); *Cambridge and its Story* (1904); and *The Christ of English Poetry*, Hulsean lectures (1905). He has edited Matthew and Mark for *The Temple Bible* (London, 1901); and *Verba Christi: Sayings of the Lord Jesus, Greek and English* (1903).

STUBBS, WILLIAM: Church of England bishop; b. at Knaresborough (16 m. n. of Leeds) June 21, 1825; d. at Oxford Apr. 19, 1901. He studied at Christ Church College, Oxford (B.A., 1848; M.A., 1851); was fellow of Trinity College, Oxford (1848–1851); of Oriel (1867–84); honorary fellow of Balliol (1876–84); honorary student of Christ Church (1878–84); vicar of Navestock, Essex (1850–67); librarian to the archbishop of Canterbury, and keeper of the manuscripts at Lambeth (1862–67); examiner in the schools of law and modern history, Oxford (1865–66); regius professor of modern history (1866–84); select preacher (1870); examiner in the school of theology (1871–72); and of modern history (1873, 1876, 1881); rector of Cholderton, Wilts (1875–79); canon of St. Paul's, London (1879–1884); member of royal commission on ecclesiastical courts (1881); became bishop of Chester (1884), and was translated to Oxford (1888). As a historian and critic he belonged in the front rank of English scholars. He was one of the foremost contributors to the *Rolls Series;* was the editor or author of *Registrum sacrum Anglicanum* (Oxford, 1858); *Chronicles and Memorials of the Reign of Richard I.* (2 vols., London, 1864–65); *Benedictus Abbas* (2 vols., 1867); *Roger Hoveden* (4 vols., 1868–71); *Select Charters* (1871); *Councils and Ecclesiastical Documents* (vol. iii., 1871); *Walter of Coventry* (2 vols., 1872–73); *Constitutional History of England* (3 vols., 1874–78); *Memorials of St. Dunstan* (1874); *The Early Plantagenets* (1876); *The Historical Works of Ralph de Diceto* (2 vols., 1876); *Works of Gervase of Canterbury* (2 vols., 1879); *Chronicles of Edward I. and II.* (2 vols., 1882–83); *Seventeen Lectures on the Study of Mediæval and Modern Church History* (1887); *The "Gesta Regum" of William of Malmesbury* (1887–89); and, posthumously, *Ordination Addresses*, ed. E. E. Holmes (1901); *Historical Introductions to Rolls Series*, collected and ed. A. Hassall (1902); *Letters, 1825–1901*, ed. W. H. Hutton (1904); *Visitation Charges*, ed. E. E. Holmes (1904); *Lectures on Early English History*, ed. A. Hassall (1906); and *Germany in the . . . Middle Ages*, ed. A. Hassall (2 vols., 1908).

BIBLIOGRAPHY: W. H. Hutton, *William Stubbs, Bishop of Oxford, 1825–1901*, London, 1906.

STUCKENBERG, JOHN HENRY WILBURN: Lutheran; b. at Bramsche (60 m. s.w. of Bremen), Germany, Jan. 6, 1835; d. at London May 28, 1903. He was educated at Wittenberg College, Springfield, O. (A.B., 1857), and at the universities of Halle (1859–61), Göttingen, Tübingen, and Berlin (1865–1867). He held Lutheran pastorates at Davenport, O. (1858–59), Erie, Pa. (1861–65), Indianapolis, Ind. (1867–68), and Pittsburg, Pa. (1868–74), being also chaplain of the 145th Pennsylvania Volunteers in 1862–63; he was professor of theology in Wittenberg Theological Seminary (1874–80), and from 1880 until his retirement from active life in 1894 was pastor of the American Church in Berlin. In theology he was a liberal evangelical, and wrote *Ninety-Five Theses for the Seventh Semi-Centennial of the Reformation* (Baltimore, 1868); *History of the Augsburg Confession from its Origin till the Adoption of the Formula of Concord* (Philadelphia, 1869); *Christian*

Sociology (New York, 1880); *Life of Immanuel Kant* (London, 1882); *Final Science* (New York, 1885); *Introduction to the Study of Philosophy* (1888); *The Age and the Church* (Hartford, Conn., 1893); *Tendencies in German Thought* (1896); *Introduction to the Study of Sociology* (New York, 1897); *The Social Problem* (York, Pa., 1897); and *Sociology: or, The Science of Human Society* (2 vols., New York, 1903). He also translated C. R. Hagenbach's *German Rationalism in its Rise, Progress, and Decline* (in collaboration with W. L. Gage; Edinburgh, 1865).

STUDENT VOLUNTEER MOVEMENT FOR FOREIGN MISSIONS: A movement originated at the first international conference of Christian college students, held at Mount Hermon, Mass., in 1886, at
Origin, Organization, Purpose. the invitation of the late D. L. Moody. Of the 250 delegates who attended, twenty-one had definitely decided to become foreign missionaries when the conference opened. Of this number Robert P. Wilder of Princeton, Tewksbury of Harvard, and Clark of Oberlin had come with the conviction that God would call from that large gathering of college men a number who would consecrate themselves to foreign missions. Before the conference closed 100 of the delegates had recorded their " purpose, if God permit, to become foreign missionaries." At the conference it was decided that a deputation should be sent among the colleges, and four students were selected for this purpose. Of the four selected, Wilder alone was able to go, and John N. Forman, also of Princeton, was induced to join him. The expenses of the deputation were borne by Mr. D. W. McWilliams, of Brooklyn. Messrs. Wilder and Forman visited 176 institutions, including a majority of the leading colleges and divinity schools of Canada and the United States. In the summer of 1888 about fifty volunteers attended the student conference at Northfield. It was there decided that some organization was necessary, and a committee was appointed by the volunteers present to effect such an organization. This committee met in Dec., 1888, and an organization was effected, taking the name of the Student Volunteer Movement for Foreign Missions which is incorporated under the laws of the state of New York. There is an executive committee, a board of trustees, and an advisory committee. This movement is in no sense a missionary board. It never has sent out a missionary, and never will. It is simply a recruiting agency. Those who become student volunteers are expected to go out as missionaries under the regular missionary organizations of the Church. It does not usurp or encroach upon the functions of any other missionary organization. It is unswervingly loyal to the Church, and has received the endorsement of every leading missionary board on the continent. It is primarily a movement of students, and it is not in any sense an organization forced upon the students. The purposes are as follows: (1) To awaken and maintain among all Christian students of the United States and Canada intelligent and active interest in foreign missions; (2) to enroll a sufficient number

of properly qualified student volunteers to meet the successive demands of the various missionary boards of North America; (3) to help all such intending missionaries to prepare for their life-work and to enlist their cooperation in developing the missionary life of home churches; (4) to lay an equal burden of responsibility on all students who are to remain as ministers and lay workers at home, that they may actively promote the missionary enterprise by intelligent advocacy, gifts, and prayer.

Student volunteers are drawn from those who are or have been students in institutions of higher learning in the United States and Canada. Each
Methods of Work. student volunteer signs the " declaration," which is as follows: " It is my purpose, if God permit, to become a foreign missionary." The work for which the movement, as an agency of the Church, is held responsible is the promotion of the missionary life and activity in the institutions of higher learning in the United States and Canada, in which more than 250,000 students are matriculated. From these should come the future missionaries and missionary leaders of the Church. Therefore no work can be more important than that of making each student center a stronghold of missionary intelligence, enthusiasm, and activity. To accomplish this a staff of secretaries is employed, offices are maintained in New York City, and conferences and conventions are held. Besides administrative secretaries, there are traveling secretaries; and this position is usually held for one year by a student volunteer ready to go to the mission field. Returned missionaries also have been employed. The number of traveling secretaries is determined by the funds at the disposal of the executive committee. The traveling secretaries visit the colleges, deliver addresses on missions, meet with missionary committees and volunteer bands, organize mission-study classes, and in every way possible promote the missionary activities of the colleges—but the chief object of their work is by public address and personal interview to lead students to give their lives to missionary service. The student volunteers in an institution are organized into a volunteer band, which has as its objects to deepen the missionary purpose and spiritual lives of the members, to secure other volunteers, and to promote missions in the college and in the college community. Once in three years an international convention is held. Six such conventions have been held; at that of 1910 there were present 2,954 students and professors representing 735 institutions.

The Volunteer Movement has reached by its propaganda nearly if not quite 1,000 institutions of higher learning in North America. In a large majority of these the work was the first
Results. real missionary cultivation which they ever received. It is the testimony of professors and other observers that even in the institutions which had already been influenced in different ways by the missionary idea, the Volunteer Movement has very greatly developed missionary interest and activity. Because the Student Volunteer Movement is a movement for foreign missions, the principal proof of its efficiency is to be found

in the going forth of its members to the foreign mission field. It is gratifying, therefore, to note that the movement has on its records the names of 4,784 volunteers who, prior to Jan. 1, 1911, had reached the mission field, having been sent out as missionaries of no less than fifty different missionary boards of the United States and Canada. About one-third of the sailed volunteers are women.

The sailed volunteers are distributed by countries as follows:

Mexico	152
Central America	28
South America	288
West Indies	146
Latin and Greek Church countries of Europe	21
Africa	503
Turkish Empire	174
Arabia	21
Persia	39
India, Burma, and Ceylon	924
Siam, Laos, and Straits settlements	79
China	1,389
Korea	219
Japan	401
Philippine Islands	145
Oceania	58
Miscellaneous	197
Total	**4,784**

In order to be of greater service to all the mission boards in helping them to secure the most capable men and women to go as missionaries, there was established in the fall of 1907 the candidate department. The work already done has demonstrated the wisdom of this forward movement. Almost every board has been aided during the past year in finding properly qualified candidates. In 1894 the movement began to promote the systematic and progressive study of missions among students. At that time there were less than thirty classes carrying on such study in all the institutions of North America. During the first year there were organized 144 classes with an enrolment of 1,400. In the year 1909–10 there were in 596 institutions 2,379 classes having an enrolment of 29,322. At the beginning of this period there were no text-books available for the classes. Since 1894 a text-book literature has been created, not only for the students, but the work, taken up by other organizations, has been pushed in the churches among young people's societies, women's missionary societies, and in the Sunday-schools, so that now the annual sales of missionary text-books by these different agencies has passed the 100,000 mark. This mission study work is developing an intelligent and strong missionary interest and is striving to make that interest permanent. It is an invaluable help in preparing missionary candidates for their life-work, is making the conditions favorable for the multiplying of the number of capable volunteers, is developing right habits of praying and giving for missions, and is equipping those who are to become leaders at home to be real citizens of a world-wide kingdom. The movement has also stimulated gifts to missions by students. When it began its work less than $10,000 a year was being contributed toward missionary objects by all the institutions of the United States and Canada. During 1909–10 29,000 students and professors gave over $133,761, of which

more than $90,000 was given to foreign missions and $37,000 to home missions. Eighty-nine institutions gave $300 or more each. Many colleges and theological seminaries are supporting entirely or in large part their own representative on the foreign field. The movement has been helpful also in raising the standards of qualifications of intending missionaries. During the past twenty years in particular it has emphasized that those who are to become missionaries should possess the highest qualifications. It invariably encourages students to take a regular and thorough college or university course and to press on to such graduate courses as may be required by the agencies under which they expect to go abroad. The leaders of the movement have always insisted that no student volunteer was prepared for his high calling unless he were spiritually qualified. Hence the movement has guided and stimulated volunteers to form right devotional habits such as that of personal Bible study, secret prayer, and the practise of religious meditation.

Great as the achievements have been, the work is not and will not be finished while there is an increasing demand for missionaries. New missionaries are needed to fill the places made vacant on the mission field by the death or retirement of the old missionaries, to reach the unevangelized millions in the countries where missions have already been established, and to occupy the countries which are at present without a single missionary, or where no work has as yet been attempted. These recruits must be found among the students.

F. P. TURNER.

BIBLIOGRAPHY: Reports of the Executive Committee and of the international conventions, published by the organization from time to time.

STUDITES. See ACŒMETI.

STUMBLING-BLOCK, STONE OF STUMBLING: The translation in the English versions of the Hebrew *mikshol, makshelah, ebhen negheph,* and the Greek *proskomma, lithos tou proskommatos, skandolon,* the fundamental idea of which is either an object in the way over which one may stumble or a weighted trap used for catching wild animals, which falls when the bait is touched. These terms may represent persons or things good in themselves, as when (I Cor. i. 23; I Pet. ii. 8) they are applied to Christ, the guilt resting upon those " which stumble at the word, being disobedient "; and moral guilt may be incurred by a Christian if, when he should uphold his faith, he weakly denies it or conceals it for fear of giving offense. On the other hand, he is always to take the ideas and feelings of others into consideration (cf. Matt. xvii. 27). An offense which involves blame to the giver does so because it leads to sin, if only by confusing the moral judgment, in the awakening of a doubt about the character of the agent or the action or about the correctness of another's habitual convictions. Sin is thus made easier, and the one who gives offense incurs the guilt of consciously or unconsciously leading another into temptation. It is from this standpoint that St. Paul exhorts the Corinthians to abstain from meat offered in sacrifice (I Cor. viii. 7–13, x. 28), laying down his principle of Christian liberty, " All things are lawful unto me, but all things are not expedient " (vi. 12, x. 23, 32).   (RUDOLF HOFMANN.)

STUNDISTS. See RUSSIA, II., § 7.

STUPA: A mound of masonry, usually domelike, employed by Buddhists to commemorate a notable event, mark a sacred spot, preserve a relic, or to serve a combination of these purposes. The terms dagoba and tope are employed to some extent as equivalents, the latter having reference to the form and the former to the purpose as protecting a relic. The shape has been explained as due to the tradition that Buddha, born among a race descended from the Scythians, directed that his remains be buried in Scythian fashion (cf. Herodotus, iv. 71, 72, 217; and the notes and plans in Rawlinson's transl., iii. 57–63, New York, 1875) under a raised mound (S. Beal, *Catena of the Buddhist Scriptures from the Chinese*, pp. 126–130, London, 1871). The period during which these structures were raised coincides roughly with the middle stage of the dominance of Buddhism in India, c. 250 B.C.– 250 A.D., though some rebuilding was done as late as the eighth century. Those best worthy of mention are (1) that at Sanchi, Bhopal, Central India, having a horizontal diameter of 106 feet and placed upon a circular platform 120 feet in diameter, and having a perpendicular radius of forty-two feet. It is constructed of bricks laid in mud covered with a layer of chiseled stone, and has a tee or flattened surface on the apex (the place where usually the relic was kept) fourteen feet in diameter. The whole is surrounded by an elaborately carved stone railing. (2) A second important example is found at Manikyala, near Raval Pindi, in the Punjab (where these structures are especially numerous). (3) The finest of all, perhaps, was that at Amravati, in the Madras Presidency, the sculptures of which are now in the British Museum. (4) One of great historic interest is twelve miles from the Lumbini Garden (the traditional birthplace of the Buddha, about 110 m. n.e. of Benares), and covered that part of the ashes of the saint which fell to his own Sakhya clan. (5) A notable series of groups are in the vicinity of Bhilsa in Bhopal, and number between twenty-five and thirty. Most of these are in a most ruinous condition, the Mohammedans and others having used them as quarries of material for later structures. The Chinese Buddhist pilgrim Hiouen Thsang (seventh century) reports that what are known to have been some of the earliest were already in ruins.   GEO. W. GILMORE.

BIBLIOGRAPHY: J. Fergusson, *Hist. of Indian and Eastern Architecture*, book I., chap. iii., London, 1891 (gives excellent cuts, one on title-page); idem, in *Royal Asiatic Society's Journal*, new series, iii (1868), 132–166; K. Ritter, *Die Stupas*, Berlin, 1838, H. H. Wilson, *Ariana Antiqua*, pp. 55–118, London, 1841; A. Cunningham, *The Bhilsa Topes*, ib. 1854; idem, in *Royal Asiatic Society's Journal*, xiii (1852), 108–114; J. Burgess, *Notes on the Amaravati Stupa*, Madras, 1882; J. Burgess, *The Buddhist Stupas of Amaravati and Jaggayyapeta*, London, 1887; and the following articles in the *Royal Asiatic Society's Journal*, new series, v (1870), 164–181 (by S. Beal), xiv (1882), 332–334 (by W. Simpson), 1902, pp. 29–45 (by J. Burgess).

STURM (STURMI) OF FULDA: Disciple of Boniface, first abbot of Fulda (q.v.), and apostle of Hesse and Saxony; b. in Bavaria in 710; d. at Fulda Dec. 17, 779. He came of a distinguished Christian family, and was sent to Boniface for instruction while the latter was in Bavaria; he accompanied Boniface on at least one of his missionary journeys, and for further education was under the care of Abbot Wigbert at Fritzlar, being made priest in 740. He was then a missionary in Hesse for three years; but, feeling a strong inclination for the monastic life, he was encouraged by Boniface to build an abbey, and after some indecision settled at Fulda, receiving a gift of the land from Carloman through the intercession of Boniface, erecting the first structure and becoming its first abbot under the Benedictine rule. After the death of Boniface, when great efforts were made to carry the body to Mainz for entombment, Sturm carried out the wishes of his master for burial at Fulda. Lullus of Mainz attempted to disregard the exemptions secured by the abbey, and Sturm was the defender; but in consequence he was charged with disloyalty to Pippin and banished to Jumièges in Normandy, 758, but was permitted to return in 760 and received into Pippin's good graces, this result being in part due to the favor in which Sturm was held throughout the Frankish kingdom. Sturm was also regarded highly by Charlemagne, and was employed by him in diplomatic affairs, and it fell to his lot to carry the Gospel to the regions brought under the Frankish's king's dominion in Saxony. His accomplishment was not merely the planting of the abbey and its erection into a strong and influential institution, but the impulse to general education and culture which he imparted and the results of this in churches and schools in central Germany.

BIBLIOGRAPHY: The fundamental source is the *Vita* by Egil, abbot of Fulda, 818–822, in *ASB*, iii. 2, pp. 269–284, with discussion of the year of death and account of the canonization by Mabillon, pp. 284–286, also in *MGH, Script.*, ii (1829), 365–377, and *MPL*, cv. 423–444; there is a Germ. transl. by W. Arndt, Berlin, 1863. Consult further: G. F. Maclear, *Hist. of Christian Missions during the Middle Ages*, pp. 211–217, Cambridge, 1863; idem, *Apostles of Medieval Europe*, pp. 132–138, London, 1888; F. J. Nick, *Der heilige Sturmius, erster Abt von Fulda*, Fulda, 1865; J. Kayser, *Der heilige Sturmi, der erste Glaubensbote des Paderborner Landes*, Paderborn, 1866; A. Ebert, *Allgemeine Geschichte der Literatur des Mittelalters*, ii. 104–106, 121, 144, Leipsic, 1880; B. Kuhlmann, *Der heilige Sturmi, Gründer Fuldas und Apostel Westfalens*, Paderborn, 1890; Rettberg, *KD*, i. 371, 607 sqq., 616 sqq.; Hauck, *KD*, vol. ii. passim.

STURM, sturm, JAKOB: German reformer; b. at Strasburg Aug. 10, 1489; d. there Oct. 30, 1553. He was educated at Heidelberg (B.A., 1503); and at Freiburg (M.A., 1505), where he studied theology in connection with law after 1506. He maintained relations with the greatest humanists of his day, and was highly esteemed by Erasmus. He was first a clerical of the lower order; occupied the position of secretary to the cathedral provost at Strasburg, 1517–23; was an earnest member of the Strasburg society of learning; and in 1522 devised a plan for the reorganization of the University of Heidelberg. In 1524 he entered the municipal service, being elected to the great council, as a member of which he represented Strasburg and other imperial cities, in the government of the empire. From 1526 he was one of the " college of thirteen," was chosen

Stadtmeister thirteen times from 1527, and soon advanced to the leadership of Strasburg statesmanship. The wise moderation of Strasburg in the Peasants' War was due to his influence. His fearless championship of the Protestant cause and his eloquence at the Diet of Speyer of 1526 (see SPEYER, DIETS OF) secured for his city the leadership in upper Germany. In the quiet movement of the Reformation at his native city, he took the ground of liberty of conscience in church matters, recognizing neither pope nor emperor in matters of faith. Hence Strasburg became a center of toleration and freedom. He held aloof from the Eucharistic controversy, declining the communion for years; but was present at the conference at Marburg (q.v.). At the Diet of Speyer in 1529 he advocated the abolition of the mass, took sides with the protesting estates, and assisted Philip of Hesse to prevail upon these not to concur in the condemnation of the Swiss. At the Diet of Augsburg (1530) he helped in drawing up the *Confessio tetrapolitana* and strove, though unsuccessfully, for unity. He participated in the deliberations before the Wittenberg Concord of 1536. Simultaneously he was employed upon ecclesiastical organization at Strasburg; he was president of the synod of 1533, and took a part in the preparation of the church order which appeared in 1534. Shortly after he succeeded in founding the Strasburg gymnasium. Since 1528 he had been one of the supervisors of public instruction. During the Interim, he humbled himself, though unconquered, to the emperor, thus parting with M. Butzer, whom he had hitherto supported; yet sustaining the dignity and Protestant freedom of the city. As a strategic point on the Rhine, he took every precaution to fortify Strasburg against the French. Sturm held the respect of all parties as well as of his opponents and of the emperor; and from 1525 to 1552 represented the city of Strasburg ninety-one times at political and religious conferences. Unsurpassed as an administrator and statesman in the history of Strasburg he was a man of deep moral and religious conviction, of circumspect wisdom and highminded Christian patriotism.

(JOHANNES FICKER.)

BIBLIOGRAPHY: Sources are: E. Winkelmann, *Urkundenbuch der Universität Heidelberg*, i. 214 sqq., Heidelberg, 1886; the *Opera* of Zwingli, passim; *Politische Korrespondenz der Stadt Strassburg im Zeitalter der Reformation*, ed. H. Virck and O. Winckelmann, vols. i.–iii., Strasburg, 1882–97; J. Strickler, *Aktensammlung der schweizischen Reformationsgeschichte, 1521–32*, 5 vols., Zurich, 1878–84; and M. Lenz, *Briefwechsel Landgraf Philipp des Grossmütigen von Hessen mit Bucer*, 3 vols., Leipsic, 1880–1891. For biographical material consult: J. Sturm, *Consolatio ad senatum Argentinensem de morte . . . Jacobi Sturmii*, Strasburg, 1553; Stein, *Jacob Sturm* (Jena dissertation), Leipsic, 1878; H. Baumgarten, *Historische und politische Aufsätze und Reden*, pp. 458 sqq., Strasburg, 1894; *ADB*, xxxvi. 5 sqq. For light on various sides of Sturm's activities consult: A. Jung, *Geschichte der Reformation der Kirche in Strassburg*, vol. i., Leipsic, 1830; T. W. Röhrich, *Geschichte der Reformation in Elsass und besonders in Strassburg*, 3 parts, Strasburg, 1830–32; A. W. Strobel, *Hist. du gymnase protestant de Strasbourg*, ib. 1838; J. W. Baum, *Capito und Butzer*, Elberfeld, 1860; H. Baumgarten, *Ueber Sleidans Leben und Briefwechsel*, Strasburg, 1878, A. Baum, *Magistrat und Reformation in Strassburg bis 1529*, ib. 1887, C. Engel, *Das Gründungsjahr des protestantischen Gymnasiums zu Strassburg*, pp. 113 sqq., ib. 1888; idem, *L'École latin et l'ancienne académie de Strasbourg (1538–1621)*, ib. 1900; M. Fournier and C. Engel, *L'Université de Strasbourg et les académies protestantes françaises*, Paris, 1894; J. W. Richard, *Philip Melanchthon*, pp. 18, 176, 185, 226, 264, New York, 1898; S. M. Jackson, *Huldreich Zwingli*, pp. 312, 324, 330, 2d ed., ib. 1903; *Cambridge Modern History*, ii. 204, 258, ib. 1904; and works on the history of Strasburg.

STURM, JOHANNES: German humanist and schoolman; b. at Schleiden (60 m. s.w. of Cologne) Oct. 1, 1507; d. at Strasburg Mar. 3, 1589. He entered, in 1521 or 1522, upon his humanistic studies at the school of St. Hieronymus at Lüttich and completed them at the University of Louvain, where he had a share in a printing-press and issued several Greek works. Visiting Paris in 1529 to sell his books, he was induced to teach dialectics and give lectures on Cicero and Demosthenes. Influenced by the writings of M. Butzer, he adopted the principles of the Reformation. After participating in the attempt to reconcile the Protestant and Roman Catholic parties in 1534, upon a new outbreak of persecution, he repaired to Strasburg to organize the new gymnasium. Dependent on Melanchthon, he followed the principle of training in rhetoric and eloquence, based upon Humanism and Evangelical piety, for the offices of the Reformation movement and the State.

Although a Protestant, Sturm had many Roman Catholic connections and always cherished the hope of a reunion. His oratorical talent and diplomatic aptitude qualified him for many embassies in behalf of Strasburg, the Protestant estates, and the king of France. He attended the conferences at Hagenau and Worms, 1540; of Regensburg, 1541; and went with Butzer to meet the elector of Cologne, 1542. After helping to negotiate peace between England and France, 1545, he again went to France, 1546, at the outbreak of the Schmalkald War, to procure the aid of Francis I. A personal friend of many French Protestants and especially of Calvin, Sturm preferred the Reformed teaching on the Eucharist, but, desiring a reconciliation, shared the attitude of Butzer and Melanchthon. He spared no sacrifice in behalf of liberty of conscience for France, even demanding German aid to the Huguenots. For this he incurred the suspicion of the Lutherans. After the death of Jakob Sturm (q.v.) and with the stricter enforcement of the Lutheran confession after 1555, Sturm became involved in continuous violent controversies. He upheld the broader views of Butzer, which formerly prevailed at Strasburg, being also influenced by his Biblical and humanistic tendency toward a non-dogmatic Christianity. This controversy, lasting more than thirty years, marks the division of the Strasburg church from its past. A consensus in 1563 on the basis of the Wittenberg Concord did not last long. Sturm was engaged to organize a number of schools upon the model of his own, among which was the gymnasium at Lauingen, 1564. In 1566 he secured an imperial privilege for an academy, which was dedicated 1567. But the complaint of the theologians against the Reformed tendencies of himself and some of his professors became ever louder. The intensely partizan Johann Marbach (q.v.) brought on an acrimonious strife over the school, which a referee decided in favor of

Sturm in 1575. But soon after, the occasion of the introduction of the Formula of Concord (q.v.) at Strasburg reopened the conflict. Coarser in method was the assault of Johannes Pappus (q.v.), who was supported by L. Osiander and Jakob Andreä (qq.v.) of Württemberg. Many virulent pamphlets were exchanged. The result was the removal of Sturm from the rectorship. He spent his last years at his rural house at Northeim. He had a sanguine, sympathetic nature, easily attracted or violently repelled, and was lacking in self-control. To this may be added his arrogance and increasing passion of temper as motives of his controversial spirit, provoked when his broad, international, humanistic attitude refused to be pressed into narrow confessional molds. His eminent capability as an organizer and teacher made the Strasburg high school world-renowned and one of the best attended of the time, and history has assigned him the fame of "the greatest of the great school rectors of the sixteenth century." (JOHANNES FICKER.)

BIBLIOGRAPHY: The book of most value is C. Schmidt, La Vie et les travaux de Jean Sturm, Strasburg, 1855 (contains list of the works of Sturm and also names the earlier literature). As sources to be consulted are: J. Camerarius, Epistolarum libri V posteriores, pp. 496–505, Frankfort, 1595; Zanchii epistolarum libri duo, passim, Hanover, 1609; Aschami familiarium epistolarum libri III, pp. 529 sqq., ib. 1610; Fecht, Hist. eccl. sæc. XVI., supplementum, pp. 836, 877, 886–896, Frankfort, 1684; A. Schumacher, Gelehrter Männer Briefe an die Könige in Dänemark, ii. 311 sqq., Copenhagen, 1758; Zurich Letters (1558–1602), Parker Society, Cambridge, 1845; the Opera of Calvin and Melanchthon in the CR; and A. L. Herminjard, Correspondance des reformateurs, 9 vols., Geneva, 1864–97. For discussions of Sturm's life and activities consult: L. Kückelhahn, Johann Sturm, Strassburgs erster Schulrektor, Leipsic, 1872; E. Laas, Die Pädagogik des Johann Sturms, Berlin, 1872; E. and E. Haag, La France protestante, ix. 318 sqq., Paris, 1859; F. von Bezold, Briefe des Pfalzgrafen Johann Casimir, 3 vols., Munich, 1882–1903; R. Zoepffel, Johann Sturm, Der erste Rektor der Strassburger Akademie, Strasburg, 1887; H. Veil, in Festschrift des protestantischen Gymnasiums zu Strassburg, ib. 1888; G. Schmid, in K. A. Schmid, Geschichte der Erziehung, ii. 2, pp. 30 sqq., Stuttgart, 1889; F. Paulsen, Geschichte des gelehrten Unterrichts, passim, 2d ed., Leipsic, 1896–97; Bourilly, in Bulletin de la société de l'hist. du protestantisme français, 1900, pp. 237 sqq., 477 sqq.; idem and Weiss, in the same, 1904, pp. 97 sqq.; G. Mertz, Das Schulwesen der deutschen Reformation, passim, Heidelberg, 1902; T. Ziegler, Geschichte der Pädagogik, pp. 73–91, 2d ed., Munich, 1904; ADB, xxxvii. 21–38; much of the literature under STURM, JACOB, especially the works there named of C. Engel, M. Fournier and C. Engel, H. Baumgarten, and T. W. Röhrich, and the Politische Korrespondenz der Stadt Strassburg.

STURM, JULIUS KARL REINHOLD: German poet and hymnist; b. at Köstritz (30 m. s.s.w. of Leipsic) July 21, 1816; d. at Leipsic May 2, 1896. He received his preparatory training at the gymnasium at Gera, 1829–37, and studied theology at Jena, 1837–41. He served as tutor at Heilbronn, 1841–44; then was tutor of Prince Henry XIV. of Reuss-Schleiz-Gera, 1844–47; and attended the prince in the gymnasia of Schleiz and Meiningen, 1847–50. His first volume of secular and religious poetry appeared with the title Gedichte (Leipsic, 1850). He served as pastor at Göschitz, 1850–57, and at Köstritz, 1857–78; was church councilor there, 1878–85; and privy councilor after 1885. Among a long series of poetic publications may be named. Fromme Lieder (1852); Zwei Rosen oder

das Hohelied der Liebe (1854); Neue fromme Lieder und Gedichte (1858); Für das Haus (1862); Israelitische Lieder (2d ed., Halle, 1867); Aufwärts (1881), and Dem Herrn mein Lied (Bremen, 1884), both collections of religious poems; and his last poems, in Freud und Leid (Leipsic, 1896).

(A. FREYBE.)

BIBLIOGRAPHY: E. Heyden, Galerie berühmter und merkwürdiger Reussenländer, Frankfort, 1858; O. Kraus, Geistliche Lieder im 19. Jahrhundert, pp. 543 sqq., 2d ed., Gütersloh, 1879; Zuppki, in Unser Vogtland, ii. 1 (1895), 2–10; R. König, in Daheim, xxxii. 37 (1896), 592 sqq.; F. Hoffmann, in R. Virchow and F. von Holtzendorff's Gemeinverständliche wissenschaftliche Vorträge, part 306, Hamburg, 1898; K. L. Leimbach, Ausgewählte deutsche Dichtungen, iv. 2, pp. 345 sqq., 13 vols., Frankfort, 1899; Julian, Hymnology, p. 1100.

STUTTGART, stut'gärt or stūt'gärt, **SYNOD AND CONFESSION OF:** The convention in 1559 which gave solemn sanction to the Lutheran doctrine of the Lord's Supper. The immediate occasion of the synod was an accusation brought against Bartholomäus Hagen, pastor at Dettingen, and preacher to the Duchess Sabina of Württemberg, mother of Duke Christopher, of being an adherent of the Swiss doctrine. At the command of the duke, Hagen was cited to appear in Apr., 1559, at Stuttgart and was given a month's time to offer a categorical explanation on the article of the presence of Christ. After this had been referred to all the superintendents and their judgments received, an extraordinary synod was summoned at Stuttgart, which consisted of four general superintendents, the clerical and lay members of the consistory, the rector, and the theological faculty of the University of Tübingen, and all the special superintendents of the country. The synod met on Dec. 13, 1559. Jakob Andreä (q.v.) was appointed to conduct the disputation with Hagen before the assembled synod, presenting, after a conference with Johann Brenz (q.v.), the same arguments on the ubiquity that appeared later in the "Confession" of the synod. Hagen was finally obliged to confess his defeat and to acknowledge the doctrine of the Württemberg Church as true and Scriptural. On Dec. 19 Brenz presented a formula which was signed by all the theologians, and published in German and Latin under the title, Confessio et doctrina theologorum et ministrorum verbi Dei in ducatu Wirtembergensi de vera præsentia corporis et sanguinis Jesu Christi in cœna dominica (Tübingen, 1560–61). The main points are here summarized: (1) In the Lord's Supper, by virtue of the Word, or institution of Christ, the true body and blood of Christ are truly and essentially given and transferred with the bread and wine to all who partake; so that both the body and the blood, as given by the hand of the minister, are received by the mouth of those who thus eat and drink. (2) The nature and substance of the bread and the wine are not transformed, but are ordained and sanctified by the Word of the Lord to serve in the distribution of the body and blood of Christ. Yet they are not merely symbols, but just as the substance of the bread and wine is present so also the substance of the body and the blood is present, and by means of those signs is truly given and received. (3) This does not imply a confusion of the bread and the wine with the body and blood of Christ, there is no spatial enclosure but only such a sacramental union of the bread and body as is described by the Word of the Lord; hence, there is no sacrament aside from the use. (4) The ascension of Christ into heaven is no obstacle to the doctrine, inasmuch as Christ in his majesty and glory at the right hand of the Father fills all things not only by his divinity, but also by his humanity, in a mysterious way conceivable not to reason but only to faith. (5) Not only the pious and worthy, but also the godless and hypocrites receive the body and blood, the latter to their judgment; therefore to be received by the godless does not detract from the glory and majesty of Christ, because as a just judge for him to punish the impenitent is as laudable as to show grace to the penitent. This " Confession," which was claimed to rest upon Scripture and to be in accord with the Augsburg Confession (q.v.) and the Wittenberg Confession submitted to the Council of Trent, was forthwith incorporated with the Württemberg church order.

The historical significance of the Stuttgart Synod lies in the fact that there, for the first time, was the difference between the Lutheran and the Calvinistic doctrines of the Lord's Supper sharply distinguished; namely, the three main points: giving and receiving by hand and mouth, partaking by the unbelieving, and the founding of the doctrine of the Lord's Supper on the teaching concerning the person of Christ and his sitting at the right hand of the Father. Epoch-making was the last, in which Brenz, in strict dependence upon Luther, coordinated the doctrine of the Lord's Supper with Christology, which occasioned a renewal of the doctrine of Ubiquity (q.v.), a name charged by the opponents but disavowed by Brenz. This synod marked a rallying of the original Lutheran doctrine at a crisis in which it had been well-nigh supplanted by the ever-spreading view of Calvin and Melanchthon. Moreover, the advancing unionistic tendency promoted by the alliance of the influences of Melanchthon and Calvin was thwarted, and for German Protestantism the cleavage was fixed. Duke Christopher vainly hoped to make the " Confession " a basis for his tireless efforts to effect union, and despatched it throughout Germany and France, but it was almost universally ignored. Within Württemberg this assertion of the conservatism of its reformer and organizer, Brenz, marked the beginning of a new scholastic theology, and proved not only exclusive to neighboring lands for a century, but also oppressive to many of the clergy at home.

(H. Hermelink.)

Bibliography: The confession is printed in *Acta et scripta publica ecclesiæ Wirtembergicæ*, ed. C. M. Pfaff, pp. 334 sqq., 340 sqq., Tübingen, 1720. Matters of importance are to be found in the *Opera* of Calvin, vols. xvi.–xix., especially xvii. 622–625, xix. 350–353 (in *CR*, xliii.–xlvii.). Consult further: J. V. Andreä, *Fama Andreana reflorescens*, pp. 94 sqq., Strasburg, 1630; C. A. Salig, *Vollständige Historie der augspurgische Confession*, iii. 424 sqq., Halle, 1735; C. F. Schnurrer, *Erläuterungen der württembergischen Kirchenreformations- und Gelehrtengeschichte*, pp. 259 sqq., Tübingen, 1798; G. J. Planck, *Geschichte der Entstehung des protestantischen Lehrbegriffs*, v. 2, pp. 398 sqq., Leipsic, 1799; J. Hartmann and K. Jäger, *Johann Brenz*, ii. 372

sqq., Hamburg, 1842; H. Heppe, *Geschichte des deutschen Protestantismus*, i. 311 sqq., Marburg, 1852; H. Schmid, *Der Kampf der lutherischen Kirche um Luthers Lehre vom Abendmahl*, pp. 226 sqq., Leipsic, 1858; B. Kugler, *Christoph Herzog zu Wirtemberg*, ii. 171 sqq., Stuttgart, 1872; *Württembergische Kirchengeschichte*, pp. 393–394, ib. 1893; W. Köhler, *Bibliographia Brentiana*, nos. 368–370, 391, 600, Leipsic, 1904.

STYLITES (PILLAR SAINTS): Anchorets who, in their desire for complete separation from the world and extreme asceticism, passed their lives on pillars. The first pillar saint was Simeon the Elder, who was born in Sisan or Sesan, in northern Syria, about 390. Originally a shepherd in the lonely mountains, he visited a church for the first time at the age of thirteen and immediately resolved to become a monk. His extreme asceticism caused the monks to expel him, and after living for three years as a hermit near Tel Neskin (Telanessa), continuing excessive mortifications, he began, about 420, his pillar life. This he selected, he said, in consequence of a divine revelation, as well as to escape the importunities of the masses. He accordingly built himself a pillar, at first only four ells high, but later reaching the altitude of thirty-six or forty ells.

The later stylites practically imitated Simeon with slight modifications. They lived on the capitals of pillars of varying height, these capitals being sufficiently large for the construction of a small cell on them. They were surrounded by a railing to keep the stylite from falling, and communicated with the ground by a ladder.

Simeon at first roused sentiments other than admiration. The Nitrian monks, fearing the loss of their prestige as incomparable patterns of monasticism, threatened him with excommunication; and the Mesopotamian abbots likewise disapproved his ascetic methods. But the purity of his life and motives soon silenced his critics, and Simeon became renowned as a worker of miracles, a healer of the sick, and a converter of the heathen. He was a powerful factor in promoting peace and in the cause of the suffering and oppressed; he also took part in church polity, as when, in 429, he induced Theodosius II. to revoke an edict which restored to the Jews of Antioch their synagogues, and, in 457, the Emperor Leo I. asked his advice concerning the troubles in Egypt, whereupon the saint espoused the cause of Chalcedonian orthodoxy in two letters to the emperor and Bishop Basil of Antioch. Until his death, in 459, Simeon remained on his pillar.

The example of Simeon Stylites was quickly imitated, at first by only a few, but later by so many that the stylites formed a regular order in the East. The immediate pupil of Simeon and his first successor was Daniel of Maratha near Samosata, who began to live on a pillar in the vicinity of Constantinople shortly after his teacher's death. Like Simeon he zealously defended the Chalcedonian creed, even leaving his pillar once for this purpose. He enjoyed the special protection of Leo I., who built for him a new pillar and later prevailed upon him to permit the construction of a tiny cell on the pillar to protect him against the elements. Daniel died in 493. In the sixth century lived Simeon the Younger. He is said to have left his father's house at the age of five and to have lived as a stylite for sixty-nine years until his death in 596 near Antioch. He sought to surpass Simeon the Elder in his austerities, against the warnings of his teacher. During the reign of Heraclius, Alyphius lived as a stylite at Adrianople in Paphlagonia. Like nearly all the stylites he reached an advanced age, though for the last fourteen years of his life he was unable to stand, lying crouched on his pillar until his death. Mention may finally be made of the stylite Lucas the Younger, who in the tenth century lived on a pillar near Chalcedon, reaching the age of 100 years. Many other stylites are known by name, and the system was flourishing in the tenth century. The last stylites known were among the Ruthenian monks in 1526.

Stylites were most numerous in Syria, Palestine, and Mesopotamia, though they were also found in Greece and in the Russian church. Only one effort is known to have been made to introduce stylitism into the West. In 585 a deacon named Wu'flaicus erected a pillar near Treves, but the bishops compelled him to descend from it and then destroyed it. Occidental antagonism to extravagant asceticism, episcopal opposition to a body of men who might easily withdraw from their control, and unfavorable climatic conditions all combined to render stylitism impossible in the West.

(G. Grützmacher.)

BIBLIOGRAPHY: Several early *Vitæ* of the earlier Simeon are collected, with commentary, in *ASB*, Jan. i. 261–286; the *Vita* by Theodoret of Kyros, *Hist. religiosa*, xxvi.; the *Acta* mistakenly ascribed to Cosmas is in S. E. Assemani, *Acta sanctorum martyrum*, ii. 268–398, cf. ib. 230 sqq. (a poem by Jacob of Sarug), Rome, 1748. Consult further: G. Lautensack, *De Simeone Stylita*, Wittenberg, 1700; F. Uhlemann, *Symeon der erste Säulenheilige in Syrien*, Leipsic, 1846; P. Zingerle, *Leben und Wirken des heiligen Simeon Stylites*, Innsbruck, 1855; H. Delehaye, in *Compte rendu du 3. congrès scientifique des catholiques à Bruxelles*, vol. v., Brussels, 1895; E. Marin, *Les Moines de Constantinople*, Paris, 1897; H. Lietzmann, *Das Leben des heiligen Symeon Stylites*, Leipsic, 1908. A *Vita* of the younger Simeon with commentary is in *ASB*, May, v. 298–401.

SUAREZ, swä′reth, **FRANCISCO:** Jesuit scholastic; b. at Granada, Spain, Jan. 5, 1548; d. at Lisbon Sept. 25, 1617. He was of noble birth; studied law at the University of Salamanca, 1561–64; but decided to enter the order of Jesuits. After his novitiate of three years he studied philosophy at Salamanca; lectured on Aristotle at Segovia and Avila after 1572, and on theology at Valladolid, 1576–78, at Rome, 1578–85, at Alcala, Spain, 1585–1592, at Salamanca for a year; and at the University of Coimbra, Portugal, 1597–1617. His lectures are said to have been sensational in their popularity. Spanish grandees came to hear the " prodigy and oracle of his age," and in an episcopal approbation of one of his writings occurs the term, " a second Augustine "; but Suarez never relinquished his modesty. He lived only for knowledge and pious exercises. He fasted three times a week and on no day took more than one pound of nourishment, and flagellated himself daily with a wire-woven scourge.

Suarez's literary activity was directed mainly to the discussion of the Aristotelian philosophy and to scholastic theology. His works were published, *Opera omnia* (23 vols., Venice, 1740–51;

28 vols., Paris, 1856–61). The last two volumes of the former of these two editions contained metaphysical disputations and a complete index to the metaphysics of Aristotle, and was so widely recognized that it formed a text-book in Protestant institutions for a long time. Vols. i.–xx. consist of disputations and comments on Thomas Aquinas. As vol. ix. represented the "congruism" of Luis Molina (q.v.), it failed to receive the imprimatur of the pope, and was not allowed to appear until 1651. In the field of morals Suarez discussed only the three theological virtues (vol. xi.), the State, religious discipline, and the duties of monks (vols. xii.–xv.). In accordance with the taste of the age and of his order, he heaped up scholastic problems without end by means of his remarkable gift of invention, and with a refined subtlety resolved them by means of dialectic. He wrote his *Defensio fidei catholicæ et apostolicæ adversus anglicanæ sectæ errores* (Coimbra, 1613) at the instance of Pope Paul V. against James I. of England and the English oath of allegiance, in which he laid down the principle that the pope had the power to depose temporal rulers for heresy and schism, and that this must be accepted as an article of faith on the ground of the power of the keys. James had the book publicly burned by the executioner in front of St. Paul's. It was also burned in Paris, but Philip II. of Spain accepted the principle as genuinely Roman Catholic, and the pope gratefully applauded the work in a personal letter to the author Sept. 9, 1613.

(O. Zöckler†.)

BIBLIOGRAPHY: The one work of importance is C. Werner, *F. Suarez und die Scholastik der letzten Jahrhunderte*, 2 vols., Regensburg, 1861. Consult further: the biography printed with the collected works; B. Sartolo, *El Doctor F. Suarez*, 2d ed., Coimbra, 1731; *KL*, xi. 923–929.

SUBDEACON: A clerical order in the Roman Catholic and Greek Churches, ranking next below the deacon. The orders in the ancient Church were only those of bishop, presbyter, and deacon (see ORGANIZATION OF THE EARLY CHURCH). From the diaconate branched the subdiaconate, not uniformly, however, as shown by its frequent absence as late as the middle of the ninth century. Pope Cornelius mentions among the clergy at Rome seven subdeacons, which goes to show the existence of the office by 250, as well as its origin at Rome. When Alexander Severus divided the city into seventeen administrative districts, Fabian, not to exceed the Apostolic number, added seven subdeacons to the seven deacons for the corresponding ecclesiastical divisions. In Spain they are mentioned in connection with the Synod of Ancyra (c. 305); in Africa, according to Cyprian, they existed at the middle of the third century, and in the East they were known at the middle of the fourth. The subdeacons performed minor functions. They might handle the holy vessels when empty; they received the oblations, had superintendence of the graves of the martyrs, guarded the church doors during the communion, and poured the water into the chalice, to which duties was added the chanting of the epistle. Gregory the Great extended the obligation of celibacy to the subdeacons, and a council under Urban II. granted them permission to become bishops.

In the Eastern Church they remained a lower order, but in the West Innocent III. decided that they constituted a higher order. Their ordination, however, differs from that of deacons; they are not presented by the archdeacon, and the ordination is the " tradition of instruments and vestments." The age of consecration fixed by the Council of Trent is the entrance upon the twenty-second year. One year must intervene before the diaconate is reached, a rule from which the bishop may depart. The office of subdeacon is assumed as transitional, and its functions are fulfilled chiefly by laymen and presbyters. In the Evangelical Church, when it occurs, the title subdeacon indicates a difference of outer rank only, not of ordination.

(E. FRIEDBERG†.)

BIBLIOGRAPHY: An adequate and authoritative historical presentation will be found both in Bingham, *Origines*, III., ii., and in *DCA*, ii. 1938–39. Consult further: H. Reuter, *Das Subdiakonat, dessen historische Entwickelung und liturgisch-kanonistische Bedeutung*, Augsburg, 1890; F. Wieland, *Die genetische Entwickelung der sogenannten Ordines minores in den ersten Jahrhunderten*, Rome, 1897.

SUBINTRATION. See TRANSUBSTANTIATION, II., § 4.

SUBINTRODUCTÆ VIRGINES (SYNEISAKTOI): A name for female ascetics who lived together with men although both parties had taken the vow of celibacy with earnest intent. It is a nickname that arose relatively late when the practise was condemned, and has had not a little influence in confusing opinions on this form of asceticism. The practise was widely prevalent throughout Christian antiquity. In Antioch Paul of Samosata had several young girls in his *entourage* (Eusebius, *Hist. eccl.*, VII., xxx. 12 sqq., *NPNF*, 2 ser., i. 315). In Cyprian's time dedicated virgins dwelt with confessors, clericals, and laymen. The rigorous Tertullian advised well-to-do Christians to take into their houses one or more widows " as spiritual consorts, beautiful by faith, endowed by poverty, and sealed by age," and stated that " to have several such wives is pleasing to God " (" Exhortation to Chastity," xii.; " Monogamy," xvi.; Eng. transl. in *ANF*, iv. 56–57, 71–72). Among heretics the chiefs of the Valentinians lived with " sisters " (Irenæus, *Hær.*, I., vi. 3, *ANF*, i. 324); the Montanistic Alexander was bound in spiritual marriage with a prophetess (Eusebius, *Hist. eccl.*, V., xviii. 6 sqq., *NPNF*, 2 ser., i. 236), and the Marcionite Apelles had two spiritual wives, one the prophetess, Philumene (Tertullian, *Præscriptione*, xxx., *ANF*, iii. 257). This spiritual marriage, springing from ascetic motives, had its real place in Monasticism in which it retained its original form, even far into the Middle Ages. In the desert, where the monk and his companion dwelt in seclusion, she frequently became his servant. It should, however, not be forgotten that the motive that drew them both into the desert was a common ascetic ideal. In the ancient Irish Church, the organization of which was built upon asceticism, men and women of distinction were permitted to participate in ecclesiastical functions. In the cloister, monks and nuns lived together until 543 (Haddan and Stubbs, *Councils*, ii. 2, p. 292). When the Irish

missionaries came to Armorica, the Gallic bishops regarded it specially censurable that they were accompanied by women who like the men exercised sacramental functions. A new form of spiritual marriage was developed as the wealthy circles in the great cities entered the Christian Church. Rich widows and maidens disdained marriage, but in order to provide a master over their houses and estates joined themselves in spiritual marriage to priests or monks. This variation did not always lead to happy results; the woman retained both the possession of her property and the reputation of unwedded chastity. No matter how seriously asceticism and the soul-tie were taken, the clerical could not escape compromise, and his position varied all the way from steward or chaplain to spiritual paramour. This was the rôle acted by the French abbé in the seventeenth and eighteenth centuries. At the time of Chrysostom (*MPG*, xlvii. 495 sqq.) the abuse was prevalent in Constantinople, and likewise in Gaul according to Jerome (*Epist.*, cxvii., *NPNF*, 2 ser., vi. 215–220). Best known is the spiritual marriage of the clergy. Marriage being disparaged, and the clergy being required to lead spiritual lives, celibacy became the rule and spiritual marriage followed. The purity of the original motive gradually declined. The spiritual bride became a mere housekeeper, suspected of being a mistress. She came to be called *mulier extranea*, received the same recognition as a maidservant, and Spanish synods about 600 ordered that she be sold as a slave and the proceeds given to the poor (e.g., Synod of Toledo, 589, capitulum 5, Hefele, *Conciliengeschichte*, iii. 51, Eng. transl. iv. 419, Fr. transl. iii. 1, p. 225). Gregory IX. distinctly prohibited clerical concubinage. Likewise in the Orient the *syneisaktos* was regarded as no more than a housekeeper of the clerical by the twelfth century. Practical exigencies had replaced the earlier common ideal. The original motive of cohabitation was the natural result of two opposing tendencies in early Christianity: fraternal love fostered in communal life; and ascetic contempt of the sexual relation, and the renunciation of marriage as sensual. The inconsistency of the social ideal of intimate community life with another that increased the distance between man and woman resulted in this unnatural combination of asceticism and fraternal love, with a form of cohabitation which in its moment of spiritual enthusiasm failed to foresee its pitfalls. Naturally, at first Christians of the highest standing, such as prophets, bishops, and confessors, lived in spiritual marriage. The " spiritual wives " were those who, as " brides of Christ," enjoyed especially honorable consideration; such were the widows, virgins, and prophetesses. The opinion of the Church regarding the institution, at first favorable, however, changed, and beginning with the Synods of Elvira, Ancyra, and the Council of Nicæa in the fourth century the edicts against codwelling with *subintroductæ* do not cease. In case of disobedience the clergy were corrected or dismissed, and the monks and laity received stern warning. The change of attitude on the part of the Church was caused by its rapid increase in the first three centuries and the absorption of elements which undermined the austerity against carnal sins. Spiritual marriages tolerable in small communities could not be entrusted to large societies of mixed elements, and the increasing sternness of the prohibitions prove the obstinate resistance to the effort at extermination. Concerning the remoteness in time of spiritual marriages, first mention occurs in the Shepherd of Hermas (*Visions*, I., i. 1, Eng. transl., *ANF*, ii. 9; *Similitudes*, ix. 11, 3, 7; x. 3, Eng. transl., *ANF*, ii. 44–47, 55). The passage I Cor. vii. 36–38 has been brought into connection with spiritual marriage (E. Grabe). In the *De vita contemplativa*, a genuine work of Philo, reference is made to the Therapeutæ in Egypt who repudiated marriage and the sexual relation and dwelt together in ascetic companionship like the later Christian ascetics, except that the element of fraternal love was there absent. It is to be concluded that spiritual marriage belongs, in the primitive life of Christianity, to an ascetic effort to replace marriage with brotherly love, and was not an outgrowth of clerical celibacy and monasticism. (H. Achelis.)

BIBLIOGRAPHY: H. Achelis, *Virgines subintroductæ. Ein Beitrag zum I Kor. vii.*, Leipsic, 1902 (cf. Jülicher, in *Archiv für Religionswissenschaft*, vii. 373 sqq.); Pseudo-Cyprian, *De singularitate clericorum* (edition of it promised in *TU*, new series, ix. 3); *DCA*, ii. 1939–1941; and the commentaries on I Cor. vii.

SUBLAPSARIANISM: The view held by moderate Calvinists, first applied to the Remonstrants (q.v.), according to which the decree to create logically preceded the decree of the fall. God determined to create the world and man notwithstanding the fact that he foresaw man's fall. Cf. Supralapsarianism and Infralapsarianism in CALVINISM, § 8.

SUBMISSION. See OBEDIENCE.

SUBORDINATIONISM. See ANTITRINITARIANISM; and CHRISTOLOGY, II., 2.

SUCCESSION, APOSTOLIC.

I. The Anglican View: The handing on of the ministerial commission and authority, given by the Lord Jesus Christ to his apostles, by a regular chain of successive ordinations. It presupposes the formation by Christ of a visible Church on earth, an organized society, the kingdom, or the embodiment of the kingdom, which the Messiah was to set up, to carry on his work by witnessing to the truth revealed, by ministering covenant gifts of grace, and by guiding and training its members in life and character. If Christianity were a philosophy scattered broadcast for men to follow as isolated individuals, there would be no need of or room for a succession of ministers. The theory of a traditional ministry is linked with the belief in a visible Church, corresponding, in its outward organization and its inward spiritual life, with the law of the Incarnation. Specialized functions belong to an organized body.

In the society which he formed, Christ ordained a particular body or order of ministers to act for him and with his authority. Out of the general company of the disciples he chose the twelve that they should be with him and then go forth in his name. By a trial mission during his own earthly ministry they were in part prepared for the commissions he gave them to represent him when he left the earth (Matt.

xxviii. 18, 19; John xx. 21–23). The twelve apostles formed a distinct company within the general society; within the body mystical, as within the body physical or social, there is a differentiation of functions. This is marked in the New Testament, e.g., by certain powers being conferred on the Seven, who preached and baptized, but apostles were sent after them to confirm (Acts viii.). Doubtless all acted as organs of the body, representing the whole society, but they were like the eye or ear in the natural body, divinely appointed and constituted organs, whose functions cannot be changed at will, nor the limitations of their several commissions enlarged. Accordingly while the officers may and should be chosen from below, they are endowed with authority from above—not merely deputed from below. This authoritative stewardship or pastorate was intended to be perpetuated in every generation. The gifts were not personal but official. God's gifts last as long as the needs which they are designed to supply. The authoritatively commissioned ministry is the normal instrumentality through which Christ, the exalted and invisible head of the Church, working by his Spirit, communicates to his people his promised gifts of grace. It is the guaranty of his presence and action.

The episcopate (see BISHOP; EPISCOPACY) is the normal organ for transmitting this authoritative ministerial commission, the organ of spiritual generation. Here certain distinctions must be made. (1) In the New-Testament writings the names " presbyters " or " elders " (see PRESBYTER) and "bishops" are apparently used to designate the same officers, the pastors of local churches. It was not till later that the title " bishop " was reserved for a single chief pastor who presided over a number of presbyters (see ORGANIZATION OF THE EARLY CHURCH). But in the New-Testament writings, though the names are interchangeably used, a difference of functions may be recognized. Timothy and Titus exercise authority over the presbyters as over the church generally in their respective districts; while others cooperate, they are responsible for ordaining men to the ministry (I Tim. iii., v.; Titus i. 5–9). The organization seen in its beginning at Ephesus and in Crete seems to have been thoroughly established in Asia Minor before St. John, the last of the original apostles, passed away, and thence it spread, if it had not already been independently adopted, generally throughout the Christian Church. (2) The " bishop " differed in two respects from the apostle proper, to whose authority in general he succeeded. The original apostles had their special function as witnesses to what they had seen and heard with the incarnate Son (Acts i. 8, 21, 22; I John i. 1–4). This, of course, could not be handed on. The bishops were limited in the exercise of their office, each to one church in a district, whereas the apostolic office had been more general. The twelve exercised a concurrent or collegiate world-wide jurisdiction. (3) It is possible that in some churches the rule by a body of presbyters continued for some time after the monarchical episcopate had been elsewhere established. But this would make no exception to the doctrine of apostolic succession rightly understood, since this is concerned not so much with the exact form of the ministry, as with the transmission of the commission to execute ministerial functions by those who have received authority to transmit it. The college of presbyters at Alexandria, to which Jerome refers, was probably a college of presbyters possessed of full ministerial power, including the right of ordaining.

All this was generally recognized in the Christian Church for 1,500 years. Where the rule was then reluctantly abandoned, this was done (as was thought) by force of necessity, as the lesser of two evils, in order to preserve a pure faith.

Two further points should be mentioned. It was to the consentient testimony of the Scriptures and of the due successors of the Apostles that Irenæus (A.D. 180) appealed against false teaching (*Hær.*, iii. 2, 3). As a matter of history the traditional faith has been linked with the traditional ministry; the one has very largely depended on and failed with the other. The episcopate with its chain of succession serves as a link of historical continuity, such as is needed in a universal spiritual society.

ARTHUR C. A. HALL.

II. The Syrian Succession: The doctrine of apostolic succession, which includes necessarily the historic episcopate as continued generation after generation in all branches of the Christian church, was scarcely ever questioned (or denied) during the conciliar and medieval ages. The first serious opposition occurred when various leaders of the several reforming movements of the sixteenth century had gained sufficient popular support to enable them to dispute the truth of the traditional Catholic teaching of an ecclesiastical hierarchy consisting of three orders, bishops, presbyters, and deacons.

Of the immediate results of the ecclesiastical conflicts of that memorable period in the progressive development of the Western church, the first, the steady and continuing weakening of the inner or spiritual authority of the Latin church, as exemplified by the increasing deviations from the accepted doctrines of the medieval theologians, was soon followed by the defiance of its outer or hierarchical authority, by the ordination of presbyters by presbyters instead of by bishops. This departure from the historic, ecumenical order of the Catholic Church was then and is even now justified by the appeal not only to the assumed presbyteral polity of the Apostolic Church, but also by the citation of the statements of certain of the Fathers and ecclesiastical historians of the primitive and conciliar ages. Although the presbyteral polity was first introduced by the German reformers into those parts of continental Europe which had generally accepted their ecclesiastical leadership, through the influence of the Genevan reformers it soon passed into Scotland and England, in which latter country it in turn gave birth to an even more radical departure from the episcopal government of the Latin church, Congregationalism or Independency. There are, as a result of these various reforming movements, in the Western church, the three distinct theories of the Christian ministry, the episcopal or monarchical, the presbyteral or collegiate, and the congregational or democratic, corresponding closely to the three

modern forms of the secular state, autocracy, limited monarchy, and democracy (see POLITY, ECCLESIASTICAL). The solution of the question of apostolic succession, or the constitution of the Christian Church, is of even greater importance to-day than during the Reformation and post-Reformation periods, because the antagonisms and polemics of those centuries are all but forgotten, and the consciousness of the weakness of the divided Western Church is inspiring an increasing longing for the suppression of sectarianism, and for the restoration, especially in America, of that imposing unity and visible solidarity which was the glory of the post-apostolic age.

It is a fundamental fact, not sufficiently recognized or emphasized in the discussions of the original constitution of the Christian ministry, that the apostolic age of the Church was a formative period during which neither the New-Testament canon, the polity, nor the ritual was defined decisively or fixed finally. Therefore it is in the post-apostolic or conciliar canons and decrees, rather than in the primitive or ante-conciliar writings descriptive of the transition state from a Judeo-Hellenic to a pan-Hellenic homogeneous ecclesia, that this debated question of the received polity of the one holy, catholic, and apostolic Church of Christ can find a satisfying historic solution of the perplexing problems involved. That monarchical episcopacy, as it has been established for many centuries in both the Latin and the Greek church, was not known in the apostolic age, is no longer authoritatively asserted by ecclesiastical historians of the present period. The earliest evidence in favor of the former, or traditional, theory, are the well-known quotations from the epistles of Ignatius of Antioch (q.v.). These impassioned pleas for the willing recognition of each parochial bishop as the only head of the Christian congregation of the city, used again and again as positive proof of the apostolic authority for a monarchical episcopacy, are now met by other equally credible citations from contemporaries and even from later writers, whose several statements suggest unmistakably that isolated peculiarities of a persisting presbyter polity were well known to them. That monarchical episcopacy, whether or not owing its final form to the Apostle John, as one tradition asserts, became slowly and silently the prevailing polity of the entire Christian Church, as is admitted by all historians, can be explained only on the assumption that the experience of the early Church with sectarianism, already evident during the apostolic age, emphasized the necessity of concentrating in the bishop, as the head of the established presbytery of parochial clergy, that spiritual authority which was formerly exercised in common by them with the itinerant prophets and other apostolic coworkers mentioned in the Pauline epistles, the Didache (q.v.), and other newly discovered authentic descriptions of the congregations and services of the primitive period. The correctness of this theory of the general adoption of episcopacy in its final form, is indicated by the fact that in the first ecumenical council of the Church, convened at Nicæa in 325, bishops from all parts of the then known world assembled as the sole representatives of their several sees, for the discussion and the definition of the fundamentals of the Christian faith, summarized in that creed of the Catholic church accepted by every separate branch which professes orthodoxy. Furthermore, among the decisions of the preparatory synod of Alexandria in 324 is one concerning the question of the ordination of presbyters by presbyters (Athanasius," Defence against the Arians," 12, 76, Eng. transl. in *NPNF*, 2 ser., iv. 107, 140). This synodal action recognizing the exclusive right of the bishops to ordain presbyters (reaffirmed in a similar case by the Council of Sardica in 347, Canon 20) was evidently not contested by any opponent during the subsequent sessions of the Nicene Council, which not only declared the accepted faith, but also decided other less vital questions affecting the ritual and the clergy in general. The authoritative canonical action of the assembled bishops in refusing to recognize the regularity of non-episcopally ordained presbyters can be rejected by any dissenting communions only by repudiating *in toto* the apostolic authority of this the first undisputedly ecumenical synod of the undivided Christian Church, in declaring definitely what is and what is not binding on all who accept the teachings of Christ and of his apostles and their successors.

This, then, should be the authority for the principle of the historic episcopate, the authority of the Catholic Church as it developed under divine direction from its formative state under the care of the apostles themselves, through various minor changes in its primitive polity necessitated by its varying needs, until, at the time of the Council of Nicæa, unity in polity and organization had been fully attained through the general acceptance of the doctrine that the bishops, as the recognized successors of the apostles, are the centers of Christian and Catholic communion. This doctrine of apostolic succession is not only Scriptural in asserting the authority of the apostles, and of their recognized successors, in exercising the plenary power of binding and of loosing (see KEYS, POWER OF THE), committed to them by Christ himself, but is also consistent throughout with the historic development of the ecclesiastical hierarchy, which recently discovered writings of the primitive periods describe in detail.

The several departures, during the troubled times of the Reformation, from the established episcopal polity of the entire Catholic Church, both East and West, have scarcely justified their introduction, in view of the division and subdivision which have resulted in every Reformed church that has rejected the historic episcopate universally accepted (until the Reformation) since the ecumenical Council of Nicæa. While, on the contrary, those Reformed churches which retained the historic episcopate, the Anglican and Scandinavian communions, have been comparatively free from sectarianism, a positive proof in modern times of the truth of the traditional Catholic teaching, that the bishops are ever the centers of unity in the Christian Church (throughout the centuries). There is this further view of the historic episcopate, considered in connection with the question of reunion, not only of the divided churches resulting from the Western Reformation,

but also of their eventual intercommunion with the older Latin, Greek, and Eastern branches of the One Holy Catholic and Apostolic Church of Christ. That the restoration of the primitive historic episcopate with its college of presbyters, assisted by the deacons and subdeacons and lower orders of laymen, developed so practically for effective pastoral service by the successors of the apostles themselves, will work marvels in regaining the wavering allegiance of the unchurched people of our free secular states by solving the pressing problems of our intricate modern civilization, can neither be doubted nor denied.

Then, if this be generally recognized, the question must naturally arise: From what source can a historic episcopate be obtained, since both the Latin and the Greek churches view with suspicion several churches developed from the reforming movements of the sixteenth century, and have repeatedly insisted that intercommunion with them can be secured only by the unreserved and unquestioning acceptance of their respective dogmatic decrees on the Catholic faith, the seven sacraments, and their ritual in its entirety? Heretofore there was no independent historic episcopate in the Western patriarchate which was not derived directly or indirectly from the Latin church of the pre- and post-Reformation periods. Therefore, all episcopal successions in the Western church are involved in the notorious apostasies, heresies, and simonies of those past centuries, filled as they were with mutual papal depositions, accusations, and counter-accusations of irregularity, invalidity, and schism, ending usually with mutual anathemas and excommunications.

But in the year 1891, the Syrian patriarch of Antioch, to whom can be ascribed as the historic successor of the first bishop of Antioch, the Apostle Peter himself, whatever preeminence and primacy of jurisdiction the leader of the apostolic college could impart to another, authorized the elevation to the episcopate of the Old Catholic priest Père Vilatte (q.v.) of Wisconsin. The solemn patriarchal bull permitting this canonical archiepiscopal consecration by eastern prelates, of a western priest, and investing him with the plenary power and apostolic authority of the primatial dignity, is given verbatim as translated from the authentic Syrian original.

" In the name of the Essential, Eternal, Self Existing, Almighty God: His servant Ignatius Peter III., Patriarch of the Apostolic See of Antioch and the East.

" We, the humble servant of God, hereby allow the consecration by the Holy Ghost of the Priest Joseph René Vilatte, elected for archiepiscopal dignity, Archbishop-Metropolitan in the name of Mar Timotheus, for the church of the Mother of God in Dykesville, Wisconsin, United States, and other churches in the archdiocese of America, viz., the churches adhering to the orthodox faith, in the name of the Father, amen; and of the Son, amen; and of the living Holy Ghost, amen.

" We stand up before God's majesty, and raising up our hands towards his grace, pray that the Holy Ghost may descend upon him, as he did upon the apostles at the time of the ascension of our Lord, Jesus Christ, by whom they were made patriarchs, bishops, and priests, and were authorized to bind and loose, as written by St. Matthew.

"We, therefore, by virtue of our authority received from God, authorize him to bind and loose, and elevating our voice, we offer thanks to God, and exclaim, ' Kyrie Eleison, Kyrie Eleison, Kyrie Eleison.' Again, we pray to God to grant him cheer of face before his throne of majesty, and that we and he may be made worthy to glorify him, now and at all times for ever and ever.

" Given on the seventeenth of Konum Kolim of the year of our Lord, eighteen hundred and ninety-one (corresponding to the twenty-ninth of December, eighteen hundred and ninety-one) from the patriarchal palace of the monastery of Mardin."

" (Signed) IGNATIUS PETER III."

The ceremony performed in conformity with this apostolic authorization was unique in the simultaneous use of both the western and the eastern rites of episcopal consecration. The Portuguese Archbishop Alvarez, himself consecrated by Syrian prelates, conferred the episcopate on Père Vilatte, according to the forms of the Latin ritual, while concurrently, the two co-consecrating Syrian metropolitans likewise conferred the episcopate according to the forms of the Syrian ritual, so that the validity of this new apostolic succession in the western patriarchate is indisputable either respecting canonical authority, intention, or rite. It will be noticed that the title of consecration of Père Vilatte is stated as archbishop-metropolitan of the archdiocese of America. This plenary canonical power was consistently conferred on Archbishop Vilatte by the patriarch of Antioch, because it is admitted by all unbiased canonists that, as the Western continent was unknown during the conciliar ages, it is obviously exempt from the exclusive jurisdiction of any patriarch, either of the eastern or western branches of the Holy Catholic Church of Christ.

There is therefore in the western patriarchate, besides the Latin succession of the Independent Catholic Church of Holland, derived in 1724 from the French Bishop Varlet, the canonical Syrian succession of Archbishop Vilatte, who has already been solemnly recognized in his archiepiscopal character not only by the Church of Holland, but even by the Holy Office of the Roman Catholic Church.

In view of this fact, the several reformed communions in the Western Church are not now dependent for a historic episcopate, either upon the disputed Anglican succession dating from the Elizabethan restoration, or upon the valid but irregular succession of the Old Catholic bishops of Europe, since there is now available this newer apostolic and canonical episcopate derived direct from that first center of Christianity itself, that oldest of all the branches of the primitive Church, the Syrian Church of Antioch.   ERNEST MARGRANDER.

BIBLIOGRAPHY. W. E. Gladstone, *Church Principles Considered in their Results*, London, 1840; W. Palmer, *A Treatise on the Church of Christ*, 3d ed., 2 vols., London, 1842; H. P. Liddon, *A Father in Christ*, 3d ed., London, 1885; C. Gore, *The Church and the Ministry*, London, 1889; J. Tod, *Protestant Episcopacy in Relation to Apos-*

tolic Succession, London, 1889; W. Earle, *The Reunion of Christendom in Apostolical Succession*, London, 1895; C. H. Waller, *Apostolical Succession*, St. Leonards, 1895; J. Brown, *Apostolical Succession in the Light of History and Fact*, London, 1898; R. C. Moberly, *Ministerial Priesthood . . . with an Appendix upon Roman Criticism of Anglican Orders*, London, 1897; T. F. Lockyer, *The Evangelical Succession, or, the Spiritual Lineage of the Christian Church*, London, 1899; R. Bruce, *Apostolic Order and Unity*, Edinburgh, 1903; W. H. M. H. Aitken, *Apostolical Succession in the Light of the History of the Primitive Church*, London, 1903; R. E. Thompson, *The Historic Episcopate*, Philadelphia, 1910; and the literature under APOSTOLIC SUCCESSION.

SUCCOTH-BENOTH: A term used in II Kings xvii. 30, evidently as the name of a deity of Babylon. The passage in which the term occurs (verses 24–41) describes the settlement in the district of Samaria of the colonists brought by Sargon from different parts of the East to replace the northern Israelites carried by him into exile after the capture of Samaria (q.v., II., 1, § 1). The phrasing of the passage is peculiar in that it is said that these settlers " made " (Hebr. *'asu*) the deities and " put them in the houses of the high places." Apparently the idea is that they made images of the deities and put them in the shrines left by the Hebrews; possibly, however, the meaning is simply that they installed the worship of these deities on the high places. At first sight the passage seems very corrupt, for out of seven deities named only one, Nergal, is certainly recognizable (see ADRAMMELECH; ANAMMELECH; ASHIMA; NIBHAZ; and TARTAK); and yet it seems to pass the bounds of probability that in a short passage from a context that is generally clear six out of seven names should be so utterly distorted as to be unrecognizable.

With slightly different vocalization the term should mean " tents of (the) daughters," yet no deity is known whose name or title could be even approximately thus represented; and Marduk as god of Babylon is the deity whose name would be expected here. The various attempts at solution offered in the commentaries and elsewhere throw little light on the subject. Selden (*De dis Syris*, ii. 7) supposed a shrine where marriageable girls (*banoth*) offered their virginity as a religious duty; Gesenius (*Thesaurus*) changed *banoth* to *bamoth* (" high places "). A number of students see in the term a corruption of *Zirpanitu* (Zirbanit), the name of Marduk's consort. No progress is made by comparison of the word with the *sikkuth* of Amos v. 26 (cf. R. V. margin). And other suggestions in the commentaries display ingenuity but give no solution which has commanded acceptance.

To be remembered is the fact that the colonists introduced by Sargon were almost certainly from the lower orders, who worshiped, in all probability, deities or spirits of an animistic sort whose names have not been transmitted. As in modern times in non-Christian lands (e.g., India) the state cults are often not those of the masses of the population (Kipling makes a countryman in *Kim* speak of " the good ' little gods' ""), so in ancient times it is demonstrable in many cases that the objects of worship were deities whose names do not appear in the official records. Some of these names may in exact or confused form be present in the text awaiting future light. At present nothing satisfactory can be made out of Succoth-benoth.

GEO. W. GILMORE.

BIBLIOGRAPHY: Besides the commentaries on Kings consult: P. Scholz, *Götzendienst und Zauberwesen bei den alten Hebräern*, pp. 407–409, Regensburg, 1877; F. Delitzsch, *Wo lag das Paradies*, pp. 215–216, Leipsic, 1881; A. Jeremias, *Das A. T. im Lichte des alten Orients*, p. 322, ib. 1904, Eng. transl., London, 1911; Nagl, in *ZKT*, 1904, pp. 417–418; *DB*, iv. 626; *EB*, iv. 4820.

SUDAILI. See STEPHEN BAR ZUDHAILE.

SUESKIND, FRIEDRICH GOTTLOB. See TUEBINGEN SCHOOL, THE OLDER.

SUEVI, swī′vai, **IN SPAIN, THE:** A branch of the Germanic people of that name which removed from the Rhine during the migration of nations. More inconstant than the other migratory peoples, the Suevi manifested six religious epochs in their history: (1) In the heathen period (409–448 or 449), under the kings Hermeric and Rechila, these tyrants occasionally came into conflict with the Roman Church; but while they plundered the property, they were indifferent to the religion of their conquered subjects. The organization of the Church remained intact in Galicia, the core of the kingdom of the Suevi. (2) During the first Catholic period (448 or 449–c. 464), the Suevi were brought into the Church under King Rechiar and remained Catholics under his successors until 463 or 464. Many, however, may have clung to their primitive forest heathenism. Rechiar, in spite of his orthodoxy, married the daughter of the Arian Visigothic King Theodoric I.; and he surpassed his heathen predecessors in love of plunder. He was vanquished and made captive at Astorga (456) by the Visigothic King Theodoric II. (3) The first Arian period (c. 464–c. 550) followed when Remismund had restored his shattered kingdom and married a Visigothic woman, perhaps a relative of Theodoric, in order to establish friendly relations with his more powerful neighbor. He went over to Arianism, and, with the help of the renegade Ajax, led over a majority of his people. Under Euric (466–485) the Suevi lost all their possessions in the southeast of the peninsula, and were driven back to Galicia, and during this dark and little-known period the diocesan organization continued. This statement is supported by an inscription found at Braga which narrates that a nun Marispalla dedicated a church under King Veremundus, implying freedom of cultus to Roman Catholics, and by the letter of Pope Vigilius of 538, to the resident bishop Profuturus of Braga, which shows that the Arian régime did not in the least disturb the Roman church organization; that free intercourse with Rome was allowed to the orthodox episcopate; that the orthodox clergy were allowed a free hand in combating all heresies, Priscillianism as well as Arianism; and that Arianism refrained from propaganda by peaceable persuasion no less than orthodoxy. (4) The second Catholic period continued from c. 550 to the collapse of the kingdom 585. About the middle of the sixth century the Arian kings were replaced by Catholic princes. Zealously orthodox kings like Theodemir (559 or 560–570) and Miro (570–583) succeeded in winning back the great majority of the people, assisted by the Pannonian Martinus (d. 580), abbot of Dumium and later metropolitan of Braga, who was known as the "Apostle of Galicia." It is disputed whether the reaction came under Carraric (550–559) or Theodemir (559 or 560–570). Miro was conquered (583) by Leovigild, the last Arian Visigoth king, and made a vassal. Leovigild took advantage of the contests for the throne that broke out after the death of Miro to incorporate the kingdom of the Suevi in his kingdom as the province of Galicia. (5) and (6) were the second Arian (585–586) and the third Romanizing (587 and 589) periods. After their absorption Leovigild, wishing to attach the Suevi to his moderate Arianism, without using measures of force, appointed Arian duplicate bishops to certain dioceses, namely, Lugo, Oporto, Tuy, and Viseu. Many Suevi adopted Arianism to please their new ruler. A little later they showed themselves just as hospitable to the opposite religious policy of Recared (586–601), and became again Roman Catholics at the command of this "Spanish Constantine." (FRANZ GÖRRES.)

BIBLIOGRAPHY: Sources are: The continuation of the Hieronymian *Chronicon* by Hydatius, in *MGH*, *Auct. Ant.*, xi (1893), 21–25, 85–93, 212 sqq., also Joannes Biclarensis, *Chronica*, and the *Hist. Gothorum* of Isidore of Seville in the same volume; Isidore of Seville, *Suevorum historia*, in his *Opera*, ed. Arevalus, vii. 134 sqq., Rome, 1803; Martin of Braga, *Formula de vita honesta*, ed. A. Weidner, in a Magdeburg *Programm*, 1872, pp. 3–10; Martin of Braga, *De correctione rusticorum*, ed. C. P. Caspari, Christiania, 1883. Consult further: J. Aschbach, *Geschichte der Westgothen*, Frankfort, 1827; F. W. Lembke, *Geschichte von Spanien*, Hamburg, 1831; P. B. Gams, *Kirchengeschichte von Spanien*, vol. ii., 3 vols., Regensburg, 1862–79; F. Dahn, *Die Könige der Germanen*, vols. v.–vi., Leipsic, 1870; L. Geley, *L'Espagne des Goths et des Arabes*, Paris, 1882; J. Dräseke, in *ZWT*, xxviii (1885), 506–508; F. Görres, in *Jahrbücher für protestantische Theologie*, xii. 132–174, and in *ZWT*, xxviii (1885), 319–325, xxxvi., 2 (1893), 542–578; E. Peréz Pujol, *Hist. de las instituciones sociales de la España Goda*, 4 vols., Valencia, 1896; J. Ortega Rubio, *Los Visigodos en España*, Madrid, 1903; R. de Ureña y Smenjaud, *La Legislacion gótico-hispaña*, Madrid, 1905; *DCB*, iii. 845–848, 924; *KL*, viii. 922–924; and literature on GOTHS.

SUFFERING: Any state of physical or mental pain. In the general view, anything detrimental to self-preservation is an evil, anything favorable to self-preservation a good. In many respects the Christian view is just the opposite. Here self-preservation is thought of not for this natural life but for life eternal. Thus, what would seem to be an evil becomes a good when viewed *sub specie æternitatis*, and similarly a good becomes an evil. Sickness, for instance, by awakening the religious consciousness, becomes a good; and riches, by encouraging worldliness, become an evil. Even from the worldly point of view suffering has value, since it develops character and enriches experience. From the Christian point of view, a good is that which promotes the attainment of the kingdom of God, which is the highest good, and an evil is that which opposes its attainment. However, it is a mistake to suppose that pain and suffering cease to be such for the faithful; if they did, they would lose their potentiality for good. It would be fantastic to deny that for the Christian real pain and evil still exist. God sends to every Christian his measure of suffering, and particularly those persecutions incident to the enmity of the world (John xv. 18–21

Matt. v. 10–12, x. 38, xvi. 24). To practise asceticism and inflict pain on oneself is not only unnecessary but antagonistic to God (Col. ii. 23). The task of the Christian is rather to bear patiently the sufferings actually sent by God and make them a means of righteousness (Heb. xii. 11; II Cor. iv. 16). For the real Christian all trials and tribulations contribute to the attainment of the highest good (Rom. viii. 26). Of course suffering may have just the opposite result, in case of a weak Christian (Matt. xiii. 21). It is the moral obligation of the Christian to take effective action against threatening reverses, and his position in the world makes this necessary. Stupid resignation is as unchristian as rank fatalism.

Pain and suffering are the means appointed by God to wean the Christian from the pleasures of the world and the flesh and bind him close to the kingdom of God. Whom the Lord loveth he chasteneth, and if he sends afflictions he sends at the same time strength to bear them or overcome them (II Cor. i. 3–8, iv. 8–9). God may send sufferings and tribulations to punish offenders (Ps. xxxviii. 5; Lam. i. 14; Ex. xx. 5), to prove and educate his children (Heb. xii. 5–12; II Cor. xiii. 5), or to glorify himself (John ix. 3, xi. 4). (L. LEMME.)

BIBLIOGRAPHY: E. Burritt, *The Mission of Great Sufferings*, London, 1866; W. G. Eliot, *The Discipline of Sorrow*, Boston, 1868; E. de Pressense, *The Mystery of Suffering*, New York, 1869; J. Hinton, *The Mystery of Pain*, Boston, 1893; C. C. Hall, *Does God send Trouble?* ib., 1894; D. O. Mears, *Inspired through Suffering*, New York, 1897; V. C. Harrington, *The Problem of Human Suffering . . . from the Standpoint of a Christian*, ib. 1899; G. Müller, *Das Leid als die Wurzel des Glückes*, Berlin, 1899; J. H. Brookes, *The Mystery of Suffering*, New York, 1903; J. Hinton, *The Mystery of Pain*, London, 1909; Père Laurent, *The Mission of Pain*, ib. 1910.

SUFFRAGAN: A title applied to certain classes of bishops (see BISHOP; BISHOP, TITULAR; and VICAR). The word does not appear to have been employed in classical Latin, but is frequent in the ecclesiastical language of the Frankish kingdom (MGH, Leg. i., *Cap. reg. Francorum*, p. 79, 1835), where it appears in the sense of " helper," and so, e.g., Amalarius of Treves (q.v.) understands it. The term becomes equivalent also to " vicar." The term ' suffragan " is applied to titular bishops who assist or substitute for diocesan bishops; also to diocesan bishops, expressing their relation to the metropolitan [cf. Bingham, *Origines*, II., xiv. 14–15]. The ordinances bearing on the relative rights of suffragans and metropolitans are collected in Gratian, *causa* III., qu. 6 and IX. 3. For suffragans in the United States see PROTESTANT EPISCOPALIANS, II., § 1. (A. HAUCK.)

SUGER: Abbot of St. Denis; b. in 1081, probably in the neighborhood of St. Omer; d. at St. Denis Jan. 12, 1151. He was the contemporary of St. Bernard and Abelard, and one of the greatest statesmen France produced during the Middle Ages. He was educated in the monastery of St. Denis, together with Louis VI.; and when the latter ascended the throne, in 1108, he immediately called the monk to his court, and made him his principal councilor. In 1122 Suger was elected abbot of St. Denis; but he remained at the court, and continued

to live as a man of the world till 1127, when he came under the influence of the reformatory movement of his time. He at once assumed the habits and practises of severe asceticism, but he continued to be a politician rather than an ecclesiastic. After the death of Louis VI., in 1137, he was appointed regent during the minority of Louis VII., and again when the latter, in 1149, made a crusade to the Holy Land; and during his lifetime hardly anything of consequence took place in French politics without his immediate intervention. His leading idea was the consolidation of the monarchy as a divinely established institution. He was planning and preparing to conduct in person a crusade when he died. His writings embrace *Libellus de consecratione ecclesiæ a se ædificatæ et translatione corporum s. Dionysii ac sociorum eius facta anno 1140; Liber de rebus in sua administratione gestis;* and *Vita Ludovici VI. Grossi sive Crassi regis Francorum († 1137), Philippi I. filii;* all of which are found most conveniently in *MPL*, clxxxvi. 1211–1340. They were also edited by A. Lecoy de la Marche, Paris, 1867.

BIBLIOGRAPHY: The early life by the monk and associate W. Suger is in *MPL*, clxxxvi. 1193–1208, and in the ed. of the "Works" by Lecoy de la Marche, ut sup., pp. 377–411. Consult further: J. Baudouin, *Le Ministre fidèle, représenté sous Louis VI. en la personne de Suger*, Paris, 1640; M. Baudier, *Hist. de l'administrati n de Suger, abbé de St. Denys*, Paris, 1645, new ed., 1660; F. A. Gervaise, *Hist. de Suger, abbé de St. Denis*, 3 vols., Paris, 1721; A. Nettement, *Hist. de Suger*, Paris, 1842; A. de Saint-Méry, *Suger, ou le France au xii. siècle*, Limoges, 1851; F. Combes, *L'Abbé Suger*, Paris, 1853; A. Huguenin, *Étude sur l'abbé Suger*, Paris, 1855; L. de Carné, *Les Fondateurs de l'unité française: Suger*, Paris, 1856; J. L. T. Bachelet, *Les Grands Ministres français*, Rouen, 1859; A. Vétault, *Suger*, Paris, 1871; P. Viollet, in *Bibliothèque de l'école des chartes*, xxxiv. 241–254, Paris, 1873; E. Ménault, *Suger . . . régent de France, père de la patrie*, Paris, 1884; A. Lecoy de la Marche, in *La France chrétienne*, 1896, pp. 148 sqq; *Hist. littéraire de la France*, xii. 361–362; *KL*, xi. 975–977; Ceillier, *Auteurs sacrés*, xiv. 373–376 et passim.

SUICERUS, swī'ser-us, **JOHANNES CASPARUS (HANS KASPAR SCHWEITZER):** Philologist, author of the *Thesaurus ecclesiasticus;* b. at Zurich June 26, 1620; d. there Dec. 29, 1684. He began his studies in the schools of his native city, and completed them at Montauban and Saumur, returning in 1643 to Zurich for his examination, and being sent as pastor to Basadingen in Thurgau; he was called to teach in Zurich, 1644; became inspector of the Alumnates and professor of Hebrew, 1646; professor of catechetics, 1649; of Latin and Greek in the Collegium humanitatis, 1656; and of Greek at the Carolinum, 1660; retired on account of failing health, 1683. He served theology well through his works in philology, many of them going through several editions. Among his published works may be named: *Sylloge vocum Novi Testamenti* (Zurich, 1648); *Novi Testamenti dictionum sylloge Græco-Latina,* issued by Hagenbuch in 1744 as *N. T. Glossarium Græco-Latinum;* the celebrated *Thesaurus ecclesiasticus* (2 vols., Amsterdam, 1682; encyclopedic); and *Lexicon Græco-Latinum et Latino-Græcum* (1683). He left other works in manuscript, among them his apparatus for a new edition of the lexicon of Hesychius. (P. SCHWEIZER.)

SUICERUS, JOHANNES HEINRICH: Swiss theologian, son of the preceding; b. in Zurich in 1646; d. in Heidelberg Sept. 23, 1705. He studied in Zurich and Geneva; was professor of Greek and philosophy in the gymnasium at Hanau 1665–67; then became pastor at Birmensdorf near Zurich; in 1683 succeeded his father at the Carolinum; and went in the spring of 1705 as first pastor and ecclesiastical councilor to Heidelberg. He caused considerable excitement by the publication of his book on Revelation (1674), and it was suppressed, but he had it and his *Lapis Lydius* printed anonymously in Holland (1676), after which he received a reprimand from the council of Zurich. Outside of his commentary on Colossians, his other works were on subjects in philosophy or church politics.

(P. SCHWEIZER.)

SUICIDE: The intentional killing of oneself, the term excluding both the shortening of life by excess or recklessness, and self-sacrifice, or the surrender of life to gain a higher moral good, since only in suicide is there a conscious and deliberate contempt for life *per se* and an entire absence of desire to attain any superior good (as in self-sacrifice) or even a greater degree of pleasure (as in excess or recklessness). The history of suicide reveals marked variations according to race and period. Among peoples of simple civilization and those with a fixed code of morals and an unshaken

History. belief suicide is very rare, and is deemed unnatural and reprehensible.

This was the view of the early Greeks, and of the Pythagoreans, Plato, and Aristotle; but with the decay of national thought and character Stoicism taught indifference to life and death as mere external phenomena, and advocated voluntary surrender of life as a means of gaining independence for the soul. This view, which failed to distinguish clearly between self-sacrifice and suicide, and was also irreconcilable with the Stoic doctrine of the virtuous man's submission to the universe, was eagerly defended by the Romans of the early Empire, particularly by Seneca (q.v.). While Biblical religion conquered this attitude of despair and the uselessness of life, neither the Old nor the New Testament contains any specific prohibition of suicide, though the principles enunciated in the sixth commandment and in such passages as Rom. xiv. 7–9, I Cor. vi. 19, and Eph. v. 29 may be extended by analogy to suicide. Even where cases of suicide are recorded, as of Saul (I Sam. xxxi. 4), Ahithophel (II Sam. xvii. 23), Zimri (I Kings xvi. 18), and Judas (Matt. xxvii. 5, Acts i. 18, 25), there is no word of condemnation of the act in itself. On the other hand, Paul once prevented suicide (Acts xvi. 27–28). The lack of express prohibition finds explanation partly in the extreme rarity of suicide among the Jews, and partly in the national abhorrence of it, the sole exception being when patriotic motives entered into the question (Judges xvi. 28–30; II Macc. xiv. 37–46; Josephus, *Ant.*, XIV., xiii. 10). Christianity worked here, not by prohibitions, but by creating a new attitude of mind, teaching the fatherly love of God (I Cor. x. 13; I Thess. v. 9), giving life a distinct ethical content (Phil. i. 22 sqq.),

and interpreting suffering as a divine dispensation (Rom. v. 3 sqq., viii. 18). The early Church firmly opposed suicide, although practically the only case in which such a tendency appeared was in the overzealous desire for martyrdom (see MARTYRS AND CONFESSORS). Whether, in time of persecution, Christian women might commit suicide to escape dishonor was a moot question, lauded by Eusebius, Chrysostom, and Jerome, but condemned by Augustine (*De civitate Dei*, i. 16 sqq.), the latter position also being taken by church councils, some of which forbade the suicide honorable burial (Orléans, 533, canon 15, Hefele, *Conciliengeschichte*, ii. 757, Eng. transl., iv. 187, Fr. transl., ii. 2, p. 1135; Braga, 563, capitulum 16, Hefele, ut sup., iii. 19, Eng. transl., iv. 385, Fr. transl., iii. 1, p. 180). The rise of the tenet of personal freedom in the period of the early Illumination wrought a marked change, although many of the earliest works advocating the permissibility of suicide could appear only posthumously, as J. Donne's *Biathanatos* (London, 1644) and D. Hume's essay on suicide in his *Two Essays* (1777). In the general literature of the eighteenth century suicide was frequently discussed as a psychological and moral question, as by Rousseau, Montesquieu, and Goethe; but while these authors advocated a less rigorous attitude, theologians and all the best philosophical writers, such as Spinoza, Wolff, Mendelssohn, Kant, and Fichte, condemned it. Modern pessimism maintains a rather indeterminate position toward the problem.

The increasing frequency of suicide had been statistically proved in the nineteenth century, the rate being at least trebled in the great civilized countries. A large number of suicides, about a third, may be traced to mental derangement, thus indi-

Conditions cating a close connection between sui-
and cide and insanity. Suicide is more fre-
Remedy. quent in cities than in the country, increasing with ease of communication and the progress of education; it is far more frequent among Protestants than among Roman Catholics, but is in inverse proportion to crimes against the person. All this does not imply that higher culture involves despair and disgust for life, but that as needs increase, the number of those increases who, unable to satisfy these needs, despair since they have within themselves no means of consolation. The highest percentage of suicides is found among the Germanic peoples, next coming the Romance peoples and the Slavs. The reasons for the excessive frequency of suicide among the Teutons has been ascribed either to the use of intoxicants or to the results of unrestricted investigation in science and religion, although it seems more probable that the true explanation lies in Germanic idealism and individualism, with a touch of sentimentalism, which is ill adapted to cope with stern and circumscribing conditions. A still more potent factor than all others, however, is the decay of religion and of moral conviction during the nineteenth century, which has deprived large masses of influences most potent in counteracting the tendency to suicide; for it is only a spiritual and inward strength which can enable the individual to stand

against the pressure and the vicissitudes of complex modern civilization; though natural elasticity and strong sense of duty may give similar results within a limited area, the only reliable foundation of a patience and a hope which do not fail even in the most desperate situations is religion. And as once Christianity brought new regard for life into a decadent civilization, so only the Gospel can heal the destructive and deadly tendencies of modern culture. The battle against suicide thus becomes, in the last analysis, identical with the validation of a Christian view of life and morality. He who knows that he has a duty to perform toward God is bound to go on, be conditions what they may; and he who is convinced that there is forgiveness for the penitent and help for the fallen can never despair. The Christian Church has naturally condemned utterly an act which she can not but regard as absolute negation of the fear of God and of trust in him, and as an insult alike to divine judgment and to divine grace. It is, therefore, inadvisable to break down the barriers erected by law and custom against the suicide, for such procedure would only invite still greater laxity of public opinion. While in some cases the suicide may deserve pity rather than blame, the act itself must uncompromisingly be regarded as morally impossible for the Christian. At the same time, it is hopeless to look for great results merely from laws and disciplinary measures; only the Gospel can create a new spirit, and thus heal the evils of modern civilization. (O. KIRN.)

BIBLIOGRAPHY: C. F. Stäudlin, *Geschichte der Vorstellungen und Lehren vom Selbstmord*, Göttingen, 1824; A. Wagner, *Die Gesetzmässigkeit in den scheinbar willkürlichen menschlichen Handlungen*, Hamburg, 1864; A. Legoyt, *Le Suicide ancien et moderne*, Paris, 1881; T. G. Masaryk, *Der Selbstmord als soziale Massenerscheinung der modernen Civilisation*, Vienna, 1881; H. Morselli, *Der Selbstmord*, Leipsic, 1881, Eng. transl., *Suicide*, London, 1881; J. J. O'Dea, *Suicide; Studies on its Philosophy*, New York, 1882; G. Garrisson, *Le Suicide dans l'antiquité et dans les temps modernes*, Paris, 1885; M. Imhofer, *Der Selbstmord*, Augsburg, 1886; C. A. Geiger, *Der Selbstmord im klassischen Altertum*, Augsburg, 1888; E. Motta, *Bibliografia del suicidio*, Bellinzona, 1890; E. Rehfisch, *Der Selbstmord*, Berlin, 1893; É. Durkheim, *Le Suicide*, Paris, 1897; H. H. Henson, *Suicide*, Oxford, 1897; F. H. P. Coste, *The Ethics of Suicide*, London, 1898; J. Gurnhill, *The Morals of Suicide*, 2 vols., London and New York, 1900; H. Rost, *Der Selbstmord als sozialstatistische Erscheinung*, Cologne, 1905; H. A. Krose, *Der Selbstmord im 19. Jahrhundert*; and *Die Ursachen der Selbstmordhäufigkeit*, 2 vols., Freiburg, 1906; W. W. Westcott, *On Suicide*, London, 1905; W. Spark, *Der Selbstmord, seine Folgen und seine Verhütung*, Freiburg, 1909.

SUIDAS, swī'das: Greek lexicographer. Nothing is known of the personal history of Suidas, even his period is only with probability assigned as that of Johannes Tzimisces, Basil II., and Constantine IX., therefore before the end of the tenth century; his home is conjectured to have been Samothrace. His Greek lexicon, probably finished c. 976, is a most important, even indispensable, reference-book for the classical philologist, and is equally valuable for the theologian and church historian. He drew upon older dictionaries and collections, upon Hesychius Milesius for facts of literary history, upon the dictionary of Harpokratio, perhaps also upon that of Photius, upon the Biblical glossators, and upon the scholiasts. His articles on secular and ecclesiastical history are derived chiefly from the book of excerpts of Konstantinos Porphyrogenitos and from George the Monk. He also read a great number of sources at first hand. From all this it is easy to explain the manifold character of Suidas' work. It resembles now a lexicon, now an encyclopedia. It is a repertorium for the study of the classics and the Bible, of secular and ecclesiastical history.

Of interest from a theological point of view are especially the Biblical glosses derived from Hesychius and such Greek exegetes as Theodoret and Œcumenius, relating to Biblical names and the more important New-Testament words and conceptions. It is still worth while to consult Suidas on such words as δικαιοσύνη, δικαίωμα, δόξα θεοῦ, ἐκστασις, εὐχαριστία, νόμος, πλοῦτος, πνεῦμα, ψυχικός. The theological and dogmatic point of view of the work may be inferred from such entries as θεός. The general scientific and philosophic interest of Suidas appears abundantly. Finally Suidas offers a large register of patristic names and choice excerpts, enriched with biographical and literary details. The notice of Hypatia's life, studies, and death may be cited. The opinion of the author and his church appears not seldom in the account. For example, Dionysius the Areopagite receives the appellation of "the most famous man," who attained the summit of Greek wisdom, and as a pupil of Paul was by him made bishop of Athens. Chrysostom is praised yet more highly. His eloquence was like the cataracts of the Nile and was never equaled; only God could count the number of his works.

The lexicon was first issued by Demetrius Chalkondylas (Milan, 1499; Aldine ed., Venice, 1514). Other editions are Cambridge, 1705, by Küster; Oxford, 1834, by Gaisford; best ed. by Bernhardy, Halle, 1853; and the reprint by Bekker, Berlin, 1854. (PHILIPP MEYER.)

BIBLIOGRAPHY: The introduction in Bernhardy's ed., ut sup.; Krumbacher, *Geschichte*, pp. 562–570, where a large list of helps is furnished; Fabricius-Harles, *Bibliotheca Græca*, vi. 389–595, Hamburg, 1795.

SUIDBERT, swid'bärt: Apostle of the Frisians; d. at what is now Kaiserswerth in Mar., 713. He was one of the twelve who under the leadership of Willibrord (q.v.) began the mission to the Frisians. He was chosen bishop by his companions and placed at the head of the undertaking, and this has given rise to many explanations of the passing over of Willibrord, the real leader; the probable reason was Willibrord's youth and Suidbert's maturity. Suidbert was consecrated by Wilfrid of York late in 692 or early in 693. Soon after his return to his field of work he abandoned it and went to labor beyond the Rhine among the Bructeri, a course probably to be explained by a difference between him and Pippin, who had the right of confirmation of bishops in his realm. The only notice of Suidbert's success is Bede's brief statement that "by his preaching he led many into the way of truth" (*Hist. eccl.*, v. 11); but this success aroused the animosity of the heathen Saxons who scattered the Christians. Suidbert was then presented with the island on which he founded the cloister of Kaiserswerth, where he passed the remainder of his life.

(A. HAUCK.)

BIBLIOGRAPHY: Early material is collected in *ASB*, Apr., iii. 802–805, March, i. 67–86; *ASM*, iii. 1, pp. 239–245; and *MPL*, cxxxii. 547–550, 557–559. Consult further: Bede, *Hist. eccl.*, v. 11; P. Heber, *Die vorkarolingischen christlichen Glaubensboten am Rhein*, Frankfort, 1858; K. W. Bouterwek, *Swidbert, der Apostel des bergischen Landes*, Elberfeld, 1859; P. P. M. Alberdingk-Thijm, *Der heilige Willibrord*, pp. 108 sqq., Münster, 1863; W. Diekamp, *Die Fälschung der Vita S. Suidberti*, in *Historisches Jahrbuch der Görres-Gesellschaft*, ii (1881), 272–287; *Analecta Bollandiana*, vi (1887), 73–76; Rettberg, *KD*, ii. 396, 460, 524; Hauck, *KD*, i. 437, ii. 367; *DNB*, lv. 155; *DCB*, iv. 745; Ceillier, *Auteurs sacrés*, xii. 218, 783.

SUIDGER. See CLEMENT II.

SULPICIANS: A congregation the foundations of which were laid by Jean Jacques Olier (q.v.) in 1642. The society arose through the promise of great usefulness afforded by the seminary founded by Olier first at Vaugirard and later moved to the church of St. Sulpice at Paris. This society received the protection of Anna, queen-regent of Austria, and being devoted principally to the cause of education was soon engaged in that work in other seminaries established in various cities of France, in Canada, and in 1790 in the United States. The Sulpicians are bound by no vows, but have been noted for their fidelity to the church which they serve and for the model of " regularity " which they have furnished. In the United States St. Mary's Seminary and St. Charles' College in Baltimore are under their care, as was the seminary of Brighton, diocese of Boston, till 1911, and they have the spiritual direction of the students of theology in the Catholic University at Washington. The events of the years 1903–06 in France (see FRANCE, I., § 5) bore with especial hardship upon this congregation, bringing its activities to an end, and leaving North America the most important field of work.

BIBLIOGRAPHY: Besides the literature under OLIER, JEAN JACQUES, consult: G. M. de Fruges, *J. J. Olier*, Paris, 1904; *Vie de Emery . . . précédée d'un precis de l'hist. du séminaire et de la compagnie de St. Sulpice*, 2 vols., Paris, 1862; J. St. Vangan, in *The Dublin Review*, 1866, pp. 22 sqq.; J. H. Icard, *Traditions de la compagnie de prêtres de St. Sulpice*, Paris, 1886; M. Siebengartner, *Schriften und Einrichtungen zur Bildung der Geistlichen*, pp. 428 sqq., 431 sqq., Freiburg, 1902; Heimbucher, *Orden und Kongregationen*, iii. 442–449.

SULZER, SIMON: Swiss theologian of Lutheran tendencies; b. in the Haslithal above Meiningen (24 m. s.s.w. of Lucerne) Sept. 23, 1508; d. at Basel June 22, 1585. He was educated at Bern under the humanist Rubellus of Rottweil and at Lucerne under Oswald Myconius (q.v.); in 1530 he was in Strasburg, where he heard lectures from Butzer and Capito, and in Basel in 1531, where Simon Grynæus (see GRYNÆUS, 1) taught him, where he also helped the printer Herwagen, taught at the Collegium, later the Pädagogium; in 1533 Capito and Butzer had him called to Bern as a teacher with occasional preaching duties and the work of inspecting six district schools; in 1536 he went to Basel to continue his studies, and the same year visited Luther at Wittenberg. From this time his Lutheran tendencies became marked. In 1538 he was again called to Bern, and in 1541 succeeded Sebastian Meyer as

leader of the Lutheran movement; then he and his following strove in vain to abolish the oath that bound the preachers to a recognition of Zwingli's doctrines and to introduce the Lutheran view of the Lord's Supper. In 1544 he succeeded Kunz as preacher, but in 1548 was deposed from his position after a quarrel which, it is supposed, he provoked in order to pose as a martyr in the Lutheran cause. He was made pastor at St. Peter's, Basel, 1549; professor of Hebrew, 1552; successor to Oswald Myconius at the minster, and antistes of the Basel church, 1553. He was happy and active in his double position, defended the persecuted Lutherans, and advocated union between Germans and Swiss. He could not conceal his anti-Zwinglian views, which ultimately became plain to everybody.

Sulzer's efforts to introduce Lutheran ideas in Basel had no lasting effect. He never dared to put aside the first Basel Confession of 1534, although he relegated it to the background. After his death, the Basel church was brought back to Zwinglianism and united to the Swiss churches. His efforts were more successful in Baden. He became acquainted with Margrave Karl II., who in 1555 began the Reformation of the lower part of his margravate. Sulzer recommended and ordained over twenty pastors, and was named superintendent of Röteln, Schopfheim, Müllheim, and Hochberg. His activity was remarkable, but his undeniable services to the schools of Bern and the churches of Basel and Baden are somewhat shadowed by his weak character and his injudicious partizan opposition to the traditional Swiss church.

(W. HADORN.)

BIBLIOGRAPHY: Hundeshagen, in F. Trechsel's *Beiträge zur Geschichte der schweizerisch-reformirten Kirche*, pp. 105 sqq., Bern, 1844; G. Linder, *Simon Sulzer und sein Anteil an der Reformation im Lande Baden*, Heidelberg, 1890; A. Fluri, *Berner Schulordnung von 1548*, Berlin, 1901.

SUMER. See BABYLONIA, V.

SUMMA DER GODLIKER SCRIFTUREN: The first clause in the title of a noted book which first appeared in Leyden, 1523. The full title reads: *Summa der Godliker Scrifturen, oft een duytsche Theologie, leerende en onderwijsende alle menschen, wat dat Christen gheloue is, waer doer wi allegader salich worden, ende wat dat doepsel beduyt, nae die leeringe des heiligen evangelijs ende sinte Pauwels episteln.* It was suppressed by the stadtholders in the name of Charles V., orders were given for its destruction as containing prohibited doctrines, all persons were forbidden to own, read, buy or sell the book, while in 1524 the publisher, Jan Zwerts, was banished for life and his fortune confiscated. Fresh editions continued to appear, however, as well as translations into other languages, although it was placed on the Index of the Church and on that of the Louvain Theological Faculty. In England various edicts issued in 1526, 1535, 1539, against the Latin original and the English version (*The Summa of Holy Scripture*, 1542, etc., five editions). The Sorbonne condemned it in 1550, in Italy it was found on all the indexes after 1549, in Spain the indexes of Valdez, 1559, and Quiroga, 1583, mention it, and it was known at the court of Charles V. It had an important part in the Refor-

History of the Work.

mation in the countries named. Having performed its mission during the Reformation, the book was forgotten until 1877, when Professor Boehmer, of Zurich, discovered in the public library a copy of the Italian version and enabled Professor Milio, of Florence, to publish it in *Rivista Cristiana* and in a special edition. Benrath found a Dutch edition of 1526, published a German translation (Leipsic, 1880), and judged that there must have been an earlier original Dutch issue in 1523. It appeared, also, that a second part was published in low German, presumably the following year, the author of which claimed the authorship of the first part, but the second part was written originally in low German, and does not appear in other languages. The first part, however, with the prologue, is a translation, and from the Latin, as Benrath surmised and Van Toorenenbergen proved, the author himself being the translator.

An edition of the Latin and the oldest Dutch translation were published by Prof. J. J. van Toorenenbergen, of Amsterdam, in 1882. The Latin, *Œconomica Christiana in rem Chris-*
The Latin. *tianam instituens, quidve creditum ingenue Christianum oportet, ex evangelicis literis eruta*, was published, Strasburg, 1527. Comparison shows that the *Summa* is much less complete than the *Œconomica*, which was evidently intended to enlighten the minds of the clergy and educated laity regarding the truths of the Gospel, and also to combat the corruptions of monastic life, and especially the illusion that the life, in itself, was sanctified. One portion is practical; the other, theoretical. The *Summa* is adapted to the popular understanding, and consequently is abridged in many places, especially those portions that refer to monastic life. The author was at first reluctant to publish the Latin original, and it is questioned whether he indorsed its publication in 1527. Van Toorenenbergen surmises that a friend of the author, Gerardus Goldenhauer, being in straitened circumstances, handed over the work to the Strasburg publisher, Christian Egenolphus. The original *Œconomica* was probably written in 1520. The author was evidently still in the Roman church and desired to reform, but not abolish, monasticism. The influence of Luther's writings is traceable, among others the " Sermon on Baptism " (1519), the " Babylonian Captivity," and " A Christian's Liberty " (1520). In the *Summa*, the Reformers also speak. In the edition of 1523 is a formula for the celebration of the Lord's Supper: *Dat Testament Jesu Christi datmen tot noch toe de misse ghenoempt heeft, verduyts(t) duer Joannem Oecolampadium to Adelenburch*, and in the edition of 1526 is an entire chapter taken almost verbatim from one of Luther's writings. In all editions prior to 1526, the twenty-ninth chapter contains a merciless condemnation of war, unless it be for the protection of subjects from foreign or internal oppression. This is evidently an almost verbatim transcript of Luther's treatise of 1526, *Ob Kriegsleute auch im seligen Stande sein können*. The author must be responsible for this change of sentiment, as no one else would have ventured to introduce it, and on the title-page of the edition of 1526 stand

the words " new and thoroughly revised edition." The author's name does not appear on either the *Œconomica* or the *Summa*. Van Toorenenbergen and Benrath both incline to ascribe the authorship to Hendrik van Bommel, a preacher in Wesel in 1557, who then acknowledged himself the author of *Summa der deutschen Theologie*, which had appeared thirty years earlier.

The *Œconomica* consists of two parts, the first containing fifteen, the second fourteen, chapters; the *Summa* contains thirty-one chapters and a prologue. The first fifteen chapters of
Contents. both works treat of the doctrine of
faith under the same headings: What is baptism; What baptism insures, and that it is not a mere sign; What Christians celebrate in baptism; What Christian faith is and what those must believe who would be saved; On the surest way of salvation; That by God's goodness alone, and not by works, are we saved; In what manner our salvation is assured by his death who gave us his Testament; How, according to the Gospel, faith is never without works; Faith stirs your souls to obey God's commands; Who is a son, and who a hireling; Two kinds of men in the Christian world; The fruits of faith; Of many beliefs mentioned in Holy Scripture; The condition of Christendom; That death should not make us sorrowful. In the fourteen chapters of *Œconomica* (second part), the author shows how all conditions of men should live according to the Gospel, and also in chaps. xvi. to xxxi. of the *Summa;* but in *Œconomica* eight chapters are devoted to monks and nuns, and in the *Summa* only four, which are materially abridged, with a special chapter on parents who dedicate their children to monastic life. Chaps. xi. and xii. of *Œconomica* deal with the rich, the married, burghers, and magistrates; chap. xiii. shows that the Gospel forbids war; chap. xiv. closes with the inquiry: " By what Gospel authority may princes levy taxes? " and discusses the corresponding duties of subjects. In the *Summa*, chap. xxii. deals with the question of married life; xxiii. with the Christian rule of children by parents; xxiv. considers the life of the middle classes; and xxv. tells how the rich should conform to the teaching of the Gospel. Chap. xxvi., which treats of worldly and spiritual rule, shows that the author was familiar with Luther's *Von weltlicher Obrigkeit*; chap. xxvii. points burgomasters, magistrates, and other officers to the Gospel; xxviii. resembles chap. xiv. of *Œconomica;* xxx. deals with the life of men- and maid-servants and day-laborers; and xxxi. with widows.

A truly remarkable work is the *Summa*, and it indicates that a wholesome spirit of reform predominated in the Netherlands earlier than elsewhere, where was, so to speak, an individual reformation, of which the *Summa* was the expression. It also bears evidence of a growing sympathy with Luther and Zwingli. In fact, the Netherlands supported and furthered the reform movement in other countries partly by the *Summa*, which spread abroad and fostered the intellectual awakening of the reform spirit. (S. D. VAN VEEN.)

BIBLIOGRAPHY: Besides the introductions to the editions named in the text, consult the articles in the *Theologi-*

sche Studien (of Utrecht), i (1883), 313–323, and ii (1884), 447–451, by H. G. Kleyn, ii (1884), 145–162, by Van Toorenenbergen; K. Benrath, in *JPT*, vii. 127 sqq.; Düsterdieck, in *GGA*, 1878, and Kattenbusch, in the same, 1883; P. Hofstede de Groot, in *De Tijdspiegel*, 1882–83; and M. A. Gooszen, in *Geloof en Vrijheid*, 1882.

SUMMENHART, KONRAD: Scholastic theologian; b. at Calw (20 m. w.n.w. of Stuttgart), Württemberg, or more probably in the village of Sommenhardt (close by Calw), between 1450 and 1460; d. at the monastery of Schuttern near Offenburg (17 m. s.s.w. of Carlsruhe), Baden, Oct. 20, 1502. He was a representative of the scholastic reaction against William of Occam's formalism, which constituted the realistic transition to humanism, and has been lauded as a precursor of the Reformation. Summenhart studied first at Paris, and in 1478 went to Tübingen, where, from 1489, he lectured on canon law, sociology, and natural philosophy. The writings left by Summenhart, mainly his Tübingen lectures, fall into three groups. The *Tractatus bipartitus de decimis* (Hagenau, **1497**) and *Septipertitum opus de contractibus pro foro conscientiæ* (1500) belong to the borderland of theology, sociology, and canon law. The second group consists of *Commentaria in summam physice Alberti Magni* (Freiburg, 1503), essaying a pious explanation of nature. The third group is composed of occasional addresses: *Oratio funebris pro Eberhardo* (Tübingen, 1498); *Quod deus homo fieri voluerit;* and *Tractatulus exhortatorius super decem defectibus virorum monasticorum* (1498), against monastic abuses.   (H. HERMELINK.)

BIBLIOGRAPHY: J. J. Moser, *Vitæ professorum Tubingensium*, pp. 36–41, Tübingen, 1718; F. X. Linsenmann, *Konrad Summenhart*, ib. 1877; K. Steiff, *Der erste Buchdruck in Tübingen*, pp. 50–53, 228–233, ib. 1881; H. Hermelink, *Die theologische Fakultät in Tübingen vor der Reformation*, pp. 156–162, 194–195, ib. 1906; *Württembergische Vierteljahrshefte für Landesgeschichte*, 1906, pp. 331 sqq.

SUMMERBELL, MARTYN: Free Baptist; b. at Naples, N. Y., Dec. 20, 1847. He was educated at the College of the City of New York (A.B., 1871), pursued a post-graduate course in New York University (1886–89; Ph.D., 1889), and was non-resident professor of pastoral theology in the Christian Biblical Institute, Stanfordville, N. Y. (1874–1901). He has held successive pastorates at the Christian Church of the Evangel, Brooklyn, N. Y. (1866–80), the First Christian Church, Fall River, Mass. (1880–1886), St. Paul's Evangelical Church, New York City (1886–88), and the College Church, Bates College, Lewiston, Me. (1888–98). He was instructor in church history at Cobb Divinity School, Lewiston, Me. (1895–98), and was elected president of the Palmer Institute, Starkey Seminary, Lakemont, N. Y., in 1898, which position he still occupies. In theology he holds to " fellowship for active Christians of every name on the basis of vital Christian piety." He has written *Special Services for Christian Ministers* (Fall River, Mass., 1885) and is joint author of *The People's Bible History* (Chicago, 1895).

SUMMERFIELD, JOHN: Methodist Episcopal; b. in Preston (28 m. n.w. of Manchester), England, Jan. 31, 1798; d. in New York June 13, 1825. He was educated at the Moravian Academy at Fairfield, near Manchester; was sent into business at Liverpool; removed to Dublin, 1813; was converted in 1817, and next year became a local Wesleyan minister. In 1819 he was received on trial in the Methodist Conference of Ireland, and in Mar., 1821, having emigrated to America, in the New York conference. He leaped into astonishing popularity by reason of his eloquence, and in 1822 he preached in Philadelphia, Baltimore, and Washington, everywhere heard by great crowds. Because of ill-health he was in France and England, 1822–24, returning to New York Apr. 19, 1824, but he was not able again to do full work. He was a founder of the American Tract Society. His *Sermons and Sketches of Sermons* was published (New York, 1842).

BIBLIOGRAPHY: Lives were written by J. Holland, New York, 1829, and W. M. Willitt, Philadelphia, 1857. Consult further: N. Bangs, *Hist. of the M. E. Church*, iii. 324–329, New York, 1860; W. B. Sprague, *Annals of the American Pulpit*, vii. 639–654, ib. 1861; and literature (under METHODISTS) on the early history of Methodism in America.

SUMMERS, THOMAS OSMOND: Methodist Episcopal South; b. near Confe Castle (18 m. e.s.e. of Dorchester), England, Oct. 11, 1812; d. at Nashville, Tenn., May 5, 1882. His early religious training was Calvinistic. He came to America, 1830, and united with the Methodist Church; joined the Baltimore Conference, 1835; was ordained deacon, 1837, and elder, 1839; was an organizer of the first Texas conference, 1840, and a missionary to Texas, 1840–43; member of the Alabama conference, 1843–76; and secretary of the Louisville Convention in 1845, at which the Methodist Episcopal Church South was organized. In 1846 he was appointed by the general conference to assist Bishop Wightman as editor of *The Southern Christian Advocate*, published at Charleston, S. C.; while there, he edited for four years the *Sunday-School Visitor.* He was the general book editor for the organization of the church, editing some 300 volumes; he removed to Nashville in 1855, where he took charge of *The Quarterly Review;* performed pastoral work in Alabama, 1862–66; in 1866 was elected editor of the Nashville *Christian Advocate;* was professor of systematic theology in Vanderbilt University, Nashville; also dean of the theological faculty and ex-officio pastor, 1874–82. He was secretary of every general conference of his church, devoted much time to hymnology, and was chairman of the committee that compiled the hymn-book, which he edited. Possessed of encyclopedic knowledge, and always abreast of the times, he was thoroughly Wesleyan and Arminian in his creed, but in hearty sympathy with all Evangelical denominations of Christians. He edited *Songs of Zion: Supplement to the Hymn-book of the Methodist Episcopal Church South* (Nashville, 1851); *Biographical Sketches of Itinerant Ministers, Pioneers within Bounds of the Methodist Episcopal Church, South* (1858); and wrote *Baptism: its Nature, Perpetuity, Subject . . . With Strictures on Howell's " Evils of Infant Baptism "* (1852); commentaries on the Gospels (1868–72), the ritual (1873), and the Acts (1874).

BIBLIOGRAPHY: O. P. Fitzgerald, *Dr. Summers, a Life Study*, Nashville, 1884.

SUMNER, JOHN BIRD: Archbishop of Canterbury; b. at Kenilworth (44 m. n.n.w. of Oxford), England, Feb. 25, 1780; d. in Addington (12 m. s.

of Charing Cross) Sept. 6, 1862. He studied at Eton, 1791–98, and at King's College, Cambridge (B.A., 1803; M.A., 1807; D.D., 1828). In 1802 he became assistant master at Eton; was rector of Maple Durham, 1820–48; became canon of Durham, 1820; bishop of Chester, 1828; archbishop of Canterbury, 1848. He was untiring in his efforts to provide for schools and to further the erection of churches, and had consecrated more than 200 new churches by 1847. He was the leader of the " evangelical party " in the Church of England, and earnestly opposed to Romanism and the Oxford movement. His primacy covered the restoration of the Roman Catholic hierarchy to England, the period of *Essays and Reviews* (q.v.), and the revival of the synodical power of convocation. His publications include commentaries on Matthew and Mark (London, 1831), Luke (1832), John (1835), on Romans and I Corinthians (1843), II Corinthians, and Galatians,

Ephesians, Philippians, and Colossians (1845), and Thessalonians (1851); also, *A Treatise on the Records of the Creation, and on the Moral Attributes of the Creator; with particular Reference to the Jewish History, and to the Consistency of the Principle of Population with the Wisdom and Goodness of the Deity* (2 vols., 1816); *The Evidence of Christianity, Derived from its Nature and Reception* (1824); *Sermons on the Principal Festivals of the Christian Church; to which are added three Sermons on Good Friday* (1827); *Four Sermons on Subjects Relating to the Christian Ministry* (1828); *Christian Charity, its Obligations and Objects, with Reference to the Present State of Society, in a Series of Sermons* (1841); *On Regeneration and Grace* (1850); *Practical Reflections on Select Passages of the New Testament* (1859); and numerous occasional sermons.

BIBLIOGRAPHY: *DNB*, lv. 168–170 (gives references to scattering notices).

SUN AND SUN WORSHIP.

I. Among the Hebrews: In the Old Testament the usual name for the sun is *shemesh*, a name which, with various vocalization, appears in most of the Semitic languages, as in Babylonian-Assyrian, Aramaic, Arabic, Phenician, and Pal-

1. Names and Titles. myrene (cf. the name of the god Shamash, BABYLONIA, VII., 2, § 4, and see below, II., 2). The signification of the word is unknown (Brown-Driver-Briggs, *Hebrew and English Lexicon*, p. 1039, Boston, 1906). The word is in the Hebrew prevailingly masculine,* but sometimes feminine (as in Gen. xv. 7), as is the Aramaic *shemsha;* the Assyrian-Babylonian form is invariably masculine, and the Arabic (*shams*) is always feminine (Albrecht, in *ZATW*, xv., 1895, p. 324). Poetical names for the sun in Hebrew are *ḥammah* (probably " the glowing one "; Job xxx. 28), and *heres* (Job ix. 7; meaning of the root of the word doubtful). In Gen. i. (where the sun is not called *shemesh*, but is spoken of as the greater of the " two great lights ") the purpose of the sun is given as " to rule the day," " to divide the light from the darkness," and " to be for signs, and for seasons, and for days, and for years "; that is, the function of the sun was conceived as being to indicate morning, noon, and evening, the seasons of the year, and therefore the religious festivals in their

recurring times. The sun as a measurer of time naturally comes into connection with both the Day and the Year (qq.v.; see also MOON; and TIME, BIBLICAL RECKONING of). The arrangement for an intercalated month in later times reveals the fact that the lunar year was made to square, at least approximately, with the solar year, at any rate in the later period of Jewish history.

The Hebrew notions regarding the sun were those of the region in which Palestine was situated, and of the period when Babylonian influence prevailed. The luminary was regarded as " going forth " in

2. General Conceptions. the morning from his pavilion at the eastern end of the heaven (cf. the seals in which the Babylonian Shamash is represented as issuing from a gate, represented by posts, in W. H. Ward, *Seal Cylinders of Western Asia*, chap. xiii., Washington, 1910) with the joy and confidence of a bridegroom (Ps. xix. 5), while his setting is called an " entering " (i. e., of gates in the West; cf. the cognate Babylonian thought, P. Jensen, *Kosmologie der Babylonier*, p. 9, Strasburg, 1890); and this involved the idea of a subterranean course in the night in order to be in his place of rising in the morning (Ps. xix. 5–7; Eccles. i. 5, the latter a conception slightly more developed). An eclipse or darkening of the sun was considered to be ominous of evil, and is one of the signs constantly associated with the Day of the Lord (q.v.; cf. Job iii. 5; Isa. xiii. 10; Joel ii. 10, iii. 15; Amos viii. 9; Matt. xxiv. 29, and often). Interference with the orderly course of the sun is conceived as within God's power (Job ix. 7), and its progress is reported to have been stayed to work salvation in battle for Israel (Josh. x. 12–13) or even reversed as a sign to Hezekiah (the shadow of the dial or steps is reversed, II Kings xx. 9–11; the sun itself, Isa. xxxviii. 8). With the

---

* An interesting question is raised with reference to the gender of *shemesh* in Gen. xxxvii. 9. The " sun and the moon and the eleven stars " [signs of the zodiac] represent Jacob, Rachel, and the eleven brethren of Joseph (cf. verse 10). But the word for " moon " is invariably masculine, and it is argued that consequently *shemesh* must here be feminine. On the other hand, the order in verse 9 is as above and the sun corresponds in place to Jacob, the moon to " thy mother," and so on. Moreover, where Semitic Babylonian influence prevails the male is the superior (note the insignificance of Babylonian female deities after Sumerian influence had become decadent; see ASSYRIA, VII., § 1), and in theology the sun takes precedence of the moon.

exegesis of these passages the present article does not deal further than to say that the attempt to relieve the earlier passage of difficulty by calling attention to its poetical character seems unnecessary because of the existence of the second and much later passage, where not merely suspension of progress but actual reversal equivalent to forty minutes in time is stated as an actual fact (if the " degrees " be of a circumference). If the Hebrews of Hezekiah's age and later could accept as historical such an event, it is not necessary to have recourse to the usual palliative explanations of a statement arising so much nearer a primitive (and more credulous) age dealing with the stopping (apparently for twenty-four hours, cf. Josh. x. 13, last clause) of the sun's progress. The effects of the sun's action on the earth were, according to Hebrew belief, in general, the production of crops (Deut. xxxiii. 14; II Sam. xxiii. 4); it was his also to give light (Gen. i.; Eccles. xi. 7; Rev. vii. 16) and heat (Ps. xix. 6). In respect to this last function it is noteworthy that the references to the scorching heat of the sun, to what may be called its malign influence, are comparatively infrequent (Ps. cxxi. 6; Isa. iv. 6, xxv. 4, xlix. 10; Jonah iv. 8; Rev. xvi. 8–9), though the conception of its malevolence comes out frequently in other lands, as in India (see below, II., 6) and in Babylonia, where Nergal was a god of destruction (see Babylonia, VII., 2, § 4). The prevailing Biblical idea of the sun was that of its might and glory as a luminary, and these naturally became the basis of poetical comparison for heroes and the faithful (Judges v. 31; II Sam. xxiii. 4; Ps. xix. 5–6; Cant. vi. 10); Yahweh is himself in metaphor called a sun (Ps. lxxxiv. 11; Isa. lx. 19), and his healing grace is in the same manner compared with a sun of righteousness (Mal. iv. 2). The passage in Isa. xxiv. 23 is noteworthy—the glory of the restored Zion and Jerusalem is to be so great that even the sun in his brightness will be abashed (there does not seem any basis for the quite common exegesis of the passage which regards the sun and moon here as demonic powers which are put away, e.g., W. von Baudissin, in Hauck-Herzog, *RE*, xviii. 519, and *Semitische Studien*, i. 118 sqq., Leipsic, 1876).

The evidence for the worship of the sun among Israelites is limited and late. II Kings xxiii. 11 records the destruction of the chariots and removal of the horses of the sun from the Tem-

3. Worship. ple at Jerusalem. Ezek. viii. 16 describes a vision of the prophet in which he saw twenty-five men at the door of the Temple worshiping the sun in the East and " putting the branch to their nose " (i.e., using a branch as symbolic of the productive powers of the sun; cf. J. G. Frazer, *Golden Bough*, passim, 3 vols., London, 1900; tree-worship often combines with the cult of the sun). With respect to the chariot and horses of the sun the most obvious source is Babylon (see below, II., and cf. Jensen, *Kosmologie*, ut sup., pp. 108 sqq.; Schrader, *KAT*, p. 368). It is hardly likely that so early as this the influence of the Persians is to be seen (cf. F. Spiegel, *Eranische Alterthumskunde*, ii. 66 sqq., Leipsic, 1873; for references to the Persian sacred horses cf. Herodotus, i. 189, vii. 55, viii. 115; Xenophon, *Cyropædia*, VIII., iii. 12;

and the *Mihir Yast*, § 13, Am. ed. of *SBE*, iii., part 2, p. 122, speaks of the " swift-horsed sun "). The idea of the chariot of the sun appears outside of these sources and the Greek myths in Enoch, lxxii. 5, lxxiii. 2, lxxv. 3, 4, 8, where sun, moon, and stars are supplied with chariots; Baruch, Apocalypse, vi.; and the Mandæans placed the seven planets in chariots. The conception of Yahweh or of the Son of Man riding on the clouds (Ps. civ. 3; Dan. vii. 13) has no relationship to this idea. Further evidence of sun-worship in Israel is furnished by the existence of sun-pillars (Hebr. *ḥammanim*, A. V., " images," R. V., " sun-images "; for representation of one to " the lord, Baal-Ḥamman," cf. Benzinger, *Archäologie*, p. 183) which the reforming kings are said to have destroyed (II Chron. xiv. 5, Hebr. verse 4, xxxiv. 4, 7) against which the exilic and post-exilic prophets speaking in Isa. xvii. 8, xxvii. 9 and Ezek. vi. 4, 6, and the priestly writer (Lev. xxvi. 30) uttered their threats.* Other evidences adduced to prove the existence of worship of the sun among the Israelites do not bear examination. Certainly the name of Samson, even though it be derived from *shemesh* (which is not altogether sure) does not show this cult; it is not at all necessary, nor is it the best explanation of the episode to regard it as a sun myth, since it is rather an accretion of legend about a character whose exploits were probably in fact just such as suit the heroic period of a nation's development. And as little faith is to be put in the assumption that the horses and chariot of fire by which Elijah was translated are those of the sun. The much later practise of the Essenes (q.v.), as given in Josephus, *War*, II., viii. 5, of directing their worship toward the sun instead of toward Jerusalem is hardly sufficient, in view of the general Pharisaic character of their beliefs and customs, to convict them of following the cult of the sun. The Mandæan practises were not Jewish but Babylonian in origin. Dr. Briggs, in his commentary on Psalms (vol. i., New York, 1906), sees in the first part of Ps. xix. a hymn to the sun.

All indications point to a late date for the importation of this cult into Israel, and also to its derivation from the peoples in the immediate environment, and (less likely) from Assyria. It is true that the Chronicles (II Chron. xiv. 3) reports that Asa suppressed this worship; but the parallel and earlier passage in I Kings xv. omits mention

4. Date of Introduction. of the pillars, though it specifies minutely the anti-idolatrous activities of that king. The same situation is repeated with reference to Josiah (II Chron. xxxiv. 4, 7; cf. II Kings xxiii.). So that apparently the earliest mention of the sun-pillars is found in Ezekiel, and this squares with the other data already examined. The mention of the horses and chariot of the sun, however, carries this feature

* The word for " sun-pillar " in these passages is the same as that found in an inscription on an altar at Palmyra and now in the Ashmolean Museum at Oxford, England (D. G. Hogarth, *Authority and Archæology*, pp. 135, 139, London, 1899), and in the name Baal-Hamman, who was a sun-deity of Carthage, as is shown by a votive pillar and by inscriptions (W. Gesenius, *Scripturæ linguæque Phœniciæ monumenta* table 21, Leipsic, 1807). Other traces of this name are quite frequent in Aramean environment.

back of the time of Josiah. It must be borne in mind that while such place-names as Beth-shemesh, Harheres, Timnath-heres, and Heres (see below, II., 4, § 1) favor the supposition that the worship of the sun had loci there, it does not follow that during Israelitic times this cult was followed. Biblical place-names in Palestine in general date back to pre-Hebraic times, and the worship at those places, if worship there was, was Canaanitic. The probable date of the introduction of such worship as is implied in the horses and chariot of the sun (II Kings xxiii. 11) and the vision of Ezekiel may perhaps be given as the reign of Manasseh (q.v.), who was a contemporary of the vigorous and aggressive Esarhaddon and Asshurbanipal. It is a priori probable that a king with so decided heathen tendencies as Manasseh would adopt a cult which was so popular as the cult of the sun was in the neighboring lands (see below, II., 3) and in Assyria, especially as his policy was pro-Assyrian and not pro-Egyptian. And there are indications of a wide-spread distrust of the power of Yahweh in the days of the declining kingdom, just before the exile, which would favor this period.

II. In Other Lands. 1. In General: That, if not in temperate, yet in tropical or sub-tropical regions the sun should from primitive times be an object of worship is no occasion for wonder. The feelings of awe which manifested themselves in early ages were only heightened as man's capacity for increased recognition, as time went on and experiences enlarged, of the influence of the sun on the earth and its contributions to the well-being of man. So that in some form, explicit or implicit, either as itself a divinity, or as the seat of deity, or as in some other way related to the gods, in probably every inhabited land the sun has received homage, influenced thought, and contributed to human development. Even in architectural matters it has had much to say, controlling the orientation of structures down into late Christian times, so that cathedrals often stand with their altars so placed that worship is directed to the East, the place of the rising sun. Some nations have found the sun's power and significance too great and his activities too varied to be expressed by homage to a single deity, and numerous sun-gods were imagined, and to each was given his own cult and worship.

A fundamental law in religious psychology is that the human mind works out into similar forms in different countries the same or similar conceptions dealing with similar material. Hence, it is not surprising that the symbols for the sun are so few yet so universal. Thus the disk or circle, with or without wings, sometimes with rays (these rays may be outside the disk or on the face of the disk; for examples of both cf. A. J. Evans, in *Journal of Hellenic Studies*, xxi., 1901, pp. 108, 161); again it is surmounted by a human figure, and often occurs with the accompaniments of serpents (see SERPENT IN WORSHIP, etc., IV., § 1), is the almost universal symbol.* Other common symbols are the eagle or

hawk, eagle- or hawk-headed figures of gods, the winged horse, the scarab, possibly the swastika. When the figure takes the human form, it usually appears as vigorous and youthful, with golden hair and often golden horns, while a rayed crown or rays of light issuing from his body serve in other cases to identify him. The benefactions attributed to him, apart from the obvious ones of light and heat, are quite commonly those of life and fertility; and in lands as disassociated as Semitic Syria and Dravidian India he is connected with wells and springs (possibly in a way similar to the popular occidental superstition which speaks of the sun as " drawing water " when its oblique rays are seen shining in the distance through rifts in the clouds; cf. for this relationship with water, W. H. Ward in *AJT*, ii., 1898, pp. 115–118). The same thing occurs in symbolism when, from the symbolic disk, there emanate not only rays of light (indicated by straight divergent lines) but also streams of water (indicated by parallel wavy lines). A representation of Shamash with streams of water issuing from his body is in A. Jeremias, *Das Alte Testament im Lichte des alten Orients*, p. 111, Leipsic, 1906; that the streams represent water and not light is proved by the fish swimming in them). In accordance with this conception, the flowers and incense offered to him are sometimes thrown into a stream. His course in the heavens is conceived as made on foot (as occasionally in India), on horseback, in a chariot, or in a boat, the form of representation depending upon the cosmological notions of the different peoples. As a deity who in his daily journey passes over the earth and looks down upon the deeds of men, it is not strange that he should be now the eye of Ouranos or Varuna (Heaven) who sees all and reports to that exalted deity, or again that he should be the judge of men and gods, or once more (as pure light) the champion of truth and an agent in ethical uprightness. Still further, occasionally the sun appears as a culture deity, conceived as giving laws to men, leading the advances of civilization, and, on the reverse side, punishing those who break the laws of gods and men. And, once more, it ought not to surprise that the sun may have two opposing aspects, that he may be regarded as kindly and as malign, so that in Babylonia (see below) he is both Shamash and Nergal, and that in India the Aryans could, while in the temperate land of the five rivers, sing gloriously in his praise and in central and southern India affirm " yon burning sun is death."

2. Babylonia: In this land, early and late, sun-gods were numerous, though the number tended ever to decrease. Chief among these was Shamash, who of this class of deities figures most frequently in inscriptions and on seals. He is the successor of or identical with the Sumerian Utu, whose principal shrines were at Larsa and Sippara (see BABYLONIA, IV., §§ 4, 11, VII., 2, § 4; a very excellent reproduction of the figure and inscription of the Sippara Shamash, with the sun's disk and light rays and water streams, is given in R. W. Rogers, *Religion of Babylonia and Assyria*, p. 84, New York, 1908). At Sippara there were horses and a chariot sacred to him, with which were associated a large number (140 in one list) of sacred objects, and to the chariot

---

* Several of these symbols are reproduced on a single page in J. B. Deane, *Worship of the Serpent*, p. 51, London, 1833; for a Phenician example cf. Benzinger, *Archäologie*, p. 180.

sacrifices were offered (in one case of a white sheep; cf. *DB*, iv. 629). With this should be connected possibly the horses and chariot of the sun mentioned in II Kings xxiii. 11 (ut sup., I., § 3). But the worship of Shamash was not confined to these places. He represents the beneficent power of the sun and the ethical side of life. He was portrayed on the monuments and seals in two postures, sitting and standing, the latter including his posture as he is represented as emerging from the gates of day (cf. W. H. Ward, *Seal Cylinders of Western Asia*, Washington, 1910; H. Gressmann, *Altorientalische Texte und Bilder*, ii. 12, cf. p. 57, Tübingen, 1909). Sometimes he journeys in a boat, and once is figured as stepping on a human-headed bull. He wears a tiara, sometimes rayed, and rays of light and sometimes streams of water proceed from his shoulders or other parts of his body. He carries a serrated sword, or a club, or both, and occasionally a battle ax. He is spoken of in the inscriptions as supreme judge, avoucher of truth, giver of oracles, bestower of life and health. The metal particularly associated with him was gold, as silver was with Sin, the moongod. In the course of history this deity became so important that he absorbed into his own personality the sun-gods of minor cities. The worshiper often brings a goat or an antelope as a sacrifice. Some noble hymns to him are extant (cf. M. Jastrow, *Religion of Babylonia and Assyria*, Boston, 1898; Germ. ed., issued in parts, Giessen, 1902 sqq.). His consort Aa often appears, sometimes as intercessor. While Marduk appears as a sun-god, his part in this sphere is unimportant. Another deity related to this luminary was Ninib, associated especially with the sun of early morning and of spring, a god of fertility and the guardian of boundaries, as well as a war-deity. In the case of Ninib, as of Shamash, the process of coalescence with other gods was protracted, so that in his person were summed up many early local gods of the field, in later theology regarded as his manifestations. Nergal was specifically the sun of high noon and of summer, hence the sun which brought destroying heat, fever, pestilence, and death, therefore belonging also to the deities of the nether world. Associated with the sun as fire was Girru, known in Assyria principally as Nusku; testimonies to him are derived mainly from the magical texts, a fact which shows what was regarded as his chief concern. In the Assyrian Asshur there was originally seen a solar deity, but his position at the head of the pantheon of the warlike Assyrians led to the entire obscuration of this significance. Nevertheless, this origin is perhaps to be discerned in his symbol, the disk, winged and surmounted by the figure of a warrior discharging an arrow (remember the Greek figure of the rays of Apollo shooting his arrows, in the first book of the *Iliad*). For Tammuz as a solar deity see the article on the subject. It may be added that Semitic solar deities seem in large part to have gained the ascendency over Sumerian lunar gods, Sin being the one marked exception.

3. Egypt: It is demonstrable that in this country worship of the sun is prehistoric. Besides the disk, plain and winged (for a fine example of the latter cf. A. Wiedemann, *Religion of the Ancient Egyptians*, p. 75, New York, 1897), a symbol largely employed was the obelisk, and pyramids and mastabas (truncated pyramids) served the same purpose. The great center of sun-worship was On (q.v.), the Greek Heliopolis and the Hebrew Beth-shemesh; there is the sacred spring connected with the Holy Family as a resting-place on their flight into Egypt, still known as " the spring of the sun." In Egypt the great importance of the Nile led to the conception that the gods made their journeys on boats over the Nile of the heaven, and the solar deity was supposed to have two, the " Madet " boat for the morning and the " Sektet " boat for the afternoon or night, and these figure largely on the monuments.

The sun-god most noted of all, and indeed the chief deity of Egypt, was Ra, portrayed as a hawk-headed man, or as a hawk, and he wears a disk encircled by the uræus or the serpent Khut. In his journeys on his boats the course was kept by numerous other gods. His nightly travel involved a conflict with the serpent Apepi, and the story of the first conflict quite closely parallels that of the conflict of Marduk with Tiamat (see BABYLONIA, VII., 3, § 4), excepting the creation of the firmament out of Tiamat's split corpse. As in Japan, the early dynasty claimed descent from the sun. In the process of amalgamation of deities so noteworthy in Egypt, Ra became combined with various other sun-gods, whose names he took. Apparently he had different names in the various parts of his daily course: " O thou who art Ra when thou risest and Temu when thou settest " . . . " I am Khepera in the morning, Ra at noonday, and Temu in the evening " (E. A. W. Budge, *Gods of the Egyptians*, i. 335, 352, London, 1904). For hymns of praise to him cf. Budge, ut sup., pp. 335–348, and Wiedemann, ut sup., pp. 40–42, 44–51, 111–118, 136. Myths concerning him are numerous, the most famous being that of Isis and the serpent (see NAMES, I., § 1). Hathor was originally the female counterpart of Ra, and in the religious texts wears on her head horns and the solar disk. She was also connected with the star Sothis (Sirius), " the second sun in heaven." Bast was identified with Rat (the feminine form of Ra), and symbolizes the heat of early and late summer. Of Horus it is difficult to speak, since one can not say how many deities of that name there were. Over twenty forms of Horus are noted by Budge. In some of these, or, to express it in another way, in some of his phases Horus was solar, and appears both as the rising and as the midday sun, often wearing in the texts the solar disk. He was also represented in the more philosophic texts as one of the chief forms of Ra, is given a hawk's head, and is reported as transforming himself into the winged disk with the uræus. His temples were apparently in all parts of the country. Next to Ra is Amen—often united with Ra as Amen-Ra, whose attributes he possesses, two hymns speaking of his " rays (shining) on all faces " and of his " sailing over the sky in peace " (Budge, ut sup., ii. 5, 7); as a crown he wears horns and the double disk. Similarly he is lord of the Sektet boat and is said to shine in the eastern and the western horizons. Apparently, however, it was only by this union with Ra that he was associated with the sun, and by it he absorbed " all the attributes of Ra and of every other ancient form of the sun-god " (Budge, ii. 11). Thus he became in the later empire the mightiest of the gods of the land. Aten (= disk of the sun) is noteworthy because of the attempt of Amenophis IV. (1375–58 according to Breasted, *History of the Ancient Egyptians*, p. 428, New York, 1908; for an account of the attempt itself cf. the same author, pp. 264 sqq.), " the heretic king," to create a monotheism by making the worship of Aten dominant in the land. Conflict with the priests of Thebes caused him to build his capital at Tell Amarna, and the revolution at his death, with the covering up of a part of the records, is responsible for the existence of the famous Amarna Tablets (q.v.). This deity is noteworthy for the portrayal of him in this reign as a disk the rays from which terminate in hands (symbolizing the blessings he bestows), and in some cases two of the hands hold out the ankh (the sign of life) to Amenophis and his consort, the handle being toward the recipients (cf. Budge, ut sup., vol. ii., chap. iv.). Solar deities were doubtless numerous in Egypt, especially local gods, such as the ancient Menthu, later Menthu-Ra and Her-shef, god of Herakleopolis, who was granted many of the attributes of Ra.

4. Aramea, Syria, and Phenicia: In the region thus designated the indications of sun-worship are numerous and persistent. In the Canaanitic portions the place names have some significance, those

1. Place Names. who deny this fact not having taken fully into account the very early habit of indicating the kind of sanctity inhering in a place by the name attached to it. The names are En-shemesh, " fountain of Shemesh " or " of the sun," Josh. xv. 7, xviii. 17; Ir-shemesh, " city of Shemesh," Josh. xix. 41; cf. Isa. xix. 18; Beth-shemesh, " house " or " temple " or " city of Shemesh," Josh. xxi. 16; Her-heres, " mount of the sun," Judges i. 35; Timnath-heres, " territory of the sun," Judges ii. 9; and possibly the Kir-heres of Jer. xlviii. 36, with which, however, cf. the Kir-hareseth or -hareseth or -hares of II Kings iii. 25; Isa. xvi. 7, 11; and Jer. xlviii. 31. It will be noticed that these names occur mainly in connection with the early history of Israel and as the names which the places had (presumably) when the Hebrews entered the land. The easiest explanation and the most likely is that the names indicate the presence of sanctuaries dedicated to the sun. Other secondary and general evidences of this cult are the use of the disk, especially on coins, both winged and plain, and particularly the disk in a crescent. In one case a coin of Baalbek has the sun mounted on a chariot, and in other instances he is on a steed (cf. e.g., L. Heuzey, in *Comptes rendus de l'académie des inscriptions*, 1902, pp. 190–200). This does not take into account the existence of the disk in inscriptions or monuments left by invaders, such as that of Rameses II. at Nahr al-Kalb, nor the many coins of late times which bear the disk, though in many cases these are evidential. It has been supposed that possibly the rayed star so frequently seen above the crescent in Syrian monumental remains and coins represents the sun,

not a star such as Venus; but the probability is that a star is meant. The cromlechs of Syria are possibly to be connected with sun-worship. One reason for this is that the Dravidians still employ these monuments in that cult, while some of these places are used in worship of the phallus with rites that differ hardly at all in many particulars from those of the sun (cf. C. R. Conder, *Heth and Moab*, pp. 218–219, London, 1883), and connections of sun and phallic worship are not difficult to find.

To these lines of evidence is to be added for this region the formation of personal names. Quite prominent in this relation is the name of Shamash

2. Personal Names. (however it was vocalized). Thus there may be adduced from Phenicia *Adon-Shmsh*, *'bd-Shmsh* (Greek *Heliodoros*, borne by a Phenician in a Greek environment, *CIS*, no. 117, 2; the Greek equivalent for Shamash is found in a Beirut inscription *Kronou Heliou bomos*—cf. Ceccaldi, *Revue archéologique*, xxiii., 1872, pp. 253–256). Yet it is noteworthy that actual worship of Shamash under that name does not appear in Phenicia, so far as monumental evidence goes; it is inconceivable, however, that Phenicians did not know its significance. The fragments of Sanchuniathon (q.v.; in Eusebius, *Præparatio Evangelica*, Eng. transl., pp. 37 sqq., Oxford, 1903) report sun-worship among the Phenicians, and this author traces the cult back to the earliest men, who called him " Baal of Heaven " (ib., p. 39). From Edessa come the names *'math-Shmsh*, " maid of Shamash," *Br-Shmsh*, " son of Shamash," *'bd-Shmsh*, " servant of Shamash " (Sachau, in *ZDMG*, xxxvi., 1882, pp. 145 sqq., 163; *Doctrina Addai*, ed. Phillips, p. 39, London, 1876, Eng. transl. in *ANF*, viii. 663). Attention has frequently been called in this work to the real significance of names into which " servant of " and " maid-servant of " enter as elements, they being regarded as proofs of the worship in the region of the deity whose name forms the second element in the compound. At the same time this may not always be assumed as evidence of worship contemporaneous with the person bearing the name, since nomenclature often persists after the recognition of its significance is lost. From Emesa, also from Maglula near Baalbek and from Palmyra, comes the name in Greek form *Samsigeramos* (*CIG*, 4511; attested also by Photius, *Bibliotheca*, 181; S. A. Cook, *Glossary of Aramaic Inscriptions*, Cambridge, 1898; M. Lidzbarski, *Ephemeris für semitische Epigraphik*, Giessen, 1906). Strabo (XVI., ii. 10–11) mentions a Samsikeramos as an officer in Emesa whose origin (?) was in Apamea; and Josephus (*Ant.*, XVIII., v. 4) knows of a king of Emesa bearing that name; while a Baalbek Latin inscription also contains it (*CIL*, iii. 14387a). From Palmyra come *Br-Shmsh*, *Tym-Shmsh* (—*'bd-Shmsh*), while inscriptions containing " to Shmsh " are frequent (cf. Cook and Lidzbarski, ut sup.); and *Klzyr-Shmsh* and *Shmsh-'dri* are found (*CIS*, nos. 87, 97). Baudissin (Hauck-Herzog, *RE*, xviii. 507) is inclined to accept the ending *sh'* as an abbreviation for the Aramaic form of the word *shemesh*, and so to increase greatly the volume of testimony; but the hypothesis can not be said to be proved.

Clermont-Ganneau (*Archives des missions scientifiques et littéraires*, 3d series, xi. 182, no. 23, Paris, 1885) describes the bronze head of a statue with rayed crown from Tripoli (cf. Gressmann, ut sup., ii. 74), and numerous evidences of the same sort might be adduced. Julian (*Oratio*, iv.) speaks of Edessa as long the sacred territory of the sun. At Emesa honey was offered in sacrifice to the same deity (Athenæus, xv., emended text). One of the deities of this city was Elagabalus, who became a solar god (he was perhaps a god of the hill-top), and his namesake the Roman emperor (see ELAGABALUS) endeavored to force his cult upon the empire as the sole legitimate worship (cf. J. H. Mordtmann, in *ZDMG*, xxxi., 1877, pp. 91–99); a conical stone stood in the temple of this deity, and this, once more, shows that between sun-worship and the phallic cult there were interconnections. The coins of Emesa often bear the image of a deity with rayed crown. For Palmyra the fact of the existence of the cult is so well-known as hardly to need additional testimony. While *Shmsh* (however vocalized) is the predominant object of worship, other deities there were brought into relations with the sun; coins of the city bear the usual head with rayed crown, and monolingual and bilingual inscriptions add further witness. The worship of Shamash appears to have been very ancient. One deity known as *Mlkb'l* ("Baal is king"?) is identified as *Sol* on an altar inscription in Rome, and the solar eagle is present (Lidzbarski, ut sup., p. 477, no. 2). The predilection for solar deities in this region is perhaps in this city most strongly represented, as is attested by the fact that the deity *Yrḥb'l* ("Moon is lord"; cf. *yareaḥ* as a name for the moon in MOON, HEBREW CONCEPTIONS OF, § 1) was identified with the sun (*CIL*, iii. 108), and a relief of this god wears the rayed crown of a solar deity (Ronzevalle, in *Comptes rendus de l'académie des inscriptions*, 1903, pp. 276 sqq.). At Baalbek the evidences of sun-worship, outside of those belonging to the Roman imperial age, are well known; among these are many evidences of Egyptian influence on the art side at least, the disk with uræus appearing in the reliefs; there are also traces of Phenician influence. The Greek name Heliopolis is indicative of the controlling worship of the place, and the bronzes and other art objects found there show both the rayed crown and gilding. The coins often carry this same crown together with an eagle, while the inscription *CIL*, iii. 14386*d*. mentions the sun. Even Balanios, originally perhaps a form of Hadad (see RIMMON) came to be accepted as solar. Farther east, at Hierapolis on the Euphrates, Lucian (*Dea Syria*, § 34) reports a temple in which was a throne for the sun-god, but no image of him; and from a place called Nizib to the north comes a bronze eagle which bears the inscription *Helios* (R. Dussaud, *Notes de mythologie syrienne*, Paris, 1903) —the connection of the eagle with the sun-god, which has been assumed in the foregoing, is made certain for the Semitic region by the very numerous occasions in which they are brought together, by the explicit identification just noted, and by the Arabian conception of an eastern and a western

Nasr (" eagle "), evidently referring to the rising and the setting sun. The same connection so common in Egypt is confirmatory, not evidential. A large number of additional witnesses might be adduced from the region south of Hermon and east of the Jordan, but most of them would be but supplementary to the testimony already cited. In the Amarna Tablets Akizzi of Katna near Emesa speaks of Shamash as the God of his fathers; the Senjirli and Nerab inscriptions name Shamash apparently as one among a number of deities; Shamash was worshiped at Gebal (Amarna Tablets, nos. 87, 65 in Winckler's numbering). There was an Amoritic deity *Sharebu*, " heat," who is perhaps to be connected with the sun (Schrader, *KAT*, p. 415); Nergal is mentioned on a Canaanitic seal cylinder at Taanach, probably as the name for a local sun-god (E. Sellin, *Tell Ta'annek*, pp. 27, 105, Vienna, 1904), and is mentioned also in the Amarna Tablets, nos. 13, 25, 37. The Egyptian deity Amon-Ra was known in North Syria and was identified with Shamash at Gebal. One of the eight temples of Gaza was dedicated to the sun.

From ancient testimony like that of Servius (an annotator of Vergil's *Æneid*, on i. 729) there is raised the presumption that in this region where the name Baal is used of a deity, the sun is meant. It has already appeared that the title of the sun-god varied, now appearing as Bel or Baal, Greek *Despotēs;* now as *Melek* or " King," Greek *Basileus,* and later as *Mar*, Syrian for " Lord." Not infrequently he received also the title " savior," especially when he was regarded as a deity of healing. Even Saturn was blended with this cult in late Roman times. The spread of the Mithra cult only emphasized the general tendency, for as a solar god he gained recognition, although the myth distinguished him from the sun and made him the subduer of that luminary and the master assigning tasks to it. Even Tammuz (q.v.) at Byblos, became a sun-deity (E. Renan, *Mission de Phénicie,* plate xxxii. 2, Paris, 1864; Macrobius, *Saturnalia,* I., xxi. 1, " Adonis is surely the sun "). As bearing on the later Nabatæan conceptions it may be remembered that in Arabia Shams was feminine, and the testimony of proper names attests the fact of worship. Aramaic names among the Nabatæans (q.v.), such as *Shmsh-grm* (see above, § 2), do not carry conclusive weight, because of the borrowing of language which characterized the Nabatæans. Yet much might be said for the original Nabatæan origin of this name. Strabo (XVI., iii. 26) reports that these people had altars to the sun on their houses, and the tendency is to see the sun in Dusares (see NABATÆANS, II., § 3; cf. J. H. Mordtmann, in *ZDMG*, xxix., 1875, pp. 99–106), especially as the epithet " invincible " so common in association with solar deities is applied to him. This solar character may, however, have been acquired after he came to Aramean soil, for the indications are plain that he was originally a god of fertility (Lidzbarski, *Ephemeris*, ut sup., p. 262).

5. The Hittites: In the present state of limited knowledge of the Hittites reserve respecting their religious ideas is eminently becoming   From the inscription of Rameses II. giving the account of the treaty with the Hittite King Khetasira (cf. W. M. Müller, *Der Bündnisvertrag Ramses II. und des Chetiterkönigs*, Berlin, 1904; W. H. Ward, *Seals*, etc., ut sup., pp. 257 sqq.), it is clear that the solar disk was employed among the Hittites (this is abundantly evident also from other remains), and there are references to a sun-god localized as "god of Arenena," but also universalized as "lord of all lands." The quite numerous seals reveal the worship of Shamash (or his Hittite equivalent; these seals show this deity in attitudes characteristically Babylonian), as well as of a deity similar to Nergal. The entire question of borrowing is here on the carpet, priority between native conceptions and the acceptance of Babylonian-Assyrian gods being hard to decide (J. Garstang, *Land of the Hittites*, p. 322, London, 1910). The series of art-remains plainly influenced by Egyptian ideas do not here come into consideration.

6. India: A distinct change is to be perceived in passing from the immediately Semitic environment. The emphasis upon the sun as an object of worship is lost, and other objects fairly divide with him the attention of devotees (only about thirty of the 1,028 hymns of the Rig Veda are to the sun-deities). In India, the land of many races and of different grades of civilization contemporaneously present, interesting features are to be discerned, one of which is that in the Vedas there can be traced the advance of the Aryan invaders as they enter the land from the northwest and advance into central and southern India. The difference in the conception of the sun in the Rig Veda and in the Atharva Veda is noteworthy; in the former the sun is the quickener and giver of life, in the latter he becomes deadly and the cause of death (E. W. Hopkins, *Religions of India*, p. 44, Boston, 1895). In early times and under favoring environment Surya, the principal Vedic deity, son of Aurora, was "the shining god, the red ball in the sky" (Hopkins, ut sup., pp. 40–41). He is also called Savitar, "the quickener or generator," and comes later to be identified with the local Brahmanic deity Bhaga and with Pushan, while in Hinduism he appears as Vishnu, who traversed the dome of heaven in three strides, thus winning the worlds for the gods, who holds the solar disk as his emblem, and has the eagle-man as his companion. In the earlier time this deity was felt as a stimulating force, author of birth, giver of life even to the gods, and donor of wealth. He drives across heaven with his seven steeds, and notes in his course all that passes. Sometimes again he is the eye of Varuna (*Ouranos*, "Heaven"), the creation of Mithra and Varuna. A little farther on in time the advance of the priestly conception is seen, and the statement is made that he is "the priest's priest," the "arranger of sacrifice" (*Rig Veda*, v. 81), and in later time his glory was as the divider of time for the sacrifice. As Pushan the bucolic deity he was bestower of a prosperity in which the rural or pastoral ideas are predominant, though those of the warrior or priest are to be seen invading. The later sun-god is Vishnu, whose hymns in the earliest collection are few, celebrating his three strides, his anchoring of the earth, and his

munificence. In the Brahmanas the sun has the power to draw forth and out a person's vitality and to cause his death; and so he is regarded often as malignant (*Satapatha Brahmana*, II., iii. 3, § 7, Eng. transl., *SBE*, American ed., ix. 343). As the priesthood developed its power, the solar gods, like the others, lost much of their divinity in the thorough anthropomorphization they underwent. Yet in the epics Surya retains much of his old grandeur and under Hinduism regained much of his eminence as creator, furnishing the rain which refreshes the earth and so acting as the provident father of his family. So in the *Bhagavad Gita* (III., iii. 36 sqq.) occurs a hymn where are chanted the 108 names of the sun, while the poet thinks "that in all the seven worlds and all the *brahma*-worlds there is nothing superior to the sun." Among the Hindu sects naturally there are some devoted particularly to the sun; and it is curious that a feature found in Egypt and elsewhere repeats itself here, since some sects direct their worship to the sun of the morning, others to that of noon, and still others to the evening sun, while some unite all in their worship as offered to a triad or trinity. The Sauras of southern India are an existing sect of this sort. In the festivals the second of the four New Year's days is sacred to Agni or Surya, and Feb. 4th to the sun. Some of the finest temples in India tell of the ardor of his worshipers. For early hymns to solar deities cf. Hopkins, ut sup., pp. 17–18, 48–50, the translations noted at vol. ii., pp. 249–250 of this work, and R. W. Frazer, *Literary History of India*, pp 49–50 (New York, 1898).

7. China and Japan: The sun in China is not marked out for especial distinction in worship. The sacrifices to him belong not in the first or highest grade into which cultic offerings are divided, but in the middle or second grade. In Peking he has a large walled park with open altar terrace outside the East Gate, where the especial sacrifices by the emperor or his representative are offered in the middle of spring. In Japan in the Shinto pantheon (see JAPAN, II., 1) the sun-goddess Amaterasu-O-Mi-Kami (or Amaterasu no Oho-Kami, "Heaven-shining-great-Deity"); or, to use the now common Chinese equivalent of her name, Tien-sho-dai-yin) is chief, bears the title "ruler of heaven," and is said to be unrivaled in dignity. It must not be understood from these expressions that there is any lordship over the other deities, nor is the idea quite that of the worshiper in Egypt, who in addressing any one deity heaped up phrases of adoration as if no other deity existed. The goddess had her supposed sphere of influence, however, and her worship is historically perhaps the most important in the island empire. The mythology of the Japanese is in spots peculiarly crude and repulsive, to say nothing of its occasional obscenity. Thus in the theogony the origin of Amaterasu is traced to the ablutions of the primitive creation deity Izanagi, who made the "descent into hell" to see his dead consort. This compelled ceremonial purification on his return, and in his ablutions as he discarded garments and washed away filth, these became deities of various grades, and the sun-goddess took form from the washings of his left eye (those from his right eye producing the moon-god). Native conceptions vary from the animistic, which induce worship of the physical sun (still to be seen), to the anthropomorphic which regards her as a deity whose sphere of control centers in the sun. She figures as a beneficent goddess whose chief care is the welfare of mankind, in the exercise of this providing them with seeds and showing them how to cultivate rice. The mirror is her emblem, and as such is in itself an object of reverence and worship, with ceremonies peculiar to itself. The sun crow, a fabulous creation, is her sacred bird and messenger (cf. the eagle-hawk of the Egyptian-Semitic-Greek deities and the ravens of Wotan or Odin). For a prayer to this deity offered in 870 A.D. cf. W. G. Ashton, *Shinto*, pp. 125–127 (London, 1905). The idea of different sun-gods for different parts of the day reappears in Japan. Waka-hirume ("young-sun-female") is the morning sun, as is also Ho-no-akari, while Ho-no-susori is the noon sun and Ho-no-wori the evening sun. Other mythical sun-gods are known, as Nigi-haya-hi ("gentle-swift-sun"), and Hiruko, the first-born of Izanagi and Izanami.

8. Western Indo-European Peoples: Among the Aryan nations of the West the cult of the sun takes a relatively unimportant place. The Greeks and Romans, it is true, were devoted to Apollo. But the mature form of this deity is the result of a long period of development, as is manifest from the diverse epithets and the variant rites employed in his worship. Amalgamation with other gods is evident, and that solar deities were among these is unquestionable. Helios (Latin, *Sol*) and Apollo were originally distinct (cf. L. R. Farnell, *Cults of the Greek States*, iv. 136 sqq., Oxford, 1907), and the merging of the two was completed only by the Romans of imperial times, so that not until the Christian era was Apollo made to ride in the chariot of the sun, and apparently not till the Roman period in Greek history did he receive the rayed crown. The identification of Helios and Apollo at the end of the second Christian century is explicitly attested by Pausanias (VII., xxiii. 8; Frazer's transl., i. 364, London, 1898), but how much earlier this had come about is uncertain. Among the gods who went into the composition of Apollo is a Cretan deity figured with rays streaming from his shoulders much like those of the Babylonian Shamash (ut sup., II., 2; cf. A. J. Evans, in *Journal of Hellenic Studies*, xxi., 1901, p. 170). The identification of Apollo had, however, been growing for centuries, and it was in part due to this phase of his being, though also to his activities as an oracle god and to his relation to music, that he was one of the most influential members of the Greco-Roman pantheon. He inspired some of the noblest productions both in art and literature (cf. the Homeric hymn to Apollo, Eng. transl. and discussion by Andrew Lang in *Homeric Hymns*, London, 1899). The early Teutons and Scandinavians undoubtedly had a cult of the sun—such antiquities as a sun chariot with six wheels and disk and horse being conclusive (cf. K. Blind, "A Prehistoric Sun-Chariot in Denmark," in *Westminster Review*, clx., 1903, pp. 552–558). Evidential also is the cycle of festivals at critical points in the year,—at the winter and summer solstices and in spring and autumn.

But the Teutonic pantheon as reflected in the Eddas and sagas seems to contain no sun-deity unless Balder be one. That he was a light-god is clear, but that he was solar is disputed.

9. Primitive Peoples : In the barbarous stage of civilization, as well as among the more advanced stages, the cult of the sun is often registered by symbolic acts which, though they do not always involve actual worship, yet are indicative of a high degree of reverence. Such are the Sioux customs of looking toward the sun when they smoke the ceremonial pipe and of presenting to him the calumet; that of the Natchez of smoking toward the east at sunrise, and that of burial of the dead facing the east as practised by Ainus, Guarayos, Yunanas, and Australians. Sometimes the evidence demonstrates worship, as is the case among many American Indian tribes which perpetuate the sun-dance, an annual ceremony performed during the first week of July. In this ceremony the sun's benefactions are remembered and he is praised as the giver of life to man and its supporter, the donor of corn and the one who makes it grow, and also as giving success in the hunt. At that time prayers are offered for continuation of his gifts and sacrifices are made to him. Primitive peoples often registered their adoration of the sun by cruel rites, especially by human sacrifice. In Central and South America the first-born was usually the sacrifice to the sun (cf. J. G. Frazer, *Golden Bough*, ii. 52 sqq., London, 1900; where cases are collected). In the Aztec region one of the great deities of the official cult was the sun-god Ometecutli ("twice lord," i.e., supreme lord), and a sort of derivative was Uitzilopochtli, the sun of spring, summer, and autumn, whose messenger was the humming bird. He was beloved, the people called themselves his children, and they delighted in praising his qualities of kindness and his benefactions. His worship was performed eight times each twenty-four hours, conducted by courses of priests. At three annual festivals his glory was celebrated, in May, August, and December. At the last was performed one of the rites which so astounded the early Roman Catholic missionaries—the making of an image of the sun-god in dough mixed with the blood of slaughtered infants, piercing it with an arrow (to typify the death of the fading sun), and then eating it in sacramental fashion. The winter sun, Tezcatlipoca, brother of Uitzilopochtli, was different in qualities, being stern where his brother was kind, a god of judgment and retribution. Among the Gonds, a Dravidian tribe of India, the sun was the chief object of worship and to him human sacrifices were offered, which were later represented by a manikin of straw. Similarly the Khonds of India offered human beings in sacrifice to him, though he was not their chief deity. The Santhals regard the sun as the highest of all spirits. Among other Dravidian tribes he was adored both as the creator and as the paradise of souls. Geo. W. Gilmore.

Bibliography: For the cult of the sun in the Semitic Egyptian-Hittite region consult: E. Renan, *Mission de Phenicie*, Paris, 1864; E. M. De Vogüé, *Mélanges d'archéologie orientale*, Paris, 1869; idem, *Syrie, Palestine, Mount Athos*, ib. 1876; C. R. Conder, in PEF, *Quarterly Statement*, 1881, 80–84; F. A. Paley, *Gold-worship in its Relation to Sun-worship*, in *Contemporary Review*, xlvi (1884)

270–277; P. Jensen, *Kosmologie der Babylonier*, pp. 108–111, Strasburg, 1890; M. Jastrow, *Religion of Babylonia and Assyria*, Boston, 1898; W. H. Ward, in *AJT*, ii (1898), 115–118; idem, *Seal Cylinders of Western Asia*, Washington, 1910; S. I. Curtiss, *Primitive Semitic Religion To-day*, New York, 1902; R. Dussaud, *Notes de mythologie syrienne*, 2 parts, Paris, 1903–05; L. Frobenius, *Das Zeitalter des Sonnengottes*, vol. i., Berlin, 1904; G. V. Schiaparelli, *Astronomy in the O. T.*, Oxford, 1906; Vollers, in *Archiv für Religionswissenschaft*, ix (1906), 176–184; A. T. Clay, *Amurru, the Home of the Northern Semites*, Philadelphia, 1910; J. Garstang, *Land of the Hittites*, New York, 1910; *DB*, iv. 627–629; *EB*, iv. 4821–22; *JE*, xi. 588–597.

For the Indo-Aryans and Eastern Asiatics consult: R. T. Griffith, *Hymns of the Rigveda*, 4 vols., Benares, 1889–1892; H. Böttger, *Sonnencult der Indogermanen . . . insbesondere der Indoteutonen*, Breslau, 1890; W. E. Griffis, *Religions of Japan*, Boston, 1895; E. W. Hopkins, *Religions of India*, Boston, 1895; R. W. Frazer, *Literary History of India*, New York, 1898; W. G. Aston, *Shinto*, chap. vii. et passim, London, 1905; L. R. Farnell, *Cults of the Greek States*, vol. iv., Oxford, 1907; and literature under BRAHMANISM; CHINA; HINDUISM; INDIA; and JAPAN.

For practises among primitive peoples consult: G. Cattin, *O-Kee-Pa; a Religious Ceremony*, Philadelphia, 1867; W. Mannhardt, *Wald- und Feldkulte*, 2 vols., Berlin, 1875–1877; A. Reville, *Native Religions of Mexico and Peru*, pp. 39 sqq., London, 1884; S. D. Peet, *Animal Worship and Sun Worship in the East and the West Compared*, in *JAOS*, 1889, pp. cclxx.–cclxxix.; D. G. Brinton, *Religions of Primitive Peoples*, pp. 138–139, New York, 1897; J. W. Fewkes, in *American Anthropologist*, xi (1898), 65–87 (on an Arizonian Indian winter solstice-ceremony); G. A. Dorsey, in *Columbian Museum Publication no. 75*, June 1, Washington, 1903; E. B. Tylor, *Primitive Culture*, London, 1903; A. L. Kroeber, *Religion of the Indians of California*, San Francisco, 1907; J. Déchelette, *Le Culte du soleil aux temps préhistoriques*, Paris, 1909.

SUNDAY.

I. History of Observance of Sunday: The earliest traces of the observance of the first day of the week in remembrance of Christ's resurrection is found in the Pauline period of the

1. The Apostolic Age. Apostolic Age. Preceding this, Christians had, after the example of Christ himself and as a continuation of the Old-Testament custom, kept the Sabbath, but with some freedom as to the method of its observance. At first daily meetings were held for the expression of thanks for salvation. But soon a movement began among gentile Christians (cf. I Cor. xvi. 2 with Acts xx. 7) to hold longer services on Sunday characterized in part by the collection of free-will offerings. The name, "the Lord's day," became a designation for it (Rev. i. 10; Ignatius, "Magnesians," ix., Eng. transl., *ANF*, i. 62; Didache, xiv.). The author of the Epistle of Barnabas (chap. xv., *ANF*, i. 147) speaks of the day as the "eighth day" and justifies its observance as celebrating the resurrection of Christ, his first appearance to the disciples, and his ascension. The day is called Sunday by Justin Martyr as commemorating the creation of light on the first day of the creation and also the awakening of Christ, the "Sun of righteousness," from the darkness of the grave. After Justin, the mention of the Lord's day as the weekly observance of the Christians becomes ever more frequent. Opposed to the claim that Christians in celebrating Sunday had indirectly appropriated a day already observed in honor of a heathen deity, it is to be considered that in addition to the motive for observing that day assigned by Justin Martyr and Barnabas, the great aversion of the early Christians to idolatry would preclude the possibility of such appropriation.

From Tertullian (*De corona*, iii., *ANF*, iii. 94) and other sources it appears that, after the Apostolic Age, since Sunday was a day of rejoicing, fasting and kneeling at prayer was not observed. Tertullian advised that the ordinary daily routine of labor be avoided, not out of respect to the Old-Testament law (Ex. xx. 8–9), but because it was in keeping with the purpose of devoting the day to a celebration of joy. This conception of

2. To the Reformation. Sunday continued for a number of centuries; as late as 538, at the Third Synod of Orléans (Hefele, *Conciliengeschichte*, ii. 778; Fr. transl., ii. 2, p. 1162; Eng. transl., iv. 208–209), the idea that meals could not be prepared on Sunday and that other like work could not be done was condemned as Jewish superstition. Sunday was first regulated by civil authority in 321, under Constantine, directing that the day be hallowed and observed appropriately. By this law juridical and industrial activities were suspended. The laws regulating Sunday observance were gradually made more comprehensive and stringent by subsequent emperors, forbidding participation in or attendance at places of public amusement and prescribing a more humane treatment of prisoners on that day. A synodical decree of 585 (canon 1, Synod of Macon; Hefele, *Conciliengeschichte*, iii. 40, Fr. transl., iii. 209, cf. note 2, Eng. transl., iv. 407) established severe punishments for the desecration of Sunday. But these strict regulations were not borrowed from Old-Testament legislation, the day being only broadly regarded as corresponding to the Old-Testament Sabbath. "Sabbath signifies rest, Sunday signifies resurrection," taught Augustine (on Ps. cl.). Not until the time of the Carolingians did the idea of substitution of Sunday for the Old-Testament Sabbath prevail in Christian Europe. Charlemagne's numerous strict Sunday regulations were explicitly based upon the Old-Testament command to keep the Sabbath day holy, and henceforth, throughout the Middle Ages, the Old-Testament idea of the Sabbath was the basis for laws regulating the observance of Sunday. And the situation in the East repeated that in the West, labor being strictly prohibited on Sunday—as by Leo the Isaurian.

After the Reformation German Protestantism turned away from the Judaizing theory back to the original conception of Sunday observ-

3. Post-Reformation Conceptions of Sunday. ance. Luther's Larger Catechism taught that one day is not essentially better than another, but that, since it is not possible to devote each day in the week to a special religious celebration, one day should be set apart for that purpose and that, to avoid the unnecessary disturbance which an innovation would occasion, it should continue to be Sunday. The Augsburg Confession (art. xxviii.) protests against the Sabbath substitution theory. However, there was not entire agreement among the early Protestants on this subject, there being a number who advocated literal adherence to the Sabbath law of the Old Testament. Others, on the contrary, held that Sunday was only a symbol of the resurrection and that no outward formal observance was required on that day. But the more commonly accepted view among Protestants sanctioned a moderately liberal observance of Sunday. Even the stringent Sunday regulations of Calvin were not the outgrowth of the substitution theory. Scotch and English Presbyterians returned to the idea that Sunday took the place of the Old-Testament Sabbath and that consequently no labor is to be permitted, the entire day being devoted to worship (Schaff, *Creeds*, i. 777–778). This doctrine found acceptance among Anglicans and had some following in Holland and Germany. However, opposition to the Puritan Sunday was present among both Anglicans and Presbyterians. In England the controversy was bitter throughout the seventeenth century. The Presbyterian theologians strongly protested against an edict of James I. in 1616 (see SPORTS, BOOK OF), allowing participation in certain pleasures on Sunday. But the edict found defenders among Anglican prelates and theologians. It may be noted that, in a revival of the dispute toward the end of that century, John Bunyan took a position favoring the freer conception of Sunday. John Milton in *On Christian Doctrine* (vol. iv. of his *Prose Works*, London, 1848–53) recorded opinions partially at variance with those of the Westminster Confession. In the controversy which was then in progress on the continent, the development of the extreme views of the anti-Sabbatarians is noteworthy. They held that Christians are not commanded to devote any particular day to a special celebration, and that everything which a Christian may do, he may do to the glory of God. Ordinary labor need not, therefore, be suspended on Sunday, provided only the hearts of the laborers are in a correct attitude toward God.

Thus three main tendencies developed regarding the observance of Sunday: the Puritanical, the extreme anti-Sabbatarian, and the moderate Lutheran. The first of these **4. Three Theories of Sunday.** positions is represented best in the strict Sunday laws of Scotland and of the New England colonies. That Sunday should be most carefully observed as a day of rest and that the State should support them in securing such an observance, was held as a fundamental right. However, there were always men of influence who opposed this view, and in America particularly the influence of the Sunday-school has tended to moderate, in some measure, the earlier Puritanical view of Sunday observance. In England there has been during the last quarter of a century, under the influence of anti-Sabbatarian and even irreligious utilitarian ideas, a reaction against the formal observance of Sunday. The Sunday League, organized July 2, 1875, at a meeting in Westminster Palace Hotel, in London, is in favor of allowing participation in harmless Sunday amusements, particularly in the larger cities. Here and there, where the influence of this organization has reached, museums, public gardens, and libraries have been opened on Sunday. A more radical tendency is that which supports public lectures on secular themes on Sunday afternoons.

In Germany there developed a strong movement about the middle of the nineteenth century in favor of a more careful observance of Sun-**5. Recent Movements in Germany.** day as a day of rest. Through a series of church conventions and by the issue of a large number of publications relating to the subject, the great extent of Sunday labor was brought to public attention, and the necessity of protecting the laborer in his right to Sunday rest. The governments of Prussia and Württemberg responded to the appeal of the Protestant church there (1850) by enforcing Sunday observance in all branches of the governmental service. The religious periodicals championed the cause with great zeal. The movement waned for a period but revived about 1874 as one of the phases of the *Kulturkampf*. In both Germany and Switzerland numerous organizations were brought into existence for the purpose of strengthening the movement, and these have been united since 1876 in an international congress. The movement has resulted in Germany in a number of recent laws enforcing the observance of Sunday as a day of rest.

(O. ZÖCKLER†.)

II. Sunday Legislation: Laws respecting Sabbath-keeping or the observing of Sunday have never been religious only, but have had also a hygienic basis. So far as the acts of observance **1. Origin and Character of the Sabbath.** have been detailed in legislation, the course prescribed has always been rest and quiet. In fact, the word " Sabbath " has never been the name of a day of the week at any time, but has always been descriptive of human conduct on the day in question. Although the spirit may be religious and distinctly Christian, the idea of physical rest and quiet is at the bottom of all the regulations in all Sunday legislation. The Mosaic annals record the command from Sinai to keep the Sabbath holy, but its details relate largely, if not wholly, to the enforcing of physical rest. It must not be assumed that these were new regulations. It was beyond doubt the writing into the Decalogue of a law previously existing and observed, whether written or unwritten. How early those regulations were first made does not appear, but it is impossible from the whole of that record to conclude otherwise than that it was a regulation for human conduct which had been given from the very origin of the human race, and that contemporary with it was the week of seven days as a division of time. So far as is known the Hebrews never had names for the days of their week, but knew them by numbers only. Aside from the Bible record, the division of time into weeks, consisting of seven days each, one of which days was by law made a rest day, appears very early in the history of oriental peoples, other than the Hebrews (see WEEK).

Upon the basis of the archeological discoveries of the last half-century it is claimed by many archeologists, with apparent justification, that the Akkadians, who inhabited North Babylonia long before the time of Abraham (see BABYLONIA,

2. The Week. V., § 1), divided time into periods of weeks, and that each week consisted of seven days, named for the sun, the moon, and five of the planets. One day of each week, or the seventh, fourteenth, nineteenth, twenty-first, and twenty-eighth days of each month, each known as *Sabatu*, was a rest day, on which all labor was unlawful, and even the king was interdicted from labor and from ordinary and royal pleasures (see WEEK). The regulations in that regard will compare in drastic repression with any of the requirements of the mythical blue-laws of Connecticut. The weekly calendar of seven days was unknown to the early Greeks. Their week consisted of ten days. The early Romans divided the year into months and the months into three unequal and varying parts, the Kalends, of thirteen to fifteen days, the Ides, of seven to nine days, and the Nones, of nine days. The Egyptians, like the Assyrians and Babylonians, were advanced astronomers, and in very remote time, but how early is not known, had their weeks of seven days each. How they came to have weeks of seven days like the Akkadians, the Assyrians, and the Babylonians is not known. Nor is it known why they also called their days for the sun, the moon, and five of the planets. This Egyptian division of time was introduced into Rome and supplanted the Roman calendar, but the time of the innovation is not certainly known; some authorities placing it in the second and others in the fourth century of the Christian era. In this Roman week of seven days, one day was named for the sun, and called "day of the sun." It is clear that this naming it after the sun was wholly distinct from and unconnected with the worship of the sun or of Apollo, who, in Greek, and later in Roman, mythology represented the sun, and was worshiped in Greece on the seventh day of each month, and in Rome on a like day, and not on the first day of the week of seven days, the day in the calendar named for the sun. With the progress of the Greek armies under Alexander many oriental customs disappeared, and with the destruction of the Jewish nation and the supremacy of the Roman empire, the general and open keeping of the Mosaic law as to Sabbath observance ended, though the Jews privately continued the observance.

Not until the Christian religion had made its converts throughout the Roman Empire, and the body of Christians had become so great as to be an element to be reckoned with, does legislation concerning the rest day again recur. The Christians had passed through the throes of persecution, and had been deprived of property and of civil rights. Constantine had ruled in Gaul and

3. Roman Legislation for Sunday. Britain, where he had ameliorated the conditions for Christians. And when he came to power in 313 A.D., he was joined by Maxentius in the celebrated edict of Milan, by which civil rights were accorded to Christians, their property restored, and general religious liberty guaranteed to all. In 321 A.D. Constantine, having become sole emperor, issued his famous edict, prohibiting certain labor and trades on Sunday. ("Let all magistrates and people of the city, and all who work as artisans, rest on the venerable day of the sun"; text and transl. of the edict given in Schaff, *Christian Church*, iii. 380, note 1). Exceptions follow as to farmers and vine-growers, who might otherwise lose their crops. However one may strain not to see in this edict of the Roman emperor any recognition of the religious element or of Christian rites, it remains clear that it was not the inauguration of a feast to the sun, or to Apollo the heathen representative of the sun, for it was not Apollo's day. Apollo never was worshiped on the first day of the week, nor on the seventh day of the week, but upon the seventh day of the month, which was his festal day. It is also beyond dispute that it was a setting apart by law for the first time of the first day of the week as a *festum*, or feast day, which day was then kept holy only by Christians, who observed it as a rest day as well as a day of worship. By the edict of Constantine the keeping of the day in the same manner as Christians kept it was enjoined by making physical labor unlawful on that day. Sixty-six years later, 387 A.D., in another Roman decree, Sunday is called "The Lord's Day." This constitutes legal recognition of the Christian name for the day, used by Christians from the middle of the first century. In 392 A.D., another Roman decree forbade on that day all exhibitions that might turn away attendance from the mysteries of the Christian religion. The Sunday legislation of the Roman empire never went backward. The decrees of Valens, Valentinian I., Gratian, Valentinian II., Theodosius the Great, Honorius, Arcadius, Theodosius II., Leo I., and Athenius, between 364 and 467, added other inhibitions, but also made from time to time exemption from certain prohibitions of the law. In the time of Justinian 685 A.D., the laws of the empire on the subject were gathered into the codes, which contained the law of the Roman empire, and from the year 800, when Charlemagne was crowned, this code was of force and effect all over the "Holy Roman Empire," that "complex Frankish empire," a State composed of many states. During the Middle Ages there were decrees and canons of popes and of councils concerning the observance of Sunday, which, though ecclesiastical, were of civil force because enforced by the civil power.

It would seem that English Sunday legislation got its impulse and initiative from the Christian religion. Such early statutes as are known followed the advent of Augustine in England and the conversion of the Saxon kings to Christianity. They appear as early as the Heptarchy. Ina reigned king of Wessex from 688 to his abdication in 725.

4. Early English Legislation. He began as a warrior, then became a statesman and law-giver, and died a religious recluse. When he had added much to his kingdom by war upon his neighbors he gave a code of laws, known as the " West Saxon code," in which was a law for observance of Sunday which prohibited all work on that day. In the east of England, the kingdom of Kent, the home of Augustine and the field of his success, it is strange that there is no earlier record of Sunday laws. Perhaps ecclesiastical canons were deemed enough. But in the time of Withred, king of Kent, in 696, a statute was enacted forbidding labor from Saturday at sunset to Sunday at sunset. This recalls an early New England custom as to the beginning and ending of Sunday observance. The same law made free the slave who worked on Sunday by his lord's command, and enslaved the free man who worked without his lord's command. Other severe penalties are mentioned. In 747 Eidelbald, king of the Mercians, enacted the observance of the Lord's day by all, and forbade all business, journeys, and meetings. Before 900, Alfred, king of Wessex, and " over-lord " of the Saxon kingdom of England, had enacted a law for Sunday observance. Earlier than 930, the kingdom of the West Saxons and Mercia having been united, Athelstan the king, also " over-lord " of the other kingdoms, by his statute forbade all merchandizing on the Lord's day. Edgar, king of the same realm 959–975, enacted a further Sunday law forbidding Sunday trading, folkmotes (meetings of the people), heathen songs, and devils games on that day, and he is said to have enacted that Sunday began at three on Saturday afternoon and continued until daybreak of Monday. Ethelred, king of the same kingdom 978–1016, enacted that all " hunting bouts," trafficking, courts, and worldly works were forbidden on Sunday; yet allowed courts to sit on occasions of necessity. Canute, the first Danish king of England, came to that throne in 1017, and reenacted Sunday laws forbidding hunting and worldly work on Sunday, and also marketing, except for necessity, and forbade capital punishment on that day. The Saxon dynasty was restored in 1040, and Edward the Confessor about 1056 enlarged the Sunday law of Canute. Lord Mansfield, in a decision of a lawsuit (Swann vs. Browne, 3 Burrow, 1599) which involved the question whether a court could make a valid judgment on a Sunday, is authority for the statement that both William the Conqueror and Henry II. ratified and confirmed the canons of the councils of Tribury and Saint Medoro and the ordinances of Edward the Confessor as to Sunday observance, and decreed that the codes of Justinian on Sunday observance were the law of England. Successive acts of parliament on Sunday observance became the law of England (e.g.: 1354 A.D., the 28th of Edward II., chapter 14; 1388 A.D., the 12th of Richard II., chapter 6; 1410 A.D., the 11th of Henry IV., chapter 7; 1428 A.D., the 6th of Henry VI., chapter 3; 1449 A.D., the 27th of Henry VI., chapter 5; 1464 A.D., the 4th of Edward IV., chapter 7; 1552 A.D., the 6th of Edward VI., chapter 3; 1603 A.D., the 1st of James I., chapter 25; 1625 A.D., the 1st of Charles I., chapter 7; 1627 A.D., the 3d of Charles I., chapter 1).

The Puritan ideas obtained ascendency in England and in 1676 A.D., 29 Charles II., chapter 7, was enacted. This statute was the most comprehensive and severe and the most detailed of any English Sunday law. Its purpose as expressed in its title was for " the better observa-

5. Legislative Results of Puritanism. tion and keeping holy of the Lord's Day, commonly called Sunday." It enacts the careful execution of all existing laws relating to the Lord's day; commands exercises public and private of piety and of religion on that day; forbids all labor, work, or business of ordinary calling, works of charity or necessity alone excepted, but exempts children; forbids the crying or exposing for sale of wares, merchandise, fruit, herbs, goods, or chattels on pain of forfeiture; forbids travel by horse or boat, except as allowed by a magistrate; relieves the parish of responsibility for robbery of a Sunday traveler; makes void all service of legal writs or proceedings, except in case of treason, murder, and breach of the peace; but its provisions are not to apply to dressing of meats in private families, or in inns, cook or victualing houses, for such as can not be otherwise provided; also the crying and selling of milk before 9 A.M. and after 3 P.M. This statute has been practically the law of England ever since. It has been modified in particulars and exceptions, and other regulations have been made by subsequent statutes, but the law remains substantially the same to-day. At the time of the American Revolution the statute of Charles II. had been for more than 100 years the law of England and of its colonies. With this history of Sunday legislation in England for more than 900 years (from 747), the Puritans came to America. They came with the traditions, civil and religious, of the mother country, particularly those which developed with the Reformation in England; their colonial regulations as to Sunday-keeping therefore could not fail of such influence. To their account has been laid the fabulous " blue-laws," the reports concerning which were an exaggeration of the facts and ridiculous in some things as applying to dumb beasts and inanimate objects. It is, however, true that there were colonial laws on the subject of Sunday-keeping which partook strongly of the religious spirit of the English laws on the same subject and that of the English Puritans who settled the colonies. They were enacted in Massachusetts Bay Colony. The Dutch authorities of the West India Colony enacted Sunday laws for the New Netherlands in 1641, 1647, 1656, 1657, and 1663. In 1665 the " duke's laws " (duke of York's laws) took effect in the English colony of New York, and they contained a provision against profaning Sunday; colonial statutes for preventing desecration of Sunday were enacted also by the general assembly of that colony in 1685, and again in 1695, which were in effect at the time of the American Revolution. When the independence of the American colonies was proclaimed, the continental congress called upon the colonies (then called states), each for itself to frame and adopt a constitution, and these constitutions all recognized liberty of conscience and freedom of worship, and also the God of the Christian, and obligation to him for all benefits. These features have been retained in the subsequent amended constitutions of the original thirteen states as well as in the constitutions of all the states later admitted into the union, until in the constitutions of all but one of the American states God and the true religion are recognized, and in twenty of them his worship is guaranteed, and in not one is any other worship guaranteed. It matters not that the federal constitution forbidding establishment of religion as a legal national institution has not " God " written in it, for that constitution is but an instrument to provide a union of the several states, all but one of which constitutionally recognizes God. And yet Sunday laws have been enacted by congress, which has forbidden the pursuit of studies at the military and naval academies on Sunday.

With such origins for the founders, such traditions for its settlers, such laws of the mother country in force in the colonies, and such recognition of the true God in the constitution of the

6. Legisla- states, it would have been strange
tion in the indeed if in the legislation of the states
Several laws for observance of Sunday had not
States. been enacted. In the several original
states, and in the many states admitted from time to time, Sunday laws followed until in all the states of the American Union except one (and that on the western frontier) laws have been enacted for the observance of Sunday, not as a day of worship, but as a day of rest and quiet. In New York they appear as early as 1788. They are not uniform in language but agree in substance, forbidding by some formula labor and work and business on that day, except for necessity or charity. Some of them limit prohibition to work, labor, or business for profit or amusement, or to secular work, and in most states make the fulfilling of a contract on Sunday unlawful, and in some the making of a contract; also the serving of legal process, or the holding of courts. In many states all noise and disorderly conduct are prohibited; also sports for purposes of money-making through admission fees. There is often in these statutes such a recognition of others who continually observe another day as holy time, as permits such to pursue their labor or calling, but in such manner as shall not disturb the quiet, repose, or worship of those who regard Sunday as a holy day. These laws have not always preserved the original language, but have from time to time been amended. Attacks are continually made upon these statutes principally on the ground that they are unconstitutional, but the laws have been uniformly upheld by the courts of the several states and by the supreme court of the United States. These attacks have come almost exclusively from Seventh Day Baptists and Jews, who have never proposed to make any other day a rest day, but have proposed only to destroy the rest day of Sunday.

But Sunday legislation in modern times has not been confined to Christian England or Christian America. The Code of Justinian remained the law of the territory of the Roman empire until legally

abrogated. Its provisions as to observance of Sunday may have become obsolete and disregarded, but the influence of the Church and
7. Condi- the decrees of councils and popes have
tions in kept it in force. It may with the
Europe. political changes and the social changes
of medieval and modern times have ceased to be observed, but the law remained, enforced or unenforced. In modern times the Sunday legislation of the countries of continental Europe has gone forward. In **France** such legislation has had a varying history. In 1793 the convention abolished the week of seven days, and with it Sunday, and all other then and now known names for days, substituting a week of ten days. The seven-day week with its names of days was restored under Napoleon. Since then, in the history of that people during the struggles with the Roman Catholic Church and with rationalism and atheism there have been attacks upon everything that has religious relationship, and hence upon Sunday-keeping. The excess of this virulence brought all workmen to demand one rest day in seven, and in 1906 a law was enacted requiring a rest of one day in seven for all workmen, preferably on Sunday, but not requiring it on that day; in practise, however, Sunday was the choice. In **Belgium**, after many years of discussion and agitation, in 1905 a law was enacted guaranteeing one day of rest in each week to all workmen, but it does not require closing of shops. In **Holland** since 1815 Sunday rest has been required by law. The statute is religious in character, and includes so many exceptions that it does not command the loyal obedience of the people. In **Germany** the claim is that after the Franco-Prussian war the German Emperor William I. was sympathetic toward Sunday legislation, but that Bismarck opposed it on the ground that the closing of factories would increase the consumption of beer on the idle day, cause deterioration in physique, and tend to disorder. No progress was made until in the reign of William II. a great reform was commenced, and in 1892 laws were enacted for what is called Sabbath rest in commerce, and Sabbath rest in industry, reducing hours of work on Sunday to five hours after 7 A.M. The hours from 9 to 11 A.M. were earlier protected for public worship. These laws, however, gave some discretion to municipalities as to limitations of the hours, and the result has been a lack of uniformity of application. In **Norway** labor in factories, opening of drinking-shops from 6 P.M. of Saturday to 8 A.M. of Monday, and the printing and publishing of newspapers are unlawful. In **Sweden** buying and selling are unlawful, and public places of amusement must be closed on Sunday. In **Russia** in 1906 a Sunday law was enacted restricting labor engaged in industry or commerce on Sunday and on holidays. The enforcement is another question. **Greece** and **Servia** are without Sunday legislation. **Rumania** enacted a Sunday law in 1907, which was abrogated the next year, and now has no Sunday statute. The dual empire of **Austria-Hungary** has for twenty-five years been struggling with the matter of Sunday legislation, and the latest statute enacted in Austria in 1905 provides for a Sabbath in commerce,

limiting work from four to six hours. In **Hungary**, since 1891, there has been a Sunday rest law. In **Switzerland**, consisting of several independent cantons united for limited purposes, the State lacks uniformity in Sunday laws. Five of the cantons have laws requiring rest in commerce. This country is such a resort of tourists that no law could be obtained to limit Sunday as regards their entertainment and amusement. In **Italy** in 1907 a Sunday law was enacted by which labor must cease and shops must be closed after noon on Sunday. In **Spain** in 1904 a Sunday law was enacted, but has since been very much changed. Bull fights on Sunday were unlawful, but the popular clamor for that brutal sport compelled the modification of the law to permit restoration of bull fights on Sunday. **Portugal** has a Sunday law, but it is practically ignored. In **Turkey** the Mohammedan keeps Friday as his Sabbath; the Jew, Saturday; the Christian, Sunday. This land has many of all these peoples, and to require physical rest or business suspension for all three would leave but four days in the week for other than religious duties. Hence, no Sunday legislation exists or can exist in the Ottoman empire.

From this survey, it is impossible to avoid the conclusion that, although the manner of Sunday-keeping is physical rest and quiet for one day in seven, yet the general and exclusive choice of Sunday for that time of rest, is due to the influence of the Christian religion. Although observation may show that Christian religious and hygienic requirements are not loyally observed and enforced by all, this does not contradict the teaching of history that its provisions are Christian. All attacks upon these laws are in violation of the best interests and assail the health and manhood of the people. Such attacks are mainly commercial, aiming to destroy any rest day whatever, and never aim to substitute another day of rest for the Sunday of rest.

RALPH E. PRIME.

BIBLIOGRAPHY: For the Sabbath as a Hebrew institution see SABBATH. On the history, theory, and ethics of Sunday observance consult. Bingham, *Origines*, XX., ii.-iii., cf. XVI., viii.; A. J. Binterim, *Denkwürdigkeiten*, vol. v., part 1, Mainz, 1829; G. Holden, *The Christian Sabbath*, London, 1825; D. Wilson, *The Divine Authority and Perpetual Obligation of the Lord's Day*, ib. 1830; J. J. Gurney, *Brief Remarks on the History, Authority, and Use of the Sabbath*, ib. 1831; J. E. Volbeding, *Thesaurus commentationum selectarum*, vol. i., Leipsic, 1847 (collects tracts by C. C. L. Francke, J. B. Albert, and D. H. Arnoldt); P. J. Proudhon, *De la célébration du dimanche*, Paris, 1848; G. Huyssen, *Die Feste der christlichen Kirche*, 2 vols., Iserlohn, 1850–59; W. B. Barter, *Tracts in Defense of the Sabbath and the Church*, London, 1851; E. W. Hengstenberg, *Der Tag des Herrn*, Berlin, 1852, Eng. transl., *The Lord's Day*, London, 1852; J. T. Baylee, *History of the Sabbath*, London, 1857; W. L. Fisher, *History of the Institution of the Sabbath Day, its Uses and Abuses*, 2d ed., Philadelphia, 1859; J. N. Andrews, *History of the Sabbath and First Day of the Week*, Battle Creek, Mich., 1887, London, 1861; N. L. Rice and others, *The Christian Sabbath: its History, Authority, Duties, Benefits, and Civil Relations*, New York, 1863; R. Cox, *The Literature of the Sabbath Question*, 2 vols., Edinburgh, 1865; J. Gilfillan, *The Sabbath*, ib. 1861, New York, 1865; W. Milligan, *The Decalogue and the Lord's Day in the Light of the General Relation of the Old and New Testament*, Edinburgh, 1866, J. S. Stone, *The Divine Rest; or, Scriptural Views of the Sabbath*, New York, 1867; G. Uhlhorn, *Die Sonntagsfrage in ihrer sozialen Bedeutung*, Leipsic, 1870; T. Hayem, *Le*

Repos hebdomadaire, Paris, 1873; T. Lefort, *Du report hebdomadaire au point de vue de la morale, de la culture intellectuelle et du progrès de l'industrie*, ib. 1873; C. M. Davies, *Unorthodox London*, pp. 51–52, 2 vols., London, 1873–76; *Orthodox London*, vol. i. passim, ib. 1873; E. Wetzel, *Ueber den Ursprung der christlichen Sonntagsfeier*, Stettin, 1874; A. Eschenauer, *Le Repos du dimanche au point de vue hygiénique*, Paris, 1876; E. Naville, *La Loi du dimanche du point de vue social et religieux*, Geneva, 1876; M. Rieger, *Staat und Sonntag*, Frankfort, 1877; A. Vinet, *Le Sabbat juif et le dimanche chrétien*, new ed., Lausanne, 1877; K. Rohr, *Der Sonntag; sein göttl. und menschl. Recht*, Schaffhausen, 1878; T. Zahn, *Geschichte des Sonntags vornehmlich in der alten Kirche*, Hanover, 1878; A. Haegler, *Le Dimanche au point de vue hygiénique et social*, Basel, 1879; R. Lauterburg, *Die Sonntagsarbeit in den grossen Industrien*, Bern, 1880; P. Niemeyer, *Der Sonntag vom hygienischen Standpunkt*, Heidelberg, 1880; L. B. Bacon, *The Sabbath Question*, New York, 1882; R. L. Dabney, *The Christian Sabbath; its Nature, Design, and proper Observance*, Philadelphia, 1882; M. J. Fuller, *The Lord's Day; or, Christian Sunday; its Unity, History, Philosophy, and perpetual Obligation*, London, 1883; A. J. Sessions, *The Lord's Day Rescued*, Boston, 1884; W. F. Crafts, *The Sabbath for Man. A Study of the Origin, Obligation, History and present State of the Sabbath Observance*, New York, 1885; *Eight Studies in the Lord's Day*, Boston, 1885; G. Elliott, *The Abiding Sabbath: an Argument for the perpetual Obligation of the Lord's Day*, New York, 1885; W. W. Everts, *The Sabbath: its Permanence, Promise, and Defence*, ib. 1885; J. Plath, *Der Sonntag, das Geschenk Gottes an die Welt*, Berlin, 1885; A. E. Waffle, *The Lord's Day; its universal and perpetual Obligation*, Philadelphia, 1885; A. M. Weston, *The Evolution of a Shadow; or, The Bible Doctrine of Rest*, Cincinnati, 1886; H. A. Köstlin, *Geschichte des christlichen Gottesdienstes*, Freiburg, 1887; T. Hamilton, *Our Rest-Day; its Origin, History, and Claims with special Reference to present-day Needs*, new ed., Edinburgh and New York, 1888; A. A. Gieguel des Touches, *Le Dimanche chez les nations protestantes*, Paris, 1889; U. Grimelund, *Die Geschichte des Sonntags*, Gütersloh, 1889; J. A. Hessey, *Sunday, its Origin, History, and Present Obligations*, 5th ed., London, 1889; J. Schwab, *The Sabbath in History*, St. Joseph, Mo., 1890; W. Spiers, *The Sabbath made for Man: an Inquiry into the Origin and History of the Sabbath Institution with a Consideration of its Claims upon the Christian, the Church, and the Nation*, London, 1890; E. J. Waggoner, *Sunday: Origin of its Observance*, ib. 1891; S. E. Warren, *The Sunday Question; or, The Lord's Day: its Sacredness, Permanence, and Value as shown by its Origin, History and Use*, Boston, 1891; J. O. Bittenger, *A Plea for the Sabbath and for Man. With Discussions of Social Problems*, ib. 1892; D. Campbell, *The Puritan in Holland, England and America*, London, 1892; A. M. Earle, *The Sabbath in Puritan New England*, ib. 1892; O. Henke, *Der Sabbatismus. Eine judaistische Reliquie in der christlichen Kirche*, 3d ed., Barmen, 1892; R. Linklater, editor, *The Lord's Day and the Holy Eucharist. Treated in a Series of Essays by various Authors*, New York, 1892; R. A. Morgan, *Bible Teaching; or, The Sanctification of one Day in Seven*, London, 1892; L. Thomas, *Le Jour du Seigneur*, 2 vols., Geneva, 1892; G. Guirey, *The Hallowed Day*, New York, 1893; S. J. Du Toit, *De Leerstukken der Sabbattariers*, Paarl, 1893; G. Godet, *Le Bon Droit du dimanche*, Neuchâtel, 1894; C. Büttner, *Die Sonntagsruhe im Gewerbebetrieb und im Handelsgewerbe* Leipsic, 1895; M. Werner, *Die Sonntagsruhe in Industrie und Handwerk*, 3d ed., Berlin, 1895; W. de L. Love, *Sabbath and Sunday*, Chicago, 1896; M. von Nathusius, *Die Mitarbeit der Kirche an der Lösung der sozialen Frage*, Leipsic, 1897; T. de Vries, *Overheid en Zondagsviering*, Leyden, 1899; J. R. Milne, *Primitive Christianity and Sunday Observance*, Norwich, 1900; S. W. Gamble, *Sunday the True Sabbath of God*, Cincinnati, 1901; H. R. Gamble, *Sunday and the Sabbath*, New York, 1902; F. Meyrick, *Sunday Observance*, London, 1902; W. B. Trevelyan, *Sunday*, New York, 1902; L. Duchesne, *Christian Worship, its Origin and Evolution*, pp. 47, 78, 228, 494, 549, London, 1904, A. Barry, *The Christian Sunday*, ib. 1905; A. W. Streane, *Sabbath and Sunday historically Considered*, New York, 1906, R. J. Floody, *Scientific Basis of Sabbath and Sunday: a new Investigation after the Manner and Methods of Modern Science, revealing the true Origin and Evolution of the Jewish Sabbath and the Lord's Day*, 2d ed., Boston, 1907; *World's Rest Day. Being an Account of the Thirteenth International Congress on the Lord's Day, held at Edinburgh 6th to 8th Oct.*, 1908, Edinburgh, 1909; A. E. Main, *Bible Studies on the Sabbath Question*, Alfred, New York, 1910; W. B. Dana, *A Day for Rest and Worship; its Origin, Development, and Present-day Meaning*, ib., 1911; *DCA*, ii. 1042–1056; *DB*, iii. 138–141, iv. 317–323; *EB*, iii. 2813–16; *JE*, x. 587–605; *DCG*, i. 251–253, ii. 540–542; Schaff, *Christian Church*, i. 476–480, ii. 201–205.

For Sunday laws consult: *Codex Theodosianus*, ed. T. Mommsen, Berlin, 1905; *Blue Laws of New Haven Colony . . . Connecticut: Quaker Laws of Plymouth and Massachusetts: Blue Laws of New York, Maryland, Virginia, and South Carolina*, Hartford, 1838; *Blue Laws of Con-*

necticut from the Code of 1650 and Public Records Previous to 1655, 5th ed., New York, 1904; H. Kingsbury, *The Sabbath: a Brief History of Laws, Petitions, Remonstrances, and Reports, with Facts and Arguments relating to the Christian Sabbath*, ib. 1840; J. H. Rigg, *The Sabbath and the Sabbath Law*, London, 1881; E. Beavan, *History of the Welsh Sunday Closing Act*, Cardiff, 1885; L. A. Govett, *The King's Book of Sports*, London, 1890; G. E. Harris, *A Treatise on Sunday Laws. The Sabbath. The Lord's Day, its History and Observance, Civil and Criminal*, Rochester, 1892; A. H. Lewis, *A Critical History of Sunday Legislation*, new ed., New York, 1902; R. C. Wylie, *Sabbath Laws in the U. S.*, Pittsburg, 1905; H. E. Young, *Sunday Laws. Paper in Proceedings of Third Annual Meeting of American Bar Association; Documents 29, 41, 46, etc., of New York Sabbath Committee*.

SUNDAY-SCHOOLS.

The Sunday-school may be defined as an assembly of persons grouped in classes, with teachers, on the Lord's Day, for the study of the Bible, for moral and religious instruction, and for the worship of God. The modern Sunday-school grew out of a movement to provide religious instruction for poor and neglected children, near the close of the eighteenth century. In its present popular form, it seeks to teach and to train all whom it can reach in the performance of the duties owing to God and to neighbor, as these duties are set forth in the Jewish and Christian Scriptures.

I. History. 1. Early Religious Instruction: Religious instruction of the young and the unlearned has, from the earliest history of the human race, been recognized as a sacred duty. In early times all primary instruction centered in the family, the father was teacher and priest of the household (Gen. xviii. 19). The more advanced education was, however, often provided in connection with temples, indicating how large a place religion had in the nations of great antiquity. The recent explorations in Babylonia, as at Sippara and Nippur, have not only shown that fully equipped schools existed in the days of Abraham and earlier, but they have also made known the methods of those schools, since multitudes of tablets have been found giving varied forms of school exercises of pupils, illustrating the pedagogical methods in the schools of Chaldea and Babylonia when Abraham and his fathers were children. Hymns and religious texts formed part of the extensive equipment used. Among the Semitic peoples, religious instruction in accord with school methods, therefore, was known and practised long before Abraham's day,

(margin: 1. Early Ethnic Religious Training.)

and the glimpses of the fact which appear in the Hebrew narratives, reveal its existence, and come out unmistakably in the record of the " first " and great commandment (Deut. vi. 4–9). And these are unexpectedly and signally confirmed by the school-tablets found in Babylonia and by a law of Hammurabi (see HAMMURABI AND HIS CODE), forbidding a lost child's recovery by its parents, when adopted and " taught " a handicraft or trade by its foster-father (§§ 188–189; Eng. transl. in *DB*, Extra Volume, p. 605).

Faithful religious instruction of the young was given by Abraham, with military training (Gen. xiv. 14; cf. Job i. 5), and was enjoined in the observance of the Passover. The Mosaic law required children and adults to come together before the Lord at certain seasons to hear the law, and to have it explained, in addition to the instruction given in the family (Deut. xxxi. 10–13; Josh. viii. 34, 35). Joshua gathered the people at Gerizim and Ebal, where the law of God was impressively proclaimed anew. The prophets, from Samuel to Elijah and Elisha, promoted religious instruction, teaching the people God's will, besides maintaining the so-called " schools " of the prophets. Jehoshaphat appointed a royal educational commission to reestablish systematic religious instruction throughout the Hebrew nation, and a similar effort was made by Josiah (II Chron. xvii. 7–9, xxxiv. 30–33). In like manner Ezra gathered the people with the children into a national Bible assembly or school, wherein the priests taught and explained the meaning of the law of God, similar to modern methods of school instruction. In New-Testament times, schools for relig-

(margin: 2. Hebrew and Jewish Religious Education.)

ious instruction were held in connection with Jewish synagogues in every city and important village of Palestine. These schools were part of an extended system of religious instruction. Lightfoot finds four kinds of schools and teaching among the Jews: (1) the elementary school; (2) the teaching of the synagogue; (3) the higher schools, as those of Hillel and Shammai; and (4) the Sanhedrin, which was a great school, as well as the great judicatory of the nation. Some have questioned the prevalence of elementary schools in the time of Christ's childhood; but, according to the Talmud, synagogue schools were of earlier origin, and had then become common. They used the Hebrew Scriptures, and, later, little parchment rolls prepared for children. The Mishna says, "At five years of age let children begin the Scripture, at ten the Mishna, and at thirteen, let them be subjects of the law." In this period a synagogue presupposed a school, as now a church implies a Sunday-school. Hence the Church and Sunday-school, not the Church and district-school, parallel the Jewish system. The methods in these schools were not unlike those of the modern Sunday-school. Questions were freely asked and answered, and opinions stated and discussed. Such a Jewish Bible school, no doubt, Jesus entered in the temple when twelve years old. Paul was "brought up at the feet of Gamaliel," a phrase which implies the customary posture of Jewish students at a school. The apostolic age was remarkable for the activity of these schools. Every town having ten men, giving themselves to divine things, was to have a synagogue; and every place having twenty-five boys, or, according to Maimonides, 125 families, was compelled to appoint a teacher, and for forty or fifty boys, two teachers. In the apostolic period teachers were a recognized body of workers quite distinct from pastors, prophets, and evangelists (I Cor. xii. 28, 29; Eph. iv. 11; Heb. v. 12). The special work of teachers in the apostolic church was to instruct the young and the inexperienced in religion and in the way of salvation through Jesus Christ.

The Christian schools were founded upon the plan of the Jewish synagogue schools. These schools or catechetical classes were to aid in preparing new converts for full church membership, and also were an important means of instructing the young and the worldly in the knowledge of God, and of salvation through Jesus Christ. Thus in the fourth century A.D., Gregory the Illuminator (see ARMENIA, III., § 2) founded Bible schools for the children throughout Armenia. The sixth general council at Constantinople (680 A.D.) required the presbyters to hold schools in country towns and villages, to teach all children sent to them without pay or reward, except as parents made them a voluntary present. Schools were effective and aggressive missionary agencies of the early churches, and are aptly termed the Sunday-schools of the first ages of Christianity. They were graded, the pupils being divided into two, three, and four classes, according to their proficiency. They committed passages of Scripture, and were taught the doctrines concerning God creation, providence, sacred history, the fall, the

3. Early Christian Schools.

incarnation, the resurrection, and future rewards and punishments. Their books were portions of the Bible, sometimes in verse, Old-Testament history and antiquities, sacred poems, and dialogues. When the ecclesiastical spirit overcame the apostolic and Gospel teaching, the study of the Bible was largely displaced by ritual ceremonies and priestly confessionals. A few faithful continued to teach the Bible, as the Waldenses and the Lollards.

Classes and schools for the religious instruction of the young were among the agencies recognized as indispensable by the Protestant Reformers. "Christian schools must be established and maintained," declared Luther, "for God maintains the church through the schools." He prepared Biblical catechisms and lessons for such schools in 1529. Calvin in 1536 issued similar catechisms in fifty-eight sections, for teaching the young in Geneva. Alarmed by the spread of the Reformation, which he strenuously opposed, Carlo Borromeo (q.v.), archbishop of Milan, gathered boys and girls for religious instruction. He separated them into two divisions, and grouped them into large classes, with a priest aided by a layman for the boys, and a matron for the girls, that they might be taught the doctrines and discipline of the Roman Catholic Church. Similar schools were established throughout his diocese by the cooperation of bishops, priests, and the Jesuits, the instruction aiming to hold the people to the Roman Catholic faith and to prevent them from accepting the Reformer's doctrines and instructions from the Bible. The religious instruction in Borromeo's schools was concentrated chiefly upon the Church's decrees and confessions, while that of the Reformers was upon Christ and the Bible. The way was further prepared for the modern Sunday-school movement by the labors of Zwingli, Beza, Melanchthon, Spener, Francke, and Zinzendorf (qq.v.) on the continent; and in Great Britain by John Knox, Baxter (qq.v.), and the English and Scottish Reformers, who recognized the school as a part of the divinely appointed mission of the Church. Luther would "that nobody be chosen as a minister if he were not before this a school-master." The Heidelberg Catechism declared as a requirement of the fourth commandment "that the ministry of the Gospel and the schools be maintained." The first Scottish general assembly directed that the second of the two public services on every Lord's Day be given to worship, and the catechizing of the young and ignorant. The Church of England as early as 1603 required "every person, vicar, or curate, upon every Sunday and holiday, for half an hour or more, to instruct the young and ignorant in the ten commandments, the articles of belief, and in the Lord's Prayer." In America early Protestant settlers regarded it as a duty of the Church and the State to maintain schools wherein religion and the Bible were taught. Some form of catechetical and religious instruction, therefore, widely prevailed in connection with the Protestant and Reformed Churches of Europe and America for more than a century before the origin of the modern popular movement. The religious influence of the schools, it is true, declined in the seventeenth and eighteenth

4. Schools in the Reformation Era.

centuries, but it was partly because the school method was misused or neglected, and greater emphasis was laid upon proclaiming and preaching than upon interlocutory teaching of the Gospel. Religion and morals suffered a sad decline in consequence. Great and godly men saw and lamented their mistakes in this respect. Thus Bishop Joseph Hall (q.v.), Henry More (d. 1687), and George Herbert (q.v.) placed catechizing in the forefront for effectively planting the Gospel in the minds of men. John Owen (d. 1683) declared that "more knowledge is ordinarily diffused among the young and ignorant by one hour's catechetical exercise, than by many hours' continual discourse."

These facts account for the fact that many places claimed to have had Sunday-schools previous to those in Gloucester, England. Among the many worthy instances only a few can be noticed. It is claimed that Sunday-schools were begun in Scotland by John Knox about 1560; in Bath, England, 1660, by Joseph Alleine; in Roxbury, Mass., 1674; in Norwich, Conn., 1676; in Plymouth, Mass., 1680; in Newton, N. Y., 1683; by Bishop Frampton, England, 1693; in Glasgow, Scotland, 1707; by the Schwenckfelders, in Pennsylvania, 1734; in Bethlehem, Conn., by Joseph Bellamy, 1740; in Ephrata, Pa., by Ludwig Häcker, 1740—a school giving gratuitous instruction, holding children's meetings and blessed by many conversions, maintained for thirty years among German Seventh Day Baptists, and broken up by the war of independence; in Philadelphia, Pa., by Mrs. Greening, 1744; in Norham, Scotland, by Rev. W. Morrison, 1757; in Brechin, Scotland, by Rev. David Blair, 1760; in Catterick, England, by Rev. T. Lindsey, 1763; by Rev. E. Wheelock, Columbia, Conn., 1763; by Miss Harrison, Bedale, England, 1765; by Oberlin, at Walbach, 1767; by Miss Hannah Ball, High Wycombe, England, 1769; by W. Galt, Doagh, County Antrim, Ireland, 1770; by Rev. J. W. Moffatt, Nailsworth, England, 1772; by Dr. Kennedy, Bright, County Down, Ireland, 1774; by Kinderman, in Bohemia, 1773; by A. Crompton, Little Levers, near Bolton, England, 1775; by David Simpson, Macclesfield, England, 1778; and by many others in the decade, 1770 to 1780. These were, in some cases, catechetical schools and classes, giving religious instruction, yet not wholly parallel with the methods of the modern Sunday-school as devoted to the study of the Bible.

5. Anticipations of Modern Sunday-school.

2. Modern Sunday-schools: The pioneer schools mentioned above, were isolated, often with catechisms as the chief text-books. They did not arouse popular interest, nor did they come into affiliation one with another, tending toward organized movement or toward a system of religious instruction, with the Holy Scriptures as the chief text-book. Of this great movement Robert Raikes, Jr. (q.v.), is justly called the founder. He was editor and proprietor of the *Gloucester Journal*, Gloucester, England, and a strange mixture of the "dandy" and of the reformer. Before he was of age, he began visiting the two prisons of Gloucester, to relieve the horrors of prison life, and to reform the prisoners.

1. The Raikes Schools.

His sympathies were widened, his charity deepened; his failures in prison reform set him thinking, until he reached the conclusion that "vice is preventable." Twenty-five years later, when he was forty-four years of age, he began a "new experiment," as he called it, of "botanizing in human nature." Going into the suburbs of the city, where many youths were employed in the factories, his heart was touched by the groups of ragged, wretched, cursing children. He knew their parents, homes, and habits; none ever entered the house of God. It was useless to appeal to such parents. He had tried to reform adults and had failed. George Whitefield had tried to reach the masses in Gloucester, but with meager results. Raikes was moved, therefore, to apply his maxim that "vice is preventable." "Begin with the child, for idleness is the parent of vice," and "ignorance is the cause of idleness"; therefore, "begin by instructing the child." These seem like trite statements now, but they were the result of long, deep thought by Raikes. Here was his mission. And the Rev. Thomas Stock, headmaster of the Cathedral School, whom he met in his walk, was the man to help him. He started his first Sunday-school in Sooty Alley in 1780, paying Mrs. Meredith for teaching the wretched little street children, whom he persuaded to come to her kitchen for instruction. Mrs. Meredith found the boys "terrible bad," and soon the pupils were transferred to Mrs. Mary Critchley's in Southgate Street, whose house extended to Grey Friars, facing the south porch of the St. Mary de Crypt Church. Raikes lived nearly opposite the church. Bad as the boys were, the "girls were worse." The children were required to come with clean hands and faces, hair combed, and with such clothing as they had, though shoes and clothes were sometimes provided. The boys were "strapped" or "caned" by Raikes himself, for misbehavior; the girls were subdued by other means. The children were to remain in school from ten to twelve, then go home; to return at one, and, after a lesson, to be conducted to church; after church service to repeat portions of the catechism; then to go quietly home about five, without playing in the streets. Attentive scholars received rewards of Bibles, Testaments, books, combs, shoes, and clothing. The head teachers were paid a shilling a day. Raikes engaged four women in his schools, and procured other employment for them as rewards of diligence, which "may make it worth sixpence more." The Rev. Thomas Stock "went around to the schools Sunday afternoon," says Raikes, "to examine the progress made, and to enforce order and decorum among such a set of little heathen." The boys were in classes of five, the advanced pupils acting as "monitors," or teachers, teaching the younger pupils their letters. The girls in a separate room, with white tippets on their shoulders and white caps on their heads, were in classes also, with "monitors" or sub-teachers over them. This was nearly ten years before Dr. Bell or Joseph Lancaster introduced the "monitorial systems" into the week-day schools of England, and his biographer, Harris, affirms that Raikes maintained these monitors without change and his schools have continued unto this day.

For about three years, Raikes looked upon his schools as an experiment. When William Fox, William Wilberforce (q.v.), and the Wesleys—John

2. Popular Interest Aroused. and Charles (qq.v.),—and Jonas Hanway, came as the guests of Raikes and his neighbors, he explained his plan, asked their counsel, and took them to the school to hear the children repeat prayers, the catechism, answer Bible questions, and sing Watts' hymns. It is recorded that they were astonished, "caught the fire," and extended the movement. Contrary to a popular notion, it is now affirmed that Raikes used "voluntary teachers," or monitors over small classes. "The system," says Harris, the latest biographer of Raikes, "was founded on, and supported by, voluntary effort; paid masters and mistresses were at first necessary, but they gradually disappeared; the monitors over classes were unpaid and voluntary from the beginning of his schools." The paid "master" and "mistress" of Raikes' schools were the superintendents; the class teachers were unpaid and voluntary, selected and directed by the paid master or mistress. When satisfied that his scheme had passed the experimental stage, Raikes published a brief notice of it in the *Gloucester Journal* of Nov. 3, 1783, which was copied into the London papers. The *Gentleman's Magazine* also published a letter of Raikes' of Nov. 25, 1783, in full, and a little later, another description by Raikes was given in the *Arminian Magazine* edited by John Wesley. These and many other published accounts extended knowledge concerning the new movement, while many pulpits repeated the story and praised the institution. By these means the knowledge and character of these Sunday-schools were rapidly diffused throughout the Christian world.

The schools of Raikes, and of the earlier promoters of the new movement, chiefly aimed to reach the children of the poor, and of those who neglected the

3. Voluntary Services of Workers. church. The scheme commended itself to thoughtful and philanthropic minds; learned and influential persons became its warm advocates. It met with criticism and opposition from some professors of religion and churchmen, who questioned its wisdom and its usefulness. The archbishop of Canterbury was moved to call together bishops and clergy to see what should be done to stop it. William Pitt seriously considered the introduction of a bill in Parliament for the "suppression of Sunday-schools." In Scotland, teaching on the Sabbath by laymen was pronounced an innovation and a breach of the fourth commandment. Sunday-schools on the new plan, however, continued to multiply in face of opposition, extending with marvelous rapidity in England, Wales, and Ireland, more slowly in Scotland, upon the continent, and in America. Experience soon proved that even paid "masters," to say nothing of paid teachers, made the system expensive, tending to limit its usefulness. If class-teachers and monitors could give their time, why might not persons competent for masters, and for all the instruction, be found to act without pay? Next, therefore, to founding the system, the most important step was to replace paid supervising "masters" and

"mistresses" and the few paid instructors by voluntary and unpaid superintendents and teachers. Raikes used unpaid class-teachers from the first, but paid superintendents. Sir Charles Reed credits Oldham, England, with having been the first Sunday-school to displace paid by gratuitous instruction. John Wesley notes Sunday-schools at Bolton, England, in 1787 "having eighty masters (teachers) who receive no pay but what they received from the great Master." The famous Stockport Sunday-school in 1794 paid only six of its thirty teachers. A Sunday-school in Passaic County, N. J., in 1794, having children from a cotton factory, gave them gratuitous instruction, and Samuel Slater, of Pawtucket, R. I., had a similar school, with unpaid teachers, for factory operatives. William Brodie Gurney introduced gratuitous instruction into several Sunday-schools in London, England, about 1796; and similar schools were promoted by Rowland Hill about the same time. Wholly gratuitous instruction speedily became a popular feature of the institution, and displaced the earlier plan of paid supervision and partly paid instruction. The adoption of the Sunday-school as a mode of religious instruction for children of the Church came more slowly into favor. But it had a remarkable growth, under the improved feature of wholly voluntary instruction and management, which adapted to the needs of poor communities and parishes in city and country.

The growth of modern Sunday-schools was phenomenal. While published reports of the membership vary widely, showing imperfect enumeration and defective census with gaps filled by mere estimates, yet the following figures give some idea of

4. Extension in Great Britain. the average progress, at different periods during the past century. Raikes, in a letter to the *Gentlemen's Magazine* in 1787, estimated the number of children in Sunday-schools at 250,000. This was evidently an over-estimate, for the same magazine in 1800 gave the number as only 156,400. A parliamentary census of England and Wales in 1818 reported 5,463 Sunday-schools, with 477,225 scholars, and 19,230 day-schools having 674,833 scholars. A similar census in 1833 reported a membership of 1,548,890. An educational census of England and Wales in 1851 reported 2,407,642 Sunday scholars, which was 260,000 more than were reported by the same census for all the public and private [secular] schools in the country at that time. At the same period it was said that there were 292,-549 Sunday scholars in Scotland, and a total in Great Britain (including Ireland and some islands) of 2,987,980 in 27,048 Sunday-schools, having 325,-450 teachers. At the Raikes centenary in 1880, reports and estimates placed the number of Sunday scholars then in Great Britain at 6,060,677, with 674,704 teachers. At the world's Sunday-school convention in 1889 it was reported that Great Britain (including Ireland) had 44,944 Sunday-schools with 704,286 teachers and 6,695,399 scholars. In 1907, at the Rome convention, Great Britain and Ireland reported 44,399 Sunday-schools, 684,342 teachers, and 7,450,374 scholars. J. Henry Harris computes that the Sunday-schools in Great Britain involve an annual expenditure of about £700,000, and including incidentals, such as excursions, socials, and other items, the amount equals £1,200,000 per annum for the schools in Great Britain alone.

The growth in America was even more phenomenal than in Great Britain. In 1825, the American Sunday-school Union reported in its connection

5. In America. 1,150 Sunday-schools with 11,295 teachers and 82,697 scholars, and computed from reliable data that there were in other Sunday-schools in this country and British America and the West Indies upward of 61,000 Sunday scholars, making a total for North America of 143,697 scholars. The reported conversions in the schools of the American Sunday-school Union were as remarkable as the growth of the schools. In 1828, the number of teachers in these schools reported as professing Christ was equal to about four per cent of the entire number of teachers. In 1829, the number of schools connected with the American Sunday-school Union increased to 5,901, with 52,663 teachers and 349,202 scholars. This rapid growth was further increased by the effort, national in scope, in 1830 to plant a Sunday-school in every needy community throughout the newly settled valley of the Mississippi. About eighty Sunday-school missionaries were employed to visit the 8,000 to 10,000 destitute settlements estimated to be in the valley; 2,867 new Sunday-schools were organized and 1,121 revived within about eighteen months, and not less than 20,000 adults and 30,000 scholars in the Union's schools professed conversion, as many as " 17,000 in a single year, it was believed." And in 1831, the semi-centennial of the founding of the system by Raikes, the American Sunday-school Union reported that the number in the United States enrolled as members of the Sunday-school may be safely estimated at upward of 600,000. In 1851 the membership in the United States and Canada was computed at 3,250,000. Meanwhile, besides the extension work of the American Sunday-school Union, which for over eighty years formed an average of three and one-half new Sunday-schools per day, the larger denominations separately began a vigorous Sunday-school extension and improvement in their respective churches. At the first international Sunday-school convention in 1875 the United States and Canada were reported to have 69,272 Sunday-schools with 788,805 teachers and 6,062,064 scholars. The latest statistics (1910–11) from the most trustworthy sources give the number of Sunday-schools held by Protestant churches in the United States and its possessions at 193,495, with 1,749,894 teachers and 15,380,694 scholars.

Schools enrolled in English-speaking lands are now computed at about 263,000, with about 2,500,000 teachers and about 24,000,000 scholars, while all the rest of the world not speaking English is to be credited with about 65,000 schools, upward of 300,000 teachers, and about 4,000,000 scholars. These facts indicate the phenomenal growth in English-speaking lands. It is also to be taken into account that in connection with this institution not less than 15,000,000 young people and adults also receive instruction. In connection with the movement is often found a " children's day," on which the services are wholly for the children and in large part consist of exercises in which they have the principal parts. The system has not made such great gains in the continental countries of Europe, as in Great Britain and America. The

5. In Denmark, Germany, and Norway. Roman Catholic and Greek churches have not placed emphasis upon instruction directly from the Bible, but from catechisms, creeds, and confessions peculiar to them. The large bodies of Protestants on the continent believe in religious instruction in their day-schools, which some there deem equal, if not superior in efficiency, to the method pursued in the modern Sunday-school. Thus, in Denmark, all between seven and fourteen years of age are compelled to attend day-school, and religious instruction is obligatory. Dissenters (numbering less than one in 100 of the population) can have their children excused from religious instruction in the State schools by showing that they are satisfactorily taught elsewhere. In 1907 it was computed that of " children's services " and Sunday-schools together, there were in Denmark about 1,000, having an attendance of about 80,000, the numbers having more than doubled in the last twenty years. In Germany, day-school attendance is compulsory and religious instruction required by the State. The kind of religious instruction thus given varies with the different views of the parish clergyman and the village teacher in charge of the school. The modern Sunday-school is there widely looked upon as designed for the lower classes. Children of the better class rarely attend. Yet Sunday-schools on the " class " or " American " system were begun in Prussia about 1834, received a new stimulus from the American Albert Woodruff about 1862, are extending among the free or dissenting churches, through the work of the centennial mission of the London Union, and are winning their way slowly into State churches. Many Evangelical Lutherans, however, say: " Luther taught us how to teach the Bible in our schools; why do we need Sunday-schools? " The State views every one as a Christian who is not a Jew, Moslem, or pagan. Some see two kinds of Sunday-schools in Germany; those in State churches and those in dissenting churches. Some of the former adopt the class system, others do not. The free churches generally welcome the modern class system in Sunday-school. The reports for 1910 give about 9,000 Sunday-schools of all kinds in Germany with about one million scholars. The modern Sunday-school system was introduced into Norway, with the free-church movement, about 1850, and is extending into the State churches, about three-fourths of all Sunday-schools in 1898 belonging to them, and they use lessons of their own. Including the " children's services " and Sunday-schools in the State churches there were in 1910 upward of 1,000 schools in Norway. Many of the free-church schools are coordinated in a union and use the International Sunday-school Lessons.

Sweden introduced Sunday-schools also into the free churches about 1851, and the system is gaining strength in the State churches (see statistical table). The first Sunday-school in Sweden was organized about 1833 in Stockholm by the daughter of an

English consul; it was followed by a few others, but continued only a short time. In 1851 P. Palmquist

7. In Other European Countries. of the same city saw the exhibit of Sunday-school work in the great exhibition at London, and began a Sunday-school for the poor children on his return, which became the germ of the system of the free (Baptist, Wesleyan, and Congregational) churches of Sweden. In 1853 Lady Ehrenburg began a similar school, which introduced the system into the State church. For twenty years the new system had a slow growth. In the first five years of this century, greater activity in extension and improvement of Sunday-schools has been secured through special missionaries, though in 1909 there were districts and provinces where Sunday-schools are unknown. Holland has a strong Sunday-school society, chiefly supported by the free and Evangelical churches, that for several years has promoted the extension and improvement of Sunday-schools, resulting in about 200,000 children in 2,000 schools. In Switzerland Sunday-schools are popular in all the German Evangelical cantons. The system has been adapted to the special conditions of the people, training of teachers, and the latest improved methods are studied in the land of Zwingli and of the Reformed churches. In the French cantons of Switzerland, the modern Sunday-school method has been in use for over fifty years. "Childrens' services" have been held, the children being grouped in classes, each class in charge of a teacher for "catechetical exercises," followed by the general address of "instruction" by the minister, the course of study being Old-Testament history and New-Testament doctrines. In the land of the Huguenots, Sunday-schools early found a footing, but not a hearty welcome. The upheaval in civil affairs, the domination of the Roman Catholic priesthood, and the disruption of Church and State in France in this century have prevented a wide extension of Bible-study. Lately there has been a revival of interest, the Protestant churches have a wide-open door, the Gospel can be extended freely by the best Sunday-school methods, and the opportunity for a large increase of the 1,200 Sunday-schools (with 74,000 members) never was brighter in France than since the separation of Church and State. Russia, under rigid laws, has hitherto frowned on Bible-study save by those only who adhered to the Greek Church. Among the few dissenting or free churches of the empire, some Sunday-schools were founded. It was reported in 1910 that there were about 1,000 schools having about 66,000 scholars in Russia, taught in different languages, on the Dnieper, Volga, and Don rivers, and along the Black Sea. The system of Bible-study by the Sunday-school method is not welcome in the Greek Church. Bohemia, the land of Huss, has about a quarter of a million of Protestants, among whom Sunday-schools find favor; the greater number of Bible scholars, however, study at home; the home department generally outnumbering those in the schools. Italy was late in receiving the Sunday-school. It has a national committee and "Union" formed in 1891, which is still doing effective work in the extension of Sunday-schools in the face of great difficulties.

In Spain the Sunday-school exists by sufferance as do all Protestant bodies, though the spirit of religious toleration is gaining strength in the Spanish mind (see SPAIN, EVANGELICAL WORK IN).

In the other countries of the world, except in India, Austria, and the Philippines and Hawaii, Sunday-school extension is dependent upon Protestant missions maintained by the missionary societies of Christian lands. The Sunday-schools are comparatively few, and can not be increased except through mission agencies. The efficiency and economy of the Sunday-school, modified to meet conditions in non-Christian lands, fit it for a far wider usefulness in propagating the Gospel than almost any other means within reach of the Church.

II. Sunday-school Societies. 1. In Great Britain: The magnitude of the task of "teaching the Bible to the world" attracted the attention of Christian philanthropists, and after several public conferences in London, William Fox, Jonas Hanway, Henry Thornton, and Thomas Raikes (brother of Robert Raikes) with three others formed The Society for the Support and Encouragement of Sunday-schools in England, Sept. 7, 1785. As its work extended beyond England, the title was changed some years later to include the British dominions. Owing to the long title, it was popularly known as "The Sunday-school Society." It leased rooms, employed teachers, and provided Bibles and books gratuitously. In 27 years it founded and aided 3,730 Sunday-schools, having 303,981 scholars, donating 8,001 Bibles, 70,537 Testaments, 329,695 spelling-books and primers, and expending £4,383 15s 4d. After 1811 its work was limited to grants of class-books and Scriptures. This society dissolved in 1864.

As the advantages of voluntary teachers and wholly gratuitous instruction became apparent, schools discontinued paid teachers altogether. Rowland Hill, pastor of Surrey Chapel,

1. London Sunday-school Union. London, England, formed a Sunday-school on this purely voluntary plan. William Brodie Gurney, a young Christian layman, fired with zeal for this service by meeting William Fox, John Howard the philanthropist, and others, proposed a conference, to consider the extension of schools with voluntary teachers only. This was held in Surrey Chapel, July 13, 1803, and resulted in the formation of the London Sunday-school Union. This society is conducted by members of different Evangelical denominations, through a general committee of fifty-four persons, who render service gratuitously. For more than a century, it has promoted the work in Great Britain by publishing suitable record and reading-books and other requisites at a low price, and by issuing cards, periodicals, and helps for teachers. *The Sunday School Teachers Monthly Magazine*, founded by its secretary, W. F. Lloyd, in 1813, was a pioneer in that line and was conducted with rare ability. *The Sunday-School Chronicle*, now issued by the London Union each week, is the foremost periodical of its class in Great Britain. The Union, by means of auxiliary unions, extended the system throughout the British dominions. It has provided a system of teachers' training-classes or institutes in which persons by study and examination have been fitted for teaching. It secured a "loan fund" from which loans were made without interest to churches and organizations erecting buildings and class-rooms, and maintains a large reference library and reading-room for teachers and others, at a subscription price of one shilling per annum for each person. Since 1864, the union has aided in maintaining special missionaries to extend Sunday-schools on the continent, in India, and elsewhere. At its centenary in 1903, it reported in its connection, through its auxiliaries, 9,584 Sunday-schools, 213,226 teachers, and 2,252,497 scholars. Affiliated with it is the International Bible Readers' Association, having 800,000 to 1,000,000 members, in nearly 100 countries, who are pledged to read an assigned portion of the Bible daily. Its chief support is from the Congregationalists, Baptists, and Presbyterians. The other dissenting bodies and the Church of England each have separate Sunday-school societies.

The Church of England Sunday-school Institute was formed in 1843, "to extend, improve, and develop the Sunday-school system in the Church of England" and "to secure efficient

2. Other Societies. teaching therein." It is directed by a committee of about 50 persons, 25 clergymen and 25 laymen. The work is promoted through branch or local associations (about 400), and through publications, institutes, teachers, examinations, and lectures. Its benevolent receipts in its Jubilee year (1893) were £2,213, and from sales of publications £10,869; in its sixtieth year (1903) the benevolent receipts were £1,339, and from sales £9,032 (about the average yearly receipts). In 1910 the number of scholars for England and Wales in its schools was 3,153,476, and of teachers, 212,712. Its total annual receipts have slightly diminished in the last twenty years. Its lessons comprise a course of five years' study, based on the Bible and Prayer Book, and conforming to the church calendar. The Wesleyan Sunday-school Union was formed in London in 1875. In seven years, it enrolled about 6,500 schools, 123,000 teachers, 830,000 scholars, with £700 annual benevolent receipts. It has steadily advanced in all branches of its operations. Its report for 1907 gave: schools, 7,566; officers and teachers, 133,108; scholars, 1,000,819. This showed a decrease of 28,858 from the previous year's report, but the members of the "pleasant Sunday afternoon classes" showed a gain of 33,271, leaving a net gain of 4,413. The Sunday-school Society for Ireland was formed in 1809. At the end of fifty years it had 2,700 schools, 255,000 members, and it is still doing a useful work. There are Sabbath-school societies in Edinburgh and Glasgow, and in several countries on the continent of Europe. The India Sunday-school Union and the Australian Sunday-school Union at Melbourne are doing an effective work, having affiliation with, or encouragement from, the London Sunday-school Union.

2. In America: Christian philanthropists abounded in America, and were early awake to the advantages of the Sunday-school. Bishop William White, Dr. Benjamin Rush, Matthew Carey, and nine others held a meeting in Philadelphia Dec. 19, 1790, which resulted in forming The First Day, or Sunday-school Society, for the "establishment of Sunday-schools." It se-

1. Early Societies Local. cured funds, rented rooms and halls for holding schools, had both paid and voluntary teachers (in 1794), and secured a charter in 1797. In 1791 it petitioned the state legislature to establish "free public schools." In ten years it expended in rents, salaries, and gifts of books about $4,000. When voluntary teachers displaced all paid "masters" in Sunday-schools, the society appropriated its funds to supply needy schools with religious literature, issued on the union principle, a benevolent work which it still continues, having granted about $40,000. The "First Day" is therefore the oldest existing Sunday-school society in the world. The changes in the modern Sunday-school movement in the beginning of the last century, such as introducing the systems into the churches, displacing all paid masters with voluntary teachers, and transferring the sessions of the schools from rented rooms and halls to the churches, and the like, checked the spread of the new movement for the first decade of that century. But organizations for promoting Sunday-schools sprang up in many parts of this country. The Union Society for the education of poor female children was formed in Philadelphia in 1804, chartered in 1808; the Evangelical Society in 1808; and half a dozen other local union societies a few years later in Philadelphia were in part the result of the zealous labors of Christian men and women. The Rev. Robert May, in 1811, also popularized a system of reward tickets, primers, and the wider adoption of small classes, under voluntary teachers. In 1815, Eleazer Lord visited Philadelphia and studied its Sunday-school methods, then returned to New York so fired with enthusiasm that two societies were at once formed there—the New York Female Sunday-school Union (Jan., 1816) and the New York (male) Sunday-school Union Society (Feb., 1816). Meanwhile the several local Sunday-school unions in Philadelphia united in founding The Sunday and Adult School Union, 1817, which became the largest in America, within seven years having over 700 affiliated schools and auxiliaries.

The New York Sunday-school Union proposed a national society as early as 1820, and this was seconded by other unions until 1824, when the Phila-

2. American Sunday-school Union. delphia Sunday and Adult School Union was changed into a national society and named the American Sunday-school Union, the various unions elsewhere becoming auxiliary to the new national union. This "Union" is composed of persons of different evangelical denominations who voluntarily unite together, "to establish and maintain Sunday-schools, and to publish and circulate moral and religious publications." The union is not therefore anti-denominational, nor undenominational (for all its members and workers are actively connected with some denomination), nor is it strictly interdenominational, since it does not aim to blend or act for organized denominations, nor do ecclesiastical bodies appoint its officers and managers; it is a voluntary " union " of individual Christians of different churches for promoting the study of the Bible and the Sunday-school cause. It is conducted by a board of officers and thirty-six managers, all laymen. It employs laymen and ministers as missionaries to found Sunday-schools in new communities and in those removed from churches, issues library books, dictionaries, commentaries, maps, records, tickets, primers, teachers' tracts, manuals, lesson helps, and Sunday-school records and requisites in great variety, and also nine periodicals. In five years after its organization, the American Sunday-school Union issued over six millions of copies of Sunday-school works, published 200 bound volumes for libraries in Sunday-schools, started a *Teachers' Magazine* and two other periodicals, was receiving and expending annually over $76,000 in promotion of the cause, had in its connection 6,000 schools with 60,000 teachers and over 400,000 scholars, and one-half its schools reported in 1833 that 2,607 teachers and 6,121 scholars had professed Christ in that year alone. Among important measures inaugurated and popularized by this union may be noted: the system of free lending or circulating libraries of religious books, the first American monthly magazine for Sunday-school teachers, 1824; the first weekly folio journal for Sunday-schools, 1831; the employment of missionaries specially to establish Sunday-schools, 1821–24 and continuously since; a world's monthly concert of prayer for Sunday-schools, 1825; a system of selected uniform Bible lessons for Sunday-schools, 1826; a national scheme to plant a Sunday-school in every needy settlement in the Mississippi valley in two years, 1830; a similar scheme for the entire south, 1833; proposing and planning the first and second national Sunday-school conventions, 1832, 1833; graded lessons and *Union Questions*, 1829; a simultaneous invitation, July 4, 1833, to all " suitable subjects of Sunday-school instruction in the United States to attend some place for Bible study, on the following Sabbath, July 7"; the issue of low-priced illustrated Sunday-school periodicals for children, providing special records and manuals for conducting and improving Sunday-schools, establishing and furnishing supplies to auxiliaries (400) in all parts of the land, which were to supply the same to Sunday-schools connected with them, below or at actual cost; and finally, organizing state Sunday-school unions from 1825; and later, teachers' normal institutes and lectures, to inform and train officers and teachers in better methods of instruction, and also of discipline in, and the conduct of, Sunday-schools.

In the first decade of the twentieth century (1901–1910) it founded 24,992 schools, with a membership of 963,412, in which were reported 98,659 professed conversions, and 1,062 churches of dif-
3. Results of this Society's Work. ferent denominations following from the schools planted, and over 305,000 copies of the Scriptures provided for those without the Word of God. The Union employed in the ten years 2,594 missionaries, exclusive of superintendents and secretaries, an average of about 260 a year. It expended in benevolent work in the decade, $2,110,000. In eighty-six years the union claims to have formed in America 121,038 Sunday-schools, with over 655,000 teachers and 4,770,000 scholars. It has preserved a detailed record of every school, its precise location, the name and address of each superintendent, and the number of teachers and scholars in each school, when it was formed and when revisited, for fifty years past. The union, from time to time, enlists students in colleges and seminaries in the work of Sunday-school extension under direction of a regular missionary. Thus, it claims to have organized an average of nearly four schools a day for every day of the last 86 years, and to have distributed Bibles and publications to the value of about $15,000,000; having responded to 335,000 requests from schools with over 20,000,000 members for aid and encouragement in the study of God's Word. The union conducts all its operations on a thoroughly systematic plan (financial, publication, including educational, and missionary extension), each feature being under direction of a standing committee. The whole country is divided into great districts with a district superintendent to counsel, aid, and direct the labors of its force of missionaries.

It reports for the year ending Mar. 1, 1910, new schools organized and reorganized, 2,366, with 93,527 members, and also 11,198 visited for aid and encouragement, having 739,495 members. Its receipts for 1910 were $224,922 (exclusive of funded bequests and gifts), and its expenditures $218,728. It employed 231 regular missionaries, who reported 9,275 professed conversions for the year, visited 178,587 homes for instruction and prayer, and distributed 40,087 copies of Bibles and Testaments, 21,663 sermons and addresses to public assemblies, 88 new churches as the outcome of these union schools, $6,200 worth of religious books and periodicals given to the needy, besides grants for special objects, as homes, hospitals, and prisons, and issuing devotional commentaries, Bible wall rolls, charts, maps, and lesson helps. The union is supported by voluntary contributions, and has invested funds, amounting to between $1,000,000 and $2,000,000, the income from which is devoted to its benevolent work, including founding and improvement of Sunday-schools, and distribution of religious literature issued by the Society as directed by the donors.

The leading denominations in America also have Sunday-school unions, societies, or publishing departments. The Massachusetts Sunday-school Union, formed in 1825 by Congregationalists, Bap-
4. Other Societies. tists, and others, dissolved in 1832. The Congregationalists then started the Massachusetts Sabbath-school Society which, after several changes, is now the Congregational Sunday-school and Publishing Society, and employs secretaries, editors, and agents to promote Sunday-schools in that denomination. The Methodist Episcopal Sunday-school Union was formed in 1827, merged with its Tract Society in 1833, reorganized in 1844, for promoting the movement in that church and publishing and distributing literature through the preachers attached to that denomination, holding training-classes and Sunday-school assemblies, and the Chautauqua (see CHAUTAUQUA INSTITUTION) has achieved a world-wide reputation.

The Protestant Episcopal Church formed a Sunday-school Union in 1827, and was warmly supported by many. Others, while conceding that Sunday-schools were useful for non-churchgoers, and those who were poor and destitute, held that the church should teach its children by its clergy, under their direction, in families, and in parish schools. Yet Sunday-schools have prospered under the fostering care of diocesan authority, and through an efficient Sunday-school commission. Courses of study and text-books are provided that are suited to the worship and articles of confession in that church. The Presbyterians (North and South) have Sunday-school boards and the Baptists (North and South) have similar boards and Sunday-school departments. Each of these employ colporteurs or agents, and provide an extensive literature for the use of their respective schools. The Reformed churches also maintain similar publishing-houses, and secretaries for promoting the efficiency of their schools in instructing the young. Besides these, there are upward of twenty-five publishing-houses of more or less prominence devoting their chief attention and energy to providing publications and requisites for Sunday-schools in every variety of form and character, so that if Sunday-schools in America do not steadily improve and attain increasing efficiency, they can not plead lack of machinery and material.

3. Conventions of Sunday-school Workers: Conventions are used to awaken public interest, to discuss methods, to gather and disseminate information, and to promote Sunday-schools.

1. Conventions to 1862. Local conferences and conventions for this purpose were held before 1820. The first delegated convention, general or national in its scope in America and representing societies from all parts of the land, was held in Philadelphia in 1824, to consider the formation of a national society, and led to the organization of the American Sunday-school Union. In 1828 another convention was held in the same city, when delegates from fourteen states considered various measures for enlarging the operations of the "National," or American Sunday-school Union. Among other measures commended were extension of Sunday-schools in communities using the German language, among seamen, the offer of premiums for suitable publications, and plans for increased contributions to sustain the cause. In 1830 conventions and meetings were held in every important city of America, in furtherance of the "Mississippi Valley" mission proposed by the American Sunday-school Union. In 1832 the American Sunday-school Union proposed a national convention for "considering the principles of the institution (Sunday-school), and improved plans for organizing, instructing, and managing Sunday-schools." At the call of the union ninety delegates from thirteen states and one territory and the District of Columbia met, and decided to call a national convention of Sunday-school workers in New York, to be composed of delegates appointed by the local unions, associations, and by schools not connected with any union. This preliminary meeting also appointed committees, and authorized the sending out of a series of seventy-eight "interrogatories" grouped under thirteen

heads, embracing organization, mode of instruction, system of lessons, libraries, infant schools, adult Bible classes, visiting, and all measures tending to improve the institution. Delegates from fourteen states and territories met, discussed the questions for two days, referred the answers to the interrogatories to a committee to collate and report later, and proposed a second convention to be held in Philadelphia in 1833. The second convention approved of the effort proposed by the American Sunday-school Union personally to invite every person on July 4, 1833, to attend some Sunday-school the following Sabbath, July 7; urged that religious instruction be given to inmates of jails, prisons, and alms-houses, favored private Sunday-schools in homes with irreligious parents, recommended that sermons be preached for teachers and members of Sunday-schools, and the training of the young in mission-work. The special report on modes of instruction, prepared by James W. Weir and published by the American Sunday-school Union, was based upon the information given in response to the seventy-eight interrogatories. The replies made a quarto volume of about 1,200 pages. A third national Sunday-school convention was held in Philadelphia in 1859. A general convention was held in London, England, in 1862, attended by about 450 delegated workers from Great Britain, Ireland, the continent, America, and Australia, and considered the history, objects, and methods, with a view to the improvement and extension of Sunday-schools at home and abroad.

A fourth national convention in America was held, 1869, in Newark, N. J., attended by 526 enrolled members from 28 states and 1 territory, besides some from Canada and abroad.

2. 1869-1910. The purpose of this convention was twofold, inspiration and instruction. The fifth convention was held in Indianapolis, Ind., in 1872, attended by 338 delegates, from 22 states, 1 territory, and Canada. Meanwhile a conference of publishers had arranged a series of "uniform lessons" as a "trial scheme" as hereafter noticed. This plan was adopted at the convention with great enthusiasm, and prepared the way for the next and first "international" convention at Baltimore in 1875, and the lesson committee through Dr. Warren Randolph made its first report. Since 1875, the international conventions have been held triennially. The second was in Atlanta, Ga., 1878, with over 400 delegates, and promoted kindly feeling between the northern and the southern states; the third in Toronto, 1881; the fourth in Louisville, Ky., 1884, when a third lesson committee was appointed and four persons added to it from Great Britain, and one from France. The fifth met in Chicago, Ill., 1887; the sixth in Pittsburg, Pa., 1890, where a quarterly temperance lesson was adopted; the seventh in St. Louis, Mo., 1893; the eighth in Boston, 1896, over 1,000 delegates present, marked by the leadership of D. L. Moody; the ninth in Atlanta, Ga., marked by the election of Marion Lawrance as general secretary; the tenth in Denver, Colo., 1902, with 1,168 delegates, when special lessons for beginners were approved; the eleventh in Toronto, 1905, with 1,988 delegates, when "advanced lessons " were adopted, and the historical exhibit illustrating the development of the Sunday-school by Dr. Edwin W. Rice, and of the educational exposition of current Sunday-school material by Dr. C. R. Blackall were marked features. The name was also changed from " International Sunday-school Convention " to " Association," and it was proposed to obtain a charter of incorporation. The twelfth convention, 1908, in Louisville, Ky., appointed a new lesson committee instructed to prepare a thoroughly graded course of lessons, in addition to the uniform course of Bible study. The thirteenth convention, 1911, met in San Francisco, Cal. The international Sunday-school convention originated in a desire for conference upon methods of organization and improvement. The leading workers in it for about twenty years did not favor assuming or claiming any continuous authority. When each convention ended, all further action devolved upon the state, county, denominational, and other organizations. Some wished to make it an organic institution with continuous power; this view finally prevailed, and resulted in an incorporated association. The delegates are appointed by state and provincial organizations, several of which also are incorporated under independent charters. The representatives in all these conventions and associations are mainly from those workers who use the international series of lessons. The Church of England, the established Church of Scotland, the Protestant Episcopal, and some branches of the Lutheran Church in the United States, and the state churches on the continent are not represented in the deliberations of these conventions beyond occasionally sending friendly greetings.

Besides the above, there have been other notable gatherings in the interest of religious education, as the world's Sunday-school conventions in London, England, 1889; St. Louis, Mo., 1893; London, 1898; Jerusalem, 1904; Rome, 1907; Washington, 1910; the next will meet in Geneva, in 1913. Denominations have held assemblies to consider Sunday-school work, and the London Sunday-school Union invited a centenary meeting, to celebrate the founding of modern Sunday-schools in London, 1880, with a session in Gloucester, and in 1903 commemorated its hundreth year by centenary meetings. The American Sunday-school Union held a series of meetings in Philadelphia in 1899, to celebrate its seventy-fifth anniversary. The Religious Educational Association in America has also held several noteworthy conferences in Chicago, Philadelphia, Boston, and Washington, bringing together representative educators to discuss measures, and tending to bring Sunday-school methods more fully into harmony with accepted modern principles of education as advocated in the twentieth century.

III. Modes of Instruction and Literature: In the modern Sunday-school movement two distinct features came into prominence, making it to differ from the preaching and children's services on the one hand, and from venerable catechetical instruction on the other. These features were: (1) grouping of persons into small classes, each class having a teacher; (2) lessons chiefly, if not wholly, from the Bible. Even in Raikes' schools there were many children that must first be taught to read (and this was done that they might read the Bible for themselves); besides teaching the catechism and prayers, and singing, the scholars were taught answers to Bible questions. Raikes took great pains to have the children understand Bible passages, so that they could " give the sense " to parents in the home. Instruction in those early Sunday-schools had the germ of a method radically different from a mere parrot-repeating of memorized lessons. Mere memorizing and reciting of the catechism and of verses was carried to excess in the catechetical schools of Scotland and elsewhere. Before the era of free public schools in America, it was a necessity to teach the children of the poor to read in the early Sunday-schools. To aid in removing a prejudice against these schools, because reading was taught in them, the founders no doubt thought a liberal use of the catechism a prudent measure, and this condition may have led to the excess. Yet it is clear, from the latest investigations of the rise of this early movement, that the aim was specially to teach children to think for themselves. Raikes repeatedly laid strong emphasis upon this feature of his plan. It was inherent in his scheme from the beginning and was bound to win its way. Free public schools spread slowly in some portions of the United States, in the early part of the nineteenth century, hence there Sunday-schools were forced to continue to teach pupils to read at a later date than in other portions. Yet the great purpose of the Sunday-school, to teach the Word of God, was steadily kept in view. The advance of free day-schools in due time relieved the Sunday-school of the apparently secular service of teaching reading. However, it widely overlapped what has been termed the " memorizing era " as the " memorizing era " overlapped that of " limited and uniform lessons." The period of excessive memorizing of lessons in the Sunday-school was approximately from 1810 to 1824, in America. This was also the period when the system was expanding from an exclusively missionary stage for the children of the wretched, ignorant, neglected poor, and began to be introduced in churches as an aid or supplement to religious instruction in Christian families. Catechetical teaching was the " old time " form in such families; and Sunday-schools in churches accepted it, thinking that if it was well to memorize catechism questions and answers, and hymns and verses in some measure, it was better to memorize as many as possible. So they offered rewards therefor, until the teachers were overwhelmed with the astounding achievements of pupils; some coming with an entire catechism, or with a whole book of the Bible for a single " memorized lesson."

Meanwhile the " monitorial " or " mutual " plan of instruction came into public prominence, popularized by the efforts of Andrew Bell, M.D., a churchman, leading to the formation of the National School Society in the established Church of England, which provided that the articles and formularies of that church should be taught to the

1. Earlier Methods.

3. Other Conventions.

exclusion of all others. This action was stimulated by a similar plan of instruction exploited by Joseph Lancaster, a Quaker, known as

2. Transition to Systematized Instruction. the Lancastrian system, on which the British and Foreign School Society was founded. His plan provided lessons from the Scriptures, but excluded lessons in denominational creeds and catechisms. This society was largely sustained by dissenters. These plans agreed in employing monitorial or voluntary teachers, but differed widely on the system of lessons and subjects of study. Lancaster's plans had a decided influence upon the instruction in Sunday-schools in Great Britain and America. Other influences followed, as the vigorous attacks of James Gall of Scotland upon the parish mode of reciting catechisms in Scotch churches. Gall also advocated what he termed the "lesson system" of instruction, which consisted in requiring the scholar to "draw" some practical "lesson" from each sentence or clause in the lesson of the day. Moreover, the Sunday-school teachers' magazines were, for two or more decades, devoting column after column in their journals to explaining and discussing the principles of education suggested by Bacon, Milton, Comenius, Locke, Pestalozzi, Francke, Froebel, Gall, Bell, Lancaster, Jacatot, Stow, and others, and sifting therefrom whatever seemed suitable or helpful in shaping lessons or methods of instruction in Sunday-schools. The diffusion of this knowledge prepared the way for better schemes of lessons, and improved methods of teaching. The idea of a system of "selected lessons" uniform for the entire school seems to have come about the same time into many minds, widely separated, in America and Great Britain. It was first put in practise, as stated in the Appendix to the *Report* for 1825 of the American Sunday-school Union (issued May, 1826), in several schools in Albany, Utica, and by fourteen schools in New York City, and a list of "Selected Lessons" was published first in a leaflet by the Union. The first year's course comprised forty-nine lessons in the Gospels, "chronologically arranged according to the most approved harmonies." "The selection is divided into four portions, each designed to occupy the Sabbaths of three months, for the convenience of a quarterly examination of the scholars." The projectors hope that this plan will be so systematized, "that every school may be furnished with the same lesson at the same time." Each lesson was limited to from "ten to twenty verses," and among the advantages claimed for the scheme were: "it promotes uniformity," and united study by teachers during the week; aids the teachers' classes "conducted by the pastor" for "expounding the selections," gives the scholar the "same lesson when he moves to another school as would have been assigned him in the school he left." Within a year after this list of "Bible lessons" had been first published, a book of questions in three grades, prepared by Albert Judson on these same "selected lessons," was published, as a help in the study of them. They were so "happily adapted to advance the scholars in an intimate and correct knowledge of the Scriptures" that it was said "the old plan of committing large portions of Scripture to memory is generally relinquished." About fifteen or twenty ministers in New York City gave weekly lectures on the lesson to teachers; churches were crowded at the public examinations held quarterly in several schools on the "select lessons," and "scholars became acquainted with the general truths of the Scriptures." Judson's questions were soon combined with another similar help, and the joint book called *Union Questions* issued by The American Sunday-school Union, and the successive volumes (12 in all) of these lesson helps covered the chief books of the Bible. These *Uniform Select Lessons* with the *Union Questions* thereon were commended, as the best then known, by the first and the second national Sunday-school conventions, 1832, 1833, and continued to be widely used for more than a generation. Special helps, notes, and explanations on the lessons were issued weekly in the (Union's) *Sunday School Journal* of Philadelphia, and in book form, the latter being a fivefold form of notes. For instruction in the doctrines peculiar to each denomination, the chief dependence continued to be catechisms; particular Sundays often being designated for this purpose, by schools using the *Union Questions* and *Uniform . . . Lessons*. After a time, many large schools began to prepare for themselves a course of Bible-study lessons each year, and some prominent in a denomination advocated or put forth a series of lessons intended to teach the doctrines peculiar to the denomination, which soon drifted into what has been termed the "Babel series" of lessons in America.

In Great Britain about 1842, the London Sunday-school Union issued a double series of Bible lessons (without the texts), one for the morning session of the Sunday-school, and another for the

3. Various Systems Tried. afternoon, giving brief explanations, doctrines, practical lessons, and questions on each lesson in a monthly tract of twelve pages, duodecimo in size, differing from the American lessons of 1826 and on, by omitting to provide for any review, either weekly or quarterly. The *Lesson System* of James Gall, the *Graduated Simultaneous Instruction* by Robert Mimpriss, the "training system" of David Stow, and the "collective system" of the London Union were popular in England about the same period. The great defects of Gall's system were said to be absence of all instruction, save as to meaning of words, and the use of direct catechizing. Mimpriss's was better, but required too much mechanism, and is limited chiefly to the Gospels. Stow's was without a book of explanations, or questions, and required separate rooms for classes, and was fitted in the most part for infant classes only; the "collective system" of 1842 was largely topical, the Bible texts were too long to be mastered, suited better for advanced Bible classes only, and failed to give a comprehensive knowledge of the entire Scriptures. Each of these systems was tried in America, and each laid aside, after it had attained a brief local popularity in different places. Meanwhile the way was being providentially prepared for the international uniform lessons. The uniform idea had been partially lost to sight, though continued in fact, in the annual series of *Union Questions*, and in the series of *Explanatory Question Books*. Orange Judd's *Lessons for Every Sunday in the Year* (1862–65), lessons of the *Sunday Teacher* of Chicago, 1866, Vincent's *Berean Lessons*, McCook's Westminster series, and Drs. Newton's and Allibone's *Union and Explanatory Lessons*, with others, indicated the features of a new system that was coming.

Representatives of the foregoing systems of lessons, and of about twenty-five Sunday-school societies and publishers met in New York in August, 1871, and appointed a committee of five, who arranged a trial list of uniform lessons for 1872. This proved so satisfactory that the national Sunday-school convention of 1872 at Indianapolis approved the system, and appointed a committee of ten (five ministers and five laymen) from five different denominations, to select a seven-years' course of study to cover the entire Bible. This committee has been since continued with some changes and modifications and the addition of the British section to the American. Latterly, persons of nine denominations serve on this committee, comprising about 32 members (12 from the United States, 3 from Canada, 15 from Great Britain, and 1 each from India and Australia). Since 1894, each course of lessons has been limited to six years. In 1902 special lessons were provided for beginners and in 1906 for advanced classes. In general, the plan of study aims to give a comprehensive knowledge of the Bible in six years, the lessons being selected from the Old and the New Testaments alternately, upon some intelligent system, presenting the important salient events, characters, doctrines, and narratives of the whole Bible in the compass of each six-years' course of study. Gradually, the " uniform " idea has been modified by the demand for graded courses of study suited to scholars of the primary department, and another for advanced Bible classes as stated above. The lessons are called " international " because they are used in different countries of the world, and probably more widely than all other current systems of Sunday-school study.

In addition to the above " Uniform Series " of study, the International Lesson Committee began, 1908, a graded series of lessons for Sunday-schools. The plan outlined is for each grade to have one year of study, and a Bible text adapted to each successive grade. It recognizes beginners' department, two courses of one year each; primary, three courses, one year each; junior, four grades, each a year; intermediate, four, and a similar number of grades for senior and advanced departments. Thus, when complete there will be from sixteen to eighteen different grades and Bible texts studied in the same school at the same time.

The Bible Study Union (Blakeslee) system of Graded Lessons has been outlined for about twenty years. Its plan provides six series of lessons to cover the whole Bible; each series has four courses issued in seven grades, as biographical, Old-Testament history, life of Christ, gospel history, apostolic leaders, and apostolic church history. The Bible texts are selected so as to give a uniform text or

4. The International Lessons.

theme of study in each department of the Sunday-school at the same time.

The Sunday-schools of the Church of England have a system of their own, adapted usually to the church year. This church system is used, it is claimed, by about one-half of the Sunday scholars in England. A similar system is used by the Sunday-schools of the Protestant Episcopal Church in the United States and in Canada. Several branches of the Lutheran Church also have a series of Bible lessons conforming to the church calendar, and many schools in Scotland and on the continent of Europe have special courses and have not adopted the international lessons.

A new institution of the magnitude of the modern Sunday-school would naturally demand a literature. There was in the eighteenth century no juvenile literature, of moment, in existence, certainly none of a religious type. Sunday-schools created a religious revival, and an intellectual awakening, which demanded a juvenile literature. It began in England with primers, and simple " hints " for forming, conducting, and teaching Sunday-schools, followed speedily by books of prayers, hymns for children, selections of Scripture for reading, and small periodicals. *Youths' Magazine* (1805), *Child's Companion, Children's Friend,* and juvenile magazines by the score sprang into existence. They were at first small leaflets, monthly, each issue having from four to twelve pages. The *Repository or Teachers' Magazine* began as a quarterly (1813) of about fifty pages, and was later continued as a monthly for nearly forty years, and followed by the *Union Magazine, The Teacher,* and by the *Sunday-School Chronicle*, London, weekly, the leading journal for Sunday-school teachers in Great Britain. The Church of England maintains a scholarly magazine for Sunday-school workers, as do the Wesleyans. Scotland and Ireland sustain similar journals worthy of note. Instructive religious books, narrative and didactic, for youth rapidly multiplied. Authors like Hannah More, Jane Taylor, Rowland Hill, and Mrs. Sherwood devoted their best thought to producing literature of this type Manuals and hand-books on teaching and principles of education were issued in abundance, beginning before 1840. Training-classes for those intending to become Sunday-school teachers have long been maintained by the London Sunday-school Union, the Church of England Sunday-school Institute and other societies. Educational writers of note prepared text-books for the instruction of these training-classes, constituting quite a body of literature, specially relating to instruction and methods of teaching. A revival of interest in this branch of the work sprang up in Great Britain and America in the first decade of the twentieth century.

In America, the literary awakening was even more significant. While Great Britain produced many religious periodicals for the young, America gave greater attention to books and a permanent rather than an ephemeral juvenile literature. Men like President Humphrey of Amherst College, and Dr. T. H. Gallaudet of Hartford, testify that in

5. British Sunday-school Literature.

the first decade of the nineteenth century, a half-dozen books for children exhausted the list of existing works that could then be classed as juvenile. The Sunday-school had the task
6. American of creating a juvenile literature and a
Literature. taste for it also. In this The American Sunday-school Union was credited with leading the way. It secured some of the most gifted of Christian writers to prepare works for the young, setting forth Gospel truths in pleasing form. The three Alexanders—father and sons— Drs. Nevin, Edwards, Judson, Sears, D. Wise, Todd, Durbin, Tyng, Hodge, Bedell, Packard, Newton, Trumbull, Schaff, Allibone, Hall, Rice, and the Guernseys, among many others, aided in producing a juvenile religious literature in America, of the foremost character and in varied types of history, biography, narrative, travel, interlocutory instruction, and discourse, which were brought out, with engravings by the most skilled artists and engravers of that day—an attractive literature, religious in tone, forceful in thought and expression, and rich in substance and variety, the most widely read, of all the literature current for two generations, in their day. Statesmen and clergymen of note here and there declared that their first taste for learning was acquired by reading the books issued by The American Sunday-school Union. Composers of music, like Hastings and Lowell Mason, prepared hymns and songs for the young. Songs of the children from Sunday-school displaced the ribald, rollicking songs and drove them from the street if not from the face of the earth. Cheap Bible dictionaries, antiquities, helps in Bible study, and libraries for Sunday reading were issued by the tens of thousands, and scattered and read in every part of America. Primers and question books were produced by advice and cooperation of leading educators, college and theological professors, and millions of copies distributed. Normal works and teachers' manuals by Trumbull, Vincent, and others followed later. The influence of this juvenile literature on the mind of the rising generation, in the first half of the nineteenth century in America, has not been surpassed by any produced since that era. The several denominational Sunday-school societies, and not a few private publishers also, have been conspicuous in providing a juvenile literature, until it was conceded that America had the most abundant supply of such literature in the world, and this was marked for the purity of its tone and teaching. The stronger denominations issue periodicals and magazines, giving, from time to time, articles and essays on topics and methods of instruction by foremost educators, and they have a wide circulation. Among them are *The Baptist Teacher*, Philadelphia; *Methodist Sunday School Journal*, New York; *Pilgrim Teacher*, Boston; *Westminster Teacher*, Philadelphia; *American Church Sunday School Magazine*, ib.; *Heidelberg Teacher*, ib.; *Sunday School World*, ib.; *Sunday School Magazine*, Nashville; *Bible Teacher*, Dayton, O.; *Sunday School Helper*, Boston; *Earnest Worker*, Richmond, Va. The medium of communication and of news, between workers of all denominations, is the *Sunday School Times*, Phila-

delphia, the recognized representative weekly Sunday-school periodical of America, which has been issued for half a century. For more than a generation the *International Lessons* have been credited with causing a great revival in Biblical investigation and research, using and taxing the abilities of the foremost Biblical scholars.

A revival of interest in summer assemblies for Sunday-school workers, in the first decade of the twentieth century, has produced a new literature in America on teacher-training and instruction. This agency for promoting Bible instruction, which was earlier known as the Chautauqua movement (see CHAUTAUQUA INSTITUTION), was begun in 1874 by John H. Vincent (q.v.). Renewed attention to teacher-training has stimulated other persons to form summer assemblies in all parts of the United States, as educational forces for students of the Bible. Several permanent Bible schools have also created special departments in methods of study and instruction, as Moody's Bible Institute, Chicago; White's Bible Teachers' Training School, New York, which have led to the issuing of special text-books and a literature suitable for normal class work. Each of the larger denominations has provided manuals, instruction books, and courses of study for intending Sunday-school teachers, and offers a diploma at the satisfactory completion of the course.

The Sunday-school movement, as to its numbers and glory, appears in this historical sketch. The weakness and defects of the movement are also
obvious. Foremost among these are:
7. Conclu- (1) The organization and machinery
sion. are often too complex and cumbersome
in proportion to the teaching and spiritual power, for its highest efficiency. (2) The emphasis is placed too much on the school idea only, to the neglect, in part, of worship and of spiritual training. (3) It fails to make adequate provision for the adolescent period, and does not satisfactorily hold the scholars passing into the adult stage. The defects, however, will be remedied in time. The Sunday-school is destined to accomplish great victories in the work of advancing the kingdom of God. The Sunday-school in the past thirty years has concentrated upon its lessons and methods of instruction a ripe scholarship, a wealth of learning, a masterful marshaling of the widest knowledge in critical investigation, stimulating explorations in Bible lands, and the production of a literature on Oriental manners, habits, and customs, and a keen discrimination in practical applications of truth to modern conduct, never before surpassed or equaled. More light has been thrown upon the interpretation and illustration of the books of the Bible for this generation than ever before in the history of the world.

IV. Statistics of Sunday-Schools.—1. United States:[*] The United States Census Bureau says of the census figures for 1905: " These figures do not include the mission Sunday-schools which are maintained by some bodies, notably the

---

[*] Compiled from the Special Report of the United States Census Bureau on Religious Bodies for 1905.

Congregationalists and Presbyterian Church in the United States of America, but which are not connected with local organizations." (These are estimated at about 3,000 schools, with 108,000 membership.)

State or Territory.	Sunday-schools.	Officers and Teachers.	Scholars.
Maine	1,657	14,811	113,596
New Hampshire	835	8,097	66,741
Vermont	902	8,429	62,624
Massachusetts	3,111	52,834	497,782
Rhode Island	506	8,330	81,791
Connecticut	1,396	19,803	182,502
New York	9,189	126,839	1,273,300
New Jersey	3,004	44,502	416,021
Pennsylvania	13,482	185,665	1,723,749
North Atlantic Division.	34,082	469,310	4,418,106
Delaware	448	5,655	50,313
Maryland	2,672	32,038	266,471
District of Columbia ...	302	5,392	57,550
Virginia	6,521	53,207	451,667
West Virginia	3,699	29,037	223,777
North Carolina	7,511	54,245	495,403
South Carolina	5,099	35,669	334,072
Georgia	8,456	52,478	474,780
Florida	2,706	15,883	127,897
South Atlantic Division	37,414	283,604	2,481,930
Ohio	9,683	114,752	967,534
Indiana	6,222	65,741	532,074
Illinois	8,713	97,318	856,526
Michigan	5,537	55,319	452,244
Wisconsin	4,381	30,406	289,187
Minnesota	4,498	32,301	291,399
Iowa	6,105	57,279	434,551
Missouri	7,599	64,158	537,622
North Dakota	1,616	7,977	64,864
South Dakota	1,765	10,128	80,763
Nebraska	3,376	27,712	210,927
Kansas	5,410	48,900	363,214
North Central Division	64,905	611,991	5,080,905
Kentucky	5,275	37,241	343,991
Tennessee	6,494	42,767	369,217
Alabama	6,917	40,904	365,868
Mississippi	6,053	33,177	290,525
Louisiana	3,493	18,681	184,410
Arkansas	4,842	30,337	248,531
Oklahoma	3,684	24,499	201,947
Texas	9,384	62,066	558,483
South Central Division .	46,142	289,672	2,562,972
Montana	508	3,454	35,226
Idaho	663	6,390	47,828
Wyoming	290	1,969	15,920
Colorado	1,407	12,351	108,736
New Mexico	409	1,924	21,257
Arizona	237	1,841	15,682
Utah............	599	10,783	90,608
Nevada	91	589	5,085
Washington............	1,810	15,064	121,778
Oregon	1,277	10,653	81,466
California	2,888	26,479	250,312
Western Division	10,179	91,497	793,898
Continental U. S.	192,722	1,746,074	15,337,811
Alaska	50	196	2,222
Hawaii	207	780	11,321
Philippines	311	1,752	15,409
Porto Rico	205	1,092	13,931
Totals for the U. S.	193,495	1,749,894	15,380,694

2. Great Britain and Ireland:*

Countries.	Schools.	Officers and Teachers.	Scholars.
ENGLAND AND WALES: Church of England...	} 44,035	} 212,712	3,153,476
Other denominations..		} 432,574	3,616,016
SCOTLAND: Church of Scotland...		{ 20,722	234,252
Scottish United Free Church	} 3,954	{ 25,221	239,049
Other denominations..		{ 11,048	117,222
IRELAND	1,221	18,037	184,156
Great Britain and Ireland, Total.........	49,210	720,314	7,544,171

3. Other Countries of the World:†

Countries.	Schools.	Officers and Teachers.	Scholars.
North America (exclusive of Cont. U. S. and Alaska)	11,191	90,186	788,803
South America	891	4,826	58,698
Central America	75	471	5,419
Europe (exclusive of Gt. Britain and Ireland) .	33,823	110,670	2,155,912
Asia	15,986	37,014	735,604
Africa	8,996	29,835	490,298
West Indies (exclusive of Porto Rico)	1,891	10,972	149,485
Oceania (exclusive of Hawaii)	12,624	68,399	748,889
Malaysia (exclusive of Philippines)	84	113	24,236
Totals.............	85,561	352,486	5,157,344
Total for world ...	328,266	2,822,694	28,082,209

EDWIN WILBUR RICE.

BIBLIOGRAPHY: (1) On the history much matter will be found in the following periodicals: *Gentlemen's Magazine*, London, vols. for 1784–87; *Evangelical Magazine*, ib. 1793–1840; *Christian Observer*, ib. 1802–50; *Cottage Magazine*, ib. 1809–32; *Sunday School Repository and Teacher's Magazine*, ib. 1813–47; *Sunday School Chronicle*, ib. 1874 sqq.; *Church Sunday School Quarterly and Magazine*, ib. 1847 sqq.; *Imperial Magazine*, Liverpool and London, vols. for 1819, 1821, 1822, 1826, 1828; *Christian Spectator*, New Haven, 1819–38; *American Sunday School Magazine*, Philadelphia, 1824–31; *Sunday School Journal and Advocate of Christian Education*, ib. 1831–58; *Sunday School Times*, ib. 1859 sqq.; *Sunday School World*, ib. 1861 sqq.

Books on the subject are: L. G. Pray, *Hist. of Sunday Schools*, Boston, 1847; S. H. Tyng, *40 Years' Experience in the Sunday School*, New York, 1860; J. C. Power, *Rise and Progress of Sunday Schools*, ib. 1863; A. Bullard, *50 Years with the Sabbath Schools*, Boston, 1876; R. S. Duncan, *Hist. of Sunday Schools*, Memphis, 1876; M. P. Hale, *Leaves from Sunday School and Mission Fields*, Boston, 1876; S. Gilbert, *The Lesson System; the Story of its Origin and Inauguration*, New York, 1879; W. A. Candler, *Hist. of Sunday Schools*, ib. 1880; D. Evans, *The Sunday Schools of Wales*, London, 1883; E. W. Rice, *Origin of Sunday Schools*, Philadelphia, 1886; idem, *Short History of the International Lesson System, with Classified List of Lessons for 33 Years*, Philadelphia, 1902; idem, *Origin and*

* Compiled from "Special Commissioner" in *London Sunday-School Chronicle*, 1910. (Roman Catholic Sunday-schools are not included.)

† Compiled from the World's Sixth Sunday-School Convention Report, 1910. Parish schools and catechetical classes are maintained for religious instruction in most of the Protestant, and in many Roman Catholic, churches of continental Europe. These are not included in this table.

Expansion of the Sunday School, ib. 1906; H. C. Trumbull, *Yale Lectures on the Sunday School*, New York, 1888; Marianna O. Brown, *Sunday School Movements in America*, ib. 1901; J. H. Harris, *Story of the Sunday School*, London, 1902; W. H. Groser, *A Hundred Years' Work for the Children*, ib. 1903; O. S. Michael, *Sunday School in the Development of the American Church*, Milwaukee, 1904; W. Paret, *Place and Function of the Sunday School in the Church*, New York, 1906; *Sunday Schools the World Around. The Official Reports of the World's Fifth Sunday-Schools Convention in Rome, 1907*, London and Philadelphia, 1908; W. H. Watson, *First 50 Years of the Sunday School*, London, n.d., and literature under RAIKES, ROBERT; and the *Records* and *Reports* or *Annual Reports* of the following societies and conventions: First Day or Sunday School Society, Philadelphia, 1790 sqq.; Sunday School Union, London; Sunday School Society for Ireland; New York Female and Male Sunday School Unions, 1816–24; Philadelphia Sunday and Adult School Union, 1818–24 (nos. 1–7); American Sunday School Union, 1825–1910; General Sunday School Convention, London, in 1862; National and International Sunday School Conventions, 1869–1910; World's Sunday School Conventions; Church of England Sunday School Institute, London.

On methods and principles consult: J. W. Alexander, *The American Sunday School and its Adjuncts*, Philadelphia, 1856; A. W. and C. E. Knox, *The Infant Sunday School*, Cincinnati, 1870; J. S. Hart, *Sunday School Idea*, Philadelphia, 1871; W. Abbott, *Our Sunday School and how to conduct it*, new ed., Boston, 1872; J. H. Vincent, *Church School and its Officers*, New York, 1872; W. F. Crafts, *Through the Eye to the Heart, or, Eye-Teaching in the Sunday School*, New York, 1873; idem, *Plain Uses of the Blackboard and Slate*, New York, 1881; W. H. H. Marsh, *The Modern Sunday School*, Philadelphia, 1874; E. W. Rice, *Organization and Classification of Sunday Schools*, Philadelphia, 1881; idem, *Handy Helps for Busy Workers*, ib. 1899; idem, *The Sunday-school; how to start and keep it*, ib. 1909; A. E. Dunning, *Sunday School Library*, Boston, 1883; B. Clarke, *The Blackboard in the Sunday School*, London, 1884; E. G. Harmer, *By-Paths of Sunday-School Work*, London, 1892; J. L. Hurlbut, *Seven Graded Sunday Schools*, New York, 1893; A. E. Winship, *Methods and Principles in Bible Study*, Boston, 1885; idem, *Organizing and Building up the Sunday-School*, New York, 1910; A. F. Schauffler, *Ways of Working*, Boston, 1895; E. Hobson, *Principles and Practice of Teaching in their Application to Sunday Schools*, London, 1896; J. Bailey, *Sunday School Teaching*, London, 1897; I. P. Glack, *Practical Primary Plan*, Philadelphia, 1898; W. H. Groser, *Sunday School Teacher's Manual*, 16th ed., London, 1898; A. P. Foster, *Manual of Sunday School Methods*, Philadelphia, 1899; P. DuBois, *Point of Contact in Teaching*, 4th ed., New York, 1900; J. E. Horrocks, *Suggestions towards Improving the Instruction in Sunday Schools*, London, 1901; H. Williams, *The Reformation of the Sunday School*, London, 1902; E. D. Burton and S. Mathews, *Principles and Ideals for the Sunday School*, Chicago, 1903; G. W. Mead, *Modern Methods in Sunday School Work*, New York, 1903; A. H. McKinney, *After the Primary—What?* New York, 1904; F. N. Peloubet, *Front Line of the Sunday School Movement*, Boston, 1904; A. R. Wells, *Sunday School Problems; practical Plans for Sunday-School Teachers*, New York and London, 1905; M. G. Brumbaugh, *Making of a Teacher*, Philadelphia, 1905; idem, *Development of the Sunday School*, Boston, 1906; M. Lawrence, *How to Conduct a Sunday School*, New York, 1905; R. F. Y. Pierce, *Pencil Points for Preacher and Teacher*, Chicago, 1906; J. Adams, *A Primer on Teaching, with Especial Reference to Sunday School Work*, Edinburgh, 1907; H. F. Cope, *The Modern Sunday School in Principle and Practice*, New York, 1907; E. A. Fox, *The Pastor's Place of Privilege and Power in the Sunday School*, Nashville, 1907; F. Johnson, ed., *Bible Teaching by Modern Methods*, London, 1907; H. T. Musselman, *National Teacher-training Institute Text-books*, Philadelphia, 1907 sqq.; M. S. Littlefield, *Hand-Work in the Sunday-school; with an Introduction by P. DuBois*, Philadelphia, 1908; G. H. Trull, *A Manual of Missionary Methods for Sunday-School Workers*, Philadelphia, 1908; G. H. Archibald, *The Sunday School of To-Morrow*, London, 1909; J. C. Gray and C. S. Carey, *The Class and the Desk. A Manual for Sunday School Teachers*, 4 vols., London, 1909; J. Gunn, *Our Sunday Schools. Studies for Teachers in Principles and Practice*, London, 1909; P. J. Sloan, *The Sunday-School Director's Guide to Success*, New York, 1909; H. H. Meyer, *The Graded Sunday-School in Principle and Practice*, New York, 1910; R. P. Shepherd, *Religious Pedagogy in the Modern Sunday School*, St Louis, 1911.

SUNDAY, WILLIAM ASHLEY: Presbyterian and revivalist; b. at Ames, Ia., Nov. 19, 1863. He received his education at the high school, Nevada, Ia., and at Northwestern University; was a professional baseball player, 1883–90; assistant secretary of the Young Men's Christian Association, Chicago, 1891–95; became an evangelist in 1896, and has since devoted himself with great success to that work, receiving Presbyterian ordination in Chicago in 1903.

SUNESOEN, ANDERS. See ANDREW OF LUND.

SUPERANNUATION. See Vol. xii., Appendix.

SUPEREROGATION, WORKS OF: A concept in Roman Catholic theology which has its place in the doctrine of indulgences was justified by the great scholastics through the notion of the organic unity of the Church. They asserted that the sum total of the merits of Christ was greater than was required for the salvation of man, and that the saints also had done more and suffered more than was absolutely required to insure their own salvation, that these superabundant merits were placed in the " spiritual treasury " of the Church, at the disposal of its visible head; that as the Church is one, in this world and the next, they may be applied to such of its members as are still lacking in the required amount of works necessary to satisfy the divine demands. This is effected by indulgences, as an exercise of judicial power for the living and *per modum suffragii* for the souls in purgatory. The doctrine is set forth in the Constitution *Unigenitus Dei filius* of Clement VI. (1343), and implicitly sanctioned by the Council of Trent in its affirmation of the doctrine of indulgences. It was further established in the condemnation of contradictory propositions of Luther by Leo X. (1520) and of Bajus by Pius V. (1567), Gregory XII. (1569), and Urban VIII. (1641), as well as by Pius VI. in the constitution *Auctorem fidei* of 1794, against the Synod of Pistoja.

The Roman Catholic doctrine of good works has a threefold basis. It rests first upon the Augustinian doctrine of grace together with the idea of the universal operation of God. Thus considered, a meritorious work in the strict sense is inconceivable; but another complementary idea comes in—that free man is bound to acquire merit before God and through it to make satisfaction for his sins. This idea, found as early as Tertullian, is the joint product of Jewish legalism and Stoic moralism. A third element comes in from the Stoic distinction between the *medium* and the *perfectum*, to say nothing of the Jewish emphasizing of special and extraordinary virtues (cf. Tob. xii. 8). An apparent sanction for the notion of a gradation in the value of works was found in Matt. xix. 16–22 and I Cor. vii. 25, 40. By degrees the doctrine of " Evangelical counsels " (see CONSILIA EVANGELICA) was developed, and took ever deeper root with the establishment of the ascetic life in the Church.

Thus, while the practical significance of works of supererogation is connected with indulgences, their theoretical basis is found in the conception of merit and of the nature of Christian perfection. Protestantism, by dissolving the association of the entire train of thought in which they find a place, did away with them altogether. If the good works of men are the product of God's free grace, the idea of merit on man's part is ruled out; if Christ is the one mediator and his death the one atonement, there can be no more talk of the possibility of satisfaction on the part of man; and if he is alone the head of the Church, such a thing as a treasure of superfluous works to be arbitrarily distributed by an earthly head becomes a figment of the imagination. (R. SEEBERG.)

SUPERINTENDENT: The title of a German ecclesiastical officer. Among later schoolmen " superintendent " was applied, as by Gabriel Biel (*Super quattuor libros sententiarum*, dist. 24, qu. 1), to bishops, in so far as they were governing officers, this translation of *episkopoi* occurring as early as Augustine (" City of God," xxix. 19) and in Jerome (*Epist.*, lxxxv.), and after them in the *Corpus juris canonici* (c. 11, C. 8, qu. 1, and D. 93, c. 24). The term was applied in Saxony to the permanent supervisory officers that were instituted after the visitations had been completed (cf. E. Sehling, *Die V Kirchenordnungen des 16. Jahrhunderts*, i. 142 sqq.). The Saxon superintendents of 1527 and later were intended to be no other than state executive officials. But at the start they officiated as subordinates to the visitation committees, and afterward to the consistories. The example of Saxony was often followed, though the term " superintendent " was not generally retained. In South Germany the designation " dean " is occasionally in vogue (as in Bavaria); in the German Reformed churches " inspector," and, locally, " metropolitan," " senior," " ephor," " provost." But this involves no material alteration. The bishops of the Evangelical State Church of Balkan Transylvania are superintendents.

Within the area of his province, the superintendent exercises supervision over the official administration and conduct of the clergy and of the inferior church servants; also at times over the conduct, and sometimes the studies, of ministerial candidates, who come to him for permission to preach in particular instances. Where pastoral vacancies occur, he must provide proper supplies, conduct the pastoral election, and induct the new pastor. In the event of disputes between pastor and congregation, he is the competent referee. He has, furthermore, oversight of administration of church property. To what extent the superintendent has the right to define disciplinary penalties, or independently to institute official suspensions, is a matter which varies according to special statutes. Various details of the superintendent's activity also involve the cooperation of the civil organism.

There are superintendents of higher and lower grades. The former class especially includes the general superintendents, whose discretion in the several state churches, however, shows very differ-

ent official features. In Old Prussia, they are spiritual consistorial directors beside the temporal consistorial president. Their sphere of action stretches over an entire province; and, if need be, they exercise very personal influence over the superintendents and pastors under their jurisdiction. Elsewhere, while certain superintendents are indeed members, as well, of the church governing boards, it is only in this attribute that they rank higher. Recent modifications in the superintendents' position have their warrant in the introduction of presbyterial and synodical constitutional arrangements, by virtue of which, in most German Evangelical state churches, the previous consistorial church organization has become a so-called mixed one.

The German Evangelical state churches have, for the most part, adopted the synodical limitation of the superintendent's office, which varies in different localities.

[The title is now substituted in the Methodist Episcopal Church for that of presiding elder (see METHODISTS, IV., 1, § 8).]   E. SEHLING.

BIBLIOGRAPHY: W. W. J. Schmidt, *Der Wirkungskreis und die Wirkungsart des Superintendenten in der evangelischen Kirche*, Quedlinburg, 1837; J. C. W. Augusti, *Beiträge zur Statistik . . . der evangelischen Kirche*, iii., no. 14, Leipsic, 1837; E. Friedberg, *Das geltende Verfassungsrecht der evangelischen Landeskirchen in Deutschland*, Leipsic, 1888; and the works on Kirchenrecht by A. L. Richter, § 72, 8th ed., ed. W. Kahl, ib. 1886, and E. Friedberg, pp. 236 sqq., 6th ed., ib. 1909.

SUPERNATURAL RELIGION: The title of a work in criticism which evoked much attention in the last part of the nineteenth century. Its author, Walter Richard Cassels, was born in London in 1826. His early ventures in authorship were poetical. His first book bore the title *Eidolon; or, the Course of the Soul, and other Poems* (London, 1850), a critic of which wrote in *The Saturday Review* (i. 236): " He must do more and also do less; and we will hazard a prediction that he will at last do something which will not be forgotten." The prediction was fulfilled when, in 1874–77, he published *Supernatural Religion* (3 vols.; latest popular ed., 1 vol., 1902). I ran through many editions, causing a stir similar to but more profound than that made by *Essays and Reviews* (q.v.).

To understand the purpose of the book and the stir it made, a word regarding the history of Bible study in England is necessary. In the eighteenth century Deism (q.v.) had made a fierce and prolonged attack on the traditional conception of the supernatural. The defense, in substance, consisted in showing that " revelation " was a republication of " reason " with divine authority, that authority being authenticated by the supernatural in two forms, (1) prophecy conceived as prediction of events in the life of Christ, and (2) miracles. For the time being the defense succeeded, in part because deism was lacking in constructive force, but mainly because of the vast revival of religion (Wesleyan and Evangelical movements; see METHODISTS; and REVIVALS). The traditional conception of Holy Scriptures was grappled to the heart of the nation. England had no constructive philosophical movement and no critical movement of her own. The entire strength of the nation went into the struggle with Napoleon and into commercial expansion. When interest in history revived, it came in the form of the Oxford movement (see TRACTARIANISM), so that the critical question was still further postponed. English orthodoxy stood entrenched and intact down to 1860. The assault was opened by *Essays and Reviews* (1860; cf. F. Harrison's brilliant sketch in *The Creed of a Layman*, London, 1907), was continued by *Ecce Homo* in 1865, and in 1874 reached its climax in *Supernatural Religion*.

The title of the book places it in close connection with eighteenth-century deism. It is an assault upon " supernatural " religion. Since that religion connected itself inseparably with miracles, the purpose of the book is to bring the " supernatural " to the ground by knocking the miraculous underpinning from beneath it.

" I contend that the historical (argument against miracles) is the necessary complement of the philosophical argument. . . . The preliminary affirmation is not that miracles are impossible, but that they are antecedently incredible. The counter-allegation is that, although miracles may be antecedently incredible, they nevertheless actually took place. It is, therefore, necessary, not only to establish the antecedent incredibility, but to examine the validity of the allegation that certain miracles occurred, and this involves the historical inquiry into the evidence for the Gospels " (preface to 6th ed., pp. v.–vi.).

The purpose is to show that the canonical Gospels are so far removed in time from the events they record that they lose all competence as witnesses to the reality of the miraculous. The author conceived that by thus lopping off the " supernatural " from the religion of Jesus, the spiritual majesty and the moral sublimity of Christ would shine forth with beauty and clarity.

" Destructive must precede constructive criticism. It is only when we clearly recognize that the Bible is not in any ecclesiastical sense the word of God, that we can worthily honor and enjoy it as the word of Man " (pref., p. lxxxii.). " We gain infinitely more than we lose in abandoning belief in the reality of Divine Revelation. Whilst we retain pure and unimpaired the light of Christian Morality, we relinquish nothing but the debasing elements added to it by human superstition " (ii. 489).

Essays and Reviews had not touched the question of the supernatural in the life of Christ, but confined its specific criticism to the Old Testament. *Supernatural Religion*, on the contrary, touched the very vitals of Christianity by assaulting the supernatural in the life of Christ. English orthodoxy had learned nothing from deism, it was not willing to learn anything from Germany. So the attack caused profound emotion and alarm. The strength of the book was due first of all to the facts that its author carried the art of the popularizer to a high pitch of perfection, and that he used his art in the interest of a dogmatic thesis. As a historical critic he took his responsibility quite as lightly as the positive dogmatist on the other side took his. His art was not cramped or confined by original learning. He was fairly well read in German critical scholarship,—an accomplishment decidedly rare in the England of that day. His book is part of the German invasion of England. But, while he massed the conclusions of German scholarship in sweeping and undiscriminating ways, he was altogether lacking in the intellectual restraints of first-hand knowledge. And he rode the argument from silence till its back was raw. HENRY S. NASH.

BIBLIOGRAPHY: M. H. Habershon, *The Wave of Scepticism and the Rock of Truth: a Reply to "Supernatural Religion,"* London, 1875; J. Kennedy, *A Brief Defence of Supernatural Christianity, being a Review of the Philosophical Principles . . . of . . . " Supernatural Religion,"* ib. 1875; C. A. Row, *The Supernatural in the New Testament Possible, Credible, and Historical,* ib. 1875; M. F. Sadler, *The Lost Gospel and its Contents; or, the Author of " Supernatural Religion " refuted by himself,* ib. 1876; J. B. Lightfoot, *Essays on . . . " Supernatural Religion,"* ib. 1889 (generally regarded as a complete rejoinder). Many of the later works on the criticism of the Gospels (see under GOSPEL AND GOSPELS) remark on the subject of this article.

SUPERNATURALISM. See RATIONALISM AND SUPERNATURALISM.

SUPERSTITION.

Superstition may be defined objectively as either the aggregate of erroneous beliefs and practises current which may be traced to a combination of errant reason with feeble will, ill-controlled emotions, and ignorance more or less complete; or, any single act or belief which bears these marks. Subjectively, it is a mental attitude, " a phyletic instinctive desire to believe in certain causal relations which have not been and can not be proved, either experientially or logically, to exist " (F. B. Dresslar, *Superstition and Education* in *University of California Publications*, V., i., p. 141, n.p., 1907). The essential error of superstition is therefore in part the misplacing of the source of causation. Psychologically, a superstition is often the result of inability or unwillingness to carry on sustained thinking, involving a consequent readiness to accept as correct certain conclusions which have been handed down without being tested as to their cogency. From this same psychological standpoint, according to scientific investigation, subjective superstition, or the tendency to accept quasi-reasoning as effective, is in part an emotional credulity inherited from earlier periods; it is a species of atavism. Inasmuch as inherited mental reactions are not easily changed, not only is there in this fact a partial explanation of the persistence of superstition even where education has in other respects produced its effects, but also a partial palliation of the individual moral culpability of those who, though educated, still entertain beliefs of this character. More specifically, and from the standpoint of religion, superstition is a belief that is erroneous in that it asserts a causal connection between supernatural powers and events, real or conceived, in the world of sense. It thus not only involves ignorance of the laws of nature, but offends the enlightened reason in that it opposes those dicta of revelation which have found the securest sanction in human experience and consciousness.

1. Definition.

Slight advance is made toward a comprehension of the subject by a study of the etymology and equivalents of the word, though a development in meaning is traceable. The Latin *superstitio* (*super* and *stare*, " to stand still over or by a thing "; cf. the Gk. *deisidaimonia*, " fear of the **2. Etymol-** gods, religious feeling "; Germ. *Aber-* **ogy; Biblical** *glaube*, for *Oberglaube*, " belief to ex- **and Other** cess," Dutch, *Biglove*) expressed " ex- **Usages.** cessive fear of the gods, unreasonable religious belief," and was opposed to *religio*, " a proper, reasonable awe of the gods " (Cicero, *De natura deorum*, i. 42, 117, ii. 28, 72). It developed so as to mean a (religious) performance over and above what custom and the nature of the case required, or one which was not recognized by proper authority. In the authorized version of the New Testament the word and its derivative " superstitious " both occur. In Acts xvii. 22, in the celebrated address of Paul on Mar's Hill at Athens, " superstitious " translates wrongly the Greek *deisidaimonesterous* (R. V., margin, " religious "). It is to be noted that an unfavorable meaning is not to be accepted here, since it is not likely that Paul would have prejudiced his case by charging his hearers, whom he wished to conciliate, with " superstition." In Acts xxv. 19, " superstition " translates the Greek original *deisidaimonia*, though exactly what term Festus employed (as he probably spoke Latin) is of course not known. But, as in the former case, Festus would hardly have gratuitously offered offense to Agrippa and the Jews by calling the religion of the latter " superstition," the word employed must have had a good sense (cf. R. V., text, " religion "). Outside these passages, the word does not occur in the English Bible. The meaning the word has taken in modern times follows a different construction of its etymological elements, and embodies the idea of " something surviving " or " something left over (from an earlier and less advanced stage of culture)." This meaning is in itself an explanation of many of the concrete facts of superstition—they are survivals from earlier usage or belief which persist against the pronouncements of an enlightened reason. At the same time it is not precluded either in fact or theory that new " superstitions " arise from time to time.

In close connection with the usage just noted is that according to which the word is employed by adherents of one faith to characterize the religious beliefs and practises of adherents of another faith, particularly those of a dead religion. **3. Historical** Tacitus (" Annals," xv. 44) speaks of **Usage in** the religion which had sprung from **Religion.** " Christus, who had been put to death by . . . Pontius Pilate " as *exitiabilis superstitio*, " pernicious superstition." On the other hand the compliment was returned when, under Christian influence a couple of centuries later, pagan rites and worship were so denominated. Thus Constantine in a law of 319, speaking of the pagan religion of Rome, says: " They who are desirous of being slaves to their superstition, have liberty for the public exercise of their worship " (*Codex Theodosianus*, IX., xvi. 1-2), only a little afterward

practically defining superstition as *præterita usurpatio*, " antiquated usage." Even within the bounds of the same religion great, indeed, irreconcilable, difference exists as to what constitutes superstition. Thus to Protestants very many Roman Catholic beliefs and observances are nothing less than superstition. Among these may be named the veneration of the Host, the adoration of images, the entire cult centering about the Virgin Mary and the saints, particularly the belief in such phenomena as many alleged to have taken place at Lourdes and Loreto (qq.v.), together with the strongly entrenched regard for relics, such as the Holy Coat (q.v.). Yet to the devout Roman Catholic some of these things belong to the very arcana of the religion, and doubt of them seems little if at all short of blasphemy. Another illustration which comes from the same region is the Roman Catholic belief concerning the liquefaction of the blood of St. Januarius (q.v.), regarded by those of that faith as a recurrent miracle, while scientists scoff at the explanation of the alleged miracle, and point to the fact that analysis of the contents of the vial is refused. Of course the guardians decline to allow decisive tests on the ground of the sanctity of the relic. Agreement upon what constitutes a superstition in many cases of this sort is unattainable. The difficulty is not relieved if one considers that Roman Catholic authorities would almost certainly denounce as superstition the belief that incubation as practised in the cult of Asklepios (cf. Mary Hamilton, *Incubation, or the Cure of Diseases in Pagan Temples and Christian Churches*, London, 1906) resulted in cures, though it is claimed that cures result from the practise as maintained in connection with certain saints in Roman Catholic churches in and near Naples, at Amalfi, and elsewhere, as well as under the Greek Church (cf. Mary Hamilton, ut sup., pp. 109 sqq.). And the case is still more complicated by the fact that psychologists maintain the entire probability of many cases of cures under both pagan and Christian auspices, and offer what they deem scientific explanation of the alleged cures.

On its subjective side or as a mental attitude superstition seems to spring from four roots: (1) Ignorance, combined with the exceedingly prevalent and characteristically primitive fallacy of post hoc propter hoc, is a fundamental cause. Man has, so **4. Bases:** far as indications show, always sought **Ignorance;** for the reasons of events, but in his **Credulity.** lack of knowledge of real causes has often linked things causally which are not so connected. Thus, to give an example of savage logic, the breaking of the fluke of an anchor cast ashore from a wreck on the western coast of Africa having been followed by the death of the man who committed the act, his associates regarded the anchor as a divinity which had been offended by the mutilation and had punished the evil-doer, and they thereafter did reverence to the anchor as to a god (cf. E. B. Tylor, *Primitive Culture*, ii. 143 sqq., London, 1877). Similarly, bathing in a pool being followed by a scrofulous affection, the natives of the region regarded the pool as the haunt of a deity which was offended by the invasion and looked upon the disease as the penalty for the breach of the divinity's rights (cf. Tylor, ut sup., ii. 209 sqq.). In like manner, the fact that contact with a chief, or with some article belonging to him, had preceded some calamity to the person who touched him led to the belief that the chief and his possessions were taboo (see Comparative Religion, VI., 1, c), from which belief has unquestionably resulted the death of many natives of Australia, New Zealand, and other regions (*Old New Zealand, by a Pakeha Maori*, pp. 83, 94–97, London, 1884; A. S. Thomson, *The Story of New Zealand*, i. 103, ib. 1859). Thus, in some respects, superstition takes the form of pseudo-science. The cases are illustrative, and also representative of an enormous body of facts in human history; they serve to open up the wide range of primitive and later superstitions, including the practises of totemism, taboo, magic, fetishism, sacrifice, and the like (see Comparative Religion; Fetishism). (2) Involved in the foregoing is a credulity from which enlightened reason offers the only escape. That primitive and early man should accept either explanations which occurred to him in accordance with the methods of logic just exemplified, or those which tradition had supplied, was to be expected. Science, in the sense of careful induction, is a very modern product, and is the acquisition even yet of comparatively few. As a consequence, credulity is one of the most persistent traits of the mass of mankind, and those who exhibit it are perhaps proportionally almost as numerous in Christendom as elsewhere. As a striking example of this it is possible to cite the testimony of a clergyman at the trial of Dr. C. A. Briggs (q.v.) for heresy in 1893 to the effect that his mother in Scotland used to lay the Bible on the doorstep to keep out the witches. This custom is not yet entirely obsolete. Still widely prevalent and productive of corresponding actions is the belief in the validity of signs and omens, such as indications of the weather drawn from the inclination of the horns of the new moon, or in prophylactics and cures of various sorts such as that which regards as a cure or preventive of rheumatism the carrying in the pocket of a stolen potato, or as a cure for warts the rubbing of the same with a piece of stolen bacon rind (which is then to be buried). No reason adequate to the alleged effects can be assigned for the assumed causes, and induction finds no invariability in such antecedents and consequences. So that credulity is to be charged with a part at least in the continuance of superstition. It is important to note in this connection that credulity is in a sense communicable. A superstitious person, who is almost invariably dogmatic in his attitude, easily communicates and diffuses his anticipations or his dread and wins new adherents for his theories.

(3) The native conservatism of the human mind lends itself to the acceptance and retention of explanations or statements when once **5. Conserv-** they have become current. The au-**atism and** thority of tradition is potent, and what **Fear as** the fathers believed is often for that **Factors.** reason alone taken as fact. So that in this aspect superstition is an externalization of the native conservatism of the race. (4) Fear is also an element. Dread of what may

happen often overcomes " common sense," and a person who lives may even in the present under this influence do that which he will in other circumstances hesitate to acknowledge. The emotions are in modern life, and with the utmost certainty have always been, the strongest element in superstition. Faith is " felt " in certain " indications " in spite of the pronouncement of reason against them and of the mandate of the will not to receive them. Thus, as stated by Dresslar (ut sup., p. 150), " the ' will to believe ' and the reason for believing are both impotent when opposed by a well-developed *feeling* to believe." In other words, the emotions may override both reason and will. It is susceptible of proof that fear, as an emotion, is in part the result of certain physical conditions. This is illustrated by the fact that at night, when what psychologists call the subnormal and more primitive psychical forces are to the front and man's rational and higher faculties are less advantageously situated, the stress of superstitious fear is accentuated. Similarly, physical or mental or moral illness produces conditions favorable to the operation of superstition. Shakespeare noted the effects along this line in his saying, " Conscience does make cowards of us all " (*Hamlet*, III., i. 83). In this respect superstition, like Ecstasy (q.v.), belongs, so far as it is religious, to the pathology of religion, and altogether to the pathology of psychology.

Only the merest suggestion, comparatively, of the all-pervasiveness and the harmful effects of superstition in history can be afforded here. A brief summary of the story is given as follows in J. G. Frazer's *Psyche's Task* (p. 1, London, 1909): " It (superstition) has sacrificed countless lives, wasted untold treasures, embroiled nations, severed friends, parted husbands and wives, parents and children, putting swords, and worse than swords, between them: it has filled gaols and mad-**6. Histor-** houses with its innocent or deluded **ical Effects.** victims: it has broken many hearts, embittered the whole of many a life, and, not content with persecuting the living it has pursued the dead into the grave and beyond it, gloating over the horrors which its foul imagination has conjured up to appal and torture the survivors." How numerous its ramifications and products have been is merely hinted in the following list of subjects given as cross-references in a public-library catalogue card: Alchemy, apparitions, astrology, charms, delusions, demonology, devil-worship, divination, evil eye, fetishism, folk-lore, legends, magic, mythology, occult sciences, oracles, palmistry, relics, second sight, sorcery, spiritualism, supernatural, totems, and witchcraft. And this list is most incomplete. This force has pervaded all provinces of life from the cradle to the grave and, as Frazer says, beyond. It establishes customs as binding as taboo, dictates forms of worship and perpetuates them, obsesses the imagination and leads it to create a world of demons and hosts of lesser spirits and ghosts and ghouls, and inspires to fear and even worship of them. It has, even under Christianity, sought and received the sanction of the Church, as in the affirmation of Thomas Aquinas (*Quodlibeta*, xi. 10) regarding Witchcraft (q.v.) and in the bull *Summis desiderantes* of Innocent VIII. issued in 1484 commanding the clergy to assist in hunting out and punishing witches, and giving papal authority to belief in succubi, incubi, and other horrible figments of the diseased imagination (text of the bull is in Reich, *Documents*, pp. 200–201; cf. further, Schaff, *Christian Church*, v. 1, pp. 879 sqq., and 2, pp. 514 sqq.). And with equal force it has made use of the State, from the time of Hammurabi (q.v., II., 2) to the Salic Law (xix. 2; Eng. transl. in F. A. Ogg, *Source Book*, p. 64, New York, 1908), and even much later (see ORDEAL, § 9). It reestablished the pestiferous distinction between white magic and black, a distinction which seems to have existed in all grades of civilization. Its deadliest power, perhaps, is that by which it acquires influence over the commonest affairs of everyday life, stifling initiative, stagnating thought, poisoning the intellect, and subjecting activities to the imagined effects of chance happenings with which they have no relation.

The statement just made may be exemplified by reference to the list of current superstitions educed by the inductive study of the subject by Dresslar in the work already cited. The study was conducted upon the basis of questions submitted

7. Present to students of normal schools (there-
Super- fore adults or adolescents) in California
stitions. in the twentieth century. Things with which superstitions were connected were named as follows: salt, bread and butter, tea and coffee, plants and fruit; fire, lightning, rainbow, the moon, the stars; babies, birds, owls, peacocks and their feathers, chickens, cats, dogs, cows, sheep, swine, horses, rabbits, rats, frogs and toads, fish, crickets, spiders, snakes, lizards, turtles, wolves, bees, dragon flies; chairs and tables, clocks, mirrors, spoons, knives and forks, pointed instruments, pins, hairpins, combs, umbrellas (mostly unlucky), candles, matches, tea-kettle, brooms, dishcloths, handkerchiefs, gardening tools, ladders, horseshoes, hay; days of the week and various festivals or fasts, especially Hallowe'en, birthdays; various numbers, counting, laughing, singing, crying; starting on a journey and turning back, two persons simultaneously saying the same thing, passing in at one door and out at another, walking on opposite sides of a post, stepping on cracks, sneezing, crossing hands while shaking hands, use of windows as exits, stumbling; itching of palm, eye, nose, ear, or foot; warts, moles; various articles of dress, shoes, precious stones, amulets and charms, rings, money; wish bones; death and funerals, dreams, spiritisms, weddings, and initials. Of course, even this long list is most incomplete and might be expanded indefinitely. The practical significance of the beliefs registered in connection with these various beliefs or actions is that activities and procedure are supposed to be governed by them—action is indicated or inhibited according as the " sign " is favorable or unfavorable. A slavery with respect to action is thus shown which ought to be anomalous in enlightened Christendom, and yet is manifested as current.

A graver fact than the preceding is involved in the slavery of thought which is a consequence of the attention paid to " signs " and " omens." The function of the Church as an educator and the large

8. Present field which is here opened bring the
Conse- subject in this aspect into view with
quences. relation to religious duty. Knowledge of the actual work of the Church warrants the statement that not sufficient attention is paid to this side of the Church's paideutic mission. The preoccupation of the mind by such superstitious faiths can but retard the acceptance not merely of scientific but of religious truth. The very springs of healthy mental and spiritual perception are poisoned while such trivialities are permitted to control the sources of action. That such effects are very far-reaching, even to the control in a measure of business concerns of immense importance, is shown by the fact that some great corporations engaged in transoceanic transportation avoid Friday as a day of sailing, this custom being undoubtedly due in considerable part to the outworn sailors' superstition as to the misfortune which surely awaits the voyagers who set out on that day. And another consequence which is not paltry is that by such beliefs imposture is encouraged, while hosts of quacks in medicine, palmists, fortune-tellers, and " wizards " flourish on the credulity of the ignorant and deluded, at the same time that these beliefs are spread because the cunning and ambiguous pronouncements of the impostors are interpreted as wisdom by the victims and new strength is furnished to superstitious growths. Of the results in loss of life in more backward communities such as Russia and even Ireland, of sacrifices and cruelties practised even in the latter part of the nineteenth century and indeed in the city of New York itself, there is not space here to treat. How terrible the current beliefs and the almost contemporary consequences are may be discovered from the accounts in the *Popular Science Monthly* for 1898–99, pp. 207–218, of murders, e.g., of helpless infants supposed to be fairy changelings in the last part of the nineteenth century. And if at such a period events can occur such as are there recounted, the imagination must fail to portray what has happened in the darker ages of human history.

It is therefore no argument for the perpetuation of superstition that some fruits of good have resulted from its existence, such as those adduced by J. G. Frazer (in *Psyche's Task*, ut sup.). Examination of savage and barbarous life reveals that,

9. Contri- for instance, the institution of taboo
butions to founded essentially upon superstition
Develop- has entrenched respect for 'certain
ment. forms of government, especially those of a monarchical type, and in this way has contributed to the development of the body politic and consequently to society at large. By this means the will of the individual has within certain lines been subjected to what is recognized as a common good, a basis for a partially altruistic practise has been laid, and the exercise of self-denial has been fostered. In a similar way respect for private property has been enforced under fear of penalty impending from supernatural powers. In certain stages of development the suggestion and protection of the rights of ownership were

necessary in order to an attitude toward communal affairs which should make progress possible. And though this end was not consciously present, the historical effects are unquestioned. Another social institution, that of the family, has experienced some degree of unfolding under the protection of certain superstitions touching the relations of the sexes. It can not be doubted that the passions and lusts of man have been restrained, in part, it is probable, under instinctive impressions that license was injurious which registered themselves as superstitions, under the influence of which what is now known to be immorality was decreased, e.g., penalties of infidelity to marriage ties were imagined which checked indulgence and the welfare of society was thereby served. In a fourth way, namely, by hedging about the life of man and by introducing the fear of taking that life because of the penalties which would follow, the respect and honor for life itself upon which in so large measure present human society is founded has gradually been built up. The superstitions which have accomplished these results are as varied as the peoples among which they have worked; and under them and out of them man has changed in character from savagery and barbarism into something higher and more ennobling. These facts are, however, no plea for the continuance of illogical or irrational practises. To end them both the Church, with all its auxiliaries, and the State, employing especially educational means and processes, are obligated; the aim is to encourage man to honor his Creator by the intelligent and rational use of his powers as against the retention of customs or beliefs which are impeached by reason and by a lofty faith in God.　　　　GEO. W. GILMORE.

BIBLIOGRAPHY: The one work discussing superstition from the modern inductive standpoint is that by Dresslar, cited in the text. The literature giving the superstitions of various peoples is extremely abundant, and no attempt is made here to exhaust the list. Only some works concretely representative of the psychology of the subject from different religions are cited. The list of works given under FETISHISM; MAGIC; and WITCHCRAFT are of course pertinent, and are not repeated here. Especially valuable for concrete statements of superstition in the Americas are the painstaking Reports and other publications of the Smithsonian Institution. Sidney Hartland's Primitive Paternity, London, 1910, a discussion of certain concrete primitive superstitions, contains a very rich bibliography which should not be overlooked; and H. Webster's Primitive Secret Societies, New York, 1908, in the footnotes refers to literature on travels which are sources of very numerous facts. Discussions of superstitions are. R. Blakeman, Philosophical Essay on Credulity and Superstition, New York, 1849; C. Meyer, Der Aberglaube des Mittelalters, Basel, 1884; A. Lang, Custom and Myth, London, 1884; idem, Myth, Ritual, and Religion, ib. 1889; C. Rogge, Aberglaube, Volksglaube, und Volksbrauch, Leipsic, 1890; L. Strümpell, Der Aberglaube, Leipsic, 1890; L. J. B. Bérenger-Feraud, Superstitions et survivances étudiées au point de vue de leur origine et de leurs transformations, 5 vols., Paris, 1895–96; F. D. Bergen, Current Superstitions, Boston, 1896; A. Lehmann, Aberglaube und Zauberei, Stuttgart, 1898; A. D. White, Hist. of the Warfare of Science and Theology in Christendom, 2 vols., New York, 1898; E. P. Evans, in Popular Science Monthly, liv (1898), 206–221; idem, Criminal Prosecution and Capital Punishment of Animals, New York, 1906; A. Wuttke, Der deutsche Volksaberglaube der Gegenwart, 3d ed., Berlin, 1900; J. D. Hirsch, Der Aberglaube, Bielefeld, 1902; C. F. Robinson, in American Journal of Religious Psychology, Aug., 1904, pp. 249 sqq.; W. Fischer, Aberglaube aller Zeiten, 5 vols., Stuttgart, 1906–07; E. Westermarck, The Origin and Development of Moral Ideas, London, 1908; T. Sharper Knowlson, Origins of Popular Superstitions and Customs, London, 1910.

Useful as source books for various superstitions are: W. Ellis, Polynesian Researches, 2 vols., London, 1829; T. Wright, Narrative of Sorcery and Magic, 2 vols., London, 1851; T. F. Campbell, Popular Tales of the West Highlands, 4 vols., Edinburgh, 1862; R. Taylor, Te Ika A Maui; or New Zealand and its Inhabitants, London, 1870; S. Matier, The Land of Charity; a descriptive Account of Travancore and its People, London, 1871; A. R. Wallace, The Malay Archipelago, 6th ed., London, 1877; S. Baring-Gould, Curious Myths of the Middle Ages, many editions, e.g., Boston, 1882; J. Grimm, Teutonic Mythology, 4 vols., London, 1888; H. Spencer, Principles of Sociology, chaps. x.–xxvi., London, 1888; T. Parkinson, Yorkshire Legends and Traditions, 2 vols., London, 1889; A. B. Ellis, The Ewe-Speaking Peoples of the Slave Coast of West Africa, London, 1890; R. H. Codrington, The Melanesians, Oxford, 1891; J. Fiske, Myths and Myth-Makers, Boston, 1891; G. B. Grinnell, Blackfoot Lodge Tales, New York, 1892; J. Curtin, Hero Tales of Ireland, London, 1894; idem, Myths and Folk-Tales of the Russians, Western Slavs, and Magyars, Boston, 1903; F. Granger, The Worship of the Romans, London, 1895; W. Crooke, Popular Religion and Folk-Lore of Northern India, London, 1896; J. Abercromby, The Pre- and Proto-historic Finns, 2 vols., London, 1898; B. Spencer and F. J. Gillen, Native Tribes of Central Australia, London, 1899; idem, Northern Tribes of Central Australia, ib. 1904; J. G. Frazer, Golden Bough, 2d ed., 3 vols., London, 1900; J. G. Campbell, Superstitions of the Highlands and Islands of Scotland, Glasgow, 1900; idem, Witchcraft and Second Sight in the Highlands and Islands of Scotland, ib. 1902; F. H. Cushing, Zuñi Folk-Tales, New York, 1901; H. G. Hutchinson, Dreams and their Meaning, London, 1901; G. F. Abbott, Macedonian Folk-Lore, Cambridge, 1903; E. B. Tylor, Primitive Culture, 2 vols., London, 3d ed., 1903; E. L. Daniels, Encyclopedia of Superstitions, Folk-lore, and Occult Sciences, 3 vols., Chicago, 1903; A. W. Howitt, Native Tribes of South-East Australia, London, 1904; E. Crawley, The Tree of Life, London, 1905; C. Partridge, Cross River Nati.es, London, 1905; A. C. Kruijt, Het Animisme in den Indischen Archipel, The Hague, 1906; C. A. Sherring, Western Tibet and the British Borderland, London, 1906; E. M. Gordon, Indian Folk-Tales, London, 1908; B. Thomson, The Fijians, a Study of the Decay of Custom, London, 1908; A. C. Hollis, The Nandi, their Language and Folk-lore, Oxford, 1909; A. Freybe, Der deutsche Volksaberglaube in seinem Verhältnis zum Christentum und im Unterschiede von der Zauberei, Gotha, 1910; T. G. Knowlson, The Origins of Popular Superstitions and Customs, New York, 1910; The Laws of Manu, in SBE, vol. xxv.

SUPRALAPSARIANISM. See CALVINISM, § 8.

SUPREMACY, ACTS OF: Acts declaring the king (or queen) of England the head (or governor) of the Church of England and abrogating therefore the authority of the pope.

Henry VIII., although bent on retaining the chief points in Roman Catholic doctrine and worship, resolved to abolish in time papal jurisdiction within his realm. The rupture with Rome, at first attempted by means of gradual steps, was definitely accomplished in Nov., 1534, by the passing of the Act of Supremacy (26 Henry VIII., chap. 1), which conferred on the king the headship of the Church of England. The sovereign became, without qualification, " the only supreme head in earth of the Church of England, called ' Anglicana Ecclesia.' " This assumption of ecclesiastical jurisdiction was relinquished by Mary, who likewise repealed all the other enactments of her father's reign antagonistic to papal authority. Elizabeth's first act, when she felt assured of her position, was to nullify all the religious restorations of her sister, Mary. Her Supremacy Act (1 Elizabeth, chap. 1) was passed in Jan., 1559. It reenacted many of the antipapal acts of Henry VIII., and it vested the fulness of ecclesiastical jurisdiction in the crown. It prescribed for all holding office in Church and State an oath recognizing the Queen as " the only Supreme Governor of this realm as well in all spiritual and ecclesiastical things or causes, as temporals," and provided penalties for those refusing to take it.

SURIUS, su′rî-us, LAURENTIUS: German Carthusian; b. at Lübeck in 1522; d. at Cologne May 23, 1578. Probably of Protestant parentage, he was educated at Frankfort-on-the-Oder and at Cologne, where he became acquainted with Petrus Canisius; was won to Roman Catholicism, and, in 1541, became a Carthusian. All his subsequent life was characterized by his zeal for the exercise of the rules of his order, and, in his writings, by his passionate enthusiasm for his church and his violent hatred of the Reformation. Among his works was a *Commentarius brevis rerum in orbe gestarum ab anno 1500 usque in annum 1568* (Cologne, 1568), which was continued by others to 1673, and was in reply to Johann Sleidan's Protestant *Commentarii de statu religionis et reirepublicæ, Carolo Quinto Cæsare* (Strasburg, 1555), a famous history of the Reformation. He also wrote *Homiliæ sive conciones præstantissimorum ecclesiæ doctorum in evangelia totius anni* (1569); and *Concilia omnia* (1567). His main work was the *Vitæ sanctorum* (6 vols., 1570–75), republished with an additional volume under the title, *De probatis sanctorum historiis* (1618; 12 vols., Turin, 1875), which was recognized by the Bollandists as the best predecessor of their own hagiology (*ASB*). (O. Zöckler†.)

BIBLIOGRAPHY: A. Räss, *Die Convertiten seit der Reformation,* ii. 338 sqq., Freiburg, 1866; *ADB,* xxxvii. 166; *KL,* xi. 999–1001; *Der Katholik,* 1863, ii. 416 sqq.

SURPLICE. See VESTMENTS AND INSIGNIA, ECCLESIASTICAL.

SURPLICE FEES. See STOLE FEES.

SUSA. See SHUSHAN.

SUSANNA, HISTORY OF. See APOCRYPHA, A, IV., 3.

SUSO (SUS, SUSE, SEUSE), HEINRICH (AMANDUS): German mystic; b. at Constance Mar. 21, 1300; d. at Ulm Jan. 25, 1366. One of the greatest of German mystics, and the inspired prophet of the religious lyric, he understood how through divine love to influence a sinful world by the power of human love and sympathy. He came of a noble family, but took the name of his mother, a godly woman, in preference to that of his worldly father, Von Berg. Being delicate, he was destined for the ministry, and was permitted to enter the Dominican monastery when only thirteen. Being dissatisfied spiritually with the monastic routine, he sought to attain higher spirituality and devoted himself to the practise of asceticism, wearing a hair shirt studded with nails and a cross a span long, pierced with nails and needles, and remained for years in utter seclusion, in order to tame his spirit and subdue his body. While studying in Strasburg and Cologne, in his twenty-eighth year, he came under the influence and teaching of Eckhart (q.v.), whom he defended from the charge of heresy. Suso

practised asceticism until his fortieth year, when his system was so exhausted that, in order to save his body, he was forced to discontinue it. Returning to his monastery he became lector and prior. He sided with the pope in his dispute with Louis of Bavaria, and was banished from Constance and sent to Diessenhoven (1339–46). Here he began work as an itinerant preacher, also hearing confessions, and in his wanderings sought out the Dominican convent of Töss (near Winterthur) and met Elsbet Stagel, daughter of a councilor of Zurich, who was the original inspirer of the publication of his biography. He subsequently retired to Ulm, passing his later years in the Dominican monastery there. At what date he was summoned before a council and his books condemned, as containing false doctrine that contaminated the whole land, is uncertain.

Among Suso's writings was the so-called *Exemplar,* a collection of four treatises with a prologue: (1) the " Biography "; (2) " Book of Eternal Wisdom "; (3) " Little Book of Truth "; (4) " Little Book of Letters," to which was added an unabridged book of letters. A fifth work is *Horologium sapientiæ;* a sixth consisted of " Sermons," and there was possibly a seventh, the *Minnebüchlein.* The date of these books is unknown. The " Biography " owed its existence to Elsbet Stagel, who wrote down all that Suso had told her of his life. On learning this, Suso destroyed a portion of the notes and expanded and revised the rest, not observing chronological order, but describing his inner life, using his career merely as a guide to the attainment of Christian perfection. He finished it shortly before his death. The " Book of Eternal Wisdom " became one of the favorite books of meditation of the Middle Ages. Suso made a free Latin translation of it, the *Horologium sapientiæ,* in order to present it to Hugo von Beaucemain, who was general of his order, 1333–41, and this fixes its probable date. The " Book of Truth " is mainly devoted to the defense of Eckhart, and to that end is directed against the Beghards (see BEGHARDS AND BEGUINES) and the Brethren of the Free Spirit (see FREE SPIRIT, BRETHREN OF THE), who distorted Eckhart's teachings.

The aim of all Suso's teaching was to point the path to perfection, as it was made plain to him in his monastic study of the writings of Solomon, during which time he had visions of Christ and of the Virgin Mary. Many of his views and speculations are derived from the great teachers of the Church, John of Damascus, Augustine, Bonaventura, and others. In certain points Eckhart's views are distinctly recognizable, as, for instance, the teaching that in aspiring to perfection man becomes one with God. Suso's aim, however, was not speculation; he sought to make religion have a practical bearing on life. (FERDINAND COHRS.)

BIBLIOGRAPHY: The writings of Suso were first edited by F. Fabri, Augsburg, 1482, then by A. Sorge, 1512, L. Surius' Lat. transl., Cologne, 1555, by H. Diepenbrock *Heinrich Susos . . . Leben und Schriften,* Regensburg 1829, 4th ed., 1884, by Denifle, Munich, 1880, and by H. E. Bihlmeyer, Stuttgart, 1907; Fr. transl. by Thirot 2 vols., Paris, 1899; and the *Briefe,* ed. W. Preger, Leipsic, 1876. Preger also edited an additional and previously unknown writing in *AMA,* III. Klasse, xxi. 2, pp

425 sqq. On Suso's life and works consult: C. Schmidt, in *TSK*, 1843, pp. 835 sqq.; F. Bricka, *Henri Suso*, Strasburg, 1854; *The Life of Blessed Henry Suso, by himself*, transl. from the German by T. F. Knox, London, 1865; the *Programm* of the Gymnasium of Duisburg for 1869 by Volkmann; L. Kärcher, in *Freiburger Diöcesenarchiv*, 1868, pp. 187 sqq.; F. Böhringer, *Die Kirche Christi in ihre Zeugen*, xviii. 1 sqq., Stuttgart, 1878; W. Preger, *Geschichte der deutschen Mystik im Mittelalter*, ii. 309 sqq., Leipsic, 1881; F. Vetter, *Ein Mystikerpaar des 14. Jahrhunderts*, Basel, 1882; K. Goedeke, *Grundriss zur Geschichte der deutschen Dichtung*, i. 212, Dresden, 1884; R. Seeberg, *Ein Kampf um jenseitiges Leben: Lebensbild eines mittelalterlichen Frommen*, Dorpat, 1889; K. Jäger, *Heinrich Seuse aus Schwaben*, Basel, 1894; H. Delacroix, *Études d'hist. et de psychologie du mysticisme*, Paris, 1908; R. A. Vaughan, *Hours with the Mystics*, i. 341 sqq., 8th ed., London, n.d.; Schaff, *Christian Church*, v. 2, pp. 233–234, 262 sqq.; *ADB*, xxxvii. 169 sqq.; *KL*, v. 1721–29.

SUSPENSION. See Jurisdiction, Ecclesiastical, I., 1, § 5.

SUTEL, sū'tel, **JOHANN:** German Reformer; b. at Altenmorschen near Melsungen (50 m. n.e. of Giessen) 1504; d. at Northeim (48 m. s.e. of Hanover) Aug. 26, 1575. In 1518 he went to Erfurt to study, and after the completion of his education became rector in Melsungen. In 1530 he was called to Göttingen as Evangelical preacher. At first he preached at the Church of St. Nicolaus; later he received the parish of St. John's as Evangelical superintendent. In 1542 Landgrave Philip of Hesse called him to Schweinfurt to introduce the Reformation there, where he formulated a church order for the city under the title, *Kirchenordnung Eines Ehrbaren Raths des heiligen Reichs Stadt Schweinfurt in Franken* (Nuremberg, 1543); but the outbreak of the Schmalkald War compelled his flight from the city in 1547. After a short activity as pastor in Allendorf (1547–48), he became again preacher in Göttingen at the congregation of St. Alban (1548–55). In 1555 he accepted a call to the Church of St. Sixtus at Northeim, where he labored until his death. He published *Artikel wider das päpstliche Volk in Göttingen* (1531); *Das Evangelium von der grausamen erschrecklichen Zerstörung Jerusalems* (Wittenberg), with a preface by Luther; *Historia von Lazaro, aus dem XI. Kapitel das Evangelii S. Johannis gezogen* (1543).

(Paul Tschackert.)

Bibliography: P. Tschackert, *Johann Sutel*, Brunswick, 1897; H. C. Beck, *Sutellius*, Schweinfurt, 1842 (good only for the Schweinfurt period).

SVERDRUP, tsvär'drup, **JAKOB LIV ROSTED:** Norwegian clergyman and statesman; b. in Christiania Mar. 27, 1845; d. in Bergen June 11, 1899. He was graduated from Nissens Skole (B.A., 1864) and from the University of Christiania (Candidate in Theology, 1867). A traveling scholarship from the government enabled him to study the people's high schools in Denmark (see Grundtvig) which proved profitable to him when he organized a like school in Sognedal. These institutions pay special attention to influencing the personality of young men and women, fostering an affection for country and mother-tongue. The attempt is not to train the pupils for any particular position in life or for examination, but to fit the pupils by general culture for whatever sphere of life they are called upon to enter. Sverdrup taught in such a school, 1871–

1878; in 1878 he was appointed parish priest for Leikanger in Sogn. He had already become a power in local politics, and in 1876 had been elected member of the Storthing, in which he held a seat until 1884.

During these years of service in the Storthing he was an active worker in the committee on ecclesiastical matters. In 1884 when Johan Sverdrup, Norway's greatest statesman, was elected prime minister, Jakob Sverdrup, his nephew, was made a member of the cabinet, and in 1885–89 he was chief of the department for ecclesiastical affairs and public instruction. To him Norway owes the adoption of two new series of pericopes (1887), and of a new liturgy and book of worship (1889). Through his efforts the State came to permit a greater latitude in using the churches. When a new ministry was formed, 1889, Jakob Sverdrup got a well-earned respite as legislator. He was appointed parish priest in Bergen, which anew elected him member of the Storthing, where he served 1892–97. After a schism in the liberal political party, he became one of the leaders of the moderate wing. Twice he was requested by the king to form a new ministry—the existing union with Sweden was the burning question—but he could not comply with the king's wishes because of political opposition at home. In 1895 he was a second time appointed member of the cabinet and chief of the department for ecclesiastical matters. With his gift of organizing, fine political intuition (a family birthright), and his great learning, he was instrumental in having passed a number of salutary measures regarding churches, cemeteries, salaries of the clergy, etc. With the resignation of the entire ministry Feb. 17, 1898, he retired from political life, and was appointed bishop of Bergen. But before he could be consecrated, a painful disease, which kept him confined after Mar., 1898, terminated his life.

Perhaps no one has worked so faithfully and aggressively to give the State Church of Norway a liberal form of self-government. He followed the plan, originated by his father, of building up the Norwegian church on a national basis true to the ideas of the Reformation. As leader of the democratic element in the western part of Norway he was a strong opponent of High-church bureaucracy as well as of the anti-Christian literary movements which were undermining the morals of the Norwegian people. An illustration of the first was his continuous opposition to the High-church conception of the office of the ministry held by J. N. Skaar, later bishop.

By his translations of French and German religious works, by his sermons, essays, debates—scattered in an immense amount of printed matter, too large to be covered here—his name is familiar to every household in Norway. He was coeditor of *Ny Luthersk Kirketidende*, 1877–81. Of special interest to the American reader is an article on the oldest Norwegian theological school in America, Augsburg Seminary, founded 1869, now quite Anglicized, in *Luthersk Kirketidende*, 1875, no. 14. Likewise his *Forklaring over Luthers lille Katekisme* (1893), an abbreviated edition of his father's epitome of Luther's catechism, which in 1898 passed through the nineteenth edition. It has been translated into English by H. A. Urseth, *Luther's Small Catechism Explained* (Minneapolis, 1900).   JOHN O. EVJEN.

BIBLIOGRAPHY: J. B. Halvorsen, *Norsk Forfatter-Lexikon*, v. 537 sqq., Christiania, 1901 (contains a complete list of his works).

SWEDEN.

Sweden is a kingdom constituting the eastern side of the Scandinavian peninsula in northwestern Europe. It has an area of 172,876 square miles and a population (1909) of 5,476,441.

I. History. 1. The Missionary Period (830–1130): In the beginning of the ninth century, the Norse religion had assumed a strong monotheistic tendency. Thor and Odin had acquired preeminence over the other gods, who, on the other hand, were multiplied in the direction of polytheism. This twofold tendency prepared the soil for the reception of Christ, and Sweden was one of the few heathen countries in which missionary activity took its initiative from the natives themselves. The belief in heathen deities was not in decadence, but the proclamation of Christ was not in the eyes of the Scandinavians necessarily inimical to their system of religion; so that everywhere old Norse representations, with little alteration, could be transplanted to the soil of triumphant Christianity. It was a matter of outward test between the strength of Christ and the ancient gods. This is why, all through the Middle Ages, old national ideas and beliefs endeavored to reshape the Roman Catholic Church. Great political interests had a share in Christianizing Sweden, influencing the sending of the first missionary, Ansgar (q.v.), in 830. Sweden became one of the northern world powers in the ninth and tenth centuries, taking part in the wars in western Europe; Denmark was at times under its control; and the Russian kingdom was established by Sweden (Rus) under Rurik about 860. Sweden was also in close relation with the Byzantine orient at this time, and of such importance as to attract missionary zeal. The missionary history falls into three periods. The first consists of incipient sporadic efforts for 150 years under the archbishop of Hamburg-Bremen. After Ansgar's death in 865 his work was carried on by Rimbert. Of the succeeding archbishops Unni seems to have been most active in the Swedish mission, and died while on a visit to Birka in 936. There were probably few Christians in this period; the mission exerted no influence upon national interests; the chief end seems to have been to bring Sweden under German domination and culture.

With the beginning of the eleventh century external conditions changed. Christianized Denmark had obtained inner stability; with the help of England King Olaf Trygvesson (995–1000) of Norway had Christianized his countrymen; and after the battle of Svoldern (1000), Svend (Sweyn I.), the redoubtable king of Denmark, who had brought England under his yoke (1014), annexed part of Norway. His son Knut the Great, or Canute, bred in England, introduced English interests. On the other hand, the archbishops of Hamburg-Bremen struggled to preserve their northern interests. The work of evangelizing was prosecuted with earnest zeal from two directions (1000–66), with the result that the kingdom was won to Christianity. In 1008 Olaf Skottkonung, with many of his nobles, was baptized at Husaby in West Gothland, in spite of the fact that he and his successors retained their office as chief defenders of the heathen worship and of the national temple at Upsala. It is disputed whether Siegfried, who baptized Olaf, was German or English, but the fact remains that West Gothland, bordering on Norway, first received Christianity from Norway, probably through the English priest, Sigurd, who is almost certainly the same as Siegfrid, and in this manner came to be one of the greatest saints of Sweden. He also preached in Småland, where he is venerated as the founder of the church in Vexiö. One effect of the leaven of Christianity among the people was the awakening of individual consciousness; there arose a desire to hand down the names of their dead to posterity. Most of the runic inscriptions date from this period; and these stones show that Christianity was now spreading to East Gothland, and as far as Svealand. But West Gothland was its head source, and the first bishopric was nominally erected there at Skara (Thurgot was first bishop of Skara, c. 1025). Those called bishops in Sweden at this time were really missionary bishops. King Olaf and his sons, Anund and Edmund, carried on a very prudent religious policy, exercising no pressure to hasten the conversions. The Swedish mission developed more rapidly after Adalbert became archbishop of Bremen, and he succeeded in maintaining the dominance of German influence; Adalvard I. and Adalvard II., ordained by him, introduced Christianity to the north, the former to Värmland, the latter to Sigtuna in Uppland, which later became the chief seat of the church of North Sweden. John the Monk was bishop of Birka, the first monastic known to have worked in Sweden after the time of Ansgar. Stenfi, another German missionary, went to Helsingland and became the apostle of the Lapps, and a rune record that Jemtland was now Christianized. The first church was built in Gothland and around it the town of Visby grew. Asmund, a relative of Sigurd who had obtained access to King Edmund, sought in Rome to obtain ordination independently of Bremen; but Adalbert thwarted his plans. The year of the Norman conquest in England 1066, witnessed the downfall of Adalbert and the severing of the relations with Germany, through the reaction of heathenism in the German colonies. All attempts, therefore, to unite Sweden with the interests of the German Empire were at an end. The pope's desire was to free the north from Bremen and attach it to his interest. Gregory VII. was the first pope to interfere directly in Swedish affairs (two letters addressed to King Inge, 1080 and 1081, inviting him to send ambassadors and contributions to Rome). Stenkil, the last king capable of holding together the kingdom, died in 1066, and the national assembly was dissolved for a century. The antagonism between the provinces became more marked (according to some, between two races, the Svea, or Swedes, and the Goths); the more prominent provinces, West Gothland, East Gothland, and Uppland, had each its royal stock, although for a short time Stenkil's successors, who were of West Gothland, maintained a certain preeminence over the rest of the country. They were Christian, but had not the wise tolerance of their predecessors; and thus the opposition to the practically heathen Svealand and the Upsala temple became more intense. The people there demanded that the king should preside over the heathen sacrificial worship. This discord was turned to good account by the missionaries in spreading the Gospel. East and West Gothland were, in 1100, the chief stronghold of Christianity, and Svealand now joined them. According to legend, David was the apostle to Westmanland, and Eskil and Botvid were the apostles to Södermanland; and they all came from England or had been educated there. Anselm, archbishop of Canterbury, who upheld the papacy, became interested in Sweden, and it was partly due to him that Lund was made the see of an archbishop of the northern countries in 1104, although Sweden's formal dependence on Bremen was not dissolved until 1150. English bishops were also sent to Skara. The downfall of the ancient gods was due to the work of the English missionaries; finally, in Uppland, where Sigtuna became the seat of a bishopric; and by 1130 Sweden may be considered a Christian country.

2. The Roman Catholic Period: A brief period (1130–64) of national dissolution closed these internal conflicts simultaneously with the weakening of English aggression by interior disturbances at Rome; this appears to have been especially favorable to plans for Roman Catholic organization in Sweden. Almost all institutions which were favorable to the Church and to the culture of the Middle Ages entered at this time or strengthened their position. Behind the work of organization was the strong hand of Archbishop Eskil of Lund (1137–78). Bishoprics were established in Skara, Linköping, Upsala (removed from Sigtuna), Strengnäs, Westerås, and later, Wexiö, first mentioned in 1183; Åbo, in Finland, the last in the Middle Ages, was founded by 1200. With Eskil's assistance the first monasteries were erected in Sweden, and they belonged to the Clairvaux branch of the Cistercian order. The most important of these were Alvastra in East Gothland, 1143, and Nydala in Småland, 1144. Pope Eugenius III. attempted to make Sweden an independent church province. As legate he sent Nicholas Breakspear, afterward Pope Adrian IV., who, after erecting Norway into an archbishopric, called the Synod of Linköping in 1152. Owing to disagreement on the primacy, the plan failed.

Archbishop Eskil received the pallium intended for Sweden, and the Danish Lund obtained the primacy over Sweden. As a token of Swedish dependence on the Church of Rome, the synod decreed the annual contribution of Peter's pence. The first missionary crusade was a sign that the Church was awakening to self-consciousness. King Eric of Uppland, the rival of King Sverker of East Gothland for the national throne, undertook a crusade, in 1150, to heathen Finland, where, in the southwestern part, a mighty work of conversion was carried on. It is impossible to determine whether there was a political motive behind this, but Eric acquired fame above all other Swedes as a warrior of God; and when, shortly after, he was assassinated by a Danish pretender to the throne, he was crowned as a martyr, and thus became patron saint of Sweden. He was revered also in Denmark and Germany. Equal reverence was accorded in Sweden to the Norwegian Saint Olaf, in the earlier Middle Ages. The establishment of an archbishopric at Upsala in 1164 was the culmination of the work of establishing the Roman Catholic Church; and Sweden became a self-governing church province. This was the result of the Gregorian policy of Alexander III., who feared the growth of large archiepiscopal dioceses; and it was a powerful obstacle to Frederick I. in attaching Sweden to German interests. But the founding of this archbishopric was important as a factor in the individual development of Sweden. The primate of Lund still retained the right to consecrate the archbishop of Upsala; but the one desire of the Swedish Church was to free itself from this vestige of foreign dependence.

The next period (1164–1305) was that of organization. Karl, the son of Sverker, soon gained recognition in Svealand, and Sweden once more became a united kingdom. The ecclesiastical system of law and organization served as prototype for the developing state system; on the other hand, it was **2. Organ-** the papal policy to support a unified **ization.** kingly rule. Such a government was indispensable to the inner organization of the newly established church with respect to the requirements of canonical law. The archbishop of Sweden became the king's main support, and Sweden's political unity was confirmed by the establishment of the archbishopric. The descendants of Sverker and Eric, reigning alternately for ninety years, both depended on the support of the Church, which, independent of their disputes, could, with their assistance, erect new edifices. The jurist pope, Alexander III., issued a number of decretals to the king and bishops of Sweden; and two letters (1171) may be considered the earliest basic laws of the Swedish Church. Ecclesiastical jurisdiction in criminal cases was demanded for the clergy, and canonical testaments were to be admitted, *in pios usus.* A conflict ensued between canonical and old Germanic legal views. By 1200 the priests were universally exempt from secular jurisdiction in criminal law. A special priestly status began. In 1219 John I., son of Sverker, placed the church property outside the royal penal levy, thus originating ecclesiastical freedom from taxation. At the instance of the popes, the establishment of cathedral chapters in the episcopal sees was begun; about the year 1200 Upsala had regular canons. This collegiate organization served as a basis for the later development of state law. During the papacy of Innocent III., the king appealed for coronation to the Church. While Germany and Denmark were making conquests in Livonia, a Swedish crusade set out for Esthonia. The long struggle for the supremacy over the Baltic now began. The reign of Eric III. (1222–50), the last of the old dynasty, was the most important period in the organization of the Church, and it would seem as if anarchy had been the best soil for its development. The prelates advanced as the most powerful figures of the regency and of the incipient institution of councils. Bishop Bengt of Skara, a man of great political foresight, visited Rome in 1220–21, and he established the chapter at Skara, probably the first secular chapter in Sweden. Bishop Bengt of Linköping, his contemporary, established a cathedral chapter in 1232, and began the erection of a magnificent cathedral in Linköping. The chapter at Abo was founded at this time. Archbishop Jarler (1236–55) restored as a secular chapter the defunct chapter at Upsala, and introduced the mendicant orders. After 1230 monastic life became a chief factor in the Swedish Church; the rising cities from the beginning of the twelfth century were closely identified with its interests. The Franciscans came to Wisby in 1233, and went from thence to various towns in 1240, and to Upsala in 1247. The Dominicans, of more importance, first established themselves firmly in Sigtuna, where their cloister became one of the most famous in Sweden, and then founded a scarcely less important one in Skennige. Many others were built in various towns. A new crusade to Finland was undertaken in 1249. This had long been a pet scheme of Gregory IX. to counteract the Palestinian politics of Frederick II. At its head was the most powerful man in the country, the king's jarl, Birger, of the old race of the Folkungar. Tavastland was now converted. King Eric on the demand of Innocent IV. gave the church legal jurisdiction over certain offenses of the laity, and exempted cathedral property from taxation. The organization of the lower clergy and the episcopal divisions were confirmed. And now Innocent IV., in accordance with his greater political schemes, sent the cardinal-bishop, Wilhelm of Sabina, who understood northern conditions, invested with great authority as cardinal-legate. He knew how to turn the internal troubles to the benefit of the Church. At a provincial synod at Skennige (1248), it was decreed that the clergy be obligated to celibacy; and that the bishops procure and study the last collection of decretals. Innocent IV. supplemented the same by an ordinance that the bishops should be chosen by the cathedral chapter, and not, as heretofore, by popular vote and the sanction of the king. This was the corner-stone of the Roman Catholic edifice. In the next half-century, celibacy was very gradually established and the canonical choice of bishops simultaneous with the universal organization of cathedral chapters. The seat of the archbishopric was transferred from Old-Upsala to Upsala in 1270, and its incumbent presided over the great

national assemblies. Political events shaped themselves in the interest of the Church. The Folkungar Magnus Ladulâs overthrew his brother, Waldemar, in 1275; but in return for the assistance of the Church in his coronation had to grant almost all the demands made by Gregory X. in a decretal to Sweden in 1274. By this means, all church property, even the diocesan churches, became exempt from taxation and the legal authority of the Church was extended. The conditions by which the king was bound were ratified at the Synod of Telje, 1277, which was the most important in the history of the Swedish Church, whose independent position in the kingdom was now complete. Under the protection of Magnus the mendicant orders took on new life and many new cloisters were built, the most important of which were the Franciscan monastery at Riddarholm in Stockholm in 1270, and the monastery of the Poor Clares at the Norrmalm in Stockholm in 1289. The Franciscans became the most influential order; mendicant monks frequently became bishops. Church instruction, carried on principally by the Dominicans in Skennige, began to improve. Swedes began to study diligently in Paris, where they had a house, 1285. Collections of books were taken to Sweden, and the first Swedish writer of any importance was Petrus de Dacia, a Dominican lector in Skennige (d. 1288). Educated at Cologne he studied under Thomas Aquinas, and was of a deep mystical nature. His language may be taken as a sample of the speech of the thirteenth century. Mysticism in Sweden began with him. In every department the Church advanced under royal promotion, which was reciprocally requited; yet the alliance bore the seed of future conflict. Progress attained to less power than in the neighboring lands. There was a tenacious adherence to the old Germanic legal point of view, retarding canonical innovation. In important questions the Church was forced to yield to King Magnus, as in the case of the long-desired canonical testament law; and thus a definite limit was set to the economic extension of the power of the Church. The Swedes maintained their ancient popular right of appointment to the lower ecclesiastical offices in a manner almost unparalleled in church history. A fruit of the political awakening was the establishment of the Swedish organic law which relatively culminated in the granting of the code of 1300. In ecclesiastical specifications this was an apparent compromise with canon law, but in general the basic Swedish character and standpoint were maintained. The last crusade (1290) effected the conversion of Karelia and occasioned the beginning of the long Russian wars. To the climax of outer and inner organization was lacking only release from the primacy of Lund but this came practically with the close of the thirteenth century when Nils Allesson, archbishop of Upsala, received the pallium.

The dominant period of the Church (1305–1448) opens with the regent administration of Marshal Torgils Knutsson who represented in Sweden the beginning of political reaction against the preponderance of the Church, which at that time was felt all over Europe, and found its principal representative in Philip the Fair. Greater restriction were placed on the Church's freedom from taxation, the ecclesiastical taxation of the peasantry was remitted, and church property was

3. The Height of Power. even confiscated; but this aroused the opposition of the prelates. The infamous King Birger, when he had attained his majority, capitulated to the lay and spiritual rulers. At the great conference at Strengnäs (1305) the prelates allied themselves with the nobles against the crown, the control of the feudal lords began, and the hierachy returned to power. The struggle between Birger and his brothers issued in a complete revolution resulting in the accession of Magnus, the three-year-old son of Duke Eric, to the throne. The government conducted by lay and spiritual lords was not advantageous to the kingdom. Finally, the demands of Magnus becoming too exacting, and a parliament being threatened, he was deposed and Albrecht of Mecklenburg was enthroned. His economic demands conflicting with the Church he lost its support and subsequently his throne. The rule of the nobles was still further confirmed by the so-called Kalmar Union of 1389. The consummation of outward power was accompanied with intense internal activity. The only bishop-saints are of this period. Matthias of Linköping, the confessor of Bridget (q.v.), was the foremost scholastic theologian in Sweden of the Middle Ages and the first to attempt a translation of the Bible, the earliest attempt at a German rendering. This period was the most active in culture in Swedish history. Religion was to a great extent robbed of its grossness, and became an ennobling power. The monks and priests now began to preach in Swedish. The rich culture of the Middle Ages became so securely planted in Sweden that it weathered all subsequent storms; philanthropy on a large scale fostered by the Church spread over country and city, and the treasures of learning were rendered available. The zenith of development in the fourteenth century is in striking contrast with the decay of the Church elsewhere in the West. St. Bridget (q.v.) was a contemporary of Wyclif, Petrarch, and Boccaccio; and she and her order, in which all church activities were concentrated, stand as evidence of this florescent period of the Swedish church. At the beginning of the fifteenth century the decline of the papacy produced more pronounced results in Sweden. Margaret and after her, Eric of Pomerania, the regents, lived in Denmark; they were in accord with the pope whenever it came to plundering the Church. Both pope and king repeatedly attempted to name the archbishop at Upsala. Their most degraded choice was the Dane, Jöns Jerkerson in 1408, who was forced to leave Sweden in 1419. These disputes resulted in the Church becoming interested in the endeavors for reform and in the growing national desire for an independent Sweden. Although, during the papal schism, Sweden had united itself to the papacy, its church took part in the reform councils, and recognized their authority over that of the pope, and preaching in Swedish came more and more into vogue. Many churches were built. Almost forty years Bishop Tavast served as the apostle of the Finns, and his work was continued by the order of St. Bridget. When the great struggle for freedom began (1434) with the uprising of the peasants under the popular hero, Engelbrecht, it found an advocate at the Council of Basel in its prominent Swedish representative, Nils Ragnaldsson, who became archbishop in 1438–1448, and steered the Swedish Church with extraordinary wisdom and piety through the political tempests. A provincial synod at Söderköping, 1441, passed several measures for the extension of a true Christianity among the lower classes, and for the foundation of an independent Swedish educational institution; but the University of Upsala was not founded until 1477.

The next period (1448–1520) is marked by the struggle of the modern ideas of state with the hierarchy following the victory of the papacy over the councils. In 1448 the Union was dissolved by the election of Charles Knutsson as

4. Struggle of the Rising Nationality with the Hierarchy. king; a domestic kingdom serving the national interest now arose. Nils dying in this year, Jöns Bengtsson Oxenstierna became archbishop. He was a typical upholder of ecclesiastical dominance, which saw the danger to the Church of a powerful royal authority. King Charles's investigations into the illegality of the church holdings incensed all the prelates (1454). Jöns led the hierarchy over to the side of the Danish union; or rather, it united with the feudal nobility in their struggles with the State. The disgrace and death of Jöns, upon his flight in 1467, put an end to his endeavors to combine all ecclesiastical and political power in his own hands. His successors with the suffragans followed in his steps. The regents Sture had to accustom themselves to the prelates as the opponents of national liberation and reorganization. An exception was Heming Gad, bishop of Linköping from 1501 and one of the few advocates of humanism in Sweden, a warrior and poet inspired by deep love of country. The pope never confirmed his election, and he was excommunicated in 1512, and gave place to Hans Brask, the last noted prince of the Swedish Church. Brask, after some vacillation, adopted the interests of hierarchy. The lower clergy, on the other hand, were frequently loyal to their fatherland, and awaited a brighter future; as, for instance, Ericus Olai (d. 1486), the most learned man in the new university. In this long struggle the Swedish hierarchy had neglected the peasantry. This caused the downfall of the inner power of the Roman Church in Sweden. None of the pre-Reformation influences elsewhere, as humanism and hostility to indulgences, were present in Sweden. The change came with a political crisis, followed by political reestablishment. Of this the Reformation was an attendant circumstance.

3. The Later Period: The great Reformer of Sweden, Olaus Petri (b. at Oerebro, 100 m. w. of Stockholm, Jan. 6, 1493; d. at Stockholm Apr. 19, 1552), studied at Upsala, Leipsic, and Wittenberg with Luther and Melanchthon, 1516–18; and became a deacon at the cathedral of Strengnäs in 1520. Eloquent, genial, and faithful, he here won to his side the old archdeacon Lorenz Andreä (q.v.), the greatest political ecclesiastic of the Swedish reformation, who introduced the new teachings to Gustavus Vasa, and was made secretary to the king,

1. The Reformation (1520-1611). and counselor. For a short period, when the feudal and unionist policy had reaped its reward in the Stockholm massacre in 1205, the whole country appeared to be crushed and lost; but the peasants of Dalecarlia arose under Gustavus Vasa to fight for national freedom. The Danish Christian II. had executed the former leaders, among them most of the bishops; in 1522 only two bishoprics were filled. The popular uprising resulted in the establishment of a national government, in 1523, in Strengnäs, and the king, as the people's choice, was invested with purely personal authority. In every department, however, the Roman Church, forming a state within a state, appeared as an obstacle, particularly on the economic side; for after the war Sweden was an impoverished, defenseless country, unless it could avail itself of the wealth of the churches and monasteries. The king at once recognized the value of the new teachings as a means to a popular national regeneration, the principle of which was to unite the whole population in the common obligation to rescue and defend their fatherland, and in the common responsibility for the execution of necessary measures and their consequences. The king was the accountable personification of this union; the entire people shared in his undertakings, and were therefore responsible to him as long as he maintained the defense and prosperity of the country. The religious life of the people formed no exception, and the king was obliged personally to conduct the whole reform, so far as it came within the interests of the State. It was Gustavus Vasa who decided on the manner of introducing the Reformation, as appeared at the decisive diet which he assembled at Westerås (1527). He compelled the decision of the diet assisted by the nobility and the military party. By this decision, the Church was freed from Rome and the rule of canonical law; its possession were placed at the disposal of the king (except the parsonages), and the nobles were bound to the throne by the acquisition on their part of the church property. It was decreed that " the Word of God should be preached purely and plainly "; formally, religious freedom for Protestantism only was introduced. There was no loud demand for religious changes. In fact, however, Protestantism had to ensue as the successor of abolished Rome. All the estates subscribed the resolutions, and in this manner the national popular government, through its king, maintained the right to watch over the development of the Church. The inner work of the Reformation meanwhile progressed slowly, guided by the wisdom and prudence of Olaus Petri, who in 1524 had been removed to Stockholm as preacher and secretary for the city. In 1526 he translated Luther's " Prayer-book," the first Reformation publication in Sweden, and the same year gave the people a translation of the New Testament, which had the same influence on the language and culture of Sweden as Luther's translation of the Bible had in Germany. He also collaborated in the publication of the first hymnal. The Roman Catholics were lacking in able defenders. Brask, who at first set up a vigorous opposition, had to flee after the Synod of Westeras and died in exile in 1538. When Gustavus Vasa supplied the vacated bishoprics by installing such men as were then available, consecration was performed by Petrus Magni, a monk of the order of St. Bridget, who had himself received episcopal consecration from the pope at Rome. Thus the so-called " Apostolic succession " was preserved. The latest writings of Olaus Petri, which were in accord with the decisions of the Synod of Oerebro (1529), in regard to outward religious forms, were the " Church Manual " (1529), the " Postil," the " Catechism " (1530), and the " Swedish Mass " (1531). Olaus Petri was aided by his brother, Laurentius, who became the first Protestant archbishop of Sweden, 1531. A Swedish translation of the whole Bible was given out by the brothers Petri in 1541, and new Reformation literature was spread abroad. Under ultra-reform influence, Gustavus attempted (1539–43) to do away with the office of bishop, to install " *superattendenten* " over the entire Swedish Church, and to establish a sort of presbyterian rule. Olaus Petri and Lorenz Andreä, on account of their opposition, were sentenced to death (1540), but were pardoned, though they did not regain their former influence (both died in 1552). The opposition of the people recalled the king to his former policy. A diet at Westerås discarded more Roman Catholic forms and usages, and a compilation of church laws, *Vadstena artiklar* (1553), drawn up probably by the archbishop, was the first attempt to make the Church a purely Protestant organization. Eric XIV., successor of Gustavus, not being able to maintain the personal character of government, the Church slipped somewhat from royal control, and its administrative forces, particularly the archiepiscopate, increased greatly in importance. The great religious war of Europe now spread to Sweden. Calvinism sought to establish a firm footing (1560–68); and Calvin himself corresponded with Eric, and his followers presented to the king a formula of belief. This movement was opposed by Laurentius Petri, and the result was an internal development through which the Church became more narrowed to Evangelical Lutheranism. A result, as well as the last work of Laurentius (d. 1573), was the church order of 1571, which prevailed for a century. A Counter-Reformation was threatened by the fact that Catherine, wife of King John III., was a Roman Catholic. In 1574 the first Jesuit came to Sweden. John, who had been under the influence of the party of Melanchthon and the development of the English Reformation, sought a safe middle path. His " Red Book," a new order of the mass, was to reunite the Swedish Church with the old true Roman Catholic Church. The papal obstinacy to the compromise put an end to Roman influence in 1580; but the controversy concerning the Red Book and cryptopapacy constituted the baptismal fire of Lutheranism and produced a generation of staunch characters, so that upon John's death (1592) it was, with the support of Duke Charles, son of Gustavus I. completely triumphant. The synod called by Duke Charles, now regent, in Upsala (1593) was the most important in the history of the Swedish Lutheran Church. The Red Book was prohibited and al-bound themselves to stand by the " pure word of God, the three symbols, and the unaltered Augsburg Confession." Calvinism was discarded, in spite of the protests of Duke Charles. At this synod the independence of the Church with reference to internal matters of faith and doctrine come to recognition; and at the same time its character as a national church, with claims on the State for the protection of its belief and dogmas, received expression. Sigismund, the son of John III., the heir-in-law to the throne, was also king of the Poles, and the great champion of the Counter-Reformation in the northeast of Europe. His endeavor was to restore Roman Catholicism in Sweden. Duke Charles, at the diet in Söderköping (1595), took the same revolutionary national stand that his father had taken; summoned the estates to their mutual responsibility to oppose the Roman Catholic plans of the legal king; and finally, by the defeat of Sigismund at the battle of Stångebro (1598), put an end to Sigismund's attempt. After 1600 he became king and reigned as Charles IX. The results of this period of the new birth of Sweden was the organic union of the independent Evangelical church with the State, concentrating its power in the crown, and the beginning of its political greatness. The external quarrels had as a consequence inner chaos. Organization was deficient, morals coarse; the monasteries as the repositories of culture had gradually become impoverished and disappeared; education was neglected. The University of Upsala was closed, but in 1595 King Charles and the Church sought to reestablish it. The Lapland mission needed workers. The Roman Catholics continued their plotting; Charles, with his political ambitions and Calvinistic tendencies, had no sympathy with the, to him, oppressive and exclusive Lutheranism. The Church had to combat, single-handed, Calvinism that was now making headway over all Europe. The cause of Lutheranism was led by Archbishop Olaus Martini (d. 1611). With the accession of Gustavus Adolphus, the Swedish Church for the first time gained an assured position in the kingdom.

A new era (1611–1718) of organization and orthodoxy now began. A younger generation took matters in hand in Church and State. Gustavus Adolphus was only eighteen when he ascended the throne, and his great coadjutor, Axel Oxenstierna, governed European politics at the age of twenty-eight; and the most celebrated generals of the Thirty Years' War had not yet attained the age of thirty. In the Church J. Rudbeckius, leading ecclesiastical personality, began his great career at twenty-three. He represented the Aristotelianism that, from 1615, prevailed in the university, and was the court and military chaplain of the king, and bishop of Westerås, 1619–46. Under him concomitant with orthodoxy a hierarchical reaction set in. The king set himself against orthodox intolerance and persecution, assisted by John Matthiä, royal chaplain and tutor from 1629, and bishop of Strengnäs from 1643. During the ceaseless foreign wars the Swedish Church was distinguished by an intense inner life and work of organization. The energy of the new

2. Ecclesiastical Organization and Orthodoxy.

faith within and its combination under Gustavus Adolphus with popular freedom explain Sweden's influence abroad. During the great wars ecclesiastical organization was left principally to the great bishops. Gustavus contemplated a universal self-government, and proposed a general consistory (1623) of representatives of the laity and the higher and lower clergy. The bishops, however, thwarted this plan. The cathedral chapter, which had languished since the time of Gustavus Vasa, now became under episcopal guidance a central organ of the administration and gained a unique and beneficent standing. The composition of the chapter was also changed, especially under Rudbeckius, from being largely prelatical to consisting of professors, while the laity gained an important part in the administration, which they still possess. The Church was somewhat represented by the spiritual estate assembled at the diets, but this was under the control of the bishops. However, under their control, led by Rudbeckius and Laurentius Paulinus Gothus at Strengnäs (1609–46) the Church made tremendous advances in administration, literature, missions, and schools. But after 1648 the great bishops disappeared, and leadership was transferred to the diet. The result of the Treaty of Westphalia (1648) was to turn interest to internal affairs. The effort was no longer toward a consistory but a unitary organization. From the political side after 1648 new territories continued to come under the crown of Sweden. Their absorption was best promoted by church activity. The erection or conquest of new dioceses necessitated closer organization in the life of the Church. Examples of these dioceses are Wiborg (1618), Karlstad (1647), Hernösand (1647), Wisby (1645), Lund (1658); in 1665 Gothenburg, and in 1678 Kalmar became bishoprics. Thus the provincial organization was complete as it has continued to the present time. A university was founded in Lund (1666), which became a theological center of great importance to the Swedish Church. The question of orthodoxy was now at its height; but the proposal of the bishop of Westerås, Olof Laurelius, that the Formula of Concord be made a part of the church law, was not pleasing to all; Matthiä was its most distinguished opponent, and he was supported by Queen Christina, and later by Charles X. Matthiä and John Terserus, bishop of Abo, the former a disciple of Comenius, the latter of Calixtus, were also " Syncretists "; the latter fought for popular and spiritual freedom against the growing power of the nobles and the bishops. On the death of Charles X. (1660), the regency being in the hands of a powerful orthodox nobility, they were deprived of their bishoprics on the charge of syncretistic heresy.

Charles XI. introduced the one-man rule in Sweden, and he did not intend to allow the Church to exist as an independent factor. The church itself had no organized central government that could protect its interests. Owing partly to orthodoxy and partly to the ceaseless wars, a spirit of superstition and a decline in morals prevailed among the people and the lower clergy. The king procured the adoption of the Book of Concord as a symbol of the Church in the great church law of 1686. This confirmed orthodoxy; it confirmed also unified organization, but reduced independence, producing a pronounced State Church. The king assumed the appointment to a large number of spiritual positions. He was energetically employed in completing the great work of organization, which served as a cloak to hide the peril to the heritage of independence and the decline of the religious and moral life. A general catechism was introduced (1689), a new church manual (1693), the celebrated hymnal (1698), a revised translation of the Bible (1703), and subsequently a large work on the Bible. A royal ordinance provided for the general instruction of children in reading and the catechism. Among the ecclesiastics of this period distinguished for clearness of thought, intense patriotism, intolerance of any deviation from the true doctrine, and a willingness to sacrifice themselves to the demands of orthodoxy and absolute monarchy were Archbishops Olof Svebilius (1681–1700), the author of the manual and the catechism; and Eric Benzelius the elder (1700–09), father of the most distinguished family of bishops in Sweden; the celebrated poet, Torsten Rudéen, subsequently bishop of Linköping, the spokesman of the clerical estate at many a diet; and the noted hymn-writers, Archbishop Haquin Spegel and Bishop Jesper Svedberg, the former striving for uniformity of worship and belief, and furthering the education of the masses, the latter stanchly opposing the abuses of orthodoxy and strongly inclined to mysticism. Upon the death of Charles XII., a new direction was given to all Swedish culture.

With the awakening of individualism in culture and politics in the " age of freedom " there entered at the same time the religious and moral influence of Pietism and the Unity of the Brethren (q.v.) among the masses of the people (1718–72). At this time the Swedish Lutheran Church probably enjoyed its greatest prosperity. During the last years of Charles XI., Pietism had entered the German possessions of Sweden, where it was opposed with orthodox intensity. It extended from thence to Finland and found a good soil in the temperament of the people under the teachings of the brothers Wegelius, but was strongly opposed by J. Gezelius (q.v.). In the early part of the eighteenth century it surrounded the Baltic Sea and reached Stockholm. But the movement first made a significant religious inroad after the return (1721) from Siberian captivity of some of the soldiers of Charles XII., who were now converted to Pietism. It now spread over a great portion of Sweden, the sane Halle Pietism, that did not antagonize the Church, being the prevailing form. A great many ecclesiastics joined the movement. Sweden's two foremost men, Eric Benzelius the younger (bishop of Linköping and archbishop), and Andreas Rydelius, the first well-known and independent philosopher of Sweden, later bishop of Lund, could not withstand it. The latter, in particular, was in sympathy with the efforts of the young convert to Pietism, Peter Murbeck of Schonen (1731–66), and placed his theological erudition and practical ability at the service of a deeper religiousness. He was especially devoted

3. The Religious Awakening.

to the education of the young. Murbeck, " the Francke of Sweden," became the head of the religious awakening in the southern part. In the north the movement was led by Eric Tollstadius (d. 1759), vicar and pastor at Stockholm, the most celebrated name in the inner church history of the time. A noble and more influential representative of the strongly mystical branch of Pietism was Sven Rosén (d. 1750). Pietism met with more opposition than appreciation from the higher authorities. Many bishops attacked it; the spiritual estate of the diet opposed it. Both Tollstadius and Murbeck were subjected to wearisome law processes. At a conventicle at Sicla outside Stockholm (1723) the government brought the principals to trial at which they set forth their views in a remarkable memorial that may be considered the creed of the Swedish Pietists. They were acquitted, but the proceedings resulted in the government allowing the well-known *Konventikelplakatet* (1726), by which all private religious meetings for edification were prohibited under severe penalties. Domestic devotions, however, were permitted, and the clergy were called upon to hold frequent house inquiries. While the edict of restriction checked Pietism, it also remained a fetter upon free religious life for 125 years. The strength of the Church over against the government was also shown otherwise. The sovereign diet of the estates erected a special " ecclesiastical deputation " in 1723, which, in view of Pietism, was intended to become a general " consistory " dependent on the diet with the function of bringing the church order into conformity with the new politics; but the spiritual estate in the diet knew how effectively to neutralize the activity of this deputation. In the tracks of Pietism followed the great tide of Roman Catholic mysticism which struck Sweden in the third decade of the eighteenth century. After 1727 the movement passed beyond bounds. Enthusiastic forms, separatism, apocalyptic, and general schism followed. The inner situation became precarious in the next decade, when help came from the Unity of the Brethren (q.v.). When the brotherhood was founded in 1727 a Swede, Assessor C. H. Grundelstierna, was associated with Zinzendorf; and from the first the brethren directed their attention to Sweden. Grundelstierna returned to Sweden to prepare the soil, 1729–39. In 1738 Arvid Gradin arrived at Herrnhut and became after 1741 the leader in Sweden. Even the mystic Sven Rosén joined the community. Under the Stockholm pastors Thore Odhelius and Jonas Hellmann the brotherhood maintained its flourishing condition in Sweden, 1739–44, with headquarters at Stockholm and West Gothland. The movement was wholesome, bringing back the enthusiasts and stimulating orthodoxy with life. Unfortunately in 1745 appeared also the morbid mystical side as the worship of the wounds of Christ, resulting in religious decline and factionalism. This phase was overcome after 1760. These special awakenings aroused the orthodox Church to turn to the needs of the masses. A series of energetic bishops and pastors came to the front, who, by a more earnest instruction and care of souls, effected profounder religious soundness and piety. Such were Sven Bälter (d. 1760), a famous preacher; Bishop Jacob Serenius (d. 1776), who introduced the rite of confirmation according to English and Danish form; and Anders Nohrborg (d. 1767), court preacher, and author of *Die Seligkeitsordnung des gefallenen Menschen*, a devotional work ranking next to the Bible for the people of Sweden. A peculiar product of the time was Emanuel Swedenborg (q.v.).

This previous period formed the transition from Sweden of the Reformation and the politics of war to the modern state; it was prolific of ideals minus fixed purposes. It prepared the way for the speculative Enlightenment, or the period of neology (1772–1817). The great religious per-

4. The Neological Period and the Nineteenth Century. sonalities were gone by 1770; the prince of the Enlightenment, Gustavus III., nephew of Frederick the Great, mounted the throne in 1772; and his French school of poets, particularly J. H. Kellgren, satirized Swedenborgianism and Pietism. German rationalism began to show its head and to influence more and more the leaders of the Swedish Church; but it never reached extremes, and in southern Sweden and other portions of the country it never gained the mastery. Almost all earnest men in the Church at this time were of the Unity of the Brethren or Swedenborgians, and these two beliefs were the salvation of the religious life of the country. The religious awakening of the middle of the century was protracted among the people, and Württemberg Pietism was spread abroad in Sweden by many revivalists, preparing the way for the epoch-making work of Henrik Schartau (q.v.). The independence of the Church in the national life did not suffer; although for a time the rationalistic royalty which had again become supreme worked some injury to the ecclesiastic conditions by its appointments. The king found, however, his match in the intellectual and powerful bishop, Olof Wallquist of Wexiö (d. 1800), as celebrated in statesmanship and finance as in church organization. He organized a new ecclesiastical office, called the "ecclesiastical expedition," by which all church business was to be prepared. It was not of long duration but paved the way for the present ministry of worship. The period lacked the power to afford the Church new impulse. The neological revision of the church-books was a failure; and the Church was too weak to aid the people in political crises. The cession of Finland to Russia in 1809 was rather a religious than a political loss. The first half of the nineteenth century was a time of restoration for the Church, when internal and foreign missions prospered, with some persistent sectarian dispersion of a subjectivistic character. Then came the non-conformist movements from England, George Scott preaching Methodism in 1840, and Anders Wiberg the Baptist doctrine from 1851, followed by the Irvingites (Catholic Apostolic Church, q.v.). The conventicle edict was recalled in 1858, and Swedish subjects were granted religious freedom in 1860. This gave impetus to the Reformed tendency even within the national Church. The most important fact in religious life was the revival after 1840 under the preaching of Dean Peter Wieselgren (noted temperance

advocate, d. 1877), the layman K. O. Rosenius (d. 1868), and the missionary Peter Fjellstedt (d. 1881). In 1863 the Church obtained its own representation at the church assembly through the change which converted the old diet into one of two chambers, whereby the position within the national state life intended by the Reformation and attempted by Gustavus Adolphus was achieved.

II. Statistics: Ninety-nine per cent. of the population belongs, formally at least, to the Evangelical Lutheran State Church. By the church law of 1686, which, with some changes and amplifications, is still in force, the confession of faith embraces, beside the three ancient symbols, the resolution of the *Upsala möte* of 1593, and the entire Book of Concord. In the constitution of 1809 the *Upsala möte* and the *Confessio Augustana* alone were mentioned, and the uncertainty whether the entire Book of Concord is symbolically in effect has not been finally decided. Any one may leave the State Church, but must join some other denomination recognized by the State. In 1900 there were 2,378 Roman Catholics; 3,912 orthodox Jews; 7,041 Methodists; 3,309 Baptists; and smaller scattered bodies. The actual number of Baptists was 40,000 and of Methodists 15,231, most of them remaining in the State Church. The most considerable sect within the State Church is the Pietistic "Swedish Missionary Union," deviating somewhat from the normal doctrine of the atonement and practising separate communion, and carrying on an extensive internal and foreign mission. This union was founded by the well-known Paul Petter Waldenström (q.v.). They numbered (1903) 84,602, with more than 1,100 churches. The State Church of Sweden embraces 13 bishoprics, to which are added the municipal consistory of Stockholm and the court consistory. The latest diocese, Luleå (1904), was established by the diet only on condition that Wexiö and Kalmar were to be combined on the death of either of the incumbent bishops. The diocese of Upsala bears the title of archbishopric, although its incumbent bears only the relationship of a *primus inter pares*. The dioceses are now Upsala (including Stockholm), Linköping, Skara, Strengnäs, Westerås, Wexiö, Lund, Göteborg, Kalmar, Karlstad, Wisby, Hernösand, and Luleå. The dioceses are divided into district, each of which contains seven to eight parishes. There are now 1,380 parishes. Each parish has its *kyrkoherde* (pastor); one of them is provost over the district. The parishes are frequently divided into sub-parishes, each with its own church, and often also with its own ordinary minister. The number of churches in 1909 was 2,576, and of ministers 2,767, and there is one minister to every 1,700 inhabitants. The king of Sweden is the highest earthly ruler of the Swedish Church, and must be an adherent of the "pure Evangelical doctrine, as adopted and explained in the unaltered Augsburg Confession and in the resolutions of the Synod of Upsala of 1593." He must, however, in the exercise of his ecclesiastical authority, "obtain information and advice" from the ecclesiastical minister, and from the rest of the council of state, the members of which must all be adherents of the pure Evangelical doctrine. In ecclesiastical legislation, the king and the diet cooperate, with the consent of the church assembly. In this manner the danger of hasty legislation is avoided, as the diet consists of two chambers, and the ordinary church assembly is to be called by the king only once in five years; but, on the other hand, it increases the difficulty of passing justifiable reforms. Changes may more easily be effected in matters that come within the king's administrative authority in ecclesiastical affairs, such as a new translation of th' Bible, the Psalter, the church manual, and the catechism, to which the consent of the diet is not necessary, but only that of the church assembly, acting by a two-thirds vote of those present. This consists of sixty members (with the diocese of Luleå of sixty-four), half clerical and half lay; and these are chosen by their respective electors, except the bishops, who are members *ex officio*. Their compensation and other expenses are defrayed by the State. The consistory of Stockholm and the cathedral chapters of the dioceses come next to the king as permanent church authorities. The bishop presides over his own chapter and his assessors are usually the cathedral provost and certain lectors of the free high-school of the bishop's see. The lay element has more representation here than the clerical. Under these ecclesiastical authorities are also the public schools. Since 1905 the higher popular educational institutions have been withdrawn. The cathedral chapter, among other duties, has to make proposals on the appointment of pastors and assistants, except in a few parishes that are in the gift of patrons; and has to issue letters patent to all appointees, except of the so-called royal pastorates, which number 494. The congregation selects its pastor from one of three candidates proposed by the chapter, after these have preached on trial before the congregation. Erring clergy may be cautioned, suspended, or removed by the chapter. The bishop, besides making visitations in person or through the district provosts, is obliged to call conventions of his clergy at least once every six years, in order to render a report and receive under consideration matters of discussion. Every parish has the right to deliberate and decide in church meeting on the affairs of the parish church and of the common schools, and to take action in regard to economic interests. The contributions for church purposes by the parishes for 1903 were $3,687,234, and for common schools, $6,423,308. The common schools are under a school council representing the parish; and the pastor presides over these councils *ex officio*. Liberals are endeavoring to dissolve this union between the Church and the schools. Popular education is at a high level. There are two complete universities, one at Lund, the other at Upsala, each having a faculty of theology. Before ordination the candidates are required to pass an examination before the philosophical faculty, next an examination in theology and in practical exercises before the theological faculty, and, finally, a clerical examination before the cathedral chapter. The church assembly of 1903 formulated the ordination vow as follows: " To proclaim the pure Word of God according to one's best understanding and conviction, as given by Holy Scripture and witnessed by the creeds of our Church." A pericope

covering three years is laid down for the public services. The liturgy otherwise is regulated by the latest church-book of 1894. The translation of the Bible, which occupied more than a century, resulted in an approved version of the New Testament in 1883; but this is again under revision. A good translation of the Old Testament, approved by the church assembly of 1903, is permissible in public worship. The completion of the new translation in 1911 makes available a new source for Bible reading. For missions in Sweden see JEWS, MISSION TO THE; LAPPS. A flourishing mission is also carried on in several large ports of Europe and Australia and among the fishermen of the North Sea.

(HJALMAR HOLMQUIST.)

III. Swedish Theology in the Nineteenth Century: At the beginning of the century rationalism was dominant, although not to such an unlimited degree as in other countries of Protestant Christendom. The influence of the Unity of the Brethren and Swedenborgianism, to a great extent, counteracted its effect, and the old form of orthodox piety had remained unshaken in the outlying country districts. Opposition to rationalism began to show its triumphant effect in the second decade, led by J. O. Wallin, archbishop of Upsala (d. 1839), who gave to Sweden a hymnal ranking with the best in Christendom; Esaias Tegnér, prince of poets; F. M. Franzen, poet and bishop of Wexiö, and E. G. Geijer (d. 1847), the historian, philosopher, poet, and musician, whose *Von falscher und wahrer Aufklärung* (1811) was strongly instrumental in turning the attention of the young men to inner spirituality. In the universities the modification of rationalism advanced as far as a rational supernaturalism. Geijer scouted both dogmatic orthodoxy and sentimental Pietism, but at the same time detected the weakness of rationalism and manifested true religious susceptibilities in his hymns. Central in his philosophical position is the idea of personality. The ultimate antithesis is not between being and not-being (Hegel), nor between the ego and the non-ego (Fichte); but between the ego and the alter-ego. The succession in the philosophy of religion proceeded through the idealism of C. J. Boström (d. 1866) to the two most famous personalities of the latter half of the century: W. Rydberg, author of *Die Lehre der Bibel von Christus*, and P. Wikner, author of *Gedanken und Fragen von dem Menschensohne*. Theology proper, however, owes its renascence to the University of Lund, and particularly to H. Schartau (q.v.) and E. M. Ahlman (d. 1844); the latter forms the connection with the new epoch of theology, which began with Kant and Schleiermacher. Among his pupils H. Reuterdahl (q.v.), the most learned theologian of the first half of the century, was a disciple of Schleiermacher, and wrote *Svenska kyrkans historia* (2 vols., Lund, 1838–1850), and an " Introduction to Theology " (1837). Hegel's philosophy was represented in Sweden by E. G. Bring (d. 1884). His contemporary was the exegete, H. M. Melin (d. 1887), whose lectures on the life of Christ, directed against Strauss, were received with great enthusiasm. In 1850–70 the theology of Lund developed in a conservative and orthodox direction. While all forms of contemporary

Protestant theology were represented in Lund, the theology of Upsala had remained more uniform. This was due to the exclusion of the new development beginning with Schleiermacher. The prevailing characteristic was a strict confessional orthodoxy, embracing a Pietistic element as well as a liberal Low-church tendency as distinguished from the High-church tendency of Lund. Among theologians at Upsala were L. Lindblad (d. 1837); the exegetes A. E. Knös (d. 1862) and O. F. Myrberg (d. 1899); and the church historians, L. A. Anjou (d. 1884), Theodore Norlin (d. 1870), and C. A. Cornelius (d. 1893). Outside of the theological faculties, J. Hallenberg wrote a distinguished commentary on Revelation (3 vols., 1800); and N. Ignell (d. 1864) wrote *Grundzüge der christlichen Sittenlehre* (1842–49), and *Mens:likliga utvecklingens historia* (Stockholm, 1855–62).　　(G. Aulén.)

Bibliography: For the political history the best work is E. Hildebrand, *Sveriges Historia*, Stockholm, 1903 sqq.; and for the organization of the state, idem, *Den svenska Statsförfattningens historiska Utveckling*, ib. 1896. On the Swedish church a good work is H. Hildebrand, *Sveriges Medeltid*, part iii., on the church, ib. 1903, to which add H. Reuterdahl's *Svenska kyrkans historia*, ut sup., Germ. transl., Berlin, 1837. For later history there is available: L. Stavenow, *Frihetstiden*, Gothenburg, 1898; idem, *Gustaf III.*, ib. 1901; H. Hjäine, *Gustaf Adolf*, Stockholm, 1901; idem, *Karl XII.*, ib. 1902. On the history of Swedish literature consult: H. Schück, *Svensk Litteraturhistoria*, vol. i., Stockholm, 1890; idem and C. Warburg, *Illustrerad svensk Litteraturhistoria*, ib., 1895 sqq. Consult further: E. Tegner, *Die Kirche Schwedens in den beiden letzten Jahrzehnten*, Stralsund, 1837; E. G. Geyer, *Hist. de la Suède*, Paris, 1840; A. G. Knös, *Die schwedische Reformation*, Berlin, 1852; L. A. Anjou, *Hist. of the Reformation in Sweden*, New York, 1859; idem, *Svenska kyrkans historia från Upsala möte 1593*, Stockholm, 1866; T. Norlin, *Svenska kyrkans historia efter reformationen (1549–1649)*, Lund, 1864–71; M. Weibull, *Lunds Universitets Historia*, Lund, 1868; A. Crichton and H. Wheaton, *Scandinavia, Ancient and Modern*, 2 vols., New York, 1872; H. Hildebrand, *Das heidnische Zeitalter in Schweden*, Hamburg, 1873; C. Annerstedt, *Upsala Universitets Historia*, Upsala, 1877; J. Weidling, *Schwedische Geschichte im Zeitalter der Reformation*, Gotha, 1882; C. M. Butler, *The Reformation in Sweden*, New York, 1883, new issue, 1900; W. Tottie, *Jesper Svedberg*, Upsala, 1885–90; G. Billing, *Ebbe Gustaf Bring*, Lund, 1886; R. Sundelin, *Swedenborgianismen i Sverige*, Upsala, 1886; C. A. Cornelius, *Svenska Kyrkans historia efter Reformationen*, Upsala, 1886; idem, *Handbok i svenska Kyrkans Historia*, 3d ed., ib. 1892; J. B. Baur, *Die Kapuziner und die schwedische Generalität im 30-jährigen Kriege*, Brixen, 1887; P. B. Watson, *The Swedish Revolution under Gustavus Vasa*, London, 1889; F. Puaux, *Hist. de l'établissement des protestants français en Suède*, Paris, 1891; H. Lundström, *Laurentius Paulinus Gothus*, Upsala, 1892–1898; O. Ahnfelt, *Utvecklingen af Svenska kyrkans ordning under Gustaf I.*, Lund, 1893; H. Hjäine, *Reformationsriksdagen i Vesterås*, Stockholm, 1893; J. A. Källström, *Bidrag till den Svenska Pietismens Historia*, Stockholm, 1894; H. Wordin, *De eklesiastika deputationerna*, Strengnäs, 1895; E. J. Ekman, *Den inre missionen historia*, Stockholm, 1896–1902; K. O. Lundquist, *De Svenska domkjapitlen under medeltiden*, Upsala, 1897; K. A. Appelberg, *Kyrkansrättskja Ställning i Sverige*, Helsingfors, 1900; F. Nippold, *Handbuch der neuesten Kirchengeschichte*, ii. 431 sqq., Berlin, 1901; H. Lundström, *Skizzer och Kritiker*, Stockholm, 1903; E. Hildebrand, *Gustaf Vasa och hans söner*, ib. 1903–04; L. M. Bâath, *Bidrag till kanoniker rättens historia i Sverige*, Stockholm, 1905; T. Höjer, *Vadstena klosters och Birgittenordens historia*, Upsala, 1905; R. Chartin, *Gustaf Vasa et la réforme en Suède*, Paris, 1906; G. Aulén, *Reuterdahl*, Upsala, 1907; R. Holm, *Terserus*, Lund, 1907; H. von Schubert, *Kirchengeschichte Schleswig-Holsteins*, Kiel, 1907; H. Holmquist, *De svenska domkapitlen 1571–1687*, Upsala, 1908; N. Jakobson, *Den svenska herrnhutismens uppkemot*, ib. 1908; E. Rodhe, *Kyrka och skole*, Lund, 1908; G. M. Williams, *The Church of Sweden and the Anglican Communion*, Milwaukee, 1910; E. Linderholm, *Rosén*, Upsala, 1911; K. B. Westman, *Birgittastudier*, ib. 1911; J Wordsworth, *National Church of Sweden*, London, 1911.

SWEDENBORG, swī'den-börg, EMANUEL.

I. Life.
　Parentage and Education (§ 1).
　Scientific Labors (§ 2).
II. His Writings.
　1. Scientific.
　2. Philosophical.
　　Philosophy of Matter (§ 1).
　　Mind and " Tremulation " (§ 2).
　　Psycho-Physiology; Correspondences (§ 3).
　　Transition to Theology (§ 4).
　　Call as a Seer (§ 5).
　3. Theological.
　　The " Internal Sense " of Scripture (§ 1).
　　Heaven, Hell, Spirits, and Revelation (§ 2).
　　Doctrines of Christ and the Scriptures (§ 3).
　　Life and Faith (§ 4).
　　The " Angelic Wisdom " (§ 5).
　　Marriage; the Planets; Summary (§ 6).
III. Close of Life; Death and Burial.
IV. Recent Honors.

I. Life: Emanuel Swedenborg (Swedberg) was born in Stockholm Jan. 29, 1688; d. in London Mar. 29, 1772. His father, Jesper Swedberg, was at the time Lutheran court chaplain, afterward professor and dean of the University of Upsala, and bishop of Skara from 1702 to his death in 1735.

1. Parentage and Education. He was distinguished for his religious zeal, his upright life, and by his extensive writings. The family were descendants of Daniel Isaacson, a mining peasant-proprietor in Fahlun, who gave the name Sweden to their property. When the family of the bishop was ennobled by Queen Ulrica Eleanora in 1719, the name Swedenborg was given it. Swedenborg's mother, Sara Behm, was also the daughter of a miner, Albrecht Behm, and therefore Emanuel inherited on both sides a bent for mining pursuits. Piously educated at home under his tutor, Dr. Moreus, Emanuel pursued his studies at the Upsala University till 1709, experiencing something of the Cartesian controversy rife at that time, and acquiring facility in the classics and in the writing of Latin verse. On leaving the university he at first, under the friendly patronage of his brother-in-law, Eric Benzelius, afterward archbishop, made a journey to England in pursuit of scientific knowledge, especially of mathematics and astronomy, meeting Flamsteed in London, and Halley in Oxford, " studying Newton daily " and acquainting himself in the workshops with various trades and arts, including the grinding of lenses. Returning to Sweden he published a book of verses, *Camena Borea*, edited a mathematical journal, *Dædalus Hyperboreus*, and, in 1716, published the first algebra produced in Sweden.

2. Scientific Labors. He devoted himself to the study of metals and mines, the action of water on the earth's surface, the discovery of longitude by the moon, and meanwhile was fertile in remarkable inventions, many of which are only at the present day coming to practical experiment, including the submarine war vessel, the flying-machine, and the machine gun. Attracted by his genius and ability, King Charles XII. called Swedenborg to his service in the college of mines and gave him an apprenticeship with the celebrated royal engineer Polhem, in whose family he became a favorite inmate. He formed a love attachment with a daughter of Polhem, which was favored by the king, but failed of marriage by the daughter's refusal, and Swedenborg remained single the rest of his life. After the death of Charles XII. in 1718, Swedenborg took his seat as the oldest son of the now ennobled family, in the house of nobles in the Swedish diet. Declining a professorship in mathematics in the university and in pursuit of his studies as a royal assessor of mines, he undertook a series of journeys through the various countries of Europe especially for the study of mines and manufactures. In these journeys he enjoyed the patronage and friendship of princes and scholars, and his explorations took him not only into mines, furnaces, workshops, laboratories, and lecture-rooms, but also to museums, galleries, churches, theaters, army garrisons, palaces, everywhere where the life and civilization of his time could be observed and studied. His *Itinerarium* or "Diary of Travel" affords a picturesque view of the actual life of the important cities of France, Italy, Germany, Belgium, and Holland at that period. Meanwhile his treatises had been appearing from time to time at home or abroad and his widely extended reputation as a metallurgist and anatomist brought him invitations to membership in the academies of science at St. Petersburg, Paris, and Stockholm. His practical achievements at home in assisting Polhem in large engineering works for the kingdom, especially in transporting galleys for fourteen miles overland at the siege of Friedrickshall in 1718, show that his life was by no means satisfied with theorizing. Courted by princes, praised by scholars, a man of the world in a wide sense, his inner life may best be known by the simple rules drawn up by himself to govern his daily conduct. These were: (1) Often to read and meditate on the Word of God; (2) to submit everything to the will of divine providence; (3) to observe in everything a propriety of behavior and to keep the conscience clear; (4) to discharge with faithfulness the duties of my office and to render myself in all things useful to society.

II. Writings: The writings of Swedenborg may be divided into three classes: (1) material and scientific, including those in mathematics and literature; (2) philosophical; (3) theological.

1. Scientific: The works produced during the first (the literary and scientific) period of his life are as follows: *Carmina Miscellanea; Camena Borea; Selectæ Sententiæ L. A. Senecæ; Itinerarium; Prodromus principiorum naturalium* (" Principles of Chemistry "); *Nova Observata circa Ferrum et Ignem* (" On Iron and Fire "); *Artificia Nova Mechanica* (" Construction of Docks and Dikes "); *Miscellanea Observata* (in geology, mineralogy, etc.); the treatises on metals and mines in the *Opera philosophica;* posthumous tracts on salt, on muds, and soils; on the height of water, etc., in *Geologica et epistolæ*, Royal Academy series no. 1.

2. Philosophical: It was in 1734 that, together with the small treatise, *De infinito*, the *Opera philosophica et mineralia* appeared in three volumes, the first part of which, *Principia* (Eng. transl. by

Dr. J. J. G. Wilkinson, London, 1840), has become widely known as embodying Swedenborg's physical philosophy or cosmology. In 1740 appeared the *Œconomia regni animalis* (" Economy of the Animal Kingdom "); in 1740, the first and second parts of the *Regnum animale;* and in 1745, the *De cultu et amore Dei* (" The Worship and Love of God ").

In this wide range of physical, physiological, and psychological studies, Swedenborg pursues what he avows to be his one quest—his "search **1. Philoso-** for the soul." Where to find her, he **phy of** asks, but in her own realm—the body? **Matter.** Hence came the term *regnum animale* —or "soul kingdom," applied to the human anatomy and physiology. In the "Chemistry" and the *Principia* he had sought the imponderable and invisible substances and forms which lie at the beginning of creation and which mark the entrance of life from the Infinite into the finite. Conceiving the origin of the universe as lying in a "conatus of motion in the Infinite," which assumes in the "natural point" an existence in time and space (in which "point" lie potentially all future forms and motions in their perfection), he traces the progress of the point through a series of finites in active and passive relation to the "elementaries" or primal auras, ethers, and atmospheres, and thence to the first forms of solid matter. These he conceives to be angular particles originating in the interstitial spaces between the spherical globules. The modern sciences of crystallography and stereo-chemistry are admitted by the best authorities to find their germ in Swedenborg's conception of elementary forms. Swedenborg conceives light as a form of ethereal motion. The series of forms, circular, spiral, and vortical, the nature and phenomena of magnetism, the evolution of the planets from a condensed ring thrown off by the central mass of the primal nebula, the position of the earth in the galaxy, are discussed in these works in lines which anticipate not only Kant, Buffon, and La Place, the supposed originators of the nebular theory, but even the most recent discoveries in radioactive and vibratory forces and motions. In method, Swedenborg proceeds inductively from experience but under the guidance of certain a priori principles. To experience and geometry there must be added the recognition of deity and the soul. Adopting Aristotle as his model rather than Plato, he, with this master, finds that intelligence can discover only what intelligence has devised, and that to all the sensitive faculties of man there descends a "somewhat from above" giving to the sensuous impressions a form and meaning.

With this survey of the material universe behind him, Swedenborg proceeds to explore the universe of mind or, as he terms it, the *regnum animale*, a term inadequately translated by "animal kingdom," meaning rather the kingdom of the **2. Mind** rational soul presiding over the entire **and "Trem-** realm of matter, not only in her own **ulation."** body, but in the universe as a kind of indefinite extension of her body. The universe is a system of tremulations moved by the divine life and communicated through recipient forms and substances in their various orders and degrees. In his introduction to the *Principia* he conceives the " true philosopher " as that primitive perfect soul which responds by a perfect innate intelligence to every tremulation of the universe. For sensation is but a succession of vibrations communicated from without through the series of subtle receptacles even to the sensory of the brain. Here action is produced by a similar series of motions reversed, originating primarily in the will and taking form in the thought and in the action of the nervous and muscular systems. As early as in 1719, he had outlined his doctrine of tremulations in a dissertation submitted to the Royal Medical College on *The Anatomy of our most Subtle Nature, Showing that our Moving and Living Force Consists of Tremulations.*

The " Economy of the Animal Kingdom " treats in part I. of the circulation of the blood and of the fetal life and in part II. of the motion of the brain,

3. Psycho-Physiology; Correspondences. the cortical substance, and the human soul. It affords a complete system of psycho-physiology. The human anatomy and organic life are treated as the theater of the soul's activity; consequently in their normal, living play of forces and mechanism. Their mechanism is so complete as to seem almost to exclude the free action of the soul and the influx of the Infinite; but the reconciliation is found in the involution of the wisdom of the Infinite in the least finite forms of motion, and this is what gives the human soul a finite sense of its own freedom. In the " Animal Kingdom," the publication of which is still incomplete, the doctrine of correspondences, forms, series, and degrees is outlined and the theory set forth that the physical world is purely symbolical of the spiritual world. But even the spiritual world in the philosophical period had a certain continuity of degree with matter, its distinction from matter being that of priority of form and simplicity of structure. It was not until Swedenborg's later experience of " things heard and seen " in the spiritual world that he learned actually the discreteness between matter and spiritual substance. His doctrine of forms and order he derived in part from Wolf, the disciple of Leibnitz, even as in his vortical theories and his doctrine of the first atomic shapes he somewhat resembles Descartes. It is not until after his illumination or alleged intromission into the spiritual world as an actual witness and participant that he sets forth in all its fulness the great doctrine of the three discrete degrees, projected now beyond nature into the vast scale that embraces God as end, spirit or the plane of conscious relation as cause, and nature as effect, and that in its assertion of two coexistent and correspondential worlds, the spiritual and the natural as given in the minor treatise, *De Commercio Animæ et Corporis* (" On Influx ") seems to have given Kant (who had interested himself in Swedenborg's two-world experiences and had declared his doctrine strangely like his own) the suggestion of his inaugural discourse at Königsberg, 1770, *De mundi sensibilis atque intelligibilis forma.* The vast and profound researches on the structure and function of the brain, its respiratory motion, the location of its several sensories, etc., are only just beginning to receive due appreciation among Europe's most learned physiologists (cf. the address of Prof. Gustav Retzius of the Royal Swedish Academy before the Congress of Anatomists in Heidelberg, 1902).

Further portions of this vast work, notably on the fibers, the generative organs, on the senses, on the soul or rational psychology, and on the brain have been posthumously published and translated into English. The *De Anima* (" The Soul, or Rational Psychology ") is in method not unlike Aristotle's *Peri Psychē*, treating of the mind in its successive planes as *animus, mens,* and *anima* (the sensitive or imaginative mind and memory; the rational mind and the pure intellect; and the soul and its state after death). The chief and permanent interest of the *Rational Psychology* lies in the subtle analysis of the process of the conversion of sensation into idea and then of ideas into thoughts and of these again back into words or motions, all in accordance with the great universal doctrine of tremulation and of series, orders, and degrees. All the remaining manuscripts of this and other works of Swedenborg are now in process of translation and publication by the Royal Swedish Academy of Sciences under the editorship of Professors Retzius, Arrhenius, Nathorst, and other eminent scholars.

The *De cultu et amore Dei* (" Worship and Love of God ") forms the bridge between the philosophical and theological periods and is a work unique

4. Transition to Theology. in literature for the boldness of its speculation and the sublimity of its conceptions. It traces the process of the creation of this planet out of the sun's nebula, the evolution of its seasons and temperatures, and of the kingdoms successively from mineral through vegetable up to man, and views the human soul as a little world of intelligences and forces by which the created universe renders up its adoration to its creator. This work is written in a style of great elegance and contains passages of poetic beauty and sublimity. In it, at the same time, the author takes leave, as it were, of his career of personal authorship and ambition to devote himself henceforward to being the simple recorder of things " revealed " and the humble proclaimer of the " second coming of the Lord."

Parts I. and II. of the " Animal Kingdom " were published in 1744, and the " Worship and Love of God " in 1745. At this point there is a sudden and strange interruption of Swedenborg's scientific

5. Call as a Seer. quest. He experiences, as he avers, a direct divine call to enter upon the higher mission of a seer and revelator of the things of the spiritual world, and simultaneously of the spiritual truth and doctrine which underlie the literal and symbolic sense of the sacred Scriptures. During the period from 1743 to 1749 (in which year he began to publish the *Arcana Cælestia,* containing the spiritual sense of Genesis and Exodus) he had not only been experiencing visions and dreams of an extraordinary character, accompanied by temptations and struggles of soul of the severest kind, a conflict between the flesh and the spirit and between intellectual ambition and the authority of a divine voice within, but he had recorded these with great frankness and in an awed sense of their deep significance, in his *Dreams* and *Spiritual Diary*. At the same time in his *Adversaria* he noted down glimpses appearing to him of an inner meaning of the Scriptures. But it is in the introduction to the *Arcana Cœlestia* that he plainly declares, after asserting that the sacred Scriptures have a spiritual sense:

> " That this is really the case in respect to the Word it is impossible for any man to know except from the Lord, wherefore it is expedient here to premise, that, of the Lord's mercy, it has been granted me now for several years to be constantly and uninterruptedly in company with spirits and angels, hearing them converse with each other and conversing with them. Hence it has been permitted me to hear and see things in another life which are astonishing and which never before came to the knowledge of any man or entered into his imagination. I have thus been instructed concerning different kinds of spirits, and the state of souls after death; concerning hell or the lamentable state of the unfaithful; concerning heaven or the most happy state of the faithful; and particularly concerning the doctrine of faith which is acknowledged throughout all heaven, on which subjects, by the divine mercy of the Lord, more will be said in the following pages."

3. Theological: Here begins, then, the period of Swedenborg's theology and spiritual philosophy, or what is called by him the " angelic wisdom," being a survey of the two worlds, natural and spiritual, and of the operation of God as end and final cause, through the spiritual world as instrumental or efficient cause, into or upon nature as the world of effect. The series of theological works was begun by *Arcana Cœlestia* (an exposition of the internal sense of Genesis and Exodus, published anonymously in Latin, 8 vols., London, 1748–56).

Of this " internal sense," Swedenborg says: " In the following pages it will be seen that the first chapter of Genesis in its internal sense treats of the new creation of man or of his regeneration in general; and specifically, of the most ancient Church; and this in such a manner that there is not a single syllable which does not represent, signify, and involve something spiritual." The first eleven chapters of Genesis are declared by Swedenborg to be strictly symbolic and to have been derived by Moses from a more ancient word given in purely correspondential language in which spiritual truths are clothed with natural figures. Beginning with Abraham, the Word is historical in form but divinely composed into a drama of the spiritual life of man in its progress from the bondage of nature and self, represented by Egypt, into the liberty of the heavenly kingdom. The temptations and struggles of the forty-years' wandering are prophetic of the Lord's temptation combats in the flesh, by which he, in the fulness of time and in fulfilment of all the prophets, overcame the power of hell and set man spiritually free. In this way the Word is shown to be everywhere in its spiritual sense descriptive of the incarnation and glorification of the divine humanity in Jesus Christ. While this minute explanation in the *Arcana* covers only the books of Genesis and Exodus, its citations from other parts of the Word are so numerous as to make it a very comprehensive Biblical exegesis. A subsequent posthumous publication gives an outline of the " Internal Sense of the Prophets and Psalms."

1. The "Internal Sense" of Scripture.

Heaven and its Wonders and Hell; and the World of Spirits; from Things heard and seen (London, 1758) is a description of heaven in its three degrees or planes and of the angelic life and its occupations, showing that angels are regenerated human beings who have lived in the natural world and are now living in a perfected civilization according to the laws of the divine order of life in the spiritual world, heaven itself being a reflection of the divine human form, in its life of related uses and neighborly service. Hell is in the opposite or reversed order of the heavens, and exhibits the divine love in its endeavor to control and restrain the wicked who are governed by the love of self, and to protect them from their own insanities. The world of spirits is the intermediate state between heaven and hell into which all souls enter immediately upon the death of the body. Here the judgment takes place and the revelation, to each one, of the nature of his own ruling loves and of his ability or inability to be happy in heaven, where the ruling love is love to the Lord and charity to the neighbor. Four smaller works are: *The Earths in the Universe; The Last Judgment; The New Jerusalem and its Heavenly Doctrines;* and *The White Horse of the Apocalypse* (London, 1758). *The Apocalypse Explained, Giving the Internal Sense of the Book of Revelation* reveals the internal history of the Christian Church, showing its decline in the two dominant evil tendencies, the " harlot " or the lust of dominion, exhibited in the Roman Catholic hierarchy, and the " dragon " or doctrine of faith alone as saving, exhibited in the Protestant sects, terminating with the judgment enacted in the world of spirits in the year 1757. This judgment, which marks the transition into a new age of the world and of the Church, is effected by the coming of the Lord to spirits and to man in the opening of his Word in its spiritual sense, which is his promised second coming. In the light of this " book of life," the false and evil spirits are cast down and the good are enabled to recognize the Lord Jesus Christ in his glorified humanity as the only God, and to follow him in the life of charity and faith combined, and so to compose the new Christian heaven. Out of this will descend to the earth more and more the holy city, New Jerusalem, by which is signified the true doctrine of faith and of life as seen in heaven in which God will himself dwell with men and be with them their God (see NEW JERUSALEM CHURCH). The *Apocalypse Explained* was not finished by the author, but was replaced later by an abridgment entitled the *Apocalypse Revealed* (Amsterdam, 1766).

2. Heaven, Hell, Spirits, and Revelation.

The Doctrine of the New Jerusalem respecting the Lord; the Sacred Scriptures; Faith; and *Life;* commonly known as the *Four Leading Doctrines* (Amsterdam, 1763) are brief treatises which embody in concise form what may be called the religion of the New Church. The Lord Jesus Christ is shown by Scripture texts to be Jehovah incarnate in a humanity born of the virgin; who, by triumphs over the hells in the conflicts of his temptation and passion on earth, set man free from the tyranny of evil which threatened the human race, and opened the way to heaven. This is redemption. The doctrine of a trinity of persons resulting in worship and prayer to three gods, and of a vicarious atonement made by one god to appease another are declared to be human inventions. The holy Trinity of Father, Son, and Holy Spirit is declared to be a trinity of person, not of persons, like that of soul and body and action in man, being essentially the trinity of the divine love and wisdom and operation in Jesus Christ glorified, " in whom dwelleth all the fulness of the godhead bodily " and who, having " all power in heaven and earth " is the only visible and true God and the only rightful object of worship in the Christian Church. In the sacred Scriptures the " books of the Word " which embrace the " law, prophets, and Psalms " of the Old Testament and the " four Gospels and Revelation " of the New are shown to have an internal sense throughout, being dictated by the divine spirit to the human writers without their intervention, and clothed in natural symbolic language exactly corresponding to the spiritual and universal truths within, just as nature is a symbolic clothing with matter of the forces and forms of the divine love and wisdom. The other books of the Bible are inspired and useful for the Church but are not the divine Word itself in the sense of the above named. By the Word man is brought into association with angelic societies in heaven who are in the spiritual sense, and by the same divine indwelling and association the holy sacraments of the church, founded in the Word, have their supernatural power.

3. Doctrines of Christ and the Scriptures.

The doctrine of life teaches that " all religion has relation to life and the life of religion is to do good." The good of life, which is charity, is defined as consisting primarily in shunning all evils as sins against God and doing faithfully the duties of one's office. The decalogue in its external and internal sense shows what evils are sins, including not only outward deed but inward motive. Particularly the sin of adultery is shown to embrace fornication and all lust and practise hurtful to the holy bond and pure marriage love between one man and one woman. Saving faith is shown to be faith in the Lord God, the Savior Jesus Christ, and in his power to save those who look to him for strength to overcome evil in obedience to the divine commandments. With those who are in this effort and are fulfilling faithfully their duty to the neighbor in a life of use according to their station, the Lord implants a good and heavenly nature in place of the evils put away, and so man is regenerated and enters the heavenly life. Acts of charity, benevolence, piety, etc., are not properly good works, since they may be done equally by the evil, but they are the signs of charity and the means of its exercise for those who are in the effort to shun evils as sins and do good from God.

4. Life and Faith.

Other works published in Amsterdam are: " Continuation Concerning the Last Judgment and the Spiritual World "; " The Angelic Wisdom Respecting the Divine Love and Wisdom " (1763); " The Angelic Wisdom Respecting the Divine Providence " (1764); " The Delights of Wisdom Concerning Conjugal Love " (1768); " A Brief Exposition of the Doctrine of the New Church Signi-

fied by the New Jerusalem in the Revelation " (1769); and, lastly, the great summary of all his theology, " The True Christian Religion or Universal Theology of the New Church " (1771).

The works entitled " Angelic Wisdom " present systematically what may be called a spiritual metaphysics and ethics in distinction from the dogmatics and the exegesis of the other works. Thus in " Angelic Wisdom Respecting the Divine Love and Wisdom " there is a spiritual philosophy of creation and of the discrete degrees by which the universe and man emanated from God without being continuous with God. It is the complement to Swedenborg's earlier cosmology, and in place of the formless infinite there is substituted the divine man, a being whose *esse* is love, whose *existere* is wisdom, and whose *procedere* is use; whose first effulgence or manifestation is through the sun of the spiritual world which emanates from himself, whose heat is love and whose light is truth; and which in succession, by its emanations, produces the auras, ethers, and atmospheres of the spiritual world. These again in their receding orbits become condensed and fixed in the forms of the material atmospheres and so of the visible and ponderable suns and earths of our universe, every particle of which is actuated and put in motion by the particles or forces of the corresponding higher atmosphere or aura of the spiritual world. In this way God, who is the only life and the source of motion and the divine Man after whose form all things are created, actuates and shapes all creation, without being himself nature; and because these degrees of creation, viz., God, spiritual world, nature, are discrete, like end, cause, and effect, and not continuous planes of matter more or less attenuated, pantheism is avoided and the human individuality is preserved. The universe is shown to be the theater of the divine altruism, the world deriving its being from love's need of an object, which can freely reciprocate that love, man in his free moral nature being that object. The reciprocation of the divine love by man is in the life of charity, that is, of love and service to the neighbor. Man's individual personality, being the reactive agent to respond to divine love, is never destroyed, and heaven is the perfect society of immortal personalities. In the " Divine Providence " the laws are set forth by which the Lord leads man in freedom by reason out of his evils into lesser evils and into good, and how the Lord's providence, looking only to eternal ends, controls everything with a view to the greatest good.

5. The " Angelic Wisdom."

In the " Conjugal Love," Swedenborg presents an ethics of marriage remarkable for its elevation and purity. The sex distinction and relation are as fundamental in the spiritual as in the physical nature of man, resulting from the relation of the volitional and the intellectual faculties of the mind, and marriage finds its high and holy source in the union of love and wisdom in the divine nature. The Christian marriage relation of one man and one woman is essentially holy and chaste and its bonds inviolable. It is " the purest pearl of human life, the most precious jewel of the Christian

6. Marriage; The Planets; Summary.

religion." In an appendix to this work, Swedenborg has written on scortatory love and its insane pleasures; showing how these are the very opposite of marriage and destructive of the holy conjugal principles and pointing out their various degrees of destructiveness. While exhorting his reader to seek alone the sacred union of marriage he warns him " to shun wandering lusts as he would the lakes of hell."

In the " Earths in the Universe," the distinguishing qualities of the inhabitants of various planets are discussed, but not, as some have supposed, from any claimed abode in the planets themselves, but from information obtained in the spiritual world from the former inhabitants of these planets.

The True Christian Religion gives the great summary of all the theological doctrines, including chapters on God, on redemption, on reformation, on regeneration, on the sacraments, on the succession of the churches or divine dispensations on the earth, from the most ancient or Adamic through the Noachic, Jewish, and Christian to the New Jerusalem of the Apocalypse; and of the second coming of the Lord in the opening of the internal sense of the Scriptures. The opening chapters on God the Creator, in their discussion of the *esse* and the *existere* of God and their respective attributes, handle the profoundest ontological concepts and afford a basis for a philosophy of revelation and of human knowing of the widest scope and validity.

III. Close of Life; Death and Burial: A noteworthy fact connected with Swedenborg's period of illumination is that far from exhibiting any signs of mental aberration during these same years in which he claimed to be in daily intercourse with the inhabitants of the other world, he was living the normal public life of a useful citizen. Rejecting the royal offer of a permanent assessorship in the Board of Mines, and asking to be retired on a half-salary, the board, on his retirement, gave expression to the honor and appreciation in which he was held; his contributions on the mining industry of Sweden were declared to be of the highest practical value, as were his contributions to finance; even so late as 1766 he published in Amsterdam his " New Method of Finding the Longitude of Places on Land and Sea." In 1771 Swedenborg went to London for the last time and took up his humble lodgings in Cold Bath Fields. He saw *The True Christian Religion* come from the press in that year. In the following year, the eighty-fourth of his age, he peacefully passed away. Before his death he devoutly received the sacrament at the hands of the Lutheran pastor, Ferelius, to whom he solemnly avowed, as his dying testimony, the truth of all that he had written. Swedenborg's remains were interred in the Lutheran Church in Princes Square, Ratcliff Highway, London, and some years later a memorial tablet was placed on its wall. In 1908, owing to the necessary abandonment of the church by its congregation and the deep interest awakened in Swedenborg among the learned men of Sweden, by consent of the British government the remains were disinterred and transferred in state on a Swedish warship to Sweden, and were deposited in the cathedral at Upsala; and here two years later, in

the presence of the king and royal family and of the dignitaries of the university and of the Church, was solemnly dedicated the memorial erected over the remains by order of the Swedish parliament.

IV. Recent Honors: Like many leaders of the world's thought, Swedenborg has required the vista of years by which to be seen in his real significance. Kant concealed his indebtedness to him under the persiflage of the " Dreams of the Spirit-Seer "; Goethe is more outspoken in his gratitude, and his *Faust* is full of the Swedenborgian world-view. Swedenborg's trinal monism, the doctrine that the One embraces in itself the three essential degrees, end, cause, effect: the grand man or the human form of society; the spiritual, as being the real, world; the spiritual meaning as the true and essential meaning of the Scriptures; God as divine Man, visible and adorable in the glorified humanity of Jesus Christ; the doctrine of the world as a vast system of tremulations set in motion by its center, the infinite divine love, and transmitted through successive spiritual and natural spheres and atmospheres; and of the kingdom of heaven as a kingdom of uses—these ideas are permeating all the newer developments of philosophic and religious thought. Early theological prejudice is giving way to profound respect; and the time seems near when Swedenborg's own prophecy, from the words of Seneca, will be realized: " There will come those who will judge without offense or favor " (*Epist.* lxxix.).

FRANK SEWALL.

BIBLIOGRAPHY: The scientific and philosophical works, letters, and archives are in course of publication in a complete monumental edition under the auspices of the Royal Academy of Sciences in Stockholm under the chief editorship of Prof. Gustav Retzius. Nearly all the unpublished MSS. have been reproduced in photo-lithograph and are deposited in the national libraries. The writings of Swedenborg have been translated and published as a whole or in part in the English, Welsh, French, German, Italian, Spanish, Norwegian, Swedish, Icelandic, Russian, Danish, Dutch, Polish, Hindi, Arabic, and Japanese languages. The chief publishing centers of his works and collateral literature are the Swedenborg Society, London, founded in 1810, located at 1 Bloomsbury Street; the Massachusetts New-Church Union, 16 Arlington Street, Boston; and the American Swedenborg Printing and Publishing Society, 3 West Twenty-ninth Street, New York. Complete editions are to be had in both Latin and English.

As literary helps use: J. Hyde, *Bibliographical Index to the Published Writings of Emanuel Swedenborg Original and Translated; from the Library of the Swedenborg Society,* supplemented *from English and Foreign Collections, public and private,* London, 1897. A very large list of entries will be found in the *British Museum Catalogue* under " Swedenborg." Note also J. F. Potts, *The Swedenborg Concordance,* 6 vols., London, 1898. On the life consult: R. L. Tafel, *Documents concerning the Life and Character of Emanuel Swedenborg,* 3 vols., London, 1875–77; B. Worcester, *Life and Mission of Emanuel Swedenborg,* Boston, 1883; G. Trobridge, *Emanuel Swedenborg, his Life, Teachings and Influence,* London, 1908; S. P. Doughty, *Life of Emanuel Swedenborg,* London, 1857; J. W. Fletcher, *Emanuel Swedenborg,* London, 1859; J. Hyde, *Swedenborg the Man of the Age,* new ed., London, 1863; W. White, *Emanuel Swedenborg: Life and Writings,* London, 1871; J. J. G. Wilkinson, *Emanuel Swedenborg,* London, 1886; J. F. Buss, *Swedenborg; his Life and Mission,* London, 1887; C. T. Odhner, *Account of the Life and Work of E. Swedenborg,* Philadelphia, 1893; G. Ballet, *Swedenborg: hist. d'un visionaire au xviii. siècle,* Paris, 1899.

On the doctrines of Swedenborg consult: J. J. G. Wilkinson, *A Sketch of Swedenborg and the Swedenborgians,* Boston, 1842; idem, *Popular Sketch of Swedenborg's Philosophy,* London, 1847; A. Clissold, *Practical Nature of*

Swedenborg's Writings, Boston, 1839; I. Kant, *Träume eines Geistersehers*, Königsberg, 1766, Eng. transl., London, 1900, see below under F. Sewall; R. W. Emerson, *Representative Men*, Boston, 1850; E. Cambefort, *Essai sur Swedenborg et ses idées eschatologiques*, Strasburg, 1857; J. Mill, *The Claims of Swedenborg*, London, 1857; A. J. Matter, *Emanuel de Swedenborg*, Paris, 1863; H. James, *The Secret of Swedenborg*, Boston, 1869; J. J. van Oosterzee, *Emanuel Swedenborg*, Amsterdam, 1873; G. Wallis, *Swedenborg and Modern Culture*, London, 1875; S. Simpson, *The Delusions and Errors of Emanuel Swedenborg*, North Walsham, 1876; W. Bruce, *Wesley and Swedenborg*, London, 1877; B. F. Barrett, *Lectures on the New Dispensation*, Boston, 1881; E. A. Beaman, *Swedenborg and the New Age*, Philadelphia, 1881; E. Swift, *Swedenborg: the Man and his Works*, London, 1883; E. Madeley, *The Science of Correspondences Elucidated*, London, 1884; W. Graham, *The Facts of Being; a concurrent Study of the Divine Word and the theological Works of E. Swedenborg*, London, 1896; G. Bush, *Statement of Reasons for Embracing the Doctrines of Swedenborg*, new issue, New York, 1898; J. E. Bowers, *Suns and Worlds of the Universe*, London, 1899; G. Trobridge, *Swedenborg and Modern Thought*, London, 1899; A. Vismara, *Emanuele Swedenborg*, Milan, 1902; J. Whitehead, *A Study of Swedenborg's Psychical States and Experiences*, Boston, 1909; F. Sewall, *Swedenborg and Dante. Essays on the New Renaissance*, London, 1893; idem, *Kant and Swedenborg*, in Kant's *Dreams of a Spirit Seer*, ib. 1900; idem, *Swedenborg and the Sapientia Angelica*, in Constable's *Philosophies Ancient and Modern*, London, 1910. To the exposition of the philosophy of Swedenborg, *The New-Church Review*, Boston, and *The New-Church Magazine* and *The New-Church Quarterly*, London, are devoted. *The New Philosophy*, Lancaster, Pa., promulgates his science and philosophy.

SWEDISH EVANGELICAL MISSION COVENANT OF AMERICA: An association of churches in the United States which is an offshoot of the free-church movement in Sweden there organized into the Swedish Covenant. The history is as follows:

In 1868 a congregation of former members of the First Swedish Lutheran Church of Chicago was organized and incorporated with a charter permitting the ordination of ministers. Other churches springing up in various towns, especially in Illinois and Iowa, united in 1873 with this congregation to form the Swedish Evangelical Lutheran Mission Synod. Another synod, the Swedish Evangelical Ansgarii Synod, was organized 1874, and the two bodies united, 1885, into the Swedish Evangelical Mission Covenant of America. The basis of the movement is the idea that each Christian church is a voluntary union of individuals upon the foundation of faith in Christ Jesus and of brotherly love and confidence, this union to be held open to every believer leading a Christian life, without considering differences of creeds as far as these do not imply a denial of the authority of the Holy Scriptures. The covenant is not, strictly speaking, a church organization, but rather a missionary society having churches as its members. The churches have in fact consolidated because their missionary spirit has led them on to missionary enterprises too large for any single church to undertake. There is at the same time a tendency, although not very pronounced, to grow into a more intimate consolidation along denominational lines. And, in theory at least, the covenant has, through its annual conferences, the same disciplinary power over any single church as the church over any single church-member.

The organization reports 185 churches, 375 ministers, 34,500 church-members, property value $143,000, income for missionary purposes $31,000.

It has three weekly periodicals, *Missionsvännan* and *Chicagobladet*, published in Chicago, and *Veckobladet*, published in Minneapolis.　　D. NYVALL.

BIBLIOGRAPHY: D. Magnus, *The Scandinavian Work in Michigan*, in *The Home Missionary*, Mar., 1885; P. Waldenström, *Genom Nordamerikas Förenta Stater*, Stockholm, 1890; idem, *Nya Färder genom Nordamerikas Förenta Stater*, Stockholm, 1902; *World's Congress of Religions*, ed. J. H. Barrows, Chicago, 1893; A. P. Nelson, *Missionsvännernes Historia*, Minneapolis, 1906.

SWEENY, JAMES FIELDING: Anglican bishop of Toronto; b. in London, England, Nov. 15, 1857. He was educated at McGill University, Montreal (B.A., 1878), and was ordered deacon in 1880 and priested in the following year. In 1880–83 he was rector of St. Luke's, Montreal, and of St. Philip's, Toronto (1883–1909), also being commissary for the bishop of Moosonee in 1901–09, domestic chaplain to the archbishop of Toronto in 1903–09, and archdeacon of York, diocese of Toronto, in 1906–09. In 1909 he was consecrated bishop of Toronto.

SWETE, HENRY BARCLAY: Church of England; b. at Bristol Mar. 14, 1835. He was educated at Gonville and Caius College, Cambridge (B.A., 1859), and was ordered deacon in 1858 and ordained priest in the following year. He was curate of Blagdon, Somerset (1858–65), All Saints', Cambridge (1866–68), and Tor Mohun, Devonshire (1869–72), and rector of Ashdon, Essex (1877–90). He was fellow of his college (1858–77); tutor (1872–1875); divinity lecturer in the University of Cambridge (1875–77); professor of pastoral theology in King's College, London (1882–90); and since 1890 has been regius professor of divinity at Cambridge, where he was Lady Margaret preacher in 1902–03. After being an honorary fellow of Gonville and Caius College in 1886–90, he was reelected fellow in the latter year, and has also been fellow of King's College, London, since 1890. He was examining chaplain to the bishop of St. Alban's from 1881 to 1890. He has written or edited: *England versus Rome: A brief Handbook of the Roman Catholic Controversy* (London, 1868); *On the Early History of the Doctrine of the Holy Spirit* (Cambridge, 1873); *Theodorus Lascaris Junior, De Processione Spiritus Sancti oratio apologetica* (London, 1876); *On the History of the Doctrine of the Procession of the Holy Spirit from the Apostolic Age to the Death of Charlemagne* (Cambridge, 1876); *Theodori Episcopi Mopsuesteni in epistolas Beati Pauli Commentarii* (2 vols., 1880–82); *The Old Testament in Greek* (3 vols., 1887–94, 4th ed. of vol. i., 1909); *The Akhmîm Fragment of the Gospel of Peter* (London, 1893); *The Apostles' Creed in Relation to Primitive Christianity* (Cambridge, 1894); *Faith in Relation to Creed, Thought, and Life* (London, 1895); *Church Services and Service Books before the Reformation* (1896); *The Gospel according to St. Mark: The Greek Text, with Introduction, Notes, and Indices* (London, 1898); *An Introduction to the Old Testament in Greek* (1900); *Patristic Study* (1902); *Studies in the Teaching of Our Lord* (1903, new ed., 1910). *The Apocalypse of St. John* (Greek text, with introduction and notes), 1906; *The Appearances of our Lord after his Passion* (1907); *The Holy Spirit in the New Testament: a Study of Primitive Christian*

Teaching (1909); *The Ascended Christ; a Study in the earliest Christian Teaching* (1910); and edited *Essays on Some Biblical Questions of the Day* (1909).

SWING, ALBERT TEMPLE: Congregationalist; b. at Bethel, O., Jan. 18, 1849. He was educated at Oberlin College (A.B., 1874), Yale Divinity School (B.D., 1877), and the universities of Berlin and Halle (1891–92). He has held pastorates at Fremont, Neb. (1878–86), Cortland, N. Y. (1886–1887), and Detroit, Mich. (1887–90). In 1890–93 he was in Europe, and since 1893 has been professor of church history at Oberlin Theological Seminary. In theology he is a liberal conservative. He is the author of *Theology of Albrecht Ritschl* (New York, 1901); *Outline of the Doctrinal Development in the Western Church* (Oberlin, O., 1904); and *Life of James Harris Fairchild, or Sixty Eight Years with a Christian College* (New York, 1906).

SWING, DAVID: American divine; b. in Cincinnati, O., Aug. 23, 1830; d. in Chicago Oct. 4, 1894. He came of blended English and German ancestry; grew up on a farm near Williamsburg, Clermont County, O., attending the district school of the village; was graduated from Miami University, Oxford, O., 1852; studied for two years in the Theological Seminary at Cincinnati, under Dr. Nathan Lewis Rice; then returned to Miami University as professor of classic languages, where he remained for twelve years. He married Miss Elizabeth Porter, of Oxford, O., in 1855, and two daughters were born in their home. In 1866 he was called to the Westminster Presbyterian church of Chicago, which was consolidated with the North Church in 1869, under the name of the Fourth Presbyterian church, Professor Swing being retained as pastor of the new organization. The church edifice was destroyed by fire in 1871, but was rebuilt the following year. Charges of heresy were filed against Professor Swing with the Chicago Presbytery in 1874, by Dr. Francis Landey Patton, editor of *The Interior*. An exciting trial ensued, the records of which are preserved in *The Trial of Rev. David Swing, Edited by a Committee of the Presbytery* (Chicago, 1874). The result was a verdict of " not proved," but upon appeal by the prosecution to the Northern Illinois synod the accused withdrew from the Presbyterian Church.

The following year, 1875, Central Church was organized with Professor Swing as pastor, $50,000 having been subscribed by citizens of Chicago to support the enterprise. It was an independent society, founded upon a simple statement of faith in Christ as the savior and leader of men. In 1880 Central Music Hall was dedicated as the home of the church, and in that spacious auditorium Professor Swing preached to a congregation of 3,000 people until his death. Professor Swing was editor of *The Alliance*, an undenominational religious weekly, 1873–82, and of *The Weekly Magazine*, 1883–85. He was much in request as a lecturer, his most popular themes being " The Useful and the Beautiful," " Overdoing," and " The Novel." His sermons, which he read, were little essays, covering a wide range of moral and spiritual topics, and written with rare delicacy and beauty of style.

Among his published works are *Truths for To-day* (2 series, Chicago, 1874–76); *Motives of Life* (1879); *Club Essays* (1880); *Sermons* (1883); *Old Pictures of Life* (1894)—two volumes of essays edited after his death.   JOSEPH FORT NEWTON.

BIBLIOGRAPHY: J. F. Newton, *David Swing: Poet-Preacher*, Cedar Rapids, Ia., 1908.

SWISS BRETHREN. See MENNONITES.

SWITHUN, swith'un (**SWITHIN, SWITHUM**), **SAINT:** Bishop and patron of Winchester; d. at Winchester July 2, 862. Of noble birth, he was educated in the Old Monastery, Winchester, where he was ordained by Bishop Helmstan, 827. Egbert, king of the West Saxons, committed his son and successor, Ethelwulf, to his care, and availed himself of his counsels. Ethelwulf, on his accession, made him his minister, especially in ecclesiastical affairs, and in 852 appointed him, with the clergy's consent, bishop of Winchester on the death of Helmstan. St. Swithun's Day is July 15, because on that day, in 971, his relics were moved from the churchyard, where he had been buried at his own request, so that his grave might be trodden on by passers-by, to the cathedral of Winchester. Owing to the fact that rain fell on the day and for a considerable period afterward, the superstition exists that a rainy St. Swithun's Day presages forty days of rain immediately afterward. Miracles are reported to have followed in great number.

BIBLIOGRAPHY: Early material, with comment, is collected in *ASB*, July, i. 321–330, Aug., i. 98–100, and in *MPL*, clv. 57–66. Consult further: J. Earle, *Gloucester Fragments*, vol. i., *Facsimiles of some Leaves in . . . Handwriting on St. Swithun*, London, 1861 (contains essay on life and times of Swithun and three early lives); *DNB*, lv. 239–241.

SWITZERLAND.

The censuses ordered by the federal government, 1850–1900, give evidence of the varied and often complicated conditions in the Church as well as in the State of Switzerland. The four divisions tabulated were the Protestant, Roman Catholic, Jewish, and " Others not specified "; but distinctions were not clearly drawn, and subdivisions were omitted. It is therefore not evident how many members of the smaller Evangelical denominations were included either in the first or fourth categories; how many Christian Catholics (Old Catholics), in the second or fourth; and how many were included in the fourth because of religious indifference or inadvertently. From a review of the census statistics of Dec. 1, 1900, it appears that the confessional distribution in Switzerland from 1880 to 1900 has undergone little alteration. The Protestants lost eight per cent, the Roman Catholics gained the same; the Jews increased from two to four per cent of the total; those of no denomination fell from four to two per cent. Of a total number of Jews of 12,263, the canton of Zurich had 2,933 and of Basel-Stadt, 1,897. Of the 7,359 non-classified Geneva had 1,928 or over twenty-five per cent of its total. The cantons of Zurich, Bern, Schaffhausen, Vaud, and Neuchâtel were (1900) over 80 per cent Protestant; Appenzell-Outer-Rohdes, over 90 per cent. The original cantons of Lucerne, Uri, Schwyz, the two Unterwalden, Zug, Appenzell-Inner-Rhodes, Ticino, and Valais were over 90 per cent Roman Catholic, with Freiburg at 84.6 per cent. Most closely divided are Graubünden, Protestant 52 per cent, and Roman Catholic 47 per cent; Aargau, 55 and 44, respectively; and Geneva, 47 and 51.

I. The Church Law: The federal constitution of May 29, 1874, placed the church conditions of all confessions on a new footing. That of 1848 had guaranteed to all adherents of the Christian confessions unmolested residence and freedom of worship; reserved to the federation and cantons the maintenance of public order and peace among the confessions and civil equality between church-members and citizens; and prohibited the Jesuits and affiliated orders. The constitution of 1874 further guarantees state primary education open to all without restriction of confessional faith or freedom of conscience, both of which are pronounced inviolable within the state. There is to be no coercion of religious affiliation, religious instruction, or of any religious performance, and no penalty on account of religious opinion. Parents or guardians exercise control of the religious instruction of children till the end of the sixteenth year, in the sense of the above-mentioned principles. The exercise of civil and political rights are not to be abridged by any prescriptions or conditions of an ecclesiastical and religious character. Religious beliefs do not exempt one from civic duties. No one is obliged to pay taxes for the special purposes of religious worship of a society to which he does not belong. The application of this fundamental principle in detail is reserved to the federal diet. Freedom of worship is guaranteed within the limits of morality and public order. Full power is secured to the federation and cantons to adopt measures for the maintenance of order and public peace among the adherents of the different religious societies as well as against the invasion of the rights of citizens by church authorities. Questions of public or private rights arising from the formation or separation of religious bodies may, by way of complaint, be submitted to the decision of the proper civic authorities. The erection of dioceses on Swiss territory is subject to the approval of the Federation. The prohibition against the Jesuits may, by act of the Federation, be extended to other religious orders whose activity may be a menace to the State, or disturb the peace of the confessions. The erection of new, or the restoration of abolished, monasteries or religious orders, is not permissible. The disposition of burial places devolves upon the civil authorities, who must see to it that every dead person is suitably buried. The civic authorities are to determine and record the civic status. The right of marriage is under the protection of the Federation, and must not be restricted either for religious or economic reasons, nor on account of previous conduct. The spiritual jurisdiction is abolished. The carrying-out of these fundamental laws might have had as a result the complete indifference of State to Church and the disappearance of the cantonal state churches; but only a few radical consequences have actually resulted. A reaction in favor of a closer union of Church and State has gradually set in. The articles on the civil status and marriage have been enacted. A statute aiming at the extension of the federal supervision of public schools by the creation of a secretary was voted down in 1882. After much deliberation the constitutional article was amended so that the cantons receive national aid for the primary school system without the sacrifice of independent control.

The effect of the operation of the constitution to date may be summed up as follows: (1) All religious instruction, in or out of school, is facultative. However, in most cantons it is given in the schools, and in many cantons it is imparted by the clergy, especially in the higher grades. (2) The clergy may not serve *ex officio* as inspectors, presidents, or members of school boards; but they may, nevertheless, be elected, which often happens in the Reformed cantons. (3) It has been questioned whether persons belonging to a religious order, and hence bound by vows other than those to the state authority, may become teachers in public schools; but the Roman Catholic cantons hold to it, and no other decision has been reached by the Federation. (4) Religious jurisdiction, especially official participation of church or priest in legal questions of marriage and paternity is prohibited; the civil marriage is obligatory, and alone legally valid; the civil register must not be conducted by priests; the church ceremony prior to the civil marriage is forbidden under severe penalties. (5) The federal diet has interfered with attempts of the Roman Catholic Church to make changes in the dioceses without reference to the Federation. (6) Ecclesiastical measures (e.g., exclusion from church voting) against those who intentionally disregard church practises like baptism, confirmation, communion, church marriage, or church burial, are not admissible in cantons where the Protestant Church is established.

II. The Reformed Church: In the course of the Reformation the only alternative to the power of the papacy was the State. The resort to this on the part of the adherents of the Evangelical Church was not opposed by Zwingli and Calvin, who sought to promote the religious moral reformation of the whole as politically organized, as well as of individuals. Only the Evangelical adherents belonged to the State in Protestant cantons; the Roman Catholics, in cantons under their control. The former were masters, the latter servants, of their governments. The council of 200 at Zurich ordered the preaching of the Word only, carried out the Reformation in doctrine and cultus, and organized the synod of clericals in 1528, including the clergy of Glarus until 1630, and those of Thurgau and Rheinthal till 1798. Similar synods were erected in St. Gall with Appenzell, Toggenburg, and Schaffhausen. Those instituted at Bern and Basel soon lapsed. In Graubünden (Grisons) the synod had almost independent conduct of church affairs. In Geneva, the choice of the clergy lay with the Compagnie des pasteurs, and the church discipline in the hands of a consistory whose members were the six pastors of the town, and twelve men chosen by the council. The entire church government in Neuchâtel lay in the hands of the Compagnie des pasteurs. In canton Vaud, the discipline and the appointment of pastors, subject to confirmation by the government, was vested in the five classes. The union of classes into synods was not invariable, and ceased in the seventeenth century. The current church administration was conducted by a board of examiners in Zurich, consisting of members of the council, pastors, and professors, presided over by the *antistes*, i.e., the pastor of the Great Minster and president of the synod. It examined and ordained candidates, offered suggestions to the council for the election of pastors, and had supervision of the clergy. Similar boards existed in Schaffhausen, Basel, and other cantons under an *antistes* or dean. The chapter of Roman Catholic times survived in the assemblies of the clergy of smaller districts, under the name of classes as in Bern and Vaud, or colloquies as in Graubünden, their presiding officer being generally called dean. In Glarus, Appenzell, and Graubünden, the congregations had the right to choose and dismiss their pastors, but in most cantons this was the prerogative of the government, or of the hitherto existing collators acting on the suggestion of the examiners or church conventions. Even from the time before the Reformation the congregations in many cantons had variously constituted and differently named administrative boards which regulated discipline and morals, the observance of festivals, attendance at church, management of church property, and charities, and formed the first court of marriage discipline. Absolute church discipline to the extent of exclusion from the communion devolved on these boards only in the cantons of Basel, Schaffhausen, Neuchâtel, and Geneva, in the last of which very severe civil penalties were associated with those of the Church, such as expulsion. The synods began to lose power, or ceased altogether in the seventeenth and eighteenth centuries, and the church interests became more and more those of the State. With the founding of the Helvetian republic, a plan was projected for a unified church organization, but was not put into effect. The Helvetian government held the highest ecclesiastical authority, the minister of arts and sciences being also minister of religion. During the intermediate period the old forms were revived. The newly formed cantons of St. Gall and Thurgau were given synods and church councils, but Aargau, only a church council. In 1830 the political changes occasioned alterations in the church constitution looking toward more independence from the State. A few church synods obtained the right of decision in purely church matters, subject to the ratification of the grand council, and the right of approval in matters not purely ecclesiastical, as in Zurich, St. Gall, Thurgau. Others, as in Schaffhausen, Appen-

zell, had only, even in purely church affairs, the right to propose measures. Mixed synods, with a limited clerical representation, were established in Bern (1852), Neuchâtel (1848), Freiburg (1854), and Glarus (1845). Popular synods, with absolute free choice, belong to a recent date. Basel-Stadt had a church council, but no synod; Basel-Land no definite church constitution. The chapter-general in Aargau had the right of decision in purely church matters; and in others the right of approval.

The cantons are independent of each other in church matters, there being no Swiss Reformed Church, in the legal sense; but only cantonal state churches. No one is obliged to belong to the established church of his canton; however,

2. Present Church Constitution. a Protestant removing from one canton to another is *ipso facto* regarded as an adherent of the state church where he takes up his residence. Between 1863 and 1903 new church laws were made in thirteen principal cantons, including Bern and Geneva (1874), and Zurich (1902). In Schaffhausen the law of 1854 is in contradiction with the constitution of 1876. Basel-Land has as yet no church law. In purely internal church affairs (worship, hymnal, liturgy, or materials for religious instruction), the organizations decide, with or without the pleasure of the State; but in mixed affairs the State decides, subject to the approval of the church organization (supervision of church properties, pay of the clergy, or division of parishes). In Glarus, Freiburg, Appenzell, St. Gall, Thurgau, the independence of the Church or of individual churches is predominant; in Basel-Stadt, Schaffhausen, Aargau, Vaud, and Geneva, the material competence of the state authorities. The churches set up no formal creed, but declare themselves members of the Christian church, or of the Evangelical church, or avow the principles of the Reformation. Some deny all confessional form as qualification for synodal rights and ecclesiastical offices. All citizen voters who belong to the Reformed faith, or submit to the church regulations, constitute a parish community. Outsiders have a church vote in Appenzell and Neuchâtel. Parishes in all the cantons may choose their pastor; in Vaud, however, they have only two nominations to the government. Most have the choice of the church governing boards; many the choice of the members of the synod; some have either the sole right with reference to worship, hymn-book, and liturgy, or the right to veto the proposals of the synod. The church board of which the pastor is member *ex officio* or advisory member, generally has supervision of the order of worship, of pastoral activity, specially of instruction, moral discipline, and official or non-official charge of the poor. The synods (consistory in Geneva) are either absolute legislative bodies, in purely church affairs, or are subject to the state authorities or to the churches. They are constituted of representatives of the parishes, or of parishes and the State combined, or election districts, or of the entire canton, or of district boards. The term is three, four, or six years, and the sessions are usually annual (monthly in Geneva). The highest board of administration, variously styled church commission or council and synodal commission or council, is either collateral, or subordinate to the government of the canton, or has a representation therefrom, and is wholly or partly or not in any way chosen by the synod. Its duty is to prepare and execute the decisions of the synod, to regulate mostly the acceptance and eligibility of the clergy, supervise the clergy, institute visitations, settle cases of discipline and dispute, and, in many cantons, to supervise the administration of church property. The intermediate district boards exist only in Zurich and Vaud. The colloquies in Graubünden and the deans of the chapters in St. Gall have similar prerogatives. The clergy of a district together form a chapter in Zurich, St. Gall, and Thurgau, and may submit matters to the action of the synod, and cooperate with it in practical and theological affairs. In Basel-Stadt and Aargau the clergy of the canton form the chapter. The Compagnie des pasteurs in Geneva and the convention of clergy at Schaffhausen and Basel-Land have a similar function. The clergy become eligible on the basis of a university course, followed by examination before appointed committees, or a diploma granted by a theological faculty. Ordination takes place in connection with a public service by the laying on of hands, and in most cantons by the taking of a vow, pledging faithfulness in the preaching of the Gospel, and the administration of the sacred ordinances, and purity of life. Geneva and Neuchâtel exclude the vow, placing every clerical on the responsibility of his own conscience. Pastors are elected for life in Vaud and Geneva; for three years in Glarus; five in Basel-Land; six in Zurich, Bern, Freiburg, Basel-Stadt, Aargau, and Neuchâtel; eight in Schaffhausen, and until dismissed in Graubünden; but these terms are usually renewable. The church councils usually deal with the suspension of delinquent pastors; the synod with dismission from office in Glarus, Freiburg, St. Gall, Graubünden; the civic council in Basel-Stadt, Vaud, Geneva, and Neuchâtel; the church council in Appenzell. Dismission can be effected only by legal sentence in Bern and Zurich. The pastors are paid by the State in nine cantons, with here and there additional free-will offerings from the Church, and in the others by the churches, and salaries average between $390 and $595, the minimum being $195, the maximum, $780–877. A pension for retired clergy is provided by law in Bern, Basel-Stadt, Zurich, Schaffhausen, Aargau, and Vaud; and in many cantons there are free institutions for old and sick clergy, and for their widows and orphans.

The Concordat of Feb. 19, 1862, relating to the "mutual admission of Evangelical Reformed clergy" is in effect in the cantons of **3. Inter-** Zurich, Aargau, Appenzell-Outer- **cantonal** Rhodes, Thurgau, Glarus, Schaff- **Arrange-** hausen, St. Gall, and from 1870 the **ments.** two Basels. These cantons together appoint an examining board, which holds office three years, and may call in professors as experts in the examinations. The usual requirements for examination are a recommendation from the church council of the canton in which the candidate has a permanent residence, a certificate affirm-

ing the sufficient gymnasium studies, and a testimonial as to morals, besides a certificate of at least two years in high-school studies for the propædeutic test, and of at least three years for the theological. Ordination is performed by the church council that recommends the candidates. The examination certificates qualify the holders to a position in any of the associated cantons, but a pastor going from one canton into another must bring a certificate of official conduct and character from the church council of the former canton. Local reasons prevented Bern and Graubünden from joining the Concordat, but free interchange is in effect in all German Switzerland. The first conference of the Evangelical church boards of Switzerland met annually, 1858–62, and resolved upon (1) Good Friday as a solemn holy day; (2) the mutual admission of pastors; (3) the arrangement of a liturgy for Evangelical field service, beside pastoral instruction, and preliminaries for a military hymn-book; (4) steps toward a common translation of the Bible on the basis of Luther's; (5) propositions to the federal authorities for the simplification of the marriage ceremony; and (6) mutual exchange of the official reports of the cantonal church boards. No conferences were held between 1863 and 1875, but in the latter year the relation of the church boards to the state law as regards the civil estate was discussed and agreement arrived at concerning general principles. The church council of Zurich was authorized to look out for matters of common importance to the Evangelical churches, and to call a conference whenever circumstances warranted. In consequence by means of a joint resolution by circular of the church boards, 1876, the federal diet was induced to adopt a provision for the securing of religious instruction to children working in factories. On the occasion of the disturbance of the celebration of the national day of prayer by a military parade, 1877, similar steps secured the assurance against its recurrence. The conferences were resumed in 1881, in order to bring the church boards into closer affiliation in matters of common interests, and have been held annually ever since. They are attended by representatives of all the boards of the cantonal Evangelical state churches. The place of meeting changes every two years. Each canton has one vote which is cast according to the instructions of its board; these decisions are not obligatory, but suggestive to the cantons, or are simply expressions of common opinion. The most important subjects that have been treated are: the membership of the state churches; the right of outsiders to vote; the right of women to vote; church statistics; the matter of baptism and confirmation; a general proclamation for the day of prayer, and Reformation day, on the first Sunday in November; appointment of Mar. 6, 1904, as Bible Sunday; celebration of the fourth centennial anniversary of Zwingli's birthday, 1884; prayers for the federal celebration of 1891; the question of the establishment of a permanent Easter day; measures against instruction in advanced education on Sunday, and for the restriction of amusements on solemn feast days, and especially the running of excursion trains on those days; a petition for the prevention of the disturbance of the celebration of the day of prayer by military assemblies; the minimum amount of material to be taught and memorized in the instruction of the young on the part of the church, and the provision of concrete materials for the same; religious instruction in the gymnasia; care of the newly confirmed; restriction of divorce; and regulations against games of chance and lotteries. In 1905 there were, in the cantons of the Reformed State Church only, 953 churches with 1,030 clerical positions. In the cantons dominated by the Roman Catholics there were 30 Reformed churches, 23 of which were organized and supported by Protestant aid associations. In the principal cities and in the canton of Bern (8) there are together 27 French churches. In cantons Vaud, Neuchâtel, and Geneva are 16 German pastorates.

Theological instruction is given by the theological faculties of Zurich, Bern, Basel, Lausanne, Geneva, and of the academy of Neuchâtel. Ecclesiastical instruction is no longer bound

4. State of Theology and Religion. to an official confession of faith in any Swiss Evangelical State Church, but rests on the general recognition of Evangelical truth, as expressed in the ordination and synodal vows, or, more or less briefly, in the provisions of the church constitutions. The use of the Reformation catechism is also not obligatory, and no longer generally employed, and in preparation for confirmation, the pastor is free in most cantons to adopt his own method, or to select from one of the many of greater or less merit that are available. Theological and religious diversities have produced severe and protracted controversies in the Swiss state churches. After the strife of supranaturalism and rationalism in the third decade of the last century had been allayed by the influence of Schleiermacher, and the constitutional conflicts of 1830 had diverted attention to the practical side of church matters, the "Life of Jesus," by D. F. Strauss, and its adoption at the Zurich high-school, led to a violent reaction, which culminated in the popular movement of Sept. 6, 1839. This was neither purely religious, nor purely political, but the outcome of deep, religious and moral emotion, blended with personal, local, and political interests. Hegel's philosophy and the critical writings of the Tübingen School led to fresh theological and ecclesiastical controversies. Thus there grew up three church parties: the Evangelical church association, representing a strict Biblical tendency; the association for free Christianity, which is at the heart of the free-thinking, or reform tendency; and, mediating between the two, the theological church society. The influence of the Ritschlian theology among the younger men in recent decades has done much to weaken and alter these tendencies. Opposition to dogmatism and intellectualism has given rise to a strong aversion here and there to the present organization and cultic institutions, without, however, practical results. The organization of free churches has restricted itself to isolated examples in German Switzerland. The principal resource for the edification and revitalizing of the Swiss Church has been

the Bible. In the German parts this is the Lutheran version. Zurich has its own since the Reformation, frequently revised and improved until 1882. Bern had the translation of Johannes Piscator (q.v.) after 1602. A revision instituted for Switzerland in 1836, resumed in 1862 by the Evangelical conference, and again in 1877, resulted in the completion of the New Testament and the Psalms (Frauenfeld, 1893); but it was not adopted by the Synod of Zurich. In Geneva the old translation authorized by the Compagnie des Pasteurs held undisputed recognition and use for a long time (see BIBLE VERSIONS, B, VI., § 3). The revisions of this of D. Martin and J. F. Osterwald circulate widely in Neuchâtel and Vaud. The Compagnie authorized new versions; namely, of the Old Testament by L. Segond (1874), and of the New by H. Oltramare (1872). Divine service consists of preaching, prayer, and singing. There is no system of pericopes. Liturgies, of which almost every canton has its own, were drawn up partly by the Reformers and based on Roman Catholic prayers or have partly originated in recent times, or have often resulted from the long and toilsome work of the synods. These liturgies, formerly strictly obligatory, can now be employed with more liberty by pastors and churches. Until the nineteenth century, church singing was restricted to the metrical version of the Psalms in four-part melodies. Hymnals have been introduced based on the German in the cantons individually. A new Swiss hymnal (1890) for universal use has been very widely adopted. Solemn holy days are Sundays, Christmas, Good Friday, Easter, Ascension Day, and Whitsuntide; with holiday seasons specially in the eastern cantons for Christmas, Easter, and Whitsuntide. Reformation Sunday is the first in November, and the third Sunday in September is a general day of national thanksgiving, penance, and prayer, celebrated since 1650. The Lord's Supper is administered three or four times a year and on solemn feast days, including the day of prayer, or on the Sunday before or after; but in Basel it is, besides, administered every Sunday in one of the four principal churches. Children's services are held everywhere, devoted either to catechetical or consecutive Biblical instruction. Confirmation usually takes place after the age of sixteen, following a course of catechetical instruction given on week-days. Free associations have exercised a beneficent influence on religious life in Switzerland. The Association of Swiss Evangelical Preachers and Theological Teachers was founded in 1839, for the furtherance, through united action, of the theological and practical interests of the church. This body meets annually at different places, and has branches in the various cantons. In addition to the cantonal assemblies the larger cantons have pastors' societies. Bible societies exist in most of the cantons, that of Basel having been organized in 1804, and also missionary associations, which partly contribute their gifts to the Basel society and partly to the general Evangelical Protestant missionary society organized in 1883. The Protestant church aid societies were founded in 1842 through the Swiss preachers' association. Under the priority of the Basel society they foster and support Protestantism in scattered places, specially Roman Catholic cantons, as well as in neighboring foreign countries. Associations of the Innere Mission have in hand a great variety of philanthropic work. Religious periodicals in Protestant Switzerland numbered (1904) twenty-nine, in Roman Catholic seven. For Free Churches of French Switzerland see IV., below. Other denominations that have gained followers are, the Methodist Episcopal, the Methodists of the Evangelical Communion, the Baptist, the Catholic Apostolic (Irvingites), the Darbyites, Swedenborgians, Salvation Army, Christian Science, the Christian Catholic Apostolic Church of Zion of Alexander Dowie, and the Mormons. Of these the Methodists and Baptists are the most numerous, the former in 1904 having 60 preachers and 9,083 regular members. Many of the adherents of these continue as members of the state churches.

III. The Catholic Churches: According to the representations of the Roman Curia the diocese of Chur (q.v.) embraces the cantons of Zurich, Uri, Schwyz, Unterwalden, Glarus, and Graubünden; the diocese of Basel, the cantons of Bern, Lucerne, Zug, Soleure, Basel-Stadt, Basel-Land, Schaffhausen, Aargau, and Thurgau; of St. Gall, the cantons of St. Gall and Appenzell; of Lausanne and Geneva, the cantons of Freiburg, Neuchâtel, Vaud, and Geneva; and the diocese of Sitten, the canton of Valais. The organization of the Roman Catholic Church in Switzerland is lax and for the most part in a state of confusion. The administration of the bishop of Chur is only provisory except in the canton of Graubünden. This does not include Zurich, the congregations in which were declared absolved from the see of Chur, and were permitted to secure episcopal means individually for themselves as needed according to their own judgment, subject to the supremacy of the State. The bishop of Basel, with his seat at Soleure, is for the time being recognized only by Zug and Lucerne. In a dispute all the other cantons save Schaffhausen pronounced the episcopal office vacated in 1873, and no reorganization has yet taken place. The latter is under the see by provisory arrangement. After violent and lengthy disputes at Bern, the Roman Catholics there organized as free associations. In the diocese of St. Gall the Roman Catholics of Appenzell assume adherence but are not formally united. In Sitten there is no church law, but the church is governed by canonical law. The canton of Ticino, according to the agreement of 1888, is nominally under the Bishop of Basel, but has its own administrator residing at Lugano and chosen by the pope, by agreement with the bishop of Basel. In consequence of a papal encyclical containing strictures on the conflict at Geneva, the papal nunciature was abolished, the federal diet declaring further papal representation inadmissible. The total number of Roman Catholic churches is given as 1,207, and of priests, 1,957. There are 32 monasteries; of Benedictines (with 165 monks), Augustinians (106), Carthusians (22), Franciscans (9), 25 Capuchin monasteries (6–12 each), and a number of hospices. Of nunner-

ies there are 45, besides numerous congregations of sisters devoted to charity and instruction. The institute of teaching sisters at Menzingen, canton Zug, has 700 teachers, who teach in 250 public schools, and care for 45 orphanages, poorhouses, and hospitals; and the congregation of the sisters of mercy in Ingenbohl, canton Schwyz, numbers 3,400 sisters, 1,350 of whom are active in Switzerland, and the rest in various Austrian institutions. There are organizations in behalf of the Roman Catholic interests, such as the Swiss student societies (600 members), the Roman Catholic associations (30,000), the Roman Catholic association for internal missions, to care for interests in Protestant cantons under the direction of the Swiss bishops, and the associated Roman Catholic men and labor unions (6,000).

After the dispute arising in the Basel diocese in consequence of the Vatican Council of 1870, Bern, Aargau, Soleure, Thurgau, and Basel rejected the doctrine of papal infallibility, and forbade their bishops to discipline priests for the non-acceptance of it. As the bishop refused to obey, he was removed, and the adherents formed the Association of Swiss Liberal Catholics. Christian Catholic churches were at once organized in the above cantons, and in the towns of Basel and Zurich. Bern and Geneva transferred the state church organization from the Roman Catholic Church to the new churches. They held their first national synod in 1875, chose a bishop, 1876, who, with all his followers, was promptly excommunicated by the pope. The synod consists of the bishop, the synodal council, all clergy in office, and delegates from the churches. It issues general regulations concerning worship and discipline, and chooses the synodal council and the bishop. The synodal council consists of five laymen and four priests, and is the administrative and executive board. At the beginning of 1905 there were 43 churches and associations and 56 priests. The most important reforms are the use of the national language in liturgy and ritual; and the abolition of enforced confession, the commandments of fasting, and the law of celibacy. The mass is regarded as the outgrowth of the celebration of the Last Supper; and the saints, it is held, can best be honored by emulating their example.

(F. MEYER.)

IV. The Free Churches of French Switzerland: Although in the same relation toward the state, these three bodies of Geneva, Vaud, and Neuchâtel are by origin, ruling principles, and historical development very different from one another. The community at Geneva is the oldest and most rigid in doctrine, organization, and discipline. Although the Free Church of Neuchâtel, which is the latest, has no bond with the government, it resembles a state church most closely, and still claims to be a national church. The Free Church of Vaud, on the other hand, holds an intermediary position between a state and a merely confessional church.

In doctrine, Vaud is the most liberal, the professors of its college of divinity being in constant touch with German theology; the Geneva community has always been very orthodox, so also that of Neuchâtel, though standing on a broader basis. The churches of Vaud and Neuchâtel each possess a general fund, a synod, and a college of divinity. The Geneva Free Church is organically quite separate from the Geneva Evangelical Society's college, although from the beginning it has been connected with it by deep spiritual bonds.

The two former owe their origin to political and religious events; the latter sprang from the réveil, that great Pietistic movement which spread throughout the whole country in the beginning of the nineteenth century. These three communities, independent of each other, were united in 1902 into a federation. In addition, the Transvaal mission, originating in Vaud and being known as Mission romande, has a budget amounting yearly to $29,250, and is supported by the three churches.

From the days of the Reformation Geneva has been a very important center of religious life for all lands of the French language. There-
1. Geneva. fore when Count Zinzendorf (q.v.) came in 1741, after the period of the barren orthodoxy of the seventeenth century, he found a favorable ground for his Bible lessons and prayer-meetings. In 1817 Robert Haldane (q.v.), Scottish Pietist, arrived at Geneva and attracted to his devotional Bible hours a group of about twenty students of divinity. Among them were H. Merle d'Aubigné, César Malan, and François Louis Gaussen (qq.v.). From the time of Zinzendorf, opposition to the Pietist movement grew until a sermon of Gaussen, emphasizing Christ's divinity, raised it to a climax. The church authorities forbade private assemblies. Guers immediately protested, refused submission, and in 1818 founded with a few friends a free congregation whose regular meetings were held at the Bourg de Four. Six years later, César Malan, having been suspended by the Compagnie des Pasteurs, founded L'Église du Témoignage, which soon became a center for Geneva Pietism, but at the same time an object for the fury of the mob, so that the government troops had frequently to protect it. Both congregations, the former Congregationalist, the latter Presbyterian, were united, 1848, under the name of Église évangélique. In 1831 the " Evangelical Society " (q.v.) was founded, which, without an organic bond with the Free Church, is, however, in intimate connection with it. Gaussen was dismissed from the Compagnie des Pasteurs and opened L'Oratoire, a hall where the principal divine services of the Free Church of Geneva are still held. The confession of faith of the Église évangélique de Genève is the so-called Apostolic Creed, and contains seventeen articles embodying the usual Evangelical orthodox doctrines. The difference in dignity between the clergymen and elders is nominal, the church being quite Presbyterian. Admission to membership is by confession of faith in the presence of two elders, and admission by confirmation is not tolerated. The church has a committee of evangelization working in different places in connection with the chapels, and several Sunday-schools numbering more than 600 scholars. From 1884 the whole body has divided into three parishes, each having its own pas-

tor. At present the congregation consists of about 700 members, has an annual budget of $5,265, and contributes $3,140 to the Mission romande.

The Free Church of Vaud, too, had its origin in the revival after the period of religious stagnation. The preparations were unknowingly
2. Vaud. laid by Dean L. A. Curtat, later a foe of the Free Church, who, by the power of his preaching and the stimulating intercourse with the students at Lausanne, revived the fundamental truths of the Gospel and the Reformation, bearing fruit in zeal for the Bible, Evangelization, and missionary associations. But the movement encountered the opposition of the government and the populace. The mission society, founded at Yverdon (1821), was suppressed, and several of the pastors were dismissed. Many young men being excluded from the state examination were obliged to gain their living abroad. In 1824 a law was promulgated against " the exalted people who are trying to found and propagate a new sect." The Pastor Bauty had to appear before the government because he had frightened his community by his preaching on the Holy Communion; another had to resign because he held a meeting of twenty people in a private house; and Alexander Vinet (q.v.) had to submit to prosecution for publishing two pamphlets on religious liberty. In 1839, by a new law, the government made itself supreme over the church, and abrogated the Helvetic Confession. Immediately eleven clergymen resigned and others soon followed. In Feb.-Nov., 1845, during a revolution, the situation grew more unbearable, the government forbidding private meetings, requiring total submission, taking no notice of a petition signed by 222 clergymen ending with these words: " We are ready to sacrifice everything to our state church but our conscience "; and ordering the reading of a proclamation (July 29) from the pulpit commending its injustice and intolerance to the people. Forty-one pastors refused to read this proclamation, and were suspended. Shortly after, 190 sent in their resignation. To escape the predicament, the government offered to those who had resigned, with the exception of twenty, the privilege of resuming their charges, but conditionally and without reservation. Forty returned; the others, like Charles Secretan and Vinet, were dismissed. A commission of seven clergymen and seven laymen asked Professors Vinet, Chappuis, Herzog, Pastor Bauty, and others to give lectures on divinity. A committee of evangelization was founded for the purpose of establishing new congregations throughout the canton, and the Free Church was born, the first synod being held June, 1847. The Free Church of Vaud comprises 42 churches and numbers not more than 5,000 members, but has over 15,000 auditors at its different services.

The Free Church of the canton of Neuchâtel had a history of quiet development. In spite of the separation, it maintains the character
3. Neu-   and the forms of a state church; such
châtel.   as confirmation, liturgy, and the vestments. In 1872 the grand council rejected a bill proposed by the government for the separation of State and Church, and then adopted

another which necessitated a complete revision of the fundamental law of the State Church. The synod, in extraordinary session, opposed the bill and almost unanimously replied to the superior council, apropos of a revision of the fundamental church law of 1848, by protesting against political competence to enact confessional statutes, and against their consolidation with so-called liberal Protestantism. It demanded the same autonomy as was given to other non-established churches, and, in the case of the revision of the organic church law, requested that such be undertaken only in consultation with the church boards and be submitted to popular vote. The government ignored the letter. The bill projected by it was in turn rejected by the synod, with only one negative vote, which declared it to be perilous to the State Church on the ground that the State exceeds its rights in prescribing the qualifications of electors and their rights in ecclesiastical matters; in claiming absolute freedom of doctrine for pastors and professors; in creating a synod which abrogated the colloquies and in pointing out *sua sponte* its attributes. Further, the identification of the ecclesiastical with the political voter, the interdiction upon the church of confessing its faith, the eligibility of any graduate citizen as a pastor without any guaranty as regards culture or morality, were pronounced measures detrimental to the State Church. To this was attached the proposition of the separation in autonomous congregations of the Evangelicals and liberal Protestants, all to share in the privileges and goods afforded by the state, or, best of all, the separation of church and state. Signed by 55 clergymen and supported by a petition of 10,300 signatures, this document was presented; nevertheless, the grand council, by a vote of 47 to 40, adopted the projected bill, further aggravated by the clause that the professors of theology should be chosen by the government and not by the synod. A second petition asking for the separation resulted in a submission to popular vote and by a majority of 16 out of 13,956 revision was lost. Nothing remained to be done but to organize a free church. Twenty-one congregations with twenty-four pastors founded the Église évangélique neuchâteloise indépendante de l'état. From that time, 1873, the Free Church of the canton of Neuchâtel has developed; the number of its members has increased from year to year; and the participation in the Evangelization of France, Belgium, Spain, and Italy and in the Mission romande is very energetic and self-denying.

C. Correvon.

Bibliography: Collections of titles are to be found in: Schaff, *Christian Church*, vol. vii.—the literature, general and special, on the Reformation is given with great fulness in this work; F. Lauchert, *Bibliographie der christlich-katholischen Kirche der Schweiz*, Bern, 1893; G. Finsler, *Bibliographie der evangelisch-reformirten Kirche in der Schweiz*, Bern, 1896. On the general history of Switzerland consult: C. Gareis and P. Zorn, *Staat und Kirche in der Schweiz*, 2 vols., Zurich, 1877–78; A. von Orelli, *Das Staatsrecht der schweizerischen Eidgenossenschaft*, Freiburg, 1885; K. Dändliker, *Geschichte der Schweiz . . . von den ältesten Zeiten*, 3 vols., Zurich, 1893–95, cf. his *Short History of Switzerland*, London, 1899; B. van Muyden, *Hist. de la nation suisse*, 3 vols., Lausanne, 1896–99; *Cambridge Modern History*, vols. i.–xii., New York, 1902–10. For history prior to the Reformation consult: E. F.

Gelpke, *Kirchengeschichte der Schweiz unter der Römer-, Burgunder- und Alemannzeit*, 2 vols., Bern, 1856–61; J. C. Moerikofer, *Bilder aus dem kirchlichen Leben der Schweiz*, Leipsic, 1864; A. Lütolf, *Die Glaubensboten in der Schweiz*, Lucerne, 1871; F. Naef, *Les Premiers Jours du christianisme en Suisse*, Lausanne, 1879; E. Egli, *Kirchengeschichte der Schweiz bis auf Karl den Grossen*, Zurich, 1893; E. Herzog, *Beiträge zur Vorgeschichte der christkatholischen Kirche der Schweiz*, Bern, 1896; J. A. Gautier, *Hist. de Genève des origines à l'année 1691*, 6 vols., Geneva, 1896–1901.

On the Reformation consult: The works of the Swiss Reformers, Bullinger, Calvin, Farel, Leo Jud, Œcolampadius, Vadianus, and Zwingli, and the literature under the articles on them in this work; Schaff, *Christian Church*, vol. vii.; S. Fischer, *Die Reformation in Bern*, Bern, 1827; J. Kuhn, *Die Reformation Berns*, Bern, 1828; A. Ruchat, *Hist. de la réformation de la Suisse*, 7 vols., 2d ed., Nyon, 1835–38; H. Bullinger, *Reformationsgeschichte nach dem Autographon*, ed. J. Hottinger and H. Vögeli, 3 vols., Frauenfeld, 1838–40; K. B. Hundeshagen, *Die Konflikte des Calvinismus, Zwinglianismus und Lutherthums in der Berner Landeskirche*, Bern, 1842; F. Godet, *Hist. de la réformation dans le pays de Neuchâtel*, Neuchâtel, 1859; W. M. Blackburn, *William Farel: Story of the Swiss Reformation*, Edinburgh, 1867; *Archiv für die schweizerische Reformations-Geschichte*, Freiburg, 1869 sqq.; E. Egli, *Die Zürcher Wiedertäufer zur Reformationszeit*, Zurich, 1878; K. R. Hagenbach, *Hist. of the Reformation in Germany and Switzerland*, Edinburgh, 1878–79; A. L. Herminjard, *Correspondance des reformateurs*, 9 vols., Geneva, 1878–97; *Actensammlung zur schweizerischen Reformationsgeschichte, 1521–32*, ed. J. Strickler, 5 vols., Zurich, 1878–84; *Actensammlung zur Geschichte der Zürcher Reformation 1519–33*, ed. E. Egli, Zurich, 1879; H. G. Sulzberger, *Geschichte der Reformation im Kanton Graubünden*, Coire, 1880; H. S. Burrage, *History of the Anabaptists in Switzerland*, Philadelphia, 1882; H. Escher, *Die Glaubensparteien in der Eidgenossenschaft*, Frauenfeld, 1882; R. Nitzsche, *Geschichte der Wiedertäufer in der Schweiz*, Einsiedeln, 1885; E. Baehler, *Le Comte de la Croix. Ein Beitrag zur Reformationsgeschichte der Westschweiz*, Biel, 1895; E. Choisy, *La Théocratie à Genève au temps de Calvin*, Geneva, 1896; E. Issel, *Die Reformation in Konstanz*, Freiburg, 1898; A. Bernus, *T. de Bèze à Lausanne, Étude*, Lausanne, 1900; *Quellen zur schweizerischen Reformationsgeschichte*, ed. E. Egli, Basel, 1901; H. Vuilleumier, *La Religion des pères*, Lausanne, 1888; idem, *L'Église du pays de Vaud aux temps de la réformation*, ib. 1902; *Cambridge Modern History*, ii. 305–341, New York, 1904; *Die Chronik des Laurencius Bosshart von Winterthur 1185–1532*, ed. K. Hauser, Basel, 1905.

On history since the Reformation use: G. Finsler, *Kirchliche Statistik der reformierten Schweiz*, Stuttgart, 1854 (valuable); J. Gaberel, *Hist. de l'église de Genève . . . jusqu'à nos jours*, 3 vols., Geneva, 1858–62; J. Cart, *Hist. du mouvement religieux et ecclésiastique dans le canton de Vaud pendant la première moitié du 19. siècle*, 6 vols., Lausanne, 1870–79; G. R. Zimmerman, *Die Zürcher Kirche und ihre Antistes*, Zurich, 1877; idem, *Die Zürcher Kirche 1519–1819*, ib. 1878; H. Fleury, *Hist. de l'église de Genève*, 3 vols., Geneva, 1879–81 (comes to 1820); G. Finsler, *Geschichte der theologisch-kirchlichen Entwickelung in der deutsch-reformirten Schweiz seit den 30 Jahren*, Zurich, 1881; J. Genoud, *Les Saints de la Suisse française*, 2 vols., Paris, 1882; E. Bloesch, *Geschichte der schweizerisch-reformirten Kirchen*, 2 vols., Bern, 1898–99; S. Grueter, *Der Anteil der katholischen und protestantischen Orte der Eidgenossenschaft an den Kämpen im Wallis, 1600–13*, Stans, 1900; W. Hadorn, *Geschichte des Pietismus in den schweizerisch-reformirten Kirchen*, Constance, 1901; F. Nippold, *Handbuch der neuesten Kirchengeschichte*, ii. 466 sqq., Berlin, 1901; W. Hadorn, *Kirchengeschichte der reformirten Schweiz*, Zurich, 1907; T. de La Rive, *La Séparation de l'église et de l'état à Genève*, Paris, 1909.

On the Free Churches consult: *Bulletin des séances du synode constituant de l'église évangélique neuchâteloise*, Neuchâtel, 1874; E. Guers, *Notice historique sur l'église évangélique libre de Genève*, Geneva, 1875; J. Cart, *Hist. du mouvement religieux dans le canton de Vaud*, vol. vi., Lausanne, 1880; L. Monastier, *Une voix de jadis sur l'origine et les premiers pas de l'église évangélique libre du canton de Vaud*, ib. 1885; *Constitution de l'église évan-*

gélique neuchâteloise indépendante de l'état, Neuchâtel, 1897; J. Favre, *Il y a cinquante ans*, Lausanne, 1897; E. Monvert, *Hist. de la fondation de l'église évangélique neuchâteloise*, Neuchâtel, 1898; R. Dupraz, *Fondation de l'église évangélique libre du canton de Vaud*, Lausanne, n. d.; the journals *Le Chrétien évangélique, 1847–97*, and *Le Messager;* and literature under VINET, ALEXANDER.

On the Roman Catholic Church consult: *Der Basler Religionsprozess vom Jahre 1884–85*, Bern, 1885; C. Woeste, *Hist. du culturkampf en Suisse, 1871–86*, Brussels, 1887; A. Büchi, *Die katholische Kirche in der Schweiz*, Munich, 1902; J. Beck, *Die katholisch-sociale Bewegung in der Schweiz*, Bern, 1903; P. G. Gschwind, *Geschichte der Entstehung der christkatholischen Kirche der Schweiz*, 2 vols., Basel, 1904–10.

SWORD, BRETHREN OF THE (*Fratres militiæ Christi*): An order founded by Bishop Albert of Appeldern in Livonia in 1202 and patterned after the Templars (q.v.). The name is derived from the fact that the members of the order wore upon their white mantle as an insignium a red sword alongside of a red cross. The purpose of the bishop was the securing of the Christian colony in Livonia and the extension of its bounds. The founding of the order was ratified by Innocent III. in 1202, and the rule prescribed was that of the Templars. There were three classes of members: knights, of noble birth and obligated to soldierly duties; spirituals, whose duty was the conduct of divine service; and serving brethren, who performed the lower duties pertaining to service in war, had household duties, and aided by using their skill as handicraftsmen. The numbers, at first small, rapidly increased under the political conditions of the time and place, and early claimed one-third of the region, the subjection of which was the object of the foundation. Campaigns were carried on in the surrounding regions, in Lithuania, Russia, and Denmark, and the result, by 1230, was to decimate the numbers of the order, while the number of accessions continually lessened. Proposals were then made for union with the Teutonic Order, and in 1237 this union was accomplished, and the fortunes of the Brethren of the Sword were thenceforth those of the Teutonic Order.

BIBLIOGRAPHY: J. Voigt, *Geschichte Preussens*, vols. i.–ii., Königsberg, 1827; K. von Schlözer, *Livland und die Anfänge deutschen Lebens im baltischen Nord*, Berlin, 1850; F. G. von Bunge, *Der Orden der Schwertbrüder*, Leipsic, 1875; idem, *Geschichte der Ostzeeprovinzen*, vol. i., Mitau, 1879; H. Hildebrand, *Livonica*, Riga, 1887; Dragendorff, *Ueber die Beamten des Deutschen Ordens in Livland während des 13. Jahrhunderts*, Berlin, 1894; Pfülf, in *Stimmen aus Maria-Laach*, lii (1897), 58 sqq.; *KL*, x. 2115–2118.

SYLLABUS OF ERRORS, PAPAL: An index or catalogue of eighty heresies condemned by Pope Pius IX., Dec. 8, 1864, on the basis of several encyclical letters and consistorial allocutions issued previously by the same pontiff. The number of heresies was probably suggested by the work of Epiphanius against the eighty heresies of the first three centuries, which were mostly of a Gnostic character. The papal document is purely negative, but indirectly it teaches and enjoins the very opposite of what it condemns as error. It is divided into ten sections. The first condemns pantheism, naturalism, and absolute rationalism; the second, moderate rationalism; the third, indifferentism and latitudinarianism; the fourth, socialism, communism, secret societies, Bible societies, and other

" pests of this description "; the fifth, errors concerning the Church and her rights; the sixth, errors concerning civil society; the seventh, errors of natural and Christian ethics; the eighth, errors concerning Christian marriage; the ninth, errors concerning the temporal power of the pope; the tenth, errors of modern liberalism. Among the errors condemned are the principles of civil and religious liberty, and the separation of Church and State. The Syllabus impliedly asserts the infallibility of the pope, the exclusive right of Romanism to recognition by the civil government, the unlawfulness of all religions other than the Roman Catholic, the complete independence of the papal hierarchy, the power of the Roman Church to coerce and enforce, and its supreme control over public education, science, and literature. It reasserts all the extravagant claims of the medieval papacy, and is a declaration of war against modern civilization and progress.

What authority attaches to this document? Cardinal Newman, in his defense of the Syllabus against Gladstone's attack, virtually denied its dogmatic force, saying (*Letter to the Duke of Norfolk*, p. 108), " We can no more accept the Syllabus as *de fide*, as a dogmatic document, than any other index or table of contents." But the Syllabus is more than a mere index, and contains as many definitions and judgments as titles. Moreover, the papal infallibility decree of 1870 makes all *ex cathedra* or official utterances of the pope on matters of faith and discipline infallible. The Syllabus is an official document, addressed to all the bishops of the Roman Catholic world, and sent to them with a papal encyclical. Its infallibility was at once asserted by Cardinal Hergenröther (cf. J. J. I. von Döllinger, *Das Papstthum*, ed. J. Friedrich, p. 281, Munich, 1892). The quotations made from it by Leo XIII. and in 1907 by Pius X. in his encyclical *Pascendi gregis* seem to confirm its infallible authority. Pius X. quotes it extensively at least twice (cf. *The Programme of Modernism*, pp. 195, 222, New York, 1908). At the opening of the Vatican Council (q.v.) a part of the program was solemnly to ratify the Syllabus (T. Granderath, *Geschichte des vatikanischen Konzils*, i. 357, Freiburg, 1903; J. Friedrich, *Geschichte des vatikanischen Konzils*, i. 749, Bonn, 1877), but this was not formally carried out. Clothed with infallible authority, and followed by the decrees of the Vatican Council, the Syllabus provoked and stimulated the so-called Kulturkampf in Germany, a pamphlet war in England about its bearing on civil and political allegiance, and led to serious conflicts between Church and State in Italy, Austria, Prussia, France, Belgium, and Brazil. Where Church and State are united, there must be collision when each claims sovereignty, and the one claims infallible authority in addition. Even in the United States, the Syllabus comes into crisp conflict with the functions of government as recognized by the statutes of the land. The State claims and exercises the right and duty of educating the people for intelligent and useful citizenship; while the Syllabus condemns all public education which is not controlled by the teaching of the Roman Church, and stimulates the

efforts of the priesthood to Romanize or to break up the public schools, or, where neither can be done from want of power, to neutralize them by parochial schools in which the doctrines and principles of Trent and the Vatican are inculcated upon the rising generation. The encyclical *Pascendi gregis* (ut sup.) sounds almost like a continuation of the Syllabus, being a condemnation of "Modernism" (q.v.). The text of the encyclical is given in *The Programme of Modernism* (ut sup.).
P. SCHAFF†.   D. S. SCHAFF.

BIBLIOGRAPHY: The text is most convenient of access in Schaff, *Creeds*, ii. 213–233; it is also in *Acta et decreta concilii Vaticani*, Freiburg, 1871, and in W. E. Gladstone, *Rome and the Newest Fashions in Religion*, London and New York, 1875 (containing three tracts of Gladstone on the subject, the text of the Syllabus, and a history of the Vatican Council). On the subject consult besides the literature named in the text: Pronier, *La Liberté religieuse et le Syllabus*, Geneva, 1870; Cardinal H. E. Manning, *The Vatican Decrees in their Bearing on Civil Allegiance*, ib. 1875 (reply to Gladstone, ut sup.); Cardinal J. H. Newman, *Letter to the Duke of Norfolk on Occasion of Mr. Gladstone's Recent Expostulation*, ib. 1875; and much of the literature under INFALLIBILITY; ULTRAMONTANISM; and VATICAN COUNCIL.

SYLVESTER.   See SILVESTER.

SYLVESTRINS: A Roman Catholic congregation under Observantine Benedictine rule, established by Silvestro Gonzelini (b. at Osimo, 9 m. s. of Ancona, 1170 or 1174; d. at his monastery on Monte Fano near Fabriano, 45 m. s.w. of Ancona, Nov. 26, 1267). After studying at Padua and Bologna and being canon in his native city, he retired, about 1227, to the Grotta fucile near Osimo. Here his piety attracted so many pupils and followers, that about 1231 he established a monastery for them on Monte Fano. The congregation was approved by Innocent IV. (June 27, 1247), and spread especially in Umbria, Tuscany, and Ancona. In 1662–67 the Sylvestrins were united with the order of Vallombrosa, and in 1688 their rule was revised, approval being given by Alexander VIII. in 1690. The congregation was directed by a general, elected by the chapter general quadrennially, and represented at Rome by a procurator-general, whom he appointed triennially. The habit is dark blue, and that of the general, who may wear episcopal vestments, is violet. The order is now very small in numbers, although it has monasteries in Rome and other parts of Italy, and an active mission in Ceylon.   (A. HAUCK.)

BIBLIOGRAPHY: S. Fabrini, *Breve Chronica della Congregazione dei Monachi Silvestrini*, Camerino, 1618, new ed., ed. A. Morosi and A. Lucantovi, Rome, 1706; the "Constitution" was printed at Camerino, 1610, and Rome, 1690; Helyot, *Ordres monastiques*, vi. 170 sqq.; Heimbucher, *Orden und Kongregationen*, i. 277–279; *KL*, xi. 1039–41.

SYMBOLICS.

I. Creeds and Confessions: The term symbol is used in a twofold sense; for the pictorial representation of religious ideas (see MYS-
1. Original TAGOGICAL THEOLOGY; SYMBOLISM,
Idea of ECCLESIASTICAL), and for the au-
Symbol. thoritative ecclesiastical formulations of religious doctrines. This article is to be restricted to the latter class of symbols, otherwise styled the church creeds or confessions. From them the theological discipline styled "symbolics" and mostly pursued in Protestantism has derived its name. The custom of designating as symbols the formulas by which Christian faith has expressed itself in history took its origin in referring to that formula as a symbol by which, in the ancient Church, the candidates for baptism were wont to confess their faith. It began with "I believe," being therefore decidedly individual and personal. Of its many names one was simply that of "the faith." In the East "the lesson" (*to mathēma*) was sometimes employed, but seldom "the confession of faith." The designation of the baptismal confession as "symbol" originated in the West; in the East it appeared relatively late. The term is first found in Tertullian (*Adv. Marcionem*, v. 1). The Latin Church borrowed the term from the secular Greek. Derived from *symballein* ("to compare"), *symbolon* may be applied to whatever signifies a means of recognition or identification, a sign, a watchword, a comparison or agreement. The equivalents in Latin are *signum, nota, indicium, tessera, pactum;* some of the older Latin theologians, such as Rufinus, rendered it by *collatio*, confusing the Greek *symbolē* and *symbolon*. The latter attached his interpretation to the legend that the primitive creed was composed jointly by the Apostles, each contributing one sentence. Cyprian (*Epist.*, lxix [lxxv.] 7; Eng. transl., *ANF*, v. 399) is a sure witness of the application of "symbol" to the baptismal confession. In what sense it was applied is open to explanation; it was probably used as a general token of recognition, although different views are held on this point, according to the diverse theories of the origin of the creed itself. The view of the present writer is that all the formulas found in the primitive Church go back to the creed known as the old Roman (designated as R in this article); that this creed was composed in Rome at one time, as the expression of the summary of faith at the period of its date, probably about 100, but rather earlier than later; and that it was composed for liturgical and catechetical purposes, but not as the outcome of polemical antagonism to heresy, as is the view advocated by A. C. McGiffert (*The Apostles' Creed*, New York, 1902). The latter considers R the fundamental formula, indeed, but one composed by the Roman Church during the struggle with Marcion. Loofs doubts the hypothesis of a single "mother-formula," and traces the custom of making the catechumens recite a creed (which was substantially the same everywhere, though not identical in phraseology) to Asia Minor, if not to the primitive churches of Palestine and Syria.
It may at least, however, be taken as proved

that the creed originally had its proper place in the solemn administration of baptism. There were different local developments of the customs of the *traditio symboli* to the catechumens shortly before baptism; a *redditio* of the same, after catechetical exposition of the several articles, as a proof of their readiness for the sacrament; and an assent to the same in the midst of the act of baptism itself; but wherever the baptismal symbol was employed, it had, notwithstanding its personal form, a liturgical character. With this is connected the signification of the formula as a *sacramentum*, no doubt partly as the oath militant of the Christians, and partly as a sacred emblem signifying by its *traditio* the setting apart, once for all, of the believer as a Christian. From the very early time of the first conflict with a contrary belief (loosely Gnosticism, perhaps in its Marcionite form), the creed came to be used in the West as the "rule of faith." That from the middle of the second century the West considered the creed as a weapon against hostile attacks, as the standard given by God himself, is demonstrable. Not so certain but probable is the theory that the East adopted it before the end of that century in Asia Minor (perhaps in connection with Polycarp's journey to Rome); but that here originally the Scriptures had occupied the position of a rule of faith. This was their position in the rest of the East, which only gradually, in some places not till the fourth century, adopted a formulated creed. Especially with Origen it appears as though there was no creed and none was desired, but it was deemed better to meet various controversial needs by expedient formulas drawn up for each occasion. This method issued in the practise of councils of preparing consistent formulas, somewhat suggestive of the symbol. In the third century and numerously in the fourth, dogmatic resolutions resembling a (or the) symbol, and in part distinctly under the subsumption of such a one, were adopted at the councils. Such definitions were never designated as "symbols," unless, as in some instances, they were applied to baptismal use. In time, especially after the legislation of Justinian, the formula attributed to the joint action of the first two ecumenical councils, the so-called Niceno-Constantinopolitan creed (C; see Constantinopolitan Creed) came to hold the rank of a "symbol." It, then, in the East, though still in ultimate association with the Scriptures and with the "exposition of the faith" made by the whole seven ecumenical councils, came to be the rule of faith, as it is to this day in the Greek Orthodox Church. (The term ecumenical, strictly speaking, applies to C only, since neither the Apostolic nor the Athanasian creed ever obtained official recognition in the East.) Even if C thus presents the highest criterion for distinguishing between orthodox and heretical doctrine, it owes its special importance to the fact that it retained its position in the public services of baptism and the Eucharist.

In the West also the idea of a "symbol" carried with it, until the Reformation, a reference to the liturgical use of a formula. The title passed from R, or the provincial "daughter-recensions" of R,

2. The Rule of Faith.

finally again to a single formula, the present text of the Apostles' Creed (q.v.) as received to-day by Roman Catholics and Protestants alike (T). It was then extended to C, which in the West also, though only gradually and within limits, became the Eucharistic creed; and to the "Athanasian" Creed (q.v., and see revised translation below; called *symbolum Quicunque* from its opening word; hence Q). The Middle Ages speak of these as "the three symbols"—the phrase is first demonstrably found in Alexander of Hales, *Summa*, III., qu. 82, m. 5, introduction. T and C were compared usually as *minus* and *major*. Ludolf of Saxony (cf. Loofs, *Symbolik*, p. 58), in the fourteenth century, defining symbol as "a compendious collection of all things which concern salvation," says that "the first symbol was made for instruction in the faith, the second for explanation of the faith, and the third for defense of the faith." Occasionally the formula of the Lateran Council of 1215, the "Definition against the Albigenses and other heretics," is called the "fourth symbol"; this professes to offer a compendium of "the whole" faith, in formal adherence to T, but makes use of C and still more of Q, besides sanctioning the new developments of the Eucharistic doctrine. It may have been the obvious following of the structure of T that allowed the name of symbol to be applied to it, though it came to no liturgical use. In the same indefinite way, the name is applied to the *Symbolum fidei a Leone IX proposium Petro episcopo*, though this formula has a certain public use, being put in the form of questions for the examination of candidates for episcopal consecration. Similarly mention is made of the *symbolum Tridentinum* by which is meant "the profession of Tridentine faith prescribed by Pius IV." in 1564, and slightly enlarged by Pius IX. in 1877; it was recited by candidates for reception into the church until 1859, and is orally confessed and subscribed by those who are entering the teaching office, especially by priests (see Tridentine Profession of Faith).

It must now be remarked that theological development in the West, unlike that of the East, differentiated increasingly the conception of the rule of faith from that of the symbol. After uncertainty had arisen in the fourth century as to the sufficiency of the symbol for the purpose of a rule of faith, and the Scriptures had begun, under the influence of the East, to be considered as part of it, Augustine not only took account of the new development, but also set bounds to it. He brought the symbol into such intimate connection with the Scriptures that he could speak of it as really representing in condensed form the whole of their teaching. Thus the Middle Ages held firmly to the thesis that the *symbolum triplex* was one and the same sum of faith in a threefold form, with varying degrees of explicitness. But while in the East the content of the Scriptures was more and more reduced to an equivalence with that of C, Augustine had shown how to get a deeper meaning from them for the words of the creed and to fill the latter with new import. Other influential

3. Western Development.

4. Change of Attitude in the West.

theologians, however, especially Vincent of Lerins (q.v.), spoke of the symbol rather as a single portion of tradition, agreeing with the Scriptures but not sufficient as a guide through them; and their view prevailed in time over Augustine's. But though the Scriptures gradually won the superior rank as the rule of faith, yet it was in conjunction with the untested ecclesiastical tradition and the operation of the episcopal or papal teaching office; so that practically the rule of faith came to be the *propositio ecclesiæ*, that which is put forth by the Church, in which the creeds have their place. In modern Roman Catholic usage the Protestant term, " symbolic books," has been adopted (*KL*, xi. 1050 sqq.). A distinction is made between symbolic writings of the first and of the second class; the former including the creeds proper, the definitions of the ecumenical councils, and *ex cathedra* papal decisions in matters of faith, while the latter are such documents as the Tridentine Profession and the Roman Catechism.

In the Reformation period the term " symbol " departed wholly from its original liturgical basis, and acquired an almost exclusively theological meaning, in spite of the fact that T and, to a certain extent, C were still employed in cultic functions. The personal character of the primitive creeds also disappeared; the formulas became professions of groups or churches. Thus a distinction begins to be made between " ecumenical " creeds and those of the Protestant communions, especially of the Lutherans. With the Reformed bodies the name " symbol " did not become customary; the term " confessions " was preferred, being better adapted to denote the formulas as the expressions of faith and the determination of doctrine on the part of the churches. The part performed by each, however, was practically the same. In the Formula of Concord (q.v.) the term symbol is first applied to the Augustana (see AUGSBURG CONFESSION AND APOLOGY) on the same plane with the ecumenical creeds, to which was added the " Apology and Articles of Schmalkald " (see SCHMALKALD ARTICLES). Neither in itself nor in the Book of Concord was the Formula included as a symbol. The history of the internal effect of the symbols upon the development of Protestantism has not yet been written. Indeed, they performed a much smaller part in orthodox dogmatism than might have been expected. The doctrine of the Bible as the only rule of faith reduced the authority of all creeds. This supremacy of Scripture was due to its own inner authority and not to that of the Church, as before. The symbols subordinated to Scripture were obligatory only in so far as they accorded with it. They were regarded not as having dogmatic value, but as polemical and political or juridical. There remained also the consciousness that they were confessions, in the sense of witnesses to Biblical truth. In the Syncretistic Controversies (see SYNCRETISM, SYNCRETISTIC CONTROVERSIES) the orthodox Lutherans were disposed to emphasize the insufficiency of all extant symbols as compared with the completeness of the entire faith; this was especially the case with regard to the ecumenical

5. Post-Reformation Creeds.

creeds, which Georg Calixtus (q.v.) and his school wished to use as a basis of union between the conflicting churches. Attempts were even made from this standpoint to formulate a new creed among the orthodox Lutherans; but the point was never actually reached. Among the Reformed, on the other hand, the production of new formulas was incessant, nor has the tendency to revision or new creation yet ceased.

The authority of the creeds, strongly enforced in the period of Pietism, declined notably under the influence of rationalism. In the history of Protestantism they belong essentially to established or territorial organizations, except in certain Reformed confessions in North America and free churches elsewhere; but the relation between Church and State was really as close in the Reformed system as in the Lutheran, only somewhat differently defined, while the " free " churches, the first type of which is the English Independent, are essentially modern. In the old political systems, which contemplated only one Church (a conception not yet entirely done away; see LIBERTY, RELIGIOUS; and UNION OF THE CHURCHES), the creeds were among the foundations of the constitution; and citizens, especially officials and most of all clericals, were strictly bound by them, at least so far as their public teaching was concerned. In what measure they should be binding upon the conscience was difficult to determine in Protestant states and churches. The nineteenth century has for the most part brought forth an unhistorical abstract idealizing of the symbols in Protestantism. A result of the methods of Schleiermacher is a confessional theology which regards itself bound in advance by the symbols, as over against the Bible. To this the *a priori* justification of symbols, of that view of the history of dogma resting upon Hegel, is to be added. The obligation of teaching with reference to them has long since been restricted to theologians, and frequently to pastors alone. The idea of this obligation, by virtue of the development assumed by theology as the science of Christianity, is everywhere in a state of uncertainty.

II. Comparative Symbolics: The symbolics of modern times is partly a substitute for, and partly an amplification of, older disciplines. The latter reverts for its origin to a department of knowledge first introduced in the seventeenth century by the Lutherans, representing it by lectures in various universities and in literature, having as its object the introduction of the symbolic books. The creator in this form was probably Leonhard Rechtenbach, author of *Encyclopædia symbolica vel analysis Confessionis Augustanæ* (Leipsic, 1612). This was followed by the *Isagoge in libros ecclesiarum Lutheranarum symbolicos* (1665) by J. B. Carpzov the elder (see CARPZOV, 2), who first used the title " symbolic books "; and an abundant literature succeeded. On the other hand, comparative symbolics takes the place of polemics. How superior in intellectual power the Roman Catholicism of the seventeenth century was is shown by the form in which the controversies were waged. It furnished the tone and presented the themes.

1. Nature, Scope, and History.

Doctrine was opposed with doctrine absolutely, without historical appreciation on either side. The attempts at union proved also futile. The irenics of the time did not possess a correcter understanding of the confessions than the orthodox polemics. The literary expansion of polemics is best illustrated by J. G. Walch's *Bibliotheca theologica*, chap. v. (19 parts, Jena, 1757–65) covering the whole history of the subject, and only in part of interest to symbolics. Pietism awakened also the life of Christians and churches alongside of doctrines, and augmented the attention to sects. The semi-orthodoxy of the first half of the eighteenth century approached matters of church and confession from the standpoint of independent understanding. The *Historische und theologische Einleitung in die Religionsstreitigkeiten* (1, *ausserhalb der lutherischen Kirche*, 3d ed., 5 vols., 1733–36; and 2, *in der lutherischen Kirche*, 5 vols., 1730–39) is a type of the learned treatment of the inner divisions of the Church, though yet from a polemical standpoint. The *Geschichte der Religionspartheyen* (Halle, 1766) by S. J. Baumgarten, representing not churches and sects, but religions, shows a broadening of the point of view. With the reappearance of an ecclesiastical interest, rationalism first produced the formation of comparative symbolics. The originator was G. J. Plank with his *Abriss einer historischen und vergleichenden Darstellung der dogmatischen Systeme unserer verschiedenen christlichen Hauptpartheyen* (1796). The term symbolics came to be applied to such comparative study by Philip Marheineke, and "comparative symbolics" has fixed itself in usage as a result of G. B. Winer's *Comparative Darstellung* (Leipsic, 1824; 4th ed. improved by P. Ewald, 1882). The new step of Plank was not the limitation of the material which he reattempted, nor merely comparison, but the sublimation of fundamental principles and their comparison. Marheineke further emphasized the peace of history and the impartial objective treatment of the spirit and the essentials in each confession. The most valuable works along this line of thought are the Protestant *Lehrbuch der Symbolik* of G. F. Oehler, issued by J. Delitzsch (Tübingen, 1876; 2d ed., T. Hermann, Stuttgart, 1891), and *Handbuch der Symbolik* by Hermann Schmidt (Berlin, 1890); and the Roman Catholic *Symbolik* (Mainz, 1834) of J. A. Möhler.

Progressive historical investigation must reveal that the symbols can not serve as adequate sources for the comparison of the confessional

2. Konfes- churches. Symbolics can form only
sionskunde. a department of the *Konfessionskunde*
(the summary of all material knowledge pertaining to the confessional churches). By lectures and literary productions it may occupy its independent position, and thus fulfil its former function of introduction to the symbols, and treat a constantly considerable part of the sources for the *Konfessionskunde*. It is undisputed that the symbols are specially adapted to afford an understanding of the Reformation and set forth sharply what should be the inner norm of an Evangelical church; but to determine at the present time what the churches are is another important problem.

It is commonly understood that the living churches can not be adequately judged historically, either merely by their "authoritative statements" or by the documents according to which they were originally distinguished. Hence it is incumbent upon *Konfessionskunde* to bring into view not only doctrines but also the cultus, constitution, morals, spirituality, and the like, of the churches. The writer of this article has therefore sought to satisfy this altered consideration by substituting the title "Comparative knowledge of confessions" (*Vergleichende Konfessionskunde*; see bibliography).

(F. Kattenbusch.)

The Guardian, London, Nov. 10, 1909, gives the following revised translation of the Athanasian Creed (q.v.), made at the request of the archbishop of Canterbury, pursuant to the twenty-ninth resolution of the Lambeth Conference of 1908, by a committee of seven, viz.: Bishop Christopher Wordsworth of Salisbury; Dean Alexander Francis Kirkpatrick of Ely; Vice-chancellor Arthur James Mason of Cambridge; Warden Walter Lock of Keble College, Oxford; Regius Professor of Divinity Henry Barclay Swete, Cambridge; Regius Professor of Ecclesiastical History Edward William Watson, Oxford; and Cuthbert Hamilton Turner, Magdalen College, Oxford.

1. Whosoever would be saved (1): before all things it is needful that he hold fast the Catholic Faith.

2. Which Faith except a man have kept whole and undefiled (2): without doubt he will perish eternally.

3. Now the Catholic Faith is this: that we worship the one God as a Trinity, and the Trinity as an Unity.

4. Neither confusing the Persons: nor dividing the Substance.

5. For there is a Person of the Father, another of the Son: another of the Holy Ghost;

6. But the Godhead of the Father, the Son, and of the Holy Ghost is one: their glory equal, their majesty coeternal.

7. Such as the Father is, such is the Son: and such is the Holy Ghost;

8. The Father uncreated, the Son uncreated: the Holy Ghost uncreated;

9. The Father infinite, the Son infinite: the Holy Ghost infinite;

10. The Father eternal, the Son eternal: the Holy Ghost eternal;

11. And yet they are not three eternals: but one eternal;

12. As also they are not three uncreated, nor three infinites: but one infinite, and one uncreated.

13. So likewise the Father is almighty, the Son almighty: the Holy Ghost almighty;

14. And yet they are not three almighties: but one almighty.

15. So the Father is God, the Son God, the Holy Ghost God;

16. And yet they are not three Gods, but one God.

17. So the Father is Lord, the Son Lord: the Holy Ghost Lord;

18. And yet they are not three Lords: but one Lord.

19. For like as we are compelled by the Christian verity (3): to confess each of the Persons by himself (4) to be both God and Lord;

20. So are we forbidden by the Catholic religion: to speak of three Gods or three Lords.

21. The Father is of none: not made, nor created, nor begotten.

22. The Son is of the Father alone: not made, nor created, but begotten.

23. The Holy Ghost is of the Father and the Son: not made, nor created, nor begotten, but proceeding.

24. There is therefore one Father, not three Fathers; one Son, not three Sons: one Holy Ghost, not three Holy Ghosts.

25. And in this Trinity none is before or after: none is greater or less;

26. But all three Persons are co-eternal one with another: and co-equal.

27. So that in all ways, as is aforesaid: both the Trinity is to be worshiped as an Unity, and the Unity as a Trinity.

28. Let him therefore that would be saved (5): think thus of the Trinity (6).

29. FURTHERMORE it is necessary to eternal salvation: that he also believe faithfully the Incarnation of our Lord Jesus Christ.

30. The right Faith therefore is that we believe and confess: that our Lord Jesus Christ, the Son of God, is at once both God, and Man;

31. He is God of the Substance of the Father, begotten before the worlds (7): and He is Man, of the Substance of his Mother, born in the world (8);

32. Perfect God: perfect Man, of reasoning (9) soul and human flesh consisting;

33. Equal to the Father as touching his Godhead: less than the Father as touching his Manhood.

34. Who, although he be God and Man: yet is one Christ;

35. One, however, not by change of Godhead into flesh: but by taking of manhood into God;

36. One altogether: not by confusion (10) of substance, but by unity of person.

37. For as reasoning (11) soul and flesh is one man: so God and man is one Christ;

38. Who suffered for our salvation: descended to the world below (12), rose again from the dead;

39. Ascended into heaven, sat down at the right hand of the Father: to come from thence to judge the quick and the dead.

40. At whose coming all men shall rise again (13) with their bodies; and shall give account for their own deeds.

41. And they that have done good will go into life eternal: they that have done evil into eternal fire.

42. THIS is the Catholic Faith: which except a man have faithfully and steadfastly believed, he cannot be saved.

The figures in parenthesis above refer to the following alternative renderings:

(1) Or desireth to be saved.
(2) Or uncorrupted.
(3) Or by Christian truth.
(4) Or severally.
(5) Or desire to be saved.
(6) Or concerning the Trinity.
(7) Or before all time.
(8) Or in time.
(9) Or rational.
(10) Or One: not by any confusion.
(11) Or rational.
(12) Or into Hades.
(13) Or must rise again.

BIBLIOGRAPHY: Sources, besides those named in the text, are: Schaff, Creeds; C. A. Heurtley, Harmonia symbolica: a Collection of Creeds belonging to the ancient Western Church and to the Mediæval English Church, Oxford, 1858; F. W. Bodemann, Sammlung der wichtigsten Bekenntnisschriften der evangelisch-reformirten Kirche, 2d ed., Göttingen, 1867; C. P. Caspari, Ungedruckte, unbeachtete und wenig beachtete Quellen zur Geschichte des Taufsymbols und der Glaubensregeln, 2 vols., Christiania, 1869–75; Die symbolischen Bücher der evangelisch-lutherischen Kirche, ed. J. T. Müller, 6 parts, Stuttgart, 1847–48, 4th ed., 1876; H. E. Jacobs, The Book of Concord, 2 vols., Philadelphia, 1893; Bibliothek der Symbole und Glaubensregeln der alten Kirche, ed. A. Hahn, 3d ed. by G. L. Hahn, Breslau, 1897 (for the early creeds); H. Denzinger, Enchiridion symbolorum, 9th ed. by J. Stahl, Würzburg, 1900 (for the Latin Church); T. H. Bindley, The Œcumenical Documents of the Faith, London, 1901; W. Townsend, Great Symbols, London, 1901; Die Bekenntnissschriften der reformirten Kirchen, ed. E. F. K. Müller, Leipsic, 1903; Thēsauros tēs orthodoxias, ed. J. Michalcescu, Leipsic, 1904 (for the Greek Church).

On the history or theory of symbolics consult: J. G. Plank, Geschichte der Entstehung, der Veränderungen und der Bildung unseres protestantischen Lehrbegriffs, 6 vols., Leipsic, 1781–1800; P. Marheineke, Christliche Symbolik, 3 vols., Heidelberg, 1810–13; P. Hall, The Harmony of Protestant Confessions, London, 1841; A. Schweizer, Die protestantischen Centraldogmen in ihrer Entwickelung innerhalb der reformirten Kirche, 2 vols., Zurich, 1854–56; W. Gass, Symbolik der griechischen Kirche, Berlin, 1872; C. G. A. von Scheurl, Sammlung kirchenrechtlicher Abhandlungen, i. 149 sqq., Erlangen, 1872; G. B. Winer, Comparative View of the Doctrines and Confessions of the Various Communities of Christendom, Edinburgh, 1873; K. G. G. von Scheele, Theologische Symbolik, 3 vols., Gotha, 1881–82; J. A. Möhler, Symbolik, 10th ed., Mainz, 1889, Eng. transl., new issue, New York, 1894; H. E. Jacobs, A Study in Comparative Symbolics. The Lutheran Movement in England during the Reign of Richard VIII. and Edward IV., and its literary Monuments, Philadelphia, 1890; G. F. Oehler, Lehrbuch der Symbolik, 2d ed., by T. Hermann, Stuttgart, 1891; F. Kattenbusch, Lehrbuch der vergleichende Konfessionskunde, vol. i., Freiburg, 1892; P. S. Liebmann, Kleines Handwörterbuch der christlichen Symbolik, Leipsic, 1893; Zeitschrift für Theologie und Kirche, iii (1893), 140 sqq. (by K. Sell), 332 sqq. (by F. Nitzsch), 427 sqq. (by J. Kaftan), x (1900), 405 sqq. (by H. Schultz); G. A. Gumlich, Christian Creeds and Confessions, New York, 1894; E. F. K. Müller, Symbolik, Erlangen, 1896; K. F. Nösgen, Symbolik oder confessionelle Principienlehre, Gütersloh, 1897; P. Tschackert, Die unveränderte augsburgische Konfession, Leipsic, 1901; idem, Die Entstehung der lutherischen und der reformierten Kirchenlehre, Göttingen, 1910; F. Loofs, Symbolik oder christliche Konfessionskunde, vol. i., Tübingen, 1902; A. G. Mortimer, The Creeds: Exposition of the Apostles', Nicene and Athanasian Creeds, London, 1902; C. W. Leadbeater, The Christian Creed, its Origin and Significance, New York, 1904; J. A. Moehler, Symbolism or Doctrinal Differences, transl. from 5th Germ. ed., by J. B. Robertson, London, 1906; C. H. Turner, Hist. and Use of Creeds . . . in Early Centuries of the Church, London, 1906; J. Cooper, Confessions of Faith and Formulas of Subscription in the Reformed Churches of Great Britain and Ireland, Especially in the Church of Scotland, Glasgow, 1907; E. C. S. Gibson, The Three Creeds, New York, 1908; A. E. Burn, The Nicene Creed, London, 1909; N. Bonwetsch, Griechisch-orthodoxisches Christentum und Kirche in der Neuzeit, A. Ehrhard, Katholisches Christentum und Kirche in der Neuzeit, and E. Tröltsch, Protestantisches Christentum und Kirche in der Neuzeit, all in Kultur der Gegenwart, 2d ed., Leipsic, 1909; DCB, iv. 523. Much relevant material will be found under DOCTRINE, HISTORY OF, and under the articles on the three principal creeds.

SYMBOLISM, ECCLESIASTICAL.

I. Symbolism in General: By ecclesiastical symbolism is meant the system of interpretation by which all objects used in connection with divine worship are made to bear a twofold interpretation—to the obvious natural meaning being added another based on some analogy with supernatural things. The Greek word symbolē from which the word "symbolism" comes originally meant tallies, the two halves of a coin or other like object which any two contracting parties broke between them; hence the derived sense of a token or ticket, and

1. Definition. consequently a distinctive mark or formula, in which sense the creeds of religious bodies are known as symbols (see SYMBOLICS). Symbolism is, within obvious limits, the science of the relations which unite God and his creation, the natural and the supernatural worlds; the science of the harmonies which exist between the different parts of the universe, constituting a marvelous whole, each part of which presupposes the other and throws light on the other. The belief of Plato that this world was nothing but the image of a divine exemplar recalls the words of Ecclesiasticus: " Look upon all the works of the most High; and there are two and two, one against another " (xxxiii. 15), or again, " All things are double, one against another; and he hath made nothing imperfect " (xlii. 24). In the words of Hugo of St. Victor (q.v.), one of the greatest of medieval symbolists, " a symbol is the comparison of the visible forms for the showing forth of the invisible " (*In hierarchiam cælestem*, II., i. 941).

The history of symbolism in a broad sense is coextensive with that of humanity; the creation of man in God's image and likeness out of the clay of the earth, and of woman from a rib of man, are

2. Symbolism Rooted in Human Nature. given their symbolic meaning. Cain's sacrifice of animal life by the side of Abel's offering of the fruits of the earth contained a symbolic reference to their respective callings. The worship of all races, as well as the idols of many pagan religions, remained symbolic until the grossest materialism prevailed; and in the family and social life of primitive peoples there was scarcely any important act but had its tinge of symbolism. " The truth is," says W. R. Inge (*Christian Mysticism*, p. 259, London, 1899), " that the need of symbols to express or represent our highest emotions is inwoven with human nature, and indifference to them is not, as many have supposed, a sign of enlightenment or of spirituality. It is, in fact, an unhealthy symptom. We do not credit a man with a warm heart who does not care to show his love in word or act; nor should we commend the common sense of a soldier who saw in his regimental colors only a rag at the end of a pole."

The most richly developed symbolism of ancient times, especially important by reason of its abundant influence on that of the Christian Church, was

3. In the Old Testament. found in the Mosaic system, in which, consonantly with the whole character of the old covenant, scarcely any religious action took place without at least the accompaniment of a symbolic meaning. To many of the prescribed rites and the objects to be used in them the signification was expressly attached at the time of their institution by divine command; but throughout the Old-Testament history there are numerous examples of action instinctively symbolic, after the manner of eastern peoples. Typical examples are the rending of Jeroboam's garment by the prophet Ahijah, to signify the separation of Israel and Judah (I Kings xi. 29);

Elisha's command to Joash to smite upon the ground with the arrows (II Kings xiii. 18); Jeremiah breaking the earthen bottle in the presence of the elders of Israel (Jer. xix. 1–11); and Ezekiel removing his household goods as a type of the captivity of Zedekiah (Ezek. xii. 3–16). There is, however, a great difference between such things as the two fundamental symbols, the Sabbath (q.v.) and the rite of Circumcision (q.v.), both representing the covenant of God with his people, and the extremely minute and fanciful interpretations put by the later students of the Law upon every detail of the temple worship—interpretations not surpassed in elaborate ingenuity by the most imaginative of medieval symbolists. Thus the Temple was interpreted as symbolic of human nature, and the two cherubim, the only images in it, of the concentration of all natural life; although Philo, attributing a cosmic meaning to the entire edifice, takes them as denoting the two hemispheres. The table with the showbread set forth the dependence of the people upon God for their sustenance. The seven-branched candlestick meant in Philo's scheme the seven planets, for later interpreters the congregation of the people of God. According to Josephus (*Ant.*, III., vii. 7), every detail of the high priest's official vestments had its own special meaning. Thus the coat symbolized the earth and the upper garment heaven; the bells and pomegranates, thunder and lightning; the ephod, the four elements; and the interwoven gold, the glory of God. The breastplate in the center of the ephod set forth the relation of the earth to the universe; the girdle was the ocean, the stones on his shoulders the sun and moon, and the twelve jewels in the breastplate the signs of the zodiac, while the miter once more represented heaven.

It is impossible within the limits of this article to give any extended account of the world-wide practise of attaching an inner meaning to the simplest

4. Comprehensiveness of Symbolism. religious acts, as it is likewise to describe in detail the far-reaching nature symbolism of the Middle Ages, which provided an emblematic meaning for everything in the visible world, regarding it as " full of sacred cryptograms." A salient instance of this kind of labored search for analogical reference is the *Physiologus* or *Bestiary* (probably a product of the allegorizing school of Alexandria, but popular and influential down to late medieval times), in which various animals are supposed to typify moral or spiritual qualities. A complete survey of this kind of analogical teaching would lead far afield, out of the domain of theological learning into that of poetry—at least such poetry as Wordsworth's, who reproaches his Peter Bell for blindness to it:

> A primrose by the river's brim
> A yellow primrose was to him—
> And it was nothing more;

who also says of himself, on the other hand,

> To me the meanest flower that blows can bring
> Thoughts that do often lie too deep for tears.

If this is true, in a greater or less degree, of all poets, it is not surprising to find it pointed out as a special method of the greatest of the medi eval poets by A. F. Ozanam (*Dante*, p. 68, Paris, 1839), who calls it " a very philosophic proceeding, since it is based upon the incontestable law of the association of ideas, and, moreover, one which is eminently poetic; for, while prose places the thought proposed immediately under the sign of the word, poetry sets there instead certain images which are themselves the signs of a more elevated thought."

This article considers only such symbolism as in the Christian Church has been deliberately introduced for the sake of the lesson conveyed, or sanctioned as a more or less officially accepted explanation of the inner meaning of such usages. The language of signs may be used either to instruct those whose understanding of words is limited, or to baffle those who are not supposed to understand them. Thus a crucifix may be as good as a sermon to an illiterate peasant; while the sign of the fish was used by the early Christians because it told their enemies nothing. This latter kind of symbolism, however, was in the nature of the case of but transitory importance, employed as it was only during the time of persecution, when it was necessary to conceal from the pagans some of the deepest truths of Christianity.

II. Christian Symbolism: In the earliest ages of the Christian Church one would look in vain for the detailed and minute symbolism of which the Middle

1. Symbolism as a Religious Need. Ages are so full, because the conditions of divine worship had not yet allowed so stately and developed a ritual; but the underlying principle was the same —the belief in a real affinity or correspondence between the visible sign and the invisible truth. Adolf Harnack truly says (*Dogma*, ii. 144): " What we nowadays understand by ' symbols ' is a thing which is not that which it represents; at that time [in the second century], symbol ' denoted a thing which, in some kind of way, is that which it signifies "; and again (iv. 289), " The symbol was never a mere type or sign, but always embodied a mystery." Thus the sacraments of baptism and the Lord's Supper (qq.v.) are symbols in this sense of the word, taking it to imply something which, in being what it is, is a sign and vehicle of something higher and better. The need of sacraments rests ultimately upon the reluctance instinctive in our nature to allow any spiritual fact to remain without an external expression, as well as upon the principle enunciated by Augustine (*Contra Faustum*, xix. 11) that " there can be no religious society, whether the religion be true or false, without some sacrament or visible symbol to serve as a bond of union." Both of these rites are symbols of the mystical union between Christ and the believer, baptism symbolizing that union in its inception, the Eucharist in its organic life.

In harmony with its natural development, Christianity took over a multitude of the old symbolic interpretations, both those of the earlier revelation and those of various surrounding peoples. But it also carried the tendency further by attaching symbolic meanings to its own proper ceremonies and external acts. Thus, early in the development of Christian worship, the exact manner of performing the more important ceremonies tended by degrees to become fixed and prescribed, in order

2. Early Tendency toward Unification. that the same belief might be everywhere taught by the action in question; although so long as the advantage of absolute uniformity was not recognized, it was possible for varying symbols to set forth different sides of the one truth. Thus in Spain in the sixth and seventh centuries, a single immersion or affusion was customary in baptism in order to assert against the Arians the single substance of the three divine Persons— " one Lord, one faith, one baptism "—while usually it was threefold, setting forth the other side of the same doctrine and corresponding to the pronunciation of the three sacred names of the Trinity. The most interesting features of early Christian symbolism are to be found in the painted and sculptured representations of the Catacombs (see CEMETERIES) and later of the most ancient churches, which were full of the fervent faith of the primitive Church. The art of Rome in the period just before the coming of Christianity had shown an increasing

3. Early Symbolism. tendency not to represent objects literally, but to employ visible forms for the representation of abstract notions. The fundamental difference, however, between classical art, as represented by the Greek, and Christian, as represented by the Gothic, is that the former dwelt contentedly on mere physical beauty, while the Christian artist, who has gained a conviction of his own spiritual nature, always tries to represent it. Clement of Alexandria (q.v.) suggested to the faithful of his day that instead of the pagan devices cut on stones and rings by Roman artists, they should have such things as a dove, symbolic of the Spirit of God within them, the palmbranch of victory, or the anchor, emblematic of their hope. Tertullian, in his *De idololatria*, though his zeal against pagan rites inclines him to object to all representations and to stigmatize the painter's art as unlawful, yet makes an exception in favor of these devices, and speaks of the Good Shepherd as depicted on chalices (*De pudicitia*, vii., x., Eng. transl. *ANF*, iv. 80, 84–85).

The sources of the early symbols are various. Those of a pictorial nature, owing to the prohibition of painted or plastic representations among the Jews, usually either spring from primi-

4. Sources and Figures Employed. tive Christian consciousness, or are adaptations of forms already at hand in the work of pagan artists. A useful illustration of the latter case is the frequently recurring figure of the Good Shepherd, which often resembles that of Hermes Kriophoros, the ram-bearer. Apart from the place which the shepherd occupies in the life and literature of ancient peoples, it is obviously unnecessary to conclude that the motive or spirit of the Christian symbol was derived from prevalent heathen thought. Not to mention the frequent references in the Old Testament to the pastoral relation of God to his people, the words of Christ himself (John x. 11–19) would naturally have been in the artist's mind; and confirmatory evidence is often present in the association with the figure of distinctively Christian symbols—the fish, the Chi Rho monogram (see JESUS CHRIST, MONOGRAM OF), or the Alpha and Omega (q.v.). The palm-branch is found equally on pagan and Christian monuments, but in the latter bears its unmistakable reference to Rev. vii. 9. The vine, again, occurs on heathen monuments with manifest reference to the worship of Bacchus, while it would at once call up in Christian minds the parabolic teaching of John xv. 18. In the absence of authentic likenesses of the Savior, his person, life, and office were set forth under symbols whose meaning was at once intelligible to all the initiated. Among the earliest and most frequently recurring is the lamb, which, with a variety of accompaniments, continued to be used until its representation was forbidden by canon 82 of the Trullan Synod in 692 (Hefele, *Conciliengeschichte*, iii. 340, Eng. transl. v. 234, Fr. transl., iii. 1, p. 573)—apparently because of mystical extravagances connected with it in some minds; the decision, however, was not accepted by the Western Church, in which the symbol of the lamb long remained an object of reverence. Of even deeper significance is the fish (Greek *ichthus*), sometimes in its pictorial representation and sometimes indicated merely by the Greek letters of its name. Wherever the word or the figure was found, rudely scratched upon the fresh mortar of the Catacombs, or more elaborately chiseled in connection with other symbols or inscriptions, or engraved upon gems in signet rings, it spoke of the precious doctrine contained in the five words for which its Greek letters stand—" Jesus Christ, the Son of God, the Savior." It connotes even more in some early mural paintings which bear distinct evidence of the eucharistic character of the feast in which the fish is the central figure. Still more permanently familiar are the cross, the Chi Rho or monogram composed of the first two Greek letters of the name of Christ, and the Alpha and Omega, referring to Rev. i. 11, xxi. 6, xxii. 13. The disciples appear also under the symbols of the dove and the fish, or as the sheep of the Good Shepherd's fold; the Church as a ship riding safely over the waves, or as the ark of Noah, to which a dove returns, bearing an olive-branch in its beak.

The other division into which the subject falls, the symbolism of ceremonial observances and accessories, is illustrated by a long series of liturgical treatises, becoming fuller and more

5. Development of Liturgical Symbolism. minute as the thirteenth century approaches. Among the earlier works, those of the Alexandrian school, with its characteristic leaning toward symbolic or allegorical interpretation of Holy Scripture, contain the most frequent instances of such treatment; Cyril of Jerusalem's catechetical instructions are also full of mystical explanations of the Church ceremonies (see MYSTAGOGICAL THEOLOGY), although when he approaches the chief of them all, the Eucharist, he is almost exclusively preoccupied with the dogmatic and devotional aspects of it. The works of the pseudo-Dionysius afforded much suggestion for the later development; and in the seventh century Bede and Isidore of

Seville (qq.v.) lead along the path which was to be so much trodden. Symbolism was reduced to a speculative science by Hugo of St. Victor; by his pupil and successor Richard of St. Victor (q.v.); by Honorius of Autun (q.v.), who, after the fashion of the time, took all knowledge to be his province; by Sicardus, bishop of Cremona (d. 1215), renowned as a historian, canonist, and liturgiologist, especially in his *Mitrale seu de officiis ecclesiasticis summa;* by Vincent of Beauvais (q.v.), after Albertus Magnus and Thomas Aquinas (qq.v.) the most distinguished Dominican theologian of the thirteenth century; by Jacobus de Varagine (q.v.), the Dominican archbishop of Genoa, in his " Golden Legend "; and most of all by Durandus (q.v.), bishop of Mende in Languedoc, the greatest of medieval liturgiologists, whose *Rationale divinorum officiorum*, written about 1284, is said to have been oftener republished during the early days of printing than any other book except the Bible.

There was no limit to the range of medieval symbolism. Hugo of St. Victor (*In hierarchiam cœlestem*, II., x. 1146) considered it possible that " intelligent minds might perhaps arrive

6. Examples of Liturgical Symbolism. at the union of everything in a beautiful harmony, visible and invisible things alike, so as to leave no single sensible object without demonstrating that it has the mission of representing something immaterial." There was no detail about a church, however insignificant to the ordinary eye in which the medieval imagination could not find a meaning, an analogy. Thus, in the very walls of the church building, where, of course, the foundation and other stones have their Scriptural interpretations (I Cor. iii. 11; I Pet. ii. 5), Durandus goes so far as to remember and interpret the cement. This, " without which there can be no stability of the walls, is made of lime, sand, and water. The lime is fervent charity, which joineth to itself the sand, that is, undertakings for the temporal welfare of our brethren; because true charity taketh care of the widow and the aged, and the infant, and the infirm; and they who have it study to work with their hands, that they may have wherewith to benefit them. Now the lime and the sand are bound together in the wall by an admixture of water. But water is an emblem of the Spirit; and as without cement the stones can not cohere, so neither can men be built up in the heavenly Jerusalem without charity, which the Holy Ghost worketh in them" (*Symbolism of the Churches*, p. 15, London, 1906). The above quotation is an instance of the pertinacity with which a meaning was sought for everything, however practical the reason for its presence. Of more importance and, for most people, of more interest are the significations attached to the essential and prominent ritual accessories of the chief act of worship in the Roman Catholic Church, medieval and modern. Candles (see LIGHTS, USE OF IN WORSHIP) burn upon the altar, to typify the true Light of the world. Incense is used at certain portions of the mass, as before the altar in heaven (Rev. viii. 3), and with the same general significance, that of prayer (Rev. v. 8). But, as in so many cases, there is no restriction to a single symbol;

meaning. Thus the Fathers delight to see in the censer the humanity of Christ, in the fire his divinity, and in the smoke his grace. The censer, says Augustine, is like the body of the Lord, and the incense like the same body offered in sacrifice for the salvation of the world and received as a sweet perfume by the Heavenly Father (*Hom. vi. in Apoc.* x. 3).

The vestments of the officiating priest and his attendants have each its reminder, either of the passion of Christ or of some virtue necessary to his ministers. The amice figures the helmet of a warrior, and reminds the priest that he is a warrior; or it is a memorial of the veil with which the eyes of Christ were bandaged by the soldiers. The alb is the white robe put upon him by Herod; the emblem of purity. The girdle brings to mind the manner in which Christ was bound, and typifies continence. The maniple, originally a kind of handkerchief intended to wipe the face during the holy offices, teaches the lesson that man must earn the bread of immortality in the sweat of his brow, and figures also the whips and scourges of the passion. The stole, even in its present diminished form, by its very name reminds us of the garment of innocence and immortality with which our first parents were clothed. The chasuble symbolizes the yoke of Christ; when he puts it on, the priest prays " O Lord, who hast said, My yoke is easy and my burden is light, grant that I may carry it in such a manner as to obtain thy grace "—and there are similar prayers alluding to the symbolic meaning with each of the other vestments. Of those peculiar to bishops, it will be sufficient here to mention the crosier or pastoral staff, in the shape of a shepherd's crook, which in his own diocese he carries with the curved part out, as a sign of jurisdiction; in that of another bishop, he turns it toward himself to express the opposite. The colors used for the sacerdotal garments under the old law were five—gold, blue, purple, scarlet, and white (linen); and as late as Gregory the Great *De pastorali cura,* ii. 3) there seems to have been a tendency to retain the consecrated sequence. The modern Roman colors, however (increasingly followed in the Anglican church), while still five according to the traditional number, are partly different. They are: white, a symbol of purity, on feasts of Christ, the Blessed Virgin, confessors (saints who were not martyrs), and virgins unless also martyred, suggesting both blood and fire, on the feast of Pentecost and of all martyrs; green, the ordinary color of nature, on Sundays and weekdays not specially set apart; violet, the somber color of mourning and penitence, during Advent and Lent; black on Good Friday and in services for the dead. See Mass, II., 7.

7. Symbolism of Vestments and Insignia.

The usages accompanying the solemn administration of the sacrament of baptism at this day in the Roman Catholic Church, most of which have come down from very early times, are an admirable illustration of the manner in which every smallest action in sacred things was supposed to teach its own lesson to the participants and spectators. The priest, wearing a violet stole, symbolic of the miserable state of fallen man, meets the child at the door of the church to signify that in its original state it has no right to enter the house of God. After the command to the devil to depart, the seal of a different Master is impressed on the child's forehead and breast with the sign of the cross; and the priest lays his hand upon its head to denote that he takes possession of it in the name of God. Salt, which preserves from corruption and gives a relish to food, is then put into the mouth, and then, lest the devil should attempt to take away the gift of Christian wisdom and the relish for divine things, he is solemnly exorcised. A strange but very ancient ceremony, mentioned by Ambrose (*De sacramentis*, I., i.) is still retained at this point. In memory of Christ's curing of a deaf-and-dumb man by touching his ears and tongue with spittle, the same is done by the priest to the ears and nostrils of the child, to symbolize the opening of its ears to the truth and its mouth to the praise of the Lord. After the formal renunciation of Satan at the font (see Renunciation of the Devil), the child is anointed with the " oil of catechumens," on the breast to make it love the yoke of Christ and on the shoulders to give it strength to carry that yoke. The actual essential ceremony of baptism proper has already been spoken of. It is followed by a fresh anointing with the sacred chrism, in token of the quality of prophet, priest, and king which has been bestowed upon the new member of Christ; and the child's head is covered with the white chrism-cloth (as the newly baptized adults in the primitive Church wore their white garments for eight days), as a reminder of the necessity of striving to preserve baptismal innocence unspotted to the end. A lighted taper is then placed in the child's hand, held by one of the godparents; and the words put into the priest's mouth express an allusion to the light which must be kept burning till the call comes to go out and meet the Bridegroom.

8. Symbolism in Baptism.

For one final illustration, the intricate ceremonies of the consecration of a church, as would naturally be expected, were in the Middle Ages, and are to-day in the Roman Catholic Church, full of an elaborate symbolism of their own, including some unique features. One is that in which the bishop, with the end of his crosier, traces the letters first of the Greek alphabet and then of the Latin in the shape of a great X from corner to corner of the church; this corresponds to the taking possession of land and marking its boundaries. While not found in the East and not attested before the ninth century in the West, this rite goes back for its origin much further, and may have been suggested by the practise of Roman surveyors, who used to trace two transverse lines on land which they wished to measure. But it was easy to regard the formation of the big X as a taking possession of the floor space of the church in the name of Jesus Christ, the great Alpha and Omega, whose monogram and title, so to speak, were written large upon the pavement by the tracing of the intervening letters. Lustration with specially prepared holy

9. Consecration of a Church.

water is a prominent part of the rite; but rather too much, it seems, has been made of the analogy drawn by L. Duchesne (*Christian Worship*, p. 413, London, 1904), following such medieval liturgists as Yvo of Chartres, between the consecration and the ceremonies of baptism. There is no attempt, however remote, to imitate the " form " of baptism; and it is safer to regard the lustration as merely a symbolized moral disinfection. It is the natural and logical order that purification should precede embellishment. Even in pagan Greece, at the annual commemoration of those who fell at Platea, the archon washed the gravestones with water before anointing them with oil. So in the rite under discussion the consecration is symbolized and made eloquent to the spiritual sense by the use of oil, typical of God's benedictions.

A. I. du P. COLEMAN.

III. Symbolism in Art.—1. Relation of Art and Symbolism: Throughout the entire history of Christian art more or less of symbolism has ever been present. This Christian art has on the one side been in agreement with the historic manifestations or forms of art in general, while on the other side religious fancy and the tongue of the Church and of Christendom have brought forth a wealth of symbols, comparisons, allegories, and types peculiarly their own which in turn have had an especially eventful influence upon art. In the early Christian period alongside of purely Christian conceptions earlier art traditions were still effective. In the discovery and interpretation of art symbols needful care has not always been exercised in distinguishing between what belongs to literature, what to literature and art combined, or what exclusively to art. Such men of the Middle Ages as Honorius of Autun, Sicard, and Durand, for example, in their symbolic interpretations concerned themselves all too narrowly with the emblematic speech of art. For the Middle Ages the most effective work has been done by such French scholars as Cahier and Didron, for the early Christian period by German Protestants.

2. The Early Period: For the period before Constantine this form of expression is limited to sepulchral monuments. The expression is essentially symbolic, and material from the Old and the New Testament is used to express the conceptions and hopes of that period, although with occasional peculiarities more or less loosely attached. Roses, branches of bloom, flowering meadows, and trees, especially the palm, represent paradise, the entrance being indicated by two pillars, or, later, by two great candlesticks. Still more significant was the lamb, standing upon a mountain from which gushed the four streams of paradise, and the Jordan also came into this connection. In very intimate connection with this was the favorite figure of the good shepherd, thought of as lord and protector of the dead, to which belonged also the sheep upon his shoulder. The sheep also appeared alone in this symbolism; the number twelve represented the apostles; the lamb stood for Christ and also for the sacrificial lamb; exceptionally upon the sarcophagus of Junius Bassus the lamb represents the

1. Primitive Forms.

wonder-working Jesus. The fish, one of the most ancient symbols, also belongs here so far as it expresses the mystical communion brought about through the Lord's Supper, the result of which is incorruption. The conversion of this into a confession as *Ichthus* (=*Iēsous Christos Theou huios sotēr*) can be proven first in the fourth century, while the designation of the Christians as *pisciculi* seems never to have been taken up into art. The vine, appearing as early as the second century, either relates itself to the Lord's Supper or represents the living community with Christ (John xv. 1 sqq.). The dove, with or without the olive branch, as the symbol of heavenly peace belongs here; it may be purely ornamental, however, or it may represent the Holy Spirit. So mention may be made here of the palm, the wreath or crown, and the anchor. The peacock was a possession of the ancient, of Jewish, and of Christian sepulchral symbolism. The same may be said of the Sirens, the Dioscuri, Eros, and Psyche. The figure of Orpheus also was used, not because there was any relation to Christ, but possibly because of the connection in the Orphic mysteries with immortality. Ship and lighthouse portrayed the voyage to eternity; the shepherd suggested the sighing of the soul for eternal peace, and was employed in baptisteries. Whether the so-called Orantes (praying figures, generally female) represented Christian prayer as such is not absolutely sure, but they do not represent the Church. Religious regard restricted representations of the deity to a hand reaching down, later surrounded by a nimbus or giving rise to rays of light. From the secular life were taken such figures as the lion, eagle, horse, balance, and instruments of labor.

With the end of the fourth century began the downfall of sepulchral figuring and loss of its symbolism, replaced by a new series of symbols. To be named here are the monogram of Christ (see JESUS CHRIST, MONOGRAM OF), the cross (see CROSS AND ITS USE AS A SYMBOL), the A and Ω, the swastika, the phenix and the eagle (both symbols of the resurrection), the cantharus from which vine branches issue (recalling the Supper), while serpents, dragons, and other monsters either lie at Christ's feet or are transfixed by the emperor's bannered spear (recalling the fall or representing the devil and his companions). Other objects introduced more or less frequently were the lizard, squirrel, cypress spring or well, dog, and ring. To be separated in category are the purely heathen symbols which owe their entrance into Christian art to purely mechanical causes, such as Eros (Cupid) with reversed torch (see MITHRA, MITHRAISM), Gorgon head, and pomegranate (an accompaniment of Persephone). A higher step in development was taken when by way of personification the human figure came to be used. So a half-figure, with a robe in folds over the head, upon which the enthroned Christ sets his foot, represents the heaven. While sun and moon appear as disk and crescent, the sun appears also as a youth going forth in his chariot with winged horses, likewise as a bust from the head of which issue rays; the moon is a woman with the sickle in her hair or with a garment blowing or falling in folds about her. Mal-

2. Advanced Development.

forms, from the pedestals of which waters issue, represented sea and rivers, especially the Red Sea and the Jordan. Nymphs of the springs appear also, while the seated matron may represent the city if she have a tesselated crown. The Codex Rossanensis introduces a new Christian creation, wisdom, or inspiration; death is presented as a half-naked youth seated upon a sarcophagus, and prayer was also personified.

3. The Middle Ages: In the Middle Ages there was a great inrush of new forms and ideas, derived not only from the influence of the Bible and the sermon, but also from the liturgy, the legends of the saints, the religious drama, and the moralities, from fable, and indeed from scholar-

1. Trinity, Christ, Mary. ship. Yet only a small part of what was available was really employed. The mystery of the Trinity was represented by the triangle, by three rings interlaced, or by a triplet of like-formed animal shapes; while about the end of the period issued a three-headed form. The number three had an important part in architecture and artistic composition. The Holy Spirit was still figured as a dove, while doves represented likewise the seven gifts of the Spirit, only exceptionally did this person of the Trinity appear in human form as a lad. The life of Jesus afforded a rich material. For the incarnation the unicorn legend was used—hunted by Gabriel and his four hounds, pity, truth, justice, and peace, the unicorn took refuge in the protection of the seated virgin. The virgin birth is connected in symbolism with the virginity of Mary, as by the use of the lily. So from the Old Testament into connection with the life of Christ were brought the burning bush, the vessel with manna, the rod of Aaron which sprouted, etc. The sufferings and death of Christ were symbolized by the lamb with the cross-banner or the stream of blood flowing from its breast. The self-sacrificing death of Christ was figured by the pelican which pierced its breast to give drink to its young. The lioness also appeared, bringing to life by breathing upon it her stillborn cub. The lion represented the evil powers and the devil. Christ's exaltation was figured by showing him seated upon a throne or a rainbow, a lily branch (grace) issuing from his head, while a sword denoted justice. The Virgin Mary was portrayed as queen of heaven with diadem, scepter, and throne, and with her were pictured sun, moon, and stars; as " mother of pity " she wore a mantle which was caught up by the wind and covered those who sought her help; to her the lily and the rose were sacred; the red rose symbolized her sufferings, the white her joy. The functions of prophets and apostles and certain doctors of the Church as teachers were represented by the book or roll which was given them in art; to some, certain definite articles gave character and distinction—the lyre to David, the keys to Peter, or the sword of martyrdom distinguished Paul; the founders of churches sometimes bore in the hand a model of the church.

Of course the Church had its figures representing itself. In the most beautiful representations of the Middle Ages the Church appeared as a royal woman, crowned, carrying the banner of victory and the

XI.—14

cup; or Christ on the cross crowned her, or she caught from his wounded side the flowing blood,

2. The Church, Virtues, and Vices. and a prophet was her companion; her significance for salvation was represented by a ship or the ark. Opposed to her stood the synagogue, unbelieving Judaism, a feminine form, in the right hand a cracked staff and in the left a table of the law falling to earth; a bandage covered her eyes, and the crown was falling from her head. The influence of the religious drama was felt here, and the popular feeling against Judaism registered itself in art by picturing Judaism under the figure of the swine. For the sacrament the cup and ears of grain had their symbolism; the cup on a gravestone indicated the priestly character of the deceased. Transubstantiation had also its symbolism in the " mill of the host." Of course, the moralizing character of the Church was displayed here, and the virtues appeared on portals, in the chancel, on memorials of the dead, and in the patterns of the carpets. Practically always they appeared as female forms: Faith had the cup and the cross, Justice had the balance, Charity (or love) protected a beggar or a child, Hope looked off in the distance or stretched out her hand for a crown, Prudence held a book, Bravery made preparation (for defense or attack), Temperance had a measuring instrument, Chastity was represented by a palm, phenix, or a nesting dove, Humility by a dove, Perseverance by a crown, Harmony by an olive branch. Naturally this symbolism induced the figuring of the opposites: Idolatry was shown by a man worshiping an idol, Desperation by a man committing suicide with a sword, Inconstancy by a monk fleeing from the monastery.

As the seasons symbolized the changing course of human life, so the wheel of fortune was especially employed for this purpose, being taken in from pre-

3. Later Forms and Conceptions. Christian art after being passed over by early Christian symbolism. It became a great favorite as a moralistic medium. The destructive might of death was set forth by the figure of a man weeding a garden or felling trees, or of a rider (Rev. vi. 8) with stretched bow, or more extensively as an emaciated old man which developed into the skeleton with sickle and hour-glass. The dance of death (see DEATH, DANCE OF), a favorite theme in art, is in origin connected with the devastation of the Black Death. The departing soul was usually pictured as a small, naked, sexless, human figure, issuing from the mouth. The last judgment was also a subject of art, in which the revenge of the monsters of hell occupied the central place, while the devil was a prominent figure. Upon the devil played all the popular richness of imagination and grotesqueness; hence developed the human figure in varied shapes, with horn of goat, hoof, bat's wings, and tail; he even appeared as a black bird inspiring Pontius Pilate. There was in connection with this theme not a little also of the humorous. There was a great revival of the antique in art as in literature. Sirens, centaurs, the Sibyl, Plato, and Aristotle are common figures. Great difficulty attends the understanding of the meaning of the scenes in which animals appear, now figuring in wild combat and again grouped in restful pose. These are found especially in Germany in many situations. Possibly in many cases the explanation is to be sought in warning against demonic powers, assaults, and sins; occasionally the decorative motive is evident; again possibly, though not probably, irony is present.

4. Byzantine Art: Byzantine art was not nearly so rich in its forms and figures as the artistic symbolism of the West, the naturally conservative tendencies of the East revealing themselves here and permitting little that was creative. In this its literature differed, employing symbols, allegories, personification, and types freely. While the West employed the human form in this region, the East remained true to its traditions in the employment mainly of animal and plant forms. The image controversy (see IMAGES AND IMAGE WORSHIP, II.) had its effects in this direction, so that the Physiologus myth had a far narrower influence upon art. Anthropomorphic symbolism was less potent in its effects. Of course the East had its own favorite symbols. Thus in the pictures of the last judgment there appears the crowned king of hell riding a sort of griffin. It had also the "Etimasia," a throne upon which rested cross, lamb, and book—representing Christ; while the empty throne stood for the majesty of God, in which the early Christian abhorrence of figuring God as a person is seen. Byzantine art remained closer to the earlier personification, as when the shepherd lad David, playing the harp, gives the key to the melody, behind a pillar in the distance the Oread Echo takes up the tone, while in the foreground the half-naked mountain-god listens. Similarly David appears as the royal singer, by his side the female forms Sophia and Prophecy and above his head the Holy Spirit as inspirer in the form of a dove.

In France, Germany, and England the Roman Catholic Church is endeavoring at present to come again into full accord with the symbolic feeling of the Middle Ages, while Italy and Spain seem to linger in the rear. There are attempts at creation, seen especially in the use of the "Heart of Jesus" and "Heart of Mary." The Protestant churches are also showing an awakening interest in symbols and their use in religious art. See ANIMALS; and PARAMENTA.   (VICTOR SCHULTZE.)

IV. Apologetics of Symbolism from the Roman Catholic Standpoint: A certain amount of symbolism is necessary in all religions, pagan, Christian, Roman Catholic, or Protestant. In all ages and places the inward feeling of devotion must be accompanied by an outward manifesta-

1. Symbolism Inevitable. tion of it. All religious actions are from their very nature symbolical and figurative. The Mussulman in his devotions must take off his shoes and kneel on his carpet facing toward Mecca. These are symbolical acts. Even the Quaker must keep on his hat and sit in a bare room in silence, to show by these symbols his vain attempt to disregard symbols. A fortiori, the Roman Catholic, whose religion is based on a sacramental system, is surrounded on all sides by symbolism, in architecture, art, and music, all contributing to the elaborate ritual

of his public worship in the holy sacrifice of the Mass, which sanctifies and applies symbolism in the highest and widest sense. The study of Roman Catholic ceremonies might be called the science of liturgical esthetics.

It may be said that a symbol is synonymous with a sacrament, inasmuch as they are both signs, something which stands for something

2. Fundamental Analogy. else; something exterior, visible, which signifies and usually conceals something interior, invisible. For instance, life, per se, in itself—vegetative, sensitive, or rational—is never really seen; it is perceived only by its effects in exterior signs and symbols which that life informs, through which it works. The best illustration of the symbolism or sacramentality of the universe is found in man himself, a microcosm, as he is called, a "sum and compendium of the universe." His body, composed of all the sensitive, vegetative, and mineral elements found in the world outside him, is the sacramental symbol of the rational soul by which it is informed; the outward and visible sign of the real invisible ego within. And man thus constituted, himself a kind of sacrament, in a world which is by its nature universally sacramental, must of necessity lead a sacramental life, both in the order of nature and of grace, i.e., because in the order of nature therefore in the order of grace; for grace does not destroy nature, on the contrary, it presupposes and perfects it; nature is the raw material for grace to work upon. Revealed religion is above natural theology, but never opposed to it. A religion purely spiritual, without the outward sign of the interior grace, would be for angels (pure spirits), not for men—at least according to Roman Catholic doctrine. Indeed, Christ himself became a sacrament, for he became man. The incarnation is the sacrament of sacraments; his humanity was the sign, the symbol of his divinity. As a teacher of men he was a symbolist, for he spoke in parables. The sacramental idea is coextensive with the Roman Catholic Church, and is the basis of ecclesiastical symbolism with all it implies, not only of the seven sacraments themselves, but of the elaborate Roman Catholic ceremonial and ritual. Every Roman Catholic theologian who admits a divinely instituted sacramental system is necessarily more or less of a symbolist. The reason for symbolism in the supernatural is according to Thomas Aquinas, the same as that required in the natural order, viz., man is composed of body and soul. Truth, which is immaterial, must be presented to him by material signs. In the natural order ideas are expressed by words; thoughts arrive to us through the senses, not that the material sense contains the essence of the immaterial idea but that it is its messenger, just as the wind carries winged seeds. "Sensation is our messenger to the intellect, our king." Similarly in the supernatural order grace is brought to men through the exterior form of sacraments and ceremonies.

Sacrament here is taken in the strict Roman Catholic, theological sense, as understood of the seven sacraments, to wit: it must be a sensible sign, it must be instituted by Christ, it must effect the grace it signifies. The matter—or materia

(*materia*)—of these sacraments was not chosen arbitrarily by Christ. "It was becoming," again to quote Thomas Aquinas, "that there be

3. Sacramental Analogies. a natural analogy between the matter of the sacrament and the grace operated by it," e.g., What is the effect of baptism? To cleanse the soul of the stain of original sin. Therefore water, which cleanses the body, is the necessary matter of this sacrament. Oil softens and strengthens, it permeates and nourishes, serves as a dressing for wounds, it is a seasoning for food, and, combined with other liquids, rises to the top; it is used for the anointing of priests and kings. It is a symbol of youth and vigor of soul. Mixed with balm it is the symbol of good example, of the good odor which the Christian soul should everywhere exhale. All these many qualities of oil are symbolic of the many and great operations of the Holy Ghost upon the soul, hence its use in the sacraments of baptism, confirmation, holy orders, and extreme unction.

Bread and wine are the matter of the sacrament of the Eucharist, because, according to the Council of Trent, Holy Communion produces in the spiritual all the effects of bread and drink in the material order, it sustains, gives growth, repairs forces, and fills the soul with a holy joy.

In *Le Symbolisme* (see bibliography), Landriot, archbishop of Reims, says in effect: Every creature, however small, is a partial and material expression of the Infinite Intelligence. Besides

4. Essential Valuation of Symbolism. its proper form, its individual character, it contains within a divine thought, a divine ideal, it bears the indelible seal of the Word, of which it is an imperfect though in a sense a true expression. Just as on a page written by a man of literary genius one can distinguish in each letter its form, individuality, material direction, typographical beauty, yet underneath the dead letter—above all in the *ensemble* of these inanimate characters—there is something else: there is the sublime, gracious, and varied thought of the master. So every object of creation corresponds to a divine ideal, it is a sign of a divine thought, a hieroglyphic of the language of heaven. Hence, Roman Catholic theology, the highest Roman Catholic philosophy, the great secret of art, consist first in knowing how to spell, then to read, then to understand this magnificent poem of the Creator, this sublime literature of God, this masterpiece of the greatest of creative artists. Thus to discover through the material element the divine side of things is to discern him who is at once the Great Unknown and supremely Intelligible Being. An activity could hardly be found more worthy than this of man's rational soul, made, as it is, after the image of its maker.

But such is the science and the philosophy of ecclesiastical symbolism, understood and applied by the Roman Catholic Church, "symbolism" in its most universal and therefore most Catholic meaning and use. STUART CHAMBERS.

BIBLIOGRAPHY: On the general subject of symbolism the reader is referred to: Rupert of Deutz, *De divinis officiis* and *De trinitate*, in his *Opera*, in *MPL*, clxviii.-clxx.; Cabrol, *Dictionnaire* (the one great modern thesaurus of the facts); W. Durand, *Rationale divinorum officiorum*, Augsburg, 1470 and often, Eng. transl. of first book, *The Symbolism of Churches and Church Ornaments*, 3d ed., London, 1906; Bingham, *Origines*, book VIII.; H. Alt, *Die Heiligenbilder*, Berlin, 1845; J. Dudley, *Naology; a Treatise on the Origin, Progress, and sacred Import of the sacred Structures . . . of the World*, London, 1846; F. Piper, *Mythologie und Symbolik der christlichen Kunst*, Weimar, 1847–51; W. Menzel, *Christliche Symbolik*, 2 vols., Regensburg, 1854; W. and G. Audsley, *Handbook of Christian Symbolism*, London, 1865; C. Cahier, *Les Caractéristiques des saints dans l'art populaire*, 2 vols., Paris, 1866–68; J. R. Thomson, *Symbols of Christendom*, London, 1867; R. St. J. Tyrwhitt, *Art Teaching of the Primitive Church*, London, 1873; C. A. Auber, *Histoire et théorie du symbolisme religieux*, 4 vols., Paris, 1874; J. W. Legg, *Notes on the Hist. of the Liturgical Colours*, London, 1882; J. P. Lundy, *Monumental Christianity; or, the Symbolism of the Primitive Church*, New York, 1882; F. A. Philippi, *Symbolik. Akademische Vorlesungen*, Gütersloh, 1883; C. Auber, *Hist. et théorie du symbolisme religieux avant et depuis le christianisme*, 4 vols., Paris, 1884; T. Inman, *Ancient Pagan and Modern Christian Symbolism*, New York, 1884; H. C. W. Philipps, *Domain of Symbolism in Religious Worship*, London, 1884; J. R. Allen, *Early Christian Symbolism in Great Britain and Ireland before the 13th Century*, London, 1887; H. Schmidt, *Handbuch der Symbolik*, Berlin, 1890; J. F. A. T. Landriot, *Le Symbolisme*, Paris, 1891; W. R. Lethaby, *Architecture, Mysticism, and Myth*, London, 1892; W. Palmer, *Early Christian Symbolism*, London, 1895; W. F. Shaw, *Chapters on Symbolism*, London, 1897; E. C. Neff, *An Anglican Study in Christian Symbolism*, Cleveland, 1898; E. M. Repullés y Vargas, *El Symbolismo en la arquitectura cristiana*, Madrid, 1898; E. Geldart, *Manual of Church Decoration and Symbolism*, Oxford, 1899; J. H. Spencer, "As Old as Adam"; first Principles in religious geometrical Symbols and alphabetical Characters*, London, 1899; F. W. Hackwood, *Christ Lore; being the Legends, Traditions, Myths, Symbols, Customs, and Superstitions of the Christian Church*, London, 1902; J. Sauer, *Die Symbolik des Kirchengebäudes und seiner Ausstattung in der Auffassung des Mittelalters*, Freiburg, 1902; H. J. Smith, *Illustrated Symbols and Emblems of the Jewish, Early Christian, Greek, Latin, and Modern Churches*, London, 1900; H. D. M. Spence, *White Robe of Churches*, London, 1900; H. Leclercq, *Manuel d'archéologie chrétienne*, Paris, 1907; J. H. Blunt, *The Annotated Book of Common Prayer*, pp. 44–80, latest impression, New York, 1908; *DCA*, ii. 1944–47; *KL*, vi. 593–600; A. E. Waite, *The Hidden Church of the Holy Graal: its Legends and Symbolism*, London, 1909; M. C. Nieuwbarn, *Church Symbolism; a Treatise on the General Symbolism and Iconography of the Roman Catholic Church Edifice*, ib. 1910; Mrs. H. Jenner, *Christian Symbolism*, Chicago, 1910; and the literature under PARAMENTA.

On symbolism in relation to art forms in general consult: the works named under ART AND CHURCH by Didron-Hemans, Piper, Lübke, Tyrwhitt, Otte, Jameson, Stokes, Cutts, Schultze, Kraus, and Michel; the literature under ARCHITECTURE, ECCLESIASTICAL; CEMETERIES; JESUS CHRIST, PICTURES AND IMAGES OF. Books dealing with art in all periods are: F. E. Hulme, *The Hist., Principles, and Practice of Symbolism in Christian Art*, new ed., London, 1908; F. Piper, ut sup.; Louisa Twining, *Symbols and Emblems of Early and Mediæval Christian Art*, London, 1860; C. Browne, *A Lecture on Symbolism and its Connection with Church Art*, New York, 1865; H. J. Grimouard de Saint Laurent, *Guide de l'art chrétien*, 6 vols., Paris, 1872–75; C. E. Clement, *A Handbook of Legendary Art*, Boston, 1881; idem, *Heroines of the Bible in Art*, London, 1900; E. P. Evans, *Animal Symbolism in Ecclesiastical Architecture*, London, 1896; A. B. Hinds, *A Garner of Saints. Legends and Emblems usually represented in Art*, London, 1900; H. Kehrer, *Die "Heiligen drei Könige" in der Legende und in der deutschen bildenden Kunst bis Dürer*, Strasburg, 1904.

For the early period read: W. D. Ward, *Hist. of the Cross; the pagan Origin and idolatrous Adoption and Worship of the Image*, London, 1871; C. Lüdtke, *Die Bilderverehrung und die bildenden Darstellung in den ersten christlichen Jahrhunderten*, Freiburg, 1874; J. E. Wessely, *Ikonographie Gottes und der Heiligen*, Leipsic, 1874; V. Schultze, *Archäologische Studien über altchristliche Monumente*, Vienna, 1880; F. X. Kraus, *Realencyklopädie der christlichen Altertümer*, 2 vols., Freiburg, 1882–86; A.

Hasenclever, *Der altchristliche Gräberschmuck*, Brunswick, 1886; H. Bergner, *Der Gute Hirt in der altchristlichen Kunst*, Berlin, 1890; A. Breymann, *Adam und Eva in der Kunst des christlichen Alterthums*, Wolfenbüttel, 1893; A. Heussner, *Die altchristlichen Orpheus Darstellungen*, Cassel, 1893; H. Detzel, *Christliche Ikonographie*, 2 vols., Freiburg, 1894–96; E. Hennecke, *Altchristliche Malerei und altkirchliche Literatur*, Leipsic, 1896; G. Stuhlfauth, *Die Engel in der altchristlichen Kunst*, Tübingen, 1897; L. Cloquet, *Eléments d'iconographie chrétienne*, Lille, 1900; K. M. Kaufmann, *Die sepulkralen Jenseitsdenkmäler der Antike und des Urchristentums*, Mainz, 1900; idem, *Handbuch der christlichen Archäologie*, Paderborn, 1905; T. Beaudoire, *Genèse de la cryptographie apostolique*, Paris, 1902; K. Michel, *Gebet und Bild in frühchristlicher Zeit*, Leipsic, 1902; H. Bergner, *Kirchliche Kunstaltertümer in Deutschland*, Leipsic, 1903–05; J. Reil, *Die frühchristlichen Darstellungen der Kreuzigung Christi*, Leipsic, 1904; J. Wilpert, *Die Malereien der Katakomben Roms*, 2 vols., Freiburg, 1904.

For the Middle Ages and modern times consult: J. M. von Redowitz, *Ikonographie der Heiligen*, Berlin, 1834; idem, *The Saints in Art*, Rome, 1898; A. N. Didron, *Iconographie chrétienne*, Paris, 1843; English transl., *Christian Iconography; or, the Hist. of Christian Art in the Middle Ages*, London, 1851; C. Cahier and A. Martin, *Mélanges* (and *Nouveaux Mélanges*) *d'archéologie, d'histoire, et de littérature sur le moyen-âge*, 10 vols., Paris, 1847–77; G. Heider, *Ueber Tiersymbolik und das Symbol des Löwen in der christlichen Kunst*, Vienna, 1849; J. E. Wessely, *Die Gestalten des Todes und des Teufels in der darstellenden Kunst*, Leipsic, 1876; H. J. Grimouard de Saint-Laurent, *Les Images du sacré-cœur au point de vue de l'hist. et de l'art*, Paris, 1880; A. Springer, *Ueber die Quellen der Kunstdarstellungen im Mittelalter*, Leipsic, 1880; H. Otte, *Kunstarchäologie des deutschen Mittelalters*, 2 vols., Leipsic, 1880–85; B. Eckl, *Die Madonna als Gegenstand christlicher Kunstmalerei*, Brixen, 1883; P. Jessen, *Die Darstellung des Weltgerichts bis auf Michelangelo*, Berlin, 1883; G. Voss, *Das jüngste Gericht in der bildenden Kunst des frühen Mittelalters*, Leipsic, 1884; N. Kondakoff, *Hist. de l'art byzantin*, 2 vols., Paris, 1886–91; E. Müntz, *Études iconographiques et archéologiques sur le moyen-âge*, Paris, 1888; F. Lauchert, *Geschichte des Physiologus*, Strasburg, 1889; C. Rohault de Fleury, *Les Saints de la messe et leurs monuments*, Paris, 1893; M. Engels, *Die Darstellung der Gestalten Gottes des Vaters in der Malerei*, Luxemburg, 1894; idem, *Die Kreuzigung Christi in der bildenden Kunst*, ib. 1899; P. Weber, *Geistliches Schauspiel und kirchliche Kunst in ihrem Verhältnis . . . an einer Ikonographie der Kirche und Synagoge*, Stuttgart, 1894; J. Strzygowski, *Der Bilderkreis des griechischen Physiologus*, Leipsic, 1899; N. Bell, *The Saints in Christian Art*, 3 vols., London, 1901–04; M. Kernarel, *Le " Livre" de Paula. Causeries familières sur l'art et le symbolisme chrétiens*, Paris, 1902; J. Sauer, *Symbolik des Kirchengebäudes . . . des Mittelalters*, Freiburg, 1902; É. Male, *L'Art religieux du xiii. siècle en France*, Paris, 1902 (crowned by the Academy); A. Venturi, *The Madonna*, London, 1902; J. E. Weis-Liebersdorf, *Christus- und Apostelbilder*, Freiburg, 1902; E. A. Greene, *Saints and their Symbols: a Companion in the Churches and Picture Galleries of Europe*, London, 1904; O. Zöckler, *Die Tugendlehre des Christentums mit besonderer Rücksicht auf deren zahlensymbolische Einkleidung*, Gütersloh, 1904; A. Muñoz, *Iconografia della Madonna*, Florence, 1905; H. O. Taylor, *The Medieval Mind*, 2 vols., New York, 1911.

SYMBOLUM APOSTOLICUM. See APOSTLES' CREED.

SYMMACHIANS: The name applied to one or more heretical sects, at least one of them centering at Rome. Philaster (*Hær.*, lxii.) speaks of them as derived from a certain Patricius, a teacher at Rome, whose chief doctrine was that the body was the handiwork of the devil, and that in consequence illtreatment of it was a duty. This was pushed by followers to its extremes of suicide and of indulgence in all lusts. Ambrosiaster (prologue to Galatians, and on I Tim. iv. 1) brings a sect of the name

into connection with Marcionites (see MARCION) and Manicheans (q.v.). Augustine (*Contra Faustum*, xix. 4, 17, *NPNF*, 1 ser., iv. 240, 246; *Contra Crésconium*, i. 31) relates Symmachians with the Ebionites (q.v.), and also (by implication) with Manicheans.

SYMMACHUS, sim'a-kus": Pope 498–514. On the death of Anastasius II. the deacon Symmachus of Sardinia and the archpriest Laurentius divided the votes; the former was consecrated in the Lateran and the latter in S. Maria Maggiore on Nov. 22, 498. Both parties agreed to submit the affair for decision to Theodoric the Great, although he was an Arian, who was then the suzerain of Rome. He decided that whoever was consecrated first, and by a majority, had a right to the papal chair; this being Symmachus, Laurentius withdrew, and apparent unity reigned. Symmachus called a synod on Mar. 1, 497, and introduced directions regarding the papal election which would render impossible such events as had occurred. This decision did not, however, prevent later schisms; moreover, the rivalry between Symmachus and Laurentius was renewed, and although the latter was made bishop of Nocera and removed from Rome, his followers continued their opposition to Symmachus, blaming him for appointing a time for the Easter festival of 501 A.D., and accusing him of adultery, of alienating church property, and various other crimes. Appeal was again made to Theodoric, who called Peter, bishop of Altinum, to Rome to investigate matters, and to take control of the church property. Symmachus, who was in Ariminum, refused to appear at the synod called by Peter in Rome, some time after Easter, 501, unless Peter withdrew and the church property were restored to his control, when he would be willing to defend himself before the synod. The bishops dared not deny the pope's request, but Theodoric demanded a new session of the synod, at which Symmachus decided to appear; but as a tumult arose during the session he refused to appear again and appealed to the king, to whom the synod also referred the matter. Theodoric, however, ordered the bishops to decide, and on Oct. 23, 501, at a fourth session they rendered the famous decision by which all accusations against Symmachus were set aside without examination, on the ground that, by reason of the exalted authority of the Apostle Peter, they did not dare to judge the pope, but left it to God, who sees the secrets of the heart. The synod followed out the conclusions of its decision, and declared those who had not favored Symmachus to be schismatics, and condemned Peter of Altinum and Laurentius. Symmachus convoked a sixth session of the synod Nov. 6, in order to prevent the interference with his election from becoming a precedent. The decision of the synod did not, however, restore harmony, and after deeds of violence, the followers of Laurentius finally resorted to literary arguments. Symmachus finally carried the day, but the opposition to Symmachus was broken only when Theodoric declared himself against the Laurentians and commanded that their church be given over to Symmachus (505 and 506 A.D.); whereupon Laurentius retired to a country place belonging to his stanch supporter, Senator Festus, and became an ascetic.

Symmachus was now firmly established as pope, and devoted himself to building and endowing churches. He entered into a dispute with the Emperor Anastasius (*Epist.*, x.), had relations with the banished Africans (*Epist.*, xi.), with Ennodius of Pavia (*Epist.*, vii., ix., xviii.), and with the Gauls (*Epist.*, xiv.) He favored the demands of the bishops of Arles, and his utterances at this time were not without influence on later views regarding the relation of spiritual to worldly authority. He died July 19, 514. (A. HAUCK.)

BIBLIOGRAPHY: Sources are: *Liber pontificalis*, ed. L. Duchesne, i. 44 sqq., 260, Paris, 1886, and ed. Mommsen, in *MGH, Gest. pont. Rom.* i (1898), 120; Theodorus Lector, in *MPG*, lxxxvi. 1, pp. 189–190; *MGH., Auct. ant.*, ix (1891), 324, xii (1894), 393 sqq.; and the " Letters " in *Epistolæ Romanorum pontificum genuinæ*, ed. A. Thiel, i. 639 sqq., Braunsberg, 1867. Consult further: Jaffé, *Regesta*, i. 96; A. von Reumont, *Geschichte der Stadt Rom*, ii. 38, Berlin, 1868; Vogel, in *Historische Zeitschrift*, i (1883), 400 sqq.; J. Langen, *Geschichte der römischen Kirche*, ii. 219 sqq., Bonn, 1885; F. Gregorovius, *Hist. of the City of Rome*, i. 317–321, London, 1894; Hefele, *Conciliengeschichte*, ii. 625 sqq., Eng. transl., iv. 49 sqq., Fr. transl., pp. 947 sqq., Bower, *Popes*, i. 296–309; Platina, *Popes*, i. 116–118; Milman, *Latin Christianity*, i. 350–351, 416–423.

SYMMACHUS: Translator of the Old Testament into Greek. See BIBLE VESRIONS, A, I., 2, § 2.

SYMPHORIANUS, sim-fōr″î-ê′nus: A Gallic martyr of the reign of Marcus Aurelius; d. probably in 180. He was a native of Autun, and is described as a youth of distinguished appearance and excellent education. Having refused to do homage to the statue of Berecynthia (Cybele), he was carried before the prefect Heraclius, who tried to subdue him by threats and torture, and finally had him beheaded outside the walls.

BIBLIOGRAPHY: The early *Acta*, with commentary, are in *ASB*, August, iv. 491–498. Consult further: C. L. Dinet, *Saint Symphorien et son culte*, 2 vols., Autun, 1861; K. J. Neumann, *Der römische Staat und die allgemeine Kirche*, i. 303–304, Leipsic, 1890; *DCB*, iv. 753; Ceillier, *Auteurs sacrés*, i. 472–473, x. 358, xii. 327, 832, 834, xiii. 21; Neander, *Christian Church*, i. 108, 115.

SYNAGOGUE.

I. The Institution: Synagogue is the term applied to the Jewish local houses of worship which arose probably during the Babylonian exile and are still in common use. In the Mishna and later
they were called " houses of assem-
1. Name, bling," or a term shortened to that.
Origins, Aramaic from that; there was also in
Purpose. use the expression " house of teaching." The Greek word *synagogē*, often employed in the New Testament, means both " assembly " and " house of assembly "; equivalent terms are " place of prayer " (I Macc. iii. 46),

simply " prayer " (cf. Acts xvi. 13), *synagōgion* and *proseuktērion* (the last two used by Philo). The need to appoint special places and to build houses for common worship seems not to have been felt before the destruction of Jerusalem by Nebuchadrezzar, that is, so long as the Temple of Solomon stood with its centralizing of the sacrificial cultus. While it may be concluded from II Kings iv. 23 that the pious on feast-days assembled at the place of dwelling of a prophet who lived in the neighborhood, it is clear that this did not become a firmly established institution. That the Targums (e.g., Pseudo-Jonathan on Ex. xviii. 20; Judges v. 9; Isa. i. 13) speak of synagogues as an early institution is an example of the habit of the Targums to attribute unhistorically to earlier times what belonged only to later. During the exile the people had neither Temple nor sacrifice. There remained only their attention to the words of Ezekiel and other men of God, the Sabbath, and prayer in common. Whether during the exile houses for such meetings were already appointed can not be determined. It may be taken as correct, however, that the need produced by the exile led up to common services of worship which did not cease after the exile had come to an end. Another motive contributed to this end. The law, transgression of which in earlier times had led to so severe punishment, became now the determinative norm, knowledge of it the one condition of the continued favor of God, its study a profitable engagement. Reading and explanation of this law was the chief business of the post-exilic assemblages of the people—prayer and instruction in the prophetic word and in history were secondary to this. The purpose of learning to know the law could be accomplished only by regular recurrence of meetings. Naturally the day chosen was the Sabbath. This regularity of meeting together led as a matter of course to the appointment of definite places. The earliest mention of synagogues is in Ps. lxxiv. 8, which may belong to the period of Artaxerxes III. Ochus (359–338 B.C.) [now usually assigned to the early Maccabean period]; the expression used in that passage can hardly be understood of anything else than of houses of assembling for divine worship, and with this agrees Acts xv. 21. Josephus mentions synagogues seldom and only casually. It may be concluded from the mention by Josephus (*War*, VII., iii. 3) of a synagogue in Antioch as first coming into existence in the time of Antiochus Epiphanes that he does not mean to claim so late an origin for them in Palestine.

At the time of Christ and the apostles there was at least one synagogue in each city of any size in Palestine (at Capernaum, Mark i. 21; Nazareth,
Mark vi. 2). In Jerusalem at least the
2. Number, more important, if not all, divisions of
Location, the city had their own synagogues.
Structure, But the Jerusalem Talmud is unhis-
Furnishings. torical in declaring (*Megilla*, iii., beginning, folio 73d) that there were 480 synagogues in the city, or 460 according to another reading. Also most of the cities of Syria, Asia Minor, Egypt, and Greece which contained any considerable number of Jews had one or more syna-

gogues. Thus there was one in Antioch in Pisidia (Acts xiii. 14), Iconium (ib. xiv. 1), Thessalonica (ib. xvii. 1), Berea (ib. xvii. 10), Athens (ib. xvii. 17), Corinth (ib. xviii. 4), Ephesus (ib. xviii. 19); there were several in Damascus (ib. ix. 2, 20), Salamis in Cyprus (ib. xiii. 5), Alexandria (Philo, *Opera*, ed. Mangey, ii. 565), Rome (ib. ii. 568–569), and certainly in Antioch in Syria, since the one which Josephus mentions (*War*, VII., iii. 3) was the chief synagogue. These were built within the cities, and so far as possible on the highest point and in such a way that the roof was above the roofs of the dwelling-houses; or it might happen that one was built upon the shore of a lake, the sea, or on the bank of a river. The Tosephta demands that the entrance be on the east side, after the pattern of the door of the Tabernacle; but this was not strictly carried out, and the matter was often determined by the varying circumstances. The individual turned himself for prayer toward the Holy of Holies, or, if he was not in Jerusalem, toward Jerusalem or toward Palestine. It was not prescribed that the synagogue should have a roof, and as late as the fifteenth century there were in the orient synagogues in which, as a rule, worship was conducted under the open sky. Of the internal arrangement only the following items are known. The holy ark or chest containing the holy books was opposite the entrance. The manuscripts of the law used in the reading, as also that of Esther used at the feast of Purim, had and still have the form of rolls, which was the customary form for books for the Jews from antiquity even down into the Christian era. The bema, or elevated platform in the midst of the synagogue from which the reading was conducted, is indeed not mentioned in the New Testament, but was doubtless already in use in the times of Christ (cf. Neh. viii. 4). The congregation sat (Matt. xxiii. 6; James ii. 3; Philo, ed. Mangey, ii. 458, 630), except during prayer (Matt. vi. 5; Mark xi. 25); he also sat who expounded the Scriptures (Luke iv. 20). But he who read the Scripture lesson stood, as did the one who rendered the passage into Aramaic. Neither Old Testament nor New nor earlier Jewish tradition knows of a separate part of the synagogue for women; the passage so often cited from Philo (ed. Mangey, ii. 476) is in the much later *De vita contemplativa*. The construction and care of the building were the affair of the congregation, though a private individual of wealth might assume the expense (cf. Luke vii. 5).

The administration was under the control of the religious community, which in Palestine coincided with the political body (non-Jews having no participation in either), and was under the control of elders. Officers named in the New Testament are:

3. Officers. the ruler, Gk. *archisynagogos* (Luke xiii. 14; Acts xiii. 15 speaks of " rulers "), also designated as *archōn tēs synagogēs* (Luke viii. 41), who was probably chosen from the elders and had the oversight of the worship, and also guarded against improprieties (cf. Luke xiii. 14), besides caring for the conduct of the service (Acts xiii. 15); the attendant, Gk. *hypēretēs*, Aram. *ḥazzan*, or *ḥazzan hakkeneseth* (Luke iv. 20, " minister "), who at worship brought the Scrip-

tures to the reader and replaced them in their receptacle, cared for the cleansing of the structure and its lighting, inflicted punishment by stripes (this taking place in the synagogue, Matt. x. 17, xxiii. 34; Mark xiii. 9), but it is not certain that he had the office of teacher of children. Alms were given at the door of the synagogue. Whether there was a special officer to care for this in the time of Christ is not known. The *shaliaḥ ẓibbur*, " deputy," was probably not a special officer, but the duties were probably assumed at special times by such as would undertake them (cf. on the subject E. Schürer, *Die Gemeindeverfassung der Juden in Rom in der Kaiserzeit*, Leipsic, 1879).

(H. L. Strack.)

II. The Service: In order that this should take the character of public worship, the attendance of not less than ten men was required, and from these one was chosen as leader. The charac-

1. Shema, Benediction, Shemoneh 'Esreh, Prayers. ter of the service was that of common prayer offered by a people deprived of political independence, but united upon the Torah delivered at Sinai and recognizing as the one living God him who had given that Torah. The liturgical effect was that of an act of confession. For the form of prayer the Psalms were the pattern, though the verse form is often displaced by prose; by the Middle Ages a large number of what may be called " forms of prayer " had developed, yet it must not be supposed that in the ancient period anything like a set form had arisen, although the outline was settled. An important part of the service was the recitation of the *shema'* (so called from its initial word), which comprised three passages: Deut. vi. 4–9, xi. 13–21; Num. xv. 37–41. The first and second of these are taken to enjoin the use of Tephillin (q.v.). The recitation of the shema, in which all joined, was preceded by two benedictions and followed by a third. At the beginning of the second century the chief prayer of the synagogue was the *Shemoneh 'esreh*, " eighteen (benedictions)," said to have come down from the time of Ezra and to have received their final redaction from Simeon ha-Pakoli c. 110 A.D. In Babylonia nineteen benedictions were used, the nineteenth against the " heretics " attributed to Simeon the Little. The recitation of the Shemoneh 'esreh was enjoined on all Israelites —women, children, and slaves—three times daily (after Dan. vi. 10), viz., in the morning, at the time of the afternoon offering (i.e., about three o'clock), and at evening. A fourth daily prayer was directed for those days when the law prescribed an offering additional (Hebr. *musaph*) to those usual. This addition was for the most part connected with the morning service, while on the Day of Atonement (see ATONEMENT, DAY OF) and fast-days a fifth time of prayer was added. Great importance was attached to the response to the benediction made by the people in the Amen (see LITURGICS, III., 1), by which they made the words of the leader their own. The priestly blessing was, according to Num. vi. 22–26, to be bestowed by the descendants of Aaron as often as an assemblage of Israelites for worship gave opportunity. For this purpose the priest took up his station between the ḥazzan (see above, I.,

§ 3) and the ark, facing the people; the leader uttered the blessing as the priest stood with hands shoulder high, while the congregation responded with the Amen at the end of each of the three parts of the blessing. Were no priest present, in ancient times the blessing was not uttered, as it was not regarded as a part of the service, but was considered as exclusively the duty of the priests.

It was regarded as a Mosaic ordinance that the Torah be read in public on the morning of all Sabbaths, new moons, feast-days and half-feasts, while it was believed that Ezra extended this reading to

2. Scripture Reading; Sermon. the mornings of Monday and Thursday and the afternoon of the Sabbath. While the prayer was uttered by the leader, it was the desire that as many as possible take part in the reading; on Sabbath morning at least seven were to take part, in the afternoon and on Monday and Thursday at least three, and no one was to read less than three verses; priests and Levites usually preceded in the reading. When the required number of scholars were not present, one officiated in their place, especially among the Hellenists. In the reading a method of cantillation was employed which is still in use. The Pentateuch was read through consecutively in the Sabbath and week-day readings, in Palestine in the course of three years (cf. A. Büchler, in *JQR*, v. 420 sqq., vi. 1 sqq.), being divided into weekly portions; these portions went by the Aramaic name of *sidra*, Hebr. *sedher*, but the general name for each section of Scripture was Parashah (q.v.). Special readings were selected for the four Sabbaths before Passover, festivals, half-festivals, new moons, and fast-days. It was the ḥazzan's duty before the service so to adjust the roll that it would open at once to the lesson, which was to be read standing. Special benedictions were pronounced by the first reader before the reading and by the last reader at the end. After each verse an Aramaic rendering (Hebr. *targum*) was given by an interpreter (Hebr. *methurgeman*), who in Palestine was bound not to use a written translation, not to allegorize, and to adhere to the traditional rendering. No independent position in divine service was held by the reading of prophetic selections (the name for a prophetic lection was *haphtarah*); in general such reading was limited to the morning of the Sabbath, festivals, and the Day of Atonement; as a rule, only a few verses were read, and this lesson was also rendered into Aramaic by an interpreter, who translated it three verses at a time. The first explicit testimony to this reading of the prophets is Acts xiii. 15, 27; cf. Luke iv. 16–17. The Hagiographa (see CANON OF SCRIPTURE, I., 1, 4c), with the exception of Esther, did not form a part of the reading in public. The official service consisted in the shema, the prayers, and the reading of Scripture; with this the sermon (i.e., exposition of Scripture (*midhrash, derash;* see MIDRASH) had nothing to do. Yet there is testimony (cf. L. Zunz, *Die gottesdienstlichen Vorträge der Juden*, pp. 342 sqq., Berlin, 1832) that especially on the afternoon of the Sabbath the service was followed by an exposition of the lesson, doubtless delivered in the "house of learning," provided the congregation

had one. In ancient times the sermon seems to have been connected directly with the prophetic selection; later this connection seems to have been severed, probably owing to the introduction of the musaph prayer. The preacher sat while he taught, and often an interpreter assisted him. A visiting teacher was preferred, otherwise local scholars officiated.

On any week-day the three seasons of prayer might be kept in the synagogue, and on Monday and Thursday morning the reading of the Torah (ut sup.), originally for the benefit of the country people coming to town. The rabbinical ob-

3. Festivals. servance of the **Sabbath** (q.v.) required abstention from all work, including the preparation of food, and limitation of travel to a distance within 2,000 cubits of the dwelling, which distance was extended, however, by a method of symbolic interpretation to double the distance (see WEIGHTS AND MEASURES, HEBREW). The synagogue service has been set forth above. Observance at home consisted in the lighting of the Sabbath lamps on the evening of Friday, arrangement of the Sabbath meals at the same time, the blessing of the wine before the eating of the first Sabbath meal; the celebration was closed on Saturday evening by a benediction upon wine, spices, and light, and a formula of blessing which praised God, who distinguished between profane and sacred. At **New Moon** only women refrained from work; in the public service there was reading of Scripture, the musaph prayer; individuals, when they first saw the moon, uttered a benediction (see MOON, HEBREW CONCEPTIONS OF THE). The first of Tishri, or **New Year** (see YEAR, THE HEBREW), was the first day of the common, Sabbatical, and jubilee years, and received a specially solemn character through the belief that it was the day when it was determined who should die during that year. In addition to the prayers, ten passages were read which dealt with the kingdom of God, remembrance of God, and the blowing of trumpets, the latter ceremony being regarded as an admonition to repentance and prayer. The **Passover** (q.v.) was the feast of unleavened bread (Nisan 15–21) during which leaven was scrupulously removed from the house. While the paschal lamb was no longer slaughtered, the paschal meal was regarded as a duty, including the drinking of four beakers of wine, the eating of unleavened bread, of bitter herbs, and of a dish of sweets, while there was also the recitation of a formula setting forth the meaning of the festival and of the Hallel (q.v.) in two parts, each concluded by a special benediction. According to *Pesaḥim* 37d two dishes of meat were used, recalling the Passover and the festival sacrifice. The leading thought of the celebration is the deliverance from Egypt. The first and seventh days were rest days, though preparation of food was permitted, the other days were half-festivals; the musaph prayer was used on all seven days, on the first and on the previous evening the Hallel was recited. **Pentecost** (q.v.) or the feast of weeks came fifty days from the day after the Passover Sabbath (Lev. xxiii. 15), was the harvest festival, and lasted for a single day on which no work was done; the musaph (i.e., additional) prayer was

said and the Hallel recited. The "Little" or "Second Passover" was celebrated on Iyyar 14 by those who had been unable to attend the celebration of the Passover (Num. ix. 10). The **Feast of Tabernacles** lasted eight days (Tishri 15–22), of which the first and last were full festivals and the others were half-festivals. The musaph prayer and the Hallel were recited each day; the distinctive features were the eating and sleeping in booths, the carrying of a palm with myrtle and willow branches and a citron. The seventh day was known as the day of willows, since on that day the floor was beaten with willow branches. In the post-Talmudic period the Jews encircled the reading-desk in procession carrying the palms, etc., and singing special songs with the refrain Hosanna. In Babylon, where the Pentateuch was read through in a year, the conclusion of the reading took place on what was there the ninth day of the festival, which gave rise to the feast of "the rejoicing of the Torah." The **Feast of Dedication** (Kislew 25–Tebet 3) was instituted by Judas Maccabeus (I Macc. iv. 59) to celebrate the rededication of the sanctuary, and, according to II Macc. i. 9, 18, ii. 10, x. 8, was generally observed by carrying branches and singing songs of praise. Ps. xxx. seems from its title to have been especially composed for this occasion. Jewish tradition enjoins recitation of the Hallel and the Shemoneh 'esreh daily, but no cessation of work or musaph prayer. Josephus calls it the "feast of lights," and in each house at least one lamp was to be lighted and placed before the house. **Purim** was celebrated on a day between Adar 11 and 15, and recalled the deliverance recounted in the book of Esther. The Shemoneh 'esreh was recited, and the universal obligation was to read or hear read the book of Esther. It was a festival marked by the giving of presents and alms. See FEASTS AND FESTIVALS, I.

On the Day of Atonement (see ATONEMENT, DAY OF; also KOL NIDRE) food, work, and anointing of oneself were prohibited during the entire twenty-four hours; the musaph and neila (the name given to the last of the services on the Day of Atonement; *JE*, ix. 214–222) prayers were recited, and confession of sin characterized the prayers of this day.

4. Fasts. The killing of a cock, now found in the ritual, is post-Talmudic in origin. Other fasts were both public and private. In Palestine the one public fast outside of the Day of Atonement was the ninth of Ab, observed in commemoration of the destruction of the Temple by the Chaldeans and the Romans and the taking of Bittir in the insurrection of Bar Kokba (q.v.). From the first of the month pleasures were eliminated, while the week in which the ninth fell was one of lamentation. On the eighth of Ab there was abstention from wine and meat, and on the ninth a total fast. In Babylonia Tammuz 17 was a public fast, commemorating the taking of Jerusalem by the Chaldeans (Jer. xxxix. 2), and the setting up of an idol in the Temple by the Romans; there, too, Tishri 3 was observed to commemorate the killing of Gedaliah (Jer. xli. 2), also Tebet 10 commemorated by a fast the day of the beginning of the Chaldean siege of Jerusalem. Clearly, after the destruction of Jerusalem by the Romans, the ancient fasts mentioned

by Zechariah (viii. 19) were revived. The fast of Adar 13, commemorating the day on which, according to the counsel of Haman, the Jews were to be destroyed, is not ancient. The Palestinians seem later to have had three fast-days after Purim (Monday, Thursday, and the following Monday), while the Babylonian Jews celebrated these in advance. Extraordinary fast-days might be appointed by a community in time of distress, but they might not fall upon the Sabbath, new moon, or a feast-day; moreover, fast-days were not to succeed each other without the interposition of other days (cf. Monday, Thursday, and Monday above). The public service of a fast was by preference celebrated in the open, and the participants had ashes on their heads. There was an exhortation to repentance, the Shemoneh 'esreh, six selections from Scripture and benedictions were interpolated; so there arose a prayer with twenty-four benedictions.

III. **The Jewish Calendar:** For the Jewish year and week see YEAR, THE HEBREW; and WEEK. The settlement of the calendar was claimed as a prerogative by Palestinian Jews, and the announcement of the new moon was made in early times by beacon fires and later by messenger, though only in the six months in which feasts fell. The most important months in the fixing of the calendar were Nisan and Tishri, since the indication of the days of celebration appointed by the law hinged upon them. Outside of Palestine, observances covered two days (except that of the Day of Atonement) because of uncertainty as to the time of beginning the month. But, owing to the matter of intercalating a month in certain years, the calendar was long in confusion, and the first fixed system was introduced by Hillel II. (c. 350 A.D.), who provided for seven leap-years in every period of nineteen years, and fixed also the years which should have six months each with twenty-nine and thirty days and what years should have five and which seven months with twenty-nine or with thirty days each. While it is usually stated that since the second century before Christ the Jews employed the Greek era, and I Macc. uses this method of dating, there were later in use in Palestine a number of eras. The method of counting from creation is medieval in origin, the year of creation being equivalent to 3761 B.C. Aids in computation of time are G. A. Jahn, *Tafeln zur gegenseitigen Verwandlung jüdischer und christlicher Zeitangaben* (Leipsic, 1856); H. Schlesinger, *Hundert Tabellen* (Creuznach, 1862); B. Zuckermann, *Anleitung und Tabellen zur Vergleichung jüdischer und christlicher Zeitangaben* (Breslau, 1893); and M. Simon and L. Cohen, *Ein neuer Maphteach* (Berlin, 1897).

(G. DALMAN.)

BIBLIOGRAPHY: Maimonides, *Hilchoth Tephilla*, in Germ. transl. of "Works," i. 257–341, 10 vols., St. Petersburg, 1850–52; L. Zunz, *Die gottesdienstlichen Vorträge der Juden*, 2d ed., Frankfort, 1892; also, *Die synagogale Poesie des Mittelalters*, 2 vols., Berlin, 1855–59; idem, *Litteraturgeschichte der synagogalen Poesie*, ib. 1865; C. Vitringa, *De synagoga vetere*, Franeker, 1696; J. Buxtorf, *Synagoga Judaica*, Hanau, 1604, and often, e.g., Leipsic, 1737; S. J. Cohen, *Historisch-kritische Darstellung des jüdischen Gottesdienstes, und dessen Modifikationen*, Leipsic, 1819; A. T. Hartmann, *Die enge Verbindung des A. T. mit dem Neuen*, pp. 225–376, Hamburg, 1831; A. Geiger, *Der Hamburger Tempelstreit*, Breslau, 1842; idem, in *Nachgelassene Schriften*, i. 203 sqq., 283–295. Berlin, 1875; idem, *Israeli-*

tisches Gebetbuch, 2 vols., ib. 1870; J. M. Jost, Geschichte des Judentums und seiner Secten, Leipsic, 1857; M. Duschak, Geschichte und Darstellung des jüdischen Cultus, Mannheim, 1866; Sieffert, in Beweis des Glaubens, 1876, pp. 3–11, 225–239; J. Hamburger, Real-Encyklopädie für Bibel und Talmud, ii. 1142–47, Strelitz, 1883; A. Edersheim, Life and Times of Jesus the Messiah, i. 430–450, London, 1884; I. Abrahams, Jewish Life in the Middle Ages, pp. 1–34, New York, 1896; Weinberg, in Monatsschrift für Geschichte und Wissenschaft des Judenthums, 1897, pp. 588 sqq., 639 sqq., 673 sqq.; L. Löw, in Gesammelte Schriften, iv. 1–71, Szegedin, 1898; J. Elbogen, Geschichte des Achtzehngebets, Breslau, 1903; idem, Studien zur Geschichte des jüdischen Gottesdienstes, Berlin, 1908; L. Stern, Die Vorschriften der Thora, 4th ed., Frankfort, 1904; A. Kistner, Der Kalender der Juden, Carlsruhe, 1905; P. Haupt, "Purim," in JBL, 1906, and Leipsic, 1906; O. Holtzmann, Neutestamentliche Zeitgeschichte, 2d ed., Tübingen, 1906; M. Rosenmann, Der Ursprung der Synagoge und ihre allmähliche Entwickelung, Berlin, 1907; W. O. E. Oesterley and G. H. Box, The Religion and Worship of the Synagogue: an Introduction to the Study of Judaism from the New Testament Period, New York, 1907; E. Schürer, Geschichte, ii. 427–463, Eng. transl., II., ii. 52–89; Nowack, Archäologie, ii. 83 sqq.; DB, iv. 636–643; EB, iv. 4832–40; JE, xi. 619–640. The subject is discussed in many of the works on the history of the Jews (see under Ahab; and Israel, History of).

On the worship consult: C. G. Bodenschatz, Kirchliche Verfassung der heutgen Juden, part ii., Leipsic, 1748; J. F. Schröder, Satzungen und Gebräuche des talmudisch-rabbinischen Judenthums, Bremen, 1851; L. M. Lewinsohn, Geschichte und System des jüdischen Kalenderwesens, 1856; F. Delitzsch, Physiologie und Musik, pp. 44–57, Leipsic, 1868; M. H. Friedländer, Beiträge zur Geschichte der synagogalen Gebete, Brünn, 1869; Rothschild, Der Synagogalkultus in historisch-kritische Entwickelung, vol. i., Alzey, 1870; A. Schwarz, Der jüdische Kalendar, Breslau, 1872; J. Dessauer, Schlüssel zum Gebetbuche, Budapest, 1878; H. Guedallah, Observations on the Jewish Ritual of the Present Time, London, 1885; J. Singer, Die Tonarten des traditionellen Synagogengesanges, Vienna, 1886; A. H. Lawatsch, Das Synagogenjahr, 2d ed., Reichenberg, 1887; L. Stern, Die Vorschriften der Thora, 3d ed., Frankfort, 1895; J. Winter and A. Wünsche, Die jüdische Litteratur, iii. 477–529, Treves, 1896; J. M. Japhet, Die Accente der heiligen Schrift, pp. 167–184, Frankfort, 1896; E. Breslaur, Sind originale Synagogen- und Volksmelodien bei den Juden . . . nachweisbar? Leipsic, 1898; L. N. Dembitz, Jewish Services in Synagogue and Home, Philadelphia, 1898 (popular); T. Schärf, Das gottesdienstliche Jahr bei den Juden, Leipsic, 1902; L. Zunz, ut sup.; also the works of Geiger, Duschak, Elbogen, Stern, Kistner, and Oesterley and Box in the preceding paragraph.

SYNAGOGUE, THE GREAT: According to Talmudic and rabbinic tradition, a council established in the time of Ezra and Nehemiah, consisting of 120 members, and lasting till the beginning of the Greek period, which was concerned principally with the law and the ordering of life according to that law. Especially to this body were attributed the settling of the Canon of Scripture (q.v., I., 1, § 2), the masoretic marginal notes, the punctuation or pointing of the text, the composition of prayers, and directions respecting prayer and the like. As support for the theory of the existence of this body, the report in Neh. viii.–x. regarding the reading of the law by Ezra was cited, together with the assembly in which the people obligated itself to keep perpetually the law. The number 120 is found there (Neh. x. 128—comprising eighty-five subscribers to the obligation, with Ezra as the eighty-sixth) and the twenty-six (Neh. viii. 4, 7), who supported Ezra at the reading of the law, together with eight Levites (Neh. ix. 5–6) who prayed and sang. That from these three chapters no cogent proof for the existence of the Great Synagogue is deducible needs no

proof. The most complete assemblage of passages from Jewish literature bearing on the subject is found in Rau, Buxtorf, and Aurivillius (see bibliography).

All testimonies for the existence and activities (as outlined above) of this body are late. The oldest passages relatively are Pirke Aboth, i. 1–2 [cf. C. Taylor, Sayings of the Jewish Fathers, pp. 124–125, Cambridge, 1877], and Baba Bathra, 15a, in the Babylonian Talmud. In the first passage " the men of the Great Synagogue " appear simply as the mediators of the law (torah) between the prophets on the one side and Antigonus of Socho and his followers on the other. Simon the Just, i.e., probably the high-priest Simon I. at the beginning of the third century before Christ, is designated as belonging to the remnant of the Great Synagogue, so that with him or soon after him the body ceased to exist. Now, since the period between the rebuilding of the Temple and the overthrow of Persian rule in Palestine (516–331) is compressed to thirty-four years, the traditional conception of a body which continued for more than a century has here no firm basis. The passage from Baba Bathra reads: " The men of the Great Synagogue wrote Ezekiel, The Twelve, Daniel, and Esther. Ezra wrote his book and the genealogies in Chronicles up to his time." Of the closing of the canon there is here no mention; the subject dealt with is only the authorship (editing?) of the books which are recognized as the latest. From the nature of the relations existing and from some indications in the Bible (such as the reference to Ezra in Ezra vii. 6 as a ready scribe in the law of Moses) it may be concluded that activities corresponding to those attributed to the Great Synagogue actually were carried on. It is a fact that since the time of Ezra Jewish life was under the domination of the law and was characterized by that very fact. So that while the Great Synagogue can not be established as historical, yet the activities attributed to it were actually in operation through some medium then authoritative, and it is upon these activities that the tradition cited was in fact based.

(H. L. Strack.)

Bibliography: The modern hypothesis regarding the existence of this body depends upon J. Buxtorf's Tiberias, chap. x., Basel, 1665, and Elias Levita's Massoreth ha-Massoreth, ed. Ginsburg, pp. 112 sqq., London, 1867. That the question is now answered in the negative is due principally to H. E. Ryle, Canon of the O. T., Excursus A, pp. 250 sqq., London, 1892, and A. Kuenen, Over de mannen der groote Synagoge, Amsterdam, 1876, Germ. transl., Ueber die Männer der grossen Synagoge, in Gesammelte Abhandlungen, pp. 125–160, Freiburg, 1894. The subject will be found treated in most of the recent larger treatises on the introduction to the O. T. and on the canon—e.g., C. A. Briggs, Study of Holy Scripture, pp. 120–122, 252 sqq., New York, 1899. Consult further: J. E. Rau, Diatribe de synagoga magna, Utrecht, 1727; C. Aurivillius, Dissertationes, ed. J. D. Michaelis, pp. 139–160, Leipsic, 1790; A. T. Hartmann, Die Verbindung des A. Ts. mit dem Neuen, pp. 120–166, Hamburg, 1831; M. Heidenheim, in TSK, 1553, pp. 93–100; L. Herzfeld, Geschichte des Volkes Jisrael, ii. 22–24, 380–396, iii. 244–245, 270–271, Nordhausen, 1855–57; J. M. Jost, Geschichte des Judenthums, i. 41–43, 91, 95–97, Leipsic, 1857; J. E. Löwy, Kritisch-talmudisches Lexikon, i. 241–261, Vienna, 1863; J. Derenbourg, Essai sur l'histoire et la géographie de la Palestine, i. 29–40, Paris, 1867; J. S. Bloch, Studien zur Geschichte der Sammlung der althebräischen Litteratur, pp. 100–132, Breslau, 1876; J. Hamburger, Real-Encyklopädie für Bibel und Talmud, ii. 318–323, Strelitz, 1883;

D. Hoffmann, in *Magazin für die Wissenschaft des Juden-thums*, x (1883), 45–63; L. Löw, *Gesammelte Schriften*, pp. 399–449, Szegedin, 1889; S. Krauss, in *JQR*, x (1898), 347–377; *JE*, xi. 640–643.

SYNAXARIUM. See Acta Martyrum, Acta Sanctorum, II., § 1.

SYNCELLUS: The title of certain high ecclesiastical officers in the Eastern Church. The name signifies literally " one who shares a cell," and was attached to monks and clergy associated with high ecclesiastics. The patriarchs and metropolitans of Constantinople had from early times one or more of these officers, the chief of the patriarch's being

called " the great protosyncellus." The (patriarchal) syncelli took precedence of the metropolitan at festivals, though later this precedence was contested. They were usually the confessors of the patriarchs, and hence were often employed as spies by the emperors, who sometimes conferred the title upon archbishops and bishops. They were not unknown in the Western Church, and a synod held by Gregory I. in 595 issued regulations concerning them. (Philipp Meyer.)

Bibliography: L. Thomassin, *De vetere et nova ecclesiæ disciplina*, I., ii., Frankfort, 1787; Milasch, *Das Kirchen-recht der morgenländischen Kirche*, Mostar, 1905; *DCA*, ii. 1947–48.

SYNCRETISM, SYNCRETISTIC CONTROVERSIES.

Syncretism refers in general to the union of opponents on a basis which they hold in common, and so applies to philosophy and organized religion; in particular, to the irenic movement arising from an effort within the Lutheran Church in the seventeenth century toward interconfessional union, the sole final result of which was the moderation of the theological spirit. Syncretistic controversies is a phrase summing up the conflict waged between the partizans and opponents of the movement.

I. Syncretism: The only mention of the term in ancient literature is that of Plutarch, who, in illustrating brotherly love, cites the example of the Cretans, stating that they make war upon one another, but in the face of attack unite against a common enemy. It was resuscitated by Erasmus (q.v.), who, in *Adagia*, criticed the practise, yet in a letter to Melanchthon (1519) proposed a common (*synkretizein*) defense of the learned against their opponents, although not wholly in accord among themselves. In a letter of Zwingli (q.v.) to Œcolampadius (q.v.) and other clerics of Basel (in Zwingli's *Opera*, ed. Schuler and Schulthess, vii. 390), the former urged a syncretistic union against the persecutions arising over the Eucharist, and soon after both term and conception became prominent in the peace negotiations of M. Butzer (q.v.), and in the vocabulary of humanists in general. Zacharias Ursinus (q.v.) applied it likewise to the wicked, speaking of their " syncretism " and conspiracy against God. In the first half of the seventeenth century the twofold value of censure and praise continued, although the term acquired an increasingly sinister significance as the unpopularity of the concord with dissenters increased during the time in which dogmas became more and more fixed. The Roman Catholic theologian Paul Windeck predicted, in *Prognosticon futuri status ecclesiæ* (1603), the speedy fall of Protestantism, and admonished those of his own church to cultivate " syncretism," which called forth the *Irenicum sive de unione Evangelicorum concilianda* (Heidelberg, 1614–15) of David Pareus (q.v.), summoning the two Protestant bodies to a peaceful conciliation against the common foe.

1. Origin of the Term.

2. Misuse of the Term.

The Jesuit Adam Contzen attacked the proposition of Pareus with *De pace Germaniæ* (Mainz, 1616) in two books, the first of which is superscribed *De syncretismus*. He omitted no effort before the Thirty Years' War to incite the Lutherans against the Reformed in order to avert an anti-Catholic union. Two years before the Synod of Dort he pointed to the alleged effort of the stricter Reformed to suppress the moderate, charging them with *syncretissare*, which, according to Titus i. 12, they had ascribed to others; and he in eighteen chapters suggested numerous reasons against fellowship with the revolutionary Reformed. In the next three decades of the war, the term as well as the thing to which it applied retired to the background.

Toward the middle of the century, however, there developed a tendency in the direction of the finality and authority of dogma, specially in the Lutheran and Roman Catholic Churches. This necessarily involved the perpetuity of differences and divisions within the Church. Against this Georg Calixtus (q.v.) protested, denouncing it as a cause for shame in Christianity, and the theology crystallized for this purpose as barbarism. He brought to recognition the differences between the more and the less fundamental doctrines, proposed to refer those basic doctrines which by common consent were less important to the schools for further development, and desired to see a closer affiliation established, at least between the Lutheran and Reformed Churches. But with the events of 1645 (see below), the irenics of Calixtus only served to irritate the Lutherans and Roman Catholics. Before the Conference of Thorn (q.v.) two published briefs from Wittenberg counseled against " syncretism." The Jesuit Voit Ebermann, in *Eirenikon catholicum* (Mainz, 1645), objected to the irenics of Calixtus, holding that there could be no more dangerous heresy than that all who could assent to the apostolic symbol should therefore feel themselves as one; because it would admit to unity those otherwise at variance, or lead to a false appearance deceiving both themselves and others. Thereby the union not only of individuals of different religions but of the discordant religions themselves would receive endorsement. Perhaps from this arose the false assumption that the demand for an alliance of partially dissenting persons on the basis of their consensus meant a jumbling together of religions. At any rate the term came to be wrenched from its original practical sense and was forcibly applied to a confused mixing of religions, and later was strained even to the extent that it was derived from *synkerannumi* (" to mix up "). The theologian J. K. Dannhauer, *Mysterium syncretismi detecti* (Strasburg, 1648), who includes all combinations of the unlike under syncretism and compares the perfection of the Lutheran doctrine with the eye that cannot stand a particle of dust, and Abraham Calovius (q.v.), raised the point against Calixtus that the term signified things irreconcilably different, such as the Lutheran and Reformed Churches. This is the only meaning implied in the term in the controversies; but even syncretists like Calixtus declined the epithet. Its original laudable meaning gradually disappeared; so that the incorrect meaning of a perverse attempt at combining unlike and irreconcilable elements of truth persisted. The recent attempts, by reason of the historical tendency in theology, to show Christianity at the beginning as syncretistic (H. Gunkel), or the old Catholic Christianity of c. 250 as a syncretistic religion (A. Harnack), has invested the term with a new importance.

II. Syncretistic Controversies: Three periods may be noted, separated by seasons of quiet: namely from the Conference of Thorn till the death of Calixtus, 1645–56; from the colloquies of Hesse-Cassel and Berlin till the order of silence to the Saxon theologians, 1661–69; and the last struggles of Calovius for the Consensus and against Johann Musæus (q.v.), until his death, 1675–86. All the efforts before 1645 to bring together the Lutheran and Reformed Churches may be considered as preliminary to the controversies. In reply to an appealed question the general synod of the French Reformed Church at Charenton in 1631 instructed, upon the basis of the essential agreement of the churches of the Augsburg Confession and the other Reformed churches and of the absence of superstition and idolatry from their worship, that in the French churches those Lutherans who approached in the spirit of friendship and peace should be admitted to the communion without abjuration; and that such could as sponsors present children for baptism, if they only promised the consistory that they would never incite those so baptized to transgress the doctrine received in those churches, and that they would bring them up in the instruction of those articles of doctrine on which there was agreement. This was approved also by many of the strictest Reformed theologians outside of France, but aroused violent attacks from the Roman Catholics in France against Protestant union. The principle of a union of the unlike upon the fundamental of faith was alleged to be the foundation of a new sect, namely, the neutralists, the worst heresy of all, because it led to the renouncing of all love for their own religion, obligated to indifferentism, and

1. The Synod of Charenton.

led to heresy (F. Véron). Others claimed to see in it an apostasy from the faith of their fathers, a violence done to the constitution, i.e., the Edict of Nantes, thus releasing Roman Catholics from the observance of the latter.

1. The First Period: Georg Calixtus (q.v.; ut sup.), by his extensive travel and acquaintance and his comprehensive studies, had acquired a broader irenic attitude toward the confessional bodies and a more real appreciation of the relative inner truth and value of the dogmas than most Lutheran theologians of his time. He looked with concern upon the crystallization of theology and the ecclesiastical authorization of fixed dogma as a menace to free investigation, the peace of the Church, and the hope of Protestantism. This variance with the trend of the times was apparent in his many writings. He naturally aroused the ill-will of the guardians of orthodoxy and self-assumed sole defenders of the Reformation and drew their attacks, such as the attempted refutation at the convention of theologians at Jena, 1621; and the polemic of Statius Büschser, later entitled *Cryptopapismus theologiæ Helmstadiensis* (1640). But the open assault of orthodoxy upon Calixtus and his Helmstedt colleagues was first occasioned by the events of 1645 and 1648. When King Ladislaus IV. of Poland issued the call for the Conference of Thorn, Calixtus not only circulated and commended the proclamation by a writing of his own, but also sought appointment as a delegate. Hereby he drew upon himself the enmity of the East Prussians, who were engaged in a struggle against union with their ruler, the Reformed elector of Brandenburg, and were led by Cölestin Myslenta (1588–1653) of Königsberg and Abraham Calovius (q.v.) of Danzig (then Polish). The latter prevented the election of Calixtus from Danzig; then, when the elector delegated him from Königsberg, Calovius succeeded in having him barred from the chairmanship of the Lutheran collocutors, a post which was secured for Johann Hülsemann (q.v.) of Wittenberg, and even from entering the conference at all as a Lutheran, as well as a representative for the towns of Thorn and Elbing. Nevertheless, Calixtus rendered the valuable service of his learning and counsel to the Reformed. Next, as Elector Johann Georg I. of Saxony had forbidden all innovations from theological conventions, the theologians of that electorate united with Hülsemann in a joint memoir (Dec. 29, 1647) accusing the theologians of Helmstedt with innovations and departures from the Augsburg Confession and with undermining the foundations of Evangelical doctrine. In reply Calixtus branded his accuser, whoever he might be, as an infamous calumniator, until he had proved his charges. This set the opposition in the succeeding years to watch for every possible deviation on the part of the Helmstedt theologians and to denounce it as a departure, inviting the inference that efforts for union were untrustworthy. In Prussia the elector replaced Calovius at Königsberg with C. Dreier, and appointed as professor of theology J. Latemann, respectively friend and pupil of Calixtus. Myslenta and his supporters invited a joint *Censuræ theologorum ortho-*

1. In Prussia.

doxorum (1648) of all opponents of the Reformed, in condemnation of their new colleagues. Calovius used the term " syncretism " as one of the springs of ruin, and hence " syncretist " fastened itself more and more to the " more moderate theologians " of Helmstedt and the tendency which they represented. The battle continued in Prussia with literary broadsides pro and con until after the death of Myslenta.

Political jealousy and strife also played their part in the controversies. For years the electorate of **2. In Electoral Saxony.** Saxony had sought to prevent the grant of an equal status to the Reformed, in favor of the other two electorates, of the Palatinate and Brandenburg; but, in the Peace of Westphalia (see WESTPHALIA, PEACE OF) its aim was defeated. Equality of religious practise was sustained. The Reformed professed themselves adherents of the Augsburg Confession as a genus to which the two bodies were as species, to which electoral Saxony objected in vain (1649). Even the assignment as director of the *Corpus Evangelicorum* (1653) could not compensate for the humiliation of Saxony. The theologians of Wittenberg and Leipsic made a report that the theologians of Helmstedt were astray not only on the necessity of good works, but also on almost every article of faith, and Johann Georg bade them to set this forth " article by article " (Jan. 21, 1648). On June 16, 1649, the elector issued an address to the three dukes of Brunswick, who maintained Helmstedt as their joint university, personally assuming all the charges against Calixtus, whom he accused of patching together a new religion and introducing violent schisms. He asked that the theologians of Helmstedt be prohibited from issuing polemics against his theologians, and invited the dukes to a proposed alliance of Evangelical states for restrictive measures, under threat of assuming protection against schism. On the other side, the dukes of Brunswick had commissioned Konrad Horneius (q.v.) to prepare an apology against the Königsberg censures (ut sup.) and requested an exposition in German of the points (1) on the authority of the ancient Church, (2) good works, (3) the New-Testament proof of the Trinity, (4) the theophanies of the Old Testament, and (5) the unity of dissidents charged as " syncretists." Calixtus elaborated the third and fourth points, *Num mysterium trinitatis e solius*, etc. (1649). Now, he furnished an apology against Johann Georg's address, and the dukes of Brunswick in joint reply to the latter (1650) offered to acquiesce in the suppression of the polemical writings of their theologians, provisionally, if he would take the same steps, and proposed a convention to devise counsels against schisms in behalf of peace, but intimated resistance to the threatened directorate, if the same implied the assertion of superiority by force. But the elector only consented to a more vehement polemic. The call of Calovius to a professorship at Wittenberg meant the concentration of forces and occurred amid fresh polemical explosions. Hülsemann issued *Dialysis apologetica problematis Calixtini num mysterium trinitatis* (1649); *Judicium de Calixtino desiderio concordiæ ecclesiasticæ* (1650); and, finally, *Der*

calixtinische Gewissenswurm (1654), a work exceeding 1,600 pages. Most active was Calovius, who produced, besides his wailing inaugural, *Consideratio novæ theologiæ Helmstadioregiomontanorum syncretistarum* (1649); and *Syncretismus Calixtinus* (1653). Ninety-eight heresies of Calixtus were collected and a conference of theologians demanded by the party of Calovius; but this effort failed owing to the wise suspicion of the dukes of Saxony, who were first invited, and the Jena theologians, that the veiled pretension concealed the design of a joint attack upon the dukes of Brunswick, their exclusion from the Lutheran body, and, consequently, a widening of the schism. At the most recent diet at Regensburg, twenty-four Evangelical estates had united in a call for a conference of peaceable theologians and state representatives and in an appeal for silence on the part of both theological factions. But Johann Georg, upon whom, as director of the *corpus Evangelicorum*, first action devolved, gave heed to neither. His theologians now clamored for the expulsion of the Helmstedt party from the Lutheran Church on the basis of the ninety-eight heresies. *A consensus repetitus fidei vere Lutheranæ* was drawn up as a new confession. In eighty-six parts, following the order of the Augsburg Confession, it was arranged, each according to the scheme of (1) the right doctrine (*profitemur*); (2) the dissidence of the Helmstedt faction (*rejicimus*); (3) proofs from the writings of the latter (*ita docet*). Subscribed first by the Leipsic and Wittenberg theologians, the signatures of others were sought by a fresh productivity of the pen of Calovius; *Harmonia Calixtina-hæretica* (1655) of 1,200 quarto pages; *Systema locorum theologicorum* (2 vols., 1655); and *Fides veterum et imprimis fidelium mundi antediluviani in Christum* (1655), in which the heresies of Calixtus were mentioned as the " excrements of Satan." But the acceptance of the confession elsewhere could not be secured, and the death of Calixtus, 1656, followed the same year by that of Johann Georg, produced a lull in the storm.

2. The Second Period: The peace of Westphalia had restored the more Lutheran parts of North Hesse to the Reformed rule of Cassel, including, practically, the control of Schaumburg and the University of Rinteln. The policy of **1. In Hesse-Cassel.** Landgrave Wilhelm VI. was broad and lenient enough under the liberal church order to effect the union of Lutheran and Reformed elements. The University of Magdeburg, reopened in 1653, was pledged to promote " the ecclesiastical peace and concord of all Protestants," and to a mediating theology. Further, to promote the union and abate partizan hatred, the landgrave called a colloquy at Cassel June 1–9, 1661. When the Wittenberg theologians, Calovius, J. A. Quenstedt, and Johann Deutschmann (qq.v.) heard of it eight months later, they issued a violent attack, *Epicrisis de colloquio Casselano Rintelio-Marpurgensium* (1662) which they despatched far and wide to the faculties and ministeria. In consequence, the three faculties of Saxony united in a representation to the theologians of Rinteln in which the repudiation of the elenchus against the Reformed and of their condemnation in worship were pressed upon them as errors, and a retraction or closer explanation was urged. Before the receipt of this the Rinteln theologians had replied with an *Epistola apologetica* (1662). For the people H. M. Eckart prepared a memoir (1662) setting forth that by schisms the Church violated its foremost mark of distinction, the commandment of love, and made itself the laughing-stock of the wicked; that it was specially incumbent upon Protestants to remove the disgrace; and, without mixing confessions or organizations, to promote amity and peace. The more violently incensed by their failure, the Wittenberg theologians now published their *Epicrisis* (1663), with a preface in which they threatened another edition of collective censures, this time against the theologians of Rinteln. This was followed by a fusillade of polemical writings, among which *De puncto discrepitatione inter Lutheranos et Calvinianos* (1664) by Andreas Kühn; and by Calovius a *Grundlicher Beweis* (1664) of 1,000 pages, to the effect that the Calvinistic error threatened the syncretistic innovation at Rinteln, followed by an *Antapologia* (Wittenberg, 1666) of 700 quarto pages, a resumé of all points of contention from Calvin to the Rinteln colloquy.

The renewal of this controversy soon brought on its revival in Prussia and Brandenburg. In Königsberg, Dreier had been protesting against the stigmatization of the efforts for church peace as syncretism, and declared that the common faith must be sought in the ancient Church and not in the sum of contents of the new confessions. The great elector of Brandenburg, Friedrich Wilhelm, following the example of his brother-in-law, Landgrave Wilhelm, in an edict (June 2, 1662) deplored the schisms and local religious demoralization, and enjoined that clergy to be appointed must be pledged to silence except as to what is edifying. He called a colloquy (Sept., 1662–May, 1663) at Berlin, of three theologians from each party. But the suspicions and over-scrupulousness of the Lutherans (instigated from Wittenberg) to relent in the condemnation of points rejected by their confessions defeated the effort. A new edict of Sept. 16, 1664, forbade the use of abusive epithets and the attributing of doctrines to their opponents not acknowledged by them. Soon after a pledge was demanded of all the clergy to this and previous edicts. In vain the Lutheran clergy of Berlin made appeal to the universities and ministeria. The elector summoned them before the consistory and demanded the pledge under pain of removal. E. S. Reinhardt and C. Lilius, and finally Paul Gerhardt (q.v.) lost their positions. By an order of June 6, 1667, the pledge was no longer demanded, but strict maintenance of the edict was now enjoined upon the consistory. A declaration of May 6, 1668, guaranteed to the Lutherans not only full religious liberty, but the peaceful discussion of disputed points.

The Wittenberg theologians meantime resumed a fresh onslaught on the syncretists. They published their great collection of *Consilia theologica Witebergensia* (1664), including the *Consensus repetitus fidei vere Lutheranæ* (ut sup.) retired since 1655. Calovius issued a special edition in 1666 with a

2. In Prussia and Brandenburg.

preface, with express reference to the syncretism at Rinteln and a " synopsis of the errors of Calixtus and his accomplices." The obvious purpose was the exclusion of all syncretists from the Lutheran Church, and, in a less degree, the binding of all other Lutherans under a new confession, including such eccentric doctrines as the knowledge of Old-Testament believers of the whole doctrine of the Trinity, the real faith of baptized infants, and the ubiquity of the human nature of Christ to all believers. The main effect of its adoption would have been the rehabilitation of the idea of the one true church, visible and invisible, namely, the Lutheran, with an absolute, unimprovable body of dogma as an exclusive ecclesiastical norm. Friedrich Ulrich Calixtus took up the defense of all his father's particular ideas, publishing *Demonstrata liquidissima* (1667), a running commentary on the Consensus, attempting sometimes to show the baselessness of the meanings attributed to his father and his followers, sometimes the accordance of these with the confessions, and sometimes the intrusion of the opinions of the authors into the Consensus as though they were doctrines of the church, thus opening the arbitrary multiplication of dogmas indefinitely. A new and professional disputant appeared at Wittenberg, Ægidius Strauch, who in a *Vindicatus* (1668) discharged a flood of mendacious invective and sophistry against the younger Calixtus. This was followed by *De Deo uno* (1667) by Deutschmann, son-in-law of Calovius, who, in turn, followed with *Locos et controversias syntagmatis antisyncretistici* (1668), in which the tabulated Calixtine errors reached the number of 120. Calixtus answered the last two with writings, and against Strauch he brought formal charges of libel. Strauch responded by a joint legal opinion of the juristic faculties of the three universities, and now the conflict was waged back and forth from behind the battlements of legal authorities, while the polemics of Strauch, said to have been prepared by Calovius, now produced in German, greatly incensed the public.

3. The Wittenberg Consensus.

Seeing that the proposed Consensus threatened the freedom of learning in the universities and might further disrupt the Lutheran Church, and jeopardized the benefits of the treaty of Westphalia over against the Roman Catholics, the university now put forth an abler champion, Hermann Conring (q.v.), who, in *Pietas academiæ Juliæ*, made reply to Strauch and others. He maintained that there was no school of Calixtus and none desired by him; that the latter regarded free inquiry as the safeguard of the Church. Helmstedt had been singled out because here the Word of God was treated as trustworthy and of itself authentic, while the confessions were treated impartially and considered valid in so far as they accord with Scripture. Calovius confounds heresy with error, whereas the Calixtine ideas do not violate express dogmas. The masses are not to be thrown into religious confusion with these controversial questions; yet the intelligent are not to be denied a voice in the acceptance of a new confession. The Consensus should first be proved by Scripture; and the princes must exercise their

4. Hermann Conring.

responsible offices for the restoration of order, for they (the clergy) who excite the tumult are not the ones to allay it. A German edition of the above, entitled *Schutzrede der Juliusuniversität*, issued shortly after by C. Schrader, summed up the judgment upon the Consensus, that (1), according to the scheme, the *profitemur* is not invariably the universal confession of the Lutheran Church; (2) *rejicimus* is opposed to liberty and promotes schism; and (3) *ita docet*, the doctrines attributed to Calixtus and Horneius are unwarranted and untruly represented. Even the pope was slow to decree new articles of belief and not until after prolonged investigation with the cardinals and councils. Calovius dismisses without notice the greater number of adherents of the Augsburg Confession, sums up the mass of disputed points, and in the heat of haste forges a number of antagonistic tenets, which henceforth are to be called Lutheran. Those who do not approve of the intruded symbols are to be thrust out of the fellowship of the saints; and this is not the end, but the process is to be perpetual. As the Galatians refused circumcision (Gal. v. 1–2), so they will decline the Consensus. These writings, scattered among courts, consistories, and universities, had the effect of arousing apprehension; for if it came to be accepted that those not recognizing the Consensus were out of the Lutheran Church, they might lose the benefits of the treaty of Westphalia, a result not far removed from the motive of Calovius. Duke Friedrich Wilhelm of Saxe-Altenburg now sought to counteract further separation and passion, and induced his brother-in-law, Elector Johann Georg III., to give audience to the theologians of Wittenberg. Their long report of Apr. 22, 1669, may be summed up as follows: (1) continuance of the refutation; or (2) a synod, or rather, since no examination of the Helmstedt doctrine is further necessary, letters of communication for sounding the opinion and binding together the orthodox; (3) that first the theologians of electoral Saxony get the consensus of other theologians before the elector refers to other potentates; (4) amendment of the code for the clerical and political ministries with a clause forbidding syncretism, the mixing of religions, ecclesiastical toleration, and spiritual affiliation with papists and Calvinists, or its equivalent, subscription to the Consensus; (5) compulsory binding of the Brunswick theologians to their old confessions without reservation, which latter "knavery" is not to be tolerated by any Christian government. Though approved by the elector, the effect of which as well as the advice of the counselors was to perpetuate the quarrel, yet the alarm sounded by Conring and the theologians of Helmstedt was not without results, for the order given in Saxony to refrain from literary polemics was heeded for several years.

An interim of quiet followed, 1669–79. Duke Ernst the Pious, successor to Friedrich Wilhelm of

5. The Counsel of Spener. Saxony, made an alliance with his son-in-law, Ludwig VI. of Hesse-Darmstadt, and conceived the preventive of a permanent college of theologians. With his three sons he gathered his clergy and ministry, together with several outside theologians, among

whom was Johann Musæus (q.v.), in a conference at Jena (Apr. 15–17, 1670). The most diverse personages, like Calovius, Spener, Quenstedt, were already being proposed for a peace court, when the measure carried to send deputations to ascertain the opinions of other Lutheran courts. These gave only friendly but evasive replies, but Ernst redoubled his efforts to remove the schism. He obtained an opinion from Spener (May 31, 1670) to the effect that it was not yet too late for the restoration of unity; because the quarrel had not yet rent the churches, and the Consensus had nowhere been introduced. As to the cause of the strife he did not exonerate Calixtus from eccentricities of doctrine and obduracy, and ascribed the disorder to " human affections." As to the measures for restoration, he advised a cooperation of Christian governments and clergy and a reformation from external sterile conformity. If a synod of all Germany was not practicable, then a consultation of earnest, enlightened men would be advisable. The question as to what Calixtus the elder and Horneius once taught should be buried with the past, and the profession and assertion by the Helmstedt theologians that their teaching was in accord with the symbols, and their declination of the charge of syncretism and adherence to the fundamental errors of Romanism, should be deemed sufficient. Whether and how far the remaining doctrines like that of ubiquity were fundamental to faith might then be easily determined. Toleration and gentleness were meet for weaker brethren and unnecessary invective without prejudice to the elenchus was to be forbidden. Ernst sent out another deputation with an outline of this to seek out the theologians and persuade them to the counsels of peace. Turning first to the electorate of Saxony, these were referred from Dresden to Wittenberg. Quenstedt and B. Meisner (q.v.) themselves complained of the radicalism and inflexibility of Calovius, who now surreptitiously inserted over his signature to the theses to be submitted to the Helmstedt theologians, two fresh points: on abandoning the errors of syncretism and on believing the mystery of the Holy Trinity in the Old and New Testaments. The three things demanded by the other theses were that the theologians should not dispute any doctrine contained in the Book of Concord; should teach according to their charter; and renounce syncretism, by which was meant only the recognition of a fundamental consensus between Lutherans and Reformed. But at Helmstedt and other places under its influence, Calovius was utterly mistrusted, and a quarrel among the rulers caused the forbidding of the Helmstedt theologians to commit themselves. Yet the negotiations allayed the strife for a few years.

3. The Third Period: In 1675 the conflict was renewed and lasted till the death of Calovius in

1. Recrudescence of Calovius. 1686. The latter knew how to take advantage of the favor of Ernst and specially of his successor, so that he felt bold to reopen hostilities. In the year in which Spener by his *Pia desideria* (1675) opened a new epoch in Christian life, Calovius again announced in programs as his unchanged life purpose,

E diaboli excrementa Calixtinas sordes exquirire. Calixtus answered with his *Pietatis officium pii viri innocentiam vindicans.* This was followed by writings pro and con, prose and verse, reaching its climax in the appearance of a farce in four acts of three or four scenes each celebrating the installation of Deutschmann into the prorectorship at Wittenberg, almost blasphemous in terms. The elector caused the printer to be fined and the author to be imprisoned. Likewise, Strauch, called to Danzig in 1669, was detained as prisoner at Küstrin by order of the elector of Brandenburg, 1675–78; and the elector of Saxony renewed the edict against writing polemics without special permission. Calovius now wrote under a pseudonym, and produced also *Systema locorum theologicorum* (vols. v.–xii., 1677), more flighty than the first four and including also the new polemic against Jena. In vain was Spener's caution to him that the effort to secure the recognition of his Consensus was both futile and injurious. Besides a quarrel with his colleague Meisner and the latter's humiliation, 1677–1680, he engaged, by sermons, disputations, and writings, in a warfare on Musæus at Jena, who won his displeasure by rendering his allegations against the syncretists void and was now being condemned as worse than they. He succeeded in having the entire faculty of Jena, including Musæus, compelled to abjure syncretism, if not to adopt the Consensus. But the limits of his accomplishment were reached. Johann Georg II. renewed the edict against polemical writing (Jan. 12, 1680), and the printers of *De syncretismo Musæi* were severely dealt with. With the accession of Elector Johann Georg III. in 1680 began a protective alliance with the great elector of Brandenburg. Calovius had to see his *Historia syncretistica* (1682), a compilation issued anonymously and without place, consisting of the blows he had dealt against syncretists together with fresh fulminations, refused circulation. This made such an impression on him that he referred two questions to his most intimate followers at Giessen: whether, in view of the political syncretism made necessary by the danger from France, a Calixtine syncretism with the papists and Reformed was still to be condemned; and whether the strife brought on by the universities of Helmstedt, Jena, and Königsberg, on account of the elector of Brandenburg and the dukes of Brunswick, should be buried with an amnesty, or the controversy over syncretism be continued. This was taken by friends and foes alike as a wavering and a sign of alinement with the court. This Calovius denied in a pamphlet relating the correspondence thereto and reiterating his anathemas against all his opponents inclusive of the Musæan syncretists. The comprehensive publications, *Apodixis articulorum fidei* (1668), and *Synopsis controversiarum cum hæreticis modernis* (1685) appeared before his death, which practically closed the controversies.

4. Final Influence: The great work with which Friedrich Calixtus closed his career, *Via ad pacem inter protestantes restaurandum* (Helmstedt, 1700), was the irenic counterbalance to the *Historia syncretistica* republished in 1685. The term syncretism

as name of a party gradually disappeared and came to recur only as incidental reference to varying combinations of the unlike. To be sure, the after-effects of the strife persisted a long time, specially in electoral Saxony. A result was the aversion to affiliation on the part of the German Lutherans and Reformed for a century to come, as seen, for example, in the indifference of the Lutherans to the French Protestants at the revocation of the Edict of Nantes (1685; q.v.). The peaceable separation of religion and theology and the adjustment of the borders between church and schools, confession and science, were not actualized, though they were frequently on the horizon of promise. According to Calovius pure doctrine is the only necessity; it is ready-made and complete, the ecclesiastical norm, admitting of neither addition nor reduction. According to Calixtus, doctrine is not only not the only necessity but it is also of varying degrees of value within itself, giving room for broad unity on essentials. The controversy left a cloud of suspicion and prejudice specially over the Lutherans, retarding the progress of these distinctions. The despotic determination to force a *Consensus repetitus*, as the only and final dogma and theology before which all investigation and progress must fall prostrate, raised up its own factional limits, and the most deplorable result, surviving to the present, is the alienation from the church of educated men, and thereby the demoralization of a great unitary spirit, for the need of which the German Evangelical Church is suffering.

(PAUL TSCHACKERT.)

BIBLIOGRAPHY: The principal source is A. Calovius, *Historia syncretistica*, 1685. Consult further: J. G. Walch, *Religionsstreitigkeiten der lutherischen Kirche*, i. 219 sqq., iv. 666, 10 vols., Jena, 1733–39; W. Gass, *G. Calixt und der Synkretismus*, Breslau, 1846; E. L. T. Henke, *G. Calixtus und seine Zeit*, vol. ii., Halle, 1856; A. Tholuck, *Akademisches Leben des 17. Jahrhunderts*, vol. ii., ib. 1854; W. Gass, *Geschichte der protestantischen Dogmatik*, vol. ii., Berlin, 1857; I. A. Dorner, *Geschichte der protestantischen Theologie*, pp. 600 sqq., Munich, 1867, Eng. transl., Edinburgh, 1871; G. W. Frank, *Geschichte der protestantischen Theologie*, ii. 4 sqq., Leipsic, 1875.

SYNEISAKTOI. See SUBINTRODUCTÆ VIRGINES.

SYNERGISM AND SYNERGISTIC CONTROVERSY: A type of Semi-Pelagianism in the sixteenth century and the dispute which arose concerning it. Synergism is the doctrine of the cooperation of human effort and divine grace in regeneration.

Opinions
of Luther
and
Melanchthon.

Luther regarded the spiritual life as monergistic, the result of the experience of a divine act. Faith is a gift of God. " Free will determined without grace has no power with respect to righteousness but is necessarily involved in sin." Justification follows " whenever we are made purely passive with respect to God with reference to interior as well as exterior acts." God's relation to man is considered as strictly predestinarian. After the Leipsic Disputation Melanchthon maintained that " man is wholly incapable of doing good "; that " in the choice of external things " there is some freedom, but internal effects are not within human power. " All things that happen, happen of necessity by divine predestination; there is no freedom of will." Conversion is possible only as an inner divine act. Dead through the law, man is " resuscitated by the word of grace." Faith is originated by " the Spirit of God renewing and illuminating " the human heart. To say that the beginning of repentance is in man, would be inverting the order; man turns to God on the ground that God first turns to man. Melanchthon later modified this view, first, by relinquishing the deterministic conception of the doctrine of predestination (*Scholia* on Colossians, 1527). The special properties of the nature with which God endowed man in distinction from the other creatures are " reason " and " choice." The natural man is capable of a " carnal and civil righteousness." The thought of God as the author of sin formerly not avoided is now repudiated. In the Commentary on Romans (Wittenberg, 1532) he teaches the universality of divine grace, and shuns all closer investigation of the mystery of divine election. Melanchthon now regards the pity of God as the cause of election, but recognizes in non-rejection a negative cause of acceptance. The development of his doctrine of free will and conversion gains momentum with his growing desire to understand the act of divine grace at the same time as a psychological process in the human consciousness and will, consistently with his explanations of the mental powers presented in his commentary on the Ethics of Aristotle (1529) and in *De anima* (1540). Besides, there was his practical motive to make man responsible for his own salvation. With respect to the former, the will is the formal power which responds, either by willing, not willing, or neutrality, to the subjects manifested by the intellect; it may follow the beckoning of the desires or the admonitions of the reason. The will produces nothing original, but assumes an attitude toward what approaches it. This power was not lost through original sin. Likewise, when the grace of God contained in his Word draws nigh, and, through the hearing of it, the Holy Spirit enters man and produces the spiritual effects of repentance and faith, there yet remains to the will the alternative attitude of acceptance or rejection. In this sense Melanchthon mentions the " three concurrent causes of good actions " in regeneration: " the Word, the Holy Spirit, and the will, not absolutely inert, but struggling against its own infirmity." In this sense he lets the definition of Erasmus hold: " Free will is the power of applying oneself to grace."

This synergism was taught in the Leipsic Interim, which affirmed among other things that God does **The Leipsic** not deal with man as with a block, but **Interim.** so regenerates him that his will cooperates. Matthias Flacius (q.v.) professed to divine in those words a papistical *meritum de congruo* and a fragment of free will. Johann Pfeffinger published Melanchthon's doctrine in two disputations: *De libertate voluntatis humanæ* (Leipsic, 1555); and *De libero arbitrio* (1555). The concurrent active causes are " the Holy Spirit moving through the Word of God, the mind in the act of thinking, and the will not resisting, but complying whenever moved by the Holy Spirit." If the attitude of man were *ut statua* when the Holy Spirit has kindled reason, will, and feel-

ing, then there would be no inner struggle to secure faith; if man was idle or " purely passive," then the distinction between pious and impious, elect and non-elect, as well as the impartiality and justice of God, would disappear. " Therefore, there was in us some cause why some assent and others do not assent." Pfeffinger's doctrine was renounced by V. Strigel and by Nikolaus von Amsdorf (q.v.), who opened the attack (1558) with a rude misrepresentation as if Pfeffinger had asserted that " man could adapt and prepare himself by free will from his natural powers for the reception of grace without the gift of the Holy Spirit."

To the defense of Pfeffinger, Flacius replied in *Refutatio*, published in *Disputatio de originali peccato et libero arbitrio*, pp. 367 sqq. (Weimar 1560). He appealed to the words of Luther and further **Conflict** asserted that in regeneration, when the **with** old man " is made into a new creature," **Flacius.** he is worse than a block or stone inasmuch as he is not only passive but " contrary, resisting, or hostile toward the work of God," like a knotty piece of wood wholly unfit for the hewer. The despised adiaphorists here received the additional denunciatory appellative of " synergists." Another polemic followed, *De originali peccato et libero arbitrio* (ut sup., pp. 398 sqq.) and a disputation at Jena Nov. 10–11, 1559. Flacius succeeded in pressing the denunciation into the second part of the " Weimar Book of Confutations," *Illustrissimi principis Jo. Friderici secundi solida et ex verba Dei sumpta confutatio et condemnatio præcipuarum corruptelarum, sectarum et errorum hoc tempore grassantium* (Jena, 1559). It denounces those who teach that by the fall man's natural powers were " not so totally perverted and corrupted that he, animated by the help and support of grace, is capable of anything in conversion by his own free will; that they ascribe to free will such grace in its arbitrary power that it can accept and follow or reject it "; and that they describe human reason and will as *synergos*, or co-agent with the Word and the Spirit of God. Against these alleged errors was affirmed that man is by nature wholly dead and his heart is petrified; that all knowledge of Christ springs from the enlightenment of the Holy Spirit; and all that pertains to will to become obedient to God must first be given and wrought by God. Melanchthon, at whom the attack was aimed, vindicated his views before the Elector August, emphasizing his ethical practical motive in turning against the deterministic delirium and investigating the problem of free will. Sinful nature retained some freedom to maintain outward discipline. In conversion the Word of God has the initiative, to condemn sin and extend pardon and grace and thereby produce fear and comfort; but God does not coerce any one to be different regardless of heeding the Word. " He who rejects God does so by his own will and God is not the cause of the will's rejecting him." Conversely, there is no regeneration, " so long as the will wholly resists." " God draws; but he draws him who is willing," was his favorite sentence. He protests against the form of speech used by Flacius referring to " compulsion of faith," as also in the disputation of Nov. 28, 1559, when he criticized the same as indicative of Manichean error and sophisms.

In the mean time Victorinus Strigel (q.v.) assumed the defense of Melanchthon at Jena. He had successively sought to prevent the severity and **Support of Strigel.** the adoption of the Book of Confutations, and now Duke Johann Friedrich called for a disputation between Flacius and Strigel, which occurred at Weimar Aug. '2–8, 1560. For Flacius conversion was the awakening in brief time of the sinner to repentance and his endowment with faith, while the will remains passive. For Strigel, conversion was the development of the state of grace continuously through life, embracing the " perpetual repentance, governance, and conservation," the beginning and growth of the spiritual life. According to Flacius a new will is originated by the " gift of faith " capable of spiritual motives. According to Strigel the human will enters into coordinate action with the inception of conversion, and to every spiritual activity there is a corresponding exercise of human will. The disputation was suspended without judgment by the duke, who thought to bring the matter before a synod. The attitude of the court, at first favorable to Flacius, underwent a gradual change, and in spite of Flacius' fanning of the flames and of his increasing clamor to secure the condemnation of his rival the duke simply demanded a declaration of doctrine from both (ut sup., pp. 322 sqq.). Before the end of 1561, Flacius and his associates were driven from Jena. In his *Declaratio* of Mar. 3, 1562 (ut sup., p. 591), Strigel distinguished between the " power " or " efficacy " (lost in the fall) to consider, will, and execute what is well-pleasing to God, and the " capacity " for the divine calling which marks the rational man from the other creatures, by which he remains capable of assenting to the Word through the Holy Spirit and of retaining the acquired blessing of grace. This was adopted and Strigel was restored to his professorship. The *Declaratio* meeting with opposition from the clergy, the visitator Johann Stoessel supplemented it by a mitigating *Superdeclaratio* requiring only conditional signature. This only served to intensify the quarrel, so that the refractory clergy were removed, and Strigel, dissatisfied with the *Superdeclaratio*, in disgust withdrew from the discussion of free will and retired to Leipsic. See further STRIGEL, VICTORINUS; STOESSEL, JOHANN; FLACIUS, MATTHIAS. With the reign of Duke Johann Wilhelm Gnesio-Lutheranism entered, and with it stress upon the " Book of Confutation " as a doctrinal norm. As the Wittenberg theologians broke off the discussions at the Altenburg Colloquy, Oct. 21, 1568–Mar. 9, 1569, the Jena theologians had to be content with a protest in writing consisting of the old objections. The Formula of Concord (q.v.) cast its decision against the Philippists (q.v.) but rejected the language of Flacius identifying original sin with substance as a Manichean error.

(G. KAWERAU.)

BIBLIOGRAPHY: Consult the articles in this work on Matthias Flacius, Martin Luther, Philipp Melanchthon, Johann Pfeffinger, Philippists, Augustus Gottlieb Spangenberg, Johann Stigelius, Johann Stoessel, Victorinus Strigel, and Will, as also the literature given thereunder. In addition to the matter thus indicated, consult: H. Heppe, *Geschichte des deutschen Protestantismus 1555–81*, 4 vols., Marburg, 1853–59; idem, *Dogmatik des deutschen Protestantismus im 16. Jahrhundert*, Gotha, 1857; A. Beck, *Johann Friedrich der Mittlere*, 2 vols., Weimar, 1858; F. H. R. Frank, *Theologie der Konkordienformel*, vol. i., Erlangen, 1858; C. E. Luthardt, *Die Lehre vom freien Willen*, Leipsic, 1863; Flotow, *De synergismo Melanthonis*, Wratislaw, 1867; E. F. Fischer, *Melanchthons Lehre von der Bekehrung*, Tübingen, 1905; F. Loofs, *Leitfaden zum Studium der Dogmengeschichte*, 4th ed., Halle, 1906.

SYNESIUS, si-nī′shi-us, **OF CYRENE:** Bishop of Ptolemais; b. at Cyrene in the Libyan Pentapolis between 370 and 375; d. before 415. He prided himself upon his descent from a royal stock, as the descendant of Eurysthenes, one of the Heraclides, who led the Dorians to Sparta. Eager for classical learning, he went to Alexandria to study poetry, rhetoric, and philosophy under Hypatia. After returning home, although still young he became the head of a deputation from the Pentapolis to the Emperor Arcadius to secure release from certain onerous conditions of taxation. About 399 or 400 he traveled to Constantinople, where the eunuch Eutropius was ruling the incompetent emperor and the empire; he remained there three years, waiting a year before he could obtain audience. He then delivered before Arcadius and the court his celebrated oration " Concerning Kingship " (*MPG*, lxvi. 1053–1108), in which he showed the difference between a tyrant and a king ruled by the fear of God, and portrayed the departure from the old Roman simplicity in affectation of oriental ostentation and ceremony. He uttered a patriotic protest against the entrusting of the empire to irresponsible and dangerous foreigners, just then emphasized by the outbreak of the Goths under Tribigild in Asia Minor, with whom Gainas made common cause soon after and compelled the banishment of three noted statesmen, among them Synesius' friend Aurelian. This situation Synesius described in a historical romance (*MPG*, lxvi. 1209–1282). By 402 he had achieved the results he sought for his native city, and returned home, describing his journey in a letter (*MPG*, lxvi. 1328 sqq.). He next visited Athens and Alexandria (402–404) for further study, and then divided his time between his home in Cyrene and his country estate, where he occupied himself in rural occupations and leisurely study, having a distaste for public occupations. At times he was engaged in defense of his estates, against the incursions of tribes from the interior. In 403 he married a Christian woman. He engaged in an extensive correspondence; though bewailing that he was in unphilosophical surroundings, he produced in his " On the Dream " (*MPG* ut sup., 1281–1320) a statement of his ideal of philosophical culture; his *Dion, ē peri tēs kath' heauton diagogēs* is a defense of the same.

It is a remarkable fact that such a man should a few years later be called to work in public as a bishop. No trace in his life or writings up to this point suggests that he was a Christian, though he knew Christianity well. He may have witnessed the fanaticism which in 392 destroyed the Serapion at Alexandria, as at Constantinople he did not escape the activities of a Chrysostom. He had sung of the Christian temples as sanctuaries of the serving gods and spirits whom the All-ruler had clothed with angel brilliancy; and in monkish theology he recognized a striving akin in mystic contemplation to philosophy. The influence of his wife may have been felt, as well as the influence coming from the interest of such theologians as Theophilus in himself, and he was in a Christian environment. To this ten hymns testify, written before he became bishop, which, though in Neoplatonic wise, speak of God as the highest unity, the monad of monads, father and mother, center of nature. Yet in the ninth hymn, the divine Son appears as the Savior, son of the Virgin, opener of the gates of Tartarus and leader of the souls to the highest heaven. He became even more Christian in tone, developing his material without changing essentially the nucleus of his religious-philosophic view of things, until in the last hymn is the pious prayer to Christ, the physician of soul and body.

In 409 (406 or earlier?) the bishop's seat at Ptolemais became vacant, and clergy and laity called Synesius, from whose influential connections much was hoped. He consented to have the affair referred to the Patriarch Theophilus, but sent with the messenger a letter to his brother Evoptius (MPG, lxvi. 1481 sqq.) which was meant for publicity. This letter, remarkable for its contents, contained the expression of his scruples and doubts in view of the duty of the priest or bishop and the high obligations which rest upon him. Moreover, the conclusions his philosophy had forced upon him might not accord with the teachings religion might demand of him— the idea of the relation of the soul to the body, the form of the doctrine of the resurrection, as he held them, were not in the shape of the beliefs held by the multitude, for philosophy is opposed to the feelings of the vulgar. There was, too, the matter of his marriage; his wife was the gift of the law, of God, and of Theophilus, and he would not separate from her openly nor yet visit her secretly. He would regret also to give up his beloved occupations and amusements, but would do so if the call seemed imperative, and would do his best in his office. After a delay of seven months Synesius received baptism and episcopal consecration, though his letters show that his heart remained heavy and his feelings divided. His letters express humility and distrust of his powers and fitness for his duties. The year 407 brought him into conflict with Andronicus, the tyrannical prefect and direst plague of the Pentapolis, whom at first in vain he tried to turn from his cruelty. Through the withdrawal of the right of asylum by Andronicus Synesius found himself in a difficult position and as a philosopher unable to handle the affair. In the very noteworthy address (MPG, lxvi. 1384–1400) in which he told of his determination to excommunicate Andronicus, he recalled the happier earlier time when such duties did not engage him. He expressed his wish that he could be relieved of his consecration, he feared to minister unworthily in the mysteries of God; he desired, if he could not be relieved of his duties, at least to have an assistant. Before the ban was pronounced, Andronicus appeared to have repented; the publication was delayed, when the prefect fell back into his old courses and the excommunication was pronounced at the close of the year 407. The

difficulties of Synesius were increased when the tribes from the interior again fell upon the unfortunate province. At first the young and capable Anysius, whom Anthemius sent as commanding officer, was able to afford protection. But a little later a change in affairs gave the barbarians free play, and Synesius even thought of leaving his fatherland; even when, a year later, the situation improved, the dominant sadness did not leave him. Of the rest of his life nothing is known, though he does not appear to have outlived Hypatia or the episcopate of Cyril of Alexandria.

(G. KRÜGER.)

BIBLIOGRAPHY: The "Works" of Synesius were edited by A. Turnebus, Paris, 1553 (incomplete), and by D. Petavius, ib. 1612; substantially the latter text was taken into MPL, lxvi. 1021–1756; the "Letters" have been published by R. Hercher in Epistographi Græci, pp. 638–739, Paris, 1873, and a critical edition is expected from W. Fritz, who has made preliminary studies on the subject (see below); of the "Hymns" the first edition was by Canterus, Basel, 1567, while others are by J. F. Boissonade, in Sylloge poetarum Græcarum, vol. xv., Paris, 1825; W. Christ and M. Paranikas, in Anthologia Græca carminum Christianorum, Leipsic, 1871, and J. Flach, Tübingen, 1875.
On the life consult: DCB, iv. 756–780 (elaborate, with many illuminative extracts from the works); Clausen, De Synesio philosopho, Copenhagen, 1831; B. Kolbe, Der Bischof Synesius von Cyrene als Physiker und Astronom, Berlin, 1850; H. V. M. Druon, Études sur la vie et les œuvres de Synésius, évêque de Ptolemais, Paris, 1859; F. X. Kraus, in TQS, xlvii (1865), 391–448, xlviii (1866), 85–129; R. Volkmann, Synesius von Cyrene, eine biographische Charakteristik, Berlin, 1869; G. A. Sievers, Studien zur Geschichte der römischen Kaiser, pp. 371–418; ib. 1870; E. R. Schneider, De vita Synesii, Grimma, 1876, E. Gaiser, Des Synesius von Cyrene ägyptische Erzählungen, Wolffenbüttel, 1886; A. Gardner, Synesius of Cyrene, London, 1886; G. Barner, Comparantur inter se de regentium hominum virtutibus auctores, pp. 47–62, Marburg, 1889; O. Seeck, in Philologus, lii (1893), 442–483; O. Bardenhewer, Patrologie, pp. 314–316, Freiburg, 1901, Eng. transl., St. Louis, 1908; W. S. Crawford, Synesius the Hellene, London, 1901; H. Koch, in Historisches Jahrbuch der Görresgesellschaft, xxviii (1902), 751–774; A. J. Kleffner, Synesius von Cyrene, der Philosoph und Dichter, Paderborn, 1901.
On the works consult: J. C. Thilo, Commentarii in Synesii hymnos, Halle, 1842–43; F. Reess, Der griechische Hymnendichter Synesius von Cyrene mit einigen Uebersetzungsversuchen, Constance, 1848; J. N. Huber, Philosophie der Kirchenväter, Munich, 1859; W. Fritz, Die Briefe des Bischofs Synesius von Kyrene, Leipsic, 1898; idem, in AMA, 1905, 329–398; idem, in Byzantinische Zeitschrift, xiv (1905), 75–86; C. Velley, Études sur les hymnes de Synésius de Cyrène, Paris, 1904; A. Baumgartner, Die lateinische und griechische Litteratur der christlichen Völker, pp. 314–81, Freiburg, 1905; W. von Christ, Geschichte der christlichen Litteratur, pp. 947–948, 4th ed., Munich, 1905.

SYNGRAMMA SUEVICUM. See BRENZ, JOHANN, § 2.

SYNOD. See COUNCILS AND SYNODS; and PRESBYTERIANS, X., § 2 (6).

SYNOD OF THE REFORMED PRESBYTERIAN CHURCH IN NORTH AMERICA. See PRESBYTERIANS, VIII., 4.

SYNODAL COURTS.

Origin (§ 1).	Further Changes (§ 3).
Addition of Jurors (§ 2).	Decline (§ 4).

Under the name of Send (from Gk. synodos, Lat. synodus), or Sendgericht, an institution grew up in Germany in the ninth century which was practically an episcopal court for the trial and punishment of misdemeanors. It developed out of the episcopal

visitations (see CHURCH VISITATIONS) which had been customary since the fourth century alike in East and West. In the Frankish king-
1. Origin. dom, Boniface had insisted on their observance, which was enforced by Carloman, Pippin, and especially Charlemagne (Capitularies of 769, 789, 802, 813; cf. canon xvii. of the Synod of Arles of 813). At these visitations each class and order was questioned as to the performance of its special duties; and the synodal court arose out of the separation from the other visitation business of the investigation and punishment of misconduct on the part of the laity. This development took place immediately after the close of Charlemagne's reign. The sixteenth canon of the Synod of Rouen (held probably under Louis the Pious) exhibits the synodal court as an independent institution, though still connected with diocesan visitation. As to the offenses subject to the jurisdiction of this tribunal, Carloman emphasized the duty of the bishops to root out all remains of pagan superstition. Charlemagne enjoined upon his bishops the investigation of " incest, parricide, fratricide, adultery, superstitious beliefs, and whatsoever other evil things are contrary to the law of God."

In the second half of the ninth century a modification was introduced in the selection of a sort of grand jury, which was to relieve the
2. Addition bishop from the necessity of depend-
of Jurors. ing wholly upon chance evidence that an offense had been committed. He chose a number of trustworthy men from the district who were bound by oath to lay charges against all offenders in those points known to them. That this usage was still unknown in the middle of the century is shown by the eighth canon of the Synod of Mainz of 852, according to which the bishop still dealt immediately with the people at large. But the *testes* or *juratores synodi* are found in the diocese of Constance between 875 and 889. This innovation was probably copied from a similar secular institution established by Charlemagne's son Pippin for Italy, and was found north of the Alps under Louis the Pious. The accusations brought by this jury were not required to be proved by them, but the accused was expected to prove his innocence. For freemen this was done by an oath, unless there were well-grounded doubts of their credibility; in that case the Ordeal (q.v.) was resorted to. In the absence of the accused, the charge might be proved by the evidence of those who were present. After the proof of the charge, the bishop (together with such priests as were in attendance) passed sentence in terms of ecclesiastical penalties. Excommunication was not an ordinary penalty, but was employed in case of stubborn refusal to attend the court or obey its rulings.

The system seems to have remained substantially the same in the eleventh century; but early in the twelfth the *testes* or *juratores* not merely appeared as accusers, but shared with the ecclesias-
3. Further tical judges in the finding of the court.
Changes. This development is explicable by the fact that at this time the participation of laymen in the decision of questions affecting legal and property questions pertaining to the Church

was becoming customary. In the course of the twelfth century the lay element gained still further strength when the choice of the jurymen was taken away from the bishop. Another innovation was even more far-reaching. With the increase of the worldly state of the bishops, they became less and less able to execute their ecclesiastical duties in person. The archdeacon gradually took the bishop's place in the synodal court. In the twelfth century the representation of the bishop by his delegate had become the usual custom; the brief of Innocent II. to Provost Gerhard of Bonn (1139) exhibits the archdeacon as possessing independent power; and under Innocent III. (1211) he is denominated *judex ordinarius* equally with the bishop. In some places the disintegration of the synodal jurisdiction went even further, and the archdeacons were represented by the archpriests, who later claimed independent jurisdiction. In consequence of the synodal courts ceasing to be strictly episcopal, the nobility began to claim exemption from them, as they were doing from the lower secular tribunals, which exemption the bishops acknowledged in the thirteenth century. The same exemption was claimed and obtained by the ministerial class in some states; and this withdrawal of subjects led in the end to the downfall of the institution.

Throughout the greater part of the Middle Ages the offenses which the synodal court was competent to try remained practically the same; but at the end of this period a notable restriction
4. Decline. became visible. Thus a synodal ordinance of Jülich-Berg in the fourteenth century names as offenses of this class blasphemy, drunkenness, unchastity, unlawful marriages, disorderly housekeeping, breach of the Sunday laws, neglect of divine worship and the sacraments, and hedge-preaching—those offenses which fell directly under the secular law being excluded. The disinclination of the laity, after they had obtained an important share in the power of the court, to be bound by its decisions came partly from the feeling of competition with the civil laws, partly from unwillingness to see ecclesiastical offenses made matter of legal proceedings. The territorial rulers also came to regard the courts as an invasion of their rights; and their importance gradually decreased. The imposition of money fines instead of the earlier penances also hurt them in the public esteem, especially when a portion of the fines went to their members and were looked upon as a source of income. At the Reformation the whole institution was reckoned among the abuses of the unreformed Church. In the Roman Catholic districts it maintained a partial existence until the eighteenth century (the synodal court of Aachen was abolished only in 1797); but its real significance ceased with the end of the Middle Ages.   (A. HAUCK.)

BIBLIOGRAPHY: C. F. Eichhorn, *Deutsche Staats- und Rechtsgeschichte*, i. 706, ii. 499, 4 vols., Göttingen, 1821–23; A. J. Binterim, *Denkwürdigkeiten*, v. 3, pp. 36 sqq., Mainz, 1829; H. F. Jacobson, *Geschichte der Quellen des Kirchenrechts*, i. 118 sqq., Königsberg, 1837; K. von Richthofen, *Friesische Rechtsquellen*, passim, Berlin, 1840; P. Hinschius, *Kirchenrecht*, v. 425 sqq., ib. 1895; R. Schröder, *Lehrbuch der deutschen Rechtsgeschichte*, pp. 577 sqq., Leipsic, 1898; E. Friedberg, *Lehrbuch des . . . Kirchenrechts*, 320 sqq., ib. 1903; Rettberg, *KD*, ii. 742 sqq.; Hauck, *KD*, ii. 733 sqq., iv. 61–62.

SYRIA.

I. Name: The name Syria is an abbreviation of Assyria, even as " Syrians " is shortened from " Assyrians," the ultimate source being the name of the Assyrian god Asshur (see ASSYRIA, IV., § 1, VII., § 2). In their earlier period the Greeks applied the designation Assyrians or Syrians in a purely political sense to all subjects of the king of Assyria; and in their view this empire, with which they came in contact after the eighth and seventh centuries, stretched from the Black Sea to the Mediterranean. When, however, the Greeks became better acquainted with Asia after the fall of the Assyrian empire, they reserved the name Assyria for the original center of Assyrian power, and termed the western provinces of the former empire Syria. This usage corresponds in general to that of the Old Testament, where Asshur generally connotes Assyria proper, exclusive of the conquered lands. By the time of Alexander the Great the Greeks had come to restrict the designation Syrians to the Semites in the western portions of the former empire of Assyria, and thus " Syrians," now an ethnographical term, became identical with " Arameans." In the Old Testament there is no mention of either Syria or Syrians, the designation there being Aram (q.v.); but in the Talmud and in Syriac, under Greek influence, the term " Syria " is found. The Arabs call the land al-Sham, " the left " (in contradistinction to South Arabia, to the right of Syria), and the Turks designate it Suristan or Arabistan (" Syrian Land " or " Arab Land ").

II. Geography: Modern Syria is practically coterminous with the land so designated from the time of Alexander, its approximate boundaries being Cilicia and the Alma Dagh on the north, the Euphrates and Syrian Desert on the east, Arabia and Egypt on the south, and the Mediterranean on the west, while a considerable portion of this territory of 108,000 square miles is occupied by Palestine (q.v.). Syria forms part of Turkey in
1. Divisions. Asia, and comprises the vilayet of Aleppo with the *livas* (" districts ") of Aleppo, Mar'ash, and Urfa (Edessa); the independent *liva* of Zor; the vilayet of Beirut with the *livas* of Ladiḳiyah, Ṭarabulus, Beirut, 'Akka, and Nablus; the independent *liva* of Lebanon; the vilayet of Suria (" Syria ") with the *livas* of Ḥama, Damascus, Hauran, and Ma'an and the independent *liva* of Jerusalem. For population and ethnology see below, IV.

The mountain ranges run from north to south. The northern portion of the narrow coastal highland is formed by a range from the Gulf of Iskanderun (or Alexandretta Bay) to the Nahr al-Kabir (the classical Eleutherus). South of the Nahr al-Kabir are Lebanon (q.v.) and Anti-Lebanon, the highest peak of the latter range being the Biblical Hermon (q.v.). The highland east of
2. Physical the plateau of al-Biḳa', which separates
Geography. Lebanon from Anti-Lebanon and finds its continuation in the Jordan valley, falls away toward the Euphrates or to the northern Syrian desert, agreeably interrupted by the oases of Damascus, Aleppo, and Palmyra. In the southeast the plateau extends over the Lejjah and Jabal Ḥauran to the Syro-Arabic desert proper. Syria has but few rivers. From the valleys of the Anti-Libanus the Nahr Barada (the Chrysorrhoas of the Greeks and the Abana or Amana of II Kings v. 12) flows to the Baḥrat al-'Ataibah, six hours east of Damascus; and from Hermon the Nahr al-'Awaj (the Pharpar of II Kings v. 12) flows into the Baḥrat Hijanah. On the plateau of al-Biḳa' rises the Nahr al-Aẓi (the classical Orontes), which flows north to Antioch, where, augmented by the discharge of the Ak-Daniz, it turns to the west and empties into the Mediterranean. The Litany (the classical Leontes) rises near the source of Nahr al-'Aẓi, flows first to the south and then to the west, and empties into the Mediterranean north of Tyre. Besides the Baḥrat al-'Ataibah, Baḥrat Hijanah, and Al-Daniz, mention may be made of the morass of al-Maṭkh near the ruins of Ḳinnasrin (the Chalcis founded by Seleucus Nicator), where the Nahr Ḳuwaiḳ debouches, and of the salt Baḥrat Jabbul and the Baḥrat Ḥomṣ (the ancient Emesa). The year is divided into the dry season or summer (May–October), and the rainy season or winter (November–April). Rain is rare by the middle of May (I Sam. xii. 17–18), but dew is plentiful in summer, except in the desert. The early rains begin in November (cf. Deut. xi. 14; Joel ii. 23), the heavy rains fall in the middle of December, and the late rains in March and April. The heat is most intense on the coast, though the sea breezes cause some moderation. In Damascus and Aleppo, where the climate is more extreme both in heat and cold, the west winds alone bring relief. The fertility of Syria is much inferior to what it was in ancient times, largely because of Assyrian and Turkish misrule. Recently, however, a marked amelioration has begun; the Hauran plateau, anciently one of the chief granaries of the East, is regaining its former renown; grapes are cultivated on Lebanon; the cultivation of the olive is reviving; there is an increasing trade in apricots in Damascus; and in northern Syria

gall-nuts promise to be rivaled by the orange as products for export. For the flora and fauna of Syria see PALESTINE.

III. History: The early history of Syria is obscure. About 2000 B.C. Arameans were found east of Syria proper, into which they penetrated about 1200, finding there a population for the most part probably Semitic. The history may most conveniently be divided into six periods: (1) to the conquest of the Aramean states by the Assyrians, or to the capture of Damascus in 732; (2) under Assyrian, Babylonian, and Persian dominion (to 605, 539, and 332 respectively); (3) under Greek dominion (to 64 B.C.); (4) under Roman dominion (to 635 A.D.); (5) under Arab dominion (to 1516); and (6) under Turkish dominion (to the present time).

1. To the Assyrian Conquest: About 2800 B.C. the North Babylonian King Sargon I. (see BABYLONIA, VI., 3, § 1) made an expedition to Syria, Palestine, and the Mediterranean, and some 700 years later Ḥammurabi (q.v.) termed himself king of Amurru (Palestine and Syria). The Arameans who crossed the Euphrates from the south found the Mesopotamian kingdom of Mitanni (cf. ASSYRIA, VI., 2) to the north and Assyria to the east, and in the fourteenth century the Assyrian King Arik-den-ilu (Pudi-Ilu) was warring against Aramean hordes. By 1400 the Hittites (q.v.) were pressing into Syria and Phenicia, their capital being Carchemish (q.v.), and their dominions extending to the northern boundaries of the later Israel. About 1270 Rameses warred against the Syrian Hittites, but was forced to conclude an offensive and defensive alliance with them. Northern Syria was tributary to the Hittites. After destroying the kingdom of Mitanni in the fourteenth century, the Assyrians attacked the kingdom of Ḥanigalbat (between the Euphrates, Taurus, and Anti-Taurus), defeated the King Shattuara, who had allied himself with the Hittites and Arameans, and seized the Aramean stronghold of Kasyar (the modern Karaja Dagh), as well as Syria as far south as Carchemish. Shalmaneser I., who had conducted these campaigns, was compelled to lead repeated expeditions against the Arameans in the Kasyar range, but with Hittite and Alarodian inroads in the twelfth century the Arameans, who had reached the Tigris during Shalmaneser's reign, were divided, one portion migrating westward to Syria and the other eastward to Assyria. Tiglath-Pileser I. kept the Arameans from Assyria proper, and also broke the Hittite power in Syria. The latter people formed a number of petty states, into which the Arameans poured.

By the time of the rise of the kingdom of Israel the Old Testament could record the existence of several Aramean states (see ARAM, §§ 1, 9), of which the most important was Damascus. David made energetic war on the Arameans (cf. II Sam. x. 6 sqq.), but with the reestablishment of Damascus a power was created which was to exercise a profound influence on the fortunes of Israel. The founder of the new dynasty was Rezon, who had revolted from Hadadezer, king of Zobah, and, making himself

2. In the Old Testament.

1. Assyro-Babylonian Period.

master of Damascus, " was an adversary to Israel all the days of Solomon " (I Kings xi. 23–25). I Kings xv. 18 also mentions Hezion, father of Tabrimmon and grandfather of Ben-hadad, this latter monarch being apparently different from the Ben-hadad of I Kings xx. In the war between the northern and southern kingdoms after Solomon's death, the latter power invoked the aid of the Arameans. Damascus, situated at the junction of the caravan routes between north and south, as well as between east and west, gladly welcomed this opportunity, and Tabrimmon concluded a treaty with the father of Asa, this being renewed between Asa and Benhadad, and so forcing Baasha (q.v.) to desist from fortifying Ramah (I Kings xv. 18–21). Aramean hostility toward Israel continued during the reigns of Omri and Ahab, and the northern kingdom accordingly made alliance with Phenicia; but since this imperiled the safety of Aramaic caravans to the Mediterranean, the Arameans, during Omri's reign, seized Israelitic cities and made bazaars in Samaria (I Kings xx. 34). It is possible that Omri was a vassal of Aram, and this was certainly the case with Ahab (I Kings xx. 3–4, 9), but I Kings xx. records the complete defeat of the Aramean by the Israelitic king. This struggle may best be dated before 854, the year in which Shalmaneser II. defeated Ben-hadad and twelve allied kings, including Ahab (q.v.).

When Tiglath-Pileser I. had overcome the Hittites, the Assyrians laid claim to northern Syria, but the Arameans took advantage of the weakness of Assyria after Tiglath-Pileser's death and founded a series of petty states in Mesopotamia and north of the mouth of the Orontes, these including Hamath, Patin, Arpad, Sam'al, Yaudi, Gurgum, Suḥi, Laki, and Bit-Adini. Shalmaneser II., however, conquered all the states of northern Syria as far as Hamath, but though in 854, as already noted, he was victorious over the confederation headed by Damascus, it was but a hollow success, as were his three subsequent campaigns in 850 (?), 849, and 846. But soon after 854 war again broke out between Ben-hadad and Ahab, this being continued by Ahab's successors. Finally, however, Ben-hadad suddenly raised the siege of Samaria (II Kings vi. 24–vii. 7) and shortly afterward was murdered by Hazael (II Kings viii. 7–15), who successfully defended Ramoth-gilead against Joram and Ahaziah (II Kings viii. 28–29), but in 842 was defeated by Shalmaneser on Hermon and unsuccessfully besieged in Damascus. Ten years later the inhabitants of Patin killed their King Lubarna II. and made Surri his successor, and when he died during the siege of Kunalua by the Assyrians, the latter crowned Sasi king of Patin. After 839 Hazael was unmolested by the Assyrians, and he became the most dreaded enemy of Judah and Israel (cf. II Kings x. 32–33, xii. 17–18, xiii. 3, 7). With Adad-Nirari III. (812–783), however, Assyrian oppression of Aram commenced again, and in one of his expeditions he beleaguered Mari, or Ben-hadad III., in Damascus, exacting from him rich tribute. In 773 Shalmaneser III. made another expedition against Damascus, and in the following year As-

3. Fortunes of the Syrian States.

shur-Dan III. marched against Hadrach, on Lebanon (Zech. ix. 1). These diversions were doubtless the factors that enabled Joash of Israel to defeat Ben-hadad III. thrice and probably to wrest from him the conquests of his father Hazael west of the Jordan (II Kings xiii. 14–19, 24–25); although the real liberator of Israel from the Arameans was Jeroboam II., who regained all the territory from Hamath to the Dead Sea. The fall of the Aramean states was the work of Tiglath-Pileser III. (745–727). Arpad was the first to yield (740), followed by other Syrian principalities in alliance with Armenia. Unki (the modern al-Amḳ) and Kullani (the Calno of Isa. x. 9) were taken in 738, and nineteen districts of Hamath were formed into the Assyrian province of Simirra. During Tiglath-Pileser's Median campaigns (737–735) Rezon of Damascus, aided by Pekah of Israel, revolted, captured Elath, and besieged Jerusalem until forced by Tiglath-Pileser to withdraw. The Assyrian king now subdued the northern parts of Israel, and in 732 Damascus was reduced and Rezon slain, while Ahaz of Judah did homage to Tiglath-Pileser in Damascus (II Kings xv. 29, xvi. 5–10). The subjugation of the remaining provinces quickly followed. In 720 Ilu-bi'di, or Yau-bi'di, of Hamath, in alliance with Arpad, Simirra, Damascus, and Samaria, revolted, but in the same year Sargon crushed them, probably simultaneously with the subjugation of Sam'al. Finally Gurgum was incorporated with Assyria in 711, and the first period of Syria's history came to an end.

2. To the Year 332 B.C.: In 625 Syria was invaded by Scythian hordes, and from the battle of Megiddo (609) to that of Carchemish (605) the land was under the sway of Pharaoh Necho, after which it came under the dominion of the Neo-Babylonian empire. With the fall of Babylon in 539 Syria was made part of the Persian province " beyond the river " (Neh. ii. 7, 9), over which a satrap ruled, apparently residing in Aleppo, though Damascus was the most important of the inland cities. Aramaic became the official language for the conquests of the Persian empire, and south of Carchemish Mabog (the Greek Bambyce and the modern Mambij) became a religious center for the worship of Atargatis, while Nebo was worshiped in such cities as Edessa and Palmyra. The general fortunes of Syria during the Persian period were evil, since the land constituted the route of the expeditions against Egypt, Phenicia, and Palestine. See MEDO-PERSIA.

3. To the Year 64 B.C.: In 332 Syria passed under Macedonian dominion, and with peculiar facility adopted Hellenic culture. The death of Alexander in 323 was followed by the dismemberment of his empire, and in 321 Seleucus I., Nicator, became ruler of Babylonia, although it was not until the death of his great rival, Antigonus, satrap of Phrygia, in the battle of Ipsus in 301 that he became uncontested lord of the greater part of Syria. He made his capital the city of Antioch on the Orontes, which he himself had founded, his eastern capital being another of his many new cities, Seleucia on the Tigris, south of Bagdad. Seleucus was succeeded by Antiochus I. (280–261), but in the reign of the latter's son, Antiochus II.

(261–246), the decay of the kingdom began. Bactria and Parthia became independent; the Attalids harried Asia Minor; Palestine and Phenicia had been ceded to Egypt in the previous reign; and for a time Ptolemy III. Euergetes, ruled the Seleucid dominions. In 198, after several reverses, Antiochus III., the Great (223–187) definitely recovered Palestine from Egypt, but his crushing defeat by the Romans at Magnesia (190) brought with it the loss of Asia Minor to the Taurus. Cappadocia and Armenia revolted, while the pro-Hellenic and anti-Jewish sympathies of Seleucus IV. (187–175) and Antiochus IV. (175–164) provoked the revolt of the Hasmoneans (q.v.), which finally detached Palestine from Syrian sway. Between 150 and 140 the Parthians won from Syria the Iranian provinces and Babylonia, and with the death of Antiochus VII. in battle against the Parthian Phraates (129) Seleucid power was restricted to Syria. Internecine strife broke out after the death of Antiochus VIII. in 112, and in 83 Tigranes II., the Great, of Armenia, made himself master of Syria. In 69 Tigranes was crushed by Lucullus, who placed the Seleucid Antiochus XIII. on the throne, but this petty king fled before Pompey, and in 64 Syria became a Roman province (for more detailed account of this period see PTOLEMIES; and SELEUCIDÆ).

4. To the Year 635 A.D.: Under the Seleucids Syria proper had apparently been divided into the four districts of Antiochia, Seleucia, Apamea, and Laodicea. The Romans, bounding the country by the Taurus, the middle Euphrates, the Gulf of Issus, Parthia, and the isthmus of Suez, divided it into the ten districts of Commagene, Cyrrhestica, Chalybonitis, Pieria, Cassiotis, Chalcidice, Apamene, Laodicea, Palmyrene, and Cœle-Syria.

1. Under the Roman Empire. There were also a number of princelings who were Roman clients: the Herodians of Palestine, a Seleucid dynasty in Commagene (until 72 A.D.), the dynasties in Chalcis (until 92 A.D.), Abila (until 41 A.D.), Arethusa and Emesa (until 72 A.D.), and Damascus and Petra (until 106 A.D.). On the death of Antiochus XII. in battle in 85 B.C., Damascus passed under Arab control, only to submit to Roman dominion. When Paul fled from the city, it was controlled by a governor appointed by Aretas (see NABATÆANS), but in the reign of Trajan it became a Roman provincial city. From 65 to 48 Syria was under the sway of Pompey, but in 56 Crassus received it, and after sharing the vicissitudes of the period, it was controlled by Mark Antony from 41 to 30, despite attempted Parthian invasions. It was one of the provinces assigned to Augustus in 27 B.C., and after the Jewish war of 66–70 was separated from Palestine. Septimius Severus (193–211) divided the district into Syria Magna and Syria Phenice, the latter including, besides Phenicia, Heliopolis, Emesa, Damascus, Palmyra, Auranitis, Batanea, and Trachonitis. As the heir of the Seleucids, Trajan (98–117), and Caracalla (211–217) took possession of the Mesopotamian regions, so that a distinction was now drawn between Osrhoene in the west, Mygdonia in the east, Zabdicene, and the district the of Arabes Scenitæ. Constantine the Great detached Commagene and Cyrrhestica from

Syria, which was included in the " province of the Euphrates "; and on the division of the Roman Empire in 394 Syria was given to Byzantium. Theodosius II. (408–450) divided what remained of Roman Syria—the eastern part had long been the prey of Arabs and Parthians—into Syria Prima, or the coast and the northern portions as far as the Euphrates, and Syria Secunda, or the country bounded by the southern course of the Orontes, the capital of the former division being Antioch, and of the latter Apamea.

The rise of the Sassanian dynasty in the third century brought new danger to the Roman power in Syria, and Sapor I. (241–272) was even able to make the Roman Emperor Valerian (q.v.) prisoner in Antioch. A little later Zenobia, queen of Palmyra, sought, in alliance with Persia, to establish a Syrian world-empire, but the exten-

2. Period of Persian Rule. sion of her domains to Syria, Mesopotamia, and part of Egypt brought her into conflict with Rome, the result being a crushing defeat by Aurelian at Ḥomṣ in 271. In the reign of Jovinian the Romans were forced to cede Nisibis, among other places, to Sapor II. (309–379); and though the *status quo* was maintained by the treaty between Theodosius II. and Yazdagird I. (399–420), war with the Romans again broke out in the reign of Kavad, the result being the treaty of 531, humiliating to the Romans. Chosroes I. (531–579) ravaged the portions of western Syria still belonging to the Romans, taking Antioch, among other cities, in 540; while in the reign of Chosroes II. (590–628) his general reduced Hamath and Edessa in 609, Aleppo in 611, Antioch, Damascus, and Jerusalem in 614, and Egypt in 618. For a brief time Heraclius (610–641) recovered the Roman territories which the Persians had held since 623, but in 635 Syria passed definitely into the hands of the Arabs.

5. To the Year 1516: Long before the Arab expansion there had been Arab kingdoms and enclaves in and near Syrian soil, such as the Laḥmid dynasty and the Nabatæans (q.v.), the latter gradually spreading their power from northwestern Arabia as far as Damascus and Palmyra. It was

1. Arab Dominion. not, however, until the Arabs had been unified and inspired by the teachings of Mohammed that the establishment of an Arab world-power was projected. The first land to yield to the immigration from the interior of Arabia was Syria, and in 635 the Byzantine Emperor Heraclius was routed by Ḥalid on the banks of the Yarmuk. Damascus was retaken in 636, Jerusalem and Antioch fell in 637, Hamath and Aleppo surrendered voluntarily, and in 640 Cæsarea was taken. Muawiya (661–750), the founder of the Omayyad dynasty, transferred the khalifate from Medina to Damascus, and a period of glory began for the city. With the rise of the Abbasid dynasty in the eighth century, power passed from Damascus to Bagdad, but learning still flourished in Syria, especially at Damascus, and through Syriac translations the writings of the Greeks became accessible to the Arabs. As the Abbasid dynasty decayed, Turkish elements commenced to make themselves felt, and while in 837 Theophilus of Byzantium dev-

astated northern Syria and Mesopotamia, in 878 the Turk Aḥmad ibn Tulun extended his power from Egypt over Syria as far as Mesopotamia. Although his dynasty was extirpated by the Abbasids in 905, the Hamdanids had meanwhile founded a double kingdom with capitals at Mosul and Aleppo. After 970 the Fatimids ruled in Damascus, and toward the middle of the eleventh century the Seljuḳs for a time ruled the greater portion of the Mohammedan East. In 1071 the Seljuk Malik-Shah took Jerusalem, reducing Damascus five years later, while in 1085 Antioch, a Greek possession since 966, was lost to the Turkish Sulaiman of Iconium.

During the period of the Crusades (q.v.) the fortunes of war at first inclined toward the Christian side. In 1098 Antioch was taken by the Franks, and a year later Jerusalem was theirs.

2. The Crusades and Turkish Ascendency. In the latter year Baldwin was lord of Edessa, but in 1144 the city was forced to capitulate to Imad-al-Din Zengi, whose son, Nur-al-Din, not only held possession of northern Syria, but made resistance to the crusaders a religious obligation. The battle of Ḥaṭṭin, near Tiberias, in 1187, where Saladin (1169–93) conquered the Franks, marked the turning-point of the crusades. Acre and Jerusalem were taken, and by the peace of 1193 the Franks were obliged to surrender the entire coast from Jaffa to Acre. Malik al-Kamil (1218–38), on the other hand, made a treaty with Emperor Frederick II. whereby Jerusalem and the coast cities were given to the Franks for ten years. In 1244 the alliance of the Franks, Nasir Daud of Karak, and Saliḥ Ismail of Damascus was defeated by the Mameluke Bibars at Gaza. With the fall of the kingdom of Chwarizm in the first half of the thirteenth century, the Turkish hordes poured into Syria, where, in the pay of the Mameluke Saliḥ of Egypt, they won Jerusalem (1244), Damascus (1245), Baalbek (1246), and Ascalon and Tiberias (1247). In 1269–70 the Mongols under Hulagu Khan overran Syria, but in the latter year they were routed by Bibars at 'Ain Jalut, near Nablus (the ancient Shechem), and all Syria now passed under Egyptian control. Bibars successfully opposed the crusaders, taking Antioch in 1268, while in 1291 al-Ashraf Ḥalil of Egypt reduced Acre, the last stronghold of the Christians in Syria. After a century of strife between Bahritic and Cherkiss Mamelukes and the Ilkhans of Hulagu's line, Syria was once more terribly devastated by the Tatar hordes under Timur in 1400.

6. From 1516 to the Present Time: In 1516 Syria was wrested from the Egyptian Mamelukes by the Osmanli Turk, Selim I. of Constantinople, and since that time the country has formed part of the Turkish empire. From 1545 to 1634 a Druse kingdom maintained itself, with a capital at Beirut, but was finally crushed by Amurath. Ali Bey of Egypt became lord of Syria in 1771, and in his Egyptian campaign Napoleon reduced Jaffa and besieged Acre, ultimately penetrating as far as Safed and Nazareth. Meanwhile, in the middle of the eighteenth century Shaikh Zahir al-Omar had gained control of Lower Galilee and a considerable portion of Upper Galilee, his capital being at Acre, while his son and successor, Jazzar Pasha, ruled from Baalbek to Cæsarea. In 1832, however, Ibrahim Pasha, son of Mohammed Ali of Egypt, aided by the Druse prince, took Acre and Damascus and defeated the Turks at Ḥoms and Bailan, although the European powers secured a peace favorable to Turkey. A rebellion broke out against the Egyptians in 1834, and though at first Ibrahim was successful, he was finally defeated by an Anglo-Austrian force. Another anti-Egyptian revolt broke out in Lebanon in 1840, and the same European allies restored Syria to the Turkish dominions. After the Arab conquest of 635 the position of the Christians was generally not unfavorable, although they were persecuted by the Fatamid Hakim bi-Amrillah and by Timur. The Turks sought to mediate between the different Christian sects, but in 1860 European interference in Syrian affairs, combined with the Indian Mutiny, led to a Christian massacre by Druses and Turkish soldiers, the result being a punitive expedition of the French against the Druses. (G. Beer.)

IV. Population: The population of Syria, which here includes the five governmental divisions of Aleppo, Beirut, The Lebanon, Damascus, and Jerusalem, was estimated in 1905 to be between three and three and a quarter millions; about 700,000 of these are in Palestine.

	All Syria	Mutessari-fat of Jerusalem.
Moslems	1,865,595	251,332
Christians		44,389
Latins	35,144	24,793
Maronites	308,740	401
Uniate Greeks	141,407	1,014
" Syrians	45,793	179
" Armenians	19,459	499
" Chaldeans........	17,865	
Syrian Jacobites	45,805	150
Orthodox Nestorians	15,300	
Orthodox Greeks	304,140	16,039
Gregorian Armenians	23,815	715
Protestants	21,520	599
	978,988	
Jews	90,382	39,866
Druses....................	151,837	
Nusairi	119,720	
Ismailî	9,000	
Foreigners	20,000	6,051
	3,235,512	

Of these it may be said that the Druses (q.v.) and Nusairî are semi-pagan; the Bedawin, nominally Moslem, are really ignorant and superstitious deists; the Maronites are devoted adherents of the papacy; the Ismailî are heretical Moslems; while the Greeks, Armenians, and Jacobites are Oriental Christians. The bulk of the population in the cities is Mohammedan, excepting Beirut, of whose population of 140,000 less than one-third are Mohammedans. The northern part of Lebanon is almost exclusively Maronite; the southern portion, south of the Damascus road, being chiefly Druse, with scattering villages of Greeks, Maronites, and Moslems. In Palestine proper the most of the villagers are Moslems, the Greeks and Uniate Greeks being dispersed in northern Palestine and on the plain of Sharon.

V. The Native Oriental Churches: These are the Orthodox Greek, the Maronite, the Uniate Greek, the Jacobite, Armenian, and Uniate Armenian. The **Greeks** number about 304,000. They are Syrians by birth and descent, and speak only the Arabic language. The doctrines and ritual are the same as in Greece and Russia. They differ from the Roman Church in (1) the calendar, (2) the doctrine concerning the procession of the Holy Spirit, (3) retaining the use of pictures and excluding images from sacred buildings, (4) rejecting of purgatory, (5) retaining communion in both kinds, and (6) in permitting the marriage of the secular clergy. The church is divided into the patriarchates of Antioch and Jerusalem, which, though nominally independent, are really under the control of the primate of Constantinople. The patriarch of Antioch governs the bishoprics of Beirut, Tripoli, Akkar, Latakîa, Hamah, Ḥoms, Saidnaya, and Tyre. The patriarchate of Jerusalem includes Palestine and Perea, and has under it the bishoprics of Nazareth, Akka, Lydda, Gaza, Sebaste, Nablus, Philadelphia, and Petra. Among these the bishop of Akka is the only one who resides in his diocese; all the others live in the convent at Jerusalem. The Greek Church allows the reading of the Scriptures by the people, hence they have become more enlightened than any other of the Syrian sects. The **Jacobites** (q.v.) use the Syriac language in church services, although it is not understood by the people. Their head is the patriarch of Mardin. Their number is small, chiefly in Sudud, Kuryetein, Ḥoms, Nebk, Damascus, and Aleppo. They are poor and industrious, and receive the Scriptures without opposition. The **Maronites** (q.v.) renounced monothelitism in 1182, and submitted to the pope. They are devoted Roman Catholics, and call their part of Lebanon the Holy Mountain. Although adhering to the pope, they still retain many of their former peculiarities. Their ecclesiastical language is Syriac; their patron saint, Marōn, is not found in the Roman calendar; they have their own church establishment, and the people regard their patriarch as not inferior to the pope; and their secular clergy marry. Their convents, numbering nearly 100, own their best estates in Lebanon, and formerly supported about 2,000 monks and nuns, with a revenue of not less than $350,000. Emigration has been steadily reducing the numbers of those entering the monasteries and convents. The people are independent, hardy, and industrious, but are left in gross ignorance, illiteracy, and superstition. Their clergy are educated at Ain Werka; and those trained in Rome are men of fair learning: but the mass of the priests are lamentably ignorant.

The **Roman Catholic** schismatic churches which are in connection with the Roman communion— Greek, Syrian, and Armenian—sprang from the missionary efforts of Roman Catholic priests and Jesuits during the past two centuries. The Greeks retain the marriage of the clergy, their Arabic service, oriental calendar, and communion in both kinds. The **Armenian** population is confined to the vicinity of Antioch and Aleppo, speaking the Turkish and Armenian languages. The **Jews** of Palestine are foreigners, numbering about 40,000, having come from every country on earth, and living chiefly in Jerusalem, Hebron, Tiberius, Safed, and the Jewish colonies. But the Jews of Damascus (5,000), Aleppo (15,000), and Beirut (5,000) are natives, speaking the Arabic, and many of them possess great wealth (see ZIONISM).

VI. Modern Protestant Missions in Syria. 1. American Presbyterian:

The first modern Protestant mission to Syria began in Jan., 1819, when Revs. Pliny Fisk (q.v.) and Levi Parsons, missionaries of the A. B. C. F. M., landed in Smyrna. In Feb., 1821, Parsons reached Jerusalem.

1. Origins and Work. In 1823 Messrs. Fisk, Jonas King, from America, and Way, of the London Jews Society, reached Beirut, and summered in Lebanon. Jerusalem and Beirut continued for years the two centers of American missionary labor, until 1843, when the American mission was withdrawn from Jerusalem, and confined to Syria proper, leaving Palestine to the Church Missionary Society. In 1871 the Syria mission of the American Board was transferred to the Presbyterian Board of Foreign Missions of the United States, owing to the then recent reunion of the two branches of the Presbyterian Church. The whole number of American missionaries laboring in Syria under these two boards from 1823 to 1910 is as follows: male missionaries, 60; female missionaries, 93; printers, 4; total, 157. The missionaries were at first directed to attempt the reform of the oriental churches, leaving the converts within the oriental communions; but it soon became necessary to organize a distinct Oriental Evangelical Church. Thirty-four native Evangelical churches have been organized, of which 14 have native ordained pastors, and 27 licensed preachers aid in the work of evangelization. The number of converts is about 2,800, of whom 1,100 are women. Eighty Sunday-schools contain about 7,000 scholars. The number of Protestant adherents is about 8,000. Medical mission work has received especial attention in a well-equipped hospital at Tripoli and in medical practise among the poor in the interior towns and villages. The first refuge and sanatorium for tuberculous patients was opened at Tunieh in 1909, with summer quarters at Shebainyeh.

The great work undertaken by the American Syria Mission, however, is not merely for the three millions in Syria, but, through the medium of the Arabic Scriptures and Christian Arabic

2. Publications; Arabic Bible. literature, for the 235,000,000 of the Mohammedan world. The work of translating the Bible from the original tongues into Arabic was begun in 1848 by Dr. Eli Smith, who labored assiduously until his death, Jan. 11, 1857. Only Genesis, Exodus, and the first sixteen chapters of Matthew had received his final revision; but he had revised and nearly prepared for the press the whole of the New Testament, and all except Jeremiah, Lamentations, and the last fourteen chapters of Isaiah, of the Old Testament. On his death, Rev. Cornelius Van Alan Van Dyck continued the work of translation. In 1860 the New Testament was completed, and issued from the press; and in 1865 the entire Bible was finished, and sent forth to the world. Dr. Smith had prepared in 1837, with the aid of Homan Hal-

lock, the punches of a new font of Arabic type, made from the best specimens of Arabic calligraphy. The type was cast by Tauchnitz, in Leipsic. This type, which at first was anathematized by the religious heads of the oriental sects, has been adopted by the Turkish government journals, the Dominican press at Mosul, the Greek, and other native presses, and the Leipsic Arabic press. Seven complete editions of the Arabic Bible have been electrotyped at the American Press at Beirut at the expense of the American Bible Society, together with many portions in various types of different books of the Old and New Testaments. Of the seven complete editions four are unpointed except where ambiguity would result without the vowels and two are completely voweled. One is a second font Reference Bible, and two editions of a first font Reference Bible have been printed from types. An entirely new edition of the largest first font Reference Bible is now in preparation, with a new set of references based upon the standard American and English editions. The adaptation of the new references was begun in 1908 by the present editor, Rev. F. E. Hoskins, D.D., and, with the making of the plates for about 1,450 pages, can not be completed before 1914. A photographic edition of the first font pointed Bible has also been issued in London by the British and Foreign Bible Society. The Arabic Bible, during the past thirty-seven years, has been distributed throughout Syria and Palestine, Mesopotamia, Egypt, in Asia Minor, Tunis, Algiers, Tripoli, Morocco, Sierra Leone, Liberia, Zanzibar, Aden, Bagdad, India, China, and wherever Syrian emigrants are found in the United States, South America, and Australia. Between July 1, 1872, and Dec. 31, 1909, there have been printed in Beirut, 158,998 complete Bibles, 210,522 complete New Testaments and 972,746 parts, making a total of 1,342,266 volumes of the Arabic Scriptures. In addition to this, nearly 500 different books have been printed at the Beirut press; comprising works on medicine, surgery, anatomy and physiology, chemistry, natural philosophy, botany, astronomy, the higher mathematics, geography with atlases, grammar, arithmetic, history, theology, homiletics, church history, evidences of Christianity, mental philosophy, hermeneutics, etc., together with religious books and tracts, and illustrated books for the young, and weekly and monthly journals. Butrus Bistany, a learned convert from the Maronite faith, who aided Dr. Eli Smith in the Bible translation, published, in 1870, a fine dictionary of the Arabic language (2 vols., 8vo, 1,200 pages) and began in 1872 an Arabic encyclopedia (12 vols., 8vo, 800 pages each), of which vol. xi. is completed. During the year 1909, 39,231,000 pages in Arabic were printed at the Beirut press, making 962,577,000 from the foundation of the press. The demand for the Beirut publications is greater in Egypt than in any other country. The Beirut press has an Arabic type foundry and electrotype apparatus, five steam presses, six hand presses, hydraulic, hot rolling, and embossing machines, and sixty-two employees. The American Bible Society and the American and London Religious Tract Societies have given substantial aid in the printing and publishing work of the mission.

Education is a prominent branch of the mission-work in Syria. The first missionaries found the people in a deplorable state of intel-

3. Educa-tional Work. lectual and moral ignorance. The only schools were the Moslem medrisehs, attached to the mosques, and the cler-ical training-school of the Maronites at Ain Wurka, Mount Lebanon. Books were to be made for read-ers, and readers for books. Drs. Thomson and Van Dyck founded a seminary for boys in Abeih in 1846, which was placed under the care of Simeon Howard Calhoun in 1849, and continued in his care until 1876. It was the highest literary institution in Syria for years, until the founding of the Syrian Protes-tant College in Beirut (see below). In the absence of any adequate public school system the mission has more than 100 day-schools gathering nearly 5,000 children from all the religious sects. It has three boarding-schools—in Beirut, Sidon, and Trip-oli—for the higher education of girls with nearly 300 pupils; four training-schools for boys—in Suk ul-Gharb, Sidon, Shweir, and Tripoli—where 500 boys are being educated along the best American lines. The Sidon school for boys, now known as Gerard Institute, has industrial training in four de-partments and on its large farm an orphanage for children from Protestant families. Several members of the mission give theological instruction to candi-dates for the Christian ministry. The total number under instruction is nearly 6,000 pupils.

2. The Syrian Protestant College: Situated on a commanding location at Ras Beirut, with its eight-een stone buildings scattered over its campus of forty acres, this college is now the largest American educational institution in the world outside the boundaries of the United States. While a direct outgrowth of the American mission and closely affiliated with its work, it is not connected with any missionary society, but is undenominational, and has an entirely independent organization. It was incorporated by the legislature of New York in 1863 and is under the control of the board of trustees residing in that state, who have charge of all the funds of the college and ultimate authority in all the affairs of the institution. The local government is vested in the faculty. The college began with a preparatory class in 1865 and the college proper opened in the fall of 1866. A medical class was formed in 1867. In the autumn of 1873 the college moved to the present location. The departments of the college are seven: preparatory, collegiate, com-merce, medicine, pharmacy, training-school for nurses, and Biblical archeology. English is the lan-guage of instruction in all the departments. The eighteen buildings furnish excellent accommodations for the present staff of 70 instructors and nearly 900 students. There are nine well-furnished laborato-ries; a library with over 15,000 volumes; the George E. Post Hall of Science contains nine museums scientifically arranged for exhibition and study; the astronomical observatory is well equipped; four new buildings accommodate the hospitals for women, children, and eye diseases, together with the training-school for nurses. The whole number of students in the college for the year 1909–10 was 845, of whom 4 were Behai, 25 Druses, 88 Jews, 104

Moslems, 160 Protestants, 85 from the Roman, and the remainder, 379, from the orthodox Christian sects of the orient. They represented at least 12 nationalities and spoke 24 different languages. The total number of graduates to the year 1909 was 1,767, distributed as follows: preparatory (since 1883), 922; collegiate (since 1870), 300; commerce (since 1902), 53; pharmacy (since 1875), 162; med-icine (since 1871), 330.

3. Irish Presbyterian Mission in Damascus: This was founded in 1843. The United Presbyterian Church of the United States soon entered upon the work, and continued to cooperate for a number of years, until the latter church concentrated its work upon Egypt. Since 1905 the Irish church has con-fined its work to Damascus and the village of Blu-dân in the Anti-Lebanon. Besides the evangelistic work of preaching, there are in Damascus a girls' boarding- and day-school and a boys' boarding- and day-school in the Christian quarter, and two similar schools in the Jewish quarter for Jews, all under the care of Irish ladies; also two day-schools in Bludân. On the rolls of these schools are about 600 pupils of various sects, including 200 Jews. Two Bible women visit about 230 homes in the Jewish quarter of the city.

4. The Church of England Missions: These, having their center at Jerusalem, embrace a vari-ety of enterprises which, while acknowledging and affiliating with the Anglican bishopric, differ in their organization and policy from each other. The historical beginnings and relations of the four main divisions are not easy to disentangle. (1) The Lon-don Society for Promoting Christianity among the Jews dates back to 1829, when its Jerusalem mis-sion was begun. The other centers now occupied are Safed and Damascus. Since 1829 various insti-tutions have been founded, many of which have passed into other hands. In 1910 there were two boarding-schools for Jewish children, with 80 schol-ars, and a day-school for girls with a regular attend-ance of 130; an industrial establishment for receiv-ing inquirers and teaching them a trade in addition to ordinary Christian instruction. The society has two workshops for carpentry and printing. A prominent feature is the medical work in the hos-pital and three dispensaries, this being the first medical mission of modern times. Christ Church, Jerusalem, was the first Protestant church built in Syria and was consecrated in 1849. There have been 659 baptisms of Hebrews since the foundation. The staff consists of two clergy and twelve lay mis-sionaries with two doctors and five English trained nurses. In connection with Jerusalem there is a small mission in Jaffa. Safed is the center of the work in Galilee. Here there are schools and a hos-pital served by two clergy, three lay missionaries, an English doctor, and three nurses. In Damascus there has been a small mission with schools and in-dustrial work among girls. (2) The Protestant bishopric of Jerusalem (see JERUSALEM, ANGLICAN-GERMAN BISHOPRIC IN) now has attached the Col-legiate Church of St. George with the status of a cathedral, a school for boys and for girls, two hos-tels, and a home for nurses, and is the main center of the Jerusalem and the East Mission whose operations are coextensive with the jurisdiction of the bishopric, which extends over the congregations and interests of the Anglican Church in Egypt, the Sudan, the region on both sides of the Red Sea, Palestine, and Syria, parts of Asia Minor, and the island of Cyprus. (3) The Society for the Propagation of the Gospel in Foreign Parts proposed a mission to the Druses of Lebanon in 1841, but it was many years later before it really entered Syria. In 1905 the society agreed to become trustees of the property of the Jerusalem bishopric, and since then has aided in many of its enterprises. (4) The Church Missionary Society's work in the Holy Land may be said to be the outcome of previous work done about the shores of the Mediterranean and the establishment of the Jerusalem bishopric. It has 11 European and 116 native workers. Its operations are mainly in Palestine, where in 28 stations and outstations it carries on an extensive educational work in 46 schools with nearly 100 teachers and an average daily attendance of 2,581 scholars. Its medical work in 4 well-equipped hospitals and many dispensaries is a great blessing to the country. The native church organizations with 10 ordained men form the Palestine Native Church Council, which aims at self-administration and ultimate financial independence. The communicants number 777 and the adherents 2,239.

5. The German Evangelical Missions: These include the following agencies: (1) The deaconesses of Kaiserswerth, whose work comprises orphan training, higher education of all nationalities, and hospital nursing, and there are 64 sisters in Beirut, Jerusalem, Bethlehem, and Haifa. They began labor in Sidon after the massacres of 1860 and then transferred their work to Beirut, where, in 1910, they have 31 deaconesses and 6 native helpers who serve in the Johanniter Hospital, the large orphanage, and their schools, which contain 320 pupils. In Jerusalem 10 of the deaconesses are nurses in the hospital, 13 serve in the Talitha Kumi Orphanage, and 6 in the magnificent new Augusta Victoria Institute on the Mount of Olives. Two serve in Bethlehem and 2 in Haifa as visiting nurses and kindergarten teachers. They represent one of the finest Christian enterprises in the world. (2) The Syrian Orphanage, commonly called Schoeller's, after its founder, at Jerusalem, is one of the most useful, varied, and successful of the enterprises which came into existence after the massacres of 1860. It has maintained and trained thousands of orphans, instructed the blind, and done much for the industrial improvement of Syria. With 21 German and 14 native workers it carries on a system of kindergarten, elementary, and higher education in the orphanage and tributary schools, which enroll 315 pupils. Its most important features have been its training workshops, where hundreds of boys have been taught printing, blacksmithing, locksmithing, tailoring, carpentry and turning, pottery and brickmaking, basket and chair making, and its agricultural departments at Bir Salem in the Plain of Sharon and near Nazareth, the latter a gift of Germans living in America. Its Protestant community embraces 118 communicants and 277 adherents. (3) The Jerusalem Stiftung, which cares for the German

congregations in the Church of the Redeemer at Jerusalem, operates schools, and maintains chaplaincies at Beirut and elsewhere. (4) The Herrnhut or Lutheran Brethren have charge of the Leper Asylum near Jerusalem, where 40 to 60 of these sad sufferers now receive Christian care from trained deaconesses. (5) The Jerusalem Verein (Berlin) was founded in 1852 to assist German evangelical institutions in the orient. It long enjoyed the royal protection of the Empress Augusta and since the present emperor's visit to the Holy Land in 1897 has received special support and encouragement. While contributing yearly to the hospitals, orphanages, leper asylum, supporting German pastors in Jaffa and Haifa, it has also provided native pastors for Arabic-speaking congregations at Jerusalem, Bethlehem, and Beit Jala. It took up independent work at Bethlehem in 1860, Beit Jala in 1870, Hebron in 1884, and Beit Sahur in 1900. (6) The Knights of St. John own the hospitals in Beirut and Jerusalem and the hospice at Jerusalem, and are to have charge of the Augusta Victoria Institute on the Mount of Olives, the largest and finest pile of buildings in the Holy Land devoted to Protestant mission work, which were dedicated with ceremony by Crown Prince Eitel Frederick Apr. 9, 1910.

6. The British Syrian Mission: This enterprise, formerly the British Syrian schools founded in 1860 by Mrs. J. Bowen Thompson and afterward conducted by her sister, Mrs. A. Mentor Mott, has completed its first half century of superb work for the girls and women of Syria and begins another period with extensive enlargements of its training-college at Beirut, where the mission aims thoroughly to train teachers for its own 38 schools, which are grouped about the main centers at Beirut, Damascus, Baalbec, Tyre, Hasbeya, Zahleh, Shemlân, and Ain Zehalteh, and also to render the largest possible assistance to the work of all other societies. Twenty English workers superintend the 38 schools, with 82 teachers and over 3,000 pupils. Fifteen Bible women visit thousands of homes and teach Christian and Moslem women to read. Two schools for the blind, one for girls and one for men, the latter with 23 pupils, teach various forms of handicraft in addition to reading and other studies.

7. The Society of Friends (English): This organization carries on work on Mount Lebanon with resident missionaries at Brumana, Beit Miri, and Ras al-Metn. In Brumana are two large boarding-schools for boys and for girls, and a hospital with 20 beds where clinics are held regularly and a number of Syrian girls have been trained as nurses. Besides these larger stations they have schools in eight villages and about 1,000 pupils under instruction, 13 English missionaries, and 35 native workers. This mission was founded in 1873 by Theophilus Waldemeier, and was carried on by a special committee until 1898, when it was taken over by the Board of the Friends' Foreign Mission Association as one of its five fields of missionary labor (Syria, India, Madagascar, China, and Ceylon). In 1896 Waldemeier left the mission and founded the Lebanon Hospital for the Insane at Asfurîyeh just outside of Beirut. After extensive journeys in Switzerland, Great Britain, and the United States,

Waldemeier proceeded with the erection of the buildings which now constitute the best-equipped home for the insane in the whole Turkish empire. The general committee of the hospital is in London, the trustees are English and American, while the executive committee is international.

The Society of Friends (American) carries on an extensive medical and educational work at Ramallah, Jaffa, and Ramleh with 4 American and 22 Syrian workers.

8. Other Enterprises: These, mentioned in the order of their founding, are: (1) The Reformed Presbyterians (Covenanters) in North America occupied Latakia in 1859 and later extended their work to Suadieh, Tarsus, Mesine, and Cyprus. They have done much for the Nusairî, really a pagan people, which the government has attempted to make Mohammedan. Twenty American missionaries with 48 native helpers in the 4 main stations and 9 outstations have gathered more than 350 communicants and 800 pupils in 15 schools. (2) The Tabeetha Mission (1863) in Jaffa, aiming to give a Christian training to Christian, Jewish, and Moslem girls, was founded and is still carried on by Miss Walker Arnott. Four foreign and 10 Syrian helpers serve a home with 44 boarders, 2 day-schools with 160 girls, and oversee an industrial work employing 500 women and girls. (3) The Church of Scotland Jewish Mission (1864) in Beirut aims to create and direct a movement among the Jews by which they may deliver themselves from rabbinical traditions and seek after God, and to infuse Christian knowledge rather than to withdraw individuals. Eight British and 12 Syrian workers maintain excellent day schools for boys and girls and a boarding home for Jewish girls, with a total of about 400 pupils. (4) Miss Taylor's orphanage for Moslem and Druse Girls (1868) in Beirut is without question the most unique work in Syria, if judged by the class of pupils and the influence exerted by Miss Taylor's impressive personality and those who have followed her. (5) The Palestine and Lebanon Nurses' Mission (1883) at Baaklin in the Lebanon for the evangelization of the Druses through the agency of a medical mission, with 5 English and 2 native workers, maintains a cottage hospital with 15 beds, a large clinic, and services and classes for Druse women and girls. (6) The Edinburgh Medical Missionary Society at Damascus (1884), after many years in hired premises, erected in 1908 its commodious Victoria Hospital, where Dr. Frank Mackinnon and another English doctor with 3 English and 2 native nurses receive and treat the sick poor of all creeds and nationalities. Their aim and object is " to preach the Gospel and to heal the sick." (7) The United Free Church of Scotland Mission has a fine hospital at Tiberias on the Sea of Galilee (1884) with 40 beds and a large outpatient department where Dr. Torrance has labored 26 years; another large hospital at Hebron, and one at Safed. In connection with the medical work are 4 schools with 330 pupils and religious services and communities. There are 12 British and 20 native workers. (8) The Dufferin and Procter Memorial Schools for boys and girls at Swheifat were founded in 1885 by Miss Louisa Procter, an Irish

lady who gave her money and 21 years of her life to the building up of two boarding-schools. At her death the work was placed in the hands of her assistant, Rev. Tanius Saad, who, in cooperation with an English and Irish committee of reference and a board of visitors, is carrying on the work successfully. Two English and 6 Syrian workers care for 173 pupils in the schools. (9) The Christian and Missionary Alliance of New York began in 1893 an undenominational work in Jerusalem among Jews, Moslems, and oriental Christians for a deepening of the religious life, and has organized a church with boarding-schools for boys and girls, sends visiting workers into the villages, and supports a day-school for girls in Hebron. (10) The Presbyterian Church of England's Mission to the Jews entered Aleppo in 1895 and aims mainly at helping the Jews while admitting a limited number of Gentiles. Three British and 9 Syrian workers care for a community of 120 Protestants with about 300 pupils in its schools. (11) The Danish Mission to the Orient in 1898 entered Syria, in 1905 took over the Kalamoon district (n.e. of Damascus, toward Palmyra) from the Irish Presbyterian Mission, and has opened work in Yabrood, Nebk, Deir Atiyeh, Hafr, and Karjasem. Eight Danish and 17 Syrian workers have opened 9 schools with 340 pupils, while plans for an extensive medical and church work are well under way. (12) The Swedish Jerusalem Society of Stockholm entered Jerusalem in 1903 and is building a hospital at Bethlehem, where Dr. Ribbing has been laboring since 1904. This society employs 4 Swedish, 2 German, 1 English, and 4 Syrian workers.

VII. Summary and Conclusion: The whole number of foreign Protestant societies now operating in Syria is 35, with not less than 500 foreign workers of whom about 150 are Americans and 200 are from Great Britain. The pupils in Protestant schools number more than 20,000. Medical missions are carried on in 28 cities and towns, with more than 40 foreign physicians and twice as many trained nurses. In addition to the Protestant educational institutions in Syria and Palestine, numerous schools have been opened by other sects, foreign and native, and the Turkish government has begun to develop a system of its own, but has apparently begun at the top with military and civil institutions instead of at the bottom with elementary education. Beirut was in the days of the Roman empire a city of schools and is so still. Out of 97 schools of all grades 36 are Moslem (mainly elementary attached to the mosques), 43 are foreign, 14 belong to the native Christian sects and 2 to the Jews. Out of the 13,256 scholars more than half are in foreign schools and more than two-thirds are in Christian schools. The highest grades of all schools are Christian.

The re-promulgation of the constitution in Turkey in 1908, the deposition of Abd ul-Hamid in 1909, and the other stirring events of the years 1907–09 gave a great impetus to all missionary operations. The new government, despite the malignant influence and activity of the reactionaries, has shown itself friendly to all educational enterprises, and men prominent in the new régime have rendered superb tributes to the foreigners who toiled amid the darkness and confusion of the past twenty-five years. Great problems confront the present administration. The politico-religious alliance between Islam and the State must certainly give way to something more suited to the modern world. Those who have fanned the fanaticism of the ignorant Moslems are guilty of awful crimes. But closer contact with European influence, the growth of education, the reading of the Bible, the phenomenal increase of newspapers, and the spread of a purer Christianity are surely leavening the minds of an increasingly larger number of Mohammedans. Diplomacy can never regenerate the East. The patient work of education, the preaching of the Gospel, the distribution of God's word among the masses, and the diffusion of Christian literature, will gradually disarm prejudice, awaken inquiry, promote social harmony, destroy polygamy, reform the oriental churches, and bring the followers of Mohammed to the religion of Jesus Christ. Thus will the press, the Church, and the school cooperate in hastening the true regeneration of this most interesting, and, until recently, so degraded land.

H. H. JESSUP†. Revised by F. E. HOSKINS.

BIBLIOGRAPHY: On the geographical and political history up to the fall of the Seleucidan kingdom the literature is fully included in the lists given under ASSYRIA; BABYLONIA; PERSIA; AHAB; ISRAEL, HISTORY OF (where such works as McCurdy's *History, Prophecy and the Monuments* deal with Assyrian and Babylonian control of Syria); PALESTINE; PTOLEMY; and SELEUCIDÆ; see also under DRUSES; and MARONITES. Consult further: G. Cormack, *Egypt in Asia. A Plain Account of pre-Biblical Syria and Palestine*, New York, 1908; Schrader, *KAT*, ed. of 1902, pp. 132–135; A. P. Stanley, *History of Syria and Palestine*, new ed., London, 1883; W. L. Gage, *Palestine, Historic and Descriptive*, London, 1887; H. Winckler, *Keilinschriftliches Textbuch zum A. T.*, 2d ed., Leipsic, 1903; idem, *Auszug aus der vorderasiatische Geschichte*, ib. 1905; A. Henderson, *Historical Geography of Syria*, Edinburgh, 1885; A. Sanda, in *Der alte Orient*, v. no. 3, Leipsic, 1902; T. Nöldeke, in *Hermes*, v. 443–468; A. Neubauer, *La Géographie du Talmud*, Paris, 1868; W. M. Müller, *Asien und Europa nach altägyptischen Denkmälern*, Leipsic, 1893; A. Müller, *Der Islam im Morgen- und Abendland*, 2 vols., Berlin, 1885–87; E. Meyer, *Geschichte des Altertums*, vols. i., iii., Stuttgart, 1884–1901; idem, *Die Entstehung des Judentums*, Halle, 1896; idem, *Die Israeliten und ihre Nachbarstämme*, Halle, 1906; W. Geiger and E. Kuhns, *Iranische Philologie*, ii. 395–604; F. Hommel, *Grundriss der Geographie und Geschichte des alten Orients*, pp. 187–194, Munich, 1904; idem, *Geschichte des alten Morgenlandes*, 3d ed., Leipsic, 1904; G. L. Bell, *Durch die Wüsten und Kulturstätten Syriens*, 2d ed. Leipsic, 1910.

On missionary work, besides the reports of the various bodies operating in Syria, consult: T. Laurie, *Historical Sketch of the Syria Mission*, New York, 1862; R. Anderson, *Oriental Missions*, 2 vols., Boston, 1872; J. S. Dennis, *Sketch of Syrian Missions*, New York, 1872; H. H. Jessup, *Women of the Arabs*, New York, 1874; idem, *Syrian Home Life*, ib. 1874; idem, *Mohammedan Missionary Problem*, Philadelphia, 1880; idem, *Fifty-three Years in Syria*, New York, 1910; E. D. G. Prime, *Forty Years in the Turkish Empire;* . . . *Memoirs of . . . W. Goodell*, New York, 1876; W. A. Holliday, *Historical Sketch of Missions to Syria*, Philadelphia, 1881; Mrs. E. R. Pitman, *Mission Life in Greece and Palestine*, London, 1881; *The Star in the East: quarterly Record of the Progress of Christian Missions within the Turkish Empire*, London, 1883; F. Conil, *Jerusalem moderne. Hist. du mouvement catholique dans la Ville Saint*, Paris, 1894; J. H. Wilson and J. Wells, *Sea of Galilee Mission of the Free Church of Scotland*, Edinburgh, 1895; M. Jullien, *La Nouvelle Mission de la compagnie de Jésus en Syrie, 1831–95*, 2 vols., Tours, 1898; A. Forder, *With the Arabs in Tent and Town; an Account of missionary Work in Moab and Edom*, London, 1902; H. J. E.,

One Hundred Syrian Pictures, illustrating the Work of the Syrian Mission, London, 1903; W. A. Essery, *The Ascending Cross. Some Results of Missions in Bible Lands*, London, 1905; Jehay, *Sujets Ottomans non-Mussulmans*, Brussels, 1906; Baedeker's *Syria and Palestine*, Leipsic, 1908.

SYRIAC LITERATURE.

Syriac literature—the literature of the language designated as " Syriac " or " Syrian " (R. V. marg. " Aramaic," " Aramean ") in the Old Testament (II Kings xviii. 26; Dan. ii. 4; Ezra iv. 7)—is of prime importance in the history of the Christian religion, though not so much for its bearing on the Bible and its exegesis as because of the high value of the Christian literature which it contains. This statement holds good both of the works originally written in Syriac by native authors, and of those works which were first composed in other languages, but which now, their original texts having been lost, are preserved only in Syriac translations. Of the latter type it is sufficient simply to allude to such recent finds as the Old Syriac Gospels from Sinai (see BIBLE VERSIONS, A, III., 1, § 3), to the Odes of Solomon (see SOLOMON, ODES OF), or to the list of " Old Syriac Versions of Early Christian Greek Literature " given by Harnack (*Litteratur*, i. 885–886).

Syriac literature may be divided (1) from the religious point of view into (a) heathen, (b) Jewish, and (c) Christian. (2) Chronologically it ranges from the beginning of the Christian era, or, if the recent discoveries of Aramaic papyri in Egypt be included, from the fifth century B.C.

1. Divisions of Syriac Literature. (3) Geographically the literature ranges to the Middle Ages; while in the nineteenth century a modern Syriac literature sprang up, largely through the agency of the American Mission at Urumiah. (3) Geographically the literature ranges from the southern frontier of Egypt and the shore of the Mediterranean across Mesopotamia to India (Kottayam in Malabar), Turkestan (Semiryeshchie), and China (Singan-fu). (4) In extent and contents Syriac literature is sufficiently rich to arouse the zeal of the scholar, without being so huge as to make him despair, as is the case, for instance, with Arabic. The new *Corpus Scriptorum Christianorum Orientalium* (Paris, 1903 sqq.) allows 125 parts for the Syriac section, or more than for any other branch; a single editor, Paul Bedjan, during recent years has published over thirty volumes, mostly *inedita;* and Paul de Lagarde (q.v.) began a *Bibliotheca Syriaca* (Göttingen, 1892).

Though mainly theological, Syriac literature covers all branches of science—history, geography, philology, medicine, law, and astronomy—and even contains specimens of the romance.

Eusebius, in various places in his *Hist. eccl.*, like Jerome and Gennadius in their *De vir. ill.*, make mention of some Syriac writers who had already become known in the West, but the chief work of this sort is the "Catalogue" drawn up by Ebed Jesu (q.v., where details will be found regarding the edition by J. S. Assemani). Among modern works mention may be made of W. Wright, *Short History of Syriac Literature*, London, 1894 (first
2. General Works on Syriac Literature. published as the article "Syriac Literature" in *Encyclopædia Britannica*, 9th ed., xii. 824–856, London, 1887); R. Duval, *La Littérature syriaque* (Paris, 1899; 2d ed., 1901); E. Nestle, *Litteratura Syriaca* (Berlin, 1888; extract from his *Syrische Grammatik*, 2d ed., giving the titles of the principal publications prior to 1888); C. Brockelmann, *Syrische Grammatik*, pp. 124–144 (2d ed., Berlin, 1905), gives a selection with additions up to 1905, and the same scholar has also treated this field in the section on the Syriac and Christian Arabic literatures in the *Geschichte der christlichen Literaturen des Ostens*, pp. 1–74 (Leipsic, 1907); J. B. Chabot, *Les Langues et les littératures araméens* (Paris, 1910); while more special topics are discussed by A. Baumstark in his "Bibliotheks- und Buchwesen der christlichen Syrier," in *Germania*, Sept. 23, 1909, and in his "Palæstinensia," in *RQS*, xx. 123–149, 157–188, and "Ostsyrisches Christentum und ostsyrischer Hellenismus," ib., xxii., pp. 17–35. For a more thorough study the catalogues of the collections of Syriac manuscripts in the libraries of Europe and the East are indispensable, since a large part of Syriac literature is still hidden in manuscripts, of which some are to be found in America (for a list of some of these catalogues see *BrGr.*,* p. 124–125; cf. also the works referred to in SYRIAC CHURCH, especially those of F. C. Burkitt, R. Duval, J. Labourt, and L. J. Tixeront).

A Judæo-pagan source is probably to be sought in the story of Ahikar the Sage, a fragment of which has been found in one of the Aramaic papyri now in the Royal Library, Berlin, while the complete version was made accessible by F. C. Conybeare, J. R.
3. Judæo-Pagan Writings. Harris, and A. S. Lewis in their *Story of Ahikar from the Syriac, Arabic, Armenian, Ethiopic, Greek, and Slavonic Versions* (London, 1898; cf. *BrL*, p. 5; F. Nau, *Histoire et sagesse d'Ahikar l'Assyrien*, Paris, 1909); and Mara bar Serapion, who, in a letter to his son (first edited by W. Cureton, in his *Spicilegium Syriacum*, London, 1855), makes the wise king of the Jews (i.e., Christ) the

* Special abbreviations employed in this article:

AB, Analecta Bollandiana, Paris and Brussels, 1882 sqq.
BO, J. S. Assemani, *Bibliotheca Orientalis*, Rome, 1719–28.
BrGr, C. Brockelmann, *Syrische Grammatik*, 2d ed., Berlin, 1905.
BrL, C. Brockelmann, in *Geschichte der christlichen Literaturen des Ostens*, Leipsic, 1907.
GA, Abhandlungen der königlichen Gesellschaft der Wissenschaften zu Göttingen, Göttingen, 1843 sqq.
NSt, Neue Studien zur Geschichte der Theologie und Kirche, ed. G. N. Bonwetsch and R. Seeberg, Leipsic, 1897 sqq.
OChr, Oriens Christianus, Rome, 1901 sqq.
PO, Patrologia Orientalis, Paris, 1903 sqq.
ROC, Revue de l'orient chrétien, Paris, 1896 sqq.
RQS, Römische Quartalschrift, Rome, 1887 sqq.

equal of Socrates and Pythagoras, was probably a pagan, not a Christian (cf. Harnack, *Litteratur* i. 763, ii. 701; E. Renan, in *JA*, IV., xix. 328; F. Schulthess, in *ZDMG*, li. 365–391).

The beginnings of the Syriac version of the Bible probably came from Syrian Jews (see BIBLE VERSIONS, A, III.; cf. also W. E. Barnes, "The Peshitta Version of II Kings," in *JTS*, vi. 220–232, xi 533–542); but a practical and critical edition of the Syriac Old Testament is still to be made (cf. E. Nestle, in *TLB*, 1910, no. 23, and the same scholar on the edition of the British and Foreign Bible Society, in *ZDMG*, lix. 31–32). To Christian or Gnostic literature, rather than to apocryphal or even Jewish, belong the Odes or Evangelion (q.v.), which were first edited by J. R. Harris (Cambridge, 1909;
4. Bible and Apocrypha. 2d ed. revised, 1911), who has also published *An Early Christian Psalter* (London, 1909; cf. A. Harnack and J. Flemming, *Ein jüdisch-christlicher Psalmbuch aus dem ersten Jahrhundert*, Leipsic, 1910). On the Syriac translations of the New Testament general reference may be made to BIBLE VERSIONS, A, III., to which may be added, as the most important subsequent publications, A. S. Lewis' *Old Syriac Gospels or Evangelion da-Mepharreshê: Being the Text of the Sinai or Syro-Antiochen Palimpsest, including the latest Additions and Emendations with the Variants of the Curetonian Text* (London, 1910) and H. K. H. von Soden's *Die Schriften des Neuen Testaments in ihrer ältesten erreichbaren Textgestalt* (§§ 331, 342, 363–368, 463, 493, 548, Berlin, 1902 sqq.), his main conclusions being that the *Diatessaron* of Tatian (q.v.) existed not only in Syriac, but also in Greek, and that the influence of both Tatian and his work was extremely great on the text of the New Testament. Among the Apocrypha of the New Testament more than usual interest attaches to the Acts of Thomas (see APOCRYPHA, B, II. (9), and cf. A. S. Lewis, in *Horæ Semiticæ*, iii London, 1904), which seems to be of Syriac origin and to belong to the school of Bardesanes (q.v.) It is also noteworthy as containing the celebrated "Hymn of the Soul," on which cf. A. A. Bevan, in *TS*, v.; *BrL*, pp. 12–15; F. C. Burkitt, *Hymn of Bardaisan* (London, 1899) and *Early Eastern Christianity*, lecture vi. (New York, 1904; Eng. transl. pp. 218–223). There is considerable doubt as to whether the original language of the "Book of the Laws of the Countries," which also belongs to the school of Bardesanes, was Greek, as is maintained by F. Schulthess, or Syriac, as T. Nöldeke holds (cf. *ZDMG*, lxix., 91–94, 555–560, 745–750; and F. Nau in *ZA*, Sept.–Oct., 1910, pp. 209 sqq.)

Excepting these few pieces which have a heathen Jewish, or Gnostic origin, and to which may be added scattered fragments of Manichean literature (see MANI, MANICHEANS; and note also MANDÆANS), Syriac literature is entirely Christian, and for the
5. Native Christian Literature. most part ecclesiastical and theological. The chief centers were Edessa and Nisibis, and at first the literature was purely national, though later came under the influence of the Greek Church, and finally was compelled to struggle against Arabic domination. As the chief authors of the

literature have already been considered in separate articles, it is sufficient here merely to allude to them, giving in addition the latest literature upon them.

The chief representatives of the earliest original Syriac literature are **Aphraates** and **Ephraem Syrus** (qq.v.), the "Homilies" of Aphraates have been edited afresh by J. Parisot in *Patrologia Syriaca* i (Paris, 1894 sqq.), while his theological point of view is discussed by P. Schwen, in his *Afrahat, eine Person und sein Verständnis des Christentums* (Berlin, 1907; cf. *TJB*, 1907, pp. 322, 327, 330; cf. further, H. Koch, "Taufe und Askese in der alten syrischen Kirche," in *ZNTW*, xii. 37–69). Ignatius Ephraem II. Rahmani's *Sancti Ephraemi Syri Hymni de Virginitate* (Beirut, 1906) is, despite its full title, only in part a first edition (cf. *TJB*, 1907, pp. 324–325). Minor successors and imitators of Ephraem were Cyrillona (c. 396; cf. Zahn, *Kanon*, i. 252; G. Bickell, in *ZDMG*, xxvii. 566–625, xxxv. 357) and Balai (c. 420), whose works were edited, together with some of Ephraem and others, by J. J. Overbeck, in his *S. Ephræmi Syri, Rabulæ Episcopi Edesseni, Balæi aliorumque opera selecta* (Oxford, 1865; on Balai cf., further, K. V. Zetterstéen, *Beiträge zur Kenntnis der religiösen Dichtung Balai's*, Leipsic, 1902; *BrGr*).

For the second period of Syriac literature, that under Greek influence, general reference may be made to F. C. Burkitt's *Early Eastern Christianity*, ut sup., and to J. Tixeront's "Théologie de langue syriaque au iv. siècle" (*Histoire des dogmes*, vol. i., chap. vii., Paris, 1909). Here the most prominent figures are **Rabbula of Edessa, Isaac of Antioch** (qq.v.), and **Barsauma of** **6. Theo- Nisibis** (flourished c. 485). Isaac's **logical** treatise *De Perfectione Religiosa* has **Literature** recently been edited by P. Bedjan, **under Greek** Paris, 1908; while the letters of Bar- **Influence.** sauma to the Catholicos Acacius have been published by P. Braun (in *Actes du x. congrès international des orientalistes*, iii. 83–101, Leyden, 1896), and a hymn ascribed to him (though others attribute it to Mar John) is given in A. J. Maclean's *East Syrian Daily Offices*, p. 226 London, 1894).

The literary importance of **Narsai (Nerses) the Great** (see NERSES) is attested both by his surname and by the publication of *Sancti Nersetis Preces xxiii linguis editæ* (Venice, 1862). To the works of Feldmann, Martin, Sachau, and Weil listed in *BrGr*, p. 135, and besides those mentioned in the bibliography of NERSES, allusion may be made to T. Grabowski, *Die Geschichte Josefs von Mar Narses* (Leipsic, 1889), and to A. Mingana's edition, *Narsai Doctoris Syri homiliæ et carmina primo edita* (2 vols., Mosul, 1905). The fifth volume of the *Homiliæ Selectæ* of Jacob of Sarug (q.v.) has been edited by P. Bedjan (Paris, 1910), this part containing homilies cxlvii.–cxcv., only one of which had previously been edited. **Philoxenus of Mabug** (see PHILOXENUS), whom Brockelmann calls "the greatest prose writer of Syria," has recently received further study. The edition of his *Discourses* by E. A. W. Budge (London, 1894) has been discussed in a Russian criticism by A. Spassky, in *Bogoslavsky Vestnik*, Oct., 1896, pp. 143–149; while A. A. Vas-

chalde's edition of certain letters (Rome, 1902) has been further considered by R. Duval, in *JA*, Jan.– Feb., 1903, pp. 168–170, and by A. Baumstark, in *OChr*, ii. 447–450. **Stephen bar Zudhaile** (q.v.) is of importance chiefly because of his connection with the literature which gathered around Dionysius the Areopagite (q.v.), the latest contribution to this subject being P. Peeters, "La Vision de Denys l'Aréopagite à Héliopolis," in *AB*, xxix. 3. Very little was known concerning **Martyrius-Sahdona** (c. 650) until H. Goussen published his *Martyrius-Sahdona's Leben und Werke* (Leipsic, 1897) and P. Bedjan edited his writings (*Sancti Martyrii qui et Sahdona quæ supersunt omnia*, Paris, 1902; cf. R. Duval, *JA*, Jan.– Feb., 1903, p. 166). When Sahdona abandoned Nestorianism, he found a bitter opponent in Ishoyabh III., the author of *Acta Martyrii Išo'sabran* (ed. J. B. Chabot, in *Nouvelles archives des missions scientifiques*, viii. 486) and *The Book of Consolations, or the Pastoral Epistles of Mar Isho-Yahb* (ed. P. Scott-Moncrieff, part i., London, 1904; these epistles have also been edited, with a Latin transl., by R. Duval, in *CSCO*, II., lxiv., 1905). Another writer whose very name was almost unknown until the present century was **Theodorus bar Koni** (or, perhaps, Kewanai), who left a large collection of annotations on the Bible (cf. J. B. Chabot, "Théodore bar Khouni et le livre des scholies," in *JA*, Jan.– Feb., 1901, pp. 170–179), the first part of which has been edited by Addai Scher in *CSCO*, II., lxv., 1910. An author long known and justly famous was **Jacob of Edessa** (q.v.), new fragments of whose correspondence have been published by F. Nau (*ROC*, 1901, pp. 1–9, 1905, pp. 3–4); and to this same period belongs **George, bishop of the Arabians** (q.v.), who worked over the "Chronicle" of Eusebius, and some of whose fragments are quoted in *BrGr*.

A new period began with the rise of Islam and the establishment of the califate in Babylonia; and Syriac literature as a whole soon yielded place to Arabic. Theological literature fell into the background, and secular branches were cul- **7. Rise of** tivated, treatises now being written **History** on astronomy, on astrology, on philos- **under Islam.** ophy, on logic, and on rhetoric. **Theophilus of Edessa** is said to have corresponded with the calif Al-Mahdi on astrological problems, and he even attempted to translate the Iliad and the Odyssey for his countrymen, although only a few fragments of his version have survived. After **Paul the Persian** had written on logic, **Antonius the Rhetor**, of Tagrit, adapted Greek rules to the Syriac language; while by translating the works of Aristotle the Syrians became the teachers of the Arabs, and thus, through them, the instructors of medieval Europe [cf. I. Pizzi, "Della Cultura creduta araba," in *Giornale arcadico*, ser. III., vol. v.]. A historical work written about 775 A.D., and embodying extracts from Eusebius, Socrates, and John of Ephesus, has preserved the chronicle of **Joshua the Stylite**, a chronicle which was long believed to be the work of Dionysius of Tell-Mahre, but of Dionysius' own history only a portion has survived. **Moses bar Kepha** (b. about 813; d. 903; bishop of Mosul, under the name of Severus, in 863) was a prolific author, although scarcely any of his writings have thus far been published (cf. O. Braun, *Moses bar Kepha und sein Buch von der Seele*, Freiburg, 1891). The work of Thomas of Marga (monk in the cloister of Beth 'Abbe in 832, secretary to the Patriarch Abraham in 837, and later bishop of Marga), *The Book of Governors, the Historia Monastica of the Bishop of Marga* (ed. and transl. E. A. W. Budge, 2 vols., London, 1893; *Liber Superiorum . . . Mar Narsetis Homiliæ in Joseph, Documenta patrum de quibusdam fidei dogmatibus*, ed. P. Bedjan, Paris, 1901), is of importance for the history of the Syrian monasteries. A contemporary of Thomas of Marga was Ishodad, whose position in the exegesis of the Old Testament has been pointed out by G. Diettrich, in the *Beihefte zur ZATW*, no. 6, 1902, while an edition and translation is promised in the near future by Margaret D. Gibson.

The eleventh century produced no great author among the Syrians, but to the twelfth belongs **Dionysius bar Salibi,** some of whose numerous works have been published in *CSCO, II.*: the explanation of the Mass (by H. Labourt, vol. xciii., 1903), the first part of the commentary on the Gospels (by I. Sedláček, vol. xcviii., 1906), and the commentary on Revelation, Acts, and the Catholic Epistles (by the same, vol. ci., 1910). In the early part of the thirteenth century there flourished Bishop Solomon of Basra, the author of *The Book of the Bee* (ed. and transl., E. A. W. Budge, in *Anecdota Oxoniensia*, vol. i., part ii., Oxford, 1886), which is full of curious legendary information concerning the Bible. To this period also belongs the poet **Giwargis Warda** of Arbela (about 1225), but the most versatile author of the century, and indeed of the whole range of Syriac literature, was **Abulfaraj** (q.v.), commonly called Bar-Hebræus. To the list of modern editions of his works given by Nestle (*Litteratura*, pp. 46–50, ut sup.) some twenty more have been added by *BrGr*, p. 159, and even this is not exhaustive (cf. J. Göttesberger, " Barhebräus und seine Scholien zur heiligen Schrift," in *Biblische Studien*, ed. O. Bardenhewer, v. 4–5, Freiburg, 1900). Abulfaraj was followed by **Ebed Jesu** (q.v.), the author of a versified list of Syriac literature, a collection of canons, and the " Paradise of Eden," an imitation of the Arabic " Seances " of Hariri. The name of the last writer of good Syriac is unknown, but he was the biographer of the Patriarch Yaballah (1281–1317), who started on a pilgrimage from China to Jerusalem and Europe, and who rose, through his relations with the Mongolian princes to whom the Syrian Church was then subject, to the dignity of patriarch. Several centuries then passed before the literature in modern Syriac began, a literature which, however, falls outside the scope of this article.

The discussion has thus far been concerned chiefly with individual authors, most of whom wrote on theology. There are, however, also numerous works the authors of which are unknown, as well as collected works (cf. the list in *BrGr*, pp. 131–134) and the rich literature of translations (*BrGr*, p. 140 sqq.), especially from Greek, though there are also some from Arabic and Persian, and a few from Latin,

8. Period of Decline.

9. Collected and Miscellaneous Writings.

such as the works of Cyprian, which probably came through the medium of Greek. Among theological works mention may here be made (cf. the more complete list in Harnack, *Litteratur*, i. 885–886) of the writings of Alexander of Alexandria, Clement of Alexandria, Clement of Rome, Dionysius of Alexandria, Eusebius, Gregory Thaumaturgus, Hippolytus, Ignatius, Irenæus, Julius Africanus, Pseudo-Justinus, Marcion, Melito, Methodius, Origen, Paul of Samosata, Peter of Alexandria, Polycarp, Sextus, and Tatian (qq.v.). Noteworthy among the collections and anonymous works are the important *Didascalia* and Apostolic Constitutions (see APOSTOLIC CONSTITUTIONS AND CANONS), the so-called " Rules of the Egyptian Church," and the Acts of Andrew, Archelaus, John, Philip, and Paul (especially the latter's correspondence with the Corinthians). Being the home of the Christological controversies, almost every important writer and document became known to the Syrians through translations, particularly Cyril of Alexandria, Athanasius, Gregory Nazianzen, and Gregory of Nyssa; while special mention is due the last great discovery in this field, the finding of the *Liber Heraclidis* of Nestorius. This treatise, the Greek version of which has been lost, has been edited by P. Bedjan (*Le Livre d'Héraclide de Damas*, Paris, 1910) and has been translated into French by F. Nau (Paris, 1910; cf. also E. W. Brooks, " La Lettre de Nestorius aux habitants de Constantinople," in *ROC*, II., v. 3; M. Brière, ib. v. i.). And a considerable literature has already arisen on the Odes of Solomon, which were first edited from the Syriac version by J. R. Harris in 1909 (see SOLOMON, ODES OF).

In the domain of philosophy the Syrians became the teachers of the Arabs, whose translations of the writings of Aristotle carried this new learning throughout medieval Europe. Here the way was led by the Nestorian **Probus,** who probably flourished in the first half of the fifth century, and he was followed by **Theodore,** bishop of Merv after 540. Here belong also Paul the Persian (see above), who resided at the court of Chosroes Anushirvan and Sergius of Ras'ain (c. 535; see the works of A. Baumstark, Friedmann, R. J. H. Gottheil, G. Hoffmann, A. van Hoonacker and N. Nagy, cited in *BrGr*, p. 140). For the grammatical treatises of the Syrians reference may be made to A. Merx, *Historia Artis Grammaticæ apud Syros* (Leipsic, 1889 [cf. also *Mâr(i) Eliâ of Ṣôbhâ, Treatise on Syriac Grammar*, ed. and transl. R. J. H Gottheil, Berlin, 1877]). Galen and Hippocrates gave to the Syrians their knowledge of medicine (cf the works of Gottheil, Merx, and H. Pognon listed in *BrGr*, p. 142). On geography J. P. N. Land published " Aardrijkskundige fragmenten uit de syrische litteratuur " in the *Verslagen en Mededeelingen der koninklijken Akademie van Wetenschappen, Afdeeling Letterkunde*, III., iii. 1886), while from R. J. H Gottheil came contributions on the history of Syriac geography in *Hebraica*, vii. 39–55, viii. 65–76, *Mitteilungen des akademisch-orientalischen Vereins zu Berlin*, no. 3, 1890, pp. 148, *JAOS, Proceedings*, May

10. Works on Philosophy and Science.

1888, pp. xvi.–xx., and F. Nau has written not only "La Cosmographie au vii. siècle chez les Syriens" in *ROC*, II., v. 3, but also, on the theme of astronomy, "Notes d'astronomie syrienne," in *JA*, Sept.–Oct., 1910.

Syriac translations from the Pahlavi include the famous "Kalilag and Dimnag" (ed. and transl., G. Bickell, with introduction by T. Benfey, Leipsic, 1876), while the Psalms, with the canons of Mar Abha, were translated from Syriac into Pahlavi (see F. C. Andreas, in *SBA*, 1910, p. 869 sqq.). [There is also reason to suppose that the Biblical fragments preserved in Pahlavi translation in the *Shikand-gumanig Vijar* were derived, as the form of the proper names shows, from a Syriac original (see BIBLE VERSIONS, B, XIII.).] The Syriac version of the Pseudo-Callisthenes (ed. and transl., E. A. W. Budge, *The History of Alexander the Great*, Cambridge, 1889) was based on the Greek original, while, on the other hand, some Syriac writings, notably of Ephraem, were rendered into Greek. A second Syriac recension of "Kalilag and Dimnag" was founded on an Arabic instead of a Pahlavi version (ed. W. Wright, *Book of Kalila and Dimna*, London, 1834; new ed., with German transl., by F. Schulthess, Berlin, 1911), and to a similar source belongs the "Story of Sindban, or, The Seven Wise Masters" (ed. and transl., F. Baethgen, Leipsic, 1879). Many Syriac works have been translated into Armenian, Arabic, and Coptic. Thus, the homilies of Aphraates were long known from their Armenian version, although, prior to the discovery of their Syriac original, they were ascribed to Jacob of Nisibis (q.v.). Still other works, such as Ephraem's commentary on the Diatessaron of Tatian, are yet lost in Syriac, and are known only through Armenian versions.

12. Juristic Literature. The juristic literature of the Syrians was concerned with both ecclesiastical and civil law, and it was especially important since the bishops and other clergy were the representatives of their people under the Iranian and Mohammedan rulers. For the earlier literature reference may be made to *BrGr*, and other publications of note are C. G. Bruns and E. Sachau, *Syrisch-römisches Rechtsbuch aus dem fünften Jahrhundert*, Leipsic, 1880; O. Braun, *Buch der Synhados*, Stuttgart, 1900; J. B. Chabot, *Synodicon orientale*, Paris, 1903; and the *Nomocanon* of Ebed Jesu (q.v.). There is also a great collection of laws, the Greek original of which appears to date from the reign of Basiliscus (475–477), while its Syriac version has been translated into Armenian, Georgian, and Arabic (cf. E. Sachau, *Syrische Rechtsbücher herausgegeben und übersetzt*, i., Berlin, 1907, containing the laws of Constantine, Theodosius, and Leo; idem, "Ueber ältere syrische Rechstliteratur der Nestorianer und im besonderen über das Buch der richterlichen Urteile des im Jahre 705 gestorbenen Patriarchen Chananischo," in *SBA*, 1904; E. Sachau and L. Mitteis, "Ueber drei neue Handschriften der syrisch-römischen Rechtsbücher" ib. 1905—also published separately; D. H. Müller, *Das syrisch-römische Rechtsbuch*, Vienna, 1905; J. Kohler, "Altsyrisches,"

in *Zeitschrift für vergleichende Rechtswissenschaft*, xix., parts 2–3; V. Aptowitzer, "Die Rechtsbücher der syrischen Patriarchen und ihre Quellen," in *Wiener Zeitschrift für die Kunde des Morgenlandes*, xxiv., parts 2–3). Much importance attaches to the Syriac translations of the canons of the early synods of the Church (see the ed. by F. Schulthess, "Die syrischen Kanones der Synoden von Nicæa bis Chalcedon nebst einigen zugehörigen Documenten," in *GA*, vol. x., part 2; cf. also F. Nau, *Ancienne littérature canonique syriaque*, iii., Paris, 1909). Among the canons of individual bishops, to which a more limited interest attaches, special mention may be made of those of Jacob of Edessa (q.v.), John bar Cursus (*BrGr*), Timotheus I. (transl., F. Labourt, *Les Canons ecclésiastiques du patriarche nestorien Timothée I.*, Paris, 1908), and Simeon of Revardeshir (c. 650; cf. A. Reicker, *Die Canones des Simeon von Rêvârdešîr*, Leipsic, 1908; see also W. Wright, *Notulæ Syriacæ*, pp. 3–11, n.p., 1887). It should also be stated that some Syriac canons are translated from the Persian.

The historical literature of the Syrians begins with the legend of King Abgar (q.v.), which Eusebius incorporated in his *Hist. eccl.* This literature includes works of great importance, among them the translation of the history of Eusebius just mentioned—a version made perhaps during the lifetime of its author. The calendar of the church at Nicomedia is preserved in the "Syrian Martyrology" (first ed. W. Wright, in *Journal of Sacred Literature*, viii. 45, 423; also by R. Graffin and L. Duchesne, in *ASB*, Nov., vol. ii., 1, pp. lii.–lv.; German transl. by H. Lietzmann, *Die drei ältesten Martyrologien*, Bonn, 1903). The **13. Historical Treatises.** Syriac *Acta Martyrum et Sanctorum*, edited or reedited by P. Bedjan, fill seven volumes (Paris, 1892–97), these including the collection of Maruthas, bishop of Maipherkat (see MARUTHAS), on the Persian martyrs. The historical and geographical knowledge that may be gained from these acts is well illustrated by G. Hoffmann's *Auszüge aus syrischen Akten persischer Märtyrer* (Leipsic, 1880). A good type of the historical legend is that of Alexis, "the man of God" (cf. A. Amiaud, *La Légende syriaque de saint Alexis, l'homme de Dieu*, Paris, 1889; T. Nöldeke, in *ZDMG*, liii. 256–258); while for a real historical biography reference may be made to that of Rabbula (q.v.). There are, besides, a large number of chronicles, largely revisions and continuations of the work of Eusebius (cf. F. Macler, "Extraits de la chronique de Maribas Kaldoyo," in *JA*, May-June, 1903, pp. 491–549). Three parts of *Chronica minora* have been edited and translated by E. W. Brooks, J. B. Chabot, and I. Guidi in *CSCO*, ser. iii., vol. iv., parts 1–3), and special value also attaches to L. J. Delaporte's *editio princeps* of *La Chronographie d'Élie bar Sinaya, métropolitain de Nisibe* (Paris, 1910). New fields of church history were opened up by the writings of John of Ephesus (q.v.); the *Chronicle* of Joshua the Stylite (ed. W. Wright, London, 1882); the "Chronicle of Edessa" (ed. and transl., L. Hallier, in his *Untersuchungen über die edessenische Chronik*, Leipsic, 1892); the church history of Zacharias

Rhetor (see ZACHARIAS SCHOLASTIKOS; Eng. transl., by F. H. Hamilton and E. W. Brooks, *The Syriac Chronicle, known as that of Zachariah of Mitylene*, London, 1899; cf. also K. Ahrens and G. Krüger, in *Scriptores Sacri et Profani Seminarii Philologici Jenensis*, iii., Leipsic, 1899; the "Life of Severus" has been edited and translated by A. Kugener in *PO*, vol. ii., part 1; cf. further, A. Kugener, in *ROC*, 1900, parts 2–3, J. Gwynn, in *Hermathena*, xi., no. 24; the Syriac text includes the legend of Joseph and his wife, Asenath; the legend of the Seven Sleepers of Ephesus (q.v.; cf. also M. Huber, *Die Wanderlegende von den Siebenschläfern*, Leipsic, 1910); a description of Rome in connection with the war of Totila; and an account of the world based on Ptolemy. Among the historical romances is the history of Julian called the Apostate (see JULIAN), which has been edited by G. Hoffmann (*Julianos der Abtrünnige*, Leiden, 1880) and, in selections, by R. J. H. Gottheil (1906); while a complicated history attaches to the so-called "Chronicle" of Dionysius of Tell Mahre (cf. H. G. Kleyn, in *Feestbuundel aan Prof. M. J. de Goeje*, pp. 57–75, Leyden, 1891; F. Nau, *Nouvelles études sur le chronique attribué à Denys de Tellmahré*, Paris, 1896; *Bulletin critique*, 1897, pp. 54–58; *JA*, viii. 2; *ROC*, 1897; the fourth part of the chronicle in question was edited by J. B. Chabot, Paris, 1895).

E. NESTLE.

BIBLIOGRAPHY: In addition to the works mentioned in the article, the following treatises may be consulted with advantage: from *PO*, *Histoire nestorienne (chronique de Séert)*, i., Arabic text, ed. Addai Scher, transl. P. Dib (vol. iv., part 3, vol. v., part 2); *Les Légendes syriaques d'Aaron de Saroug, de Maxime et Domèce, d'Abraham, maître de Barsoma et de l'empereur Maurice*, ed. and transl. F. Nau (vol. v., part 5); *James of Edessa, the Hymns of Severus of Antioch and Others*, ed. and transl. E. W. Brooks (vol. vi., part 1; cf. W. E. Barnes, in *JTS*, xii. 304–305); *Traité d'Išaï le docteur et de Ḥnana d'Adiabène sur les martyrs le vendredi d'or et les rogations, suivis de la confession de foi à réciter par les évêques avant l'ordination*, ed. and transl. Addai Scher (vol. vii., part 1); also F. Nau, "Hagiographie syriaque," in *RCO*, II., v., no. 1; id., *La Version syriaque de la première lettre de Saint-Antoine: Analyse du traité de Denys bar Salibi contre les Nestoriens*, Paris, 1909; Ignatius Ephraem II. Rahmani, "Documenta de antiquis hæresibus," in *Studia Syriaca*, part iv., 1909; H. W. Codrington, "Liturgia præsanctificatorum Syriaca," in χρυσοστομικά, *Studi e ricerche intorno a S. Giovanni Crisostomo*, pp. 719–729, Rome, 1908; A. Baumstark, "Die Chrysostomusliturgie und die syrische Liturgie des Nestorius," ib. pp. 771–857; J. B. Chabot, "L'Autodafé des livres syriaques au Malabar," in *Florilegium . . . à M. le marquis Melchior de Vogüé*, Paris, 1909; B. Charon (pseudonym for C. P. Karalevsky), *Histoire des patriarcats melkites . . . depuis le schisme monophysite du vi. siècle jusqu'à nos jours*, Rome, 1909–10; A. Rabbath, *Documents inédits pour servir à l'histoire du christianisme en orient*, Beirut, 1910; S. Euringer, "Abyssinien und die heilige Stuhl," in *TQS*, xcii. 329 sqq.; Addai Scher, "Episodes de l'histoire du Kurdistan," in *JA*, X., xv. 119–139; id., "Joseph Hazzâyâ, écrivain syriaque du viii. siecle," in *Rivista degli studi orientali*, iii.; G. Levi della Vida, "Pseudo-Beroso siriaco," ib.; G. Richard. *Two Syriac-Arabic Glosses of Ishô' bar 'Ali*, Rome, 1910; R. Duval, *Les Homiliæ cathedrales de Sévère d'Antioche*, Paris, 1907 (cf. *JTS*, viii. 465–467); J. Lebon, *Le Monophysisme sévérien*, Louvain, 1909 (cf. *Revue d'histoire et de littérature religieuses*, xi. 85–93); E. A. W. Budge, *Coptic Homilies* (London, 1910; contains the Syriac text, with translation, of John the Faster's homily; and also the text and transl. of portions of a homily of Alexander, the twelfth patriarch of Alexandria); I. Pizzi, "La Dottrina dell' apostolo Addai," in *Giornale arcadico*, ser. iii., vol. iv.

SYRIAN CHURCH: This organization, in spite of its importance, particularly in the earlier period, has by historians and investigators been sadly neglected. There is yet no really critical edition of its Bible, and no work devoted to the history of the church. Yet it has been noted by Harnack (*Mission und Ausbreitung des Christentums*, ii. 126, 2d ed., 2 vols., Leipsic, 1906, Eng. transl., *Mission and Expansion of Christianity*, 2d ed., London, 1908) that it is a church to which protection by the State has never been granted, while J. F. Bethune-Baker (*JTS*, viii. 123) remarks upon the Nestorian branch that its magnificent history, its endurance under unparalleled persecution, its undoubted loyalty to the faith received from the Fathers, and its Eastern character combine to give it a unique postion.

In a sense its history begins when the apostles were in Damascus and Antioch, and each of the Gospels alludes to the Syrians (Matt. iv. 24; Mark vii. 26; Luke iv. 27; John xii. 20). It would appear that there were Christians at Damascus in the days of Origen, and the bishop of the city was present at Nicæa, though nothing is known concerning the number of Christians there. In the time of Chrysostom the inhabitants of Antioch were proud of the fact that there "the disciples were called Christians first" (Acts xi. 26); according to Ephraem Syrus the Gospel of John was written there; this city had its own bishops (although the list is not without variations), among them Ignatius, who termed Antioch "the Church of Syria." The national Syrian Church began, however, in Edessa (q.v.). It is possible that the Syriac translation of the Old Testament was at least in part a Jewish production, but Christianity did not become the dominant factor in Edessa until the early part of the third century. By the time of the first pilgrims to Palestine Edessa had come to be regarded almost as a part of the Holy Land, a fame which it retained through out the period of the Crusades. The earliest certain names in the history of the church at Edessa are those of Bardesanes (q.v.) and his son, Harmodius, and their antagonist, Ephraem Syrus (q.v.)

Syriac literature (q.v.) is almost entirely Christian, and, indeed, theological (cf. BIBLE VERSIONS A, III.; HARMONY OF THE GOSPELS, I, §§ 2–3), including a large number of Apocrypha, such as the *Testamentum Domini nostri Jesu Christi* (q.v.) and *The Gospel of the Twelve Apostles, together with the Apocalypses of each one of them* (ed. J. R. Harris, Cambridge, 1900), while the Bible manuscripts frequently contain III Cor., but have neither the Catholic epistles nor the Apocalypse, for which they sometimes substitute the *Testamentum Domini* and the six books of Clement.* The art displayed in these manuscripts is an important factor in the determination of the influence of Syrian art on the occident and of the significance of Syrian individuals and colonies in Italy and Gaul. There were Syrian popes: Anicetus, John V., Sergius, Sisinnius, Constantine I., and Gregory III. A new period in the history of the Syrian Church began when

---

* [The *Testamentum Domini*, in two books, together with six other books of church law, forms the "Clementine Octateuch," used both by Nestorians and by Jacobites.]

Greek influence commenced to be predominant in theology and Church shortly after the time of Aphraates (q.v.) in the fourth century, while political bonds with the empire were dissolved. It was then that the Christological controversies of the Eastern Church raged with greater fury in Syria than in their own land, ultimately causing not only transformation and schism, but well-nigh resulting in destruction. Much of this struggle is discussed in the articles MONOPHYSITES; and NESTORIANS. The great extension of the Syrian church may be seen from its inscriptions, which are found as far south as India (Cottayam, in North Travancore), as far east as China (the famous inscription of Sing-an-fu of 781; see NESTORIANS, § 2), and as far north as Semiryeshchie. Syrian influence is shown in Central Asia by the Mongolian script, which is from top to bottom in the early Syrian fashion, and still more clearly by the manuscripts discovered in Turkestan in Estrangelo script (though in a number of different languages), these texts, however, being mainly concerned with Manicheism. Syriac literature is exceedingly extensive, the comprehensive character being shown by the four series contemplated and begun in *CSCO*. Its relation to monasticism is close, and its martyrology is voluminous, much of which is being utilized in the *Analecta Bollandiana*.

Since the Syrian church stood very close, both in place and language, to the primitive Church, it is evidently very important for the history of liturgy and organization, especially since such sources as the *Didascalia* are more ancient than the corresponding documents of the West. The Nestorian liturgy is most nearly akin to that of Dionysius the Areopagite (q.v.), yet it contains neither renunciation of the devil (see RENUNCIATION) nor a creed (the latter omission scarcely being original). Valuable data for the history of canon law may also be drawn from Syriac literature, as from the *Nomocanones* of Barhebræus, Ebed Jesu, and Jacob of Edessa, or the Syro-Roman code of the fifth century edited by K. G. Bruns and E. Sachau (*Syrisch-Römisches Gesetzbuch*, Leipsic, 1880).

The twenty-five metropolitans once possessed by the Nestorian church are now reduced to the patriarch and metropolitan, with three bishops in Persia and seven in Turkey, some of the dioceses being merely nominal. An active propaganda has been carried on among the Nestorians by the Jesuits at Beirut, the Dominicans at Mosul, and the Roman Catholic mission in Malabar. Comparatively little has been accomplished by the archbishop of Canterbury's Assyrian (East Syrian) Mission or by American Protestant missionaries at Urumiah (see JERUSALEM, ANGLICAN-GERMAN BISHOPRIC IN). No statistics, even approximate, can be given concerning the present numbers, divisions, or institutions of the Syrian Church. (E. NESTLE.)

The foregoing outline should be read in connection with a series of articles in this work (mainly by the same author) exclusive of those named in the text. These articles, which illumine particular epochs and practically display the entire history of the church, deal with Abgar, Apollinaris of Laodicea, Ebed Jesu, Ibas, Jacob of Edessa, Jacob of Nisibis, Jacob of Sarug, Jacobites, John of Dara, John of

Ephesus, Isaac of Antioch, Maruthas, Rabbula, Stephen bar Zudhaile, Syriac Literature, and Theodore of Mopsuestia.

BIBLIOGRAPHY: For sources the first place is taken by *CSCO*. Other sources are indicated in the articles (and attached bibliographies) referred to in the text. Eng. transls. of various documents are to be found in *ANF*, vols. viii. and ix., and in *NPNF*, 2 ser., xiii. 117 sqq.; W. Cureton, *Ancient Syriac Documents*, London, 1864; *Ein Brief Georgs an den Presbyter Jesus, aus dem Syrischen*, Gotha, 1883; Thomas of Marga, *The Book of Governors; the Historia monastica*, Eng. transl. by E. A. W. Budge, 2 vols., London, 1893; *Das Buch der Synhados*, Germ. transl. by O. Braun, Stuttgart, 1900; Michael the Syrian, "Chronicle," ed. J. B. Chabot, Paris, 1900 sqq.; *Lettre du catholicos Mar-Aba II. aux membres de l'école patriarcale*, ed. and transl. J. B. Chabot, Paris, 1896; *La Légende de Mar Bassus*, ed. and transl. J. B. Chabot, Paris, 1893; *Jesusdena, La Livre de chasteté*, ed. and transl. by J. B. Chabot, Paris, 1896; *Vie de Jésus-Sabran, écrite par Jésus-Yahb d'Adiabiène*, ed. J. B. Chabot, Paris, 1897; *Regulæ monasticæ sæc. VI. ab Abrahamo et Dadjesu conditæ*, ed. and transl. J. B. Chabot, Paris, 1898; *The Book of Consolations. Pastoral Epistles of Mâr Ishô Yahbh*. Syriac text, with Eng. transl. by P. S. Moncrieff, London, 1904.

For discussion and history consult: F. C. Burkitt, *Early Christianity outside the Roman Empire*, Cambridge, 1899; idem, *Early Eastern Christianity*, New York and London, 1904; J. B. Chabot, *L'École de Nisibe*, Paris, 1896; idem, *Pierre l'Ibérien, évèque de Mayouma*, ib. 1896; idem, *Vie de Mar Youssef I., patriarche des Chaldéens*, ib. 1896; E. S. A[ppleyard], *Eastern Churches*, London, 1850; A. d'Avril, *La Chaldée chrétienne*, Paris, 1864; C. B. Benni, *Tradition of the Syriac Church of Antioch*, London, 1871; *Jacobites of Ceylon. By a Missionary Apostolic*, Colombo, 1889; R. Duval, *Hist. d'Edesse*, Paris, 1892; L. Hallier, in *TU*, ix. 1 (1892); A. J. Maclean and W. H. Browne, *The Catholicos of the East and his People*, London, 1892; G. M. Rae, *Syrian Church in India*, Edinburgh, 1892; R. Graffin, *Patrologia Syriaca*, Paris, 1894; O. H. Parry, *Six Months in a Syrian Monastery*, London, 1895; J. G. Gregson, *Among the Syrian Christians in Travancore*, London, 1897; idem, *The Reformed Syrian Church in Malabar*, ib., 1899; P. Perdrizet and C. Fossey, *Voyage dans la Syrie du Nord*, in *Bulletin de correspondance*, xxi (1897), 66 sqq.; G. Voisin, *L'Apollinarisme*, Louvain, 1901; S. Jamil, *Genuinæ relationes inter sedem apostolicam et Assyriorum orientalium seu Chaldæorum ecclesiam*, Rome, 1902 (Lat. and Syr.); W. Bauer, *Der Apostolos der Syrer*, Giessen, 1903; R. H. Conolly, in *JTS*, vi (1904), 422–439; A. Harnack, *Expansion of Christianity in the First Three Centuries*, 2d ed., 2 vols., London and New York, 1908; H. Labourt, *De Timotheo I., Nestorianorum patriarcha (728–823)*, Paris, 1904; W. A. Shedd, *Islam and the Oriental Churches; their historical Relations*, Philadelphia, 1904; I. Silbernagl, *Verfassung und gegenwärtiger Bestand sämmtlicher Kirchen des Orients*, Regensburg, 1904; J. R. Harris, *The Cult of the Heavenly Twins*, chaps. xii.–xiv., Cambridge, 1906; E. Buonajuti, *Lucian of Samosata and the Asiatic and Syriac Christianity of his Times*, in *New York Review*, July, 1906; Bernard Ghobaïra al-Ghaziri, *Rome et l'église Syrienne Maronite d'Antioche (517–1531)*, Beirut, 1906; De L. O'Leary, *The Syriac Church and Fathers*, London, 1909; G. D. Malech, *Hist. of the Syrian Nation and the Old Evangelical-Apostolic Church of the East*, Minneapolis, 1911. Of the highest value is the detailed literature named under the articles to which attention is called above.

SYRO-HEXAPLAR VERSION. See BIBLE VERSIONS, A, I., 1, § 6.

SYROPULUS, sai-rep'u-lus **(SGUROPULUS), SILVESTER:** Historian of the Council of Ferrara-Florence (q.v.); lived in the first half of the fifteenth century. He was one of the five high dignitaries under the patriarch in Constantinople. He was a passionate adherent of his church and averse to all Latin tendencies; but circumstances forced him to take part in the pressing movement for church union under the leadership of Emperor Johannes. At the synod he belonged to the party of

Marcus Eugenicus of Ephesus, a strictly orthodox anti-unionist. According to his own account, he detested the whole journey, did not expect success, became involved in conflict with the patriarch and even the emperor, and obstinately refused his assent to the agreement; only the demand and threat of the emperor induced him to sign, and this he counted a weakness. After his return to Constantinople his concessions at the synod occasioned bitter attacks. He then retired from his activity and gave an account of this important experience in a work bearing perhaps the title as " Recollections of the Council of Florence." It is of great value as a source, being the work of a participant in the events. Though partizan, it reveals a series of relationships and developments which otherwise would have remained unknown. The author tries to prove that a real harmony could not be attained, but that the leading personalities, the pope, Bessarion, the patriarch, and the emperor, together with some other spokesmen, approached each other more closely until the urgent position of the Greeks decided the issue. Syropulus justly calls the result a mediating pact, instead of a union.

In 1642 Claudius Serrarius, the learned senator in Paris, had the work of Syropulus copied from a codex of the Bibliotheca regia (N. 1247) and sent the manuscript to Isaak Vossius for publication. The English minister, Robert Creighton, chaplain at the court of Charles II. and subsequently bishop of Bath, was entrusted with the work; he undertook the publication of the Greek text together with a Latin translation under the title, *Vera historia unionis non veræ inter Græcos et Latinos, sive Concilii Florentini exactissima narratio græce scripta per Sylvestrum Sguropulum* (The Hague, 1660). Unfortunately the edition is incomplete since the whole of the first book was missing in the Paris codex, but the beginning may perhaps still be supplied from manuscript. (PHILIPP MEYER.)

BIBLIOGRAPHY: L. Allatius, *In R. Creyghtoni apparatum . . . ad historiam concilii Florentini*, part i., Rome, 1665, also 1674; Fabricius-Harles, *Bibliotheca Græca*, xi. 711, Hamburg, 1808; Hefele. *Conciliengeschichte*, vol. vii. passim; idem, in *TQ*, xxix (1847); O. T. Frommann, *Kritische Beiträge zur Geschichte der Florentiner Kircheneinigung*, Halle, 1872; A. C. Demetracopulos, *Græcia orthodoxa*, p. 109, Leipsic, 1872; *KL*, xi. 1154-55.

SZEGEDINUS. See KIS, STEPHANUS.

T

TABERNACLE: The term used in the Middle Ages for the outer vessel in which the host is preserved, the inner being named the pyx (see VESSELS, SACRED). The word also designates the baldaquin above the altar, and the ciborium (see ALTAR, II., 1, § 1).

TABERNACLE CONNECTION. See METHODISTS, I., 2.

TABERNACLE, THE MOSAIC.

" Tabernacle " is the term used in the English versions of the Biblical account of the exodus to name the structure serving in the wilderness wanderings as the dwelling-place of God, to which the people assembled. It represents several Hebrew phrases—'*ohel mo'edh*, '*ohel Ha'edhuth*, *mishkan*, *mishkan ha'edhuth*, which, translated literally, mean "tent of meeting," "tent of testimony," but it is not to be taken as a place in which men met. In structure it was a temple in the form of a tent.

The tent itself consisted of a wooden structure of acacia boards covered with curtains. The boards were forty-eight in number, each one ten cubits long and one and a half wide. They

1. The Tent. were distributed in such a way that there were twenty boards each on the north side and the south side, eight boards at the west or rear; the front, on the east, remained open. Inasmuch as the boards were closely joined to make a real wall, the length of the structure was thirty cubits, the width twelve cubits, and the height, corresponding to the length of the boards, ten cubits. The boards were connected with each other and with the floor by tenons and sockets. The sockets were of silver, and each board had two such sockets, *i.e.*, probably holes into which the tenons were put. The rear wall had, besides the six boards that were like the others, two corner boards of a different kind, but it is not clear from Ex. xxvi. 24 wherein their peculiarity consisted. The boards were fastened together with five bars for each side that were thrust through rings of gold; the boards were covered with gold as were the bars, which were made of acacia wood.

This wooden structure became a " tabernacle " or " tent " only through the curtains spread over it (Ex. xxvi. 1 sqq., xxxvi. 8 sqq.) which were so essential to it that one of them, the byssus curtain, could be called the tabernacle (xxvi. 1

2. The Curtains. 6, etc.). The lowest covering, the so-called byssus curtain, consisted of ten pieces each twenty-eight cubits long and four wide, of twined byssus, therefore probably of white as the ground-color, interwoven with patterns of blue, purple, and scarlet cherubim. Five of these ten pieces were fastened together so as to make two large curtains twenty-eight cubits long and twenty cubits broad. Each of these curtains had fifty loops of purple yarn through which were thrust golden taches, fastening the whole into one covering. Over this curtain, to which the name " tabernacle " was given, there was spread for its protection a curtain of goats' hair, called " tent." It consisted of eleven pieces, each thirty cubits long and four wide, so connected as to make two curtains, one of five, the other of six of the smaller pieces. In the larger of these two the sixth piece was to be doubled in the forefront of the tabernacle. These were coupled together by the fifty loops on the edge of each curtain by means of fifty taches of brass put through the loops. The curtain hung over the three sides of the tabernacle. This curtain of goats' hair was protected by a covering of rams' skins dyed red, and this again by a covering of *taḥash* skins. *Taḥash* probably denotes the sea-cow which frequents the Red Sea, the skin of which furnishes a strong leather.

The interior was divided into the holy place and the most holy place by means of a " veil " (Ex. xxvi. 31 sqq., xxxvi. 35 sqq.) The veil was of the same material as the byssus curtain and hung on four gilded pillars of acacia wood with silver sockets. It was adorned with patterns of cherubim and was fastened on the pillars with golden nails. Behind the veil was the most holy place, a cube of ten cubits, containing only the ark (see ARK OF THE COVENANT). On the side of the veil toward the entrance was the holy place, ten cubits wide and high and twenty cubits long. It contained the table of showbread, the candlestick, and the altar of incense. On the north side of the holy place stood the table of showbread (Ex. xxv. 23 sqq.), made of acacia wood, overlaid with gold, two cubits long, one broad, and one and a half high. Round about the table was an ornament in the form of a wreath, likewise a border extending around the table connecting its four feet; this also was adorned with a wreath. The account does not show how these were fastened. The enclosing border had rings of gold through which staves were thrust to carry the table. On the table were dishes, spoons, and bowls of gold. On the opposite side of the holy place, opposite the table, stood the candlestick (Ex. xxv. 31 sqq., xxxvii. 17 sqq.). It was beaten work, of pure gold throughout. From the stem or central stock proceeded six branches, three on each side, each one of which ended in a bowl made like an almond, each bowl having a knob and a flower; the stem had four such bowls. Each of the three lower knobs of the stem was under a pair of side branches. While the Biblical description does not assert that the branches and stem were in one plane, Jewish tradition makes that to be the case. According to Ex. xxvii. 20 sqq; Lev. xxiv. 1 sqq., the lamps were to burn the whole night. This is presupposed also by the story of Samuel, I Sam. iii. 3. But according to Josephus (*Ant.*, III., viii. 3) three of the lamps burned also in the daytime. From I Sam. iii. 3 it is not improbable that in the law the older idea and custom are reflected; but as in private houses lights were burned day and night, it may be assumed that in the course of time the custom of private houses was transferred to the sanctuary. Various symbolical meanings were attached to the candlestick. The ancients recognized in it a symbolical representation of the seven planets (Josephus, *War*, V., v. 5; *Ant.*, III., vi. 7, vii. 7). Philo interpreted the middle lamp, also the central stem, as representing the sun. Its resemblance to a conventionalized tree is evident, while the connection with light is, of course, on the surface (cf. Ps. xxxvi. 10).

Around the tabernacle extended a spacious court (Ex. xxvii. 9 sqq., xxxviii. 10 sqq.), exactly as in temples the shrine proper is surrounded by a courtyard for the congregation as it sacrificed and celebrated. The court was a hundred cubits long and fifty wide; and instead of walls there was a portable barrier consisting of sixty pillars, placed at intervals of five cubits, on which were hung byssus curtains. The most important piece of furnishing in the court was the altar, generally known as the altar of burnt offering, a portable object, thus in accordance with the design of the whole sanctuary. It was five cubits long, five broad, and three high, and had horns on its four corners; it was of wood covered with brass. The utensils which went with it, such as pans, shovels, etc., were of brass. For half its height the altar was surrounded with a network of brass, undoubtedly to protect it from desecration. On the four corners of the network there were fastened rings by the aid of which the altar could be transported on staves. Beside the altar there is mentioned in Ex. xxx. 17 sqq. also a laver of brass in which the priests used to cleanse themselves when they entered the sanctuary.

There is no reason to doubt the authenticity, in its essential points, of the tradition respecting the tabernacle as it is recorded in Ex. xxxiii. 7 sqq. According to this account, Moses pitched the tabernacle without the camp and called it the tabernacle of the congregation. Whenever one desired a revelation from Yahweh he went out to the tabernacle; for there " the Lord spake unto Moses face to face, as a man speaketh unto his friend." It would naturally be expected here that mention would be made of the ark, since the tent was merely a covering or protection for some object within (cf. II Sam. vi. 17). While there is no reason to doubt the existence of a Mosaic tabernacle, it is another question whether it is identical with the tabernacle described in Ex. xxv. sqq. In the first place it is to be mentioned that the account (by E) in Ex. xxxiii. 7 sqq. regards the tent as outside of the camp, not, as is the case with the tabernacle of Ex. xxv. sqq., in the midst. The older tradition of E evidently gives an idea of the Mosaic tent other than that afforded by the later tradition of P; the historical Mosaic tent, therefore, was of another kind than that of the narrative of P. After this fact is made evident, the account of P will appear in a different light. The great amount of precious materials and metals in possession of a migrating people in the desert, the artistic execution of all these objects there, the difficulties of transportation, and the like, have been cited to show the historical improbability of the account in Ex. xxv. sqq. Many of these objections may be answered as not pertinent, but even were all difficulties of this kind solved, there would still remain the fact mentioned that the Mosaic tabernacle of the older tradition is quite different from that of Ex. xxv. sqq. How then did the account of Ex. xxv. sqq. originate or how did it pass into tradition if according to genuine Biblical tradition it does not assume to be the historical Mosaic tabernacle? In the first place it may be said that, if this tabernacle is not the historical tabernacle, it must owe its origin to the idea of a later time; the account of P tells how, at a later time, the Mosaic tabernacle was conceived. If the description of the temple of Solomon be compared with that of the tabernacle of Ex. xxv. sqq., it appears that the tabernacle is rather the temple of Solomon in a portable condition. It is the prototype of the temple of Solomon transplanted into the wilderness. People of the later time who knew the temple of Solomon could not imagine the divine service of Israel without it (or its equivalent). That the tabernacle of Ex. xxv. sqq. was imagined after the model of the temple and not vice versa appears from the fact that certain peculiarities of the tabernacle are explicable only as being transferred from the temple, where they had a proper place, to the tabernacle in a form adaptable for use in the desert and in the portable sanctuary, and were even estranged from their proper purpose. To mention only one instance, the stately altar, as required for the burnt offerings of the temple, had to be either of stone or of brass; the altar of the tabernacle of Ex. xxv. sqq., however, was a wooden structure with a covering of brass. Such an altar had the one quality which was required for the Mosaic tabernacle, portability; but it lacked every other quality of an altar in the proper sense. It was unusable for the sacrifices for which it was assumably intended, especially of whole oxen. There can be no doubt that such an altar did not exist; it is not the original of that other altar, but an imaginary idea proceeding from it. Portable altars, indeed, are well known to history; but the altar in question was intended for the great burnt offerings of the Mosaic cultus.

The conclusion is warranted that a "tabernacle" as a protection for the ark existed in early times, but that the description of it in Ex. xxv. sqq. contains little of a historical character. Since David

6. Conclusion; Later History. according to II Sam. vi. 17 erected a tent for the ark, it is evident that in his time the old tabernacle no longer existed. It may, therefore, be supposed that it had been lost or destroyed at the time of the capture of the ark, if in that time it still existed, i.e., in the time of Eli. But this seems to be contradicted by the fact that the place of the ark in Shiloh during Samuel's youth (I Sam. i. 7, 9, iii. 3) is called "house" (not "tent") and even "temple" while in I Sam. iii. 15, i. 9 its "doors" and posts are mentioned. It is, therefore, to be assumed that at that time there existed a permanent structure. There remains then only the notice of Josh. xviii. 1, which relates that the Mosaic tabernacle was erected in Shiloh. What is related here of the Mosaic tabernacle is made probable by the fact that Shiloh was for a long time the place of the ark. The old tabernacle may have been preserved for a time, but in the course of time was replaced by a more solid structure. See HEXATEUCH, § 14. (R. KITTEL.)

BIBLIOGRAPHY: The earlier literature may be regarded as having but historical interest. Consult the commentaries on the principal passages cited in the text, many of which contain excursuses on the subject; especially important is much of the critical and conservative literature cited under HEXATEUCH, since the two schools are at variance concerning the historicity of the Biblical account. Further material is in F. Friedrich, Symbolik der mosaischen Stiftshütte, Leipsic, 1841; Kamphausen, in TSK, 1858, pp. 97 sqq., 1859, pp. 110 sqq.; W. Neumann, Die Stiftshütte in Wort und Bild, Gotha, 1861; J. Popper, Der biblische Bericht über die Stiftshütte, Leipsic, 1862; R. Newton, The Jewish Tabernacle and its Furniture in their Typical Teachings, New York, 1863; K. H. Graf, Die geschichtliche Bücher des A. T., pp. 51 sqq., Leipsic, 1866; C. J. Riggenbach, Die mosaische Stiftshütte, Basel, 1867; K. C. W. F. Bähr, Symbolik des mosaischen Kultus, vol. i., Heidelberg, 1874; E. E. Atwater, Hist. and Significance of the Sacred Tabernacle of the Hebrews, New York, 1875; H. Ewald, Antiquities of Israel, pp. 317–333, Boston, 1876; A. E. Webb, The Tabernacle and the Temple, London, 1882; J. E. Hawkins, Lectures on the Tabernacle, ib. 1883; J. Ritchie, The Tabernacle in the Wilderness, ib. 1884; F. Whitfield, The Tabernacle, ib. 1884; J. J. Chase, The Jewish Tabernacle, Cincinnati, 1884; J. Wellhausen, Prolegomena, 6th ed., Berlin, 1905; Eng. transl. of earlier edition, pp. 38 sqq., Edinburgh, 1885; T. O. Paine, Solomon's Temple . . . , and Tabernacle, Boston, 1886; D. A. Randall, Ham-Mishkan, The Wonderful Tent, Cincinnati, 1886; J. F. K. Keil, Manual of Biblical Archæology, 2 vols., Edinburgh, 1887–1888; B. F. Westcott, Epistle to the Hebrews, pp. 233 sqq., London, 1889; C. Schick, Die Stiftshütte der Tempel in Jerusalem, Berlin, 1896; A. H. Klostermann, in NKZ, viii. (1897); M. Rainsford, The Tabernacle in the Wilderness, London, 1897; R. L. Ottley, Aspects of the O. T., pp. 261 sqq., ib. 1897; W. Brown, The Tabernacle and its Priests and Services, 6th ed., London, 1899; J. Adams, The Mosaic Tabernacle, Edinburgh, 1900; W. S. Caldecott, The Tabernacle, its Hist. and Structure, ib. 1904; B. Jacob, Der Pentateuch, pp. 134–346, Leipsic, 1905; M. Dibelius, Die Lade Jahves, Göttingen, 1906; H. Gunkel, Die Lade ein Thronsitz, Heidelberg, 1906; K. Budde, in TSK, 1906, pp. 589–607; Benzinger, Archäologie, pp. 336–339; Nowack, Archäologie, vol. ii.; Driver, Introduction, pp. 128, 153; DB, iv. 653–688 (elaborate); EB, iv. 4861–75; JE, xi. 653–656.

TABERNACLES, FEAST OF: A festival of the Hebrews, known in the Old Testament also as the "feast of ingathering" (Ex. xxiii. 16) and more simply as "the feast" (I Kings viii. 2), or "the feast of Yahweh" (Lev. xxiii. 39); it is mentioned also in the New Testament and in II Macc. x. 6. For the historical development see FEASTS AND FESTIVALS, I. It was one of the chief festivals of the Hebrews, and in the codes it is coordinated with the two other great feasts and connected with the harvest. In the latter connection it was the festival of thanks for the yield of the earth (Ex. xxiii. 16; Deut. xvi. 13), in early times celebrated at some sanctuary (I Sam. i. 3). The corresponding Canaanitic feast appears in Judges ix. 27, the first mention of it as Israelitic is Judges xxi. 19 sqq. as a yearly celebration at Shiloh. In the early regal period it seems to have taken place in the eighth month, though Solomon is said to have connected it with the seventh month (I Kings viii. 2, cf. vi. 38) and with the consecration of the Temple. The earliest laws prescribe no definite time, Ex. xxiii. 16 giving simply autumn. Deuteronomy requires its celebration at the central sanctuary for a period of seven days (cf. I Kings viii. 66). The Deuteronomic regulations are expanded in Lev. xxiii. and the manner of the feast prescribed (the prescription as to date is by a later hand). It was to continue seven days, on the first of which the participants were to take boughs of trees (to make booths) and were to dwell in the booths during the feast. The text enacts that only Israelites shall participate; but Bertholet shows that the reading is probably a late refinement. The regulations suit an agricultural, not a nomadic, environment, and point to an original feast celebrated in vineyards and gardens, in accordance with the modern Palestinian custom.

After Deuteronomy had made the festival universal, to be kept at the Temple, a definite dating became necessary, and such fixation appears first in Ezekiel (xlv. 25) for the fifteenth day of the seventh month of the later reckoning, where the offerings are also prescribed. The final step appears in Lev. xxiii. and the date is that of Ezekiel, but an additional day was added to the duration, each day having its offering, while the first and eighth days were marked by convocations of the people and abstinence from labor. The method of the first celebration after the promulgation of the new law is described in Neh. viii. 14 sqq., the booths being erected on the roofs, in the temple court and private courts, and in the streets. The Chronicler depends upon this latest code, and consequently ascribes to Solomon a celebration lasting eight days in the seventh month (II Chron. vii. 8 sqq., cf. I Kings viii. 66). The importance of the festival for post-exilic times is indicated by Zech. xiv. 16 sqq., where not to attend yearly is regarded as a grievous sin. The interest in the festival is shown in the development of attendant customs (cf. II Macc. x. 7; Josephus, *Ant.*, III., x. 4, XIII., xiii. 5; *Mishna*, tract Sukkah), tending to greater minuteness in details. Thus prescription was given as to the kind of branches to be carried in the right and in the left hand, the altar of burnt offering was to be encircled once daily and seven times on the seventh day, and a special libation of water was made. A high point was reached in the night between the first and the second day. The priests and Levites erected in the front court of the women a double gallery for the spectators. In the middle of the front court was placed a great candlestick with four golden cups to serve as lamps, and then a torch dance took place while the Levites sang psalms, this continuing till first cock-crowing, when two priests stationed at Nicanor's gate gave on the trumpet the signal to cease. The Psalms sung at the feast were xxix., l. 16 sqq., xciv. 16 sqq., and 8 sqq., lxxxi. 7 sqq., lxxxii. 5 sqq., lxv., cxiii.–cxviii.   (F. BUHL.)

BIBLIOGRAPHY: The Bible Dictionaries; *JE*, xi. 656–662; C. F. Kent, Student's Old Testament, vol. iv., New York, 1907; and the full literature under FEASTS AND FESTIVALS.

TABLE OF THE NATIONS.

The chapter containing the so-called " Table of the Nations," Gen. x., is composed of two parts which go back to the documents J and P. To the latter belong verses 1a, 2–7, 20, 22, 23, 31, 32, the chief divisions of which are marked by the formulas: " the sons of Japheth are. . .," " . . . of Ham," " . . . of Shem "; with similar formulas for the subdivisions; while the close of each division is marked by the formula: " these are the sons of . . .,

after their families, after their tongues," etc., with a variation for the end of the whole in verse 32.

This forms the basis of the exposition
1. Literary by the redactor; the pieces from J are
Analysis. interwoven. But other materials are clearly intruded, as where verse 9 breaks the thread between 8 and 10 to complete the picture of Nimrod. So verse 24 gives a different account of Eber from that in 21 and 25 sqq.; in the former he is great-grandson of Shem, in the latter he is the son. The remainder of the chapter belongs to J.

The material taken from J in verses 8–20, dealing with Ham, diverges in form from P in that the items are not bound together with the word " son," which
has in Hebrew a wider sense than in
2. The English, but by the expression " he
J Source. begat " or the passive " were born." J derives Babel and Asshur from Cush, while P in 22 derives Asshur from Shem. This difference has been ascribed to an error of the redactor, who equated the *Kasshu* of the cuneiform inscriptions with the African Cushites (see ASSYRIA, VI., 2, § 1; BABYLONIA, VI., 5). A better explanation is that which makes J refer Cush here to the Arabian district of that name (see CUSH and NIMROD). Verses 13–14 differ in form from verse 8; the latter uses the singular, the former the plural, a fact explained by Gunkel as due to the fact that 13–14 are later parts of the document J. Among the seven sons of Egypt (Mizraim) Lud (singular of Ludim) is mentioned in Ezek. xxvii. 10, xxx. 5; Isa. lxvi. 19; Jer. xlvi. 9, and is to be regarded as a people who were neighbors to Egypt; the same is true of the Anamim. The Pathrusim were no doubt the inhabitants of Pathros (Isa. xi. 11; Jer. xliv. 1, 15; Ezek. xxx. 14), especially of Upper Egypt; the Egyptian *pata-res* means southland. Erman suspects that for " Naphtuhim " the text should read " Pathmahim," which corresponds to Pathrusim and means " northland." Nothing is known of a people corresponding to the Gasluhim; but the Caphtorim are generally connected with Crete. Verses 15–19 deal with Canaan. Comparison of verses 8 and 15 show that the redactor united passages in which different magnitudes were comprehended: Cush is the name of a people and a land; Nimrod is the name of a legendary person; Canaan, of a land; Sidon, of a city; Heth, of a people (see CANAAN; PHENICIA; and HITTITES). Verses 16–18a are a later insertion, aiming to enumerate the Canaanites more completely (see AMORITES; JEBUS, JEBUSITES; CANAAN; and PHENICIA for treatment of the peoples named). The Hamathites were inhabitants of the city and kingdom of Hamath on the Orontes (see SYRIA). Verses 18b–19 deal with the spread of the Canaanites southward to Gerar, and are a later part of the J source. The completest selection from J is found in verses 21–30; Shem is designated as the father of all the children of Eber, and this last name has here a wide connotation, covering not only the line of Peleg which leads to Abraham, but also the line of Joktan. The name Eber may be connected with the expression *'ebher hannahar*, " beyond the river," of Isa. vii. 20, the land beyond the Euphrates,

regarded as the home of the Israelitic branch of the Hebrews in the Old Testament. For Peleg the best assonance is found in the place-name Phalga at the confluence of the Chabor with the Euphrates; the narrator makes a word-play on the name with the meaning " divide ",(cf. Gen. xi. 1–9), but does not carry his line further, because in later passages the development is followed out (cf. Gen. xi. 10 sqq., xii. sqq.), and the Moabites and Ammonites, Arameans Ketureans, Ishmaelites, and Edomites are touched on in later chapters. In verses 26–29 the descendants of Joktan are named, and thirteen South Arabian stocks are given, though probably originally there were but twelve. Little is known of the settlement of the individual areas of the different tribes.

This review of the data derived from J shows that it is nowhere complete. The transition is lacking from Shem to Eber (verse 21 sqq.), and nothing is said of Japheth. Possibly the beginning of the table of J is to be found in ix. 18–19 and x. 1b, where is found the same order-**3. Character** ing of the brethren as in P (x. 1), and **of the J** x. 21 shows that Japheth follows Shem. **Narrative.** It appears that the order " Shem, Ham, Japheth " is late. The older J thinks of all mankind as springing from one family, that of Noah, who stands at the head of the new race after the flood, and so divides the whole into three branches derived from the three sons. But according to Gen. ix. 20–27 Noah was the original settler in Canaan, the founder there of agriculture and viticulture, while his sons represented the inhabitants of that region. The difference can not now be explained. The representation in the " table of the nations " does not have the usual purpose, viz., to trace the relationship of nations by speech and descent. J was concerned with the Hebrew races in their widest extent and with the South Arabian stocks. The mention of Ham raises great difficulties. But it is not to be understood that the author brings together not only the Egyptians and neighboring peoples, but also Canaan, the Hittites, and even the Assyrian-Babylonians with Cush all under Ham under the relationship of blood and of speech; rather it is political and geographical relationships that influence him. He counts Israel as belonging to Shem, the Canaanites to Ham, although Israel spoke the speech of Canaan. If Cush (verse 8) belongs to South Arabia, it may be that the matter of verses 26–29 was derived from a tradition of early wanderings no longer in existence. Ham in the Old Testament is used for Egypt (Ps. lxxviii. 51, cv. 23, 27, cvi. 22); the word may correspond to the native name for the land, *kam-t*, Coptic *kemi*, *khemi*. The purpose of the narrative is ethnographic—to give a review of the peoples in the little world of the author; but the material employed is not all of a kind; names of persons, cities, and peoples are commingled. The material dates from a time when Assyria and Babylon were known, when Assyria was the ruling power and had not gone down under the Medes and Babylonians. The most important people in Canaan were the Phenicians, while the Hittites had still importance for Palestine, and their cities were not yet overcome

by the Assyrians. The knowledge of the South Arabians is a consequence of the commerce under Solomon, a relation which was broken off when the Edomites got their freedom, c. 845. The age of this source, therefore, can not be lower than the eighth century, with parts still older.

Concerning Japheth the redactor used material only from P, possibly because the data of J no longer suited the situation. Japheth had seven sons. Of these Gomer corresponds to the Cimmerians of the **4. Japheth** Odyssey (xi. 14) and Herodotus (iv. **in the** 11–12), the Gimir of the Assyrian in-**Narrative** scriptions, dwelling to the north of the **of P.** Black Sea and west of the Don, who migrated in the eighth century to Thrace, thence with Thracian tribes to Asia Minor c. 709 B.C., where about 650 they came into conflict with the Lydians and were driven back to the highland of the Halys. To Gomer are assigned three sons, Ashkenaz, Riphath, and Togarmah. Ashkenaz has been taken to mean the Phrygian Ascanians; but Winckler (*Altorientalische Forschungen*, i. 484 sqq., Leipsic, 1893) would read Ashkuz instead of Ashkenaz, and see in them the Scythians, designated in the cuneiform documents Ashkuza. This is a possibility, but the mistake in writing is hardly a probability. In Jer. li. 27 Ashkenaz is named in an Armenian environment, or on the upper Euphrates and about the Araxes. Bochart and Lagarde look for Riphath in the Ribantians on the River Ribas in Bithynia not far from the Bosporus, while Josephus equates them with the Paphlagonians. Togarmah (cf. Ezek. xxvii. 14, xxxviii. 6) is by scholars brought into connection with the Armenians, who once stretched down into the Taurus and Antitaurus, who derived their descent from Haik, son of Thorgom. The locus indicated for Gomer and his sons is, therefore, chiefly in the neighborhood of Cappadocia and Armenia. The second son of Japheth, Magog, is first mentioned in Ezek. xxxix. 6 in close connection with Gog (see Gog and Magog). For the third son of Japheth, Madai, see Medo-Persia. Javan (q.v.) designates the Greeks in general (cf. verse 5), though in Ezek. xxvii. 13; Isa. lxvi. 19, Javan appears along with Tubal and Meshech, cf. verse 4, where the sons of Javan are Elishah, Tarshish, Kittim, and Dodanim (q.v.). The Kittim were originally the inhabitants of the city Citium in Cyprus, then, generally, of Cyprus. Tarshish, the Greek-Roman Tartessus, was the Andalusian plain on both sides of Guadalquivir in Spain; Elisha is either Carthage or Sicily. Since these four names (of verse 4) stood originally in connection with the Phenicians, their arrangement under Javan is a surprise, to be explained by the consideration, however, that the expression " son " does not necessarily express derivation, but rather a relationship of influence, whether through cult, politics, or commerce. Hence for P what once was Phenician is now Greek, the latter having gained the hegemony of the Mediterranean Sea after about 700 B.C., Carthage alone remaining distinctly Phenician. Tubal and Meshech (verse 2) are in the Old Testament often named together (Ezek. xxvii. 13, xxxii. 26, etc.). The former (Assyr. *Tabali*) are the Tibareni, and

Meshech (Assyr. *Mushki*) are the Moschi of Herodotus (III., xciv., VII., lxxviii.), according to Assyrian data of the ninth century north of Cilicia; Herodotus places the Moschi between the upper Phasis and Kyros, the Tibareni east of Thermodon in the later kingdom of Pontus. Either the Assyrians or the Cimmerians drove them from their old settlements. For Tiras one would look somewhere in the neighborhood of Tubal and Meshech; the Tyrrheni seem to be too far to the west. The peoples named in verses 2–5a are all assigned to Japheth, and dwell northward from the Taurus, eastward as far as Media, westward to the isles and coasts of the Mediterranean, with the exception of Crete (see above). The Persians do not appear—are they included under the Medes? A satisfactory explanation of the name Japheth has not yet been given.

Under Ham P first names Cush (q.v.). By this name the Old Testament usually means the land and people south of Egypt. Originally the Cushites dwelt in the land rich in gold east of the Nile; later, Syene was their northern boundary. They were usually despised by the Egyptians, who under the twelfth dynasty subdued their northern tribes,

5. Cush in P. was an Egyptian province. By 1000 B.C. the land was lost to Egypt, and in the eighth century the Cushite or Ethiopian kings subjected Egypt. Their chief city was Napata, the present Merawi between the third and fourth cataracts, and their culture was Egyptian. The So of II Kings xvii. 4 has been identified with Shabako of the twenty-fifth dynasty (Ethiopian); Winckler understands rather Sib'i (Shabi), the general of Pir'u, king of Muẓri in northwestern Arabia (see ASSYRIA, VI., 3, § 10, and 2, § 1). Another king of this dynasty is mentioned in II Kings xix. 9. Several prophecies of Isaiah (xix., xxx. 1–5, xxxi. 1–3) relate to this people, whose rule over Egypt was broken by the campaigns of Esarhaddon and Asshurbanipal (see ASSYRIA, VI., 3, §§ 13–14). Probably the campaign of the Persian Cambyses (see MEDO-PERSIA) resulted in the fall of Merawi and the assumption of Meroe as the capital of the Cushites under a priesthood which fell at the beginning of the third century. The queen mother was the real power and had the title Candace (cf. Acts viii. 27 sqq.).

To Cush P gives five sons and two grandsons, among them Havilah and Seba, whom J assigns to Joktan (verses 28–29). Seba was frequently identified with Meroe (Josephus, *Ant.*, I., vi. 2), though

6. The Sons of Cush. Meroe is never called by this name. Strabo (XVI., iv. 8) and Ptolemæus (IV., vii. 7–8) knew of a seaport Saba, near the present Massowa, which may have its name from a Cushite tribe of that name, living between the Nile and the sea. Havilah was probably a considerable territory in South Arabia, is named with Ophir (q.v.) in verse 29; in the course of the centuries it had various tribes as its inhabitants and consequently is in verse 29 reckoned to Joktan and in verse 7 to Cush; in Gen. xxv. 8 it seems to indicate a region in northern Arabia, and the name is known in both the northern and the southern part of the Arabia of

to-day. Whether it had any connection with the *kolpos Ayalites* and the *Abalitai* on the African coast near the straits of Bab al-Mandeb named by Ptolemæus and Pliny can not be made out. Glaser connects Sabtah (verse 7) with the city Saphtha named by Ptolemæus (VI., vii. 30) not far from the western coast of the Persian Gulf; others think of the old Arabian city Sabbatha or Sabota, the central point for the commerce in spices. Nothing certain is known of Sabtecha. Raamah has been newly found on Sabæan inscriptions as a place-name within the region of the early Minæans north of Maryab. Sheba, one of the sons of Raamah, is no doubt the people often mentioned in the Old Testament and in early writers as the Sabæans, who dwelt in Southwest Arabia and were connected always with gold and incense material (Isa. lx. 6) and with the commerce from India; their chief city, Sheba or Maryab, lay three days' journey from San'a, and numerous inscriptions show that their speech was Semitic. Little is known of their history; they rendered tribute to Tiglath-Pileser III., and Sargon the Assyrian. Of the extent of their territory and their relations to the Minæans almost nothing is certain. The fact that in the Old Testament they are now reckoned to Cush, now to Shem, and then to Joktan the son of Keturah (Gen. xxv. 3), is not to be construed as meaning three separate stocks, but simply as implying change of settlement and of relationships, and that alongside the settled Sabæans there were those who lived a nomadic life and that groups broke away and led a separate existence. Dedan appears (Jer. xlix. 8; Ezek. xxv. 13) as being on the southern border of Edom; the present writer may have had in mind a part which wandered to the south and came into relations with the Sabæans. The arrangement of the districts named under Cush in verse 7 shows that the writer did not limit Cush to Africa but extended it to the west coast of Arabia, whose inhabitants had connections with the regions of the Upper Nile, and he was not governed by the matter of language, since he included Sheba. The arrangement of Sheba as a son of Ramaah proves that he dealt with a late period. The Phut of verse 6 refers to the land of Punt, designating the coast east of the Nile and north of the region of the Cushites and the region opposite in Arabia. The connecting of Canaan with Cush, Egypt, and Phut again shows that the matter of language did not control the narrator. Ham meant for him the people on the southern Nile and the adjacent coast of the Red Sea; why Canaan is brought in here is not clear, but perhaps it was the opposition between Israel and Canaan and also that the center of Phenician power in his time was transferred from the Phenician to the African coast at Carthage. With this J in verses 15–19 hardly agrees. If the division " Shem, Ham (instead of Canaan), and Japheth " issued first from P, the use of earlier pieces necessarily involved dissimilarity and contradiction. The relations of Cush imply the twenty-fifth dynasty; were earlier data used, or were there migrations to us unknown?

The data of P concerning Shem are in verses 22–23. For Elam and Asshur see ELAM; and As-

SYRIA. Since Bochart Arphaxad has been identified with the district of Arrhapachitis of Ptolemæus (VI., i. 2) on the Upper Zab, the Armenian Aghbak and Kurdish Albak. But the last **7. Shem.** consonants remain unexplained by this name, and the identification has by many been given up; Cheyne and Jensen compound the word of '*rpd* and *ksd*, the first part being (Cheyne and Winckler) the Assyrian city and province of Arabha west of Elam and between the Tigris and the Median mountains; Jensen retains the early explanation. Hommel explains the name as equivalent to " Ur of the Chaldees " in Gen. xi. 28. Lud is generally accepted as the Lydians of Asia Minor, who were subjected by the Persians under Cyrus in 546 B.C. Here again is shown the fact that language does not govern the arrangement, since the Lydians did not use a Semitic language. If language were considered, Elam and Lud would not be found among the Semitic peoples. An east-to-west arrangement of lands and peoples does not appear if verse 23 is taken into account. With Elam and Lud the Hebrews were not acquainted till late, with Lud probably not till the conquest by the Persians in the sixth century. Lud may be a portion of the Persian kingdom, and the governing consideration here may be political relations. That the regions and stocks known to early Israel are not named here may be due to the lateness of the author, the older groups of the Arameans having been lost. The name Shem is often brought into connection with the Hebrew *Shem*, " name," " repute," and explained as an abbreviation for *Bene Shem*, " noble race." Others prefer the meaning " high," as deriving the race from a heaven-god or as referring to the lofty homeland of Semites. Yet none of these is entirely satisfactory.

The field of vision of P is quite extensive; it reaches in the north the sources of the Euphrates and the Black Sea, in the west the Straits of Gibraltar, in the south the present Nubia and South Arabia, and in the east Elam and Media. J shows exact geographical knowledge of South Arabia.
8. General Review. The larger horizon of P speaks in general for the later date of that document, though use of older sources is not excluded. Verses 20 and 31 are clear in their expression of the fact that the editor has united under his three groups not only diverse stocks, lands, and peoples, but also diverse languages; consequently the basis of division is not to be sought in linguistic relationship or in diversity of ethnical relationship. While the modern distinction into Semitic and Hamitic languages goes back to this chapter, there is a similar product of comparative linguistics which does not derive its standards from antiquity. The proposition has been advanced that a geographical view-point governed the writer, that Japheth represents the peoples of the north, Ham those of the south, and Shem those between; but in that case why are Elishah and Tarshish under Japheth, Canaan under Ham, the distant Lud under Shem? Moreover, J would not have put the South Arabian tribes under Shem if he had seen in the Semites the peoples of the middle region. In details and incidentally, geographical considerations did govern. But it seems forbidden, if one would understand the arrangement of peoples and lands, to regard P, still more than J, as governed by historical and political relationships. Strictly scientific principles do not appear; the geographical or the historical view-point is used as one or the other seems best to P. Hence on political grounds Lud is placed under Shem, on geographical grounds the peoples of Asia Minor generally are placed under Japheth. He may have been governed, also, by reports or legends regarding the derivation of the nations. We can not follow the learned of early times, because our science and theirs seldom coincide, indeed often conflict. This " table of nations " can not be regarded as a complete review of all the nations known to Israel or of all the peoples of the world, although this was the view of Jewish and Christian scholars who saw in the list seventy peoples, thirty-four in P and thirty-six in J. But apart from the artificiality of the number, the most that could be said is that the redactor who united the sources had this number in mind, and even that does not appear probable. For an estimate of the whole it is essential to keep completely within the view the analysis of the chapter; and on this account the data of the " table of nations " do not fit on one chart.

In its present connection the " table " serves as the bridge from the universal history of mankind to the history of the patriarchs of Israel. All men go back in origin to Noah and Adam (Gen. i. 26, ix. 6; cf. Job xxxi. 15); but the history of these people is not that of the salvation which God is preparing for mankind. That salvation begins with the patriarchs of Israel, through whose mediation the blessing is to come upon all peoples (Gen. xii. 2–3). This connection belongs to P, possibly also to the compilation of J, but whether to the original J is doubtful. (H. GUTHE.)

BIBLIOGRAPHY: The earliest interpretations are to be found in Josephus, *Ant.*, I., vi.; and the Book of Jubilees, viii.–ix., Eng. transls. by G. H. Schodde, Oberlin, 1888, and by R. H. Charles, London, 1902. The chief modern material is in the commentaries on Genesis (named under Hexateuch), best by S. R. Driver, London, 1904, and J. Skinner, ib., 1910. Consult further: A. Knobel, *Die Völkertafel der Genesis*, Giessen, 1850; P. de Lagarde, *Gesammelte Abhandlungen*, pp. 254 sqq., Göttingen, 1866; De Goeje, in *ThT*, iv (1870), 233 sqq.; D. Chwolson, *Die semitischen Völker*, Berlin, 1872; F. Delitzsch, *Wo lag das Paradies?* Leipsic, 1881; F. Hommel, *Die semitischen Völker und Sprachen*, ib. 1883; idem, *Die altisraelitische Ueberlieferung in inschriftlicher Beleuchtung*, Munich, 1897; J. Halévy, in *Revue des études juives*, xiii (1886), 147 sqq.; E. Glaser, *Skizze der Geschichte und Geographie Arabiens*, ii. 323 sqq., 387 sqq., Berlin, 1890; A. H. Sayce, *Races of the O. T.*, London, 1891; idem, *The " Higher Criticism " and the Monuments*, ib. 1894; W. M. Müller, *Asien und Europa nach altägyptischen Denkmälern*, Leipsic, 1893; H. Winckler, *Altorientalische Forschungen*, ib. 1893 sqq.; idem, *Die Völker Vorderasiens*, ib. 1902; idem, in Schrader, *KAT*; A. Jeremias, *Das A. T. im Lichte des alten Orients*, 2d ed., Leipsic, 1906; A. R. Gordon, *Early Traditions of Genesis*, Edinburgh, 1907; M. E. Kern, *The Distribution of the Races; a Commentary on Gen. x.*, College View, Neb., 1907; *DB*, extra vol., pp. 72–83.

TABOO. See COMPARATIVE RELIGION, VI., 1, c.

TABOR LIGHT. See HESYCHASTS.

TABOR, MOUNT. See PALESTINE II., § 6.

TABORITES. See HUSS, JOHN, HUSSITES, II., §§ 3–7.

TACHÉ, tā"shē, ALEXANDRE ANTOINE: Roman Catholic archbishop; b. at Rivière-du-Loup, Canada, July 23, 1823; d. at Winnipeg, Canada, June 22, 1894. He was educated at the College of St. Hyacinth and the Seminary of Montreal, entered the order of the Oblates of Mary Immaculate, and began missionary activity among the Indians of the Red River. He was ordained to the priesthood in 1846, and five years later was consecrated titular bishop of Arath. He now made Ile-à-la-Crosse the center of his labors, and in 1853 became bishop of St. Boniface. He sought in vain to induce the Canadian government to remedy the grievances of the Métis in 1869, but on his return from the Vatican Council he was requested by the government to use his good offices in quieting the insurrection which had meanwhile arisen, and in this he was successful. In 1871 St. Boniface was erected into a metropolitan see, and Taché became its archbishop. He was the author of *Esquisse sur le nord-ouest de l'Amérique* (Montreal, 1869; Eng. transl., *Sketch of the Northwest of America*, by D. R. Cameron, 1870) and *Vingt ans de missions dans le nord-ouest de l'Amérique* (1866).

TADMOR (TAMAR): A city named in the Bible only in I. Kings ix. 18 (*keri*) and II Chron. viii. 4, as built by Solomon and generally identified by geographers and historians with Palmyra (150 m. n.e. of Damascus). Practically the whole tendency of modern criticism, however, is to disconnect Solomon from any relationship with Tadmor (in both Biblical passages "Tamar" is doubtless right; the other places named there are in southern Palestine). Inherently, the probability is against any connection of Solomon with a place so far to the northeast of his kingdom. Its site was originally an oasis formed by springs or streams from the neighboring hills, and in the time of Pliny (*Hist. nat.*, v. 24) it was a considerable town, which formed an independent state between the Roman and Parthian empires. In the second century it seems to have been beautified by the Emperor Hadrian, the name being changed to Hadrianopolis. Under Septimius Severus it became a Roman colony, and received the *jus Italicum*, but it was ruled by its own laws. The most interesting period in the history is the time of Odenatus and Zenobia. The Emperor Valerian being captured by the Persians, Odenatus, perhaps a man who had attained the position of prince of Palmyra, revenged the wrongs of the fallen emperor and vindicated the majesty of Rome. The services thus rendered to Rome were so great, that Odenatus was given the title of Augustus (264 A.D.). He enjoyed his dignity but a short time, being murdered only three years afterward. Zenobia, his widow, succeeded him as queen of the East, and ruled the country during a period of five years. In 272 the Emperor Aurelian turned his arms against her; and having defeated her in two pitched battles invested Palmyra. Zenobia attempted to escape, but was captured and taken to Rome to grace the triumph of Aurelian. Palmyra never recovered its former opulence. It eventually became the seat of a bishop, but never attained importance. When the successors of Mohammed extended their conquests beyond the confines of Arabia, Palmyra became subject to the califs, and from that period seems to have fallen into decay. In 1173 it was visited by Benjamin of Tudela, who found there a considerable Jewish population, besides Mohammedans and Christians. It was again visited in 1751 by R. Wood, and since the beginning of the eighteenth century by many travelers. The inscriptions recovered at the place have exceptional interest and value.

GEO. W. GILMORE.

BIBLIOGRAPHY: R. Wood, *The Ruins of Palmyra*, London, 1753 (highly valuable); L. de Laborde, *Voyage de la Syrie*, pp. 10–22, Paris, 1837; E. M. de Vogüé, *Syrie centrale*, Paris, 1865–77; idem, *Syrie, Palestine, Mount Athos*, ib. 1876; Von Sallet, *Die Fürsten von Palmyra*, Berlin, 1866; Barthélemy, *Reflexions sur l'alphabet et sur la langue . . . à Palmyra*, Paris, 1874; P. V. N. Myers, *Remains of Lost Empires, Sketches of the Ruins of Palmyra . . .*, New York, 1875; L. Double, *Les Césars de Palmyre*, Paris, 1877; E. Ledrain, *Dictionnaire des noms propres palymyréniens*, Paris, 1886; B. Moritz, *Zur antiken Topographie der Palmyrene*, Berlin, 1889; *CIS, Inscriptiones Aramaicæ*, 2 parts, Paris, 1889–93; Deville, *Palmyre. Souvenirs de voyage et d'hist.*, Paris, 1894; W. Wright, *Palmyra and Zenobia*, London, 1895; E. Gibbon, *Decline and Fall*, ed. J. B. Bury, i. 372, 306 sqq., London, 1896; J. H. Mordtmann, *Palmyrenisches*, Berlin, 1899; M. Sobernheim, *Palmyrenische Inschriften*, Berlin, 1905; Baedeker's *Palestine and Syria*, pp. 339–348, Leipsic, 1906; *DB*, iv. 673; *EB*, iv. 4886; *JE*, ix. 507; Vigouroux, *Dictionnaire*, fasc. xxx. 2070–72.

TAFFIN, JEAN: Dutch Reformer and preacher; b. at Tournai probably in 1528; d. at Amsterdam July 15, 1602. He came of a well to-do-family, but of his education and youth almost nothing is known. He first becomes known as secretary or librarian to Granvelle, bishop of Utrecht, but how he came to break with the Roman church is not known. He may have studied under Calvin and Beza at Geneva before the founding of the university there. He was in Amsterdam at the end of 1557, where in the controversy between Gaspar van der Heyden and Adrian van Hæmstede he took part against the latter. Thence he seems to have gone to Aachen and worked in the Walloon congregation, which sent him in 1559 to Worms, and from Aachen to Strasburg in 1561, and thence as preacher to Metz, where he stayed till 1565. For a short time he worked in Tournai, but went the same year to Antwerp, where he preached secretly, and his arrest was ordered on the ground that he was " a great heretic and might do much harm." But he avoided arrest, and when the prince of Orange sanctioned public preaching, Sept. 2, 1566, he became preacher to the Walloons in the "Round Temple." But Protestant worship was precluded by agreement, and Taffin went to Metz again, where in Apr., 1569, Charles IX. closed the church; then Taffin settled at Heidelberg as preacher for the Walloon church there. He attended the Synod of Emden in 1571, and was deputed to convey a message to the next synod of the Reformed Church of France. In Heidelberg Taffin formed a close and lasting friendship with the prince of Orange, by whom he was sent on a confidential mission to Germany in Dec., 1576. He also assisted in promoting the marriage of the prince to Charlotte of Bourbon. Taffin was associated with the prince as court chaplain, representing the interests of the Dutch church. With the prince's other chaplain, De Villiers, he presided at the Walloon synods, and also represented the Walloon interests in the synods of the Dutch churches at Dort in 1574 and 1578, and in Middelburg in 1581. The Antwerp synod decreed in 1578 (art. 3): "Inasmuch as the court is in residence where there is a French church, the town church and that of the court shall become one church: the court chaplains combining with the other preachers to serve the united church as ministers of the same. Messieurs De Villiers and Taffin shall accordingly be considered ministers of Antwerp, and shall minister to the court, and should the court absent itself, the church of this town shall be obliged to provide it with one of these two, or some other chaplain, until the next synod." Taffin thus became preacher to the Walloon congregation. Owing to his French sympathies, the prince was obliged to leave Antwerp in July, and when the town was yielded to Parma by treaty, in 1585, Taffin also left and went to Emden, but the following year became preacher to the Walloon congregation in Haarlem until 1590, when he went to Amsterdam and preached there till his death.

Taffin was noted for his probity and eminent piety. He showed his moderation and forbearance in the controversy regarding Arminius, and in so doing roused suspicion of his own orthodoxy; though as a Calvinist he opposed the views of Arminius. Of his earlier writings nothing is known, although he is mentioned in the Antwerp *Index* of 1570 among "authors of the first rank." He was prominent as a practical theologian. A little work entitled *Des marques des enfans de Dieu et des consolations en leurs afflictions* went through more than nine editions (1606, etc.; Dutch transl., 1593, etc.; Eng. transl., *The Markes of the Children of God*, London, 1590). He issued also four pamphlets bound in one, entitled *Instruction contre les erreurs des Anabaptistes* (Haarlem, 1589); an instructive treatise *Vermaninghe tot liefde ende aelmoese ende van de schuldige plicht ende troost der armen* (1591); the *Traité de l'amendement de vie* (1594), is his best-known work, and was translated into Dutch in 1595 with fresh editions in 1628 and 1659; published in Latin in Geneva in 1602; and in Eng. transl., *The Amendment of Life*, London, 1595.

(S. D. VAN VEEN.)

BIBLIOGRAPHY: C. Rahlenbeck, in *Bulletin de la commission des églises wallones*, vol. ii., The Hague, 1887; C. Sepp, *Drie Evangeliedienaren uit den tijd der Hervorming*, pp. 1–80, Leyden, 1879; idem, *Polemische und irenische Theologie*, pp. 81–94, ib. 1881; H. Heppe, *Geschichte des Pietismus und der Mystik in der reformirten Kirche, namentlich der Niederlande*, pp. 95 sqq., ib. 1879.

TAGG, FRANCIS THOMAS: Methodist Protestant; b. at Union Mills, Md., June 2, 1845. He was educated in Carroll Academy, in his native town, where he was a teacher and principal until 1870, when he became a Methodist Protestant minister. After holding various pastorates in Maryland and Washington until 1884, he was chosen missionary secretary of his denomination, and organized its mission work in Japan. Since 1892 he has been editor of the *Methodist Protestant*. He was president of the general conference of the Methodist Protestants in 1904, and has been a delegate to such bodies as the Ecumenical Conference of Methodism, London, 1901, the Church Federation Conference, New York, 1905, and the Federal Council of Churches of Christ in America, Philadelphia, 1907.

TAGGERT, ROBERT BREWSTER: United Presbyterian; b. at East Palestine, O., Sept. 16, 1842. He was educated at Westminster College (B.A., 1865) and at Xenia United Presbyterian Theological Seminary, from which he was graduated in 1868. He began preaching as a missionary in New York City, and later held pastorates in North Kortright, N. Y., Washington, Ia., Mount Pleasant, Pa., Clinton, Pa., and Harriman, Tenn. He was one of the founders of Temperance (later American) University, Harriman, Tenn., where he was professor of ancient languages. He likewise taught in Ruskin College, Trenton, Mo., and in 1884–86 was professor of Greek in Westminster College. Theologically he describes himself as "independent, Judeo-Christian, with the Bible and sanctified reason as basis."

TAGORE, DEVENDRANATH: Hindu theist; b. in May, 1817; d. Jan. 19, 1905. His father, Dwarkanath Tagore, was a distinguished and wealthy Bengal lawyer and a merchant, a friend of Raja Rammohan Roy (see RAMMOHAN ROY), and a co-laborer with him in the religious reform movements of that day. The eldest son Devendranath grew up under the special instruction of his father's mother, who was a devout believer in idolatry. He attended the school founded by Raja Rammohan Roy, gaining a knowledge of Sanskrit, Persian, and English, besides his vernacular Bengali. In his autobiography he recognizes the temptations that wealth brought him, leading him to forget his higher duties in the pleasure of the moment. At the age of eighteen, however, his mind passed through a change. While watching by his dying grandmother at the river bank, a strange sense of the unreality of all things entered his mind and he was filled with the ecstasy of the feeling of God's presence, followed, however, for a time by sadness and despair. At the age of twenty-one he picked up a torn leaf of a Sanskrit book which proved to be a verse from the *Ishopanishad*, and through it he was induced to make a deeper study of the Upanishads. He became absorbed in these studies, and decided to become a religious teacher. In order to make known his views to sympathetic friends, he established a society called the Tatwabodhini Sabha, to which finally even elderly and influential men were attracted. In 1842 he was first brought into contact with the Brahmo Somaj, which had been founded by Rammohan Roy, but since the death of its founder, in 1833, had been languishing. Devendranath's religious devotion, his talents, and wealth gave new life to the society. "Henceforth," says his biographer, Mr. Muzoomdar, "he was not only the leader, but the absolute all of the society; the committee was his making; he ruled it; the bulk of the expenses he paid; the monthly journal he controlled." The Tatwabodhini Sabha and the Brahma Somaj were amalgamated. Devendranath, perceiving that the members had not absolutely given up idolatry, introduced a Brahmi covenant, which every member was asked to sign. This covenant changed the Somaj from a mere platform for the discussion of reformed views to a fraternity based on a creed. In 1845 a heated discussion with Dr. Duff, in which the members were charged with being believers in the infallibility of the Vedas, led Devendranath and his followers to reexamine their faith. The result was the pronouncement of their belief that no ancient writings are infallible guides and that reason and conscience alone are of supreme authority. The doctrine of the infallibility of the Vedas being abandoned, the rationalistic wave in the society rose so high that Devendranath, becoming alarmed and finally disgusted, retired in 1856 to the Himalayas, where he spent his time in the study of Indian and Western philosophical books, returning only after an absence of a year and a half. While he was absent, in 1857, Keshav Chandra Sen (see SEN, KESHAV CHANDRA) joined the Somaj. His energy and enthusiasm attracted Devendranath, and with close affection the two worked in the interests of the Sabha. But the conservatism of Devendranath and the radicalism of young Keshav led in time to a rupture. In 1865 Keshav withdrew and in 1866 founded the Brahmo Somaj (q.v.) of India. Devendranath then named his faction the Adi-Brahmo Somaj. The defection of Keshav disheartened Devendranath and he retired from the activities of life to solitary meditation, after the ideals of a Hindu rishi. For nearly half a century he lived in this retirement, but was visited by those who reverenced his piety, and who wished to listen to the words of wisdom that fell from his lips.   JUSTIN E. ABBOTT.

BIBLIOGRAPHY: *In Memoriam, Maharshi Devendranath Tagore,* Calcutta, 1905; *The Adi Brahma Samaj, its Views and Principles,* ib. 1870; Sivanath Shastra, *The New Dispensation and the Sadharan Brahma Samaj,* Madras, 1881; *The Offering of Srimat Maharsha Devendranath Tagore,* Lahore, 1890; and the literature under INDIA.

TAI-PING ("Great peace"): The name given to a Chinese religious sect established by Hung Siu Tsuen (b. in a village thirty miles from Canton, 1813; d. at Nanking July 19, 1864). While on a visit to Canton to attend the official examinations, he received from I. J. Roberts, an American missionary, a package of tracts in Chinese. Five years afterward he fell sick, and had visions, in which an old man with a golden beard commanded him to destroy the demons (i.e., the idol-gods) of his countrymen. He then read the tracts; and associating the man in his visions with Christ, and catching up several Christian ideas, he abandoned the Chinese religion, and began to preach his new faith. He retired to the mountains, and by 1840 gathered many converts, whom he styled "God-worshipers." He carried out his supposed commission, and destroyed some Buddhist idols. This brought him into conflict with the government, so that he again retired to the mountains. In 1850 he engaged in a new enterprise. The time was ripe for rebellion; and he proclaimed himself as sent by heaven to drive out the Tatars and set up a native Chinese dynasty. His standard was pushed victoriously forward. Nanking was captured in 1852. The Tai-ping dynasty was founded, with himself as the first emperor under the title Tien-Wang (" the heavenly

king "). The struggle continued against the imperial troops with slow but continuous gains for the rebels, until Shanghai was menaced and foreigners—English and French—were engaged. In 1863 Charles George Gordon took charge of the imperial forces, and within fourteen months the rebellion was so far suppressed that the leader despaired of his cause and with his wives committed suicide.

Hung Siu Tsuen's religious views were a mixture of Christian and Chinese elements. He considered Christ the oldest of the sons of God, and himself one of the younger. In his manifestos he grouped God the Father, Jesus Christ, himself, and his son, whom he styled the " Junior Lord," as the coequal rulers of the universe. He adopted baptism, but rejected the Lord's Supper, allowed polygamy (he had himself a hundred and eighteen wives), and punished adultery and opium-smoking with death.

BIBLIOGRAPHY: L. Brine, *Taeping Rebellion,* London, 1862; A. Wilson, *The " Ever Victorious Army." A History of the Chinese Campaign under . . . C. G. Gordon,* ib. 1868; C. G. Gordon, *Gordon's Diary in China,* ib. 1885; A. E. Hake, *Events of the Tai-Ping Rebellion,* ib. 1892; C. Spielmann, *Die Taiping-Revolution in China, 1850–64,* Halle, 1900; and the general histories of China.

TAIT, ARCHIBALD CAMPBELL: Church of England, archbishop of Canterbury; b. in Edinburgh Dec. 22, 1811; d. at Addington (11 m. s.s.w. of Charing Cross, London) Dec. 3, 1882. After passing through the high school and academy of Edinburgh, he studied at Glasgow University, 1827–30; and at Balliol College, Oxford (B.A., 1830; fellow, 1834); became tutor, 1835; and was ordained, 1836. He took a prominent part in opposing Tractarianism (q.v.), and was one of the four tutors who entered a protest against *Tract No. 90* (see NEWMAN, JOHN HENRY). In 1842 he was appointed headmaster of Rugby school. In 1850 Tait accepted the deanery of Carlisle, and became well known as a hard-working parish clergyman, and in 1856 was appointed bishop of London. Tait initiated the scheme for raising a million pounds to meet the deficiency of church accommodation in London. In 1868 he was raised to the see of Canterbury. He was a representative of Low-church views, and managed with great courtesy and excellent judgment the conflicting relations of the ritualists, and ecclesiastical law of England. He was a man of sound piety and practical common sense rather than of preeminent literary attainments. His works embrace *Suggestions Offered to the Theological Student, under Present Difficulties* (London, 1846); *An Historical Sketch of Carlisle Cathedral. A Lecture* (Carlisle, 1855); *The Dangers and Safeguards of Modern Theology* (London, 1861); *The Word of God and the Ground of Faith* (sermons; 1863–64); *Harmony of Revelation and the Sciences* (Edinburgh, 1864); *The Present Position of the Church of England* (3rd. ed., London, 1873); *Some Thoughts on the Duties of the Established Church of England as a National Church* (1876).

BIBLIOGRAPHY: R. T. Davidson (Tait's son-in-law) and W. Benham, *Life of Archibald Campbell Tait,* 2 vols., London, 1891; W. Benham, *Memorials of Catherine and Craufurd Tait,* new ed., ib. 1882; A. C. Bickley, *Public Life of the Late Archbishop of Canterbury,* ib. 1883; F. W. Cornish, *The English Church in the Nineteenth Century,* 2 vols., passim, ib. 1910; *DNB.* lv. 292–299.

TALBOT, EDWARD STUART: Church of England, bishop of Southwark; b. in London Feb. 19, 1844. He was educated at Christ Church College, Oxford (B.A., 1866), of which he was senior student in 1866–70 and honorary student since 1899. He was ordered deacon in 1869 and ordained priest in the following year. He was warden of Keble College, Oxford, 1870–88, and vicar of Leeds, 1889–95. In 1895 he was consecrated bishop of Rochester, and in 1905 was translated to his present see of Southwark. He was commissary to the bishop of Colombo in 1881–91, chaplain to the archbishop of Canterbury in 1883–89, honorary chaplain to the Queen in 1890–94, chaplain in ordinary in 1894–95, and was select preacher at Oxford in 1871–72, 1883–85, and 1906, as well as rural dean of Boroughbridge in 1890–95 and dean of St. Saviour's, Southwark, since 1897. He has written *Influence of Christianity on Slavery* (Oxford, 1869); *Preparation for the Gospel in History* in *Lux Mundi* (London, 1889); *Some Titles and Aspects of the Eucharist* (1894); *Sermons preached in Leeds Parish Church* (1896); *Vocation and Dangers to the Church* (1899); *Some Aspects of Christian Truth* (1905); *Sermons in Southwark* (1905); and *The Church's Stress* (1907).

TALBOT, ETHELBERT: Protestant Episcopal bishop of Central Pennsylvania; b. at Fayette, Mo., Oct. 9, 1848. He was graduated at Dartmouth, 1870, and at the General Theological Seminary, New York City, 1873; became rector of St. James', Macon, Mo., 1873; missionary bishop of Wyoming and Idaho, 1887; and bishop of Central Pennsylvania, 1897.

BIBLIOGRAPHY: W. S. Perry, *The Episcopate in America*, p. 301, New York, 1895.

TALBOT, PETER: Roman Catholic archbishop of Dublin; b. 1620; d. in Newgate prison, Dublin, 1680. He joined the Jesuits in Portugal in 1635; was ordained in Rome; and taught moral theology at Antwerp. He was in Ireland during part of the civil war and espoused the royalist cause. In 1654 he made the acquaintance of Charles II. at Cologne, whom he is reported to have reconciled to Roman Catholicism. Eventually he severed connections with the Jesuit order. Harsh things have been said of him on account of his alleged duplicity and machinations with political conspirators. He was consecrated archbishop of Dublin at Antwerp in May, 1669. His preferment was mainly due to his opposition to the "Remonstrance" of Peter Walsh, which was considered derogatory to papal authority. He was forced to leave Ireland in 1673. Returning in May, 1678, he was imprisoned on the charge of being implicated in the "popish plot." Although Talbot's diplomatic affairs claimed much of his attention, he published numerous works displaying ability and learning. *Erastus Senior* (London, 1662), aiming to disprove the vindications of Anglican orders advanced by Mason, Heylin, and Bramhall, has been reprinted several times; *Primatus Dubliniensis* (Lille, 1674) was an attempt to show the precedency of the see of Dublin over Armagh; *Blakloanæ hæresis confutatio* (Ghent, 1675) and *Scutum inexpugnabile fidei* (Lyons, 1678) were directed against the peculiar opinions of Thomas White (q.v.). While in exile, Talbot wrote a letter to the Roman Catholics in Ireland, *The Duty and Comfort of Suffering Subjects* (Paris, 1674).

TALIANI, tal-ya´nî, EMIGDIO: Cardinal; b. at Montegallo (a village in the diocese of Ascoli-Piceno), Italy, Apr. 18, 1838; d. there Aug. 24, 1907. He was ordained to the priesthood in 1861, and in 1869 was appointed secretary to the papal nuncio at Madrid. From 1875 to 1880 he occupied a similar position at Paris, after which he was made a canon of the Lateran. Consecrated titular archbishop of Sebaste in 1896, he was sent to Vienna as papal nuncio, and in 1903 was created cardinal priest of San Bernardo alle Terme.

TALLIS, THOMAS: English musical composer; b. probably about 1510; d. Nov. 23, 1585 (buried in Greenwich). He was organist of Waltham Abbey before 1540, and soon after of the Chapel Royal, under Queen Elizabeth, and has been styled the "father of English cathedral music." Five of his anthems were included in John Day's *Certain Notes Set Forth in Four and Three Parts . . .* in 1560, and eight of his tunes in Archbishop Parker's *Psalter* in 1567. With his pupil William Byrd he published *Cantiones Sacræ* in 1575. In 1641 his *First Service* in the Dorian mode, besides a litany, responses, and canticles, appeared in Barnard's *Selected Church Music*, but by far the most remarkable of his works was the motet for forty voices "Spem aliam non habui" edited by Mann in 1888. The seven-voiced *Miserere* was an extraordinary piece of canonic writing, and it was in the Latin church music that Tallis displayed his contrapuntal ingenuity. His instrumental music was only mediocre.

BIBLIOGRAPHY: H. Davey, *Hist. of English Music*, pp. 126–148, 479, London, 1895; *DNB*, lv. 348–351.

TALMAGE, THOMAS DEWITT: Presbyterian; b. near Bound Brook, N. J., Jan. 7, 1832; d. at Washington, D. C., Apr. 12, 1902. He studied at the University of the City of New York (special diploma, 1853), and was graduated from the Theological Seminary, New Brunswick, N. J., 1856. He was pastor of the Reformed Dutch Church at Belleville, N. J., 1856–59; at Syracuse, N. Y., 1859–62; of the Second Church, Philadelphia, Pa. 1862–69; Central Presbyterian Church, Schermerhorn Street, Brooklyn, N. Y., 1869–70. In 1870 the congregation erected on the same street, near the old site, a new and much larger church, known as the "Tabernacle." It was burned Dec. 22, 1872; rebuilt 1874; dedicated, Feb. 22, 1874, and burned Oct. 13, 1889. A new structure was erected on Green Ave., in 1891, and burned May 13, 1894. Talmage then preached a few months in the Academy of Music, 14th Street, New York; and in 1895 became associate pastor with Dr. Byron Sunderland of the First Presbyterian Church, Washington, D. C., and then sole pastor, but retired in 1899 from all active pastoral work, continuing the issue of his sermons in the weekly journals; indeed, his sermons were widely published in America and Europe, weekly, for thirty years. Talmage edited *The Christian at Work*, New York, 1873–76; *The Advance*, of Chicago, 1877–78; *Frank Leslie's Sunday Magazine*, 1880–90; and *The Christian Herald*. He was the author of *Crumbs Swept Up* (Philadelphia,

1870); *Abominations of Modern Society* (New York, 1872); *Sermons* (4 vols., 1872–75); *One Thousand Gems* (1873); *Around the Tea Table* (Philadelphia, 1874); *Masque Torn Off* (Chicago, 1879); *Brooklyn Tabernacle Sermons* (New York, 1884); *New Tabernacle Sermons* (1886); *Marriage Ring; Discourses* (1886); *From Manger to Throne; a New Life of Jesus, and a History of Palestine* (Philadelphia, 1891); *From the Pyramids to the Acropolis:*

Sacred Places seen through Biblical Spectacles (1892); besides many other volumes of sermons, the contents of most of which were first disseminated by the daily and weekly press.

BIBLIOGRAPHY: C. F. Adams, Jr., *Life and Sermons of T. DeW. Talmage*, Chicago, 1902; C. E. Banks, *Life and Works of T. DeW. Talmage*, New York, 1902; L. A. Banks and Others, *T. DeWitt Talmage, his Life and Work*, Philadelphia, 1902; W. C. Wilkinson, *Modern Masters of Pulpit Discourse*, pp. 33–54, New York, 1905.

TALMUD, THE.

I. History: The Babylonian exile was for the history of the Jews a turning-point of moment. The subjects of the kingdom of Judah had lost not only their political independence and their home, but also, through the destruction of the Temple, their one legitimate place of sacrifice,

1. Situation Created by the Exile. the center of the whole worship of Yahweh. But the hope of restoration was still strong; they had for it a support in the words of Yahweh communicated through Jeremiah that the Chaldean sway should last but seventy years, after which God would be again found of his people, who were to return into their own land (Jer. xxv. 11, xxix. 10 sqq.; Dan. ix. 2). The one condition to all this was that the people seek their God with their whole heart (Jer. xxix. 13). This could not then be done by sacrifice nor through the ordinary ordinances of worship; the only way was by keeping of the sabbath and by honoring God's word—that which was written as well as that which was spoken during the exile—especially by regarding the will of God as laid down in the Pentateuch. Special devotion to the law was suggested by the result of the search after the cause of the calamity to the people chosen by God, by the hope of restoration of the cultus and of independence, and by the resolution not to sink again into the past course of iniquity. Consequently there arose in the exile the class of men learned in the law to which Ezekiel belonged (V. Ryssel, in *TSK*, 1887, pp. 149–182). This development was favored by the vanishing of prophecy and the gradual disuse of the Hebrew language, the vehicle of the law and of the revelation of God in the past. Ezra was already described as " a ready scribe in the law of Moses " (Ezra vii. 6, 11), who had " prepared his heart to seek the law of the Lord . . . and to teach it " (Ezra vii. 10), and took with him to Jerusalem " men of understanding " (i.e., teachers; Ezra viii. 16), while the Levites were instructors of the people (Neh. viii. 4 sqq.).

The written Pentateuchal law was closed at least from the time of Ezra, and could not submit to addition or other change. Nevertheless, new relations in life called ever for new pronouncements; so from Ezra's period there must have been some organized power to preserve the law and apply it to practical life. From this fact and in view of Neh. viii.-x.

sprang up the theory of the Great Synagogue (q.v.). Decisions, rules, and Halakoth were delivered as the times and special cases required,

2. Beginnings of Oral Law. and thus grew up an oral common law (cf. the works of Brück and Bloch in the bibliography). The immediate origin of these deliverances being forgotten, they came to be regarded as early, indeed as given to Moses at Sinai (cf. *Pirke Abhoth*, i. 1). Later men resorted to explanations or interpretations of the written law, which served as an extension of the latter, and this oral method came to be acknowledged as authoritative. It came to be the ordinary belief of the faithful Jew that an oral law transmitted by tradition had existed alongside of that which was written in the Pentateuch. But this receives, of course, no historical support and is negatived by lack of mention in Scripture, by the lack of even traditional support, and by the false chronology used to support it. How feeble the support for this may be illustrated by the fact that the whole system of rules for ritual slaughter is made to depend on the words " as I have commanded thee " in Deut. xii. 21. All this constantly increasing material of additions to the Torah (the Law) was for a long time transmitted orally. Philo, in a fragment preserved in Eusebius (*Præparatio Evangelica*, VIII., vii. 6; Eng. transl., ii. 388, Oxford, 1903), speaks of " countless . . . unwritten customs and usages "; while Josephus (*Ant.*, XIII., x. 6) declares that " the Pharisees have delivered to the people a great many observances by succession from their fathers, which are not written in the law of Moses; wherefore the Sadducees reject them and declare that those observances are obligatory which are in the written word, but not those which are derived from tradition." Many other such references there are, but none of the early period suggest fixation of this body in writing. The first reduction of this matter to writing took place in the first half of the second century of our era, and was arranged both topically and according to the order of the passages explained. It may be assumed that the existence of the canon of the New Testament had some influence.

The two forms which this new collection took were, then, the topical or Mishna form and the exegetical or Midrash (q.v.). Mishna (from *shanah*,

" to repeat," " to learn and teach [the content of doctrine]) " means oral teaching and its study.

3. The Mishna; Origin and Growth. It comes to mean the total content of the material of oral tradition which had gathered by the end of the second century of our era, or the total content of the teaching of individuals active in this work (the " Tannaim "), or their single deliverances (in this sense *Halakah* is also used), then any collection of such deliverances. It means, *par excellence*, the collection made by Judah ha-Nasi. In opposition to the sixty (sixty-three) tracts of this collection the term Baraitha was applied to other collections, as also to single pronouncements not contained in it. Among these collections were those called Tosephta, of which one is extant (ed. M. S. Zucker, *Tosefta*, Pasewalk, 1880, supplement volume, Treves, 1882). An Aramaic equivalent of " Mishna " is *Mathnitha* (from *teni* or *tena'*, " to teach "), while *tanna*, pl. *tannaim*, is the designation of the Mishnaic doctors, and also of the later " wandering librarians " who had memorized Mishnaic deliverances and in the discussions of the Amoraim or lecturers on the Mishna served in place of texts. In the Talmud the Mishna is cited with the formula " we learned." The attempt has been made to prove that before the destruction of the Temple a Mishna collection was made by the schools of Shammai and Hillel (D. Hoffman, *Die erste Mischna*, Berlin, 1882); but if Josephus (ut sup.) is to be relied upon, this could have been only oral. But before Judah ha-Nasi there were halachic collections. It is probable that many revered tannaim made halachic collections and books of Haggada both to aid the memory and in the preparation of their lectures, though these might not be used during the actual course of instruction. Such collections, relating to special departments of traditional material, may have been used by the redactors of the Mishna, and to this may have been due the attribution of certain tracts to this or that noted teacher of early times. There is good testimony to work of this kind by Rabbi Akiba (first third of the second century), as in *Zabim* 678, and upon this the work of Rabbi Meir rested. These collections laid the foundations for the more comprehensive labors of Judah ha-Nasi. That a collection was really made at this time seems certain, though that the Mishna in its present form could have originated so early is not to be doubted. It has in the course of time received numerous additions, such as those in which the first assumed author's name is mentioned with his views, and differing views by his contemporaries, and the like. Later authorities than he are seldom named. The text of the Mishna exists in three recensions: that in the manuscripts or editions of the Mishna; that in the Babylonian Talmud, in which the work of the Amoraim follows short excerpts or single pronouncements of the Mishna; that in the Palestinian Talmud, in which the Gemara follows each whole chapter of the Mishna and so that the initial word of the explanatory Mishna sentence is repeated in the corresponding place. Of this third recension for a number of centuries there were known only the first four series and of the sixth series only Nidda 1–4 (cf. W. H. Lowe,

The Mishnah on which the Palestinian Talmud Rests, London, 1883; based on the Cambridge Ms. Add. 470, 1). The relation of these recensions to each other needs investigation.

The development of the Halacha in the earlier period was altogether independent of the written (Pentateuchal) laws; only later were the citations added. Yet, in relation to the present Mishna the form of the midrash (or exegesis) is in many passages more or less significantly to be recognized as the older (for examples cf. Hauck-Herzog, *RE*, xix. 320). The extant Tosephta in many cases is the Mishna in midrash form. Here should receive mention, at least, the fact which is of interest to the Christian reader, that the Pentateuchal passages to which the traditional material brings explanation, extension, and the like are not directly cited but are set forth as thoroughly known. Variations from the arrangement which the name of the tract would lead one to expect are due to the fact that for the sake of relieving the memory deliverances which are alike on one point only are cited, even though they differ on other things. The links of association are of many kinds. Dissimilarities in the handling of the material are sometimes due to the reception into the collection of not a few tracts, apart from additions, essentially in the shape in which their collectors left them. There is also great lack of systematic arrangement. Originally a controlling factor in the arrangement was the length of the tracts, partly due to the teacher's desire to utilize the zeal of the student in mastering the longer treatises while he was fresh to the subject. The Mishna rabbis soon deserted all other Mishna collections for the one which had the approval of the Amoraim. In elucidating the Mishna, the same rules were employed as on the written law of Moses. The relation of the Amoraim to the Mishna was very like that of the Tannaim to the Torah.

4. The Material Described.

Manuscripts are: (1) at Parma, MS. 138, according to De Rossi of the thirteenth century, half of it pointed; (2) at Berlin, Orient. Fol. 567, orders II.–IV., with the commentary of Maimonides in Hebrew translation; Orient. Qu. 566–574, with the Arabic commentary of Maimonides (no. 568 was written in 1222, eighteen years after the death of Maimonides); (3) at Hamburg, no. 18, orders I.–III. with the Hebrew commentary of Maimonides, dated 1416; (4) at Oxford, nos. 393–407, with the Arabic commentary of Maimonides; nos. 408–409, 2662, with Hebrew translation; nos. 2661, 2662–2669 contain fragments of a somewhat higher antiquity; (5) at London, in the British Museum, the Mishna with Arabic commentary of Maimonides—Cod. Orient. 2217–26, 2391–94, Add. 27588; (6) at Cambridge the MS. Add. 470 published by Lowe ut sup.; (7) at Budapest there is a valuable old codex.

II. Divisions: The extant Mishna and the Babylonian Talmud consist of six parts called *sedharim*, " orders," and from the initials of the Hebrew for this expression (*shisshah sedharim*, " six orders ") arose the Hebrew mnemonic for Talmud, " shas." Of the Palestinian Talmud only the first four orders and a part of the sixth are extant. Each order has a number of tracts (from seven to twenty-two) called *massekhtoth* (sing. *massekheth*, " web "), and the tracts fall into chapters (*perakim*) which are divided into paragraphs or sentences (each of which is called a *mishnah*, or, in the Palestinian Talmud, *halakah*). The names of the orders are: *zera'im*, "seeds"; *mo'edh*, "festivals"; *nashim*, "women"; *nezikin*, "injuries"; *kodhashim*, "holy things"; and *teharoth*, "purifications." The names of the tracts are old, testimony to some comes from the middle of the second century of our era; some of them are derived from the contents, some from the first word, and some have in use a double nomenclature. The present number of the tracts is sixty-three. Originally the three first tracts of the fourth order constituted but one, and the fifth tract of the same order was formerly the conclusion of the preceding tract. Consequently the number of tracts was formerly but sixty. The arrangement of the tracts within the separate orders is not universally the same, but the length of the tracts has been the most general governing principle. The division into chapters is also ancient. In the Gemara many chapters are cited by the names (the initial words) still in use. An alphabetical index of the chapter-headings is found in many editions of the Babylonian Talmud in the appendix to the tract *Berakhoth;* it may be found also in J. Buxtorf, *De abbreviaturis Hebraicis,* at the end (Basel, 1613); J. C. Wolf, *Bibliotheca Hebræa,* ii. 724–741 (Hamburg, 1721); and best in W. H. Lowe, *The Fragment of Talmud Babli Pesachim . . . in the University Library,* pp. 50–59 (Cambridge, 1879). The number of chapters is 523.

III. Contents of the Sixty-three Mishna Tracts:
First Order, eleven tracts (1) Berakhoth, "blessings," is on blessings and prayers, especially those for daily use. (2) Pe'ah, "corner," deals with the corners of the field in agriculture and the rights of the poor (cf. Lev. xix. 9, 20, xxiii. 22; Deut. xxiv. 19–22). (3) Dammai (also pronounced Demay), "doubtful (fruits)," deals with fruits of which it is uncertain whether the tithe was given to the priests. (4) Kil'ayim, "of two sorts," deals with forbidden mixtures of things (cf. Lev. xix. 19; Deut. xxii. 9–11). (5) Shebhi'ith, "sabbatical year" (Ex. xxiii. 11; Lev. xxv. 1–7; Deut. xv. 1 sqq.), of which it treats. (6) Terumoth, "heave (offering)," deals with the offerings noted in Num. xviii. 8 sqq., 25–26. (7) Ma'asroth (or Ma'aser rishon), "tithes" (or "first tithe"), treats of the matter of Num. xviii. 21–24. (8) Ma'aser sheni, "second tenth," deals with the tithe which was to be eaten at Jerusalem (Deut. xiv. 22 sqq.). (9) Hallah, "Cake," having to do with the dough of Lev. xv. 18–21. (10) 'Orlah, "foreskin (of trees)," treats of the prohibition to eat the fruit of trees during the first three years after planting (Lev. xix. 23). (11) Bikkurim, "first fruits," on the laws in Ex. xxiii. 19; Deut. xxvi. 1 sqq.
Second Order, twelve tracts. (1) Shabbath, "Sabbath," on the laws connected with observance of the Sabbath, enumerates the thirty-nine chief kinds of work forbidden. (2) 'Erubhin, "mingling," treats of three methods of avoiding the especially burdensome requirements of the Sabbath laws. (3) Pesahim, "Passover festivals," treats of the ordinances respecting Passover. (4) Shekalim, "shekels," dealing with the tax of Ex. xxx. 12–16 for the support of the Temple. (5) Yoma, "day of (atonement)," treats of that fast. (6) Sukkah, "booth," on the feast of tabernacles. (7) Bezah or Yom tobh, "egg" or "feast day," named after the initial word, treats of the observances of festivals, and on the distinction between these and the Sabbath. (8) Rosh ha-Shanah, "new year's feast," deals with festivals of the new moon and the new year. (9) Ta'anith, "fasting," treats of fasts and times of mourning. (10) Meghillah, "roll," principally on the Esther roll read at Purim in the synagogue. (11) Mo'edh katan, "half-feast," deals with the days between the first and last days of the Passover and feast of tabernacles observances. (12) Haghigah, "feasting," has to do with the observances of the three chief feasts.
Third Order, seven tracts. (1) Yebhamoth, "widows obligated to a Levirate marriage," has to do with the levirate marriage (see FAMILY AND MARRIAGE RELATIONS, HE-

BREW, § 12). (2) Kethubboth, "marriage contracts," deals with the duties of husband and wife. (3) Nedharim, "vows," considers vows and their annulment. (4) Nazir, "Nazirite," on the Nazirite vow (see NAZIRITES). (5) Gittin, "divorce papers," on the dissolution of marriage. (6) Sotah, "woman suspected of adultery," on the subject treated in Num. v. 11–31 (see ORDEAL). (7) Kiddushin, "betrothal," has to do with the conditions of legal marriage (see FAMILY AND MARRIAGE RELATIONS, HEBREW).
Fourth Order, ten tracts. (1) Babha kamma, "first gate," deals with injuries, and follows Ex. xxi. 33, xxii. 5–6, giving four chief kinds of injuries of this kind. (2) Babha mezi'a, "middle gate," treats of sales, leases, things found, and interest. (3) Babha bathra, "last gate," considers matters dealing with property rights, sales, and inheritance. (4) Sanhedrin, "court of justice," treats of the various courts of law, the four methods of capital punishment, and of those who shall have part or no part in the future world. See LAW, HEBREW, CIVIL AND CRIMINAL; STONING; SANHEDRIN. (5) Makkoth, "blows," deals with stripes as a method of legal punishment. This and the preceding tract were originally one. (6) Shebhu'oth, "oaths," on the regulations respecting oaths (cf. Lev. v. 4 sqq.). (7) 'Edhuyyoth, "evidences," is a collection of testimonies by later teachers to earlier deliverances; many of the sayings occur elsewhere in the Mishna under other subjects. (8) 'Abhodhah zarah, "idolatrous worship," treating of idolatry and idols. (9) Abhoth, "fathers" (also Pirke abhoth, "sayings of the fathers"), aims to show the continuity of tradition and its reliability, and then to give practical instruction. This tract is very often reprinted, and is commonly found in Jewish prayer-books. (10) Horayoth, "decisions," deals with religious and legal decisions erroneously followed.
Fifth Order, eleven tracts. (1) Zebhahim, "sacrifice," —the name indicates its subject. (2) Menahoth, "meat offerings," the title of which also denotes its subject. Hullin, "profane," has to do with the killing of animals not designed for sacrifice and like matters. (4) Bekhoroth, "first-born" (on various firstlings). (5) 'Arakhin, "valuations," deals with equivalents to be paid instead of persons dedicated to deity. (6) Temurah, "exchange," refers to substitution for dedicated animals. (7) Kerithoth, "extirpations," treats of the excommunication or cutting of one off from the congregation, and the expiation for a fault so punishable. (8) Me'ilah, "trespass," has to do with the subject prescribed for in Num. v. 6–8. (9) Tamidh, "the daily (morning and evening) offering,"—the title denotes the subject. (10) Middoth, "measures," expounds the furnishing of Temple and sanctuary. (11) Kinnim, "birds' nests," has to do with the bringing of birds (doves) as offerings.
Sixth Order, twelve tracts. (1) Kelim, "utensils," treats of the various kinds of ceremonial impurity which vessels may acquire. (2) 'Ohaloth, "tents," deals with the defilement incurred through connection with a corpse. (3) Negha'im, "leprosy," is concerned with that disease. (4) Parah, "red heifer," has to do with the ceremony of purification by the ashes of a red heifer (Num. xix.). (5) Teharoth, "purities"—the name is a euphemistic expression for "impurities," and the tract deals with minor defilements. (6) Mikwa'oth, "ritual baths," treats of the bathing of the defiled. (7) Niddah, "menstruous woman," —the name indicates the subject. (8) Makhshirin, "predisposings," has to do with the predisposition to defilement caused by contact with various fluids. (9) Zabhim, "sufferers from discharges," deals with the subject of Lev. xv. 2 sqq. (10) Tebhul yom, the title means one who has taken a ritual bath on the day of defilement, and therefore remains defiled till sunset. (11) Yadhayim, "hands," treats of ceremonial defilement and purification of the hands. (12) 'Ukzin, "stems," deals with the relations of fruit to stems, skins, and seeds with reference to the mutual impartation of defilement.

IV. The Palestinian Talmud: Two early names of this collection are "Talmud of the land of Israel" and "Jerusalem Talmud." Talmud itself means: (1) study, especially in the expression Talmud torah; (2) teaching, especially in connection with proof texts; (3) explanations coming from the time of the Amoraim dealing with deliverances of the earlier Tannaim (in this sense it is supplanted by

TABLE OF THE TRACTS IN MISHNA, TALMUDS, AND TOSEPHTA.

Vol.	Order.	Babylonian Talmud 1697 sqq.	Since 1606.	Maimonides.	Names of Tracts.	Number of Chapters.	Munich Codex.	Mishna Ed. Lowe.	Palestinian Talmud.	Tosephta.		Mishna Ed. 1559.
										Vienna Codex.	Erfurt Codex.	
i.	Zera'im	1	1	1	Berakhoth	9	[1]	1	1	1	1	1
		2	2	2	Pe'ah	8	2	2	2	2	2	2
		3	3	3	Dammai (Damay)	7	3	3	3	3	5	3
		4	4	4	Kil'ayim	9	4	4	4	6	7	4
		5	5	5	Shebhi'ith	10	5	5	5	5	6	5
		6	6	6	Terumoth	11	6	6	6	4	3	6
		7	7	7	Ma'asroth	5	7	7	7	7	8	7
		8	8	8	Ma'aser sheni	5	8	8	8	8	9	8
		9	9	9	Hallah	4	9	9	9	10	10	9
		10	10	10	'Orlah	3	10	10	10	9	4	10
		11	11	11	Bikkurim[2]	3	11	11	11	11	11	11
ii.	Mo'edh	1	1	1	Shabbath	24	1	1	1[3]	1		1
		2	2	2	'Erubhin	10	2	2	2	2		2
iii.		3	3	3	Pesahim	10	3	3	3	3		3
iv.		11	11	4	Shekalim	8	9[4]	5	5	4		12
		9	8	5	Yoma	8	7	5	4	5		4
		10	9	6	Sukkah	5	6	6	6	6		5
iii.		4	5	7	Bezah (Yom tobh)	5	8	7	8	7		6
iv.		7	7	8	Rosh ha-Shanah	4	5	8	7	8		7
		8	10	9	Ta'anith	4	11	9	9	9		8
		12	12	10	Meghillah	4	10	10	10	10		9
iii.		6	6	11	Mo'edh katan	3	12	12	12	11		11
		5	4	12	Haghiga	3	4	11	11	12		10
v.	Nashim	1	1	1	Yebhamoth	16	1	1	1	1		1
		2	2	2	Kethubhoth	13	2	2	3	2		2
vi.		5	6	3	Nedharim	11	5	3	4	3		5
		6	7	4	Nazir	9	6	4	6	4		6
		4	4	5	Gittin[5]	9	4	5	5	6		3
		7	5	6	Sotah	9	7[6]	7	2	5		7
v.		3	3	7	Kiddushin	4	8	6	7	7		4
vii.	Nezikin	1	1	1	Babha kamma	10	1	1	1	1		1
		2	2	2	Babha mezi'a	10	2	2	2	2		2
viii.		3	3	3	Babha Bathra	10	3	3	3	3		3
ix.		5	4	4	Sanhedhrin	11	4	4	4	4		4
		6	5	5	Makkoth	3	5	5	5[7]	5		5
		7	6	6	Shebhu'oth	8	6	6	6	6		6
		9	7	7	'Edhuyyoth	8	9	7	..	7		10
viii.		4	8	8	'Abhodhah zarah	8	8	8	7	8		7
ix.		10	9	9	Abhoth[8]	5	[9]	9	..	..		9
		8	10	10	Horayoth[10]	3	7	10	8	9		8
x.	Kodhashim	1	1	1	Zebhahim	13	1	1	1	1[11]		1
		2	2	2	Menahoth	13	1	1	1	1		1
xi.		4	3	3	Hullin	12	3	3	3	2		12
x.		3	4	4	Bekhoroth	9	4	4	4	4		12
xi.		5	5	5	'Arakhin	9	5	5	5	5		3
		6	6	6	Temurah	7	6	6	..	6		4
		7	7	7	Kerithoth	6	8	7	..	8		5
		8	8	8	Me'ilah	6	7	8	..	7		6
		10[13]	9	9	Tamidh[14]	7	9	10	..	..		7
		11	10	10	Middoth[15]	5	10	9	..	..		9
		9	11	11	Kinnim	3	11	11	..	..		8
xii.	Teharoth	2	9	1	Kelim	30	1	1	..	1		14
		3	4	2	'Ohaloth	18	2	2	..	2		6
		4	5	3	Negha'im	14	3	3	..	3		7
		5	2	4	Parah	12	4	4	..	4		8
		6	8	5	Teharoth	10	5	5	..	7		9
		7	1	6	Mikwa'oth	10	6	6	..	6		1
		1	7	7	Niddah	10	7	7	1[16]	5		2
		8	11	8	Makhshirin	6	8	8	..	8		10
		9	6	9	Zabhim	5	9	9	..	9		11
		10	10	10	Tebhul yom	4	10	10	..	11		12
		11	3	11	Yadhayim	4	11	11	..	10		3[12]
		12	12	12	'Ukzin	3	12	12	..	12		12

[1] The Munich Ms. has Berakhoth between orders 2 and 3; the Mishnayoth of the first order (without Berakhoth) and of the sixth order (with Niddah) stand after the fifth order in Maimonide ' arrangement. [2] A fourth chapter of many Mishna eds. and of many eds. of the Talmud do not belong to the Mishna, but is taken from the Tosephta and extended. [3] The Palestinian Gemara to Shabbath chaps. xxi.–xxiv. is no longer extant. [4] With the Palestinian Gemara, which is printed with this tract also in eds. of the Babylonian Talmud. [5] Lippmann, Heller, and Levi ben Gershon place Gittin after Sota. [6] After this Niddah, followed by the order Nezikin. [7] Makkoth, chap. iii. here is without Gemara. [8] A later addition is the section Kinyan ha-Torah or Perek R. Me'ir reckoned as the sixth chap. of Abhoth. [9] Stands after the Mishnayoth of the sixth order at the head of the so-called little tracts. [10] The Mishna of Naples, 1492, transposes Abhoth and Horayoth. [11] The Erfurt (Berlin) MS. contains only orders I.–IV. and Zebhahim chaps. i.–iii. [12] Hullin and Bekhoroth are in the fourth and fifth places in order VI. [13] In Tamidh chaps. i., ii., and iv. alone have Gemara. [14] In Lowe's ed. of the Mishna chaps. vi.–vii. form one chapter. [15] The Naples Mishna transposes Tamidh and Middoth. [16] Mishna chaps. i.–iv., Gemara to chaps. i.–iii. and the first three lines of Gemara to chap. iv.

" Gemara," which means acquired learning); and (4) Talmud is the comprehensive term for the Mishna and the explanations it contains. Amoraim is a term which means " speaker " and refers to the Jewish scholars who were active from the period of the closing of the Mishna till toward the end of the fifth century. The most celebrated of the Amoraim was Johanan bar Nappaha (d. 279; cf. *JE*, vii. 211–213). Of later date were Mani bar Jonah, head of the school in Sepphoris, and Jose bar Abin. The close of the Palestinian Talmud took place in the next generation in the beginning of the fifth century. In the Palestinian Talmud there are evidences of several redactions: in the first and second orders there are many Tannaitic sayings attributed to Samuel (of Nehardea; see below, V.), but none in the third and fourth; on the other hand there are many notes of controversy between Mani and Abin in the third and fourth, in the first and second they are few. Against compilation by one author may be adduced the great number of repetitions; thus from the first book there are thirty-nine long excerpts in the second, sixteen in the third, ten in the fourth. The editions of the Palestinian Talmud contain only the first four orders and the Mishna of four chapters of Niddah (sixth order) with the Gemara of three chapters and a few lines beside. In the second order there are lacking the four last chapters of the Gemara to Shabbath, in the fourth the last chapter of the Gemara to Makkoth and all of Abhoth and 'Edhuyyoth. This results from the condition of the Leyden Codex upon which the first edition (Venice, 1523–24) was based, and there are witnesses to the existence of some of these parts. The Mishna of the Palestinian recension is complete in the Cambridge manuscript already noted. This Talmud as extant has Gemara to thirty-nine tracts, the Babylonian to only thirty-seven; yet the latter is three times as extensive. The Babylonian Talmud was authoritative, and in case of conflict was preferred to the Palestinian.

Manuscripts are (1) the Leyden Codex Scaliger 3, dated 1289 A.D., used for the first edition (ut sup.); (2) at Oxford, no. 365, Berakhoth with commentary, no. 2671, Mo'edh ḳaṭan, 2672, Babha kamma, no. 2674, Berakhoth; (3) at London, British Museum, Codices Orient. 2822–24, Zeraim and Sheḳalim; (4) at Rome, Codex 333 contains Zera'im and Soṭah; (5) a Lewis-Gibson manuscript of one leaf from Giṭṭin is described in *JQR*, 1897, 117–119.

V. The Babylonian Talmud: In the beginning of the second century Nehardea was a seat of Jewish learning, and under Mar Samuel (d. 254) it was at the height of its prosperity. Contemporaneous with

1. Origin; Celebrated Authorities.

this was the academy at Sura under Rab (d. 247). After the destruction of Nehardea in 259 Judah bar Ezekiel, a disciple of Samuel and Rab, founded the school at Pum Beditha, noted for the activities of Babbah bar Naḥmani (d. 331), a keen dialectician, of Joseph bar Hiyya (d. 333), who because of his comprehensive knowledge of the law was called Sinai, and of Abaye (d. 338), the pupil of the two named just before him. Raba bar Joseph bar Hama (d. 352) taught in Mahuza on the Tigris, and after him Nahman bar Isaac (d. 356) was the head of the academy restored at Pum Beditha. Papa (375) founded the school at Neresh

near Sura, and after his death the school at Sura acquired new importance. The deliverances of Joseph and Raba form a large part of the Babylonian Talmud, and to these is added material brought from Palestine. Through Ashi, for half a century head of the school at Sura, the accumulated material during two centuries was arranged. A spur to the making of this collection was the persecution of the Jewish religion in Persia, 439–457. Rabbina bar Huna (d. 499) was the last of the Amoraim, those coming after used the work of those who preceded as a basis. As early as Tanna Judah ben Il'ai mention is made of mnemonic signs, and these were used in manuscript for convenience and for saving of time and space; collections of these abbreviations were employed by the Tannaim, also the abbreviations themselves were used by those who collected and arranged the Babylonian Talmud. In the manuscripts these gradually fell away, partly because they became superfluous and partly because they were no longer understood. Of the sixty-three tracts of the Mishna twenty-six are without the Babylonian Gemara; these were, no doubt, discussed in the Babylonian schools in the fourth century, but the discussions were probably never digested or reduced to writing. A great part of the contents of many of these tracts can not have been employed outside of Palestine, while that of others went under other tracts; 'Edhuyyoth and Abhoth could from their subject matter have had no Gemara. The first mention of the Babylonian Talmud entire occurs in the second half of the eighth century.

Of manuscripts the following may be mentioned: (1) at Munich, Codex Hebr. 95, the one extant manuscript of the entire Babylonian Talmud, written in 1343; Codex Hebr. 6, containing Pesahim, Yoma, and Haghigha; Codex Hebr. 140–141, which contains five tracts or parts of tracts; (2) at Rome according to the brothers Assemani thirty-one codices contained fifty-seven tracts of the Talmud and some of the so-called lesser tracts; (3) at Oxford no. 366 contains two tracts, no. 367 has two, 368 has one, 369 one, 370 four, 373 one, 375 one, while other fragmentary codices are nos. 2661, 2666, 2667, 2671, 2673–78, some of them important, the oldest dated 1123 (cf. S. Schechter and S. Singer, *Talmudical Fragments in the Bodleian Library*, Cambridge, 1896); (4) in London, British Museum Harley 5508 contains eight tracts, and Add. 25, 717 contains three in whole or part; (5) in Florence the National Library contains the second-oldest of known dated Talmud manuscripts (1176 or 1177), with seven tracts. (6) in Hamburg no. 165 of the year 1184 contains three tracts. (7) at Göttingen Codex Heb. 3 contains five tracts in whole or part; (8) at Carlsruhe a manuscript contains Sanhedrin; (9) at Paris the National Library has no. 671 with Berakhoth, no. 1337 with three tracts, and no 1313 with a part of Babha Bathra; (10) in New York Columbia University has a South Arabian manuscript written in 1548 which contains four tracts; (11) at Cambridge is the manuscript described in W. H. Lowe, *The Fragment of Talmud Babli Pesachim* . . . (Cambridge, 1879).

The fewness of early manuscripts is in some degree compensated by the numerous citations in early authorities, such as the Talmud compendium

2. Censorship; Consequent Changes.

of Isaac ben Jacob Alphasi (between 1013 and 1103), the Talmud dictionary of Nathan ben Yehi'el of the eleventh century, and the Talmud commentaries of Rashi and the Tosephtists. There is need of a critical commentary of the Talmud (the Mishna and the two Talmuds), and this need is the greater because of the mischief wrought through Christian censorship (or the fear of it) both in manuscripts and in editions. The evidence both of this censorship and its results is abundant. In 1631 a Jewish assemblage in Poland issued a circular (cf. C. Leslie, *A Short and Easy Method with the Jews*, pp. 2–3, London, 1812) which directed under pain of excommunication that in the issue of editions of Mishna or Gemara all references to Jesus of Nazareth be expunged and marked with a circle (which the rabbis would know how to explain); this was in consequence of the interest of Christians in Jewish literature and was intended to avoid persecution and charges against Jews by Christians. Russian censorship has forbidden attention to be called to omissions by the existence of blank spaces. An example of this censorship is the edition of the Talmud of Basel, 1578–81; the tract 'Abhodhah zarah is wholly omitted, in place of " Talmud " " Gemara " appears, " Sadduceans " or " Epicureans " displaces " Jewish Christian " or " heretic," " Samaritan " or " Cushite " displaces the word for " non-Jew," " Rome " is transposed into " Babylon," " Roman " becomes " Aramean " or " Persian " or " Babylonian," and other even graver changes are made. In matters of this sort not only Christians but Jews have been deceived, as when portions belonging to the second century make mention of Sadducees, whose existence ceased after the destruction of the Temple, and, similarly, mistakes have been made in the understanding of the word rendered " Jewish Christian " or " heretic." On the censorship of Jewish books light is thrown by L. Zunz, *Die Ritus des synagogalen Gottesdienstes*, pp. 147–149, 222–225 (Berlin, 1859); H. Reusch, *Der Index der verbotenen Bücher*, vol. i. (Bonn, 1883); A. Berliner, *Censur und Confiscation hebräischer Bücher im Kirchenstaate* (Frankfort, 1891); W. A. Popper, *The Censorship of Hebrew Books* (New York, 1899). Some of the passages either stricken out or changed through this censorship are collected in books mostly anonymous (with Hebrew titles; one issued at Königsberg, 1860) and in the *Dikduke sopherim* of Rabbinovicz (1868–88).

VI. Evaluation of the Talmud: As respects the contents of the Talmud, distinction is to be made between halachic and haggadic material. The meaning of Halacha (Halakah) is (1) conduct regulated by the Torah, (2) the law according to which conduct is regulated, or legal regulations.

1. Halacha and Haggada. The plural is used to express both individual regulations of a religious sort and also the collections of such regulations. Halacha means, in its implications, what has been immemorially regarded as fixed, then what a majority has decided in a recognized assembly (of scholars), and finally what has been taught by prevailing authority. In the Mishna conflicting opinions are often adduced without indicating which prevailed. The Gemara gives the impression of a salon or of a collection of records of discussions by the Amoraim concerning Tannaite deliverances. Relatively seldom can one determine from the Talmud itself what is Halacha or definitive requirement; this is to be reached by investigation and use of the rules found in the

halachic part of the *Sedher Tannaim we-'Amor'aim*, or by the employment of the *Yadh ha-Ḥazaḳa* of Maimonides, *the Sepher ha-Miẓwoth* of Moses of Coucy, and the *Shulḥan ha-'Arukh* of Joseph Karo, and with these last the commentaries should be used. Haggada (*Haggadhah*) now denotes in general the non-halachic contents of the Talmud; it comes from a word employed in the sense " to teach," and was formerly employed in the sense " the Scripture teaches." Haggadic material in the Talmud is inserted in the body of halachic material, and often the connection is loose; sometimes there is no connection at all. Long haggadic pieces which may be specifically referred to are Berakhoth 54a–64a, Shabbath 30a–33a, Meghillah 10b–17a, Giṭṭin 55b–58b, Sanhedrin 90a–113b.

Few literary products have educed so contradictory estimates of their value as has the Talmud. To it have been given overweening praise and calumnious blame. A calm estimate requires first the consideration of the foregoing distinction between Halacha and Haggada. Next there must be taken into account the political relationships and the religious views of the Jews both in Palestine and in Babylonia during the first five centuries of the Christian era and the circumstances under which these relations and views arose. There will then be explained the hostility of the Jews, which here sometimes finds expression, to their oppressors and to the forms of religion and irreligion and heathenism and unethicality which pervaded the regions and actions of that period. While the forms of this hostility will not thus be justified, they will at least be understood.

(H. L. STRACK.)

VII. Explanation and Translation of the Page from the Talmud.

The text is the matter in large print in the center of the page; the Rashi (commentary) is immediately on the left of the text, and the Tosafot (" additions ") immediately on the right. The material on the margins are condensed biographical notes (not translated), and that on the lower right hand and bottom margin relates to another page and is also not translated. The question under discussion on the preceding pages (not reproduced here) has to do with the saving of a scroll of the law in case of fire by means of passing into a closed lane, and in the discussion the query arises, what is a closed lane? The various answers to this appear in the first part of the translation which follows (which is given very literally, preserving so far as possible the order of the words).

Text: R. Ashi, however, said: three partitions and one stake form a closed lane; three partitions without a stake form an open lane; and even R. Eliezer, who says that two stakes are required, that is only for (moving thither) provisions and beverages, (admits that) for a scroll of the Law one stake is sufficient.

Mishna: One may save food for three meals, that which is fit for human beings (may be saved) for men, and that which is fit for cattle (may be saved) for cattle. How so? If a conflagration happen on a Friday night one may save food for three meals; on Saturday morning, for two meals in the afternoon, for one meal. R. Jose says one may always save food for three meals.

Gemara: Since (a man) is troubled about what is permitted, why should not he save more? Said Rabba, because a man is anxious for his possessions, and were he allowed he would go so far as to extinguish (the fire). Ahaye said to him: We have previously learned that a man upon whose roof a barrel becomes broken may bring a vessel to put underneath; but may not bring a vessel to intercept (the flowing), nor put a vessel alongside (the roof). What precautionary measure can be (devised) in that case (to prohibit it)? Here there is also the precaution against his bringing a vessel through public ground. The text reads: A man upon whose roof a barrel becomes broken, may bring a vessel and put it underneath; but he may not bring a vessel to intercept (the flowing), nor put a vessel alongside (the roof). Should he happen to have guests he may bring a vessel to intercept or put a vessel alongside. He should not, however, intercept first and then invite guests, but should invite guests first and then intercept: no artifice should be used in order to circumvent the law. It is reported in the name of Jose ben Judah that an artifice may be used. Is the clash of opinions not the same as that of R. Eliezer and R. Joshua in the following teaching: An animal and its offspring that have fallen into a pit (on a holy day)? R. Eliezer says that one may bring up one to be killed, while the other is to be left where it is, but provided with food that it may not starve. R. Joshua says that one may (supposedly) bring up one with the intention of killing it, but on some pretext may not kill it, and may bring up the other and then kill either one. No, it is possible that R. Eliezer says so only in the case when it (the remaining animal) can be fed, but not here in our case; on the other hand, it is possible that R. Joshua says so only when the suffering of a living being is involved, but not in our case where there is no suffering of a living being.

The rabbis taught: If one has saved fine bread, one is not allowed to save afterward coarse bread, but if one has saved first coarse bread, he may save afterward fine bread. One may save on the Day of Atonement (food) for Sabbath, but not on Sabbath for the Day of Atonement, and still less on Sabbath for holy days, or for the next Sabbath. The rabbis taught: If a man has forgotten bread in the oven and the sanctity of the day (i.e., the sacred day) begins, he may save of it for three meals, and tell to others that they may come and save for themselves. He should not, however, take it with a baker's shovel, but with a knife. Why, did not R. Ishmael teach " In it thou shalt not do any work " (Ex. xx. 10), except blowing of the horn and taking out bread because these belong to science and not labor? So far as it is possible to do it (i.e., such a piece of work) in another way (than as it is performed in the week-days) we are under obligations to do it (in that other way). R. Hisda said: A man should always make his preparations for the Sabbath early, for it is said: and it shall come to pass, that on the sixth day they shall prepare that which they bring in (Ex. xvi. 5), at once. One must break on Saturday two loaves, because it is said: " Twice as much bread " (verse 22). R. Ashi said: I have seen R. Kahana keeping in his hands two loaves and break only one, stating that it is said, they gathered (twice, but did not break). R. Zera used to break a large piece that sufficed for the whole meal. Said Rabina to R. Ashi, did it not look like gluttony? The latter answered him: Since he did not do it every day it did not look like gluttony? R. Ami and R. Assi, when they happened to have the bread that was used for making an *Erub,* would begin the meal with it, for they said that because one religious duty had been fulfilled with that bread, it should be used to fulfil another religious duty.

How so? If a conflagration happen, etc.* The rabbis taught: How many meals is one obliged to eat in Sabbath? Three. R. Hidka says four. Both opinions are deduced from the same verse " And Moses said, eat that to-day; for to-day is a Sabbath unto the Lord: to-day ye shall not find it in the field " (Ex. xvi. 25). R. Hidka holds that the thrice repeated " to-day " means three (meals) besides that of the evening, while the rabbis hold that therein is included the evening meal. We have learned: If a conflagration happen on Friday night . . . . . .

Rashi (on the left): *R. Ashi, however, said, etc.†* Both the sages and Ben Bethera are of the opinion of R. Eliezer that generally three partitions and two stakes are required, but the sages say that in the case of a scroll of the Law even R. Eliezer admits that one stake is sufficient, while Ben Bethera says that in this case R. Eliezer admits that no stake is needed. *One stake is sufficient:* this refers to the opinion of the sages.

Mishna: *A Conflagration happen on Friday night:* before the meal. *In the Morning:* before breakfast. *One may always save:* it being such a day (i.e., when fasting is prohibited) and he is troubling himself about what is permitted, for food is an article that by itself is allowed to be moved and it (is carried) to a court provided with an *Erub,‡* he' would have been allowed to save more, were it not for the precautionary measure, as explained in the Gemara.

Gemara: Since he is troubling himself about what is permitted: things which are allowed by themselves to be carried and (removed) to a court provided with an *Erub. If he were allowed:* In busying himself with so much saving, he might forget the Sabbath in his state of anxiety and might proceed so far as to extinguish the fire. *Intercept:* the flow that is falling through the air. *Put alongside:* near the roof as a receptacle, though it can not draw because the roof is flat and the wine is not in a hole. He, therefore, places a vessel near the

---

* The abbreviated form used here and elsewhere arises from the fact that only the initial words of well-known formulas were used in stating a case or beginning a discussion.

† This is cited from the first paragraph above. It will be noted that the commentary takes up successive portions of the text, first citing in abbreviated form (printed in italics) the part on which comment is to be offered.

‡ The technical term for " a symbolical act by which the legal fiction of community or continuity is established." M. Jastrow, *Dictionary of the Targumim,* . . . , p. 1075, London and New York, 1903.

roof that it should drip from the roof into the vessel which he holds in his hands. *What precautionary measure can be, etc.:* Since it is permitted (to carry wine in private ground), why should he not be allowed to intercept or to put (a vessel alongside the roof)? *Against his bringing a vessel through public ground;* in looking so much after vessels he may forget and bring. *He should not intercept and invite afterward:* for while intercepting he does not need guests. *No artifice should be used:* who do not wait to taste, in order that they should leave. *Fallen into a pit:* on a holy day. The mother and its offspring may not be killed on the same day (since this is prohibited by Mosaic Law). *May not kill it:* for he might use the pretext that the other is fatter. *R. Eliezer says so only:* that no artifice is to be used. *One has saved fine bread:* sufficient for three meals. *One is not allowed to save afterward coarse bread:* coarse bread made of the seconds; for it is not a fitting pretext that this is better for him. *But not on Sabbath for the Day of Atonement:* as, for instance, when the Day of Atonement falls on a Sunday. As one is not allowed to eat before the day is over, he is compelled to prepare in the evening. *And still less on a Sabbath for a holy day:* because one can prepare it on the same day. *Baker's shovel:* an instrument with which the bread is moved and separated from the walls of the oven to which it cleaves, one should not take out with the baker's shovel because that is the every-day way of doing. *A man should . . . early:* to busy himself on the eve to prepare that what is needed for the Sabbath. *They should prepare that which they bring, at once:* to prepare at the moment of bringing, and that the bringing should be early is deduced from the verse " and they gathered it every morning " (early). *Break:* to pronounce the benediction of ha-Mozi. *Keeping two:* he took them in his hands. *It is said: "They gathered";* which shows that two have to be kept, but it is not said that two must be broken: *To break a big piece that sufficed for the whole meal:* A big piece that was enough for that meal. He did it in honor of the Sabbath, showing thereby that the Sabbath meal was so dear to him that he is going to make effort to eat much. *When happening:* sometimes when the *Erub* was made in their house, and sometimes when it was made in the house of somebody else. *Would begin:* that is, to pronounce on it the benediction of " ha-Mozi " which is the beginning of eating. *Begin:* start. *Thrice repeated " to-day":* [The repetition here] comes (to show) the number of meals.

Tosafot (on the right): *We have previously learned that a man upon whose roof a barrel became broken:* R. Porat queried: Why did he (Abaye) not ask his question from the Mishna which is at the beginning (of the chapter entitled) " Hobit," where we have learned: A barrel that became broken one may save from it enough for three meals, and may say to others, come and save for yourselves, only one should not use a sponge? He answered: There one can say that the barrel was in a marked-off plot in a public thoroughfare (where articles are not allowed to be moved) and there was reason to fear that one would carry the vessel to a distance of four cubits, while here in this Baraitha is expressly said " on

the roof " (private ground). The Ri answered: There it is stated that the wine was spilled on the ground and there was reason to fear the using of a sponge. R. Samuel said in the name of R. Tam that (this prohibition) is only in the case when the barrel is broken, but when the barrel is only cracked and it drips, one may bring vessels to intercept or to put alongside, for then the man would not be so greatly confused as to bring vessels through the public thoroughfare, as (he might be) if it were entirely broken.

A vessel to intercept or a vessel to put alongside: The Ri said that there is meant here " not only this, but even that," not only to intercept, when it is evident that one is saving, but even to put alongside when it is noticeable that one is saving, is also prohibited.

If one has saved fine bread one is not allowed to save afterward coarse bread: The Ri said that when one has baked on the Passover unleavened bread from fine flour sufficient for the holy days, one may not bake afterward unleavened bread from seconds; but he may bake first from seconds and afterward from fine flour.

But not on a Saturday for the Day of Atonement: The commentaries explain for the evening following the Day of Atonement (for there is no need of food for the Day of Atonement which is a fast-day). But if thou shalt ask: Is it not a matter of course, what difference is there between the evening following the Day of Atonement and that following the Sabbath? One may answer that it is a religious duty to eat on the evening following the Day of Atonement, as explained above (folio 114b), and also because one fasted in the day he would believe that it is allowed. It is also possible that it is meant for the Day of Atonement itself, to give food to the children.

Did not R. Ishmael teach: "You shall do no servile work" (Lev. xxiii. 8. As one may see, the Tosafists had here another reading): If thou shouldst ask, why is quoted here the verse of " no servile work " which refers to holy days, since on Sabbath to which refers the verse " thou shalt not do any work," in general, without saying " servile work," one may also blow the horn and take out bread from the oven according to the Mosaic Law, as we see it here where it is quoted in reference to Sabbath? R. Samuel explained that in fact the correct reading here is " Thou shalt not do any work." The Rashba explained that it is true that the exceptions of blowing the horn and taking bread from the oven are derived from the verse "Any servile work," and we (apply what is) deduced from what is said about the holy days to the Sabbath, because there is no other difference between holy days and Sabbath than the preparation of food (which is allowed on holy days) as is said: " Save that which every man must eat " (Ex. xii. 16).

Because these belong to science and not labor: And since they are allowed by the Mosaic Law, though it is prohibited by the sages, as is said in the treatise *Rosh ha-Shanah:* " One does not prevent children from blowing the horn, but one prevents women from doing so," here one has to allow (the taking out of bread) for the sake of three meals (that are needed).

BIBLIOGRAPHY: Of the Mishna the first ed. was issued at Naples, 1492, with the (Hebr.) commentary of Maimonides; another ed. was that of Riva di Trento, 1559; and the latest that of Lowe named in the text. The first complete ed. of the Babylonian Talmud was that of Bomberg, Venice, 1520–23; others are Venice, 1531 and 1546–51; Lublin, 1559 sqq. (incomplete), 1617–39 (entire text); Basel, 1578–81 (censored); Cracow, 1602–05, 1616–20; Frankfort, 1697–99 and 1720–22 (the basis of most later eds.); Amsterdam, 1644–48 and 1714–19. Of modern editions those which are perhaps best worthy of note are: Berlin, 1862–68; Wilna, 1886 (the largest, with many aids to study); and the ed., with Germ. transl. and notes, by L. Goldschmidt, Berlin, 1896 sqq. (in progress vol. v., fasc. 1 issued Leipsic, 1910). Of the Palestinian Talmud the editio princeps is that of Venice, 1523 sqq.; later ones are Cracow, 1609; Krotoschin, 1866; Jitomir, 1860–67 (complete with commentary); and that of Piotrkow, 1898–1902. For other editions of both Talmuds cf. JE, xii. 23–24. Space can not be given here to editions of parts of the Talmud and of single tracts. A partial list is given in Hauck-Herzog, RE, xix. 315, and a further source for recent issues is the Schlagwort Katalog of C. Georg, Hanover, 1889–1909, under the caption "Talmud." There is an Eng. transl. of the Babylonian Talmud by M. L. Rodkinson, 10 vols., New York, finished 1906, but it is not altogether scholarly; a French transl. of the Palestinian Talmud is by M. Schwab, 11 vols., Paris, 1878–90, while a French transl. of the Babylonian was begun by J. de Pavly, Orléans, 1900; in German there are: A. Wünsche, Der jerusalem. Talmud in seinem haggadischen Bestandteilen . . . ins Deutsche übertragen, Zurich, 1880; idem, Der babylon. Talmud in seinem haggad. Bestandteilen . . . übersetzt und erläutert, 5 vols., Leipsic, 1886–89.

For commentaries on the Talmud the reader is referred to the article in JE, xii. 27–28, where a history of the subject and a list of commentaries down to 1905 are furnished.

As helps to the Talmud the following stand out—among dictionaries: J. Levy, Neuhebräisches und chaldäisches Wörterbuch, 4 vols., Leipsic, 1876–89; idem, Chaldäisches Wörterbuch über die Targumim, ib. 1886; M. Jastrow, Dictionary of the Targumim, Talmud Babli and Yerushalmi, and Midrashic Literature, 2 vols., London, 1886–1903; S. Krauss, Griechische und lateinische Lehnwörter im Talmud, Midrasch, und Targum, Berlin, 1898–99; idem, Talmudische Archäologie, vol. i., Leipsic, 1910; G. Dalman, Aramäisch-neuhebräisches Handwörterbuch, Frankfort, 1901; and cf. JE, iv. 580–585. For grammars: I. Rosenberg, Das aramäische Verbum im babylonischen Talmud, Marburg, 1888; C. Levias, A Grammar of the Aramaic Idiom Contained in the Babylonian Talmud, Cincinnati, 1900; G. Dalman, Grammatik des jüdisch-palästinischen Aramäisch, Leipsic, 1905; M. L. Margolis, Lehrbuch der aramäischen Sprache des babylonischen Talmuds, Munich, 1910, Eng. transl., Manual of the Aramaic Language, London and New York, 1910; and cf. further JE, vi. 67–80. Other kinds of helps are: J. Lightfoot, Horæ Hebraicæ et Talmudicæ, in Eng. transl. in the Works, 2 vols., London, 1684 (the great thesaurus for English readers); Isaak ben Samuel Lampronti, Paḥaḥ Yiẓḥak, 14 vols., printed at various places, 1750–1888 (the most comprehensive encyclopedia of facts relating to the Talmud); J. Hamburger, Real-Encyklopädie für Bibel und Talmud, 3 vols., new ed., completed Leipsic, 1901; JE, viii. 609, 618, xii. 1–39.

In matters of introduction, on the origin consult: N. Brüll, in Jahrbücher für jüdische Geschichte, ii (1876), 1–123; D. Hoffmann, Die erste Mischna und die Controversen der Tanaim, Berlin, 1882; J. S. Bloch, Einblicke in die Geschichte der Entstehung der talmudischen Literatur, Vienna, 1884; I. A. Rosenthal, Ueber den Zusammenhang der Mischna. Ein Beitrag zu ihrer Entstehungsgeschichte, 2 vols., Strasburg, 1890–92, 2d ed. of vol. i., 1909; idem, Die Mischna, Aufbau und Quellenscheidung, ib. 1903–06; H. L. Reich, Zur Genesis des Talmuds, Vienna, 1892; S. Funk, Die Entstehung des Talmuds, Leipsic, 1910. On other matters of introduction such as the history, etc., consult: H. L. Strack, Einleitung in den Talmud, 4th ed., Leipsic, 1908; M. L. Rodkinson, The History of the Talmud from the Time of its first Formation, about 200 B.C., to the Present Date, New York, 1904; J. C. Wolf, Bibliotheca Hebræa, ii. 657–993, iv. 320–456, Hamburg, 1721–1733; A. G. Wähner, Antiquitates Hebræorum, i. 231–584, Göttingen, 1743; H. S. Hirschfeld, Halachische Exe-

gese. Ein Beitrag zur Geschichte der Exegese und zur Methodologie des Talmuds, Berlin, 1840; W. Bacher, Die Agada der babylonischen Amoräer, Strasbourg, 1878; idem, Die Agada der Tannaiten, 2 vols., ib. 1884–90; idem, Die Agada der palästinischen Amoräer, 3 vols., ib. 1892–99; idem, Die Agada der Tannaiten und Amoräer—Bibelstellenregister, ib. 1902; M. Joel, Blicke in die Religionsgeschichte zu Anfang des 2. christlichen Jahrhunderts, Breslau, 1880–83; idem, Der Aberglaube und die Stellung des Judenthums zu demselben, ib. 1881; E. Schreiber, Der Talmud vom Standpunkte des modernen Judenthums, Berlin, 1881; W. H. Lowe, The Mishna on which the Palestinian Talmud Rests, Cambridge, 1882; M. Ehrentheil, Der Geist des Talmuds, Budapest, 1887; M. Schwab, Le Talmud de Jerusalem traduit, pp. i.–lxxxiii., Paris, 1890; E. O. M. Deutsch, The Talmud, Philadelphia, 1895; A. Edersheim, Life and Times of Jesus the Messiah, Appendices III., V., VIII., XVII., XVIII., 8th ed., London and New York, 1896; M. Flügel, Spirit of the Biblical Legislation; the Mosaic and Talmudical Codes, Baltimore, 1896; D. A. Friedman, Rabbis of Ancient Times; biographical Sketches of the Talmudic Period, Rochester, 1896; I. Halévi (or Halevy), in REJ, xxxiii (1896), 1–17, xxxiv (1897), 241–250; idem, Die Geschichte und Literatur Israels, vol. ii., Frankfort, 1901, vol. iii., Pressburg, 1897; A. Darmesteter, The Talmud, Philadelphia, 1897; S. Bernfeld, Der Talmud. Sein Wesen, seine Bedeutung und seine Geschichte, Berlin, 1900; L. Ginsburg, Die Haggada bei den Kirchenvätern, ib., 1900; S. Funk, Die Juden in Babylonien 200–500, 2 vols., ib. 1902–08; M. Mielziner, Introduction to the Talmud, New York, 1903; B. von Schottenfeld, Was muss Man von Talmud wissen? Berlin, 1904; A. Wünsche, Monumenta Judaica, Vienna, 1906–07; idem, Aus Israels Lehrhallen, Leipsic, 1907 sqq.; J. Gossel, Was ist und was enthält der Talmud? Frankfort, 1907; J. Bassfreund, Zur Redaktion der Mischna, part i., Berlin, 1908; M. S. Zuckermandel, Tosefta, Mischna und Boraitha in ihrem Verhältnis zu einander, oder palästinensische und babylonische Halacha, 2 vols., 1908–09; L. Rosenthal, Ueber den Zusammenhang der Mischna. Ein Beitrag zu ihrer Entstehungsgeschichte, part i., Strasburg, 1909; S. Kraus, Talmudische Archäologie (vol. i., Leipsic, 1910; vol. ii., Stuttgart, 1911); F. W. Farrar, Life of Christ, excursuses II., XII. 13th ed., London, n. d.

The materials in the Talmud have been practically digested in monographs. Some of these are: On geography: J. Derenbourg, Essai sur l'hist. et la géographie de la Palestine d'après les Talmuds et les autres sources rabbiniques, vol. i., Paris, 1867; A. Neubauer, La Géographie du Talmud, ib. 1868; A. Berliner, Beiträge zur Geographie und Ethnographie Babyloniens im Talmud und Midrasch, Berlin, 1883. On life as regulated by the Talmud: J. Stern, Die Frau im Talmud, Zurich, 1879; A. Rohling, Le Juif selon le Talmud, Paris, 1889; A. Katz, Der wahre Talmudjude. Die wichtigsten Grundsätze des talmudischen Schriftthums über das sittliche Leben, Berlin, 1893; L. Vial, Le Juif sectaire; ou, la tolérance talmudique, Paris, 1899. Law as affecting phases of life: H. B. Fassel, Das mosaisch-rabbinische Civilrecht, 2 vols., Gross-Kanisha, 1852–54; J. L. Saalschütz, Das mosaische Recht, nebst den vervollständigten thalmudisch-rabbinischen Bestimmungen, Berlin, 1853; S. Mayer, Die Rechte der Israeliten, Athener, und Römer, 2 vols., Leipsic, 1862–66; S. Mendelsohn, The Criminal Jurisprudence of the Ancient Hebrews, Baltimore, 1891; M. Bloch, Die Civilprocess-Ordnung nach mosaisch-rabbin. Rechte, Budapest, 1882; idem, Der Vertrag nach mosaisch-rabbin. Rechte, ib. 1893; A. Schwarz, Die hermeneutische Analogie in der talmudischen Litteratur, Carlsruhe, 1897; idem, Der hermeneutische Syllogismus in der talmudischen Litteratur, ib. 1901; idem, Der Mischnah-Thorah. Ein System der mosaisch-talmudischen Gesetzlehre, ib. 1905; J. Fromer, Der Organismus des Judentums, Charlottenburg, 1909; M. Duschak, Das mosaisch-talmudische Eherecht, Vienna, 1864; M. Mielziner, The Jewish Law of Marriage and Divorce, Cincinnati, 1884; M. Bloch, Das mosaisch-talmudische Erbrecht, Budapest, 1890; idem, Die Vormundschaft nach mosaisch-talmud. Recht, ib. 1904; D. W. Amram, The Jewish Law of Divorce, Philadelphia, 1896; T. André, L'Esclavage chez les anciens Hébreux, Paris, 1892; M. Mielziner, Slavery among the Ancient Hebrews, Cincinnati, 1895; D. Farbstein, Das Recht der unfreien und der freien Arbeiter nach jüdisch-talmud. Recht, Bern, 1896. On education: M. Duschak, Schulgesetzgebung und Methodik der alten Israeliten, Vienna, 1872; B. Spiers, The School System of the Talmud, London, 1882;

B. Strassburger, *Geschichte der Erziehung und des Unterrichts . . . von dem talmud. Zeit bis auf die Gegenwart*, Strasburg, 1885. On various scientific matters: E. Grünebaum, *Die Sittenlehre des Judenthums*, Strasburg, 1878; M. Jacobson, *Versuch einer Psychologie des Talmud*, Hamburg, 1878; A. Wünsche, *Neue Beiträge zur Erläuterung der Evangelien aus Talmud und Midrasch*, Göttingen, 1878; J. Bergel, *Studien über die naturwissenschaftlichen Kenntnisse der Talmudisten*, Leipsic, 1880; A. Hahn, *The Rabbinical Dialectics*, Cincinnati, 1881; F. Weber, *Jüdische Theologie auf Grund des Talmud und verwandter Schriften*, Leipsic, 1897; W. Bacher, *Die exegetische Terminologie der jüdischen Traditionslitteratur*, 2 vols., Leipsic, 1899–1905; B. Zuckermann, *Materialien zur Entwicklung der altjüdischen Zeitrechnung*, Breslau, 1862; idem, *Das jüdische Maasssystem*, ib. 1867; idem, *Das Mathematische im Talmud*, ib. 1878; P. Rieger, *Technologie und Terminologie der Handwerke in der Misnah*, vol. i., Berlin, 1894; H. Vogelstein, *Die Landwirtschaft in Palästina zur Zeit der Misnah*, vol. i., ib. 1894; J. Krengel, *Das Hausgerät in der Misnah*, vol. i., Frankfort, 1899; R. J. Wunderbar, *Biblisch-talmudische Medizin*, 2 vols., Leipsic, 1850–60; J. M. Rabbinowicz, *Einleitung in die Gesetzgebung und die Medizin des Thalmuds*, Leipsic, 1883; W. Ebstein, *Die Medizin im Neuen Testament und im Talmud*, Stuttgart, 1903. Illustrative of Christianity: R. T. Herford, *Christianity in Talmud and Midrash*, London, 1903; G. Aicher, *Das A. T. in der Mischna*, Freiburg, 1906; A. Marmorstein, *Talmud und Neues Testament*, Vincovci, 1908; Miss A. Lucas, *Talmudic Legends, Hymns, and Paraphrases*, London, 1908; A. Marmorstein, *Die Bezeichnungen für Christen und Gnostiker im Talmud und Midras*, Skatschau, 1910; W. Knight, *The Golden Wisdom of the Apocrypha . . . and an Appendix Containing some of the Proverbial Wisdom of the Talmud*, London, 1910; S. Rapaport, *Tales and Maxims from the Talmud*, ib. 1910.

TAMMUZ-ADONIS.

In Ezek. viii. 14, in a chapter in which the prophet relates the idolatries of the Jews as seen by him in a vision, it is stated that before the north door of the Temple women sat weeping for Tammuz. This

1. Tammuz in the Old Testament. statement opens up the history of a cult which, in the light of a certain identification presently to be established, persisted through several millennia, arising among the Sumerian inhabitants of pre-Semitic Babylonia, passing into the worship of their Semitic conquerors, and proceeding by way of Cyprus to become the possession of Aryan peoples—the Greeks and the Romans. The story of Tammuz-Adonis is thus in more than one sense one of the romances in the history of religion. Other references to the cult than the one cited above which this scholar or that has seen in the Old Testament are, with two exceptions (Dan. xi. 37 and Isa. xvii. 10–11), not to be allowed, the explanations which bring them into connection with Tammuz being forced rather than natural.

Amos viii. 10 can hardly be related with the mourning for this deity; Jer. vi. 26 is no more germane, while the passage Zech. xii. 10 has already been explained as giving another meaning (see HADAD-RIMMON). It is very likely that the phrase "the desire of women," in Dan. xi. 37 has reference to Tammuz-Adonis, for the sense requires some deity honored by women, and this cult was especially feminine. The apocryphal Epistle of Jeremiah may possibly have in mind the Adonis cult, though it is noticeable that in this case it is the priests and not the women who mourn and shave their heads and beards. For Isa. xvii. 10–11 see below, § 13.

The name Tammuz represents the Sumerian *Dumuzi* (variant forms *Tauuzu, Ta'uzu, Da'uzu, Duzu;* full form *Dumuzi-abzu;* the form *Tammuz,* with doubled m, seems to have originated in the

2. Name; Mention in Early Inscriptions. Hebrew, perhaps on account of the short vowel in the first syllable), the meaning of which is still under discussion. Zimmern (latest in J. Hastings, *Encyclopædia of Religion and Ethics,* ii. 313, New York, 1910; cf. Schrader, *KAT,* p. 397) renders the full form "real child of the water depths"; Prof. J. D. Prince (in a private communication) gives as the rendering "young life"; the usual translation has been "son of life." In Babylonian (Sumerian) literature Tammuz makes his appearance as early as Urukagina, Gudea, and Siniddina (see BABYLONIA, VI., 3, §§ 3, 5), and if the identification of Tammuz and Adonis be regarded as made out (see below, § 8), the final traces of his cult do not disappear till late in the Christian era, indeed, it seems not to have received its coup de grâce until the Mohammedan conquest of the Aramean region. Tammuz appears in the inscriptions and documents of the pre-Semitic period in a variety of ways. Testimony to his early existence in the pantheon is given by tablets from Telloh which bear names in which his name form one element (H. Zimmern, *Abhandlungen* of the Saxon Academy, xxvii. 721–722, Leipsic, 1909). Witness to him comes from Shirpurla and Kish in the times of the kings named above and of Eannatum, and from Larsa under Siniddina, when mention is made of "the month of the celebration of the god Tamuz." Consequently, he rightly claims a place among the oldest of the well-attested deities of the Sumerian pantheon, though in those times there seems not to exist any hint of his relations with the Sumerian Ishtar. After the Semites gained control he drops out of sight, except for the name of his month, in official records, and that in the quite numerous hymns and in the epics he still has mention, also that he appears among the very minor deities who seem to have stalls in some Assyrian temples.

He figures in the Babylonian myths named after Adapa and Gilgamesh, and in the "descent of Ishtar" (these are most easily accessible to the English reader in *Assyrian and Babylonian Literature, Selected Translations, . . .* by R. F. Harper, pp. 314 sqq., New York, 1901; for mention of Tammuz cf. pages 316–317, 338, 413). In all this Babylonian literature the story is by no means complete as judged by the myth as it appears from Greek sources; the references are quite obscure, though for the most part the details are in accord with, or at least do not contradict, the fuller story as recovered from Greek and Roman sources; so that it is possible to infer that in these latest records the essential features of the original are preserved. In the Adapa myth Tammuz is associated with the deity Gishzida apparently as guardian of the gate of heaven, and the two become the successful advocates before Anu of Adapa, who has offended Anu by breaking the wings of the south wind. To this story Tammuz, though in a subordinate position with respect to Anu, seems to be independent, is not connected with Ishtar, and with his companion is spoken of as having disappeared, apparently much to the surprise of the two gods themselves. In the Gilgamesh epic there appears a feature which is not easily explained and does not come out in the western form of the story. When Ishtar tempts Gilgamesh with her love the hero answers her:

3. In Adapa and Gilgamesh Epics.

" Where is thy husband Tammuz, who was to be forever?
What, indeed, has become of the Allallu bird . . . ?
Well, I will tell thee plainly the dire result of thy coquetries.
To Tammuz, the husband of thy youth,
Thou didst cause weeping and didst bring grief upon him
    every year.
The Allallu bird, so bright in colors, thou didst love;
But its wing thou didst break and crush . . ."

In this passage two things are significant: (1) Tammuz and Ishtar are brought into close relationship—he is her " husband " (lover?), and this is one of the enduring features of the myth which accompanies the cult in all its travels; (2) Gilgamesh accuses Ishtar of herself working ill upon those she loves—concerning Tammuz yearly grief and weeping are specified. This second and later feature does not appear in the western and later forms; although the god comes to his death because of Ishtar's love for him, that death is caused by other means than the goddess herself, while here the charge is plainly brought home to her, parallel with the breaking of the wing of the Allallu bird.

For the descent of Ishtar to " the land of No-Return," so far as the epic itself relates, the motive has to be supplied. But the object is by most Assyriologists asserted to be the rescue of Tammuz from the world of the dead. During the absence of Ishtar, who was detained by Allatu, her sister and the goddess of the lower world, desire ceased among all on earth, man and beast, and the allurements of love were no more. Hence Ea created a man who entered the lower world and demanded drink from Allatu from her water-skin. The very demand (its full significance is not known) brought about the return of Ishtar (and presumably of Tammuz). Then comes mention of Tammuz " the husband of Ishtar's youth " and of his " day " on which the sad sounds of the flute and the wailing of male and female mourners mingle and incense is burned. There seems to be implied also the washing, anointing, and clothing of the figure of Tammuz (see below, § 13).

4. The " Descent of Ishtar."

There is also a considerable body of hymns to Tammuz in the Sumerian language (cf. Zimmern,

Abhandlungen, ut sup., pp. 723–726; F. A. Vandenburgh, *Sumerian Hymns,* New York, 1908; St. Langdon, *Sumerian and Babylonian Psalms,* pp. 299–341, Paris, 1909; T. Pinches, *Memoirs . . . of the Manchester Literary and Philosophical Society,* xlviii., 1904, no. 25), which go very far toward completing the picture of the Babylonian deity. These hymns speak of the " stormy weeping " for the god, who is " lord of the year, . . . of the name of life, . . . of the word of judgment, of the eye of precious stones, the artificer, the light of my heaven, . . . the shepherd, . . . him of stormy weeping "; his sister is goddess of the wine of heaven (J. D. Prince, in *American Journal of Semitic Languages,* xxvii. 1, 1910, pp. 84–89). In another hymn apparently Ishtar sings the lament for " my mighty one, . . . my spouse, . . . great god of the heavenly year, . . . lord of the lower world [!], . . . of vegetation, artificer, the shepherd [a very constant element in the activities attributed to him], the lord, the god Tammuz who liveth no more." And from the further mutilated text it seems to be deducible that he was producer of wine and lord of fructification, and he is compared with a mighty bull (a common oriental symbol of strength), and is the " power of the land, . . . the word which overcometh disease," giver of food and of water, strengthener of the maid and the warrior, in contrast with Ninib, who is the destroyer (Prince, in *JAOS,* xxx. 1, 1909, pp. 94–100).

Noteworthy is the fact that in Babylonia Tammuz does not appear as the god of any large city.* In the Adapa myth, while his standing is independent, it is subordinate—he is doorkeeper and pleader with Anu. So far as records in hand show, he played no heroic part and achieved no noteworthy deed. He is connected with fertility, productiveness, and strength; but the epic passages have the sound of artistic and forced poetic laudation and lack the tone of sincere attribution of power. Even in the hymns, in spite of the many epithets, his death and the mourning for him are the notable features, together with his relations with Ishtar. And still further, it is not his death that effects decline of fertility, it is the absence of the goddess that causes passion and desire to cease.

5. Unimportance in Babylonia.

Summing up the apparent facts as gathered from Babylonian sources, Tammuz was a deity who, at one time regarded as a gate-keeper of heaven, came to be associated with Ishtar as her beloved. Each year he died and passed to Hades, the realm of Allatu or Ereshkigal. He was mourned (in the month named after him, occurring just before the summer solstice) not only by Ishtar, but by male and female mourners and with the accompaniment of flutes. His mistress journeyed to the lower world, seemingly in quest of him; and since her absence caused the absence of love, Ea sent a messenger and

* Zimmern (*Abhandlungen,* ut sup., pp. 718–721) cites inscriptions from a very early period, showing apparently a temple to him in a suburb or a subject town of Lagash and in a fortress named Bad-urud-nagar or Dur-gurgurri. Eridu and Erech (ib., p. 720) seem also to have had temples in which he was present.

secured her release from " the land of No-Return," and presumably also that of her lover.

Outside of Babylonian literature and Ezek. viii. 14, the references to Tammuz under that name are few, but fortunately significant. Thus the Syrian lexicographer Bar Bahlul reports that Tammuz, a shepherd and hunter, was beloved by Balthi (Balti),

6. Tammuz in other Literature. whom he carried off and whose husband he slew, but was in turn killed by a wild boar. Consequently in his month a season of mourning for him was observed. The reference here is doubtless to the myth current and the practise in vogue in Byblus (see below, §§ 7, 13), and the effect is to give the equation Tammuz = Adonis, while Balthi can be no other than Ishtar (cf. D. Chwolson, *Die Ssabier und der Ssabismus*, ii. 206–207, St. Petersburg, 1856, and the same author's *Ueber Tammuz und die Menschenverehrung bei den alten Babylonier*, ib. 1860). Melito (*Apol.*, i., Eng. transl., in *ANF*, viii. 752) reports that " Balthi, queen of Cyprus . . . fell in love with Tamuz, son of Cuthar, king of the Phenicians, and . . . came and dwelt in Gebal (Byblus; see Phenicia, Phenicians, I., § 7). . . . Also, before Tamuz, she had fallen in love with Ares, and committed adultery with him; and Hephaistos, her husband, caught her, and his jealousy was roused against her, and he came and killed Tamuz in Mt. Lebanon as he was hunting wild boars; * and from that time Balthi remained in Gebal. And she died in the city of Aphiki (Aphaka, see below, § 7) where Tamuz was buried." The data here are sufficient to establish the connection between the Babylonian Tammuz, the beloved of Ishtar, and Adonis, the beloved of Aphrodite. Similarly, the statement that Balthi was the consort of Hephæstus and had a liaison with Ares, identifies her with Aphrodite, while the fact that she loved Tammuz identifies her with Ishtar, giving the equation Balthi = Ishtar-Aphrodite-Venus. It is to be noted, however, that the scene of action is no longer Babylonia, but the Lebanon and Phenicia, particularly Byblus or Gebal and Aphaka.

Strabo (XVI., i. 18) and Lucian (*De dea Syria*, §§ 6 sqq.) report that at Byblus there was a great sanctuary of Aphrodite where the worship of Adonis was conducted, and the former declares that the

7. Byblus and Nahr Ibrahim. city was sacred to him and to Kinyras his reputed father. The Nahr Ibrahim, which had its mouth a short distance south of the city, in early times bore the name of Adonis (Lucian, ut sup., viii.; E. Renan, *Mission de Phénicie*, pp. 282 sqq., Paris, 1864), and the discoloration of its waters at the time of the freshets was attributed to the blood of the deity. For suitability to the rites which were associated with the Aphrodite and Adonis cults, as well as for romance and beauty, the glen of the river is remarkable (Robinson, *Researches*, iii. 603–609). At the head of the glen in the mountains is Afka, the ancient Aphaka, where was a grove of Astarte and a temple (to " Venus ") at the spot

where Adonis and Aphrodite are said to have met, where also he was said to be buried (Melito, ut sup., *ANF*, viii. 752; Eusebius, " Life of Constantine," iii.ʹ55, Eng. transl. in *NPNF*, 2 ser., i. 534–535; Sozomen, *Hist. eccl.*, ii. 5, Eng. transl., *NPNF*, 2 ser., ii. 262). At Ghineh, one point of the glen, there is a recess or tablet carved in the rock on which is the figure of a hunter (identified as Adonis) with a spear awaiting the onset of a bear (not of a boar); and a little distance away is a female figure in a posture of mourning, identified by many as the sorrowing Aphrodite (cf. Macrobius, *Saturnalia*, I., xxi. 5; Renan, *Mission*, ut sup., plates xxxiv., xxxviii.; a reproduction from a photograph is in A. Jeremias, *Das Alte Testament im Lichte des alten Orients*, p. 90, Leipsic, 1904). Other sculptures are known along the glen, as at Mashnaka. To put the matter briefly, Byblus and the course of the Nahr Ibrahim to Aphaka formed the locus of a cult whose objects were Adonis and Aphrodite, and are proved (see below, § 10) to have been the center for diffusion of that cult in a considerable part of the Mediterranean basin.

The continuation of the combined cult of Tammuz and Ishtar in Greek surroundings depends upon the answer to the question whether the worship of

8. Tammuz and Adonis. the deities at Byblus and along the Nahr Ibrahim is the same (under changed names as transmitted through non-Semitic sources) as that in Babylonia. It must be premised that (1) no clear indications exist of a path by which such a cult passed from the lower Euphrates to the Mediterranean—traces of Syrian Adonis worship are post-Christian and may well have spread from Byblus eastward; (2) the usual indications in names of places and persons compounded of the divine name Tammuz are altogether lacking in Phenician environment. That Tammuz and the Adonis of Byblus were regarded as the same is asserted in numerous sources. This is the testimony of Origen (commentary on Ezekiel at viii. 14) based on apparently early tradition, of Jerome (*Epist.*, lviii. 3, in *NPNF*, 2 ser., vi. 120, and in his commentary on Ezekiel at the passage cited), of Cyril of Alexandria (commentary on Isa. xviii. 1, in *MPG*, xcii. 329), of Aristides (*Apol.*, Eng. transl. in *ANF*, ix. 272), and of Macrobius (*Saturnalia*, I., xxi. 1), who asserts the Assyrian origin of the Adonis cult and makes clear the relation of Ishtar and Aphrodite-Venus by mentioning the descent to the lower world for the purpose of rescuing Adonis from " Persephone." Lucian does useful service in connecting the Adonis of Byblus, not indeed by direct identification, but by his account of the celebrations in the great temple of " Aphrodite "—celebrations which included flagellation, mourning, sacred prostitution, shaving of the head, and offerings to one who was regarded as dead. The express identification already cited is confirmed by several facts: in both environments the god occupies a subordinate (in the Phenician a passive) position; the assumed death of the god is in both regions the occasion of formal mourning, chiefly by women, and this is the principal characteristic of the rites; and in both there is seen in the significance of the deity some reference to death and

---

* The connection of Adonis with hunting is so constant as hardly to need citation ; but cf. Apollodorus of Athens, *Peri theon*, III., xiii. 4, IX., lxiv. 401; Propertius, III., xiii. 53–54; Ovid, *Metamorphoses*, x. 535 sqq.

decay, whether of the sun of the springtime or of vegetation (see below, § 15). In view of this wealth of explicit and authoritative testimony to the identity of Tammuz and Adonis, combined with inferential evidence including the coincidence in the two centers of principal features in myth and ritual, the identification must stand against the doubts of Chwolson (*Die Ssabier*, ut sup., ii. 510), Renan (*Mission de Phénicie*, pp. 216, 235), and Baudissin (Hauck-Herzog, *RE*, xix. 376). The argument of the last-named that the identification argues separateness falls before the apparent fact that the separateness is no more than difference in name in a different environment. The duality is only apparent.

The identification, however, raises two questions: (1) the transmission of the cult from Babylonia to Phenicia (see below, § 16), and (2) the origin of the name Adonis. There can be no doubt that the latter is the common West Semitic *Adon*, " lord," occurring frequently in the Hebrew in

9. The Name Adonis. the form *Adonai*, translated " my lord " or " Lord " in the A. V. (cf., e.g., Gen. xviii. 12; Ezek. vi. 3). The way had already been prepared in Babylonia for the application of such a title of address to Tammuz when he was addressed as Bel (" lord "; see above, § 4); and it requires no imagination to see that this title might become a proper name in a cult, just as Baal did in Canaan. It is curious that, in spite of the wealth of testimony to this worship at Byblus, there is no monumental or inscriptional testimony in Phenicia to the name as applied to this particular deity. Yet the name was applied to other deities, as is shown by numerous inscriptions—to Baal-Shamem, Melkarth (both of Cyprus and Tyre), Reseph, Hamman, Esmun, Shamash, and others (cf. *CIS*, vol. i. passim; M. Lidzbarski, *Epigraphik*, Berlin, 1898, and *Ephemeris*, Giessen, 1900 sqq.). Zimmern (in Schrader, *KAT*, p. 398, note 2) remarks on a number of compounds in the Assyrian cuneiform, but of Phenician origin, in which the form *Aduni* occurs, giving such characteristic combinations as " Aduni has given a son," " Aduni is brother," " Aduni is my rock "; but no certainty exists that Aduni is here more than an appellative. By the Greeks, however, the term was regarded as a proper name and adopted as such, being taken into the scheme of declension of nouns. It seems beyond doubt, therefore, on the basis of the preceding, that the Adonis of the Greeks and the Tammuz (Tamuz) of the Babylonians are one, and that their meeting-place was Byblus (on the Phenician coast about 32 m. n. of Sidon). It was no secret to the Greeks that Adonis came to them from the Semites (Strabo, XVI., ii. 18–19), especially from Byblus, " sacred to Adonis," and the coins of the city contain the epithet " sacred," but do not name the deity.

That the Greeks adopted Adonis very early is evinced by the quotation from Hesiod (8th century B.C.; in *Hesiodi quæ ferunter omnia*, ed. A. Rzach, fragment 41, Leipsic, 1884) and by a fragment of Sappho (c. 600 B.C.; cf. T. Bergk, *Poetæ lyrici Græci*, iii. 897, Leipsic, 1843; Pausanias, IX., xxix. 8). The transfer came about through the Phenicians, and the locations of the temples in which Adonis

had a part (with Aphrodite) are in some degree indicated by Phenician settlements. Before naming these it is proper to remark that the

10. Distribution of the Cult. cult was established in Antioch in Syria—Ammianus Marcellinus (XXII., ix. 15, Eng. transl., by C. D. Yonge in Bohn's *Classical Library*, p. 297, London, 1887) reports that on the occasion of Julian's visit to Antioch the festival of Adonis, the beloved of Venus, was being celebrated. In Cyprus, early settled by the Phenicians, on the south coast was Amathus, where Astarte-Aphrodite had a sanctuary, and Adonis was worshiped (Pausanias, IX., xli. 2; confirmed by Stephen of Byzantium, *Ethnika*, s.v. " Adonis "). Paphos in the southwest was a notable center, and coins of the Roman period picture the sanctuary with doves (the bird sacred to the goddess) over the façade. There is an interesting model of a shrine of just this pattern recovered at Mycenæ (*Journal of Hellenic Studies*, ix., 1888, pp. 210–213), and if there is a connection—which it is tempting to see—the history of the shrine is carried back to c. 1100 B.C. The cone and pillar, so characteristic of the Ishtar-Astarte-Aphrodite cult, were present, and the custom obtained of requiring of the native women submission as a religious duty to strangers once in a lifetime, as at Babylon, Baalbek, and elsewhere. Photius (*MPG*, ciii. 632) quotes Ptolemy Hephæstion to the effect that Aphrodite found the body of Adonis in " Argos, a city of Cyprus "; and Pausanias (II., xx. 5) remarks upon the wailing for Adonis by the women of the city. It will be remembered that Melito makes Balthi a queen of Cyprus, asserting that she changed her residence to Byblus and Aphaka. Pausanias also quotes Apollodorus (III., xiv. 3–4) as making Adonis son of Kinyras, founder of Paphos in Cyprus. There is similar testimony for Aphrodisias in Cyprus—if the name is not enough. This island seems to have been covered by the cult. At Alexandria the celebration was elaborate, and is described by Theocritus in one of his celebrated Idyls (the fifteenth, named the *Idoniazusæ*), which relates the part taken in the festival by Ptolemy Philadelphus and his queen. The story as current in the West connects closely with Byblus (see below, § 11). Canopus in Egypt was another center. Concerning Athens there can be no mistake, for Plutarch (*Alcibiades*, xviii.) states that when the ill-fated expedition against Sicily in 415 was departing, the celebration of the Adoneia (the local name for the mourning) was in progress, and the ill omen was noted after the event. Evidence can be adduced for the celebration in Alexandria of Caria, Perga of Pamphylia, Samos (cf. O. Gruppe, *Griechische Mythologie und Religions-Geschichte*, p. 275, note 6, p. 291, note 1, Munich, 1902), Laconia, and Dion in Macedonia. These names of places are representative, not exhaustive. The earliest explicit witness for the celebration among the Romans is Ovid (43 B.C.–18 A.D.; *Ars Amatoria*, i. 75); but an Etruscan mirror bears the name *Atunis*, suspected to mean Adonis (A. Falratti, *Corpus inscriptionum Italicarum*, Turin, 1867), and this suggests a much earlier footing in the Italian peninsula. The cult was favored by Elagabulus (q.v.). Certainly to be attributed to a late period and probably through Greek, not Semitic, agencies, came the establishment of the cult at Bethlehem, where, according to Jerome (*Epist.*, lviii. 3, Eng. transl. in *NPNF*, 2 ser., vi. 120), there was a grove to Tammuz-Adonis, and in the cave of the nativity " lamentation was made for the paramour of Venus." The extinction of the cult in certain parts of Syria, notably at Aphaka, under Constantine is reported by Sozomen (*Hist. eccl.*, ii. 5, Eng. transl. in *NPNF*, 2 ser., ii. 262); yet the reports from Arabic sources by Chwolson (*Die Ssabier*, ut sup.) show its continuance much later.

It was not to be expected that a myth and a cult which wandered so widely as these of Tammuz-Adonis would retain everywhere their original forms. It is a law of the diffusion of religions that observances of a religious character in trans-

11. Forms of the Myth. plantation to a new locus take on naturally, and, so to speak, unconsciously, something of the local character in order to domicile themselves and to become acceptable to the new clientele.* The scholia to classical authors make mention, too frequently for citation here, of the details of the cult. So the story and the rites of this deity, while faithful in the main to the Semitic originals so far as these can be made out and also often preserving the consciousness of this origin, yet in different localities differed in the minutiæ. This has already been illustrated by the story of the finding in the Cypriote Argos of the body of the god, while the Phenician form locates the event in the Lebanon near Aphaka. The many epithets applied to Adonis illustrate the same fact —Kiris or Kirris (in Laconia), Memnon, Serach, Koarē or Koros, Itaios, Abobas (in Pamphylia, from the Semitic *abub*, " flute "), Gingras, Hoies or Aoos or Ao (among the Dorians), Gauas, Pygmaion (in Cyprus; cf. Hesychius, s.v. " Pygmaion "), Luchnos, Pherektes (cf. for many of these O. Gruppe, ut sup., s.v. " Adonis "). Each of these applied to Adonis probably has reference to or suggestion of local peculiarity of observance or conception. The genius of Greek mythology required that a father be found for the deity, the Babylonian conception being lost in the distance both of space and time. The principal story in the West was that Aphrodite, in revenge for a slight upon her beauty by the queen of Kinyras, king of Cyprus, in declaring her daughter more fair than the goddess, inspired the unfortunate girl with an illicit passion for her own father, which for twelve nights she contrived to indulge. When the father discovered the identity of his companion, in horror he pursued her with drawn sword, and the girl was saved from him only by being metamorphosed into a myrtle-tree (Apollodorus, III., xiv. 4). The story of the birth then assumes various forms—the father cleaves the tree, and Adonis is born; or in ten months the tree parts of itself to give birth to the beautiful young god; or a boar (one of the constant elements of the myth) rips the bark with his tusk and so brings the boy

* Of course it is not to be forgotten that the story and cult of Adonis were bound up with that of the goddess with whom he was associated, and that the accounts of him underwent variations more or less concordant with those of Aphrodite in different environments.

to birth (Apollodorus, *Bibliotheca*, iii. 182, ed. R. Wagner, Leipsic, 1894; Ovid, *Metamorphoses*, x. 298–502; Vergil, *Eclogues*, x. 18; and the glossator on the same author's *Æneid*, v. 71). Both the father and the mother are variously connected with both Cyprus and Phenicia. The father is Agenor, or Phoinix (an evident recollection of the derivation of the cult from Phenicia), or Theias (Panyasis, fifth century B.C., cited in Apollodorus, III., xiv. 4; Athenæus, X., lxxxiii. 456, ed. W. Dindorf, 3 vols., Leipsic, 1827); the mother is Aoa or Metharme (in Cyprus) in place of Myrrha, or Alphesiboia (so Hesiod, ut sup.); and Adonis has as children Amymone, Golgos, Melos, Priapos, and Zariadres (Theocritus, *Idyl*, xv.; glossator on Vergil's *Eclogues*, viii. 37; cf. *SBE*, xxiii. 80). The accounts of the death vary also—Ares (or Hephæstus) caused it by means of the boar, or one or the other transformed himself into that animal, or Apollo did it in revenge for the blinding of his son Erymanthos by Aphrodite when by him she was seen bathing. The place of the death was variously located in the Lebanon, at Argos in Cyprus, and at Idalim. Once more the duration of the stay of Adonis in Hades is differently given. The principal thread of the Greek myth records that on his birth Aphrodite received him and hid him in a chest which she gave to Proserpine to guard. But his beauty won the love of the latter, and she refused to give him up to Aphrodite. Appeal was then made to Zeus, who adjudged possession of him for a third of the year to Proserpine, another third to Aphrodite, while the rest of the year was at his own disposal, and he gave it to Aphrodite. Other accounts divide the year equally between the two goddesses, or give the larger part to Proserpine.

It is not at all improbable that at many places where the Adonis cult became domesticated there was already a worship not alien in character. This would prove the solution of a number of problems which arise. It is not merely probable but certain that other cults of a kind not antagonistic in idea came in upon the Adonis worship and fused with it or modified it. Thus confusion came to

12. Identification with Other Deities. exist as to the particular deity in whose honor the rites were performed, or the deities were identified. Among those with whom Adonis was either confused or identified were Apollo, Apsyrtos (O. Gruppe, ut sup., p. 576 note), Epaphos (Apollodorus, II., ix.; Mnaseas, in R. and T. Müller's *Fragmenta*, iii. 155, no. 37), Phæthon (Timon, in Müller, ut sup., iv. 522, no. 3). But of especial note were Attis and Osiris. The closeness of relationship of these may be seen in a somewhat overemphasized form in J. G. Frazer's *Adonis, Attis, and Osiris*, passim (London, 1906). The connection with Osiris comes out particularly in the story of the body of Osiris, or his head, later rationalized into a letter, which was yearly committed to the sea at Alexandria and made its way to Byblus (M. H. Ohnefalsch-Richter, *Kypros, die Bibel und Homer*, pp. 219–220, Berlin, 1893). The mourning of Isis for Osiris, to say nothing of that of the farmers who called on Isis as they cut the first sheaf of grain (Diodorus Siculus, I., xiv. 2), as well as the search for the body of Osiris and the burial, suggested a relationship between the two deities who caused their loves so great sorrow, and the identification was indeed made. The emphasis upon the cult of Adonis at Alexandria (see below, § 13) and Byblus and the similarity of ideas for which the two deities stood, whatever that may be, made the identification easy (Damascius, in *Vita Isidori*, cited by Photius, *Bibliotheca*, ccxlii., in *MPG*, ciii. 1276; Hippolytus, *Hær.*, v. 4, in *ANF*, v. 4, but cf. v. 56, where the "thrice desired Adonis" is the Assyrian, i.e., Syrian, name for Attis; Stephen of Byzantium, *Ethnika*, s.v. "Adonis"). So the myths of the two overflowed and mingled at the meeting-places of Byblus and Alexandria, just as those of Attis and Adonis did in Cyprus, so near to Phrygia. Attis was a Phrygian deity whose myth relates that he was either killed by a boar or bled to death from self-castration, and orgiastic rites and mourning marked his cult; in this case also a goddess, Cybele the "Great Mother," was the objective of the worship (J. G. Frazer, ut sup., and *Golden Bough*, i. 296–301, London, 1900). Rather less obvious is the relationship of Adonis and Dionysus, yet Plutarch testifies explicitly (*Symposiaca problemata*, IV., v. 3) that "they regard Adonis not as another (deity) but as Dionysus" (cf. also "Orphic Hymn," xlii.). This identification of Adonis with other gods was not confined to the Greeks. In Babylonia Tammuz was the same as an early god Shulgur (M. Jastrow, *Religion of Assyria and Babylonia*, p. 58, New York, 1898), and Zimmern (*Abhandlungen*, ut sup., pp. 705–709) gives a list of names applied to Tammuz several of which involve identification of him with others. It is indisputable that in Babylonia, Syria, Egypt, Asia Minor, and Greece there were conceptions of deities so alike in their main features, having to do with the decay of power—whether solar or vegetational (see below, § 13)—that confusion and merging were to be expected. Whether in the writings of Sanchuniathon (q.v.) in Eusebius, *Præparatio evangelica*, i. 4 (Eng. transl. by E. H. Gifford, i. 41, Oxford, 1903) the "Elioun" and "Beruth," the former of whom died in an encounter with wild beasts, are Adonis and Aphrodite is not certain.

Just as the myth and conceptions concerning the deity varied in different localities, so the details of

13. The Rites.
the celebration differed in accordance with the genius of place and people. The salient feature was the mourning, principally by women, and generally accompanied by the mournful strains of the flute. In the Adapa epic but nowhere else the mourning seems to have included Gishzida. The mourners beat their breasts and in some cases shaved their heads, the hair going to the temples as a part of the perquisites of the shrine. From notices as cited above respecting the observances at Byblus, Alexandria, and Athens it is gathered that an effigy or image of Adonis was made, washed, dressed, incensed, and laid on a couch or bier (at Alexandria an image of Aphrodite was made and laid on a couch by that of Adonis, and the observance celebrated the wedding of the two deities). Where classic influences prevailed, the image represented a beauti-

ful youth. The image was surrounded by fresh flowers and plants, and at Alexandria also with the early fruits, the "gardens of Adonis," myrrh, and cakes of honey, meal, and oil, and after this was done the wailing and singing of dirges began (Sappho, fragment 6). After the wailing and on the second day, the image was carried away and cast into the river or the sea, or was given burial, the women accompanying the procession with bared breasts and singing an ode which besought prosperity for the coming year. At Harran the story went that the "lord of Adonis" slew him and ground his bones in a mill, and then scattered the fragments; hence the women of that region during the celebration ate nothing that had passed through the mill (Frazer, *Adonis*, etc., p. 131, citing Chwolson). At Byblus, after the wailing a sacrifice was offered to Adonis "as to one who was dead," therefore it was a holocaust and piacular (Lucian, *De dea Syria*, § vi.; Smith, *Rel. of Sem.*, p. 411). In Cyprus it was customary to build a pyre for Adonis and to cast therein live doves (the bird of Aphrodite). Apparently with the mourning for Tammuz there was combined lamentation for departed friends and relations, so that the occasion was a sort of "All Souls' Day" (Jastrow, ut. sup, pp. 575, 599, 682). A unique institution was the "gardens of Adonis" (Plato, *Phædrus*, 276B; Theophrastus, *De historia et causis plantarum*, VI., vii. 3; Hesychius, s.v. "Adonidos kēpoi"). These were shallow receptacles much like fern dishes, filled with earth, sowed with various kinds of seeds, and for a few days before the festival carefully tended by the women. Under the warm eastern sun the seeds germinated quickly, but when left unwatered, the same sun quickly dried the shallow earth and the growth withered. The "gardens" were then carried to a spring, river, or the sea and thrown in. That this was an old charm intended to promote the growth of vegetation is practically certain (Frazer, *Adonis*, etc., pp. 137–159, where early authorities are cited, to which add the Emperor Julian, "The Cæsars," xxv., in E. Talbot's Fr. transl., p. 285, Paris, 1863; and R. Rochette, *Revue archéologique*, viii. 1, 1851, pp. 97–123; a picture of these "gardens" is given in A. Jeremias, *Das Alte Testament*, etc., ut sup., p. 88).* It is concordant with this interpretation that the mourning was followed on the next day by a festival which typified the return of the god from the dead (Origen and Jerome on Ezek. viii. 14, and Cyril of Alexandria, on Isa. xviii. 1–2; *MPG*, lxx. 440–441). This feature, perhaps not a part of the original rites in Babylonia, has always mystified the narrators and students, some of them assuming strangely that the incensing of the effigy was supposed to effect revivification. But on that hypothesis why should burial or the casting of the effigy in river or sea

---

* There are several good reasons for thinking that in Isa. xvii. 10–11 the prophet had these "gardens of Adonis" in mind. The surface meaning gives just the usual order of procedure and the results of making these "gardens," while "the day of grief and desperate sorrow" certainly looks like the mourning. The word rendered "pleasant" (*na'amanim*) —probably containing a double reference to the anemone (sacred to Adonis) and to the meaning "darling," an epithet often applied to him—seems to make the reference to Adonis (or Tammuz) quite certain.

follow? In accordance with the naive magic of early times, persisting after its original meaning had been forgotten, the revival to life can be understood as expected after the ceremonial of casting " garden " or effigy into the supposed sources of fertilization.

The date of the festival has caused no little discussion. For Babylonia the month Tammuz (June-July) is indubitably indicated, and about July 15 is implied by Maimonides and Makrizi as cited by Chwolson (*Die Ssabier*, ut sup., ii. 202 sqq.) for a

14. Date of the Festival. late period in the Christian era; for Harran the date is also July (ib., ii. 27, and *Ueber Tammuz*, ut sup., p. 38). Jerome (ut sup.) seems to imply June as the date for the death of Tammuz.

The feature of the " gardens " as just related suggests surely the heat of summer. According to Frazer (*Adonis*, etc., p. 7), relying upon W. R. Smith, the month Tammuz does not absolutely fix the time of year, inasmuch as the Syrian calendars varied considerably. Jastrow (ut sup., pp. 547, 682), speaking for Babylonia and adjacent regions, sets the time at just before the summer solstice. For Antioch the data afforded by Ammianus Marcellinus (XXII., ix. 15) in connection with Julian's visit to the city necessitates a time before Aug. 1. The description in Theocritus, *Idyl*, xv., implies a date sufficiently late in the summer for certain fruits to have ripened (cf. W. Mannhardt, *Antike Wald- und Feldkulte*, p. 277, Berlin, 1875–77). The data from Byblus are confusing. Lucian (*De dea Syria*, vi. sqq.) gives the time as when the Nahr Ibrahim runs red, which seems to imply the season of spring freshets, the color being locally attributed to the blood of the god who is slain annually; but this is against most other indications, which imply midsummer, though an alternative supposition is that sandstorms caused the discoloration. There was a spring festival at Byblus, which, however, had no connection with Adonis, and Lucian may have confused his references. On the other hand, the scarlet anemone blooms at this time of the year, and the legend derived its color from the blood of the god either as springing from it or being stained by it. The Arabs still call the flower " the wounds of Na'aman " (*na'aman* being an epithet of Adonis; W. R. Smith, in *Historical Review*, ii., 1887, p. 307). Yet somewhat inconsistent with this in the same region the color of the red rose, blooming in June, is attributed to the blood from Aphrodite's feet wounded by a thorn as she went to meet her lover. In Attica the date is fixed for midsummer by the departure of the expedition to Sicily (ut sup.; cf. Thucydides, vi. 30). At Hierapolis in Syria there was an annual festival at the beginning of spring at which trees were cut down and planted in the temple court, animals and birds were hung on them as sacrifices, and then fire was set and the whole consumed. This may have been wrongly brought into connection with the Cypriote festival described above and have influenced the conception of the date. General indications from many incidental allusions suggest the beginning of the harvest season, which for Syria, Greece, and Egypt varies from the end of March to the end of June (see AGRICULTURE). The dating in spring may be due to confu-

sion of the Adonis celebration with one to Aphrodite. The final conclusion will in some degree rest upon the solution of the question of the significance of Tammuz-Adonis.

What Tammuz-Adonis stood for in the popular mind was as variously answered in antiquity as now. Macrobius (*Saturnalia*, I., xxi. 1 sqq.) says that he was considered to be a sun-god; and Martianus

15. Significance of the Deity. Capella (*De nuptiis*, ii. 192) gives " Byblius Adon " as one of the names of Sol. Ammianus Marcellinus (XIX. i. 11; Eng. transl. ut sup., p. 186) speaks of " the solemn festival of Adonis, which the mystical doctrines of religion show to be some sort of image of the ripened fruits of the earth . . . cut down in their prime." Porphyry (cited in Eusebius, *Præparatio evangelica*, III. xi., Eng. transl., i. 120) also asserts that " Adonis was the symbol of the cutting of the perfect fruits," Attis representing the early blossoms which drop off unfertilized. Origen (ut sup.) makes him represent the seed corn placed in the earth and fructifying; Jerome on the same passage reports that the common idea related the celebration to the death and resurrection of the seeds; and Smith (*Rel. of Sem.*, p. 318) connects it with the harvest. Jastrow (ut sup., pp. 547–548) lends his weighty authority to the idea that Tammuz was a local solar deity— a god of spring approaching the summer solstice. Zimmern (Schrader, *KAT*, p. 397) calls him the " god of spring vegetation." Frazer (*Adonis*, etc., passim) also makes him a deity of vegetation. His position is strong, though allowance has to be made for the thesis which underlies his volume. A. Jeremias (*Das Alte Testament*, etc., pp. 114 sqq.) shows that Tammuz is a form which admits identification with sun, moon, or star, since he represents dying and reviving life. The Babylonian relations do little to clear up the question, since Tammuz appears now in the circle of Ea, now in that of Anu, again in that of Shamash (cf. Zimmern, *Abhandlungen*, ut sup., p. 715), as well as with such deities of vegetation as Gishzida and Ningirsu. The " gardens " might turn the scale in favor of the vegetational theory did they not seem a late intrusion. Baudissin's contention (Hauck-Herzog, *RE*, xix. 336–337) that the midsummer date best attested for the festival is against a solar significance falls with the consideration of specialized " seasonal suns " which ruled a part of the year, and these existed in Babylonian as well as in Egyptian thought. Were Tammuz the god of the spring sun, the summer solstice would be the time of his death. To be sure, the rôle of solar and vegetational deity are not exclusive (see SUN AND SUN WORSHIP, II., 1); and where great deities like Shamash emerge with definite solar functions, it is not uncommon to find lesser and local deities having originally the same relation relegated to subordinate functions. This may be the solution of the question. That later philosophical conceptions should advance beyond these was to be expected. So Hippolytus seems to regard Adonis as typifying the soul (*Hær.*, v. 7, Eng. transl. *ANF*, v. 56–58). The triple conception Adonis-Osiris-Dionysus was regarded as giving a hope for a future life. The life substance of Adonis was connected with myrrh, which was supposed to arrest decay and so was used in embalming (cf. John xix. 39). The Orphic hymn cited above makes Adonis hermaphrodite, and this recalls the fact that some Sumerian data raise the question whether Tammuz was not feminine.

The question of the origin of Tammuz-Adonis may be regarded as settled. It is no longer possible to regard him as Cypriote in derivation (W. H. Engel, *Kypros*, ii. 643, Berlin, 1841), a theory revived in part in Pauly, *Realencyklo-*

16. Sumerian Origin of Tammuz. pädie (ed. G. Wissowa, vol. i., Stuttgart, 1893), which conceives him as coming under Phenician influence and then traveling eastward; nor even as Semitic (Baudissin, in Hauck-Herzog, *RE*, xix. 378–377). Had he been Semitic, a more general popularity among that people would have been expected. The deity is clearly pre-Semitic Sumerian, attested by the early mention in the Sumerian texts, especially in the Sumerian hymns, as well as by the fact that the later hymns clearly imitate the earlier. Under the Sumerians Tammuz had some importance; with the Semites that disappeared, he became one of the popular as contrasted with the official gods; and but for the popular celebration and the epics he almost drops out of sight. Among the Assyrians he had no position of note in the national worship. His festival may have been celebrated among the Assyrians, but in that case all traces have been obliterated. As Adonis he reappeared at Byblus and along the Nahr Ibrahim to Aphaka. The explanation of this curious leap across the desert is difficult, possibly reached only by the help of two hypotheses. If the Phenicians came from the Persian Gulf (see PHENICIA, I., § 2; cf. Herodotus, i. 1–8, vii. 8–9, and Rawlinson's note to i. 1 in his translation), they might have brought the cult with them. Still the difficulty rises, why was not the cult more general among the Phenicians? The second hypothesis is what has already received notice—a pre-Phenician local cult a some features akin to that of Tammuz. For the first of these suppositions there is evidence; the second has only indirect support in the facts of similar cases in Egypt and Cyprus.

The influence of the myth of Tammuz was widely felt. In Bœotia in the cults of Artemis and Dionysus the mourning and mock burial were repeated.

17. Influence of the Tammuz Myth. The wailing reappears in the story of Laodameia and Protesilaos, and in that of Artemis for Hippolytus and for Endymion. The relation of Adonis to myrrh passed over into the stories of the later Dionysus in the epithets applied to him, such as *myrrha, smyrnē, myrinē, myrto;* and the plant was sacred both to Aphrodite and to Artemis, whose relations with their lovers were so alike. The element of the boar comes out strongly in Greek and Roman literature from Bion (Ode i. of the "Idyls," cf. lines 7–8) to Augustine ("City of God," vi. 7, Eng. transl. in *NPNF*, 2 ser., ii. 116); and Macrobius (*Saturnalia*, I., xxi. 4) interprets this element as typifying winter. It is well known that Syria the swine was a tabooed or "sacred" animal (Lucian, *De dea Syria*, liv.), and in Greece was

sacred to Aphrodite. Its part in the stories about Attis has already been noticed, and in the Dionysus cycle it also appears. But one may discard the interpretations of Jeremias (*Das Alte Testament*, etc., passim) regarding the influence of the myth on the Old Testament, especially when he sees " Tammuz-motives " in the history of Abraham, Joseph, David, and other Hebrew heroes. Still less basis of fact can be found for the astral interpretations of E. Stucken, *Astralmythen der Hebräer, Babylonier und Ægypter* (Leipsic, 1896 sqq.).   GEO. W. GILMORE.

BIBLIOGRAPHY: The principal literature is cited in the text; the older literature among that which follows is of value chiefly for its citation of the passages in the classics and elsewhere from which the data are collected   J. Selden, *De dis Syris*, pp. 254–264, Amsterdam, 1680; C. Moinichen, *Hortulus Adonidis*, Copenhagen, 1702; Bayle, *Dictionary*, s.v. Adonis, i. 113–116; C. F. Dupuis, *Origine de tous les cultes*, pp. 156–163, Paris, 1795; F. C. Movers, *Die Phönizier*, i. 191–253, 2 vols., Bonn, 1841–56; H. Brugsch, *Adonisklage und Linoslied*, Berlin, 1852; Greve, *De Adonide*, Leipsic, 1877; A. Jeremias, *Die babylonisch-assyrischen Vorstellungen vom Leben nach dem Tode*, ib. 1877; P. Scholz, *Götzendienst und Zauberwesen bei den Hebräern*, pp. 217–238, Regensburg, 1877; W. W. von Baudissin, *Studien zur semitischen Religionsgeschichte*, i. 298–304, Leipsic, 1878; W. H. Roscher, *Lexikon der griechischen und römischen Mythologie*, i. 69–77, ib. 1884; A. H. Sayce, *Religion of Ancient Babylonia*, pp. 221–250, London, 1887; *Journal of Hellenic Studies*, ix (1888), 210–213; F. Baethgen, *Beiträge zur semitischen Religionsgeschichte*, pp. 41–44, Berlin, 1889; P. Jensen, *Die Cosmologie der Babylonier*, passim, Strasburg, 1890; idem, *Assyrisch-babylonische Mythen und Epen*, pp. 81 sqq., 95 sqq., 169, 560, Berlin, 1900; Ball, in *PSBA*, xvi (1894), 195–200; W. L. King, *Babylonian Religion and Mythology*, pp. 178–183, London, 1899; T. K. Cheyne, *Bible Problems*, pp. 71–95, London, 1904 (cf. A. Jeremias, *Babylonisches im Neuen Testament*, p. 34, Leipsic, 1905; Cheyne finds a North Arabian form of the myth of Adonis in the tale of Dusares—see NABATÆANS, II., § 3); C. Vellay, *Le Culte et les fêtes d' Adonis-Thammouz dans l'orient antique*, Paris, 1904 (the student can not afford to pass this book); idem in *RHR*, xlix (1904), 154–162; R. Dussaud, *Notes de mythologie syrienne*, ii. 148–155, ib. 1905 (also important); M. J. Lagrange, *Études sur les religions sémitiques*, pp. 40, 295, 309, 348–349, ib. 1905; O. Gruppe, *Griechische Mythologie und Religionsgeschichte*, Index " Adonis " and "Tammuz," Munich, 1906; and especially the works of Zimmern noted in the text and his *Sumerisch-babylonische Tamuzlieder*, in the *Berichte* of the Saxon Academy, lix (1907), 201–252.

TANCHELM, tan'kelm (**TANCHELIN**): Opponent of the medieval Church; killed at Antwerp 1115 (or 1124). He is said to have assailed the entire hierarchy and all their ecclesiastical functions, and to have defamed the Church, claiming that his followers were the true Church, that the efficacy of the sacraments depended upon the worthiness of the ministers, and that he himself was filled with the Holy Ghost and was, therefore, God, even as Christ had been. He is also said to have married an image of the Virgin, and to have given water in which he had bathed to his followers as a sacrament bringing salvation to body and soul. This account, of which the chief source is a letter written about 1112 by the Utrecht clergy to the archbishop of Cologne (ed. P. Fredericq, *Corpus documentorum inquisitionis Neerlandicæ*, i. 15 sqq., Ghent, 1889), is evidently inspired by hostility. Probably Tanchelm was little else than one of those who, in the medieval Church, demanded that the Church should be holy, and who often attacked the hierarchy. He doubtless believed himself to be inspired, and he was apparently influenced by political motives, seeking to detach a part of the diocese of Utrecht and to unite it with the neighboring French bishopric of Terouanne. He preached to thousands, assuming considerable pomp and finding many adherents among women and the lower classes. At this time his chief center was Utrecht, but later he is found at Antwerp and Bruges, the authority for his activity in the former city being the *Vita Norberti*, xvi. (*MGH, Script. xii.*, Hanover, 1856). In Antwerp the unworthiness of the only priest stationed there gave Tanchelm such following that neither prince nor bishop dared molest him. He was finally killed by a priest, but his adherents maintained themselves until the coming of Norbert in 1124.　　(A. Hauck.)

Bibliography: U. Hahn, *Geschichte der Ketzer im Mittelalter*, i. 459, Stuttgart, 1845; J. J. I. von Döllinger, *Beiträge zur Sektengeschichte des Mittelalters*, i. 104 sqq., Munich, 1890; P. Fredericq, *Geschiedenis der Inquisitie in de Nederlanden*, i. 20, Ghent, 1892; H. C. Lea, *History of the Inquisition of the Middle Ages*, i. 64–65, New York, 1906; Hauck, *KD*, iv. 88 sqq.

TANNER, BENJAMIN TUCKER: African Methodist Episcopal bishop; b. at Pittsburg, Pa., Dec. 25, 1835. He was educated at Avery College, Alleghany, Pa., and the Western Theological Seminary, though without graduating from the latter institution, and, after holding various pastorates in his denomination, was appointed, in 1867, editor of the *Christian Recorder*, its official organ. This position he held for sixteen years, after which he was editor of the *African Methodist Quarterly Review* (1884–1888) until he was chosen bishop in 1888, with special jurisdiction in Canada, Bermuda, and the West Indies. Since 1892 he has had charge of the First District, comprising New York, New Jersey, and eastern Pennsylvania, and in 1901 was a delegate to the third Ecumenical Methodist Conference at London. Among his publications may be mentioned his *Apology for African Methodism* (Philadelphia, 1867) and *The Negro's Origin; and, Is the Negro Cursed?* (1869).

TAOISM. See China, I., 2.

TARGUM. See Bible Versions, A, V.

TARPELITES: A word occurring only in Ezra iv. 9, apparently as the name of one of the tribes settled by the Assyrians in Samaria (II Kings xvii. 24), but otherwise unknown. G. Hoffmann (*ZA*, ii. 54 sqq., 1887) sees in the word the Persian *taraparda*, "beyond the bridge," and takes it as qualifying the names "Rehum" and "Shimshai" in the sense of "(the provincials) across the Euphrates." Jensen (*TLZ*, 1895, p. 509) would translate it "couriers." See Apharsachites.

TARSHISH. See Commerce, § 2; Navigation, § 3; Ophir; and Table of the Nations.

TARSUS. See Asia Minor, IX.

TARTAK: The name of a deity mentioned in II Kings xvii. 31 as belonging to the Avvites settled in Samaria by Sargon. For the general condition of the passage see Succoth-benoth. An identification of this deity with any so far known is as yet most uncertain. No reliance can be placed upon the late rabbinical statement that this god had the form of an ass (*Sanhedrin*, 63a-b). P. Jensen (*Die*

Kosmologie der Babylonier, pp. 49 sqq., Strasburg 1890) mentions Tartaku as a name for Antares an perhaps connected with the deity Ninib (see Babylonia, VII., 2, § 9), but this requires a change from k to ḳ which is unlikely. Hardly more probable i the derivation from the name of the deity (A)tar gat(is), originally perhaps Derketo (cf. Schrader *KAT*, p. 484, note 4); or from the name of a storm god Tarku (Baudissin, Hauck-Herzog, *RE*, xix 381); and Cheyne's suggestion (*EB*, iv. 4903) tha the word is a corruption of *Jerah(meel)* does no command support. The possibility exists that th name will sometime be found as that of a folk deit who did not obtain entrance into any official pan theon, except perhaps that of the city from whic the Avvites were brought. What that city was i not known, and the ascertaining of this datum ma be a condition precedent to a final explanation the name.　　Geo. W. Gilmore.

Bibliography: Besides the commentaries on Kings, con sult: J. Selden, *De dis Syris*, ii. 253, Amsterdam, 168C F. Lenormant, *La Magie chez les Chaldeens*, pp. 10, 11C Eng. transl., *Chaldean Magic*, London, 1877; P. Scholz *Götzendienst und Zauberwesen bei den alten Hebräern*, 400, Regensburg, 1877; Nagl, in *ZKT*, 1904, pp. 412–42 *DB*, iv. 689; *EB*, iv. 4903; *JE*, xii. 66.

TASCHEREAU, ELZÉAR ALEXANDRE: Roma Catholic cardinal; b. at Sainte-Marie-de-la-Beauce Quebec, Feb. 17, 1820; d. at Quebec Apr. 12, 1898 He was educated at the Seminary of Quebec and a Rome (D.C.L., 1856), and was ordained to th priesthood in 1842. He was then appointed pro fessor of moral philosophy in the Seminary of Que bec, and held this position until 1854, displaying a attitude in marked contrast with ultramontanism In 1856–59 he was director of the Petit Séminaire and of the Grand Séminaire in 1859–60, bein also a member of the Council of Public Instructio for Lower Canada. He was appointed superio of the Grand Séminaire and rector of Lava University in 1860, and two years later becam vicar-general of the diocese of Quebec. Shortl after his return from the Vatican Council, he wa chosen, on the death of Archbishop Baillargeon, on of the two administrators of the archdiocese, and i 1871 was raised to metropolitan rank. In 1886 h was created cardinal, being the first Canadian t receive that dignity, and in 1894 he retired fro active life. He was the author of *Discipline d diocèse de Quebec* (2d ed., Quebec, 1895).

TASCODRUGITES (PAXILLONASONES): Th nickname of a heretical sect first mentioned in th fourth century by Epiphanius and Jerome. Th designation occurs in widely variant forms, and is b Epiphanius (*Hær*, xlviii. 14) derived from th Phrygian *taskos*, "wooden nail or stake," an *drungos*, "nose"; whence the sect bore the Gree name *Passalorhynchites* and the Latin *Paxillono sones*. The designation was bestowed on ther because of a peculiarity in their worship, or becaus they prayed with one finger on the nose, or thrust finger in their mouth for a sign of strictest silenc in reference to Ps. cxli. 3. Epiphanius obscure connects them with the Montanists, Theodor (*Hæreticorum fabularum compendium*, i. 9–10) wit the Gnostics. Jerome (commentary on Galatian book ii., preface) and Epiphanius place the sect i

Galatia, whence it seems to have spread over Asia Minor and into Syria. Imperial laws came in to forbid the sect's assemblages. Theodore the Studite (*Epist. xl. ad Naucratium*, in *MPG*, xcix. 1051) in the ninth century is the latest to testify to its existence. Philastrius (*Hær.*, lxxv.), who had no independent knowledge of the sect, confused them with the Ascites who kept the consecrated blood in a sack (*askos*) and had a cult resembling that of Bacchus.   G. GRÜTZMACHER.

BIBLIOGRAPHY: The principal sources are named in the text. Consult further: Augustine, *Hær.*, lxiii.; Timothy of Constantinople, in J. B. Cotelerius, *Ecclesiæ Græcæ monumenta*, iii. 377 sqq., 4 vols., Paris, 1677–92; J. H. Blunt, *Dictionary of Sects* . . . , p. 590, London, 1874; T. Zahn, *Geschichte des neutestamentlichen Kanons*, ii. 437, Leipsic, 1891.

TASKER, JOHN GREENWOOD: Wesleyan Methodist; b. at Skipton (22 m. n.w. of Leeds), Yorkshire, England, Jan. 20, 1853. He received his education at Hawkshaw House School, Garforth, Leeds, and at Richmond College; was assistant tutor at Richmond College, 1876–80; was at Cannstatt, Germany, also pastor of English Church at Stuttgart, 1880–84; returned and served again as assistant tutor at Richmond College, 1884–87, then as classical tutor, 1887–91; superintendent of the Manchester (Longsight) circuit, 1891–92; as Biblical and classical tutor at Handsworth College, 1892–1904, and as theological tutor, 1904–10, when he became principal. He delivered' the Fernley Lecture in 1901, with the title *Does Haeckel Solve the Riddle?* in *Is Christianity True?* (London, 1904); has written *Spiritual Religion: a Study of the Relation of Facts to Faith* (1901); and has contributed to Hasting's *Dictionary of the Bible, Dictionary of Christ and the Gospels*, and *Encyclopedia of Religion and Ethics*.

TASMANIA. See AUSTRALIA.

TAST, HERMANN (HARMEN, HERMEN): Reformer in Sleswick-Holstein; b. at Husum (21 m. w. of Sleswick) c. 1490; d. there May 11, 1551. At some time after 1514 he held the vicarage of St. Michael in the Church of our Lady in Husum. The Reformation was felt there at an early time; as early as 1518 two students from that flourishing borough studied at Wittenberg, others followed from the vicinity, and all returned zealous friends of the new truth. Tast is said to have arrived at his better knowledge by reading the works of Luther, and about 1522 he dared to announce the truth openly. He found many adherents; but as the majority of the priesthood and of the congregation clung to the old traditions, he was excluded from the church, and his life was endangered. But Mathias Knudsen, a neighbor, protected him and opened his house for the gathering of his adherents. When it could no longer hold them, Tast preached in the churchyard. The Reformation developed further under the protection of Frederic I., who in 1524 is said to have required of both parties mutual toleration in a formal and general edict of toleration. Tast found an efficient assistant in Theodoricus Pistorius (Becker), father of Johannes Pistorius (q.v.), a true pupil of Melanchthon. After 1526 the young Duke Christian, as temporary stattholder and

XI.—18

regent of the duchies, and the king not only tolerated, but advanced, the cause of the Reformation. Tast prepared the way in Flensburg, so that in advent season, 1526, the first Evangelical sermons were delivered in the two principal churches of the town by Geert Slewert and Nikolaus Johannis. About the same time Husum was won for the Reformation. In 1527 Tast was appointed pastor, Pistorius and Hamer first and second chaplains. Roman Catholic masses and vigils were prohibited, and an Evangelical church service was introduced. Baptism was administered in accordance with Luther's *Taufbüchlein;* the school of the monastery was reorganized, and H. Bokelmann of Brunswick, a pupil of Luther, was placed at its head.

At the colloquy of Flensburg, which was held on April 8, 1529, with Melchior Hoffmann (q.v.) Tast was the chief spokesman of the Lutheran party. The controversy turned principally about the Lord's Supper, which Hoffmann interpreted spiritually. It was impossible to convince Hoffmann, and the colloquy ended with his banishment. In the winter of 1536–37 Tast assisted in the elaboration of a church order for the territories of Christian III., which appeared under the title, *Ordinatio ecclesiastica regnorum Daniæ et Norwegiæ et ducatuum Slesv., Holsat.*, etc. (1537). After its issue Tast was entrusted with the provostship of the old Nordstrand with its more than twenty churches, and soon afterward also with that of Eiderstedt and with the inspection of the churches in the district of Husum. After 1540 he was one of the four (five) superintendents in the duchy of Sleswick. In 1542 he, together with the other superintendents, assisted Bugenhagen in drawing up the church order of Sleswick-Holstein, issued on March 9, 1542. In accordance with this church order Tast lost his privileges as superintendent in favor of the new Lutheran bishop or superintendent of Sleswick, and, in consequence of the division of the country in 1544, also his provostships (1545, 1547–48).

Tast earned the reputation of a highly educated and studious thinker, diligent, zealous, courageous, and earnest in the performance of all his duties.

(E. MICHELSEN.)

BIBLIOGRAPHY: J. Möller, *Introductio ad hist. ducat.*, Leipsic, 1699; idem, *Cimbriæ literatæ prodromus*, vol. i., Copenhagen, 1744; A. Heimreich, *Nordfresische Chronik*, 3d ed. by N. Falck, vol. i., Tondern, 1819; C. Kortholt, *Hist. eccl.*, Leipsic, 1697; L. von Seckendorf, *Historia Lutheranismi*, ib. 1694; Eggers, *H. Tastii Memoria* (Husen Programm), 1817; O. Kallsen, in Meyn's *Schleswig-holsteinischer Hauskalendar* for 1880; *ABD*, vol. xxxvii.; H. F. Rördam, in *Dansk biografisk Lexikon*, vol. xvii., Copenhagen, 1887 sqq.

TATE, NAHUM: Hymnist, and poet laureate; b. in Dublin 1652; d. in the Mint at Southwark, London, Aug. 12, 1715. He was educated at Trinity College, Dublin (B.A., 1672); went to London, and in 1692 became poet laureate. He is remembered by *A New Version of the Psalms of David*, made in collaboration with Nicholas Brady (q.v.), which appeared in 1696 (see HYMNOLOGY, IX., § 3, for development). Tate is supposed to have been the better poet, and to have shown it chiefly here. The psalter made its way slowly but surely in popular acceptance, not entirely driving out Sternhold and Hopkins till the nineteenth century was somewhat advanced, and being, in turn, displaced by the greatly increased supply and use of hymns in the Church of England. In one section, at least, of this country, it was largely used in preference to the New England version, or Bay Psalm Book (q.v.), many editions appearing in Boston between 1750 and 1800. It contains some fairly poetical portions, many that are still well adapted to public worship where metrical psalms are preferred, and a few that are able to hold their own simply as hymns. The *Supplement to the New Version* (1703) is supposed to be the work of Tate alone; it contains versions of the *Te Deum*, Lord's Prayer, Creed, Commandments, and other passages of Scripture or Prayer-Book. Some of these are well done, and have been largely used in the English Church; and one, " While shepherds watched," is in nearly universal use. In 1702 Tate was named historiographer-royal. In 1677 he published a volume of poems, and in 1678 his drama *Brutus of Alba* (London); he also wrote some versions of Shakespeare's dramas. His best original poem was *Panacea—a Poem on Tea* (London, 1700); and his translations include *The Life of Louis of Bourbon, Late Prince of Condé* (1693), and *Cowley's History of Plants* (1695).

BIBLIOGRAPHY: W. S. Austin and J. Ralph, *Lives of the Poets-Laureate*, pp. 196–222, London, 1853; S. W. Duffield, *English Hymns*, pp. 428, 610, New York, 1886; Julian, *Hymnology*, pp. 799–802, 919–920; *DNB*, lv. 379–380; and the literature on English hymns under HYMNOLOGY; and PSALMODY.

TATIAN, tê′shi-ȧn.

I. Life.   II. Writings.

I. Life: Concerning the date and place of birth of Tatian nothing is known except what he himself tells in his " Address to the Greeks," chap. xlii. (*ANF*, ii. 81–82), viz., that he was born in " the land of the Assyrians "; and neither the date nor place of his death is known. He enjoyed a good education and became acquainted with Greek culture. Extensive travels led him through different countries and showed him the nature of Greek education, art, and science. He himself states that he studied the pagan religions. Finally he came to Rome, where he seems to have remained for some time. Here he seems to have come for the first time in touch with Christianity. According to his own representation, it was primarily his abhorrence of the heathen cults that led him to spend thought on religious problems. By the Old Testament, he says, he was convinced of the unreasonableness of paganism. He adopted the Christian religion and became the pupil of Justin. It was the period when Christian philosophers competed with Greek sophists, and like Justin, he opened a Christian school in Rome. It is not known how long he labored in Rome without being disturbed. The later life of Tatian is to some extent obscure. Since the " Address to the Greeks " was written probably in Greece, it may be inferred that he tarried in that country for some time. Epiphanius relates that Tatian first established a school in Mesopotamia, the influence of which extended to Antioch in Syria, and was felt in Cilicia and especially in Pisidia, but these statements can not be verified. The later activity of Tatian is attested by the history of the Diatessaron (see below). Irenæus remarks (*Hær.*, I., xxviii. 1, *ANF*,

i. 353) that Tatian after the death of Justin separated from the Church and taught Encratitic heresy, also a doctrine of eons related to that of Valentine. Such statements are to be received with caution; for the Occident regarded as heretical much which the Orient judged orthodox. The ascetic character which Syriac Christianity bore as late as the time of Aphraates was not impressed upon it by Tatian, but has roots that reach deeper. The importance of Tatian lies neither in his protest against Hellenism in his " Address to the Greeks " (see below), nor in his work on Jewish antiquity, but in his service for the church in Syria. He was the first to give the Syriac congregations the Gospel in their own language. The Syrian church possessed and used the Gospel from the very beginning until the time of Rabbula only in the form of the Diatessaron; it is probable, therefore, that Tatian not only brought the Diatessaron into Syria, but also developed there a successful missionary activity in the last quarter of the second century. A later age did not realize that the Syrian ascetic tendencies had been transmitted from Semitic primitive Christianity, hence it regarded Tatian as a sectarian, the head of the Encratites.

II. Writings: His " Address to the Greeks " tries to prove the worthlessness of paganism, and the reasonableness and high antiquity of Christianity. It is not characterized by logical consecutiveness, but is discursive in its outlines. The carelessness in style is intimately connected with his contempt of everything Greek. No educated Christian has more consistently separated from paganism; but by overshooting the mark, his scolding and blustering philippic lost its effectiveness because it lacks justice. But Tatian was praised for his discussions of the antiquity of Moses and of Jewish legislation, and it was because of this chronological section that the " Address " was not generally condemned. For his *Diatessaron*, see HARMONY OF THE GOSPELS.

In a lost writing, entitled *On Perfection according to the Doctrine of the Savior*, Tatian designates matrimony as a symbol of the tying of the flesh to the perishable world and ascribed the " invention " of matrimony to the devil. He distinguishes between the old and the new man; the old man is the law, the new man the Gospel. The early development of the Syrian church furnishes a commentary on the attitude of Tatian in practical life. Thus for Aphraates baptism conditions the taking of a vow in which the catechumen promises celibacy. This shows how firmly the views of Tatian were established in Syria, and it supports the supposition that Tatian was the missionary of the countries around the Euphrates. The starting-point of Tatian's theology is a strict monotheism which becomes the source of the moral life. Originally the human soul possessed faith in one God, but lost it with the fall. In consequence man sank under the rule of demons into the abominable error of polytheism. By monotheistic faith the soul is delivered from the material world and from demonic rule and is united with God. God is spirit (*pneuma*), but not the physical or stoical *pneuma*; he was alone before the creation, but he had within himself potentially the whole crea-

tion. The means of creation was the *dynamis logikē*
(" power expressed in words "). At first there proceeded from God the Logos who, generated in the
beginning, was to produce the world by creating
matter from which the whole creation sprang.
Creation is penetrated by the *pneuma hylikon*,
" world spirit," which is common to angels, stars,
men, animals, and plants. This world spirit is lower
than the divine *pneuma*, and becomes in man the
psychē or " soul," so that on the material side and
in his soul man does not differ essentially from the
animals; though at the same time he is called to a
peculiar union with the divine spirit, which raises
him above the animals. This spirit is the image of
God in man, and to it man's immortality is due.
The first-born of the spirits fell and caused others to
fall, and thus the demons originated. The fall of
the spirits was brought about through their desire
to separate man from God, in order that he might
serve not God but them. Man, however, was implicated in this fall, lost his blessed abode and his
soul was deserted by the divine spirit, and sank into
the material sphere, in which only a faint reminiscence of God remained alive. As by freedom man
fell, so by freedom he may turn again to God. The
Spirit unites with the souls of those who walk up-
rightly; through the prophets he reminds men of
their lost likeness to God. Although Tatian does not
mention the name of Jesus, his doctrine of redemption culminates in his Christology. Other (lost)
writings of Tatian are a work written before the
" Address to the Greeks " and treating the nature
of man as contrasted with the nature of the animals,
and a *Problēmatōn biblion*, which aimed to present a
compilation of obscure Scripture sayings.

(E. Preuschen.)

Bibliography: On Tatian: H. A. Daniel, *Tatianus der
Apologet*, Halle, 1837; J. Donaldson, *Critical Hist. of
Christian Literature and Doctrine*, iii. 3 sqq., Oxford, 1866;
A. Hilgenfeld, *Ketzergeschichte des Urchristentums*, pp. 384
sqq., Leipsic, 1884; T. Zahn. in *Forschungen zur Geschichte
des neutestamentlichen Kanons*, i. 268 sqq., Erlangen, 1881;
Harnack, in *TU*, ii. 1–2 (1886); idem, *Litteratur*, i. 485
sqq., ii. 1, pp. 284 sqq.; idem, in *Encyclopædia Britannica*,
9th. ed., xxiii. 80 sqq., cf. K. Lake, in 11th ed., xxvi. 450–
451; F. R. Wynne, J. H. Bernard, and S. Hemphill, *Literature of the Second Century*, London, 1881; F. X. Funk,
Kirchengeschichtliche Abhandlungen, ii. 142 sqq., Paderborn, 1899; O. Bardenhewer, *Geschichte der altkirchlichen Literatur*, i. 242 sqq., Freiburg, 1902; Krüger,
History, pp. 117–121; *DCB*, iv. 783–803; *KL*, xi. 1233 sqq.
　Editions of the " Address " are: the *editio princeps* by
Frisius and Gessner, Zurich, 1546; by J. C. T. Otto, in
Corpus apologetarum Christianorum, vol. vi., Jena, 1851;
and the independent one by E. Schwartz, in *TU*, iv. 1
(1888). There is an Eng. transl. in *ANF*, ii. 65–83. For
discussions, besides the introductions to the editions and
in the treatment of Tatian's life and work, consult: C. E.
Freppel, *Les Apologistes chrétiens au ii. siècle*, Paris, 1860;
B. Aubé, *De l'apologétique chrétienne au 2. siècle*, ib. 1861;
H. Dembowski, *Die Quellen der christlichen Apologetik*,
part i., Leipsic, 1878; W. Steuer, *Die Gottes- und Logos-
lehre des Tatians*, ib. 1893; B. Ponschab, *Tatians Rede an
die Griechen*, Metten, 1895; R. C. Kukula, *Tatians soge-
nannte Apologie*, Leipsic, 1900; J. Dräseke, in *ZWT*, xliii
(1900), 603 sqq.; H. U. Meyboom, in *ThT*, xxxvii (1903),
440 sqq.
　For the Diatessaron it is to be noted that all earlier
works are discounted by the careful reconstruction by T.
Zahn, in *Forschungen zur Geschichte des neutestamentlichen
Kanons*, vol. i., Erlangen, 1881, cf. ii. 286 sqq., and also
Zahn's *Geschichte des neutestamentlichen Kanons*, ii. 2, pp.
530 sqq., Leipsic, 1891. The fragments found in later
writers have been collected by H. Goussen, in *Studia theologica*, vol. i., Leipsic, 1895, and by J. R. Harris, *Fragments of the Commentary of Ephrem Syrus upon the Diatessaron*, London, 1895. The Arabic working over was issued
by A. Ciasca, *Tatiani Evangelicæ harmonicæ Arabice*,
Rome, 1888 (with a Latin transl., which is rendered
into English, with an introduction by J. H. Hill, *The
Earliest Life of Christ ever Compiled from the Gospels,
Being the Diatessaron of Tatian*, Edinburgh, 1894, 2d ed.,
1910, and an Eng. transl. of the Arabic is furnished in
ANF, ix. 9–138; all of these are provided with critical
apparatus). The *Codex Fuldensis* was edited by E.
Ranke, Marburg, 1868. The early German version has
been edited by J. A. Schmeller, Vienna, 1841, and by E.
Sievers, Paderborn, 1892. Discussions other than those
above indicated are: A. Harnack, in *ZKG*, iv (1881),
471–505; J. P. P. Martin, in *Revue des questions historiques*, xxxiii (1883), 349 sqq., xliv (1888), 5 sqq.; S.
Hemphill, *The Diatessaron of Tatian*, London, 1888;
J. R. Harris, *The Diatessaron of Tatian*, ib. 1890; idem,
in *Contemporary Review*, 1893, pp. 800 sqq.; M. Maher,
*Recent Evidence for the Authenticity of the Gospels; Tatian's
Diatessaron*, ib. 1893; B. W. Bacon, in *AJT*, 1900, pp.
770 sqq.; C. H. Turner, in *Journal of Theological Studies*,
iii (1902), 110 sqq.; F. C. Burkitt, *Early Eastern Christianity*, London, 1904; A. Hobson, *The Diatessaron of
Tatian and the Synoptic Problem*, Chicago, 1904; K. Lake,
in *Expository Times*, 1906, p. 286. See also Harmony
of the Gospels.

TATTAM, HENRY: Orientalist; b. in Ireland
Dec. 28, 1789; d. at Stanford Rivers (7 m. n.e. of
Charing Cross, London) Jan. 8, 1868. He was educated at Trinity College, Dublin, and at the universities of Göttingen and Leyden; held the benefices
of St. Cuthbert's, Bedford, 1822–49, and of Great
Woolstone, near Newpont Pagnell, 1831–49. He
was archdeacon of Bedford, 1845–66, and from 1849
till his death, rector of Stanford Rivers, and also
chaplain-in-ordinary to the queen. His fame rests
upon his labors on Coptic, in which he was an authority. He discovered in the Nitrian convent, and
secured for the British Museum, a splendid collection
of ancient Syriac manuscripts. He edited in Arabic
and Coptic the Gospels (London, 1829); the Coptic
Apostolic Constitutions (1848; with English translation); the Book of Job (1846; with translation);
the minor and major prophets (1836–52; with
Latin translation); and the New Testament in Coptic and Arabic (1847); and he was the author of
*A Compendious Grammar of the Egyptian Language
as Contained in the Coptic and Sahidic Dialects, with
Observations on the Bashmuric . . .* 3 pts. (1830);
and *Lexicon Ægyptiaco-Latinum, ex veteribus linguæ
Ægyptiacæ monumentis, et ex operibus La Crozii,
Woidii . . . congestum* (Oxford, 1835).

TAULER, tau'ler, JOHANN: Dominican mystic
(see Friends of God); b. at Strasburg about 1300;
d. there June 16, 1361. More would be known of
　　　　　　　　the circumstances of his life, if the
Life. 　" master of the Holy Scriptures " ap-
　　　　　　　　pearing in the " *Meisterbuch* of the
Great Friend from God of the Highlands " (issued
by C. Schmidt under the title, *Nicolaus von Basel
Bericht von der Bekehrung Taulers*, Strasburg, 1875)
of Rulman Merswin (see Friends of God) could be
identified with Tauler. This was long assumed, but
conclusively disproved by H. S. Denifle (*Taulers
Bekehrung*, Strasburg, 1879. Attracted by the
ascetic life of the Dominicans, Tauler joined that
order at Strasburg at an early age. It is not impossible that during his eight years of study there
he heard Meister Eckhart (q.v.) preach, whose stay

at Strasburg is determined at least for the year 1314. Also he must have been reached by the influence of the mystic Johann Sterngasser, lector at the Dominican monastery at Strasburg (1317–24). If it be assumed, with W. Preger, that Sermon·l. was preached at Cologne (which is not established), Tauler may have been at the stadium generale of the order in that city while Eckhart was lecturer (1326–27). Possibly he witnessed, at the same time, the closing events of the latter's life, and in that case met Heinrich Suso (q.v.). At any rate he was acquainted with Suso, having received from him as a gift his *Horologium sapientiæ.* Beyond doubt Nicholas of Strasburg (q.v.), whom he may have known at his native city, was one of his teachers at Cologne. He probably returned to Strasburg at the conclusion of his studies and reappears toward the close of the fourth decade in the correspondence of Henry of Nördlingen (q.v.) with Margareta Ebner (q.v.). During Lent 1339 he appears at Basel, driven from Strasburg, together with the other Dominicans, in consequence of suspending mass pursuant to the interdict of John XXII. (q.v.). He is known to have been there at the beginning of 1346, and with Henry of Nördlingen was the center of a numerous body of Friends of God. In 1347, or 1348 at the latest, he was preaching at Strasburg, and Christina Ebner (q.v.) writes of his "fiery tongue that has kindled the horizon." Rulman Merswin chose him as his confessor. To this activity at Strasburg must have belonged his open opposition to pope and interdict mentioned by the chronicler Daniel Speckle (Specklin), an account which has been variously disputed. A coincidence of a sermon (102d) preached on the twentieth Sunday after Trinity in honor of St. Cordula (Oct. 22) leads W. Preger to the conclusion that about 1357 Tauler stayed for a considerable period at Cologne, and that his extant sermons belonged to this period. That they were preached at Cologne is shown by internal references and by the mention of the ancient Cologne manuscript (see below), which locates them at St. Gertrud, of that city; yet the arrangement, according to the church year, points to a later date. The sermons may presuppose a long sojourn in Cologne, and there is nothing to be said against this being in the sixth decade.

With reference to the works ascribed to Tauler, the following is to be said: (1) *Nachfolgung des armen Lebens Christi* (Frankfort, 1621; Eng. transl., *The Following of Christ,* London, 1886), published by Denifle with the more accurate title,

Works. *Das Buch von der geistlichen Armut* (Munich, 1877; Eng. transl., *Golden Thoughts from the Book of Spiritual Poverty,* Glasgow, 1897), formerly ascribed to Tauler, has been proved by Denifle to be ungenuine, by the difference of doctrine from the sermons; and A. Ritschl showed that it is a compilation; (2) the *Medulla animæ* (Frankfort, 1644) contains the material appended in seventy-seven chapters to " Sermons " (Cologne, 1543). The title intended for chapters i.–xxxix. only originated with Christian Hohburg, who issued this separate edition. These are merely compilations, and of the rest of the collection even Preger would claim as genuine only several of the

epistles in xl.–lxvi., and chapter lxxii. *Golden Thoughts on the Higher Life* (Glasgow, 1897) consists of selections from (1) and (2) translated into English. (3) *Betrachtūg und erklerung des leidens und sterbens Jhesu Christi* (Cologne, 1567; Berlin, 1856) was shown to be ungenuine by C. Schmidt. (4) Several hymns have been ascribed to Tauler (cf. P. Wackernagel, *Das deutsche Kirchenlied,* numbers 457–67, ii. 302 sqq., Leipsic, 1863–77); but even the one most generally held to be genuine, " Es kumt ein schif geladen," Preger has declared not by him. (5) There remained the " Sermons " of which no edition scientifically adequate has been produced, and there is scarcely the beginning of a critical examination of the manuscripts. The first redaction, *Sermon des gross gelarten in gnadē erlauchtē doctoris Johannis Tauleri* (Leipsic, 1498; reprint, *Sermones von latein in teütsch gewendt,* Augsburg, 1508), consisted of eighty-four sermons. The second redaction, *Predige* (Basel, 1521; another ed. with preface by Johann Arndt, Hamburg, 1621), adds forty-two, " recently found," to the first, of which several in the opinion of the publisher were not from Tauler. It further affixes sixty-one sermons and literary pieces from other teachers, in particular, Meister Eckhart. The third redaction (Cologne, 1543) drops the latter and instead adds twenty-five sermons, which are genuine in the judgment of the editor, but certainly are not all by Tauler. This edition, based upon the manuscript found at St. Gertrud, Cologne, in 1542, which is the first to distribute the sermons according to the church year, became the basis of all those following. L. Surius translated and paraphrased it into Latin, *Opera oīia ex Germanico nunc primum idiomate in Latinū transfusa sermonem* (Cologne, 1548; German retransl., Frankfort-on-the-Main, 1622–1621; another ed., with preface by P. J. Spener same place, 1681; Germ. Roman Catholic retransl. Cologne, 1660; and retranslations into Italian, Dutch, and French). Recent editions, going back to the old prints, are, *Johann Tauler's Predigten Nach den besten Ausgaben und in unverändertem Text in die jetzige Schriftsprache übertragen,* with an excellent introduction (Frankfort-on-the-Main, 1826; Eng. transl., *The History and Life of the Reverend Doctor John Tauler,* by Susanna Winkworth, with preface by Charles Kingsley, London, 1857 and New York, 1907; rev. ed., J. Hamburger Frankfort, 1864); and *Predigten* (Berlin, 1841) It can scarcely be presumed that most of the sermons were preached at St. Gertrud. In form they are rather dissertations than sermons; they proceed in a quiet, orderly way, but often rise into dramatic energy. Scripture is employed in most fanciful allegory. The sermons, contrary to the misunderstood titles of the first redaction, were delivered in German.

The sermons are to form here the only basis upon which to determine Tauler's doctrines. A disciple of Eckhart, he was more practical **Practical** hence his sermons lack in real consist-**Teachings.** ency. This practical side, which came to the attention of Luther, who in his day frequently extolled him, made him famed among Protestants as a forerunner of the Reformation. It may be shown, however, that this Evangelical tone appears prominently in the popular parts of his preaching. Sifted down to his elemental speculations these impressions disappear. That immediacy and personal experience of the divine in the place of dead formalism and works was Evangelical can not be gainsaid. This does not imply that he had wholly overcome traditional views; he revered the saints, but direct communion with God stood first (sermon xxxiii.). Sometimes this communion seems to be mediated through the work of Christ (death on the cross), and the acceptance of it by faith (lxv., lxxxiii.). While it appears that the conception of faith as assenting to the truth of the promise of forgiveness is advanced, yet the other idea, of trust, is the essential and avails with God. To this the fundamental significance of Scripture receives the supreme emphasis, likewise in the Evangelical sense, as the ultimate source of truth. Tauler also warns against the contemplative life and impractical quietism, and values, though in the lowest degree, the works of the earthly vocation; and he ascribes full worth to deeds of loving service (lxxxvii.). He counsels his hearers to shun lofty speculations, such as the mystery of God, but to know themselves in spirit and nature and maintain a pure and simple faith (liv.).

However, the interest in the practical appears always as one of expedience and somewhat strained, while his tendency is ever backward to the deep and mysterious ground of things, a field which he regards as reserved for the speculative select. He deplores that the masses of the people

Speculative pass through their lifetime with the
Doctrines. help of the grace of God, and yet, like
blind fowls, remain ignorant of what lies concealed within (cxix.). He has reference here, with Eckhart, to the speculative fundamental essence of the soul, which is essentially the core of his doctrine and rests upon his views of the divine and the human. The former is the divine darkness to the whole understanding of man and angel. But as God the heavenly Father, in self-knowledge begetting his beloved Son, or speaking by his eternal Word, proceeded out of himself, indeed in such manner that Father and Son remained one, joined in a new unity, and sent forth from them both the Holy Spirit, in an indescribable compass, as the love of both—so has he also further poured himself out to the creatures (lxxx.). What man, created, is in himself he was uncreated from eternity in God (cxix.). By laying aside every appetency to the lower, or animal, alienated from all sense and sorrow, man returns not only to a vision of the essence of the soul as a rational image of its source (xciii.), but also to behold with raptures the abyss of God, who now first emerges from the darkness. This image is not a picture or resemblance of the divine, but it is that in which God loves, knows, and enjoys himself, and acts within himself. In this unity God and the soul are one. It would be difficult to acquit Tauler of pantheism in this light. As to the final estimate of these pensive speculations, the gradual union of the divine and human is illustrated (xxvi.) by the grape-cluster and the sun. In the first stage must be overcome the man who exerts

himself in sensuous tasks and works of fasting, watching, and prayer; but who, unable to realize his essence purely, regards himself with sensuous satisfaction, or pleasure and displeasure. In the second stage is to be discarded the man who has despised all temporal things and overcome the coarser instincts. As the weeds are removed, the divine sun begins to shine upon the ground.

In the third stage, just as the sunshine clasps the grape, when the leaves are cut away, so all images of saints, as well as knowledge, works, and prayer fall away; man is absorbed in God like a drop of water in a cask of wine; all differences disappear. But where in this deification reaching to " annihilation," to " actless passivity " (xlix.), has he left behind his regard for the practical, the earthly vocation, the service of love, and, above all, the redemptive work of Christ? While the renewal of grace by the acceptance of Christ through the sacrament, taking into account his suffering and death, and union with the Father through him as prototype (cxxviii., lxxii.), are emphasized; yet the basis of grace is not in the restored relation of love between man and God, but the essence of the soul. It is but a figure for Tauler to say that man is born in Christ of the Father and with the Son returns again into the Father to become one with him (lxix.). To remove Christ and his work from Tauler's views would not alter his fundamental conceptions. At bottom the entire interpolation of Christian thoughts and modes may be designated as an accommodation to the churchly and Christian mode of speech. That he did not see clearly how, though with the best intentions, he clothed his mystical ideas in Christian form is certain; that he also sometimes felt the necessity of distinguishing himself as a Christian preacher from the adherents of a false mysticism is likewise shown (xxxi.). In this he severely censures those brethren of the free spirit who mistake idle inertness for unity with God; the latter is not possible, and no one is free without the keeping of the commandments, good works, and divine love and aspiration. The difference was not inherent in the doctrines but in the attitude toward the teaching of the Church and the different spirit in which Tauler proclaimed them. At bottom he was in accord with the libertine trend. Likewise in his attitude to the revealed Word, he is no more entitled to the name of forerunner of the Reformation. In particular instances he insisted upon the fundamental importance of the Scriptures (lxxxviii., xci.), but at the same time he placed the inner Word, or Christ enthroned within obedient man, as of higher authority (lxxxii.). As to the Church he is so prepossessed by his estimation of the personal relation to God that he loses all appreciation for the ordinances, in spite of incidental recognition of them (cxxxi.). To him the Friends of God, who are in immediate contact with God, take the place of the Church (cxiii., cxxvii., cxxxi.) The visible Church has only a preliminary pedagogical worth, to be forsaken as soon as the inner Word is perceived.

(FERDINAND COHRS.)

BIBLIOGRAPHY: Works of Tauler recently made accessible in English are A. W. Hutton, *The Inner Way, 36 Sermons for Festivals by John Tauler,* Transl. *with Introduction,* London, 1905; and *Conferences and Sermons of John Tauler;*

being his *Spirit Doctrine; first complete Translation* by Rev.
W. *Elliott*, Washington, D.C., 1911. Consult J. Quétif and
J. Échard, *Scriptores ordinis prædicatorum*, i. 677 sqq.,
Paris, 1719; R. Hoffmann, *Johann Tauler*, Rixdorf, 1833;
C. Schmidt, *Johann Tauler*, Hamburg, 1841; idem, *Die
Gottesfreunde im 14. Jahrhundert*, ib. 1854; A. G. Rudel-
bach, *Christliche Biographie*, pp. 187 sqq., Leipsic, 1849; F.
Bähring, *Johann Tauler und die Gottesfreunde*, Hamburg,
1853; W. Edel, *Tauler*, Strasburg, 1853; *Hist. and Life of
Rev. Doctor John Tauler . . . ; Transl. with twenty-five
of his Sermons from the German with additional Notices of
Tauler's Life and Times, by Susanna Winkworth . . . and
a Preface by C. Kingsley*, London, 1857, new ed., New
York, 1907; E. Böhmer, *Nicolaus von Basel und Tauler*,
in *Damaris*, 1865, pp. 148 sqq.; W. Preger, in *ZHT*, 1869,
pp. 109 sqq.; idem, in the *Abhandlungen* of the Bavarian
Academy, xiv. 1; idem, *Geschichte der deutschen Mystik
im Mittelalter*, part III., Leipsic, 1893; idem, in *ADB*,
xxxvii. 453–465; O. Billhorn, *Tauleri vita et doctrina*,
Jena, 1874; Nicolaus von Basel, *Bericht von der Bekehrung Taulers*, ed. C. Schmidt, Strasburg, 1875; J. Nobbe,
in *Zeitschrift für lutherische Theologie*, 1876, pp. 637–663;
H. S. Denifle, in *Historisch-politische Blätter*, lxxv (1875),
18 sqq.; idem, *Taulers Bekehrung kritisch untersucht*,
Strasburg, 1879; idem, in *Zeitschrift für deutsches Altertum*, xxiv. 200 sqq., 280 sqq., xxv. 101 sqq.; M. Jundt,
Les Amis de Dieu au 14. siècle, Paris, 1879; idem, *Rul-
man Merswin et l'ami de Dieu de l'Oberland*, ib. 1890; P.
Strauch, *Margaretha Ebner*, Tübingen, 1882; M. Arnold,
in *Nineteenth Century*, xxi (1887), 499–506; F. A. Bevan,
Three Friends of God, London, 1887; J. E. Erdmann,
Grundriss der Geschichte der Philosophie, i. 504 sqq., 4th ed.,
1896, Eng. transl. of earlier ed., London, 1893; Schaff,
Christian Church, v. 2, pp. 256 sqq., and literature under
FRIENDS OF GOD. A new ed. of his *Predigten*, ed. F.
Velter, appeared Berlin, 1909.

TAUSEN, HANS: Danish Reformer; b. in the
village of Birkende on the island of Fünen, 1494;
d. at Ribe (154 m. w.s.w. of Copenhagen) Nov. 11,
1561. He received his early education at the schools
of Odense in Fünen, and Slagelse in Zealand, and
in the monastery of the Knights of St. John near
Slagelse. In 1516 he entered the University of Rostock, where he lectured in 1520; from 1520 to 1521
he probably studied in Louvain and Cologne, and in
October, 1521, he was called home to lecture at the
University of Copenhagen. In 1523 he entered the
University of Wittenberg and heard Luther, but
because of his enthusiasm for the Reformation was
recalled. Having advocated the doctrine of justification by faith in one of his sermons, he was imprisoned in a monastery and subsequently sent to
Viborg in Jutland where the prior of the monastery
of the Knights of St. John vainly endeavored to
win him back to the old faith. Tausen was protected by Peder Trane, the burgomaster of Viborg,
while Jakob Skjönning, rector of the school and
priest of the Church of St. John, yielded his pulpit
to Tausen; the crowds which soon assembled compelled him to hold services in the open air; later
the citizens of Viborg, embittered by the resistance
of the clergy, broke open the Franciscan church,
and Tausen preached there twice every Sunday
afternoon and introduced singing in the Danish
tongue. On the arrival of King Frederic I. at Aal-
borg in 1526, Tausen induced him to issue a letter
of protection. An armed assault by the Roman
Catholic bishops in Jütland evoked the protection
of the people, and the Reformation in Viborg began
to make progress. In 1528 Tausen published a baptismal formula for Evangelical church services.
From Viborg the Reformation spread to other cities
of Northern Jutland. Tausen became pastor of the

Franciscan church, but in 1529 went to Copenhagen,
where his sermons had the same effect as in Viborg.
At the diet of 1530 held at Copenhagen, under the
leadership of Tausen, there was laid before the assembly a confession of faith, " the forty-three articles of Copenhagen," an independent counterpart
of the Augsburg Confession, and on July 14, 1530,
freedom was granted for Evangelical preaching.
Tausen defended his Evangelical doctrine in a
learned work which in Dec., 1530, was submitted
to the council of the empire and printed six months
later. In Copenhagen also the reformatory movement was the occasion of violent disturbances. On
Dec. 27 the citizens, headed by their burgomaster,
invaded the Church of Our Lady and there demolished pictures and relics. Tausen, naturally conservative, disapproved of this iconoclasm and practised moderation in regard to the old usages of the
Church. Nevertheless, the hatred against him increased, and on the death of Frederic I. in 1533 his
position was very insecure. He was accused at the
diet in 1533, but was allowed to continue his activity. He took part in the compilation of the Danish
church ordinance of 1537 and in the same year became lector in Hebrew at the university. In 1542
he was consecrated bishop of Ribe. Under the
Evangelical Christian III., Tausen continued his
work unhindered. He translated the Pentateuch
into Danish (Magdeburg, 1535), and edited a Danish liturgy and a collection of sermons on the Gospels and epistles (1535). In 1543 Christian III.
granted him a privilege for twenty years to furnish
a Danish translation of the whole Bible as continuation of the five books of Moses, but Tausen was not
able to carry out this plan. He was also a composer of hymns.   (F. NIELSEN†.)

BIBLIOGRAPHY: A selection from Tausen's smaller works
was edited by H. J. Rördam, Copenhagen, 1870. Con-
sult: F. Wedel, in *ThT*, vols. vi.–vii., 1888–89; D.
Schäfer, *Geschichte von Dänemark*, vol. iv., Gotha, 1893;
L. Schmitt, *Johann Tauser, oder der dänische Luther*,
Cologne, 1894 (Roman Catholic).

TAVERNER BIBLE. See BIBLE VERSIONS, B,
IV., § 4.

TAVERNER, RICHARD: Translator of the
English Bible; b. at Brisley (20 m. n.w. of Norwich), England, 1505; d. at Wood Eaton (4 m. n. of
Oxford) July 14, 1575. He studied first at Corpus
Christi College, Cambridge, and then at Cardinal
College, Oxford (B.A., 1527; then M.A., Cambridge,
1530). After teaching at Cambridge and studying
abroad, he began to study law in 1533, and in 1536
he became, at Cromwell's recommendation, clerk
of the privy seal; he was licensed to preach, 1552;
served as justice of the peace, 1558; and as high
sheriff of Oxfordshire, 1569. He published the
following translations: *The Flowers of Services
Gathered out of Sundry Writers by Erasmus in Latine*
(London, 1547); also from Erasmus *A Ryght Frute-
full Epystle . . . in Laude of Matrymony* (1530?);
and *The Confessyon of the Fayth of the Germanes*
(1536). He was the author of *The Garden of Wyse-
dome Conteynyng Pleasaũt Floures, that is to Saye,
Propre and Quycke Sayinges of Princes, Philosophers
and other Sortes of Men . . . 2 pts.* (1539). He is
remembered for his edition of the English Bible

(London, 1539), commonly called Taverner's Bible. It appeared both in folio and quarto, the latter edition in parts, so that all might be able to secure a portion of the Scriptures. It was really a revision of Matthew's Bible. In 1539 he also issued two editions of the New Testament. See BIBLE VERSIONS, B, IV., § 4.

BIBLIOGRAPHY: Besides the literature on the history of the English Bible noted in vol. ii. p. 141 of this work, consult: A. à Wood, *Athenæ Oxonienses*, ed. P. Bliss, i. 419–423, London, 1813; *DNB*, lv. 393–396.

TAXATION.

I. Hebrew.
    For Sacred Purposes (§ 1).
    For Secular Purposes (§ 2).
II. Ecclesiastical.
    The Primitive Custom (§ 1).
    Rise of Taxation of Clergy (§ 2).
    Feudal Principles Applied (§ 3).
    Development from the Fourteenth Century (§ 4).
    Present System (§ 5).

I. Hebrew: The Hebrew language has no general term for taxes. Dues collected for the temple, priests, and sacred purposes in general are designated by *terumah*, " oblation," " offering," " heave offering "). The first-born, the first-

1. For Sacred Purposes. fruits, and the Tithes (q.v.), which belonged to Yahweh as Israel's king, may be considered the first class of such sacred taxes. In II Kings xii. 4–12, xxii. 3–7 mention is made of money paid into the temple treasury, which consisted in part of " the money imposed by estimation," i.e., of the tax fixed by law for the redemption of persons devoted to God by a vow (Lev. xxvii. 1–13), and in part of voluntary contributions. Ex. xxx. 11–16 (P) treats of a tax for the regular service, and this Mosaic legislation was used in later time to justify the assessments necessary for the sanctuary (cf. II Chron. xxiv. 6, 9); the revenue thus derived was to be used for the temple service, but not for the building of the sanctuary. The sum imposed upon " every one that passeth among them that are numbered " was " half a shekel after the shekel of the sanctuary "; rich and poor were taxed alike (verse 15). The post-exilic period developed from this single poll-tax an annual temple-tax. Under Nehemiah the community agreed to an annual contribution of one-third of a shekel for the service of the house of God (Neh. x. 32; cf. Ezra vi. 9; I Macc. x. 39–41; II Macc. iii.). The money current at this time was the Babylonian silver coinage, in which the shekel was divided into thirds. In the time of the Maccabees Phenician money was introduced, which divided the shekel into halves, and the temple tax was then half a shekel, i.e., a double drachma Matt. xvii. 24, 27). Since Exodus xxx. 13 required payment in the ancient sacred coinage, money-changers found entrance into the temple Matt. xxi. 12). Jews living outside of Palestine also sent the temple tax to Jerusalem after they became twenty years of age (Mishna, *Shekalim*, ii.–iv.; Josephus, *Ant.*, XVIII., ix. 1).

Of secular tributes the tenth is mentioned as one of the royal privileges in the address which is put into the mouth of Samuel when the Israelites asked for a king (I Sam. viii. 10–18). From this it has been inferred that such a tax was known to the people under the kings, and it is not impossible that the taxation of families which is implied in I Sam. xvii. 25 refers to the tenth.

2. For Secular Purposes. The mention of " king's mowings " (Amos vii. 1) points to a claim of the king upon the first cutting of cultivated crops suitable for fodder for his horses (I Kings xviii. 5). From I Kings iv. 7–19, although the text is corrupt, the following may be inferred concerning tribute at the time of Solomon: all Israel was divided into twelve districts, each of which was under a governor; on the basis of this division the corvée was arranged (I Kings v. 13–18; cf. xi. 28), and the burdens of taxation were fixed. That the latter intended payment in kind is evident from I Kings iv. 7, where it is said that each of these governors provided food for the king and his household, each man his month in a year. The other revenues of Solomon were derived from his expeditions to Ophir (I Kings ix. 28, x. 22), with which an export trade was probably connected; from the trade in horses, which were bought in Egypt and sold to the kings of the Hittites and of Syria (I Kings x. 28–29); and from the imposts collected from the caravans passing through his kingdom to Phenicia (I Kings x. 15). All these taxes were entirely new and were necessitated by Solomon's splendid court, as may be seen from the fact that upon his death the people complained of the burdens as something unusual. His predecessors had probably no need to levy such tribute. Saul maintained no costly court. In the time of David revenues derived from tributes of homage and justice had probably greatly increased. At any rate, David's property had become considerable, and, according to I Chron. xxvii. 25–34 (cf. II Chron. xxvi. 10), he owned crown lands of large extent. Added to this were the rich spoils of war (II Sam. viii. 11–12, xii. 30), and the regular tributes of the subjugated nations (II Sam. viii. 2; cf. I Kings v. 1; II Kings iii.). It is probable that the census by David (II Sam. xxiv.) was intended to serve as a basis for taxation, on which account evil results were expected from the innovation. The tax systems were most likely the same under the kings of the two kingdoms as under Solomon. According to I Kings xxi. 1–16, the crown demains seem to have been increased by confiscating in certain cases the property of those who were condemned; I Sam. viii. 12 also implies real estate over which the king could appoint his officers (cf. Ezek. xlvi. 17). But there is no mention of land tax in the time of the divided kingdom, and a poll-tax (which is not mentioned in the description of the royal privileges, I Sam. viii. 10–18) was exacted only in extraordinary cases, as when a war-contribution was to be paid to foreign despots (II Kings xv. 20, xxiii. 35). In the post-exilic period, the Jews as subjects of the Persian kingdom had to pay customs, " tolls," and " tributes," no doubt a direct money-tax and probably a capitation-tax (Ezra iv. 13, 20, vi. 8; Neh. v. 4); the priests and temple-attendants were exempt (Ezra vii. 24). Owing to the bitter feeling of servitude (Neh. ix. 36–37) the burden of taxation seemed harder than it really was; yet the Persian governors occasionally practised extortion (Neh. v.

15). For the Greek and Roman periods, see
TAXES, TAX-GATHERERS (PUBLICANS).

VICTOR RYSSEL†.

II. Ecclesiastical: The cost of maintaining the
ecclesiastical organization is defrayed partly from
the endowments which it possesses in land and capital, partly by subsidies from the State, and partly
by the contributions of its members.

1. The In primitive times the Church de-
Primitive frayed its expenses from the voluntary
Custom. oblations of its members, consisting
of oil, wine, bread, incense, and the
fruits of the earth. The Jewish custom of presenting the first-fruits was early adopted; and by the
time of Tertullian (d. 215) contributions of money
are mentioned. Gradually the custom grew up of
paying tithes, partly as a substitute for the oblations in kind; but before the end of the sixth century only scattered notices of it are found. The
clergy, as they became a distinct class, were exempted from these payments, though from the end
of the fourth century they were not at liberty to
alienate from the Church the property they acquired.

The first traces of a real taxation of the clergy
occur at the end of the sixth century. First, an
annual tax was paid by all the churches in a diocese
to the cathedral. It is first met in
2. Rise of Spain (council of Braga, 572; of To-
Taxation ledo, 646), where it was paid in money.
of Clergy. In the Frankish empire, where it was
paid in kind, it is mentioned in a capitulary of Charles the Bald, 844; in Italy it appears
as an almost universal custom under Innocent III.
(d. 1216) and Honorius III. (d. 1227). According
to the Council of Trent, its payment is regulated by
the diocesan synod. Next, a fee was paid by one
appointed to a benefice to the bishop who installed
or ordained him. In the East this is mentioned as
a custom in 546; the amount can not have been
small, since it is stipulated that it shall not exceed
a year's income of the benefice. In the West, a
Roman council declared in 595 that voluntary gifts
to the ordaining bishop and his assistants were not
simoniacal; but a synod at Paris in 829 and Ivo of
Chartres (q.v.) in one of his letters complain of the
magnitude of the gifts which the Curia expected
from prelates consecrated in Rome. When in the
ninth century metropolitans were compelled to apply to Rome for their pallium, a somewhat similar
tax was attached, which had become so heavy by
1027 that Canute requested a remission of it for the
English archbishops. Similar objections were later
raised elsewhere, especially in Germany. Finally,
it was considered (again first in Spain, 589 and 646)
the duty of the clergy to entertain the bishop on his
visitations. This obligation (called procuration)
was afterward commuted for a money payment.
The eighth century witnessed a further development. The task of church-building was systematically regulated; and dispensations were granted
by popes and bishops on payment of a contribution
for some pious end. Regular fees to the pope appear first under John XXII. (d. 1334), and they
were systematized under Alexander VI. Fees, voluntary, indeed, but fixed by custom, paid to the
clergy for certain sacraments and sacramentals

must have arisen about the same time, since the
fourth Lateran Council (1215) speaks of them as a
laudable custom (see STOLE FEES).

As the constitution of the Church more and more
assumed the character of a feudal monarchy, ecclesiastical taxation developed in the same direction.

Secular rulers paid tribute to the pope
3. Feudal in token of feudal allegiance; the
Principles "Peter's Pence" collected from every
Applied. household seems to have had a similar
character. The same may be said of
the protection-money paid by monasteries and
exempt bishoprics from the reign of Alexander III.
(d. 1181). With the decay of the secular importance of the Church, most of these have disappeared.
Two, however, are still worth mentioning—the *sub-
sidium charitativum* and the *jus deportuum*. The
former is a tax which the bishop was empowered to
levy, in case of extraordinary need, on all the beneficed clergy of his diocese; it is first mentioned at the
beginning of the thirteenth century. A variant
form is the *ingressus* or *entrata*, which the bishop
might levy on entering his see city; this is still
preserved in Bavaria. Allied to it also is the tithe
of all ecclesiastical incomes which the pope asserted
his right to take in case of great need. The *jus deportuum* (annates), mentioned under Honorius III.
(d. 1227) and Boniface VIII. (d. 1305), was the
right by which the bishop was entitled to collect
the first year's income of every benefice in his diocese from a new incumbent. Sometimes it appears
as a special privilege accorded by the pope for extraordinary needs of a certain year, sometimes as a
fixed and permanent right. Both bishops and popes
at times claimed this right. Sometimes the popes
exacted it only from the benefices to which they
had reserved the right to present. Out of this right
developed the later papal annates strictly so called.
To the class of feudal payments belong those which
were levied on the estate of a deceased cleric, when
in the fourteenth century the clergy gained liberty
to dispose of their property by will. Sometimes the
clergy were required to leave a fixed proportion to
the Church; in other cases to submit their wills to
the rural dean for probate and pay a fee to him.

The decay of church life after the fourteenth century gave rise to a number of new forms of payment or modifications of existing ones. To this
period belongs the absence-money
4. Develop- paid to the bishop for dispensation
ment from from the obligation of residence, gen-
the Four- erally by clerics who possessed more
teenth than one benefice. The pope, when-
Century. ever as metropolitan or patriarch he
consecrated a bishop, claimed the *ob-
latio* spoken of above. In fourteenth-century documents such payments occur under various titles, or
servitia cameræ papæ, servitia communia, and by
the end of that century they are fixed at a maximum of a year's income. From this time, in addition, the popes claimed (at first occasionally and
then definitely) the *jus deportuum* to the extent of
half the first year's income from all benefices the
appointment to which was reserved. As this class
of benefices was always increasing, opposition to
this payment developed in more than one national

Church, particularly in the German. In England the papal annates were transferred to the crown at the Reformation; in the reign of Anne they were formed into a fund (Queen Anne's Bounty; q.v.) for the augmentation of the poorer livings. As regarded Germany, the arrangements were regulated at the Council of Constance in 1418, the provisions of which resulted in the practical abolition of annates in Germany, as well as in Belgium, France, and Spain. The so-called *quindennia*, whose collection every fifteen years was decreed by Paul II., also never became practically operative there; these were payments in compensation for the loss of annates from such reserved benefices as had been incorporated with others, in which therefore no vacancies ever occurred. The *servitia*, however, both the *communia* and the smaller chancery fees connected with them, were still to be paid to the pope; and these in common parlance often took the name of annates. The Council of Basel, in agreement with the German princes, talked of abolishing them entirely; but the Concordat of Vienna in 1448 left the matter where the Council of Constance had left it, except that after that time the tax gradually rose in amount, and was paid in one sum instead of two. In the later concordats and bulls of circumscription (see CONCORDATS AND DELIMITING BULLS), the annates are usually retained and their amount designated. It became customary, however, in later times for an individual agreement to be reached at the appointment of each new bishop, by which a lump sum was paid considerably smaller than that named in the older documents. The whole subject was considered at the Council of Trent. The result was partly the regulation of the older imposts, partly the creation of a new one, which the bishop was authorized to levy on all the beneficed clergy in his diocese, using the proceeds to found and maintain the clerical seminaries which the council wished to see established. This is called *alumnaticum* or *seminaristicum*.

The payments which remain nowadays of all this complicated system may be classified according as they are paid by all members of the Church or only
5. Present by the clergy, or again only by the
System. beneficed clergy; those which are received by all the clergy, or the bishop, or the pope alone; those which are properly called taxes, and those which are rather fees. In the Roman Catholic Church at present those paid by all members include surplice (see STOLE FEES) and dispensation fees, the former received by all the clergy, the latter by the bishop or pope; tithes, payments for church-building, and the voluntary offerings whose amount is more or less fixed by custom; and, in certain countries, especially some of the German states, a tax regulated by the government for the support of public worship. The clergy, again, pay fees for their letters of orders, letters dimissory and of approbation, dispensations, etc. The taxes formerly levied on the clergy are not now (with the exception of a possible universal tax in case of necessity, as described above) prescribed by the common law of the Church; local laws provide for procurations, inheritance duty, the *alumnaticum*, and the *annus carentiæ* (q.v.). The

State formerly exercised a supervision in many places over these taxes, that they might not fall too heavily on any subject. See IMMUNITY.

(E. FRIEDBERG†.)

BIBLIOGRAPHY: On I., besides the literature under TITHE; and TAXATION, consult: J. Wellhausen, *Prolegomena*, 4th ed., pp. 149 sqq., Berlin, 1895, Eng. transl. of earlier ed., Edinburgh, 1885; B. Stade, *Biblische Theologie des A. T.*, i. § 84, Tübingen, 1905; Benzinger,⊥*Archäologie*, pp. 382–386; Nowack, *Archäologie*, vol. ii.; *EB*, iv. 4905–16; *JE*, xii. 69–70. On II. consult: L. Thomassin, *Vetus et nova ecclesiæ disciplina circa beneficia*, III., ii. 32 sqq., Paris, 1728; G. Phillips, *Kirchenrecht*, v. 235, 238, vii. 438, 7 vols., Regensburg, 1852–72; P. Woker, *Das kirchliche Finanzwesen der Päpste*, Nördlingen, 1878; A. Gottlob, *Aus der Camera Apostolica des XV. Jahrhunderts*, Innsbruck, 1889; L. König, *Die päpstliche Kammer unter Clemens V. und Johann XXII.*, Vienna, 1894; E. Friedberg, *Kirchenrecht*, §§ 171–173, 5th ed., Leipsic, 1903; J. P. Kirch, *Die päpstlichen Annaten in Deutschland während des 14. Jahrhunderts*, Paderborn, 1903.

TAXES, TAX-GATHERERS (PUBLICANS):

The earliest notice of a species of taxes in the Old Testament is I Kings x. 15, as derived as toll from commerce in return for protection; a standing impost is mentioned (Ezra iv. 13, 20, vii. 24). Such taxes were levied by the Persians, Ptolemies and Seleucidæ (qq.v.), and Romans in the subjected countries upon exports and imports, and were collected not immediately by the State but through those who bid for the privilege for certain periods, a yearly sum being contracted for yearly, all excess going into the collector's purse and deficiencies being supplied from the same. Little is known of Palestinian tax-gatherers of the time of Christ. Palestine was in three districts, at the frontiers of which probably toll was collected for the respective rulers. So Levi (Matt. ix. 9) at Capernaum collected for Herod Antipas, and Zaccheus at Jericho (Luke xix. 1–2) for the Romans. Among the Romans companies of the equestrian order often united for the purpose, and the office had no necessary taint, except for the lower ranks of officials; but among the Jews it was despised, the official was regarded as on an equality with incendiaries and bandits, and his entire family suffered under social and religious ostracism. This was due to the facts that the native Jewish impost was laid for purposes of religion only, that the impost of the ruling power tended to protect and continue foreign domination, and that it was the means of oppression, the collectors often becoming rich. Tax-gatherers and sinners were classed together. The graciousness of Jesus toward tax-gatherers was shown not to the office, but to the person, and gained for him the hatred of the Jews. The two striking cases are Matthew and Zaccheus (Luke v. 27 sqq., xix. 1–10). Compare TAXATION.

(R. ZEHNPFUND.)

BIBLIOGRAPHY: L. Herzfeld, *Handelsgeschichte der Juden des Altertums*, pp. 160–163, Brunswick, 1879; Rémondière, *De la levée des impôts en droit romains*, Montauban, 1884; J. Marquardt, *Römische Staatsverwaltung*, ii. 261–270, 289–293, Leipsic, 1885; A. Edersheim, *Life and Times of Jesus the Messiah*, i. 514 sqq., New York, 1896; Schürer, *Geschichte*, i. 473–479, Eng. transl., I., ii. 65–71; *DB*, iii. 172–173, extra volume, pp. 394–396; *DCG*, ii. 455; *JE*, x. 265–266; and literature under TAXES.

TAYLOR, BARNARD COOK:

Baptist; b. at Holmdel, N. J., May 20, 1850. He was educated at Brown University (B.A., 1874) and Crozer Theological Seminary (1877). With this institution he has since been connected as instructor in Hebrew (1877–80), associate professor of Biblical interpretation (1880–83), and professor of Old-Testament literature and exegesis (since 1883). He has written *Outline Analysis of the Books of the Bible* (Philadelphia, 1892) and *Historical Books of the Old Testament* (1895).

TAYLOR, CHARLES: Church of England; b. in London May 27, 1840; d. at Nuremberg, Germany, Aug. 12, 1908. He was educated at St. John's College, Cambridge (B.A., 1862; M.A., 1865); was ordained priest 1867; became a fellow of his college, 1864, and master, 1881. He was an examiner at St. David's College, Lampeter, Wales, 1874–1877; vice-chancellor of Cambridge, 1887–88; and alderman of the borough of Cambridge, 1889–95. He was select preacher at Cambridge in 1887, 1893, 1899, and after 1876 was an honorary fellow of King's College, London. His works embrace: *The Gospel in the Law, a Critical Examination of the Citations from the Old Testament in the New* (London, 1869); *The Dirge of Coheleth Discussed and Literally Interpreted* (1874); *Sayings of the Jewish Fathers, including Pirke Aboth, etc., in Hebrew and English, with Critical and Illustrative Notes* (1877; second enlarged edition, with a Cairo Fragment of Aquila's Version of the Old Testament, 1897; appendix, 1899); *The Teaching of the Twelve Apostles, with Illustrations from the Talmud* (Cambridge, 1886); *The Witness of Hermas to the Four Gospels* (1892); *The Oxyrhyncus Logia and the Apocryphal Gospels* (London, 1899); *The Wisdom of Ben Sira, Portions of Ecclesiasticus from Hebrew Manuscripts in the Cairo Genizah Collection now at Cambridge* (in collaboration with S. Schechter; Cambridge, 1899); *Cairo Genizah Palimpsests, including a Fragment of Psalm xxii. according to Origen's Hexapla* (1900); *Shepherd of Hermas* (2 vols., London, 1903–06); and *The Oxyrhyncus Sayings of Jesus* (1905).

TAYLOR, DAN: Founder of New Connection of General Baptists; b. at North Owram (2 m. n. of Halifax), Yorkshire, England, Dec. 21, 1738; d. in London Dec. 2, 1816. He began work as a miner with his father at the age of five, came under Methodist influences when fifteen, joined the Wesleyans in 1759, began to preach for them in 1761, but withdrew in 1763, and was immersed in 1763, taking the pastorate at Wadsworth of the General Baptist Church, the same year. He became dissatisfied with the Unitarian drift in this connection, and sought to arrest it. Failing, he, together with the Barton Independent Baptists, formed, in June, 1770, the New Connection of General Baptists (see BAPTISTS, I., 3, § 3). He preached at Halifax from 1772, where a church was organized in 1782, of which he became pastor 1783; in 1785 he became a colleague at Church Street, Whitechapel, London, and in 1794 sole pastor. He was a tutor in the General Baptist Evangelical Academy at Mile End, London, 1798–1813, retaining his pastorate meanwhile. He wrote copiously and ably on the theological questions of the day, and also shaped the course of his denomination. He was its leading spirit for nearly half a century, founded its college in 1797, and started

and edited its magazine, 1798. His chief literary works are: *Compendious View of Christian Baptism* (London, 1772); *Fundamentals of Religion in Faith and Practice* (Leeds, 1775); *Dissertations on Singing in the Worship of God* (2 parts, London, 1787); *Eternity of Future Punishment* (1789); and *Essay on the Truth and Inspiration of the Holy Scriptures* (1790).

BIBLIOGRAPHY: A. Taylor, *Memoirs of Rev. Dan Taylor*, London, 1820; W. Underwood, *Life of Rev. Dan Taylor*, ib. 1870; *DNB*, lv. 405–406. References will be found also in the literature on Baptists dealing with this period.

TAYLOR, GEORGE BOARDMAN: Baptist; b. at Richmond, Va., Dec. 27, 1832. He was educated at Richmond College (A.B., 1850), and, after teaching and studying law (1850–52), studied at the University of Virginia (1852–54). He has held pastorates at the Franklin Square Church, Baltimore (1854–55), and at Staunton, Va. (1855–73), being also a confederate chaplain in the Civil War. He was twice appointed chaplain of the University of Virginia (1869–71 and 1885–87). In 1873 he was sent by the Foreign Mission Board of the Southern Baptist Convention to take charge of their mission in Italy, which position he held until 1904, while since 1901 he has been professor of systematic theology in the Baptist Theological School at Rome. In theology he is a progressive conservative. He has written *Baptists—Who They are and what They have Done* (4 vols., Philadelphia, 1872–73); *Italy and the Italians* (1898); and *Manuale di Teologia Sistematica* (Florence, 1906).

TAYLOR, GRAHAM: Congregationalist; b. at Schenectady, N. Y., May 2, 1851. He was graduated from Rutgers College (A.B., 1870) and from the New Brunswick Theological Seminary (1873). He was pastor of the Reformed Church, Hopewell, N. Y. (1873–80), and the Fourth Congregational Church, Hartford, Conn. (1880–92); professor of practical theology at the Hartford Theological Seminary (1888–92); was appointed professor of sociology at the Chicago Theological Seminary in 1892, professorial lecturer at the University of Chicago in 1903, and director of the Chicago Institute of Social Science in 1906, all of which positions he still holds. He founded The Commons, a sociological settlement in Chicago, and has exerted a wide influence as arbiter in labor troubles.

TAYLOR, ISAAC: English lay theologian; b. at Lavenham (28 m. e.s.e. of Cambridge) Aug. 17, 1787; d. at Stanford Rivers (7 m. n.e. of Charing Cross, London) June 28, 1865. Early in life he entered the Established Church; after following for a while the profession of engraver and artist, he turned his attention to literature and inventions. He invented a very ingenious engraving machine which was eventually used for patterns upon rollers for calico-printing. His intellectual activities were largely in the Baconian and patristic lines of study, and as an author he was very prolific and original. His works embrace *Elements of Thoughts* (London, 1822); *History of Transmission of Ancient Books to Modern Times* (1827); *The Process of Historical Proof* (1828); *Natural History of Enthusiasm* (1829); *New Model of Christians Missions to Popish,*

Mahomedan and Pagan Nations Explained (1829);
Fanaticism (1833); *Spiritual Despotism* (1835);
Physical Theory of Another Life (1836); *Ancient
Christianity, and the Doctrine of the Oxford Tracts
for the Times* (1839); *Loyola and Jesuitism in its
Rudiments* (1849); *Wesley and Methodism* (1851);
The Restoration of Belief (1855); *Logic in Theology
. . . Essays* (1859); *Ultimate Civilization . . .
Essays* (1860); *Spirit of Hebrew Poetry* (1861);
and *Considerations on the Pentateuch* (1863).

BIBLIOGRAPHY: A fundamental source for a life is his own
Personal Recollections, London, 1864; and his *Memorials
of the Taylor Family of Ongar*, 2 vols., ib. 1867. Consult
further: Sir J. Stephen, *Essays in Ecclesiastical Biography*, pp. 585–633, ib. 1868; *DNB*, lv. 417–419.

TAYLOR, JAMES HUDSON: Founder of the
China Inland Mission; born at Barnsley (18 m. s.
of Leeds), Yorkshire, England, May 21, 1832; d. at
Changsha (340 m. n. of Canton), China, June 3,
1905. His father was an eloquent and able Methodist local preacher and his mother a woman of more
than ordinary sweet and patient spirit. Hudson
Taylor combined the ability of his father with the
gentle disposition of his mother. He was converted
through the reading of a tract at the age of fifteen,
and not long afterward passed through a remarkable
experience, at which time he dedicated himself to
God for whatever service might be appointed. Unknown to himself, his father, who had been deeply
interested in China, had prayed that his son might
go to that land as a missionary, and very early,
through the reading of Walter Henry Medhurst's
China (London, 1838), the thoughts of young Taylor
were directed to that country.

With a view to preparing himself for his lifework, he engaged as assistant to a physician at
Hull, and subsequently studied medicine at the
London Hospital. The great interest awakened in
China through the Taiping rebellion, which was
then erroneously supposed to be a mass movement
toward Christianity, together with the glowing but
exaggerated reports made by Carl Friedrich August
Gutzlaff concerning China's accessibility, led to the
founding of the China Evangelization Society, to
the service of which Hudson Taylor offered himself
and on Sept. 19, 1853, he sailed for China before the
completion of his medical studies. The six years
from 1854 to 1860 were spent in Shanghai, Swatow,
and Ningpo, working sometimes in company with
older missionaries of other societies and especially
with William Chalmers Burns of the English Presbyterian Mission. During this period he retired from
the China Evangelization Society, which subsequently ceased to exist, and continued as an independent worker, trusting God to supply his need.
His experiences of God's faithfulness in meeting his
own personal needs and the needs of a hospital at
Ningpo, of which he had taken charge, had much to
do with the subsequent step of founding the China
Inland Mission. While at Ningpo he married Miss
Maria Dyer, daughter of the Rev. Samuel Dyer of
the London Missionary Society. Of the children
born by this marriage, three survive their father's
decease, and two are to-day missionaries in China.

Invalided home in 1860, he spent the next five
years in England, and, in company with the Rev.

Frederick Foster Gough of the Church Missionary
Society, completed the revision of a version of the
New Testament in the colloquial of Ningpo for the
British and Foreign Bible Society, and also finished
his medical course. To arouse interest in the great
Middle Kingdom he published a book entitled
China, its Spiritual Need and Claims (London, 1865,
8th ed., 1890), which has been much used in calling
forth sympathy for China and volunteers for the
field, who began to go out in 1862, the first being
James J. Meadows. In 1865, at Brighton, Taylor
definitely dedicated himself to God for the founding of a new society to undertake the evangelization
of inland China. In May, 1866, he, with his wife
and children and a party of sixteen missionaries,
sailed for China. Thus was definitely launched that
organization which, on Jan. 1, 1911, had 968 missionaries (including wives) connected with it, and
in the support of which more than £1,471,000 had
been contributed in answer to prayer and without
public or private solicitation of funds. From the
founding of the mission in 1865 Taylor's time became more and more occupied as general director
of a growing work. His duties necessitated extensive journeys in China and frequent visits to the
home country. In 1888 a wider ministry was commenced through the formation of a home center in
North America. This arose through Taylor's presence at the Northfield Convention (see MOODY,
DWIGHT LYMAN). Two years later another center
was founded in Australasia. Various visits to the
continent of Europe led to the inception of associate missions, which recognized Taylor as their general director on the field. In Jan., 1911, these associate missions had 216 workers on the field.

The constant pressure and increasing strain inseparable from such a work frequently threatened
a serious breakdown; but Taylor, though far from
strong as a child, manifested remarkable recuperative powers. In 1900, however, at the New York
Conference, the first serious signs of failing health
began to manifest themselves. Having already associated Dixon Edward Hoste with himself in the
directorate of the mission, he slowly resigned his
great responsibilities, still seeking to assist the work
as consulting director while living quietly in retirement in Switzerland. His second wife (née Faulding), to whom he had been married in 1871, and by
whom he had two children, died in the summer of
1904. Early in 1905 Taylor determined, though
extremely feeble, to pay another visit to China.
After visiting various centers he reached Changsha,
the capital of the previously anti-foreign province
of Hunan, where he suddenly and peacefully passed
from his labors. His remains were interred at
Chinkiang, by the side of his first wife and those of
his children who had died in China.

As a Bible student Taylor was unique. Holding
firmly to the plenary inspiration of the Scriptures
and putting them to daily test in his life and work,
he became a most helpful and remarkable expositor,
his Bible readings being greatly appreciated at the
various conventions held in Europe and North
America. As a leader of men and careful organizer
he had preeminent gifts. Being convinced of his
duty, every detail was carefully thought out and

arranged for, and then no subsequent difficulty or opposition was allowed to daunt him. Gifted with the power to command sleep whenever needed, he labored night and day, resting only when exhausted nature compelled him. No day, however, was entered upon without a period of quiet prayer and Bible study. James Hudson Taylor was, to quote the pregnant words of Prof. Gustav Warneck, " A man full of the Holy Ghost and of faith, of entire surrender to God and his call, of great self-denial, heart-felt compassion, rare power in prayer, marvelous organizing faculty, energetic initiative, indefatigable perseverance, and of astonishing influence with men, and withal of child-like humility." Taylor was the author of: *Union and Communion* (London, 1893); *A Retrospect* (1894); *Separation and Service* (1898); and *A Ribband of Blue, and other Bible Studies* (1899).   MARSHALL BROOMHALL.

BIBLIOGRAPHY: M. G. Guinness, *Story of the China Inland Mission*, 2 vols., London, 1893; M. Broomhall, *Pioneer Work in Hunan*, ib. 1906; idem, *The Chinese Empire, a General and Missionary Survey*, ib. 1908; idem, *Faith and Facts as Illustrated in the Hist. of the China Inland Mission*, ib. 1909.

TAYLOR, JEREMY: English bishop, theologian, and devotional writer; b. at Cambridge Aug. 15, 1613; d. at Lisburn (8 m. s.w. of Belfast), Ireland, Aug. 13, 1667. He studied at Gonville and Gaius College, Cambridge (B.A., 1630–31; M.A., 1633–34; D.D., Oxford, 1642); by doing occasional duty for Thomas Risden, divinity lecturer at St. Paul's, London, he attracted the attention of Archbishop Laud, who sent him to Oxford, 1635, and procured for him a fellowship, 1636, made him his chaplain, and probably secured for him appointment as royal chaplain; he was made rector of Uppingham, Rutland, 1638; probably in 1642 he accompanied the king to Oxford, and it is likely that he was then (though not formally till 1644) deprived of his living; in 1643 he was made rector of Overstone, Northamptonshire; in 1644 he was a prisoner with the army of the Commonwealth. In 1645 he became one of the principals in a school at Newton Hall, Carmarthenshire, also chaplain to Richard Vaughan, earl of Carbery. This period was one of the most fruitful in his life; then he published his *Theologia eklektike; a Discourse of the Liberty of Prophesying* (1646), a plea for deprived Episcopal clergymen; his *Great Exemplar . . . Life and Death of . . . Jesus Christ* (1649); *Rule and Exercises of Holy Living* (1650); *Rule and Exercises of Holy Dying* (1651). The two last named with his *Worthy Communicant* (not published till 1660) are among the most noted and worthy devotional books in the English language. A number of sermons followed, including his *Discourse on Baptism* (1652); to this period is chargeable also *The Real Presence and Spirituall of Christ in the Blessed Sacrament Proved . . . against Transubstantiation* (1654), and *Polemical and Moral Discourses* (1657). Meanwhile he had resumed relations with London in 1653, preached there occasionally in 1654, and for reasons unknown, he was a prisoner in Chepstow in 1654 and again in 1655; in 1657–58 Taylor ministered to a small body of Episcopalians in London. The next year he was invited to accept a weekly lectureship at Lisburn, County Antrim, Ireland, which after

some hesitation he accepted, receiving from Cromwell papers for his protection, but in 1660 he was again in London, where he published his *Doctor dubitantium or the Rule of Conscience*, favorably noticed by Hallam as an " extensive and learned work on casuistry "; the work was dedicated to Charles II. On the restoration of episcopacy he was raised in 1660–61 to the bishopric of Down and Connor, to which Dromore was afterward added, but found his course difficult as a bishop, the Presbyterians especially furnishing trouble to which he replied by frequent depositions of those who refused to recognize episcopal jurisdiction. He desired translation to an English see, but his request was passed by, and he was left to finish his life in uncongenial surroundings. Besides the works named above, special mention should be made of his *Discourse of Friendship* (1657); he also issued a large number of sermons. His *Whole Works* were edited by Reginald Heber (15 vols., London, 1822; revised edition by C. P. Eden, 10 vols., 1847–52). The *Works*, ed. T. S. Hughes (5 vols., 1831), consist of sermons and the *Holy Living* and *Holy Dying*. *Poems and Verse Translations*, ed. A. B. Grosart, was issued 1870.

Taylor has been called " the Chrysostom of England," surpassing in brilliancy of imagination his Greek antetype. For succeeding generations his fame rests on the three devotional works especially noted above.

BIBLIOGRAPHY: The best of the earlier lives, perhaps absolutely the best, is that by Heber, as revised by Eden, in the *Whole Works*, ut sup. Consult further: H. K. Bonney, *The Life of . . . Jeremy Taylor*, London, 1815; R. E. A. Willmott, *Bishop Jeremy Taylor, his Predecessors, Contemporaries, and Successors*, London, 1847; A. Barry, *Jeremy Taylor, the English Chrysostom*, in J. E. Kempe, *Classic Preachers of the English Church*, 2 ser., London, 1877; F. W. Farrar, in A. Barry, *Masters in English Theology*, London, 1878; W. H. D. Abrams, *Great English Churchmen*, London, 1879; E. H. May, *Dissertation on the Life, Theology, and Times of Jeremy Taylor*, London, 1892; W. E. Collins, ed., *Typical English Churchmen*, London, 1902; E. Gosse, *Life of Jeremy Taylor*, London and New York, 1904; D. Merriman, *Jeremy Taylor and Religious Liberty in the English Church*, Worcester, Mass., 1906; G. Worley, *Jeremy Taylor; Sketch of his Life with a popular Exposition of his Works*, new ed., London, 1907; E. George, *Seventeenth Century Men of Latitude. Forerunners of the new Theology*, London and New York, 1908; *DNB*, lv. 422–429; Julian, *Hymnology*, p. 1118.

TAYLOR, JOHN: Unitarian theologian and Hebrew scholar; b. at Scotforth (2 m. s. of Lancaster) 1694; d. at Warrington (20 miles e. of Liverpool), Lancashire, Mar. 5, 1761. His first theological studies were made in 1709, under Thomas Dixon, who had just established, at Whitehaven, a non-conformist academy for the preparation of students for the Presbyterian and Congregational ministries. Here he began to acquire that knowledge of Hebrew which was destined one day to bear rich fruit. Leaving Whitehaven, he studied under Thomas Hill, near Derby, perfecting himself especially in classical knowledge. Before being ordained to the ministry he became connected, Apr. 7, 1715, with a non-conformist chapel at Kirkstead, Lincolnshire; he was ordained Apr. 11, 1716, by dissenting ministers in Derbyshire. In 1733 he became the colleague of the Presbyterian minister, Peter Finch (d. Oct. 6, 1754), in Norwich, and in 1757 he was appointed to the divinity chair at Warrington Academy. Here his health broke down, owing in great part to the disputes in which he became engaged. He had serious differences with the rector, John Seddon, and wrote strongly against the scheme which the latter was advocating of introducing fixed liturgical forms into non-conformist worship.

It was not until Taylor had passed middle life that a radical change in his theological views seems to have taken place. Shortly after undertaking his new post at Norwich, he read the *Scripture Doctrine of the Trinity*, by Samuel Clarke (q.v., 4). As a consequence his belief in that central dogma suffered eclipse, and in *A Paraphrase with Notes on the Epistle to the Romans*, etc. (London, 1745, Dublin, 1746), he freely discloses his Arian sentiments. Naturally enough he abandoned the Calvinistic view of human nature; and his work, *The Scripture Doctrine of Original Sin* (London, 1740, 4th ed., enlarged, 1767), which called forth the famous reply of the elder Edwards, was more instrumental than any work of its kind in undermining the root ideas of the Calvinistic system both in England and in the American colonies. Deviating as far as he did from the forms of traditional orthodoxy, his treatise on prayer (*The Scripture Account of Prayer*, London, 1761, 2d ed., 1762), written at the close of his life, would seem to negative the description of Wesley that Taylor's views were " old deism in a new dress." Some of his other works not mentioned above are: *The Scripture Doctrine of Atonement* (London, 1751); and *The Lord's Supper Explained upon Scripture Principles* (London, 1756). Especially noteworthy is *The Hebrew Concordance* (2 vols., folio, London, 1754–57), adapted to the English Bible and disposed after the manner of Buxtorf, which held first rank among works of its kind for almost a century, and is an enduring monument to the author's accuracy and industry.

BIBLIOGRAPHY: E. Harwood, *Sermon Occasioned by the Death of . . . J. Taylor, with Some Account of his Character and Writings*, London, 1761; E. Taylor, in *Universal Theological Magazine*, July, 1804; *Monthly Repository*, 1826, pp. 482–483; L. Stephen, *English Thought in the Eighteenth Century*, ii. 418–419, New York, 1881; *DNB*, lv. 439–440 (has references to scattering notices).

TAYLOR, NATHANIEL WILLIAM: Congregationalist preacher, teacher, and author; b. at New Milford, Conn., June 23, 1786; d. at New Haven Mar. 10, 1858. He was graduated at Yale College in 1807; studied theology with President Dwight, and became pastor of the First Church in New Haven in 1811, which office he resigned in 1822, to take the chair of dogmatic theology in the theological department of Yale College, where he continued to teach until his death. As a preacher he was singularly impressive, combining solidity and clearness of thought with a remarkable eloquence. Unusual results followed upon his sermons, especially in connection with Revivals (q.v.). From early youth deeply interested in the problems of theology, and endowed with metaphysical talents of a very high order, he worked out, on the basis of the previous New England theology, an elaborate system, which gained numerous adherents, and powerfully affected theological thought and preaching in America beyond the circle of its professed

advocates. For his labors, views, and influence in this direction see NEW-ENGLAND THEOLOGY. His most noted sermon was the *Concio ad Clerum* (New Haven, 1828), though he had previously issued others, e.g., one on *Regeneration* (1816). After his death his *Practical Sermons*, ed. Noah Porter, were published (New York, 1858); also *Lectures on the Moral Government of God* (2 vols., 1859); and *Essays and Lectures upon Select Topics in Revealed Religion* (1859).

BIBLIOGRAPHY: G. P. Fisher, *Discussions in History and Theology*, New York, 1880; W. Walker, in *American Church History Series*, iii. 355–361, New York, 1894; idem, *Ten New England Leaders*, pp. 398–402 et passim, ib. 1901; B. N. Martin, in *New Englander*, vol. xvii.; N. Porter, in *New Englander*, vol. xviii.; F. H. Foster, *Genetic Hist. of New England Theology*, Chicago, 1907.

TAYLOR, WALTER ROSS: United Free Church of Scotland; b. at Thurso (80 m. n.e. of Inverness), Caithness, Apr. 11, 1838. He was educated at the University of Edinburgh and New College, Edinburgh, from which he was graduated in 1861. He was minister of East Kilbride Free Church in 1862–1868 and since 1868 has been minister of Kelvinside Free Church, Glasgow. He is convener of the committee of the Glasgow United Free Church Theological College, chairman of the Glasgow United Free Church Normal College, and vice-president of the National Bible Society of Scotland. His theological position is liberal, and he is an advocate of the union of churches and the revision of the creed. He has written *Religious Thought and Church Life in Scotland in the Nineteenth Century* (Edinburgh, 1900).

TAYLOR, WILLIAM: Methodist Episcopal missionary bishop; b. in Rockbridge County, Va., May 2, 1821; d. at Palo Alto, Cal., May 18, 1902. He went from his father's farm and tanyard into the ministry, 1842; was regular itinerant, 1842–49; missionary in California, 1849–56; evangelist in the Eastern States and Canada until 1862, when he went to Europe, engaging in evangelistic work; he traveled over the continent, then to Egypt, the Holy Land, Australia, Africa, the West Indies, and India. He organized many self-supporting churches in India, and as a result of his work the South India conference and Madras conference were organized. Later he visited Central and South America. He was elected a bishop in 1884, and going again to Africa he established a chain of mission stations on the Congo and elsewhere. His works embrace *Seven Years' Preaching in San Francisco* (New York, 1857); *California Life Illustrated* (1858); *Christian Adventures in South Africa* (London, 1867); *Four Years' Campaign in India* (New York, 1875); *Our South American Cousins* (1878); and *Ten Years of Self-supporting Missions in India* (1882).

TAYLOR, WILLIAM MACKERGO: Congregationalist; b. at Kilmarnock (20 m. s.w. of Glasgow), Scotland, Oct. 23, 1829; d. in New York Feb. 8, 1895. He was graduated from the University of Glasgow, 1849, and from the United Presbyterian Theological Seminary, Edinburgh, 1852; became pastor of the parish of Kilmaurs, Ayrshire, 1853; of Derby Road Church, Liverpool, England, 1855; visited the United States in 1871, and became pastor of the Broadway Tabernacle (Congregational), New York, 1872. He was Lyman Beecher lecturer in Yale Seminary, 1876 and 1886; L. P. Stone lecturer in Princeton Seminary, 1880; and editor of *The Christian at Work*, 1876–80. He was a preacher in the front rank, and enjoyed an international reputation. He was compelled by a stroke of paralysis to retire in 1893. He was the author of *Life Truths: Being Discourses on Christian Doctrine and Duty* (Liverpool, 1862); *The Miracles: Helps to Faith, not Hindrances* (Edinburgh, 1865); *The Lost Found, and the Wanderer Welcomed* (1870); *David, King of Israel* (New York, 1875); *Elijah the Prophet* (1876); *The Ministry of the Word* (Yale Lectures; 1876); *Peter the Apostle* (1876); *Daniel the Beloved* (1878); *Moses the Lawgiver* (1879); *The Gospel Miracles in their Relation to Christ and Christianity* (Princeton lectures; 1880); *The Limitations of Life, and Other Sermons* (1880); *Paul the Missionary* (1881); *Contrary Winds, and other Sermons* (1883); *John Knox, a Biography* (1885); *The Parables of our Savior; Expounded and Illustrated* (1886); *Joseph, the Prime Minister* (1886); *The Scottish Pulpit from the Reformation to the Present Day* (1887); *The Miracles of our Savior, Expounded and Illustrated* (1890); *Ruth, the Gleaner; Esther, the Queen* (1891); *Paul the Missionary* (1892); and *The Boy Jesus, and Other Sermons* (1893).

TE DEUM: The title of the so-called Ambrosian hymn, taken from the opening words: Te Deum laudamus. This hymn has been regarded from early times as the classic expression of Christian faith and placed on a par with the liturgical confessions. In the Roman hymnals it bears the designation: " Hymn in honor of the Holy Trinity " and " Hymn of St. Ambrose and St. Augustine," the former in reference to its contents and the latter in agreement with the legend that, at the time of the baptism of Augustine, in 387, Ambrose intoned the hymn and sang it alternately with Augustine. That Ambrose and Augustine were the originators of the hymn, in the sense of the legend that, carried away by the inspiration of the incident, they improvised it, can not be held, though it is possible that the memory of a real event on that memorable occasion endured, especially if it was a hymn new to the community and one that had been borrowed by Ambrose from the Eastern Church, and was first used in public on that occasion.

The hymn in its present form is no original and strictly uniform creation. Verses 1–21 are composed in rhythmic prose and the other verses in ordinary prose (Lejay, in *Revue Critique*, 1893, i. 192). Verses 1–21 are therefore probably of earlier date than the rest. It is consequently no mistake to regard these verses (as far as *numerari*) as the foundation of the Te Deum, which then appears as a psalm with an antiphon, in about the following form:

1. *Te Deum laudamus, te Dominum confitemur.* 2. *Te æternum patrem omnis terra veneratur.* 3. *Tibi omnes angeli, tibi cœli et universæ potestates,* 4. *Tibi Cherubim et Seraphim incessabili voce proclamant,* 5. *Sanctus, sanctus, sanctus Dominus Deus Sabaoth.* 6. *Pleni sunt cœli et terra majestatis tuæ.* (7. *Te gloriosus apostolorum chorus,* 8. *Te prophetarum laudabilis numerus,* 9. *Te martyrum candidatus laudat exercitus.*) 10. *Te per orbem terrarum sancta confitetur ecclesia,* 11. *Patrem immensæ majestatis.* 12.

Venerandum tuum verum unigenitum-Filium, 13. *Sanctum quoque paraclitum Spiritum.* 14. *Tu rex gloriæ Christe.* 15. *Tu Patris sempiternus es filius.* 16. *Tu ad liberandum suscepturus hominem non horruisti virginis uterum.* 17. *Tu devicto mortis aculeo aperuisti credentibus regna cœlorum.* 18. *Tu ad dexteram Dei sedes in gloria Patris.* 19. *Judex crederis esse venturus.* 20. *Te ergo quæsumus nobis tuis famulis subveni quos precioso sanguine redimisti.* (Antiphon:) 21. *Æterna fac cum sanctis tuis in gloria numerari.*

Verses 22 to the end are derived from the Scriptures (Ps. xxvii. 9, cxlv. 2, cxxiii. 3a, xxxiii. 22, xxxi. 2a), and Dom Pothier believes that the verses were originally a kind of preces in the matins, such as are still recited in the Roman offices at prime and compline, and that only later were they incorporated in the Te Deum (*Der gregorianische Choral*, p. 229, Tournai, 1881). If the melody of the words *Æterna fac cum sanctis tuis . . . æternum*, as well as the close: *In te Domine*, was taken from an introit of an old Greek mass of Dionysius the Areopagite, which has been sung up to modern times at St. Denis near Paris during the octave of the festival of this saint, to the words: *Kyrie theos basileu ouranie pater pantokratōr*, it would be natural to seek the origin of the Te Deum in the Eastern Church, even though no hymn has been found in the Greek language which can be determined to be the Greek original of the Te Deum. The Greek versions mentioned in Julian (*Hymnology*, pp. 1125 sqq.) are evidently translations into Greek of the already existing Latin hymn, made at the beginning of the sixth century. It is possible that it may have been present to the mind of the poet Prudentius (q.v.) in his *Apotheosis*, lines 1019–20, where he connects the verbs *suscipere, liberare, horrere*, precisely in the same way as in verse 16 of the hymn. If the words of Cyprian of Carthage (*De mortalitate*, xxvi.): *Illic apostolorum gloriosus chorus, illic prophetarum exultantium numerus, illic martyrium innumirabilis numerus*, are either an intentional or unintentional allusion to verses 7–9, the original form of the hymn must have been familiar to the Church of the third century. It may have been a psalm of thanksgiving which guided the newly baptized from baptism to the Eucharist. Nicetas of Remesiana and Ambrose of Milan (qq.v.) may share in the honor of the liturgical adaptation and the introduction of the hymn.

The Te Deum belongs to the service of hours; the Benedictine rule concludes therewith the third nocturn on all Sundays and festivals. In the Roman offices it has its place in the matins after the ninth lesson, as a prayer of thanksgiving on all days wherein the festival celebration is a joyous one, therefore on all Sundays (except from Septuagesima to Easter), on all festivals (except the festivals of the Holy Innocents), on the festival octaves and during the entire Easter time. Besides this, it was employed on special occasions " to render thanks to God for the bestowal of great blessings." A German translation existed as early as the ninth century, and there is a prose translation of 1389, and one in Low German. Poetical versions first appeared after Luther's example (see below). The German translation of the text gradually led to its transformation into the form of the song. All others were supplanted by the so-called German Te

Deum: " Grosser Gott, wir loben Dich," which has become an ecclesiastical popular song and has found its way into the Evangelical church. The text is by Ignaz Franz (b. at Prozau, in the district of Frankenstein, Oct. 12, 1719; d. Aug. 19, 1790). Among the melodies which were composed for this text that one has remained the most popular which first appeared in Vienna in 1774, in the " Catholic Hymnal." For Luther, the Te Deum was indispensable, since he wished to see matins and vespers preserved, and the Te Deum seemed of special value to him. Prose translations such as Luther found in the earlier hymnals did not satisfy him. He, therefore, translated the hymn into German, and his version first appeared in the " Hymnal " of Klug, 1529, justly supplanting all others, for " the Latin original was completely transformed into a German poem by Luther, both as to the sense and as to the form." The melody is admirably adapted, and the original character and form of the hymn have been reverently preserved. In the congregational music of the Evangelical church, the " Ambrosian hymn," in spite of Luther's masterly rendering, was forced later to yield its place to the hymn of Martin Rinckart (q.v.) " Nun danket alle Gott," as the German Te Deum of the Evangelical church.

The character and contents of the Te Deum and more especially its liturgical use as a psalm of thanksgiving, were determining factors in the transformations to which it has been so often subjected. In this work musical art has, on the one hand, confined itself to increasing the brilliancy and impressiveness of the Gregorian chant by means of a fuller harmony and the use of many voices, or by the addition of instrumental accompaniment, so that the chant was either simply adapted to several voices or was made the foundation of an elaborate polyphonic symphony. On the other hand, the text was treated in an entirely free and independent manner, and the single verses and the imagery presented by them were transformed into well-rounded and connected sentences. In this way the Te Deum was developed into an antiphon on a grand scale, with a varied combination and graduation of solo and choral passages, and was also embellished with all the splendid coloring of modern orchestration, and so it became a magnificent musical solemnization of thanksgiving. In the Greek Church the place of the Te Deum is taken by the *hymnos akathistos* (i.e., " hymn to be sung standing "), a hymn of thanksgiving for the preservation of city and State from the hands of the Avars (626), addressed to Mary, to whose supplications this preservation was attributed. See AMBROSE, SAINT, OF MILAN; AMBROSIAN CHANT.   H. A. KÖSTLIN†.

BIBLIOGRAPHY: Julian, *Hymnology*, pp. 1119–1134 (elaborate); W. E. Tentzel, *Exercitationes sacræ*, Leipsic, 1692 (still referred to); B. Gavantus, *Thesaurus sacrorum*, ed. C. M. Merati, ii. 147–153, Venice, 1744 (discusses Ambrosian-Augustinian authorship); J. M. Thomasius, *Opera*, ii. 345 sqq., iii. 614 sqq., Rome, 1747 (gives texts and textual variations); W. Palmer, *Origines liturgicæ*, i. 226 sqq., Oxford, 1832; H. A. Daniel, *Thesaurus hymnologicus*, ii. 276–299, Halle, 1844; W. Maskell, *Monumenta ritualia*, ii. 12–14, 229–232, London, 1847 (contains early English versions); E. Thompson, *A Vindication of the Hymn Te Deum laudamus*, London, 1858 (valuable for the versions it gives); F. A. March, *Latin Hymns*, pp. 20–21, 231, New York, 1874 (Latin text and notes);
J. Pothier, *Der gregorianische Choral*, Tournay, 1881; E. C. S. Gibson, in *Church Quarterly Review*, xviii (1884), 1–27 (able and learned); E. Challier, *Grosser Lieder-Katalog*, Giessen, 1886–87; S. Kümmerle, *Encyklopädie der evangelischen Kirchenmusik*, 4 vols., Gütersloh, 1886–1895; J. W. Legg, *Some Imitations of the Te Deum*, London, 1891; S. A. Blackwood, *Te Deum laudamus*, London, 1892; G. M. Dreves, in supplement to *Stimmen aus Maria Laach*, lviii (1893); P. Lejay, *Revue critique*, 1893, i. 192 sqq.; F. Kattenbusch, *Das apostolische Symbol*, i. 404 sqq., Leipsic, 1894; G. Morin, *Revue bénédictine*, Feb., 1894 (names Nicetas of Remesiana as author); H. Kretschmar, *Führer durch den Konzertsaal*, ii. 1, pp. 287–300, Leipsic, 1895; T. Zahn, in *NKZ*, v (1896), 106 sqq.; A. E. Burns, *Introduction to the Creeds and the Te Deum*, London, 1899; idem, *Niceta of Remesiana, his Life and Works*, Cambridge, 1905; J. Wordsworth, *The Te Deum, its Structure*, 2d ed., London, 1903; W. A. Merrill, *Latin Hymns*, pp. 6–7, Boston, 1904 (Latin text); F. Spitta, *Ein feste Burg ist unser Gott. Die Lieder Luthers in ihrer Bedeutung für die evangelische Kirche*, Göttingen, 1905; *KL*, x. 1282–84; *DCA*, ii. 1949–51. Much will be found in the literature under LITURGICS; and SEQUENCES.

TEACHING ORDERS, ROMAN CATHOLIC. See THEOLOGICAL EDUCATION, III.

TEELLINCK, til′link: A family of Dutch Reformed theologians, conspicuous for their labors in behalf of Pietism.

1. Eewoud Teellinck: The eldest member of the family; b. at Zierikzee (31 m. s.w. of Rotterdam), in the island of Schouwen, about 1570; d. at Middelburg (48 m. s.w. of Rotterdam), in the island of Walcheren, 1629. He studied law, in 1598 and 1602 was burgomaster of his native town, and in 1603 was made treasurer general of Zeeland. After 1607 he was elder of the Reformed church at Middelburg, yet found time to write a number of devotional books. Under the pseudonym Alexius Philopator he is said to have written *Querela patriæ: Dat is, Clachte des vaderlants over de teghenwoordighe swaricheden* (Amsterdam, 1617); his regular pen-name was Ireneus Philalethius, signed, e.g., to his *De ereupele bode brengende seeckere tydinge uyt Boemen, met een christelycke wærschouwinge daerover* (Amsterdam, 1621). His writings lament the controversies of the time, which he feared might act to the detriment of practical piety; he urged the necessity of a godly life, exposing himself to the suspicion of stressing unduly good works.

2. Willem Teellinck: Youngest brother of the preceding; b. at Zierikzee Jan. 4, 1579; d. at Middelburg Apr. 8, 1629. He studied law at St. Andrews and Poitiers, and then went to England, where he was profoundly influenced by pietistic Puritans. After studying theology at Leyden for a short time, he was installed minister of Haamstede and Burcht (near his native town) in 1606, where he remained until 1613, when he accepted a call to Middelburg. Here he became a potent factor in religious life, exercising a still wider influence by his numerous writings. He may be said to have begun as a Pietist and to have ended as a mystic, as may be seen from his *Het nieuwe Jerusalem, vertoont in een 'tsamensprekinghe tusschen Christum ende Mariam, sittende aen sijn voeten* (Middelburg, 1635). In an age of controversy he gave many what they needed far more than dogmatic treatises, especially as his own orthodoxy was unimpeached, except by a few of the overzealous, who accused him of caring everything for life and nothing for doctrine. The theme of his sermons, which were essentially simple and practical, and purely Biblical in character, was repentance. He championed the cause of Sabbath observance in his *De rusttijdt ofte tractaet van d'onderhoudinge des christelijken rust-dachs, die men ghemeynlyck den Sondach noemt* (Rotterdam, 1662), and he was the first Reformed pastor in Holland to advocate foreign missions, as shown in his *Ecce Homo, ofte ooghen-salve voor die noch sitten in blintheydt des ghemoedts* (Middelburg, 1622) and *Davids danckbaerheyt voor Gods weldadicheyt* (Amsterdam, 1624). Some of his sermons, etc., were translated into English, such as his *Paulus klacht over zijne natuurlijke verdorvenheid* (Middelburg, 1653; Eng. transl., *Paul's Complaint against his Naturall Corruption*," by C. Harmar, London, 1621). He exercised an influence far beyond Holland, and with his brother Eewoud may be styled the forerunner of the Dutch pietists of the seventeenth and eighteenth centuries.

3. Maximiliaan Teellinck: Eldest son of the preceding; b. at Angers (190 m. s.w. of Paris) 1606; d. at Middelburg Nov. 26, 1653. At the age of twenty he was made minister of the English congregation at Flushing, whence he was called in the following year (1628) to Zierikzee, while from 1640 until his death he was Reformed minister at Middelburg. He published many of his father's works, among them *De worstelinghe eenes bekeerden sondaers* (Flushing, 1631; with a dedication valuable for its biographical material) and *Laetste predikatien* (Amsterdam, 1647). He himself was best known for his political and polemic writings, although mention should be made of his *Verclaringhe ende toeeygheninge over de thien gheboden ende het ghebedt des Herren* (in the second edition of his father's *Huysboeck*, Middelburg, 1650) and *Christelicke onderwijsinge in de leerstukken des geloofs* (1652).

4. Jan Teellinck: Youngest brother of the preceding; b. at Middelburg; d. at Leeuwarden (70 m. n.e. of Amsterdam) May 7, 1674. He resided for a considerable time in England, being minister at Maidstone, and in 1641 was called to the church at Wemeldinge, Zeeland. In 1646–48 he was supply to the English congregation at Middelburg, and in 1649 he was called from Wemeldinge to Flushing, where he remained until 1654, when he became minister at Utrecht. Here he so stubbornly resisted the right of secular authorities to interfere with church affairs, especially in the controversy over benefices, that in 1660 he was forbidden to remain in the city or province of Utrecht. He at once became minister in Arnemuiden, near Middelburg, and in the following year was called to Kampen, whence he went as minister to Leeuwarden in Apr., 1674, a month before his death. Together with his brother Theodorus (d. 1660), he began an edition of his father's works, of which three volumes appeared between 1659 and 1664, and wrote, besides a sermon, *Den vrugtbaermakenden wynstok Christus* (3 parts, Kampen, 1666–67). His spirit and tendency were essentially identical with those of his father and uncle.   (S. D. VAN VEEN.)

BIBLIOGRAPHY: Material on all named in the text is in P. de la Rue, *Geletterd Zeeland*, pp. 169 sqq., 331 sqq., Middleburg, 1734; and B. Glasius, *Godgeleerd Nederland*, sub voce, 3 vols., 's Hertogenbosch, 1851–56, In addition on 1 consult A. Ritschl, *Geschichte des Pietismus*, i. 124 sqq., Bonn, 1880. On 2: W. J. M. Engelberts, *Willem Teellinck*, Amsterdam, 1898; H. Heppe, *Geschichte des Pietismus und des Mysticismus . . . der Niederlande*, pp. 106 sqq., Leyden, 1879; Ritschl, ut sup., pp. 124 sqq.; F. Nagtglas, *Levensberichten van Zeeuwen*, vol. ii., Middelburg, 1893. And on 4: G. Brolikhert, *Vlissingsche Kerkhemel*, pp. 123–130, Vlissingen, 1758.

TELEOLOGY: The term expressing the doctrine that the activity in nature is with reference to ends. Its interest for the religious consciousness lies in its bearing on the theistic proof—the teleological argument. This, the most ancient of all the theistic proofs, received classic expression in Paley's *Natural Theology*, and the *Bridgewater Treatises* (see PALEY, WILLIAM; and BRIDGEWATER TREATISES). The argument to be valid would have to run as follows (cf. I. Kant, *Critique of the Pure Reason*, pp. 536–539, London, 1897): (1) the universe is full of adjustment of parts and of adaptation of means to ends unspeakably rich in content and infinite in extent; (2) the various elements so coordinated and adjusted have in themselves no tendency to the results described, but are related and arranged by a rational (external) disposing principle according to certain ideals and aims; (3) this arrangement can be explained only by reference to an (external) intelligent cause acting freely; (4) the unity of the cause can be certainly inferred from the unity of the reciprocal relations involved in experience and analogy. This argument presupposes that the genera and species of all living beings were created with complete organs and fixed functions, as, e.g., eye and ear. In Christian theology it has been accepted as the teaching of the Scriptures and hence final for rational thought. The effort was made to verify the argument by appeal to existing world facts. While the principle of this proof has never been invalidated, yet in its classical form it has been found liable to serious if not fatal objections. (1) From the changed interpretation of the Genesis story. (2) At best it proves not a creator, but an external and arbitrary contriver (cf. J. Caird, *Introduction to the Philosophy of Religion*, pp. 139–153, London, 1880). (3) Since every individual end is an integral part of the final end, and the final end is hidden from thought, a perfect teleology is impossible (cf. F. Paulsen, *Introduction to Philosophy*, pp. 158–180, New York, 1898). (4) The existence of sin has never been reconciled with a teleological view of the world. The theory of evolution has invalidated the traditional form of the argument, but it has reinstated it in a far more significant and impressive form. It has infinitely increased the evidence of ends and adaptations in nature; it has proposed a new theory of the way in which these ends are realized; it has indefinitely lengthened the processes of this adaptive activity; it has transferred the scene of the activity from that of externality to that of immanence—the teleology is essential and is best illustrated in the animal organism. Whether the cause thus active is infinitely self-conscious with purposeful forethought, can not be fully ascertained by the teleological argument alone. Its task is far more modest. It is not demonstrative but indicative. It first inquires if there is evidence of cosmic activity toward ends, and secondly, if such evidence is forthcoming, this is referred to intelligence.   C. A. BECKWITH.

BIBLIOGRAPHY: J. McCosh and G. Dickie, *Typical Forms and Special Ends in Creation*, Edinburgh, 1855; J. Frohschammer, *Ueber die Aufgabe der Naturphilosophie*, Munich, 1861; P. Wetzel, *Der Zweckbegriff bei Spinoza*, Leipsic, 1873; A. Stadler, *Kants Teleologie*, ib. 1874; P. Janet, *Les Causes finales*, Paris, 1876, Eng. transl., *Final Causes*, 2d ed., Edinburgh, 1883; R. Schellwien, *Das Gesetz der Kausalität in der Natur*, Berlin, 1876; E. F. W. Pflüger, *Die Teleologische Mechanik der lebendigen Natur*, Bonn, 1877; F. V. Baerenbach, *Gedanken über die Teleologie in der Natur*, Leipsic, 1878; G. J. Romanes, *Candid Examination of Theism*, London, 1878; A. Mühry, *Kritik und kurze Darlegung der exacten Naturphilosophie*, 5th ed., Göttingen, 1882; W. B. Carpenter, in *Modern Review*, 1884; P. F. Fitzgerald, *A Treatise on the Principle of Sufficient Reason*, London, 1887; E. Domet de Vorges, *Cause efficiente et cause finale*, Paris, 1889; R. Flint, *Theism*, 7th ed., London, 1889; B. Liebermann, *Der Zweckbegriff bei Trendelenburg*, Meiningen, 1889; F. Erhardt, *Mechanismus und Teleologie: eine Abhandlung über die Principien der Naturforschung*, Leipsic, 1890; W. M. W. Call, *Final Causes: a Refutation*, London, 1891; A. Kohlschmidt, *Kant's Stellung zur Teleologie und Physikotheologie*, Jena, 1894; J. Stier, *Theismus und Naturforschung in ihrem Verhältnis zur Teleologie*, Frankfort, 1896; E. Haughton, *The Evidence of Design in the Constitution of Nature*, London, 1897; C. Brockdorff, *Kants Teleologie*, Kiel, 1898; N. Kaufmann, *Philosophie naturelle d'Aristote: étude de cause finale*, Paris, 1898; P. N. Cossmann, *Elemente der empirischen Teleologie*, Stuttgart, 1899; E. Ebrillard, *Études philosophiques sur les causes premières et les causes finales*, Paris, 1900; E. Ferrière, *La Cause première d'après les données expérimentales*, ib. 1900; J. M. Baldwin, *Development and Evolution*, New York, 1902; S. Prudhomme and C. Richet, *Le Problème des causes finales*, Paris, 1902; J. B. Pettigrew, *Design in Nature*, New York, 1908; A. R. Wallace, *The World of Life*, ib., 1911.

TELESPHORUS, tel″es′fer-us: Pope 127–137. Irenæus (*Hær.*, III., iii. 3, *ANF*, i. 416), followed by Eusebius (*Hist. eccl.*, IV., x., *NPNF*, 2 ser., i. 182), states that he was a martyr; but Eusebius contradicts himself as to the year of Telesphorus' death, saying in his *Hist. eccl.* (ut sup.) that it was in the first year of Antoninus Pius (138), and in his "Chronicle" putting it in the eighteenth year of Hadrian (135). The tradition that this pontiff established the forty days of Lenten fasting and the celebration of the midnight Christmas mass is erroneous. See LITURGICS, III, § 2.   (A. HAUCK.)

BIBLIOGRAPHY: *Liber pontificalis*, ed. Mommsen, in *MGH*, *Gest. pont. Rom.*, i (1898), 12; Jaffé, *Regesta*, p. 6; R. A. Lipsius, *Chronologie der römischen Bischöfe*, pp. 170, 184, 190, Kiel, 1869; J. Langen, *Geschichte der römischen Kirche*, i. 103 sqq., Bonn, 1881; Harnack, *Litteratur*, ii. 1, p. 144; Bower, *Popes*, i. 11; Platina, *Popes*, i. 24–25.

TELFORD, JOHN: English Wesleyan; b. at Wigton (11 m. s.w. of Carlisle), Cumberland, Oct. 5, 1851. He was educated at Didsbury College, Manchester, and at London University, and, after holding various pastorates and being, in 1904, one of the secretaries of the committee which prepared the Methodist Hymn Book, he became, in 1905, editor for the Wesleyan Methodist Connection. He is also editor of the *Wesleyan Methodist Magazine* and of the *London Quarterly Review*. Among his numerous publications mention may be made of his *Life of Charles Wesley* (London, 1886), *Life of John Wesley* (1886), *Two West-End Chapels: or, Sketches of London Methodism from Wesley's Day* (1886), *The Story of Moses and Joshua: Its Lessons for To-Day* (1893), *Makers of our Missions* (1895), *Women in the Mission Field* (1895), *History of Lay Preach-*

ing in the Christian Church (1897), *Story of the Upper Room* (1905), *A Sect that moved the World: Three Generations of Clapham Saints and Philanthropists* (1907), *Man's Partnership with Divine Providence* (1908), and *The Life of James Harrison Rigg* (1909).

TELLER, ROMANUS: German Lutheran; b. at Leipsic Feb. 21, 1703; d. there Apr. 5, 1750. He was educated at the university of his native city (1719–23), and in 1723 was appointed catechist at the Peterskirche in Leipsic. In 1730 he was called to Merseburg, but in the following year returned to the Peterskirche as preacher and first catechist, in 1737 becoming subdeacon at St. Thomas's. He was made deacon there in 1739, and, after again officiating at the Peterskirche after 1740, was chosen pastor of the Thomaskirche in 1745. Meanwhile he was also active in academic circles. He had been appointed associate professor of theology in 1738, and had advanced to a full professorship in 1740; while in 1745 he was made a canon, and in 1748 assessor of the consistory. He is best known for his " English Bible," bearing the title *Die heilige Schrift . . . nebst einer vollständigen Erklärung derselben, welche aus den auserlesensten Anmerkungen verschiedener engländischer Schriftsteller zusammengetragen und zuerst in französischer Sprache an das Licht gestellt* (19 vols., Leipsic, 1749–70), a work of distinctly Reformed tendency, but of which Teller himself was able to edit only two volumes.

(P. WOLFF.)

BIBLIOGRAPHY: A " programm " of the University of Leipsic, *Memoria Telleri*, is given by J. E. Kapp in *Actis historico-ecclesiasticis*, ii. 377, Weimar, 1747. A number of references to biographical lexicons and similar works is given in Hauck-Herzog, *RE*, xix. 475.

TELLER, WILHELM ABRAHAM: German Lutheran and rationalist; b. at Leipsic Jan. 9, 1734; d. at Berlin Dec. 8, 1804. He was educated at the university of his native city (1749–53), and was Sunday evening preacher at the university church (1753–55), catechist at the Peterskirche (1755–60), and Sunday evening preacher at the Nicholaikirche (1760–61). He had published several studies in textual criticism and had already manifested a rationalistic tendency when, in 1761, he was called to Helmstedt as professor of theology, pastor, and general superintendent. He now drew a distinction merely of degree between the Biblical writers and profane poets, denied verbal inspiration, and posited a twofold inspiration of matter and words, dividing the former into dogmatic, prophetic, and historical. His reputation as a leader of the Enlightenment was won by his *Lehrbuch des christlichen Glaubens* (Helmstedt, 1764), in which he prepared the way for rationalistic dogmatics. He laid great stress on method and maintained that divine revelation was intelligible to man, so that forced theological interpretations were to be rejected. He accordingly contrasted the " simple " Gospel with the teachings of the Church, and, manifesting marked Socinian influence, he referred the doctrine of God and divine perfection to natural religion, treated justification somewhat synergistically, refused to discuss the twofold nature of Christ, and ignored the doctrines of the Trinity and original sin. The book evoked a storm of disapproval, so that, though he had powerful friends, he ceased his lectures on dogmatics and in 1767 gladly accepted a call to Berlin as supreme consistorial councilor and provost of Kölln.

At Berlin, in the reign of Frederick the Great, Teller was in his element. He was elected to the Academy of Sciences in 1786, and though he was unsuccessful as a preacher, his printed sermons influenced wide circles. In 1772 he published at Berlin the first edition of his *Wörterbuch des Neuen Testaments zur Erklärung christlicher Lehre*, in which he held that Christianity was designed to be merely " the wisest counsel to an ever ascending blessedness," and that many things must be altered to harmonize with riper religious concepts and changed conditions, so that " kingdom of heaven " means " the Christian Church," " to repent " is " to improve oneself," and " atonement " is " the union of the Jews with other peoples, and thus of all mankind in one religion." This work, which naturally evoked orthodox hostility, and called forth several analogous books of an opposite tendency, received a supplement in his *Religion der Vollkommnern* (Berlin, 1792), in which he urged the abandonment of a number of doctrines, including that of justification, and the furtherance of a practical knowledge of God and of his blessings for the benefit of man, this knowledge leading to good conduct and beneficent activity, while all dogma was to be excluded from sermons, which should be devoted simply to practical Christianity. In this same spirit Teller edited for ten years the *Neues Magazin für Prediger*, which he founded in 1792, and he likewise wrote upon classical and Germanic philology, his *Vollständige Darstellung der deutschen Sprache in Luthers Bibelübersetzung* (2 vols., Berlin, 1794) still being a book of value. Special mention should also be made of his *Anleitung zur Religion überhaupt und zum Allgemeinen des Christentums besonders* (Berlin, 1792), *Sammlung einiger Gebete zum Gebrauch bei öffentlichen Gottesdiensten* (1793), and *Opuscula varii argumenti* (Frankfort-on-the-Oder, 1780).

With the death of Frederick the Great, Teller's position became precarious. Long before he had tried to mold the religious views of the heir-apparent by his anonymous *Valentinian der Erste, oder geheime Unterredungen eines Monarchen mit seinem Thronfolger über die Religionsfreiheit der Unterthanen* (Brandenburg, 1777), and when the famous religious edict of Johann Christian Wöllner (q.v.) was issued in 1788, he sought in a pamphlet to weaken its force. For several years he was more or less involved in a controversy, which he himself had started, regarding the admission of Jews to Christianity with the avowed purpose of securing civic equality with Christians, Teller's sole requirement being that such persons should state that Christ was the founder of a better religion than the one to which they had formerly belonged. In 1791 he defended the course of the notorious and rabid rationalist, Johann Heinrich Schulz, pastor at Gielsdorf, who had attacked the elements, not only of Christianity, but of all religion; and for this position Teller was sentenced to suspension from office for three months, his salary during this time being confiscated for the benefit of the lunatic asylum.   (P. WOLFF.)

BIBLIOGRAPHY: *Nova acta historico-ecclesiastica*, v. 132–133, Weimar, 1764; J. E. Troschel, *Gedächtnispredigt auf Teller*, Berlin, 1805; F. Nicolai, *Gedächtnisschrift auf Teller*, ib. 1807; G. W. Mayer, *Geschichte der Schriftererklärung*, vols. ii.–v. passim, Göttingen, 1809; I. A. Dorner, *Geschichte der protestantischen Theologie*, pp. 700, 710, 713, Munich, 1867; W. Gass, *Geschichte der protestantischen Dogmatik*, iv. 83, 86, 206–207, 446, Berlin, 1867; M. A. Landerer, *Neueste Dogmengeschichte*, pp. 20–21, 34, 52, 97, 130, Heilbronn, 1881.

TEMPLARS (KNIGHTS-TEMPLARS): A military order founded in Jerusalem in 1119. The Templars formed under the Augustinian rule one of the spiritual orders of chivalry that owed their origin to the Crusades (q.v.)—a knightly society on a spiritual basis and for spiritual ends. Under King Baldwin II. of Jerusalem, Hugo de Payens and Godfrey of St. Omer, along with six fellow knights, united under a solemn vow to protect the pilgrims faring from the coast to Jerusalem. Baldwin gave to them quarters in his palace, called " Solomon's Temple," whence came their designation as " Poor Knights of the Temple." During their initial years, the knights plied their calling with unassuming simplicity. Expansion, firmer organization, and papal approbation, were first obtained through the Synod of Troyes, in 1128. Through Bernard of Clairvaux the order received official sanction from Pope Honorius II. The draft of a new set of statutes was entrusted to Bernard. According to this rule, the Knights were bound to observe the canonical hours, or, if prevented, to repeat a number of paternosters; meals were in common, accompanied with spiritual reading; the fare was plain, and every tenth loaf was to be given to the poor. According to the oldest rule, the garb was a white cloak, in token of purity of the heart. Pope Eugenius III. supplemented the Templars' mantle with a red cross; the attendants wore a black robe. No knight was to have more than three horses and one servant. All needs of the members were supplied by the order; and the individual must refer his wants to the master; the latter, in turn, was bound to punctual obedience. No brother was allowed to write letters or to receive them; conversation with women was strictly to be avoided. The penalty for grave delinquency was exclusion from intercourse with the brethren; stubborn impenitence involved expulsion. After the Synod of Troyes, Hugo de Payens visited France, England, and Spain in the interests of the order, receiving everywhere stately welcome and powerful support. As the order grew, its aim became enlarged, and the Templars came to be the standing host of the Church in the East. But the spiritual and monastic side of the order receded more and more into the background, ever more obtruding the predominance of the knightly side.

The most considerable manifestation of papal favor was derived from Pope Alexander III. By the bull *Omne datum optimum*, June 18, 1163, the order was authorized to institute its own clergy, which was to be consecrated by any bishop whatever. Under the papal favor, the order became a rich and powerful league of nobles. Its stations in the East were divided into five chief provinces; Jerusalem, Tripolis, Antioch, Cyprus, and Romania-Morea. In the West, its headquarters were France, the Spanish kingdoms, Portugal, and England. It was not so strongly represented in Germany, nor had it any possessions in the northern lands. The larger stations were called "temple courts," "preceptories of the Templars," priorates preceptories; the smaller ones, commanderies and bailiwicks. Owing to the papal privileges, the order became a firmly cemented institution, with extensive property holdings, dynamic organization, vast range of administration, and its own corps of clergy, so that it aroused the jealousy of bishops and the enmity of princes. As appears from extant statutes (arts. 77–685, which date from the twelfth and thirteenth centuries), the order's constitution had expanded still further. According to these data, the core of the order was composed of the knights, who were to be of noble birth, of pure wedlock, guilty of no grave crime, mentally and bodily sound. Reception into the order was not subject to novitiate; it was accorded by the presiding dignitary, in chapter assembled, in solemn form, and exclusive of outsiders. The knights wore the white mantle with an octagonal red cross. They were attended by the serving brothers, of lower rank. From the time of the bull of Alexander III. (1163) the chaplains of the temple formed the third class in the order.

At the head of the order stood the grand master, with princely rank, who had the power of appointment to the inferior offices. His authoritative position was limited by the chapter general, in which alone lay the right over war and peace with the Saracens. During a vacancy in the office of grand master, the order was directed by the grand commander. The grand master was chosen by majority vote of thirteen duly qualified electors. The knight's vocation ill consorted with the monk's task of prayer; and consequently the statutes disclose a continually emphasized subordination of the latter duty. What passed in the chapter had to be kept strictly secret. The penalties imposed for the member's transgressions were generally milder than in other monastic orders. Offenses, however, such as simony, murder of a Christian, theft, sodomy, perjury, riot, cowardly flight from the enemy, desertion to the Saracens, involved exclusion from the order. The order evinced both unselfishness and valor in the prosecution of its allotted task of defending the Holy Land. Not a single real betrayal of the Christian cause can be brought against it; though in the thirteenth century complaints were produced on account of arrogancies and extravagances. Hence in 1291, when Acco, the last position in the Holy Land, succumbed, this defeat was unwarrantably charged to the rivalry between the Templars and the Knights of St. John; and Pope Nicholas V. was desirous that the two orders be united. After the conquest of the Holy Land, the Templars, from 1291 on, made their headquarters in Cyprus, which was transformed into a stronghold that was intended to check the

Growth, Power, and Constitution.

Organization and Character.

onset of Mohammedanism on its passage to the West.

The Templars in France were a formidable obstruction against centralization of power in the hands of the king. After the victory of Philip IV. (1285–1314) over Pope Boniface VIII., the French king designed to establish himself in the opulent possessions of an order so little to his convenience, and directly after the enthronement of Clement V. at Lyons, in Nov., 1305, he planned action against the Templars. On June 6, 1306, the masters of the orders of St. John and of the temple were invited by Clement to a conference at Avignon, with reference to a projected crusade. The grand master of the Templars, Jacques de Molay, accepted this invitation but, in a later interview in 1307, declined a proposition to fuse the Hospitallers and the Templars. Pope Clement then consented to an investigation of the charges against the Templars. But before the investigation had come to pass, Philip, Sept. 14, 1307, resolved upon the arrest of the Templars and the seizure of their goods. Throughout all France, the Templars were therefore arrested, Oct. 13, 1307. The charges against the order were the denial of Christ by spitting upon the crucifix, indecent kisses, and the sufferance of revolting immorality. On Oct. 15, 1307, the grand master, with several knights, confessed to several accusations; then Philip felt so secure that he addressed letters to the princes of Christendom urging them to imitate his example. Inquisitorial processes went on in France under the warrant of Sept. 14; those who confessed received pardon on returning to the faith of the Church, the others were sentenced to death. Clement protested against the king's action, Oct. 27, requesting the surrender of certain knights and their goods to himself, doubtless with a selfish object. By the bull *Pastoralis præeminente,* Nov. 22, however, he made common cause with the king, and commanded all princes to seize the Templars and their goods. But in Feb., 1308, he again attempted to check proceedings by suspending the inquisitors' powers, and in May Philip convened an assembly to rally the national support to himself against the pope. In August, the pope and the king agreed upon measures against the order, the bull *Faciens misericordiam,* Aug. 12, 1308, convened a council at Vienne to make final disposition of the matter, the council to meet Aug. 1, 1310. General proceedings against the order went on throughout Europe and Cyprus from Aug. 7, 1309, till May 26, 1311; 127 test questions were proposed to the members; but previous admissions were retracted as extorted by torture. However, fifty-four Templars were burned at the stake as backsliding heretics by order of the archbishop of Sens, May 12, 1310; thereafter the spirit of the order was broken and whatever was asked was admitted. Wherever outside France governments and bishops opposed torture, the pope quashed the opposition. Confession was extorted by the rack; but in Portugal, Sicily, Cyprus, and parts of Germany the innocence of the accused came to light.

The Council of Vienne, opened Oct. 16, 1311, declared the order entitled to vindication; but the

Destruction of the Order.

pope abrogated the order by right of his absolute power and as a prudential measure for the general good, assigning its possession to the Knights of St.
John, the official orders to this effect

Final being the bulls of Mar. 22, and May 2, **Dissolution.** 1312. In France and in England the property of the order enriched the king and government. Dionysius of Portugal, a friend of the Templars, founded the Order of Christ, to which the possessions of the Templars were made over while the Portuguese Templars joined the new order. The grand master, with other high officers, was sentenced to perpetual imprisonment; but he declared that the charges were false, and so he and Godfrey de Charney, the French inspector, were burned at the stake Mar. 11, 1314, still affirming the order's innocence.

The motive for the annihilation of the order was twofold; the French king's avarice, and his desire to crush the powerful organization of the Templars within the kingdom. He took advantage of Clement's weakness and of episcopal jealousy of the order. The general guilt and sacrilege charged to the Templars as a whole are incredible, and their downfall is the result of shameless violence on the part of the despotic Philip V.   G. GRÜTZMACHER.

BIBLIOGRAPHY: Original documents are given in Reich, *Documents*, pp. 196–197, 311–313; and Thatcher and McNeal, *Documents*, pp. 492–496. For other basic material consult: D. Wilkins, *Concilia Magnæ Britanniæ et Hiberniæ*, ii. 313 sqq., London, 1727; F. J. M. Raynouard, *Monumens historiques relatifs à la condamnation des chevaliers du Temple*, Paris, 1813; C. Maillard de Chambure, *Règles et statuts secret des Templiers*, ib. 1840; *Documents Illustrative of English Hist. in the 13th and 14th Centuries*, ed. H. Cole, pp. 139–230, London, 1844; W. Dugdale, *Monasticon Anglicanum*, new ed., by J. Caley, H. Ellis, and B. Bandinel, vi. 813–854, 6 vols., ib. 1846; J. Delaville le Roulx, *Documents concernant les Templiers*, Paris, 1882; R. V. Taylor, in *Journal of the Yorkshire Archeological and Topographical Association*, vii. 429–452, viii. 259–299, ix. 71–98, London, 1882–86; H. de Curçon, *Règle du Temple*, Paris, 1886; A. Knöpfler, in *Historisches Jahrbuch der Görresgesellschaft*, 1887, pp. 666 sqq. (best edition of the earliest " rule "); J. Gmelin, *Die Regel des Tempelordens*, in *Mittheilungen des Instituts für österreichische Geschichtsforschung*, xiv (1893), 193–236.

Consult further: D. G. Moldenhauer, *Prozess gegen den Orden der Tempelherren*, Hamburg, 1792; J. Michelet, *Procès des Templiers*, 2 vols., Paris, 1841–51; W. Havemann, *Geschichte des Ausgangs des Templerordens*, Stuttgart, 1846; C. G. Addison, *Hist. of the Knights Templars*, 3d ed., London, 1852 (still the best in English); F. Wilke, *Geschichte des Ordens der Tempelherren*, 2 vols., 2d ed., Halle, 1860; E. Boutaric, *La France sous Philippe le Bel*, Paris, 1861; J. Kenrick, *A Selection of Papers on Archeology and Hist.*, pp. 1–68, London, 1864; J. Loiscleur, *La Doctrine secrète des Templiers*, Orléans, 1872; F. C. Woodhouse, *The Military Religious Orders of the Middle Ages*, London, 1879; M. Bruguera, *Historia de la Orden de los Caballeros de Temple*, vol. 1, Barcelona, 1882; F. Jacquot, *Defense des Templiers contre la routine des historiens*, Paris, 1882; H. Hagenmeyer, *Le Procès des Templiers*, ib. 1885; B. Jungmann, *Dissertationes selectæ*, vi. 79–149, Regensburg, 1886; G. Lambert, *Templars. A Short Paper on the Order*, London, 1887; H. G. Prutz, *Malteser Urkunden zur Geschichte der Tempelherren*, Munich, 1883; idem, *Geschichte des Tempelherrenordens*, Königsberg, 1887; idem, *Entwicklung und Untergang des Tempelherrenordens*, Berlin, 1888; idem, *Die geistliche Ritterorden*, ib. 1908; K. Schottmueller, *Der Untergang des Templerordens*, 2

vols., Berlin, 1887; J. Y. A. Morshead, *The Templars' Trials*, London, 1888; F. Naef, *Recherches sur les opinions religieuses des Templiers*, Nîmes, 1890; J. J. I. von Döllinger, *Akademische Vorträge*, iii. 245 sqq., Munich, 1891; J. A. Froude, *The Spanish Story of the Armada*, pp. 250–310, new ed., London, 1892; J. Gmelin, *Schuld oder Unschuld des Templerordens*, Stuttgart, 1893; A. Grange, in *Dublin Review*, 1895, pp. 329–346; J. Miret y Sans, *Cartaral dels Templers de les Comandes de Garden y Barbens*, Barcelona, 1899; G. Salvemini, *Studi storici. L'Abolizione dell'Ordine dei Templari*, Firenze, 1901; L. Keller, *Die Tempelherrn und die Freimaurer*, Berlin, 1905; H. C. Lea, *Hist. of the Inquisition of the Middle Ages*, i. 16, iii. passim (consult Index), New York, 1906; H. Finke, *Papsttum und Untergang des Tempelordens*, 2 vols., Münster, 1907 (contains new documénts from Spain); C. Perkins, in *American Historical Review*, Jan., 1910; Bower, *Popes*, iii. 66 sqq.; and literature under CLEMENT V.; and PHILIP IV.

TEMPLE, FREDERICK: Archbishop of Canterbury; b. at Leukas, in Santa Maura (one of the Ionian Islands), Nov. 30, 1821; d. in London Dec. 23, 1902. He studied at Blundell's School, Tiverton, and at Balliol College, Oxford (B.A., 1842; M.A., 1846; B.D., 1858). He was made fellow of his college and tutor in mathematics 1842, ordained deacon 1846, and priest 1847. He became principal of Kneller Hall Training College, near Twickenham, in 1848, government inspector of schools in 1855, headmaster of Rugby in 1858, and about the same time chaplain to Queen Victoria. Under his administration Rugby regained much of the prestige which the school had enjoyed under Thomas Arnold. In 1860 he acquired a reputation for rationalism by contributing an essay on *The Education of the World* to the famous *Essays and Reviews* (q.v.). The suspicion of heterodoxy clung to him, and when Gladstone, whose Irish disestablishment measure he had supported, offered him the bishopric of Exeter, in 1869, a strong protest was made against the appointment. He was consecrated Dec. 21, 1869, was translated to the see of London in 1885, and was made archbishop of Canterbury in 1896. By the firmness and justice of his rule as bishop and archbishop he completely overcame the early prejudices against him. One of his last official acts was the crowning of Edward VII. Aug. 9, 1902. Besides the essay already referred to, single sermons, and addresses, he published *Sermons Preached in Rugby School Chapel* (3 series, London, 1861–71); *The Relations between Religion and Science* (1884), the Bampton lectures for 1884; *Responsio archiepiscoporum Angliæ ad litteras apostolicas Leonis Papæ XIII.* (1897; Eng., French, and Gk. transls., 1897), an able reply by Temple and W. D. Maclagan, archbishop of York, to a papal encyclical denying the validity of Anglican orders; and *Helps to Godly Living* (ed. J. H. Burn, 1898), being extracts from various sermons.

BIBLIOGRAPHY: *Memoirs of Archbishop Temple, by seven Friends*, ed. E. G. Sandford, 2 vols., London, 1906; W. F. Aitken, *Frederick Temple*, ib. 1901; C. H. Dant, *Archbishop Temple*, ib. 1903 (popular); F. J. Snell, *Early Associations of Archbishop Temple*, ib. 1904; F. E. Kitchener, *Rugby Memoir of Archbishop Temple, 1859–69*, ib. 1907; E. G. Sandford, *The Exeter Episcopate of Archbishop Temple*, ib. 1907; literature under ESSAYS AND REVIEWS.

TEMPLES, HEBREW.

I. Solomon's Temple: Among the great services which David rendered to the Hebrew nation was that of securing a capital which served as a center not only for political life but also for religion. Here he placed the sacred ark, rescued from the forgetfulness in which Saul's superstition had involved it. The Bible further relates that it was his purpose to provide for it a stately habitation, but was deterred by prophetic injunction from carrying out that purpose (II Sam. vii.), while I Chron. xxii. sqq. asserts that he made provision for its erection. The building of this structure was held by Solomon to be one of his urgent duties. The question is raised here whether Solomon conceived it to be his duty to destroy other sanctuaries; the answer must be that he did not, and that such a purpose is not in evidence prior to Deuteronomy (see HIGH PLACES, § 5). But the paling of the other sanctuaries was the natural effect of the splendor and beauty of the Temple, with its costly sacrifices and imposing priesthood, and of the fact that it was the royal sanctuary and so gained exceptional prestige, illustrated by the number of pilgrims who soon came to worship there. The measures of Jeroboam I. to establish rival sanctuaries at Bethel and Dan show how powerful had become the central attraction of the Temple. The question as to the site of the Temple must be decided from a study of the topography of the situation (see JERUSALEM, V., §§ 1-5). The location of the Temple according to unbroken tradition, supported by the topographical character of the locality, was upon the hill extending eastward between the Tyropœon and the valley of the Kidron. This is the " hill of Zion." Since this hill fell away abruptly to the south as well as on both sides, it was necessary, in order to obtain a horizontal level for building, to construct a kind of terrace. This part of the hill still shows its artificial character, and is known as Haram al-Sherif. The spot where the Temple stood is marked by the Mosque of Omar at the highest point of the hill. The Temple extended from east to west; the altar being in front, to the east of the entrance. The orientation does not imply that Solomon's Temple was built to a sun-god, but it is probable that a sun-temple was the model. The state buildings of Solomon must have been connected with the Temple to the southward. The remaining space of the level plain toward the Kidron was occupied partly by the fore-court of the Temple (I Kings vi. 36) which surrounded the Temple proper, and partly by the great court that surrounded the entire Temple and palace district (I Kings vii. 12). Adjoining the Temple, or " inner " court was the " other " court, to the south, which surrounded the palace itself, while the state buildings—hall of justice, throne-room, and house

1. Importance, Site, Arrangement.

of Lebanon, lying farther south—were surrounded only by the great court that embraced everything within its walls. The palace, therefore, in accordance with the topography, lay somewhat lower than the Temple.

In his building-operations David had availed himself of foreign workmen, sent by Hiram of Tyre (II Sam. v. 11), and Solomon continued this policy, a treaty providing for this and for barter of materials being compacted between the two kings. According to I Kings ix. 10-14, the cost of Solomon's building-operations was so great that he was finally obliged to cede to Hiram twenty Galilean cities, having obtained also 120 talents of gold from the Tyrian king. Solomon impressed 30,000 laborers for his undertaking, whom he divided into three shifts, each shift having to work one month on Lebanon and two months at home. There were besides 70,000 burden-bearers and 80,000 stone-masons in the Jewish mountains who worked under 3,300 overseers. These figures are possibly exaggerations. The text of the passage describing the construction of the Temple (I Kings vi.–vii.) is corrupt. The original account seems to have been written by a priest who was familiar with the details of the structure, but this was modified or added to by editors who no longer understood some of his technical terms and wished, moreover, to magnify the splendor of the holy building. In the course of time, too, doubtless, many changes were made in the structure itself. As an aid to the reconstruction of Solomon's Temple there exists, besides what textual criticism and archeology offer, the description by Ezekiel (chaps. xl. sqq.) of his ideal temple, in imagining which he must have been influenced by the Temple with which he was familiar.

2. Provisions for Construction.

The Temple building may be described in its three chief parts: the Temple proper, its surrounding structure, and the fore-courts. The Temple proper or house of God was an oblong sixty cubits long, twenty wide, and thirty high, interior measurement. The thickness of the walls is not given; in Ezekiel's ideal temple this was six cubits. The partition between the holy place and the holy of holies may have been of thin wood, notwithstanding II Chron. iii. 14. On the eastern side in front of the Temple there was a stately porch twenty cubits by ten and probably of equal height with the temple. Its side walls were in line with the long walls of the Temple and were probably of the same thickness. The height of 120 cubits given in II Chron. iii. 4 is obviously an exaggeration. There was probably a flight of steps rising to the porch. The other three sides of the building, north, south, and west, were not open to the view of the

3. Structure of the Temple Proper.

spectator, but were concealed by a structure fifteen to twenty cubits high. This was in three stories and contained a great number of small rooms or cells, each five cubits high; those on the ground floor were five cubits wide, those on the second floor six, and those on the third, seven. The approach to the whole was on the south side and the ascent from lower floor to upper was by means of a stairway. Ezekiel mentions thirty-three rooms on one floor, which would show them to have been very small— probably for storing paraphernalia, votive offerings, and the like. The Temple proper was divided into two chambers, the holy place and the holy of holies. The door to the latter was of olive wood, the lintel above forming with the posts a pentagon. The entrance door to the holy place was of cedar and cypress, very wide, double, and each door was in two parts. The holy place was forty cubits long and twenty wide. It was the room for the officiating priests and the vestibule to the holy of holies. The latter, which was the real shrine, inaccessible to the ordinary mortal and even to the priest, was a cube of twenty cubits and was accordingly ten cubits lower than the holy place, and there must therefore have been a room ten cubits high above it, as in the Temple of Herod. From this the light was completely excluded, while the holy place was but dimly lighted. Both chambers were wainscoted and paneled with cedar and cypress. The windows are not described (I Kings vi. 4), but were probably along the upper third of the walls. Light was obtained from candles. In the holy of holies stood the Ark of the Covenant (q.v.); in the holy place, the table of showbread, the candlesticks, and the altar of incense (see below, IV.).

The account reports ornamentation by means of carved cherubs, palms, and flower garlands. Everything, moreover, is said to have been covered with gold-leaf (I Kings vi. 20 sqq., 28 sqq., 4. Orna- 35), though the texts are not in com- mentation. plete accord. There is some question as to whether the treasures and trophies hung on the walls were of gold. It seems likely that Solomon ornamented certain parts of the interior with gold-leaf, though there is no positive evidence of the fact. On the other hand, it seems certain that there were in the time of Ezekiel figures engraved on the walls. This is suggested by II Kings xii. 8 sqq., xvi. 10 sqq., xxiii. 4, 11 sqq. The roof is not described. II Kings xxiii. 12 shows that the kings of Judah had placed altars there, and a gloss affirms that Ahaz built an upper story for this reason. It must be inferred that the roof was flat. In the porch stood two bronze pillars, eighteen cubits high, twelve in circumference, and four fingers thick, which were surmounted by capitals five cubits high, covered with checkered work. The capitals were formed like lilies, and two rows of 100 pomegranates each ran along each, in the form of garlands over the checker-work. The description is vague, especially as to the relation of the checker-work to the lilies. The pillars stood to the right and left of the portal, that on the right being called Jachin, and that on the left, Boaz. The meaning of the names and the significance of the pillars are obscure. The purpose here may have been purely architectural,

but the pillars are probably to be related to the obelisks and pillars that were characteristic of Phenician and Canaanitic temples (see ALTAR, I., § 3; ASHERAH; GROVES AND TREES, SACRED; MEMORIALS AND SACRED STONES).

Solomon's Temple can hardly have been of native design. Solomon was obliged to import not only material, but workmen. There was apparently no native architectural art in Israel.

5. Architec- The bronze work was entrusted to **ture.** Huramabi, a Tyrian artificer, and it seems probable that both execution and conception of the plan of the Temple were strongly influenced by Phenicia. But it seems unlikely that the Phenicians originated the style of architecture employed; they were better imitators than inventors. The type is common in Egypt, where a chamber of columns corresponds to the holy place, and the pylon to the porch, while in front of the pylon stand two pillars or obelisks. The home of the peculiar style employing wooden columns must be sought in the Lebanon district, in northern Syria; but it probably goes back still further, to Egypt. The Temple represents, then, a mixture of styles. The Temple proper with its firm, square construction corresponds to the native Phenician-Canaanitic style. It was essentially Phenician in origin, though details were borrowed from Mycene and Egypt. The arrangement of the holy of holies, cells, vestibule, and walled court is ultimately of Egyptian origin, further developed in northern Syria under Phenician and Hittite influence.

II. Zerubbabel's Temple: The most important source for the origin of the Temple which took the place of Solomon's, which was destroyed by Nebuchadrezzar, is the book of the prophet Haggai. This says nothing of the opposition of the Samaritans, who, according to Ezra iii.–iv., prevented the early completion of the structure on which a beginning was made two years after the return. Haggai attributes the delay of construction to the lukewarmness of the congregation itself. The building was begun about the middle of the year 520 B.C., and the corner-stone was laid on the twenty-fourth day of the ninth month. Haggai says nothing of a former attempt, and it must be assumed that the returned exiles had merely raised an altar, as narrated in Ezra iii. 1 sqq. Hag. ii. 14 has a similar implication. The accounts, Biblical and other, give unfortunately scarcely any information as to the character of the Temple that was built in 520 under Zerubbabel and the high priest Joshua. It may be assumed that it occupied the site of Solomon's. From Hag. ii. 4 it appears that the new building made a sad impression on those who had seen the earlier. It was, in all probability, inferior not so much in its dimensions, for the plan of Solomon's Temple was probably followed, but in its construction, appointments, adornment, and surroundings. But according to Ezra vi. 3–4, Cyrus ordered a building sixty cubits high and sixty wide, much larger, therefore, than Solomon's Temple. If Cyrus issued this order, it evidently was not executed. Hecateus is probably right (Josephus, *Apion*, i. 22) in giving the dimensions of the fore-court as 475 x 142 feet. It was entered by a folding-door. The altar for burnt-offerings stood inside, of the same size as that of Solomon's Temple and, according to I Macc. iv. 44 sqq., of unhewn stone. There must have been an outer court in which there were the oft-mentioned cells (Ezra viii. 29, x. 6, etc.). The laity, up to the time of Alexander Jannæus, had free access to the inner court in all its parts. The ark having disappeared, its place in the holy of holies was taken by a flat stone called the *shetiya*, upon which the high-priest on the day of atonement placed the censer. There was a curtain between the holy place and the holy of holies, and the entrance to the holy place seems also to have been hung with a curtain. In the holy place were found a golden candlestick, the table of showbread, and the gilt altar of incense. The Temple contained besides, at least in later times, rich ornaments.

The absence of the ark resulted in a change in the conception of the Temple; God was no longer thought of as actually present in the holy of holies. Although the sacrifices continued, they were not gifts to God as present, but symbols of the heart's devotion. The priesthood took on increased importance. Religion became more and more the exclusive business of the priesthood and the (ecclesiastical) State. Of the later history of this Temple, it is reported (Ecclus. l.) that Simon II. repaired the Temple and raised the outer walls. Antiochus Epiphanes plundered and desecrated it; Judas Maccabæus restored and purified it, after which it was newly decorated and fortified. It was stormed by Pompey, who penetrated to the holy of holies, and again by Herod.

III. The Temple of Herod: About 20–19 B.C. Herod conceived the plan of erecting a new temple at Jerusalem; but his motives were political rather than religious, as he aimed to conciliate the pious Jews, whom he had formerly outraged, and to rival the magnificent temples of Greece. Josephus (*Ant.*, XV., x.) and the Mishna tractate *Middoth* are the chief sources of information concerning this Temple. The area covered was twice that of the old. The present Haram is essentially the work of Herod. The whole resembled a great fortress with towers and battlements. The chief gates were on the west and south sides. Josephus mentions four gates, one of which connected with the city by means of a bridge, and another by a stairway. The two "Hulda" gates were on the south. The great outer court, or court of the gentiles, was surrounded by magnificent pillared halls, the most splendid of which, the royal hall, contained 162 Corinthian marble columns in four rows; on the other three sides the columns were in two rows. There were, no doubt, also rooms for the priests and a chamber for the Sanhedrin. A short flight of steps led up to the inner court in the northern half of the area. Bronze tablets forbade any but Jews to enter on pain of death, and one of these was discovered in 1871 by Clermont-Ganneau (for the text cf. Schürer, Eng. transl., II., 1. 266). This court was divided into three parts the court of women, the court of men, and the court of the priests, the last surrounding the Temple. The altar stood in the innermost court, the laity being allowed to view the ceremonies only from a distance, the women

farther removed than the men. Outside the men's and women's courts ran pillared halls, and, adjoining these, were chambers for paraphernalia. Sentinels guarded the vestibules—Levites on the outside, and priests inside. The altar of burnt-offerings, in the innermost court, was 32 cubits square at the bottom, contracting to twenty-four at the top. The blood of the sacrifices was drained away through two holes, a canal conducting it to the Kidron. The altar was approached by a stairway sixteen cubits wide and thirty-two long, of unhewn stone, like the altar itself. Behind the altar was a bronze laver, approached by twelve steps, and north of the altar was the slaughtering-place, behind which were pillars and marble tables for the preparation of the sacrifices.

The Temple proper, gleaming with gold and marble, was approached by twelve steps. The vestibule was 100 cubits high, 100 wide, and twenty deep. Through its gateless entrance over which Herod had placed an eagle, afterward torn down by the people, could be seen the door to the holy place, hung on the outside with a great Babylonian curtain, and ornamented with golden vines with grapes. The holy place was an oblong forty cubits long and twenty wide, containing the table of showbread, the seven-branched candlestick, and the altar of incense; only the priests might enter. The holy of holies was a cube of twenty cubits. The high priest alone entered it on the day of atonement to offer incense and place the sacrificial blood on the stone that had taken the place of the ark. A double curtain forty cubits long and twenty wide separated it from the holy place. A three-story structure, as in Solomon's Temple, containing thirty-eight cells ran around three sides of the Temple, as high as the interior of the holy place; which consequently must have been dark. Over the holy place was an attic, and probably a double-attic over the holy of holies.

IV. The Temple Furniture: In the Hebrew of I Sam. xxi. 6 the expression commonly rendered "showbread" is "bread of the face," i.e., that placed before Yahweh; it was called also "hallowed bread," and later other names

1. The Table of Showbread. were given. This bread corresponded to the food offerings in other systems of religion, and the offering itself goes back to the times when the gods were thought to need sustenance, and it might in early times be eaten only by persons ritually clean. At Nob this bread was probably placed on a table, and such a table is to be assumed for the Mosaic Tabernacle. But historically such a piece of furniture is provable first for the Solomonic Temple (I Kings vi. 20), where it was an altar of cedar overlaid with gold (cf. I Kings vii. 48); according to the Chronicler (I., xxviii. 16; II., iv. 8, 19) there were ten such tables in Solomon's Temple; Ezekiel (xli. 22) makes the (one) table two cubits square and three high. Like other altars, it probably had horns or projecting corners. Comparison of the Solomonic article with that described in Ex. xxv. 23 sqq. shows a difference of construction, of size, and of proportions. It was probably destroyed when Nebuchadrezzar took Jerusalem, as it is not mentioned with the booty. The second Temple also had a table (I Macc. i. 22) which was among the costly articles that excited the cupidity of Antiochus Epiphanes, and was replaced later (I Macc. iv. 49). For the Herodian table the directions of Ex. xxv. were probably followed (see TABERNACLE, THE MOSAIC), though the representation on the Arch of Titus suggests some departures in details. The description by Josephus (*Ant.*, III., vi. 6) of the table in the Tabernacle corresponds with the Exodus description, except that he places feet on it; Josephus places the rings differently from that on the Titus Arch and from that in Exodus.

At Shiloh in the night light was furnished by a lamp with enough oil to last till morning (I Sam. iii. 3). This implies that the sanctuary must have been adequately lighted by windows.

2. The Candlestick. Only a little natural light entered the holy place (ut sup.) of Solomon's Temple, and artificial illumination was necessary. Accordingly, mention is made of ten golden candlesticks, placed on both sides of the entrance (I Kings vii. 49). Though the passage is a later addition, it is not justifiable to reject these candlesticks as unhistorical; they were, however, probably of bronze. Josephus (*Ant.*, III., vii. 7) makes the sevenfold candlestick consist of seventy pieces, and sees in them seventy symbols through which the seven planets pass. The symbolism may be old and true, but applies more appropriately to seventy lights than to seventy scarcely distinguishable parts of a single candlestick. It corresponds, moreover, to the ten candelabra of seven lights each placed by Solomon in his Temple. The Chronicler (I., xxviii. 15; II., iv. 7, xiii. 11) varies between one and ten in his account. It follows from the foregoing that the candlesticks were intended for use in the daytime. The reference in II Chron. xiii. 11 is to the time of lighting, not to its duration. The Temple of Zerubbabel contained only one candlestick, and that was comparatively large. It was carried off by Antiochus Epiphanes, restored by Judas Maccabæus, and by Herod placed in his Temple. It was also carried off by Titus, and is figured on the arch. Vespasian placed it in the Temple of Peace, and it can be traced till 534 A.D., when it was taken from Carthage to Constantinople. Subsequently it was taken to Jerusalem and destroyed at a plundering of the city.

In the Temple of Solomon stood a circular basin (" sea ") of bronze, ten cubits in diameter, five in height, and a handbreadth in thickness; its brim was slightly curved, like the petals of a lily. Under the edge were two rows of bronze cucumbers as ornamentation. It stood on twelve oxen in groups of three, each of which groups faced toward a cardinal point. It was con-

3. Other Articles. structed out of copper taken as booty (I Chron. xviii. 8). It is said to have served the priests in ceremonial cleansing, but was ill adapted for such a purpose. The expression "sea" recalls that Babylonian, Egyptian, Syrian, and Phenician temples were also provided with " seas," symbolic of the deity subduing the sea-dragon. King Ahaz made use of the oxen to pay tribute to the king of Assyria. The basin was

finally carried to Babylon by Nebuchadrezzar. In the Temple of Zerubbabel no " sea " seems to have existed, though there were means for ceremonial washing. In the Temple of Herod stood a fine laver, with brass pedestal, for the priests for the washing of hands and feet before officiating.

In Solomon's Temple were ten peculiar pieces, the " bases " (I Kings vii. 27) not otherwise mentioned. Vessels found in Cyprus seem to aid the description, and to show that on four wheels was a frame, on which figures of animals and cherubim were depicted. Upon this frame was a cylinder, into which a kettle was fitted. As these articles were movable, they were possibly for washing the sacrificial animals. (R. KITTEL.)

V. Other Hebrew Temples. A new chapter in the history of Hebrew worship and temples has been opened by the investigations in Egypt. For the Onias temple see LEONTOPOLIS. It is now known that a temple for worship and sacrifice existed at Elephantine, Egypt. The Aramaic papyri discovered there (see SEMITIC LANGUAGE AND LITERATURE; cf. E. Sachau, *Abhandlungen der königlich-preussischen Akademie der Wissenschaften*, 1907, partial Eng. transl. and discussion in *Annual Report of the Smithsonian Institution*, 1907, pp. 605–611; A. H. Sayce, *Aramaic Papyri Discovered at Assouan*, London, 1906) show that in the fifth century a Jewish community possessed an imposing temple, which in 408–407 B.C. had already existed for a considerable period. The Persian control of Egypt had been favorable to the community and its temple, but through the machinations of Egyptian priests the temple had recently been destroyed and its treasures and vessels appropriated. Two of the documents are an appeal for the reconstruction of this temple, while the third implies that the request was granted. The net result of the documents is to show that at least two temples in which sacrifice was offered to Yahweh in Egypt. A suggestion which is made in connection with the critical opinions concerning Isa. xix. 18 is that in view of the known numerous settlements of Hebrews in Egypt, the discovery of other temples there would now hardly be a surprise. It is interesting to note that partly as a result of the discovery and verification of the existence in Egypt of these Jewish temples, Ezek. xx. is interpreted as referring to an inquiry by the " elders of Israel " (verse 1) respecting the erection of a temple to Yahweh in Babylonia. The answer, on this interpretation, was an emphatic negative (verses 39–41). GEO. W. GILMORE.

BIBLIOGRAPHY: On the topography of the site of the Temple consult the abundant literature under JERUSALEM, and the following: G. Rosen, *Der Haram von Jerusalem und der Tempelplatz des Moria*, Gotha, 1866; F. Adler, *Der Felsendom und die heutige Grabeskirche zu Jerusalem*, Berlin, 1873; C. Schick, *Beit el Makdas oder der alte Tempelplatz*, Stuttgart, 1887; idem, *Die Stiftshütte, der Tempel in Jerusalem, und der Tempelplatz der Jetztzeit*, Berlin, 1896; C. Mommert, *Topographie von Jerusalem*, 3 parts, Leipsic, 1903–05; A. Kümmel, *Materialen zur Topographie des alten Jerusalem*, Halle, 1904–06.

On the different temples in Jerusalem consult: J. F. von Meyer, *Der Tempel Salomos*, Berlin, 1830; C. F. Kiel, *Der Tempel Salomos*, Dorpat, 1839 (still of value); C. C. W. F. Bähr, *Der salomonische Tempel*, Carlsruhe, 1848; G. Williams, *The Holy City*, ii. 296 sqq., London, 1849; J. T. Bannister, *The Temples of the Hebrews*, ib., 1861; J. Fergusson, *The Temples of the Jews*, ib. 1875; T. H.

Lewis, *The Holy Places of Jerusalem*, ib. 1880; W. Warren, in *TSBA*, vii (1880), 309 sqq.; F. Spiess, *Das Jerusalem des Josephus*, Berlin, 1881; idem, *Der Tempel . . . nach Josephus*, ib. 1881; H. Pailloux, *Monographie du temple de Salomon*, Paris, 1885; T. O. Paine, *Solomon's Temple and Capitol*, Boston and London, 1886; T. Friedrich, *Tempel und Palast Salomos*, Innsbruck, 1887; T. Newberry, *The Tabernacle and the Temple*, London, 1887; E. C. Robins, *The Temple of Solomon; a Review of the various Theories respecting its Form und . . . Architecture*, ib., 1887; O. Wolff, *Der Tempel . . . und seine Masse*, Graz, 1887; G. Perrot and C. Chipiez, *Le Temple de Jérusalem*, Paris, 1889; Büchler, in *JQR*, x (1898), 678 sqq., xi (1899), 46 sqq.; E. Schmidt, *Solomon's Temple in the Light of other Oriental Temples*, Chicago, 1902; W. Sanday, *Sacred Sites of the Gospels*, pp. 106–117, Oxford, 1903; E. Babelon, *Manual of Oriental Antiquities*, chap. vii., London, 1906; A. Wünsche; *Salomos Thron und Hippodrom*, Leipsic, 1906; W. S. Caldecott, *Solomon's Temple, its History and Structure*, London, 1907; idem, *The Second Temple in Jerusalem. Its History and its Structure*, ib. 1908; A. Edersheim, *The Temple. Its Ministry and Services as they were at the Time of Jesus Christ*, ib. 1909; Benzinger, *Archäologie*, pp. 329 sqq.; *DB*, iv. 695–716; *EB*, iv. 4923–4956; *JE*, xii. 81–101; *DCG*, ii. 708–713; Schürer, *Geschichte*, i. 15–17, 392–393 (for literature), and passim for discussion, Eng. transl., consult index; the *Quarterly Statements* of PEF for the reports on the various discoveries resulting from excavation; and the commentaries on Kings, Chronicles, and Ezra-Nehemiah.

On the temples in Egypt consult: E. Sachau, *Drei aramäische Papyruskunden aus Elephantine*, Berlin, 1908; L. Belleli, *An Independent Examination of the Assuan and Elephantine Aramaic Papyri*, with eleven plates and two appendices on sundry items, London, 1909; *JBL*, xxviii. pp. 71–81 (an excellent article reviewing the Assouan papyri and recent literature on it).

TEMPORAL POWER. See CHURCH AND STATE; PAPAL STATES.

TEMPTATION: The most general expression for every motive that incites man, especially the Christian, to sin (Buddeus, *Institutiones theologiæ dogmaticæ*, III., ii. 30, 1724). The Bib-

Origin and Meaning.

lical usage, however, is less definite. In the Old Testament the word is from *nasah* (Gk., *parazein* [Gen. xxii. 1; Ex. xvii. 2; Deut. vi. 16]), and *bahan* (of the people tempting God, Ps. xcv. 9; Mal. iii. 15; Gk. *dokimazein* in Ps. xxvi. 2, lxvi. 10, lxxxi. 7, in the sense of II Cor. xiii. 5). The root meaning of these two verbs is to test or prove, as rendered in most of the passages. However, there is a distinction between proving and tempting, in the modern sense. To prove is to establish a matter of fact, either known or assumed, or to augment its certainty. To tempt means simply to make an attempt, and this with the application of power, with which is combined more or less indefinitely, in personal reference, the collateral concept of enmity (I Kings x. 1). A circumstance of temptation without a personal tempter is unknown in the Old Testament; but this occurs frequently in the New, hence the perspicuity of the term *peirasmos*. This is implied in advance in the idea of incitement to sin, prepared in the New Testament by the efforts to entrap Jesus unwarily into some fatal assertion. Theology limits this New-Testament term by distinguishing precisely temptation from proving and enticement. Faith or the ethical motive is tested by suffering in order to come to assurance (Jas. i. 12–13; Rom. v. 3–4; II Cor. viii. 2). On the contrary the susceptible will is tempted with the possible result that it turns to evil, or if purpose may

be admitted, with the design of inducing it to turn to evil. But inasmuch as that result does not necessarily follow, and because so long as there is temptation that result is not actualized, temptation is to be distinguished from enticement. Evident design or plotting may be a special mark of the latter (Matt. xxiv. 4, 5, 11, 24; Eph. iv. 4; II Cor. xi. 3). In the Lord's Prayer the relation of man to sin is presented from the standpoints of guilt and temptation (Luke xi. 4), and the latter is given a broad significance. Sin is not the consequence of constraint, but occasioned, not always by the perceptible action of a tempting being, rather by circumstances in which the human subject happens to be (Jas. i. 2; Matt. xxvi. 41; I Pet. iv. 12). Yet the peril is according to the constituent character of the one affected. With reference to the persons tempted the New Testament speaks of disciples, but the statements of Jesus do not imply the regenerate in the dogmatic sense; James (i. 13–15), who points to the person's own lust as the source of temptation, does not give this any special Christian application; and Paul looks upon the Jews as special prototypes of tempted Christians (I Cor. x. 1–13). Therefore, temptation may be assumed to have universal reference. It occurs in different degrees in individual cases, coming into consciousness in the awakened conscience and being heightened by resistance. The Bible nowhere calls the experience of the first parents a temptation, but rather an enticement, according to the distinction previously made; yet quite generally and properly the fall as well as the trial of Jesus in the Synoptical narrative are held to be types of temptation. The question arises whether the principle laid down by James applies also to them; or, in other words, whether temptation merely brings to light sin existing already before the act (Rom. vii.). Neither Gen. iii. nor Rom. v. 12, nor the Synoptic account postulates that a perverted desire determines and defiles the inner self of the tempted. Yet the presumption of Scripture that sin is in no wise of God and consequently not necessarily due to the conditions of finite existence is only to be dogmatically established. Even the sinlessness of Jesus is a dogma.

The desire responds to a proffered good. Jesus reminds of the weakness of the flesh, as occasion to the tempting passion (Matt. xxvi. 41); the tempting power of the circumstances of the passion is specially emphasized in the New

Social Temptation; the Tempter.

Testament (Luke xxii. 40; Matt. xiii. 21); yet the typical temptation of Christ shows that sensuous desire and avarice are no less prominent (cf. I Cor. vii. 5). The division into temptations through lust and through passion is also justified. Apart from evil and temptation by passion, which is the exercise of the moral government of this world, there certainly remains no proneness to evil in the possibility for the appropriation of some good and in the experienced stimulus. The fall, therefore, appears in Scripture as enticement, and not as merely arising from circumstances; and the temptation of Christ not only presupposes the " sin of the world " but comes from the " tempter." The influence of the existent immorality is thus joined with the inciting circumstances. This leads to the Biblical conception of snare or stumbling-block, used in the Old Testament of idolatry (Ex. xxiii. 30); Jesus applies it to the social complexity of human life (Matt. xviii. 6–9, xvi. 23). An act innocent of itself may by example be occasion for stumbling to another (I Cor. viii. 9–13, x. 28–29); the point here is that life qualified by sin every-where confronts the insecure human being with its snare, and unintentionally society is involved by reciprocal activity in occasions of guilt. This is in reference to the solidarity of human evil. The personal originator of temptation with reference to Christ is the devil (Luke iv. 13; John xiv. 30), represented by the serpent in paradise (cf. II Cor. xi. 3; Rev. xii. 9); the accuser (Rev. xii. 10) is the motive power of the tempting persecutions (I Pet. v. 8–9; Rev. ii. 10), with the fear of death as means (Heb. ii. 14–15, 18), and sinful desire (I Cor. vii. 5). None of these passages refers to an immediate inner influence. Of Judas Satan takes possession not by virtue of temptation, but gradually after successful enticement by avarice (John xii. 6). However, all occasions for sinning are subject to the omnipotence of God, and the one tempted is prone to refer that which is tempting in his situation to Providence and thus attempt to escape responsibility (Jas. i. 13). Yet it is fundamentally certain that God is not the author of evil, and does not tempt, so far as this may refer to the origination of evil (ut sup.). To God is only attributed induction into the tempting circumstance brought upon oneself (Luke xi. 4). How this fact is to be reconciled with the Christian consciousness belongs to theodicy. However, the dependence of sin upon temptation conditionally mitigates its guilt, and at the same time postulates the salvation of the sinner.

The concept of temptation belongs, in the first instance, to dogmatics, more definitely, to the doctrine of sin, signifying that the origin of sin in humanity as a whole and in individuals

Dogma and Christian Ethics. is to be so explained as not to appear as malice, but far more as pardonable failure, without, however, canceling responsibility. Not less important is the knowledge of temptation for theological ethics, if this is not regarded as released from relation to real life. On the one hand the full seriousness of the battle presupposes power to resist, and on the other, the Christian least of all sees beyond the conflict. A special phase of the Christian life is the conflict of the new man against the old, facing the peril of relapse, bringing to the front a special category of sins, and necessitating sober vigilance. This involves self-discipline, the soul of which is active faith. In the deepest sense temptations here become challenges to faith, and doubts which cause the convictions of salvation to waver enter the moral point of view, since they undermine the standpoint of the combatant. In this the temptation of Christ was again typical in that it had the denial of humble faith as its objective. Similar temptations are those of the self-security of the victor (Matt. xii. 43–44). To the episodes of this inner sphere of conflict is given the term " as-

saults " upon the Christian life. The essential result is the confirmation of faith (Jas. i. 2–3; I Pet. i. 6–7; Heb. ii. 18; cf. Luke viii. 13). The more intelligible then becomes the background of the " wicked enemy " against the kingdom of God (Matt. xiii. 39, 41; II Cor. ii. 11).

(M. KÄHLER.)

TEMPUS CLAUSUM ("Closed Time"): A canonical term applied to those days on which noisy festivities, especially the merry-makings usually incidental to marriage, are not allowed. These prohibitions had their origin, in part, at least, in the theories that governed the introduction of fasts. At quite an early period, prayer and continence are commended by way of preparation for a worthy observance of feast days. The Council of Trent inaugurated a modified restriction in this matter; and ruled (session XXIV., chap. 10, de reform. matrim.): " From the Advent of our Lord until the Day of Epiphany, and from Ash Wednesday until the octave of Easter, inclusively, let the ancient prohibitions of nuptial celebrations be diligently observed by all." In Constitutio LXXX., Benedict XIV. communicated a declaration of the Congregatio concilii, stating: " Even during the times expressed in chap. 10, session XXIV., marriage may be contracted before the parish priest; only the nuptial celebrations, feasts, escorting processions, and carnal intercourse are forbidden." Thus it appears that so-called " quiet weddings " may take place in the prohibited season, though not without episcopal dispensation, save in so far as in extraordinary instances the priest is permitted to officiate at a marriage even without a dispensation, as in articulo mortis.

The German Evangelical church retained the forbidden season as a catholic custom; and the church orders of the sixteenth century also, to some extent, recognize the same expressly. But from the beginning both legislation and usage produced great variations. The Eisenach Conference (q.v.) gave some attention to this matter in the year 1857; and published, in its minutes, full particulars of the aspects of the situation as then it stood (cf. Moser, Allgemeines Kirchenblatt für das evangelische Deutschland, 1857, pp. 325–326, 1858, pp. 197–198). The result of the deliberations at Eisenach was as follows: " The Conference recognizes the Tempus clausum Quadragesimæ as a salutary instructive institution of the Church, and must accordingly recommend the careful maintenance of what still survives of this institution in the several churches; yet can but refer the question, what may be done toward bringing about a satisfactory status in this connection, to the discretion of the particular church executives." E. SEHLING.

TEN ARTICLES, THE: A series of articles sanctioned by both English convocations, and passed by parliament in 1536, advancing the Reformation in England. The first five relate to doctrine, and (1) make Scripture the basis and summary of Christian faith, (2) affirm the necessity and regenerating grace of baptism, (3) declare penance (including contrition, confession, and reformation) necessary to salvation, (4) take the position that the body and blood of Christ are present in the Eucharistic elements, and (5) affirms that justification (remission of sin and reconciliation to God) is by the merits of Christ, though good works are still necessary. The second five deal with ceremony, define images as means of remembrance and not objects of worship, teach that saints are patterns of living and objects of prayer, and hence may be invoked as intercessors, declare ceremonies to be mystically significant, and sanction prayers for the dead. The articles are embodied in *Institution of a Christian Man* (commonly called " The Bishops' Book," London, 1537).

BIBLIOGRAPHY: J. H. Overton, *The Church in England*, i. 389, London, 1897; W. Clark, *The Anglican Reformation*, pp. 103–104, New York, 1897.

TEN COMMANDMENTS. See DECALOGUE.

TENEBRÆ: The name given the matins and lauds usually sung on Wednesday, Thursday, and Friday of Holy Week. The *Gloria Patri* is omitted, as are the hymns, the antiphons of the Blessed Virgin, etc., in conformity with the sorrowful aspect of the season. When the office is begun, fifteen lighted candles are placed on a triangular candlestick, and one is extinguished at the end of each Psalm, only one being left lighted. The candles on the high altar are likewise extinguished during the singing of the *Benedictus;* and at the antiphon after the *Benedictus* the one lighted candle is hidden at the epistle end of the altar until the completion of the office, when a peculiar wooden clapper is sounded.

The gradual extinction of the candles in the office typifies the growing darkness of earth after Christ, " the Light of the World," was taken away, though the hiding and subsequent bringing out of the one lighted candle shows that the divine light could not really be extinguished. The sound of the clapper represents the confusion which followed the death on the cross.

TENISON, THOMAS: Archbishop of Canterbury; b. at Cottenham (6 m. n. of Cambridge), England, Sept. 29, 1636; d. at Lambeth (3 m. s. of Charing Cross, London) Dec. 14, 1715. He studied at Corpus Christi College, Cambridge (B.A., 1657; M.A., 1660; fellow, 1662; incorporated at Oxford, 1664; B.D., 1667; D.D., 1680). In 1662 he became tutor and in 1665 was appointed university reader at Cambridge. He was ordained about 1659; became vicar of St. Andrew the Great, Cambridge, 1665; preacher at St. Peter Mancroft, Norwich; rector of Holywell and Needingworth, Huntingdonshire, 1667; upper minister of St. Peter Mancroft, 1674; was rector of St. Martin-in-the-Fields, London, 1680–91; minister of St. James, Piccadilly, 1686–92; became archdeacon of London, 1689; bishop of Lincoln, 1692; and archbishop of Canterbury, 1695. He showed great administrative power, for which he was more remarkable than for pulpit eloquence. He was an active Churchman, and busy in matters connected with the Revolution of 1688. In favor with William III., he held various political posts during that reign, but his favor ended with the accession of Queen Anne, whom he crowned, 1702. It was as president of the upper house of convocation that he had the most arduous duties to discharge. The lower house was chiefly composed

of High-churchmen, unfriendly to the Revolution (which Tenison cordially approved), and advocating the independence of the ecclesiastical establishment in a way which he condemned. Aiming at church reform, he manifested a steadiness of purpose and an invincibility of calm resistance, which won for him the name of the " rock-like " Tenison. He erected the first public library in London; it was for his parish in Castle Street, Leicester Square. As archbishop he gave great support to the religious societies, and in particular to the Society for the Propagation of the Gospel, of which he was the continued benefactor and to a large degree the founder. His publications were sermons and controversial tracts.

BIBLIOGRAPHY: *Memoirs of the Life and Times of . . . T. Tennison, late Archbishop of Canterbury*, London, 1715; C. J. Abbey, *The English Church and its Bishops, 1700–1800*, 2 vols., ib. 1887; J. H. Overton, *The Church in England*, vol. ii. passim, ib. 1897; W. H. Hutton, *The English Church . . . (1625–1714)*, ib. 1903; *DNB*, lvi. 57–60.

TENNENT: A family of ministers illustrious in the history of the American Presbyterian Church.

1. William: Presbyterian and educator; b. in Ireland 1673; d. at Neshaminy, Bucks County, Pa., May 6, 1746. Being graduated probably from Trinity College, Dublin, in 1704, he entered the ministry of the Episcopal Church of Ireland, but came to America, and entered the Presbyterian synod of Philadelphia, 1718. In 1720 he settled at Bedford, Westchester County, N. Y., and in 1726 became pastor at Neshaminy, Pa., although he was never formally installed. Impressed by the lack of educational facilities for the young men growing up around him, he erected, in 1728, a log-house, the famous " Log College," wherein he taught three of his four sons and a number of other youth, several of whom afterward rose to eminence in the church. Log College was the first of the literary and theological institutions of the Presbyterian Church in America. Tennent withdrew from active labor about 1742. His publications were mostly sermons. Knowledge of his life and college is in good part derived from Whitefield's journal, which shows his apostolic character.

2. Gilbert: Presbyterian, eldest son of the preceding; b. in County Armagh, Ireland, Feb. 5, 1703; d. in Philadelphia July 23, 1764. He came to America with his father, 1718; was educated by him; after a year's study of medicine he turned to theology and was licensed by the presbytery of Philadelphia, 1725; he acted as tutor in Log College for a year; preached for some time at Newcastle, Del.; and was ordained and installed pastor in New Brunswick, N. J., 1726. Like his father, he was an ardent admirer of Whitefield, and, at Whitefield's solicitation, he accompanied him to Boston on a preaching-tour. By his fiery zeal, deep moral earnestness, spirituality, no less than by his logic and his argumentative ability, he produced everywhere a profound impression; his popularity was second only to Whitefield's. But he was lacking in tenderness and consideration for those who differed from him. At that time many Presbyterian ministers were conscientiously opposed to the methods adopted by the revival preachers. Tennent had no appreciation of such scruples, but set them down to a lack of vital religion. Moreover, Log College was openly criticized by the synod of Philadelphia, because of the type of piety there fostered, and its educational defects. Tennent naturally resented these attacks, and, under what he deemed sufficient provocation, preached in 1740 his famous " Nottingham sermon," in which he dealt vigorously with his opponents. Largely as a result of this sermon and of Tennent's impetuous course came the division of the Presbyterian Church. Although he then contributed so largely to the disruption, he was as active later in effecting the reconciliation of 1758. In 1743 Tennent was called to the Second Presbyterian Church of Philadelphia, then just formed, made up of the admirers of Whitefield and the friends of the revival. But, although he remained their pastor till his death, he did not repeat in his second charge the triumphs of his first; he was faithful and highly useful; but his preaching was quieter, and his delivery much less impassioned. In 1753 he raised in Great Britain some £1,500 for the College of New Jersey. Besides a memoir of his brother John (Boston, 1735), he published a volume of sermons (Philadelphia, 1743), and occasional sermons and pamphlets.

3. William: Presbyterian, and brother of Gilbert; b. in County Antrim, Ireland, Jan. 3, 1705; d. near Freehold, N. J., Mar. 8, 1777. He came to America with his father, who gave him a preparatory course; he then studied theology under his brother Gilbert in New Brunswick; was licensed by the presbytery of New Brunswick; ordained pastor of the church now known as "The Old Tennent Church" near Freehold, 1733, and held the position throughout his life. He was the subject of a trance which has given him great celebrity. While preparing for his examination for licensure, he fell sick, and had a trance which lasted three days, during which time he was, as he believed and declared, in heaven, and heard " unutterable things." His friends thought he was dead, and were upon the point of burying him, notwithstanding the protestations of his physician, when he revived. He regained his health in a year, but had lost all his knowledge of reading and writing, much more, all his previous learning. After a time, however, his knowledge began rapidly to return. " For three years," he said, " the sense of divine things continued so great, and everything else appeared so completely vain, when compared to heaven, that, could I have had the world for stooping down for it, I believe I should not have thought of doing it." Tennent was a remarkable character, full of resource, and indefatigable in Christian labors.

4. John: Presbyterian, and third son of William, the first; b. in County Antrim, Ireland, Nov. 12, 1706; d. near Freehold, N. J., Apr. 23, 1732. He came to America with his father, and received both classical and theological training at the Log College; in 1729 he was licensed to preach; and was pastor near Freehold, N. J., 1730-32. He was very earnest and successful.

5. Charles: Presbyterian, and fourth son of William, the first; b. at Colerain, County Down, Ireland, May 3, 1711; d. at Buckingham, Md., 1771. He came to America with his father; was educated

at Log College; licensed to preach, 1736; was pastor at Whiteclay Creek, Del., and later at Buckingham, Md.

6. William, the third: Presbyterian, and son of William, the second; b. near Freehold, N. J., 1740; d. at Charleston (?), S. C., Aug. 11, 1777. He was graduated from the College of New Jersey, 1758; was licensed to preach, 1762; ordained, 1763; junior pastor of the church in Norwalk, Conn., 1765-72; pastor of an Independent Church in Charleston, S. C., 1772-77. He was an eloquent preacher and of clear judgment.

BIBLIOGRAPHY: The list of writings by the Tennents will be found accurately described in C. Evans, American Bibliography, vols. ii.-vi., Chicago, 1904-10. Notices of all but Charles will be found in W. B. Sprague, Annals of the American Pulpit, pp. 23 sqq., 41 sqq., 52 sqq., 264 sqq., New York, 1858. Consult further: E. H. Gillett, Hist. of the Presbyterian Church, vol. i. passim, Philadelphia, 1864; C. A. Briggs, American Presbyterianism, passim, New York, 1885; G. P. Hays, Presbyterians, pp. 89-92, New York, 1892; R. E. Thompson, in American Church History Series, vol. vi. passim, New York. 1895. On 1 consult also: A. Alexander, Biographical Sketches of the Founder and . . . Alumni of the Log College, Princeton, 1845. On 2: The funeral sermon by President S. Finley was published with a " Funeral Eulogy," Philadelphia, 1764; Life of the Rev. William Tennent, with an Account of his Being three Days in a Trance, New York, 1847. On 3: E. Boudinot, Memoir of William Tennent, New York, 1847. On 4: G. Tennent (his brother), wrote a memoir in connection with A Discourse on Regeneration, Boston, 1735.

TENT. See TABERNACLE, HEBREW.

TEPHILLIN (PHYLACTERIES): Boxes containing inscriptions in Hebrew worn by Jews for ceremonial purposes. The boxes are constructed from the skin of a clean animal and sewed upon a strong leather foundation; they contain definitely prescribed passages from the Pentateuch. They are worn during prayers during the week, being fastened to the forehead and the left arm by means of straps. The rabbinical command to wear phylacteries rests upon a literal construction of Deut. vi. 6-8 [cf. xi. 18; Ex. xiii. 9, 16; Matt. xxiii. 1 sqq.]. A metaphorical sense has been seen in the passage by some Jews and by Christians, but the passage favors a literal reading. The tephillin for the head differ from those for the arm. The former consist of four compartments, each of which contains a passage from the Bible (Ex. xiii. 1-10, 11-16; Deut. vi. 4-9, and xi. 13-21) written on a strip of parchment, which is rolled up and tied with a hair. On two sides on the outside of the phylactery is placed the letter Shin, one with four and the other with three prongs. The arm phylacteries have but one cell in which the same Biblical sections are contained on one roll of parchment. The tephillin for the head during prayer are firmly placed on the forehead below the hair, between the eyebrows. The knot of the loop that passes around the head must lodge on the neck behind, and the straps must be long enough to fall over the shoulders and hang down in front below the breast. The hand-tephillin are so fastened that the box is turned inward toward the heart, the seat of the feelings. The straps are wound seven times around the arm and then three times around the middle and ring finger. The single compartment of the hand-tephillin symbolizes the unity of God; the four compartments of those for the head, his sway over the four corners of the earth.

At the putting on of the tephillin for the head, the benediction, " Blessed art thou Yahweh, our God, king of the universe, who hast hallowed us by thy commandments and hast commanded us to wear the tephillin," is pronounced. When assuming the hand-tephillin the benediction is only slightly different. There are minute injunctions as to who may wear them, where and when they may be worn, etc. They are first put on by boys at confirmation at the age of thirteen, but are not worn on the Sabbath or on holidays.

The Talmud lays great stress on the tephillin ceremonial, and carries its prescriptions into the minutest details, which are assumed to be Mosaic. The practise of the ceremony was looked upon as a kind of altar service. Whoever puts on the tephillin and reads the *Shema* (Deut. vi. 4–5) may be considered as one who has built an altar and laid a sacrifice upon it (Rosh ha-shanah 3, 15a). God himself is said to wear them. He himself revealed them to Moses and taught him how to place the knot behind the head. The tephillin were supposed to guard their wearer from witchcraft and sin, and were worn as amulets. Some teachers went beyond the Biblical injunction and wore them all day. Nevertheless, there were persons and sects who discarded or made light of the articles, especially in later centuries.

Minute directions are given for the preparation of these articles. They must be made by Jews. The words on the parchment may be written from memory, but no letter may run into another or stand out more than another. No erasures or corrections may be made. The name of God must be written by the scribe with reverence and full appreciation of its significance. (AUGUST WÜNSCHE.)

BIBLIOGRAPHY: M. Margoliouth, *Fundamental Principles of Modern Judaism*, pp. 1–49, London, 1843; Z. Frankel, *Ueber den Einfluss der palästinischen Exegese auf die alexandrinische Hermeneutik*, pp. 90 sqq., Leipsic, 1851; L. Zunz, *Gesammelte Schriften*, ii. 172–176, Berlin, 1876; G. Klein, in *JPT*, 1881, pp. 666–689; M. L. Rodkinson, *Ursprung und Entwickelung des Phylacterien-Riten*, Pressburg, 1883; idem, *Hist. of Amulets, Charms, and Talismans*, New York, 1893; M. Friedländer, *Jewish Religion*, pp. 331–334, London, 1900; idem, *Der Antichrist in den vorchristlichen jüdischen Quellen*, pp. 155–165, Göttingen, 1901; M. Grünbaum, *Gesammelte Aufsätze*, pp. 208 sqq., Berlin, 1901; Schürer, *Geschichte*, ii. 484 sqq., Eng. transl., II., ii., iii. sqq.; Benzinger, *Archäologie*, p. 387; *DB*, iii. 869–874; *EB*, ii. 1566–67; *JE*, x. 21–28; Vigouroux, *Dictionnaire*, fasc. xxxi. 349–353; and the commentaries on the Scriptural passages cited.

TERAPHIM: The name of an image or object apparently used specifically for divination. The term occurs in nine passages in the Old Testament. Though plural in form, the usage in I Sam. xix. 13–16 shows that it was, at any rate, at times singular in meaning, just as was (for the most part) *Elohim*, " God," though the use of the plural " gods " by Laban when speaking of the teraphim suggests a real plural. Some explain the use of the word as a plural of majesty; others, however, regard it in the same way as they do *Elohim*, the linguistic evidence being that the object connoted was at one time plural. In Gen. xxxi. 19, 34, 35 (E) the size was evidently not great, since it could be hidden in the camel's litter, and the context (verse 30) suggests that it was an image or idol (" my gods " as above). I Sam. xix. 13–16, on the other hand, gives the impression that it might be as large as a man, and both passages seem to involve use in the household, not in a temple. From Judges xvii. 4–5, xviii. 17, 18, 20, 30, it evidently differed from both a " graven " and a " molten " image, and does not appear to have been an object of worship, since Judges xviii. reports again and again that the Danites set up (for worship) the graven image which Micah had made, but of the teraphim it alleges only that they took it from Micah and carried it with them. The use of the object as a means of divination is settled by Ezek. xxi. 21, where it is described as employed by the king of Babylon among other means for determining the future; and by Zech. x. 2, where the parallelism is: " teraphim have spoken vanity, diviners have seen a lie."

In I Sam. xv. 23 (R. V.; the A. V. obscures the original), one of the later (Deuteronomistic) portions of the book, the teraphim is implicitly condemned; according to II Kings xxiii. 24 it was among the things which were abolished in the reformation of Josiah. It is not improbable that in Gen. xxxv. 2, 4 (by E, the writer of Gen. xxxi. 19 sqq.) the teraphim are included in the " strange gods " which were to be put away (see DEMON, § 4). On the other hand, in Hos. iii. 4, it is among the things (which may be classed as official) deprivation of which was to be a part of the punishment of unfaithful Israel, viz., king, priest, sacrifice, pillar, and ephod, and it was therefore by that prophet not regarded as inconsistent with the worship of Yahweh. Consequently, the total effect of all the Old-Testament passages is to indicate that the size of the teraphim was variable; that it might be kept in a house or a temple or shrine; that it is to be distinguished both from a molten and a graven image, but that its form is not known;* that it was probably an importation from abroad (Gen. xxxi.), both Laban and the king of Babylon making use of it; that its employment came under condemnation at least as early as 621 B.C., possibly considerably earlier, if Gen. xxxv. 2 intends to include it among the " strange gods," though in the time of David and probably of Hosea its use was regarded as legitimate; and, finally, it does not appear, except from the mention by Hosea, to have belonged to the public official cult, but rather to have been employed in private or household practise in divining. To be noted is the fact that there is no statement outside of the Genesis passages or even necessary implication that the teraphim was an object of worship, although the contrary hypothesis has ruled in exegesis.

By the best authorities the derivation of the word is still regarded as doubtful (Brown-Driver-Briggs, *Hebrew and English Lexicon*, s.v.); many connect the word with *repha'im*, " shades " (cf. Isa. xiv. 9, R. V. margin), and regard the thing itself as associated with ancestor worship. It is impossible to say whether the translators of the Septuagint were entirely unacquainted with the object or knew so

---

* It does not follow from I Sam. xix. that the form was more than approximately human, though its size in that case must have corresponded to that of a man.

well its form, etc., as not to think of it as requiring explanation. They usually transliterate the word, now as a singular, again as a plural. In I Sam. xix. 13, 16, they render by *kenotaphia*, the only possible meaning of which in the passage is image, the usual sense, "empty tomb," giving no adequate sense. Symmachus renders by *eidōlon* or *eidōla*. The Vulgate is very varied in its rendering, sometimes simply transliterating, sometimes translating by *idola*, *idololatria*, *figuræ idolorum*, *statua*, *simulacrum*. The Syriac sometimes renders by the word equivalent to the Hebr. *ẓelem*, "image" (Gen. i. 26), also by other words which have a connection with soothsaying. Rabbinic tradition varies between some undefined medium used in divination, the semblance of a human head, or a mummified head such as was reported as in use by Hauranians for oracular purposes (cf. D. Chwolson, *Die Ssabier*, ii. 19 sqq., 150 sqq., St. Petersburg, 1856). This would lead naturally to the conclusion that it was employed as an ancestral oracle, which has indeed been a common method of explanation, comparison being made with the Roman *Lares et penates* (cf. F. Schwally, *Das Leben nach dem Tode*, pp. 35 sqq., Giessen, 1892; H. Schultz, in his *Old Testament Theology*, p. 119, calls the teraphim "household *palladia*").   GEO. W. GILMORE.

BIBLIOGRAPHY: Jerome, *Epist.*, xxix.; J. Buxtorf, *Lexicon Chaldaicum, Talmudicum*, etc., pp. 2660 sqq., Basel, 1632; D. Chwolson, *Die Ssabier*, ii. 19 sqq., 150 sqq., 388 sqq., St. Petersburg, 1856; H. Ewald, *Antiquities*, pp. 223–225, Boston, 1876; P. Scholz, *Götzendienst und Zauberwesen bei den alten Hebräern*, pp. 127 sqq., Regensburg, 1877; B. Stade, *Biblische Theologie des alten Testaments*, i. 121, 224, 262, Tübingen, 1905; *Geschichte des Volkes Israel*, i. 467, Berlin, 1887; H. Schultz, *O. T. Theology*, i. 93, 119, 149, 284, Edinburgh, 1892; G. F. Moore, *Commentary on Judges*, pp. 379 sqq., New York, 1895; H. P. Smith, *Commentary on Samuel*, p. xxxiv. and at the passages cited, ib. 1899; T. C. Foote, in *JBL*, xxi (1902), 27 sqq.; Nowack, *Archäologie*, ii. 23; Benzinger, *Archäologie*, pp. 328, 333, 347; *DB*, iv. 718; *EB*, iv. 4974–75; *KL*, xii. 108–109.

TERCE: The service for the "third hour" in the Breviary (q.v.), recited normally about 9 A.M., usually in monastic houses immediately before the community mass, and in pontifical functions just before the bishop goes to the altar. Its special note is the commemoration of the descent of the Holy Ghost, for whose guidance and inspiration the hymn (invariable except at Pentecost) prays. There is a short general introduction, and then after the hymn follow three sections of Ps. cxix., the chapter, which is the same as that for lauds and vespers of the day, a short responsory, and the collect for the day, sometimes (as in Lent and on vigils) preceded by a long series of versicles and responses said kneeling.

TERMINARE: A term used to designate the begging of the so-called mendicant orders. Every mendicant cloister or hospice had its definite district (*terminus*), within which it was obliged to confine its operations. The cloistral collectors of alms were called "terminators."

TERMINISM, TERMINISTIC CONTROVERSY: The doctrine of a definite period of grace for man within which alone he can effectually achieve his conversion, and the controversy pertaining to the same. While the concept was not exactly created

by the Pietistic movement, it was nevertheless projected by it into its full significance. Already J. C. Dannhauer (q.v.), on the basis of Heb. iii. 7, had distinguished between the "times of vengeance" and of "visitation" (*Hodosophia Christiana*, p. 876, 1649), and mentions a denial of grace "peremptorily" in the former (*Katechismusmilch*, vi 206, 1657–78). From him Philip Jakob Spener adopted both the idea and the term, stating repeatedly that "although the purpose of grace commonly lasts with sinners till the end of this life nevertheless it can be virtually cut off in the course of life, by the judgment of obduracy" (*Das Gericht der Verstockung*, pp. 24 sqq., Frankfort, 1701) Terminism attained to greater importance first through the tract of a Sorau deacon, J. G. Böse (b. at Oschatz, 31 m. e.n.e. of Leipsic, about 1662 d. at Sorau, 95 m. s.e. of Berlin, Feb., 1700). He studied at Leipsic, notably under J. B. Carpzov, and came to Sorau in 1690. Here he soon experienced an inner conversion, which caused him to give much more serious heed to his official duties, particularly the confessional. Above all he took offense at the frivolity of "death-bed conversions." A penitential sermon on Rom. ii. 4–5, as well as his total behavior, occasioned manifold conflicts with members of the congregation, and chiefly with his clerical brethren both within and without the town. The situation grew still more acute upon the publication of the tract, *Terminus peremptorius salutis humanæ* (1698; 2d ed., Frankfort, 1701). An opinion from Rostock, in 1699, was unfavorable to Böse but a second Leipsic review, by the time the Pietistic members had gained the control of the faculty supported him. In Jan., 1700, he was suspended and died the following month. The second Leipsic review was opposed at Wittenberg. Two of its established professors became bitterest enemies and chief antagonists in the dispute. The one was Adam Rechenberg (1642–1721), son-in-law of Spener; the other was Thomas Ittig (1643–1710), the local superintendent. Of outside faculties Wittenberg (J. G. Neumann, Johann Deutschmann), and Rostock (Johannes Fecht, A. J. Krakevitz) interposed on the anti-terministic side. In a short time, the number of controversial tracts exceeded that of any previous ecclesiastical dispute, theologians from all quarters of Germany taking a part. After 1702 Rechenberg and Ittig withdrew more or less from the controversy, but this continued until 1704, and was renewed occasionally thereafter.

As with Spener in Pietism so with Böse, the motive of his terminism was thoroughly practical; he desired to have an effective weapon for shattering the security of wanton sinners. He was led, however, to a position beyond this which gave grave cause for doubt. On one occasion he affirmed that for every human being, and not merely for hardened sinners, only one defined season of grace was set for conversion within this present life; and then he appeared to base the same wholly upon the free will of God, without regard to human conduct. Yet in point of fact, Böse applied his theory of the denial of the term of grace only to those who hardened themselves; nor would it seem that he ever became clear whether the ultimate cause for obduracy and thus for the appointment of the " peremptory limit " rests in man or God. In contrast, Rechenberg restricted the entire proposition to the " utterly hardened," leaving no doubt that obduracy was to be referred not to an absolute decree of God, but to the human attitude. For presentation and elucidation both terminists and anti-terminists employed the scheme of the orthodox doctrine of " antecedent " and " following grace." Both agreed that antecedent grace was universal, and fixed no definite limit. On the other hand, the terminists would have it that following grace, with which they included reclaiming grace, becomes particular grace during the lifetime of man, at the moment when obduracy becomes final. But on the opposing side it was affirmed that " reclaiming grace " is as universal as " calling grace "; and that the term of grace appointed by God lasts with every man, irrespectively of his actual moral and religious condition, until his death. R. H. GRÜTZMACHER.

BIBLIOGRAPHY: J. G. Walch, *Einleitung in die Religionsstreitigkeiten der evangelisch-lutherischen Kirche*, ii. 850–892, 10 vols., Jena, 1733–39; A. C. von Einem, *Kirchengeschichte des 18. Jahrhunderts*, ii. 337, Leipsic, 1783; G. Frank, *Geschichte der protestantischen Theologie*, ii. 175 sqq., ib. 1865; F. H. Hesse, *Der terministische Streit*, Giessen, 1877; A. Ritschl, *Geschichte des Pietismus*, ii. 210 sqq., Bonn, 1884; *KL*, xi. 1361–62.

TERRITORIALISM: A theory of church government which came in with the Reformation according to which the ruler of a country has a natural right to control the ecclesiastical affairs of the people. Enlightened Humanism first applied the concept of organized association to the State Church. Assuming that the primary civil contract includes the ecclesiastical, this theory views the adherents of the State Church as partners, the State Church as an association church, and thus shows that in course of time there may grow up in this church a representative constitution such as has already partly emancipated it from the State, and seems likely to carry the process further. This result has come about through collegialistic modifications (see COLLEGIALISM).

Territorialism, as represented by, e.g., Hugo Grotius and Christian Thomasius (qq.v.), pushed into the Evangelical praxis without difficulty. The church had been governed through state boards of control; only now the standpoints governing the process since the Reformation became gradually modified, and the alteration was unostentatiously effected step by step. A similar process marked the beginning of collegialistic modifications. Collegialism and territorialism are not essentially antithetical; both presuppose the primary civil contracts, and the distinction between them rests always in what they assume to be the measure of the respective concessions or reservations by the contracting parties; indeed, both have grown up on parallel fundamental hypotheses. But territorialism draws its boundary lines of the State's " right in sacred things " so wide that scarcely anything is left for the free play of " partnership." Collegialism first clearly restricted the State to its rights of general supremacy, and sharply distinguished from these the rights of society. And though this theory concedes to sovereign authority the matter of régime

in the Church by virtue of a tacit or implicit compact, yet this is allowed with the understanding that the attribution conveys to the civil sovereignty, over and above its proper sovereign rights, the further power of an association as such. Therefore something becomes conveyed which is extraneous to the State's own authority, and this may be taken away from it by a new compact. The territorialists ascribe to the State alone the right to draw the boundary lines between civil power and the power of associations; collegialism claims the rights of association in favor of the particular association as ultimate or original, not as derived from civil favor. The collegial system shows not only a quantitative but also a qualitative advance.

Every state which, assuming social problems as such to be problems of State, subordinates itself to society and becomes thereby identified with the social fabric, must assume the charge of ecclesiastical social tasks, as well, and is of necessity committed to the territorial polity. The most pronounced example of this is France. The French constitution of 1791 unconditionally instituted the State according to the social points of view, and, at the same time, the " Civil Constitution of the Clergy " of July 12, 1790, dissolved the ecclesiastical organism in terms of the political. The proclamation of a distinct state religion was only a step further in the same course. And though the Prussian general statute law qualifies clergymen as indirect or collateral servants of State, it does not go to the length of that " Civil Constitution," but contains, in its collegialistic features, the germs of that constitutional development which transcended territorialism. On the other hand, both in literature and also for a good while in practise, territorialism continued potent. See CHURCH AND STATE, I., § 7.

E. SEHLING.

BIBLIOGRAPHY: K. S. Zachariä, *Die Einheit des Staates und der Kirche mit Rücksicht auf die deutsche Reichsverfassung*, n.p., 1797; H. Stephani, *Ueber die absolute Einheit der Kirche und des Staates*, Würzburg, 1802; R. Rothe, *Die Anfänge der christlichen Kirche und ihrer Verfassung*, Wittenberg, 1837; K. Schmitthenner, *Ueber das Recht der Regenten in kirchlichen Dingen*, Berlin, 1838; E. W. Klee, *Das Recht der einen allgemeinen Kirche Jesu Christi*, 2 parts, Magdeburg, 1839–41; Schaff, *Christian Church*, vi. 683 sqq.

TERRY, MILTON SPENSER: Methodist Episcopalian; b. at Coeymans, N. Y., Feb. 22, 1840. He was educated at Troy University and Yale Divinity School (graduated, 1862). He has held pastorates at the Methodist Episcopal churches of Hamden, N. Y. (1862–63), Delhi (1864–67), Peekskill (1867–69), Poughkeepsie (1870–73), Eighteenth Street Church, New York City (1873–76), and Kingston (1876–79). From 1879 to 1883 he was presiding elder of New York City and Westchester County. He has been professor of Hebrew and Old-Testament exegesis and theology in the Garrett Biblical Institute, Evanston, Ill., since 1884. In theology, he " holds the Wesleyan Arminian system of theology as against the Calvinistic system and accepts the main positions of the modern critical school, but with firm adherence to the fundamentals of Protestant Evangelical Christianity." He has written: *Commentary on Judges, Ruth, First and*

Second Samuel (New York, 1873); *Commentary on Kings, Chronicles, Ezra, Nehemiah, and Esther* (1875); *Biblical Hermeneutics* (1883); *Commentary on Genesis and Exodus* (1889); *The Sibylline Oracles* (1890); *The Prophecies of Daniel Expounded* (1893); *The Song of Songs: An Inspired Melodrama* (Cincinnati, 1893); *Rambles in the Old World* (1894); *The New Apologetic* (New York, 1897); *Biblical Apocalyptics* (1898); *Moses and the Prophets* (1901); *The New and Living Way* (1902); *The Mediation of Jesus Christ* (1903); and *Primer of Christian Doctrines* (Cincinnati, 1906).

TERSTEEGEN, ter-stê′gen, **GERHARD (GERRIT TER STEEGEN):** German Reformed mystic and hymn-writer; b. at Mörs (17 m. n.n.e. of Düsseldorf) Nov. 25, 1697; d. at Mülheim-on-the-Ruhr (15 m. n.n.e. of Düsseldorf) Apr. 3, 1769. He early came under the influence of a mysticism which was at least indifferent to the recognized Church, and before long he renounced a mercantile career to live as a hermit, giving to the poor all that was not absolutely necessary for his scanty needs, yet troubled for a time with grave doubts. Somewhat later he abandoned such excessive asceticism, and was now able to devote his evenings to writing, the days being spent in ribbon-weaving. His first work was the *Unpartheiischer Abriss christlicher Grundwahrheiten in Frage und Antworten* (Duisburg, 1801), though his first publication was a translation of the *Manuel de piété* of Jean de Labadie (1725). In 1727 he completed his *Wahre Theologie des Sohnes Gottes* (not published until 1821), and composed his *Zeugnis der Wahrheit*, as well as his first collection of hymns and rimed apothegms entitled *Geistliches Blumengärtlein inniger Seelen* (Frankfort, 1729) and *Der Frommen Lotterie* (Eng. transl., by Lady E. A. Durand, *The Spiritual Lottery*, London, 1874). His largest work was his *Auserlesene Lebensbeschreibungen heiliger Seelen* (3 vols., 1733–53), which conveyed to many the false impression that he entertained Roman Catholic tendencies. In 1736 he published at Duisburg a second edition of the *Vermehrte Glaubens- und Liebesübung* of Joachim Neander (the fourth and subsequent editions being entitled *Gottgeheiligtes Harfenspiel der Kinder Zion*), which contained fifty-nine of his own hymns.

After 1725 Tersteegen became a leader in private devotional meetings, and three years later he found himself obliged to give up his trade and devote himself to quasi-pastoral duties, deriving his support from the contributions of friends. He established at Otterbeck a semi-monastic community, and his influence gradually extended far and wide, not only throughout Germany, but even to Denmark, Sweden, and Pennsylvania, while after 1732 he regularly visited Holland, the results of this prestige being in part recorded in his *Geistliche und erbauliche Briefe* (2 vols., Solingen, 1773–75). Toward the Moravians his attitude was unfavorable, and he was unable to sympathize with Zinzendorf. In 1740 new legislation rendered it impossible for Tersteegen to conduct his devotional meetings elsewhere than in Holland, but ten years later they could again be held, and Tersteegen continued to address them every one or two weeks until, in 1756,

he became physically incapable of addressing large audiences. These addresses were later published as *Geistliche Brosamen, von des Herrn Tisch gefallen* (4 parts, Duisburg, 1769–73; Eng. transl. of selections by S. Jackson, *Spiritual Crumbs from the Master's Table*, London, 1837). Apparently at the suggestion of the supreme consistorial councilor, Johann Julius Hecker, Tersteegen set forth his views on faith, justification, etc., in the first appendix to his *Weg der Wahrheit* (1750; stereotyped ed. by J. F. Steinkoff, with life, Stuttgart, 1905), and it may also have been Hecker who inspired him to write his *Gedanken über eines Anonymi Buch, genannt: Vermischte Werke des Weltweisen zu Sanssouci* (2d ed., Schaffhausen, 1763), in which he very aptly criticized the attitude of Frederick the Great toward religion.

While Tersteegen was a decided mystic, and continued to the end of his life outside the Reformed Church, he was in no sense of the term the founder of a sect, even his separatism being mainly due to his abhorrence of merely formal orthodoxy. In this spirit he wrote *Beweis, dass man demjenigen, der von Gott in seinem Gewissen zurückgehalten wird, mit offenbaren Weltkindern und Gottlosen nicht zum Abendmahl zu gehen, seine Gewissensfreiheit ungekränkt lassen müsse* (1768) and *Vom Separatismus und der Herunterlassung* (Essen, 1842). His chief fame, however, is due to his hymns, which have given him an importance second to no other hymn-writer in the Reformed Church. These hymns, 111 in number, were first incorporated in Pietistic and separatistic collections, but after 1829 the regular churches accepted them in increasing proportion. [The hymns have been edited not only in his *Gesammelte Schriften* (8 vols., Stuttgart, 1844–45), but also by W. Nelle (*Geistliche Lieder*, Gütersloh, 1897, with a life and the story of his poems); and many of them have been translated into English (see Julian, *Hymnology*, pp. 1142–45), as by Mrs. F. Bevan in her *Hymns of Ter Steegen, Suso, and Others* (London, 1895), and by Lady E. A. Durand in her *Imitations from the German of Spitta and Tersteegen* (1873).] Among the best-known are "Brunn alles Heils, dich ehren wir " (" Thee, Fount of blessing, we adore," by Miss Catherine Winkworth), " Gott ist gegenwärtig " (" Lo, God is here! Let us adore," by John Wesley,) " O Gott! O Geist O Licht des Lebens! " (" O God, O Spirit, Light of all that live " by Miss Winkworth), " O Majestät wir fallen nieder " (" O Lord our God, in reverence lowly "), and " Verborgne Gottesliebe du " (" Thou hidden love of God, whose height," by John Wesley)

(E. SIMONS.)

BIBLIOGRAPHY: Besides the lives in the editions of Terstee gen's *Schriften* and *Weg der Wahrheit* noted in the text consult: G. Kerlen, *Gerhard Tersteegen*, Mülheim, 1851 M. Goebel, *Geschichte des christlichen Lebens in der rhein isch-westfälischen evangelischen Kirche*, iii. 289–447, Cob lenz, 1860; A. Ritschl, *Geschichte des Pietismus*, i. 455–494, Bonn, 1880; S. W. Duffield, *English Hymns*, pp 177–178 et passim, New York, 1886; H. E. Govan, *Lif of Gerhard Tersteegen, with Selections from his Writings* new ed., London, 1902; Julian, *Hymnology*, pp. 1142–1145; *ADB*, vol. xxvii.

TERTIARIES (TERTIUS ORDO DE PŒNITENTIA): The name of the members of a spiritual as sociation, men or women, who, whether in the world or in close associations, lived according to " the third rule " of certain orders. The institution first arose among the Minorites (see FRANCIS, SAINT, OF ASSISI, AND THE FRANCISCAN ORDER), then was imitated in the preaching order, and later, under various names, arose also in other orders, such as the Augustinians, Servites, and Trappists (qq.v.).

(O. ZÖCKLER†.)

BIBLIOGRAPHY: Consult the lists of works under the articles in this work on the orders named in the text; also J. G. Adderly and C. L. Marson, " *Third Orders.*" A *Translation of an ancient Rule of the Tertiaries, together with an Account of some modern " Third Orders,*" Oxford, 1902.

TERTULLIAN, ter-tul′i-an, **QUINTUS SEPTIMIUS FLORENS.**

I. Life: Quintus Septimius Florens Tertullian, the first great writer of Latin Christianity and one of the grandest and most original characters of the ancient Church, was born at Carthage about 150 or 160, and died there between 220 and 240. Of his life very little is known, and that little is based upon passing references in his own writings, and upon Eusebius, *Hist. eccl.*, II., ii. 4 (Eng. transl. in *NPNF*, 2 ser., i. 106, with the notes of A. C. McGiffert), and Jerome, *De vir. ill.*, liii. (Eng. transl. in *NPNF*, 2 ser., iii. 373). His father held a position (centurio proconsularis, " aide-de-camp ") in the Roman army in Africa, and Tertullian's Punic blood palpably pulsates in his style, with its archaisms or provincialisms, its glowing imagery, its passionate temper. He was a scholar, having received an excellent education. He wrote at least three books in Greek, to which he himself refers; but none of these are extant. His principal study was jurisprudence, and his methods of reasoning reveal striking marks of his juridical training. He shone among the advocates of Rome, as Eusebius reports. His conversion to Christianity took place about 197–198 (so Harnack, Bonwetsch, and others), but its immediate antecedents are unknown except as they are conjectured from his writings. The event must have been sudden and decisive, transforming at once his own personality; he himself said that he could not imagine a truly Christian life without such a conscious breach, a radical act of conversion: " Christians are made, not born " (*Apol.*, xviii.; *ANF*, iii. 33). In the church of Carthage he was ordained a presbyter, though he was married—a fact which is well established by his two books to his wife. In middle life (about 207) he broke with the Catholic Church and became the leader and the passionate and brilliant exponent of Montanism (see MONTANUS, MONTANISM), that is, he became a schismatic. The statement of Augustine (*Hær.*, lxxxvi.) that before his death Tertullian returned to the bosom of the Catholic Church is very improbable. His party, the Tertullianists, still had in the times of Augustine a basilica in Carthage, but in that same period passed into the orthodox Church.

XI.—20

Jerome says that Tertullian lived to a great age. In spite of his schism, Tertullian continued to fight heresy, especially Gnosticism; and by the doctrinal works thus produced he became the teacher of Cyprian, the predecessor of Augustine, and the chief founder of Latin theology.

II. Writings: These number thirty-seven, and several Latin tracts are lost (cf. *ANF*, iii. 12–13) as well as those written in Greek. Tertullian's writings cover the whole theological field of the time—apologetics against paganism and Judaism, polemics, polity, discipline, and morals, or the whole reorganization of human life on a Christian basis; they give a picture of the religious life and thought of the time which is of the greatest interest to the church historian. Their general temper is austere, their purpose practical; they are full of life and freshness. In his endeavors to make the Latin language a vehicle for his somewhat tumultuous ideas, the author now and then becomes strained and obscure; but, as a rule, he is quick, precise, and pointed. He is always powerful and intrepid, commanding, not begging, the attention of the reader; with reference to earlier literature and customs he is a master of wit and sarcasm and is always original. He has been likened to a fresh mountain torrent, tumultuous, and making its own path.

The chronology of these writings is in part determined by the Montanistic views that are set forth in some of them, by the author's own allusions to this writing or that as ante-dating others (cf. Harnack, *Litteratur*, ii. 260–262), and by definite historic data (e.g., the reference to the death of Septimius Severus, *Ad Scapulam*, iv.). In his work against Marcion, which he calls his third composition on the Marcionite heresy, he gives its date as the fifteenth year of Severus' reign (*Adv. Marcionem*, i. 1, 15). The writings may be divided with reference to the two periods of Tertullian's Christian activity, the Catholic and the Montanist (cf. Harnack, ut sup., ii. 262 sqq.), or according to their subject-matter. The object of the former mode of division is to show, if possible, the change of views Tertullian's mind underwent. Following the latter mode, which is of a more practical interest, the writings fall into two groups: (1) apologetic and polemic, e.g., *Apologeticus, De testimonio animæ, Adv. Judæos, Adv. Marcionem, Adv. Praxeam, Adv. Hermogenem, De præscriptione hereticorum, Scorpiace*, to counteract the sting of Gnosticism, etc.; (2) practical and disciplinary, e.g., *De monogamia, Ad uxorem, De virginibus velandis, De cultu feminarum, De patientia, De pudicitia, De oratione, Ad martyras*, etc. Among the apologetic writings the *Apologeticus*, addressed to the Roman magistrates, is the most pungent defense of Christianity and the Christians ever written against the reproaches of the pagans, and one of the most magnificent legacies of the ancient Church, full of enthusiasm, courage, and vigor. It first clearly proclaims the principle of religious liberty as an inalienable right of man, and demands a fair trial for the Christians before they are condemned to death. Tertullian was the first to break the force of such

1. General Character.

2. Chronology and Contents.

charges as that the Christians sacrificed infants at the celebration of the Lord's Supper and committed incest; he pointed to the commission of such crimes in the pagan world, and then proved by the testimony of Pliny that Christians pledged themselves not to commit murder, adultery, or other crimes; he adduced also the inhumanity of pagan customs, such as feeding the flesh of gladiators to beasts. The gods have no existence, and thus there is no pagan religion against which Christians may offend. Christians do not engage in the foolish worship of the emperors; they do better, they pray for them. Christians can afford to be put to torture and to death, and the more they are cast down the more they grow; " the blood of Christians is seed " (chap. l.). In the *De præscriptione* he develops as its fundamental idea that, in a dispute between the Church and a separating party, the whole burden of proof lies with the latter, as the Church, in possession of the unbroken tradition, is by its very existence a guaranty of its truth. The five books against Marcion, written 207 or 208, are the most comprehensive and elaborate of his polemical works, invaluable for the understanding of Gnosticism. Of the moral and ascetic treatises, the *De patientia* and *De spectaculis* are among the most interesting, and the *De pudicitia* and *De virginibus velandis* among the most characteristic.

III. Theology: Though thoroughly conversant with the Greek theology, Tertullian was independent of its metaphysical speculation.

1. General Character. He had learned from the Greek apologies, and forms a direct contrast to Origen. Origen pushed his idealism in the direction of Gnostic spiritualism. Tertullian, the prince of realists and practical theologian, carried his realism to the verge of materialism. This is evident from his ascription to God of corporeity and his acceptance of the traducian theory of the origin of the soul. He despised Greek philosophy, and, far from looking at Plato, Aristotle, and other Greek thinkers whom he quotes as forerunners of Christ and the Gospel, he pronounces them the patriarchal forefathers of the heretics (*De anima*, iii.). He held up to scorn their inconsistency when he referred to the fact that Socrates in dying ordered a cock to be sacrificed to Æsculapius (*De anima*, i.). Tertullian always wrote under stress of a felt necessity. He was never so happy as when he had opponents like Marcion and Praxeas, and, however abstract the ideas may be which he treated, he was always moved by practical considerations to make his case clear and irresistible. It was partly this element which gave to his writings a formative influence upon the theology of the post-Nicene period in the West and has rendered them fresh reading to this day. He was a born disputant, moved by the noblest impulses known in the Church. It is true that during the third century no mention is made of his name by other authors. Lactantius at the opening of the fourth century is the first to do this, but Augustine treats him openly with respect. Cyprian, Tertullian's North African compatriot, though he nowhere mentions his name, was well read in his writings, as Cyprian's secretary told Jerome.

Tertullian's main doctrinal teachings are as follows: (1) The soul was not preexistent, as Plato affirmed, nor addicted to metempsy-

2. Specific Teachings. chosis, as the Pythagoreans held. In each individual it is a new product, proceeding equally with the body from the parents, and not created later and associated with the body (*De anima*, xxvii.). It is, however, a distinct entity and a certain corporeity and as such it may be tormented in Hades (*De anima*, lviii.). (2) The soul's sinfulness is easily explained by its traducian origin (*De anima*, xxxix.). It is in bondage to Satan (whose works it renounces in baptism), but has seeds of good (*De anima*, xli.), and when awakened, it passes to health and at once calls upon God (*Apol.*, xvii.) and is naturally Christian. It exists in all men alike; it is a culprit and yet an unconscious witness by its impulse to worship, its fear of demons, and its musings on death to the power, benignity, and judgment of God as revealed in the Christian's Scriptures (*De testimonio*, v.–vi.). (3) God, who made the world out of nothing through his Son, the Word, has corporeity though he is a spirit (*De præscriptione*, vii.; *Adv. Praxeam*, vii.). In the statement of the Trinity, Tertullian was a forerunner of the Nicene doctrine, approaching the subject from the standpoint of the Logos doctrine, though he did not fully state the immanent Trinity. In his treatise against Praxeas, who taught patripassianism in Rome, he used the words, " Trinity and economy, persons and substance." The Son is distinct from the Father, and the Spirit from both the Father and the Son (*Adv. Praxeam*, xxv.). " These three are one substance, not one person; and it is said, ' I and my Father are one ' in respect not of the singularity of number but the unity of the substance." The very names " Father " and " Son " indicate the distinction of personality. The Father is one, the Son is one, and the Spirit is one (*Adv. Praxeam*, ix.). The question whether the Son was coeternal with the Father Tertullian does not set forth in full clearness; and though he did not fully state the doctrine of the immanence of the Trinity, he went a long distance in the way of approach to it (B. B. Warfield, in *Princeton Theological Review*, 1906, pp. 56, 159). (4) In soteriology Tertullian does not dogmatize, he prefers to keep silence at the mystery of the cross (*De patientia*, iii.). The sufferings of Christ's life as well as of the crucifixion are efficacious to redemption. In the water of baptism, which (upon a partial quotation of John iii. 5) is made necessary (*De baptismate*, vi.), we are born again; we do not receive the Holy Spirit in the water, but are prepared for the Holy Spirit. We little fishes, after the example of the *ichthys*, " fish," Jesus Christ (having reference to the formula *Jesus Christus, theou uios sotēr*, the initials of which make up the Greek word for " fish "), are born in water (*De baptismate*, i.). In discussing whether sins committed subsequent to baptism may be forgiven, he calls baptism and penance " two planks " on which the sinner may be saved from shipwreck—language which he gave to the Church (*De penitentia*, xii.). (5) With reference to the rule of faith, it may be said that Tertullian is constantly using this expression and by it means now the authoritative tradition handed down in the Church, now the Scriptures themselves, and perhaps also a definite doctrinal formula. While he nowhere gives a list of the books of Scripture, he divides them into two parts and calls them the *instrumentum* and *testamentum* (*Adv. Marcionem*, iv. 1). He distinguishes between the four Gospels and insists upon their apostolic origin as accrediting their authority (*De præscriptione*, xxxvi.; *Adv. Marcionem*, iv. 1–5); in trying to account for Marcion's treatment of the Lucan Gospel and the Pauline writings he sarcastically queries whether the " shipmaster from Pontus " (Marcion) had ever been guilty of taking on contraband goods or tampering with them after they were aboard (*Adv. Marcionem*, v. 1). The Scripture, the rule of faith, is for him fixed and authoritative (*De corona*, iii.–iv.). As opposed to the pagan writings they are divine (*De testimonio animæ*, vi.). They contain all truth (*De præscriptione*, vii., xiv.) and from them the Church drinks (*potat*) her faith (*Adv. Praxeam*, xiii.). The prophets were older than the Greek philosophers and their authority is accredited by the fulfilment of their predictions (*Apol.*, xix.–xx.). The Scriptures and the teachings of philosophy are incompatible. " What has Athens to do with Jerusalem? " he exclaims, " or the Academy with the Church? " (*De præscriptione*, vii.). Human philosophy is a work of demons (*De anima*, i.); the Scriptures contain the wisdom of heaven. The rule of faith, however, seems to be also applied by Tertullian to some distinct formula of doctrine, and he gives a succinct statement of the Christian faith under this term (*De præscriptione*, xiii.).

IV. Moral Principles: Tertullian was a determined advocate of strict discipline and an austere code of practise, one of the leading representatives of the Puritanic element in the early Church. These views led him to adopt Montanism with its ascetic rigor and its belief in chiliasm and the continuance of the prophetic gifts. In his writings on public amusements, the veiling of virgins, the conduct of women, and the like, he gives expression to these views. On the principle that we should not look at or listen to what we have no right to practise, and that polluted things, seen and touched, pollute (*De spectaculis*, viii., xvii.), he declared a Christian should abstain from the theater and the amphitheater. There pagan religious rites were applied and the names of pagan divinities invoked; there the precepts of modesty, purity, and humanity were ignored or set aside, and there no place was offered to the onlookers for the cultivation of the Christian graces. Women should put aside gold and precious stones as ornaments (*De cultu*, v.–vi.), and virgins should conform to the law of St. Paul for women and keep themselves strictly veiled (*De virginibus velandis*). He praised the unmarried state as the highest (*De monogamia*, xvii.; *Ad uxorem*, i. 3), called upon Christians not to allow themselves to be excelled in the virtue of celibacy by vestal virgins and Egyptian priests, and he pronounced second marriage a species of adultery (*De exhortatione castitatis*, ix.). If Tertullian went to an unhealthy extreme in his counsels of asceticism, he is easily forgiven when one recalls his own moral vigor and his

great services as an ingenuous and intrepid defender of the Christian religion, which with him, as later with Luther, was first and chiefly an experience of his own heart. On account of his schism with the Church, he, like the great Alexandrian Father, Origen, has failed to receive the honor of canonization. (P. Schaff†.)　D. S. Schaff.

Bibliography: Editions of the works of Tertullian are numerous. The *editio princeps* by Beatus Rhenanus appeared at Basel, 1521, 3d ed., 1539. Others are by M. Mesnarts, Paris, 1545; S. Gelenius, Basel, 1550; R. L. de la Barre, Paris, 1580; J. von Wouwer, Frankfort, 1603 and 1612; J. Pamelius, Paris, 1608 and elsewhere later; J. A. Semler, Halle, 1770–76; E. F. Leopold, Leipsic, 1839–41; in *MPL*, vols. i.–ii.; one of the best is by F. Oehler, 3 vols., Leipsic, 1853–54; another is in the *CSEL*, Reifferscheid and G. Wissowa, Vienna, 1890 sqq., continued by A. Kroymann in new ed., 1906 sqq., who is also issuing editions of separate works, Tübingen, 1907 sqq.; cf. the latter's *Quæstiones Tertullianæ*, Innsbruck, 1898. Eng. transl. of the " Works " in *ANF*, vols. iii.–iv. editions of separate works are too numerous to give here.

Works dealing more or less closely with the life of Tertullian are: Grotemeyer, *Ueber Tertullien's Leben und Schriften*, Kempen, 1863–65; J. Kaye, *The Ecclesiastical History of the Second and Third Centuries*, new ed., Cambridge, 1889; G. Boissier, *La Fin du paganisme*, i. 259 sqq., Paris, 1891; H. Leclercq, *L'Afrique chrétienne*, vol. i., Paris, 1904; W. Walker, *Greatest Men of the Christian Church*, Chicago, 1908; *DCB*, iv. 818–864 (by Pusey; elaborate); Schaff, *Christian Church*, ii. 818–833 et passim; Neander, *Christian Church*, vol. i., passim; and in general the works on the church history and history of doctrine of the period.

On his writings and doctrine consult: J. A. Nosselt, *De vera ætate ac doctrina scriptorum Tertulliani*, Halle, 1768; W. Münscher, *Darstellung der moralischen Ideen des Clemens von Alexandrien und des Tertullian*, Helmstedt, 1796; F. C. H. Schwegler, *Der Montanismus*, Tübingen, 1841; K. Hesselberg, *Tertullian's Lehre entwickelt aus seinen Schriften*, vol. 1, *Leben und Schriften*, Dorpat, 1848; J. A. W. Neander, *Antignosticus oder Geist des Tertullian und Einleitung in dessen Schriften*, Berlin, 2d ed., 1849; G. Uhlhorn, *Fundamenta chronologiæ Tertullianæ*, Göttingen, 1852; A. Crès, *Les Idées de Tertullien sur la tradition ecclésiastique*, Strasburg, 1855; P. Daurès, *Étude sur l'apologétique de Tertullien*, Strasburg, 1855; F. A. Burckhardt, *Die Seelenlehre des Tertullian*, Budissin, 1857; C. Viala, *Tertullien considéré comme apologiste*, Strasburg, 1857; H. Mauchon, *Exposition critique des opinions de Tertullien sur l'origine et la nature du péché*, Strasburg, 1859; V. Bordes, *Exposé critique des opinions de Tertullien sur la rédemption*, Strasburg, 1860; P. Gottwald, *De montanismo Tertulliani*, Breslau, 1862; J. Donaldson, *Critical Hist. of Christian Literature and Doctrine*, 3 vols., London, 1864–66; J. Pelet, *Essai sur l'Apologeticus de Tertullien*, Strasburg, 1868; C. A. H. Kellner, in *TQ*, lii (1870), 547–556, liii (1871), 585–609; K. Rönsch, *Das neue Testament Tertullians aus den Schriften des Letzteren reconstruirt*, Leipsic, 1871; C. E. Treppel, *Tertullien*, 2d ed., Paris, 1872; F. Boehringer, *Die Kirche Christi*, 2 vols., 2d ed., Zurich, 1873; K. Leimbach, *Beiträge zur Abendmahlslehre Tertullians*, Gotha, 1874; G. Caucanus, *Tertullien et le montanisme*, Genève, 1876; G. N. Bonwetsch, *Die Schriften Tertullians*, Bonn, 1878; A. Harnack, in *ZKG*, ii (1878), 572–583; idem, *Die griechische Uebersetzung des Apologeticus Tertullians*, Leipsic, 1892; idem, *Litteratur*, i. 667–687, ii. 2 passim; F. Oehninger, *Tertullian und seine Auferstehungslehre*, Augsburg, 1878; J. de Soyres, *Montanism and the Primitive Church*, London, 1878; F. Nielsen, *Tertullian's Ethik*, Copenhagen, 1879; G. R. Hauschild, *Die rationale Psychologie und Erkenntnistheorie Tertullians*, Frankfort, 1880; G. N. Bonwetsch, *Die Geschichte des Montanismus*, Erlangen, 1881; W. Belck, *Geschichte des Montanismus*, Leipsic, 1883; G. Ludwig, *Tertullian's Ethik*, Leipsic, 1885; L. Atzberger, *Geschichte der christlichen Eschatologie der vornicänischen Zeit*, Freiburg, 1886; L. Lehanneur, *Le Traité de Tertullien contre les Valentiniens*, Caen, 1886; M. Klussmann, *Curarum Tertullianearum particulæ*, Halle, 1887; T. Zahn, *Geschichte des neutestamentlichen Kanons*, i. 51 sqq., 105 sqq., 585 sqq., ii. 449 sqq., Leipsic, 1889–92; P. Corssen,

Die Altercatio Simonis Iudæi . . . auf ihre Quellen Geprüft, Berlin, 1890; C. A. H. Kellner, *Chronologiæ Tertullianæ supplementa*, Bonn, 1890; E. Noeldechen, *Tertullian*, Gotha, 1890; G. Rauch, *Die Einfluss der stoischen Philosophie auf die Lehrbildung Tertullians*, Halle, 1890; F. Cabrol, *Tertullien selon M. Courdaveaux*, Paris, 1891; H. G. Voigt, *Eine verschollene Urkunde des antinomistischen Kampfes*, Leipsic, 1891; M. Klussmann, *Excerpta Tertullianea in Isidori Hispalensis etymologiis*, Hamburg, 1892; K. H. Wirth, *Der " Verdienst "-Begriff bei Tertullian in der christlichen Kirche entwickelt*, Leipsic, 1892; C. T. Cruttwell, *Literary Hist. of Early Christianity*, 2 vols., London, 1893; G. Esser, *Die Seelenlehre Tertullians*, Paderborn, 1893; J. E. B. Mayor, *Tertullian's Apology* in *Journal of Philosophy*, xxi (1893), 259–295; H. Gomperz, *Tertullianea*, Vienna, 1895; E. Rolffs, in *TU*, xii. 4 (1895); K. Werber, *Tertullians Schrift De spectaculis in ihrem Verhältnis zu Varros Rerum divinarum libri*, Teschen, 1896; M. Winkler, *Der Traditionsbegriff des Urchristentums bei Tertullian*, Munich, 1897; P. Wolf, *Die Stellung der Christen zu den Schauspielen nach Tertullians Schrift De spectaculis*, Vienna, 1897; E. M. Gaucher, *L'Apologie de Tertullien*, Auteuil, 1898; J. Stier, *Die Gottes- und Logos-Lehre Tertullians*, Göttingen, 1899; F. Kattenbusch, *Das apostolische Symbolum*, ii. 53 sqq., Leipsic, 1900; P. Monceaux, *Hist. littéraire de l'Afrique chrétienne*, vol. i., Paris, 1901; E. von der Goltz, *Das Gebet in der ältesten Christenheit*, pp. 279 sqq., Leipsic, 1901; A. Bigelmair, *Die Beteiligung der Christen am öffentlichen Leben in vorkonstantinischer Zeit*, Munich, 1902; C. H. Guignebert, *Tertullien. Étude sur ses sentiments a l'égard de l'empire et de la societé civile*, Paris, 1902; K. J. Neumann, *Hippolyt von Rom in seiner Stellung zu Staat und Welt*, vol. i., Leipsic, 1902; A. d'Alès, *Theologie de Tertullian*, Paris, 1905 (excellent); W. Vollert, *Tertullians dogmatische und ethische Grundanschauung*, Gütersloh, 1905; B. B. Warfield, in *Princeton Theological Review*, 1905, pp. 529–555, 1906, pp. 1–36, 145–167; K. Adam, *Der Kirchenbegriff Tertullians*, Paderborn, 1907; Krüger, *History*, pp. 256–280 et passim; Bardenhewer, *Geschichte*, pp. 39, 41, 310 sqq., 365; idem, *Patrologie*, pp. 157–167, Eng. transl., St. Louis, 1908; Ceillier, *Auteurs sacrés*, ii. 1–86.

TESCHENMACHER, tesh'en-māн''er, **WERNER:** Reformed pastor and Annalist; b. at Elberfeld (25 m. n.n.e. of Cologne) Sept. 13 (old style), 1590; d. at Xanten (32 m. n.n.w. of Düsseldorf) Apr. 2, 1638. He was educated at the Reformed schools at Herborn, 1601–06, and received his master's degree at Heidelberg in 1609; was pastor of a circuit of churches in the government of Jülich, 1611–13; at Sittard in the Netherlands, 1613–15; at Elberfeld, 1615–17; at Cleves, 1617–23; and court preacher at Emmerich for the government of Brandenburg, 1623–32. After the Spanish occupation the Reformed in the vicinity of Jülich, Berg, and Wesel were driven from their churches in consequence of an edict of Nov. 3, 1625, and Teschenmacher was instrumental in gaining an intervention on the part of the Netherlands states-general, and the restoration of the churches. Two of Teschenmacher's works were printed: *Repetitio brevis catholicæ et orthodoxæ religionis* (Wesel, 1635), containing brief historical and dogmatic parts; and *Añales Cliviæ Juliæ Montiium . . .* (Arnheim, 1638). His most valuable work was *Annales ecclesiastici reformationis ecclesiarum Cliviæ, Juliæ, Montium*. The original manuscript, dedicated under date of 1633, has disappeared, but was used by J. D. von Steinen, who incorporated more than one-fourth into his *Beschreibung der Reformationsgeschichte des Herzogthums Cleve* (1727). A copy of the manuscript is preserved in the royal library at Berlin. The work, though lacking in perspective and a knowledge of political surroundings, yet is distinguished by learning and conscientiousness, and the immediate use of rare manuscript sources; and it is of much local interest.

(E. Simons.)

BIBLIOGRAPHY: W. Harless, in *Zeitschrift des bergischen Geschichtsvereins*, xxviii. 207 sqq.; idem, in *ADB*, vol. xxxvii.; E. Simons, in *Theologische Arbeiten aus dem rheinischen wissenschaftlichen Prediger-Verein*, new series, iii (1899), 70 sqq.; A. Lorenz, *Die alte reformierte und die neue evangelische Gemeinde*, pp. 68 sqq., Grevenbroich, 1905.

TESSEN-WESIERSKI, FRANZ VON: German Roman Catholic; b. at Berent (30 m. s.w. of Danzig), West Prussia, Dec. 22, 1869. He was educated at the University of Breslau (Lic. Theol., 1894), where he became privat-docent in 1895, first for church history and later (1897) for apologetics. Since 1899 he has been associate professor of the latter subject in the same institution, and in 1900 was given charge of the courses in philosophical and theological propædeutics. He has written *Die Grundlagen des Wunderbegriffs nach Thomas von Aquin* (Paderborn, 1899); and *Der Autoritätsbegriff in den Hauptphasen seiner historischen Entwickelung* (1907).

TEST ACT: The name commonly applied to an act of parliament passed in 1673, formally entitled " An Act to Prevent Dangers from Popish Recusants," which extended the provisions of the Corporation Act (q.v.) to public offices in general. It disqualified for all offices, civil or military, those who had not taken the oaths of allegiance and supremacy, received the sacrament according to the rites of the Church of England, and renounced the doctrine of transubstantiation. It was partly the result of intrigues within the Cabal, forwarded by Shaftesbury with the intention of driving Clifford from office, and partly aimed at the duke of York (later James II.), who was then high admiral. William of Orange declared in favor of its principle, and it was maintained by both whigs and tories, until both acts were repealed in 1828 on the motion of Lord John Russell.

TESTAMENTS OF THE TWELVE PATRI-ARCHS. See Pseudepigrapha.

TESTAMENTUM DOMINI NOSTRI JESU CHRISTI: A church order of the fifth century. The Testament was written originally in Greek, but is not extant in that language. A Syriac translation from the Greek was made by Jacob of Edessa in 687. An Arabic version exists, taken from a lost Coptic translation. Analogous to the Arabic is an Ethiopic translation. Fragments of the liturgy may be looked for in many manuscripts, since a few prayers were long in use, partly to the present time. A fragment, the description of Antichrist, exists in Latin, which may, however, antedate the Testament. In the Arabic and Syriac the Testament appears as the first part of an octateuch entitled *Clementia*. The division into eight books was in imitation of the Apostolic Constitutions which apparently it was to replace, and as such found place among the books of the Bible in manuscripts. Nothing certain is known of the age and origin of the octateuch; it was received in various oriental legal collections.

The contents of the Testament are arranged in three parts, loosely connected: an apocalypse, i.

3–14; directions concerning church building, i. 19; and a church order, specifying the duties of the clergy and of the laity, i. 20–ii. 25. To instructions for the consecration of bishops a long liturgy is appended. There are other liturgical parts, e.g., i. 32, 34–35. Noteworthy are the canons on widows, i. 40–43; there are female clerics, ranking above the deaconesses. The sources of the work are as various as its parts. The Apocalypse is no doubt borrowed; chaps. xix.–xxii. correspond to chaps. xxxv.–xxxviii. of the Arabic Didascalia; yet the Testament is probably the prior source. From i. 20 there is so much resemblance to the Egyptian church order that this main part may be considered as an elaboration of the same. Here and there occur analogies to the Apostolic Constitutions and the " Canons of Hippolytus," and T. Zahn points out verbal agreements with the prayers of the Gnostic " Acts of Peter." These desultory parts are held together by the literary fiction to which the Testament owes its name. After the resurrection, it is represented, Christ appears to the apostles, imparts to them the Holy Spirit, and, at the request of Peter and John, gives them a description of the end, i.e., the Apocalypse (i. 1–15). John, Peter, and Matthew wrote down the New Testament and sent it into the world through Dositheus (perhaps Erastus of Aristarchus), Silas, Magnus (perhaps Manaën), and Aquila. Further on, the author does not take pains to sustain the disguise. In the form of the Testament of Christ may be seen the culmination of the apostolic fiction that attaches to church orders from the beginning. In the conviction that church orders were derived from the apostolic tradition, all books on the subject since the Didache were ascribed to the apostles. The fiction increases in the Apostolic Church Order and the Apostolic Constitutions, viii (see APOSTOLIC CHURCH DIRECTORY; APOSTOLIC CONSTITUTIONS AND CANONS) where each apostle in turn is made to give his directions verbally; finally, in the Testament all is put into the mouth of Christ himself. This form was facilitated by the apocalyptic introduction. Even the eschatological address of Macc. xiii. 5 sqq., Revelation, and the Apocalypse of Peter are represented as spoken or communicated by Jesus. It can not be doubted that the falsification was generally accepted in good faith. The Apocalypse seems to have originated in Syria, as this (i. 10) stands at the head of the lands that are to suffer from Antichrist. Zahn suggests that it might have originated in a separatist church, having first in mind the Audians (q.v.); A. Baumstark ascribes it to the Monophysites; A. Harnack and P. Drews refer it to Egypt, as the formulas and usages are Egyptian. The time of its production is assumed by most to have been the fifth century; it is already cited in the " Theosophy " of Aristocritus, at the end of the fifth century, as a pseudepigraphical work.

(H. ACHELIS.)

BIBLIOGRAPHY: The first edition was by Lagarde in *Reliquiæ juris ecclesiastici antiquissimæ Syriace, Græce,* pp. 2–19, 80–89, Leipsic, 1856, from a ninth-century manuscript; and the complete edition was by I. E. Rahmani, patriarch of Antioch, Mainz, 1899. There is an Eng. transl. by J. Cooper and A. J. Maclean, Edinburgh, 1902 (cf. Nestle in *AJT,* vii. 1903, pp. 749 sqq.). Consult: A. Ehrhard, *Die altchristliche Litteratur und ihre Erforschung 1884–*
1900, pp. 532 sqq., Freiburg, 1900; Harnack, in *SBA,* 1899, pp. 878 sqq.; Achelis, in *Theologische Literaturzeitung,* 1899, pp. 704 sqq.; Zahn, in *NKZ,* 1900, pp. 438 sqq.; Baumstark, in *TQS,* 1900, pp. 1 sqq.; Drews, in *TSK,* 1901, pp. 141 sqq.

TETRAGRAMMATON. See JEHOVAH; YAHWEH.

TETRAPOLITAN CONFESSION: The Confession presented by the four cities of Strasburg, Constance, Memmingen, and Lindau to the Diet of Augsburg, and properly speaking the first confession of the Reformed Church. The call of the Diet by the emperor at Augsburg, Apr. 8, 1530 (see AUGSBURG CONFESSION AND ITS APOLOGY, § 1), declaring for an open discussion and final reconcilement, though met with misgiving in upper Germany, where the delegates were advised rather to work for a future free general council, yet encouraged electoral Saxony and several imperial cities in southern Germany to prepare arguments in writing for the defense of their respective beliefs and forms. By Apr. 26, Wolfgang Capito (q.v.) was at work at Strasburg. However, the instructions to the delegates, Johannes Sturm (q.v.) and Matthis Pfarrer, aimed at two things; the avoidance of the disunion of the Protestant states, and of the examination of the meaning of doctrines. When they arrived at Augsburg this policy proved impracticable, because Johann Eck's 404 articles included the Strasburg party in its attack; because there were present a number of Lutheran theologians holding themselves entirely aloof; and in the opening address the demand of a written presentation and defense in Latin and German was made of each constituent. Again and again the delegates sent back to Strasburg for theologians, but no invitation or freedom of passage having been assured, the council hesitated to send Martin Butzer and Capito for fear of their arrest. Meanwhile the two had started and arrived June 23 and 26, but for three weeks longer they deferred their public appearance. It was already certain that the princes would not admit the cities dissenting on the doctrine of the sacrament to a subscription of their Confession (Augsburg); and only by the sacrifice of those dissenting on the sacrament, Melanchthon hoped to save the cause of the Evangelicals, since it was known that the emperor would not submit the corporeal presence in the Eucharist to question. Simultaneous with the arrival of Butzer, it happened that Landgrave Philip of Hesse, in spite of scruples as to the article on the sacrament, signed the Saxon Confession. The Strasburg theologian, therefore, had to prepare in haste his own confession. In substance it followed as closely as possible the Confession of the princes. Accordingly, in the article on the sacrament it is declared that " the Lord in this sacrament according to his Word gives to his followers his true body and true blood to eat and drink, to the nourishment of their souls and to eternal life, that they may remain in him and he in them." Zwingli's influence appears in the twenty-three articles in the first place given to the Scripture-principle, followed by Christ and his grace as the chief content and the critical measure of ecclesiastical tradition. Zwinglian also is the stress on the Church invisible as the " Bride of Christ." The sacraments are so called not only because they are visible tokens of grace, but also because they are acts of homage to Christ; hence a reversal of the accent of the Augsburg Confession, viii. The use of images is rejected, though " in themselves, when not honored and worshiped, they are unobjectionable." Denunciation of abuses is more severe than in the Confession of the princes, the mass being termed " a horrible carding mart" and an "unendurable abomination."

While the theologians were thus busy, the delegates were endeavoring to induce other cities to sign, but met with little success. Only Constance, Memmingen, and Lindau declared themselves willing, if the article on the sacrament were abbreviated. After a second unsuccessful effort to present the Confession in the emperor's presence, it was received by his chancellor on July 9. The emperor demanded next (July 14) that all protesting cities should declare their faith, with the result that, besides Nuremberg and Reutlingen, also Heilbronn, Kempten, and Windsheim joined the Saxon Confession. The adherents of the Tetrapolitana, now more isolated, surmised correctly that they were to be pressed to a more positive avowal of the Zwinglian idea of the sacrament; hence, they made no further statements, referring to their Confession as neither Lutheran nor Zwinglian, but in obedience to Christ's command according to Scripture. For a considerable time they heard only uncertain rumors concerning the reception of their document. Evidently the emperor was playing arbitrary treatment against them in order to gain the Lutheran estates. However, the first decree (Sept. 22) favoring common counsel and common cause against those not holding to the real corporeal presence in the sacrament and against Anabaptists, was declined by the Lutheran estates with the expressed hope that the former might be reconciled in common with the Christian churches. This reference had in mind, doubtlessly, the pending efforts of Butzer and Capito to bring together Luther and Zwingli. At any rate the principal effect of the decree was to spare the cities holding the Zwinglian doctrine the peril of a joint Roman and Lutheran antagonism, and led to a decisive break between the emperor and the Lutheran estates, tending to draw the protesting groups into closer community. On Oct. 13, the party of Strasburg ventured to apply to the Saxons for admission into the Evangelical league and were not unfavorably met. Meanwhile the Tetrapolitan Confession had been submitted to the committee of theologians, which was already occupied with a confutation of the Saxon Confession. The confutation prepared by Eck, Johannes Faber (q.v.), and Johannes Cochlæus (q.v.) was in the hands of the emperor, Aug. 10. In the confutation of the Tetrapolitana there is less monotonous citation of tradition than against the Saxon and more reference to Biblical proof, consonant with the Zwinglian Scripture-principle. The tone is very severe, and, without warrant, fables of mockery of the host are alleged, against which Sturm promptly replied with a brief and dignified exoneration. The four cities declared (Oct. 30) that they were open to conviction through a general council, " according to the divine Scripture"; and, for the rest,

avowed their allegiance. This unyielding firmness perplexéd the emperor. Nothing remained but to ignore the cities till the prorogation of the diet. The decree of the emperor turned more sternly against the " Zwinglian cities" than against the Lutherans; and he threatened to visit severe measures upon the grave error against the sacrament as against iconoclasm and the like. Naturally, the four cities declined the decree; but they had all the more reasoñ to seek cloŝer relations with the Lutherans. They were present at Schmalkald, and their signatures appear in the document of the league of Feb. 27, 1531 (see SCHMALKALD ARTICLES). Thus a development arose which turned aside the Tetrapolitana. The Swiss, to whom it was represented as a bridge to the Lutherans, would not exchange their clear doctrine on the sacrament for vague words. The Confession of the League was the Augustana, to which the Tetrapolitana became secondary, as in substance the same; and the party of Strasburg admitted at the Diet of Schweinfurt in 1532, that they recognized the Augustana alongside of theirs, but were not willing to abandon their own.

Soon after the reading of the confutation, the Strasburg delegates secured a secretly taken copy, and Butzer set to work to prepare an apology, which, with the Confession, was published, *Bekandtnuss der vier Frey- und Reichstätt* (Strasburg, 1531; Zweibrücken, 1604). A Latin translation of the Tetrapolitana appeared (Strasburg, 1531).

(E. F. KARL MÜLLER.)

BIBLIOGRAPHY: T. Keim, *Schwäbische Reformationsgeschichte*, Tübingen, 1855; F. Dobel, *Memmingen im Reformationszeitalter*, parts iv.–v., Augsburg, 1878; Virck, in *ZKG*, 1888; A. Pätzold, *Die Konfutation des Vierstädtebekenntnisses*, Leipsic, 1900; J. Ficker, in *Theologische Abhandlungen für H. Holtzmann*, Tübingen, 1902; K. Müller, *Die Bekenntnisschriften der reformirten Kirche*, Leipsic, 1903. The 404 theses of Eck are translated in *Papers of the American Society of Church History*, 2 ser., ii. 21–81, New York, 1910.

TETRARCH: The title primarily of a military and later of an administrative official. In its military sense it denoted the commander of a cavalry squadron of four companies or sixty-four men. In the administrative sense a tetrarch was the ruler of a tetrarchy, originally the fourth part of a country; as was the case among the Thessalians and, at one time, among the Galatian Celts of Asia Minor (cf. also the four " tribes " of Attica previous to the time of Cleisthenes). Later he was simply a tributary or petty prince, and in this sense the title was applied by the Romans to the many princelings of Syria, only the most important being officially styled " king."

The best example of tetrarchs is furnished by the Herodian dynasty. In 41 B.C. Herod and his brother Phasæl received the title of tetrarch from Antony. In 40 the former had the title of king at Rome, and in 20 his younger brother Pheroras was made tetrarch of Peræa. On the death of Herod (4 B.C.), his dominions were divided among his sons, Archelaus having the preeminence as " ethnarch," while his brothers Antipas and Philip were tetrarchs. Agrippa I. received from Caligula (37 A.D.) the title of king together with the tetrarchies of Philip and Lysanias; and his son, Agrippa II., was already king of Chalcis when he was given the tetrarchies of his father. The New Testament registers the popular disregard of these official distinctions; in Matt. ii. 22, Archelaus is " king " instead of his father, and Matt. xiv. 9, as contrasted with xiv. 1, and Mark vi. 14 sqq. term Herod Antipas " king." Only Luke observes the exact nomenclature (Luke iii. 1, 19, ix. 7; Acts xiii. 1).

(E. VON DOBSCHÜTZ.)

BIBLIOGRAPHY: W. M. Ramsay, *The Church in the Roman Empire*, pp. 41, 45, 55, London and New York, 1893; S. Mathews, *Hist. of N. T. Times in Palestine*, pp. 145–146, New York, 1899, 2d ed., 1910; Schürer, *Geschichte*, i. 423–424, ii. 197, iii. 77–78, Eng. transl., I., ii. 7–8; *DB*, iv. 725–726; *EB*, iv. 4978; *JE*, xii. 120; *DCG*, ii. 717.

TETZEL, JOHANN: b. at Leipsic between 1450 and 1460; d. there in July, 1519. He studied theology and philosophy at the university of his native city, entered the Dominican order in 1489, achieved some success as a preacher, and was in 1502 commissioned by the pope to preach the jubilee indulgence, which he did throughout his life. In 1509 he was made inquisitor, and in 1517 Leo X. made him commissioner of indulgences for all Germany. He acquired the degree of licentiate of theology in the University of Frankfort-on-the-Oder, 1517, and that of doctor of theology, 1518, by defending, in two disputations, the doctrine of indulgences against Luther. The impudence with which he sold full forgiveness for sins not yet committed, caused great scandal; and when Luther in the confessional became aware of the evil effect of his doings, he began to preach openly against him. He was also condemned (though later pardoned) for immorality. It became necessary to disavow Tetzel; and, when he discovered that Miltitz was aware of all his frauds and embezzlements, he withdrew, frightened, into the Dominican monastery in Leipsic. He died at the time of the Leipsic disputation in 1519. In C. H. H. Wright and Charles Neil's *Protestant Dictionary* (London, 1904), pp. 294 sqq., is a facsimile of a Tetzel indulgence.

BIBLIOGRAPHY: G. Hecht, *Vita J. Tetzeli*, Wittenberg, 1717 (Protestant); J. Vogel, *Leben des . . . Tetzel*, 2d ed., Leipsic, 1721 (Protestant); F. G. Hofmann, *Lebensbeschreibung des Ablasspredigers Tetzel*, Leipsic, 1844 (Protestant); V. Gröne, *Tetzel und Luther, oder Lebensgeschichte und Rechtfertigung des . . . Johann Tetzel*, 2d ed., Münster, 1860 (Roman Catholic); Kayser, *Geschichtsquellen über den Ablassprediger Tetzel*, Annaberg, 1877; F. Körner, *Tetzel der Ablassprediger*, Frankenberg, 1880 (Protestant); E. Kolbe, *Johann Tetzel*, Steyl, 1882 (Roman Catholic); K. W. Herrmann, *Johann Tetzel*, 2d ed., Frankfort, 1883 (Roman Catholic); G. A. Meijer, *Johann Tetzel*, Utrecht, 1885 (Roman Catholic); G. Kawerau, *Sobald das Geld im Kasten klingt*, Barmen, 1890 (Protestant); J. B. Röhm, *Zur Tetzel-Legende*, Hildesheim, 1890; P. Majunke, *Johann Tetzel, der Ablassprediger*, Erfurt, 1899; U. Paulus, *Johann Tetzel, der Ablassprediger*, Mainz, 1899; J. Janssen, *Hist. of the German People*, iii. 89 sqq., St. Louis, 1900 (Roman Catholic); *Cambridge Modern History*, ii. 121, 130, 134, 204, New York, 1904; Schaff, *Christian Church*, vi. 151–155 et passim, and, in general, literature on Martin Luther and on the beginnings of the Reformation.

TEUTONIC ORDER (Domus Hospitalis S. Mariæ Theutonicorum in Jerusalem). An order originally of the hospitaler type and later chivalric, subsequent in origin to the Knights of St. John and the Templars and probably not inferior to them in lasting importance. It differed from these two orders in that it was purely German. The beginning of the order is to be discerned in a field hospital which was established during the siege of Acre, begun in Aug., 1189, which, after the conclusion of the siege, was transferred to the imperial chaplain Konrad and the chamberlain Burkhard; these with others united to form a fraternity after the rule of the Knights of St. John and named it the " Hospital of St. Mary of the Germans in Jerusalem." In its origin, therefore, the order was purely a brotherhood for the care of the sick, at the head of which stood an ecclesiastic, the above-mentioned Chaplain Konrad, who appears in a document of 1191 as *Præceptor hospitalis Alemannorum*. After the conquest of Acre in July, 1191, the brotherhood erected there a hospital and a church.

Clement III. in 1191 and Celestine III. in 1196 gave formal sanction to the order, which found powerful protectors in Duke Frederick of Swabia and the Emperor Henry VI. From the latter it received, in 1197, a hospital at Barletta, its first possession in the West, and the wealthy monastery of the Holy Trinity at Palermo. The favor of the emperor proceeded largely from his desire to make the order an instrument for the prosecution of his plans in Europe, and this led to the assumption of the military character. In 1198 the brotherhood made military service according to the rules of the Templars a part of its work, and a knight was chosen as the first grand master. Confirmation by Innocent III. followed in Feb., 1199. The insignia of the order was a white mantle with a black cross potent. Though progress under the first grand masters was not rapid, the order gained a foothold in Germany, where a number of hospitals at Halle, Coblenz, Nuremberg, and other places came into its possession. The oldest province was Thuringia; the province of Austria was created in 1203. The Emperor Frederick II. and Pope Honorius III. gave the knights their protection, and the latter, in a bull of Jan., 1221, placed the order on an equal footing with the Knights of St. John and the Templars.

Under its fourth grand master, Hermann of Salza (1210–39), the order entered upon a rapid development. In his time occurred the most important event in the history of the order, its establishment in Prussia. The planting of Christianity in that region had been effected after many attempts by Christian, a Cistercian monk of Oliva, who, in 1212, was made bishop of Prussia. A pagan reaction in the country induced Bishop Christian to ask aid of the Teutonic Order, which received from pope and emperor the promise of the absolute possession of all the lands it might conquer. In the spring of 1230 an army of the order entered Masovia. The cities of Kulm, Thorn, and Marienwerder were founded and the conquest of Prussia proper was begun. Reenforcements poured in from Germany, where the crusade against the heathens was being preached and there resulted the steady acquisition of the Prussian territory, the possession of which was secured by the erection of castles and the establishment of cities. By 1283 the power of the order was definitely established. As early as 1237 the Teutonic Order had succeeded in achieving what every other order failed to accomplish, the erection of an independent state. After the fall of Acre in 1291 the capital of the order was removed to Venice, and in 1309 to Marienburg in Prussia.

The spread of the Christian religion and the germanization of the land were carried on simultaneously. Peasants from Lower Saxony and Westphalia transformed the lands into fertile grain fields, and by the side of the castles of the order arose numerous towns with a German population, which grew rich through an extensive commerce. Between the knights and the inhabitants of the cities cordial relations prevailed and the order itself derived great wealth from its trade. The strength of the order was due to its rigorous discipline and its excellent organization. At its head was the grand master, who was limited in the exercise of his powers by a council of the other high officials, among them the chief hospitaler and the treasurer. The supreme power was vested in the grand chapter of the order which elected the grand master and exercised its power of punishment and deposition. Each house of the order was under the authority of a commendator (*Komthur*) and a number of houses constituted a province at the head of which stood the *Land-Komthur*. Eligible to membership in the order were Germans only of legitimate birth, showing the arms of four ancestors, pure in morals and unstained in honor. The discipline in the houses was strict, the life simple. Unquestioning obedience to superiors was the highest duty and every transgression was punished severely. Flight in battle or intercourse with the heathen was punished by expulsion. The order also embraced clerical brethren for the performance of religious duties, and sisters, whose work lay especially in the hospitals. The principal hospital in Prussia was situated at Elbing and in Germany at Nuremberg.

The order attained the height of power in the second half of the fourteenth century. In the peace of Kalisch Little Pomerania was acquired from Poland and with the acquisition of the Danish possessions in Esthonia its authority extended along the entire Baltic coast. It became also the great power in the Baltic sea. In 1398 its fleet took Gotland from the Vitalian Brethren and in 1404 it acquired Wisby. By the purchase of Neumark its connection with the empire was established. In this very time of glory, however, powerful forces of decay had begun to work. In place of the rigorous discipline and simplicity of old appeared luxury and ostentation. Party strife sapped the strength of the order and the relations of friendship between knights and citizens had disappeared. Moreover, with the rise of Poland appeared a formidable rival to the German influence. In 1386 Jagello, Grand Prince of Lithuania, became king of Poland. War soon broke out with the knights, and on June 15, 1410, on the plain of Tannenberg the forces of the order were crushingly defeated; all its great officers perished, and the power of the order was annihilated at one blow. It was saved from destruction by the heroism of Count Henry of Plauen, who held Marienburg against the Poles to such good effect that the peace of Thorn in 1411 left the possessions of the order almost unimpaired. Internal anarchy, how-

ever, hastened the end. In 1440 a part of the knights and the cities organized the Prussian League in opposition to the main order and in a civil war which followed the league gained possession of more than fifty towns and offered to place the country under the suzerainty of Poland. Finally, by the peace of Thorn in 1466, West Prussia was incorporated with Poland, while East Prussia was granted to the grand master as a Polish fief. In Germany, too, decay had overtaken the order so that no help could be derived for the defense of the possessions in Prussia. In 1525 Albert of Prussia (q.v.), elected grand master of the order, transformed its possessions into a hereditary duchy, held of the king of Prussia. In 1561 Gerhard Kettler, following the example of Albert, received Livonia as a fief from Poland with the title of duke of Courland and Semigallia.

The subsequent history of the order, restricted to its possessions in Germany, Austria, and the Netherlands, possesses little interest. By the treaty of Pressburg in 1805 the presidency of the order was vested in the house of Austria, and within the next few years its territories in South Germany and on the Rhine were transferred by Napoleon to the governments within which they lay. As a purely Austrian order it was reorganized in 1809 and confirmed by Pius IX. in 1871. Its activity is now restricted to its original service, the care of the sick in war and in peace. (G. UHLHORN†.)

BIBLIOGRAPHY: For list of periodical articles consult: O. Rautenberg, *Ost- und Westpreussen. Ein Wegführer durch die Zeitschriftlitteratur*, Leipsic, 1897. Consult further: E. Hennig, *Die Statuten des deutschen Ordens*, Königsberg, 1806; *Scriptores rerum Prussicarum*, i. 3 sqq., 291 sqq., Leipsic, 1861; *Codex diplomaticus ordinis S. Mariæ Theutonicorum*, ed. J. H. Hennes, 2 vols., Mainz, 1846–51; K. von Schlözer, *Die Hansa und der deutsche Ritterorden*, Berlin, 1851; J. Voigt, *Geschichte des deutschen Ritterordens*, 2 vols., Berlin, 1857–59; B. Dudik, *Des Lohen deutschen Ritterordens Münzsammlung in Wien*, Vienna, 1858; A. L. Ewald, *Die Eroberung Preussens durch die Deutschen*, 4 vols., Halle, 1872–85; F. C. Woodhouse, *Military Religious Orders of the Middle Ages*, London, 1879; F. de Salles, *Annales de l'ordre teutonique*, Paris, 1887; M. Perlbach, *Die Statuten des Deutschordens*, Halle, 1890; M. Oehler, *Geschichte des Deutschen Ritterordens*, vol. i., *Die Anfänge des Ordens bis zum Eintritt in den Preussenkampf*, Elbing, 1908.

TEUTSCH, GEORG DANIEL: German Lutheran; b. at Schässburg (290 m. e.s.e. of Budapest), Transylvania, Dec. 12, 1817; d. at Hermannstadt (72 m. s.s.e. of Klausenburg) July 2, 1893. He studied at Vienna and Berlin, 1837–39; was instructor at the Evangelical gymnasium at Schässburg, 1842–1850; and rector, 1850–63; preacher at Agnetheln and dean of the ecclesiastical district of Schenk, 1863–67; and Evangelical bishop in Hermannstadt, 1867–93. Teutsch was the leader for German institutions among the Saxons in Transylvania, particularly in education and religion. He was instrumental in defending and maintaining the autonomy of his church and its schools against the encroachments of the Roman Catholic and Greek Churches, and the Magyar influence; and he was active, both before and after becoming bishop, in its internal organization and promotion. As a preacher he was eloquent and persuasive. He wrote *Urkundenbuch der evangelischen Landeskirche in*

Siebenbürgen (Hermannstadt, 1862); *Synodal-verhandlungen der evangelischen Landeskirche in Siebenbürgen bis 1600* (1883); and *Geschichte der siebenbürger Sachsen* (3d ed., 1899). (F. TEUTSCH).

BIBLIOGRAPHY: The memorial address by F. Teutsch was published at Hermannstadt, and contains a list of literature. Consult the biography by F. Teutsch, Hermannstadt, 1909; and *ADB*, vol. xxxvii.

TEXTUS RECEPTUS. See BIBLE TEXT, II., 2, § 2.

THADDEUS. See JUDAS.

THAMER, tä'mer, THEOBALD: German convert to the Roman Catholic Church; b. at Oberehnheim (15 m. s.w. of Strasburg) at the beginning of the sixteenth century; d. at Freiburg May 23, 1569. He received his education at Rosheim, and at the University of Wittenberg, where he studied 1535–39. He then went to Frankfort-on-the-Oder, and in 1543 was called to Marburg by Landgrave Philip of Hesse as professor of theology and preacher at St. Elizabeth's Church. Thamer had been hardly a year in Marburg when his bristling defense of the Lutheran doctrine as to the Lord's Supper brought him into collision with his colleague, Andreas Hyperius; but the landgrave admonished the Marburg theologians, Oct. 14, 1544, to refrain from strife. At the beginning of the Schmalkald War, Thamer was appointed army chaplain by the landgrave, and thereby gained opportunity to make observations that were decisive on his subsequent life. His experiences and the unhappy issue of the war moved him to questions regarding the causes of the Reformation; and thus began his doubts touching the correctness of the Evangelical doctrine of repentance and justification. Thamer was not the man to conceal these conflicts and what stirred him became known to all Marburg and set the town in commotion. The government at Cassel interposed, and summoned Thamer, Draconitas, and Adam Kraft to Cassel. Thamer here declared that he could not hold the doctrine " by faith alone " as sound and Evangelical, but promised to abstain from further attacks on the Lutheran teaching. At Easter, 1549, however, he started the conflict anew, and was suspended, on Aug. 8, 1549, after the synods at Ziegenhain and Cassel, till the return of the landgrave. At the close of 1549 he became second preacher at St. Bartholomew's in Frankfort-on-the-Main, but because of his sharp attacks on Lutheranism, he was dismissed from this post; he then turned to Landgrave Philip, and requested a regular examination of the errors charged against him. Philip resolved on the extraordinary step of procuring him the opportunity of conferring in person with the most eminent theologians of that age. So he journeyed to Jena to meet Erhard Schnepf, then to Melanchthon at Wittenberg, next to Superintendent Daniel Gresser at Dresden, and finally to Bullinger at Zurich. But none of these theologians could pronounce in his favor. Thamer then went to Rome, and there passed over to the Roman Catholic Church, probably in 1553 or 1554. Two years later he returned to Germany and was appointed preacher in Minden. Thereafter he obtained a canonry at Mainz, where he issued his *Apologia* in 1561. The same year he received a theological instructorship

at the University of Freiburg which he held till his death. CARL MIRBT.

BIBLIOGRAPHY: J. A. W. Neander, *Theobald Thamer, der Repräsentant und Vorgänger moderner Geistesrichtung in dem Reformationszeitalter*, Berlin, 1842; *Historische politische Blätter*, ed. G. Phillips and G. Görres, x. 341–363, Munich, 1842; C. W. H. Hochhuth, *De Theobaldi Thameri vita et scriptis*, Marburg, 1858; idem, in *ZHT*, 1861, part 2, pp. 165–278; H. Schreiber, *Geschichte der Albert-Ludwigs-Universität in Freiburg im Breisgau*, ii. 293–296, Freiburg, 1859; A. Räss, *Die Convertiten seit der Reformation*, i. 236–297, ib. 1866.

THANK OFFERING. See SACRIFICE.

THANKSGIVING DAY: A day specially appointed for the expression of a sense of obligation for divine favor, instituted in New England, in much the same way as Fast-day (q.v.). One was often appointed to offset the other. At first a day of thanksgiving was observed in gratitude for unusual mercies, and became regular only in the last half of the seventeenth century. There is evidence to show that the first Thanksgiving Day of the Pilgrims was on Dec. 20, 1620, upon their first arrival, but the distinction is usually given to the thanksgiving week celebrated in company with the Indians in the autumn of 1621 after the first crops had been gathered in. The first civil Thanksgiving in the Massachusetts Bay colony was observed July 8, 1630, after all the ships of Winthrop's company had arrived; and other thanksgivings followed special providences. On Oct. 12, 1637, all New England celebrated the overthrow of the Pequots. The first Thanksgiving Day of the Connecticut river towns, appointed on account of an abundant harvest, was held Sept. 18, 1639. The northern settlements of New England naturally followed the example of Massachusetts. Rhode Island thanksgivings were private affairs of churches and individuals until Governor Andros made the observance of the day compulsory throughout New England.

The annual Thanksgiving Day in celebration of harvest became regular in Connecticut after 1649, in Massachusetts Bay about 1660, and in Plymouth in 1668. Rhode Island delayed its final adoption until the time of the Revolution. It had become a regular institution in all the New England states by the end of the eighteenth century. Thanksgiving Day has always been distinctively a home festival, but its religious character was not obscured in the days of the fathers, especially in Connecticut and Massachusetts. Until well into the eighteenth century two church services were held, sermons were read at the family hearth, and the mercies of God were recounted; but the social functions of the day in time crowded out the second church service, and the day became a feast day, with a grand dinner for the united family, and with general merrymaking as its accompaniment. This latter development became common after the Revolution.

The struggle for independence drew the colonies together, and they all joined in a general thanksgiving on Dec. 18, 1777, after the downfall of Burgoyne. Similar celebrations were observed regularly during the war, and on special occasions up to 1815, but they did not become a permanent national custom. Meantime the idea was growing in favor through the country. In 1817 New York began its regular observance. New England's influence was felt through the emigration of its people to the West, and by the middle of the nineteenth century nearly all the states of the Union had adopted it. President Lincoln appointed a special thanksgiving on Aug. 6, 1863, to celebrate the victory of Gettysburg, and on Nov. 26 of the same year a harvest festival was observed likewise. From that time Thanksgiving Day has become a national occasion of rejoicing, and is appointed regularly by the president for the last Thursday of November, and the governors of the several states also appoint the same day.   HENRY K. ROWE.

BIBLIOGRAPHY: Consult the literature under FAST-DAY, and E. H. Hughes, *Thanksgiving Sermons*, New York, 1910.

THAYER, JOSEPH HENRY: Congregationalist, New Testament lexicographer; b. in Boston, Mass., Nov. 7, 1828; d. at Cambridge, Mass., Nov. 26, 1901. He was graduated from Harvard College, Cambridge, Mass., 1850, and from Andover Theological Seminary, Mass., 1857; was pastor at Salem, Mass., 1859–64; chaplain Fortieth Massachusetts Volunteers, 1862–63; professor of sacred literature in Andover Theological Seminary, 1864–82; and from 1884 professor of New Testament criticism and interpretation in the Harvard Divinity School. He translated the 7th ed. (Lünemann's) of Winer's *Grammar of the New Testament Greek* (Andover, 1869); A. Buttmann's *Grammar of the Greek New Testament* (1873); and with revision and enlargement the 2d ed. of Grimm's Wilke's *Clavis Novi Testamenti*, under title, *A Greek-English Lexicon of the New Testament* (New York, 1886); and edited a new edition of Sophocles' *Greek Lexicon: Roman and Byzantine Periods* (1887). These publications established his reputation in the first rank in New-Testament and patristic scholarship, especially in textual criticism. He was one of the New Testament company of American revisers of the Bible.

BIBLIOGRAPHY: C. H. Toy, in *Harvard Graduates' Magazine*, x (1902), 363 sqq.; C. J. H. Ropes, in *AJT*, vi (1902), 285 sqq., and in *Biblical World*, xix (1902), 248 sqq.; W. N. Stearns, in *Biblical World*, ib. pp. 226 sqq.

THEATINES: An order of regular clergy founded in Italy in the beginning of the sixteenth century. It was in a way a precursor of the Society of Jesus in that it compassed noteworthy results in battling with " heresy," in connection with the incipient Reformation in Italy. The Theatine organization had its point of departure in Rome under Leo X. and his successors, when it grew out of the Oratory of the Divine Love (q.v.), the fundamental ideas of which Gaetano of Tiene (b. at Vicenza in 1480; d. 1547) designed to apply in a more comprehensive activity. He first founded, in Verona, a fraternity (of Hieronymites) having similar aims; he then returned to Rome, renounced his prebends, and joined with Bonifazio da Colle, Paolo Consiglieri, and Giovanni Pietro Caraffa (see PAUL IV.) in creating the order, which was confirmed by Clement VII. The name which the common people gave the new order, *Chietini*, shows that they deemed not Gaetano, but Caraffa to be the actual founder or leader, their ascription referring to the see of Chieti, which had been occupied by Caraffa. The

bull of confirmation approves the rendering of the three vows, the election of a provost for terms of three years, administration of the daily routine, and conveys to the order all privileges of canons of the Lateran.

One of the four joint organizers owned a house in Rome, which was fitted up for the order. Material subsistence was to be secured through purely voluntary donations. High value was attached to diligent preaching; but fostering care was also given to the sick. As the membership increased, a larger house was occupied; but when the sack of Rome, in 1527, drove the Theatines away in the general exit, there succeeded two other settlements, one in Venice, 1527, and one at Naples, 1533. The Roman settlement was renewed in 1536. The biographer of Paul IV., Antonio Caracciolo, accounts it as chief merit of the Theatines that by means of their social connections at Naples, as likewise by cleverly utilizing what information the confessional afforded, they discovered the evil plant of heresy, and eradicated the same. And the measures devised by Gaetano at Naples, from 1538 forward, against the fellow sympathizers of a Juan de Valdés, against Pietro Martire Vermigli and Bernardino Ochino (qq.v.), he repeated àt Venice, from 1541.

Caraffa, as pope, assigned to the order, in 1,555, the church and cloister of San Silvestro, and there the Theatines' headquarters remained until they erected the convent and church of S. Andrea della Valle. Meanwhile the order had spread over all Italy, crossed the Alps, and found acceptance in Spain, France, Germany, and Poland (Munich, Vienna, Prague, Paris, etc.). Its founder was beatified in 1629, and canonized in 1660. Two sisterhoods were also organized under his name, that of the " Immaculate Conception," and that of the " Hermitage." In the articles of both, emphasis is laid on the adoration, day and night, of the blessed sacrament.   K. BENRATH.

BIBLIOGRAPHY: Helyot, *Ordres monastiques*, iv. 71 sqq.; Heimbucher, *Orden und Kongregationen*, iii. 258–269 (with very full literature); Ranke, *Popes*, i. 131–133; The *Vita of Gaetano*, by A. Caracciolo, Cologne, 1612, and Caracciolo's *Vita Pauli IV.*, ib. 1612; R. de Maulde de la Clavière, *Saint Gaetan (1480-1547)*, Paris, 1902.

THEBAN LEGION: The theme of a legend centering about the town of St. Maurice (31 m. e. of Geneva), in the canton of Valais, Switzerland, but found also elsewhere in Switzerland, in Italy, and on the lower Rhine. In its oldest and simplest form, according to a *passio* attributed to Eucherius, bishop of Lyons (q.v.), the Emperor Maximian (285–310) had under his command a legion called the Theban, consisting of 6,600 men sent from the East. They were all Christians and refused to obey the imperial command to take part in the persecution of their fellow Christians. Maximian, then encamped at Octodurum (Martigny at the foot of the Great St. Bernard), twice had the legion decimated, and when the survivors at the exhortation of their leader Maurice (Mauritius) remained steadfast, had all put to death. Among the martyrs is placed St. Gereon, in whose honor a church existed at Cologne in the seventh century. Later versions of the legend simply add details.

The legend has given rise to a long controversy.

The " Magdeburg Centuries " declared Maurice an " idol " although he is the patron saint of the city, and Protestants generally have denied the credibility of the story. Roman Catholics have been more inclined to accept it. It is found in the biography of the abbot Romanus, probably written shortly after his death in 460, and a monastery then existed on the alleged site of the martyrdom and formed the goal of pilgrimage. The legend is several times mentioned in the sixth century, and Gregory of Tours knows it in its original form and also mentions Thebans who suffered martyrdom on the lower Rhine. That it originated before the middle of the fifth century and that the Theban martyrs were honored thus early must be admitted. Against the authenticity of the legend it may be alleged that almost a century and a half intervened between its supposed occurrence and the oldest record of it, while contemporaries and earlier authors make no reference to it. The tradition also suffers from inherent improbability. No Theban legion is known to have existed at that time, and it is improbable that a general like Maximian, however great his hatred of the Christians, would have put to death an entire legion at a time when he needed his soldiers to keep the barbarians and rebels in check. The chief objection to the legend, however, is that it can not be brought into harmony with the history of the Diocletian persecution. The oldest accounts themselves are at variance as to the time and place. It was not until 296 or 297 that Christians began to be removed from the army, thus preparing the way for the general persecution. If, however, the date be laid after 296, the presence of Maximian in Valais is extremely improbable, for he was then most of the time in Africa and on the Lower Rhine. Moreover, Christian soldiers were given their choice between offering sacrifice or being discharged, and executions were rare. The view of Eucherius that the martyrdom took place during the Diocletian persecution lacks historical support, since it presupposes that Christian soldiers were put to death in large numbers. No such massacres occurred, however, in the West, where the persecutions ceased altogether with the abdication of Diocletian and Maximian on May 1, 305.

(G. Uhlhorn†.)

Bibliography: The principal forms of the *Passio sancti Mauritii et sociorum*, with commentary, are in *ASB*, Sept., vi. 308–349, 895–926, and partly in *MPL*, clxxi. 1625–30. A full list of editions and literature is in Potthast, *Wegweiser*, pp. 1472–73; and in A. Hirschmann's contribution to *Historisches Jahrbuch der Görres-Gesellschaft*, xiii (1892), 783–798. Consult further: J. A. Dubordieu, *Historical Dissertation upon the Thebæan Legion*, London, 1696 (adverse; this book is usually cited in the Fr. translation, Amsterdam, 1705); J. de l'Isle, *Defense de la verité du martyre de la légion thébéenne, autrement de S. Maurice et de ses compagnons, pour répondre à la dissertation du ministre du Bourdieu*, Nancy, 1741; P. de Rivaz, *Éclaircissements sur le martyre de la légion thébéenne*, Paris, 1779; J. W. J. Braun, *Zur Geschichte der thebäischen Legion*, Bonn, 1855; E. F. Gelpke, *Kirchengeschichte der Schweiz*, i. 50–86, Bern, 1856; O. Hunziker, in M. Büdinger, *Untersuchungen zur römischen Kaisergeschichte*, ii. 117–284, and Excursus II., 265–272, Leipsic, 1868; E. Aubert, *Trésor de l'abbaye de Saint-Maurice d'Agaune*, Paris, 1872; A. Allègre, *Le Culte de S. Maurice à Caromb*, Avignon, 1881; S. Beissel, *Geschichte der Trierer Kirchen*, i. 19–31, Treves, 1887; Ducis, *Saint Maurice et la légion thébéenne*, Annecy, 1887; J. Bernard, *S. Maurice et la légion thébéenne*, 2 vols., Paris, 1888; J. B. de Montmélian, *Saint Maurice et la légion thébéenne*, 2 vols., Paris, 1888; P. Allard, *Le Persécution de Dioclétien*, i. 17–34, ii. 335–364, Paris, 1890; F. Stolle, *Das Martyrium der thebäischen Legion*, Breslau, 1891; R. Berg, *Der heilige Mauricius und die thebäische Legion*, Halle, 1895; *DCB*, iii. 641–644 (valuable); Friedrich, *KD*, i. 101–141; Rettberg, *KD*, i. 94–111; *KL*, vii. 1615–28; Lichtenberger, *ESR*, xii. 89–91.

THECLA AND PAUL, ACTS OF. See Apocrypha, B, II.

THEINER, tai'ner, **AUGUSTIN:** Roman Catholic Church historian; b. at Breslau, Germany, Apr. 11, 1804; d. in Rome Aug. 10, 1874. He studied theology, and afterward canon law, at the university of his native city, and published, together with his brother, *Die katholische Kirche Schlesiens* (Altenburg, 1826), also *Die Einführung der erzwungenen Ehelosigkeit bei den christlichen Geistlichen, und ihre Folgen* (2 vols., 1828; new ed., 3 vols., Barmen, 1892), which was put on the Index. In 1833 he entered the Jesuit order; became a member of the Congregation of the Oratory, and was in 1855, by Pius IX., appointed conservator at the papal archives. But during the Vatican Council he was accused by the Jesuits of procuring documents from the archives for the bishops in opposition, and was removed from his position in 1870. He was a very industrious writer; his works embrace *Geschichte des Pontificats Clemens XIV.* (2 vols., Leipsic, 1853); *Annales ecclesiastici* (3 vols., Rome, 1856); *Vetera monumenta historica Hungariæ* (2 vols., 1859–60); *Vetera monumenta Poloniæ et Lithuaniæ* (4 vols., 1860–64); *Codex diplomaticus* (3 vols., 1861–62); *Vetera monumenta Slavorum meridionalium* (1863); *Vetera monumenta Hibernorum et Scotorum* (1864); *Acta . . . concilii Tridentini* (Leipsic, 1874).

Bibliography: H. Gisiger, *Theiner und die Jesuiten*, Mannheim, 1875; H. Brück, *Geschichte der katholischen Kirche in Deutschland*, iii. 344, Mainz, 1896; *KL*, xi. 1486–88.

THEISM.

The Term (§ 1).   In Modern Thought (§ 4).
In Ancient Thought (§ 2).   Relation to Scientific Reason
In Medieval Thought (§ 3).   (§ 5).

The terms " theist " and " theism " apparently originated as opposites of " atheist " and " atheism " in England during the seventeenth century, when " deistic " and " deism," as general terms indicating simply the belief in God, had lost their reputation with the adherents of the Church. Ralph Cudworth (q.v.), in the interest of Platonic rationalism, and Pierre Bayle (q.v.) used theism in contradistinction to atheism, but as deism was similarly used by the latter and others, a closer definition was required. Kant, who was also of the opinion that the differentiation of deist and theist originated in England, gave it precision, thus: " The deist believes that there is a God; the theist that there is a living God." Theology he held to be the knowledge of the original being, which is derived either by pure reason or by revelation. The former represents God by pure transcendental concepts, and is called transcendental theology, or by a concept of supreme intelligence derived from nature, to be called natural theology. A deist is an adherent of the first, and one who, in addition,

1. The Term.

accepts the second is a theist. More definitely, the deist concedes the rational cognizance of an original being, but denies that a closer determination is possible than the concept of a universal cause inclusive of all reality. The theist, on the other hand, asserts a closer determination of God, according to nature (the human soul), as a being who by intelligence and freedom, as originator of the cosmos, contains within himself the ground of all things. Transcendental theology gives rise to the cosmological and ontological proofs of the existence of God; natural theology, to the teleological and moral proofs. Kant did not include the idea of personality in the term theism, much less in deism, a term by which later theology distinguishes theism from other philosophies of the universe, which, beside self-consciousness and self-activity, is demanded as an attribute of God by the religious man, and makes the actual relations of person with person seem possible. Furthermore, theism regards God not merely as the creator who, as assumed in deism, withdrew from the world after giving it laws, but as its ruler, perhaps even changing its course.

Theism may be monistic, dualistic, or even polytheistic; but dualism is very frequently noted as theistic. Although Plato made the idea of the good equivalent to reason and again to deity, which in turn from goodness creates the universe, yet his deity or *nous* falls short of the attributes adequate to theism, particularly in self-consciousness. Aristotle is often regarded as the founder of scientific and speculative theism, although omitting in form the main attribute of modern theism, the personality of God. God he represents as pure thinking spirit. He is unchangeable and, as absolute energy, immutable, in contrast with the absolute potency, or matter, which is able to take up into itself all forms or concepts. God is one and indivisible. The subject of his thought is the best, i.e., himself, and the content is composed of the concepts, which as universals are immanent in the things of the phenomenal universe. This thinking is the highest, best, and happiest life, and life is the energy of the spirit. It may be seen that self-consciousness and feeling are ascribed to deity, which is in effect an implication of personality. God is the prime mover in the universe, but he moves without working or constructing. His activity is wholly in thought. As the good and the object of all movement, he remains unmoved. How the forms may be both transcendent and immanent, or how being passes over into becoming, remains the unsolved difficulty, present also in most other philosophic systems, monotheism not excluded. The dualism of Aristotle was not adopted by his successors. The Christian philosophers, ancient and modern, very positively represented theism from the monistic point of view. God, the infinite and omnipotent, can not be limited even by an inactive principle, such as matter. He not only designed but created the world, according to the Fathers; and, according to Clement and Origen, creation is by an eternal act. He did not find matter ready at hand, but created it out of nothing. As spirit, according to Origen, God is active in the material

2. In Ancient Thought.

universe as the soul is in the body. His successors followed all his doctrines except the eternal creation.

A principal representative of theism was Augustine. To him God was *summa essentia*, and the various things created out of nothing were charged with being of different degrees. God created by a free act, not of necessity, only by virtue of his goodness. Nothing is opposed to him, not even the world, save nonentity and evil issuing from it. Matter he made and the goodness imparted to it constitutes its form and order. Hence Augustine may scarcely be called a dualist. As creative substance God is in the whole world, and creation is a continuous process by which the universe is upheld; but it is eternal only in the counsel of God. God is inconceivable, yet a long array of attributes is produced by Augustine, by no means exhaustible, to give expression to his aspirations. Some of these are, finitely at least, mutually contradictory and even exclusive; such as always working yet ever at rest, or seeking yet possessing all things. This with his sense of immanence indicates a strain of mysticism and resembles pure pantheism; yet Augustine stands fast by his transcendentalism, maintaining the beginning and ending of the world and the eternity of God alone with the souls of men and angels. Scholasticism was strongly theistic in spite of sundry pantheistic tendencies. Anselm taught that the world, as contingent existence, presupposes absolute existence which is of itself and in itself. The contingent was not made of the absolute but by it, and of nothing. The continuous presence of God is necessary to sustain the world; hence in Anselm can be shown clearly neither dualism nor deism. In the determination of deity he approximates anthropomorphism. Besides metaphysical attributes are the ethical—justice, mercy, and love. Love in man has its foundation in living faith which involves submission and an aspiration toward its object with the hope of its attainment. Albert the Great (see ALBERTUS MAGNUS) followed the views of Augustine. Thomas Aquinas adhered more closely to Aristotle. The fact that the world as well as matter was created was philosophically demonstrable; the beginning of the world in time was a matter of faith. Preservation was a continuous creation. Following Aristotle, he considers God as absolute, simple, form, pure actuality, unchangeable. His essence is self-knowledge, implying the knowledge of all things. Therefore as the absolute good he must will himself; he wills not to attain a good thing, but for the sake of the good, to give it from love. The divine joy is his supreme self-satisfaction. With reference to man's relation to God, apart from his continuous preservation, the highest moral goal can not be reached without divine help. The perfect happiness of man consists in the intuition of the divine being. Descartes thought that he had found more certain proofs for the existence of God than those used in mathematics. Dualism is ascribed to him either because he conceived God in contrast with the world, or he opposed exclusively against each other the two created substances, the thinking and the extended, needing

3. In Medieval Thought.

nothing else for their existence and maintenance but God. It is evident that this is not dualism proper. If it be observed also that God is absolute perfection, producing the natural light or understanding in man, and that one of his first attributes is truth, Descartes may seem to be a theist. God is transcendent, yet in the most intimate relation with the world and man. Personality is also involved with veracity; yet Descartes is more deist than theist. The universe is a mechanism set in operation by a transcendent first cause; all things are moved by secondary cause and effect and the quantity of energy is invariable, which together with the validity and persistence of material law seems to be derived from the unchangeableness of God. According to Leibnitz, God is the highest monad, which is absolutely perfect. He creates all the other monads, which become self-existent and have God as the object of their aspiration. The world is a mechanism into which God does not again interfere; otherwise it would not be the best. So far Leibnitz is a deist. Besides, he maintains the belief in revelation and miracle, by the doctrine of the superrational in contradistinction to the counterrational. Only contingent happenings, such as the natural events, can be altered by God who is their ground. With this interference in the unity of nature Leibnitz passed from deism to theism. Transcendence is not sustained, but immediate divine contact with the universe is assumed, amounting to immanence in the religious and metaphysical spheres. Wolff follows Leibnitz closely and the Enlightenment is deistic.

Kant, whose definition is given above, postulates the existence of God from the infinite relation of virtue and happiness. The agreement of the latter with the former is to be assumed *a priori* as necessary, and as its ground is to be postulated a moral cause subsisting in reason and will and transcending nature, namely, the existence of God.

4. In Modern Thought. For the theoretical reason the assumption of God is merely hypothetical; for the practical reason, it is purely a matter of rational faith. In moral philosophy this faith is based on conscience in the form of a dual personality of defendant and judge. The latter must be an omnipotent being, God; but whether this be an actual or ideal person remains uncertain. In the " Critique of Judgment," the existence of God is postulated by the telic conception. The presence of contingent design in the multiplicity of nature and its subordination by reason to an unconditioned highest being involves a final objective in creation which is transcendent to nature, and its ground is in supreme intelligence. Man as a moral being must be accepted as this objective, affording the main condition upon which to observe the unity of the world, and a principle by which to consider the nature and attributes of such a cause. With reference to the highest good, namely, the existence of rational beings under moral laws, such a primal being must be omniscient, to whom all minds are open. He must be omnipotent, to adapt all nature to this purpose; all-merciful and just as conditions of a supreme cause of a world under moral laws. All the rest of the transcendental attributes follow, such as eternity and omnipresence, as presumptions to such a final purpose. On the side of the cognizance of God, Kant is neither deist nor theist; on the side of rational faith as just illustrated he is theist. Yet he disavows a personal intercourse with God as expressed in prayer. Among his followers who inclined mostly to pantheism in various forms, this view of the " Critique of Judgment " in the main prevailed; namely, Herbart and M. W. Drabisch (*Religionsphilosophie*, Leipsic, 1840). Schleiermacher, in spite of his tremendous religious influence, can not be considered a theist, but wavers between deism and pantheism. He does not represent a personal God, but a living deity; and the customary attributes appear not as properties of his being but reflections of his activity in the religious consciousness. Decidedly in behalf of speculative theism is to be reckoned the series of philosophers including T. Hoffman and C. H. Weisse, and of theologians like A. Neander and R. Rothe (qq.v.) who withstood the pantheism of Hegel and united in the establishment of the *Zeitschrift für Philosophie und spekulative Theologie*, issued chiefly by I. H. Fichte. The latter in his individual writings, in the interest of an ethical theism, advances to a doctrine of absolute personality. Lotze replaces the metaphysical infinite by the concept of God, constituting a sort of ontological proof. As the ground of reality for the finite, God possesses the metaphysical attributes of wisdom, justice, and holiness. An indispensable assumption must be personality, since the living, self-subsisting, and self-enjoying ego is the necessary presupposition and the only possible seat of the good and of all good things. At all events, the contradistinction with the external world is not essential for personality, but this is to be realized on the basis of an immanent sense of self and existence for self. Otherwise the being of God is to be in a certain measure super-personal; but by this personality itself may disappear. With God who conditions man's being, he is united by the religious sense of himself as a divine being. Here Lotze approximates Spinoza's pantheism, as also in his view that his monads are modifications of the absolute universal ground, and that reciprocal activity presupposes a common propinquity in substance. More or less under the influence of Lotze are many present-day philosophers. Of these G. Class represents God (*Phänomenologie und Ontologie des menschlichen Geistes*, Erlangen, 1896; *Realität der Gottesidee*, Munich, 1904) as personal and absolute spirit. Ludwig Bosse (*Philosophie und Erkenntnisslehre*, Leipsic, 1894) maintains that the inseparable constituents of reality rest upon a simple absolute ground, God. Guenther Thiele (*Philosophie des Selbstbewusstseins*, Berlin, 1895) affirms that the concept of God resolves itself in the absolute Ego. G. Glogau (*Religionsphilosophie*, Kiel, 1898) places the existence of God at the apex of philosophy; derives from it the ideas of the true, the good, and the beautiful; and, in mystical fashion, makes the sense and experience of God and the ideals of principal importance. According to H. Siebeck (*Religionsphilosophie*, Freiburg, 1893), God is proved by metaphysics and experienced as a living power in the religious person. English theists, like J. Martineau (q.v.), C. B. Upton, and E. Caird, supplement transcendence with immanence, thus representing a theism approximating pantheism.

On the question of its justification, it is to be admitted that a theistic view can not claim scientific validity. Scientific thought does not yield to the assumption of a personal God clothed with ethical attributes. A universal or an unconditioned being must of necessity be postulated. To the highest being universal attributes, such as 5. Relation omnipresence and unity, must be to Scientific ascribed. Omniscience is doubtful Reason. inasmuch as it implies the spiritual, which may not be attributed to unconditioned being without the presumption of a philosophic view that does not need to obtain universal validity. However, not only reason but the yearnings of the soul crave to be satisfied. The devout human being requires above all things a living God, not only omniscient, but also all-wise. He must be a person, who is at the same time love, by which he is willing to make man, whose needs he understands, contented and happy; exercising at the same time justice, and being about to bring happiness in agreement with virtue, either in this world or the next. These are attributes that may be multiplied according as man qualifies himself toward him, and may be called ethical. They bring deity near to man, or God down amidst the phenomenal, by attributing to him qualities magnified, which are inconsistent with the nature of the infinite and universal. Science, if indeed unwilling to protest against the anthropomorphizing of the highest, can do nothing to support it, and can not concur with theism in desiring to attribute these properties to God. Faith must, therefore, maintain what reason may not afford, and thus embrace theism. See DEISM; GOD; and RATIONALISM AND SUPERNATURALISM.   (M. HEINZE†.)

BIBLIOGRAPHY: S. Clarke, A Demonstration of the Being and Attributes of God, London, 1705–16; I. Kant, Kritik der reinen Vernunft, Riga, 1781 (see under KANT for Eng. transls.); F. W. J. Schelling, System des transcendentalen Idealismus, Tübingen, 1800; A. H. Ritter, Ueber die Erkenntniss Gottes in der Welt, Hamburg, 1836; J. U. Wirth, Die speculative Idee Gottes, Stuttgart, 1845; H. L. Mansel, Limits of Religious Thought, London, 1850; J. Croll, Philosophy of Theism, ib. 1851; Abbé Gratry, Philosophie de la connaissance de Dieu, 2 vols., Paris, 1853; W. M. Gillespie, The Necessary Existence of God, London, 1855; J. Tulloch, Theism, Edinburgh, 1855; I. H. Fichte, Ueber den Unterschied zwischen ethischen und naturalistischen Theismus, Halle, 1856; E. Steere, Essay on the Existence and Attributes of God, London, 1856; F. W. Newman, Theism, Doctrinal and Practical, ib. 1858; J. W. Hanne, Die Idee der absoluten Persönlichkeit oder Gott und sein Verhältniss zur Welt, insonderheit zur menschlichen Persönlichkeit, 2 vols., Hanover, 1861; M. Carrière, Gott, Gemüth und Welt, Stuttgart, 1862; W. Cooke, The Deity, Edinburgh, 1862; R. A. Thompson Christian Theism, new ed., London, 1863; F. Pecaut, De l'avenir du théisme chrétien considéré comme religion, Paris, 1864; M. Kähler, Der lebendige Gott, Leipsic, 1867; E. Herwig, Ueber den ontologischen Beweis, Rostock, 1868; A. Riedel, Ueber das Dasein Gottes, Augsburg, 1869; A. Robertson, The Existence of God, London, 1870; H. von Brucken, Das Wesen Gottes und der Welt, 2 vols., Berlin, 1871; H. Ulrici, Gott und die Natur, Leipsic, 1875; E. Castan, De l'idée de Dieu, 2 vols., Paris, 1877; G. J. Romanes, A Candid Examination of Theism, London, 1878; B. P. Bowne, Studies in Theism, New York, 1879; idem, Philosophy of Theism. rev. ed., ib. 1902; C. C. Mairae, Historical Sketch of Theism,

London, 1879; J. T. Doedes, Inleiding tot de leer van God, 2d ed., Utrecht, 1880; C. J. Ellicot, The Being of God, London, 1880; J. L. Diman, The Theistic Argument, Boston, 1882; J. Hamburger, Gott und seine Offenbarungen in Natur und Geschichte, Gütersloh, 1882; G. Runze, Der ontologische Gottesbeweis, Halle, 1882; J. J. Lias, Is it possible to know God? London, 1883; F. Vidal, De la croyance philosophique en Dieu, 2d ed., Paris, 1883; R. Flint, Theism, 5th ed., Edinburgh, 1885; F. E. Abbot, Scientific Theism, Boston, 1886; R. A. Armstrong, Man's Knowledge of God, London, 1886; idem, God and the Soul, 2d ed., ib. 1898; J. G. Cazenave, Historic Aspects of the a priori Arguments concerning the Being and Attributes of God, ib. 1886; R. T. Smith, Man's Knowledge of Man and of God, Edinburgh, 1886; J. S. Van Dyke, Theism and Evolution, London, 1886; T. V. Tymms, Mystery of God, ib. 1887; A. W. Momerie, Belief in God, 2d ed., Edinburgh, 1888; A. de Anglement, Dieu et l'être universel, Paris, 1889; S. Harris, The Self-revelation of God, 2d ed., New York, 1889; idem, The Philosophical Basis of Theism, 2d ed., ib. 1894; D. B. Purinton, Christian Theism, its Claims and Sanctions, ib. 1889; H. H. Moore, The Anatomy of Theism, London, 1890; C. A. Row, Christian Theism, ib. 1890; J. G. Schurman, Belief in God, its Origin, Nature, and Basis, New York, 1890; G. de Alviella, Origin and Growth of the Conception of God, London, 1892, Fr. ed., Paris, 1892; R. F. Clarke, A Dialogue on the Existence of God, ib. 1892; A. Drews, Die deutsche Spekulation seit Kant mit besonderer Rücksicht auf das Wesen des Absoluten und die Persönlichkeit Gottes, 2 vols., Berlin, 1892; E. Caird, The Evolution of Religion, 2 vols., London, 1893; W. L. Davidson, Theism as Grounded in Human Nature, London and New York, 1893; W. Knight, Aspects of Theism, ib., 1893; J. Orr, The Christian View of God and the World Centering in the Incarnation, Edinburgh, 1893; J. R. Illingworth, Personality Human and Divine, London, 1894; idem, Divine Immanence, ib. 1898; R. Ottley, The Doctrine of the Incarnation, 2 vols., ib. 1894; A. J. Balfour, The Foundations of Belief, London and New York, 1895; H. Baynes, The Idea of God and the Moral Sense, 2 vols., London, 1895; A. C. Fraser, Philosophy of Theism (Gifford lectures, 1st series, 1894–95), Edinburgh and London, 1895; G. W. F. Hegel, Philosophy of Religion. With Proofs of Existence of God, London, 1895; G. Jamieson, The Great Problem of Substance and its Attributes, ib. 1895; R. A. Meincke, Die Beweise für das Dasein Gottes, Heidelberg, 1895; E. Melzer, Der Beweis für das Dasein Gottes, Neisse, 1895; J. R. Seeley, Natural Religion, 4th ed., London, 1895; C. Voysey, Theism as a Science of Natural Theology and Natural Religion, ib. 1895; idem, Lectures on the Theistic Faith and its Foundations, ib. 1895; Duke of Argyll, Philosophy of Belief, London, 1896; O. Berger, Les Origines de la philosophie réele (l'athéisme spiritualiste), Brussels, 1896; L. Buchner, Gott und die Wissenschaft, Leipsic, 1896; F. Drion, Preuve philosophique de l'existence de Dieu, Brussels, 1896; G. Allen, The Evolution of the Idea of God, London and New York, 1897; J. M. Baldwin, Social and Ethical Interpretations in Mental Development, New York, 1897; E. B. Gamble, The God-Idea of the Ancients, New York and London, 1897; W. James, The Will to Believe and Other Essays, New York, 1897; J. Royce, The Conception of God, New York, 1897; J. Lindsay, Recent Advances in Theistic Philosophy, Edinburgh, 1897; R. M. Wenley, Contemporary Theology and Theism, ib. 1897; P. Bard, Das Dasein Gottes, Schwerin, 1898; C. Bensow, Ueber die Möglichkeit eines ontologischen Beweises für das Dasein Gottes, Rostock, 1898; L. T. Cole, The Basis of Early Christian Theism, New York, 1898; J. B. Heinrich, Der kosmologische Gottesbeweis und Kant's Kritik der reinen Vernunft, Mainz, 1898; E. Rolfes, Die Gottesbeweise bei Thomas von Aquin und Aristoteles, Cologne, 1898; R. de Cléré, Nécessité mathématique de l'existence de Dieu, Paris, 1899; C. F. D'Arcy, Idealism and Theology, London, 1899; J. Geyser, Das philosophische Gottesproblem, Bonn, 1899; J. Iverach, Theism in the Light of Present Science and Philosophy, New York, 1899; J. P. Brisset, La Science de Dieu, Paris, 1900; L. Désers, Dieu et l'homme, Paris, 1900; J. T. Driscoll, Christian Philosophy: God, New York, 1900; J. H. Kennedy, Gottesglaube und moderne Weltanschauung, Berlin, 1900; J. Martineau, A Study of Religion, London, 1900; P. Schwartzkopff, Beweis für das Dasein Gottes, Halle, 1900; M. Valentine, Natural Theology, or Rational Theism, New York, 1900; J. E. Alaux, Dieu et le monde, Paris, 1901; A. Caldecott,

The *Philosophy of Religion in England and America*, Edinburgh and New York, 1901; idem, *Selections from the Literature of Theism. Some principal Types of Religious Thought*, Edinburgh, 1907; J. A. Leighton, *Typical Modern Conceptions of God*, New York, 1901; Archibald Robertson, *Regnum Dei*, New York and London, 1901; R. Rocholl, *Der christliche Gottesbegriff*, Göttingen, 1901; G. Spicker, *Versuch eines neuen Gottesbegriffs*, Stuttgart, 1901; H. Walter von Walthofen, *Die Gottesidee*, Vienna, 1901; J. Fiske, *Cosmic Philosophy*, Boston, 1902; J. J. Tigert, *Theism*, London, 1902; A. Eleutheropulos, *Gott, Menschen*, 2d ed., Berlin, 1903; J. Rülf, *Wissenschaft der Gotteseinheit*, Leipsic, 1903; B. Baentsch, *Altorientalischer und israelitischer Monotheismus*, Tübingen, 1906; F. J. McConnell, *The Diviner Immanence*, New York, 1906 (distinguishes theism from pantheism); K. Müller, *Christentum und Monismus*, 1906; W. L. Walker, *Theism and a Spiritual Monism*, New York, 1906 (proposes a spiritual monism as against the material monism of Haeckel); R. de Bary, *The Spiritual Return of Christ within the Church. Papers on Christian Theism*, London, 1907; A. Drews, *Der Monismus*, vol. i., Jena, 1907; B. Wilberforce, *New Theology. Thoughts on the Universality and Continuity of the Doctrine of the Immanence of God*, London, 1907; F. Ballard, *The True God; a modern Summary of the Relations of Theism to Naturalism, Monism, and Pluralism*, London, 1907; O. Flügel, *Monismus und Theologie*, 3d ed., Cöthen, 1908; A. C. Pigou, *The Problem of Theism, and Other Essays*, New York, 1908; C. C. Everett, *Theism and the Christian Faith*, New York, 1909; A. D. Kelly, *Rational Necessity of Theism*, London, 1909.

THEMISTIUS, THEMISTIANS. See MONOPHYSITES, § 15.

THEODORE: Name of two popes.

1. Theodore I: Pope 642–649. He was the son of a bishop; born at Jerusalem; was consecrated, Nov., 642; and was an opponent of the Monothelites (q.v.). When Paul II. announced his election to the patriarchate of Constantinople, in a communication concealing Monothelite views behind orthodox phrases, Theodore ordered him to depose his fallen Monothelite predecessor Pyrrhus by a synod and that the imperial ecthesis be vacated. After Pyrrhus, in consequence of a disputation with the Abbot Maximus Confessor (q.v.) in North Africa, had returned to Rome professing his conversion to Diothelitism, he was ceremonially recognized as patriarch of Constantinople by Theodore. The abjuration of Pyrrhus, however, proved to have been only with the design of regaining his see; for at Ravenna, after consultation with the imperial exarch, he espoused anew the doctrine of the one will in Christ. Upon this the pope assembled a synod at Rome and excommunicated Pyrrhus (646 or 647). After summoning Paul by appeal to the orthodox faith in vain, Theodore also deposed him, an act which was futile in effect. Paul, however, approached the pope half-way, if it may be accepted that he influenced the emperor to issue the edict which enjoined silence on the questions in dispute, but at the same time vacated the ecthesis. Theodore died May 14, 649.　　(A. HAUCK.)

BIBLIOGRAPHY: *Liber pontificalis*, ed. Mommsen in *MGH, Gest. pont. Rom.*, i (1898), 178; *Theophanis chronographia*, i. 509, Bonn, 1839; Mansi, *Concilia*, x. 702 (the letters), also catalogued in Jaffé, *Regesta*, i. 228 sqq.; R. Baxmann, *Die Politik der Päpste*, i. 173 sqq., Elberfeld, 1868; B. Jungmann, *Dissertationes selectæ*, ii. 415 sqq., Regensburg, 1881; J. Langen, *Geschichte der römischen Kirche*, ii. 520, Bonn, 1885; F. Gregorovius, *History of City of Rome in the Middle Ages*, ii. 139, London, 1894; M. Hartmann, *Geschichte Italiens im Mittelalter*, ii. 219–220, Gotha, 1903; Mann, *Popes*, i. 369–384; Milman, *Latin Christianity*, ii. 274–275; Bower, *Popes*, i. 441–446; Platina, *Popes*,

i. 152–153; Hefele, *Conciliengeschichte*, iii. 186 sqq., Eng. transl., v. 70 sqq., Fr. transl., iii. 1, pp. 398 sqq.

2. Theodore II.: Pope 897. He occupied the papal chair only twenty days (Nov.–Dec.). He exerted himself to restore to the Church the peace which had been disturbed by the inquest in regard to Pope Formosus (q.v.). He caused the corpse of that pope to be reinterred ceremonially and the consecrations performed by him to be recognized by a synod as canonical.　　(A. HAUCK.)

BIBLIOGRAPHY: The tractate of Auxilius in Mabillon, *Analecta*, p. 43, Paris, 1723, and his *Libellus in defensione sacræ ordinationis papæ Formosi*, in C. Dümmler, *Auxilius und Bulgarius*, p. 72, Leipsic, 1866; Jaffé, *Regesta*, p. 441; F. Gregorovius, *History of . . . Rome in the Middle Ages*, iii. 230, London, 1895; Mann, *Popes*, iv. 88–90; Bower, *Popes*, ii. 302; Platina, *Popes*, i. 239–240.

THEODORE (THEODULUS): Local saint of Valais and bishop of the fourth century. That the Christian religion took deep root very early in the valley of the Rhone is quite probable, especially in view of the importance of the Pennine Pass for communication between Italy and Gaul. Martigny, situated at the point where the Alpine road first strikes the course of the Rhône, after clearing the summit of St. Bernard, the ancient Octodurum, was the seat of the bishopric as well as the capital of Valais; but with the second half of the sixth century it lost its ecclesiastical importance by the removal of the see up the valley to Sitten. Here is an inscription of the year 377, showing the Christian monogram, dedicated by the first magistrate, which points doubtlessly to the establishment of the imperial prætorium. To the same period belongs the first bishop, Theodore. In 381 he appears as *episcopus Octodurensis* in the documents of the Synod of Aquileia, among the zealous upholders of orthodoxy in opposition to the Arianism of the accused Bishop Paladius, and his name is included among the Gallic, not the Italian bishops. But *Theodulus Episcopus*, who signs at a small synod held at Milan in 390, can not be located. The *Passio Agaunensium martyrum*, attributed to Eucherius (in *ASB*, Sept. vi. 342–349), represents that the latter obtained his oral legend concerning the Theban Legion (q.v.) from Bishop Isaac of Geneva, who received it from Theodore; and that the latter first erected a church at Agaunum (Saint-Maurice) on the site of the alleged scene. A Valais legend, however, tells of a Bishop Theodulus, a contemporary of Charlemagne. According to Ruodpert, a " foreign monk," the biographer of this saint, the emperor conferred upon Theodulus the prefecture of Valais, with temporal authority over the entire country. This donation of Charles proved important to the bishopric Sitten in the later Middle Ages, on the one hand against the House of Savoy, planted in lower Valais, and on the other against the encroaching demands of a tithe on the part of the people of upper Valais. However, as early as the sixteenth century, this account came to be questioned by the historians of Valais. But in the eyes of the people of Valais this Theodulus, celebrated Aug. 16 (the historic Theodore, Aug. 26), is the real saint of the land; he is " St. Jodern," around whom local legend is spun. A critical illumination of the confusion of the historical personality with the non-historical legendary figure was first attempted in *ASB* (Aug. v., vi.), after printing Ruodpert's *Vita Theoduli episcopi* (iii.).

(G. MEYER VON KNONAU.)

BIBLIOGRAPHY: Besides the literature under THEBAN LEGION, consult: E. F. Gelpke, *Kirchengeschichte der Schweiz*, i. 90 sqq., 120 sqq., ii. 95 sqq., Bern, 1856–61; E. Egli, *Kirchengeschichte der Schweiz*, p. 132, Zurich, 1893; M. Besson, *Recherches sur les origines des évêchés de Genève, Lausanne . . .* , Geneva, 1906.

THEODORE OF ANDIDA. See MYSTAGOGICAL THEOLOGY.

THEODORE OF CANTERBURY. See THEODORE OF TARSUS.

THEODORE OF MOPSUESTIA: Foremost exegete of the school of Antioch; b. at Antioch c. 350; d. at Mopsuestia in Cilicia in 428. He was of a distinguished wealthy family, brother of Bishop Polychronius of Apamea. He spent **Life.** from forty-five to fifty years in teaching and was bishop of Mopsuestia, 392–428. The earliest reliable information is contained in two letters, *Ad Theodorum lapsum* (*MPG*, lxvii. 277–316), no doubt by Chrysostom, who a generation later, when in exile, thanks Theodore for his tried and true friendship (*MPG*, lii. 669). The second of these letters complains that Theodore, who then had scarcely attained his twentieth year, had turned his back on the ascetic life which he had commenced with such zeal, and was occupying himself with household matters and forming plans of marriage. Chrysostom entreats him to return to the monastic community. The first letter addressed to one not mentioned by name represents the latter as in love with a certain Hermione and sunk in the smudge of sensuality and the depths of despair. That this epistle was from Chrysostom and addressed to Theodore has been disputed, though not conclusively. That Theodore heard the rhetorician Libanius is more than probable, but that he did so contemporaneously with Chrysostom and renounced the world at the same time with the latter seems highly improbable, considering the difference in their ages and silence on the part of Chrysostom. It must, therefore, be assumed that Theodore's renunciation of the world and subsequent " fall " belongs to the period when Chrysostom was living as a monk in the mountains about Antioch. It is an old and credible tradition that the counsels of Chrysostom induced Theodore to return to the monastic life. That Theodore was a disciple of Diodorus is evident from his theology and exegesis, as well as from the direct testimony of the historians; and the testimony of Theodoret that this was in companionship with Chrysostom may, for at least a period, be credited. Afterward both were disciples of Flavian, bishop of Antioch, who undoubtedly consecrated Theodore presbyter in 383. In 394 Theodore took part in a synod at Constantinople, on which occasion possibly it happened that the Emperor Theodosius (q.v.), as is said, was impressed by his preaching. During this period he wrote a mass of exegetical and polemical works. He entered into the Pelagian discussion and in 420 received Julian of Eclanum (q.v.) and his associates. His fame extended far beyond the boundaries of his diocese; and he died at peace with the Church, though not before suffering some individual antagonisms.

Of his numerous works only a few commentaries are preserved more or less intact; of the rest only meager fragments are extant. A list of the works is given by Ebed Jesu (d. 1318; cf. J. S. Assemani, *Bibliotheca orientalis* III., i. 30–35, Rome **Works.** 1719–28). Theodore wrote Commentaries on Genesis, Psalms, the major and minor prophets, Job (dedicated to Cyril of Alexandria), Samuel, Ecclesiastes, and on all the books of the New Testament excepting Mark, the Catholic Epistles, and Revelation. Of those on the Pauline Epistles an old Latin translation has been issued together with the Greek fragments by Swete. Of all the commentaries only that on the minor prophets is wholly extant in the original and a Syriac version of the commentary on John has been issued by Chabot. *De sacramentis* was most probably identical with the *Liber arcanorum* mentioned by a contemporary of Ebed Jesu, and with *Sermones mystici* (Hesychius), and *Codex mysticus* (Facundus); and *De fide* was probably identical with the *Catechismus* cited by Marius Mercator, *Ad baptizandos* cited by the council of 553, and *Ad baptizatos* cited by Facundus. The most frequently cited dogmatic work was *De incarnatione* (*Peri tes enanthrōpeseōs*), in fifteen books, against the Apollinarians and Anomians, written while he was presbyter (Gennadius, *De vir. ill.*, xv.), thirty years before the *De assumente et assumpto*. This was evidently also on the incarnation, bearing on the " two sons " as alleged of the Antiochians. Hence, this work is no doubt identical with *De Apollinario et ejus hæresi*, from the introduction of which, dealing with the reproach of the " two sons," Facundus preserved a large fragment. Fragments in citations are preserved of two books *Adversus Eunomium*, and of two *Adversus asserentem peccatum in natura insitum esse;* one fragment is preserved of the five books of *Adversus allegoricos* probably identical with *De allegoria et historia contra Origenem* dedicated to Cerdo; two fragments perhaps remain of the *Liber margaritarum*, " in which his letters are collected." Ebed Jesu mentions also a book *Pro Basilio* which others have regarded as a part of *Adversus Eunomium* (ut sup.), the work having possibly become dismembered in its Syriac form (Fritzsche, pp. 96–97). In its original, the work entitled, " In Behalf of Basil, Against Eunomius," consisted of twenty five books (Photius codex 4) or even twenty-eight (Photius, cod. 177; cf. Leontius, *Adversus Eutychianos et Nestorianos*, iii.; *MPG*, lxxxvi. 1384). Works wholly lost are two works *De spiritu sancto; De sacerdotio;* two books *Adversus magiam*, the content of which is somewhat discussed by Photius; *Ad monachos; De obscura locutione; De perfectione operum;* and *Sermo de legislatione*. Ebed Jesu professed to give a complete catalogue, and what is preserved elsewhere may have been contained in the works named in this list. Such remainders are a fragment of Exodus, four of Canticles, and four of Mark, all of which have been published, and unpublished fragments exist of catenæ on Leviticus, Numbers, Deuteronomy, Judges, Ruth, Kings, and the Catholic

Epistles. The authenticity of the unprinted fragments is by no means certain, and what actually comes from Theodore was not necessarily derived from a commentary on the book to which the catena refers. Thus some genuine fragments from Canticles may have descended from a letter; but that they were taken from a commentary is improbable, for Theodore regarded Canticles as a profane love-song and, therefore, esteemed it of little value (Leontius iii. 16). He certainly did not comment on the Catholic Epistles (ib., p. 1365) and that he wrote a commentary on Mark is not probable in view of the list of Ebed Jesu and his own references exclusively to the interpretations of the other Gospels. The fragment of *De interpretatione symboli 318 patrum* (*MPG*, lxvi. 1016; Swete, ii. 327) and the symbol of Theodore (*MPG*, lxvi. 1016–1020; Swete, ii. 327–332) may without hesitation be referred to the work *De fide*. Only three printed fragments remain unassigned to the works mentioned by Ebed Jesu; namely, the hymn (E. Sachau, p. 58), the *Liturgia Theodori* (E. Renaudot, *Liturgiarum orientalium collectio*, ii. 616–621, Rome, 1716), and the citation from a work "On the Miracles" (*MPG*, lxvi. 1004; Swete, ii. 339). The hymn is from Ephraem; the citation may not be genuine; and the liturgy, though accepted by Leontius (iii. 19) and Swete as genuine on account of language and thought, yet may be of Nestorian origin and merely referred to Theodore even as early as the time of Leontius.

Theodore was the classical representative of the school of Antioch. For his christology see NESTORIUS; for Nestorius represented the same ideas, and, apart from the incipient antagonism to the *theotokos* ("mother of God"), more prudently than Theodore. The exegetical method of the Antiochians, however, is best represented by Theodore, although his most important hermeneutical work is lost (*Adversus allegoricos*). Photius states of him that "avoiding the tendency of allegory, he made his interpretation according to history" (codex 38; *MPG*, ciii. 72); and this statement is corroborated by theoretical discussions on the part of Theodore himself (Swete, i. 73 sqq.). The Old Testament he treated in the way which he assumed Paul followed; not by discarding its history, but by setting forth the resemblance of this to New-Testament materials in order to make it profitable for the present. He recognizes few direct messianic prophecies. The prophets and psalms are first explained with reference to their own times; but, convinced of the preparatory nature of the Old-Testament economy, he frequently asserts that what was reported in the Old first reached its full meaning in the New. The complaint of Leontius (iii. 15) that Theodore rejected the superscriptions to the Psalms, in historical interest, is scarcely exaggerated. His depreciation of Canticles as a profane love-song (*MPG*, lxvi. 699–700) was due to his aversion to allegorizing; and his inability to appreciate the poesy of Job, to his prosaic historic interest (Leontius, xiii. 1365). His attitude to the canon did not exclude the relative value of books (cf. *MPG*, lvi. 697); it is probable that he rejected

XI.—21

Esther and the Apocrypha (Kihn, § 54, pp. 64–65), but scarcely credible that he excluded Chronicles, Ezra with Nehemiah (Leontius, xvii. 1368), and that he rejected from the canon Canticles and Job (iii. 16, xiii. 1365) is improbable from the fact that he wrote a commentary on Job. Theodore appears to have had the ancient Syrian canon, which contained only the Gospels, the Acts, and the Pauline Epistles (see CANON OF SCRIPTURE II., § 6). The high recognition of Theodore did not long continue undiminished after his death, although he had enthusiastic adherents even after the condemnation of Nestorius, wherever the Antiochian tradition prevailed, and his repute as exegete had not wholly subsided in the orthodox Church of the succeeding century, as proved by Photius and the catenæ. Soon after the Council of Ephesus (431), which condemned his creed without mention or censure of him, he was included in the condemnations of Nestorius. Independently of each other Marius Mercator, stirred by Theodore's attitude toward the Pelagian controversy, and Rabulas of Edessa, the apostate of the Antiochians, opened the attack. The latter called the attention of Cyril of Alexandria to the charge that Theodore was the father of the Nestorian heresy. Indeed Cyril had before 435 contracted ill-feeling toward Theodore, as is shown by his letters lxvii.-lxviii., lxxi.-lxxii. (*MPG*, lxxvii. 351 sqq.); further, he wrote *Adversus Diodorum et Theodorum*, of which a few fragments are preserved (Liberatus, *Breviarium*, x., *MPL*, lxviii. 991; cf. *MPG*, lxxvi. 1437–1452). The name of Theodore was henceforth involved in the partisan strife of the period, resulting in the final tragical transaction instigated by the polemics of the Scythian monks (Maxentius, *MPG*, lxxxvi. 85; Leontius iii. 7 sqq., *MPG*, lxxxvi. 1364 sqq.); Justinian condemned with the Three Chapters (see THREE CHAPTER CONTROVERSY) the person and writings of Theodore, and in spite of the resistance of the West pressed this anathema through the council of 553.   (F. LOOFS.)

BIBLIOGRAPHY: The most complete collection of the "Works" of Theodore is in *MPG*, lxvi. 1–1020, derived from the earliest of the following named works: *Fragmenta patrum Græcorum*, ed. F. Münter, vol. i., Copenhagen, 1788; *Scriptorum veterum nova collectio*, ed. A. Mai, vols. i., vi., vii., Rome, 1825–35, and the same author's *Nova patrum bibliothecæ*, vol. vii., ib. 1854; *Theodori Antiocheni, Mopsuestini episcopi quæ supersunt*, ed. A. F. V. von Wegnern, vol. i., Berlin, 1834; *Theodori episcopi Mopsuestini in Novum Testamentum*, ed. O. F. Fritzsche, Zurich, 1847, the same scholar's ed. of the *De incarnatione Filii Dei*, ib. 1847–48; J. B. Pitra, *Spicilegium Solesmense*, vol. i., Paris, 1852; *Theodori . . . commentarii nuper detecti*, ed. J. L. Jacobi, Halle, 1855–58; P. de Lagarde, *Analecta Syriaca*, Leipsic, 1858; *Theodori Mopsuestini fragmenta Syriaca . . . ed. . . . E. Sachau*, ib. 1869; *Theodori in epistolas . . . Pauli commentarii*, ed. H. B. Swete, 2 vols., Cambridge, 1880–82; F. Baethgen, in *ZATW*, 1885, pp. 53–101; his commentary on John, ed. J. B. Chabot, Paris, 1897; Prologue to a possible commentary on Acts by E. von Dobschütz, in *AJT*, ii (1898), 353–387; J. Lietzmann, in *SBA*, 1902, pp. 334–344; G. Dittrich, *ZATW*, Beihefte, vi (1902).

On the life early accounts are: Chrysostom, *Epist. ad Theodorum lapsum*; Theodoret, *Hist. eccl.*, V., xxxix.; Socrates, *Hist. eccl.*, VI., iii.; Gennadius, *De vir. ill.*, xii., Eng. transl. in *NPNF*, 2 ser., iii. 338. Consult further: *DCB*, iv. 934–948 (minute, searching, and comprehensive); Leo Allatius, in *MPG*, lxvi. 77–104; Tillemont, *Mémoires*, xi., xii. 433–453, 673–674; Fabricius-Harles,

Bibliotheca Græca, x. 346–362, Hamburg, 1807; A. Mai, *Nova collectio*, i., pp. xviii.–xxx., and vi., pp. v.–xxii.; idem, in *MPG*, lxvi. 120–123; R. E. Klener, *Symbolæ litterariæ ad Theodorum . . . pertinentes*, Göttingen, 1836; O. F. Fritzsche, *De Theodori Mopsuesteni vita et scriptis commentatio*, Halle, 1836; W. C. H. toe Water, *Specimen observationum de Theodoro . . . XII. prophetarum minorum interprete*, Amsterdam, 1837; F. A. Specht, *Der exegetische Standpunkt des Theodor von Mopsuestia . . .*, Munich, 1871; H. Kihn, *Theodor von Mopsuestia und Junilius Afrikanus als Exegeten*, Freiburg, 1880; W. Sanday, in *Expositor*, June, 1880; T. K. Cheyne, in *The Thinker*, iii (1893), 496–498; J. Fessler, *Institutiones patrologiæ*, ed. B. Jungmann, vol. ii., part 2, Innsbruck, 1896; T. Zahn, in *NKZ*, xi (1900), 788–806; Bardenhewer, *Patrologie*, pp. 279–282, Eng. transl., St. Louis, 1908; and the introductions to the various editions noted above.

THEODORE THE STUDITE: Monk of the Eastern Church, and abbot of Studium; b. perhaps no the paternal estate on the east coast of the Sea of Marmora, near the modern Brusa (57 m. s.s.e. of Constantinople), in 759; d. in exile on the island of Chalcis Nov. 11, 826. Theodore was instructed by his uncle Plato, abbot at Saccudium, became priest 784 or 787, and head of the monastery in 794. A raid by Arabs drove the monks to the city of Constantinople, where they entered the Studium, which under Theodore's leadership attained great celebrity and its pinnacle of greatness. Yet Theodore passed only half of the twenty-eight years of his abbacy in the monastery, being in frequent exile because of his participation in the controversies of the times.

Theodore's genius was rather practical than speculative; he had a good education, and wrote exceedingly well. The most important of his writings are monastic addresses and letters. One work is dogmatic—that on the image controversy (*MPG*, xcix. 327–426), marked not so much by a wealth of knowledge as by clear argumentation. Theodore's significance lies rather in his ecclesiastical statesmanship, he being a worthy champion of ecclesiastical freedom; indeed, he is the one Greek theologian who contended for the separation of Church and State. The canons were to be enforced even against the emperor's will. This is the fundamental tone in the so-called Mœchianic strife over the emperor's divorce and remarriage. He renewed the controversy after the death of Constantine when the Emperor Nicephorus raised a layman to the patriarchal chair; he felt himself, a mere abbot, the defender of the Church, sparing not even the patriarch. While Roman Catholics claim him as a supporter of papal primacy, his letters show him to have regarded the pope merely as the patriarch of the West. His position led to trouble later, when the monks, after 843, were drawn into schism, under the Patriarch Methodius, but were subdued on the principle that monks were subject to the priests.

Theodore was essentially the abbot, and as such a reformer of monasticism. The iconoclastic controversies (see IMAGES AND IMAGE WORSHIP, II.) had impaired monastic discipline, and Theodore went back to the rule of Basil, so fastening the regulations upon the Greek monasteries that the modern rules practically perpetuate his own, which are to-day the basis of Russian monasticism. The two catechisms still in use in the monasteries bear witness to his pastoral care of the monks, the smaller containing a selection of his extempore addresses and the longer three series of sermons. Even while in exile he maintained his discipline by means of letters instructing the administrator, showing a truly apostolic disposition and command. His ministrations extended beyond the cloister, as when he organized an association for the burial of the poor. Another activity of Theodore was in hymnology, a large number of hymns being accredited to him, and these of high emotional and intellectual quality. He also revived the art of making epigrams, which he used with exceeding richness. His reputation in the Greek Church has not equaled his capacity or his desert. His was a master mind, but worked principally in the cloister.   (E. von Dobschütz.)

BIBLIOGRAPHY: The "Works" are best consulted in *MPG*, xcix.; 277 letters and a large number of discourses are given in A. Mai, *Nova patrum bibliotheca*, viii.–ix., Rome, 1871–88; the *Parva Catechesis*, ed. Zacharias, appeared at Hermupolis, 1887, and ed. E. Auvray and A. Tougard, at Paris, 1891; the *Magna Catechesis*, ed. A. Papadopou los-Kerameus, at St. Petersburg, 1904. Early sources are most conveniently collected in *MPG*, xcix. 49–328, 803–850, 883–1670, 1813–49, in the shape of early lives, treatises, and his own letters and other materials. Consult also: Krumbacher, *Geschichte*, pp. 147–151, 712–715 et passim; J. J. Müller and J. V. Beumelling, *De studio cœnobio Constantinopolitano*, Leipsic, 1721; Fabricius-Harles, *Bibliotheca Græca*, x. 434–474, Hamburg, 1807; J. Richter, in *Katholik*, liv. 2 (1874), 385–414; K. Schwarzlose, *Der Bilderstreit*, pp. 123 sqq., Gotha, 1890; A. Tougard, *La Persécution iconoclaste d'après la correspondance de St. Théodore Studite*, Paris, 1891; C. Thomas, *Theodor von Studion und sein Zeitalter*, Osnabrück, 1892; Schievitz, *De S. Theodoro*, Breslau, 1896; L. Vigneron, *L'Image sainte. Hist. byzantine du viii. siècle*, Paris, 1896; K. Holl, in *Preussische Jahrbücher*, 1898, pp. 107 sqq.; A. Ferradou, *Des Biens des monastères à Byzance*, Paris, 1896; P. J. Pargoire, in *Byzantinische Zeitschrift*, viii (1899), 98–101; G. A. Schneider, *Der heilige Theodor von Studion, sein Leben und Wirken*, Münster, 1900; Alice Gardner, *Theodore of Studium, His Life and Times*, London, 1905; C. Diehl, *Figures byzantines*, Paris, 1906; Harnack, *Dogma*, iv. 328 sqq.; Ceillier, *Auteurs sacrés*, xii. 298–320; *DCB*, iv. 955–956.

THEODORE OF TARSUS: Seventh archbishop of Canterbury, and the "first to whom the whole English church made submission" (Bede, *Hist. eccl.*, iv. 2); b. at Tarsus in Cilicia, about 602; d. at Canterbury, Sept. 19, 690. In 667 he was in Rome when the pope, Vitalian, was searching for a primate for the English Church, Archbishop Deusdedit (q.v.) having died in 664 and Wighard, who came to Rome for consecration, having also died shortly after his arrival there. Theodore was recommended by Hadrian, abbot of a monastery near Naples; Bede describes him (iv. 1) as "well-trained in secular and sacred learning, familiar with both Latin and Greek literature [he had studied at Athens and was really a learned man], of high character, and of venerable age, being sixty-six years old." He was only a monk at the time, but was ordained subdeacon in November, and was consecrated archbishop, Mar. 26, 668. He left Rome in May, accompanied by Hadrian and Benedict Biscop (q.v.), spent the winter at Paris with Bishop Agilbert, and reached Canterbury, May 27, 669. The English church was much in need of organization and discipline. The bishoprics, with one or two exceptions, were vacant, and were large, unwieldy, and shifting. The Roman party had prevailed over the Celtic at the Synod of Whitby (q.v.) in 664, but the result was yet to be made effective and ill feeling was still strong. Theodore visited all parts of the island, introduced uniformity in worship and customs, filled vacant bishoprics, created new ones, and made Canterbury a center of learning. On Sept. 24, 673, he held at Hertford a synod, which is regarded as the first English national assembly; articles were then agreed upon for the government of the church. A second synod was held at Hatfield in 680. Theodore's character and ability are shown by the success of his plans, and his services to the English church and English learning can hardly be overestimated. He is supposed to have written a *Penitential*, but if so, it is not now known. A work by another hand, embodying his views, is in Haddan and Stubbs, *Councils*, iii. 173–213.

BIBLIOGRAPHY: Bede, *Hist. eccl.*, iv. 1–3, 5, 6, 12, 17, 21, v. 3, 8; Haddan and Stubbs, *Councils*, iii. 114–227; William of Malmesbury, *Gesta pontificum*, book i.; Gervase of Canterbury, *Acta pontificum*, in Stubbs, ut sup.; *ASB*, Sept., vi. 55–82; *ASM*, ii. 985–993; W. F. Hook, *Lives of the Archbishops of Canterbury*, i. 145–175, London, 1860; J. R. Green, *Making of England*, 2 vols. passim, ib., 1897; J. H. Overton, *The Church in England*, i. 71–80 et passim, ib., 1897; W. Bright, *Chapters in Early English Church History*, pp. 251–262, 273–284, 318–321, 357–361, 394–396, 3d ed., ib. 1897; G. F. Browne, *Theodore and Wilfrith*, ib., 1897; W. Hunt, *English Church . . . (597–1066)*, passim, ib. 1899; *DNB*, lvi. 122–126; *DCB*, iv. 926–932.

THEODORE AND THEOPHANES (GRAPTOI): Illustrious martyrs of the iconoclastic controversies (see IMAGES AND IMAGE-WORSHIP).

1. Theodore was born at Jerusalem, 775 (?), and died in prison near Chalcedon (7 m. s.e. of Constantinople) in Asia Minor, Dec. 27, 840 (?). With his father Jonas and his brother Theophanes, he entered the Sabaite monastery and came to Constantinople most probably under Michael Rhangaba, where the brothers contended and suffered in behalf of the images under Leo the Armenian. Under Michael Balbus they dwelt at Soothenion on the Bosporus. Theophilus banished them to the island of Aphusia. On July 18, 836, they had their foreheads branded with twelve iambic verses (whence the name *graptoi*). Theodore died in prison. The *logoi* of Theodore on the image-cult, mentioned by biographers as *kunolukes*, have not been recovered. Several writings belonging to the Patriarch Nicephorus have been erroneously attributed to him, also a biography of Nicephorus (q.v.).

2. Theophanes, brother of Theodore, was born at Jerusalem, 778; and died at Nicæa, Oct. 11, 845 or 851 (?). He survived the restitution of orthodoxy under Theodora and was made archbishop of Nicæa. His remains were interred in the Chora cloister. Theophanes was one of the most prolific and famous religious poets of the Church. W. Christ counts among the *menœa* (*menœon:* a book containing the *troparia* or short hymns for the immovable feasts of the month the name of which stands on the title-page) in print 151 *canones* (groups of nine odes each) of Theophanes. The authenticity of most of them awaits critical investigation. One of them is to his brother to be sung on his day. (E. VON DOBSCHÜTZ.)

BIBLIOGRAPHY: The sources for a life are two biographies, one by Simeon Metaphrastes and another by Theodora Cantacuzena Palaiologina, ed. A. Papadopoulos-Kerameus, in *Analecta Ierosolumitikês*, iv. 185–223, cf. v. 397–399, Leipsic, 1897; cf. *MPG*, cxvi. 653–684; the writings of Michael

Syncellus in *MPG*, iv. 617–668, xcvii. 1504–21, and two lives of him, ed. T. Schmidt, Kahri Djami, 1906; *Acta sanctorum Davidis, Symeonis, et Georgii*, ed. Delehaye, in *Analecta Bollandiana*, xviii. 239 sqq.; E. von Dobschütz, in *Byzantinische Zeitschrift*, xviii (1908), 84–92. Consult: Fabricius-Harles, *Bibliotheca Græca*, xi. 186 sqq., Hamburg, 1808; Krumbacher, *Geschichte*, pp. 73, 166, 586, 677, 707; S. Vailhé, in *Revue de l'orient chrétien*, vi (1901), 313–322, 610–642.

THEODORET, the-od′o-ret: Bishop of Cyrrhus and member of the School of Antioch (q.v.; see also EXEGESIS OR HERMENEUTICS, III., § 3); b. at Antioch in 393 (Tillemont); d. either at Cyrus or
Cyrrhus (" about a two-days' journey
Life. east of Antioch "); eighty Roman
miles), or at the monastery near Apamea (54 m. s.s.e. of Antioch) about 457. The following facts about his life are gleaned mainly from his " Epistles " and his " Religious History " (*Philotheos historia*). His mother having been childless for twelve years, his birth was promised by a hermit named Macedonius on the condition of his dedication to God, whence the name Theodoret (" gift of God "). He was brought up under the care of the ascetics and acquired a very extensive classical knowledge, and, according to Photius, a style of Attic purity. That he was a personal disciple of Theodore of Mopsuestia and listened to Chrysostom is improbable. He early became a lector among the clergy of Antioch, tarried a while in a monastery, was a cleric at Cyrrhus, and in 423 became bishop over a diocese about forty miles square and embracing 800 parishes, but with an insignificant town as its see city. Theodoret, supported only by the appeals of the intimate hermits, himself in personal danger, zealously guarded purity of the doctrine. More than 1,000 Marcionites were reclaimed in his diocese, beside many Arians and Macedonians; more than 200 copies of Tatian's Diatessaron he retired from the churches; and he erected churches and supplied them with relics. Extensive and varied were his philanthropic and economic interests: he endeavored to secure relief for the people oppressed with taxation; his inheritance he divided among the poor; out of his episcopal revenues he erected baths, bridges, halls, and aqueducts; he summoned rhetoricians and physicians, and reminded the officials of their duties. To the persecuted Christians of Persian Armenia he sent letters of encouragement, and to the Carthaginian Celestiacus, fleeing before the Vandals, he gave refuge.

The life of Theodoret stands out prominently in the christological controversies aroused by Cyril (see NESTORIUS; EUTYCHIANISM). Theodoret shared
in the petition of John of Antioch to
The Nestorius to approve of the term
Nestorian *theotokos* (" mother of God "), and upon
Controversy. the request of John wrote against
Cyril's anathemas.
He may have prepared the Antiochian symbol which was to secure the emperor's true understanding of the Nicene Creed, and he was member and spokesman of the deputation of eight from Antioch called by the emperor to Chalcedon. To the condemnation of Nestorius he could not assent. John, reconciled to Cyril by the emperor's

order, sought to bring Theodoret to submission by entrenching upon his eparchy. Theodoret was determined to preserve the peace of the Church by seeking the adoption of a formula avoiding the unconditional condemnation of Nestorius, and, toward the close of 434, strove earnestly for the reconciliation of the East. But Cyril refused to compromise and when he opened his attack (437) upon Diodorus and Theodoret, John sided with them and Theodoret assumed the defense of the Antiochian party (c. 439). Domnus, the successor of John, took him as his counselor. After the death of Cyril, adherents of the Antiochian theology were appointed to bishoprics. Irenæus the friend of Nestorius, with the cooperation of Theodoret, became metropolitan of Tyre, in spite of the protests of Dioscurus, Cyril's successor, who now turned specially against Theodoret; and, by preferring the charge that he taught two sons in Christ, he secured the order from the court confining Theodoret to Cyrrhus. Theodoret now composed the *Eronistēs* (see below). In vain were his efforts at court at self-justification against the charges of Dioscurus, as well as the countercharge of Domnus against Eutyches of Apollinarianism (see APOLLINARIS OF LAODICEA). The court excluded Theodoret from the council at Ephesus (449) because of his antagonism to Cyril. Here, because of *Epist.* cli. against Cyril and his defense of Diodorus and Theodore, he was condemned without a hearing and excommunicated and his writings were directed to be burned. Even Domnus gave his assent. Theodoret was compelled to leave Cyrrhus and retire to the monastery of Apamea. He made an appeal to Leo the Great, but not until the death of Theodosius II. (450) was his appeal for a revocation of the judgments against him granted by imperial edict. He was ordered to participate in the Council of Chalcedon (451), which created violent opposition. He was first to take part only as accuser, yet among the bishops. Then he was constrained (Oct. 26, 451) by the friends of Dioscurus to pronounce the anathema over Nestorius. His conduct shows (though hindered from a statement to that effect) that he performed this with his previous reservation; namely, without application beyond the teaching of two sons in Christ and the denial of the *theotokos*. Upon this he was declared orthodox and rehabilitated. The only thing known concerning him subsequent to the Council of Chalcedon is the letter of Leo charging him to guard the Chalcedonian victory (*MPG*, lxxxiii. 1319 sqq.). With Diodorus and Theodore he was no less hated by the Monophysites (q.v.) than Nestorius himself, and held by them and their friends as a heretic. The Three Chapter Controversy (q.v.) led to the condemnation of his writings against Cyril in the second Council of Constantinople (553).

In literature Theodoret devoted himself first of all to exegesis. The Scripture was his only authority, and his representation of orthodox doctrine consists of a collocation of Scripture passages. The genuineness and relative chronology of his commentaries is proven by references in the later to the earlier. The commentary on Canticles, written while he was a young bishop, though not before 430,

precedes Psalms; the commentaries on the prophets were begun with Daniel, followed by Ezekiel, and then the Minor Prophets. Next that on **Works:** the Psalms was completed before 436; **Exegetical.** and those on Isaiah, Jeremiah, and the Pauline Epistles (including Hebrews), before 448. Theodoret's last exegetical works were the interpretations of difficult passages in the Octateuch and *Quæstiones* dealing with the books of Samuel, Kings, and Chronicles, written about 452–453. Excepting the commentary on Isaiah (fragments preserved in the catenæ) and or Gal. ii. 6–13, the exegetical writings of Theodoret are extant. Exegetical material on the Gospels under his name in the catenæ may have come from his other works, and foreign interpolations occur in his comments on the Octateuch. The Biblical authors are, for Theodoret, merely the mouthpieces of the Holy Spirit, though they do not lose their individual peculiarities. By the unavoidable imperfection of the translations he states, the understanding is encumbered. Not familiar with Hebrew, Theodoret uses the Syrian translation, the Greek versions, and the Septuagint. In principle his exegesis is grammatical-historical; and he criticizes the intrusion of the author's own ideas. His aim is to avoid a onesidedness of literalness as well as of allegory. Hence he protests against the attributing of Canticles to Solomon and the like as degrading the Holy Spirit. Rather is it to be said that the Scripture speaks often " figuratively " and " in riddles." In the Old Testament everything has typical significance and prophetically it embodies already the Christian doctrine. The divine illumination affords the right understanding after the apostolic suggestion and the New Testament fulfilment. Valuable though not binding is the exegetical tradition of the ecclesiastical teachers. Theodoret likes to choose the best among various interpretations before him, preferably Theodore's, and supplements from his own. He is clear and simple in thought and statement; and his merit is to have rescued the exegetical heritage of the school of Antioch as a whole for the Christian Church.

Among apologetic writings was the *Ad quæstiones magorum* (429–436), now lost, in which he justified the Old Testament sacrifices as alternatives in opposition to the Egyptian **Works:** idolatry (question 1, Lev., *MPG*, lxxx. **Apologetic,** 297 sqq.), and exposed the fables of **Historical.** the Magi who worshiped the elements (*Hist. eccl.* v. 38). *De providentia* consists of apologetic discourses, proving the divine providence from the physical order (*cap.* i.–iv.), and from the moral and social order (*cap.* vi.–x.). The " Cure of the Greek Maladies or Knowledge of the Gospel Truth from the Greek Philosophy," of twelve discourses, was an attempt to prove the truth of Christianity from Greek philosophy and in contrast with the pagan ideas and practises. The truth is self-consistent where it is not obscured with error and approves itself as the power of life; philosophy is only a presentiment of it. This work is distinguished for clearness of arrangement and style. The " Church History " of Theodoret, which begins with the rise of Arianism and closes with the death of Theodore (429), falls far behind those of Socrates and Sozomen. It contains many sources otherwise lost, specially letters on the Arian controversy; but it is defective in historical sense and chronological accuracy, and on account of Theodoret's inclination to embellishment and miraculous narrative, and preference for the personal. Original material of Antiochian information appears chiefly in the latter books. Theodoret's sources are in dispute. According to Valesius these were mainly Socrates and Sozomen; A. Güldenpenning's thorough research placed Rufinus first, and next to him, Eusebius, Athanasius, Sozomen, Sabinus, Philostorgius, Gregory Nazianzen, and, least of all, Socrates. N. Glubokovskij counts Eusebius, Rufinus, Philostorgius, and, perhaps, Sabinus. The " Religious History," with an appendix on divine love, contains the biographies of thirty (ten living) ascetics, held forth as religious models. Upon the request of a high official named Sporacius, Theodoret compiled a " Compendium of Heretical Accounts " (*Hæreticarum fabularum compendium*), including a heresiology (books i.–iv.) and a " compendium of divine dogmas " (v.), which, apart from Origen's *De principiis* and the theological work of John of Damascus, is the only systematic representation of the theology of the Greek Fathers.

Among dogmatic treatises Theodoret mentions (*Epist.* cxiii. cxvi.) having written against Arius and Eunomius, probably one work, to which were adjoined the three treatises against the Macedonians. There were, besides, two **Works:** works against the Apollinarians, and of **Dogmatic.** the *Opus adversus Marcionem* nothing has been preserved. The treatises " On the Trinity " and " On the Divine Dispensation " (cf. *Peri theologias kai tēs theias enanthrōpēseōs; Epist.,* cxiii.), assigned by A. Ehrhard to the work " On the Holy and Life-giving Trinity " and " On the Incarnation of the Lord " of Cyril of Alexandria, certainly belong to the Antiochian School and to Theodoret. To the same belong *cap.* xiii.–xv., xvii., and brief parts of other chapters of the fragments which J. Garnier (*Auctarium*) included under the title, " Pentology of Theodoret on the Incarnation " as well as three of the five fragments referred by Marius Mercator to the fifth book of some writing of Theodoret. They are polemics against Arianism and Apollinarianism. Theodoret's " Refutation " of the twelve anathemas of Cyril is preserved in the antipolemic of Cyril (*MPG*, lxxvi. 392 sqq.). He detects Apollinarianism in Cyril's teaching, and declines a " contracting into one " of two natures of the only begotten, as much as a separation into two sons (*Epist.* cxliii.). Instead of a " union according to hypostases," he would accept only one that " manifests the essential properties or modes of the natures." The man united to God was born of Mary; between God the Logos and the form of a servant a distinction must be drawn. Only minor fragments (cf. *Epist.* xvi.) of Theodoret's defense of Diodorus and Theodore (438–444) have been preserved (Glubokovskij ii. 142). His chief christological work is the *Eranistēs etoi polymorphos* (" Beg-

gar or Multiform ") in three dialogues, representing the Monophysites like beggars passing off their doctrines gathered by scraps from diverse heretical sources and himself as the orthodox.

God is immutable also in becoming man, the two natures are separate in Christ, and God the Logos is ever immortal and impassive. Each nature remained " pure " after the union, retaining its properties to the exclusion of all transmutation and intermixture. Of the twenty-seven orations in defense of various propositions, the first six agree in their given content with Theodoret. A few extracts from the five orations on Chrysostom were preserved by Photius (codex 273). Most valuable are the numerous letters (Eng. transl., *NPNF*, 2 ser., iii. 250–348).   (N. BONWETSCH.)

BIBLIOGRAPHY: The editions of the works of Theodoret to be noted are: P. Manutius (Latin only), Rome, 1556; J. Birckman, Cologne, 1573 (also Latin); J. Sirmondi, 4 vols., Paris, 1642 (Greek and Latin), vol. v. by J. Garnier, 1684, reissued with corrections and additions by L. Schulze and J. A. Nösselt, 5 vols., Halle, 1769–74, reproduced in *MPG*, lxxx.–lxxxiv.; Eugenius Diaconus, 5 vols., Halle, 1768–78 (Greek only). His " Church History " was first edited by Frobenius, Basel, 1535; afterward by R. Stephens, Paris, 1544, Geneva, 1612; by H. Valesius, Paris, 1673–74; by Reading, Cambridge, 1720; and by T. Gaisford, Oxford, 1854; Eng. transls. have been issued in London, 1612, 1843, in *Bohn's Ecclesiastical Library*, 1854, and (best) in *NPNF*, 2 ser., vol. iii. His *Sermones de providentia* also appeared in English as *The Mirror of Divine Providence*, London, 1602.

Consult: *DCB*, iv. 904–919 (detailed); Tillemont, *Mémoires*, xv. 207–340; J. G. Walch, *Historie der Ketzereien*, vols. v.–vii., Leipsic, 1770 sqq.; Fabricius-Harles, *Bibliotheca Græca*, vii. 277 sqq., Hamburg, 1802; F. A. Holzhausen, *De fontibus quibus Socrates . . . ac Theodoretus . . . usi sunt*, Göttingen, 1825; J. G. Dowling, *Introduction to the Critical Study of Ecclesiastical Hist.*, pp. 34 sqq., London, 1838; F. C. Baur, *Die Epochen der kirchlichen Geschichtsschreibung*, pp. 7–32, Tübingen, 1852; F. A. Specht, *Der exegetische Standpunkt des . . . Theodor von Kyros*, Munich, 1871; J. H. Newman, *Historical Sketches*, iii. 307–362, London, 1873; A. Bertram, *Theodoreti . . . doctrina christologica*, Hildesheim, 1883; C. Roos, *De Theodoreto Clementis et Eusebii compilatore*, Halle, 1883; A. Ehrhard, in *TQS*, 1888; A. Güldenpenning, *Die Kirchengeschichte des Theodor von Kyrrhos*, Halle, 1889; N. Glubokovskij, in Russian, Moscow, 1890; G. Rauschen, *Jahrbücher der christlichen Kirche unter . . . Theodosius*, pp. 559 sqq., Freiburg, 1897; J. Raeder, in *Rheinisches Museum*, lvii (1902), 449 sqq.; F. Loofs, *Nestoriana*, Halle, 1905; Harnack, *Dogma*, vols. iii.–iv. passim; Neander, *Christian Church*, vol. ii. passim; Schaff, *Christian Church*, iii. 881–883 et passim; Hefele, *Conciliengeschichte*, ii., passim, Eng. transl., vol. iii. passim, French transl., vol. ii. passim.

THEODORIC: Antipope, 1102. See PASCHAL II.

THEODORUS ASCIDAS. See ORIGENISTIC CONTROVERSIES; and THREE CHAPTER CONTROVERSY.

THEODORUS, thē-o-dō′rus, **LECTOR** (ANAGNOSTES): Greek church historian. That he lived in the sixth century is known from the fact that he brought his history down to 527. Of his authorship it is known only that, at the suggestion of a friend in Gangra, he compiled a work of excerpts from the church histories of Sozomen, Socrates, and Theodoret in four books entitled, *Ekloge ek tōn ekklesiastikōn historiōn*, commonly known as *Historia tripertita* (manuscript, first part mutilated, in library of St. Mark, Venice). The history covers the period from the twentieth year of Constantine to the death of Constantinus

II. (361). The work was never printed, but an extract was much used by later chronographers. Theodorus' method was to select, with verbal faithfulness, from the narratives in common the clearest and best in style and note the agreements in the margin, while the parts peculiar to each were also used and as such specially pointed out. Theodorus continued this work in a church history of his own, beginning with the death of Theodosius II. and ending with the reign of the elder Justin (518); but this work is lost with the exception of a few excerpts and citations in the works of subsequent authors and in the acts of the seventh council (cf. *MPG*, lxxxvi. 157–2280).

(ERWIN PREUSCHEN.)

BIBLIOGRAPHY: The earlier literature is indicated in U. Chevalier, *Répertoire des sources historiques du moyen âge*, i. 2171, Paris, 1894 sqq.; on the MSS. consult De Boor, in *ZKG*, vi (1883–84), 489 sqq., 573 sqq. Consult further: Ն. Allatius, in *MPG*, lxxxvi. 1, cols. 157 sqq.; Fabricius-Harles, *Bibliotheca Græca*, vii. 435 sqq., Hamburg, 1801; G. Dangers, *De fontibus* . . . *Theodori Lectoris et Evagrii*, Göttingen, 1841; Nolte, in *TQS*, xliii (1861), 569; Bardenhewer, *Patrologie*, pp. 486–487, Eng. transl., St. Louis, 1908; *DCB*, iv. 954; Ceillier, *Auteurs sacrés*, xi. 103–105.

THEODOSIUS OF ALEXANDRIA. See MONOPHYSITES, § 13.

THEODOSIUS I., thĭ"o-dō'shi-ʊs, **FLAVIUS:** Roman emperor (379–395); b. probably at Cauca (29 Roman miles from Segovia), Spain, in 346; d. at Milan Jan. 17, 395. His father, Count Theodosius, was one of the last of the great generals of the western empire, and to him the future emperor owed his military training. Theodosius early had a command of his own in Mœsia; but he renounced public service upon the execution of his father through intrigue, after the death of Valentinian I. (373), and lived with his wife, a woman of noble family, both being orthodox Christians. In 375 Gratian, in dire straits by reason of a new inundation of barbarians, recalled Theodosius from private life and in 379 proclaimed him Augustus of the East. Theodosius thereupon made Thessalonica the center of his operations against Goths, Alans, and Huns. Early in 380 he fell ill and desired baptism, which was administered by the venerable Bishop of Acholios. Theodosius then issued at Constantinople, Feb. 27, 380, the explicit *Edictum de fide catholica* as a law of the empire, wherein the catholic faith is solemnly acknowledged and heretics are threatened with incisive penalties. This edict strikes the keynote of the emperor's religious policy, clearly indicating the course of its further activities.

The war with the Goths came to an end at the close of 380, and Theodosius triumphantly entered Constantinople Nov. 24. The ecclesiastical situation was then controlled by the Arians, and the emperor's immediate effort was to convert them in the spirit of his edict. Bishop Demophilus forsook the city two days after the emperor's arrival, declining to acknowledge the Nicene Creed as the indispensable condition to his further activity. The emperor appointed as his successor Gregory Nazianzen (q.v.), and the same policy was pursued in a series of edicts. On Jan. 10, 381, the pretorian prefect, Eutropius, was directed to expel the anti-Nicene heretics from the towns and cities, while

Sapor was dispatched to the East to eject the Arian bishops. On July 19, the heretics were forbidden to build new churches. These two edicts were also incisively summarized in a third edict of July 30, the same year, while decrees were issued against the Manicheans. These measures may probably be taken as threats intended to have restraining effect.

To this period belongs the ecumenical Council of Constantinople (381), at which the Prætor Nectarius, a layman, was elected bishop of Constantinople, after Gregory Nazianzen had abdicated that see. This incident sealed the downfall of the Arians in the East (see ARIANISM, I., 4, § 8; COUNCILS AND SYNODS, § 3). In the prosecution of the religious policy, Theodosius from the outset deemed it important to act independently of the West. In the year 382, there was a pause in legislation adverse to heretics. Thereafter, in June 383, according to Socrates and Sozomen, Theodosius undertook to settle matters by means of a religious conference at Constantinople, whereto invitations were issued to leaders of both orthodox and heretical parties. But the conference proved fruitless, and decrees of July 25 and Sept. 25 resumed interdiction of religious assemblings of heretics; including the Apollinarists and the Macedonians, while ordination of heretical ecclesiastics was forbidden. In the autumn of 383, the emperor was wholly preoccupied with the treacherous assassination of Gratin, at Lyons, on Aug. 25, and the usurpation of the Spaniard Maximus in Gaul, who was not fully conquered until the summer of 388. Thereupon legislation to strengthen the Church was vigorously resumed, and sharp measures were passed against paganism. Probably in 388 the Pretorian Prefect Cynegius was dispatched to Egypt and Asia Minor with the commission of effacing Hellenism by destruction of the pagan temples and inhibition of idolatrous rites. As a result, in many places, bloody tumults arose, especially in Alexandria, where Bishop Theophilus, in cooperation with the civil power, demolished the Serapium. Also on Semitic soil vehement conflicts occurred; and though the detailed facts have not been transmitted, the elegy of Libanius, *Peri tōn hierōn*, discloses a great devastation in which the monks played a leading part. After the emperor's sojourn at Milan (389 or 390), his religious policy against the believers in the gods was exercised with great firmness, finding distinct expression in a ruling addressed to the pretorian prefects on Feb. 24, 391: "No one shall pollute himself with sacrifices. No one shall slaughter an innocent sacrificial beast. None shall set foot in a heathen sanctuary, nor visit a pagan temple. None shall look up to an idol made with human hands." A law of Nov. 8, 392, places animal sacrifice and soothsaying on a footing with high treason. While the edict was running its course, the West had once again fallen into a dangerous crisis, which required the emperor's prompt intervention. Theodosius, on leaving the West, had appointed the Frankish Arbogast as mentor to the youthful Augustus. But this gave rise to difficulties which culminated in the assassination of Valentinian at Vienne, May 15, 392. Arbogast elevated in his place Eugenius, who reluctantly assumed the hazardous dignity, and was soon constrained, against his Christian conviction, to make concessions to the importunate friends of the gods. Thus paganism revived once more. But on Sept. 6, 394, Eugenius was slain in a fierce battle along the Frigidus, near Aquileia. There duly followed the suppression of pagan superstition: Theodosius himself took direct control of the imperial sovereignty and found it possible to carry out a stronger policy of action. It was under him, especially, that the religion of antiquity vanished from public life and came to be styled " paganism." And with all this went regard for the advancement of the moral and religious tasks of the Church. The emperor also upheld firmly the cause of the State, and made it the means of control of ecclesiastical abuse. His policy toward the Jews opposed mixed marriages between Christians and Hebrews, and forbade the latter to hold Christian slaves. But he insisted on the observance of the law which insured religious freedom to the Jews, and threatened severe penalties against any violence to their synagogues.

Some significance attaches, in the life of the emperor, to his relations with Ambrose. According to the account of Ambrose the following was the course of events. (1) The assassination, by the infuriated rabble, of the local commander, Rotherich, moved Ambrose to intercede with the emperor, who could not be induced to commit himself to a definite promise. (2) On the contrary, under the influence of his counselor Rufinus, Theodosius ordered a rigorous chastisement. (3) The brutal and underhand manner whereby the sentence was executed does not permit the emperor to be held accountable for this feature of the case. (4) Ambrose failed to make allowances and demanded penance. (5) The emperor thereupon submitted to public penance before the assembled congregation.

The name of Theodosius is linked with an eventful period in the final stage of the Eastern and Western Roman Empire. He was a leader who combined clear insight with determination and energy. The combination of prince and soldier in Roman imperial history found its last successful embodiment in the person and deeds of Theodosius. What seemed the impossible task of pacifying the Goths was accomplished. A benevolent plan of legislation was prosecuted consistently to counteract evils of chronic transmission within the political fabric and the social organism. The piety of Theodosius was deep and sincere, and strongly independent as against hierarchical pretensions. In all his imperial dealing he had the conscience of a Christian prince.

VICTOR SCHULTZE.

BIBLIOGRAPHY: L. S. Le N. de Tillemont, *Histoire des empereurs*, vol. v., 6 vols., Paris, 1700–38; J. H. Stuffken, *Dissertatio de Theodosio Magno*, Leyden, 1828; M. Fléchier, *Hist. de Theodose le Grand*, Paris, 1860; W. Fröhner, *Les Médaillons de l'empire romain*, Paris, 1878; A. Güldenpenning and J. Island, *Der Kaiser Theodosius der Grosse*, Halle, 1878; W. Unger, *Quellen der byzantinischen Kunstgeschichte*, vol. i., Vienna, 1878; H. Schiller, *Geschichte der römischen Kaiserzeit*, vol. ii., Gotha, 1887; V. Schultze, *Geschichte des Unterganges des . . . Heidentums*, 2 vols., Jena, 1887–92; G. Rauschen, *Jahrbücher der christlichen Kirche unter dem Kaiser Theodosius dem Grossen*, Freiburg, 1897; W. K. Boyde, *The Ecclesiastical Edicts of the Theodosian Code*, New York, 1905; Gibbon, *Decline and Fall*, chaps. xxvi.–xxvii.; Schaff, *Christian Church*, iii. 63 sqq. et passim; Neander, *Christian Church*,

ii. 94–99 et passim; and in general the works on the history of the period. The Theodosian Code was edited by Mommsen, Berlin, 1905.

THEODOSIUS ZYGOMALAS: Greek theologian of the sixteenth century; b. in 1544. He held the position of first secretary to the Constantinopolitan patriarch, Jeremias II. Considerable is known of him through Stephen Gerlach, who at that time was chaplain to the German embassy at Constantinople. Gerlach brought about a literary intercourse between Theodosius and certain scholars at Tübingen. The *Turcogræcia* (Basel, 1584) of Martin Crusius, a valuable source of information regarding the Christian orient of the sixteenth century, is largely compiled from communications of Theodosius. From the literary remains of Gerlach, Crusius copied the two brief works entitled *Geographica de monte Sinai, Atho, aliisque Græciæ locis*. In 1578 he sent Gerlach communications containing information regarding the bishops, priests, and monasteries collected from almost the entire domain of the orthodox churches. His position under the ecumenical patriarch as collector from the dioceses of the alms by which the poll-tax for the Greek Christians living under the Turkish yoke was paid to the sultan, afforded him exceptional opportunities for gathering reliable information. He is important for the West chiefly as the author of the replies of the patriarch to the Württemberg theologians (see JEREMIAS II.). (PHILIPP MEYER.)

BIBLIOGRAPHY: Besides the *Turcogræcia* of Crusius named in the text, consult: *Stephan Gerlachs des Aelteren Tagebuch*, ed. S. Gerlach, Frankfort, 1674; E. Le Grand, *Notice bibliographique sur Jean et Theodosi Zygomalas*, Paris, 1889; P. Meyer, *Die theologische Litteratur der griechischen Kirche im 16. Jahrhundert*, Leipsic, 1899.

THEODOTION. See BIBLE VERSIONS, A, I., 2, § 3.

THEODOTUS THE TANNER. See MONARCHIANISM, III., §§ 1–2.

THEODULF, thī′ō-dulf, **OF ORLÉANS:** Poet and theologian at the court of Charlemagne; b. apparently in Spain, c. 760; d. in exile at Angers (190 m. s.w. of Paris) Sept. 18, 821. Of Gothic descent, unable on account of troubles to remain in his own country, he was received by Charlemagne, and the king made him bishop of Orléans, a dignity which he occupied as early as 798. To this several abbeys were added, probably St. Mesmin and St. Fleury on the Loire, and at least Aignan. He proved himself worthy of the trust. A collection of ecclesiastical regulations has come down in a twofold series of forty chapters and a longer capitulary, relating to the duties of priests and synods and the welfare and discipline of the laity, and, particularly, to the Carolingian policy of public schools in villages and towns. To secure co-workers he peopled St. Mesmin with Benedictines and introduced monastic reforms, and he established a hospice for strangers. In 798 he was entrusted by Charlemagne with a mission to Septimania and Provence. He described this journey in a worthy poem. He offers a word of solemn warning to the Frankish judges against official temptations (*Carmen* xxviii.), and adds that in comparison with the Mosaic, the Frankish law was exceedingly strict. His leniency in the judgment of Leo III. secured him the pallium. The relation between Theodulf and Alcuin was cordial, but Alcuin made an effort to secure Theodulf's aid in the Adoptionist controversy (see ADOPTIONISM) against Felix of Urgel. Theodulf became more prominent in theology after Alcuin's death, following in the latter's scientific method and taking part in the dispute over the procession of the Holy Spirit, being prompted by the commission of the emperor. His proof of the Western doctrine was a series of citations from the Fathers, later entitled, *De spiritu sancto veterum patrum sententiæ, quod a patre filioque procedat*. His reply to Charlemagne's circular inquiry of 812, concerning the faithful administration of baptism, manifests solid learning and thorough and skilful familiarity and thoughtfulness regarding his official duties. What especially commended him to the emperor and to posterity was his esthetic endowment. He was an industrious student of the Fathers, the philosophers, the grammarians and poets, and the Latin classics in particular. For a much admired church building at Germigny in Neustria he brought the model from Aix-la-Chapelle. The Bible manuscripts illustrated under his direction are still admired as rarities of art. He was wont to preface a valuable codex with a personal autograph in verse.

Along this line he had masterful descriptive powers; and he was easily the first poet of the Carolingian period. Only fragments remain of his great didactic poem on the revelation and acts of Christ, on rewards and punishments beyond, the battle on earth with evil, and on the duties of bishops (i., ii.). Most charming of all, even to the present day, are his epistolary poems; they penetrate the society at the court, attach striking characteristics to friend and foe, reflect on every hand the historical events of the day, and continue tireless in their praises of the overtowering greatness and the peculiar services of Charles in State and Church (xxv., xxvii.). The great monarch liked to avail himself of the poet's muse, when, for instance, at the death of the queen, 794, Theodulf composed the epitaph; and likewise upon the death of Pope Hadrian I. The confidential relations between him and the emperor were never interrupted. He was honored as one of the witnesses to the emperor's will in 811. He himself lauds eloquently the latter's zeal for the moral promotion of the whole people. Upon the king he looks as the lord of the Church (xxxii.). After the death of Charlemagne he hastened by courier to offer his homage to Louis the Pious, and received him with great pomp. From 818, however, his favor waned. Theodulf was among the bishops who supported the insurrection of King Bernard of Italy against his uncle. With its suppression, Theodulf's fate was removal from his see and retirement to the monastery. He wandered to Angers, giving poetic vent to the protesting of his innocence and to wrath against the incompetent judgment. The Palm-Sunday hymn, " Gloria, laus et honor," is ascribed to him (many versions in English, one by J. M. Neale, " All glory, laud and honor ").

(FRIEDRICH WIEGAND.)

BIBLIOGRAPHY: The first collection of the writings of Theodulph was by J. Sirmond, Paris, 1646; the most convenient source to consult is *MPL*, cv. 187–380; the *Versus contra judices*, ed. H. Hagen, appeared Bern, 1882; for supplementary sources use J. Mabillon, *Vetera analecta*, i. 383 sqq., Paris, 1723, Sirmond, *Opera varia*, ii. 665–892, Venice, 1728, and Dümmler, in *MGH, Poet. Lat. ævi Carol.*, i (1881), 437–581. Consult: J. C. F. Bähr, *Geschichte der römischen Litteratur im karolingischen Zeitalter*, pp. 91–95, Carlsruhe, 1840; L. Bannard, *Théodulphe évêque d'Orléans*, 1860; B. Hauréau, *Singularités historiques et littéraires*, Paris, 1861; S. Abel, *Jahrbücher des frankischen Reichs unter Karl dem Grossen*, ed. B. Simson, passim, Munich, 1866; B. Simson, *Jahrbücher des fränkischen Reiches unter Ludwig dem Frommen*, i. 114 sqq., Munich, 1874; E. Rzehulka, *Theodulf Bischof von Orléans*, Breslau, 1875; A. Ebert, in *Berichte über die Verhandlung der königlichen sächsischen Gesellschaft der Wissenschaft*, ii (1878), 95 sqq.; idem, *Allgemeine Geschichte der Literatur des Mittelalters*, ii. 70–84, Leipsic, 1880; E. Dümmler, in *NA*, iv (1879), 241–250; C. Port, *L'Hymne Gloria laus*, Angers, 1879; idem, *Encore l'hymne Gloria laus*, ib. 1879; Liersch, *Die Gedichte Theodulfs Bischofs von Orléans*, Halle, 1880; C. Cuissard, *Théodulphe évêque d'Orléans*, Orléans, 1892; S. Berger, *Hist. de la Vulgate*, pp. 145–184, Paris, 1893; L. Delisle, in *Bibliothèque de l'école des chartes*, xl. 1–47; *Histoire littéraire de la France*, iv. 459–474; Hauck, *KD*, ii. 491 sqq. et passim.

THEOGNOSTUS, thĭ"eg-nos'tus: Alexandrian catechist of the second half of the third century. According to an anonymous excerpt from the " Christian History " of Philip of Side (q.v.), Theognostus was the successor of Pierius in the conduct of the Alexandrine catechetical school; but the information in the excerpt is subject to serious doubts, which are in part capable of substantiation. Georgius of Corcyra named Theognostus as one of the distinguished teachers, and from the time of Dionysius and Pierius it has been concluded that he was more probably the predecessor of the latter. His time of activity may be presumed to have been between 247–248 and c. 280. Theognostus was author of a kind of compendium of dogmatics in seven books, no doubt intended for use in the school and entitled *Hypotypōseis*. A bare report of the work was given by Photius (*Bibliotheca*, codex 116). Fragments have been preserved, two by Athanasius, accompanied with lavish praise for Theognostus, one by Gregory of Nyssa, and one in the Venetian Codex of St. Mark. The work followed closely the Origenistic views, and defended against Neoplatonism the non-eternity of matter, the possibility of a Son of God, and the incarnation. Of the time of its issue nothing can be proximately determined. (ERWIN PREUSCHEN.)

BIBLIOGRAPHY: The remains are in *MPG*, x. 235–242; and with commentary, ed. F. Diekamp, in *TQS*, lxxxiv (1902), 481 sqq.; as well as by Harnack, in *TU*, ut inf. An Eng. transl. is to be found in *ANF*, vi. 155–156. Besides the literature under ALEXANDRIA, SCHOOL OF, consult: U. Chevalier, *Répertoire des sources historiques du moyen-âge*, i. 2182, Paris, 1894–99, and *ANF*, Index volume p. 70 (for older authorities); L. B. Radford, *Three Teachers of Alexandria*, Cambridge and New York, 1908; Bardenhewer, *Geschichte*, ii. 195–198; Harnack, *Litteratur*, i. 437 sqq., ii. 2, pp. 66 sqq.; idem, *Dogma*, iii. 96 sqq., 134, iv.; idem, 45, 331; idem, in *TU*, xxiv. 3 (1903); Krüger, *History*, p. 217.

THEOLOGIA GERMANICA: A mystical work of the end of the fourteenth century. It has attained its fame chiefly because it was discovered and first published by Luther. First he came into possession of a small fragment which he published under the title, *Ein geystlich edles Buchleyn* (1516). Afterward he obtained a complete manuscript which he published under the title, *Eyn deutsch Theologia* (Wittenberg, 1518), reprinted under the title,

Theologia Teütsch (Augsburg, 1518). The edition of Luther found a large circulation. In the earliest years there were eight known reprints, and in the sixteenth century at least fourteen further editions in High German, the most important among which was that of Johann Arndt (1597), appended by P. J. Spener to the *Predigten* (Frankfort, 1681, and often) of Johann Tauler (q.v.). In the next three centuries, until 1842, there were at least twenty-eight known editions in High German. Besides, there were translations into Low German, Flemish, English, Latin, and French. The two manuscripts which Luther used are unfortunately lost, but another manuscript, dating from 1497, came to light in the middle of the last century, on the basis of which F. Pfeiffer published what is regarded as the standard edition, *Theologia deutsch* (Stuttgart, 1851; Eng. transl., *Theologia Germanica*, London, 1854, 1874, and 1893). In the preface to the fragment Luther had advanced the supposition that Johann Tauler was the author of the work, an assumption which has been refuted by the complete edition, in which Tauler is quoted as authority. In the complete edition Luther appended a note to his preface according to which the author of the work was " a priest and custodian in the house of the Teutonic masters at Frankfort." The same note is found also in the manuscript published by Pfeiffer and hence proved authentic. From a passage announcing his purpose it is evident that the author belonged to the so-called Friends of God (q.v.), and that he wrote at a time when this community had to clear itself from the charge of connection with the sect of the " false free spirits " who tried to protect themselves with the name of the Friends of God, i.e., toward the end of the fourteenth century.

The work purports to be a guide to the perfect life, which in a mystical way is to be found in the union with God. Opening with the passage, " When that which is perfect is come, that which is in part shall be done away " (I Cor. xiii. 10), the work points out that this unity is conditioned by the coming of God into human nature in the manner of the incarnation of Christ and by suffering in human form. On man's part the will and desire of the creature, which produce a false freedom, must be thoroughly repudiated; and by love and obedience the true freedom must be attained, which is God's will in man, and the vision of the eternal. Thus man moves out of self into blessed union with God. The booklet is a compound of various elements: alongside of deeply religious practical thoughts lie occult speculations of a decidedly pantheistic color; alongside of suggestions of Evangelical impulses, there are relics of medieval piety. The work was placed on the Index in 1621; but this as well as the claim that its author was a forerunner of the Reformation was wholly superfluous, since it is now conceded as containing nothing antagonistic to the Roman Catholic Church. It originated in a transition period when the germs of the new were sprouting in the old, and when, therefore, in individual personalities, there occurred a singular mixture of simple faith with obscure speculation. Hence, it appealed to a variety of men: to Johann Denck, to fructify his specula-

tive mystical Anabaptist ideas, the same on account of which Calvin warned the Frankfort church in 1559; to the Pietists Spener and Arndt; and to Luther for its Evangelical motives, particularly, the yearning for God and the fundamental tone of humility as well as the denial of self, by submission to God and union with him through Christ.

(Ferdinand Cohrs.)

Bibliography: B. M. Mauff, *Der Religionsphilosophische Standpunkt der . . . deutschen Theologie*, Jena, 1890; K. Jürgens, *Luthers Leben*, iii. 267 sqq., Leipsic, 1847; F. G. Lisco, *Die Heilslehre der Theologia deutsch*, Stuttgart, 1857; F. Reifenrath, *Die deutsche Theologie des Frankfurter Gottesfreundes*, Halle, 1863; J. Bach, *Meister Eckhart*, Vienna, 1864; C. Ullmann, *Reformers before the Reformation*, ii. 213–232, Edinburgh, 1867; L. Keller, *Die Reformation und die älteren Reformparteien*, Leipsic, 1885; idem, *Johann von Staupitz und die Anfänge der Reformation*, ib. 1888; W. Köhler, *Luther und die Kirchengeschichte*, i. 242 sqq., Erlangen, 1900; J. Köstlin, *Martin Luther*, i. 111 sqq., Berlin, 1903; Schaff, *Christian Church*, vi. 141–143.

THEOLOGICAL EDUCATION.

I. History: The rise of theological education in the early Church was slow, even being excluded so long as the heads of congregations were chosen simply for their spiritual gifts. Up to the end of the second century religious teachers seem

1. Before the Rise of Monasticism. to have been self-appointed, laymen speaking in divine worship and also promulgating their teachings elsewhere. The first official required to possess a modicum of learning appears to have been the reader. This neglect of theological training, due to confidence in the divine choice of suitable men to teach the churches and in their spiritual equipment with the requisite gifts and knowledge, would doubtless have been otherwise had the bishop been considered, from the first, the proper and necessary teacher of his people. Though he was generally so regarded, he did not actually acquire this dignity generally until the third century, and he was not necessarily a learned man. Christian schools appear after the close of the second century, such as the catechetical school at Alexandria; yet even they were devoted rather to apologetics than to the education of clergy, nor were those intending to enter clerical ranks either required or accustomed to attend such institutions. The first conscious beginnings of a regular clerical training were connected with the rise of the clerical orders (see Apostolic Constitutions) in the third century, wherein the lower orders became schools of preparation for the higher. Zosimus (*Epist.*, xi.) required five years for the lower orders, four years for the sub-deacon, and five for the deacon; and the African Church, following Cyprian (*Epist.*, xxix.), advanced no one from one order to another without examination. The practical training thus afforded was supplemented, doubtless even at an earlier date, by the *diatribe*, or close personal association with the bishop for the instruction of the younger clergy. By the end of the fourth century this practise had become more definitely organized, especially in Africa, where, with the help of monasticism, Augustine formed a sort of clerical school, though designed for the further perfection of clergy already officiating rather than for the training of candidates for the priesthood. The school of Augustine was the model for the schools of his pupils, bishops Alypius of Tagaste, Evodius of Uzalis, Profuturus of Cirta, Severus of Mileve, and Urbanus of Sicca, as well as for similar institutions in Spain and southern Gaul in the fifth and sixth centuries, such as Lerinum and Arles.

These institutions, of whose courses, organization, and history little is known, which must, however, have varied greatly according to local conditions, were in great part destroyed by the inroads of the barbarians; and what prepara-
2. Monastic tions were still made for clerical train-
Schools. ing harked back to older usages. A radical change, however, came about through the monasteries, whether primarily from the Benedictines or from Cassiodorus (qq.v.), when the cloisters came to consider as a part of their duties the training of recruits for the Church, and began the foundation of monastic schools for boys. While sporadic beginnings may have been made here and there, especially as the reception of oblates, or children brought to the monasteries in tender years, presupposed religious training, the first certain traces of systematic monastic schools are to be found in the English Church, whence Boniface and Alcuin (qq.v.) transplanted the plan to Germany and France, thus leading Charlemagne, about 790, to issue his *Constitutio de scholis per singula episcopia et monasteria instituendis.* Instruction began with the Psalter, which was committed to memory, as were the Apostles' Creed and the Lord's Prayer. This was followed by the Athanasian Creed, the exorcism, penitential office, etc., as well as by the evangelary and the homilies for Sundays and holy days. Instruction in reading was supplemented by a knowledge of writing, church music, calculation of religious festivals, and Latin grammar. Those more advanced studied the *Regula pastoralis* of Gregory the Great, the *De officiis ecclesiasticis* of Isidore, and the pastoral epistle of Gelasius, canons being required also to study the *Regula de vita canonica* and monks the Benedictine rule. Such was the chief ecclesiastical training, which might be acquired, if need be, in the parish schools. Those who desired still further knowledge might study the " seven liberal arts," which were divided into the *trivium* of grammar (including the reading of the " Distichs " of Cato and the poems of Vergil and Ovid, or of the Christian Juvencus and Sedulius), rhetoric (based chiefly on Cicero's *De inventione*, but little used except in law), and dialectics;

and into the *quadrivium* of arithmetic (including the reckoning of the church calendar), geometry (which would now rather be termed geography), music, and astronomy (often including the mystic properties of numbers). Side by side with these arts, which individually were reckoned un-Christian except in so far as they bore directly upon theology, were patristic, canonical, and (above all) exegetical studies, Augustine, the *Canones conciliorum*, and the *Decreta pontificum* being widely read.

After the rise of Universities (q.v.) in the twelfth and thirteenth centuries, it became more and more customary to seek theological training in them. The
3. The monastic orders were rivals in their desire for learning, and many princes
Middle and cities made certain benefices de-
Ages. pend upon the possession of academic degrees. Thus, although the highest offices were filled rather by the influence of personal favor or money, the chief officials and counselors of bishops and other prelates were mostly men trained in theology and canon law. Attempts to rectify a tendency to neglect the practical requirements of pastoral care through absorption in theoretical scholastic studies appear in homiletic aids and compends for the sacrament of confession, and in such works on pastoral theology as the *Manipulus curatorum* of Guido de Monte Rotherii (written in 1330) and the writings of Ulrich Surgant of Basel (about 1500). In the fifteenth and sixteenth centuries, through the influence of humanism, theological education was endowed with new life, and the study of the Bible increasingly supplanted scholasticism.

With the rise of a new church system after the Reformation came the demand that pastors should submit to an examination to prove their fitness. Thus the Lutheran *Unterricht der Visitatoren* (1527)
4. Lutheran required each candidate for the minis-
Methods. try to be examined by the superintendent. This provision, however, was only temporary, and the articles of visitation of the electorate of Saxony (1529; 1533) directed that the prospective pastor be examined at the court, while the *Reformatio Wittebergensis* (1545) entrusted the examination to the theological faculty. The church order of the Saxon electorate (1580) made the chief ecclesiastical authorities the examining board, a system adopted by the majority of the Lutheran national churches. Both Luther and Melanchthon, themselves university men and teachers in universities, desired the clergy to have university training. In the first decades of the Reformation this often proved impractical, owing to the lack of a sufficient number of educated candidates for ordination, so that it became necessary to employ those possessed of but meager attainments. In the earliest period, indeed, the examination seems to have been essentially the exaction of a promise to preach pure Evangelical doctrine. But the insistence on a trained clergy soon became more pressing, and in 1544 Leipsic required all candidates for the ministry to study at least for a time at a university, except in rare cases where practical training had been received. The least training of the average pastor was

that of the Latin schools, but in these religious and theological instruction were important factors, and the lectures of the teachers in these schools, who were even termed professors of theology, gradually developed into compends of dogmatics. In fact, dogmatics was the dominant subject in the theological education of the period, even to the relative neglect of the Bible. Württemberg occupied a distinct position in the Lutheran lands. In 1547 Duke Ulrich, in establishing the "stipendium" at his national university, gave it the Augustinian monastery at Tübingen; and Duke Christopher transformed thirteen monasteries into cloister schools in which boys of fourteen or fifteen were received after passing the necessary examinations at Stuttgart. There they were trained in the usual courses of the Latin schools and in the rudiments of Greek, made thoroughly acquainted with the New Testament in Latin translation, introduced into the Psalter and the pericopes, and trained in singing. They then entered one of the four monastic schools of Bebenhausen, Herrenalb, Hirschau, and Maulbronn, where they studied in addition the Old Testament, dialectics, and rhetoric. At the age of sixteen they entered the University of Tübingen, passing through the arts course in two years, and in the third devoting themselves entirely to theological training.

From the very first the Reformed laid equal stress on theological education, Zwingli changing the Grossmünsterstift into a theological
5. The Reformed Church. seminary and creating his so-called "prophecy," whereby he hoped to revive the mutual prophetic instruction of the early Church recorded in I Cor. xiv. This "prophecy" was held twice almost daily, Zwingli presiding over the interpretation of the Old Testament in the Grossmünsterkirche in the morning, and Myconius over New Testament exegesis at the Frauenmünsterkirche in the afternoon, while the canons, theological students, and all the clergy of the city attended. By 1532, however, more stringent rules for theological education were adopted at Zurich, these serving as models for the Reformed generally. The examining-board consisted of the antistes as president, four members of the council, the theological professors, and two pastors; and more stress was laid than by the Lutherans on a thorough knowledge of the Bible, the Reformed system of training being decidedly more practical from the start.

The Thirty Years' War brought anarchy into theological education, and conditions remained almost unchanged from the Reformation period during the seventeenth century. But after peace had again been secured, special attention was accorded the problem of the training of the clergy. It was
6. Effects of Pietism and Rationalism. Pietism which most insisted on better education of the ministry, a demand reiterated by Philipp Jacob Spener (q.v.), and most fully developed by August Hermann Francke (q.v.) in his *Idea studiosi theologiæ* (Halle, 1712), in which he emphasized the necessity of a knowledge of Greek and Hebrew for true understanding of the Bible, dogmatics, polemics, symbolics, and church history. Most important of all, however, was the

insistence on the practical side, which was to be kept in mind throughout. In consequence of the views thus advanced, several national churches revised their examination requirements, among them Prussia (1718), electoral Saxony (1732), and Hanover (1735). The examination was placed at the termination of the student's university career, though it might be held by the faculty, the consistory, or a special committee. Many churches retained also the examination on the candidate's entrance upon his ministry, the second examination usually being held by the consistory. If from the Prussian requirements it may be seen how great emphasis was laid both on a wide range of theological knowledge and on personal faith, as well as on homiletic, pastoral, and catechetic ability and devotion, rationalism likewise was careful for the training of its ministers. Thus the requirements for candidates for the ministry in Baden-Durlach, drawn up in 1756, exact not only a trial sermon, but also a technical thesis in Latin, besides a knowledge of theology, church history, logic, metaphysics, philosophy, ethics, and languages. Despite these careful and exacting requirements, theological education declined during the second half of the eighteenth century; but though the reaction of rationalism against Pietism contributed to this decline, it was rationalism which earnestly labored to raise the standard of the clergy.

The present general conditions governing Lutheran theological training in Germany are as follows. Two theological examinations are required: the first, *pro licentia concionandi* or *pro candidatura*, at the close of the candidate's term of study; and
7. Present Lutheran Requirements. the second, *pro ministerio, pro munere*, or *pro ordinatione*, before appointment to a church, though in practise it is now taken a year or two after the first examination. Three years' study in a university is everywhere required, except in Württemberg, Bavaria, and Strasburg, where four years are demanded, and in Baden, where five semesters is considered sufficient. The first examination is generally conducted by representatives of the faculty, and the second by members of the consistory or of the active clergy. The first examination is, on the whole, technical, and the second practical, though in the former examination a specimen sermon and catechizing are also required, while the final examination includes homiletics, catechetics, liturgics, and often music. The universities have recognized in increasing measure the practical side of theological training, while the development of theology itself has made additional demands on the students, as in the augmentation of exegesis by introduction and Biblical theology, or of dogmatics by the history of dogma. An important place is also taken by the written portion of the examinations; only rarely, as in Baden, is there a simple oral examination, except for the specimen sermon and the catechetical exercise. The Lutheran Church pays little heed to candidates for the ministry before they have passed their double examination, but from that time on, especially in recent years, more adequate provision is made for the furtherance of their special training. In Luther's

opinion the best preparation for a clerical career was pedagogy, and, as a matter of fact, the early Lutheran pastors had invariably been teachers, a profession to which many of them returned when better salaries were offered, while many more were employed in both professions simultaneously. In Hesse pedagogy was a necessary step to the ministry, but such a system became impractical with the increasing demands on the clergy and the development of public school teachers. Nevertheless, the close connection between the two professions still continues, and the pedagogic activity of young theologians from early times is now represented by their employment as private tutors or instructors in private schools.

The earliest recognition of the fact that the interval between the completion of study and installation should be devoted to practical work was contained in the Saxon church order of 1580, which required of all pastors a preliminary deaconate under regular pastors for securing practical training in the various forms of pastoral care.

8. Practical and Advanced Training.

A like purpose was the object of the "preachers' societies" or "preachers' colleges" after the beginning of the seventeenth century. It was not, however, until the commencement of the eighteenth century that institutions were seriously organized in behalf of theological candidates. In 1735 the consistory of Hanover directed that "seminaries" be established for theological candidates who had passed their first examination, their duties there being essentially those of the deaconate. In like manner the Dresden consistory, in 1788, placed the candidates for the ministry under the supervision of the superintendent. This led to the present Saxon system whereby the candidates are formed into a society over which the superintendent presides, meetings being held at which assigned subjects are discussed. Another method of theological training is the vicariate, a system peculiar to Württemberg. Immediately after passing their first examination, candidates are employed in practical church work, being first ordained. They are now called vicars and are made assistants to some pastor, who is required to supervise their theoretical and practical progress. They then receive parishes of their own, under the supervision of an older pastor, or are appointed assistant pastors in larger churches with a relative degree of independence, though required, until they receive definite charges, to report regularly on their progress to the ecclesiastical authorities. This system has been imitated in other branches of the Lutheran Church, as in Baden, Hesse, Schwarzburg-Sondershausen, Prussia, and Hanover. The vicariate lasts a year, and usually ceases with the second examination. In addition to these two systems, a number of national churches have established special preachers' seminaries for the further training of candidates for the ministry. The first traces of these institutions date from the time of Pietism. As early as 1677 a number of theological candidates were received at the hospice of Loccum, where they were to assist in the cloister school and occasionally in preaching. This aided in the establishment of the oldest true Evangelical seminary, that of Riddagshausen near Brunswick, whose constitution is dated Sept. 27, 1690. Though its statutes contain nothing specifically Pietistic, the close relations of the contemporary duke of Brunswick, Rudolf August, with Spener, as well as passages in the writings of Veit Ludwig von Seckendorf (q.v.) and Spener, imply that Riddagshausen was essentially a foundation of Pietism. The seminary contained twelve candidates of superior ability, who were to remain at least a year, and, if proved suitable, two or three years. The canonical hours were observed regularly, time was given daily to Biblical exegesis, and each Tuesday evening was devoted to disputations, while sermons alternated with catechizings. The seminary lived on, with many vicissitudes, until 1809, when it was destroyed by the French invasion. Another seminary was founded at Dresden in 1718 by Valentin Ernst Löscher (q.v.), but it succumbed in the troublous period of the Seven Years' War. In 1735 yet another pietistic seminary was established at Frankfort under the supervision of the senior of the clergy.

Rationalism, with its love for the practical, accepted the seminary; and its influence is apparent in the rescript of Charles Frederick of Baden (1769), in which provision is made not only for thorough study of the Bible with the help of antiquities and church history and for preaching and catechizing, but also for classics, the history of Baden, mathematics, physics, agriculture, and botany. The transformation of Loccum into a seminary for preachers and the foundation of the seminary in Hanover also date from the rationalistic period. In 1800 the courses in the former institution were revised by Abbot Salfeld, who placed a "director of studies" at the head of the seminary and organized the criticism of the exercises partly by the director and partly by the students themselves. This reorganization was taken as the basis of the courses drawn up in 1820, when the modern development of the institution began. After long negotiations the seminary at Hanover was established in 1816, its model being Loccum, though it contained at most only five members and had a director for only a brief time. It was reorganized in 1854, and in 1891 was transferred to Erichsburg near Markoldendorf. While opposition to seminaries was not lacking, doubtless due in part to the rationalistic interest in such institutions, many of the conservatives favored them. Thus Frederick William III., in a special cabinet order of May 27, 1816, insisted on the need of such seminaries and urged the establishment of additional ones. The sole result of his appeal, however, was the foundation of the seminary at Wittenberg, in part compensation for the city's loss of its university, in 1817. It was not until 1854 that the matter of seminaries was again taken up in Prussia, when the royal Domkandidatenstift was founded at Berlin. This was followed by the establishment of the Kandidatenkonvikt at Magdeburg in 1857 for the training of teachers of religion in secondary schools, and by the seminaries of Soest (1892), Naumburg-on-the-Queis (1898), and Dembowalonka (1899; now called

9. Theological Seminaries.

Wittenburg), the ultimate intention being that each province of Old Prussia shall have at least one seminary.

Other national churches have founded seminaries. To this number belong the seminaries of Herborn in Nassau (1818), Munich (1833), Wolfenbüttel in Brunswick (1836; a revival of the seminary at Riddagshausen), Friedberg in Hesse-Darmstadt (1837), Heidelberg (1838),

10. Types of Seminaries. the Predigerkollegium of St. Paul's in Leipsic (1862), Altenburg (1883; with courses in practical theology as early as 1834), Hofgeismar in Hesse-Kassel (1891), Preetz in Sleswick-Holstein (1896; a similar institution had existed at Hadersleben since 1870 to train pastors for Danish-speaking churches), and Schwerin in Mecklenburg (1901). These seminaries fall into three groups: obligatory of the old type (Herborn, Friedberg, and Heidelberg); optional (all the seminaries of Old Prussia and Hanover, the Prediger-kollegium at Leipsic, and the seminaries of Munich, Altenburg, Hofgeismar, and Wolfenbüttel); and obligatory of the new type (Preetz with Haders-leben and Schwerin). Attendance at the seminaries of the first and third groups is required of all candidates for admission to the second examination, the difference between the two groups being that those of the old type treat those who attend them essentially as pupils, while those of the new type, like the optional institutions, allow wider scope for independent practical work and substitute conferences of the candidates for lectures. In consequence of their more elastic organization seminaries of the second, or optional, group may also admit such theological candidates as have already passed their second examination. In Wittenberg and Hofgeismar it is the rule to include candidates for pastorates among their members, while the Domkandi-datenstift in Berlin and the Predigerkollegium in Leipsic accept, generally speaking, only those who are awaiting a call to a parish, this being adopted as a principle at Wolfenbüttel. In Sleswick-Holstein, since 1906, all candidates are required, after completing their courses at Preetz or Hadersleben, to officiate for a year as vicars.

In the Roman Catholic Church theological education received a new impulse in the sixteenth century when the Council of Trent decided upon the training of future clergy in ecclesiastical institutions, thus requiring the establish-

11. Roman Catholic Training in Germany. ment of seminaries for priests. The future clergy were to attend these seminaries from the age of twelve, and in them were to receive their entire training, except the most elementary, which was required as a condition of entrance. The establishment of such seminaries was made the special duty of bishops, and many institutions of this character were soon erected, probably the first being those founded by Cardinal Amulio de Rieti and by Bishop Martin of Schaumberg in 1564. Others soon followed in Benevento, Verona, Larino, Brixia, and Osimo. The pope often gave funds for establishment, thus giving rise to the " papal seminaries," Gregory XIII., for instance, founding six seminaries at Rome for the Eastern Church, the

Helvetic seminary at Milan, and two seminaries at Venice. The Jesuits, however, relieved the Church in great measure of the burden of theological education, nor was it until the suppression of the order that the ruling of the Council of Trent required earnest attention. In Germany Roman Catholic clergy are either trained from boyhood in episcopal seminaries, where they may remain until their ordination, or they first attend a public gymnasium, then complete the three years' course at a university, and, finally, before ordination, take a course in a seminary, the latter institution being essentially dependent on the sanction of the State. Prussian seminaries for Roman Catholic priests now exist in Treves, Kulm, Gnesen, Ermland, Hildesheim, Osnabrück, Fulda, and Limburg. Cologne, Münster, Paderborn, and Breslau have each two seminaries; there are theological faculties in Bonn, Paderborn, and Breslau, lyceums in Braunsberg, Fulda, and Gnesen, and an academy in Münster. Saxony has a Wendish seminary in Prague, while the province of the Upper Rhine and Alsace-Lorraine have one seminary each in Mainz, Strasburg, and Metz, and two each in Freiburg and Rottenburg. There are theological faculties in Freiburg and Rottenburg. Each of the Bavarian dioceses possesses a seminary for priests, while Munich-Freising has two; there are royal lyceums in Freising, Dillingen, Regensburg, Passau, Bamberg, and Eichstätt, and theological faculties in Munich and Würzburg, as well as a large number of seminaries for boys, mostly connected with seminaries for priests.

The development of Roman Catholic theological education gained fresh impetus from the reform of studies in Austria in the eighteenth century. The various departments of church history and the ancillary Biblical sciences were then introduced into theological education, pastoral theology was separated from moral theology and canon law, and systematic lectures on dogmatics and moral theology were inaugurated. The Austrian course of studies, covering three years, has been adopted everywhere in Germany and is still in force.

(FERDINAND COHRS.)

II. Supplementary: The earliest Christian training was by means of personal contact and instruction, such as Jesus gave to his disciples and Paul to his companions. Not until the simpler faith

1. Ante-Nicene Practice. crystallized into doctrine and a canon of Scripture called for interpretation did it become necessary to establish theological schools. Before the end of the second century the debates with Gnostics and pagan philosophers made it clear that the leaders of Christianity must be well-trained in theology and interpretation. Catechetical schools became the nurseries of Christian converts and seminaries for the clergy. The oldest and most prominent of these was that of Alexandria. Pantænus (q.v.) was its first known teacher (c. 180), and the school was made famous by Clement and Origen (qq.v.). A school was begun at Cæsarea by Origen (231). Antioch had its school about 290, where some of the most illustrious of the Church Fathers received their training. Cyril of Jerusalem has left a treatise on catechetical instruction that has made him famous as a teacher. Other renowned schools of that day were Edessa and Nisibis in the East, and the Patriarchum at Rome in the West. The germs of episcopal schools for prospective clerics are also found in the instruction given by leading presbyters or bishops to young men of promise.

The disorders of the fourth and fifth centuries altered many established customs. Theological students of the Middle Ages came to depend for their education on the cloister schools of the **2. The** monasteries and the episcopal schools **Middle** of the bishops. Cassiodorus in Italy, **Ages.** Cassian and others in Gaul, and unknown founders in England and Ireland established monastic schools in the fifth and sixth centuries; the Benedictine order made famous such schools as St. Gall (q.v.) and Bobbio on the continent, and Iona and Lindisfarne in Great Britain; and the missionaries of the period, both Irish and Saxon, accomplished for learning by the founding of monasteries what modern missionaries achieve by the founding of schools. It became customary for each cathedral also to have its episcopal school, and in 814 this was made compulsory. Education was on the decline in the seventh and eighth centuries, but Charlemagne encouraged both episcopal and monastic schools, and at his own palace school set an example which inspired others. The episcopal schools of Orléans and Reims became far-famed in the ninth century. In the tenth century Liége was the most renowned school; in the eleventh century Le Bec in Normandy held that position. In such schools as these the few great scholars of that era, such as Alcuin, Bede, Lanfranc, and Anselm (qq.v.), studied and taught. None of these institutions did much more than give elementary instruction; higher education, when there was any, was directed to the Scriptures and the Fathers. Many pupils were so poor that they were forced to receive aid. The rationalistic tendency stimulated learning in the twelfth century, and resulted in the disputations of the Schoolmen and the establishment of the universities. Theological schools became a part of the university system from the thirteenth century. The Universities (q.v.) sprang up independently of the monastic and cathedral schools, but they became the centers of all learning, and theological faculties took their place in them beside the faculties of medicine and law. Several of the greatest universities, like Paris and Oxford, became most renowned for their theological instruction. At Paris in the twelfth century ten years were required for the completion of the theological course. Biblical interpretation and dogmatics made up the bulk of the instruction, and the methods used included lectures and disputations. Among other famous theological schools founded before 1500 were Rome (1303), Prague (1347), Padua (1363), Erfurt (1379), Heidelberg (1385), Leipsic (1409), Louvain (1431), Freiburg (1457), and Tübingen (1477).

The Renaissance and the Reformation had a great influence on theological education. The revival of the classical Latin and Greek, the new knowledge of the East, especially of the Semites, and the expansion of the realms of science and philosophy, all quickened and broadened men's minds; and when the spiritual awakening liberated thought from its time-worn channels theology **3. The** received a new impulse that has not **Renaissance** ceased to be felt. After the Roman **and Refor-** Catholic Church saved itself by the **mation.** Counter-Reformation, the education of its priesthood passed largely into the hands of the Jesuits, and they established numerous seminaries all over Europe. Its educational system of to-day includes both theological faculties in the universities and separate theological seminaries. Scores of these seminaries are to be found all over Europe, and even in England there are nearly thirty. German humanism became transformed into a spiritual reform, and it was natural that most of the German universities should proceed to teach Lutheran theology. Melanchthon at Wittenberg impressed his ideas upon all Germany. The study of Biblical interpretation in the original languages formed the basis of educational work. Time brought a decline in spirituality, and philosophy assumed a larger place in the universities. The Pietist movement and the founding of the University of Halle (1694) were a protest against this. Unfortunately the influence of the Pietists was not in favor of a scientific theology, and it is not strange that the reaction against them went to the extreme of rationalism. Göttingen (1731) is a representative of the latter tendency. Nineteenth-century theology in Germany has been dominated by modern scientific thought. Ferdinand Christian Baur (q.v.) at Tübingen, Eduard Reuss (q.v.) at Strasburg, and Albrecht Ritschl (q.v.) at Bonn have each made a marked impress upon the theological education of their time. All departments of instruction have felt the new force; church history has had to be rewritten; dogma has been thoroughly reviewed and in some measure recast. Thorough and scientific investigation is constantly demanded of students. Not alone among Germans has this influence gone forth, but to the other Protestant countries of Europe and to America the ideas and expressions of the German lecture-rooms have made their way. All northern Europe felt the impulse of the Renaissance of the fifteenth century, and everywhere Protestant universities are to be found in the sixteenth with their theological faculties. Among the older universities are Upsala in Sweden (1477), Copenhagen in Denmark (1479), Basel in Switzerland (1460), Groningen (1614) and Utrecht (1634) in the Netherlands, Glasgow (1451) and Edinburgh (1583) in Scotland, and Oxford and Cambridge in England, both dating back to the twelfth century. Theological strife has more than once stamped itself upon their history. Calvin made Geneva the center of French Protestant education; Calvinism maintained itself in the Netherlands at Groningen and Utrecht against Arminianism at Leyden; in Scotland, St. Andrews, Glasgow, and Aberdeen have clung to the same Calvinism, while Edinburgh has been more open to liberal influences. In England Oxford and Cambridge have regularly offered theological instruction, but they have no separate theological department. Cambridge has been more progressive, feeling the influence of Puritan and rationalistic movements, while Oxford has preserved its peaceful way, little aroused until the Tractarian movement began. Besides the universities, the Anglican church has more than twenty theological seminaries. The national churches of European Protestantism have made no provision for the theological education of Non-conformists, so that separate schools have sprung up of necessity. Baptists, Methodists, and Congregationalists have their own institutions in Germany and Scandinavia, and also in Great Britain.

In America the need of theological education made itself felt acutely as soon as the first generation of university men passed on. Harvard (1636) was founded "for Christ and the **4. America.** Church," and half its graduates during its first century entered the ministry. In the eighteenth century several colleges were founded along the Atlantic seaboard, and the prevailing motive was the preparation of an educated ministry. Chairs of divinity were established at Harvard in 1638 and at Yale in 1741, but the most practical training that students for the ministry received was the experience and individual instruction gained in the homes of the leading ministers of the colonies. The first theological school established was that of the Dutch Reformed Church at New Brunswick, N. J. (1784). The early years of the nineteenth century produced seminaries of nearly all denominations, and before 1860 these numbered more than fifty. The growth of the West and the necessity of teaching the freedmen in the South have increased the number rapidly in the last half-century. See THEOLOGICAL SEMINARIES. The schools that form a department of a university are most popular to-day, and the present tendency is toward the affiliation of separate schools with a neighboring university when practicable. The regular course of instruction is offered to those who are qualified, preferably to college graduates, and occupies three years. The fundamentals of theological instruction are the literature of the Bible and its interpretation, systematic theology, homiletics, and church history; but the present emphasis on a practical Christianity has resulted in the addition of courses in ethics, sociology, missions, and religious pedagogy. The tendency of the age toward specialization has made it necessary to introduce seminary and post-graduate courses; and America may be expected continually to increase her contributions to scientific theological literature.   H. K. ROWE.

III. Roman Catholic Teaching Orders: The great orders and congregations which had their origin in the old world and were founded with the express purpose of engaging in the work of education are now conducting schools, academies, colleges, and theological seminaries in the United States. The rise and aim of many of these communities are described elsewhere in the pages of this Encyclopedia (see ROMAN CATHOLIC PAROCHIAL SCHOOLS and special articles on the separate orders). In addition to those which receive separate treatment may be mentioned several congregations of women, having numerous establishments in several states. The Congregation of the Sisters of St. Joseph was founded in 1650 at Le Puy, France, for the Christian educa-

tion of children. During the upheaval of the French Revolution the congregation was suppressed, several of the sisters being guillotined during the reign of terror. The order was restored in 1807 under Napoleon, and so rapid was the increase in its numbers that it soon extended its activities, not only into other countries of Europe, but even into Africa and Asia. The first foundation in America was made in 1836 at Carondelet, a town near St. Louis, Mo., by a colony of nuns from the mother house at Lyons, France. The community is now engaged in all forms of educational work in every part of the country. The Sisters of Notre Dame de Namur were founded in 1803 at Amiens, France. Their first establishment in America, made at Cincinnati, Ohio, in 1840, readily became the center of an extensive system of schools and academies throughout the west. The sisters conduct schools also in the eastern states, including Trinity College in Brookland, D. C. A branch of the Notre Dame sisters was introduced in Coesfeld, Germany, in 1851, but the members were forced by the Prussian Government to form themselves into a separate community, independent of any foreign authority. When the Kulturkampf (see ULTRAMONTANISM) broke out, the sisters were expelled. They emigrated to the United States in 1874 on the invitation of the bishop of Cleveland. The community now conducts schools and academies in several dioceses. It is a fact worthy of mention that the accession to this country of many religious communities has been due to the estrangement between Church and State in the old countries. New institutes have been introduced thus and those already established have had their ranks recruited by members exiled from their native lands.

The School Sisters of Notre Dame are a branch of the Congregation of Notre Dame, founded in France by St. Peter Fourier in 1597. They were introduced into the United States in 1847. The Presentation Nuns and various congregations bearing the title of Sisters of Providence conduct numerous schools in different parts of the country. Other congregations mentioned under WOMEN, CONGREGATIONS OF, have found a home in the United States, such as the Daughters of Jesus. A full list of the communities engaged in teaching is given with statistics in *The Official Catholic Directory and Clergy List* (Milwaukee and New York, 1911, pp. 794–835).

In regard to the United States it is to be noted that conditions have rendered it imperative for congregations which were not originally intended for the purpose to engage in the labor of education. The Sisters of Charity, although originally founded by St. Vincent de Paul (q.v.) to minister to the needs of the sick and the poor, are principally engaged in this country in conducting parochial schools. As the communities that were modeled upon the older foundations of Europe found it incumbent to adapt their work to different conditions, so in like manner have some new congregations spontaneously arisen here and there to meet the demands of the time and place. The teaching institute of the Sisters of Loretto at the Foot of the Cross had its rise in an effort made in 1812 by Miss

Mary Rhodes of Maryland to establish a school at Hardin's Creek, Marion County, Ky. The schoolhouse was a log cabin. She gathered about her a small band of companions who were organized into a religious community by Father Nerinckx, a Belgian priest, who fled to the United States in 1804 in order to elude the order of arrest issued against him by the French Directory. The institute was approved by the pope in 1816. The community prospered, and at an early period established branches in neighboring and distant states. Its activities extended to missionary labor among the Indians of Kansas and New Mexico. Another community having its origin in Kentucky was the Sisters of Charity of Nazareth. Under the supervision of Father David, a Sulpician, an institute was formed in 1813 with Catherine Spalding as its Mother Superior. Its members were composed of the daughters of pioneer settlers. The institute eventually adopted the rules of the Daughters of St. Vincent de Paul. It prospered and spread from Kentucky into other western states. The Sisters of Charity of the Blessed Virgin were organized in Philadelphia in 1834. In the early forties they removed to Dubuque, Ia., and have had an important part in educational work in the west. Especially noteworthy is a recent institute known as the Sisters of the Blessed Sacrament, founded at Philadelphia in 1889 by Miss Katherine Drexel and formally approved in 1907. The sisters devote themselves exclusively to the needs of the Indian and colored races, and besides many other forms of activity conduct schools, academies, and orphanages. The income which the foundress derives from her father's estate is employed in maintaining the projects of the institute. The influx into the United States of so many foreigners who do not speak English demands that special provision be made for the instruction of their children, and sometimes new teaching communities are formed to provide for their religious as well as secular training. The Sisters of St. Casimir, for instance, were established at Chicago in 1908 for the education of children of Lithuanian birth or descent.

BIBLIOGRAPHY: The literature on the history of the Church and that on the principal figures in the development of church life contains much in scattered form which would repay perusal. See also that under UNIVERSITIES; also THEOLOGICAL SEMINARIES. A very large and useful literature on the subject of education at large is indicated also in G. K. Fortescue's Subject Index . . . to the Library of the British Museum, London, 1902, 1906. Consult: S. M. Vail, Ministerial Education in the M. E. Church, Boston, 1853; Augusta T. Drane, Christian Schools and Scholars, or Sketches of Education from the Christian Era to the Council of Trent, 2d ed., London, 1881, new ed., New York, 1910; O. Ritschl, Cyprian von Karthago und die Verfassung der Kirche, Göttingen, 1885; F. A. Specht, Geschichte des Unterrichtswesens in Deutschland . . . bis zur Mitte des 13. Jahrhunderts, Stuttgart, 1885; A. Harnack, in TU, ii. 5 (1886); H. J. Icard, Traditions des prêtres de Saint Sulpice pour la direction des grands séminaires, Paris, 1886; G. Uhlhorn, Die praktische Vorbereitung der Kandidaten der Theologie, 2d ed., Stuttgart, 1887; C. Braun, Geschichte der Heranbildung des Klerus in der Diöcese Wirzburg, Würzburg, 1889; D. Curry, Christian Education, New York, 1889; P. Durieu, Traité de l'administration temporelle des séminaires, Paris, 1890; J. B. Aubry, Essai sur la méthode des études ecclésiastiques en France, 2 vols., Lille, 1891–92; A. de Sylvia, Séminaires et séminaristes, Paris, 1892; F. A. Bourne, Diocesan Seminaries, London, 1893; G. Compayré, Abelard and the

Origin and Early Hist. of the Universities, London and New York, 1893; G. Schmidt, Die Notwendigkeit und Möglichkeit einer praktischen Vorbildung der evangelischen Geistlichen, Berlin, 1893; G. R. Crooks and J. F. Hurst, Theological Encyclopædia and Methodology, pp. 46 sqq., New York, 1894; H. Zschokke, Die theologischen Studien der Kirche in Osterreich, Vienna, 1894; A. Cave, Introduction to Theology, pp. 1–46, 2d ed., Edinburgh, 1896; F. Paulsen, Geschichte des gelehrten Unterrichts, 2 vols., Leipsic, 1896–97; E. Sachsse, Die Lehre von der kirchlichen Erziehung, Berlin, 1897; H. Bavinck, Theologische School en vrije Universiteit, Kampen, 1899; E. W. Blatchford, The Theological Seminary from a Layman's Standpoint, Chicago, 1899; W. Moeller, Hist. of the Christian Church, iii. 421–427, London, 1900; M. Siebengartner, Schriften und Einrichtungen zur Bildung der Geistlichen, Freiburg, 1902; A. Grüllich, Unsere Seminararbeit, Meissen, 1904; W. Diehl, Die Schulordnungen des Grossherzogtums Hessen, 3 vols., Berlin, 1905; P. Drews, Der evangelische Geistliche, Jena, 1905; H. Hering, Die Lehre von der Predigt, Berlin, 1905; F. X. Eggersdorfer, Der heilige Augustinus als Pädagoge, Freiburg, 1907; C. L. Drawbridge, Religious Education, how to Improve it, London, 1908; H. Schreiber, Die religiöse Erziehung des Menschen, Leipsic, 1908; C. L. Drawbridge, The Training of the Twig: Religious Education of Children, London, 1909; A. C. Flick, Rise of the Mediæval Church and its Influence on the Civilization of Western Europe, pp. 317, 356, New York, 1909; L. H. Jordan, The Study of Religion in the Italian Universities, London, 1909; Robert, Les Écoles et l'enseignement de la théologie pendant la première moitié du xii. siècle, Paris, 1909; T. F. Gailor, The Christian Church and Education, New York, 1910; F. P. Graves, A History of Education during the Middle Ages and the Transition to Modern Times, New York, 1910; Schaff, Christian Church, v. 2, chaps. viii.–ix.

THEOLOGICAL LIBRARIES.

I. Early and Medieval Libraries.
II. In Germany.
III. In the United States and Canada.

I. Early and Medieval Libraries: The causes which originated ancient Christian literature, viz., " the regulation of the increasing disciplinary, organizing, and dogmatic needs, the struggle with heresy, the necessity of defending religion, and the ineradicable desire for knowledge," led to the founding and enlarging of ecclesiastical libraries in ancient Christendom in all pe.⁙ods of the Church's history, especially after periods of decay. Through the instrumentality of Origen the library at Cæsarea was founded, enlarged by Pamphilus, and given to the church there. From the end of the fourth century the larger churches had their archives and libraries, and for many centuries there was no difference between archives and libraries of the churches, though it arose later. In the Middle Ages the church libraries differed from those of earlier times in that they included Greek and Roman heathen classics; the keen Christian opposition had moderated, and men perceived that there was much in classical literature which ministered to knowledge, particularly to theology. These classics, therefore, found a place alongside the literary productions of the teachers of the Church. Yet by the end of the Middle Ages, many church and monastic libraries had fallen into decay. This is illustrated by the remark of Pohle (KL, ii. 790) that with the general neglect of literary studies in the fourteenth and fifteenth centuries ignorance and indolence had taken hold of the monks of St. Gall.

II. In Germany: Luther, in the last part of his Schrift an die Bürger und Ratsherrn aller Städte Deutschlands, dass sie christliche Schulen aufrichten remarked that neither care nor money should be spared to establish good libraries, especially in the large cities. This admonition was particularly taken to heart by Johann Bugenhagen (q.v.) in the church ordinances for congregations; he discovered ways and means for bringing about these objects. Rules for the care of libraries are found in the Evangelical church ordinances of the sixteenth and seventeenth centuries, and the libraries were often most liberally supplied through the free-will offerings of the people. The general decline of national and ecclesiastical self-consciousness in Germany in the last half of the eighteenth century caused not only a neglect and a partial decay of the larger public archives and libraries, but also the dissolution of church libraries and archives. With the newly awakened church life after the war of liberation (1813–15) interest in church libraries was again aroused, and this interest has not abated. When the Reformers of the sixteenth century espoused the cause of libraries, they had in mind the benefit not only of clergy and teachers, but of the congregations, as may be inferred from, e.g., the Hessian church ordinances, of 1537. This demand was fully in harmony with the general tendencies of the Reformers, who advocated the establishment of schools for the general education of the people. The church ordinances of the sixteenth century, in advocating the founding of libraries, only supplemented the general principles of the Reformation, which demanded general education. On this account, the church libraries of the sixteenth, seventeenth, and eighteenth centuries were mostly public for the benefit of clergy and laity. The necessity for establishing people's or parish libraries, in the narrower sense, was occasioned, especially after the middle of the nineteenth century, by the newer legislation which granted to the people a larger share in public and ecclesiastical affairs, by the need of education and reading which this participation and the growing success of national education awakened, and in no small degree also by the effort to erect a bulwark against the intrusion of literature destructive of the best in State, Church, and society. In this development of the library the leading position has been maintained in England and America.

T. O. RADLACH.

III. In the United States and Canada: The unusually rich development of theological institutions in America, many of them possessing large endowments, and having a large roll of alumni among whom have developed in some instances special interests which have fostered the collection of books upon particular topics that have eventually come into the possession of the institutions—all this, together with special needs, has led to the formation in many cases of libraries which have been highly specialized, which consequently afford the very best opportunities for investigators in particular lines of theological work. The data given below are the result either of inquiries in person or of information from the librarians of the institutions named. It may be said, in general, that theological seminaries usually possess fairly adequate resources for the pursuit of the studies in the curriculum, while in addition the history and polity

of the denomination with which they are affiliated will be most strongly represented in their libraries. As a rule, in the following only those collections have been regarded as special which have retained their identity as collections, though in a few cases the exigencies of library administration have led to distribution. The institutions which possess these special collections are noted in alphabetical order.

Alfred Theological Seminary, Alfred, N. Y.: The Sabbath Collection contains 450 volumes on the Sabbath question, with books and pamphlets on the Seventh-day Sabbath, and rare tracts on Albigensian and Waldensian doctrines; a copy of the Rogers Bible, 1549.

Auburn Theological Seminary, Auburn, N. Y.: The Porter Collection of rabbinic and patristic literature contains the Greek and Latin Fathers in original and translation, the Migne Patrology; quarto edition of Erasmus, 11 vols.; Ugolini's Thesaurus in 34 vols., and the *Acta conciliorum*, 13 vols., Paris, 1715.

Cambridge Episcopal Theological School, Cambridge, Mass.: There is here a special collection of pamphlets relating to the *Tractarian Movement*.

Chicago Theological Seminary, Chicago, Ill.: In this institution are: a collection of works on missions; facsimiles of the leading codices; Gunsaulus Collection on the Rise of Congregationalism, about 175 volumes, chiefly of seventeenth and eighteenth centuries, includes Baylie's *Certamen religiosum* (1649) and *Metamorphosis Anglorum* (1653); the Curtiss Collection on Old Testament and Semitics, rich in Old-Testament criticism and exegesis and philological material, contains J. Bartoloccius, *Bibliotheca magna rabbinica*, 1675–93, the London Polyglot, Poole's *Synopsis criticorum* (1684–86), Ugolini's *Thesaurus* (1769), the Surenhusius Mishna, and S. *Hieronymi Stridonensis . . . Opera*, 11 vols., 1734–43; Egyptology collection presented by E. M. Williams; Africa Collection of manuscripts of papers prepared for the Chicago Congress on Africa, 1893.

Chicago, Divinity School of the University of, Chicago, Ill.: a large number of libraries or collections have been purchased and distributed through the departments, especially the 280,000 volumes and 120,000 pamphlets purchased from S. Calvary & Co., Berlin. Besides this there are: The Hengstenberg Collection, from the library of Ernst Wilhelm Hengstenberg (q.v.), strong in theology, commentaries, history of the Jews, of the Middle Ages, and of the modern period, the Church Fathers, and Medieval and Reformed theologians, also in German hymn-books; The Anderson Collection of Hymnology of 200 volumes; The Northrup Collection in systematic theology and ethics, 1,050 volumes and 350 pamphlets; Library of the American Bible Union, approximating 6,000 volumes, collected largely by T. J. Conant (q.v.), rich in Biblical texts, versions, and commentaries. Among the noteworthy items in the last are the Complutensian, Paris, and London polyglots, the *Psalterium Sextuplex* (1530), *Psalterium Octaplum* (Geneva, 1516), and David Wolder's *Biblia sacra* (Hamburg, 1596); Hebrew Bibles are the Bomberg (Venice, 1521), the Basel edition (1546), *Pentateuchus et Megilloth* (Venice, 1551), Plantin's Hebrew-Latin (1571),

Buxtorf (4 vols., Basel, 1618–20), and J. Leusden's (Amsterdam, 1667), besides many eighteenth and nineteenth century editions of the Hebrew, including that of J. H. Michaelis (Halle, 1720). New-Testament texts found are one of Erasmus (3d ed., 1522), the " O mirificam " of R. Stephens (Paris, 1546), the " editio regia " (1550), and an edition by the younger Stephens (24mo, 1569), several of Beza's texts, one by Joseph Scaliger (Geneva, 1620), an Elzevir of 1624, and two of Curcellæus (Amsterdam, 1658 and 1675). Of notable Bible versions are a Coburger Latin (1520), a Stephens (1546), *Die Bibel in Niedersächsischen* (doubtless the first of its kind), *Das neuw Testament recht grüntlich teutscht* (Strasburg, 1524), and a Roman Catholic version from the Latin into Dutch (1548). There are also a large number of modern English versions, versions for use in modern mission fields, and those in Indian dialects.

Colgate University, Hamilton, N. Y.: The Colgate Baptist Historical Collection is perhaps the most complete collection of Baptist historical material in the country. It is rich in historical articles, pamphlets, catalogues, reports, addresses, histories of local churches, anniversary sermons and addresses, biographical material, minutes of conventions, the transactions of missionary and benevolent societies, and the like. The Davis Collection on Baptism consists of about 500 volumes.

Crozer Theological Seminary, Upland, Pa.: This institution possesses a large number of unique and valuable books and pamphlets on Anabaptist and Baptist History.

Cumberland University, Theological Seminary of, Lebanon, Tenn.: The Murdock Library consists of over 1,000 volumes relating to church history, including Erasmus' first edition of Ambrose, the *Magnum bullarium Romanum,* and Breithaupt's Latin translation of Solomon Jarchi's commentary on the Old Testament.

Drew Theological Seminary, Madison, N. J.: The Creamer Collection of Hymnology contains about 1,000 volumes and is particularly strong in Wesleyan and Methodist hymnals; there are a Sternhold and Hopkins (1579), Buchanan's paraphrase (1648), a first edition of Toplady's *Psalms* (1759), and a copy of Perronet's poems, supposed to be the only copy outside the British Museum; there is a supplementary collection on the history of hymns, with books on liturgies. There is also a Collection of Bibles, of nearly 900 volumes, including a Latin Bible (Venice, 1478), the Antwerp and London polyglots, a Stephen Hebrew Bible (Paris, 1548), and copies of the editions by Hutter (1599 and 1603); in this collection are a number of early Greek New Testaments, e.g., an Elzevir (1633), Beza (1642), Mills (1707), Wetstein (1751), and, notably, an Erasmus (3 vols., Paris, 1540), one of Thomæ Anshelmi Badensis (The Hague, 1521; not usually noted in lists); and one of Strasburg, 1526, which must be the fourth (not, as usually called, the third). Among English versions are the Bishop's Bible (1575), " Breeches " (Genevan) Bible (1589, 1601, 1602, 1610), King James's (1611), and the Macklin Bible (1800, a fine example of the printer's art). There are a number of American

imprints, and about 60 volumes of missionary Bibles. The Tyerman Collection of Pamphlets on Early Methodism approximates 10,000 pamphlets bound in about 300 volumes, collected by Luke Tyerman for his works on the Wesleys, Whitefield, and Fletcher. The Osborn Collection of Pamphlets relates chiefly to John Wesley. The Osborn Collection Relating to British Methodism is rich in rare editions of John Wesley's works, and in Wesleyan biography, as well as in literature on the minor Methodist denominations. These three last-named collections are the nucleus of a literature on Methodism numbering about 10,000 volumes, including very complete files of minutes of conferences and works on discipline. The Sprague collection of pamphlets was gathered by William B. Sprague for his Annals of the American Pulpit, and of this about 30 bound volumes are found here (see below, PRINCETON THEOLOGICAL SEMINARY). The Collection of Books on Missions numbers about 6,400 volumes, while related is the Bishop Hartzell Collection on Africa, the Africans, and Slavery.

General Theological Seminary, New York, N. Y. Especially noteworthy are the collections of patristics, the history of the councils, the histories of the Protestant Episcopal Church, and a very complete collection of diocesan journals. The library of the Assyriologist Eberhard Schrader (q.v.) was acquired in 1909. The Collection of Liturgies contains about 3,000 volumes, including a complete set of the standard editions of the American Book of Common Prayer. The Collection of Bibles includes the Copinger Collection of Latin Bibles (the largest in the world), over 1,200 editions in about 2,400 volumes, 93 polyglots, 96 editions of the Hexapla, 302 editions of the New Testament, and missionary versions, including John Eliot's Indian Bible (Cambridge, Mass., 1685), a Mazarin Bible (1453; cost $15,000; and an ed. of 1483, believed to be unique so far as public libraries are concerned), and many other rare fifteenth-century editions; the copy of the Antwerp Polyglot is perfect, and there is a Hutter Polyglot. Of 124 known editions of Latin fifteenth-century Bibles 86 are in this collection, and of 562 from the next century, 438 are here. Of first editions of English Bibles worthy of note are the Coverdale (1535), Matthew's (1537), Great Bible (1539; also the rare ed. of 1541), Genevan (1560), Bishop's (1568), and the two issues of the King James's (1611). There are also numerous editions of the Greek Testament.

Lutheran Theological Seminary, Gettysburg, Pa.: The Collection on Symbolics is noteworthy for its comprehensiveness and for its rare volumes on Lutheran symbolics, dealing with the history of the Augsburg Confession, the Lutheran symbolical books and commentaries on them, Schlusselburg's *Catalogi hæreticorum* (13 vols.), the *Corpora doctrinæ* from 1560, Augsburg Confession and Apology (1st ed., 1531, the second ed. of the same year; also ed. of 1540), the *Concordienformel* (1st ed., 1580), and a first Latin edition of the Formula (1580).

Hillsdale College, Hillsdale, Mich.: The Hull Collection of Bibles includes over 100 volumes —the Geneva (1599, 1613), Bishop's (1600), a Latin Bible of 1547, a Beza New Testament (1599); also numerous seventeenth and eighteenth century editions.

Hartford Theological Seminary, Hartford, Conn.: The Arabic Collection includes the Müller Semitic Library of about 1,100 Arabic books and several hundred pamphlets besides 200 other volumes added and 150 Arabic manuscripts. There are many editions of the Koran, great strength in native lexicography and grammar, Ibn Challikan's " Biographical Dictionary," and other rarities. The Collection of Bibles is wealthy in Hebrew and Greek printed texts; in polyglots it has the Complutensian, Antwerp, Heidelberg, Paris, and London; in Hebrew Bibles it has a Bomberg ed., Felix Pratensis (Venice, 1517–18), a Münster's Hebrew-Latin (2 vols., Basel, 1546), four Plantin Bibles (three editions of 1566; and Hebrew-Latin, 1571), a Hutter (Hamburg, 1596), a Buxtorf Rabbinic Bible (1618–1619), Athias edition (1661) and Leusden edition (1667), a Jablonski (Berlin, 1699), Van der Hooght's (2 vols., 1705), Opitz's (Kiel, 1709), the Mantuan (1742–44), Foster's Oxford quarto (1750), and the leading critical texts of the last fifty years. Of Greek New Testaments it has an Erasmus (of Basel, 1516) and a third edition (1522), two of Robert Stephens (1546, 1550), Beza's of 1565, 1589, 1598, Elzevirs of 1624 and 1633, and Bengel's first edition (1734). The Paine Hymnological Collection, as made by Silas H. Paine, contained over 5,000 titles (to which constant additions are being made in all branches of hymnology), besides first-hand information, including manuscript correspondence, gathered by the collector. The annotations of the hymnologists David Creamer and Daniel Sedgwick in the collection at Drew (see above) are transcribed. The principal modern works on hymnology are included, while of rarities mention may be made of Timotheus Gateensis, *In Hymnos ecclesiasticos brevis elucidatio* (Venice, 1582), *Pseaumes de David* (Paris, 1562), several editions of Marot's *Pseaumes de David* (e.g., 1668, 1680); and Latin hymnals of the sixteenth and seventeenth centuries. There is a large number of English and American hymn-books, including a Sternhold and Hopkins of 1584, an Ainsworth *Book of Psalmes or Hymnes* (Amsterdam, 1611), a copy of Knox's Liturgy (1615), G(eo.) S(andys), *A Paraphrase upon the Psalms of David* (London, 1636), and many rare first editions. A collection of Lutherana includes a very complete set of editions of Luther's works, among them the standard editions and first and other rare editions of fugitive writings, and the collection is probably not exceeded in value by any other in America. The collection on Missions is of prime importance because of its wide range and the wealth of auxiliary collections on ethnology, comparative religion, and travel.

McCormick Theological Seminary, Chicago, Ill.: The Collection on Patristics is worthy of mention because of its completeness, including the Migne Patrology and Mansi's Concilia. The Warrington Collection of Hymnology consists of about 450 volumes, chiefly modern.

Lutheran Theological Seminary, Mt. Airy, Philadelphia, Pa.: The archives of the Ministerium of Pennsylvania are located here, and contain the rec-

ords since the founding of the ministerium in 1748, besides correspondence and journals of leaders of Lutheranism and transcripts of documents in the archives at Halle. Though not in a special collection, the works on the early history of Lutheranism in America are worthy of mention. Lutherana are specially represented by many first editions of Luther's sermons, the program of the Leipsic disputation, controversial tracts, Eck's " Four Hundred and Four Theses " (1530), the first English edition of the " Harmony of the Confessions " (1586), a first edition of the " Book of Concord " (Dresden, 1580). The Bible collection is strong in German and English editions, including the London Polyglot. Of Latin Bibles there is a Nuremberg (1483), Basel (1491), and four volumes of the 6-vol. edition, 1498–1502. Of English Bibles there are two (mutilated) Matthews (1549, 1551), Geneva (1st ed., 1560); also later editions, Cranmer's (1562 and later), Bishop's (1572). Luther's version is in several editions (a 1st ed. of the Pentateuch, 1523); and of the second part of the Old Testament (1524); Dietenberger's Roman Catholic version (1534 and 1567), and *Bibel Teutsch* (Augsburg, 1518). Erasmus is represented (editions of 1519, 1522, 1527), also Beza (1st ed., 1565). There are fascimiles of the principal codices, and of Wyclif's and Coverdale's Bibles and Tyndal's New Testament. Catechisms are represented by about 200 volumes, besides a very complete set of American editions of Luther's catechisms. The liturgical collection is made up of several collections brought together, and is particularly rich in materials on the Lutheran liturgy, German church orders and agenda. There are about 1,000 volumes, which include Durand's *Rationale divinorum officiorum* (1493), *Manuale parochialum sacerdotum* (1494), *Ordo rerum sacrarum agendarum in orthodoxa Christi ecclesia* (1553), Casalius' *De veteribus sacris Christianorum ritibus* (1647), and works in this department by Duranti, Martene, Renaudot, Burius, Muratori, Cavalieri, and Zaccaria. Breviaries are well represented, missals (Nuremberg, 1484; Bamberg, 1499), facsimiles, and more modern works. German liturgies give the distinctive character to this collection, among them a manuscript (illuminated) of the fifteenth century, Luther's first liturgical work, *Ordnung des Gottesdienst in der Gemeinde* (1523), Bugenhagen's Mass (1524), Osiander's *Taufordnung* (1524), and Spangenberg's *Cantiones ecclesiasticæ* (1545). The development of the American Lutheran service is traceable from the material here. In this department musical settings have received attention.

Princeton Theological Seminary, Princeton, N. J.: The Library of the Society of Inquiry is the nucleus (1,092 volumes, 1,200 pamphlets) of a selection of works on missions. In the general library there are collections on Semitics, patristics, and also facsimiles of the leading codices of the Bible. The Sprague Collection of Pamphlets consists of about 20,000 pamphlets collected by William B. Sprague (q.v.) for his *Annals of the American Pulpit*, bound in 1,093 volumes, with additions. Sermons on election and fast days in Massachusetts, Connecticut, and Vermont before the governor and general court, before the Ancient and Honorable Artillery Company (1701–1829), before other bodies, ordination sermons, funeral addresses and sermons, and many other varieties of pulpit discourse are here. Controversial tracts are abundant, such as those on the Trinitarian-Unitarian controversy, on baptism, episcopacy, Quakerism, Roman Catholicism, the Calvinistic-Arminian controversy, and the like. Local church disputes are also registered by entries, and the anti-slavery movement. The collection of contemporaneous pamphlets on the Synod of Dort contains over 500 pamphlets, and furnishes perhaps the best collection of sources in America. The Hinschius Collection on Kirchenrecht (" Church law ") consists of over 2,000 numbers. The Agnew Collection on the Baptist Controversy consists now of over 2,000 volumes and 3,000 pamphlets, and the range of selection is very wide. The collection of Puritan literature comprises about 2,000 volumes of English and American Puritan writings of the seventeenth and eighteenth centuries, theological, controversial, biographical, and exegetical, very many of the numbers being rare if not unique in this country.

Protestant Episcopal Divinity School, Philadelphia, Pa.: The liturgical collection comprises over 500 volumes for the most part on Anglican and Protestant Episcopal usage, but includes such works of wider scope as those of Goar, Renaudot, Martin Gerbert, and Bartolomeo Gavanto, as well as the *Missale Romanum.* It contains the publications of the Henry Bradshaw Society and the Surtees Society, editions of the Book of Common Prayer, and pamphlets on the revision of the American Book of Common Prayer.

Rochester Theological Seminary, Rochester, N. Y.: The general library contains the library of Neander, the church historian, including the manuscript of his " Church History." The Baptist history collection is perhaps the richest in America on the Anabaptists, and on the English and continental Baptists since the early sixteenth century it has very many works.

Union Theological Seminary, New York, N. Y.: This institution has a wealth of collections in many departments, among which may be named in general 430 incunabula, 37 valuable manuscripts, 1,246 titles of Reformation literature in original editions, over 4,200 volumes in church history, patristics, and canon law, the comprehensive Samuel Macauley Jackson collection on Zwingli and the Reformation at Zurich, a selection on the dogma of the immaculate conception, and a large number of editions of Greek New Testaments. The Gillett Collection of American Theology and History abounds in general and local history, ecclesiastical and secular, and in biography. The Field Collection consists of a large number of pamphlets on early American religious history. The McAlpine Collection of British Theology and History is rich in material from the seventeenth century, its materials being surpassed in this department only by the Bodleian and British Museum; there are rare volumes from the Roman Catholic controversies of the Reformation period, on the early Baptists, Brownists, Independents, and obscure sects; especially valuable is that part which contains the religious and controversial works of the Puritan and Westminster divines and those which deal with the deistic and ecclesiastical controversies of the eighteenth century. The Hymnological Collection has for its nucleus the library of the late Frederic Mayer Bird (q.v.) and now numbers over 5,000 volumes, accessible through a card catalogue. It embraces foreign worship collections, in which are found the Herrnhut *Gesangbuch* of 1741, the French Psalm books of Marot and Beza (Geneva, 1607); Greek paraphrases of the Psalms; a line of Latin hymns among which may be noted the *Poemata sacra* of L. Torrentius (1594), the *Enchiridion scholasticorum* of F. Le Tort (1586), *Lyricorum libri* (1645), Jacob Balde's *Sylvæ lyricæ* (1646) as well as George Buchanan's *Poemata quæ extant* (1687) and *Psalmorum Davidis paraphrasis poetica* (1725). The department of English worship collections is classified according to denominations, and has many early specimens, some of them exceedingly rare. The minor denominations are well represented. Of very high value is that part which contains the Psalm versions, in which are a first and several later editions of the Bay Psalm Book (q.v.), a copy of the *editio princeps* of Tate and Brady (1696), and many other rarities. General treatises are well represented, of anthem books an unusually rich assemblage, nearly one hundred by Lowell Mason, and about sixty by Thomas Hastings. Sources are also richly present, noticeable among which is a first edition of Toplady's *Poems on Sacred Subjects* (1759).

Wesley Hall, Nashville, Tenn.: This institution has a collection of Methodist disciplines, from the first (1784) up to the present.

Western Theological Seminary, Chicago, Ill.: The Hibbard Egyptian Library comprises about 1,500 volumes, to which additions are constantly made, on Egyptology, comparative religion, archeology of the Bible and the orient.

Yale Divinity School, New Haven, Conn.: The Lowell Mason Library of Church Music is a collection of about 8,000 titles in about 4,000 volumes gathered by Lowell Mason, unusually complete in early publications in America, and presenting the development of American musical taste up to the time of Dr. Mason's death. The Foreign Mission Library approximates 8,000 volumes, the hope being to assemble " the entire foreign missionary literature of the Protestant nations of the world." The nucleus consists of copies of all translations of the Scriptures published or sold by the American Bible Society. It therefore includes: translations of the Bible or parts of it made by missionaries, with dictionaries and grammars in the various languages, with other works prepared by missionaries; histories of missionary organizations and encyclopedias; histories of modern missions, including early Jesuit missions; missionary biographies and autobiographies; files of the reports of many of the Protestant missionary societies, and of the principal American and European missionary periodicals; reports of work among Jews and Mohammedans.

In Canada may be named: **Presbyterian College,**

Montreal: The Sieveright Collection contains old and curious books, including a few incunabula. The Bibaud Collection contains 25 volumes of historical and biographical manuscripts. The institution possesses, besides, the Bampton Lectures (q.v.), the Migne Patrology, the Complutensian and London Polyglots, the Bomberg Rabbinic Bible, and a small collection of other Bibles.

Wesleyan Theological College, Montreal: The Ferrier Collection consists of the works of Samuel, John, and Charles Wesley.

McMaster Theological Seminary, Toronto, possesses collections of patristics, and classic editions of history and theology of the medieval and Reformation periods.

Victoria College, Toronto, has a collection of pamphlets, reports, and minutes of conferences, and of manuscript material on the history of Canadian Methodism.   W. H. ALLISON.

BIBLIOGRAPHY: Literature on general libraries is indicated in G. K. Fortescue, *Subject Index of the . . . British Museum,* London, 1903, 1906. Consult further: M. Faucon, *La Librairie des papes d'Avignon,* vol. i., Paris, 1886; E. Müntz, and P. Fabre, *La Bibliothèque du Vatican au xv. siècle,* Paris, 1886; T. Gottlieb, *Ueber mittelalterliche Bibliotheken,* Leipsic, 1890; F. A. Gasquet, *Notes on Mediæval Monastic Libraries,* Yeovil, 1891; J. W. Clark, *Libraries in the Medieval and Renaissance Periods,* Cambridge, 1894; T. G. Jackson, *The Libraries of the Middle Ages,* London, 1898; K. O. Meinsma, *Middeleeuwsche Bibliotheken,* Zutphen, 1903; F. Simpson, *Syllabus for a Course of Study in the Hist. of the Evolution of the Library in Europe and America,* Champaign, Ill., 1903, J. W. Clark, *The Care of Books; an Essay in the Development of Libraries from the earliest Times to the End of the Eighteenth Century,* New York, 1909; D. Cuthbertson, *The Edinburgh University Library; An Account of its Origin, with a Description of its rarer Books and Manuscripts,* Edinburgh, 1910; Schaff, *Christian Church,* v. 1, pp. 543 sqq.

THEOLOGICAL SCIENCE, AMERICAN CONTRIBUTIONS TO: For books embodying contributions on religion, see supplement to RELIGION; on the doctrine of God, see supplement to GOD; for particular systems of theology, see DOGMA, DOGMATICS, also supplement to THEOLOGY; for New England Theology until 1870 see NEW ENGLAND THEOLOGY. A classification of treatises on theology since 1890 according to denominational point of view is here added. Baptist: E. H. Johnson, *Outline of Christian Theology* (Philadelphia, 1891); E. G. Robinson, *Christian Theology* (Rochester, 1894); W. N. Clarke, *An Outline of Christian Theology* (New York, 1898); A. H. Strong, *Systematic Theology* (New York, 1907 sqq.). Congregationalist: J. H. Fairchild, *Elements of Theology* (Oberlin, 1892); L. F. Stearns, *Present Day Theology* (New York, 1893); W. DeW. Hyde, *Outlines of Social Theology* (ib. 1895); C. A. Beckwith, *Realities of Christian Theology* (Boston, 1906); J. W. Buckham, *Christ and the Eternal Order* (ib. 1906); W. D. Mackenzie, *The Final Faith* (New York, 1910). German Reformed: E. V. Gerhart, *Institutes of the Christian Religion* (ib. 1894). Lutheran: H. E. Jacobs, *A Summary of the Christian Faith* (Philadelphia, 1905). Methodist: J. Miley, *Systematic Theology* (New York, 1892–94); H. C. Sheldon, *System of Christian Doctrine* (ib. 1903); O. A. Curtis, *The Christian Faith Personally Given in a System of Doctrine* (ib. 1905). Presbyterian: F. R. Beattie, *The Presby-*

terian Standards (Richmond, 1896); R. V. Foster, *Systematic Theology* (Nashville, 1898); E. D. Morris, *Theology of the Westminster Symbols* (Columbus, 1900); W. A. Brown, *Christian Theology in Outline* (New York, 1906). Protestant Episcopalian: F. J. Hall, *Dogmatic Theology,* 10 vols. (New York, 1907 sqq.; in progress). Unitarian: M. J. Savage, *Our Unitarian Gospel* (New York, 1898); E. Emerton, *Unitarian Thought* (New York, 1911). For works on the Trinity, see TRINITY.

The contributions of American thought to theological science even from the beginning have been mainly anthropological. Until the latter part of the eighteenth century the prevailing **The Early** theology of New England was strict **Period.** Calvinism (q.v.) with its five points: unconditional election, limited atonement, total impotence of the fallen will, irresistible grace, and perseverance of the saints. The younger Jonathan Edwards declared that his father, President Edwards, and those associated with him had made no less than ten improvements in the Calvinism of the time: (1) concerning the ultimate end of the creation; (2) as to liberty and necessity, against Arminians, Pelagians, and Socinians wherein natural is distinguished from moral ability; (3) as to true virtue or holiness conceived as benevolence; (4) as to the origin of moral evil; (5) as to the atonement not as payment of a debt, but as maintenance of the divine government; (6) as to imputation of Christ's righteousness and Adam's sin; (7) as to the state of the unregenerate, use of means, and exhortations to be addressed to the impenitent; (8) as to the nature of experimental religion; (9) as to disinterested affection in religion; (10) as to regeneration (J. Edwards, *Works,* i. 481–492, Boston, 1842). These so-called improvements are significant not so much for what they contain as for what they suggest and prophesy. They are a symbol of a constant condition of American theological thought. Whatever the theme of discussion, the real subject is less theological than anthropological. The " five points " might be true, and it was believed they were, but, if so, they must stand or fall not by way of authority, even that of the Scriptures, but as able to maintain themselves through the most rigorous rational and psychological inquiry. It was also inevitable that a thoroughgoing endeavor be made to reconcile Calvinism with the demands of the ethical consciousness. Furthermore, conclusions had to be adjusted to the facts of Christian experience.

The main discussion centered in the doctrine of sin, and for a hundred years the high debate continued. According to Samuel Hop- **Sin.** kins (q.v.) every man's sin is an effect of Adam's sin by a divine constitution, and yet it is his own free act. Nathanael Emmons (q.v.) held that, on account of Adam's sin, when God forms the souls of infants he produces in them by divine efficiency those moral exercises in which moral depravity essentially consists. He agreed with Edwards in the assertion that God is not thus made the author of sin, since sin lies not in its cause but in its nature, but differs from him in holding that infants have knowledge of moral law as condition of moral action. According to Timothy Dwight (q.v.) God permits but does not create sin. Leonard Woods (q.v.) in distinction from the Westminster Catechism (*Letters*, Boston, 1822) denies the imputation of any sinful disposition or act to man which is not strictly his own; this may, however, begin with the life of the soul (ib. p. 305). The other aspect of sin discussed was the divine permission of sin. Here the fundamental position was that sin is the necessary means of the greatest good. This is the position of Hopkins, Bellamy, Emmons, and Wood. Nathaniel William Taylor (q.v.) assumed divine decrees in the Calvinistic sense, and, on the other hand, natural ability to obey God as the basis of accountability, together with a propensity to sin which was in some sense sinful; he, however, denied imputation. According to him, there is no hereditary but only voluntary sin, arising in a disposition which becomes sinful only when the soul yields to it. Looking back over the course of this discussion, it is seen to issue in four great affirmations, all of which modified the strict Calvinism of an earlier day: (1) original sin is incompatible with the nature of infants, and with adult accountability. (2) Moral action is certain, but is coupled with " power to the contrary." (3) Concerning the divine permission of sin, or whether sin was the necessary means of the greatest good, the affirmation was that God could not wholly prevent sin in a moral world; and that sin was never either a good or necessary. (4) Sin may be forgiven by reason not of Christ's payment of a debt but of his maintenance of the divine government. Here are indeed great gains over the positions of Edwards, but in the reasonings by which they are reached one is reminded of the Judaic, medieval, and Lutheran scholasticism.

In the following presentation of more recent thought it is not assumed that contributions of the same nature and even of similar value have not been made by English and continental **Anthro-** writers. Attention is, however, di-**pology.** rected to the American field. Taking up in order the subjects which have been enriched by American scholars, outside of those to which reference has been made in the first paragraph above, there is first the doctrine of man. Expansion has taken place in three directions, two of which are diametrically opposed to each other, while a third, although unpremeditated, has not been less effective. More than to any other source the conception of the inherent, immeasurable, and indefeasible worth of the soul has owed its initiative and defense to Unitarian thinkers, to W. E. Channing (q.v.) first (cf. *Works*, " Sermon Preached at the Installation of Jared Sparks in Baltimore, 1819," Boston, 1875). On the other hand, Calvinism, even the most extreme, tended to the same result by a wholly different path. It ostensibly robbed man of his essential glory and abased his pride in the dust; but since it made him the highest creature in the universe, subject of the divine decrees, in whose interest the entire machinery of redemption was set in operation, thus engrossing the whole consciousness and purpose of God, he was inevitably exalted to a position of the highest significance (cf. J. Edwards, *Freedom of the Will;* also H. Bushnell, q.v.,

" Dignity of Human Nature seen in its Ruins " in *Sermons for the New Life*, New York, 1858). Moreover, the previous development of the doctrine of sin and the general advance in humanitarian spirit, quickened partly by the lofty ethical idealism of Kant (q.v.), partly by the spiritual philosophy of Coleridge (q.v.), and partly by the great moral reforms which agitated the first six decades of the nineteenth century, raised the entire conception of man to a higher level. From the point of view of evolution two contributions of great value have been made, neither by theologians, but both uniting in the religious interest, J. Le Conte, *Evolution and its Relation to Religious Thought* (New York, 1894), and J. Fiske, *The Destiny of Man Viewed in the Light of his Origin* (Boston, 1884). The works which deal with immortality, including conditional immortality, are among the most fruitful additions to American thought on this subject (see IMMORTALITY, VIII.). Outside of the writings of Universalism (see UNIVERSALISTS) future probation was advocated in *Progressive Orthodoxy* by professors in Andover Theological Seminary (ib. 1886), who maintained that since the final judgment is Christian judgment, the opportunity to accept this must come consciously to every soul.

The person of Christ has received attention from two different interests—his character and his essential nature. Chief among the treatises **Christology.** on his character are, W. E. Channing, *Works*, " The Imitableness of the Character of Christ " (ib. 1875), H. Bushnell, *Nature and the Supernatural*, " The Character of Jesus " (New York, 1858), J. A. Broadus (q.v.), *Jesus of Nazareth* (ib. 1890), C. E. Jefferson (q.v.), *The Character of Jesus* (ib. 1908), N. Schmidt, *Prophet of Nazareth* (ib. 1907). The principal attempts to reconstruct the doctrine of the inner nature of Christ have been made by H. Bushnell, *God in Christ* (ib. 1849), in which the content of Jesus's consciousness is declared to be divine, the form human, and by H. M. Goodwin, *Christ and Humanity* (ib. 1875), which finds the eternal humanity in God the principle of the incarnation—a view not unlike that presented by G. A. Gordon (q.v.) in *The Christ of To-day* (Boston, 1895). The consubstantiality of God and man offers a clue to other presentations of the person of Christ: H. Van Dyke (q.v.), *The Gospel for an Age of Doubt*, lect. IV. (New York, 1896); T. De Witt Hyde (q.v.), *Social Theology*, p. 60 (1895); F. Palmer, *Studies in Theologic Definition* (1895).

Significant contributions have been made to the doctrine of the atonement. In addition to those referred to in the articles on atonement and satisfaction which defend traditional positions, **Atonement.** five works require attention: H. Bushnell, *The Vicarious Sacrifice* (ib. 1865), in which love is suggested as the secret of Christ's sacrifice; H. C. Trumbull (q.v.), *The Blood Covenant* (ib. 1885), which presents sacrifice as an original form of blood-covenanting, blood-brotherhood between God and man effected by transfusion of blood, and God and man united in the blood of Christ; professors in Andover Theological Seminary, *Progressive Orthodoxy* (Boston, 1886), in which God is seen to be propitiated by man's repentance, and

Christ's " sympathetic repentance " in his work is a " substitution of humanity *plus* Christ for humanity *minus* Christ "; C. C. Everett, *The Gospel of Paul* (ib. 1893) which represents the curse on sin as removed on account of Paul's view of Christ's death on the cross outside of the walls of the Holy City; and E. D. Burton and others, *The Biblical Idea of the Atonement* (Chicago, 1909), where the atonement is for the first time brought into line with the social consciousness of sin and salvation.

For contributions on the Spirit of God see SPIRIT OF GOD; on conversion and religious experience, see CONVERSION, also Supplement to RELIGION, PSYCHOLOGY OF.

In Apologetics (q.v.) the most notable contributions have been by Henry B. Smith (q.v.), *The Re-* *lations of Faith and Philosophy* (New York, 1877); Horace Bushnell, *Nature and the Supernatural* (ib., 1858); John Fiske, *The Idea of God* (Boston, 1886), and *Through Nature to God* (ib. 1899); **Apologetics.** W. A. Brown, *The Essence of Christianity* (New York, 1902); G. W. Knox (q.v.), *The Direct and Fundamental Proof of the Christian Religion* (ib. 1903); G. B. Foster, *The Finality of the Christian Religion* (Chicago, 1906); and G. A. Gordon, *Religion and Miracle* (Boston, 1909).

The foregoing presentation has not aimed to be exhaustive, some subjects having been omitted and only few books on each subject named, but the main lines have been indicated and leading works suggested.   C. A. BECKWITH.

THEOLOGICAL SEMINARIES.

I. Baptist.
  1. Divinity School of the University of Chicago.
  2. Colgate.
  3. Crozer.
  4. Kansas City.
  5. Newton.
  6. Rochester.
  7. Southern.
  8. Southwestern.
  9. Virginia Union.
II. Free Baptist.
  1. Hillsdale.
III. Congregational.
  1. Andover.
  2. Atlanta.
  3. Bangor.
  4. Chicago.
  5. Hartford.
  6. Oberlin.
  7. Pacific.
  8. Yale.
IV. Disciples of Christ.
  1. Bible.
  2. Drake.
  3. Eugene.
V. Evangelical Association.
  1. Naperville.
VI. Jewish.
  1. Hebrew Union College.
  2. Jewish Theological Seminary of America.
VII. Lutheran.
  1. Augsburg.
  2. Augustana.
  3. Chicago.
  4. Columbus.
  5. Concordia (St. Louis).
  6. Concordia (Springfield, Ill.).
  7. Gettysburg.
  8. Hamma.

  9. Hartwick.
  10. Luther.
  11. Mount Airy.
  12. Columbia (formerly Mount Pleasant).
  13. Saint Anthony Park.
  14. Susquehanna.
  15. Wartburg.
  16. Wauwatosa.
  17. Western.
VIII. Methodist Episcopal.
  1. Asbury.
  2. Boston.
  3. Drew.
  4. Garrett Biblical Institute.
  5. German.
  6. Nast.
  7. Swedish.
  8. Taylor.
  9. Vanderbilt.
IX. Methodist Protestant.
  1. Adrian.
  2. Westminster (Tehuacana, Tex).
  3. Westminster (Westminster, Md.).
X. New Jerusalem Church.
  1. Cambridge.
XI a. Presbyterian (Northern).
  1. Auburn.
  2. Bloomfield.
  3. Lane.
  4. Lincoln.
  5. McCormick.
  6. Northwest.
  7. Omaha.
  8. Princeton.
  9. San Francisco.
  10. Union (New York).
  11. Western.
XI b. Presbyterian (Southern).
  1. Austin.

  2. Columbia.
  3. Kentucky.
  4. Southwestern.
  5. Union (Richmond, Va.).
XII. Reformed Presbyterian.
  1. Pittsburg.
XIII. United Presbyterian.
  1. Xenia.
XIV. Protestant Episcopal.
  1. Berkeley.
  2. Cambridge.
  3. General.
  4. Nashotah.
  5. Pacific.
  6. Philadelphia.
  7. Seabury.
  8. Virginia.
XV a. Reformed (German).
  1. Central.
  2. Lancaster.
  3. Plymouth.
XV b. Reformed (Dutch).
  1. New Brunswick.
  2. Western.
XVI. Christian Reformed.
  1. Grand Rapids.
XVII. Roman Catholic.
  1. St. Patrick's.
  2. St. Thomas of Villanova.
VIII. Unitarian.
  1. Meadville.
  2. Pacific.
XIX. Unity of the Brethren.
  1. Bethlehem.
XX. Universalist.
  1. Canton.
  2. Crane.
  3. Ryder.
XXI. Undenominational.
  1. Harvard.

[In the preparation of the present article every possible effort has been made to secure completeness, and to that end a letter was sent by the editors to some person of authority in each theological seminary of every religious communion in the United States. In the interests of strict accuracy it has been deemed best to give accounts of those institutions only from which replies were received. Accordingly, non-mention of a seminary in the article implies that the editors received no response to their request for information.]

I. Baptist.—1. Divinity School of the University of Chicago: This institution, formerly known as "The Baptist Union Theological Seminary," was founded by " The Baptist Theological Union, located at Chicago," when, in 1865, W. W. Cook of Whitehall, N. Y., and Lawrence Barnes and Mial Davis of Burlington, Vt., subscribed an annual joint sum of $1,500 for five years, thus making possible the organization of the work of instruction. Some preliminary work was done in 1865–66, when a few students received training from Dr. Nathaniel Colver and Rev. J. C. C. Clark, but organized teaching was not actually begun until 1867, when Dr. George W. Northrup, professor of church history in Rochester Theological Seminary, was made professor of systematic theology, and Dr. John B. Jackson, pastor in Albion, N. Y., was made professor of church history. The number of students the first year was twenty, and the first building of the seminary, including lecture-rooms, dormitories, and four residences for professors, was dedicated in July, 1869, in which year Dr. G. W. Northrup was made president of the institution. In 1873 a Scandinavian department was organized which later developed into the Swedish Theological Seminary and the Danish-Norwegian Theological Seminary, these two seminaries in 1910 having sixty-three students. Aften ten years of work in the city, during which the annual attendance of students had increased from twenty in 1867–68 to above eighty in 1876–77, the seminary was transferred from its location in Chicago to the suburb of Morgan Park, where it remained until 1892, prospering during these fifteen years in all departments of its work. Beginning with endowment funds of $50,000 in 1877, it had increased these to $250,000 in 1892, while the number of students so grew that in 1891–1892 it reached 190.

The University of Chicago opened its doors to students Oct. 1, 1892, and by an agreement between the boards of trustees of the university and of the seminary the latter became " The Divinity School of the University of Chicago," so that, on the opening of the university, it transferred its work to the buildings of that institution in the city. In connection with this transfer Dr. G. W. Northrup, who had conducted the affairs of the seminary with distinguished ability, resigned the presidency and was succeeded by Dr. Wm. Rainey Harper (q.v.), president of the university, whose incumbency continued until his death in 1906, when he was succeeded by Dr. Harry Pratt Judson, the new president of the university. On the union of the seminary with the university in 1892 and the retransfer of its work to Chicago as " The Divinity School of the University of Chicago," Dr. Eri B. Hulbert (q.v.), who had occupied the chair of church history for eleven years, was made dean of the school, and continued to fill this position until his death in 1907. By the terms of the union of the two institutions, under which the divinity school has prospered greatly, the seminary became the sole divinity school of the university, the president of the university became the president of the school, the board of the school turned over to the university the conferring of degrees, the department of Old Testament and Semitic studies was transferred to the university, the board of trustees of the school retained the supervision and direction of matters pertaining to instruction, and the university agreed to confirm the election of all professors and instructors in the school when and to the extent that the funds available for the school should admit. Ample dormitories have been built for the divinity school on the university grounds, and its work has been conducted in the buildings of the university, except that the Scandinavian departments have occupied one of the former buildings of the school at Morgan Park. The number of students has rapidly increased, and during the year 1909–10 was 423, this large attendance being in part accounted for by the four-quarter system which was instituted on the union of the school with the university. There are four quarters

in the school year — the summer, autumn, winter, and spring quarters — of approximately twelve weeks each. Students may take their vacation in any one of these quarters, or, by taking no vacations, except the annual one in September of a full month, may complete the three-years' course in two years. Students may, with the approval of the dean, take courses in other departments of the university, and so close is the union that the opportunities of a great university are thus open to the students of the divinity school. The libraries belonging to the divinity school are that of Prof. E. W. Hengstenberg (q.v.), late of the University of Berlin, that of Dr. George B. Ide, the Colwell library of the American Bible Union, and other collections of books of history, science, sociology, literature, and theology, to which a thousand or more volumes are added yearly, while the libraries of the university, containing 400,000 volumes, are also open to divinity students. The two men who have made the greatest financial contributions to the institution are E. Nelson Blake and John D. Rockefeller, who have made possible the securing of the present productive endowment funds of the school, which, including $100,000 held for it by the university, aggregate $350,000. The income of this fund being insufficient to carry on the work of the school, a large sum is appropriated annually by the university toward the current expenses.

The more prominent of the professors who have been connected with the school are the following: Drs. George W. Northrup, John B. Jackson, A. N. Arnold, Wm. Hague, Edward C. Mitchell (q.v.), R. E. Pattison, Thomas J. Morgan, James R. Boise, Wm. R. Harper (q.v.), Ira M. Price (q.v.), Eri B. Hulbert (q.v.), Justin A. Smith, John A. Edgren, Nels P. Jensen, Galusha Anderson (q.v.), Franklin Johnson (q.v.), Adoniram Sage, Ernest D. Burton (q.v.), Charles R. Henderson, Shailer Mathews (q.v.), George B. Foster (q.v.), John W. Moncrief, Edgar J. Goodspeed, Henrik Gundersen, Carl G. Lagergren, Harry P. Judson, Andrew C. McLaughlin, Theodore G. Soares, Edward Judson, Alonzo K. Parker, Gerald B. Smith, Allan Hoben, Shirley J. Case, and Benjamin A. Greene. Dr. Shailer Mathews was appointed junior dean of the school in 1899, and was made sole dean in 1908. The board of trustees consists of fifteen members, divided into three classes of five members each, and holding office three years, when successors are elected by the corporation of " The Baptist Theological Union," located at Chicago."

Among the principles for which the divinity school of the University of Chicago has stood are liberty of teaching, the historical method in the study of the Bible, and the practical application of Christianity to the immediate needs and problems of modern social life. In methods of work it has introduced the four-quarter system and the employment during the summer quarter of eminent professors from other institutions of this and other countries, thus affording to pastors and teachers of other institutions large opportunities for additional study and training. It has issued two periodicals, *The Biblical World* since 1893, and *The American Journal of Theology* since 1896.

THOMAS WAKEFIELD GOODSPEED.

2. Colgate: This institution, the oldest Baptist theological seminary in America, had its historic beginning in " thirteen men, thirteen prayers, and thirteen dollars," and the resulting organization, in Sept., 1817, of the Baptist Education Society of the State of New York, incorporated in 1819, with the purpose of establishing an institution which should afford opportunity for a thorough theological education, including a full literary and scientific course of training and culture. The first student, Jonathan Wade, later renowned in missionary annals, was received in 1818, but it was not till 1820 that the school was definitely organized, at Hamilton, N. Y., which became known as " The Hamilton Literary and Theological Institution." Rev. Daniel Hascall, one of the founders, was the first professor, while among other members of the faculty in the earlier years, Nathanael Kendrick, Barnas Sears (q.v.), Joel S. Bacon, George W. Eaton, and Thomas J. Conant (q.v.) acquired national reputations as scholars and educators. Of the present faculty, the following, who have rendered fifteen or more years of service, are well known in the Baptist world: William H. Maynard, Sylvester Burnham, Arthur Jones, David F. Estes (q.v.), George R. Berry, and William Newton Clarke (q.v.). In 1839, the institution admitted students not having the ministry in view, which led naturally to the organization of a college, which in 1846 was incorporated under the title of Madison (since 1890, Colgate) University. The attempt, finally defeated in 1850, to remove the two institutions from Hamilton created a perilous crisis out of which both moved into increasing prosperity. Three successive compacts (1847, 1853, 1893) between the Education Society and the university have been the basis of the administrative and educational control of the seminary. While the latter has itself no funds, it is the chief beneficiary of the Education Society, the productive endowment of which at the present time (1910) exceeds $770,000. Its library is merged in that of the university, which contains over 55,000 volumes besides periodicals and pamphlets; and the Samuel Colgate Baptist Historical Collection, which is endowed, is the most complete of any in this country in materials relating to the history of the Baptists in England and America. Already the Theological Seminary of Colgate University, to use the present name, has sent out nearly 1,400 students and graduates, of whom nearly 100 have rendered missionary service on foreign fields. The courses of instruction at present cover three years; the senior class spends one term in New York City where it studies the religious and social problems of the large city and methods of religious work. In 1907, an Italian department was opened in Brooklyn for the training of Christian workers among the Italians in America.

WILLIAM H. ALLISON.

BIBLIOGRAPHY: *Jubilee Volume: First Half Century of Madison University*, n.p., n.d. (probably published at Hamilton, N. Y., 1872).

3. Crozer: Crozer Theological Seminary is located just outside the limits of Chester, Pa., in the borough of Upland, Delaware Co. On Nov. 2, 1868, the widow and seven children of John Price Crozer endowed the seminary with land, buildings, and in-

vested funds amounting to $275,000, and on Apr. 4, 1867, the institution was incorporated by act of legislature. Its trustees and faculty are Baptists, but students of any denomination are admitted. Its earliest instructors were Henry G. Weston (q.v.; president and professor of pastoral theology), G. D. B. Pepper (q.v.; professor of theology), Howard Osgood (q.v.; professor of Hebrew and church history), and Lemuel Moss (professor of New-Testament literature). The seminary was formally opened Oct. 2, 1868, and graduated its first class of eight students in June, 1870. Since then 696 men have been graduated, including the class of 1910, and 437 others have pursued studies without graduation. Though the youngest of Baptist theological schools, Crozer's roll of alumni includes many of the foremost men in the denomination. It has always stood for the best possible training of every man who is called to the ministry, and among its prominent instructors have been George R. Bliss, professor of Biblical interpretation; John C. Long, professor of church history; Elias H. Johnson (q.v.), professor of systematic theology; and James M. Stifler, professor of New-Testament exegesis.

The seminary has a faculty of twelve professors and instructors and a board of twenty trustees who elect their successors; is empowered to confer degrees in theology; and confers the degrees of B.D. and Th.M. for work done (no honorary degrees). The first president, Henry G. Weston, died Feb. 6, 1909, after a service of forty-one years, and Prof. Milton G. Evans was chosen his successor in June of the same year. In 1910 there were eighty-nine students enrolled (among them being one Methodist and one Disciple), including six resident graduates and one special student. The productive endowment is $600,400, and the number of books in the library is nearly 23,000.   HENRY C. VEDDER.

BIBLIOGRAPHY: *Historical Sketch of Crozer Theological Seminary*, Chester, Pa., 1898. A brief history of the institution is prefixed to its catalogue each year.

4. Kansas City: The Kansas City Baptist Theological Seminary, located at Kansas City, Wyandotte Co., Kan., was founded in 1901 to meet the need of the Baptists of the Middle West for an institution devoted exclusively to ministerial education, none such then existing west of Chicago and Louisville. Rev. E. B. Meredith, missionary secretary of the Kansas Baptist State Convention, was president of the board of trustees, and on his retirement in 1902, Rev. S. A. Northrop, of Kansas City, Mo., took his place. Rev. B. W. Wiseman was financial secretary, and others influential in the founding of the school were Rev. I. N. Clark and Rev. S. M. Brown, both of Kansas City, Mo., Rev. J. F. Wells, of Kansas City, Kan., and Prof. M. L. Ward, of Ottawa University, Kan. Mrs. Charles Lovelace, of Turner, Kan., gave 115 acres of land as the " Merrick K. Barber Foundation," in honor of her deceased husband, and this property, now worth from $75,000 to $115,000, formed the nucleus of the school's resources. The seminary is under the control of the Baptist denomination; seven-eighths of its trustees must be Baptists, and the Convention of each contributing state may nominate at least one trustee to represent it on the board, and may appoint yearly a visiting committee. Instruction began Oct., 1902, with five students and the following faculty: Rev. James F. Wells, acting executive and professor of church history and English scriptures; Rev. A. C. Rafferty, systematic theology; Rev. F. L. Streeter, New-Testament Greek; and Rev. P. W. Crannell, homiletics and pastoral theology. In May, 1903, Dr. Crannell became president, and in Sept., 1903, the chairs of Hebrew (Prof. Henry T. Morton) and public speaking (Prof. P. K. Dillenbeck) were added, while in 1908 the departments of Christian sociology and religious pedagogy (Prof. W. E. Raffety) were created. The seminary seeks, on the basis of an intelligent conservatism, and a profound faith in the deity of Christ and the inspiration of the Scriptures, to furnish a broad, scholarly, well-balanced, and emphatically practical training for the pastorate. While its curriculum covers all phases of the minister's preparation, special attention is paid to the English Bible, homiletics, pastoral theology, evangelism, pedagogy, and sociology, in which latter departments it is one of the pioneers, while missions is also one of its specialties. It seeks to supply especially the Middle West, although its student body is drawn from every part of the Union and from several foreign countries. Of its hundred graduates and former students, chiefly settled in Kansas, Missouri, and Oklahoma, many are found in other states, principally in the West. Its classes are freely open to women, either as special or as regular students. It has (1910) twenty-one trustees, from Kansas, Missouri, Oklahoma, Iowa, Colorado, and Nebraska; seven instructors (six regular, one special); two field secretaries; and fifty-one students from nine colleges and from thirteen states and countries. Its resources are $170,000, including an endowment of $97,000, and its library contains 3,500 volumes. Rev. Philip Wendell Crannell is president, and Rev. B. R. Downer (professor of Hebrew) is secretary of the faculty, while Rev. J. F. Wells is field secretary, and Rev. B. W. Wiseman is associate.   E. T. JILLSON.

5. Newton: Newton Theological Institution is located on the summit of a beautiful hill in Newton Centre, Mass., and occupies fifty-two acres, including well-kept paths, lawns, shrubbery, and athletic grounds. The institution was founded in 1825, and is the oldest seminary established exclusively as such by American Baptists for the purpose of providing college graduates with a suitable course of theological instruction occupying three years. Courses are offered in the oriental and Greek languages, the history and interpretation of the Old and New Testaments, church history, theology, homiletics and pastoral duties, sociology and social reform, missions, religious psychology and Sunday-school pedagogy, and church music. While the privileges of the institution have been intended primarily for college graduates, students who can present evidence of equivalent training and of maturity of mind are received in special instances. The institution is controlled by a board of forty-eight trustees, including both ministers and laymen.

The work of the seminary began with a single professor, Rev. Irah Chase (q.v.), with whom Rev.

Henry J. Ripley was associated in 1826; in 1834 Rev. James D. Knowles was added to the faculty; and in 1836 Rev. Barnas Sears (q.v.). Professor Knowles died in 1838, after a short period of brilliant service; and in 1839 Rev. H. B. Hackett (q.v.) was made professor of Biblical literature and interpretation. All of these were eminent scholars and teachers; and the institution, though financially weak, prospered under their care. From 1839 to 1846 the number of professors was four; in 1846 an assistant instructor in Hebrew was added; and from 1868 to 1908 there were five regular professors, one of them the president, and a teacher of elocution. After years of service as a professor, Rev. Alvah Hovey (q.v.) was chosen president of the seminary in 1868, and continued in that office for thirty years. With the inauguration of President George E. Horr (q.v.) in 1908, the curriculum was enlarged to include instruction in sociology, religious psychology and pedagogy, and church music. The permanent board of instruction includes: in the Biblical departments, Professors Charles R. Brown (q.v.), Frederick L. Anderson, and Winfred N. Donovan; in church history and sociology, President Horr and Prof. Henry K. Rowe (q.v.); in theology, Prof. George Cross; in homiletics, Prof. John M. English (q.v.); and in elocution, Prof. Samuel S, Curry. Additional lecturers are appointed from year to year to supplement the regular staff, and a weekly convocation of faculty and students brings many other speakers to the seminary.

There are registered in the present year (1910) ninety-two students, of whom thirteen are postgraduates (candidates for the degrees of B.D. and S.T.M.), seventy-four are undergraduates, and five are young women preparing for foreign missionary service after a year's resident study. Students come from all parts of the United States and Canada, from England, Germany, Sweden, and the Far East, and thirty-seven colleges and universities are represented. A summer school is held in June of each year, and in 1910 fifty-seven students were in attendance. The Gordon School, a training-school for Christian workers, with twenty years of history and with sixty students in attendance, is affiliated with the institution, although located in Boston. The institution has a well-selected library of about 30,000 volumes, and a commodious reading-room. The library is open to students fourteen hours every day, except Saturday evening and Sunday, and has an income of approximately $16,000 for the purchase of books and periodicals. To meet other expenses the institution has an endowment of $800,000, besides forty-six scholarships involving a total of $120,000 for the benefit of indigent students. It has six principal buildings: Colby Hall, containing the chapel and lecture-rooms, Farwell Hall and Sturtevant Hall, which are heated by steam and have rooms comfortably furnished for seventy students, besides the dining-hall and the reception rooms, the Hills Library and Hartshorn Reading-room, a President's house, and a gymnasium. About 1,500 students have been connected with the institution, although some of them have not taken the full course. One hundred and twenty have gone from it to be missionaries in foreign fields, and more than half as many have been made presidents and professors in colleges and theological seminaries, though most of its graduates have become pastors in America. HENRY K. ROWE.

6. Rochester: The Baptist theological seminary in Rochester, N. Y., was established in 1850 by "The New York Baptist Union for Ministerial Education." A fund of $130,000 was raised, largely through the efforts of Rev. Pharcellus Church and John N. Wilder, and Oren Sage, while five professors, accompanied by many of their students, transferred their activity from Hamilton (now Colgate) University and Seminary to Rochester, two of the professors, Thomas J. Conant (q.v.) and John S. Maginnis, joining the faculty of the new seminary, while the others became instructors in the equally new University of Rochester, which, though also under Baptist influence, has no organic connection with the seminary. The first class graduated from the seminary numbered six, and in 1851–52 there were two professors and twenty-nine students. Among the distinguished members of its faculty have been Ezekiel G. Robinson (president, 1868–72), John H. Raymond, George W. Northrup, Howard Osgood (q.v.), Albert Henry Newman (q.v.), Benjamin O. True, and Henry E. Robins (q.v.). In 1852 a German department was added to the seminary, its curriculum being entirely distinct from that of the seminary itself, since it is designed especially for the training of German Baptists who, without full college education, may desire to enter the ministry of their denomination. Apart from the early years, when the difficulties naturally inherent in the nascent undertaking were increased by some tension with the older sister institution, Hamilton, the record of the Rochester seminary has been one of steady growth. Its aim has been to make its graduates not merely students and preachers, but men of thinking ability and practical force, and it has done much to give an aggressive, independent tone to the Baptist ministry.

In 1910 the seminary had a faculty of eleven (Augustus H. Strong, president) and a board of thirty-three trustees, eleven of whom are elected each year by the New York Baptist Union, which from the very first has maintained and controlled the institution. It had in 1910, 167 students, of whom seventy-seven were in the German Department, and its courses are open to members of all denominations. Its total assets in 1910 were estimated at $2,117,242, and its productive endowment at $1,689,095, from which sums generous provision is made for scholarships for needy students, as well as for fellowships. The library contains over 3,700 volumes, including the entire collection of the church historian J. A. W. Neander, which was presented to the seminary by Roswell S. Burrows in 1853, and the beginnings of a museum of Biblical geography and archeology have been made.

BIBLIOGRAPHY: A. H. Strong, *Historical Discourse, Delivered as a Part . . . of the Fiftieth Anniversary of Rochester Theological Seminary*, Rochester, N. Y., 1900; *Sixtieth Annual Catalogue of the Rochester Theological Seminary*, pp. 76–84, Rochester, 1909.

7. Southern: The Southern Baptist Theological Seminary, now located in Louisville, Ky., was established in 1859 by the Southern Baptist Convention—a step which had been decided in May, 1857, at an educational convention of Southern Baptists at Louisville. The leading spirit in the foundation of the seminary was James P. Boyce (q.v.), who was ably assisted by John A. Broadus (q.v.), these two together with Basil Manly, Jr., and William Williams, constituting the first faculty. The seminary was started at Greenville, S. C., but during the Civil War it was forced to close, its professors supporting themselves by preaching and other religious work. In the fall of 1865 the institution, badly crippled in finances, reopened its doors and maintained a precarious existence in Greenville until 1877, when in hope of endowment from states that had suffered less from the war, and in receipt of overtures from Kentucky Baptists, it was removed to Louisville. Here its tenure was equally uncertain until 1880, when a large donation from Joseph E. Brown, of Georgia, put it on a footing which assures it life and growth.

The seminary stands for the highest conservative-progressive scholarship in the education of the ministry, and its curriculum is designed to make its graduates practically efficient in pastorates, in the pulpit, and in all forms of denominational leadership. It was the first theological institution to adopt the elective system in its course of study, and the first to open its doors to men without college training, as well as among the first to include Sunday-school pedagogy in its regular curriculum. Among the prominent members of the faculty in the past may be mentioned Rev. William H. Whitsitt (q.v.) and Rev. E. C. Dargan (q.v.; resigned) and Rev. F. H. Kerfoot (deceased). All the present faculty, nine in number, are prominent in denominational life, and include Edgar Y. Mullins (q.v.; president and professor of theology), John R. Sampey (Old-Testament interpretation), A. T. Robertson (q.v.; New-Testament interpretation), W. J. M'Glothlin (church history), W. O. Carver (comparative religion and missions), George B. Eager (Biblical introduction and pastoral theology), B. H. De Ment (q.v.; Sunday-school pedagogy), C. S. Gardner (homiletics and ecclesiology), and T. M. Hawes (elocution). The trustees, elected from three nominations made for each vacancy by the Southern Baptist Convention, number sixty-seven, and represent the southern states, the number from each state depending on the amount of money contributed to the endowment fund of the institution from the state in question. This board of trustees meets annually in connection with the meeting of the Southern Baptist Convention, and an executive committee elected by the board has general charge of affairs between the annual meetings. The management of endowment funds is vested in a financial board elected annually by those who have contributed $1,000 or more toward the endowment, this election being ratified by the board of trustees. The majority of the students, who in 1910 numbered upward of 300, come principally from the southern states, though many are from the North, and some every year are from foreign lands. The great majority of the students are Baptists, but the classes of the seminary are open to members of any denomination who are properly recommended. The invested funds now amount to about $625,000, apart from grounds and buildings; the library contains about 23,000 bound volumes.

EDGAR YOUNG MULLINS.

BIBLIOGRAPHY: John R. Sampey, *Southern Baptist Theological Seminary, The first Thirty Years*, Baltimore, 1890; F. H. Kerfoot, *Southern Baptist Theological Seminary, The first Forty Years*, Louisville, Ky., 1900.

8. Southwestern: The permanent home of this institution since Oct., 1910, has been Forth Worth, Tarrant Co., Tex. The seminary was founded in 1901 as the Theological Department of Baylor University, Waco, Tex., and originated in the desire of Dr. B. H. Carroll, one of the most eminent preachers, denominational leaders, and theologians of the Southern Baptists, to supply the 1,000,000 Baptists of the Southwest with an educated ministry. Dr. Carroll had been for nearly thirty years pastor of the First Baptist Church, Waco, and president of the board of trustees of the university, and was at that time secretary of the educational commission of the Texas Baptist Convention. To aid in the development of this department of the university Prof. Albert Henry Newman (q.v.), at that time a member of the theological faculty of McMaster University, Toronto, Canada, was induced to accept a position in Baylor University, and with him was associated Prof. R. N. Barrett. Dr. Carroll soon became dean of the theological faculty and began giving comprehensive courses of lectures on the English Bible, and a reasonably full course of theological studies was provided from the beginning.

Dr. Barrett died in 1903 and was succeeded by Dr. B. H. De Ment (q.v.; now professor in the Southern Baptist Theological Seminary), who in turn was succeeded in 1904 by Dr. L. W. Doolan. By 1905 it had become practicable, through the efforts of Dr. Carroll, to enlarge the faculty. Dr. Calvin Goodspeed, an eminent Canadian theologian, was called to the chair of systematic theology, apologetics, and polemics, and Dr. C. B. Williams to that of New-Testament Greek, while Dr. Carroll retained the chair of English Bible, Dr. Newman that of church history and history of doctrines, and Dr. Doolan that of Hebrew and cognate languages and literatures. In 1907 Dr. J. D. Ray was appointed professor of homiletics, missions, and pastoral duties, and in 1908 Dr. L. R. Scarborough became professor of evangelism and field secretary, and Dr. J. J. Reeve succeeded Dr. Doolan. From 1905 the designation " Baylor Theological Seminary " was employed.

By the autumn of 1907 the conviction had been reached that the interests of both seminary and university demanded the separation of the two institutions and the removal of the former to another city, and university and seminary officials cooperated in securing the concurrence of the State Convention in measures to that end. The Convention (Nov., 1907) appointed a board of trustees and arranged for securing a charter from the state of Texas, and this was accomplished in March, 1908, the title " Southwestern Baptist Theological Seminary " having been previously adopted. The sessions 1908–09 and 1909–10 were, however, conducted in the buildings of Baylor University.

In Oct., 1909, the trustees of the seminary accepted the offer of the Baptists and others in Fort Worth to contribute $100,000 or more for the erection of a building with ample grounds, if the authorities would choose Fort Worth as its habitat. A building costing nearly $150,000 has been erected, and lands, in addition to the site, supposed to be worth at least $100,000 have been deeded to the trustees.

As already intimated, the seminary is under the control of the Baptist denomination and aims to assist in providing a thoroughly educated, reverent, conservative, consecrated ministry for the home and foreign field. The trustees, twenty-five in number, appointed by the state convention, with provision for additional members to be appointed by other southwestern state conventions, constitute the governing body, but the internal management is almost entirely in the hands of the faculty.

The charter provides also for a Woman's Training School, and provision has been made for the immediate inauguration of this department of work, the seminary professors being the chief instructors, and a number of special courses by other lecturers having been arranged for. The number of students enrolled for the session 1909–10 was 201. With few exceptions the students are Baptists, though the institution is freely open to Christian students of all evangelical denominations. Thirteen states and four foreign countries (England, Persia, Portugal, and Mexico) were represented in the student body. Besides the Fort Worth building lots mentioned above, a cash endowment of over $200,000 and a considerable sustentation fund have been subscribed through the efforts of Drs. Carroll and Scarborough, and others.   A. H. NEWMAN.

9. Virginia Union: This school, which is, properly speaking, the theological department of Virginia Union University, is located at Richmond, Va., and is a union of three schools established for freedmen immediately after the Civil War: Dr. Edward Turney's school, opened in Washington, D. C., in 1865, and sustained for the most part by the National Theological Institute and University; Wayland Seminary, opened in Washington, D. C., in 1866 by the American Baptist Home Mission Society, and united with Dr. Turney's school in 1869 under the name of Wayland Seminary and under the presidency of Dr. G. M. P. King; and a school in Richmond, Va., first conducted for a year (1865–66) by Dr. J. G. Binney under the American Baptist Home Mission Society, reopened in 1867 by Dr. Nathaniel Colver under the National Theological Institute and University, but transferred to the American Baptist Home Mission Society in 1869, presided over for thirty years (1868–98) by Dr. Charles H. Corey, and called successively Colver Institute (1867–76), Richmond Institute (1876–86), and Richmond Theological Seminary (1886–99). In 1899 it was united with Wayland Seminary under the name of Virginia Union University, and entered a group of fine granite buildings on the northern borders of Richmond. Gen. T. J. Morgan, Secretary of the American Baptist Home Mission Society, and Dr. Malcolm McVicar, the first president of the university, were the chief agents in securing the union of the schools and the erection of the buildings.

All three original schools were established primarily for the training of negro preachers, and secondarily for the training of other negro Christian workers, especially teachers. The very elementary instruction of the early years was gradually supplemented by more and more advanced studies, secular and theological, until in 1897 Wayland Seminary began regular work in a Bachelor-of-Arts course, and in 1886 Richmond Theological Seminary limited itself entirely to students for the ministry, and inaugurated a full three-years' theological course, although a very elementary ministers' course, extending over two years, is still provided for those who can not prepare for a more thorough course. An English theological course, and a full theological course, including Hebrew and Greek interpretation, are also given.

The institution stands for a moral, intelligent, evangelical Christian ministry among the negroes. It aims to give the negro preacher who is prepared for it practically the same theological training as that which is given to white men, believing that a broad and thorough education will be needed by the religious leaders to meet all kinds of errors, to guide the people to a higher life, and to win the respect of the increasingly intelligent young negro people.

A board of sixteen trustees, about equally divided between Northern white men, Southern white men, and negroes, controls the school. The theological department has five professors, whose salaries are partly paid by an endowment of about $85,000, the American Baptist Home Mission Society paying the rest. Of the university library of 12,000 books, about 7,000 may be said to belong to the theological department. The students enrolled in 1910 number thirty, and there are seventy others in the university looking forward to the ministry who have not yet entered upon their theological course. About 1,000 negro preachers have received their training in this school from 1865 to 1910. GEORGE RICE HOVEY.

BIBLIOGRAPHY: C. H. Corey, *Reminiscenses of Thirty Years' Labor in the South*, Richmond, Va., 1895; *Jubilee Volume of the American Baptist Publication Society*, New York, n.d.

II. Free Baptist.—1. Hillsdale: This seminary forms one of the departments of Hillsdale College, situated in Hillsdale, Mich. It was founded in 1870, and is affiliated with the Free Baptist denomination. In 1869 the Free Baptist Education Society gave to Hillsdale College the sum of $17,000, on condition that a theological department be organized in accord with certain requirements accompanying the gift, and these stipulations having been satisfactorily met upon the part of the board of trustees, the seminary was opened on Sept. 1, 1870. The principal agent in its foundation was the Rev. Ransom Dunn (q.v.), and he and the Rev. J. J. Butler were the first teachers. From the time of its establishment until the present the department has been continuously at work, and with no little degree of success, when one considers the small amount of its endowment and the relative size of its denominational constituency. It has strengthened its courses of study, has disbursed thousands of dollars to needy students, and has imparted instruction to hundreds of young men. The department stands for the cultivation of the moral and spiritual life on a foundation of thorough scholarship and efficient Christian service. Believing that the Bible is the supreme source for the religious life, the department aims to make its students earnest, devout, and scholarly interpreters of the word. At the same time, recognizing the activity of the Spirit of God in the history of the world, this source of divine truth is not neglected in the endeavor to trace the unfolding purpose of God, all of which helps the student better to solve the problem of to-day in the light of history. Mere acquisition is considered of less value than training and a correct method, and the class work is conducted with a view to interest the student in independent investigation and to develop a capacity for it.

The department has exerted a wide-spread and highly beneficial influence upon the Free Baptist denomination. Its graduates are found as pastors of many of the most influential churches of the denomination, and more than half of the Free Baptist workers in the mission fields are graduates of Hillsdale, while a considerable number of its alumni are to be found in important positions in other denominations. Prominent among its instructors have been the Rev. Ransom Dunn, the Rev. J. J. Butler, the Rev. A. T. Salley, the Rev. Charles D. Dudley, and the Rev. J. S. Copp; and its present corps of instructors is composed of the Rev. Delavan B. Reed, the Rev. J. T. Ward, and the Rev. Leroy Waterman. The seminary is under the supervision of thirty-five trustees, assisted by a theological advisory board of nine, nominated by the executive committee of the General Conference of Free Baptists and elected by the trustees. In 1910 the number of students was twenty-six, coming from New York, Ohio, Wisconsin, and Michigan, and including, besides Free Baptists, Methodists, United Brethren, and Congregationalists. The endowment is about $83,000, and the library contains some 2,000 volumes, the students also having access to the general college library of 17,000 volumes.

DELAVAN B. REED.

III. Congregational.—1. Andover: In the year 1807 a plan was formed for the establishment of a theological seminary in Andover, Mass., which should be connected with Phillips Academy, where for years students had been trained for the ministry by resident pastors. While the projectors of this school were maturing their plans, they heard of another and similar institution which was to be established at Newbury, less than twenty miles distant. Eliphalet Pearson (q.v.) was most prominent among the promoters of the Andover institution, and Samuel Spring (q.v.) among the Newbury group; the Andover men were " moderate Calvinists," so called, and the Newbury men styled themselves " consistent Calvinists," though they were usually called " Hopkinsians." It was so obviously undesirable that two Calvinistic theological schools should be founded so near together that efforts were at once made to combine them, and after prolonged struggles a union of the two projects was effected. To provide a theological platform for the seminary, the two parties united in a creed, representing in its modifications from the Westminster Assembly's

Catechism a compromise of the two wings of Calvinism, and destined to constitute what has been known as the Andover theology. This creed has remained unaltered from the first, but since 1900 formal subscription to it has not been demanded of the professors, either at their inauguration or at five-year intervals, as formerly. The seminary was established at Andover, as a branch of Phillips Academy, and under the management of its Board of Trustees; and a Board of Visitors was established which should represent the theological views and protect the interests of the Associate Founders, as the Newbury men were called. At the formal opening, Sept. 28, 1808, thirty-six students were in attendance, and the summary of the attendance during one hundred years is as follows: graduates in the regular course, 2,170; non-graduates, 1,066; students in the special course (1869–82), 45; resident licentiates, 509; advanced class (1882–93), 108; graduate students (1901–07), 11; or a total of 3,538 students, of whom 1,082 are supposed to be living. Of the total number, 3,031 were ordained, 2,378 of them as Congregationalists, 373 as Presbyterians. Foreign missionaries numbered 247; college presidents, 96; college professors, 271; seminary professors, 132. The seminary, always holding graduation from college as a condition of graduation, has made exception only in the cases of ninety-nine men. A special examination of the figures of the second fifty years shows that three-fourths of the graduates of that period, entering the service of the churches as pastors, remained directly and technically in their service for life, or until the present. Including the professions for which a seminary training is the natural preparation, ninety-five per cent of the graduates have carried out faithfully the purpose which brought them to the seminary. Since the year 1899, the degree of S.T.B. has been conferred upon the graduates.

The list of the faculty contains many noted names, some of which may be mentioned. Eliphalet Pearson was the first professor of sacred literature, but only for a year (trustee until 1826). Leonard Woods (q.v.) was the first professor of theology, holding the position for thirty-eight years, and his theological attitude and personal influence were important factors in securing the union of the two enterprises at the outset. Other well-known names of men now deceased are Moses Stuart (q.v.), Edward Robinson (q.v.), Bela Bates Edwards (q.v.), Calvin Ellis Stowe (q.v.), Elijah Porter Barrows, and Joseph Henry Thayer (q.v.), in the department of Biblical literature; Edwards A. Park (q.v.) in theology; in history, James Murdock (q.v.), Ralph Emerson, William G. T. Shedd (q.v.), and Egbert Coffin Smyth; and in sacred rhetoric, Edward Dorr Griffin (q.v.), Ebenezer Porter (q.v.), Thomas Harvey Skinner (q.v.), Austin Phelps (q.v.), and Charles Orrin Day (q.v.). Prof. J. Wesley Churchill, serving the seminary for thirty years in the department of elocution, occupied a unique and enviable position among teachers of his art. The history of the seminary has been identified with many religious and philanthropic movements of the country. The students' secret missionary society, " The Brethren," and the insistent zeal of Judson, Newell, Nott, and

Hall had prominent place in the organization of the A. B. C. F. M., while the American (now Congregational) Education Society, the American Temperance Society, the American (now Congregational) Home Missionary Society, the American Tract Society, the Andover House (now the South End House, a social settlement in Boston), and the plan for the first religious newspaper in the U. S., had their origin in whole or in large part on Andover Hill. The Andover press was noted for nearly a century in the publication of religious works. The *American Biblical Repository* was published here from 1831 to 1838, and the *Bibliotheca Sacra* from 1844 to 1883; and the *Andover Review* was edited by Andover professors during the ten years of its publication, 1884–93.

In the eighties there were several changes in the faculty, and prolonged theological controversies, involving questions as to the prerogatives of the Board of Visitors in the administration of the seminary. The legal questions were carried to the supreme court of the commonwealth in a protracted trial, and the controversies extended, in a train of deplorable results, to the relation of the seminary and its students to the churches, and especially to the A. B. C. F. M. During the same decade, and later, the classes became very uneven, with marked diminution in numbers, until from 1900 (when several other faculty changes occurred) they numbered no more than six men. It became increasingly difficult to secure men to fill the vacancies in the teaching force, for reasons obvious from the recital above, and from the isolated situation of the seminary. After prolonged deliberation covering several years, and in the exercise of powers expressly vested in the trustees, in the year 1908 the seminary was removed to Cambridge. Already in 1907 the general feeling on the part of friends of academy and seminary, that the interests of both schools demanded separate boards of control, had led to the incorporation of the seminary as a separate institution, with gradual changes in the membership of the board of trustees. The extensive, though somewhat antiquated, plant at Andover was readily sold to the academy, which needed the buildings.

The relations established between Harvard University and the seminary, and especially between the divinity school and the seminary, are as novel and as interesting as was the establishment of the seminary a century previous. The terms of affiliation provide for the maintenance of the seminary as a separate organization, with its own trustees, faculty, buildings, registration of students, catalogue, and degrees. The two institutions agree to avoid rivalry and unnecessary duplication, and to develop the resources of each in such way as to offer to students the best possible training. Vacancies in the faculty have been filled, and a building is in process of erection, to be occupied in 1911. More recent negotiations in the spirit of the terms of affiliation provide for the combination of the libraries of the two schools in the new Andover building, as the Andover-Harvard Theological Library, comprising at the outset over 100,000 volumes.

OWEN H. GATES.

2. Atlanta: This divinity school is situated in the

southern suburbs of Atlanta, Ga., with a beautiful campus of thirteen acres on the crown of a large hill overlooking the city. It was founded in 1901, when a company of ministers, under the lead of the Rev. Frank E. Jenkins, purchased the property that has since been its home. The institution was established, and has since been sustained, by the Congregationalists, although its privileges have always been offered, without charge, to all denominations. Funds for its maintenance have come largely from the North, and its control is in the hands of a board of trustees, thirty in number. During the first four years, Rev. J. Edward Kirbye was its president; and from the beginning leading educators of the South have been represented among its teachers. At present (1910) there are forty-one men enrolled, coming from a dozen states, and eight are to be graduated, from as many commonwealths. The seminary-extension work has increased in even larger measure, this being an effort to reach by home-study students who can not attend. The library of 10,000 volumes is free to all teachers and pastors in the South, the beneficiaries paying postage. An effort is being made to increase the endowment, now amounting to $10,000. The faculty consists of five professors, the Rev. E. Lyman Hood being president. Their purpose is to train consecrated men to become spiritual interpreters of the Scriptures, forceful preachers of the Gospel, and helpful pastors of the churches.   E. LYMAN HOOD.

3. Bangor: Bangor Theological Seminary is located in Bangor, Penobscot Co., Me., and was chartered by Massachusetts in 1814. The persons named in the charter as trustees were Revs. John Sawyer, Kiah Bailey, Eliphalet Gillet, William Jenks, Mighill Blood, Asa Lyman, David Thurston, Harvey Loomis, Hon. Ammi R. Mitchell, and Samuel E. Dutton. The first president of this board was Rev. Edward Payson (q.v.), and the first instructors were Mr. Jehudi Ashmun (afterward colonial agent in Liberia) and Rev. Abijah Wines. The seminary was designed to provide an evangelical ministry for the state (then the district) of Maine, for at that time Andover was the only other Congregational seminary in existence, and it could not supply the needs of the region. Bangor Seminary was originally located at Hampden, but in 1819 it was removed five miles up the Penobscot River to its present location. During the ninety-four years of its existence the seminary has sent out 879 graduates and has educated, for one or more years, 300 other students. It has numbered among its instructors men eminent for piety, scholarship, and influence. Not to name any still living, mention may be made of Enoch Pond (q.v.), to whom, more than to any other man, the success of the institution was due, who for fifty years was connected with it as professor and president; Dr. Pond's successor in the chair of history, Levi L. Paine (q.v.), a stimulating master of his classroom; the scholarly Leonard Woods, Jr. (q.v.), afterward president of Bowdoin College; and his successor in teaching Biblical literature, Daniel Smith Talcott, a ripe scholar; George Shepard, eminent as a pulpit orator; Samuel Harris (q.v.), who began his career of teaching theology by twelve years of instruction in Bangor; and Lewis

F. Stearns (q.v.), a worthy occupant of the same chair, whose early death was a loss to the country at large. The names just given indicate that, although the seminary is Congregational, it has never been partizan in spirit. Its position is fairly comprehensive, as indicated by the denominations represented by its student body. According to its latest catalogue, of its 44 students, 28 were Congregational, 11 Methodist, 2 Baptist, 2 Presbyterian, and 1 Lutheran, and of these 31 came from the United States, 7 from Canada, 3 from Great Britain, 1 from Macedonia, 1 from Asia Minor, and 1 from Japan. At present its staff numbers 7 professors, 5 giving instruction, 2 instructors, and 7 lecturers, and it is governed by a self-perpetuating board of trustees, whose number is usually fifteen. It has productive funds amounting to $300,000, and the value of the buildings is set at $100,000, while its library numbers more than 27,000 volumes.   F. B. DENIO.

BIBLIOGRAPHY: E. Pond, *Historical Address,* Bangor, Me., 1870; *Historical Catalogue,* Bangor, Me., 1901.

4. Chicago: The Chicago Theological Seminary, located at 20 North Ashland Boulevard, Chicago, Ill., was organized Sept. 27, 1857, by delegates from Congregational churches in Michigan, Indiana, Illinois, Iowa, Wisconsin, and Missouri, was incorporated Feb. 15, 1855, and began work Oct. 6, 1858. Its full corporate name is "The Board of Directors of the Chicago Theological Seminary." Among the names of its founders were Stephen Peet, Philo Carpenter, Truman Post, A. S. Kedzie, and G. S. F. Savage, and the earliest professors were Joseph Haven, Samuel C. Bartlett (q.v.), and Franklin W. Fisk. Among their successors were G. N. Boardman (q.v.), S. I. Curtiss (q.v.), H. M. Scott (q.v.), E. T. Harper, and W. D. Mackenzie (q.v.), while among the present professors are President Ozora S. Davis, Graham Taylor (q.v.), C. A. Beckwith (q.v.), and F. W. Gunsaulus (q.v.). The institution is organized as the seminary and its institutes, and its administration consists of the triennial convention, the board of directors, the faculty, the board of instruction (consisting of all regularly appointed teachers in the institution and the librarian), and the board of examiners. The seminary is unique in its relation to the churches of the Middle West, since it has continued to be governed as at first by a Triennial Convention, composed of delegates from each of the sixteen states west of Ohio and east of the Rocky Mountains, and including the board of directors and the faculty. The Triennial Convention elects the twenty-four directors who are chosen for six years, half appointed each three years, from members of the Congregational or other evangelical churches within the constituency. The faculty are elected by the board of directors, while the board of examiners are appointed annually from the same states which send delegates to the Triennial Convention. Associated with the seminary are three institutes: German, established 1882, Danish-Norwegian, founded 1884, and Swedish, begun in 1885, all of which were reorganized as institutes in 1893, their aim being to provide a trained ministry for foreign-speaking peoples. In 1902 the Chicago School of Church Music was established, to give practical training in the conduct of music in public worship, and in 1909 the Department of Seminary Extension was organized, which, through correspondence and lectures, offers training in theological study to ministers and others. The plant consists of Fisk Hall, with administration offices, lecture-rooms, parlor and reception room, dormitories, and gymnasium; Keyes Hall, with lecture-rooms and dormitories; Carpenter Memorial Chapel and Hall with music and other rooms; and Hammond Library. The library contains 30,000 volumes, collections on Egyptology and on the rise of Congregationalism, and a museum of Christian antiquity, while within easy access of the students are the city libraries, aggregating 900,000 volumes.

As defined by its charter of incorporation, the aim of the seminary is " to furnish instruction and the means of education to young men preparing for the Gospel ministry, and . . . be equally open to all denominations of Christians " for this purpose. Accordingly, the seminary is a high-grade institution providing training along approved lines to meet the demands of the churches for an educated ministry. Located in the heart of a great cosmopolitan city, it offers through its department of social economics an unequaled opportunity for first-hand observation of actual conditions and for personal conferences with specialists at work. Under the leadership of the head of the department of social economics is the Chicago Commons, a settlement for social and civic betterment, and the Chicago School of Civics and Philanthropy. In 1910 there were 24 directors and 2 honorary directors, 2 professors emeritus, 21 instructors and teachers, and 72 students, while in addition there were 43 students in seminary extension courses. The institution has a productive endowment of about $800,000.   C. A. BECKWITH.

5. Hartford: Hartford Theological Seminary, which until 1885 was entitled " The Theological Institute of Connecticut," the fourth Congregational seminary established in the United States, was founded in 1834 at East Windsor Hill, Conn., the organizing body being a voluntary association known as the Pastoral Union of Connecticut, and the leading spirit in the enterprise being Rev. Bennet Tyler (q.v.), who served as first president until 1857. In 1865 the institution was removed to Hartford, where, after a period in temporary quarters, in 1879 it received from Mr. James B. Hosmer the gift of its present large and convenient buildings, including chapel, recitation-rooms, dormitories, etc., besides a separate gymnasium. To the main building, Hosmer Hall, was added in 1893 a superior fireproof library building, the gift of Mr. Newton Case, and called, in memory of his wife, the Case Memorial Library. The government of the seminary is in the hands of thirty trustees, one-third chosen annually for three years, elected by the Pastoral Union. This latter body is self-perpetuating, and comprises about 175 ministers (not limited to Connecticut or to Congregationalists), who, with the trustees and the professors, give assent to the creed which is part of the constitution of the Union.

The present faculty (1911) includes eleven full professors, the librarian, two associate professors, and nine instructors. Since 1900 the curriculum has been arranged under five main groups of prescribed studies, varied so as to give emphasis respectively to the Old Testament, the New Testament, church history, systematic theology, and practical theology, and amounting in each case to two-thirds of the 1,260 hours required for graduation; the remaining one-third is open to elective choice from a very large list of courses in all departments. Since 1901 the Hartford School of Religious Pedagogy (see RELIGIOUS PEDAGOGY, HARTFORD SCHOOL OF) has been closely affiliated with the seminary, and many of its courses are taken by seminary students. Instruction is provided, especially in polity, to students of other denominations than the Congregational, and among many lectures annually given are those provided by the Carew Foundation, on various subjects, and those on the Hartford-Lamson Foundation, on the religions of the world. There are two fellowships for foreign study, and two for graduate study at Hartford. The library at present (1911) numbers about 95,000 volumes and over 50,000 pamphlets, being specially strong in apparatus for textual criticism, patristics, Reformation history, Arabic and other Semitic literatures, missions of every class, liturgics, hymnology, current periodicals, etc., so that it is one of the largest and most serviceable theological libraries in the world. The seminary is the custodian of the large missionary and ethnological museum of the American Board of Foreign Missions, which, with its own valuable collections, is adequately arranged for study. The total number of full graduates (to 1910) is 676, besides about 285 who have taken less than the full course. About 75 of the more than 550 living alumni are engaged in foreign missions. Since 1889 women have been admitted on the same terms as men, going forth as missionaries, Bible teachers in colleges, leaders in Y. W. C. A. work, and the like. The present roll of students numbers 65, including 5 fellows and 10 graduate students.

After the resignation of President Tyler in 1857 the leadership of the institution devolved upon Prof. William Thompson (q.v.) as dean of the faculty, until in 1888 Prof. Chester D. Hartranft (q.v.) was made president. He continued in office for twenty-five years, profoundly stimulating the entire life of the institution by his varied scholarship, his lofty ideals, and his practical enthusiasm. In 1903 he was succeeded by Dr. William Douglas Mackenzie (q.v.), who came from Chicago Theological Seminary, and immediately proved himself a worthy successor. Among the professors who have won distinction by long service, and usually through publication as well as instruction, are the following:—Bennet Tyler, 1834–57 (systematics), William Thompson, 1834–81 (Hebrew), Robert G. Vermilye, 1858–75 (systematics), Matthew B. Riddle (q.v.), 1871–87 (New Testament), Chester D. Hartranft, 1878–1903 (history), Edwin C. Bissell (q.v.), 1880–92 (Hebrew), Ernest C. Richardson (q.v.), 1883–90 (librarian), Williston Walker (q.v.), 1889–1901 (history), Alfred T. Perry, 1890–1900 (librarian), and, of those in the present faculty who have served ten years or more, Waldo S. Pratt (q.v.), from 1882 (music and hymnology), Clark S. Beardslee (q.v.), from 1888 (Biblical dogmatics and homiletics), Arthur L.

Gillett, from 1888 (apologetics), Melanchthon W. Jacobus (q.v.), from 1891 (New Testament), Edwin K. Mitchell, from 1892 (early church history), Alexander R. Merriam (q.v.), from 1892 (homiletics and sociology), Lewis B. Paton (q.v.), from 1892 (Old-Testament literature), Duncan B. Macdonald (q.v.), from 1892 (Semitic languages), Edward E. Nourse (q.v.), from 1895 (Biblical theology), and Curtis M. Geer, from 1900 (history).

The only general catalogue of the alumni is one issued in 1881, which naturally includes accounts of the earlier graduates only. There is no general history of the seminary, but at the fiftieth anniversary, in 1884, there was published a *Memorial of the Semi-Centenary Celebration of the Founding of the Theological Institute of Connecticut*, which contains considerable historical matter. In 1890 the *Hartford Seminary Record* began to be issued, at first as a bimonthly, and later as a quarterly, under the editorship of a committee of the faculty; this periodical, which completed its twentieth volume in 1910, regularly contains a large number of articles on theological, critical, and practical topics, and also includes much information about the current life of the institution and of its alumni. In connection with the seventy-fifth anniversary in 1909 a sort of *Festschrift* was published under the editorship of Prof. L. B. Paton, with the title *Recent Christian Progress* (New York), to which trustees, professors, and alumni of the seminary contributed a series of over eighty succinct summaries of the advances in all principal branches of theological scholarship and practical effort since 1834. The annual series of Hartford-Lamson Lectures is also being published in uniform style.   WALDO S. PRATT.

6. Oberlin: Oberlin Theological Seminary is the post-graduate department of Oberlin College, the term " College " being used to cover all the work of the various departments of the institution. It is located in Oberlin, Lorain Co., O., and was founded in 1833 by the first settlers of the town, who proposed to found at the same time both a town and a college. The college, including the theological seminary, has never had organic connection with any ecclesiastical organization, although during most of its history it has been associated more largely with Congregationalists than with the members of any other denomination. The purpose of its founders was to establish a Christian institution for the evangelization of the Mississippi Valley and the regions beyond, and the originators of the idea were Rev. John J. Shipherd, pastor of the Presbyterian church of Elyria, O., and Philo P. Stewart, who had been a missionary to the Indians in Mississippi. The first president was Asa Mahan (q.v.), and the earliest instructors in the theological seminary were Charles G. Finney (q.v.), John Morgan, John P. Cowles, Henry Cowles (q.v.), and the president. The original plan of the founders in 1833 included a theological department, a scheme which was unexpectedly developed in 1835 by the arrival of a considerable number of students from Lane Theological Seminary in Cincinnati, who brought with them Professor Morgan, and induced Charles G. Finney to come from New York City to be their professor of theology. The seminary was very early open

to all races and to both sexes. Largely through the influence of President Finney, its life has been characterized by keen interest in the philosophical aspects of theology, together with a deep and constant devotion to practical evangelism, and large numbers of its graduates have been missionaries. During anti-slavery days Oberlin was so strongly committed to the anti-slavery movement that its graduates were not acceptable to the board of foreign missions that would naturally have commissioned its missionary graduates. Consequently there was founded in Oberlin a missionary organization which later merged with others to form the American Missionary Association, and for many years the latter drew largely upon Oberlin students for its teachers and preachers. In the early decades of its history the theology of Oberlin was considered radical, and its general trend has always been what its friends like to call " progressive orthodoxy."

The following are the teachers whose terms of service were longest, not including those now actively connected with the work of the seminary: Charles G. Finney, John Morgan, Asa Mahan, Henry Cowles, James H. Fairchild (q.v.), Elijah P. Barrows, Henry E. Peck, Judson Smith (q.v.), Hiram Mead, Albert H. Currier, George F. Wright (q.v.), William B. Chamberlain, William G. Ballantine (q.v.), Frank H. Foster (q.v.), and Owen H. Gates, while among those connected with the faculty for shorter periods were John Henry Barrows (q.v.), George S. Burroughs, and Julius A. Bewer. At present (1911) Henry Churchill King (q.v.) is president of the college and professor of systematic theology in the theological seminary. The seminary has eight professors, and in addition has the use of certain courses in the College of Arts and Sciences; twenty-four trustees (who act for all departments); and eighty students, including ten in the Slavic department, which trains preachers for the Slavic peoples in the United States. These students, who are members of fifteen denominations, come as graduates from forty-one colleges, and represent nineteen states and four foreign countries. The theological library is a part of the general library of the college, which numbers about 200,000 bound and unbound volumes. The seminary shares in the general endowment of the college, which amounts to about $2,000,000 of productive endowment and $1,000,000 invested in grounds and buildings, while the amount of productive endowment specifically set apart for the seminary is about $400,000. The seminary is governed by its faculty, whose action is subject to the approval of the general faculty of the entire college, while in certain cases its authority is limited to the power of recommendation to the general council of the college and to the board of trustees.   EDWARD INCREASE BOSWORTH.

BIBLIOGRAPHY: J. H. Fairchild, *Oberlin, its Origin, Progress, and Results*, Oberlin, 1871, and *Oberlin, the Colony and the College*, ib., 1883; D. L. Leonard, *Story of Oberlin*, Boston, 1898; W. G. Ballantine, ed., *Oberlin Jubilee 1833–83*, ib., 1884.

7. Pacific: This theological seminary is located in Berkeley, Alameda Co., Cal., the seat of the state university, and originated in view of the difficulty of obtaining an educated ministry sufficient in numbers and adapted to meet the conditions of a new country. Effort was first made by a number of leading Congregationalists to secure an interdenominational institution; but this plan failed, and a denominational institution was projected, among its notable founders being Rev. J. A. Benton, Rev. George Mooar, Rev. I. E. Dwinell, Rev. W. C. Pond, Mr. Edward Coleman, Dr. J. C. Holbrook, Mr. Edward Smith, and Mr. Enos Sargent. The foundations were laid by the General Association of the Congregational Churches of California, in 1866, in which year a theological association was incorporated, a board of trustees elected, and the beginning of an endowment secured. In 1869 Rev. J. A. Benton assumed the first professorship, and instructional work opened in San Francisco, and in 1871 a spacious property was secured in Oakland. In 1870 Rev. George Mooar was elected professor, and in 1884 Rev. Israel E. Dwinell. In 1901 the seminary moved to Berkeley and was established beside the state university. During the earlier period of its history the seminary was chiefly distinguished by the personalities of its three leading instructors, Drs. Benton, Mooar, and Dwinell, men of unusual strength of character, breadth of culture, and influence. In 1894 Rev. John Knox McLean was elected president, and under his administration the seminary has advanced chiefly in the line of higher standards of scholarship and of more efficient service to the churches and the community, an important factor in this direction being the establishment of the E. T. Earl Lectureship, through which men of wide reputation and influence have made important contributions to the thought and life of the Pacific Coast. Among the most significant acts in its life is the seminary's unreserved committal to the policy of close affiliation with the life of the university, thereby influencing other denominations to take the same step, and thus creating a circle of theological schools closely cooperating with one another and affording opportunity for broad and varied theological education. Four institutions are now associated with Pacific Seminary, representing the Congregational, Disciple, Baptist, and Unitarian denominations.

Prominent among the instructors of Pacific Seminary have been Prof. Frank H. Foster (q.v.), now of Olivet, Mich.; Prof. Charles Sumner Nash, since 1891 professor of homiletics; Prof. John Wright Buckham; and Prof. William Frederic Bade. The institution has at present the largest number of students and most promising outlook in its history. It has a faculty of five professors and three instructors, and an associate faculty consisting of professors in the university and in other seminaries, beside two annual lecturers. It has a governing board of sixteen trustees, of which the president of the seminary is ex-officio president, and it has forty-six students, of whom sixteen come from affiliated seminaries. The creedal affiliations of the students are: Congregationalists 22, Baptists 13, Methodists 4, Presbyterians 2, Disciples 2, Unitarian 1, Episcopalian 1, and Mennonite 1. The Seminary has an endowment of $528,000 and a library of 10,000 volumes.

JOHN KNOX McLEAN.

8. Yale: Yale Divinity School is a coordinate department of Yale University, located in New Haven, Conn., and is undenominational in character. It was organized as a distinct school of the university in 1822, though one main purpose of Yale from its foundation, in 1701, had been training for the ministry, and definite graduate instruction had been given since the establishment of a professorship of divinity in Yale College in 1755. The earliest professors of the divinity school were Nathaniel W. Taylor (q.v.), Eleazar T. Fitch, Josiah Willard Gibbs, Chauncey A. Goodridge, and James L. Kingsley, the four first named constituting its faculty for more than thirty years. The school was founded in a period of wide-spread theological discussion, in which its first professor of theology, Nathaniel W. Taylor, was a leader. It represented the modified Edwardsean Calvinism known as the "New Haven Theology." Originally well attended, the deaths of its early instructors and the scanty endowment of the school led to a great diminution in the number of its students; still it renewed its strength during the period from 1858 to 1870 by the growth of a new faculty, eminent in which were Timothy Dwight (q.v.), George P. Fisher (q.v.), Leonard Bacon (q.v.), and George E. Day, to whom Samuel Harris (q.v.) was soon after added. Under their leadership large increase in endowment was obtained, the present buildings of the school were begun, in 1870, and the number of students rapidly and permanently grew. The theological position of the school now became broadly and progressively mediating. Without being controversial, as in the earlier period, the school emphasized, and has continued to illustrate, an earnest evangelical type of faith, in hearty sympathies with what it deems the more progressive developments of theological and Biblical science in this country and in Europe.

The course of study was originally three years, the successful completion of which has led, since 1866, to the degree of Bachelor of Divinity. Since 1879 a fourth-year study has been offered, and constantly increasing cooperation with other departments of the university, notably the graduate school, has led to a great broadening of the field of instruction. In 1910, the school was divided into four departments, each having a specific type of Christian activity in view—those of pastoral service, missionary service, religious education, and practical philanthropy. The school stands for efficient practical training, thorough scholarship, and untrammeled investigation of truth. It is under the conduct of the Corporation of Yale University, by which its instructors are appointed and its interests administered, though its immediate government is by the faculty. At the present time (1910) it is served by eleven professors, three instructors, and six lecturers, with the cooperation of twenty-three additional instructors more immediately connected with other departments of the university. There are 106 regular students enrolled in the school, and 131 under instruction. Of the regular students Connnecticut is the home of 35, Massachusetts of 6, Nebraska of 7, Canada of 5, Ohio of 5, Indiana, Wisconsin, and Pennsylvania of 4 each, Turkey of 3, Georgia, Maryland, Missouri, New Hampshire,

New Jersey, New York, Virginia, Tennessee, and Sweden of 2 each, while one student each is from Alabama, Arkansas, British Guiana, England, Illinois, Iowa, Italy, Japan, Michigan, Minnesota, Mississippi, North Carolina, Oregon, West Virginia, and Washington. Its students represent a wide variety of Protestant religious bodies, though a majority are Congregationalists, as might be expected from the historic affiliations of the school. The endowment amounts to about $833,000. The library is principally merged in that of Yale University, though the separate departmental collections of the school, largely of the nature of a working reference library, contain 18,500 volumes.

WILLISTON WALKER.

BIBLIOGRAPHY: *The Semi-Centennial Anniversary of the Divinity School of Yale College*, New Haven, 1872; W. L. Kingsley, *Yale College*, New York, 1879, ii. 15–60.

IV. Disciples of Christ.—1. Bible College: The College of the Bible, affiliated with the Disciples (Christian) Church, and the oldest theological seminary of that body, is located in Lexington, Fayette Co., Ky. It was founded in 1865 as a department of Kentucky University (now Transylvania University), but in 1875 it was severed from that institution and was reorganized under separate management. In that year it had three professors and thirty-seven students, while it has now (1910) a faculty of seven professors, and during the session of 1909–10 enrolled 180 students, of whom nine were women. It was founded by Robert Milligan and John W. McGarvey (q.v.), the former of whom was its first president, while at the time of its reorganization Robert Graham became its president, and he, John W. McGarvey, and Isaiah B. Grubbs constituted its faculty. The institution is devoted entirely to the training of preachers, missionaries, and religious workers, and has exerted a wide influence, more than half of the prominent preachers of the Disciples Church having received instruction in its classrooms. Its students during the session of 1909–10 came from twenty-two states of the United States and from England, Japan, Canada, Denmark, and Australia. Its present faculty is John W. McGarvey, president; Isaiah B. Grubbs, professor emeritus; W. C. Morro, dean, and professor of Christian history and doctrine; Benj. C. Dewesse, professor of Biblical introduction and exegesis; Samuel M. Jefferson, professor of philosophy; Hall L. Calhoun, professor of Hebrew and Old Testament; and Wm. F. Smith, professor of Bible-school pedagogy. It has eighteen trustees, all of whom are members of the church with which the institution is affiliated. Its present profit-bearing endowment is $175,000, with an additional $100,000 not now yielding the institution an income, but which will be available within the next few years. It now has a library of 4,000 volumes.

WILLIAM C. MORRO.

BIBLIOGRAPHY: J. W. McGarvey, *The College of the Bible*, Lexington, Ky., 1905.

2. Drake: This seminary, located at Des Moines, Ia., and founded in 1881, forms part of Drake University, which, although considered undenominational, was built up and is supported by the Disciples of Christ. It had its origin in an unsuccessful attempt to remove the denominational school known as Oskaloosa College from Oskaloosa, Ia., to Des Moines, and it owed its foundation chiefly to the late Gov. F. M. Drake, aided by his brother-in-law, George T. Carpenter (formerly president of Oskaloosa College), and D. R. Lucas, then pastor of the Central Church, Des Moines. The early instructors in the seminary were George T. Carpenter and Norman Dunshee, and its student body has grown until in 1910 it reached nearly 175. Drake Seminary stands for a thorough knowledge of the Bible and all lines of Christian work, and maintains that denominationalism is an abnormal condition, contrary to New-Testament standards. While it does not see its way clear to follow the so-called assured results of modern Biblical study, it criticizes extreme conservatism, and strives to reconstruct the old lines of thought with the purpose of eliminating errors and incorporating new truth. Probably the most important movement connected with the seminary is the Bell Bennett Mission (so named from an intending foreign missionary student, who was accidentally drowned), which has been instrumental in sending out many to the foreign mission field. Among the more prominent of the seminary's instructors, besides the two already mentioned, are Dr. D. R. Dungan, B. J. Radford, A. I. Hobbs, Robert Mathews, H. W. Everest, Oscar Morgan, Dr. Clinton Lockhart, Walter Stairs, A. D. Veatch, Sherman Kirk, Dr. F. O. Norton, W. S. Athearn, and A. M. Haggard. In 1910 the seminary had five instructors, and its trustees, about twenty in number, were the same as those of the university. The government of the seminary consists of a dean, responsible to the president of the university, who, in turn, is responsible to the board of trustees. The larger number of the students are from Iowa, Missouri, and the neighboring states, and eight or ten usually come each year from the Pacific Coast, as well as from Colorado. In 1910 there were about thirty students from Australia and New Zealand, about ten from England, six or eight from the Philippines, and a few from Canada, China, and Japan. As a rule other denominations than the Disciples are represented among the student body. The endowment fund amounts to $100,000.

ALFRED MARTIN HAGGARD.

3. Eugene: Eugene Bible University (known, until 1908, as "Eugene Divinity School"), located at Eugene, Lane Co., Ore., was founded by Eugene C. Sanderson in 1895, largely through the generosity of Judge J. W. Cowles and Hon. T. G. Hendricks. Its first instructors were Eugene C. Sanderson and Morton L. Rose. The institution was opened in a rented building, Oct. 6, 1895, but within a year the foundation of the Bushnell Library had been laid and land had been purchased, on which have been erected three buildings adjacent to the University of Oregon, with which its relations are most cordial. More recently a branch, the Pullman Bible Chair, has been established adjacent to the campus of the state college at Pullman, Wash. Besides this chair, the university comprises the Bible college, schools of music and oratory, the department of art, the chair of Bible-school science and pedagogy, and a preparatory department; and its students are also entitled to all courses offered in the University of

Oregon. The purpose of the school is to give its pupils a proficiency which shall be both scholarly and practical for all departments of Christian work. Among its more prominent instructors have been Eugene C. Sanderson, David C. Kellems, James·S. McCallum, and Ernest C. Wigmore. In 1910 the institution had, in all departments, twelve instructors. The number of trustees is nineteen, elected partly by the board in annual meeting, and partly by the denominational conventions of Oregon, Washington, and Idaho. The executive board consists of the president of the university and the president, vice-president, treasurer, and secretary of the board of trustees. The number of students has increased from seven the first year to seventy-four (117 in all departments) in 1910. The value of the school property is about $80,000, and its endowment is about $50,000, while its library contains 3,400 volumes.   J. A. BUSHNELL.

V. Evangelical Association.—1. Naperville: The Evangelical Theological Seminary is located at Naperville, Du Page Co., Ill., and was founded in 1873 as the " Union Biblical Institute," a name which it retained until 1909, when its name was changed to " The Evangelical Theological Seminary." The institution was established by several Western conferences of the Evangelical Association, Illinois taking the lead, other conferences gradually joining, until their number now is thirteen. The first principal of the seminary was Bishop J. J. Esher (1876–1879), and the senior professor, S. L. Umbach, has occupied the chair of historical and practical theology since 1878. Two courses of study are offered in the seminary: a diploma course and a degree course, the latter emphasizing the study of the Bible in the original, presupposing a college course with at least three years of preparatory Greek, and leading to the degree of B.D. In 1910 a graduate school was established under the direction of the seminary faculty. The courses offered in this school may be taken in non-residence, and on completion the degree of S.T.D. is conferred. Women desiring a theological training for Christian work of any kind or for the foreign mission field are admitted to the seminary on the same terms as men. The institution holds that theology is a growing science, and that the sources of knowledge are nature, human consciousness, and the Bible; and it maintains that, although the Bible is the ultimate authority, there is need of all the light of nature and of human reason to interpret it properly.

In 1910 the seminary had three regular professors: S. J. Gamertsfelder (principal and professor of exegetical and systematic theology), S. L. Umbach (historical and practical theology), and C. B. Bowman (apologetics and Biblical instruction); and in addition to their instruction, prominent men from this and other denominations are secured as lecturers on various subjects before the students. The institution is controlled by thirteen trustees, one from each of the annual conferences interested in the seminary, together with one member of the board of bishops of the denomination. The latter, appointed by his board, holds office for four years, the others, elected by the members of their respective conferences, for three. The number of students in 1910 was

twenty-five, five of whom were graduated at the close of the seminary year.   S. J. GAMERTSFELDER.

VI. Jewish.—1. Hebrew Union College: This institution was founded by Isaac Mayer Wise, rabbi of Congregation Bene Jeshurun, at Cincinnati, O., in 1875, after several unsuccessful attempts at creating theological schools for the Jewish communities in America had been made in Philadelphia and New York, and also in Cincinnati. Finally, convinced that only through a union of congregations could a college be permanently established which would meet the demands of progressive American Israel for American-bred rabbis imbued with the spirit of American life and liberty, Dr. Wise agitated for the formation of such a union. In 1873 the Union of American Hebrew Congregations was organized with the view of establishing an institution for the training of ministers for the Jewish pulpit and for the promotion of Jewish learning, and on Oct. 3, 1875, the Hebrew Union College was opened with an enrolment of seventeen students who formed the first preparatory class. After four years the collegiate department was opened with Dr. Moses Mielziner of New York as professor of Talmud; in 1881 a permanent home for the college was acquired and dedicated; and in 1883 the first four rabbis were graduated and ordained. Dr. Wise, the first president, remained in office until his death on Mar. 26, 1900, when Dr. Mielziner, the senior member of the faculty, was appointed to take his place. After the latter's death, and for some time during his illness, Dr. Gotthard Deutsch became the acting president. On Feb. 26, 1903, Dr. Kaufmann Kohler (q.v.) of New York was elected president with the express understanding that " the Hebrew Union College shall forever continue to be the exponent of American Reform Judaism as taught and expounded by its immortal founder, Isaac M. Wise, and his illustrious coworkers," and on Oct. 18, 1903, he was inducted into office.

The institution is administered by a Board of Governors consisting of twenty-four members (ten of whom are residents of Cincinnati), appointed by the executive board of the Union of American Hebrew Congregations. The college is composed of two departments, the preparatory, which extends over a course of four years, into which high-school students are admitted; and the collegiate, which extends over a course of five years, into which only university students or graduates admitted. Graduates from the preparatory department receive the degree of bachelor of Hebrew literature, while the rabbinical diploma is conferred upon the graduates from the collegiate department, though only after they have been graduated from the University of Cincinnati or some other university of recognized standing. The post-graduate course leads to the degree of D.D., which is also conferred *honoris causa* on theologians of distinction. The subjects taught are Hebrew and Aramaic; Bible exegesis with Hebrew commentators; Midrash and Targum; Mishnah and Talmud with some of the medieval codes; apocryphal, apocalyptic, and Hellenistic literature; Jewish philosophy, chiefly of the middle ages; Jewish liturgy; history and literature of the Jewish people from Biblical to modern times; the history of Judaism and its sects; systematic and practical theology, and comparative religion; Jewish ethics and pedagogy; homiletics and applied sociology. The faculty as at present constituted consists of the following members: Dr. Kaufmann Kohler (president and professor of theology, homiletics, and Hellenistic literature), Dr. Gotthard Deutsch (Jewish history and literature), Dr. Louis Grossmann (q.v.) ethics and pedagogy), Dr. David Neumark (Jewish philosophy), Dr. Jacob Z. Lauterbach (Talmud), Dr. Moses Buttenwieser (Biblical exegesis), Dr. Julian Morgenstern (Bible and Semitic languages), Dr. Henry Englander (Bible exegesis and Biblical history), and Dr. Boris B. Bogen (special instructor in sociology with relation to Jewish philanthropy).

The Hebrew Union College library has grown steadily from small beginnings, and now comprises about 30,000 volumes extending over the entire range of Biblical and Rabbinical Hebrew, and modern Jewish, Hellenistic, philosophical, Samaritan, Karaite, English, German, and French literature, besides periodicals and pamphlets. It includes the libraries of Dr. Samuel Adler, M. Kayserling, and others; and contains many rare editions. One hundred and thirty rabbis have been graduated from the college, most of whom occupy prominent pulpits in the various Jewish communities of America. The present college building being no longer adequate to its demands, the ground for a new college edifice and an adjoining library building has been purchased in the vicinity of the University of Cincinnati. The corner-stone has just been laid, and it is expected that by the close of the scholastic year of 1912 the two massive structures will be completed.   KAUFMANN KOHLER.

2. Jewish Theological Seminary of America: This is a rabbinic seminary of conservative tendency founded in New York City in 1886, mainly through Dr. Sabato Morais of Philadelphia, and conducted by him until his death in 1899, when for a time Dr. A. Kohut, the professor of Talmud, conducted the institution. Upon his death the position of the seminary became precarious, until it was reconstituted in 1902 by a new organization which was endowed with a fund of over $500,000, to which contributions were made by Leonard Lewisohn, Daniel Guggenheim, and others, including Jacob H. Schiff, who also donated a special building on University Heights. It received a charter from the State of New York in the same year, with the right to confer the degrees of rabbi, doctor of divinity, and doctor of Hebrew literature, whereupon Dr. Solomon Schechter (q.v.), reader in rabbinics in the University of Cambridge, England, and the well-known discoverer of the Hebrew original of Ecclesiasticus, was elected president of the faculty, and a number of scholars were brought over from Europe to carry on the work of the seminary under the new direction. The seminary moved, in 1903, into its new building at 531–535 West 123d Street, which contains in its highest story ample room for the fine library which has been collected since that date, and which now (1911) amounts to 39,000 books and 1,500 manuscripts,

the greatest collection of Jewish works in any Jewish institution in the world. This includes the libraries of the late M. Steinschneider, David Cassel, and M. Halberstam, and a large number of works presented by Judge Mayer Sulzberger.

The number of students is at present about seventy, of whom thirty-two are in the senior class, all graduates of American colleges or possessing an equivalent degree. The course of study extends over a period of four years, and includes training in Bible, Talmud, Jewish history and literature, theology, homiletics, and Semitics. Connected with the seminary is a teachers' institute, which provides training for teachers of Sabbath and religious schools. The seminary publishes a series of scientific works on Jewish literature entitled *Texts and Studies of the Jewish Theological Seminary*, and three volumes have already appeared, edited by Prof. L. Ginzberg (New York, 1910 sqq.).

JOSEPH JACOBS.

VII. Lutheran:—1. Augsburg: Augsburg Seminary, the oldest Norwegian Lutheran divinity school in America, is controlled by the Norwegian Lutheran Free Church of North America, was organized in 1869, and began its work at Marshall, Wis., whence it was moved, in 1872, to its present situation in Minneapolis, Minn. Prof. A. Weenaas was the first president, and he was succeeded in 1876 by Prof. George Sverdrup, who served up to his death in 1907, when Prof. Sven Oftedal, the senior professor of the seminary, who had been connected with it since 1873, became its president. On the death of Prof. Oftedal in 1911, Prof. George Sverdrup succeeded him in the presidency. In the forty years of its existence, 346 young men have graduated from its theological department, almost all serving as ministers in Lutheran churches in New York, Pennsylvania, Michigan, Illinois, Wisconsin, Iowa, Minnesota, Kansas, Nebraska, South Dakota, North Dakota, Washington, Oregon, and British Columbia, while many of its theological graduates have been, and are, engaged in missionary work, principally in Madagascar. The aim of Augsburg Seminary is to educate pious and devoted ministers qualified for the hard and self-sacrificing life of the pioneers of a free church for a free people. While adhering strictly to the Lutheran confession, and laying great stress on personal Christian experience, Augsburg Seminary takes a view of the education of ministers different from what is considered the standard in the European state churches with their Latin schools and universities. The governing ideas of the seminary are as follows: Ministers should be Christian workers trained for their calling in religious institutions, not in secular colleges; they should be so educated as not to become a caste estranged from the people in general, and especially not from the believers in the Church; the essential medium for the spiritual development of young men being educated for the ministry should not be the Greco-Roman classical literature, imbued as it is with pagan ideas and immorality, but the Word of God.

Augsburg Seminary is not, therefore, a combination of a secular college and a theological seminary, but a strictly religious institution for the education of ministers through a seven-years' course, of which the first four are preparatory for theological study proper. In the theological course much more time is given to Biblical and historical than to dogmatic theology, the idea being that Christianity is not a philosophical system, but a personal life. The history of Augsburg Seminary has been one of continual struggle, partly on account of the financial difficulties with which an institute of this kind must contend among poor and struggling immigrants, and partly because the principles of the seminary have been the object of many and persevering attacks from those who were more or less interested in continuing in the new country the ideas prevailing in the state churches in regard both to the education of ministers and to the relation between the clergy and the common people in the churches.

GEORGE SVERDRUP, JR.

2. Augustana: Augustana Theological Seminary, under the control of the Evangelical Lutheran Church, was established in 1860 at Chicago, whence it was removed, three years later, to Paxton, Ill., and thence, in 1875, to Rock Island, Ill., where it is now permanently located. It had its origin in the need of providing ministers for the Swedish immigrants, and among its founders were Rev. L. P. Esbjörn, Rev. T. N. Hasselquist, and Rev. Erland Carlsson, while its earliest professors were the two first named and Dr. A. R. Cervin, T. N. Hasselquist being also first president until his death in 1891. In 1890 two additional professors were appointed, and the course of study was changed on the adoption of the university plan, the courses offered now numbering twenty. The number of graduates of the seminary, inclusive of the year 1909, is 698, and the instruction corresponds to the best requirements of well-equipped seminaries, the diploma being recognized by the Church of Sweden. The seminary has also a post-graduate department offering twenty-four courses. Students may receive the B.D. degree, and all who have acquired A.B. and B.D., and pass satisfactory examinations in eight subjects of the post-graduate courses, receive the degree of C.S.T. by continued studies and on the completion of an accepted and printed thesis on some theological subject. The degree D.D. may be conferred if the scholarship of the candidate and his standing are such that he may be recommended. The seminary stands for Lutheran orthodoxy, evangelical Christianity, and true theological culture, and its influence on its own denomination has been to extend the work of Augustana Synod throughout the United States and to encourage missionary activity in foreign lands. Standing for true conservatism, true liberalism, and faithfulness to the Augsburg Confession, it has done much to strengthen the Lutheran Church in the United States. There are, however, no special movements that have originated in the seminary except the Augustana Foreign Mission Society. All the professors of the seminary have been more or less prominent, and among them special mention should be made of T. N. Hasselquist (who was also one of the founders of the Augustana Synod), O. Olsson (q.v.; president of the institution from 1891 to 1900), and R. F. Weidner (q.v.; now president

of the Lutheran Seminary at Chicago). The regular professors are four in number: C. E. Lindberg (acting president and professor of systematic theology, liturgics, and church polity), N. Forsander (q.v.; historical theology, Swedish homiletics, and pastoral theology), S. G. Youngert (philosophy, Greek New Testament, exegesis, New-Testament introduction, and catechetics), and C. A. Blomgren (Hebrew, Old-Testament introduction and exegesis, propædeutics, and English homiletics). There are eighteen trustees of the institution, which is governed by the Evangelical Lutheran Augustana Synod; and it had in 1910 fifty-eight students, all of whom are Lutherans, from almost every state in the Union. The endowment is about $380,000, this being for the entire institution of Augustana College and Theological Seminary, and the library of 24,000 volumes likewise belongs to the institution as a whole. A new library building known as the Denkmann Memorial Library, costing over $200,000, was dedicated in 1911. Since 1901 the president has been Dr. Gustav Andreen, who for some years has been relieved from teaching in order to raise additional funds for the college and seminary.

CONRAD EMIL LINDBERG.

3. Chicago: This seminary, officially known as " The Theological Seminary of the Evangelical Lutheran Church at Chicago, Ill.," received its charter July 29, 1891, was opened Oct. 1 of the same year, and is now located in Maywood, a suburb of Chicago. The directors, originally appointed by the officers of the General Council of the Evangelical Lutheran Church, are self-perpetuating, and elect their successors from synods in strict harmony with the doctrinal position of the seminary " as set forth in the *Fundamental Principles of Faith and Church Polity* as declared by the General Council (1867) at Fort Wayne, Ind." The first president of the board (to 1894) was the Rev. W. A. Passavant (q.v.), by whose zeal and liberality the seminary was founded. So far but five professors have been connected with the seminary: Rev. R. F. Weidner (q.v.; dogmatics and exegesis since 1891; elected president in 1893), Rev. H. W. Roth (practical theology and church history, 1891–97), Rev. G. H. Gerberding (practical theology since 1894), Rev. E. F. Krauss (New-Testament exegesis since 1900), and Rev. Alfred Ramsey (historical theology since 1904). The aim of the institution is to prepare men for the ministry of the Gospel, especially in connection with the Evangelical Lutheran Church, and is open to all students of the Evangelical Lutheran Church and to all pastors thereof, as well as to any others, whether students or pastors, who, having the proper gifts and education, give evidence of Christian character and experience. All the sciences included in theology, some thirty or more, are logically arranged so as to be comprised in twenty-one distinct and independent courses covering seventy-two hours' instruction weekly, and each subject, except Greek and Hebrew exegesis, may be completed in one year. A student of average ability can graduate in three years (sixteen courses), and in four years can take the degree of B.D. (twenty-one courses). Twenty-four different courses are also offered to post-graduates by correspondence.

In addition to the regular professors, five or more instructors are appointed each year to give instruction from three to twelve hours weekly. On an average forty students have been enrolled as resident students for the last fifteen years, and on an average over a hundred as non-resident students since 1900. There are about 10,000 carefully selected books in the library.

REVERE FRANKLIN WEIDNER.

BIBLIOGRAPHY: *Student's Handbook of the Theological Seminary of the Evangelical Lutheran Church at Chicago, Ill.*, Chicago, 1908.

4. Columbus: The Evangelical Lutheran Seminary at Columbus, O., the oldest educational institution of the Lutheran Church west of the Alleghany Mountains, was established in Canton, O., in 1830 by the Lutheran Synod of Ohio and Adjacent States, generally known as the Joint Synod of Ohio, an organization of German and English Lutheran pastors and congregations dating back to the year 1818. About two years after the founding of the school, it was removed to Columbus, O., where it has since, with some slight interruptions, continued its work of furnishing a goodly percentage of German and English pastors to the Lutheran congregations of Ohio and states farther west. It represents doctrinally the status of the Joint Synod, which is that of conservative and confessional Lutheranism, and is an exponent of the theological thought of the Lutheran Church of Germany during its orthodox period. Its first instructor was Prof. Wilhelm Schmidt, a graduate of the University of Halle, who for ten years remained its only teacher, and among his successors the most influential have been Prof. Wilhelm H. Lehmann and Prof. M. Loy, now professor emeritus. The institution has been largely influential in making Western Lutheranism confessional and orthodox, and hundreds of its graduates have been, and still are, active in the work of establishing congregations especially among the settlers throughout the West who come from the Lutheran countries of Europe. A unique feature is that its instruction is bilingual, theological lectures in German alternating with those in English, and perhaps seventy-five per cent of its graduates are able to preach in both languages. The trustees, eleven in number (eight clergymen and three laymen), are all selected from the membership of the Joint Synod, and are elected at the biennial convention of this body. The faculty numbers five of whom one, as emeritus, is no longer engaged in active work. The dean is Prof. F. W. Stellhorn (q.v.) and the secretary is Prof. George H. Schodde (q.v.). The student body, which in some years runs up to fifty, was in 1910 thirty-eight, namely, eighteen in the senior, ten in the middle, and ten in the junior class. Although originally incorporated as " The German Theological Seminary," by act of legislature this name was changed several years ago to " Theological Seminary," as both German and English are entitled to exactly the same rights in the work of the school. GEORGE H. SCHODDE.

BIBLIOGRAPHY: G. H. Schodde, *The Lutheran Seminary at Columbus, Ohio*, Columbus, O., 1905; P. A. Peter and W. Schmidt, *Geschichte der allgemeinen evangelisch-lutherischen Synode von Ohio und anderer Staaten*, Columbus, 1900.

5. Concordia (St. Louis): This institution, the largest of its denomination in the United States, was founded as a classical college and school of theology in 1839 by Lutheran emigrants from Saxony, who were fleeing from the persecutions of a rationalistic state-church to the land of religious liberty. Its first home was in the forests of Perry Co., Mo., at the village of Altenburg, and its first building was a log-hut constructed by members of the first faculty, which consisted of the candidates of theology C. F. W. Walther (q.v.), J. F. Buenger, O. Fuerbringer, and Th. Brohm. After the organization of the German Evangelical Lutheran Synod of Missouri, Ohio, and Other States in 1847, the institution was, in 1849, removed to St. Louis, and the synod elected Walther, at that time pastor of the Lutheran congregation at St. Louis, its first professor of theology. He remained with the institution as its foremost teacher and president until his death in 1887. In 1861 the classical (preparatory) department was removed to Fort Wayne, Ind., while the " Practical Theological Seminary," with Professor Craemer, was transferred from Fort Wayne to St. Louis, and was united with the " Theoretical Seminary " under the presidency of Professor Walther. The two seminaries remained united until 1875, when the " Practical Seminary " was removed to Springfield, Ill. During Walther's presidency the teachers were A. Biewend, G. Schick, Alex. Saxer, G. Seyffarth, R. Lange, Laur. Larsen, A. Craemer, E. A. Brauer, Th. Brohm, E. Preuss, F. A. Schmidt (q.v.), G. Schaller, M. Guenther, and F. Pieper (q.v.). By synodical action Professor Pieper, after the death of Walther, succeeded to the presidency and the chair of systematic and pastoral theology, and with him the following have been holding theological professorships since 1887: G. Stoeckhardt (exegesis), A. Graebner (d. 1904), E. A. W. Krauss (history), O. Fuerbringer (isagogics), F. Bente (symbolics), G. Mezger (homiletics), and W. Dau (English dogmatics). With the number of resident students steadily growing, the capacity of the college buildings had to be increased from time to time. The erection of a large main building in 1883, at the cost of $150,000, raised the capacity to 200, and an annex, built in 1907, to 300 resident students.

The doctrinal position of Concordia Seminary is understood from the position to which its founders were led under severe struggles of an awakened conscience crying for sure grace and truth. Its founders had emerged from the rationalism of a degenerated state-church, and had overcome very pronounced hierarchical tendencies in their own midst: they had firmly grasped, and they deeply impressed upon their students, the principle that, as regards doctrine and discipline, there is only one conscience-binding authority, viz. the Word of Christ, which is given to the Church in the Holy Scriptures. All matters not determined by this Word (adiaphora) are to be adjusted, not by the rulings of " church authorities," but by the mutual consent of Christians themselves, church councils, synods, etc., having only advisory power in such matters. As regards doctrine, in particular, Concordia Seminary inculcates in its students the following principles: The doctrine to be taught in the Church must be divine doctrine, not only in the sense that it treats of divine matters, but, above all, in the sense that it exhibits God's own thoughts, to the exclusion of all human views and opinions. Christian doctrine is nothing but what God himself thinks and proclaims about these matters in Holy Scripture, and Christian doctrine regarding Holy Scripture is not what men hold it to be, but what Christ and his apostles taught us that it is, viz., the infallible Word of God, given by inspiration. The various parts of Christian doctrine form a harmonic whole to such an extent that an aberration in one doctrine affects, by consequence, the whole body of doctrine, especially the doctrine of justification, and whatever lacunæ appear in the body of Christian doctrine are not to be filled up by human speculation, but must be left open, to be filled by the perfect knowledge of eternity. This principle explains the position which Concordia Seminary occupies over and against Calvinism on the one hand and Arminianism or Synergism on the other. Concordia Seminary retains both the teaching of *universalis gratia* and *sola gratia*, claiming that Scripture teaches both, and it finds a correct restatement of Biblical doctrine over against error in the *Confessions* of the Lutheran Church, while holding that later Lutheran theologians have in some points deviated from the accuracy of Scriptural teaching, as on the relations of Church and State, Sunday, conversion, and predestination. By rigidly adhering to these principles the institution has been instrumental in educating a homogeneous Christian ministry, which is modern in equipment—only graduates of classical colleges are admitted—and acquainted with modern doctrinal liberalism, while rejecting and combating doctrinal looseness in every form as unbiblical and unscientific. Its graduates are at work in all the states of the Union, and in Canada, South America, Australia, India, and Europe (London, and the Lutheran Free Churches in Germany and Denmark).

Concordia Seminary registered in 1910 285 students, and seven professors, who lecture in German, English, and Latin. It is governed by a board of trustees composed of three lay and two clerical members who are elected by the Missouri Synod for a term of three years. All the students are Lutherans and, with some few exceptions, are graduates of the Synod's classical schools at Bronxville, N. Y., Fort Wayne, Ind., Milwaukee, Wis., St. Paul, Minn., Concordia, Mo., and Winfield, Kan. The supply of young men upon whom the Synod may levy for making up losses in, and for enlarging, its ministry is practically unlimited, since 2,123 parochial schools are in operation within the Synod. Concordia Seminary carries no endowment, and all expenses are defrayed from the synodical treasury, which is kept solvent by voluntary contributions of the congregations and by the proceeds of the Synod's book concern, the Concordia Publishing House. The number of books in the library of the seminary is 15,000.   FRANZ A. O. PIEPER.

BIBLIOGRAPHY: *Der Lutheraner*, xxxviii.-xxxix.; F. Pieper, *Lehrstellung der Missouri-Synode*, St. Louis, Mo., 1897.

6. Concordia (Springfield, Ill.): This institution, now situated in Springfield, Ill., and officially entitled " Concordia College," owes its origin to Rev. J. C. W. Löhe (q.v.) of Neuendettelsau, Bavaria, who, touched by the religious distress among the emigrated Germans, founded a seminary for practical preparation for the ministry at Ft. Wayne, Ind., in 1846. Löhe sent over eleven young men, together with a talented candidate of theology, Roebbelen, as instructor, and, under the supervision of Dr. W. Sihler (q.v.), the school was opened in an upper chamber of the parsonage. The earliest instructors of this " Practical Seminary of the Missouri Synod " were Dr. W. Sihler and Profs. A. Wolter and A. Biewend (1846–50). The vacancy caused by Biewend's call to the St. Louis Seminary was filled in 1850 by Prof. A. Craemer, who for forty-one years was an untiring and zealous laborer in behalf of the " Practical Seminary." A radical change occurred in 1861, when the classical department of Concordia Seminary, St. Louis, was removed to Ft. Wayne, while the " Practical Theological Seminary," with Professor Craemer, was transferred from Ft.Wayne to St. Louis to be united with the " Theoretical Seminary " under the supervision of Dr. C. F. W. Walther (q.v.). Until 1875 all the professors lectured to the students of both seminaries, but now another important change was to take place. In Springfield, Ill., the Illinois State University had passed into the hands of the General Council. This synod was desirous of selling the institution, and, largely through the agency of Rev. W. A. Passavant (q.v.) and of Rev. H. Katt (now of Terre Haute, Ind.; then assistant pastor at Springfield), it was purchased by the Missouri Synod in 1873. The following year the " Proseminary " (established in 1852), with Professor Kroening, was removed from St. Louis to Springfield, and in 1875 the " Practical Seminary " followed, with Professor Craemer as president. Here the seminary has found a permanent home. Prof. H. Wyneken was called in 1876, and Prof. J. S. Simon in 1881. Wyneken resigned in 1890 on account of failing health, Craemer died in 1891, and Kroening was called to Milwaukee in 1892, their successors being Prof. R. Pieper (elected to the presidency in 1891), Prof. J. Herzer, and Prof. F. Streckfuss (1892). In 1892 an English theological professorship was founded and filled by the appointment of Prof. L. Wessel. Professor Simon resigned in 1904, and was succeeded first by Prof. T. Schlueter (now at Watertown, Wis.) and then by Prof. O. Boecier (1909). As quite a number of Slovak students pursue their studies here, Prof. S. Tuhy was appointed in 1910 to instruct them in their mother-tongue.

The whole course embraces two departments: the proseminary (two years) and the seminary (three years), in the latter of which the usual branches of exegetical, systematic, historical, and practical theology are taught. Since the ministers must be enabled to officiate in German and in English, instruction is imparted in both languages. The institution stands for sound Lutheranism, and no teaching contrary to the Book of Concord is tolerated, and for a thoroughly conservative position in respect to Biblical criticism and " scientific theology." Over 700 ministers have graduated here.

The campus comprises eight and one-half acres with modern and commodious buildings, and the seminary is entirely sustained by the Missouri Synod. The student body (1910) numbers 216, and comes from all parts of the United States and Canada, while six are from Australia, two from Brazil, and one from New Zealand. The library contains about 4,500 volumes.   LOUIS WESSEL.

BIBLIOGRAPHY: *Fünfzigjähriges Jubiläum des Concordia-Seminars zu Springfield, Ill., 1846–96*, St. Louis, Mo., 1869.

7. Gettysburg: This institution, officially designated " The Theological Seminary of the General Synod of the Evangelical Lutheran Church in the United States," is located in Gettysburg, Adams Co., Pa., where it occupies a site of over forty acres on the historic Seminary Ridge, overlooking the town. It was founded in 1826 by the General Synod, which at its first meeting in 1820 appointed a committee to report on the feasibility of establishing a theological school. The project was deemed impracticable, but it was revived, chiefly through a sermon preached by the Rev. S. S. Schmucker (q.v.) of New Market, Va., at the meeting of the Maryland and Virginia Synod, Oct. 17, 1824, and the General Synod in consequence reconsidered the matter a year later, taking steps at once for the organization of the seminary. Rev. S. S. Schmucker was elected the first professor in 1826, and for forty-six years he remained its head, during the greater part of this period being the most potent factor in the building of the Lutheran Church, and for the first four years of the existence of the seminary being its only professor. During the great battle of July, 1863, the old seminary building was considerably damaged by shells, besides being used as a hospital, and the institution also passed through the stress of ecclesiastical controversy in the sixties, resulting in the resignation of several professors, the establishment of another Lutheran seminary in Philadelphia in 1864, and the organization of the General Council in 1866.

The seminary has been attended by 1,100 students, most of whom have entered the Lutheran ministry, though a small minority have become ministers in other denominations. It has also prepared many professors for colleges and seminaries, as well as missionaries for the home and the foreign field. The doctrinal basis is the Word of God as contained in the canonical Scriptures of the Old and the New Testaments as the only infallible rule of faith and practise, and the Augsburg Confession as a correct exhibition of the fundamental doctrines of the divine word. The institution occupies a conservative, orthodox position, in accord with the evangelical character of the Lutheran Church in America. This seminary, being the oldest purely theological Lutheran institution in America, and the largest in the General Synod, has exerted a correspondingly wide influence, and during the first half of its existence, before other Lutheran seminaries were founded, nearly all the leading ministers and educators were trained there. Among past instructors the following may be mentioned: Drs. S. S. Schmucker (q.v.), E. L. Hazelius, H. I. Schmidt, C. A. Hay, Charles P. Krauth (q.v.), Charles F. Schaeffer (q.v.), J. A. Brown, M. Val-

entine (q.v.), E. J. Wolf, C. A. Stork, and J. W. Richard. In 1910 the number of professors was five, besides whom there are occasional lecturers on doctrinal and practical subjects. The institution is governed by a board of directors, whose maximum number does not exceed fifty, chosen by district synods which contribute toward its support. There are now fifty-three students in attendance, all of whom are Lutherans, all except two being college graduates. Three-fourths of them are from Pennsylvania, one from Germany, and the rest from adjacent states. The endowment amounts to about $260,000, and the real estate is worth $250,000. The libraries contain 20,000 volumes, including the valuable collection of 3,000 of the Lutheran Historical Society.   J. A. SINGMASTER.

BIBLIOGRAPHY: E. J. Wolf, *The Lutherans in America*, New York, 1889; H. E. Jacobs, *History of the Evangelical Lutheran Church in the United States*, New York, 1893; *Lutheran Quarterly*, vi., xiv.

8. Hamma: This institution is located in Springfield, Clark Co., O., and was known as the Wittenberg Theological Seminary until, in 1905, its name was changed to Hamma Divinity School in recognition of Dr. and Mrs. M. W. Hamma, who had just given almost $200,000 for the endowment and extension of the institution. The school was established in 1845, and has always been affiliated with and controlled by the General Synod of the Evangelical Lutheran Church, its founder being the Rev. Ezra Keller, who had come from Maryland at the call of the scattered Lutherans in Ohio. Among the early teachers were Dr. Keller (president of both college and seminary), Dr. Samuel Sprecher (q.v.; for twenty-five years president and for thirty-five years instructor), Dr. F. W. Conrad (afterward editor of *The Lutheran Observer*), Dr. J. H. W. Stuckenberg (q.v.), and Dr. Samuel A. Ort, for eighteen years president and for thirty years instructor. The school stands for the conservative theology of the historic Lutheran Church. It believes strongly in the creeds of the church, is opposed to all the so-called liberalizing tendencies of radical theology, and teaches heartily that the Bible is the Word of God, but at the same time it is progressive, and looks forward hopefully to the time when there may come a union of the Lutheran forces in America. The influence of the school has been strongly felt throughout the general body to which it belongs, and it is safe to say that no other theological school has had more influence during the last twenty years in shaping the policies and affecting the development of the General Synod.

The present faculty is made up as follows: Charles G. Heckert (president), Leander S. Keyser (Christian theology and ethics), David H. Bauslin (q.v.; ecclesiastical history), V. G. A. Tressler (q.v.; New-Testament philology), Loyal H. Larimer (Old-Testament language and exegesis), and J. L. Neve (symbolics and practical theology). The board of directors numbers forty-two, and is the same as that controlling Wittenberg College. The student body has been slowly increasing in numbers during the past five years, and the enrolment for 1910, in which Germany and Norway are represented, is thirty-four. The endowment is about $300,000, much of which has been given during the last ten years, and there is also a special endowment for library and art purposes. The library contains about 18,000 volumes. The only printed history of the seminary is that contained in a history ·of Wittenberg College published in Springfield in 1887 by Rev. G. G. Clark.   CHARLES G. HECKERT.

9. Hartwick: This institution, which is the oldest Lutheran classical and theological school in America, is located near Cooperstown, Otsego Co., N. Y., where it was founded in 1797 by Rev. John Christopher Hartwick, for the purpose of educating the American Indians who at that time occupied a ¹arge portion of the state of New York, and to furnish missionaries to labor among those tribes. Funds were secured by Hartwick from the sale of some 16,000 acres of land which he had bought from the Indians in 1754. The first instructor in theology was Dr. John A. Kunze, and this department has been maintained uninterruptedly from 1797 to the present time. In 1815 the first seminary building on the present site was erected, and Dr. E. L. Hazelius was elected principal and professor of theology. Though Hartwick's Indian scheme proved a failure, his seminary has been a factor in Lutheran theological education for more than a century. For twenty-nine years it was the only school of its denomination in the United States, and in its early history it frequently had students from all parts of the country between Canada and South Carolina. It met a distinct need in American Lutheranism by furnishing English-speaking pastors for the Anglicized descendants of the Palatines who early settled in the Hudson, Schoharie, and Mohawk valleys, and the existence of the older English-speaking Lutheran congregations in New York State may be traced directly to Hartwick Seminary.

The institution is under the control of the General Synod of the Lutheran Church, and has always stood for the pietistic type of Lutheran theology, two of its most distinguished professors being of Moravian ancestry. Among its prominent instructors have been Drs. John C. Kunze, E. L. Hazelius, G. B. Miller, William D. Strohil, William N. Scholl, and James Pitcher. At present (1911) three professors give instruction in theology, and there are eight students who are candidates for the ministry. The faculty is composed of J. G. Traver (principal), Alfred Hiller (q.v.; theology), J. L. Kistler (Greek and mathematics), G. B. Hiller (natural sciences), and two assistant teachers. The school is governed by a board of twelve trustees elected (since 1911) by the Lutheran Synod of New York for the term of four years. The amount of endowment is $63,000, and the library contains 6,300 volumes.
ALFRED HILLER.

BIBLIOGRAPHY: *Hartwick Seminary Memorial Catalogue*, Cooperstown, N. Y., 1888, 1897; *Hartwick Seminary Monthly*, 1909.

10. Luther: This institution, the " Practical Seminary " of the Lutheran Joint Synod of Ohio and Other States, was founded in 1884 under the direction of Rev. E. Böhme, who was also its first instructor. It originally formed part of what is now the " Theoretical Seminary " at Columbus, O.,

but in its very first year it was transferred to Afton, Minn., and from this year, in which the proseminary was also established, Dr. H. Ernst has been president. The growth of the institution created a necessity for more commodious quarters, and in 1892 it was accordingly removed to its present location in St. Paul, Minn., where its further development has resulted in plans for additional buildings now being under consideration. The seminary has thus far sent out 200 graduates, who have formed the nucleus of several districts of the Joint Synod, particularly those of Minnesota, Wisconsin, Kansas-Nebraska, and Canada. In 1910 the institution had five instructors and seventy students (all Lutherans) coming from fifteen states, as well as from Germany, Canada, Australia, Russia, and Austria-Hungary; and it is under the supervision of a board of seven trustees. The endowment is about $15,000, and the library contains some 2,000 volumes.
K. G. BUSCH.

11. Mount Airy: This institution, officially entitled " The Theological Seminary of the Evangelical Lutheran Church at Philadelphia," is situated at Mount Airy, a suburb of Philadelphia, and was established in 1864. As early as 1749 Henry Melchior Mühlenberg had purchased ground for such an institution; but its foundation was delayed until 1864, when the Ministerium of Pennsylvania elected Rev. Drs. C. F. Schaeffer (q.v.), W. J. Mann (q.v.), and Charles Porterfield Krauth (q.v.) full professors, and Rev. Drs. C. W. Schaeffer (q.v.), and G. F. Krotel (q.v.) associate professors, all being installed Oct. 4, 1864. In 1889 the seminary removed from the center of Philadelphia to its suburbs at Mt. Airy, north of Germantown, where, on a plot of five acres, an administration building, a large dormitory, a church, and five residences now stand, besides the Krauth Memorial Library, for whose erection and equipment a friend has contributed over $100,000. The Ministerium of New York, the Synod of New York and New England, and the Pittsburg Synod (all belonging to the General Council) have united with the Ministerium of Pennsylvania in its support and control. Previous to 1893 its property was held under the charter of the Ministerium of Pennsylvania, but since then it has been constituted a separate corporation. It is administered by a board of thirty-six members, and its professors, upon nomination by the directors, are elected by the Ministerium of Pennsylvania. The charter declares: " The seminary shall rest on the Divine Word of the Old and New Testament Scriptures, as the absolute Rule of Faith, and the confessions of the Evangelical Lutheran Church set forth in the Book of Concord, as in conformity with that Rule, and all its teachings shall be in accord with said Rule." The standard of educational preparation for admission is that of college graduation, exceptions being possible only by a unanimous vote of the faculty. The instruction is through the medium of the English language, supplemented by special courses in which German is used for those less familiar with English.

The faculty consists at present of Drs. H. E. Jacobs (q.v.; chairman, 1883), J. Fry (1891), G. F. Spieker (q.v.; 1894), Henry Offerman (1910), E. T.

Horn, T. E. Schmauk, and L. D. Reed (all 1911), and there are also two instructors and four lecturers, while the library is administered by a librarian and three assistants. The alumni list numbers 808, while about 200 have taken partial and post-graduate courses. The number of students in attendance during 1910–11 is 55. Dr. Adolph Spaeth (q.v.), for thirty-seven years a professor, and for fourteen years the chairman of the faculty, died June 25, 1910. Graduates of the seminary are serving in all parts of the Lutheran Church, all parts of the country, and in many languages, as well as in other denominations. *The Lutheran Church Review*, a theological quarterly, published by the alumni, is edited by Rev. Theodore E. Schmauk, president of the board of directors, assisted by the faculty. HENRY E. JACOBS.

12. Columbia (formerly **Mount Pleasant**): This theological seminary of the United Synod of the Evangelical Lutheran Church in the South was located at Mt. Pleasant, Charleston Co., S. C., until 1911, when it was removed to Columbia, S. C. It was founded in 1831 as a classical and theological institute to provide ministers for Lutheran churches, especially in South Carolina and the adjacent states. It was created by the action of the Evangelical Lutheran Synod of South Carolina, under impulse given by the Rev. John Bachman, of Charleston, S. C., and the first professor was the Rev. John G. Schwartz, who died shortly after the inception of the institution. Temporarily located in Newberry County, S. C., the classical and collegiate institute was more permanently situated, in 1833, at Lexington, S. C., with Ernest L. Hazelius as the chief professor. In 1859 it was removed to Newberry, S. C., and became Newberry College, but its operations were crippled by the war, and the theological department was separated from the college and became the Theological Seminary of the General Synod (South) of the Lutheran Church in 1867. Its work was carried on at various places until, in 1872, it was located at Salem, Va., with Rev. E. A. Repass and Rev. T. W. Dosh as professors. In 1884 the seminary was discontinued, but two years later it resumed its life as the theological department of Newberry College, under the control of the South Carolina Synod. In 1892 it was adopted as the theological seminary of the United Synod of the Evangelical Lutheran Church in the South, which was formed in 1886, and which superseded the General Synod (South). The institution continued at Newberry, S. C., until 1898, when it was removed to its present location at Mt. Pleasant, in the vicinity of Charleston, S. C. It stands for confessional Lutheranism according to the basis of the United Synod, and its chief influence has been to strengthen Lutheran consciousness and to promote homogeneity in the Lutheran Church in the South Atlantic States. The most prominent of its instructors was Dr. E. L. Hazelius, although Dr. J. P. Smeltzer and Dr. E. A. Repass were also men of note.

In 1910 the teaching force of the seminary consisted of two regular professors and three lecturers, and it is governed for the United Synod by a board of fourteen directors, elected by that body. In 1910 fourteen students were in attendance, all Lutheran,

from the states of Virginia, North Carolina, South Carolina, and Georgia. The amount of endowment is $50,000, and the library contains 5,000 books.
A. G. VOIGT.

BIBLIOGRAPHY: J. F. Schirmer, *Historical Sketches of the Evangelical Lutheran Synod of South Carolina*, Charleston, S. C., 1875; W. B. Sprague, *Annals of the American Pulpit*, vol. ix., New York, 1869; " Century Memorial Number " of *The Lutheran Visitor*, 1900.

13. Saint Anthony Park: This seminary, which is affiliated with the United Norwegian Lutheran Church, is located in St. Anthony Park, St. Paul, Ramsey Co., Minn., and was founded in 1890. It is under the direct control of the Annual Meeting of the United Norwegian Lutheran Church, which elects the professors and the board of trustees of the seminary, prescribes the course of study, holds title to all real estate, and has control of all funds. The institution was originally known as "Augsburg Seminary," and was located, from 1890 to 1893, in the buildings of the older institution of the same name, at Minneapolis, Minn., which have remained under the auspices of the Norwegian Evangelical Lutheran Synod of North America, and which still constitute Augsburg Seminary. From 1893, the new seminary occupied temporary quarters until Jan., 1902, when it was removed to its present permanent home. The aim of the institution is to educate men in the various branches of theology so as to fit them for the public ministry of the Gospel in the Norwegian Lutheran Church of America, and for the foreign mission field. The confessional basis is the same as that of the United Norwegian Lutheran Church: "The canonical books of the Old and New Testament are the revealed Word of God, and, therefore, the only source and rule of faith, doctrine, and life "; and it also holds that the Apostles', Nicene, and Athanasian Creeds, and the unaltered Augsburg Confession and Luther's Smaller Catechism, are true and clear embodiments of the doctrine of the Word of God. Both the Norwegian and the English language are used in instruction, and the seminary course takes three years, the preparatory training for admission being the usual college course with the classical languages, although this latter requirement may exceptionally be waived.

The equipment of the seminary consists of about nine acres of land, on which are the main building (erected at a cost of nearly $100,000), the Muskego Church (the first church erected, at Muskego, Wis., in 1844, by Norwegian Lutherans in the United States; removed to the seminary grounds in 1905; and serving to house articles of interest from Norwegian church history in America), and two professors' houses. In 1910 there were five professorships, four held by M. O. Böckman (New-Testament exegesis and isagogics; president since 1893), E. K. Johnsen (Old-Testament exegesis and Hebrew), F. A. Schmidt (q.v.; dogmatics and symbolics), C. M. Weswig (church history and homiletics), the professorship of practical theology and missions being vacant. There are also four instructors. There have thus far been 363 graduates, and the enrolment in 1910 was 62. The total value of the property of the seminary is $140,000, and its endowment is $121,600, besides which it receives annual appropriations from the United Norwegian

Lutheran Church. Its library contains about 5,000 volumes. Carl M. Weswig.

14. Susquehanna: The School of Theology of Susquehanna University, at Selinsgrove, Pa., is a part of the school founded in 1858 by Rev. B. Kurtz. It has always been under Lutheran control, and was known as "Missionary Institute," until its incorporation with Susquehanna University in 1894. Its special object as the Institute was to prepare men for both home and foreign mission work, and students were received without regard to age or domestic ties, and ordinarily with less than a college education. The course was three years, and was practical rather than theoretical, but since 1894 it has required as preparation a full college training. Among its theological teachers have been Drs. B. Kurtz, H. Ziegler, P. Born, J. B. Foehh, C. M. Heisler, and J. Zutzy. In 1910, the faculty numbered four: C. T. Aikens, F. P. Manhart, D. B. Floyd, and H. M. Follmer, and there were twelve students, while the library of the entire university contained 11,500 volumes. Frank P. Manhart.

15. Wartburg: This seminary, which is situated at Dubuque, Ia., is the theological institution of the Evangelical Lutheran Synod of Iowa and Other States. It was founded by Rev. George Grossmann, at Dubuque, Ia., in Sept., 1853, supported by the Lutheran church of Germany, under the leadership of Rev. Wilhelm Löhe, of Neuendettelsau, Bavaria, after Grossmann had withdrawn from the Bavarian settlements, near Saginaw, Mich., to prevent schism in that territory because the cooperation of Löhe was no longer desired by the Missouri Synod. From 1858 to 1876 the faculty consisted of George Grossmann, Sigmund Fritschel, and Gottfried Fritschel. In 1857 the seminary was removed to St. Sebald, Ia., where the necessities of life were raised on a farm, but in 1874 it found more spacious quarters at Mendota, Ill., whence it was transferred, in 1889, to its permanent home at Dubuque, Ia. It stands for the principles represented by the Iowa synod, namely, a conservative, positive Lutheranism, avoiding, on the one hand, a laxity which surrenders the peculiarities of the Lutheran tenets, and, on the other hand, a rigorous extreme which makes no distinction between essentials and nonessentials. It emphasizes the absolute superiority of the Scriptures in all matters of faith, and finds these expressed in the Lutheran confessions. No new movements have originated in this seminary, but the old Lutheran methods of preaching the Gospel purely have been practised. The brothers Fritschel mentioned above, two of the leading Lutheran theologians, have exerted an influence far beyond the bounds of the Iowa synod, Sigmund especially as the representative at the meetings of the General Council, and Gottfried also as author.

In 1911 there were four professors and sixty-eight students. A board of trustees elected at the triennial sessions of the synod controls the financial affairs, while the professors are elected by a special board. The students live together in the seminary building, and board is furnished by the institution. The internal affairs are regulated by the students and the faculty. The nine months' work closes with final examinations before a synodical board,

and the graduates are entitled to positions in the synod. The course of instruction provides for three years' work in a "theoretical" section for college graduates, and a "practical" section for others. All branches of Lutheran theology are taught in the curriculum, partly in German, and partly in English. For its support the institution depends upon the liberality of the Iowa synod congregations, although an endowment fund of $73,214 has accumulated. The present student body comes from the following states and countries: Germany (7), Bohemia (1), Illinois (7), Iowa (17), Kansas (1), Michigan (1), Missouri (2), Nebraska (4), North Dakota (4), Ohio (4), Wisconsin (1), and Texas (7). The library has about 12,000 volumes, among which a collection on Lutheran polemics and irenics, bequeathed by Prof. Sigmund Fritschel, is worthy of mention, being the most complete in its line on this continent.

Geo. J. Fritschel.

Bibliography: J. Deindörfer, Geschichte der evangelisch-lutherischen Synode Iowa, Chicago, 1897; G. J. Fritschel, Geschichte der lutherischen Kirche in Amerika, Gütersloh, 1896-97.

16. Wauwatosa: The Lutheran theological seminary, now located at Wauwatosa, Milwaukee Co., Wis., was founded in 1865 by the Evangelical Lutheran Synod of Wisconsin and Other States, at Watertown, Wis., as part of the Northwestern University established at that place, its purpose being to train young men for the ministry of the Lutheran Church. Rev. E. Moldehnke was the first teacher of the seminary, but was succeeded in 1867 by Rev. A. Hoenecke, who was thereafter connected with the seminary until his death in 1908. When, in 1870, Hoenecke accepted a call to one of the churches of Milwaukee, the work of the seminary was suspended until 1878, when the institution was reestablished at Milwaukee, still under the charter of the Northwestern University. Hoenecke was appointed to the presidency, and Prof. A. L. Graebner and Prof. E. Notz were the other members of the new faculty. When Prof. Graebner, in 1887, accepted a call to Concordia Seminary, at St. Louis, Mo., Rev. G. Thiele was chosen as his successor. In 1901, Prof. J. P. Koehler took the chair of church history made vacant by Prof. Thiele's resignation, and Prof. Notz having died in 1903, Rev. A. Pieper was appointed in his place. In the mean time, the seminary had been moved from the city of Milwaukee to its present suburban location within the limits of Wauwatosa, and the new building was dedicated in 1893. Soon after, the Synod of Wisconsin transferred the control of the institution to the Joint Synod of Wisconsin, Minnesota, Michigan, and Other States, then newly formed, of which the Wisconsin synod had become an integral part on its establishment. The faculty continued unchanged until Dr. A. Hoenecke died on Jan. 3, 1908, his place being taken, in September of the same year, by Prof. J. Schaller.

The seminary stands for positive Lutheran theology in the strictest sense, as closely following the teachings of the Bible, which, being verbally inspired by the Spirit of God, is the last and only authority in questions of doctrine. Among the instructors who have been attached to the institution,

Professor Hoenecke stands preeminent for far-reaching influence as a dogmatician. In the year 1910 the faculty of the seminary consisted of Prof. J. Schaller (president, and professor of dogmatics, pastoral theology, and homiletics), Prof. J. P. Koehler (church history, and New-Testament exegesis), and Prof. Aug. Pieper (Old-Testament exegesis, symbolics, and isagogics). The enrolment of students for 1910 was fifty-one, with fifteen graduates who entered the ministry, and most of the students are drawn from the territory covered by the Joint Synod above named. A board of managers is the connecting link between the institution and the synod, and the school is supported by voluntary contributions from the church-members of the entire body embraced in the Joint Synod, excepting a small endowment, the proceeds of which are used to defray the expenses of indigent students in the way of board, etc. The library contains some 5,000 volumes. J. SCHALLER.

17. **Western**: The Western Theological Seminary, the first and only seminary of the General Synod west of the Mississippi, is located at Atchison, Atchison Co., Kan., where it was founded, in 1895, by the Board of Education of the General Synod of the Evangelical Lutheran Church in the United States of America, by the authority of the General Synod held at Hagerstown, Md., in June, 1895; and it originated in the urgent demand to secure the full equipment of young men for the Gospel ministry in the territory where they expected to labor. Rev. Frank D. Altman, the first president, was installed in Nov., 1895, and other instructors have been Drs. Jacob A. Clutz, J. Howard Stough, J. L. Neve, Holmes Dysinger, and M. F. Troxell. The doctrinal basis of the seminary is "the Word of God, as contained in the canonical Scriptures of the Old and New Testaments, the only infallible rule of faith and practise, and the Augsburg Confession, a correct exhibition of the fundamental doctrines of the Divine Word, and of the faith of our Church founded upon that word"; and it is the purpose of the seminary to provide the churches with pastors in harmony with the above basis. The seminary has a productive endowment of about $21,000, and 3,500 volumes in its library. It has thus far been attended by 127 students, 72 of whom have satisfactorily completed the course of instruction and have received their graduation diploma. In June, 1910, the government was assumed by the trustees of Midland College, and Dr. M. F. Troxell is president of the combined institutions.

FRANK D. ALTMAN.

VIII. **Methodist Episcopal.**—1. **Asbury**: This college is situated at Wilmore, Jessamine Co., Ky., where it was founded in Sept., 1890, by Rev. J. W. Hughes for the promotion of true education and, through it, of Christian holiness for all the world. The institution is affiliated with the Methodist Episcopal denomination, although its trustees, fifteen in number, are selected with regard to their moral, spiritual, and business fitness rather than with respect to their church relations. It began its work with two teachers and eleven pupils in a four-room cottage, but in 1903 it was deemed best for it to pass from personal control into the hands of a board of trustees. The school emphasizes the Wesleyan type of experimental religion—conversion and entire sanctification as conscious experiences of grace and holy living in all walks of life—and each year of its history has witnessed a revival of religion. Any use of liquor or tobacco is forbidden its pupils, as are card-playing and intercollegiate games. Higher criticism is frowned upon. The institution believes in the inspiration and authenticity of the Scriptures and a full Gospel; it endeavors to build up clean manhood and womanhood; it strives to promote civic righteousness and the speedy evangelization of the world; and it stands for prohibition. It has, accordingly, exercised an influence on many churches for a more definite Christian experience and life, and its alumni may already be found in Korea, Japan, Persia, India, the Philippines, Cuba, the West Indies, Africa, and other fields. In 1910, Asbury College had seventeen instructors (Rev. H. C. Morrison, president), and during recent years its student body, of both sexes, has averaged 250, about one-half of whom are from Kentucky, and the remainder from some twenty or thirty states. The attendance was reduced by a disastrous fire in Mar., 1909, but new and better buildings have since been erected, and an effort is now being made to add an industrial plant. The library contains about 2,000 volumes, but the college is entirely without endowment. L. L. PICKETT.

BIBLIOGRAPHY: A. Johnson, *A Glimpse of Twenty Years*, in preparation.

2. **Boston**: The school of theology attached to Boston University is the oldest theological seminary of the Methodist Episcopal Church, and dates from the action of a convention of New England friends of improved theological training, held in Boston, Apr. 24–25, 1839, the first centennial anniversary of universal Methodism. In the absence of endowments it was started by the small gifts of a large number of interested parties, and until 1866, the year of the first centennial of American Methodism, was wholly maintained by small donations and by collections in the churches of the adjacent annual conferences. Instruction was first provided in 1841, when it was offered as a distinct course in connection with an older Conference academy at Newbury, Vt., but six years later this theological department of the academy was transferred to Concord, N. H., and by charter was independently incorporated as "The Methodist General Biblical Institute." In 1867 the institute was removed to Boston, and was reorganized under a Massachusetts act of incorporation as the "Boston Theological Seminary," and four years later, by a new act of the Legislature, it became the earliest department of the then newly chartered Boston University. In Newbury, for lack of funds, the school had no independently organized faculty, but at Concord, under considerable personal sacrifice, instruction was given by John Dempster (1847–52), Charles Adams (1847–49), S. M. Vail (1849–67), David Patten (1853–67), Bishop O. C. Baker (1854–67), and J. W. Merrill (1854–67). At Boston, the seminary teachers have been David Patten (1867–80), W. F. Warren (q.v.; since 1867), L. T. Townsend (q.v.; 1867–93), J. W. Lindsay (1868–84), J. E. Latimer (1869–85), H. C. Sheldon

(q.v.; since 1874), H. G.Mitchell (q.v.; 1883–1906), M. D. Buell (q.v.; since 1884), M. J. Cramer (1885–1886), Daniel Steele (q.v.; as supply, 1886–89, 1892–1893), O. A. Curtis (1890–95), G. K. Morris (1894–1900), M. B. Chapman (1898–1905), J. M. Barker (since 1898), S. L. Beiler (since 1905), A. C. Knudson (since 1906), and G. C. Cell (since 1908). The school was the first in this country to employ upon its staff representatives of differing Christian confessions, so that, between 1870 and 1878, Presidents Woolsey (q.v.), of Yale; McCosh (q.v.), of Princeton; Hopkins (q.v.), of Williams; Robinson, of Brown; Harris (q.v.), of Bowdoin; and Anderson (q.v.), of Rochester; with other scholars of non-Methodist affiliations, gave courses of lectures in the institution. It was the first to have a permanent chair of comparative religion, and also the first to employ annually a lecturer to give a course on the history, theory, and practise of Christian missions. As early as in 1868–1869 it offered courses of lectures in five different languages—Latin, English, French, German, and Italian. It was the first to open to men and women alike the advantages of a full and free Biblical and theological education with promotion to the appropriate degrees after full qualification. Up to the year 1911 about 3,000 candidates for the ministry have been trained here. These graduates have served nineteen different denominations, and a large number have become foreign missionaries. In the enrolment of 1910 172 of the 217 students were college graduates, and the graduating class of 1909, believed to be the largest ever sent out by any American theological seminary, numbered fifty-eight, all but four of whom were college graduates. Six graduates have been elected bishops; twelve, presidents of universities or colleges; and at least half a hundred, professors in theological and collegiate institutions.

The present number of instructors is fourteen; of trustees, thirty-four, these governing the school as one department of the university; and of students 210, of whom seventeen are pursuing post-graduate courses. The present student body comes from twenty-seven states of the Union, and from the following countries: Armenia, Bulgaria, Canada, China, Germany, India, Italy, Japan, Syria, and Turkey. They represent fifty-nine colleges and universities, and four theological seminaries, and, as usual, several nationalities and religious denominations are reported. The endowments of the school are an undivided part of the general endowment of the university, the university having covenanted to support the seminary at the time it accepted it in 1871 as its earliest organized department. The library of the school, and the collection of the adjoining general theological library (the latter subsidized by the university and open to the students), include 40,000 volumes, while the Boston Public Library, located but a short distance away, gives access to nearly a million more.

WILLIAM FAIRFIELD WARREN.

BIBLIOGRAPHY: A. W. Cummings, *Early Schools of Methodism*, New York, 1886, pp. 369–379; W. F. Warren, "Historical Address," in *First Quarter-Centennial of Boston University*, Boston, 1898, pp. 30–49. An illustrated history of the institution during its Concord period, by J. W. Merrill, is preserved in manuscript in the archives of the New England Methodist Historical Society, Boston.

3. Drew: This seminary, which is situated at Madison, Morris Co., N. J., was founded in 1866 by Daniel Drew, who gave $250,000 to purchase the Gibbons property, consisting of ninety-six acres and a fine old colonial mansion, and who proposed to give an equal amount for endowment, though financial reverses prevented the consummation of his plans. Under the presidency of Dr. John McClintock (q.v.), the seminary was opened in 1867, and under the care of his successors, Drs. Foster and Hurst (q.v.) passed successfully through the formative period, and also sustained the trial of the great financial panic in which the founder's private fortune disappeared. After the election of Drs. Foster and Hurst to the bishopric, Dr. Henry A. Buttz (q.v.) became president in 1880, continuing also to fill the chair of New-Testament exegesis. During his administration the productive endowment of the seminary has increased to $600,000, and buildings for library, administration, dormitories, and gymnasium have been erected to the same amount. The library contains 114,000 volumes, and more than 100,000 pamphlets. The seminary is under the control of the Methodist Episcopal Church, whose bishops constitute a board of supervision, and nominate its professors, who are elected by a board of trustees consisting of thirty-nine members, all of whom, both lay and clerical, must be members of the same church. The faculty consists of seven professors, who are assisted by two instructors and a librarian. The professors must be members of the Methodist Episcopal Church, and are required to subscribe annually to its doctrines. The number of its students (1910) is 175, and it has over 1,300 graduates engaged in pastoral or mission work throughout the world. The seminary was fortunate in its early professors, who filled large rôles in the Church, and made many contributions to its literature, among them being John McClintock, James Strong (q.v.), John Miley, and George R. Crooks (q.v.). Though closely attached to the Methodist Episcopal Church, the seminary has exercised much influence upon other denominations, and has always freely admitted to its student body members of any Evangelical church, being never without representatives of other Protestant bodies.   ROBERT W. ROGERS.

4. Garrett Biblical Institute: This institution is located at Evanston (a suburb of Chicago) Cook Co., Ill., and was incorporated by the general assembly of the state as a theological seminary of the Methodist Episcopal Church, the incorporators named in the charter being Orrington Lunt, John Evans, Philo Judson, Grant Goodrich, and Stephen P. Keyes. More than a year before the charter was obtained, a building was secured sufficient to accommodate forty students, and the school opened Jan., 1854, under charge of Rev. John Dempster, Rev. William Goodfellow, and Rev. William P. Wright. Four students were present at the beginning of the first term, but sixteen were enrolled before the close. In 1857, Rev. Daniel P. Kidder Rev. Henry Bannister, and Rev. Francis D. Hemenway were added to the faculty. The control of the institute is with a board of six trustees, three laymen and three ministers, elected by the annual conference within the bounds of which the school is located. The trustees have power to elect and remove the teachers as they see fit, and the board of instruction may, with the trustees, elect a president. During the first twenty-five years the senior professor acted as president, but in 1879, Dr. William X. Ninde was elected to that office and served until 1884, when he was elected bishop. In 1885, Dr. Henry B. Ridgaway was made president, and upon his death, in 1895, Dr. Charles J. Little, the present incumbent, succeeded him in office. There were in 1910 seven professors and one assistant professor. The property of the institute consists of a portion of the campus of the Northwestern University which is leased in perpetuity. Two buildings at present occupy this ground, Heck Hall, a dormitory capable of accommodating 100 students, and Memorial Hall, which contains the chapel, the lecture-rooms and studies of the professors, and the library annex. This annex is a fire-proof building, the gift of William Deering, and contains, besides the library, a museum of Christian archeology, given as a memorial of the late Prof. Charles W. Bennett. The library has over 27,000 volumes, including probably the most extensive and valuable collection of the literature of Methodism in the world. The productive endowment of the institute is not far from $750,000, and consisted at first of a large property, improved and unimproved, in the city of Chicago, given by the will of Mrs. Eliza Garrett, after whom the institute is named.

Garrett Biblical Institute stands for thorough instruction in all those studies which are usually taken in theological seminaries, and which are deemed necessary to an accomplished minister of the gospel, and the doctrines taught conform to the acknowledged standards of the Methodist Episcopal Church. While urging the great importance of a thorough collegiate training as a condition of admission to its classes, this institute has never rejected any candidate for the Christian ministry who, upon examination and trial, evinced a sufficient preparatory training to pursue one of its courses of study with a fair measure of success. The total number of graduates is over 1,000, and three times that number have for a time enjoyed the privileges of the school. For no considerable period has there ever been a noteworthy falling off in the numbers in attendance. The registration for the last four years has been 173 in 1907, 199 in 1908, 221 in 1909, and 194 in 1910. These students have come from all parts of the United States, and not a few from foreign lands. They have gone forth to minister in nearly every state and territory of the Union, and more than ninety of the graduates have gone as missionaries to South America, Africa, India, the Philippine Islands, China, and Japan. Most of the graduates are still living and acting as pastors of churches, many of them occupying conspicuous pulpits with marked ability, while not a few have been chosen editors of religious journals, secretaries of benevolent organizations, professors and presidents of colleges, and bishops of the Methodist Episcopal Church.   MILTON S. TERRY.

BIBLIOGRAPHY: *Memorial Volume of Semicentennial of Garrett Biblical Institute*, 1906.

5. German: This seminary forms a department of Central Wesleyan College, located at Warrenton, Warren Co., Mo., and founded by German Methodists in 1864, for the purpose of educating the youth of the land and of training young men for the ministry. In 1878, Dr. J. L. Kessler was appointed professor of theology; in 1884 two professors were elected; and since 1900 there has been a faculty of four, with Otto E. Kriege as president. In this year the theological department, reorganized as Central Wesleyan Theological Seminary, was recognized by the bishops of the Methodist Episcopal Church as an official seminary. In 1909 the German College at Mt. Pleasant, Ia., was united with Central Wesleyan College at Warrenton, Mo., and the theological department is now known as German Theological Seminary. There are two three-year diploma courses, a four-year classical-theological course, leading to the B.A. degree, and a three-year theological course, leading to the B.D. degree. The number of students is about forty. Of the 657 alumni of Central Wesleyan College, 197 entered the ministry, and 157 became teachers, while probably a hundred more, who did not graduate, are serving the church as ministers or missionaries. It has been the aim of the seminary to meet the new conditions of the German Methodist Episcopal Church by supplying well-equipped bilingual ministers, since many German churches to-day need men who can use the German language in the morning services and the English tongue equally well in the evening services. The two patron German conferences depend almost wholly upon the output of the German Theological Seminary for their new supply of ministers, and the supply does not equal the demand. A number of graduates have entered English conferences, and a few are serving with honor in other denominations. A board of trustees elected by two German conferences of the Methodist Episcopal Church governs both the college and the seminary. The endowment of the seminary is $50,000, and its library contains 2,000 volumes.

OTTO E. KRIEGE.

6. Nast: Nast Theological Seminary is located at Berea, Cuyahoga Co., O., and is in reality a part of German Wallace College, since there is no special charter nor trustee-board for the seminary, the charter of the college including the seminary. The institution was founded in the year 1863, the names of the members of the first board of trustees and incorporators of the college and seminary being: Dr. W. Nast, Rev. W. Ahrens, F. Fischer, R. A. W. Bruehl, Rev. E. Wunderlich, P. Pinger, D. Mallow, J. Kraft, Rev. F. Schuler, J. Wettstein, W. Mack, J. C. Schupp, and Anton Hasenpflug. Among the earliest instructors were Dr. W. Nast, Rev. J. Rothweiler, P. W. Mosblech, Dr. Albert Nast, Miss Mary Hasenpflug, Rev. A. Loebenstein, Rev. C. F. Morf, Dr. C. Riemenschneider, Rev. P. Wacker, Rev. J. O. Berr, Rev. C. F. Paulus, and Prof. V. Wilker. The seminary was founded by, and is affiliated with, the German Methodist Church, and its purpose is the education of the sons and daughters of German Methodism, and the training of ministers for the German Methodist Church. The seminary is strongly conservative in its theology, and aims to be very thorough in its methods and courses. A very large

percentage of the ministers of the German Methodist Church were educated in this seminary. The
names of some of its professors are well known
throughout this country and in other countries, as,
for example, Dr. C. F. Paulus, Dr. C. Riemenschneider, Prof. V. Wilker, and Bishop John L. Nuelsen
(q.v.).

The school has been enabled to do its excellent
work partly through its connection with Baldwin
University, also located at Berea, O. A contract
with this university permits students of German
Wallace College and Nast Theological Seminary to
pursue, without payment of tuition, class-work in
Baldwin University, and students of Baldwin University are permitted to do the same in German
Wallace College. The institution has now (1911)
250 students, 23 instructors, 24 trustees, $300,000
endowment, and about 9,000 volumes in the library,
while the campus and buildings are valued at about
$150,000. A magazine, *Zeitschrift für Theologie
und Kirche*, is published bimonthly by the faculty
of the seminary. ARTHUR L. BRESLICH.

7. Swedish: The Swedish Theological Seminary
of the Methodist Episcopal Church, now located at
Evanston (a suburb of Chicago), Ill., was organized
in Galesburg, Ill., in Jan., 1870, for the purpose of
educating ministers for the Swedish Methodist
churches in America; and the pastor in Galesburg,
Rev. N. O. Westergreen, being elected its teacher,
began his work with three students. Some years
afterward the school was moved to Galva, Ill., where
it was located two years, with Rev. C. A. Wiren as
teacher, until Jan., 1875, when it was moved again,
this time to Evanston, Ill., where it is still located,
and where it became affiliated with Garrett Biblical
Institute of the Northwestern University.

Rev. Wm. Henschen, of Upsala, Sweden, now
became its president, and served in this capacity till
1883, when he was succeeded by Rev. Albert Eric-
son, who was its president until 1909. In the year
1883 a suitable building was erected, at a cost of
$8,000, on the shore of Lake Michigan, near the
Northwestern University, but since this building
stood on leased ground the trustees of the seminary
bought, in the year 1908, a half block of land on
Orrington Ave. and Lincoln St., in Evanston, and
erected a commodious building, at a cost of $35,000.

The institution is now owned and maintained by
the five Swedish conferences in America through a
board of directors consisting of eleven members.
The current expenses are raised by an annual collection in the different conferences and by interest
from an endowment fund of about $50,000. In
1910 the faculty consisted of three professors, C. G.
Wallenius (president), J. E. Hillberg, and F. A.
Lundberg, and for the last ten years the registration
has varied between twenty-five and thirty. The
course of study extends through a period of four
years, the first two comprising an academic course
for those who have not completed their academic
education, while the last two years are devoted to a
thorough study of the theological branches. Since
its organization the school has graduated more than
two hundred students who are ministers in different
parts of America and Sweden. The seminary has
a library of about 1,500 bound volumes (chiefly

theological and historical works), and 500 pamphlets. C. G. WALLENIUS.

BIBLIOGRAPHY: C. G. Wallenius, *Svenska Metodismen i Amerika*, Chicago, 1895.

8. Taylor: Taylor University, under the control
of the Methodist Episcopal Church, is located at
Upland, Grant Co., Ind., and had its origin in 1846
through the union of Fort Wayne College and Fort
Wayne Female Academy, its first president being
Hon. Alexander C. Heustis. The institution remained at Fort Wayne until 1893, when, largely
through the efforts of Rev. John C. White, of Logans-
port, Ind., it was removed to Upland, its name now
being changed to Taylor University. The seminary,
which forms part of the university, stands for the
old Bible, full salvation, sanctification as a work of
grace subsequent to regeneration, and for every
truth taught in the Bible, and it is opposed to destructive criticism and to every form of worldliness
and sin. It has been largely influential in helping
to uphold the Wesleyan doctrine of entire sanctification, and it is a noteworthy missionary center,
not only sending many into the foreign mission field,
but also training many from foreign lands to return
to their native countries as missionaries. Among its
prominent instructors have been T. C. Reade, C. W.
Winchester, H. N. Herrick, and B. W. Ayers. In
1910 the university had thirteen professors and
four instructors, and about 160 students, coming
from twenty states and from eleven countries, including the West Indies, Russia, Bulgaria, Persia,
Africa, and Canada, and representing not only the
Methodist denominations, but also the United
Brethren, Friends, and Baptists. The institution
is governed by twenty-one trustees elected by the
National Local Preachers' Association of the United
States. It possesses no endowment, but receives
annually a considerable sum from regular and voluntary contributions of friends. The library contains 6,000 volumes. M. VAYHINGER.

9. Vanderbilt: This seminary constitutes one of
the seven departments of Vanderbilt University, at
Nashville, Tenn., which derives its origin from a
gift of $500,000 by Cornelius Vanderbilt, of New
York, to an institution just projected and chartered
as "The Central University of the Methodist Episcopal Church, South." He later doubled this gift,
and when the university was opened in Sept., 1875,
the name was changed to Vanderbilt University.
The "Central University" had been chartered June
29, 1872, by several ministers and members of the
Methodist Episcopal Church, South, and the first
board of trust represented eight annual conferences
of the denomination, located in Tennessee, Kentucky, Arkansas, Mississippi, and Alabama, these
conferences being termed "patronizing conferences,"
and each having representatives on the board. In
1898 these conferences transferred their rights in the
ownership and government of the university to the
General Conference of the denomination, and the
institution has since been regarded as connectional in
character, being held in trust by its board for the
entire denomination, from any part of which this
board of trust, thirty-three in number, is chosen.
The leading motive in the founding of the university
was to provide the best possible equipment for train-

ing men for the ministry of the Methodist Episcopal Church, South, and since it was deemed wise that such students should not be separated from those preparing for other avocations, the seminary was designedly made a department of the university itself. During the history of the university over a thousand students for the ministry have been enrolled, the number in the seminary (or Biblical department) being 110 in 1910 (the largest attendance thus far reached), and seventeen in the academic department. Nearly 700 alumni are in the active work of the ministry, chiefly in the Methodist Episcopal Church, South (forming at least a tenth of the entire ministry of the denomination), as well as in the foreign mission fields of Mexico, Cuba, Brazil, China, Japan, and Korea. In 1902, a correspondence school, under the direction of the theological faculty, was organized, which in 1910 had about 1,000 students, chiefly young ministers of the Methodist Episcopal Church, South. Work done in this school may be credited to the extent of one-third of the total amount required for a diploma or degree, residence being required for the remainder, and degrees being given only to those already having the B.A., those not having it receiving merely diplomas.

The first chancellor of the university was Dr. L. C. Garland, who was succeeded in 1893 by the present chancellor, Dr. James H. Kirkland; while the first dean of the theological faculty was Dr. Thomas O. Summers (q.v.), who was succeeded, at his death in 1882, by Dr. A. M. Shipp (q.v.). Among the other noteworthy members of the faculty have been Bishops John J. Tigert (q.v.) and J. C. Granbery (q.v.). The work of the Biblical department is now organized in nine schools, each under one of the following faculty: J. H. Stevenson (q.v.; Old-Testament language and literature), Thomas Carter (New-Testament language and literature), H. B. Carré (Biblical theology and English exegesis), O. E. Brown (Biblical and ecclesiastical history), Wilbur F. Tillett (q.v.; systematic theology; dean), J. A. Kern (q.v.; practical theology), G. W. Dyer (practical sociology), A. M. Harris (public speaking), and J. L. Cuninggim (religious education). The department is supported partly from the original general endowment of the university, and partly from the income of about $150,000, especially contributed to the department, the whole income available for it being about $20,000 annually. Besides this, the general conference at Asheville, N. C., in May, 1910, inaugurated a plan whereby the department may receive the additional sum of $12,000 or $15,000 annually from a general assessment levied on the entire denomination. The library contains about 10,000 volumes, and the department publishes an annual bulletin. The correspondence school issues a similar bulletin, and, in addition, a small monthly journal, entitled *The Correspondence Reporter*.

WILBUR F. TILLETT.

IX. Methodist Protestant.—1. Adrian: This theological school is connected with Adrian College, which is located at Adrian, Lenawee Co., Mich., where it was founded in the year 1860 or 1861. It was at first affiliated with the Wesleyan Methodist Church, but in 1867 it was transferred to the Methodist Protestant Church, which continues to operate the school, aiming to meet the needs of the denomination with which it is now associated. Prominent among its instructors have been the late Rev. Asa Mahan (q.v.), and Rev. G. B. McElroy and Rev. Luther Lee. The school, until recently, was under the management of the president of Adrian College (Rev. B. W. Anthony), but had its own dean (Rev. H. L. Feeman), who was responsible for the course of study, etc. In the year of 1909–10 the school offered a full seminary course, but in the spring of 1910 President Anthony recommended that it be placed under separate and distinct management, and be known as the Adrian Theological Seminary, with its former dean as its president. This recommendation was unanimously adopted by the board of trustees, and the school now has only an affiliated relation to its former college. It is a graduate school, receiving none excepting those who have the bachelor's degree.

Its course of study has been chosen after the most careful examination of the courses offered by the best seminaries in the country, and it is governed by a board of three directors chosen by the board of trustees of Adrian College. The school is without endowment, but has a very good working library. Prof. H. C. Renton is associated with Dr. Feeman in the management of the institution. The classes are naturally small, owing to the fact that it is a graduate school; but the seminary has opened with great promise for future success.

B. W. ANTHONY.

2. Westminster (Tehuacana, Tex.): The Westminster College of Theology, located in Tehuacana, Limestone Co., Tex., was founded in the fall of 1895 under the supervision of the Methodist Protestant Church, largely through the efforts of Rev. J. L. Lawlis, assisted by Rev. T. L. Garrison, both members of the Texas Annual Conference of the Methodist Protestant Church. In the early years of the work, Dr. Lawlis was assisted in the theological department by Prof. C. O. Stubbs. The institution was established to meet a need of the Methodist Protestant Church in the Southwest, and its founders were especially desirous that young men who were called to the ministry should have an opportunity to prepare themselves for their lifework in the section in which they resided and expected to labor. The seminary is evangelical in faith, and stands on the broad doctrines of the church which has it under its supervision. It was opened in connection with the College of Arts and Sciences in the town of Westminster, Collin Co., Tex., and in the summer of 1902 both colleges were moved to Tehuacana, where they are now located. Dr. Lawlis died in the fall of 1902, and in 1903, Rev. Harry Heffner Price was elected to the presidency of the College of Theology. In 1906, the College of Theology and the College of Arts and Sciences were united under one president, the Rev. Mr. Price, and the theological work was arranged as a department of the main college work. Professors H. H. Price and R. F. Day have been most prominent in developing the course of instruction.

The department has three instructors and several assistants, while eight members, elected by the Texas Annual Conference, constitute the board of regents, which is the governing body and determines the general policy of the institution. The executive officer of the board is the president of the faculty, who has authority to act in matters that pertain to the policy and government of the institution in the interval between the board meetings. In the year 1909-10 ten students were enrolled in the theological department—all Methodist Protestants—two from Oklahoma, one from Arkansas, and seven from Texas. The endowment amounts to $4,000, and the number of books in the library is about 500.

HARRY HEFFNER PRICE.

3. Westminster (Westminster, Md.): This seminary was founded in 1882 at Westminster, Md., and had its inception in a resolution adopted by the Maryland Annual Conference of the Methodist Protestant Church in March, 1881, appointing a committee to mature some plan by which systematic theology might be taught those graduates of Western Maryland College who were preparing for the Christian ministry. This committee reported to the conference in 1882, recommending that a department of theology be established in the college and that a minister of the conference be placed at the head of that department, to be styled the principal of the School of Theology. The conference adopted this recommendation, but at a special meeting of the board of trustees, held in May, 1882, to confer with the principal upon the organization of the department of theology, and upon the recommendation of the principal (Dr. T. H. Lewis), it was resolved that it was impracticable to establish such a department in the college, and that an independent theological institution should be organized. To aid in this design the board purchased and presented to the school of theology a tract of land adjoining the college, and offered to indorse a loan for the purpose of erecting a building thereon for the use of the school. This was carried out, and work was begun in 1882, while in Jan., 1884, at the recommendation of the principal, the institution was incorporated by the Maryland Legislature. The earliest instructors of the seminary were Drs. J. T. Ward, T. H. Lewis, J. T. Murray, and L. W. Bates, while other prominent teachers on its faculty have been Drs. B. F. Benson and J. D. Kinzer. The institution stands for evangelical Christianity with a progressiveness that is not radicalism, and a conservatism that is not stagnation; and among its alumni are pastors of prominent churches, professors and presidents of Methodist Protestant colleges, and missionaries in China and Japan. In 1910 there were five instructors (Rev. Hugh Latimer Elderdice, president), and a governing board of ten (five ministers and five laymen). To this board three ministers and two laymen are elected by the Maryland Annual Conference of the Methodist Protestant Church every fourth session succeeding the session of 1884, while two ministers and three laymen are elected by the General Conference of the Methodist Protestant Church, and hold office for four years. This board holds the property, elects the faculty, and exercises general supervision over the interests of the seminary. There is also a board of visitors, composed of one minister and one layman, appointed by each patron Annual Conference—i.e., each conference appropriating a collection to the seminary. In 1910 there were forty students from thirteen annual conferences, all Methodist Protestants excepting one. The endowment amounts to about $8,000, and the number of books in the library is about 2,500.   H. L. ELDERDICE.

X. New Jerusalem Church.—1. Cambridge: The New Church Theological School was established in the year 1866, and was incorporated May 17, 1881, by members of the General Convention of the New Jerusalem in the United States of America. During the first twelve years it was located at Waltham, Mass., but in 1878 it was removed to Boston, and in 1889 to Cambridge, Mass., where a convenient and ample property was secured in the immediate neighborhood of Harvard University. The first president and instructor in theology was the Rev. Thomas Worcester, and others early connected with the school were the Rev. Samuel F. Dike and the Rev. T. O. Paine (q.v.). Among its more recent instructors have been the Rev. John Worcester (q.v.) and the Rev. T. F. Wright (q.v.). The purpose of the school and its distinctive work is the preparation of ministers for the New Church, giving them thorough instruction in the Sacred Scriptures and in the doctrines of the New Church as unfolded from the Word in the writings of Emanuel Swedenborg. Twelve managers and fourteen directors, with the president and treasurer, care for the spiritual and material welfare of the school, which had in 1910 five professors, four students, and an endowment of $266,825.74.

WILLIAM L. WORCESTER.

XI a. Presbyterian (Northern).—1. Auburn: This institution is located in Auburn, Cayuga Co., N. Y., where it was founded in 1818. The proposal to establish such a seminary under the control of the local presbyteries was made in the Presbytery of Cayuga, in Jan., 1818, was adopted in the same year by the Synod of Geneva, and, after approval by the General Assembly in 1819, was chartered in 1820 and opened for students in the following year. Its work has since been continuous, except in 1854-55. The seminary had its origin in the religious revivals that swept through the new settlements early in the last century, and in the consequent quickening of missionary work and the increasing demand for ministers. Foremost among the founders of the institution was Rev. Dirck C. Lansing, and the first faculty consisted of him and of M. L. Perrine, H. Mills, and J. Richards. Originally there were four chairs of instruction, one for each of the departments now known as exegetical, historical, dogmatic, and practical theology. In 1867 the exegetical department was enlarged by establishing the chair of Hebrew language and literature, and in 1893 the faculty was strengthened, especially in the department of practical theology, by the election of a president, who is also professor of pastoral theology, church polity, and sacraments. In 1903, the assistant professorship in the New-Testament department was created, in 1904 the chair of theism and apologetic, and in 1907 the assistant professorship in the Old-Testament department. In 1909, the assistant professor in the New-Testament department became professor of New-Testament language and criticism, and the assistant professor in the Old-Testament department became professor of Semitic languages and religions. The seminary stands for the largest and best scholarly, practical, and spiritual preparation and character of young men for the work of the ministry. It encourages liberty of investigation and expression, both in professors and students, and aims to equip its students in all respects for the skilful and efficient discharge of the duties of their high profession. It was in this institution that many of the ministers received their training who were exscinded from the Presbyterian Church in 1837–38 and formed the New School Presbyterian Church, and it was one of the chief sources of supply of ministers for that church until the reunion of the Old and New School churches in 1870. Since then it has been recognized as one of the foremost of the seminaries of the reunited denomination. It was here that the Auburn Convention was held, on Aug. 17, 1837, which framed the Auburn Declaration (q.v.), which played such an important part in the division of the church at that time, and which furnished a basis for the reunion in 1870. As this seminary has always emphasized the importance of preparing its students for the active work of the ministry, it has been generally recognized as the leader in all those modifications of seminary curricula which tended toward making more practical such training; and it was the first of the seminaries to introduce, among other subjects, the teaching of English Bible, missions, Sunday-school, and pedagogy. Prominent in its faculty, in addition to its original professors, are found the names of Samuel Hanson Cox (q.v.), Laurens P. Hickok (q.v.), Samuel Mills Hopkins, William G. T. Shedd (q.v.), Ezra A. Huntington, Edwin Hall, Willis J. Beecher (q.v.), Herrick Johnson (q.v.), Ransom B. Welch, Anson J. Upson, Henry M. Booth. In 1910 its faculty numbered ten, and it is governed by twenty-eight directors, eighteen of whom are elected by the eighteen presbyteries in the state of New York, one from each, the remaining ten being elected by the board itself, the president of the seminary being *ex officio* one of the ten. All of these directors, except the president, are elected for a term of three years. This board is an independent and self-governing body, and its acts are not reviewable. There were, in 1910, seventy-one students, twenty-eight from New York State, with representatives from sixteen other states, as well as from Asia Minor and Japan, these students being attached to the following denominations: Presbyterian (52), Baptist (1), Christ's Church in Japan (6), Union Church in Japan (1), Congregational (2), Armenian Presbyterian (1), Methodist (4), Italian Presbyterian (1), A. M. E. Zion (1), and Disciples (2). The endowment of the institution is $550,000, and its library contains 33,472 volumes.　　GEORGE B. STEWART.

2. Bloomfield: This German Presbyterian theological seminary was established at Newark, N. J., in 1869, by the Presbytery of Newark, and is regularly affiliated with the Presbyterian Church of the United States of America. Its charter was granted in 1871 and amended in 1873; and by a general act of the legislature of New Jersey it received collegiate standing in 1909. Its foundation is largely due to the efforts of the Rev. D. W. Poor, and the school was organized by the Presbytery of Newark, among whose members were two German pastors, the Rev. J. U. Guenther and the Rev. George C. Seibert, who clearly saw the necessity of establishing an institution for educating clergymen to labor in the American spirit among the German immigrants. The earliest instructors were the Rev. George C. Seibert and the Rev. J. U. Guenther in German, and the Rev. Joseph Fewsmith and the Rev. Charles A. Smith in English branches. At its inception the school had nine students living in a dormitory next to the parsonage of the First German Presbyterian Church of Newark and a faculty of four teachers had been provided, giving a total of twenty-two lectures per week, instruction in German preponderating. The first outline of studies comprised an academic and theological course, and the faculty were required to subscribe annually to the standards of the Presbyterian Church. In 1872 the institution, then having twenty students, was transferred to Bloomfield, N. J., where it has since been located, and where 149 ministers of the Gospel have been graduated and a number of lay workers have been educated. In the fall of 1873 the Rev. Chas. E. Knox, secretary of the board of directors since its organization, was elected president and professor of homiletics, church government, and pastoral theology, and remained in that position until his death in 1900, and the Rev. George C. Seibert was elected professor of Biblical exegesis and theology, and held that position until his death in 1902. In 1895 the Rev. Henry J. Weber, now chairman of the faculty, was elected professor of Hebrew exegesis and church history, and he and the Rev. Chas. T. Hock have remained members of the faculty to date, while in 1902 the Rev. Arnold W. Fismer was elected professor of New-Testament exegesis and ethics. In 1890 a special course for Bohemian and Italian students was added to the German course, but, for lack of support, was discontinued in 1895. In 1904, however, at the suggestion of the General Assembly, the institution undertook polyglot work, extended the course to nine years, and adopted a curriculum to impart instruction to students of other nationalities in addition to the German. The seminary has at present (1910) eleven instructors and twenty-three directors, who are elected by the Presbytery of Newark, the General Assembly having a veto power as regards the election of directors and professors. The number of students in 1910 was fifty-seven: 25 Germans, 12 Magyars, 11 Italians, 5 Hebrews, 3 Ruthenians, and 1 Syrian. Of these students, one is affiliated with the Lutheran Church, one with the Evangelical Synod, two with the Reformed, and fifty-three with the Presbyterian Church. The endowment of the school amounted in 1910 to $206,826.46, and the library consists of 7,350 books.　　HENRY J. WEBER.

BIBLIOGRAPHY: C. E. Knox, *The German Problem and the Solution Offered by the German Theological School of Newark, N. J.*, New York, 1874; G. C. Seibert, *The Germans in America and their Need*, ib. 1874 (these appeared as *Addresses at the Inauguration of the German Theological School of Newark*).

3. Lane: This institution, which is located at Cincinnati, O., was founded in 1829 through the efforts of a number of Presbyterian ministers and laymen interested in providing an adequately educated ministry in and for the West. Its original endowment consisted of several thousand dollars donated by Ebenezer Lane and his brother, who were Baptists, and of sixty acres of land on Walnut Hills, given by members of the Kemper family. It was at first proposed to establish an academic as well as a theological institution, and a preparatory school was opened in Nov., 1829; but, after an experiment of five years, this department finally closed. The theological institution was established in Dec., 1832, when Drs. Lyman Beecher (q.v.) and T. J. Biggs were formally inducted into office. Dr. Calvin E. Stowe (q.v.) entered its service in the following July; and Baxter Dickinson in Oct., 1835, retiring in 1839. Dr. Beecher resigned in 1850, and Professor Stowe shortly after. Among those who have served the seminary since its organization the most distinguished, next to Beecher, was D. Howe Allen, and others of note have been George E. Day, J. B. Condit, Llewelyn J. Evans (q.v.), E. Ballantine, Henry A. Nelson (q.v.), Thomas E. Thomas, Henry Preserved Smith (q.v.), Z. M. Humphrey, James Eells, John De Witt (q.v.), A. C. McGiffert (q.v.), H. M. Hulbert, D. Schley Schaff (q.v.), Henry Goodwin Smith (q.v.), J. A. Craig (q.v.), Kemper Fullerton, William Henry Roberts (q.v.), D. P. Putnam, and Edward D. Morris (q.v.).

Lane has always been, in a broad and free sense, Presbyterian, and its charter provides that all professors, tutors, teachers, and instructors shall be members of the Presbyterian Church in good standing. After 1837 it sided with the New-School branch, but entered heartily into the union of 1869. It has a spacious campus, commodious buildings, a fair though inadequate endowment, considerable scholarship and library funds, and an excellent library of nearly 20,000 volumes, and is well equipped for useful service to the Church. Its present faculty consists of William McKibbin (q.v.; president and professor of systematic theology), Alexander B. Riggs (q.v.; New-Testament exegesis and introduction), Edward Mack (Hebrew and Old-Testament literature), and Selby Frame Vance (church history). The Theological Seminary of the South (Cumberland), having lost its location in Lebanon, Tenn., through an adverse legal decision, is by advice of the General Assembly (1910) transferred to Lane for the present, two of its professors, J. V. Stephens and F. H. Farr, being added to the faculty. About fifty students are enrolled.

E. D. Morris.

4. Lincoln: This theological seminary, the first to be founded in the United States for the higher Christian education of negroes, is located at Lincoln University, Chester Co., Pa. Its germ thought was an ordination service in 1849, in New London, Pa., when Rev. John Miller Dickey, while assisting in the ordination of James L. Mackey, a white man, as a missionary to Africa, determined to establish an institution where negroes could be trained for a like purpose. Four years later the New Castle Presbytery requested and secured the approval of the General Assembly for the establishment of such a school, which took legal form in a charter from the State of Pennsylvania in 1854 as Ashmun Institute. On Jan. 1, 1857, a small three-story building opened its doors to four students, and from 1857 to 1865 Rev. John Pym Carter, and, following him, Rev. John Wynn Martin, combined president and faculty each in his own person, while during this time the Board of Foreign Missions established a presbytery in Liberia with three missionaries from the school. In 1865 Dr. Martin resigned, and was succeeded by Rev. Isaac N. Rendall, who presided over the institution until 1906, when Rev. John B. Rendall was elected president. In 1866 the legislature approved the petition of the trustees, amended the charter, and changed the name to Lincoln University. From 1865 both a college and seminary course have been in operation, and in 1871 the charter was again amended, placing the seminary under the oversight of the General Assembly. During its existence the institution has graduated 674 ministers of all denominations, twenty-seven of whom have been missionaries to Africa.

Among the earliest instructors were Drs. Isaac N. Rendall, Ezra E. Adams, Edwin R. Bower, Lorenzo Wescott, Gilbert T. Woodhull, Aspinwall Hodge, and Benjamin T. Jones. In 1910 there were nine professors, twenty-one trustees, and sixty-two students, chiefly from North and South Carolina, Pennsylvania, Virginia, and Maryland, together with eight from the West Indies and three from South America, while in 1909 three South Africans and in 1908 three Zulus were graduated and returned as missionaries to their native lands. The students in 1910 are chiefly Presbyterians (28), Baptists (14), and Methodists (11), with nine of various other denominations. The property and endowment of the seminary amount to $419,783, and the institution also shares in the use of some of the public buildings of the university, while the library of 18,000 volumes is used likewise jointly by both university and seminary.   J. B. Rendall.

5. McCormick: This theological seminary, now located at Chicago, Ill., was founded in 1829 through the efforts of Rev. John Finley Crowe, at Hanover, Ind. Partly as a result of the revival of 1827–28, Hanover Academy, on its own initiative, was adopted as a synodical school by the Synod of Indiana on condition that a theological department be connected therewith. Agreeably to this provision, Rev. John Matthews was called to the chair of theology, and with him Rev. John W. Cunningham, Rev. George Bishop, and Rev. James Wood served at different times as professors. The institution was then called the Indiana Theological Seminary, but in 1840 it was moved to New Albany, Ind., and renamed the New Albany Theological Seminary, with the hope that it would thereby have an increased constituency, while in addition Mr. Elias Ayers offered for endowment what was then considered a large sum of money. Its success in this location was not great, and it became manifest that removal was essential to its growth. In 1857 the last class at New Albany was graduated, and for the next two years the question of its future home was actively discussed, until the General Assembly received a proposition from the board of directors by which the seminary was to be transferred from synodical to assembly supervision, the matter of location being left to the assembly. Mr. Cyrus H. McCormick had offered an endowment of $100,000, on condition that the seminary be moved to Chicago, and the assembly accordingly voted for this site and elected new professors and a board of directors of what was now called the Presbyterian Theological Seminary of the Northwest. From 1859 to 1881, the seminary maintained its position in spite of difficulties and limited endowment, but in the latter year reconstruction took place, and from that date onward new professorships were established and enlarged endowments obtained, new dormitories and a library building were erected, and a large increase was secured in the number of books. In 1886 the name was changed to the McCormick Theological Seminary of the Presbyterian Church. The institution stands for the largest and broadest theological culture, the deepening and strengthening of the intellectual and spiritual life of the students, and the promotion of all that will fit them for efficient work both at home and abroad. The men who have filled its chairs or been prominent in its board of directors have been leaders in the councils of the church in many important crises. The first theological student association in the country was organized at McCormick in 1897, and became one of the important factors in the development of the theological section of the Student Department of the Y. M. C. A. Prominent among its instructors, now deceased, were Drs. John Matthews, E. D. MacMaster, Nathan L. Rice, R. W. Patterson, Charles Elliott, William M. Blackburn, and Leroy J. Halsey.

The number of instructors in 1910 was fifteen, and there are forty directors, consisting of an equal number of ministers and elders, who control all affairs pertaining to the institution, and have not only the choice and election of professors, but also of trustees who are responsible for the care of the property. An annual report is made to the General Assembly, which has the right of veto on appointment to board or faculty. The number of students in 1910 was 141, coming principally from the states west of the Alleghanies, although Brazil, Canada, Cuba, Italy, Mexico, Persia, and Syria are also represented. The great majority are Presbyterian by training, with a few of other denominations. The amount of endowment is $1,981,234, and the number of books in the library is 34,290.

A. S. CARRIER.

BIBLIOGRAPHY: L. J. Halsey, *History of the McCormick Theological Seminary*, Chicago, 1893; D. W. Fisher, *McCormick Theological Seminary, Historical Sketch*, Chicago, 1910.

6. Northwest: This institution, formerly known officially as " The German Presbyterian Theological School of the Northwest," reincorporated in 1911 as the Dubuque German College and Seminary, is located in Dubuque, Ia., where it was founded in 1852 by the Rev. Adrian Van Vliet. The German immigrants had begun to pour into the Mississippi Valley, and large numbers of them were cut off from religious services because they could not understand the preaching in the American churches. The school commenced in a small way in the pastor's study, where a few German boys were trained for work among their countrymen. The enterprise rapidly

developed, a second teacher, Rev. Godfrey Moery, was secured, and a building adjoining the church was purchased and fitted up for the school, for which the Presbytery of Dubuque, in Iowa, and the Presbytery of Dane, in Wisconsin, both under the care of the old School General Assembly of the Presbyterian Church, became responsible. When the Old School and New School churches united, the German Seminary came under the care of the General Assembly of the Presbyterian Church in the United States of America, and in 1871 a well-appointed school building was bought. Among other early professors may be mentioned Rev. Jacob Conzett, Rev. A. J. Schlager, Rev. Adam McClelland, Rev. A. Van der Lippe, and Rev. N. M. Steffens. The seminary has for its object the education of a ministry of foreign speech for the immigrant population, and in this work it is the pioneer in the Presbyterian Church. It was found that it was impossible to supply the churches with an imported ministry, and that where such ministers were secured they were not desirable. Hence Van Vliet planned to send out young men of immigrant families, trained as the American minister is trained to take the gospel to their countrymen; and as this necessitated not only theological, but classical and scientific education, the school was organized into three departments, academy, college, and seminary. This plan has met with the cordial approval of the Assembly, and the work for foreign-speaking people is undertaken on this method, its success being witnessed by over a hundred churches organized by its graduates among the Germans. This aspect of the activity of the seminary has so extended that a well-equipped Bohemian department has been added, while the school has many other races among its students— Dutch, Slovak, Russian, Mexican, Jewish, Rumanian, Bulgarian, Hungarian and Japanese.

In 1907 the growing work entered a new and large building with an extensive campus. Already the collegiate department had been erected into the German Presbyterian College, and the scope had been broadened so that a classical education is offered to those who do not intend to enter the ministry. The number of students in the year 1911 was 119, coming from all parts of the United States as well as from Germany, Russia, Austria-Hungary, Servia, Monaco, Japan, and Mexico. The present faculty numbers twelve: C. M. Steffens (president), W. O. Ruston (q.v.; dean), Albert Kuhn, W. C. Laube, John Zimmerman, Daniel Grieder, Alois Barta, F. T. Oldt, John A. McFadden, H. S. Ficke, Paul A. Walz, and Justus H. Brandan. The school is governed by twenty-four regular and four life directors, who are nominated by the board and approved by the General Assembly, and who operate under the care and with the review of the General Assembly. The interest-bearing endowment amounts to $200,000, and the amount invested in campus and buildings is $129,000, a total of $266,000, while the library contains 5,000 volumes.

W. O. RUSTON.

7. Omaha: This seminary, located at Omaha, Neb., was founded Feb. 17, 1891, by clergymen and laymen from the Synods of Nebraska, Iowa, Missouri, Kansas, and South Dakota, and is the only theological institution of the Presbyterian Church, for English-speaking students, between Chicago and San Francisco. The first board of directors consisted of twenty ministers and twenty laymen, and the faculty of Drs. Wm. W. Harsha (systematic theology), Stephen Phelps (homiletics and pastoral theology), Matthew B. Lowrie (New-Testament literature), John Gordon (q.v.; ecclesiastical history), and Charles G. Sterling (Hebrew). The seminary opened in Sept., 1891, with nine students, and has thus far enrolled 200 students and graduated eighteen classes. Many of these men have become leaders in the religious movements of the west and south, and several of the classes have representatives in the foreign field. By the provisions of its charter the institution is under the control of the General Assembly of the Presbyterian Church, U. S. A., and stands for the inculcation of the cardinal doctrines of the Presbyterian Church, although, while the institution is distinctly Presbyterian, and was established for the purpose of teaching the doctrines and the polity of the Presbyterian Church, its doors are open to all young men, whatever their theological opinions, who desire training for the ministry. Free discussion is allowed, and none are compelled to adopt Presbyterian views. Its professors seek to know and teach the results of the best modern scholarship. Nothing is retained just because it is old. The changing conditions of society receive special consideration, and such methods of service are commended as these conditions seem to demand. The seminary was established to increase the supply of ministers for the great mission field within the bounds of which it is located. Its founders have not been disappointed in the results, for more than half of its graduates have entered that field, and through their labors thousands have been added to the membership of the Church. The opportunities and advantages of the institution are also extended to laymen who desire to equip themselves for Christian work.

The development of the institution has been gratifying to its founders and friends, and it has always had the hearty commendation of the Presbyterian General Assembly. At the present time its student body represents ten synods and four denominations. The faculty consists of Albert B. Marshall (president and professor of methodology), Matthew B. Lowrie (homiletics, pastoral theology, and English Bible), Joseph J. Lampe (Hebrew and Old-Testament literature), Daniel E. Jenkins (didactic and polemic theology), Charles A. Mitchell (New-Testament literature), and Charles Herron (ecclesiastical history, church polity, and missions). Through the generosity of friends, especially Mrs. William Thaw, Thomas McDougall, and John H. Converse, the seminary possesses a desirable site and a modern building ample for all its present requirements. Its endowment fund, with other holdings, amounts to $225,000, and its library contains 6,000 volumes.

A. B. Marshall.

8. Princeton: This seminary, which is located at Princeton, Mercer Co., N. J., was founded in 1812 by the General Assembly of the Presbyterian Church in the U. S. A., which created it and controls it. Its official name is "The Theological Seminary of the Presbyterian Church in the U. S. A." The assembly of 1810 decided "immediately to attempt to establish a seminary." That of 1811 adopted a plan or constitution for the seminary. That of 1812, after an agreement with the trustees of the College of New Jersey, located the seminary in Princeton. On May 3, 1812, the assembly elected the first board of directors, consisting of twenty-one ministers and nine ruling elders, as at present, and on June 2 the Rev. Dr. Archibald Alexander (q.v.) was elected professor of didactic and polemic theology. On Aug. 12 the seminary was formally opened with one professor and three students. The classes were first held in Dr. Alexander's house. Those most influential in the inception of the seminary were Rev. Drs. Ashbel Green (q.v.), who wrote the plan; Archibald Alexander, Samuel Miller (q.v.), Jacob J. Janeway, and President Timothy Dwight (q.v.), of Yale College. The General Assembly of 1813 made Princeton the permanent site of the seminary, and the Rev. Dr. Samuel Miller was added to the faculty. The number of students increased rapidly, and it was found necessary to hold the classes in the college buildings. The first seminary building was occupied in 1817. In 1822 Dr. Charles Hodge (q.v.) was elected a professor. In a large measure the seminary owes what it has been and what it has always stood for to its three earliest teachers.

In 1822 the trustees were incorporated by the New Jersey legislature, with control over the material interests of the seminary. The original charter fixed the number at twenty-one, twelve of whom should be laymen and citizens of New Jersey. In 1877 the board was authorized to add twelve to its number. This it has not yet done. The division of the Presbyterian Church, in 1837, into two branches raised the question to which branch the seminary should belong. The courts decided in favor of the Old School branch [and to that branch the seminary adhered]. Until 1835 the faculty consisted of three professors. The next most important additions were J. Addison Alexander (q.v.) in that year, William Henry Green (q.v.) in 1851, and Caspar Wistar Hodge (q.v.) in 1860. In 1871 a new chair of Christian ethics and apologetics was erected. In 1877 Archibald Alexander Hodge was associated with his father in the chair of dogmatics, and in 1880 Francis Landey Patton (q.v.) was called to the chair of the relation of philosophy and science to the Christian religion. In this latter year there were seven professors and two instructors in the faculty. Dr. Charles Hodge celebrated his professorial jubilee in 1872, and Dr. William Henry Green celebrated his in 1896. A new chair of Biblical theology was founded in 1891. In 1836–37 there were 137 students, the high-water mark of the early period; in 1858–59, 181; and 263 in 1894–95, the largest number in any one year. The total number of students, up to 1910, was 5,742, of whom 3,076 were living, while 367 have become foreign missionaries.

Princeton Seminary has always stood for a divinely inspired Bible and its perfect authority in all matters of faith and practise. It has maintained and inculcated the doctrines of the recognized standards of the Presbyterian Church, believing them to be contained in the Scriptures. It has always practised and encouraged a reverent and scientific study of the Bible, and has been ready to subject it to the keenest scrutiny in the spheres of the lower and the higher criticism.

As the oldest of the Presbyterian seminaries in the United States, it has largely influenced the character of the others. Of its students, 108 have become teachers in the Presbyterian schools of theology in the United States, and fifty-five have been moderators of the General Assembly. The *Biblical Repertory and Princeton Review*, founded by Charles Hodge in 1825, wielded a powerful influence upon the theological thought of its time. Its successors have continued, except during the years 1877–80, until the present *Princeton Theological Review*. Some seventeen other religious weeklies and quarterlies have been controlled or edited by alumni of the seminary. The publications of its professors have been noteworthy and most influential, particularly the *Systematic Theology* of Dr. Charles Hodge, and his other works, and those of Archibald Alexander, Samuel Miller, J. Addison Alexander, William Henry Green, and Archibald Alexander Hodge (q.v.).

The faculty in 1910 consisted of ten professors, two assistant professors, and five instructors. There are a librarian and an assistant librarian. There are two endowed lectureships, six fellowships, and five prizes. Besides a broad curriculum there are extra courses leading to the degree of B.D'. The governing boards are a board of directors and a board of trustees, the one electing the professors and assigning their duties, and controlling the educational interests of the seminary, subject to the revision of the General Assembly, the other having the care of its material interests and the appointment of the librarian. Until 1902 the senior professor was the recognized head of the faculty; but in that year provision was made for a president of the seminary, and Dr. F. L. Patton was elected to this office, and still retains it. The president is *ex officio* a member of both the governing boards.

There were 151 students in the seminary in the year 1909–10, coming from thirty-three states and territories, from Canada, Brazil, Ceylon, China, Ireland, and Japan. As to denomination, there were 111 Presbyterian, 9 Reformed, 4 United Presbyterian, 3 Reformed Presbyterian, 3 Methodist, 3 Congregationalist, 3 Lutheran, 3 United Evangelical, 3 Church of Christ in Japan, and 9 scattering. The library contains 87,700 bound volumes and 32,500 pamphlets, distributed in two buildings. The real estate of the seminary is valued at $628,000, and the total value of all its other holdings is $3,225,000. There are on the campus three dormitories, two library buildings, a recitation building, a chapel, a gymnasium, a power house, and nine professors' houses. The present faculty is as follows: Francis Landey Patton, D.D., LL.D., president and professor of the philosophy of religion; Benjamin Breckinridge Warfield (q.v.), D.D., LL.D., Charles Hodge professor of didactic and polemic theology; John D. Davis (q.v.), D.D., LL.D., Helena professor of orien-

tal and Old-Testament literature; John DeWitt (q.v.), D.D., LL.D., Archibald Alexander professor of church history; William Brenton Greene, Jr. (q.v.), D.D., Stuart professor of apologetics and Christian ethics; Geerhardus Vos (q.v.), Ph.D., D.D., Haley professor of Biblical theology; Robert Dick Wilson, Ph.D., D.D., William Henry Green, professor of Semitic philology and Old-Testament criticism; William Park Armstrong, A.M., professor of New-Testament literature and exegesis; Charles Rosenbury Erdman, professor of practical theology; Frederick William Loetscher, Ph.D., professor of homiletics; James Oscar Boyd, Ph.D., assistant professor of oriental and Old-Testament literature; Caspar Wistar Hodge, Ph.D., assistant professor of didactic and polemic theology; Henry Wilson Smith, A.M., instructor in elocution; Kerr Duncan Macmillan, instructor in church history; John Gresham Machen, instructor in the New Testament; Oswald Thompson Allis, A.M., instructor in Semitic philology; Joseph Heatly Dulles (q.v.), A.M., librarian; Paul Martin, registrar and secretary of the faculty; William Boyd Sheddan, assistant librarian.

JOSEPH HEATLY DULLES.

BIBLIOGRAPHY: *Charter and plan of the Theological Seminary of the Presbyterian Church, Princeton, N. J., etc.* (with all changes up to date); *Minutes of the General Assembly of the Presbyterian Church*, 1808 sqq.; *A Brief Account of the Rise, Progress, and Present State of Princeton Theological Seminary*, Philadelphia, 1822; J. H. Dulles, " Princeton Theological Seminary," ch. 25 of *United States Bureau of Education Contributions to American Educational History*, no. 23, Washington, 1899; J. F. Hageman, *History of Princeton and its institutions*, 2 vols., Philadelphia, 1879; *The Princeton Book*, Boston, 1879; A. Nevin, *Encyclopædia of the Presbyterian Church in the U. S. A.*, Philadelphia, 1884; *Addresses before the Alumni Association of Princeton Theological Seminary*, Philadelphia, 1876; C. Hodge, *Princeton Theological Seminary: a discourse, etc.*, Princeton, 1874; J. H. Dulles, *Biographical Catalogue of Princeton Theological Seminary*, Trenton, 1909; *Necrological Reports and Annual Proceedings of the Alumni Association of Princeton Theological Seminary, 1875–1909*, 3 vols., Princeton, 1891–1909; C. A. Salmond, *Princetoniana. Charles and A. A. Hodge, etc.*, New York, n. d.; *The Life of Ashbel Green*, New York, 1849; J. W. Alexander, *The Life of Archibald Alexander*, New York, 1854; Samuel Miller, *The Life of Samuel Miller*, 2 vols., Philadelphia, 1869; H. C. Alexander, *The Life of Joseph Addison Alexander*, 2 vols., New York, 1870; *Proceedings Connected with the Semi-Centennial Commemoration of the Professorship of Rev. Charles Hodge, April 24, 1872*, New York, 1872; A. A. Hodge, *The Life of Charles Hodge*, New York, 1880; *Celebration of the Fiftieth Anniversary of the Appointment of William Henry Green as an Instructor in Princeton Theological Seminary, May 5, 1896*, New York, 1896; F. L. Patton, *Caspar Wistar Hodge. A Memorial Address*, New York, 1892; idem, *A Discourse in Memory of Archibald Alexander Hodge*, Philadelphia, 1887; *William Miller Paxton. In Memoriam, 1824–1904: Funeral and Memorial Discourses*, New York, 1905; *Catalogue of the Theological Seminary . . . at Princeton, 1909–10*, Princeton, 1910.

9. San Francisco: This seminary is located in San Anselmo, Cal., and was founded in 1871, being placed under the care of what was then known as the Synod of the Pacific of the Presbyterian Church. It sprang from a conviction that the peculiar needs of the Pacific Coast demanded a ministry trained upon the field, and its founders were the Rev. William A. Scott and Rev. William Alexander (q.v.), who, with the Rev. George Burrowes and Rev. Daniel W. Poor, were its earliest instructors. It was located for years in the city of San Francisco, where the old City College and St. John's Presbyterian Church furnished a temporary habitation. More permanent quarters were secured by the erection of a suitable building in 1880, and in 1890 the present site at San Anselmo was presented by Mr. A. W. Foster, of San Rafael. Here, through the munificence of Mr. Alexander Montgomery, of San Francisco, and others, there were erected, in 1892, two spacious stone buildings, one the library and recitation hall, the other the dormitory. To these was later added the beautiful Montgomery Memorial Chapel, and there are also commodious residences on the grounds for all the professors. The location is sufficiently near the city to enable the students to avail themselves of its advantages and to engage actively in missionary and other church work. The aim of the seminary is to prepare men for a practical and efficient ministry and for missionary work in other lands. For nearly twenty years of its history the endowment was small, and the professors were pastors, giving to the seminary such time as they could spare from their pastoral duties. The number of students during this period was small. For the past twenty years, owing to the increase in endowment, which now amounts altogether to about $500,000, the faculty have devoted their entire time to seminary work, and the number of students has increased. Its graduates constitute twenty-five per cent of the active Presbyterian ministry of California, and they are also ministering in considerable numbers in other coast and eastern states, and in nearly every large missionary field of the world. Among the eminent men who have served as instructors have been Rev. William A. Scott (q.v.), Rev. James Eells, and Rev. Henry C. Minton (q.v.), each of whom was moderator of the General Assembly of the Presbyterian Church.

The seminary is at present in excellent condition. There are six full professors and one instructor, and its library contains 18,000 volumes. The board of management consists of twenty-six directors, an equal number of ministers and laymen, eighteen of whom are elected by the Synod of California, six by the Synod of Oregon, and two by the Synod of Washington. The directors elect five of their number as a board of trustees, in compliance with the laws of California, who direct the financial affairs of the institution. While it is under the immediate control of the Synod of California, it bears the same relation to the General Assembly as all the other seminaries of its denomination. The average number of students is twenty-five. They are all connected with the Presbyterian Church, and about sixty per cent of them come from Pacific Coast churches.

WARREN HALL LANDON.

BIBLIOGRAPHY: J. Curry, *History of the San Francisco Theological Seminary of the Presbyterian Church*, Newark, Cal., 1907.

10. Union (New York): Union Theological Seminary, in the City of New York, was founded by a group of Christian ministers and laymen of the Presbyterian Church, who believed that it was wise to plant a training-school for ministers in a great city. They first met Oct. 10, 1835, and, after three intermediate meetings, constituted a board of directors by the election of ten ministers and fourteen laymen, Nov. 9–16, 1835. This board of directors held its first meeting Jan. 18, 1836, when it chose its officers, appointed its committees, adopted the preamble, and proceeded to further business. Jan. 18, 1836, is, therefore, regarded as the official date of the founding of the seminary. The seminary was opened for instruction on Monday, Dec. 5, 1836. The Legislature of the State of New York passed the act of incorporation Mar. 27, 1839, and this was accepted by the board of directors Dec. 20, 1839. The founders of the seminary were Presbyterians of the broader type represented in the New-School branch of the church, and had many affiliations with New England Congregationalism. They had in view a service of wider boundaries than those of the Presbyterian Church alone. They not only believed in freedom of thought, but in the widest possible cooperation with other Christians in the practical work of the church. The Old-School men, on the other hand, were advocates of strict control both in matters of thought and practise. These differences were reflected in the training given in the seminaries of the church, all of which were at this time under ecclesiastical control. Union Seminary owes its origin to the dissatisfaction of the New-School men with this state of affairs, and to the desire to create a new institution which should more perfectly reflect their own ideals. The seminary has been from the outset independent of any ecclesiastical control, except for a period of twenty-two years. On May 16, 1870, a few months after the reunion of the Old- and New-School wings of the Presbyterian Church in the United States of America, it conceded to the General Assembly of that church the right of veto on the election of its professors. This action was taken in the interests of harmony within the church and in order to secure similarity of standing for all its theological seminaries. This concession was withdrawn on Oct. 13, 1892, as a result of the difference of opinion which arose between the seminary and the General Assembly in connection with the transfer of Dr. Briggs (q.v.) to the newly established Edward Robinson chair of Biblical theology. The General Assembly interpreted this transfer as a new appointment, and, under the influence of the excitement caused by Dr. Briggs's inaugural address, by an overwhelming majority disapproved the action of the board. The directors on their part maintained that the appointment of Dr. Briggs was a simple transfer involving no change of duties, and hence was not subject to review by the Assembly. This led to an examination by the seminary authorities of the legal aspects of the matter, and they were advised that the concession had been *ultra vires*. On all grounds, therefore, they felt that they must reconsider their action. Since 1892 Union Seminary has been ecclesiastically independent, according to the plan of its founders and the provisions of its charter. For many years the directors and professors gave their assent to the Westminster Standards, the exact formula varying from time to time. Since 1905 this requirement has ceased, and a new form of declaration has been provided, which secures the Christian character of the institution in more comprehensive terms. At the present time the board of directors and the faculty include representatives of the Presbyterian, Congregational, Protestant Episcopal, Baptist, and Methodist Episcopal Churches.

The principles underlying the foundation of the seminary were expressed by the preamble composed by Dr. Erskine Mason and adopted by the board at its first meeting on Jan. 18, 1836. They were as follows. In the first place, the founders expressed their belief that a great city furnishes peculiar facilities and advantages for conducting theological education. In the second place, while providing for instruction in the doctrine and discipline of the Presbyterian Church, of which they were members, they declared their purpose to furnish the means of a full and thorough education in all the subjects taught in the best theological seminaries in this and other countries. In the third place, they emphasized the importance of practical training for an efficient ministry. They believed that it was not enough to be pious and scholarly; one must know how to express his faith and apply his knowledge in action. Accordingly, they proposed that their students identify themselves with the various churches of the city, actively engage in their services, and become familiar with all the benevolent efforts of the city and of the time. In the fourth place, they proposed to train men not only for the Christian ministry, but for every form of Christian service, whether educational, philanthropic, or religious. Finally, they wished to provide an institution of truly catholic spirit, or, in other words, to use their own memorable language, one around which " all men of moderate views and feelings, who desire to live free from party strife and to stand aloof from all extremes of doctrinal speculation, practical radicalism, and ecclesiastical domination, may cordially and affectionately rally." The charter provides that " equal privileges of admission and instruction, with all the advantages of the institution, shall be allowed to students of every denomination of Christians." In fact, instruction is given not only in the doctrine and polity of the Presbyterian Church, but also in those of other leading Protestant churches. The student body at the present time is made up of members of eighteen different Christian bodies. All of these are urged to retain their original connection, and to enter the ministry of their respective churches. The endeavor is made to provide them all with what they need for effective service to their own people.

The first seminary building was at No. 9 University Place, and was dedicated Dec. 12, 1838. Four professors' houses were also erected on Greene Street, but, owing to the financial embarrassments of the institution, these houses were sold some four years later. Two of these, together with the house and lot adjoining at the corner of Greene and Eighth Streets, were subsequently acquired in order to provide the students with dormitories. In 1884 the seminary moved to its second home on Lenox Hill, where its important group of buildings, with the main entrance at 1200 (afterward 700) Park Avenue, was dedicated Dec. 9, 1884. The generous benefactions of ex-Governor Edwin D. Morgan, supplemented by large gifts from D. Willis James, Morris K. Jesup, and others, made this move possible. In 1910 the seminary moved, for the third

time, to its present quarters on Morningside Heights. This removal was made possible through the princely generosity of D. Willis James, then vice-president of the board, to which, after his death, Mrs. James made large additions. The work of constructing the building was begun in 1908; the building was opened for instruction in Sept., 1910; and the formal service of dedication took place Nov. 29, 1910. The buildings, which are of English perpendicular Gothic, occupy the double block bounded by Broadway, Claremont Avenue, 120th and 122d Streets, and form a large rectangle enclosing a quadrangle of approximately 360 feet long and 100 feet wide. They consist of an entrance tower, an administration building, a library building, a memorial chapel given by Mrs. James in memory of her husband, a dormitory for students, a house for the president, and an apartment house with accommodations for ten professors.

The library of the seminary, on account both of its great size and the value of its collections, offers unusual opportunities to scholars and investigators. On May 1, 1909, it contained about 97,000 volumes, 55,000 pamphlets, and 186 manuscripts. The beginning of it was the library of Leander Van Ess, consisting of over 13,000 volumes, including such rare and valuable works as 430 incunabula, from 1469 to 1510 A.D.; 1,246 titles of Reformation literature, in original editions; 37 manuscripts; 4,209 volumes in church history, patristics, canon law, etc.; and about 200 editions of the Vulgate and of German Bibles (the earliest being 1470). Valuable additions have been made from the collections of the late Drs. Robinson, Field, Marsh, Gillett, Smith, Adams, Hatfield, Hitchcock, Schaff, Prentiss (qq.v.), and others.

Special mention may be made of a collection of nearly 800 Greek Testaments gathered by the late Dr. Isaac H. Hall (q.v.), and presented in 1898 by Mr. David H. McAlpin; of the hymnological library of Prof. Frederick M. Bird (q.v.), consisting of some 5,000 volumes, presented in 1888 by the late Henry Day, Esq., and of an almost exhaustive collection of Zwingliana presented in 1901 by the Rev. Prof. Samuel Macauley Jackson, D.D., LL.D. The Gillett Collection of American History (endowed in 1884 by the late David H. McAlpin), and the Field and other collections of pamphlets contain useful material for the study of the civil and religious history and the theology of America. Most valuable of all is the McAlpin Collection of British History and Theology (endowed in 1884 by Mr. McAlpin), gathered under the supervision of Professor Briggs. It contains thousands of rare and important books and pamphlets relating to the early Puritans, to the Westminster Assembly, and to the deistic, trinitarian, and ecclesiastical controversies of the eighteenth century, as well as a large collection of general and local histories of Great Britain and her churches.

The original plan of the seminary contemplated the meeting of the necessary expenses by an annual subscription from the friends of the institution, but this proved impracticable. The first permanent fund was obtained in 1843 by the gift of $25,000 from Mr. James Boorman for the endowment of the theological chair. A further sum of $30,000 was received some five or six years later by a bequest of Mr. James Roosevelt. During the years from 1853 to 1871 the funds of the institution were further increased by $650,000, of which the greater part was obtained by general subscription. Three years later the institution was further strengthened by a generous gift of $300,000 from Mr. James Brown, as a result of which the original corps of professors was increased from three to seven, and the funds of the professorships from $25,000 to $80,000 each. These funds were subsequently increased by gifts from Mr. D. Willis James, Mr. William E. Dodge, Jr., Mr. Morris K. Jesup, and Mr. John Crosby Brown. At the present time the seminary has ten professorships fully endowed, most of which bear the names of their several founders or of funds designated by them. In the order of their foundation they are the following: The Davenport Professorship of Hebrew and the Cognate Languages, the Roosevelt Professorship of Systematic Theology, the Washburn Professorship of Church History, the Baldwin Professorship of Sacred Literature, the Brown Professorship of Homiletics, the Skinner and McAlpin Professorship of Practical Theology, the Edward Robinson Professorship of Biblical Theology, the Jesup Graduate Professorship of Practical Theology, the Marcellus Hartley Professorship of Philosophy and the History of Religion and Missions, and the Professorship of Christian Ethics. In addition to these there is an endowment for the Department of Applied Christianity, at present used for the director of Christian work and headworker of the Union Settlement. Other professorships and associate and assistant professorships are not yet endowed. The endowment of the seminary includes provision also for certain instructorships and lectureships, the most important of which are the Harkness Instructorship in Vocal Culture and Elocution and in Sacred Music, the Ely Lectureship on the Evidences of Christianity, the Morse Lectureship on the Relations of the Bible to the Sciences, and the Parker Lectureship on the Laws of Health.

On the rolls of the seminary may be found the names of many men prominent in philanthropic and religious life. Its founders were actively interested in, and many of them officers of, the leading missionary societies of the country. Among its directors were such clergymen as Absalom Peters, Erskine Mason, Albert Barnes (q.v.), Samuel Hanson Cox (q.v.), Edwin F. Hatfield (q.v.), and Jonathan French Stearns; and such laymen as Knowles Taylor, Richard T. Haines, William M. Halsted, Charles Butler, the Hon. William E. Dodge, Norman White, D. Hunter McAlpin, D. Willis James, John Crosby Brown, William E. Dodge, Jr., and Morris K. Jesup. The first president of the board was the Rev. Thomas McAuley, D.D., who was succeeded in 1840 by Richard T. Haines, who served until 1871. Charles Butler was president from 1871 to 1898, and John Crosby Brown from 1898 until 1909. The present president is Robert C. Ogden. No less notable is the roll of the faculty. The first professor of sacred literature was Edward Robinson (q.v.), the Nestor of American Biblical scholarship, and in other departments the seminary

has commanded the services of such men as Henry B. Smith (q.v.), and W. G. T. Shedd (q.v.) in theology, Philip Schaff (q.v.) and Roswell D. Hitchcock (q.v.) in church history, Thomas H. Skinner (q.v.), William Adams (q.v.), George L. Prentiss (q.v.), and Charles Cuthbert Hall (q.v.), in practical theology. Thomas McAuley, the first president of the board, acted also as president of the faculty. He was succeeded in 1840 by the Rev. Joel Parker, D.D. In 1842 the presidency of the faculty lapsed, but was revived in 1873, when William Adams, pastor of the Madison Square Church, and chairman of the New School Committee of Reunion, became president. He was succeeded in 1880 by Roswell D. Hitchcock, who was followed in 1887 by Thomas S. Hastings (q.v.). On his resignation in 1897, Dr. Charles Cuthbert Hall was chosen president and served until his death in 1908, when he was succeeded by Dr. Francis Brown (q.v.).

From the first the faculty have recognized their responsibility to the cause of productive scholarship. In the long list of their publications mention may be made of Robinson's monographs on the geography of Palestine, and his translation of Gesenius' *Dictionary;* Schaff's edition of the *Creeds of Christendom,* and his *Church History;* the *International Theological Library* and *Critical Commentary,* edited by Dr. Briggs, in cooperation with Dr. Salmond, and with Canon Driver and Dr. Plummer respectively; and the Hebrew Lexicon of Drs. Francis Brown and Briggs, in cooperation with Canon Driver; also of McGiffert's *Apostolic Age,* W. Adams Brown's *Christian Theology in Outline,* and Thomas C. Hall's *History of Ethics within Organized Christianity.* The spirit of the teachers has descended upon the scholars, and among the 3,501 alumni of the seminary no less than 74 have been college presidents, 222 teachers in colleges, and 99 in seminaries. In the curriculum of the seminary the original languages have always held a prominent place, and were formerly required of all graduates. A distinction is now customarily made between the diploma and the degree of the seminary, an acquaintance with the original languages being required only of candidates for the latter. In recent years the range of subjects included in the curriculum has greatly increased, and the freedom of election has been widely extended. At the present time no less than 141 courses are offered by the faculty, the division by departments being as follows: Old Testament, 22; New Testament, 21; church history, 17; philosophy of religion, 10; apologetics, 4; systematic theology, 6; Christian ethics, 11; practical theology, 25; religious education, 6; theological encyclopedia and symbolics, 11; vocal culture, 3; sacred music, 5. In thirty years the curriculum has been increased threefold. In addition to its own courses, through an arrangement entered into with Columbia and New York Universities, the seminary is able to offer to its students the advantage of university courses in philosophy, sociology, and other subjects of value for the student of religion. A graduate department of the seminary which now embraces some forty students has for some years been in operation. The scholarships of the seminary are administered on a merit basis.

Through two fellowships the seminary offers to the best student in each class the opportunity of two years of graduate study under the direction of the faculty in this country or abroad. In addition, the seminary offers the degree of D.D. to advanced students.

From the first the students have been active workers in the churches, Sunday-schools, and other religious and philanthropic institutions of the city and its vicinity. The supervision of these activities has recently been entrusted to the Department of Christian Work, through which students are assigned to different fields and counseled as to the best methods of dealing with the problems they present. In this connection attention may be called to the Union Settlement in East 104th Street, founded in 1895 by a group of Union Seminary alumni. While not officially connected with the seminary, the settlement is an expression of its social spirit. The seminary's director of Christian work is at the same time head worker of the settlement, and many of the students are engaged in its activities. The practical interest of the seminary appears further in its provision for university extension. The Department of Religious Education, recently organized under the leadership of Professor Coe, offers especial facilities for the training of lay workers. The foundation lectureships of the seminary are open to the general public, and many of the courses deal with topics of popular religious interest. A Sunday service is maintained in the chapel for the residents of the neighborhood, and the Union School of Religion provides a model Sunday-school for their children. In addition, attention should be called to the various conferences organized by the seminary from time to time, such as the Conference on an Efficient Ministry, held in 1908 for the pastors of the neighboring churches; the Conference on the Training for the Ministry, conducted by the students of the seminary in cooperation with the students of Hartford and Yale seminaries; and the Quiet Day for social workers. Specially noticeable has been the strong missionary interest among the students. From the first a large number of its graduates have found their way to the foreign field, and the number of foreign missionaries now on the seminary roll amounts to 251. This missionary interest was greatly stimulated by the two visits of the late President Charles Cuthbert Hall to the East as Barrows Lecturer. Provision has recently been made by a friend of the seminary for a similar lectureship, to be filled in 1911–12 by Prof. George William Knox (q.v.). WILLIAM ADAMS BROWN.

BIBLIOGRAPHY: G. L. Prentiss, *Union Theological Seminary in the City of New York: Historical and Biographical Sketches of its First Fifty Years*, New York, 1889; idem, *Union Theological Seminary in the City of New York: Its Design and another Decade of its History*, Asbury Park, N. J., 1899; *General Catalogue of the Union Theological Seminary in the City of New York* (four editions; 1876, compiled by E. F. Hatfield, 1886, 1898, 1908, compiled by C. R. Gillett); *The Seminary: Its Spirit and Aims* (addresses by Dr. Thomas C. Hall, Dr. Francis Brown, Rev. Henry Sloane Coffin, President Charles Cuthbert Hall), New York, 1907.

11. Western: This seminary was founded at Allegheny (now part of Pittsburg), Pa., in 1827, after the General Assembly had determined in 1825,

when the need for such an institution for the West had been felt for several years, to establish a training-school for Presbyterian ministers. The first instructors were Rev. Joseph Stockton and Rev. Elisha P. Swift, and among the distinguished members of its faculty have been Luther Halsey, John W. Nevin (q.v.), Alexander T. McGill, Melanchthon W. Jacobus (q.v.), William S. Plumer (q.v.), William M. Paxton, A. A. Hodge (q.v.), S. J. Wilson, S. H. Kellogg, B. B. Warfield (q.v.), David Gregg (q.v.), and M. B. Riddle (q.v.). The spirit and policy of the seminary are admirably expressed in the fundamental principle which was incorporated by its founders in the "plan": "That learning without religion in ministers of the Gospel will prove injurious to the Church, and religion without learning will leave the ministry exposed to the impositions of designing men, and insufficient in a high degree for the great purposes of the Gospel ministry." In accordance with this, a combination of learning and piety, of erudition and earnestness, of intellectual discipline and practical efficiency, is the standard which has been set up, while the institution has always been distinguished for its strong missionary spirit. While the seminary is a Presbyterian institution, it is not sectarian; students of all denominations are cordially welcomed and are entitled to scholarship aid; and representatives from bodies other than the Presbyterian Church are always found among the students. Recently the curriculum was thoroughly revised to meet modern demands, by the introduction of the elective system and by laying greater emphasis on sociological studies. The regular course extends over three years, a fourth year of study entitling a student to the degree of B.D. In 1902 a special department was organized for the training of ministers for the immigrant peoples among whom the Presbyterian Church labors, and extension courses of lectures are conducted by the faculty in the churches of Pittsburg and vicinity.

The total number of matriculants is 2,126, of whom 117 have been foreign missionaries, and the average number of students for the last five years has been eighty, the enrolment for 1911 being seventy-nine. The faculty consists of seven professors and four instructors, all of whom, with the exception of the instructors in music and elocution, must be ministers of the Presbyterian Church in the United States of America. On induction into office the professors are required to subscribe to the Westminster Catechisms and Confession.

The government of the seminary is vested in a board of directors and a board of trustees; the former consisting of forty members (twenty-eight ministers and twelve ruling elders), one-fourth of whom are chosen annually. The board of directors have power to elect, suspend, and remove professors, such election and removal being subject to the veto of the General Assembly. They superintend the curriculum, inspect the fidelity of the professors, and watch over the conduct of the students. The board of trustees, incorporated by the legislature of the state of Pennsylvania on Mar. 29, 1844, consists of twenty-one members, "nine of whom shall at all times be laymen citizens of the State of Pennsylvania," and to them is committed the management and disbursement of the funds of the institution. Each board elects its own members, subject to the approval of the General Assembly.

The institution now has two halls, a library, and four professors' houses, and plans have been laid for a complete new plant, to consist of a dormitory, administration building, and chapel. The buildings are valued at $250,000, and the endowment is $733,807, the chief benefactors being Rev. C. C. Beatty, James Laughlin, James Laughlin, Jr., S. P. Harbison and his estate, S. S. Marvin, and David and John Robinson.   JAMES A. KELSO.

XI b. Presbyterian (Southern).—1. Austin: This institution is located at Austin, Travis Co., Tex., where it was founded in 1884, practically as an independent movement, under the control of no ecclesiastical body, though it was recognized and indorsed by the Synod of Texas of the Presbyterian Church in the United States. Under the title of "The Austin School of Theology," it continued in operation until 1895, when it was compelled to suspend because of lack of sufficient funds with which to carry on the work. The actual revival of its activity took place in 1898, when the Synod of Texas appointed a board of trustees, with full power to open the institution, and ordered that its name should be "The Austin Presbyterian Theological Seminary," and that it should be regarded as the successor to the Austin School of Theology. The Synod of Texas adopted a constitution in Oct., 1901, and ordered the board to open the institution for students as soon as $100,000 should have been raised. This was done at once, and the seminary resumed its work in Oct., 1902. The founders of the seminary, in 1884, were the Rev. Richmond K. Smoot and the Rev. Robert L. Dabney (q.v.), while its revival was under the administration of the Rev. Thornton R. Sampson, its first president, the first faculty consisting of the Rev. Samuel A. King, as professor of systematic theology, and the Rev. Robert E. Vinson, as professor of Old-Testament languages and exegesis. Later, the Rev. Dr. Smoot was added to the faculty. The institution is now under the control of the Synods of Texas, Arkansas, and Oklahoma of the Presbyterian Church in the United States, and during the last period of eight years the seminary has given to the ministry of the Presbyterian Church in Texas, Oklahoma, and Arkansas about thirty men, trained in whole or in part under its instruction. The office of the first president of the seminary having terminated, according to the constitution, when the faculty reached the number of four, from 1904 to 1908 the institution was governed by the faculty under the direction of the board of trustees, appointed by the controlling synods. In 1908 the board, with the consent of the controlling synods, determined to make the office of president a permanent part of the administration of the seminary, and elected to this position the Rev. Robert E. Vinson, D.D.

This seminary stands for the type of theology which is presented in the Westminster Confession of Faith and Catechisms, and was founded for the avowed purpose of furnishing an adequate ministry in both supply and equipment for the rapidly developing home-mission territory of the Southwest. Among its instructors the best-known, perhaps have been the Rev. Robert L. Dabney, the Rev. Thomas Carey Johnson, the Rev. Samuel A. King, the Rev. R. K. Smoot, and the Rev. T. R. Sampson. In the year 1910 the seminary had five instructors, thirty-four students, a library of about 2,500 volumes, buildings to the value of $100,000, and endowments to the value of $200,000; it is governed by a board of fifteen trustees, appointed by the three controlling synods. In the student body there are four denominations represented: Presbyterian (31), Disciples of Christ (1), Baptist (1), and Episcopalian (1).   ROBERT E. VINSON.

2. Columbia: The Theological Seminary of the Synods of South Carolina, Georgia, Alabama, and Florida, popularly known as Columbia Seminary, is located in Columbia, Richland Co., S. C., and was founded in 1828 by the Presbyterians of the then Synod of South Carolina and Georgia. The institution had its origin in the conviction that if the Presbyterian churches of the cotton belt were to have an adequate supply of educated ministers, they must not only be raised up from the churches themselves, but must be trained for the ministry somewhere within this territory. From 1828 to 1831 the faculty of the seminary consisted of but a single professor, Dr. Thomas Goulding, but in 1831 Dr. George Howe and in 1833 Dr. A. W. Leland were added to the faculty. While it has had its share of vicissitudes, Columbia Seminary has a record of service not only to the churches of the cotton belt, but to the entire Presbyterian Church in the United States, popularly known as the Southern Presbyterian Church. It has numbered among its faculty such men as James Henry Thornwell (q.v.), B. M. Palmer (q.v.), J. B. Adger, James Woodrow (q.v.), William S. Plummer (q.v.), J. R. Wilson, John L. Giradeau, and Samuel Sparr Laws. Its alumni took a conspicuous part in organizing the Presbyterian Church in the United States, and were largely influential in determining its distinctive character and in shaping the lines along which its life and activities have developed. Dr. J. Leighton Wilson (q.v.), one of the first graduates of the seminary, shaped the foreign-mission policy of the Southern Presbyterian Church, while its home-missionary activities have been largely under the direction of alumni of the same seminary, and its interest in and work for the negroes have been stimulated and directed by such alumni as Dr. C. C. Jones, John L. Giradeau, and Charles A. Stillman (q.v.). In addition to supplying the denomination with many of its best preachers, Columbia Seminary has given it a considerable number of its theological professors, not to mention its other educators. Of the thirty-nine moderators of the General Assembly, nineteen have been alumni of this institution.

The faculty in the year 1910 consisted of four professors, with two chairs vacant—those of natural science in its relation to revelation, and of pastoral theology, English Bible, and homiletics. The institution is owned and controlled by the Synods of South Carolina, Georgia, Alabama, and Florida, their control being exercised through a board of directors, six of whom are elected from the Synod of South Carolina, four from the Synod of Georgia, four from the Synod of Alabama, and two from the Synod of Florida. From year to year the directors submit their minutes to the synods for approval, and also send to the General Assembly a report for its information. There were in 1910 twenty students in attendance, nine of whom were from South Carolina, four from Georgia, five from North Carolina, and two from Tennessee. All of these were candidates for the Presbyterian ministry. The endowment of the seminary amounts to $275,000, and its library contains 2,400 volumes.

W. M. McPheeters.

Bibliography: *Memorial Volume of the Semicentennial Volume of the Theological Seminary at Columbia, S. C.,* Columbia, 1884.

8. Kentucky: This institution, located at Louisville, Ky., was formed in 1901 by the consolidation of the Danville (Ky.) and the Louisville (Ky.) theological seminaries. The Danville seminary was founded at Danville, Ky., in 1853, by the General Assembly of the Presbyterian Church (Old School), and had a notably successful career until the beginning of the Civil War, attracting a large number of students. Its most widely known professors were Robert J. Breckenridge (q.v.), Edward P. Humphrey, Stuart Robinson (q.v.), Stephen Yerkes, and Nathan L. Rice (q.v.), and its influence on the Southwest through its alumni has been marked and enduring. In 1893, the Synods of Kentucky and Missouri, in connection with the Presbyterian Church in the United States, founded the Louisville Seminary at Louisville, Ky., and by reason of its strong faculty and its location in a large city the institution at once took high rank, and in its fourth session enrolled sixty-seven students. The original endowment was $100,000, mostly in subscriptions, and for three years the instruction was given in the rooms of the Second Presbyterian Church. In the first session Mr. A. J. Alexander gave real estate to the value of $75,000 to endow a chair in memory of his son, while temporary endowment by annual subscriptions and the gift of their services as professors by three pastors of the city enabled the seminary to meet its expenses. By the generosity of Mr. W. N. Haldeman, proprietor of the *Courier-Journal,* a permanent location was secured in 1896, and in 1901 the Danville and Louisville seminaries were united at Louisville, under the name of the Presbyterian Theological Seminary of Kentucky. Under the terms of the agreement for consolidation the seminary is under the control of the Synod of Kentucky in connection with the Presbyterian Church in the United States of America, and of the Synods of Kentucky and Missouri in connection with the Presbyterian Church in the United States, this control being exercised through a board of twenty-four directors, who elect the professors. Annual reports of the work of the seminary are submitted to the controlling synods and to the two General Assemblies, and the election of directors and the election or transfer of professors are subject to veto by the respective assemblies. Under the charter and constitution of the seminary the instruction " shall at all times be in accordance with those standards which are now common in both of said [Presbyte-

rian] churches, and with such modifications thereof, if any, as may hereafter be made and adopted by both of said churches." The synods of both the Presbyterian denominations concerned represent the same type of theology and ecclesiology, and the faculty are divided almost equally between the two, agreeing thoroughly in making the teaching and spirit of the institution conservative in theology and in Biblical criticism. The faculty of instruction consists of eight professors: Charles R. Hemphill (q.v.; president and professor of New-Testament exegesis and practical theology), John M. Worrall (practical theology, emeritus), William H. Marquess (Biblical introduction, English Bible, and Biblical theology), Henry E. Dosker (q.v.; church history), Robert A. Webb (q.v.; apologetics and systematic theology), Jesse L. Cotton (Old-Testament exegesis), and Thompson M. Hawes and J. G. McAllister (assistants).

The courses of study are organized into distinct schools, and cover all the subjects of theological discipline, with special attention to preparation for the practical demands made on the modern minister. Students are received from any Evangelical Church, and are ordinarily expected to have a literary degree from a reputable college. The only degree conferred is B.D., given after examination on the completion of a three-years' course. In 1910 the institution had an attendance of fifty-eight, twelve of whom were ministers pursuing special graduate courses. The grounds and buildings of the seminary represent an outlay of $220,000, while the invested funds embrace $500,000 for endowments, $40,000 for scholarships, and a small library fund. The principal benefactor of the seminary was Mr. William T. Grant, of Louisville, a director of the institution, who left a bequest of $300,000 to the seminary, probably the largest gift ever made in the South to theological education. The library includes about 20,000 volumes, and nearly 6,000 unbound pamphlets.   Charles R. Hemphill.

4. Southwestern: This institution, which is located at Clarksville, Montgomery Co., Tenn., and is under the control of the Presbyterian Church in the United States, was founded in 1885 through the combined efforts of the Synods of Alabama, Mississippi, Arkansas, Texas, Memphis, and Nashville, to establish a school for the education of young men for the ministry within their bounds. Its earliest instructors were Drs. John L. Waddel (chancellor and professor of church polity), Joseph R. Wilson (theology and homiletics), J. B. Shearer (Hebrew and New-Testament Greek), and Robert Price (ecclesiastical history). The history of the seminary from its foundation has been one of uniform, uninterrupted, and successful work. It stands for the conservative interpretation of the standards of the Calvinistic system of doctrine, for the Presbyterian form of church government, and for the highest standard of sacred learning and personal piety in the ministry. It has supplied a large number of the most useful ministers of the Southern Presbyterian Church, both in home and in mission fields.

In 1910 the seminary had four instructors and twelve trustees. It constitutes a department of the Southwestern Presbyterian University, and its students are subject to the government and discipline of the university. Its support is derived from the university endowments, and for its library it depends on that of the university, which contains some 15,000 volumes.   WILLIAM DINWIDDIE.

5. Union (Richmond, Va.): This institution, officially known as "Union Theological Seminary in Virginia," is located at Richmond, Va., and was founded in 1812. In April, 1806, the Presbytery of Hanover resolved to establish at Hampden-Sidney College a theological library and a fund for the education of young men for the ministry, and appointed Rev. John Holt Rice a special agent to solicit books and money for this purpose. In 1807 Rev. Moses Hoge was elected president of Hampden-Sidney College, and in accordance with the plan of the presbytery began at the same time to instruct in theology the candidates for the ministry, although it was not till 1812 that the Synod of Virginia officially adopted the infant seminary and formally appointed Dr. Hoge its professor of theology. He continued the work for the remaining eight years of his life, sending about thirty young men from his classes into the ministry. When he died in 1820, the synod, after trying in vain for two years to fill his place, transferred the seminary with its funds to the Presbytery of Hanover. This presbytery in 1822 reorganized the seminary, appointed a new board of trustees, and elected as professor of theology Rev. John Holt Rice, pastor of the First Presbyterian Church of Richmond, to whom, more than to any other man, the success of the institution is due. Dr. Rice began his instructions on Jan. 1, 1824, with three students. There were as yet no buildings for the seminary, and its whole endowment amounted only to about $10,000, but funds for both purposes were now rapidly raised. In 1826, the seminary was placed under the care of the General Assembly, the trustees of that body taking charge of the funds; and in 1827 the Presbytery of Hanover surrendered the institution to the joint management and control of the Synods of Virginia and North Carolina. In commemoration of this copartnership its name was changed to Union Theological Seminary. By 1831, the year in which Dr. Rice died, the institution had acquired buildings sufficient for its needs at that time, had gathered a fair library, and had secured three instructors and about forty students. A fourth professorship was added in 1856, and a fifth in 1891.

The seminary has had the following professors: in theology, Moses Hoge (1812–20), John Holt Rice (1824–31), George A. Baxter (1831–41), Samuel B. Wilson (1841–59), Robert L. Dabney (q.v.; 1859–1883), Thomas E. Peck (1883–93), Clement R. Vaughan (1893–96), and Givens B. Strickler (q.v.; since 1896); in ecclesiastical history and polity, Stephen Taylor (1833–38), Samuel L. Graham (1838–39, 1849–50), Robert L. Dabney (1853–59), Thomas E. Peck (1860–83), James F. Latimer (1884–92), and Thomas C. Johnson (q.v.; since 1892); in Hebrew and Old-Testament interpretation, Hiram P. Goodrich (1830–39), Samuel L. Graham (1839–49), Francis S. Sampson (1849–54), Benjamin M. Smith (q.v.; 1854–89), Walter W. Moore (q.v.; since 1884), James Gray McAllister

(adjunct professor, 1904–05), and A. D. P. Gilmour (associate professor, since 1908); in Biblical literature and New-Testament interpretation, William J. Hoge (1856–59), Henry C. Alexander (1869–91), Charles C. Hersman (1891–1908), and Thomas R. English (since 1908); in English Bible and practical theology, Thomas C. Johnson (1891–92), Thomas R. English (1893–98), and Theron H. Rice (since 1908). There were in 1911 seven instructors and ninety-four students, representing twenty states and countries, and three religious denominations, though the great majority are Presbyterians. The total attendance of students from the beginning to the present time has been 1,489. This seminary has educated more of the ministers of the Presbyterian Church in the South than any other, having furnished about three-fourths of all the ministers in the Synod of Virginia, about one-half of those in the Synod of North Carolina, and a goodly proportion of those in the other Southern synods as well, besides about half of all the missionaries who have been sent by this branch of the church to foreign lands.

The seminary is under the care of the synods of Virginia and North Carolina, and the board of directors is composed of twenty-four members, twelve from each of the synods to which the board reports. The General Assembly of the Presbyterian Church in the United States also has a right of general superintendence, and may advise and recommend, but may not originate, measures for the management of the institution. The plan of the seminary is thoroughly Biblical, and the Bible is the chief classbook in all departments, while the institution stands for the theology of the Westminster Confession of Faith. Although insisting upon thorough scholarship, and requiring for its degree of B.D. a grade equal to that of the professional schools of the University of Virginia, the chief aim of the seminary is to give men practical training for the actual work of the ministry, and especially to make them effective preachers. Throughout its history it has been characterized by a remarkably strong and steady missionary spirit. Its Society of Missionary Inquiry was organized in 1818, and in 1831 its founder, Dr. Rice, dictated from his deathbed the overture to the General Assembly which led to the organization of the Presbyterian Board of Foreign Missions.

In 1898, by order of the controlling synods, the seminary was removed from Hampden-Sidney to Richmond. Its property now consists of forty-five acres of land in Ginter Park, Richmond, nine substantial buildings, all erected within the last twelve years, valued at $261,000, and productive endowments of $533,000, besides unproductive assets of $25,000. Its principal benefactors have been Cyrus H. McCormick of Chicago, Henry Young of New York, Joseph Blair Wilson of Rockbridge Co., Va., William W. Spence of Baltimore, and George W. Watts of Durham, N. C. The library, which is unusually select, numbers 23,307 volumes, carefully housed in a fireproof building.   W. W. MOORE.

BIBLIOGRAPHY: *Centennial Catalogue of Union Theological Seminary in Virginia, 1807–1907,* Richmond, 1907 (containing a history of the institution and sketches of all its alumni).

XII. Reformed Presbyterian.— 1. Pittsburg: This institution is located in Pittsburg, Pa., in the North Side, formerly Alleghany, and was founded in 1810, although it has been in its present site only since 1856. It is in connection with the Reformed Presbyterian Church (Old School), and was formed by the action of that body. The purpose of the denomination to institute a seminary goes back to 1807, but it was not formally organized until May 25, 1810, with a board of superintendents consisting of Rev. John Black, Rev. Alexander McLeod, and Rev. Gilbert McMaster; and with Rev. Samuel Brown Wylie as teacher of theology. The seminary then constituted was in Philadelphia, and Dr. Wylie continued as professor of theology till 1827, with some years of intermission from 1817 to 1823, during which time the students were taught by pastors, four years' instruction being required. There was a similar interruption from 1827 to 1836, but from this period on, with little break, the students of theology were taught by professors elected by the synod, though the location was changed several times from East to West, until, in 1856, it came to its present place. The professors during this shifting period were James Renwick Willson and Thomas Sproull (q.v.). The seminary stands for the Reformed theology as embodied in the Westminster standards, and in the Act and Testimony of the Reformed Presbyterian Church, which covenanted in 1871 át Pittsburg, Pa., and is bound to witness politically against national atheism, to seek a Christian constitution, to testify against secret oath-bound orders, and to promote total abstinence and other reforms.

There are four instructors in the seminary, and eight members of the board of superintendents, who meet annually at the close of the session and pass upon the work, and hear discourses from the students. They report annually to the synod, who control the election of professors. The number of students enrolled in 1909–10 was ten, all in the membership of the denomination. One came from Massachusetts, two from New York, two from Pennsylvania, one from Illinois, two from Iowa, one from Missouri, and one from Colorado. The endowment of the seminary is about $90,000, and the number of books in the library is about 3,600.

D. B. WILLSON.

BIBLIOGRAPHY: W. B. Sprague, *Annals of the American Pulpit*, vol. ix., New York, 1869; J. M. Wilson, *Presbyterian Historical Almanac*, vol. ix., Philadelphia, 1867; W. M. Glasgow, *Historical Catalogue of the Theological Seminary of the Reformed Presbyterian Church in America*, Beaver Falls, Pa., 1898.

XIII. United Presbyterian.— 1. Xenia: This seminary is located at Xenia, Greene Co., O., and is an institution of the United Presbyterian Church, under the control of the Second Synod of the West and of the synods of Illinois, Iowa, Kansas, and Nebraska of the United Presbyterian Church. Its immediate control is committed to a board of managers, twenty-five in number, and a board of nine trustees, while the terms and course of study are determined by the General Assembly. The seminary was founded by the Associate Presbyterian Synod of North America in 1794, and was at first located at Service, Beaver Co., Pa., where a build-

ing was erected and a library of about 800 volumes was collected, and Rev. John Anderson was elected professor of theology, the first and only teacher for some twenty-five years. For 117 years it has labored to equip men for the ministry of the Gospel. It is probably the oldest Protestant theological seminary on the continent. Professor Anderson resigned, 1819, and soon thereafter the Associate Synod decided to remove it from Service to Canonsburg, Pa., which was done, and Rev. James Ramsay was chosen professor of theology. In due time other professors were added to the teaching force and the course of study was enlarged. In 1855 the synod agreed to another removal of the seminary, and it was transferred to Xenia, O., where it has prosecuted its work now for fifty-six years.

The Associated Reformed Church, one of the two branches forming the United Presbyterian Church, established a theological seminary at Oxford, O., in 1839, and Rev. Joseph Claybaugh, a local pastor, was appointed professor of theology. In 1857 this institution was removed from Oxford, O., to Monmouth, Ill., where it remained till 1874, when it was consolidated with the Xenia Seminary, its library and funds forming a part of Xenia's equipment.

The amount of endowment, including the value of buildings and grounds, is about $200,000, and the library contains between 7,000 and 8,000 volumes, besides a large collection of pamphlets and periodicals. The faculty consists of the following members: Joseph Kyle (systematic theology, history of doctrine, homiletics), Jesse Johnson (ecclesiastical history and apologetics), John E. Wishart (Hebrew exegesis, O. T. literature, pastoral theology), J. Hunter Webster (Greek exegesis and N. T. literature), Melvin G. Kyle (permanent lecturer on Biblical theology as illustrated by archeological research), Peter Robertson (voice culture), and William G. Moorehead (English Bible).

WILLIAM G. MOOREHEAD.

XIV. Protestant Episcopal.— 1. Berkeley: This divinity school is located in Middletown, Middlesex Co., Conn., and had its beginning in a theological department informally organized in Trinity College, Hartford, in 1851, by the president of the college, the Rt. Rev. John Williams (q.v.), assistant bishop of the Episcopal Church in Connecticut. Three years later a charter was granted for the school as a separate institution under its present name, to be located at Middletown, where a large building, which had been the residence of the Rev. Dr. Jarvis, was given for its use. Bishop Williams removed his residence to that city, and was dean of the school for forty-five years, until his death in 1899. The first resident professors were Rev. Edwin Harwood and Rev. Thomas F. Davies; and the bishop was also assisted by Rev. Dr. Thomas W. Coit and other lecturers. The Jarvis House, earlier called the Washington Hotel, served as a residence, dormitory, chapel, and library for several years, but in 1860 another dormitory was built; in the next year a beautiful stone chapel, erected by Mrs. Mary W. Alsop Mütter, in memory of her husband, was consecrated; and in 1868 an adjacent colonial dwelling was purchased which serves as a refectory. In 1896 a handsome and spacious library, with provision for lecture-rooms, was built, bounding another side of the grounds and serving as a special memorial of the founder of the school. Generous provision has been made from time to time for the support of the institution in the form of professorial and scholarship endowments, as well as gifts to the general funds; and the alumni have provided a fund of $10,000 for the maintenance and enlargement of the library. Under the guidance of Bishop Williams and of his successors, the Berkeley Divinity School has had a strong and widely extended influence in the life of the Episcopal Church for more than half a century. Among its most eminent instructors have been the Rev. Dr. John Binney, who still holds the professorship to which he was called in 1874, and who was dean from 1899 to 1908; Rev. Dr. Samuel Fuller, professor for thirty-six years; Rev. Dr. Frederic Gardiner (q.v.), whose professorship covered twenty-one years, and Rev. Dr. John Humphrey Barbour, who died at the end of eleven years of service. The number of its students has never been very large; in fifty-five years it has graduated about 500 men, all of whom have taken holy orders. Of these twenty-two, with three non-graduates, have been consecrated bishops, and five have been called to the headship of other theological seminaries. The living alumni, 341 in number, are about one-seventeenth of all the Episcopal clergy of the country, while of the members of the House of Bishops one-fifth are graduates of Berkeley.

The corporation consists of thirteen trustees, eight clergymen and five laymen, vacancies in their number being filled by the Diocesan Convention or by the remaining trustees. There are, in 1910, five full professors and several instructors and lecturers. The number of students, including graduates engaged in advance work and some special students, is thirty-five; nine are undergraduates in full standing, all of these, with one exception, having college degrees. The students come from different parts of the country, and the alumni are widely distributed, about one-fifth being in Connecticut and one-fifth in the State of New York. The endowment funds amount in all to about $485,000, and there are about 28,000 volumes in the library. SAMUEL HART.

2. Cambridge: This theological school, which is located in Cambridge, Mass., was founded in 1867 by Benjamin Tyler Reed, a wealthy merchant of Boston, who was much interested in the progress of the Episcopal Church, of which he was a member, and was strongly desirous that it should remain true to its evangelical traditions. He accordingly founded this school, making only one requirement of its instructors, that they should maintain the doctrine of justification by faith. Dr. John S. Stone was made the first dean of the school, and associated with him in the work of instruction were Dr. A. V. G. Allen (q.v.), and Dr. P. H. Steenstra (q.v.), who composed for a time the teaching force, Dr. Francis Wharton and Dr. Elisha Mulford (q.v.) being added later. Friends of the founder and of the dean erected buildings. Amos Adams Lawrence built a dormitory, John Appleton Burnham a refectory, and Robert Means Mason a chapel, while a building for a library and for lecture-rooms was called Reed Hall in honor of the founder of the school, who, in addition to his initial gift, made the institution the residuary legatee of his estate. Thus established, the school has ever since stood for liberal and progressive scholarship in the Episcopal Church.

The seminary in 1910 had seven full professors and two instructors, and is governed by a board of seven lay trustees, originally appointed by the founder, and self-perpetuating, who manage the finances of the school, the responsibility for the teaching resting upon the faculty. Thus the school in its government follows the plan which prevails in the American parish, the trustees corresponding to the vestry. There are forty students, of whom fifteen belong to Massachusetts, and eight to New York, others being from Pennsylvania, Rhode Island, Maine, Michigan, Washington, Tennessee, Texas, Canada, and China. The endowment is $1,000,000, half of which is in land and buildings, and the other half in productive funds. There are 12,000 books in the library. A second dormitory was added to the original group of buildings, and named for Hon. Robert C. Winthrop, then president of the board of trustees; and Mrs. George Zabriskie Gray, widow of the second dean, gave a deanery, while a library building, now in process of construction, is the gift of John G. Wright. GEORGE HODGES.

3. General: This seminary, by far the largest under the jurisdiction of the Protestant Episcopal Church, is located in New York City, where it was founded in 1817. Soon after the opening of the nineteenth century there became manifest, in various parts of the American Episcopal Church, a strong desire for, and belief in, a more systematic, thorough, and disciplined training for the ministry, as opposed to the previous isolated classes of candidates under the tuition of a single clergyman, or the inconvenient recourse to English universities. This feeling manifested itself in diocesan resolutions, pastoral addresses of bishops, and the formation of such societies to promote and aid theological education as the Protestant Episcopal Theological Society founded in New York in 1806. Bishops Bowen of South Carolina, Hobart (q.v.) of New York, and White (q.v.) of Pennsylvania were especially active in the movement, and as a result of the agitation the General Theological Seminary was founded by the General Convention of the church on May 27, 1817, and instruction began in New York two years later. It was the intention of the founders, as expressed in their resolutions of 1817, that the seminary should " have the support of the whole Church in these United States, and be under the superintendence and control of the General Convention." This breadth of plan became, and still is, a characteristic of the seminary, part of its governing trustees being still chosen by the General Convention, and its professors and students representing all sections of the country as well as foreign missionary districts. In 1819 when the seminary opened, there were but two professors, Rev. S. F. Jarvis, and Rev. S. H. Turner (q.v.), and six students. Among the latter, however, were two men—G. W. Doane and Manton Eastburn—who by their distinction later, as bishops of New Jersey and Massachusetts respectively, foreshadowed the future work of the institution in train-

ing leaders of the church as well as the rank and file of the clergy; and with the passing of fourscore years and ten nearly seventy bishops had been students at the seminary—almost a fourth of the entire American episcopate from 1784 to 1910. In the same period had been graduated 1,722 men, of whom over 1,000 are living and in the ministry to-day— almost a fifth of the present total number of the American Episcopal clergy.

Despite the encouragement with which the seminary opened, it temporarily languished, and even for a brief period (1820–22) removed to New Haven, Conn. It received new material life, however, with the bequest, in 1821, of about $60,000 from Jacob Sherred, and the gift of an extensive tract of land in what was then the upper part of New York City, from C. C. Moore (q.v.). In this location was erected the first building in 1825, and there now stand the present seminary buildings. Gifts to the institution during its first half-century were many, but its present admirable equipment of buildings, etc., may be said to date very largely from the beginning of the deanship of the late Very Rev. E. A. Hoffman (q.v.), in 1879. The buildings occupy what is known as Chelsea Square, the block bounded by Ninth and Tenth Avenues, and 20th and 21st Streets, and are a very notable group architecturally, harmonious and dignified in their outward fabric as well as distinctive in the quiet and reserve of their old-world atmosphere. The library contained in 1910 51,386 volumes and several thousand pamphlets and is especially strong in the history of the Anglican and the American Episcopal Church, patristics, liturgics, and conciliar history. It contains the Copinger Collection of Latin Biblical texts, presented in 1893 by Dean Hoffman and Cornelius Vanderbilt, which at the time of its acquisition was one of the three largest collections of Latin Biblical texts in the world, and also the private library of the eminent Assyriologist Eberhard Schrader. Among its other treasures are a valuable collection of Babylonian tablets, and several Biblical manuscripts.

Entering students are presupposed to have been admitted as candidates for orders in the Episcopal Church or to have been graduated at a " recognized university or college." Under the terms of an affiliation agreement with Columbia University, they may take courses in the latter institution and use its library. With the purpose of elevating and broadening the standard of theological education, especial effort has been made to foster advanced and graduate work. The five fellowships now maintained, with provision for study abroad or at the seminary, and the certainty of an increase in their number at a later date have served to sustain this effort, and the number of graduate students has largely increased in the last decade. In addition, a number of scholarships are available for worthy undergraduates. The total number of students at the seminary in the year 1910–11 was 126, exclusive of several non-resident graduate students.

The publications of the seminary include, in addition to its catalogues and proceedings of trustees, a series of alumni publications issued by the associate alumni and the Paddock Lectures. The latter,

a series of volumes issued since 1881, contain the lectures delivered annually at the seminary by well-known scholars and theologians, among the more recent lecturers being Rt. Rev. A. C. A. Hall (q.v.), bishop of Vermont; Rt. Rev. C. H. Brent (q.v.), bishop of the Philippines; Rt. Rev. G. H. S. Walpole, bishop of Edinburgh; Rev. F. J. Hall (q.v.), Rev. W. P. Du Bose (q.v.), and Rev. W. R. Inge (q.v.), of Cambridge University, England. The present endowment of the seminary is $2,112,115.81, exclusive of the site occupied by the institution, its buildings, and adjoining land owned by the seminary valued at $2,138,263.25. The faculty at present is as follows: W. L. Robbins (q.v.; dean), W. J. Seabury (q.v.; ecclesiastical polity and law), J. C. Roper (dogmatic theology), H. M. Denslow (pastoral theology), C. N. Shepard (Hebrew and cognate languages), C. C. Edmunds (New Testament), L. W. Batten (Old Testament), A. P. Hunt (Christian ethics), A. W. Jenks (ecclesiastical history), F. B. Blodgett (adjunct professor of Old Testament), W. H. P. Hatch (adjunct professor of New Testament), and C. H. Boynton (adjunct professor of homiletics and pedagogy). The professorship of Christian apologetics is at present vacant by death. In addition to the regular faculty, there are three special lecturers, three resident instructors, and a librarian.   EDWARD HARMON VIRGIN.

4. Nashotah: This seminary, officially known as " Nashotah House," is situated at Nashotah, Waukesha Co., Wis., and was founded in 1841 by James Lloyd Breck, William Adams, and John Henry Hobart (q.v.), under the Rt. Rev. Jackson Kemper, Episcopal bishop of the Territories of the Northwest. At first it was an associate mission, but very shortly it became a training-school for men desiring to give themselves up to missionary work in the great Northwest. From this point of departure Nashotah House soon became a recognized seminary of the Protestant Episcopal Church, and after its incorporation in 1847 it grew until, to-day, it is the second largest training-school for priests in the American Church. Among the earlier instructors, besides those whose names have already been mentioned, were the Rev. A. D. Cole, Rev. Lewis A. Kemper, Rev. T. M. Riley, Rev. A. W. Jenks, and Rev. H. E. W. Fosbroke. The seminary has always stood unqualifiedly for the principles of the Catholic revival as championed by the leaders of the Oxford movement in England, and firmly holds to that position at the present time. Though the institution has never mothered any great movement, it has, each year since its incorporation, sent out men strong champions of Catholic faith and practise, who, working as they have in nearly every diocese and missionary district of this country and in almost every part of the world, can not but have done much to push forward that great movement which arose at Oxford in the middle of the last century.

At the present time the institution numbers sixty students, eight professors and instructors, and a board of trustees of twenty-one members. The buildings, including three houses used as homes for members of the faculty and a new library building, number ten. The endowment of the institution is at present $450,000. The library, already rich with material in certain directions, and consisting of about 15,000 volumes, has now the possibility of a brilliant future, due to recent bequests.

GEORGE T. LASCELLE.

5. Pacific: The "Church Divinity School of the Pacific" is located at San Mateo, San Mateo Co., Cal., and was founded in 1893 through the generosity of George W. Gibbs of San Francisco and J. Pierpont Morgan of New York City. It is under the charge of Rt. Rev. William Ford Nichols (q.v.), bishop of California, who is also its dean and sole trustee. It possesses at present (1910) three buildings, but it is hoped that it will ultimately be possible to remove the whole institution to San Francisco and there make it part of the quadrangle of the cathedral close. The present faculty consists, in addition to Bishop Nichols, of J. O. Lincoln, H. H. Powell, F. C. Murgotten, and two lecturers, E. L. Parsons and A. B. Shields. To the end of 1908 the seminary had had forty-seven students, of whom seventeen were specials. The enrolment for 1908–09 was twelve, the great majority being from the diocese of California, with two from Los Angeles, and one each from Western Colorado and Tonga. The library contains over 6,000 volumes, and the institution is characterized by a strong missionary spirit. JAMES OTIS LINCOLN.

6. Philadelphia: This school, officially designated "The Divinity School of the Protestant Episcopal Church in Philadelphia," is located in Philadelphia, Pa., and was incorporated in 1862 after an informal training-school for candidates for holy orders had already existed for some years previously under the direction of Bishop Alonzo Potter (q.v.). This prelate, who must be regarded as the real founder of the school, set forth its purpose as follows: "The divinity school is founded upon a national and Catholic basis and doctrine. Its object is to raise up large-hearted, earnest-minded, well-instructed, and common-sense ministers of the Word and sacraments, and to send them forth, trained practically as well as theoretically, to fill up the ranks of our foreign and domestic missionaries, and to serve as men of power and godliness at home." The present buildings of the seminary were erected in 1882, and to them were added a chapel in 1885 and a library in 1907. The faculty consisted in 1910 of six professors: of systematic divinity; of liturgics, church polity, and canon law; of New-Testament literature and language; of Old-Testament literature and language; of homiletics and pastoral care; and of ecclesiastical history; and there is also an instructor in voice culture and elocution. The faculty is well equipped for its work and offers instruction in Semitic, Greek and Latin, German, French, and Italian. The school has had students from Canada, the West Indies, China, Japan, Haiti, and Liberia, and from all parts of the United States. Out of over 500 students matriculated, its graduate alumni number nearly 400, of whom three are bishops, while two others have declined the episcopate. The number of students living in the building is between thirty and forty, and an average of about fifty additional pursue post-graduate work for degrees. Arrangements have been made whereby students of theology can take courses of special study at the University of Pennsylvania, and a system for exchange of credits

has been adopted, these exchangeable credits falling within the departments of Hebrew, New-Testament Greek, and ecclesiastical history. Students who desire to become acquainted with the missionary and institutional features of the Church's work have an excellent opportunity through their services as lay readers in the institutions, churches, and missions in Philadelphia. The library contains over 20,000 volumes, including valuable theological works that are daily consulted by students from the neighboring seminaries and institutions of learning; and students of the divinity school may also use the extensive library of the University of Pennsylvania. THOMAS J. GARLAND.

7. Seabury: This divinity school, the corporate name of which is "Bishop Seabury Mission," is located in Faribault, Rice Co., Minn., and was founded in 1858 by Rev. James Lloyd Breck. It was and is affiliated with the Episcopal Church, and confines itself to the training of men for that church's ministry. It originated in the desire to found a school which would send forth clergymen equipped to meet the pioneer condition of the new Northwest, which was then just opening to settlement. Among its earliest instructors, in addition to its founder, were Bishop H. B. Whipple (q.v.), Rev. Solon W. Manney, Rev. (later bishop) E. S. Thomas, Rev. Thomas Richey, and Rev. J. S. Kedney (q.v.). In the second year of the school's existence, Bishop Whipple came to Faribault, and made it his residence, this not only bringing the students into personal contact with the great "apostle to the Indians," but also enabling him to keep a close watch over the school and to provide for its needs. Dr. Breck began the school in the most primitive way, by the erection of a frame dormitory for the students who attended recitations in his home. Later on a stone building was built, but this was burned in 1872, and the present main building (named Seabury Hall) was erected in 1873, near the site of Dr. Breck's former residence. Dr. Breck moved to Benicia, Cal., in 1867, and after a brief interval Dr. Richey became head of the school, a position which has since been held by eight other clergymen. In 1886 a second building for the library and recitation-rooms was built and named Johnston Hall, after the father of the donor, Mrs. Shumway.

During the years of the school's existence, more than 300 men have received their theological education, wholly or in part, within its walls. It has contributed largely to the growth of the Episcopal Church in the Northwest, the majority of its alumni giving their best years to missionary work in that part of the country. It stands for conservative churchmanship, sound learning, and practical training. In the year 1910 there were seven instructors in active work; the trustees are twenty in number, and are a self-perpetuating body; and the administrative officer is the warden. There are at present twenty-eight students in attendance (the school's capacity being thirty-one), coming from eleven different dioceses in eight different states. The seminary has an endowment of about $450,000, and a library of about 11,000 volumes.

F. A. McELWAIN.

BIBLIOGRAPHY: G. C. Tanner, *History of the Diocese of Minnesota*, St. Paul, 1909.

8. Virginia: This divinity school, officially termed "The Protestant Episcopal Theological Seminary in Virginia," is situated in Fairfax Co., Va., overlooking the Potomac River, three miles west of Alexandria. It was founded in 1823, and was at first located in Alexandria, whence it was removed to its present site in 1827. It owes its inception to a resolution of the Diocesan Convention of Virginia, which met in 1815, recognizing the great necessity for a supply of candidates for holy orders, and of a school for training them. A theological class was, accordingly, established in the college of William and Mary at Williamsburg, Va., in 1821, but the students were transferred to Alexandria in 1823, when the history of the seminary really begins. Chief among its founders were the Rev. William Hawley of Washington, D. C., the Rev. William H. Wilmer of Alexandria, the Rev. William Meade (q.v.; afterward bishop of Virginia), Dr. Thomas Henderson of Washington, and Francis Scott Key, the author of "The Star-Spangled Banner." Its first professors were the Revs. Revel Keith, William H. Wilmer, and Oliver Norris. The seminary has had a most interesting history, centering to a large extent around the missionary life of the Episcopal Church. Ecclesiastically it has stood, from the beginning, for the principles known as "evangelical" in the Episcopal Church, and for simplicity in ritual and in the appointed forms of worship. But it maintains its position in no spirit of narrow exclusiveness, and recognizes that "evangelical," in its best sense, refers to the historic faith as contained in the New Testament and set forth by the ancient creeds; so that clergymen of all schools of thought have been educated within its walls. The influence of the seminary has been unquestionably great as a conservative and spiritual force throughout the Episcopal Church, holding fast, as it does, to the essential principles of the English Reformation. Its chief glory, however, is the great contribution it has made to the development of missionary work in the Episcopal Church. It has founded all its foreign missions except where, in recent years, that church with other communions has followed the flag in the colonial possessions of the United States.

The seminary has a list of more than 1,000 alumni, many of whom have held, and now hold, distinguished positions in all parts of the United States. About seventy-five have become foreign missionaries, and thirty have been consecrated bishops. Among the most noted of these are the Rt. Rev. William J. Boone of China, the first missionary bishop sent forth by the Episcopal Church in 1844; Bishops Henry C. Potter (q.v.), of New York; Phillips Brooks (q.v.), of Massachusetts; Thomas U. Dudley (q.v.), of Kentucky; and James Addison Ingle, of Hankow, China. Among living bishops, Rt. Rev. A. M. Randolph (q.v.), of Southern Virginia, holds a prominent position in his Church. The most noted professors have been the Rev. Revel Keith, the Rev. Joseph Packard, and the Rev. William Sparrow (q.v.). The seminary had in 1910 six professors and seventeen trustees, five of whom are bishops, five presbyters, and seven laymen, the

president being the bishop of Virginia. This is a self-perpetuating body, chosen from the three dioceses within the limits of the states of Virginia and West Virginia, with the exception of two who are called alumni trustees, elected by the alumni, and permitted to be residents of other dioceses. The government of the seminary is vested in the board of trustees while the general administration as relating to the students is in the hand of the dean and faculty. The present number of students is forty-six, coming from twenty dioceses. Of these, twenty-seven are from the South, ten from the Middle States, one from the North, six from the West, and one from Hankow, China. The seminary has a well-selected library, containing about 35,000 volumes. The buildings are of brick, with a beautiful chapel, the choir and chancel of which were given by the late Bishop Henry C. Potter (q.v.).

SAMUEL A. WALLIS.

XV a. Reformed (German).—1. Central: This institution of the Reformed Church in the United States (formerly the German Reformed Church) is located at Dayton, O., and was formed by the union of two theological seminaries, Heidelberg Theological Seminary (formerly located at Tiffin, O.), and Ursinus School of Theology (formerly located at Collegeville, Pa., and later at Philadelphia, Pa.). The former institution was founded by the Ohio Synod of the Reformed Church in the United States, after several efforts had already been made to establish a theological seminary, as at Canton, O., in 1838, with Rev. J. G. Buettner as professor, and at Columbus, O., in 1848, under Rev. A. P. Freeze. Finally, in 1850, the synod decided to found Heidelberg College, at Tiffin, O., and also, in connection with it, a theological seminary which should bear a similar name. For ten years there was only one professor at a time, Rev. E. V. Gerhart (q.v.; 1851–55) and Rev. Moses Kieffer (1855–61), but in 1861 another professor, Rev. Herman Rust, was added, and in 1869 Rev. J. H. Good was elected professor in Dr. Kieffer's place. Later other professors were added, among them Rev. A. S. Zerbe, Rev. D. Van Horne (q.v.), Rev. E. Herbruck, Rev. J. I. Swander, and Rev. H. J. Christman, and the faculty usually had four professors. From 1853 to 1907 the seminary had graduated 345 students, the attendance being usually from twelve to twenty. Its plan contemplated five professors, and it had an endowment of about $90,000, but it had no buildings of its own as long as it was at Tiffin.

The Ursinus School of Theology was part of Ursinus College, which was located at Collegeville, Pa., and which had three departments—theological, collegiate, and academical. Instruction began about 1871, and the first class was graduated about 1873. It was organized and controlled by that element in the Reformed Church of the United States which was opposed to the liturgical tendencies of the theological seminary established first at Mercersburg, Pa., and later at Lancaster, Pa. Though it was not under the direct control of any synod of the denomination, it was officially recognized by the General Synod of the Church in 1872, and in 1878 the Eastern Synod, within whose bounds it was located, gave it a vote of recommendation. Its first professor was Rev. J. H. A. Bomberger (q.v.; president of Ursinus College), with whom were associated Rev. H. Super, J. Van Haagen, M. Peters, G. Stibitz, J. I. Good, J. H. Sechler, and W. Hinke. In 1898 it was removed to Philadelphia, Pa., where it remained until 1907, during which time Revs. Ph. Vollmer and E. R. Bromer joined its faculty, the number of active professors being usually four. At Collegeville it used the buildings of the college as dormitories and for recitations, and never had any endowment separate from that of the college, but while in Philadelphia it purchased a building of its own. The number of its students ranged from ten to thirty-five, and from its beginning to 1907 it had about 300 graduates.

In 1906 negotiations were begun between the Ohio Synod and the board of directors of Ursinus College, looking toward a union of these seminaries, and the plan was consummated in 1907. The united seminary was located at Tiffin for one year (1907–08), but in 1908 Dayton, O., was made its permanent location. Its faculty is composed of the united faculties of both seminaries, and numbers seven. It has an endowment of about $100,000, and property worth $35,000, on which a theological building is soon to be built, costing about $50,000. Its course is that which is usually presented in the theological seminaries of the United States, and its aim is to be both scholarly and Biblical, and to combine the fixed theological course with the elective by granting a number of electives each year. It now has a large constituency, and its students, who come from all over the church, usually number from thirty to thirty-five. A post-graduate course has also been arranged which usually has a dozen students. Since 1908 the seminary has graduated twenty-eight. The theological position of the seminary is that of the Heidelberg Catechism—mildly Calvinistic, but over against the modern higher critical movement it stands for the old Evangelical orthodoxy.

JAMES I. GOOD.

2. Lancaster: This seminary, which is located at Lancaster, Pa., was established by the Synod of the Reformed (German) Church convened at Bedford, Pa., in 1824, and at the same time Rev. Lewis Mayer, then pastor at York, Pa., was elected as the first professor of theology. The synod accepted the generous offer of accommodations from the authorities of Dickinson College, Carlisle, Pa., and the first session of the seminary opened in a room in that institution on Mar. 11, 1825, with a class of five students and one professor. It was the first institution of higher learning founded by the Reformed Church in the United States, and has been ever since under the supervision of one or more of its synods and conducted in its interests. Since its foundation the seminary has been located successively in Carlisle, Pa. (1825–29), York, Pa. (1829–37), Mercersburg, Pa. (1837–71), and Lancaster, Pa. (1871 to date). The following have occupied the several professorships up to the present time: Systematic theology, Lewis Mayer (1825–39 , John W. Nevin (q.v.; 1840–1851), Bernard C. Wolf (1854–64), Henry Harbaugh (q.v.; 1863–67), Emmanuel V. Gerhart (q.v.; 1868–1904), and Christopher Noss (1904–09); church history and exegesis, Daniel Young (1830–31), Fred-

erick A. Rauch (q.v.; 1832–41), Philip Schaff (q.v.; 1844–62), Elisha E. Higbee (1865–71), and Thomas G. Apple (1871–98). In 1857 a theological tutorship was founded, and during the twelve years of its actual existence (1861–73) there were three tutors —William M. Reily, Jacob B. Kerschner, and Frederick A. Gast (q.v.). In 1873 the tutorship was abolished, and in its stead the chair of Hebrew and Old-Testament theology was established, to which Professor Gast was chosen in May, 1874. In 1891 the Synod of the Potomac endowed a fourth professorship, New-Testament exegesis, of which John C. Bowman was the first incumbent (1891–1904). A fifth professorship, practical theology, was added by the Pittsburg Synod in 1893, and was first occupied by William Rupp (1893–1904). By the concurrent action of the three synods John I. Swander was appointed Associate Professor of Systematic Theology. In 1893 the original charter was amended so as to vest the control of the seminary in the three eastern (English) synods of the Reformed Church—the Eastern Synod, the Pittsburg Synod, and the Synod of the Potomac, each synod being represented on the two boards, the board of visitors and the board of trustees, in proportion to its numerical strength. The board of visitors consists of twelve ministers and supervises the instruction and the internal affairs of the institution, while the board of trustees, composed of eighteen laymen, holds and controls property and funds.

The faculty for 1910–11 is constituted as follows: John C. Bowman (president, and professor of practical theology), William C. Schaeffer (New-Testament science), George W. Richards (church history), Theodore F. Herman (systematic theology), John I. Swander (associate professor of systematic theology), Frederick A. Gast (emeritus professor of Hebrew and Old-Testament science), Irwin Hoch DeLong (Hebrew and Old-Testament science), and John M. Chambers (instructor of sacred oratory). The number of students enrolled for the year 1910 is 46—seniors 13, middlers 16, and juniors 13, with 4 graduate students; 43 are members of the Reformed Church, and 3 of the United Evangelical Church. The students come from the following states: Pennsylvania, 42; Maryland, 1; West Virginia, 1; Iowa, 1; and North Carolina, 1. The estimated value of buildings and grounds is $200,000; the endowment fund is $200,000; and the library contains 12,500 books, besides pamphlets and periodicals.

By the first professors of the seminary the distinctive genius and doctrines of the Reformed Church in the United States, formerly the German Reformed Church, whose confessional standard is the Heidelberg Catechism, were interpreted and promulgated in American Protestantism; and the system of philosophy and theology originated and expounded under the leadership of Drs. Rauch, Nevin, and Schaff came to be known as the "Mercersburg Theology" (q.v.).

GEORGE W. RICHARDS.

BIBLIOGRAPHY: T. Appel, *Beginnings of the Theological Seminary*, Philadelphia, 1886; J. H. Dubbs, *Reformed Church in Pennsylvania*, Lancaster, Pa., 1902; *Mercersburg Review,* Jan., 1876.

3. Plymouth: This seminary, or, rather, "mission house," is located near Plymouth, Sheboygan Co., Wis., and was founded by the Sheboygan Classis of the Reformed Church in the United States in 1860, to provide ministers for the settlers who emigrated to Wisconsin and the Northwest from Switzerland and Germany, for whom it was impossible to procure ministers either from Europe or from the eastern part of the United States through the board of missions of this church. The first instructors were Rev. H. A. Muehlmeier and Rev. J. Bossard. The seminary has, from the beginning, been an integral part of the mission house, but its formal organization as a school separate from the preparatory departments, college and academy, did not occur till 1875, when the Synod of the Northwest, to which the school had been transferred by Sheboygan Classis in 1867, passed resolutions to that effect, and founded the various chairs of theology. In 1881 the Central Synod was organized in Ohio, and this new German synod, as also, in 1886, the German Synod of the East, received a proportional interest in the institution, so that the mission house is now the property of the three German synods of the Reformed Church in the United States. The seminary has adhered faithfully to the confession of the church, the Heidelberg Catechism; and in the liturgical conflict of the sixties and early seventies it, together with the great majority of the German ministers of the church, occupied a middle ground, inclining neither to ritualism nor to the so-called new measures. Among the instructors Dr. Bossard (b. 1885) was known and acknowledged in Germany as an authority in philology, especially in Greek and Hebrew grammar; Rev. H. Kurtz (d. 1889) was an authority in classic church music, and many of his anthems and other compositions, published by the Central Publishing House, Cleveland, O., are sung throughout the church; and Dr. H. J. Ruetenik, still living, ranks high as editor and author. The seminary is under the control of a board of trustees elected by the synods. In 1910 there were three professors and twenty-six students, all of this church and from various states. The endowment, which is slowly increasing, amounts to $40,000, and annual collections from the congregations affiliated with the school cover the running expenses. The library of the mission house contains 16,000 volumes, of which about half are theological.

FRANK GRETHER.

BIBLIOGRAPHY: D. W. Vriesen, *Geschichte des Mission-Hauses,* Cleveland, O., 1885; L. Praikschatis and H. A. Meier, *Das Mission-Haus,* ib., 1897.

XV b. Reformed (Dutch).—1. New Brunswick: This institution, officially designated "The Theological Seminary of the Reformed (Dutch) Church in America at New Brunswick, New Jersey," is located, as its name indicates, in New Brunswick, Middlesex Co., N. J. Its origin was due to the need of the Dutch churches in New York and New Jersey for educated ministers when conditions made it no longer possible to obtain them in Holland. In 1784, the "General Body," afterward the General Synod, appointed as its professor of theology the Rev. John H. Livingston (q.v.), minister of the Protestant Reformed Dutch Church of New York City. This

professorship he held until his death in 1825, and his students attended his lectures in New York for twelve years, when, on account of the expense to students of city life, he removed them to Flatbush, L. I., though the next synod directed their return to New York. After having graduated about ninety students there, the seminary was removed to New Brunswick, N. J., in 1810, where its work was carried on in the buildings of Queens College (since 1825 Rutgers College), an institution founded by the Dutch churches, and at that time under the control of their General Synod. In 1856 a separate and spacious campus was acquired by the synod, which is the present home of the institution, and now contains three large halls and six residences. The first professor of languages, Rev. H. Meyer, was appointed by the synod also in 1784, and in 1812 Rev. John M. Van Harlingen became the first professor of ecclesiastical history, while in 1815 pastoral theology was formally provided for, in connection with the historical chair. In 1865 practical theology became a distinct department under Rev. D. D. Demarest, and in 1884 the department of languages was divided. In 1905 a lectorship in Biblical history and theology was established, and instructors in oratory and music are also regularly employed.

The seminary has had a large influence in the life of the church to which it belongs, and has sent many strong men into the pulpits, the seminaries, and the missions of other churches. It is the birth-place of the Arabian Mission. Its average number of students is thirty-five, of whom one-third are from the Middle West. It has five professors, a lector, and two instructors, an endowment, aside from scholarships, of $525,000, and a library of 49,000 volumes. There is no corporate body apart from that of the General Synod, which owns the property, chooses the professors, supervises their work through a board of superintendents, and dictates the curriculum. The institution thus stands, in fact and in principle, for the complete control by the Church of the training of the Church's ministry. In its actual work, it stands for a theology resting on Holy Scripture as a positive and authoritative revelation, which centers around the doctrine of the gracious sovereignty of God, and it aims to produce a scholarly and evangelical ministry of catholic and aggressively missionary spirit.   J. P. SEARLE.

BIBLIOGRAPHY: *Centennial Discourses,* New York, 1877; E. T. Corwin, *Manual of the Reformed Protestant Dutch Church in North America,* 4th ed., New York, 1902; D. D. Demarest, *Reformed Church in America,* New York, 1889.

2. Western: This seminary, which is under the control of the Reformed Church in America, is located at Holland, Ottawa Co., Mich., and was formally organized by the General Synod of the church in 1869, after special instruction had already been given in theology for three years in connection with Hope College, and a class of seven was ready to graduate. The necessity for such a school grew largely out of conditions arising from the settlement of a large colony from the Netherlands, whose attachment to the Reformed Church in their native country led to their uniting with the Reformed Church in America. The desire to extend its own influence in the West, where many of its members were settling, and the appeal of these fellow Christians resulted in the organization of Hope College in 1866, and of the Western Theological Seminary in 1869. In 1867 the Synod elected the Rev. C. E. Crispell professor of didactic and polemic theology, and invited other professors in Hope College to act as lectors; but the lack of endowment and the heavy demands made upon the teachers, who were giving instruction in both college and seminary, proved too great a burden, and in 1877 the synod resolved to suspend its operation, at the same time assuring the churches that it would be resumed as soon as the necessary endowment could be secured. In 1884 the work of endowment had so far advanced that the synod elected the Rev. Nicholas M. Steffens professor of didactic and polemic theology, with the Rev. Peter Moerdyke as lector in Greek and the Rev. Henry E. Dosker (q.v.) as lector in church history. Work was resumed the following December, with one student in the middle class and four in the junior class. Other professorships have been established as follows: in 1888 exegetical theology, with the Rev. John W. Beardslee as professor; in 1894 historical theology, with the Rev. Henry E. Dosker as professor; and in 1907 practical theology, with the Rev. James F. Zwemer as professor. In 1895 Mr. Peter Semelink erected a fine brick building containing lecture-rooms, a chapel, and room for a library. The "Chambers Library" had its beginning in a small donation of money and the library of the Rev. Anson DuBois, and has been supplemented by the valuable donations of many others, until it has become a good working library.

The seminary stands for the great principles, doctrinal and ecclesiastical, so strenuously contended for in the Reformation in the Netherlands, seeking always to follow the leading of God's Spirit and providence in adapting those principles to present conditions. It insists upon an educated ministry and a vigorous missionary effort at home and abroad, and seeks to commend the Gospel as the only adequate basis for the individual, society, and the State in their efforts to reach the best results in life. In organization it is directly subject to the General Synod, which controls its finances and elects its professors and board of superintendents, who make annual reports to the synod. Its present status (1910) is four professors, twenty-six students, a board of superintendents consisting of twenty members, building and real estate worth $50,000, an endowment of $120,000, and a library of about 10,000 volumes.   J. W. BEARDSLEE.

BIBLIOGRAPHY: E. T. Corwin, Manual of the Reformed Protestant Dutch Church in North America, 4th ed., New York, 1902; idem, History of the Reformed Church in America, New York, 1895.

XVI. Christian Reformed.—1. Grand Rapids: This seminary is located at Grand Rapids, Mich., and was founded in 1876, its origin lying in the difficulty of obtaining ministers from the Netherlands, especially as the people were poor, and some of the leaders of the churches in the Netherlands did not approve of what was termed the secession of 1857. In 1865 the classis appointed a local minister, D. J. Van der Werp, instructor, and he served without a fixed salary, using his study as a classroom. On his resignation in 1876 the synod elected as professor

Rev. G. E. Boer, who opened the school with seven students, while the course was divided into a literary department of four years and a theological department of two years. In 1884 Rev. G. K. Hemkes, and in 1888 Rev. Geerhardus Vos, was elected, and the theological course was extended to three years, while in 1900 the literary course was made five years (an additional year being added in 1906), and was opened to students aiming at other vocations than the ministry. Among other instructors of the seminary have been H. Beuker (1894–1900), W. Heyns (1902–06), F. M. Ten Hoor (since 1900), L. Berkhof (since 1906), and G. D. De Jong (since 1908). All instruction in the institution must be in harmony with Reformed principles, and the various branches of study are considered in the light of Calvinism as a life and a world-view.

In 1910 the seminary had four instructors and thirty-one students, few outside the Christian Reformed denomination being found either in seminary or in college. The entire institution is controlled by a " curatorium," or board of trustees, twenty-two in number (two from each of the eleven classes), who supervise the whole school and are empowered to declare graduates of the seminary eligible for the ministry. The instructors both in college and in seminary are elected by the synod. The endowment amounts to $40,000, and additional support is secured by an assessment laid on the congregations by the synod. The library contains 4,000 volumes.   GABRIEL DOOITZES DE JONG.

BIBLIOGRAPHY: Gedenkboek van het vijftigjarig jubileum der Christelijke Gereformeerde Kerk, Grand Rapids, Mich., 1907, pp 49–71, 87–125.

XVII. Roman Catholic.*—1. St. Patrick's: This training-school for the Roman Catholic priesthood is located at Menlo Park, San Mateo Co., Cal., and was established in 1898 through the efforts of the Most Reverend Patrick William Riordan, Archbishop of San Francisco. The institution is conducted, under the archbishop, by the Sulpician Fathers, and is intended solely for boys and young men who desire to devote their lives to the service of God in the Roman Catholic priesthood. It takes the boy from the parochial school and leaves him a priest at the altar. The period of preparation is twelve years: first, a classical course of six years, then two years given to the study of mental philosophy and the natural sciences, and, finally, four years devoted to theology and the other branches which are special in clerical training, such as Sacred Scripture, Hebrew, canon law, church history, homiletics, liturgics, apologetics, and sacred music. In the intention of its founder, Saint Patrick's is to serve as the ecclesiastical training-school for all the Roman Catholic dioceses of the Pacific Coast. It has at present a corps of sixteen professors and a roster of about one hundred students, principally from the states of California, Oregon, and Washington. It has already educated students for the dioceses of San Francisco, Los Angeles, and Sacramento, Cal.; Portland and Baker City, Ore.; Seattle, Wash.; Pittsburg, Pa.; Victoria, B. C.; Helena, Mont.; Boisé City, Ida., and Santa Fé, New Mex. The present institution represents the third at-

_____
* See the paragraph at the head of this article.

tempt to establish a school of this kind in California. The first attempt was made at the old Mission Dolores in San Francisco in 1853, soon after the close of the war with Mexico and the ceding of California to the United States; and the second attempt was made in 1883 at the old Mission San Jose; but in both instances events proved that conditions were not yet ripe for such a foundation. The present institution faces brighter prospects, and gives every promise of permanence and success.

H. A. Ayrinhac.

Bibliography: J. M. Guinn, *History of the State of California*, Chicago, 1904, pp. 1435–1436; *San Francisco Monitor*, " Seminary Number," Sept. 17, 1898, and " Jubilee Number," Jan. 23, 1904.

2. St. Thomas of Villanova: This seminary, officially known as " The House of Studies of the Brotherhood of Hermits of the Order of Saint Augustine for the American Province of St. Thomas of Villanova," was established by brief of Pope Gregory XVI., Dec. 22, 1843, and is located at Villanova, Delaware Co., Pa. The studies are under the direction of a regent, who is subject immediately to the prior-general of the order at Rome. Among the earliest instructors were Fr. William Harnett, Fr. Patrick Stanton, and Fr. Peter Crane. The purpose of the study house is to train members of the brotherhood in Scripture, theology, history, and canon law for parish, mission, and college work, the field mainly of the order's activities in the United States. In 1910 there were four professors, thirty-eight professed cleric students, and seven novice cleric students.

Francis E. Tourscher.

Bibliography: T. C. Middleton, *Historical Sketch of Villanova College*, Villanova, Pa., 1893; idem, *Directory of the Augustinians in the United States*, ib., 1910.

XVIII. Unitarian.—1. Meadville: This school was established in 1844 in Meadville, Crawford Co., Pa., its founders being Harm Jan Huidekoper, a native of Holland, and his son Frederic (see Huidekoper, Frederic), who became its first professor. Dr. Rufus P. Stebbins was its first president; and associated with Dr. Stebbins and Mr. Huidekoper, as members of its first faculty, were Elder David Millard and Dr. George W. Hosmer. Founded and endowed by Unitarians for the special purpose of providing ministers for the new western Unitarian churches, the school has always received students from all denominations on equal terms, and during its early years had among its trustees, faculty, and students many representatives of the Christian Connection. Dr. Stebbins' successors in the presidency have been Dr. Oliver Stearns (1856–63), Dr. Abiel A. Livermore (q.v.; 1863–90), Dr. George L. Cary (q.v.; 1890–1902), and Dr. Franklin C. Southworth (q.v.; since 1902). The number of students at the opening was five, and it increased the second year to twenty-three. In 1872 the comparative study of religion was introduced by Prof. H. H. Barber (q.v.), and this work has since been carried on under the direction of Profs. George R. Freeman and Henry Preserved Smith (q.v.). The Clarke professorship of church history was established in 1899, with Dr. Francis A. Christie (q.v.) as incumbent of the chair, and the Ballou lectureship of practical Christian sociology was founded in 1892. In 1895 the school became a pioneer in introducing sociology into the

theological curriculum, through the establishment of the Hackley professorship of sociology. This chair is held by Prof. Nicholas P. Gilman, and the school has in recent years sent a number of its graduates into the field of religious philanthropy. The school was also a pioneer among American seminaries in applying, under Dr. Cary, the methods of the higher criticism to the study of the New Testament. In all, the school has sent out 307 graduates, of whom 163 are now in the Unitarian, 16 in the Universalist, 9 in the Episcopal, and 6 in the Christian Connection ministry, and it has also sent 127 students into the ministry after a partial course.

At present the school has seven professors, one professor emeritus, a librarian, and instructors in elocution, music, and physical culture. Its governing body is a self-perpetuating board of thirty trustees, and the alumni association has the privilege of making nominations to fill vacancies in the board. The school is, and has been from the beginning, entirely free from ecclesiastical control, and it is provided in the charter that " no doctrinal test shall ever be made a condition of enjoying any of the opportunities of instruction." It assures absolute freedom of inquiry both to teacher and student, and applies the same canons of criticism and interpretation to sacred Scriptures as to secular, approaching the problems of theology in the same spirit in which it would approach problems of science. The students number twenty-eight, and represent eight different nationalities and thirteen different states in the Union; and though the majority of them are Unitarians, they come from five different church fellowships. The German Evangelical Protestant churches of the Central West are establishing (1911) a German professorship at the school, for the special training of their own ministers. On the Cruft traveling fellowship one graduate may be sent abroad each year for further theological study. The school has an endowment of $792,800, and a library of 35,000 volumes.

Franklin C. Southworth.

Bibliography: G. W. Cooke, *Unitarianism in America*, Boston, 1902; F. and F. B. Tiffany, *Harm Jan Huidekoper*, Cambridge, 1904.

2. Pacific: This institution, officially designated " Pacific Unitarian School for the Ministry," is located at Berkeley, Alameda Co., Cal., and was founded in 1904 (chartered 1906) by Mr. and Mrs. Francis Cutting of Oakland, and Mr. and Mrs. Horace Davis of San Francisco. During its first two years it was located at Oakland, but in 1906 it removed to Berkeley in order to take advantage of opportunities for cooperation with the University of California and with three other divinity schools located there. It was organized by Dr. Earl Morse Wilbur, who is president and professor of practical theology, while the Rev. William Sacheus Morgan is professor of systematic theology. The instruction given in the school itself is supplemented by that offered in the Pacific Theological Seminary and other divinity schools at Berkeley, and in the University of California; and its courses are reciprocally recognized by the other schools, as well as for higher degrees at the university.

The school is affiliated with the Unitarian denomination, and was originally designed for the training of Unitarian ministers on the Pacific coast; but it receives students of both sexes from all sources without distinction, and it stands for free and progressive scholarship of high order, with an especial view to the practical requirements of the modern ministry. It offers a three-year degree course for college graduates, and a four-year certificate course for others, and furnishes excellent opportunities for post-graduate study. The school is governed by a board of fifteen trustees, whose appointment must be approved by the directors of the American Unitarian Association. It had in 1911 three professors and two instructors, and six regular and eleven special students. Its library contains about 7,500 volumes and about 3,000 pamphlets, and is especially rich in the history and literature of the Unitarian movement. It owns property valued at $50,000, but until its endowment of $300,000 becomes available, its support is derived chiefly from annuities. EARL MORSE WILBUR.

XIX. Unity of the Brethren.—1. Bethlehem: This institution is situated in Bethlehem, Northampton Co., Pa. The founding of a school for training teachers and ministers to serve in the schools and congregations of the Moravian Church in America engaged the attention of a conference held in 1802, composed mainly of ministers representing the work of the Moravian Church in five states of the Union. Such a project had previously been urged by leaders of the church, particularly by Rev. Jacob Van Vleck, principal of Nazareth Hall, an academy for boys at Nazareth, Pa., and Rev. Christian Lewis Benzien, stationed at Salem, N. C., but the plan was not actually realized until Oct. 2, 1807, when the institution was formally opened for the reception of students. The origin of the institution is attributable to the devotion of Moravians to their church, and to their conviction that the Moravian Church, whose activity in America had begun in 1738, had function and opportunity in the United States. The first professors were Ernst Lewis Hazelius, later prominent in Lutheran theological seminaries, and John Christian Bechler, later a bishop of the church. Originally connected with Nazareth Hall academy, the institution bore the character of a normal school as well as that of a theological seminary; but in 1838 the connection with Nazareth Hall was severed, and thenceforward the institution has enjoyed independent existence. Gradual development of the two departments made reorganization possible in 1858, under the name of Moravian College and Theological Seminary, the college offering complete classical and, since 1896, Latin-scientific courses, and the theological seminary affording a curriculum of studies that does not materially differ from that of other theological schools. The institution was chartered by the legislature of Pennsylvania in 1863, and, after having led a somewhat migratory existence for half a century, was finally located in Bethlehem, Pa., in 1858. The relation between the institution and the Moravian Church in America has always been vital as regards aggressive, educational, home-missionary, and foreign-missionary activity. The scheme of the seminary is thoroughly

Biblical, and the Bible is the chief class-book in all departments, while the principle of the fathers of the Unitas Fratrum, or the Moravian Church, " In essentials unity, in non-essentials liberty, in all things charity," has ruled from the beginning. Every professor is pledged to faithfulness to the doctrinal and disciplinary standards of the church. Since 1858, the official title of the head of the institution has been " president," and Rev. L. F. Kampmann, Rev. Lewis R. Huebener, Rev. Edmund de Schweinitz (q.v.), and Rev. Augustus Schultze (q.v.) have, in the order named, worn this dignity.

The number of students connected with this institution during the first century of its existence (1807–1907) was 500, a large proportion of whom have been ministers and teachers of the church and professors in this and other institutions of learning, while an uncommonly large percentage have been missionaries to the heathen. In 1910 the number of students was fifty-six, five of whom came from northwestern Canada, five from southern states, and the remainder equally from the eastern and western states in which the Moravian Church is represented. With few exceptions the students were members of the Moravian Church, and about sixty per cent were candidates for the ministry. Five professors devote their entire time to teaching each in both the college and seminary department of the institution. The faculty is organized, and, together with the board of trustees, composed of sixteen members representing the northern province of the Moravian Church in America and five advisory members representing the Southern Province of the Church, controls the institution. Both bodies are responsible to the Synod of the Northern Province of the Moravian Church in America and to the governing board which that synod elects. The endowment fund of the institution amounts to $125,207, and the special endowments, including real estate and buildings, total $106,794. The library numbers 10,000 volumes and many hundreds of unbound pamphlets. W. N. SCHWARZE.

BIBLIOGRAPHY: W. N. Schwarze, *History of the Moravian College and Theological Seminary*, Bethlehem, Pa., 1910.

XX. Universalist.—1. Canton: This institution forms the theological school of St. Lawrence University, which is located at Canton, St. Lawrence Co., N. Y. It was founded in 1856 by an organization called " The Educational Society," appointed by the New York Universalist State Convention, which still elects its trustees. The first president was Rev. Ebenezer Fisher, and among its earliest instructors were Rev. Massena Goodrich, Rev. J. S. Lee, and Rev. Orello Cone (q.v.). The students of the seminary have numbered about 360, this figure being due to the establishment of other theological schools in the denomination. Its work has gone on steadily without marked crises. Founded for the purpose of supplying Universalism with an educated ministry, it has from the first devoted special attention to fitting men for intelligent pulpit work and practical pastoral administration. Its professorships have been filled by men representative of progressive tendencies, and it has exerted a distinctly liberalizing effect upon the opinions of its denomination.

In 1910 the seminary had four instructors and fifteen students, all Universalists, and coming from states as remote as Maine and Louisiana. It is governed by a board of nine trustees. Its invested funds and property have increased to about $300,-000, while the separate endowment of the seminary is $165,000; and it also shares an undivided interest in grounds and buildings with the College of Letters of St. Lawrence University. The library contains 12,000 volumes.　　ALMON GUNNISON.

2. Crane: This theological school is a department of Tufts College, which is located at Tufts College, Middlesex Co., Mass. It was recognized as a separate department in 1869, and arose from perception of the fact that a general college training needed to be supplemented by specific professional work for the proper training of ministers. The first foundation was given by Mr. Sylvanus Packard, and the largest gift was made in 1906 by Mr. Albert Crane, of Stamford, Conn., in fulfilment of the expressed intention of his father, Mr. Thomas Crane, of New York. The school is not under denominational control, but is Universalist in sympathy. The first instructor was Rev. Thomas J. Sawyer. The history of the institution has been entirely uneventful so far as matters of outside change or controversy are concerned. It has stood steadily for the application of sound scholarship to the materials of religious knowledge, for serviceable and practicable preaching, and for a type of religious thinking in close contact with the realities and problems of daily life. It has always held scholarship above convention, truth above tradition, and life above creed, but at the same time it has realized the importance of orderly and well-regulated thought as the basis of right living. It has emphasized the human relations of the minister's work, and has sought to strengthen the hold of its students upon reality by identifying them as closely as possible with the general life of the college, so that the theological students are not a class apart, but are associated with the general student body as an integral part of the college community. The Crane Theological School has shared with the sister school at St. Lawrence University the intellectual leadership of the Universalist denomination, not in rivalry but in generous emulation; and it has done much to prevent the thinking of the denomination from becoming stereotyped and to keep its life thoroughly modern. The special movement of most significance which originated under its influence was that which made Universalism a creedless church, by transforming the Winchester Profession and its later alternative, the Boston Declaration, into simple statements of things commonly accepted among Universalists, and abrogating all subscription requirements. Its more prominent instructors have been Dr. Thomas J. Sawyer, its first dean; his successor, Dr. Charles H. Leonard; Dr. Hinckley G. Mitchell (q.v.), in Old Testament; Dr. William G. Tousey, a teacher of ethics and logic; Dr. George M. Harmon, its professor of New-Testament literature and criticism; and Dr. George T. Knight (q.v.), professor of systematic theology.

The number of professors directly assigned to the school by the catalogue for 1909–10 is five, but the relations of the school to the college bring the students under instruction of the teaching force of the School of Liberal Arts, twenty-three in number. The school is under the absolute control of the thirty trustees of Tufts College, twenty of whom are self-perpetuating, while ten are elected by the graduates. No other supervision or control exists. The president of the college has the general direction of the school, which is organized with a dean and a department faculty. There were in the school in 1910 fifteen students, all Universalists, the majority from the New England states, and one Englishman. The separate endowment of the seminary, including grounds and buildings, amounts to $345,000, although its close relations to the college are of great financial advantage to it, and it also uses the college library, which numbers 61,000 volumes and 46,000 pamphlets.

　　FREDERICK WILLIAM HAMILTON.

3. Ryder: This divinity school constitutes the theological department of Lombard College, Galesburg, Knox Co., Ill., and was opened Sept. 5, 1881, being established to meet the needs of the Universalist denomination in the Middle West. In 1890 its trustees voted to change its name to Ryder Divinity School in honor of the late Rev. William Henry Ryder, whose gifts to the institution amounted to more than $50,000, another generous benefactor being Hon. A. G. Throop, of California, The school is open to all candidates for the Christian ministry, although its main work has been training men and women for the Universalist denomination. Among its noteworthy instructors have been Nehemiah White, E. H. Chapin (q.v.), and Isaac Parker. It has never been a large school, having had but about 150 students throughout its entire history. Of these about forty have graduated with a degree, and about fifty are now engaged in active ministerial work.　　LEWIS B. FISHER.

XXI. Undenominational.—1. Harvard: This seminary is located in Cambridge, Mass., and was so closely associated with Harvard College that no special year can be named as that of its foundation, since one of the objects of Harvard from the very beginning was the training of men for the ministry. The earliest instruction for theological students apart from the regular college courses, however, was in 1811, and classes were conducted in this way until 1819, when a distinct faculty of theology was established. With this establishment J. T. Kirkland (q.v.), then president of Harvard, had probably more to do than any other man, and the original faculty consisted of Henry Ware, Sr. (q.v.), Sidney Willard, Levi Frisbie, and Andrews Norton (q.v.). The initial constitution of the school, as made in 1816, provided " that every encouragement be given to the serious, impartial, and unbiased investigation of Christian truth; and that no assent to the peculiarities of any denomination be required either of the students, or professors, or instructors." The distinct organization of the school was legally due to the formation in 1816 of the Society for the Promotion of Theological Education in Harvard University, and from 1824 to 1830 the school was under the direct oversight of the directors of this society, though they acted under the corporation of Harvard

College, to which it transferred its property in Dec., 1830. This society, however, which was later incorporated, still exists and holds property in trust for the divinity school. In 1869 the previous requirements for admission to the school were lowered to accommodate the students of the short-lived Boston School for the Ministry, but they were soon raised, and since 1899 no student has been admitted to the school who has not already received a degree in arts or its equivalent. No degree was conferred for graduation in the school until 1870, and then only to those who passed special examinations, but since 1875 there has been no graduation without this degree. Throughout its history the school has stood for the principles already quoted from its constitution; and it has maintained the impartial, critical, and scientific study of theology in its broadest sense. Among its best-known instructors have been the two Henry Wares, Andrews Norton, John G. Palfrey, George R. Noyes (q.v.), Ezra Abbot (q.v.), Charles Carroll Everett (q.v.), and Joseph Henry Thayer (q.v.). Although formally committed to non-sectarianism, the institution was for many years practically identified with Unitarian Congregationalism, since as a rule its graduates were welcomed by no other denomination; but in 1878, in connection with an appeal for increased endowment, the undenominational aspect of the school was emphasized anew, and at the present time its faculty contains three Trinitarian and three Unitarian Congregationalists, and one Baptist. In 1910 it had a faculty of eleven and a student attendance of fifty-one, sixteen of whom were graduates. In addition the institution has conducted, since 1899, a brief summer school, attended in 1909 by fifty-nine men and five women. The elective system is carried throughout the course, and the seminary students have the right to attend lectures in other departments of Harvard University, and in Andover Theological Seminary now located at Cambridge and affiliated with Harvard University. The special library of the school contains about 38,000 volumes and 11,000 pamphlets, besides which the general university library is also available.

ROBERT SWAIN MORISON.

BIBLIOGRAPHY: J. Quincy, History of Harvard University, Cambridge, Mass., 1840; The Harvard Book, Cambridge, 1875 pp. 197–211; G. G. Bush, History of Higher Education in Massachusetts, Washington, 1891, pp. 137–147.

THEOLOGY AS A SCIENCE.

I. History of the Idea: The name and even the notion of theology, to some extent, extends back into the scientific usage of the Greeks. In the Christian Church it appears first not in the New Testament but in the apologists. Taken over from Greek science it soon won features of its own.

1. Early Use and Meaning of the Term. In Aristotle's "Metaphysics" (VI., i. 19, cf. XI. vii. 15) there are distinguished three branches of theoretical philosophy—mathematical, physical, theological. In Clement of Alexandria the expression "metaphysics" is identified with theology as conceived by Aristotle (Strom. i. 28). Aristotle appears to have thought of the doctrine of God as among the questions of fundamental philosophy: "The terms theologos, theologein (theologia) have in Aristotle . . . the fixed meaning . . . of poetical (mythical) narratives of the gods (Göttersage), corresponding to the expressions mythologos, mythologia, mythologein (Natorp, in Philosophische Monatshefte, no. xxv., 1888); thus it was a prescientific stage of reflection concerning things. According to Natorp, the Stoa was the creator of the idea of a science of theology. With the theology of the poets came their philosophical (physical) interpretation as philosophical theology. Neoplatonism (q.v.), of importance for the theology of Christianity, was the first to impress the Platonic and Aristotelian philosophy upon theology. At the outset Neoplatonism developed a view of the world on the foundation of religious notions in philosophical form and with philosophical methods. Before Scholasticism (q.v.), however, there were only side movements ruled by Neoplatonism. It was common even into the fifth century to designate the ancient poets (Orpheus, Hesiod, Musæus, Homer) as theologians. Athenagoras distinguishes between a "worldly" and a "theological" wisdom (Suppl., x.). For Clement of Alexandria the "philosophy which really is philosophy" is identical with "true theology" (Strom., v. 9). Augustine speaks of a "natural theology," i.e., especially in distinction from mythology (City of God, viii. 1, Eng. transl., NPNF, 1 ser., ii. 144). For Christian reflection, the men of the Bible took the place of the "poets" and assumed the rôle of "theologians." To Philo, Moses was the theologian par excellence. How early and in what respect John became specifically the "theologian" is not certain (cf. G. A. Deissmann, Licht von Osten, pp. 252–253, Tübingen, 1908). The ancient Church's allegorical science of the Bible influenced by Philo belongs with the ancient (Stoic) myths which the theologians of an earlier time used. The theology of the philosophers became the foundation of the apologists. Whether the apologists or the Gnostics are to be regarded as the creators of a peculiar Christian theology may be left undecided.

Harnack with justice repeatedly indicates (cf. Dogmengeschichte, 123 sqq., Freiburg, 1898, Eng. transl. of earlier ed., vol. i., Boston, 1895) that the establishing of a specific religious doctrine is a singular and at bottom a surprising act of the Christian community. This is ultimately connected with the influence of Paul. For **2. Development till Schleiermacher.** it was this apostle who necessarily had theories in order to render the Gospel intelligible and who in particular had to create a Christology. By an inner necessity piety was impelled to fashion a view of the world which corresponded to itself. Here the facts, especially of the life of Jesus, could not be drawn out to mere allegories, for this depended too much on the actuality of the same as events. Christology and soteriology took account of realities in the life of Jesus. But how Jesus as the Christ was essentially to be considered was a problem in which allegory had no place. The solution was found in the use of a theologizing on the person of the Lord which never submitted itself to mere "philosophy." In Justin's consideration of the predicate *theos* as belonging to Jesus as Messiah (*Dialogue* 5, 6) is the foundation for that religious doctrine which became the religious center of Christian dogmatics, completing itself in the doctrine of the Trinity which in the early Church received the title of *theologia* in the restricted sense. With this came as a second foundation of Christian doctrine the incarnation of the Logos for the redemption of man. In the early Church, however, the term "theology" was not used as in present custom to designate all Christian doctrine. In the Middle Ages *sacra doctrina* was the name for Christian doctrine as a whole; *theologia* was and remained the term for the doctrine of God in the narrow sense. Gradually the title "theology" came to include the complex of the church disciplines which are in any way concerned with God. The Reformation brought no discussion concerning the scientific idea or scope of theology (see ENCYCLOPEDIA, THEOLOGICAL, § 4). Granted that the doctrine was drawn from legitimate sources and rightly defined, it remained only to ask what doctrine meant and did not mean for the faith, but this was not condensed into a theology. At the time of the consolidation of Evangelical doctrine into a new orthodoxy, in another tendency was essentially reproduced what the Middle Ages had already worked out in the universities (cf. E. Troeltsch, *Vernunft und Offenbarung bei Johann Gerhard und Melanchthon*, Göttingen, 1891; E. Weber, *Die philosophische Scholastik des deutschen Protestantismus im Zeitalter der Orthodoxie*, Leipsic, 1907; O. Ritschl, *Dogmengeschichte des Protestantismus*, vol. i., Leipsic, 1908). What was new as introduced by the period of the Enlightenment (q.v.) was at first weighty and fruitful when rationalism and with it the mere recourse to the reason and natural religion retreated.

The significance of Schleiermacher (q.v.) for theology consists in this, that relying on philosophy which had outgrown dogmatism, after long critical disintegration of the idea of the Bible

3. Schleiermacher, De Wette, and Strauss.
as the "sure book of God's revelation," he prepared an end for the remainder of dogmatism in dogma, and for faith in certain universal religious ideas, anchored in the reason, innate, in such a way, however, that he established for faith a separate spiritual function—a new basis for theology—from which the character of all modern theology is determined. Theology originates in a science of God and of faith; and theology ceased to believe in philosophy. For his method of organizing theology with reference to "Encyclopedia," see ENCYCLOPEDIA, THEOLOGICAL, § 4 (cf. Schleiermacher's *Kurze Darstellung des theologischen Studiums*, Berlin, 1811). For Schleiermacher theology

has always a "given" object, wherein he agrees with the orthodox conception. There lie in the background conceptions as to faith and dogma which require examination before his theory of theology can be accepted. Of real importance for this is the final section of the introduction to *Der Christliche Glaube* with the heading "Of the Relation of Dogmatics to Christian Piety," especially § 15. In § 17 Schleiermacher expressly discusses the worth of the dogmatic propositions and affirms that these are of a double nature—ecclesiastical and scientific, but points out only the scientific. As the foundation of theology he laid down a discipline which he named "philosophical theology." This can take its point of departure only with reference to Christianity in the general notion of the pious community. With this proposition Schleiermacher unites theology and general science. W. M. L. de Wette's *Ueber Religion und Theologie* (Berlin, 1815) presents thoughts which are really not far from those of Schleiermacher, yet they have a peculiarity which is not without subsequent influence. Schleiermacher points back to Kant, Spinoza, and Goethe, De Wette to Fries and Herder; yet both are independent theologians. The view of De Wette (q.v.) concerning the nature of theology as science is founded on a double or threefold way of persuasion—the understanding which produces science; the ideal-esthetic which presents itself as faith and as feeling. Religion is faith and likewise feeling. Religion is an inner life which has been historically formed for us through Christ in a long process of spiritual church dogmas. It rests on revelation, which theology conceives in ideas and esthetic symbols. De Wette reflected on a philosophical theology which was to be nothing else than a description of human nature or anthropology. D. F. Strauss (q.v.) as scholar of Hegel formed a type of theology. In his closing discussion of his *Life of Jesus*, and especially in his introduction to his *Dogmatic* (1840), he allots to theology no other task than its transformation into a philosophy of religion. Biedermann with affecting love for Christianity as such has more completely than Strauss sought to realize his program for dogmatics. Recently F. R. Lipsius (*Kritik der theologischen Erkenntnis*, Leipsic, 1904), with other means than Strauss, presented as aim for theology that it transform itself into (monistic) philosophy.

II. Scientific Presentation: Every theory of theology is accompanied by presuppositions. To Gottschick ecclesiastical Christianity appears as a simple reality, and he undertakes to prove that this

1. Relation to Religion.
is both an undoubted and an underived fact of consciousness which must be scientifically isolated; hence theology may be set forth as a science *sui generis*. But as yet a scientific understanding of the nature of Christianity has not been attained, and this is beset by greater difficulties than were formerly conceived (cf. Kattenbusch, *Die Lage der systematischen Theologie in der Gegenwart*, in ZTK, 1905, pp. 103–146; idem, in *Christliche Welt*, no. 22, 1901). The most significant factor in the recent history of theology must be seen in the widening of the perspective for the historical considera-

tion of Christendom. Few will object if theology be defined as "science of Christianity." But it is perhaps more difficult than ever to answer the question, What is the essence of Christianity as religion? All theologians will so far agree in the designation of Christianity simply as religion. But the question immediately arises what religion is and what notes in particular characterize the Christian religion, both as piety and as content of the Church; it is debated in what degree the "experiences" of the individual or of the community come into consideration; whether the foundation of religion is reached by the simple observation of the "being" of religion or at the same time—if not instead of this—of the "obligation" in it; whether a determination of what is empirical in piety or of the self-judgment of the same according to a norm must take the lead. One may perhaps say that all are to be combined. With Schleiermacher (certainly with De Wette) it was always a common conviction that religion and theology were to be held apart. This has led to regarding theology as a specific discipline—only a branch of general science, hence as not belonging to the church (cf. G. Krueger, *Die unkirchliche Theologie*, in *Christliche Welt*, no. 34, 1900; F. Traub, *Kirchliche und unkirchliche Theologie*, in *ZTK*, vol. xiii., pp. 39 sqq., 1903; J. F. Gottschick, *Die Entstehung der Lösung der Unkirchlichkeit der Theologie*, in the same, pp. 77 sqq.). It is admitted that theology as a university study should serve the Church, hence no one will deny a pedagogical place to theologians in its instruction. One must, however, make it clear to himself that the expression "church" has two strata—the legal, the religious community, and the religious, not only believing individuals, but a "society of faith and of the Holy Spirit." The task of theology concerns the latter.

To many the religious historical method appears to involve the treatment of Christianity by theology on the same lines as all religions. As a religion

2. Christianity, Other Religions, the Individual. Christianity does indeed belong with the other religions in some one sense under a common thought, and it has been realized in the hearts of men in wholly distinct historical connections. But it is a prejudgment that it is therefore to be treated as all religions are. If one will be taught by Christianity how it regards and judges itself, he can not help admitting that it knows itself as over against the other religions and ascribes to itself a suprahistorical basis. Science can neither simply accept nor simply ignore the self-judgment of Christianity; it tests the matter even if it ends with a *non liquet*. In this way it may perhaps be convinced that Christianity and the other religions have at bottom even common experiences and perceptions. The Church will not deny the reference to Rom. i. 19–20, yet this does not prevent the Christian religion from "perhaps" standing by itself according to its essence and truth (cf. S. Dunkmann, *NZ*, xix. 255 sqq., 1908; H. Mulert, in *ZTK*, xviii. 325 sqq., 1908). A peculiar turn of the discussion concerning the character of theology in relation to religion has lately been occasioned by W. Herrmann (cf. *Kultur der Gegenwart*, Teil I, Abt. 4, *Die Christliche Religion*, 2d half, *Sys-*

tematische christliche Theologie, Leipsic, 1906). Pious men could agree only concerning what religion or faith is and by what means it is established. For every man the inner meeting with the Christ of the New Testament is the moment where he learns to know the ethical power which can indeed bring him to full subordination in perfect freedom and so to faith in God. Faith need not renounce fixing in thought every thing which it experiences, but no one should declare the result as normative; since every one experiences the same thing differently.

Another series of questions emerges in a comparison of theology with the philosophy of religion. In whatever sense one sets up a formula for the essence of religion or of Christianity, he touches

3. Philosophy of Religion, Apologetics. the problems of epistemology, psychology, metaphysics, ethics. Naturalism and idealism, monism and dualism, pantheism and personal theism are associated with theology and philosophy. The notions of the soul, freedom, and immortality vibrate between theology and philosophy. Within theology itself, in the questions concerning methods and legitimate theological judgments all kinds of points of view meet. The complexity of the present situation is evinced by the premature reemergence of the apologetic problem—now indeed the ruling one. The so-called modern "positive" theology is predominantly apologetic (cf. K. Beth, *Die Moderne und die Prinzipien der Theologie*, Berlin, 1907; G. Wobbermin, *Theologie und Metaphysik*, Berlin, 1901; G. Vischer, *Ist die Wahrheit des Christentums zu beweisen?* Tübingen, 1902; R. Otto, *Naturalistische und religiöse Weltanschauung*, ib. 1904; A. Titius, *Religion und Naturwissenschaft*, ib. 1904; A. W. Hunzinger, *Zur apologetischen Aufgabe der evangelischen Kirche in der Gegenwart*, Leipsic, 1907; idem, *Probleme und Aufgaben der gegenwärtigen systematischen Theologie*, ib. 1908). The discussion of the theses of religious faith and the ethical consciousness, especially those theses which are Christian with opposing antitheses, will be carried on under favorable auspices only when the theses at least are plainly formulated. That this is now the case no one will assert.

When theology seeks to be fundamental, it moves under much uncertainty in three directions. (1) Schleiermacher's psychological conception of religion as a purely natural *datum* in the human spirit is still influential. This feeling of "absolute

4. Lines of Advance. dependence" is a perceptible element of the soul, but it is no more than just this. The religious feeling can be combined with the other feelings and elements of the soul; in itself it can be only "clearer," not richer in content, than it is, so far as it points to a source. It is involved in the notion of absolute dependence that it works out in the consciousness of man together with the all—as a piece of it, not so much "to live" as "being lived." Religion is the profoundest, though it is a mere, aspect of becoming conscious. Thus it is fundamentally rational. Theology will be formed in the concrete community partly positively, partly philosophically. Naturally the psychology of religion can be scientifically developed in a far more concrete manner than by Schleiermacher, and religious historical investigations will be of great service especially if coupled with religious psychopathology (for the relation of the confessional school of theology to Schleiermacher, cf. F. Kattenbusch, *Von Schleiermacher zu Ritschl*, 3d ed., Giessen, 1903). In the Erlangen school, the feeling of absolute dependence has been reinterpreted by the thought of " experience " of " regeneration." " Faith " as a special " organ " of the spirit reminds of De Wette. Finally, endeavors to press theology on the path of psychology can appeal to Schleiermacher (cf. W. Vorbrodt, *Zur Religionspsychologie: Prinzipien und Pathologie*, in *TSK*, 1906, pp. 237 sqq.; W. James, *Varieties of Religious Experience*, New York, 1902; J. O. Scheel, *Die Moderne Religionspsychologie*, in *ZTK*, xviii. 1 sqq., 1908; E. W. Mayer, *Ueber Religionspsychologie*, in the same, pp. 293 sqq.). (2) Over against the mere psychological conception of religion, A. Ritschl's can be conceived as merely historical. Ritschl's idea, however, orients itself not in one's own " feeling " or even " experience," but in a closed revelation, i.e., the objective content of the Gospel or the person of Jesus. With the making of the personal quality of God as strong as possible, there is affirmed a contact of the human spirit with a supramundane reality susceptible of personal experience but never universally demonstrable. Because rationalizing has been avoided, the reproach of idiosyncrasy has had to be met. The absoluteness of Christianity has gained a sharpness which is often conceived as a return of the old " dogmatism." The followers of Ritschl have tried to guard against misunderstanding of his thought (cf. W. Herrmann, *Die Religion im Verhältnis zum Welterkennen und zur Sittlichkeit*, Halle, 1879; idem, *Der Glaube an Gott und die Wissenschaft unserer Zeit*, in *ZTK*, 1905, pp. 1 sqq.; O. Kirn, *Glaube und Geschichte*, Leipsic, 1900; J. Kaftan, *Die Einheit des Erkennens*, Tübingen, 1908). (3) For Tröltsch it is a postulate of historical science to regard even religion as a steadily developing reality. Even Christianity will not be the final form of religion, but only a contribution to its history. The epochs of Christianity are more or less different aspects of it which have to be considered when one discusses its nature (cf. *Die Absolutheit des Christentums und die Religionsgeschichte*, Tübingen, 1902; idem, *Psychologie und Erkenntnistheorie in der Religionserkenntnistheorie*, 1905). All religions have an absolutely fixed point in mystical " experiences," but Tröltsch attempts no formula for these as did Schleiermacher; to the pious it is a vital certainty of experience, but for others it is in itself irrational and debatable. God's influence on the spirit is always combined with the entire content of the spirit in contemporary culture. Christian theology has three essential tasks: (1) the purely historical psychological reception of Christianity in the frame of its development and of universal religious history; (2) the treatment of its experiences and notions in connection with all elements of the spiritual life, especially with the highest ideals and convictions to be reached in philosophy, therein confirming its right; (3) the thorough blending of its world-view with that of modern science. Tröltsch's judgment concerning the Gos-

pel is not supported by an investigation which is due from a theologian. The next task of theology lies in a comprehensive consideration of the Gospel which naturally shall not be partial.

(F. KATTENBUSCH.)

III. British and American Theology: In Great Britain and America until a recent period Protestant theology followed the Reformation program both in its point of view and in its order of topics.

1. Three Divisions. The three doctrinal divisions have been the Calvinist, the Arminian, and the Socinian. To whatever school of philosophy theologians belonged, they never doubted that metaphysics was a valid handmaid of theology. For the Calvinists and Arminians the Scriptures were the supreme authoritative source of doctrine and their principles of interpretation were in agreement. A secondary authority, often scarcely less than the first, was attributed to creeds and great names. Among the earlier Socinians the Scriptures were accepted as authoritative, the difference between them and the Calvinists and Arminians being in the method of interpretation; gradually, however, the Trinitarian and other traditional views came to be regarded as extra-Biblical and greater reliance was placed on the reason as an independent source of religious truth. During the eighteenth century the previous distinction between Socinians and Arminians was obscured and Socinian notions appeared under the general name of " Arminian." During the last century these were again differentiated, the Socinians being gradually identified with the Unitarians and Universalists (qq.v.), the Arminians swinging back into the Evangelical ranks under the lead especially of the Methodist church, and becoming a powerful leaven even in the Calvinist bodies (see ARMINIANS AND ARMINIANISM; NEW ENGLAND THEOLOGY).

Two general characteristics of English and American theology are to be noted: first, lack of thoroughgoing systematizing or strict unfolding of doctrine from an ideal principle. This is due in part to a practical interest; the Anglo-Saxon mind cares less for absolute theoretic consistency than for the pragmatic value of ideas. Secondly, during the last three-quarters of a century perhaps the most quickening and influential contributions to theology have been not the systematic presentations of theologians but suggestions lodged in sermons or embodied in discussion of particular subjects (cf. works by F. W. Robertson, Horace Bushnell, Henry Drummond, John Fiske, and Joseph LeConte).

The past century, like other ages of the Church, has been a transitional one. Many endeavors have been made to unite the old and the new in varying proportions in one presentation. Some

2. Tendencies in Dogmatics. have indeed continued steadfastly in the traditional paths, making the least possible concessions to modern thought and with only a polemic interest in its conclusions (C. Hodge, *Systematic Theology*, Philadelphia, 1865; W. G. T. Shedd, *Dogmatic Theology*, New York, 1888). Others, although yielding a modified assent to evolution, to the sufficiency but not the inerrant infallibility of the Scriptures, and to some form of divine immanence, still represent essentially the traditional positions (cf. J. Orr, *The Christian View of God and the World*, New York, 1893; H. C. Sheldon, *System of Christian Doctrine*, ib. 1903; J. A. Beet, *A Manual of Theology*, London, 1906; M. S. Terry, *Biblical Dogmatics*, New York, 1907; A. H. Strong, *Systematic Theology*, Philadelphia, 1907–08). On the other hand, several tendencies have appeared which propose modifications in the traditional modes of conceiving the realities of the Christian faith. (1) A Christocentric basis for theology has been advocated from two points of view, either constituting Christ as the heart and controlling principle of interpretation (advocated but not carried out by H. B. Smith, *System of Christian Doctrine*, New York, 1890, and by L. F. Stearns, *Present Day Theology*, ib. 1893), or regarding the consciousness of Christ as the norm of theological construction (A. M. Fairbairn, *The Place of Christ in Modern Theology*, New York, 1893; W. N. Clarke, *An Outline of Christian Theology*, ib. 1898; idem, *The Use of the Scriptures in Theology*, ib. 1905). (2) A reconstruction of theology has been indicated which rises out of the Ritschlian background and has for its immediate aim a fresh evaluation of faith, especially as affected from the historical and social side (H. C. King, *Reconstruction in Theology*, New York, 1901; idem, *Theology and the Social Consciousness*, ib. 1902). (3) Among the attempts to relate theology to a vital religious experience as interpreted through its history both in the Scriptures and the Church may be mentioned G. B. Stevens, *The Christian Doctrine of Salvation* (New York, 1905); O. F. Curtis, *The Christian Faith, Personally Given in a System of Doctrine* (ib. 1905); C. A. Beckwith, *Realities of Christian Theology* (Boston, 1906); W. A. Brown, *Christian Theology in Outline* (New York, 1906). This method finds in experience its immediate source of theology and in history the form which that experience has taken in its rational development, and accordingly devotes particular attention to these two aspects of life. (4) In the doctrine of the immanence of God lies the basis for several discussions in theology, as, e.g., by R. J. Campbell, *The New Theology* (London, 1907), and by Sir Oliver Lodge, *The Substance of Faith Allied with Science* (ib. 1907). The point of view is that of an essentially pantheistic monism, characterized by two significant bearings—a tendency to eliminate the fact of sin, and a firm emphasis on the social aspect of Christianity. Endeavors to adjust the claims of monism to the ethical demands of consciousness have been made by J. Caird, *An Introduction to the Philosophy of Religion* (London, 1880), by J. Royce, *The World and the Individual* (vol. ii., Boston, 1901), and by B. P. Bowne, *Theism* (ib. 1902), and *The Immanence of God* (London, 1905; cf. God, IV.). (5) Evolution has been accepted by most recent theologians as on the whole the method of God in his cosmic action. Some have so described the redemptive purpose as to isolate this from the uniform activity of God in the creation (cf. C. Hodge, ut sup.); others, as W. N. Clarke and A. H. Strong, have admitted evolution but with reservations; while others have adopted this as the constant mode of God's working, not only in creation and provi-

dence, but also in redemption, and have made it the key to their entire presentation (L. Abbott, *The Theology of an Evolutionist*, Boston, 1897; E. Griffith Jones, *Ascent through Christ*, London, 1901). (6) Psychology occupies a far more definite and influential place in theology than at any previous period. While Augustine and Edwards had unequaled insight into the nature and workings of the religious consciousness and expressed themselves with a subtilty and force never surpassed, yet as theology has busied itself with the human side of divine grace, it has been compelled to make a greater use of psychology in its discussions of man and sin, of the person and work of Christ, of conversion and sanctification, of future punishment, and not least of all in its determination of the character of God (for a single aspect of this subject, see CONVERSION, supplement; and in addition to the works there indicated, cf. G. B. Cutten, *The Psychological Phenomena of Christianity*, New York, 1908). (7) The so-called " positive theology " has for its key-note the " primacy of the given." There is an objective content of revelation. Christ was in relation to God what he himself and his first disciples thought him to be. In him, in his cross God redeemed the world. This action was not merely a saving influence but a saving deed; it changed God's relation to men objectively and once for all. This fact is creative of Christian experience. It is not, however, mediated by the Bible as authoritative, nor is it assured by historical criticism. A present-day experience which involves the supernatural offers a firm basis for the existence of the supernatural in the New-Testament times and in the New Testament itself. With reference to this objective gospel faith is not something which the Christian shares with Christ in imitation of him, but is directed to him as the one in whom the objective revelation centered and was declared (cf. D. S. Cairns, *Christianity in the Modern World*, New York, 1906; P. T. Forsyth, *Positive Preaching and the Modern Mind*, ib. 1907; S. Mathews, *The Church and the Changing Order*, ib. 1907; R. Seeberg, *The Fundamental Truths of the Christian Religion*, London, 1908). (8) The " critical " theology seeks the revelation of God in the orderly processes of the natural world and in the rational consciousness. The supernatural is the natural regarded from its divine causative ground; the natural is the regular method of God's activity. Hence no conflict arises between the scientific and the religious view of the world. The traditional apologetic in defense of miracles is thus unnecessary; the true apologetic is the actual adaptedness of Christianity to the social needs of men. Redemption emptied of its miraculous content is an ethical emancipation. The power of the cross lies in its capacity to quicken in the souls of men a spirit of sacrifice and service like that of Jesus (cf. G. B. Foster, *The Finality of the Christian Religion*, Chicago, 1906).

In the foregoing description no attempt is made at an exhaustive account of any one of the various treatises referred to. In all of these the lines of tendency cross and recross and each shares to some degree in all the features of the modern spirit. The purpose is to indicate only the dominant notes in the respective presentations. The aim of theology to-day, whether consciously or not, is, as it has always been, to relate its findings to the actual as well as the ideal Christian life; in this endeavor it is powerfully aided by many interests which have not been available at any previous time.

C. A. BECKWITH.

BIBLIOGRAPHY: The subject is discussed in the works named in the article on ENCYCLOPEDIA, THEOLOGICAL. So, too, the manuals and treatises on systematic theology (see under DOGMA, DOGMATICS) treat the matter. The most important literature is named in the text. Consult further: A. E. Biedermann, *Christliche Dogmatik*, 2d ed., 2 vols., Berlin, 1884–85; A. Ritschl, *Theologie und Metaphysik*, 2d ed., Göttingen, 1887; C. A. Bernoulli, *Die wissenschaftlichen und die kirchlichen Methoden in der Theologie*, Tübingen, 1897; P. Lobstein, *Einleitung in die evangelische Dogmatik*, Freiburg, 1897; G. Wobbermin, in *Zeitschrift für Theologie und Kirche*, x (1900), 375 sqq., and O. Ritschl, in the same, xii (1902), 202 sqq., 255 sqq.; J. Kaftan, *Zur Dogmatik*, Tübingen, 1904; M. Reischle, *Theologie und Religionsgeschichte*, Tübingen, 1904; N. H. Marshall, *Theology and Truth*, London, 1906; K. Beth, *Die Moderne und Prinzipien der Theologie*, Berlin, 1907; M. Schian, *Zur Beurtheilung der modernen positiven Theologie*, Giessen, 1907; P. Wernle, *Einführung in das theologische Studium*, Tübingen, 1908; A. Eckert, *Einführung in die Prinzipien und Methoden der evangelischen Theologie*, Leipsic, 1909; A. W. Hunzinger, *Probleme und Aufgaben der gegenwärtigen systematischen Theologie*, Leipsic, 1909; A. Miller, *The Problem of Theology in Modern Life and Thought*, New York, 1908; R. Seeberg, *Zur systematischen Theologie*, Leipsic, 1909; F. Traub, *Theologie und Philosophie. Eine Untersuchung über das Verhältnis der theoretischen Philosophie zum Grundproblem der Theologie*, Tübingen, 1910; E. Melzer, *Der Beweis für das Dasein und seine Persönlichkeit mit Rücksicht auf die herkömmlichen Gottesbeweise*, Neisse, 1910; *KL*, xi. 1555–1571.

THEOLOGY, MONUMENTAL. See MONUMENTAL THEOLOGY.

THEOLOGY, MORAL, ROMAN CATHOLIC VIEW OF.

Notion (§ 1).
Division (§ 2).
Sources (§ 3).
History till Thirteenth Century (§ 4).
Till the Renaissance (§ 5).
The Modern Period (§ 6).

Divine revelation has at all times contained, in addition to truths to be believed and accepted as
coming from God, certain precepts to
1. **Notion.** be submitted to as the expression of
his will. These divine commands, emphasizing the natural law and supplementing it in view of the higher condition to which man has been raised and of the means vouchsafed for the attainment of his ultimate supernatural end, constitute, when arranged in logical and systematic order, the science of Christian ethics (see ETHICS; MORALISTS, BRITISH; MORALITY, MORAL LAW), or, as it is commonly called in the schools, moral theology. It includes in principle, besides the precepts of the natural and divine law, the ordinances emanating from ecclesiastical and civil authority, and covers the entire field of moral and religious duty. In a broad sense it is sometimes made to include what is known as ascetic and mystic theology, but, strictly speaking, it has for its object the laws of right and wrong that should govern the Christian life, while ascetic and mystic theology deal with the laws of Christian perfection and with the higher processes of the spiritual union of the soul with God. The importance attached to this branch of ecclesiastical science in

Roman Catholic theological schools is based on the conviction that nothing is so practically essential to the Christian as a right knowledge of his duty toward God and his fellow men, on the proper discharge of which depends his eternal salvation.

Moral theology is generally divided into two parts. In the first are treated the general or fundamental questions pertaining to man's ultimate end,
the true nature and norm of right and
2. **Division.** wrong, the morality of human acts, law and authority, conscience, and the like. In the second, which is called special, various categories of means are discussed, viz., the different Christian virtues (theological and moral, with the precepts of the Decalogue, q.v.), the obligations pertaining to particular occupations or states of life, and likewise the sacraments, since they are the recognized sources of the graces necessary for the proper (i.e., supernatural) fulfilment of all Christian duties.

The sources of moral theology are in the main the same as those of Roman Catholic theology in
general, viz., Holy Writ, ecclesiastical
3. **Sources.** tradition and authority, and reason.
Scripture being the chief depository of divine revelation is naturally the most important source of moral science, for " all Scripture, inspired of God, is profitable to teach, to reprove, to correct, to instruct in justice, that the man of God may be perfect, furnished to every good work " (II Tim. iii. 16, 17). The Scriptures indeed abound in moral instruction in the form of both precept and example. It goes without saying that in making use of the Old Testament for the purposes of moral as well as dogmatic theology, account must be taken of the constantly progressive character of divine revelation, and, consequently, isolated texts and precepts, to be of real value, must be considered in the light of this doctrinal and ethical evolution. Moreover, the ceremonial and judicial precepts of the Jewish law, being of a temporary nature, are considered as abrogated under the new dispensation, and, while the moral precepts and the concrete examples of virtue retain a true value, they must nevertheless be used with discretion and with due regard for the higher ideals of Christian ethics. Even as regards the New Testament, a certain doctrinal and ethical progression must be admitted, though naturally in a far less degree; and, finally, the principle of progressive development, under the guidance of the Holy Ghost abiding in the Church, is recognized during the ages that have elapsed since the close, with the death of the apostles and inspired writers, of what may be termed the final era of authentic or official revelation. It should be noted also in connection with the ethical significance of the New Testament, that it contains, besides formal precepts which oblige under pain of sin, counsels of perfection (e.g., Matt. xix. 16–21), and, although these are sometimes set forth in mandatory terms, they should not be confounded with the former; hence in moral theology the distinction between evangelical precept and counsel. The final determination of what belongs to each of these lies with the authority of the Church, and the general consensus of tradition and of the theologians. In

like manner is also determined which of the New-Testament precepts have a universal and permanent binding force, and which are only of a temporary or local character (cf. Acts xv. 28–29). Here, as in matters of faith, the Scriptural data are interpreted officially, when necessary, by the teaching Church, aided by the testimony of tradition and by the expert opinions of recognized theologians. Thus papal and conciliary decrees, condemned propositions, and similar authoritative pronouncements become sources of moral theology. Chief among the Roman Catholic congregations which, with the approval of the pope, render decisions bearing on the subject-matter of moral science, are the Congregation of the Council, the Congregation of the Inquisition, and the *Sacra Penitentiaria*. The first is empowered to interpret officially the decrees of the Council of Trent (q.v.) in disciplinary matters. Its decisions relative to the meaning of these decrees are binding and apply to all cases which they cover, but its application of a decree to a particular case does not necessarily oblige in all similar contingencies. The Congregation of the Inquisition has jurisdiction in matters of heresy and schism, apostasy, abuse of the sacraments, and the like, and it has issued many decrees bearing on the moral as well as the dogmatic aspect of these questions. The doctrinal authority of this congregation is very great, but its decisions are not considered irreformable unless so indorsed by the pope as to make them his own in a special bull or brief. The *Sacra Penitentiaria* does not deal with speculative moral questions or controversies. Its function is to settle practical and concrete cases of conscience, and its decisions, while useful, do not of themselves possess a legal binding force. The place occupied by the writings of the Church Fathers and theologians as sources of moral theology is much the same as in doctrinal matters. Their consensus as witnesses of a constant tradition is more important than as exponents of their own views, and their testimony is, in all cases, subject to the authoritative rulings of the official Church. Finally, since God is the author of human reason as well as of revelation, and since even the revealed precepts should be reasonably understood, moral theology makes extensive use of the ethical principles of natural law by way of comparison, illustration, and proof. Indeed, these principles can never be in real opposition to the revealed expressions of the divine will, though they are supplemented and elevated by them. Likewise the enactments of civil authority are utilized as remote and secondary sources of moral science.

While the value of human reason is duly recognized by theologians and the teaching Church in questions of moral science, its independence in the rationalistic sense is consistently denied; it remains amenable to the higher light of divine revelation properly understood or interpreted by church authority. Besides the great utility of rational ethics in the study of moral theology, other branches of science have an important though less direct bearing on its various problems. Among these may be mentioned psychology both speculative and experimental, sociology, political economy, civil jurisprudence, and history.

In outlining the history of moral theology in the Christian Church it is customary to distinguish between the period of the Fathers and that of the theologians. The first extends from the earliest moral treatises down to the time of

4. History till Thirteenth Century. Bernard of Clairvaux (q.v.), who is called the last of the Fathers. The ethical history of this period, however, belongs rather to the history of the patristic sources of moral theology, for the Fathers made no attempt to expound either doctrine or morals in a systematic or scientific manner, and further reference to it may be omitted here (cf. A. Tanquerey, *Synopsis theologiæ moralis*, vol. ii., pp. xxx.–xl., New York, 1906). The period of moral theology properly so called begins with the early schoolmen in the twelfth century. Their work was preparatory to the great development of scholastic science in the century following—called the golden age of scholasticism. Suffice it to mention the monastic school of Bec in Normandy (see BEC, ABBEY OF), founded by Lanfranc (q.v.) and made illustrious by Anselm (q.v.), who was one of the first to introduce the scholastic methods; the school of Abelard (q.v.), who, in his *Introductio ad theologiam* sets forth a summary of theology in general, and in his *Scito teipsum* traces a compendium of ethics from the standpoint of human reason; the school of St. Victor in Paris, which though more mystical than didactic, contributed not a little to the progress of moral science. Foremost among the writers of this school is Hugo of St. Victor (q.v.), who in his treatises *De sacramentis* embodies a brief discussion of nearly all topics pertaining to moral theology. The most famous doctor, however, of this period was Peter Lombard (q.v.), professor of theology and later bishop of Paris. In the *Quatuor libri sententiarum* he discusses in scholastic form the entire cycle of moral as well as dogmatic theology derived from the Scriptures and the writings of the Fathers.

In the thirteenth century the monastic schools were superseded by the great universities, and a powerful impetus was given to the

5. Till the Renaissance. study of theology which in its comprehensive treatment absorbed nearly all the other branches of knowledge. Its practical or moral aspect was not yet so sharply differentiated from the speculative as in later times, and thus the great dogmatic theologians of the epoch were also the great masters of moral science. This period was marked by the rise of the great rival theological schools of the Dominicans (see DOMINIC, SAINT) and the Franciscans (see FRANCIS, SAINT, OF ASSISI). Among the Dominican theologians two deserve special mention: Albertus Magnus (q.v.) and Thomas Aquinas (q.v.). The former, who was professor successively in Paris and Cologne, besides discussing many of the fundamental questions pertaining to moral theology in his *Summa theologiæ*, has much bearing on the same subject in his *Summa de creaturis*. Thomas Aquinas, who taught philosophy and theology in Paris and in some of the Italian universities, is considered the greatest of all the medieval theologians. He was the first to apply successfully the Aristotelian philosophy to the systematic elucidation of revealed truths, and his lucid logical order and clearness of exposition have never been equaled by any of the Schoolmen. His greatest work is the *Summa theologica*, which has remained a classical standard in Roman Catholic theological schools down to the present time. The second part of the *Summa* is devoted to moral theology in its highest and broadest as well as its more practical aspects. In treating of the virtues he does not confine the discussion merely to what constitutes right or wrong (sin), but deals equally with the higher ideals of Christian perfection, thus combining moral and ascetic theology. Among the illustrious masters of the Franciscan school may be mentioned, besides Alexander of Hales (q.v.), who joined the order when already advanced in years, the mystical St. Bonaventura (q.v.) and Johannes Duns Scotus (see DUNS SCOTUS), whose moral as well as doctrinal principles, speculatively considered, are often divergent from those of Aquinas, whence many animated and subtile controversies between the representatives of the Dominican and Franciscan schools. The secular clergy of this epoch is well represented by writers such as William of Paris (d. 1249), who composed divers treatises on moral subjects, e.g., *Summa virtutum et vitiorum*, *De fide et legibus*, *De remediis tentationum*, *De claustra animæ*, *De pænitentia*, and others. During the ensuing period covering the fourteenth and fifteenth centuries scholasticism suffered a marked decadence due to various causes, chief among which may be reckoned the rivalry and controversies between the schools, particularly the disputes concerning nominalism and realism, and the great schism with its demoralizing influences. The broad, synthetic treatment of theological questions was abandoned and scholastic discussion became overcharged with inane subtleties and hair-splitting distinctions. Moral theology shared in the general decadence and no works of importance were produced during these two centuries.

Roman Catholic theologians were again aroused to activity by the satire of the Humanists and still more by the aggressive doctrinal controversies incidental to the Protestant Reformation. Moral science also received a fresh impetus which lasted until nearly the close of the seventeenth century. Among the distinguished writers on this and other subjects during this period may be mentioned Cardinal Thomas Cajetan (q.v.), Fr. de Victoria (d. 1546), Bartholomew Medina (d. 1581), Domingo de Soto (q.v.), Petrus de Soto (q.v.), Joannes a S. Thoma (d. 1664), J. B. Gonet (d. 1681), and Joannes Martinez Prado (d. 1668), all Dominicans. The Franciscan school was represented by Antonius Cordubensis (d. 1578), Em. Rodriguez (d. 1613), Martinus de S. Josepho (d. 1649), J. M. de Castilento (d. 1653), and Petrus Marchant (d. 1661). The order of the Jesuits produced many illustrious theologians and moralists, among whom may be mentioned Petrus Canisius (q.v.), Francis Tolet (q.v.), E. Sa (d. 1596), Luis Molina (q.v.), Gregory of Valentia (d. 1603), Johannes Azor (d. 1608), Francisco Suarez (q.v.), Gabriel Vasquez (d. 1604), Thomas Sanchez (d. 1610), Johann Martinez de Ripalda (d. 1648), and, perhaps the greatest of all

6. The Modern Period.

as a moral theologian, Cardinal Johannes de Lugo (d. 1660). Among the moralists of the Benedictine order were Ludovicus Blosius (d. 1566), J. Graffius (d. 1620), and Joseph Saenz de Aguirre (q.v.). The secular clergy was represented during this period of revival by such writers as Carlo Borromeo, bishop of Milan (q.v.), and St. Francis de Sales, bishop of Geneva (q.v.), who labored so strenuously for the reform of ecclesiastical discipline and Christian morals. Toward the end of the seventeenth century and onward the science of moral theology again declined, because of the prevailing tendency in the schools to reduce it to mere casuistry. Discussion of the underlying principles was lost sight of and undue attention was given to the solution of concrete cases of conscience with the result that this branch of theology lost much of its dignity and scientific character. It was now completely separated from ascetic theology and was almost exclusively occupied in drawing a line between what should be considered sinful and what could be tolerated as free from sin, and in defining the degree of sin (mortal or venial) involved in a given act of transgression. Discussion of the virtues and the principles of Christian life and perfection was passed over as pertaining to either dogmatic or ascetic theology. Not a few of the casuists were accused of laxity in their decisions, and the situation was not helped by the long and bitter controversies between rigorists, probabiliorists, and probabilists (see PROBABILISM). Hence the obloquy that has come to be attached to the word casuistry. During this last period of the history of moral theology no writer has arisen comparable with the great masters of previous epochs. The one who comes nearest to this standard, though yet far distant, is Alphonso Maria di Liguori (q.v.), the founder of the Redemptorist order. His works comprise a complete treatise of moral theology and other practical treatises for the use of confessors, viz., *Praxis confessarii*, *Homo apostolicus*, *Examen ordinandorum*, etc. Seeking a *media via* between the probabiliorists and the ultra lax exponents of probabilism, he evolved a system known as equiprobabilism. On this account and because of the recognition bestowed on his works by the official Church, his writings and their interpretation have been the subject of not a little controversy. The last half-century has been fertile in the production of condensed manuals of moral theology chiefly of the practical or casuistic type for the use of confessors and theological students. Among the more popular may be mentioned those of Jean Pierre Gury (q.v.), Augustinus Lehmkuhl, Edward Genicot, and two remarkable treatises, *De theologia morali fundamentali* and *De virtutibus theologicis*, by Thomas J. Bouquillon (d. 1902), professor at the Catholic University of America.

JAMES F. DRISCOLL.

BIBLIOGRAHY: J. B. Hogan, *Clerical Studies*, pp. 197–249, Boston, 1898; A. Tanquerey, *Synopsis theologiæ moralis*, vol. ii., pp. xxi.–lii., New York, 1906; S. Alphonsus Liguori, *Theologia moralis*, pp. xxvii.–cxlviii., Mechlin, 1845; T. Bouquillon, *Theologia moralis fundamentalis*, Introductio, §§ 1–14, Bruges, 1893; Paul de Broglie, *La Morale sans Dieu*, Paris, 1886; *Catechismus Conc. Trident*, Tournai, 1890; Charles Gay, *La Vie et les vertus chrétiennes*, Paris, 1876; J. Perrone, *De virtutibus fidei, spei et caritatis*, Regensburg, 1865.

THEONAS, thê-ō'nas (**THEON**): Arian bishop of Marmarica, in the Egyptian province of Cyrenaica, in the fourth century. He is mentioned in the synodal letter of Bishop Alexander (given in Athanasius, *Select Works and Letters*, in *NPNF*, 2 ser., iv. 69 sqq.) as an adherent of Arius. He and Secundus of Ptolemais were the only two Egyptian bishops who sided with Arius; and it is probable that their line of conduct was regulated by political rather than by theological reasons. At all events, they absolutely refused at the Council of Nicæa (325) to condemn Arius, and were consequently deposed and banished.

BIBLIOGRAPHY: Theodoret, *Hist. eccl.*, i. 7, Eng. transl. in *NPNF*, 2 ser., iii. 43–46; Socrates, *Hist. eccl.*, i. ix., Eng. transl., ut sup., ii. 12–17; Epiphanius, *Hær.*, lxix. 8; Tillemont, *Mémoires*, vi. 2.

THEOPASCHITES, the-ō-pas'kaits: A term designating in its widest sense all Christians who recognize as correct the formula " God has suffered " or " God has been crucified." In very early times (Ignatius, *Ad Eph.*, i. 1, *Ad Rom.*, vi. 3; Tertullian, *De carne Christi*, v.) naïve expressions like the " blood of God," the " suffering of God " were used. Then came Modalism (q.v.) and Patripassianism (see CHRISTOLOGY, II., §§ 1–2; MONARCHIANISM), and finally theopaschitic terms became suspicious to pious ears since they could be used in a Sabellian sense. They had some attractiveness, however, for those who spoke of Mary as *theotokos;* if God could be born, why could he not die? What from the standpoint of the Trinity was unendurable was not so from a christological point of view. As an ecclesiastical matter occasion for controversy came from Peter the Fuller's (see MONOPHYSITES, §§ 4 sqq.) addition to the Trisagion (q.v.), making it read " Holy God, Holy the Mighty One, Holy the Immortal One who was crucified for us." The Patriarch Calandion attempted to relieve the baldness of the expression by preceding it with the words " O Christ the King." Of the preceding events in Antioch no reports have come down, since the letters of Felix from Rome, of Acazius from Constantinople, and of other bishops, to Peter are falsified, though they have value as showing how in certain circles the new expression was decided; the situation both with reference to the Trinity and to incarnation was missed. The history of the Monophysitic controversy shows that the unionists decided otherwise, and they are justified from the point of view of the Henoticon (q.v.). But Harnack is right in asserting (*Dogma*, iv. 231) " That attempt (to extend the Trisagion in a theopaschitic sense) was rejected because it involved an innovation in worship and because it could be interpreted in a Sabellian sense."

After the death of Anastasius the theopaschitic controversy broke out again. At the beginning of the year 519 there appeared in the capital many monks (called in the sources Scythic monks, who in the great schism between Rome and Constantinople had held with Rome) with the motto " one of the Trinity has suffered in the flesh," which seems to have called forth opposition. But they found support for their formula in the sentences of the Henoticon. At Constantinople at that time all thoughts were directed to the consummation of union with Rome. After the stoppage of negotiations under Anastasius, Justinian did not rest until he had reached an agreement with Hormisdas; at the time of the monks' coming, the pope's legates were expected, and after their arrival on Mar. 25, 519, the schism ended. The monks alienated in various ways the sympathy of the papal legates, who, however, acted upon the direction of the pope not to become involved in anything except that which was their only concern, the matter of union. The legates also took the position that they could receive only what the four councils had settled and what Leo's letters contained; their leader, Dioscurus, expressed his opinion against the formula of the monks. But these despatched to Rome partizans to plead their case before the pope—Johannes Maxentius, Leontius, Achilles, Mauritius, and perhaps others. Their leader, in a writing directed to the legates, had traversed the position of Dioscurus cutting off additions to statements of belief, and supporting the monks' position by citing Cyril, Augustine, Flavian, Proclus, and others. He saw neither a trinitarian nor a christological problem; but sought to illustrate a long-fixed article of faith. Letters from the legates and Justinian to the pope, however, put the monks in an unfavorable light, and Justinian demanded that they be sent home. The pope found himself in a dilemma; he did not care to disavow his legates in favor of the monks nor to come to a disagreement with Justinian; on the other hand, he did not care to dismiss the monks. He therefore temporized; a letter from Justinian in July he answered on Sept. 2 to the effect that he was awaiting the return of the legates, and to the latter he said that he was referring the matter to John of Constantinople, while the legates repeated their accusations (of the monks). Meanwhile Justinian was coming to think that the monks were being treated badly, but did not wish to mix in a dogmatic affair and anew wrote the pope to decide, for the matter was one of words or terms only, and the monks need not fear to return home. In December the pope wrote his legates, and letters from Justinian (Jan. 19, 520) and from the pope (end of March) show that the whole question was trinitarian. The monks appealed to the senate and also sought support outside Rome, where they gained a point in confirmation of the orthodoxy of their position. In a letter to the African Bishop Possessor, then in Constantinople, the pope expressed his dejection over the querulous spirit manifested, which drew a bitter reply from Maxentius and is the last trace of the Scythic monks. On July 9, 520, Justinian had appealed again for a decision from the pope, calling the attention of the pope to the fact that it was ambiguous to speak of " one of the Trinity " without prefixing the name of Christ. Not till Mar. 25, 521, did Hormisdas reply, and then avoided committing himself on the point in controversy; yet he asserted that according to the conclusions reached in the synods against Nestorius and Eutyches and according to the pronouncements of Pope Leo, new dogmatic distinctions were not feasible. While this was the pope's last word, Justinian did not give the case up; the monks' formula seemed to him worthy, he used it as a means to win over the Severians and received the sentence into the confession of faith incorporated into the codex which in 533 he sent to Pope John II., which that pope (534) and his successor Agapetus I. (536) confirmed, while the Acoimetes monks were excommunicated by John, and the fifth ecumenical council at Constantinople pronounced excommunication against those who did not confess that " the Lord Jesus Christ, crucified in the flesh, was true God and lord of glory and one of the holy Trinity." The right to the admission of the now widely accepted sentence in the trisagion was not expressed. The extension of the trisagion remained a peculiar possession of the Monophysites, and in 692 the Trullan council anathematized it (canon 81).   (G. KRÜGER.)

BIBLIOGRAPHY: The literature of DOCTRINE, HISTORY OF, and MONOPHYSITES discusses the matter—also that under the articles to which cross reference is made in the text. Consult further: H. de Norris, *Historia Pelagiana*, appendices, Louvain, 1702; C. W. F. Walch, *Historie der Ketzereien*, vii. 232–261, Leipsic, 1776; F. Loofs, in *TU*, iii. 3–4 (1885); A. Knecht, *Die Religionspolitik Kaiser Justinians I.*, pp. 71–91, Würzburg, 1896; Harnack, *Dogma*, vol. iv. passim; and the literature on the church history of the period.

THEOPHANES, the-ef′a-nîz, **OF BYZANTIUM.—**
1. Theophanes the Confessor: Byzantine chronographer; b. c. 758; d. in Samothrace c. 817. On the eve of his marriage he bound himself and his bride to continence, then became a monk, and soon after founded the monastery " of the great field " near Sigriane on the Sea of Marmora. He advocated image worship at the Second Council of Nicæa in 787, and as a partizan of image worship was imprisoned in Constantinople under Leo the Armenian in 814–815 and then was banished to Samothrace. He wrote his chronography between 810–811 and 814–815 at the request of Georgius Syncellus (d. 810), continuing the latter's chronicle. It comprises the years 284–813 and incorporates material from Socrates, Sozomen, and Theodoret as found in an epitome by Theodorus Lector; also a Constantinopolitan chronicle. Theophanes' work has the faults of an ascetic turned historian and writing in haste, yet it is better than most of the Byzantine chronicles. A Latin translation by Anastasius Bibliothecarius made between 873 and 878 was much used in the West during the Middle Ages.

2. Theophanes Prokopovich: Bishop of Pskov and archbishop of Novgorod; d. 1736. He was Peter the Great's right hand in his ecclesiastical reforms and wrote theological text-books which were long in use in Russia. He was opposed to Rome and had sympathies with Lutheranism.   (N. BONWETSCH.)

BIBLIOGRAPHY: On 1: The " Chronography " was edited by J. Goar and issued by Combefis, Paris, 1655; is in *CSHB*, 2 vols., 1839–41; in *MPG*, cviii.; and ed. C. de Boor, 2 vols., Leipsic, 1883–85. Consult C. de Boor, in *Hermes*, xvii (1882), 489–490, xxv (1890), 301 sqq.; in *ZKG*, vi (1884), 489–490, 573 sqq.; J. N. Sarrazin, *De Theodoro Lectore Theophanis fonte præcipue*, Jena, 1881; H. Gelzer, *Sextus Julius Africanus und die byzantinische Chronographie*, ii. 1, pp. 176 sqq., Leipsic, 1885; E. W. Brooks, in *Byzantinische Zeitschrift*, viii (1899), 82–97; Krumbacher, *Geschichte*, pp. 342–347 (contains list of literature).

THEOPHANY: A manifestation or appearance of deity. The pagan Greeks understood by theophany (*theophania*), in the narrower sense, the appearance of a god (as at the festivals at Delphi); in the broader sense, every sensuous sign whereby deity revealed its approach, particularly its beneficent proximity. In the ancient Church the term *theophaneia*, the same as *epiphaneia*, was almost exclusively restricted to the manifestation of God and the divine glory in Christ. The application of *theophania* or *epiphania* to designate Jan. 6, is proof that by the above was implied principally the manifestation of God in the incarnation of the Logos. Indeed, *hē theophania* was occasionally applied to the baptism of Christ; yet decisive was the distinction between the epiphanies as the manifestation and self-witness of God at the baptism of Christ (heightened to the impartation of deity by some of the Gnostics), and the theophanies, namely, the festival of the birth of Christ. The latter name was maintained, even after the removal of the festival of the birth to Dec. 25, while for Jan. 6, as the festival of the baptism, and, further, the manifestation of the glory of Christ to the heathen, the name of epiphany was retained. F. L. Steinmeyer in *Christologie* (vols. ii.–iii., Berlin, 1881–82) restores the order of the ancient Church by designating, as epiphanies in the life of the Lord, the baptism, the temptation, and the transfiguration; while as theophanies in the life of the Lord he names the cleansing of the temple, the walking on the sea, and the entrance into Jerusalem. A third instalment follows on the christophanies of the glorified Christ. From the New Testament the restriction of the concept of the theophany to the incarnation of the Logos is amply justified by such passages as John i. 14, xiv. 9; Col. i. 15, 19, ii. 9. Not less did the testimony of Paul, I Cor. x. 4, and the practise of the Greek Fathers from Justin Martyr, who identified the " angel of the Lord " with the Logos, furnish excuse for conceiving also the theophanies of the Old Testament as christophanies. The Logos thus became universal as medium of manifestation. The later Biblical theological as well as the secular scientific terminology has, however, returned to the conception of theophany in the wider sense, every extraordinary manifestation of God reported by the Biblical authors, apprehensible by the human senses; but especially, in the narrower sense, those manifestations of God in which, equipped with the attributes of his divine glory, he appears upon earth, to command, aid, or punish. In the widest possible sense, according to the above, within the scope of theophanies would come generally all the manifestations of God which result in a direct impartation of his will and Word. The illustrations of theophanies would then coincide with the modes of revelation. Such an extension of the conception would be inapplicable, since in the innumerable manifestations of God by Word and spiritual operation the entrance of his person into the sphere of human realization is out of question. Theophany in reality presupposes that somehow the person of God enters into relation with man in terms of space. Assuming this, classes of theophanies appear in the Biblical accounts; those reported as historical facts, those depending on prophetic vision or announcement, and those which serve simply as literary integument or introduction to religious truths.

Of the historically reported are, first, those where the fact is simply stated without elaboration (Gen. xii. 7, xxvi. 2). To this category belong also the accounts of dreams (xv. 1, xx. 3, 6), where there is an underlying suggestion of God's form (further Ex. iv. 24; I Sam. iii. 21; I Kings iii. 5). Next follow the manifestations more or less in human form (Gen. xviii. 1 sqq.; cf. ANGEL). The Biblical narrators were here conscious of the distinction between the real being of God unapproachable to man, and his temporary manifestation; thus, in the passage Ex. xxxiii. 20, whatever of the person of God enters the visible represents only a partial revelation of his being as adaptable to human weakness and limitation. In Ex. xiv. 19, the angel, though distinct from God, is yet representative of him, inasmuch as he bears "the name" with its peculiar efficacy (see NAMES). In a similar sense in Ex. xxxiii. 14, the face of God is to guide the people. Here a distinction is implied between the complete personality and the outward appearance, just as in the more definitely detailed historical theophanies, the majority of which occurred in the legislation of Sinai and the journey through the wilderness, the pillar of fire or of cloud, which is an outward accident of the inner fire, is employed to hide the full majesty of God (Ex. xix. 9, 16, 21, cf. xxiv. 12 sqq., and xxxiv. 29 sqq.). Upon the erection of the tabernacle, this became the scene of the theophanies. Only here the accounts vary. According to one the cloud descends immediately after its completion to prevent the entrance of Moses, because the glory of God filled the tabernacle (xl. 34 sqq.). According to other and older passages the cloud descends when Moses enters and it remains stationary at the door (xxxiii. 9; cf. Lev. ix. 23; Num. xi. 25, xiv. 10). Although the theophany is referred to in Ex. xvi. 10, xxiv. 17, and again on extraordinary occasions (Lev. ix. 6, 23; Num. xiv. 10, xvi. 19), as the appearance of the glory of Yahweh, yet this is not to be understood as an advance beyond the concealment of the divine majesty in the cloud. Originally the "glory of Yahweh" referred to the halo visible to sight and emanating from Yahweh himself when he appeared in the storm or cloud at Sinai; but this, like "angel of God," was afterward reduced to apply to the revelation of his being, to the majesty of God in its operations which was to fill all the earth (Num. xiv. 21–22; Ps. lxxii. 19). That this was not to be absolutely identified with the fulness of the divine majesty is apparent from I Kings viii. 11; the glory of Yahweh in the form of a cloud filled the house when the ark was brought in, yet the heaven and heaven of heavens (verse 27) can not contain God, much less the house. No more can a theophany of another sort, i.e., of the absolute disclosure of the divine being, be inferred from the passages which represent Moses as conversing with God face to face (Deut. xxxiv. 10; "as a man speaketh unto his friend," Ex. xxxiii. 11; "mouth to mouth," Num. xii. 8).

That only an intermediate intercourse is meant in these instances is shown in Ex. xxxiii. 18 sqq.,where direct vision of the glory is denied and only an after glimpse is permitted when Yahweh has passed by. The more remarkable is therefore the one instance

(Ex. xxiv. 9–10) in which no mention of concealment or mediate manifestation of the divine majesty occurs. The writer, aware (verse 11) of the injunction that no man shall see God and live, seems to have been under the impression that at this most pregnant moment of the history of the theocracy, immediately after the sprinkling with the blood of the covenant (verses 6 sqq.), an exception, though indeed relative, was granted.

Beside those in connection with the account of the journey through the desert, only two other theophanies receive special mention; the covenant sacrifice of Abraham (Gen. xv. 17 sqq.), and the episode on Horeb, where the presence of God is announced to Elijah (I Kings xix. 11 sqq.). In both cases the representation is restricted to the outer form of the appearance.

In the prophetic theophanies a distinction must likewise be drawn between general announcements of the appearance of God for judgment (Isa. ii. 21; Zech. ii. 8) or redemption (Isa. xl. 10), and such proclamations as involve a closer proximation to an actual appearance; such as for judgment on the heathen (Isa. xix. 1, xxx. 27 sqq., lxiii. 1; Nah. i. 3 sqq.), of desired vengeance (Isa. lxiv. 1 sqq.), even on Israel (Mic. i. 9). In almost all the instances the accompaniment is some element of a storm, as lightning or hail, or the earthquake; and the glory of God is always enveloped in the cloud. Instruments of war and weapons of God are suggested (Nah. ii. 4–5; Isa. lxvi. 15), and in further detail (Hab. iii. 8–9, 11, 15), with the representation of Yahweh as a man of war (Ex. xv. 3; Isa. xlii. 13; Ps. xlvi. 8–9; cf. II Kings vi. 17; Ps. lxviii. 17). Among prophetic theophanies relating to visions some are sparing of detail (I Kings xxii. 19 sqq.; Amos vii. 7, ix. 1), while others afford more elaborate delineation (Isa. vi. 1 sqq.; Ezek. i. 4 sqq.; cf. iii. 12 sqq., viii. 4 sqq., x. 1 sqq., 18, xliii. 2 sqq.). In Dan. vii. 9 sqq., the Ancient of days is pictured in human form.

Theophanies in literary description (always in the introduction of the descriptions of God's works of redemption and judgment) almost invariably appear in some form of the storm symbol; to sustain his own against foes (Judges v. 4; Ps. xviii. 7–8, lxviii. 7–9, lxxvii. 16 sqq.), and for vengeance desired (cxliv. 5 sqq.); likewise to judge his people (Ps. l. 3), or reason with his accuser (Job xxxviii. 1). As point of departure for the theophanies in the instances quoted the heavens are sometimes expressly named as the permanent location of the throne of God (Ps. xviii. 9, cxliv. 5), and sometimes Sinai as the mountain of God and the scene of his earlier revelations to Israel (Deut. xxxiii. 2; cf. Judges v. 4–5 and Hab. iii. 3). For the post-Biblical construction of theophanies, namely, of the efforts in the times of the Septuagint and of Philo to replace the immediate operation of God by secondary causes, and thus get rid of anthropomorphisms, see *Jüdische Theologie* by F. Weber (issued by F. Delitzsch and G. Schnedermann, Leipsic, 1897).   (E. KAUTZSCH.)

BIBLIOGRAPHY: Besides the commentaries on the passages cited in the text, consult: C. J. Trip, *Die Theophanien in den Geschichtsbüchern des A. T.*, Leyden, 1858; Kosters, in *ThT*, 1875, pp. 369–415; C. A. Briggs, *Study of Holy Scripture*, pp. 337, 542 sqq., New York, 1889; H. Gressmann, *Der Ursprung der israelitisch-jüdischen Eschatologie*, pp. 8 sqq., Göttingen, 1905; P. Volz, *Der Geist Gottes und der verwandten Erscheinungen im A. T. und im anschliessenden Judentum*, Tübingen, 1910; *EB*, iv. 5033–36; *JE*, xii. 137–138; also the works on the Biblical theology of the O. T.

THEOPHILANTHROPISTS: A French religious organization of the Revolutionary period. In Sept., 1796, during the reign of the Directory, a small pamphlet appeared in Paris, under the title *Manuel des Theophilanthropes*, by Chemin. The divine worship described in that book had originated as a kind of family worship. During the period when all religious service was positively prohibited, five house fathers used to gather together their families for common prayer, singing of hymns in honor of God, and listening to moral and patriotic speeches. The basis of the whole organization was pure deism, the last trace left of true religion among the aberrations of atheism. The first public meeting took place on Jan. 5, 1797, in a house in Rue St. Denis. God, virtue, and the immortality of the soul formed the three articles of the Theophilanthropist creed; and any one who agreed on those three points could become a member of the association, even though he belonged to some special sect with respect to the further details of his creed.

The movement met at first with great success; Thomas Paine was a member, while Reveillère Lepeaux of the Directory was its leader; and the Directory granted it the use of ten churches in Paris. The service it instituted was very simple; the walls of the churches were ornamented with some few moral maxims; the altar was a plain table covered with flowers or fruit; the ministering officer was any one who felt disposed; and the ceremonies were reduced to a minimum of forms. The Christian baptism became a mere presentation and naming of the child; Christian wedding, a mere announcement of the civil marriage contracted, accompanied with congratulations and admonitions. New members were admitted after a short catechization upon the three articles above mentioned. As the Theophilanthropists considered their religion the only true universal religion, because the only true natural religion, they were averse to all kinds of propaganda, but they took much care of the education of their children, and their instruction in good morals.

During the first and second years of their existence the Theophilanthropists formed associations also in the provinces. But by degrees, as the Christian feeling became reawakened in the French people, the Theophilanthropist movement died away, and in 1802 the First Consul Bonaparte deprived them of their churches, which he restored to the Roman Catholics.

BIBLIOGRAPHY: H. Grégoire, *Hist. des sects religieuses*, 2 vols., Paris, 1810; N. M. D., *La Mort des Théophilantropes*, ib. 1799; *Recueil de cantiques, odes, et hymnes . . . des Théophilantropes*, ib. 1797; *Hymns on Natural Moral, and Theological Subjects, for . . . the Theophilanthropist Society*, Glasgow, 1816; R. Carlile, *The Deist; or, Moral Philosopher*, vol. i., London, 1819.

THEOPHILUS OF ALEXANDRIA: Patriarch of Alexandria from 385 to 412; d. at Alexandria Oct. 15, 412. Of the events of his life before his elevation to the archiepiscopate nothing certain is known, but soon after this event he was consulted

by the Emperor Theodosius with regard to the adjustment of the differences between the Alexandrine and Roman reckonings of Easter, 387, a matter which Theophilus was able to arrange to the emperor's satisfaction, especially as he prepared a paschal cycle for 418 years, besides reckoning the days on which Easter would fall for the century 380–480. About 389 Theophilus either obtained permission from Theodosius to destroy the pagan temples at Alexandria, or, according to other accounts, was granted the privilege of building a church on the site of a temple of Dionysus. At all events the patriarch incurred the bitter hostility of the pagans by public insults to their sacred emblems, and, after working vengeance on the Christians, they made a stand in the famous Serapeum of the city. When the pagans surrendered in terror at the shouts acclaiming the receipt of an imperial edict for the destruction of all pagan shrines, Theophilus and his followers were enabled to enter the Serapeum, where he caused the image of Serapis to be cut down, this being followed by wide-spread demolition of temples of the ancient faith, only one image (that of an ape, preserved for obvious uncomplimentary reasons) being spared.

In 391 or 392 Theophilus was appointed by the Council of Capua to arbitrate in the controversy between Flavian of Antioch (q.v.) and Evagrius, which he ultimately decided, following the lead of Chrysostom and some time after the death of Evagrius, in Flavian's favor in 398 (see MELETIUS OF ANTIOCH). In 394 he was at Constantinople, attending a council in which he urged that depositions from the episcopate should be pronounced not merely by three bishops (the number required by the canons of the Council of Nicæa for a consecration), but, if possible, by all bishops of a province.

With the year 395 the character of Theophilus, under the sinister influence of the Origenistic Controversies (q.v.), underwent a lamentable change. He had himself been in sympathy with Origen's revolt against anthropomorphism, and in his paschal letter of 399 had insisted sharply that the divine nature must not be construed in anthropomorphic fashion. This aroused the violent antagonism of the Scetic monks, and before their open threats the patriarch descended to ambiguous phrases more politic than honorable. With this change of attitude there would even seem to be connected personal antipathy for certain of his old friends, notably Isidore, whom he had proposed for the see of Constantinople in 398, and some of the " Long Brothers "—all these being in sympathy with Origenism. Late in 399 or early in 400 he convened a synod at Alexandria at which Origenism was condemned, following up his attack in his paschal letter of 401. In this same year, fortified by an imperial edict forbidding any monk to read Origen, Theophilus proceeded to Nitria and secured the expulsion of all those monks who would not subscribe to entire anthropomorphism. The accounts of this procedure are, unfortunately, so at variance that it is difficult to say whether it was carried out with violence, as Theophilus' bitter enemy, Palladius (q.v.), asserts, or, as Theophilus himself declared in a synodical letter (transl. by Jerome, *Epist.* xcii., Eng. transl. in *NPNF*, 2 ser., vi. 185–186), after a further weighing of the obnoxious tenets of Origen. Late in the year some of the exiled monks made their way to Chrysostom at Constantinople, entreating him to use his good offices in their behalf that they might be permitted to return to Egypt. Chrysostom accordingly wrote to Theophilus, but the result of the correspondence, still further complicated by the injudicious activity of the monks, was that the patriarch of Alexandria became bitterly hostile to his fellow patriarch of Constantinople. Theophilus accordingly urged Epiphanius to secure a synodal condemnation of Origenism, and the reading of any of the writings of Origen was accordingly forbidden in Cyprus. Meanwhile, however, the exiled monks at Constantinople had not been idle, but had induced the emperor, Arcadius, to summon Theophilus for trial before the patriarch of Constantinople, while the charges lodged against the monks were pronounced baseless. After a deliberate delay in obeying the summons, Theophilus finally landed at Constantinople late in June, 403, and, after flouting Chrysostom openly, practically secured his deposition and banishment at the synod *ad Quercum*, then accepted a perfunctory apology from the " Long Brothers," the most important of whom were dead. But the people would have none of Theophilus, and soon Chrysostom was recalled, while Theophilus sailed in haste for Egypt. Within two months the patriarch of Constantinople was again in imperial disfavor, and his old enemy was urged to make a fresh attack upon him. He declined, however, to come in person, but his creatures worked his will, and Chrysostom was again sent into banishment, from which he was never to return (for further details see Chrysostom, §§ 4–5).

In his paschal letter of 404 Theophilus, while not mentioning Chrysostom's name, returned to his attack upon Origenism. He now informed Pope Innocent that he had deposed Chrysostom, but the pontiff ignored the sentence and directed that a new synod be convened to try the entire case with fairness. All was in vain — the commands of the pope and the appeal of Honorius, emperor of the West, to his brother Arcadius, who stubbornly upheld Theophilus.

Of the remainder of Theophilus' life little is known, and of his writings comparatively scanty portions have survived, the most convenient edition being in *MPG*, lxv. 33–68. Here belong the paschal letters of 401, 402, and 404, preserved only in Latin translation by Jerome and sharply attacking Origenism, as well as ten "'canons" dealing with ordination and the sexual relations of the clergy; but his most important work, the treatise " Against Origen," like his "Against the Anthropomorphites " (both recorded by Gennadius, *De vir. ill.*, xxxiv., Eng. transl. in *NPNF*, 2 ser., iii. 392), has disappeared.

Bibliography: *DCB*, iv. 999–1008 (detailed, indispensable); A Gallandi, *Bibliotheca veterum patrum*, vii. 601–602, 14 vols., Venice, 1765–81; Fabricius-Harles, *Bibliotheca Græca*, vii. 108 sqq., Hamburg, 1801; B. Czapla, *Gennadius als Litterarhistoriker*, p. 73, Münster, 1898; Ceillier, *Auteurs sacrés*, vii. 438–447 (also consult Index); *MPG*, lxv. 33–68; *KL*, xi. 1579–81.

THEOPHILUS, the-of′i-lus, **OF ANTIOCH:** Bishop of Antioch in the second century. His birthplace was not far from the Euphrates and Tigris and he did not become a Christian till he had reached mature years, while his mother tongue and education were Greek. He was sixth bishop of Antioch, successor of Eros and predecessor of Maximinus or Maximus (Eusebius, *Hist. eccl.*, IV., xx., xxiv. 3). The only determined chronological datum is that he wrote his third book to Autolycus not before 181 (cf. A. Harnack, *Die Zeit des Ignatius und die Chronologie der antiochenischen Bischöfe*, pp. 42–43, Leipsic, 1878; idem, *Litteratur*, ii. 208 sqq.).

Theophilus developed a many-sided literary activity and for a time his works (sometimes ascribed to Theophilus of Alexandria) were much read and used. After the fourth century they were forgotten. They included (Eusebius, *Hist. eccl.*, IV., xxiv.) three books to Autolycus, polemical writings against Hermogenes and Marcion, and certain books of instruction and edification; further (Jerome, *De vir. ill.*, xxv.), commentaries on the Gospels (see Œcumenius) and Proverbs, and a work in several books of which Theophilus himself cites the first as *Peri historiōn*. Only the three books to Autolycus are preserved and these in but a single manuscript. The first book is apologetic, defending the Christian faith against the derision of Autolycus, an old heathen friend of Theophilus. The second is polemic, declaring the popular religion of the heathen as well as the specuations of philosophers and poets absurd or, in so far as true at all, taken from the prophets. The third book compares the Christian Scriptures with heathen literature to the disparagement of the latter. The genuineness of this work is commonly acknowledged. On the other hand, the commentary on the Gospels is regarded by later scholars with the exception of Zahn (*Forschungen*, vol. ii., Erlangen, 1883) as not the work of the Antiochian bishop of the second century. Harnack assigns the work to the early Middle Ages (c. 500) and thinks it consists of excerpts from the older Latin Fathers (cf. Bornemann in *ZKG*, x., 1889, pp. 169 sqq., and Hauck in *ZKW*, v. 561 sqq.). The commentary does not belong to Theophilus of Antioch and is a compilation from older writings made before 700.   (A. Hauck.)

Bibliography: The text was edited by J. Frisius-Gesner, Zurich, 1546; by J. Fell, Oxford, 1684; and by C. Otto, in *Corpus Apologetarum*, vol. viii., Jena, 1861; and there is an Eng. transl. with introductory note in *ANF*, ii. 85 sqq. Consult: P. Pasquet, *Essai sur les trois livres à Autolycus de Théophile d'Antioche*, Strasburg, 1857; L. Paul, in *JPT*, 1875, pp. 546–559; A. Harnack, *Die Zeit des Ignatius von Antiochen*, pp. 42–44, Leipsic, 1878; idem, *TU*, i. 1–2 (1882), 282–298, and 4, pp. 97–175; idem, in *ZKG*, xi (1889), 1–21; idem, *Litteratur*, i. 496–502, 845, ii. 2, pp. 208–213, 319–320, 534–535; C. Erbes, in *JPT*, v (1879), 464–485, 618–653, xiv (1888), 611–632; W. Sanday, in *Studia Biblica*, i (1885), 89–101; W. Bornemann, in *ZKG*, x (1888), 169–292; G. Karabangeles, *Die Gotteslehre des Theophilus von Antiochen*, Leipsic, 1891; A. B. Cook, in *The Classical Review*, 1894, pp. 246–248; O. Gross, *Die Weltentstehungslehre des Theophilus von Antiochen*, Jena, 1895; idem, *Die Gotteslehre des Theophilus von Antiochen*, Chemnitz, 1896; A. Pommrich, *Die Gottes- und Logoslehre des Theophilus von Antiochia*, Leipsic, 1904; Bardenhewer, *Patrologie*, pp. 58–60, Eng.

transl., St. Louis, 1908; idem, *Geschichte,* i. 278–290; T. Zahn, *Kanon,* vols. ii.–iii.; Krüger, *History,* pp. 132–135; *DNB,* iv. 993–999 (detailed); Ceillier, *Auteurs sacrés,* i. 475–480. A very full list of literature is given by Richardson in *ANF,* Bibliography, pp. 35–36.

THEOPHYLACT, the-of'i-lakt: Archbishop of Achrida (the modern Ochrida in Albania, 100 m. n. of Janin). He was a native of Eubœa and for his great learning was chosen teacher of the young Prince Constantine, son of Emperor Michael Ducas (1071–78), to whom he dedicated a treatise on the "Education of a Prince" (*Opera,* iii. 529–548). About 1078 he became archbishop of Achrida and he survived the accession of Alexius Comnenus (1081), but by how many years is not known. Theophylact was a many-sided representative of the Byzantine churchman. He was a disciple of Michael Psellus (q.v.) and learned from his master no small degree of classical culture. As archbishop he ruled in large measure independently of Constantinople and he grappled faithfully with the difficulties of an arduous position; in his letters he often complains of the rude ways and the wickedness of the rough Bulgars who composed his flock. He was far from narrow-minded and judged leniently in the controversies between East and West. As exegete he was skilful and sensible; though dependent in his views on the earlier Fathers like all medieval Greek commentators, he conceived rightly the aim and method of exegesis, and the precision of his interpretation makes his commentaries still worthy of consideration. They treat of the entire New Testament with the exception of the Apocalypse, and of portions of the Old Testament. An edition of Theophylact's "Works," in Greek and Latin, was published in four volumes at Venice, 1754–63 (reprinted in *MPG,* cxxiii.–cxxvi.). It includes, besides the commentaries (vols. i., ii., and part of iii.), certain homilies, of which those on the adoration of the cross and the presentation of Mary in the Temple (iii. 460 sqq.) are the best. An account of the fifteen martyrs of Tiberiopolis (iii. 477 sqq.) uses old sources. There are also a noteworthy panegyric on the Emperor Alexius (iii. 549 sqq.) and 130 letters (iii. 559 sqq.) to important and well-known personages of his time.   (PHILIPP MEYER.)

BIBLIOGRAPHY: Fabricius-Harles, *Bibliotheca Græca,* vii. 586–598, Hamburg, 1801; Krumbacher, *Geschichte,* pp. 133–135, 463–465; K. Prsechter, in *Byzantinische Zeitschrift,* i. 399–414, and J. Dräseke, in the same, x. 515–529; and the dissertation by B. M. de Rubeis, most accessible in *MPG,* cxxiii. 9–137.

THEOSOPHY.

I. Doctrines: The main teachings of Theosophy (Gk. *theosophia,* "divine wisdom"), which are at the same time religious, philosophic, and scientific, may be summed up as follows: it postulates one eternal, immutable, all-pervading principle, the root of all manifestation. From that one existence comes forth periodically the whole universe, manifesting the two aspects of spirit and matter, life and

form, positive and negative, "the two poles of nature between which the universe is woven." Those two aspects are inseparably united, therefore all matter is ensouled by life while all life seeks expression through forms. All life being fundamentally one with the life of the Supreme Existence, it contains in germ all the characteristics of its source, and evolution is only the unfolding of those divine potentialities brought about by the conditions afforded in the various kingdoms of nature. The visible universe is only a small part of this field of evolution. As ether interpenetrates the densest solid, so matter, still subtler, interpenetrates ether, and these different grades of matter constitute seven distinct regions, spoken of as the seven great planes of the universe. The physical is the densest; the one next to it is called astral; still subtler than the astral plane is the mental. The four higher spiritual planes are as yet mere names to all except initiates and adepts. The materials being thus prepared, the divine life begins the evolution of consciousness, building for itself forms on the various planes, passing slowly through the elemental, mineral, vegetable, and animal kingdoms, and finally reaching self-consciousness and individualization, when it passes into the human stage.

2. Man. Man, being a part of the whole, is also evolving toward the perfect manifestation of the divine characteristics latent in him. That perfection, however, implies not only the attainment of sainthood, but also the possession of divine power and full knowledge of the universe, visible and invisible. As he needs a physical body to work with on the physical plane, so does he need bodies composed of the matter of those higher planes, in order to cognize them, and the organizing of such bodies is the task upon which men are engaged, consciously, in the more advanced members of the race, but unconsciously in the vast majority. The physical body, then, is not the only one man uses, even during this physical life. In connection with it and interpenetrating it, even as the planes of the universe interpenetrate each other, he has an astral body, by means of which he feels and desires, a mental body, by means of which he thinks. The higher four spiritual bodies are still unorganized at the present stage of evolution, save in rare instances. But the three just mentioned are already fairly developed and constitute the normal working instruments of man. This does not mean that the astral and mental bodies are as yet organized so as to take direct cognizance of the planes to which they belong by constitution; in the majority, they work only in connection with the physical body. But some individuals have already developed the senses belonging to those higher bodies. The phenomena of clairvoyance, telepathy, prophetic dreams, etc., are merely manifestations of the activity of those finer senses. Unreliable at first, like the infant's vision, they can be developed and trained, until the subtler worlds stand as an open book before the man. This constitutes the evolution of the form, which proceeds *pari passu* with the evolution of the consciousness, the activities of which in the subtler bodies may be termed the soul.

As the soul grows in power, love, and wisdom, it needs a better form in which to manifest itself; as the form grows in perfection, it becomes a better instrument for the soul. Here again evolve side by side the two poles of the universe, life and form, spirit and matter.

This unfoldment of man's powers is slow and gradual; hence the necessity of repeated incarnations, each life on earth being like a day in school. At death, man drops his physical body,

3. Reincarnation. and, clothed in his subtle bodies, lives a life of purification, rest, and bliss, rich and full in proportion to his stage in evolution and the deeds of the life just ended. This is the time when he assimilates the experiences of that life, changing them into faculties. As this work is being done, he drops one after the other his worn-out astral and mental bodies, and, finally, having enjoyed all the bliss to which his achievements entitle him, he clothes himself in new bodies and returns to earth to take up the work where he had left it, each life being thus a progress on the preceding one. The fact that man does not remember his past incarnations is no proof against their reality, for the memory of those lives is stored up in the soul and not in the brain, which belongs to the present incarnation only and therefore can not have kept the record of experiences it never went through. But man is so absorbed by earthly interests and ambitions that he identifies himself with the body and has no time to listen to the " still small voice " within. As soon as he turns his attention inward and knows himself as the soul, then his long past will lie unrolled before his vision, as it has done in the case of the sages of all times. But even at the present stage, that past shows itself in the accumulated faculties and powers of the man and the voice of conscience, which is but the effort of the soul to guide its lower nature along lines found by experience to be the best.

Evolution proceeds under a law as unerring as any well-established scientific law, namely, that of *karma* or the law of cause and effect. Each action, each desire, each thought, produces its result with unfailing certainty. " As a man

4. Karma. soweth, so shall he also reap." This makes perfection possible, for knowledge is power, and when man knows the law and works with it, he can produce any result he chooses, he becomes master of his destiny. Thought is the most potent factor in the creation of causes. Each thought affects the mental body for good or evil, and as mental faculties are the powers of the soul working in the mental body, the mentality shown in any one life is the result of repeated thinking in past lives. Hence the splendid mental apparatus of the man of genius is not a gratuitous gift, but is due to hard work in the past. Thought is also the parent of action, and its subtle vibrations, traveling through space, affect others, awakening similar thoughts in the minds attuned to the same key. Many a thought has thus urged other men to actions, good or evil, in which the thinker has his share of responsibility. As thoughts evolve the mental body, so desires evolve the astral body, and also influence others by their far-reaching vibra-

tions. By controlling his desires, purifying them, turning them toward spiritual things, man refines his astral body and rises above his animal instincts. Actions, speaking broadly, determine future physical surroundings; those surroundings are favorable or unfavorable, according as the man has made others happy or unhappy. Reincarnation and karma explain the apparent injustice in the world, the mental and moral differences among men, and the inequality of mental, moral, and physical conditions amid which men are placed.

But a time will come when man, having reached the full perfection attainable in the human stage, shall need no longer these earth-experiences, and shall pass on to spheres of usefulness

5. Liberation. whose glory is beyond our conception. One of the missions of theosophy is to proclaim anew the possibility of treading the " ancient narrow path " which leads to adeptship and liberation, when a man need not return to earth unless he choose to remain and help his less-advanced brothers. The more advanced members of humanity, a mere handful as yet, have already reached that level, and from their lodge come forth from time to time the great founders of religions, the spiritual teachers of the race. This common source explains the oneness of fundamental teachings in all religions; the form only varies, according to the needs of the times and peoples. Now, as in olden times, these Elder Brothers are willing to accept as pupils those who possess the necessary qualifications. Those qualifications are: a conviction of the impermanence of mere earthly aims, a perfect indifference to the fruit of one's own actions; perfect control of mind and conduct; tolerance; endurance; confidence in the master and himself; balance, and desire for liberation. But his motive for seeking liberation must be an intense desire to help humanity, for only when this complete forgetfulness of self is attained, can a man's powers be safely developed. So long as selfishness lurks in his heart, there is danger of his becoming a curse to the race, instead of the helper he should be.

II. Theosophical Society in America: The teachings are not new; they represent a body of traditions preserved from time immemorial. Reincarnation was taught in the earliest history of India and Egypt, in Greece even before Pythagoras; it is found in the teachings of Plato, Plotinus, the Cabala (q.v.), the early Christians, the Alexandrian Gnostics, Neoplatonists (see NEOPLATONISM), Paracelsus, and Giordano Bruno (q.v.). During the Middle Ages traces of it appeared in Freemasonry and among the Rosicrucians. In modern times, this wisdom-tradition was revived by Helena Petrovna Blavatsky (q.v.), who had been for years the pupil of great oriental adepts or sages. Aided by Henry Steel Olcott, she founded the Theosophical Society in New York City, Nov. 17, 1875. For the development see III., below.

The three objects of the society are: (1) to form a nucleus of the universal brotherhood of humanity, without distinction of race, creed, sex, caste, or color; (2) to encourage the study of comparative religion, philosophy, and science; (3) to investigate the unexplained laws of nature and the powers latent in man. Assent to the first of these objects is required for membership, the remaining two being optional. " The Society has no dogmas or creed, is entirely non-sectarian and includes in its membership adherents of all faiths and of none, exacting only from each member the tolerance for the beliefs of others that he would wish them to exhibit toward his own." In 1895, William Quan Judge, then vice-president of the society, led a secession movement which resulted in a separation therefrom of a large number of the American and some of the European members. The seceding body, however, soon divided into two bodies, one of which is known as the Universal Brotherhood and Theosophical Society (see III., below). The other body, known as the Theosophical Society in America, again subdivided; one division located at 244 Lenox Avenue, New York City, now publishes *The Word*, a monthly magazine, and the other division, headed by Charles Johnston, 159 Warren Street, Brooklyn, N. Y., publishes the *Theosophical Quarterly*. The parent society is international, with headquarters at Adyar, Madras, India. The last yearly report of its president, Mrs. Annie Besant, shows in Dec., 1907, a total of 655 branches all over the world, 77 of which are in America. A large literature has grown up within the society, including the regular publication of forty-seven magazines. The general secretary of the American section is Weller Van Hook, 103 State Street, Chicago, Ill.   MARIE POUTZ.

III. Universal Brotherhood and Theosophical Society: The original name of the society founded by Madame Blavatsky in New York, 1875, was The Theosophical Society. In this she held no official position except that of corresponding secretary, but nevertheless she possessed the highest authority, and was the inspiration and heart of the movement. Through her the teachings of theosophy were given to the world, and without her the theosophical movement could not have been. In 1878 she visited Great Britain and India, in both of which countries she founded branch societies. The parent body in New York became later the Aryan Theosophical Society and has always had its headquarters in America; and of this William Quan Judge was president until his death in 1896. In 1888 Madame Blavatsky, then in London, on the suggestion of Judge, founded the Esoteric School of Theosophy for students, of which she wrote that it was " the heart of the Theosophical Movement," and of this she appointed Judge her sole representative in America. This is only one of the evidences of Madame Blavatsky's regard for Judge, a regard which continued undiminished until her death, in 1891, when he became her successor. In 1893 there openly began what had been going on beneath the surface for some time, a bitter attack ostensibly against Judge, but in reality against Madame Blavatsky. This attack threatened to disrupt the whole society and to thwart the main purpose of its existence, the cause of universal brotherhood. Finally, the American members decided to take action and, at the annual convention held in Boston in 1895, reasserted the principles of theosophy as laid down by Madame Blavatsky, and elected Judge president for life, the majority of the active members

throughout the world concurring in this action, which relieved the society of those who had joined it for purposes other than the furtherance of universal brotherhood. One year later, 1896, Judge died, leaving as his successor Katherine Tingley, who had been associated in the work for some years. Mrs. Tingley put into actual working practise the ideals of theosophy for which Madame Blavatsky and Judge had laid the foundations. To safeguard the work, a further reorganization of the society was adopted at the annual convention at Chicago, 1898. The full title of the organization is now the Universal Brotherhood and Theosophical Society. " The principal purpose of this organization is to teach brotherhood, demonstrate that it is a fact in nature and make it a living power in the life of humanity. The subsidary purposes are: to study ancient and modern religion, science, philosophy, and art; to investigate the laws of nature and the divine powers in man."

In 1898 Mrs. Tingley established the International Brotherhood League, the department of the Universal Brotherhood for practical humanitarian work, and under its auspices rendered aid to soldiers at Montauk after the close of the Spanish-American war. Later she took a relief expedition into Cuba, the United States government affording her free transportation for physicians, nurses, and supplies. Thus began her work in Cuba, which resulted in the establishment of Raja Yoga schools at Santiago and Pinar del Rio and now on San Juan battlefield, which she has recently purchased. Other Raja Yoga schools besides that at Point Loma have been established by her in the New Forest, England, also on the Island of Visingsö, Sweden. In 1900 the headquarters were moved from New York to Point Loma, which is now the international center of the theosophical movement throughout the world. This organization is unsectarian and nonpolitical; none of its officers or workers receives any salary or financial recompense.   J. H. FUSSELL.

BIBLIOGRAPHY: The authoritative writings of modern theosophy are the following by Madame H. P. Blavatsky, all published in London unless otherwise noted, and editions, some of them noteworthy, of the principal works of Blavatsky and Judge have been issued at Point Loma, Cal., 1907–10: *Isis Unveiled*, 2 vols., New York, 1877; *Voice of the Silence*, 1899; *The Secret Doctrine*, 3 vols., new ed., 1897, index to vols. i.–ii., 1899; *The Key to Theosophy*, 1893; and *Studies in Occultism* (an edition at Point Loma, 1910); by Annie Besant, all published in London: *Building of the Kosmos*, 1894; *Path of Discipleship*, 1895; *The Ancient Wisdom*, 1897; *Four Great Religions*, 1897; *Reincarnation*, 3d ed., 1898; *Evolution of Life and Form*, 1899; *Man and His Bodies*, 2d ed., 1900; *Religious Problems in India*, 1902; *Thought Power, its Control and Culture*, 1903; *A Study in Consciousness*, 1904; *Theosophy and the New Psychology*, 1904; *Changing World*, and *Lectures to Theosophical Students*, 1909; and *Popular Lectures on Theosophy*, 1910; by Annie Besant and C. W. Leadbeater, *Thought Forms*, London, 1905; by C. W. Leadbeater, all published in London except the last; *Clairvoyance*, 1899; *Invisible Helpers*, 1901; *Dreams*, 2d ed., 1903; *The Astral Plane*, 4th ed., 1904; *The Christian Creed*, 2d ed., 1904; and *Man Visible and Invisible*, New York, 1903; G. R. S. Mead, *Fragments of Faith Forgotten*, London, 1900; A. P. Sinnett, *The Occult World*, London, 1882; idem, *Esoteric Buddhism*, ib. 1888; idem, *Growth of the Soul*, ib. 1896. Also Mabel Collins, *Light on the Path*. London, new ed., 1896; H. S. Olcott, *Old Diary Leaves*, 3 series, New York, 1895–1904; Katherine Tingley, *Mysteries of the Heart Doctrine*, 2d ed., Point Loma, 1903; idem and others, *Pith and Marrow of Some Sacred Writings*, ib. 1905; and W. Q. Judge, *Echoes from the Orient*, 3d ed., New York, 1893; idem, *Epitome of Theosophy*, Point Loma, 1908; J. H. Fussell, *Incidents in the Hist. of the Theosophical Movement*, Point Loma, 1910; *Theosophical Manuals*, ib., 1910 (18 numbers).

Other works, for and against, are: J. C. F. Zoellner, *Transcendental Physics*, London, 1882; W. J. Colville, *Universal Theosophy*, Chicago, 1888; J. H. Dewey, *The Way, the Truth, and the Life*, Buffalo, 1888; C. Behre, *Spiritisten, Mystiker und Theosophen*, Leipsic, 1890; J. L. Harder-Hickey, *La Théosophie*, Paris, 1890; W. R. Old, *What is Theosophy?* London, 1891; J. Murdoch, *Theosophy Exposed: or, Mrs. Besant and her Guru*, Madras, 1893; idem, *The Theosophic Craze: its History; how Mrs. Besant was befooled and deposed*, Madras, 1894; J. A. Anderson, *Reincarnation*, San Francisco, 1894; L. L. de Rosny, *Le Bouddhisme éclectique*, Paris, 1894; C. F. Wright, *Outline of the Principles of Modern Theosophy*, Boston, 1894; H. Goering, *Theosophische Schriften*, 30 parts, Brunswick, 1894–96; W. Kingsland, *The Esoteric Basis of Christianity*, London, 1895; A. Lillie, *Madame Blavatsky and her " Theosophy,"* London, 1895; J. W. Boissevain, *Inleiding tot de Theosophie*, Amsterdam, 1902; C. Bleibtreu, *Die Vertreter des Jahrhunderts*, vol. iii., *Theosophy*, Berlin, 1904; W. Bruhn, *Theosophie und Theologie*, Glückstadt, 1907; A. B. Kingsford and E. Maitland, *The Perfect Way or the Finding of Christ*, New York, 1908; G. Sulzer, *Moderne indische Theosophie und Christentum*, Leipsic, 1909; C. Bragdon, *Theosophy and the Theosophical Society*, Rochester, N. Y., 1909; J. H. Fussell, *Mrs. Annie Besant and the Moral Code*, Point Loma, 1909; G. F. Moore, *Notes from India, Theosophy and Co-Masonry*, ib. 1910; R. Steiner, *Theosophy; an Introduction to the supersensible Knowledge of the World and the Distinction of Man*, New York and Chicago, 1910.

THEOTOKES, the-ot′o-kîz **(THEOTOKIS), NICEPHORUS:** Greek scholar and distinguished preacher, archbishop of Catharinoslav [Slavensk and Kherson] and of Astrachan; b. on the island of Corfu Feb., 1731 (so Strahl; others 1736); d. in Moscow May 31, 1800. He began his studies at a school of his native island, and continued them in Bologna and Padua. After returning to his fatherland he became hierodiakonos in 1748 and hieromonachos in 1753. Until 1765 he was preacher and teacher in the school of Corfu, where he had studied. He was then preacher in Constantinople and resided in Germany for some years from 1770; school-director at Jassy, 1774–77, after which he joined his friend Eugenios Bulgaris (q.v.) in Russia, whom he succeeded as archbishop of Catharinoslav in 1779, and in 1786 was translated to Astrachan. In 1796 he was removed and thenceforth lived in retirement in the Danielovski monastery in Moscow.

Theotokes' most cherished wish was to elevate his people religiously and spiritually. He therefore cultivated learning and used the modern Greek speech in his writings, with no slight literary skill. He is to be classed with Adimantios Korias and Eugenios Bulgaris and among the most influential Greeks of the eighteenth century who prepared the way for Hellenic independence, though he differed from these in that he held more closely to the traditional orthodoxy. In the West he is known chiefly in connection with the modern interest in the Catenæ (q.v.). He edited, though not critically, the so-called *Catena Lipsiensis* (2 vols., 1772–73; cf. H. Karo and J. Liezmann, *Catenarum Græcarum catalogus, Nachrichten der Gesellschaft der Wissenschaften zu Göttingen, phil.-hist. Klasse*, 1902) from a manuscript of the eleventh century containing the entire Oktateuch which he found in the library of

Prince Ghikas and another manuscript of the year 1104 which he obtained from Constantinople. Another work more widely known in the West is Theotokes' edition of the Greek translation of the ascetic works of Isaac of Nineveh (q.v.; cf. Fabricius-Harles, xi. 120) made by the monks Patricius and Abraamius (Leipsic, 1770). He also translated the " Golden Book " of Rabbi Samuel (Leipsic, 1769). This work, said to have been written in Arabic and translated into Latin by a Spaniard, Alfonsus Bonosus, presents Samuel, a rabbi of Morocco, writing to Rabbi Isaac and expressing his fear that Jesus was the Messiah, basing the apprehension on the thousand years' duration of the oppression of the Jews, the Old Testament, and the Talmud. It was as preacher, however, that Theotokes was best known to his contemporaries, and his influence on the future development of Greek preaching was great. His sermons have been collected (5 vols., vol. i., Leipsic, 1766, vols. ii.–v., Moscow, 1796–1808). Theotokes' general repute was such that questions of dogmatics and practical problems in the cure of souls were often referred to him for answer. In this way a number of minor writings arose which are highly esteemed by the orthodox and exist in both Greek and Russian translation. A collection of letters of this sort was published at Athens in 1890 by Johannes Sakkelion under the title " Unpublished Works." He also left works on mathematics and geography. [*An Evangelical and Exegetical Commentary upon Select Portions of the New Testament Founded on the Writings of Nicephoras Theotoces*, by S. Nicolaides, was published in London in 1860.]   (PHILIPP MEYER.)

BIBLIOGRAPHY: P. Strahl, *Das gelehrte Russland*, Leipsic, 1828; A. C. Demetracopulos, *Græcia orthodoxa*, ib. 1872; A. D. Kyriakos, *Geschichte der orientalischen Kirchen*, ib. 1902. The literature in Greek is given in Hauck-Herzog, *RE*, xix. 673.

THEOTOKOS, thî-ot′ō-kɵs ("God-bearing"): A term applied in the early Church to Mary the mother of Christ in order to lay the strictest emphasis upon the incarnation in opposition to those who taught that God could not be born of a human parent and in defense of the doctrine that the birth of Christ involved his two natures. It was adopted at the Councils of Ephesus (431) and Chalcedon (451) against Nestorianism (see NESTORIUS; also NESTORIANS). The term is now a favorite designation in the Greek Church for the Virgin Mary.

THERAPEUTÆ, ther″a-piū′tî or pū′tê: Name of a reputed sect of ascetics. A treatise attributed to Philo has come down, entitled *Peri biou thēorētikon* (F. C. Conybeare, *Philo: about the Contemplative Life*, Oxford, 1895), in which the Therapeutæ are represented as ascetics, learned in Scripture, dwelling in colonies, and following the contemplative life. Though scattered in many parts of the world, the majority were said to be in Egypt with headquarters near Alexandria beyond Lake Mareotis. There they dwelt securely in separate huts collected in villages; and in each dwelling there was a sacred chamber (*semneion* or *monasterion*), where, wholly secluded from the world, the mysteries of the perfect life were realized. Into these they took neither food nor drink, but only the law, the prophecies, songs of praise, and the like. All day they contemplated the (Old Testament) Scriptures, deciphering the hidden sense from the words assumed as symbols. As models they had also the writings of " ancient men," or the memorials of their founders. Besides, they had songs and hymns in different meters. Their devotional chambers they left only after sunset for food and sleep, without crossing, as a rule, the threshold of the house. Fasting was carried on from three to six days in the week. On the seventh day as well as the forty-ninth and fiftieth, after anointing themselves with oil, they assembled in common celebration, the sexes being separated by a partition. On such days, they arrayed themselves in white garments and partook of a common meal, prescribed to consist of bread, salt, hyssop, and water. The leader delivered a discourse, which was followed by philosophizing on the part of the members, interspersed with singing. Then the holy table was brought in, containing the most sacred viands, leavened bread and salt. The allegorical significance referring to the table in the temple and the distinction of the holy ones (priests) from others is obscure. Then followed an all-night vigil, consisting of exhilarating choral song and dance, in imitation of that of Miriam upon the deliverance from the Red Sea (Ex. xv. 1–21).

The first to mention this writing was Eusebius (*Hist. eccl.*, II., xvi.–xvii.; Eng. transl., *NPNF*, 2d ser., i. 116–119), who, professing to quote from Philo, regarded the Therapeutæ as the oldest Alexandrine Christians, and they and their practises were to him the weightiest proof that the Christian asceticism of his day, the philosophizing monasticism, was original Christianity itself. This was a strong support to the conception of Christianity which prevailed in the Church at the time. Philo rose in estimation and Jerome placed him among the illustrious men of the Church, a dignity which remained unchallenged for a thousand years. Protestant criticism easily overturned this assumption, and declared the Therapeutæ to have been a society of philosophizing Jews. Until recently this verdict prevailed, and the appearance of the Therapeutæ in the time of Christ was industriously employed to illustrate the diversification of the Jews in Alexandria. They were presumed to be the Alexandrine parallel to the Palestinian Essenes. H. Graetz first pointed out that they must be Christian monks of the third century (*Geschichte der Juden*, iii. 463 sqq., 2d ed., Leipsic, 1882). The result of the reinvestigation of P. F. Lucius (*Die Therapeuten und ihre Stellung in der Geschichte der Askese*, Strasburg, 1879) was as follows: the work was produced not long before the two of Eusebius by a literary philosophic author of ascetic temperament as a panegyric of asceticism; and to secure the weight of antiquity and authority he attached Philo's name. That the existence of the sect was most improbable among the Jews of the Alexandrine period was shown on internal grounds. Besides, although represented to be scattered world-wide no writer before Eusebius mentioned them, nor did Philo in any other of his writings. Philo could neither have intended nor composed it as an appendix to the

Quod omnis probus liber. Not only the details but the philosophic-ascetic ideals of the author with their rude attacks upon Plato and Hellenism are inconsistent with Philo's sympathy for Hellenic culture. That it was a Christian work of about the year 300 was shown because (1) Eusebius, who knew Christian monasticism, rediscovered Christian monks in the Therapeutæ; (2) sects based on the Old Testament but who stripped off the Jewish national character are unknown in Judaism; (3) if Christian monks are at the basis, the writing can not be earlier than the middle of the third century. In conclusion, Lucius, from his thorough acquaintance with monasticism before Constantine, was able to point out the detailed correspondence of the Therapeutæ to Christian monks, even after the author had veiled unequivocal Christian marks. Nevertheless, if this prove conclusive, yet the writing would open glimpses in many points into an ancient Christian monasticism hitherto unknown. At least not in every respect would it stand isolated to modern knowledge (see Hieracas, Hieracites); it would locate itself in some offshoot from Origen, but in detail would contain much that is new and striking, since reference to Gnostic communities is not to be thought of. But new light has been brought to bear on the work by F. C. Conybeare, and by P. Wendland (*Die Therapeuten*, Leipsic, 1896). The latter showed that the work accords philologically with the genuine tracts, and points out, from traditional historical considerations, that it was already in existence by the middle of the third century. He made it seem probable, further, that the inconsistency with other works of Philo does not necessarily invalidate unity of authorship; and that the tract was a continuation of the description of the Essenes, and therefore a part of the lost *He hyper Judaiōn apologia*, which is identical with the *Hypothetika*. If, until further proof to the contrary, the work is to obtain as genuine, then the Therapeutæ are to be recognized as a circle of Jewish contemplative students of Scripture settled on Lake Mareotis. If the whole is literally true, Philo has introduced much that is extra-Jewish and strange; and that he is silent about them elsewhere remains striking. With the Essenes the Therapeutæ have no connection.

(A. Harnack.)

Bibliography: The completeness of the edition of Philo's *De vita contemplativa* by F. C. Conybeare noted in the text, including the commentary and a most comprehensive series of excursuses covering all questions respecting the Therapeutæ, together with the annotated bibliography (pp. 391–399), makes unnecessary here a list of works. Investigation of this subject should not be undertaken without a mastery of what Conybeare has offered. Later discussions do little beside traverse his work. Cf. W. Bousset, *Die Religion des Judentums*, pp. 443 sqq., Berlin, 1903; *DCB*, iv. 368–371.

THEREMIN, LUDWIG FRIEDRICH FRANZ: Distinguished preacher and professor in Berlin; b. at Gramzow (55 m. n.e. of Berlin) Mar. 19, 1780; d. in Berlin Sept. 26, 1846. He studied at Halle, and was ordained in Geneva in 1805. From 1810 he lived in Berlin, first as French preacher of a Reformed congregation, after 1814 as (German) court preacher. He became superior consistorial councilor and member of the department of education in 1824 and professor of homiletics in the University of Berlin in 1839. His preaching was characterized by scrupulous adherence to purity and correctness of form, with earnest striving to enforce the truth by all the arts of eloquence; its content was the Biblical Christ, the pure Evangelical truth. Ten volumes of sermons (Berlin, 1818 sqq., in repeated editions and various forms) preserve his discourses, and *Die Beredsamkeit eine Tugend, oder Grundlinien einer systematischen Rhetorik* (Berlin, 1814; Eng. transl. by W. G. T. Shedd, *Eloquence a Virtue*, Andover, 1850, new ed., 1872) expounds his homiletical principles. In *Die Lehre vom göttlichen Reiche* (Berlin, 1823) Theremin seeks to develop the entire moral and dogmatic basis of Christianity from the concept of the kingdom of God. *Adalberts Bekenntnisse* (Berlin, 1828; Eng. transl., *Confessions of Adalbert*, London, 1838) is apologetic in character, presenting the story of a life long restless and troubled because of devotion to the world and unbelief, then by providential leading and subjective receptivity brought to faith and Christian fellowship. *Abendstunden* (3 vols., Berlin, 1833–39) was Theremin's most popular work; it is a collection of religious poems, stories, letters, and the like, often showing more rhetoric than true poetic form, yet containing many meritorious productions. His last publication was *Demosthenes und Massillon, ein Beitrag zur Geschichte der Beredsamkeit* (Berlin, 1845). (C. VON PALMER†.)

BIBLIOGRAPHY: *ADB*, xxxvii. 724.

THERESA, te-rî′sɑ or tê-rê′sā (**TERESA DE JESUS**), **SAINT:** Spanish mystic and monastic reformer; b. at Avila (53 m. n.w. of Madrid), Old Castile, Mar. 28, 1515; d. at Alva Oct. 4, 1582. The deeply pious and ascetic ideal after the example of saints and martyrs was early instilled in her by her father, the knight Alonso Sanchez de

    Cloister   Cepeda, and especially by her mother,

    Life.   Beatrix d'Avila y Ahumada. Leaving
her parental home secretly one morning in 1534, she entered the monastery of the Incarnation of the Carmelite nuns at Avila. In the cloister she suffered much from illness. Early in her sickness she experienced periods of spiritual ecstasy through the use of the devotional book, *Abecedario espiritual*, commonly known as the " third " or the " spiritual alphabet " (published, six parts, 1537–1554). This work, following the example of similar writings of the medieval mystics, consisted of directions for tests of conscience and for spiritual self-concentration and inner contemplation, known in mystical nomenclature as *oratio recollectionis* or *oratio mentalis*. Besides, she employed other mystical ascetic works; such as the *Tractatus de oratione et meditatione* of Peter of Alcantara (q.v.), and perhaps many of those upon which Ignatius Loyola based his *Exercitia*, and not improbably this *Exercitia* itself. She professed, in her illness, to rise from the lowest stage, " recollection," to the " devotions of peace " or even to the " devotions of union," which was one of perfect ecstasy. With this was frequently joined a rich " blessing of tears." As the merely outer and void Roman Catholic distinction between mortal and venial sin dawned

upon her, she came upon the secret of the awful terror of sinful iniquity, and the inherent nature of original sin. With this was correlated the consciousness of utter natural impotence and the necessity of absolute subjection to God. The intimation on the part of various of her friends (c. 1556) of a diabolical, not divine, element in her supernatural experiences led her to the most horrible self-inflicted tortures and mortifications, far in excess of her ordinary asceticism, until Francisco Borgia, to whom she had made confession, reassured her. On St. Peter's Day of 1559 she became firmly convinced that Christ was present to her in bodily form, though invisible. This vision lasted almost uninterruptedly for more than two years. In another vision, a seraph drove the fiery point of a golden lance repeatedly through her heart, causing an unexampled, as it were, spiritual-bodily pain. The memory of this episode served as an inspiration in determining her long struggle of love and suffering, from which emanated her life-long passion for conformation to the life and endurance of the Savior, to be epitomized in the cry usually inscribed as a motto upon her images: " Lord, either let me suffer or let me die."

The incentive to give outward practical expression to her inward motive was inspired in Theresa

                  by Peter of Alcantara (q.v.). Inci-

  Activities   dentally, he became acquainted with

as Founder   her early in 1560, and became her spiri-

  and Re-   tual guide and counselor. She now re-

  former.   solved to found a Carmelite monastery
for nuns, and to reform the laxity which she had found in the Cloister of the Incarnation and others. Giumara de Ullon, a woman of wealth and a friend, supplied the funds. The absolute poverty of the new monastery established in 1562 and named St. Joseph's, at first excited a scandal among the citizens and authorities of Avila, and the little house with its chapel was in peril of suppression; but powerful patrons like the bishop himself, as well as the impression of well-secured subsistence and prosperity, turned animosity into applause. In Mar., 1563, when Theresa removed to the new cloister, she received the papal sanction for her prime principle of absolute poverty and renunciation of property, which she proceeded to formulate into a " Constitution." Her plan was the revival of the earlier stricter rules, supplemented by new regulations like the three disciplines of ceremonial flagellation prescribed for the divine service every week, and the discalceation of the nuns, or the substitution of leather or wooden sandals for shoes. For the first five years Theresa remained in pious seclusion, engaged in writing. In 1657 she received a patent from the Carmelite general, Rubeo de Ravenna, to establish new houses of her order, and in this effort and later visitations she made long journeys through nearly all the provinces of Spain. Of these she gives a description in her *Libro de las Fundaciones* (a late ed., Madrid, 1880; Eng. transl., *Book of the Foundations*, London, 1871). Between 1567 and 1571, reform convents were established at Medina del Campo, Malagon, Valladolid, Toledo, Pastrana, Salamanca, and Alba de Tormes. After her spirit and example,

a similar movement for men was begun by Juan de la Cruz. Another friend, Geronimo Gracian, Carmelite visitator of the older observance of Andalusia and apostolic commissioner, and later provincial of the Theresian reforms, gave her powerful support in founding convents at Segovia (1571), Veas de Segura (1574), Seville (1575), and Caravaca in Murcia (1576), while the deeply mystical Juan, by his power as teacher and preacher promoted the inner life of the movement. In 1576 began a series of persecutions on the part of the older observant Carmelite order against Theresa, her friends, and her reforms. Pursuant to a body of resolutions adopted at the general chapter at Piacenza, the " definitors " of the order forbade all further founding of convents. The general condemned her to voluntary retirement to one of her institutions. She obeyed and chose St. Joseph's at Toledo. Her friends and subordinates were subjected to greater trials. Finally, after several years her pleadings by letter with Philip II. secured relief. As a result, in 1579, the processes before the Inquisition against her, Gracian, and others were dropped, and the extension of the reform was at least negatively permitted. A brief of Gregory XIII. allowed a special provincial for the younger branch of the discalceate nuns, and a royal rescript created a protective board of four assessors for the reform. During the last three years of her life Theresa founded convents at Villanueva de la Xara in northern Andulusia (1580), Palencia (1580), Soria (1581), Burgos, and at Granada (1582). In all seventeen nunneries, all but one founded by her, and as many men's cloisters were due to her reform activity of twenty years. Her final illness overtook her on one of her journeys from Burgos to Alba de Tormes. Forty years after her death she was canonized, and her church reveres her as the " seraphic virgin." The Cortes exalted her to patroness of Spain in 1814, and the university previously conferred the title *Doctor ecclesiæ* with a diploma. The mysticism in her works exerted a formative influence upon many theologians of the following centuries, such as Francis of Sales, Fénelon, and the Port Royalists.

The kernel of Theresa's mystical thought throughout all her writings is the ascent of the soul in four stages (" Autobiography," chap. x.–xxii.). The first, or " heart's devotion," is that of devout contemplation or concentration, the withdrawal of the soul from without and specially the devout observance of the passion of Christ and penitence.

Her Mysticism. The second is the " devotion of peace," in which at least the human will is lost in that of God by virtue of a charismatic, supernatural state given of God, while the other faculties, as memory, reason, and imagination, are not yet secure from worldly distraction. While a partial distraction is due to outer performances such as repetition of prayers and writing down spiritual things, yet the prevailing state is one of quietude. The " devotion of union " is not only a supernatural but an essentially ecstatic state. Here there is also an absorption of the reason in God, and only the memory and imagination are left to ramble. This state is characterized by a blissful peace, a sweet slumber of at least

the higher soul faculties, a conscious rapture in the love of God. The fourth is the " devotion of ecstasy or rapture " a passive state, in which the consciousness of being in the body disappears (II Cor. xii. 2–3). Sense activity ceases; memory and imagination are also absorbed in God or intoxicated. Body and spirit are in the throes of a sweet, happy pain, alternating between a fearful fiery glow, a complete impotence and unconsciousness, and a spell of strangulation, intermitted sometimes by such an ecstatic flight that the body is literally lifted into space. This after half an hour is followed by a reactionary relaxation of a few hours in a swoon-like weakness, attended by a negation of all the faculties in the union with God. From this the subject awakens in tears; it is the climax of mystical experience, productive of the trance.

Theresa's writings, produced for didactic purposes, stand among the most remarkable in the mystical literature of the Roman Catholic Church:

Her Writings. the " Autobiography," written before 1567, under the direction of her confessor, Padro Ibañez (*La Vida de la Santa Madre Teresa de Jesus*, Madrid, 1882; Eng. transl., *The Life of S. Teresa of Jesus*, London, 1888); *Camino de Perfecion*, written also before 1567, at the direction of her confessor (Salamanca, 1589; Eng. transl., *The Way of Perfection*, London, 1852); *El Castillo Interior*, written in 1577 (Eng. transl., *The Interior Castle*, London, 1852), comparing the contemplative soul to a castle with seven successive interior courts, or chambers, analogous to the seven heavens; and *Relaciones*, an extension of the autobiography giving her inner and outer experiences in epistolary form. Two smaller works are *Conceptos del Amor* and *Exclamaciones*. Besides, there are the *Cartas* (Saragossa, 1671), or correspondence, of which there are 342 letters and 87 fragments of others. Theresa's prose is marked by an unaffected grace, an ornate neatness, and charming power of expression, together placing her in the front rank of Spanish prose writers; and her rare poems (*Todas las poesías*, Munster, 1854) are distinguished for tenderness of feeling and rhythm of thought. Of complete editions of Theresa's works should be noted: *Obras, novísima edicion* (6 vols., Madrid, 1881), by V. de la Fuente; and for beauty and accuracy of style, the French translation by Arnauld d'Andilly, *Les Œuvres de Sainte Thérèse* (Paris, 1855, new ed., 1867–69).

(O. Zöckler†.)

BIBLIOGRAPHY: The " Life " by Theresa's father confessor, F. de Ribera, was first issued, Madrid, 1590, exists in Fr. transls. issued at Paris, 1632, 1645, 1867, 2 vols., 1884. Her autobiography, preserved in the monastery of S. Lorenzo in the Escurial, was issued anew, Madrid, 1882, and is in Fr. transl., Paris, 1691, 1857, 1880, Germ. transl., Aachen, 1868, Regensburg, 1868, Eng. transl., London, 1905. A very full collection of early material is in *ASB*, Oct., vii. 109–790. Later lives are by Diego Yepes, Madrid, 1599; Juan de Jesus Maria, ib. 1605; G. Gracian, ib. 1611; A. de S. Joaquin, 12 vols., ib. 1733–66; F. a S. Antonio, Venice, 1754; M. de Traggia, Madrid, 1807; J. B. A. Boucher, 2 vols., Paris, 1810; F. B. Collombet, Lyons, 1837; J. H. Hennes, 2d ed., Frankfort, 1866; Luis de Leon, *Biographieen aus der Geschichte der spanischen Inquisition*, p. 356, Halle, 1866; Ida, Countess Hahn-Hahn, Mainz, 1867; P. Rousselot, *Les Mystiques espagnols*, pp. 308–378, Paris, 1867; E. Hofele, Regensburg, 1882; J. Loth, Rouen, 1883; Mme. Estienne d'Orves,

Paris, 1890; Prinz von Oettingen-Spielberg, Regensburg, 1899; H. Joly, 2d ed., Paris, 1901; M. G. Liszt, Munster, 1901; W. Fairweather, London, 1907; Helen H. Colvill, *Saint Teresa of Spain*, London, 1909. Consult further: O. Zöckler, *Petrus von Alcantara, Teresia von Avila, und Johannes de Cruce*, in *Zeitschrift für lutherische Theologie und Kirche*, xxvi (1865), 68–106, 281–303; H. Heppe, *Geschichte der quietistischen Mystik in der katholischen Kirche*, pp. 9–22, Berlin, 1875; G. Hahn, *Les Phénomènes hysteriques et les révélations de S. Thérèse*, Brussels, 1883, Germ. transl., Leipsic, 1906; A. Barine, in *RDM*, lxxv (1886), 549–579; L. de Sau, *Étude pathologico-théologique sur S. Thérèse*, Louvain, 1886 (answers Hahn); H. Delacroix, *Études d'hist. et de psychologie du mysticisme*, Paris, 1908; *Saint Theresa: the History of her Foundations.* Transl. *from Spanish by Sister Agnes Mason*, London, 1909.

THESSALONICA, thes″a-lo-nai′ca: A city of Macedonia, the modern Saloniki, situated at the northeast corner of the Thermaic Gulf. Its original name was Therma, or Thermē, " Hot Bath," so called from the hot salt-springs found about four miles from the present city. Its later name was probably given to it by Cassander, king of Macedonia, who rebuilt it in 315 B.C., and called it after his wife. Being well situated for commerce, it was a town of importance from very early times. It was taken from the Macedonians, and occupied by Athenians, about 432; restored soon after; repeopled by Cassander, 315; became the great Macedonian naval station; surrendered to the Romans after the battle of Pydna, 168, and was made the capital of the second of the four divisions of Macedonia, or *Macedonia Secunda*, between the Strymon and the Axius; and when the four were reduced to one province, under the jurisdiction of a proconsul, it was the virtual metropolis, and there the proconsul lived. There Cicero lived from April till Nov., 58, during his exile; and there the party of Pompey and the senate had their headquarters during the first civil war, 49. It took the side of Octavius (Augustus) against Sextus Pompeius (42–39), and in reward was made a free city. At the opening of the Christian era it was the capital of the whole country between the Adriatic and the Black Sea, and the " chief station on the great Roman road, called the Via Egnatia, which connected Rome with the whole region to the north of the Ægean Sea." Before Constantinople was built, it was virtually the capital of Greece and Illyricum, as well as of Macedonia, and shared the trade of the Ægean with Ephesus and Corinth. In the middle of the third Christian century it was made a Roman colony, soldiers being settled there in order to increase its strength as a bulwark against the Gothic hordes. In 390 A.D., in a sedition there, the prefect Botericus was murdered; in dreadful revenge, nearly 7,000 persons were massacred by Theodosius I. (q.v.; cf. AMBROSE, SAINT, OF MILAN). From the fourth to the eighth century Thessalonica withstood many attacks from Goths and Slavs. On July 30, 904, it was taken by the Saracens; on Aug. 15, 1185, by the Normans of Sicily, and by the Turks in 1380; it was ceded to the Greek Emperor Manuel, 1403, sold to the Venetians by Andronicus, and finally taken by the Turks from the Venetians, 1430. The modern city had in 1907 a population of 150,-000. Its commerce is extensive, and it retains its ancient importance.

The apostle Paul introduced Christianity into Thessalonica upon his second missionary journey. He came with Silas and Timothy, preached for three Sundays in the synagogue there, and, as the result of the work, a church was gathered, principally composed, however, of Gentiles. Among the converts were Caius, Aristarchus, Secundus, and perhaps Jason (Acts xvii. 1–13, xx. 4, xxvii. 2; cf. Phil. iv. 16; II Tim. iv. 10). Paul wrote to the Thessalonian Church two epistles from Corinth (see PAUL, II., 2, §§ 1–2). In striking proof of the minute accuracy of Luke, upon the arch of the Vardar gate, so called because it leads to the Vardar, or Axius, there occurs the word πολιταρχούντων (politarchs) as the designation of the seven magistrates of the city, a word unmentioned in ancient literature, yet the word which Luke employs to designate them (Acts xvii. 8).

From Thessalonica the Gospel spread quickly all around (I Thess. i. 8). " During several centuries this city was the bulwark, not simply of the later Greek Empire, but of Oriental Christendom, and was largely instrumental in the conversion of the Slavonians and Bulgarians. Thus it received the designation of the ' Orthodox City ' " (Howson). Its see had well-nigh the dignity of a patriarchate; and it was because Leo the Isaurian severed the trans-Adriatic provinces, which had been under its immediate jurisdiction, from the Roman see, that the division between the Latin and Greek in great measure caused. It was the see-city of Eustathius of Thessalonica (q.v.). From 1205 to 1418 there were Latin archbishops in Thessalonica. At the present day it is the seat of a Greek metropolitan, and contains numerous churches and schools of different denominations. Many of the mosques were formerly churches.

BIBLIOGRAPHY: T. L. F. Tafel, *Dissertatio de Thessalonica*, Berlin, 1839 (the chief authority); G. F. Bowen, *Mount Athos, Thessaly, and Epirus*, London, 1852; H. F. Tozer, *Geography of Greece*, p. 204, London, 1873; W. Smith, *Dictionary of Greek and Roman Geography*, ii. 1170–1174, London, 1878; W. M. Ramsay, *Church in the Roman Empire*, passim, London, 1893; idem, *St. Paul the Traveller and the Roman Citizen*, chap. x., ib. 1896; Abbe Belley, in *Mémoires de l'académie des inscriptions*, xxxviii. 121–146; *DB*, iv. 749–750; *EB*, iv. 5046–48; *KL*, x. 658–660; and, in general, the works on Paul the Apostle, the introductions to the commentaries on Thessalonians and the commentaries on Acts.

THEUDAS, thū′das: A Jewish factionary named by Gamaliel, Acts v. 34–39. A Theudas is named also by Josephus (*Ant.*, XX., v. 1), who states that this man was a magician who in the time of Fadus the procurator (44–46 A.D.) claimed to be a prophet, drew many people after him, promising to divide the waters of the Jordan for their passage, but that his company was dispersed by a troop which Fadus sent against them; many of them were killed, while Theudas was caught and beheaded. This Theudas was anterior in time to Judas, according to Gamaliel, therefore before 6–7 A.D., so that Gamaliel could not on this basis have meant the same person as Josephus, whose affair took place ten years later than Gamaliel's speech. Since the time of Origen (*Contra Celsum*, i. 6) many have sought to see two Theudases, though a Theudas of the period indicated by Gamaliel is not known, and arbitrary identifications of others with the Theudas of Acts fail to convince. Blass conjectures a father or grandfather of the Josephan Theudas and of the same name, relying upon ancient custom, but without any testimony to the fact. Again Blass conjectures that, while many regard Josephus as the basis of Luke in Acts, some one has inserted Theudas in the text of Josephus, basing his supposition in part upon a variant reading in Codex D. Some scholars like B. Weiss, Clemen, and Hilgenfeld suppose the reference to time in Acts is due to an editor whose chronology was wrong.

Recently the passage is newly adduced to show Luke's dependence upon Josephus. Josephus follows his report of Theudas with one of the revolt of the sons of Judas under Quirinius. Moreover, there are verbal coincidences between the narrative of Luke and that of Josephus; both also name Judas, though Josephus knows his origin; both speak of Quirinius' taxing. These lead to the conclusion of interdependence. On the other hand, Luke knows the number of the adherents of Theudas, Josephus speaks of " a great part of the people," though his narrative shows that a squadron of cavalry (about 500 men) broke up the combination; Luke has employed little of the detail of Josephus. In that case Luke must have misunderstood Josephus, assumed the relative order in Josephus' narrative as historical, and transferred the events from Judas' sons to the father. Schmiedel supposes that Luke had made notes, meager, however, from Josephus, not noting the dates of the events, indeed reading hastily the account of Josephus, and so misplaced the events. But this is all conjecture. Acts does not show traces of such a method. While the notice of Judas goes back upon *Ant.*, XVIII., i. 1, other events mentioned by Luke come from other sources, and follow other traditions than those of Josephus.

It is better to consider that in the case under consideration Luke was not dependent upon Josephus, that the coincidences of the two writers depend upon the common tradition of the period, that the two cases were connected in Luke's mind as those of revolts, and that the chronological coincidence in order is accidental. (P. Feine.)

Bibliography: Sonntag, *TSK*, 1837, pp. 622–652; K. T. Keim, *Aus dem Urchristenthum*, i. 1–27, Zurich, 1878; C. C. Clemen, *Chronologie der paulinischen Briefe*, pp. 66–69, Halle, 1893; M. Krenkel, *Josephus und Lucas*, pp. 162–174, Leipsic, 1894; A. Hausrath, *Neutestamentliche Zeitgeschichte*, iv. 239–243, Heidelberg, 1877, Eng. transl., London, 1895; W. M. Ramsay, *Was Christ born at Bethlehem*, pp. 252–260, London, 1898; Cross, in *Expository Times*, 1899–1900, pp. 538–540; P. Feine, *Theologisches Literaturblatt*, 1900, pp. 60–61; *DB*, iv. 750; *EB*, iv. 5049–57; *JE*, xii. 140; and commentaries on the Acts.

THIEME, tî'me, **KARL:** German Protestant; b. at Spremberg (53 m. s.s.w. of Frankfort), Saxony, July 20, 1862. He was educated at the University of Leipsic (Ph.D., 1887; lic. theol., 1889), where he became privat-docent in 1890, and associate professor of systematic theology in 1894. In theology he is a moderate liberal, and has written, *Glauben und Wissen bei Lotze* (Leipsic, 1888); *Die sittliche Triebkraft des Glaubens* (1895); *Eine katholische Beleuchtung der augsburgischen Konfession* (1898); *Luthers Testament wider Rom*

(1900); *Der Offenbarungsglaube im Streit über Bibel und Babel* (1903); *Die christliche Demut* (vol. i., 1906); *Jesus und seine Predigt* (Giessen, 1908); *Die Theologie der Heilstatsachen und das Evangelium Jesus* (1909); and *Zu Wundts Religionspsychologie* (Leipsic, 1910).

THIERSCH, tîrsh, **HEINRICH WILHELM JOSIAS:** German Irvingite; b. at Munich Nov. 5, 1817; d. at Basel Dec. 3, 1885. He studied philology at Munich (1833–35; chiefly under his father, but also heard Schelling and Görres), theology at Erlangen (1835–37, where he heard Olshausen and Harless), and at Tübingen (1837–38); became repetent at Erlangen (1839), privat-docent (1840) and professor of theology at Marburg (1843); meanwhile, as early as 1836 he had become interested in Irvingism, and received that faith (1847), and resigned his professorship in 1850 in order to labor in the interests of the Catholic Apostolic Church (q.v.) which was then being organized in Germany by " evangelists " from England. Among these the Apostle Carlyle exercised the deepest influence upon him. Thiersch received ordination from the Irvingites, and subsequently resided successively in Marburg, Munich, Augsburg, and Basel, exercised a general ministry over the scattered Irvingite congregations, was privat-docent at Marburg (1853–58), but in general his university life was closed with his acceptance of Irvingite principles. During the later years of his life he corresponded frequently with Döllinger and other Old Catholic leaders.

Thiersch was a man of sincere and profound piety, of rare classical, theological, and general culture, an enthusiastic teacher, and might have become the successor of Neander in Berlin; but, in obedience to what he believed to be a divine call, he sacrificed a brilliant academic career to his religious convictions. He lived in poverty and isolation. He was lame; but had a very striking, highly intellectual and spiritual countenance, and an impressive voice and manner. He was the most distinguished German convert to Irvingism. He sincerely believed that the Lord had restored the apostolic office and the prophetic gifts of the Apostolic Church in the Irvingite community; and, notwithstanding the apparent failure of the movement, he adhered to it till his death.

His chief writings are: *Versuch zur Herstellung des historischen Standpunkts für die Kritik der neutestamentlichen Schriften* (Erlangen, 1845; against the Tübingen school of Baur, who answered in *Der Kritiker und der Fanatiker, in der Person des Herrn H. W. J. Thiersch. Zur Charakteristik der neuesten Theologie*, Stuttgart, 1846); *Vorlesungen über Katholicismus und Protestantismus* (2 vols., Erlangen, 1846; able, written in an irenic spirit, and in elegant style); *Die Kirche im apostolischen Zeitalter* (Frankfort, 1852; Eng. transl. by Carlyle the Irvingite, London, 1852); *Ueber christliches Familienleben* (1854); *Döllinger's Auffassung des Urchristenthums beleuchtet* (1861); *Die Gleichnisse Christi* (Frankfort, 1867); *Die Bergpredigt Christi* (Basel, 1867); *Die Strafgesetze in Bayern zum Schutz der Sittlichkeit* (1868); *Luther, Gustav Adolf*

und Max I. von Bayern (Nördlingen, 1868); *Das
Verbot der Ehe innerhalb der nahen Verwandtschaft
nach der heiligen Schrift und nach den Grundsätzen
der christlichen Kirche* (1869); *Die Genesis* (Basel,
1869; Eng. transl., *The Book of Genesis*, London,
1878); *Ueber den christlichen Staat* (1875); *Christian Heinrich Zeller's Leben* (2 vols. Basel, 1876);
*Die Anfänge der heiligen Geschichte, nach dem 1.
Buche Mosis betrachtet* (1877); *Ueber die Gefahren
und die Hoffnungen der christlichen Kirche* (1877);
Blicke in die Lebensgeschichte des Propheten Daniel
(1884); *Inbegriff der christlichen Lehre* (1886; posthumous, contains a manual of Christian doctrine
and Christian life which he used in his catechetical
instruction).   (P. Schafff†.)   D. S. Schaff.

Bibliography: P. Wiegand, *H. W. J. Thiersch's Leben*,
Basel, 1888 (partly autobiographical); Hauck-Herzog,
RE, xix. 684–692; *ADB*, xxxviii. 17.

THIETMAR, tît'mār **(DITHMAR):** Bishop of
Merseburg; b. July 25, 975; d. Dec. 1, 1018. He
was a Saxon, son of Count Sigefrid of Walbeck, and
related to the imperial family. He studied in the
abbey of Quedlinburg and in Magdeburg, and became bishop of Merseburg in 1009. Starting with
the intention of writing a history of his diocese, he
produced a "Chronicle" (ed. J. M. Lappenberg,
MGH, Script., iii., 1839, pp. 723–871; re-ed. F.
Kurze, *Script. rer. Germ.*, 1889) which is in fact a
history of the empire with the neighboring Germanic and Slavic states, and forms the most important source for the later Saxon emperors. A
manuscript preserved in Dresden [published in
facsimile by L. Schmidt, Dresden, 1905] written by
Thietmar himself shows how he worked, amending
and adding to the original draft with untiring industry. Naturally this method creates the impression
that Thietmar did not fully master his subject;
his judgment and opinions are narrow, and his style
is dry. But he knew and saw much, was a lover of
truth, and was devoted to his fatherland. For the
manners and customs of his time he has almost the
same importance as Gregory of Tours for the
Merovingian period.   (A. Hauck.)

Bibliography: W. Maurenbrecher, *De historiæ decimi seculi
scriptoribus*, Königsberg, 1870; idem, *Forschungen der
deutschen Geschichte*, xiv. 347 sqq.; Kurze, in *NA*, xiv.
593 sqq., xvi. 459 sqq.; W. Grundlach, *Heldenlieder*, i.
114 sqq., Innsbruck, 1894; Hauck, *KD*, iii. 949–950;
ADB, xxxviii. 26.

THILO, tî'lō, **JOHANN KARL:** Professor in
Halle; b. at Langensalza (19 m. n.w. of Erfurt),
Thuringia, Nov. 28, 1794; d. in Halle May 17, 1853.
He studied at Schulpforte 1809–14, then in Leipsic,
and a final semester in Halle. In 1817 he became
teacher in the Latin school of the Halle orphan
asylum and also in the Royal Pedagogium of
Franke's foundations, and filled the position five
years. From 1819 he was privat-docent in theology
in the university and in 1822 became professor.
Thilo lectured on the history of dogma, church
history, symbolics, patristics, and the New Testament, taking up the last-named subject after the
death of his father-in-law, G. C. Knapp (q.v.).
He early gave attention to the New Testament
apocrypha, to elucidate which his studies and
knowledge peculiarly fitted him, and planned a

comprehensive edition of the entire series of writings
with two volumes of comment; but in spite of much
labor he published only the Acts of Thomas (Leipsic,
1823), Peter and Paul (1838), Andrew and Matthew
(1846), fragments of the Acts of John by Leucius
Charinus (1847), and *Codex apocryphus Novi
Testamenti*, vol. I., containing the gospels (1832).
His last great undertaking, a *Bibliotheca patrum
Græcorum dogmatica*, also remained incomplete;
only one volume (*Sancti Athanasii opera dogmatica
selecta*, Leipsic, 1853) having appeared. Certain
dissertations (*Eusebii Alexandrini oratio*, Halle,
1834; *De cælo empyreo commentationes iii*, 1839–40;
Commentationes in Synesii hymnum ii, 1842–43)
were the fruit of deep studies of the Neoplatonists.
In German Thilo published a *Kritisches Sendschreiben an Augusti über die Schriften des Eusebius von
Alexandrien und des Eusebius von Emisa* (1832)
and an introduction to an edition of Knapp's
Vorlesungen (2 vols., 1827). He belonged to none
of the theological parties of the first half of the nineteenth century, though he often pronounced
Schleiermacher the greatest theologian of the German Church since Luther, and he maintained cordial
relations with the two schools into which teachers
and scholars in Halle were dividing in his time,
desiring most of all to study with mind ever open to
receive new truth.   (E. Henke†.)

Bibliography: The funeral oration by H. L. Dryander
was published at Halle, 1853. Consult further *ADB*,
xxxviii. 40 sqq.

THIRLWALL, therl'wōl, **CONNOP:** English bishop and historian; b. in London Feb. 11, 1797;
d. at Bath July 27, 1875. He displayed such remarkable precocity, that in 1809 he published, under
his father's direction, a volume of essays and poems
entitled *Primitiæ*. He was educated at the Charterhouse and Trinity College, Cambridge (B.A., 1818;
fellow, 1818); entered Lincoln's Inn, 1820, and was
called to the bar 1825; abandoned law and returned
to Cambridge, 1827; was ordained deacon, 1827,
and priest 1828. He then took a full share of
university and college work, and was assistant tutor,
1832–34; was vicar of Over, 1829; rector of Kirby
Underdale, Yorkshire, 1835–40, and bishop of St.
David's, 1840–74. He was an active member of
the Old Testament Revision Company. He translated with J. Hare from Niebuhr vols. i. and ii. of
The History of Rome (London, 1828 sqq.); and was
the author of *A History of Greece* (8 vols., 1835–47);
Our Works (1845; vol. i. of Watson and Crosthwaite's *Practical Sermons*, 1845–46); *The Irish
Church. A Speech delivered in the House of Lords*
(1869); *Remains Literary and Theological* (3 vols.,
1877–78); and *Letters Literary and Theological*
(1881).

Bibliography: A *Memoir* by Rev. Louis Stokes is prefixed
to the *Letters*, ut sup. Consult further: F. W. Cornish,
The English Church in the 19th Century, passim, London,
1910 (quite full); *DNB*, lvi. 138–141 (gives references to
scattered allusions).

THIRTLE, JAMES WILLIAM: English Nonconformist; b. at Lowestoft (40 m. n.n.e. of Ipswich), Suffolk, Jan. 23, 1854. He was privately
educated and was on the editorial staff of the
Staffordshire Sentinel (1875–84) and the *Torquay*

Times (1885–87). Since 1888 he has been one of the editors of *The Christian*, and has written *Titles of the Psalms* (London, 1904) and *Old Testament Problems: Critical Studies in the Psalms and Isaiah* (1907).

THIRTY-NINE ARTICLES, THE.

Earliest Attempts to Formulate an English Creed (§ 1).
The Forty-two Articles (§ 2).
Formulation and Adoption of the Thirty-nine Articles (§ 3).
Content and Character of the Articles (§ 4).
Interpretation (§ 5).
The Protestant Episcopal Church (§ 6).

The Thirty-nine Articles differ from the more elaborate confessions of the sixteenth century in form, but agree with them in spirit. As compared with the later canons of the synod of Dort and the Westminster Confession, they are more genial in tone and lack the metaphys-
1. Earliest ical element so prominent in the latter.
Attempt to The Ten Articles of 1536 (q.v.), and the
Formulate Six Articles of 1539 (q.v.) issued in
an English the reign of Henry VIII., prepared
Creed. the way for a final statement of
doctrinal controversies. King Henry VIII. was hardly a Protestant, but he advanced the English Reformation by abolishing the jurisdiction of the pope in England and pronouncing his authority to be no greater than that of any other bishop, as well as by suppressing a large number of English monasteries and sequestrating their revenues. The positive Reformation was first fairly introduced during the reign of Edward VI. (1547–53) under the lead of Archbishop Cranmer. Cranmer at first entertained the noble but premature project of framing an Evangelical catholic creed, in which all the Reformed churches could agree in opposition to the Church of Rome, then holding the Council of Trent, and he invited the surviving continental Reformers—Melanchthon, Calvin, and Bullinger—to London for the purpose. Calvin was willing to cross ten seas for such a work of Christian union, and so replied to Cranmer in 1552 (the correspondence is in Cranmer's *Works*, Parker Society ed., ii., 430–433, 1846). But political events prevented the conference, and so the formulation of the doctrinal consensus of the Reformed churches.

Failing in this scheme, Cranmer framed, with the aid of his fellow Reformers, the Forty-two Articles of Religion for the English reformed church. As
2. The early as 1549 he had drawn up a series
Forty-two of articles which were submitted to
Articles. licentiates before licensure. These he
revised and the council submitted them to a commission consisting of Grindal, Horne, John Knox, and others for examination. They were completed in their final form Nov., 1552, and published in 1553 by " royal authority." The title-page states also that they had the official sanction of convocation. But Cranmer stated at a later time that this was not true (cf. Dixon, 514 sqq.; J. Gairdner, *A History of the English Church from Henry VIII to Mary*, p. 311, London, 1903). The reestablishment of the papacy under the short reign of Mary (1553–58) set them aside.

Under Elizabeth (1558–1603) the Articles were

reduced to thirty-nine, and brought into the form which they have retained ever since in the Church of England. The Latin edition was prepared under the supervision of Archbishop Parker, with the aid of Bishop Cox of Ely (one of the Marian exiles) and Bishop Guest of Rochester, approved by convocation, and published by the royal
3. Formula- press, 1563, but with art. xxix. stricken
tion and out by Elizabeth. The English edi-
Adoption of tion, slightly differing from the Latin,
the Thirty- and containing the omitted art. xxix.,
nine Articles. was adopted by the two convocations in 1571, and issued under the editorial care of Bishop Jewel of Salisbury the same year. Seven of the forty-two articles were omitted (those bearing on the descent of Christ into Hades, the blasphemy against the Holy Spirit, the Millenarians, the sleep of the soul after death, etc.). Four new articles concerned the procession of the Holy Spirit, the administration of the cup to the laity, the failure of the unworthy to partake of Christ's body in the Lord's Supper, and a list of homilies. They were made binding on all ministers and teachers of religion, and students in the universities, but subscription was not always enforced with rigor. The Non-conformists, who had objections to the political articles, complained bitterly. The Act of Uniformity (see UNIFORMITY, ACTS OF) under Charles II. (1662) imposed greater stringency than ever; but the Toleration Act (q.v.) of William and Mary gave some relief by exempting dissenting ministers from subscribing to arts. xxxiv., xxxvi., and a portion of xxvii. Subsequent attempts to relax or abolish subscription resulted at last in the University Tests Act of 1871, which exempts all students and graduates in the universities of Oxford, Cambridge, and Durham, except divinity students, fellows, professors, and heads of colleges, from subscription, and throws these institutions open to Dissenters.

The Thirty-nine Articles are among the most important doctrinal formulas of the Reformation period. They cover nearly all the heads of the Christian faith, especially those which were then under dispute with the Roman Catholics. They
affirm (1) the catholic doctrines of the
4. Content Trinity and incarnation, and the three
and Charac- early creeds—the Apostles', Nicene,
ter of the and Athanasian; and (2) the Protes-
Articles. tant doctrines on the authority of the
Scriptures, " justification by faith only," the distinction between the visible and invisible Church, and the sacraments of baptism and the Lord's Supper. In common with other Protestant formularies, they condemn the doctrine of supererogatory works, purgatory, the worship of relics, the invocation of saints, clerical celibacy, the adoration of the host, and the mass. The errancy of general councils is affirmed. The bishop of Rome is declared " to have no jurisdiction in England." They are borrowed, in part, from Lutheran standards; namely, the Augsburg Confession (1530) and the Württemberg Confession (1552); but on the sacraments, especially the much-disputed doctrine of the real presence in the Eucharist, they follow the Swiss reformers, Bullinger and Calvin. The

doctrine of transubstantiation is declared to be " repugnant to the plain words of Scripture." The decree of reprobation is not referred to and in the statement of the decree of election the more mild form of the Second Helvetic Confession is imitated. In the political sections they teach the Erastian doctrine of the spiritual as well as temporal supremacy of the sovereign as the supreme governor of the Church of England. They have, therefore, an eclectic and comprehensive character, which distinguishes the Anglican Church from the Lutheran and the strictly Calvinistic churches of the continent and Scotland, and from the dissenting denominations of England.

The Thirty-nine Articles must be understood in their plain grammatical sense; and, when this is doubtful, the private writings of Cranmer and other English Reformers and the Elizabethan divines must be called to aid. The leaders of the tractarian movement disparaged the Thirty-nine Articles, and John Henry Newman in Tract 90, *Remarks on Certain Passages in the Thirty-nine Articles,* tried to show that art. xi., on justification by faith only, does not exclude the doctrine of justification by works, that art. xxv. does not deny that the five sacraments are sacraments in some sense, that arts. vi. and xx., on the authority of Scripture, do not exclude the doctrine of the authority of Catholic tradition, etc. The doctrinal decisions in the Gorham (see GORHAM CASE), Bennet, and other controversies, favor great latitude in their interpretation. High-churchmen give to the Articles a place subordinate to the Book of Common Prayer, which is followed when the Articles really are, or seem to be, in contradiction to it, as in the implications it allows in the doctrines of baptismal regeneration, the real presence in the Eucharist, and the sacerdotal character of the ministry.

5. Interpretation.

The Protestant Episcopal Church in the United States, after effecting an independent organization and episcopate in consequence of the American Revolution, formally adopted the Thirty-nine Articles of the mother-church at the general convention held in Trenton, N. J., Sept. 12, 1801, but with sundry alterations and omissions in the political articles (xxi., xxxvii.) which the separation of Church and State made necessary. The American revision omits all allusion to the Athanasian Creed (Art. viii.), which is also excluded from the American edition of the Prayer-Book. By this omission the Episcopal Church in the United States has escaped the agitation of the English Church on that creed.

6. The Protestant Episcopal Church.

(PHILIP SCHAFF†.) D. S. SCHAFF.

BIBLIOGRAPHY: The text (Latin and English, with the American changes) is given in Schaff, *Creeds,* iii. 486–516, cf. i. 592–657. Consult: Thomas Rogers, *Exposition of the Thirty-nine Articles,* London, 1579, Cambridge, 1854; Gilbert Burnet, *History of the Reformation of the Church of England,* London, 1679–1715 and often; idem, *Exposition of the Thirty-nine Articles,* Oxford, 1715 and often; R. Laurence, *An Attempt to Illustrate those Articles of the Church of England which the Calvinists improperly consider as Calvinistical,* Bampton Lectures, 3d ed., Oxford, 1838; J. Lamb, *An Historical Account of the Thirty-nine Articles,* Cambridge, 1835; E. H. Browne, *An Exposition of the Thirty-nine Articles,* London, 1850 and often (the most useful commentary, Am. ed. by J. Williams, Bishop of Connecticut, New York, 1869); C. Hardwick, *A History of the Articles of Religion,* Cambridge, 1851, rev. ed. by F. Procter, London, 1876; W. S. Perry, *Journals of the General Convention of the Protestant Episcopal Church in the United States, 1785–1835,* i. 279 sqq., New York, 1861; A. P. Forbes, *An Explanation of the Thirty-nine Articles,* 2 vols., London, 1867–68; W. White, *Memoirs of the Protestant Episcopal Church in the United States of America,* Philadelphia, 1820, ed. B. F. Da Costa, New York, 1880; R. W. Dixon, *History of the Church of England,* iii. 520 sqq. London, 1885; E. T. Green, *The Thirty-nine Articles to the Age of the Reformation,* London, 1896; E. F. K. Müller, *Die Bekenntnisschriften der reformierten Kirche,* pp. xl.–xliii., 505–522, Leipsic, 1903; A. J. Tait, *Lecture Outlines on the Thirty-Nine Articles,* London, 1910.

THIRTY YEARS' WAR, THE: The great religious struggle of the seventeenth century (1618–1648) between the Protestants and the Roman Catholics, Germany being the chief area of conflict. Of how mixed a character the whole affair was, may be seen from the circumstance that, though Roman Catholics on the one side (headed by Austria, Spain, and Bavaria), and Protestants on the other side, under various leaders (Bohemia, Denmark, and Sweden), always formed the groundwork of the party position, Roman-Catholic powers, as, for instance, France, would at times ally themselves with the Protestants, and Protestant princes with the Roman Catholics, as, for instance, the electors of Brandenburg and Saxony.

The war began in Bohemia. In 1617 Ferdinand of Styria, a brother of the Emperor Matthias, a pupil of the Jesuits, and a fanatical enemy of Protestantism, was crowned king of Bohemia; and persecutions were immediately instituted against the Protestants. But the Protestants, under the leadership of Count Thurn, penetrated into the castle of Prague, threw the imperial commissioners out of the window (May 23, 1618), organized a general rising throughout the country, entered into alliance with Bethlen Gábor, prince of Transylvania, and the Evangelical Union in Germany; and as Matthias died on Mar. 20, 1619, and Ferdinand shortly after succeeded him as emperor, they declared the Bohemian throne vacant, and offered it to the young elector-palatine, Frederick V., a son-in-law of James I. of England. He accepted the offer, but was very unfortunate. The Protestant army was completely routed in the battle at the White Hill, just outside the walls of Prague, Nov. 8, 1620, by Tilly, the commander of the imperial army, which chiefly consisted of the contingent of the Holy League; and Bohemia was speedily reduced to order; that is, more than thirty thousand families belonging to the Lutheran or the Reformed denomination were driven out of the country, and their property, valued at more than forty million crowns, was confiscated. Next year the Palatinate was invaded by a Spanish army under Spinola; and at the diet of Regensburg, March 6, 1623, Frederick V. was put under the ban of the empire, and the Palatinate was given to Maximilian of Bavaria. In 1625 the Protestant princes of Germany again rallied under the head of Christian IV., king of Denmark; but he was utterly defeated in the battle at Lutter, Aug. 27, 1626, by Tilly. The

Danish peninsula was flooded with imperial troops; and the peace of Lübeck, May 22, 1629, made an end of the direct participation of Denmark in the war. In June, 1630, Gustavus Adolphus, king of Sweden, landed in Germany; and in a very short time conquered Pomerania and Mecklenburg. Gustavus Adolphus was a Christian hero, a great general, and a great statesman. The hope of conquest, of making the Baltic a Swedish sea, was, no doubt, one of his motives in taking up the cause of the Protestants in Germany, but his conviction of the justice of that cause was as surely another, and perhaps the stronger one. His army was a model of an army, infinitely superior in moral character to the armies of Tilly and Wallenstein. The Swedish soldiers of Gustavus Adolphus resembled the Ironsides of Cromwell. Tilly was defeated at Brietenfeld, and on the Lech. In the latter battle he was killed and his army scattered. But Ferdinand charged Wallenstein with the formation of a new army, which encountered that of Gustavus Adolphus at Lützen. Wallenstein was defeated; but Gustavus Adolphus fell, and the emperor found breathing-room again. Though Wallenstein remained inactive in Bohemia, where he finally was assassinated at Eger, Feb. 25, 1634, the standard of the Swedish army rapidly sunk after the death of Gustavus Adolphus; and the Protestant army suffered a severe defeat at Nördlingen, Sept. 6, 1634, after which the electors of Brandenburg and Saxony deserted the Protestant cause, made peace with the emperor, and turned against the Swedes.

Nevertheless, the position of the emperor continued to be very critical, and his prospects of final success were very small. Richelieu, whose whole foreign policy turned upon the humiliation of the house of Austria as its true pivot, and who for that very reason had subsidized the Swedes from the very beginning, now took the army of Duke Bernhardt of Saxe-Weimar into the French service; and the war against Austria and her allies was carried on with a fierceness and cruelty hitherto unheard of. In 1646 no less than a hundred villages were burned down in Bavaria, and the inhabitants driven away. And at the same time the Swedish general Torstenson developed an activity which seemed to threaten the very existence of the Hapsburg dynasty. He defeated one Austrian army under Piccolomini at Brietenfeld, Nov. 2, 1642, and another, under Hatzfeld, at Jankow, Mar. 6, 1645; and he actually approached Vienna in order to form a connection with Prince Rakoczy of Transylvania, and laid siege to the city. The immediate danger drifted away by the somewhat peculiar proceedings of Rakoczy. But Austria was completely exhausted and the peace of Westphalia (see WESTPHALIA, PEACE OF), Oct. 24, 1648, was as necessary to her as it was welcome to Germany, which lay prostrate, and cruelly devastated from one end to the other.

BIBLIOGRAPHY: The best bibliography is that in Dahlmann-Waitz, *Quellenkunde der deutschen Geschichte*, 7th ed. by E. Brandenburg, Leipsic, 1905–06. On the bibliography consult B. Erdmannsdörfer, in *Historische Zeitschrift*, xiv (1865). Note also the very extensive classified list in *Cambridge Modern History*, iv. 801–953, New York, 1906. The most important collection of sources is *Briefe und Akten zur Geschichte des dreissigjährigen Kriegs*, begun in Munich in 1873, the 2d series issued at Leipsic and Munich (vols. viii. and xi., 1910). The best book for the English reader is the volume in the *Cambridge Modern History* already referred to. Consult further: A. W. Ward, *The Thirty Years' War*, London, 1869 (popular); S. R. Gardiner, *The Thirty Years' War*, ib. 1874 (admirable summary); E. Shebek, *Die Lösung der Wallensteinfrage*, Berlin, 1881; F. Des Robert, *Campagnes de Charles IV., duc de Lorraine*, 2 vols., Paris, 1883; J. W. De Peyster, *The Thirty Years' War. With Reference to the Operations of the Swedes*, Philadelphia, 1884; A. Gindely, *Illustrirte Geschichte des dreissigjährigen Krieges*, 3 vols., Prague, 1884, Eng. transls., *History of the Thirty Years' War*, 2 vols., London, 1885 (based on original documents); G. B. Malleson, *Battlefields of Germany from the Outbreak of the Thirty Years' War*, London, 1884; J. C. F. von Schiller, *Histoire de la guerre de trente ans*, Paris, 1884; J. Buehring, *Venedig, Gustav Adolf und Rohan*, Halle, 1885; A. Gaedeke, *Wallensteins Verhandlungen mit den Schweden*, Frankfort, 1885; T. V. Bilek, *Beiträge zur Geschichte Waldsteins*, Prague, 1886; R. C. Trench, *Gustavus Adolphus in Germany*, London, 1886 (gives social aspects); A. C. Hennequin, *Tilly, 1618 à 1632*, Lille, 1887; G. Droysen, *Das Zeitalter des dreissigjährigen Krieges*, Berlin, 1888; A. Ledieu, *Esquisses de la guerre de trente ans*, Lille, 1888; M. Ritter, *Deutsche Geschichte im Zeitalter der Gegenreformation und des dreissigjährigen Krieges*, 3 vols., Stuttgart, 1889–1908 (authoritative); A. Weskamp, *Das Heer der Liga in Westfalen, 1622–23*, Münster, 1891; O. Klopp, *Der dreissigjährige Krieg bis zum Tode Gustav Adolfs, 1632*, 3 vols., Paderborn, 1891–96; G. Winter, *Geschichte des dreissigjährigen Krieges*, Berlin, 1893; W. Leinung and R. Stumvoll, *Aus Magdeburgs Sage und Geschichte*, Magdeburg, 1894; W. Struck, *Johann Georg und Oxenstierna. Von dem Tode Gustav Adolfs, Nov. 1632, bis 1633*, Stralsund, 1899; G. Egelhaaf, *Gustav Adolf in Deutschland, 1630–32*, Halle, 1901; F. Lippert, *Geschichte der Gegenreformation im Oberpfalz-Kurpfalz zur Zeit des dreissigjährigen Krieges*, Freiburg, 1901; J. Wagner, *Die Chronik des J. Wagner über die Zeit der schwedischen Okkupation in Augsburg, 1632–35*, Augsburg, 1902; C. Jahnel, *Der dreissigjährige Krieg in Aussig*, Prague, 1903; C. Jacob, *Von Lützen nach Nördlingen 1633–34*, Strasburg, 1904; W. Stubbs (Bp. of Oxford), *Lectures on European History. Europe during the Thirty Years' War*, London, 1904; H. Teitga, *Die Frage nach dem Urheber der Zerstörung Magdeburgs 1631*, Halle, 1904; J. B. Mehler, *General Tilly, der Siegreiche*, Munich, 1905; F. Pieth, *Die Feldzüge des Herzogs Rohan im Veltlin und in Graubunden 1635–37*, Bern, 1905; E. Noel, *Gustav Adolf, King of Sweden*, London, 1905.

THISTED, WALDEMAR ADOLPH: Danish poet; b. in Aarhus (100 m. n.w. of Copenhagen), Denmark, Feb. 28, 1815; d. in Copenhagen Oct. 14, 1887. He became a teacher in 1845; a minister in Sleswick, 1855; and, in 1862, in Tömmerup, Zealand. His romances and stories were very popular; he was the author, under pseudonym of Rowel, of *Breve fra Helvede* (Copenhagen, 1866; English translation, *Letters from Hell*, 2 vols., London, 1866; 1 vol., New York, 1885); and, under the pseudonyms of Em. Saint Hermidad and Herodion, of many other publications.

THOBURN, JAMES MILLS: Methodist Episcopal bishop; b. at St. Clairsville, O., Mar. 7, 1836. He was educated at Alleghany College, Meadville, Pa. (A.B., 1857); was circuit preacher in Ohio (1857–1859); went to India as a missionary, being stationed successively at Naini Tal, Pauri, Moradabad, Lucknow, Calcutta, and Simla from 1859 to 1886. He was then presiding elder of the Indian conference in the United States (1886–88), and in 1888 was elected missionary bishop of his church, with residence at Calcutta until 1896 and subsequently at Bombay. His jurisdiction extends over the Philippines. He is the author of *My Missionary Apprenticeship* (New York, 1884); *Missionary Sermons* (1888); *India and Malaysia* (1893); *The Deaconess and her Vocation* (1893); *Light in the East* (1894); *The Christless Nations* (1895); *The Church of Pentecost* (1899); *Life of Isabella Thoburn* (1903); *The Christian Conquest of India* (1906); and *India and Southern Asia* (1907).

BIBLIOGRAPHY: W. H. Crawford, ed., *Thoburn and India*, New York, 1909.

THOLUCK, tō′luk, **FRIEDRICH AUGUST GOTTREU:** German divine and pulpit orator; b. at Breslau Mar. 30, 1799; d. at Halle June 10, 1877. Descended from very humble parentage, he first learned a trade, but by the assistance of friends attended the gymnasium of his native city, and the university of Berlin. When he left college, he delivered an address on " The Superiority of the Oriental World over the Christian," which was chiefly a eulogy on Mohammedanism. But during his university course he was thoroughly converted from his pantheism and skepticism, under the influence of the lectures of Schleiermacher and Neander, and more especially by personal intercourse with Baron Ernst von Kottwitz, a member of the Moravian brotherhood, who combined high social standing and culture with an amiable type of piety. In 1821 he was graduated as licentiate of theology, and began to deliver lectures as privat-docent; in 1824 he was appointed extraordinary professor of oriental literature. In 1825 he made a literary journey to Holland and England at the expense of the Prussian government, and in 1826 was called to the university of Halle as ordinary professor of theology, which position he occupied till his death, with the exception of a brief period (1827–29), which he spent in Rome as chaplain of the Prussian embassy. In Halle he had at first to suffer much opposition and reproach from the prevailing rationalism of his colleagues (Gesenius and Wegscheider), but succeeded in effecting a radical change; and the whole theological faculty of Halle later became decidedly Evangelical. On Dec. 2, 1870, his friends celebrated the jubilee of his professorship. The university and magistrate of Halle and delegates of several universities and of all schools of theology took part in it; and his pupils in Europe and America founded a seminary adjoining his own home, for beneficiary students of theology, as a perpetual memorial of his devotion to students. He was always in delicate health, but by strict temperance and great regularity of habits he managed to do an unusual amount of work till within the last years of his life. He was incessant in his lectures, preached regularly as university chaplain, and found time to write many books.

His principal works are as follows: *Die Lehre von der Sünde und dem Versöhner, oder die wahre Weihe des Zweiflers* (Berlin, 1823, and often; Eng. transl., *Guido and Julius. The Doctrine of Sin and the Propitiator*, London, 1836; and *The Two Students, Guido and Julius*, 1855), written in answer to De Wette's *Theodor, oder des Zweiflers Weihe* (Berlin, 1822); *Blüthensammlung aus der morgenländischen Mystik* (1825), a collection of translations from the mystic poets of the East; Commentary on

Romans (1825; Eng. transl., Edinburgh, 1834–36, 1848), the first exegetical fruit of the new Evangelical theology; on John's Gospel (Hamburg, 1827; Eng. transl. Edinburgh, 1836, Philadelphia, 1859), less thorough and permanent, but more popular, and better adapted for students, than his other commentaries; on the Sermon on the Mount (1835; Eng. transls., 2 vols., Edinburgh 1834–37, 1860), his most learned, elaborate, and valuable exegetical production; on Hebrews (1836; Eng. transl., Edinburgh, 1842); and on Psalms (1843; Eng. transl., Philadelphia, 1858); *Die Glaubwürdigkeit der evangelischen Geschichte* (1837), a vindication of the Gospels against the mythical theory of Strauss; and *Stunden christlichen Andacht* (1840; several Eng. transls., *Hours of Devotion*, London, 1853, 1870, Edinburgh, 1873), containing several original hymns. In this book he pours out his fervent Evangelical piety with all the charm of fresh enthusiasm. He was one of the most eloquent German preachers of his day, and published a series of university sermons (collected in 5 vols., 3d ed., Gotha, 1863–64, Eng. transl. of one volume, *Light from the Cross, Sermons on the Passion of our Lord*, Philadelphia, 1858). He issued also two very interesting vols. of " Miscellaneous Essays " (1839). His last works were contributions to German church history since the Reformation, derived in part from manuscript sources; namely, *Lutherische Theologen Wittenbergs im 17. Jahrhundert* (Hamburg, 1852), *Das akademische Leben des 17. Jahrhundert* (2 vols., Hamburg, 1852, 1854), and *Geschichte des Rationalismus* (part i., Berlin, 1865, never finished). A complete edition of his works appeared 1863–72, in 11 vols. He also republished the commentaries of Calvin on the Gospels and Epistles, and his *Institutio Christianæ religionis*. He conducted for several years a literary periodical, and contributed largely to the first edition of the *Realencyklopädie für protestantische Theologie und Kirche* of Herzog.

Tholuck was one of the most fruitful and influential German theologians and authors during the second and third quarters of the nineteenth century, and better known in England and America than any other. He was original, fresh, brilliant, suggestive, eloquent, and full of poetry, wit, and humor. He can not be classed with any school. He was influenced by Pietism, Moravianism, Schleiermacher, Neander, and even Hegel. His elastic mind was ever open to new light; and his heart was always right, and never shaken from faith and love to Christ. He had an extraordinary talent for languages, studied nineteen foreign tongues before he was seventeen, and spoke English, French, Italian, Greek, Arabic, and several other tongues, ancient and modern, almost like a native. His learning was extensive rather than thorough and exhaustive. He was one of the regenerators of German theology, leading it from rationalism to the Scriptures and the literature of the Reformation. His commentaries broke a new path. His personal influence was as great and good as that exerted by his works, and yields only to that of Neander among his contemporaries. He was gifted with personal magnetism, and brilliant powers of conversation. Having no children, he devoted all his paternal affection to his students, and was nobly assisted by his second wife, a most amiable, refined Christian lady. He loved, as he said, candidates for the ministry more than the ministers, and students more than candidates, because he was more interested in the process of growth than in the results of growth. His life was a life with the young, fruitful in blessings. He was in the habit of taking long walks with two or three students every day from eleven to twelve, and from four to five: he invited them freely to his house and table, tried experiments on their minds, proposed perplexing questions, set them disputing on high problems, inspired and stimulated them in the pursuit of knowledge, virtue, and piety. He had great regard for individuality, and aimed to arouse in every one the sense of his peculiar calling rather than to create a school. His chief aim was to lead them to humble faith in the Savior, and to infuse into them that love which was the ruling passion of his own heart. He adopted, as he says, Zinzendorf's motto, " I have but one passion, and that is He, and He alone." His lecture-room was truly a school of Christ. And herein lies his chief significance and merit. Thousands of students from different lands owe to him their spiritual life. To Americans he was especially attached, and a most useful guide in the labyrinth of German theology. He was very intimate with Edward Robinson, Charles Hodge (who studied at Halle in 1827, and was daily in his company), Henry B. Smith, George L. Prentiss (who studied there in 1840), and Edwards A. Park of Andover. He was invited to the General Conference of the Evangelical Alliance in 1873, and promised to come (with the humorous remark, " I am afraid of your American mobs, your hot cakes for breakfast, *and especially of your kindness* "). But his feeble health prevented him; and he sent one of his favorite pupils, Leopold Witte, as his representative, with a modest sketch of his labors and the condition of theology in Germany. It is the last public document from his pen (except some letters), and gives a faithful idea of this lover of youth, who loved them for Christ's sake.

(PHILIP SCHAFF†.) D. S. SCHAFF.

BIBLIOGRAPHY: His *Lehre von der Sünde*, ut sup., is in part autobiographical, Guido representing him. Letters will be found in the biography of Charles Hodge by A. A. Hodge, New York, 1880, in that of H. B. Smith, by Mrs. H. B. Smith, ib, 1880, cf. that of Philip Schaff by D. S. Schaff, passim. The authorized " Life " is by L. Witte, 2 vols., Bielefeld, 1884–86; an autobiographical sketch with a paper by Witte is in the *Proceedings of the Evangelical Alliance Conference of 1873*, pp. 85–89, New York, 1874. Consult further: P. Schaff, *Germany; its Universities, Theology, and Religion,* chap. xxvi., Philadelphia, 1857; idem, in *Presbyterian Review,* 1871, pp. 295–300; M. Tholuck, *Erinnerungen an Tholuck's Heimgang,* Leipsic, 1892; M. Kähler, *August Tholucks Gedächtnis,* ib. 1899; idem, *Erinnerungen an August und Mathilde Tholuck,* ib. 1899.

THOMA, tō′mä, **ALBRECHT:** German Protestant; b. at Dertingen (a village near Wertheim, 20 m. w. of Würzburg), Baden, Dec. 2, 1844. He was educated at the universities of Heidelberg (1865–67) and Jena (1867–68), and at the seminary for preachers at Heidelberg (1868–69); after which he was curate in Baden (1869–71), Bremen (1871–1872), Neunkirchen (1872), Freiburg (1872–73), Lörrach (1873–75), and Mannheim (1875–80).

Since 1880 he has been professor of German and history at the normal school in Carlsruhe. In theology his position is liberal. Among his numerous writings mention may be made of his *Geschichte der christlichen Sittenlehre in der Zeit des Neuen Testaments* (Haarlem, 1879); *Die Genesis des Johannes-Evangeliums* (Berlin, 1882); *Dr. Luthers Leben fürs deutsche Haus* (1883); *Ein Ritt ins Gelobte Land, Land und Leute in Palästina vor 3,000 Jahren* (1887); *Das Leben Gustav Adolfs fürs deutsche Volk* (Carlsruhe, 1894); *Unterm Christbaum, Weinachtsgeschichten* (1895); *Philipp Melanchthons Leben* (1897); *Geschichte des Klosters Frauenalb* (Freiburg, 1898); *Katharina von Bora* (Berlin, 1900); *Konrad Widerholt, der Kommandant von Hohentwiel* (Munich, 1903); *Bernhard von Weimar* (Weimar, 1904); *Der Sternensohn. Geschichtliche Erzählung aus der Zeit des Kaisers Hadrian* (Bielefeld, 1908); and *Jesus und die Apostel* (Gotha, 1910).

THOMAS À BECKET. See BECKET, THOMAS.

THOMAS À JESU: Portuguese Augustinian ascetic, brother of Didacus (Diogo) Andrada (q.v.); b. at Lisbon 1529; d. among the Moors in North Africa Apr. 17, 1582. He entered the Augustinian order in 1548; studied philosophy and theology at Coimbra, and then went to Lisbon, where he became master of novices; he developed a tendency toward extreme asceticism, for the furthering of which he proposed to found a monastery under stricter rules, though this met with opposition; he carried out his own ideal in person at Penhaferma, where he became a preacher; he was taken as field chaplain to Africa by King Sebastian in his campaign against the Moors, by whom he was wounded and taken prisoner, and in prison wrote his *Trabalhos de Jesus* (Lisbon, 1602), which was translated into several European languages. He was sold as a slave, but was released through the efforts of the Portuguese ambassador, but preferred to stay in Morocco to minister to the needs of other prisoners and the poor, for the accomplishment of which he sought and obtained the help of the wealthy. His last illness was contracted while engaged in these works of mercy. He wrote also a " Life " of Louis de Montroya (Lisbon, 1618); *Praxis veræ fidei* (Cologne, 1629); and also *De oratione Dominica* (Antwerp, 1623).

BIBLIOGRAPHY: His " Life " by A. de Menezes is prefixed to an edition of the *Trabalhos,* published at Lisbon, 1733. Cf. *KL,* xi. 1671–73.

THOMAS À KEMPIS. See KEMPIS.

THOMAS THE APOSTLE: In the Synoptic lists of the apostles (Matt. x. 3; Mark iii. 18; Luke vi. 15) Thomas is paired with Matthew, but in the Acts (i. 13) with Philip. The name (translated into the Greek Didymus, John xi. 16, xx. 24, xxi. 2) means " twin " and was doubtless the personal name of the apostle, most likely as recalling the facts at his birth, possibly given after the death of the other twin. It surely was not given by Jesus on account of Thomas's native disposition toward doubt. Thomas does not figure in the Synoptic Gospels outside of the lists of the apostles, while in the Fourth Gospel he stands out clearly with marked characteristics (xi. 6, xiv. 5, xx. 25–28). His nature is positive, like Peter's, but with contrary leanings, since Peter was optimistic and Thomas pessimistic. He is noted for his desire for certain and experiential knowledge, without which he was uncertain and undetermined (cf. John xiv. 5), as when he wished personal and irrefutable experience of the fact of Jesus' resurrection (John xx. 25–28).

All extra-Biblical reports are untrustworthy, including those which identify him with other Biblical personages especially in the Syrian Church. The Curetonian and Sinaitic Syriac furnish examples of identification with Judas in John xiv. 22, others are in the Syriac Didache, Abulfaraj (*Chron. eccl.*, iii. 2), Ephraem Syrus (cf. Burkitt, in *TS*, vii. 2, 4), Eusebius (*Hist. eccl.*, i., xiii., Syriac text). The defense of this identification by Resch (*TU.*, x. 3, pp. 824 sqq.), who explains Judas-James as brother of James and sees the other twin in James-Alpheus and distinguishes Lebbæus-Thaddeus from Judas-James, has no foundation. Still more startling is the identification of Thomas with Judas son of Joseph and brother of Jesus, which makes him the twin brother of Jesus; this occurs first in the Acts of Thomas [§ 31], at the basis of which is probably a Syriac original, but outside the Syrian Church is found only in Priscillian, who in this twin brother sees the apostle (John xx. 26 sqq.) and the author of I John (cf. Zahn, *Forschungen*, v. 116, 123, vi. 346 sqq.). As untrustworthy as these suppositions is the statement that Thomas was a native of Paneas in Galilee (cf. R. A. Lipsius, *Apokryphen, Apostelgeschichten und Apostellegenden*, i. 246, Brunswick, 1883). Similarly the reports of ecclesiastical tradition are pure fiction. The earliest form of this sends him to work in Parthia (Eusebius, *Hist. eccl.* III., i., and often elsewhere), and his grave was sought in Edessa (S. J. Assemani, *Bibliotheca orientalis*, i. 49, Rome, 1719) and his death naturally was located there (Clement of Alexandria, *Strom.*, IV., ix. 73), while this report brings him into connection also with the Abgar legend (see ABGAR). A later development in the beginning of the fourth century sends him to India, where he suffers a martyr death. This is brought into relation with the Edessa story by reporting the carrying of his body back to Edessa, a story without historical foundation (in spite of W. Germann, *Die Kirche der Thomaschristen*, pp. 20 sqq., Gütersloh, 1877). The source of these later stories is the Gnostic Acts of Thomas (ed. M. Bonnet, *Supplementum codicis apocryphi*, vol. i., Leipsic, 1883). A later redaction of this legend dates from the seventh century, affirming that Thomas converted Parthians, Medes, Persians, and Indians and died a martyr in Calamine in India (J. J. Grynäus, *Monumenta patrum orthodoxagrapha*, ii. 589, Basel, 1569). The Thomas Christians (see NESTORIANS) have a tradition, conditioned by the Gnostic Acts of Thomas, which makes him a martyr in Mailapur.   (E. SIEFFERT.)

BIBLIOGRAPHY: The sources are quite fully indicated in the text. The reader is referred to the Bible dictionaries, notably: *DB*, iv. 753–754; *EB*, iv. 5057–59; *DCG*, ii. 728–729. McGiffert discusses the early accounts in his transl. of Eusebius, *Hist. eccl.*, in *NPNF*, 1 ser., i. 100, 101, 104, 132, 156, 171. The fullest account of the legends concerning Thomas are in the work of Lipsius named in the text, i. 225–347. Consult further W. Wright,

Apocryphal Acts of the Apostles, London, 1871; T. Schermann, *Propheten und Apostellegenden*, Leipsic, 1907; F. Wilhelm, *Deutsche Legenden und Legendare*, ib. 1907. The apocryphal Gospel according to Thomas was edited by C. Tischendorf in *Evangelia Apocrypha*, Leipsic, 1853, 2d ed., 1876, and an Eng. transl. is furnished by B. H. Cowper, *The Apocryphal Gospels*, pp. 118–170, London, 1867; and by A. Walker, *Apocryphal Gospels, Acts, and Revelations*, pp. 78–99, ib. 1873, who gives also transl. of the Acts of Thomas, pp. 389–422. The text of the Acts of Thomas are in C. Tischendorf, *Acta Apostolorum apocrypha*, pp. 190–234, cf. pp. lxiii.–lxix., 235–242. For Eng. transl. of the "Preaching" and "Martyrdom" of St. Thomas" cf. Agnes Smith Lewis, *Horæ Semiticæ*, iv. 80–99, London, 1904. B. Pick, in *Apocryphal Acts*, pp. 222–362, Chicago, 1909, gives Eng. transl. of the Acts of Thomas. Consult also A. E. Medlycott, *India and the Apostle Thomas: an Inquiry; with a critical Analysis of the Acta Thomæ*, London, 1905.

THOMAS AQUINAS.

The birth-year of Thomas Aquinas is commonly given as 1227, but he was probably born early in 1225 at his father's castle of Roccasecca (75 m. e.s.e. of Rome) in Neapolitan territory. He died at the monastery of Fossanova, one mile from Sonnino (64 m. s.e. of Rome), Mar. 7, 1274.

1. Life. His father was Count Landulf of an old high-born south Italian family, and his mother was Countess Theodora of Theate, of noble Norman descent. In his fifth year he was sent for his early education to the monastery of Monte Cassino, where his father's brother Sinibald was abbot. Later he studied in Naples. Probably in 1243 he determined to enter the Dominican order; but on the way to Rome he was seized by his brothers and brought back to his parents at the castle of S. Giovanni, where he was held a captive for a year or two and besieged with prayers, threats, and even sensual temptation to make him relinquish his purpose. Finally the family yielded and the order sent Thomas to Cologne to study under Albertus Magnus (q.v.), where he arrived probably toward the end of 1244. He accompanied Albertus to Paris in 1245, remained there with his teacher, continuing his studies for three years, and followed Albertus at the latter's return to Cologne in 1248. For several years longer he remained with the famous philosopher of scholasticism, presumably teaching. This long association of Thomas with the great polyhistor was the most important influence in his development; it made him a comprehensive scholar and won him permanently for the Aristotelian method. In 1252 probably Thomas went to Paris for the master's degree, which he found some difficulty in attaining owing to attacks, at that time, on the mendicant orders. Ultimately, however, he received the degree and entered ceremoniously upon his office of teaching in 1257; he taught in Paris for several years and there wrote certain of his works and began others. In 1259 he was present at an important chapter of his order at Valenciennes. At the solicitation of Pope Urban IV. (therefore not before the latter part of 1261), he took up his residence in Rome. In 1269–71 he was again active in Paris. In 1272 the provincial chapter at Florence empowered him to found a new *studium generale* at such place as he should choose, and he selected Naples. Early in 1274 the pope directed him to attend the Council of Lyons and he undertook the journey, although he was far from well. On the way he stopped at the castle of a niece and there became seriously ill. He wished to end his days in a monastery and not being able to reach a house of the Dominicans he was carried to the Cistercian Fossanova. There, first, after his death, his remains were preserved.

Thomas made a remarkable impression on all who knew him, as represented in contemporary biographies. He was placed on a level with Paul and Augustine, receiving the title *doctor angelicus.*

2. Personality and Character. In 1319 the investigation preliminary to canonization was begun and on July 18, 1323, he was pronounced saint by John XXII. at Avignon. Thomas is described as of large stature, corpulent, and dark-complexioned; he had a large head and was somewhat bald in front. His manners and bearing accorded with his noble birth; he was refined, affable, and lovable. In argument he maintained self-control and won his opponents by his superior personality and great learning. His tastes were simple and his requirements few. His associates were specially impressed by his power of memory; but the passion of his soul was the search for the truth involving the inner struggle for the knowledge of God. Absorbed in thought he often forgot his surroundings. His admirers honestly believed him to be inspired, and it was reported that Peter, Paul, and Christ instructed him in visions. What he attained by such strenuous absorption he knew how to express for others systematically, with remarkable clearness and simplicity. In his writings he does not, like Duns, make the reader his associate in the search for truth, but he teaches it authoritatively. Thomas became the teacher of his church and has always remained such. The consciousness of the insufficiency of his works in view of the revelation which he believed to have received was often to him an oppressive burden.

The writings of Thomas may be classified as, (1) exegetical, homiletical, and liturgical; (2) dogmatic, apologetic, and ethical; and (3) philosophical. Among the genuine works of the first class were: Commentaries on Job (1261–65); on Psalms i.–li., according to some a

3. Writings. *reportatum,* or report of oral deliverances furnished by his companion Raynaldus; on Isaiah; the *Catena aurea* (1475, and often; Eng. transl., ed. by J. H. Newman, 4 vols., Oxford, 1841–45), which is a running commentary on the four Gospels, constructed on numerous citations from the Fathers; probably a Commentary on Canticles, and on Jeremiah; and wholly or partly *reportata,* on John, on Matthew, and on the epistles of Paul, including, according to one authority, Hebrews i.–x. Thomas prepared for Urban IV., *Officium de corpore Christi* (1264); and the following works may be either genuine or

reportata: Expositio angelicæ salutationis; Tractatus de decem præceptis; Orationis dominicæ expositio; Sermones pro dominicis diebus et pro sanctorum solemnitatibus; and L. Pignon knows *Sermones de angelis,* and *Sermones de quadragesima.* Of his sermons only manipulated copies are extant. In the second division were: *In quatuor sententiarum libros,* of his first Paris sojourn; *Questiones disputatæ,* written at Paris and Rome; *Quæstiones quodlibetales duodecim; Summa catholicæ fidei contra gentiles* (1261–64); and the *Summa theologiæ.* To the dogmatic works belong also certain commentaries, as follows: *Expositio in librum beati Dionysii de divinis nominibus; Expositiones primæ et secundæ decretalis; In Boethii libros de hebdomadibus;* and *Præclaræ quæstiones super librum Boethii de trinitate.* A large number of *opuscula* also belonged to this group. Of philosophical writings there are calatogued thirteen commentaries on Aristotle, besides numerous philosophical opuscula of which fourteen are classed as genuine.

The greatest work of Thomas was the *Summa* and it is the fullest presentation of his views. He worked on it from the time of Clement IV. (after 1265) until the end of his life. When he died he had reached question ninety of part iii., on the subject of penance. What was lacking was afterward added from the fourth book of his commentary on the "Sentences" of Peter Lombard as a *supplementum,* which is not found in manuscripts of the thirteenth and fourteenth centuries. The *Summa* was translated into Greek (apparently by Maximus Planudes, c. 1327), into Armenian, into many European tongues, and even into Chinese. It consists of three parts. Part i. treats of God, who is the "first cause, himself uncaused" (*primum movens immobile*) and as such existent only in act (*actu*), that is pure actuality without potentiality and, therefore, without corporeality. His essence is *actus purus et perfectus.* This follows from the fivefold proof for the existence of God; namely, there must be a first mover, unmoved, a first cause in the chain of causes, an absolutely necessary being, an absolutely perfect being, and a rational designer. In this connection the thoughts of the unity, infinity, unchangeableness, and goodness of the highest being are deduced. The spiritual being of God is further defined as thinking and willing. His knowledge is absolutely perfect since he knows himself and all things as appointed by him. Since every knowing being strives after the thing known as end, will is implied in knowing. Inasmuch as God knows himself as the perfect good, he wills himself as end. But in that everything is willed by God, everything is brought by the divine will to himself in the relation of means to end. Therein God wills good to every being which exists, that is he loves it; and, therefore, love is the fundamental relation of God to the world. If the divine love be thought of simply as act of will, it exists for every creature in like measure: but if the good assured by love to the individual be thought of, it exists for different beings in various degrees. In so far as the loving God gives to every being what it needs in relation

4. The Summa, Part i.; Theology.

to the whole, he is just: in so far as he thereby does away with misery, he is merciful. In every work of God both justice and mercy are united and, indeed, his justice always presupposes his mercy, since he owes no one anything and gives more bountifully than is due. As God rules in the world, the " plan of the order of things " preexists in him; i.e., his providence and the exercise of it in his government are what condition as cause everything which comes to pass in the world. Hence follows predestination: from eternity some are destined to eternal life, while as concerns others " he permits some to fall short of that end." Reprobation, however, is more than mere foreknowledge; it is the " will of permitting anyone to fall into sin and incur the penalty of condemnation for sin." The effect of predestination is grace. Since God is the first cause of everything, he is the cause of even the free acts of men through predestination. Determinism is deeply grounded in the system of Thomas; things with their source of becoming in God are ordered from eternity as means for the realization of his end in himself. On moral grounds Thomas advocates freedom energetically; but, with his premises, he can have in mind only the psychological form of self-motivation. Nothing in the world is accidental or free, although it may appear so in reference to the proximate cause. From this point of view miracles become necessary in themselves and are to be considered merely as inexplicable to man. From the point of view of the first cause all is unchangeable; although from the limited point of view of the secondary cause miracles may be spoken of. In his doctrine of the Trinity Thomas starts from the Augustinian system. Since God has only the functions of thinking and willing, only two *processiones* can be asserted from the Father. But these establish definite relations of the persons of the Trinity one to another. The relations must be conceived as real and not as merely ideal; for, as with creatures relations arise through certain accidents, since in God there is no accident but all is substance, it follows that " the relation really existing in God is the same as the essence according to the thing." From another side, however, the relations as real must be really distinguished one from another. Therefore, three persons are to be affirmed in God. Man stands opposite to God; he consists of soul and body. The " intellectual soul " consists of intellect and will. Furthermore the soul is the absolutely indivisible form of man; it is immaterial substance, but not one and the same in all men (as the Averrhoists assumed). The soul's power of knowing has two sides; a passive (the *intellectus possibilis*) and an active (the *intellectus agens*). It is the capacity to form concepts and to abstract the mind's images (*species*) from the objects perceived by sense. But since what the intellect abstracts from individual things is a universal, the mind knows the universal primarily and directly, and knows the singular only indirectly by virtue of a certain *reflexio* (cf. Scholasticism). As certain principles are immanent in the mind for its speculative activity, so also a " special disposition of works," or the *synderesis* (rudiment of conscience), is inborn in the

" practical reason," affording the idea of the moral law of nature, so important in medieval ethics.

The first part of the *Summa* is summed up in the thought that God governs the world as the " universal first cause." God sways the intellect in that he gives the power to know and impresses the *species intelligibiles* on the mind, and he sways the will in that he holds the good before

5. The Summa, Part ii.; Ethics.
it as aim, and creates the *virtus volendi*. " To will is nothing else than a certain inclination toward the object of the volition which is the universal good."

God works all in all, but so that things also themselves exert their proper efficiency. Here the Areopagitic ideas of the graduated effects of created things play their part in Thomas's thought. The second part of the *Summa* (two parts, *prima secundæ* and *secundæ secunda*) follows this complex of ideas. Its theme is man's striving after the highest end, which is the blessedness of the *visio beata*. Here Thomas develops his system of ethics, which has its root in Aristotle. In a chain of acts of will man strives for the highest end. They are free acts in so far as man has in himself the knowledge of their end and therein the principle of action. In that the will wills the end, it wills also the appropriate means, chooses freely and completes the *consensus*. Whether the act be good or evil depends on the end. The " human reason " pronounces judgment concerning the character of the end, it is, therefore, the law for action. Human acts, however, are meritorious in so far as they promote the purpose of God and his honor. By repeating a good action man acquires a moral habit or a quality which enables him to do the good gladly and easily. This is true, however, only of the intellectual and moral virtues, which Thomas treats after the manner of Aristotle; the theological virtues are imparted by God to man as a " disposition," from which the acts here proceed, but while they strengthen, they do not form it. The " disposition " of evil is the opposite alternative. An act becomes evil through deviation from the reason and the divine moral law. Therefore, sin involves two factors: its substance or matter is lust; in form, however, it is deviation from the divine law. Sin has its origin in the will, which decides, against the reason, for a " changeable good." Since, however, the will also moves the other powers of man, sin has its seat in these too. By choosing such a lower good as end, the will is misled by self-love, so that this works as cause in every sin. God is not the cause of sin, since, on the contrary, he draws all things to himself. But from another side God is the cause of all things, so he is efficacious also in sin as *actio* but not as *ens*. The devil is not directly the cause of sin, but he incites by working on the imagination and the sensuous impulse of man, as men or things may also do. Sin is original. Adam's first sin passes upon himself and all the succeeding race; because he is the head of the human race and " by virtue of procreation human nature is transmitted and along with nature its infection." The powers of generation are, therefore, designated especially as " infected." The thought is involved here by the fact that Thomas, like the other scholastics, held to creationism, therefore taught that the souls are created by God. Two things according to Thomas constituted man's righteousness in paradise—the *justitia originalis* or the harmony of all man's powers before they were blighted by desire, and the possession of the *gratia gratum faciens* (the continuous indwelling power of good). Both are lost through original sin, which in form is the "loss of original righteousness." The consequence of this loss is the disorder and maiming of man's nature, which shows itself in "ignorance, malice, moral weakness, and especially in *concupiscentia*, which is the material principle of original sin." The course of thought here is as follows: when the first man transgressed the order of his nature appointed by nature and grace, he, and with him the human race, lost this order. This negative state is the essence of original sin. From it follow an impairment and perversion of human nature in which thenceforth lower aims rule contrary to nature and release the lower element in man. Since sin is contrary to the divine order, it is guilt and subject to punishment. Guilt and punishment correspond to each other; and since the "apostasy from the invariable good which is infinite," fulfilled by man, is unending, it merits everlasting punishment.

But God works even in sinners to draw them to the end by "instructing through the law and aiding by grace." The law is the "precept of the practical reason." As the moral law of nature, it is the participation of the reason in the all-determining "eternal reason." But since man falls short in his appropriation of this law of reason, there is need of a "divine law." And since the law applies to many complicated relations, the *practicæ dispositiones* of the human law must be laid down. The divine law consists of an old and a new. In so far as the old divine law contains the moral law of nature it is universally valid; what there is in it, however, beyond this is valid only for the Jews. The new law is "primarily grace itself" and so a "law given within," "a gift superadded to nature by grace," but not a "written law." In this sense, as sacramental grace, the new law justifies. It contains, however, an "ordering" of external and internal conduct, and so regarded is, as a matter of course, identical with both the old law and the law of nature. The *consilia* (see CONSILIA EVANGELICA) show how one may attain the end "better and more expediently" by full renunciation of worldly goods. Since man is sinner and creature, he needs grace to reach the final end. The "first cause" alone is able to reclaim him to the "final end." This is true after the fall, although it was needful before. Grace is, on one side, "the free act of God," and, on the other side, "the effect of this act, the *gratia infusa* or *gratia creata*, a *habitus infusus* which is instilled into the "essence of the soul," "a certain gift of disposition, something supernatural proceeding from God into man." Grace is a supernatural ethical character created in man by God, which comprises in itself all good, both faith and love. Justification by grace comprises four elements: "the infusion of grace, the influencing of free will toward God through faith, the influencing of free will respecting sin, and the remission of sins." It is a "transmutation of the human soul," and takes place "instantaneously." A creative act of God enters, which, however, executes itself as a spiritual motive in a psychological form corresponding to the nature of man. Semipelagian tendencies are far removed from Thomas. In that man is created anew he believes and loves, and now sin is forgiven. Then begins good conduct; grace is the "beginning of meritorious works." Thomas conceives of merit in the Augustinian sense: God gives the reward for that toward which he himself gives the power. Man can never of himself deserve the *prima gratia*, nor *meritum de congruo* (by natural ability; cf. R. Seeberg, *Lehrbuch der Dogmengeschichte*, ii. 105–106, Leipsic, 1898). After thus stating the principles of morality, in the *secunda secundæ* Thomas comes to a minute exposition of his ethics according to the scheme of the virtues. The conceptions of faith and love are of much significance in the complete system of Thomas. Man strives toward the highest good with the will or through love. But since the end must first be "apprehended in the intellect," knowledge of the end to be loved must precede love; "because the will can not strive after God in perfect love unless the intellect have true faith toward him." Inasmuch as this truth which is to be known is practical it first incites the will, which then brings the reason to "assent." But since, furthermore, the good in question is transcendent and inaccessible to man by himself, it requires the infusion of a supernatural "capacity" or "disposition" to make man capable of faith as well as love. Accordingly the object of both faith and love is God, involving also the entire complex of truths and commandments which God reveals, in so far as they in fact relate to God and lead to him. Thus faith becomes recognition of the teachings and precepts of the Scriptures and the Church ("the first subjection of man to God is by faith"). The object of faith, however, is by its nature object of love; therefore faith comes to completion only in love ("by love is the act of faith accomplished and formed").

The way which leads to God is Christ: and Christ is the theme of part iii. It can not be asserted that the incarnation was absolutely necessary, "since God in his omnipotent power could have repaired human nature in many other ways": but it was the most suitable way both for the purpose of instruction and of satisfaction. The *Unio* between the Logos and the human nature is a "relation" between the divine and the human nature which comes about by both natures being brought together in the one person of the Logos. An incarnation can be spoken of only in the sense that the human nature began to be in the eternal hypostasis of the divine nature. So Christ is *unum* since his human nature lacks the hypostasis. The person of the Logos, accordingly, has assumed the impersonal human nature, and in such way that the assumption of the soul became the means for the assumption of the body. This union with the human soul is the *gratia unionis* which leads to the impartation of the

6. The Summa, Part iii.; Christ.

gratia habitualis from the Logos to the human nature. Thereby all human potentialities are made perfect in Jesus. Besides the perfections given by the vision of God, which Jesus enjoyed from the beginning, he receives all others by the *gratia habitualis*. In so far, however, as it is the limited human nature which receives these perfections, they are finite. This holds both of the knowledge and the will of Christ. The Logos impresses the *species intelligibiles* of all created things on the soul, but the *intellectus agens* transforms them gradually into the impressions of sense. On another side the soul of Christ works miracles only as instrument of the Logos, since omnipotence in no way appertains to this human soul in itself. Furthermore, Christ's human nature partook of imperfections, on the one side to make its true humanity evident, on another side because he would bear the general consequences of sin for humanity. Christ experienced suffering, but blessedness reigned in his soul, which, however, did not extend to his body. Concerning redemption, Thomas teaches that Christ is to be regarded as redeemer after his human nature but in such way that the human nature produces divine effects as organ of divinity. The one side of the work of redemption consists herein, that Christ as head of humanity imparts *ordo*, *perfectio*, and *virtus* to his members. He is the teacher and example of humanity; his whole life and suffering as well as his work after he is exalted serve this end. The love wrought hereby in men effects, according to Luke vii. 47, the forgiveness of sins.

This is the first course of thought. Then follows a second complex of thoughts which has the idea of satisfaction as its center. To be sure, God as the highest being could forgive sins without satisfaction; but because his justice and mercy could be best revealed through satisfaction he chose this way. As little, however, as satisfaction is necessary in itself, so little does it offer an equivalent, in a correct sense, for guilt; it is rather a " superabundant satisfaction," since on account of the divine subject in Christ in a certain sense his suffering and activity are infinite. With this thought the strict logical deduction of Anselm's theory is given up. Christ's suffering bore personal character in that it proceeded " out of love and obedience." It was an offering brought to God, which as personal act had the character of merit. Thereby Christ " merited " salvation for men. As Christ, exalted, still influences men, so does he still work in their behalf continually in heaven through the intercession (*interpellatio*). In this way Christ as head of humanity effects the forgiveness of their sins, their reconciliation with God, their immunity from punishment, deliverance from the devil, and the opening of heaven's gate. But inasmuch as all these benefits are already offered through the inner operation of the love of Christ, Thomas has combined the theories of Anselm and Abelard by joining the one to the other.

The doctrine of the sacraments follows the Christology; for the sacraments " have efficacy from the incarnate Word himself." The sacraments are signs, which, however, not only signify sanctification but also effect it. That they bring spiritual gifts in sensuous form, moreover, is inevitable because of the sensuous nature of man. The *res sensibiles* are the matter, the words of institution the form of the sacraments. Contrary to the Franciscan view that the sacraments are mere symbols whose efficacy God accompanies with a directly following creative act in the soul, Thomas holds it not unfit to say with Hugo of St. Victor that " a sacrament contains grace," or to teach of the sacraments that they " cause grace." The difficulty of a sensuous thing producing a creative effect, Thomas attempts to remove by a distinction between the *causa principalis et instrumentalis*. God as the principal cause works through the sensuous thing as the means ordained by him for his end. " Just as instrumental power is acquired by the instrument from this, that it is moved by the principal agent, so also the sacrament obtains spiritual power from the benediction of Christ and the application of the minister to the use of the sacrament. There is spiritual power in the sacraments in so far as they have been ordained by God for a spiritual effect." And this spiritual power remains in the sensuous thing until it has attained its purpose. At the same time Thomas distinguished the *gratia sacramentalis* from the *gratia virtutum et donorum*, in that the former in general perfects the essence and the powers of the soul, and the latter in particular brings to pass necessary spiritual effects for the Christian life. Later this distinction was ignored. In a single statement the effect of the sacraments is to infuse justifying grace into men. What Christ effects is achieved through the sacraments. Christ's humanity was the instrument for the operation of his divinity; the sacraments are the instruments through which this operation of Christ's humanity passes over to men. Christ's humanity served his divinity as *instrumentum conjunctum*, like the hand: the sacraments are *instrumenta separata*, like a staff; the former can use the latter, as the hand can use a staff. For a more detailed exposition cf. Seeberg, *ut sup.*, ii. 112 sqq. Of Thomas' eschatology, according to the commentary on the " Sentences," only a brief account can here be given. Everlasting blessedness consists for Thomas in the vision of God: and this vision consists not in an abstraction or in a mental image supernaturally produced, but the divine substance itself is beheld, and in such manner that God himself becomes immediately the form of the beholding intellect; that is, God is the object of the vision and at the same time causes the vision. The perfection of the blessed also demands that the body be restored to the soul as something to be made perfect by it. Since blessedness consist in *operatio*, it is made more perfect in that the soul has a definite *operatio* with the body, although the peculiar act of blessedness (i.e., the vision of God) has nothing to do with the body.

For two gifts before all others is Thomas to be praised; namely, his great talent for systematizing and his power of simple and lucid exposition. To be sure the work of preceding generations, especially of Alexander of Hales, had lightened his task as concerns the selection and ordering of the material;

7. The Sacraments.

but on the other hand it had added to the number of problems and expanded the learned apparatus enormously, thereby impairing the

8. Estimation. unity and clarity of the progress of thought. It was Thomas who made a single connected and consistent whole of all this unwieldy mass of stuff. Next his decided Aristotelianism, not without an admixture of Neoplatonic elements, must be noted. He owed not only his philosophical thoughts and world-conception to Aristotle, but he also took from him the frame for his theological system; Aristotle's metaphysics and ethics furnished the trend of his system. Herein he gained the purely rational framework for his massive temple of thought, namely of God, the rational cause of the world, and man's striving after him. Then he filled this in with the dogmas of the Church or of revelation. And at all points he succeeded in upholding the church doctrine as credible and reasonable. This is the final characteristic of Thomas to be noted, his blameless orthodoxy. For opposition to Thomas and the reaction in the fifteenth century, see SCHOLASTICISM, III., 2, § 2. This position as the teacher of the church has grown ever stronger from Leo X. to Leo XIII.; and even to-day the Roman Catholic Church preserves the inheritance of the ancient world-conception and the old church dogmas in the form which Thomas Aquinas gave them. For the relation of theology to philosophy and the sphere of the former and its sources, see SCHOLASTICISM.

(R. SEEBERG.)

BIBLIOGRAPHY: Editions of the *Opera* may be noted as follows: 17 vols., Rome, 1570–71; 17 vols., Venice, 1593–1594; 19 vols., Antwerp, 1612; 23 vols., Paris, 1636–41; 20 vols., Venice, 1775–78; 25 vols., Parma, 1852–72; 34 vols., Paris, 1871–80; and the new ed. begun under the auspices of Leo XIII., Rome, 1882 sqq. For a compact statement of the principal editions of single works consult Baldwin, *Dictionary*, iii. 1, pp. 513–514. Eng. translations to be mentioned are: *Doctrines of . . . Aquinas on the Rulers and Members of Christian States*, London, 1860; *Memoranda of Angelical Doctrine; from Lady Day to the Ascension*, ib. 1867; *Homilies of St. Thomas . . . upon the Epistles and Gospels*, ib. 1867, 1873; *St. Thomas Aquinas on the Two Commandments of Charity and the Ten Commandments of the Law*, ib. 1880; his commentary on the Lord's Prayer, ib. 1880 and 1893; *The Maxims of St. Thomas Aquinas and the Prayers*, ib. 1890; *The Venerable Sacrament of the Altar*, ib. 1871, 1890, 1893; *Aquinas Ethicus; or, the moral Teaching of St. Thomas. A Transl. of the principal Portion of the second Part of the Summa Theologia with Notes by J. Rickaby*, vols. i.–ii., ib. 1896; *The Religious State, the Episcopate and the Priestly Office*, ib. 1902; *An Apology for the Religious Orders by St. Thomas Aquinas*, ib. 1902; *New Things and Old in St. Thomas Aquinas. A Translation of various Writings and Treatises of the Angelic Doctor*, ib. 1909.

For the earliest accounts of the life of the saint (e.g., that by Bernard Guido), miracles, etc., consult the collection in *ASB*, March, i. 657–747, and cf. *Histoire littéraire de la France*, xix. 238–266. Biographies are by A. Pietro, Venice, 1543; P. Frigerio, Rome, 1668; A. Touron, Paris, 1757; E. J. de Lecluze, *Grégoire VII., Saint François d'Assise et Saint Thomas d'Aquin*, 2 vols., Paris, 1844; M. Carle, Paris, 1846; H. Hörtel, Augsburg, 1846; E. D. Hampden, London, 1848; D. Mettenleiter, Regensburg, 1856; K. Werner, Regensburg, 1858; J. F. Bareille, Paris, 1859; R. B. Vaughan, 2 vols., Hereford, 1871–72; F. J. V. de Groot, Utrecht, 1882; Mme. E. Desmousseaux de Givre, Paris, 1888; R. Majocchi, Modena, 1889; P. Cavanagh, London, 1890; M. Didiot, Louvain, 1894; J. Jansen, Kevelaer, 1898.

On his philosophy, theology, etc., consult: G. H. Bach, *De l'état des âmes après la mort, d'après S. Thomas et*

Dante, ib. 1836; H. R. Feugeray, *Essai sur les doctrines politiques de S. Thomas*, Paris, 1857; C. Jourdain, *La Philosophie de S. Thomas d'Aquin*, 2 vols., ib. 1858; J. N. C. Oischinger, *Die speculative Theologie des Th. v. Aquinas*, Landshutt, 1858; H. E. Plassmann, *Die Lehre des heiligen Thomas von Aquin über die Bescheidenheit und Demuth*, Paderborn, 1858; A. Rietter, *Die Moral des heiligen Thomas von Aquinas*, Munich, 1858; C. M. G. Brechillet-Jourdain, *La Philosophie de S. Thomas d'Aquin*, Paris, 1858; J. Walker, *Essay on the Origin of Knowledge according to the Philosophy of St. Thomas*, London, 1858; E. Naville, *Étude sur l'œuvre de St. Thomas d'Aquin*, Paris, 1859; A. Schmid, *Die thomistische und scotistische Gewissheitslehre*, Dillingen, 1859; A. Goudin, *Philosophie suivant les principes de S. Thomas*, Paris, 1864; J. Delitzsch, *Die Gotteslehre des Thomas von Aquino kritisch dargestellt*, Leipsic, 1870; A. Reali, *S. Thomas d'Aquin et l'infaillibilité des pontifes romains*, Paris, 1870; M. Glossner, *Die Lehre des heiligen Thomas vom Wesen der göttlichen Gnade*, Mainz, 1871; F. X. Leitner, *Der heilige Thomas von Aquin über das unfehlbare Lehramt des Papstes*, Freiburg, 1872; A. Murgue, *Questions d'ontologie: études sur S. Thomas*, Lyons, 1876; E. Lecoultre, *La Doctrine de Dieu d'après Aristote et Thomas d'Aquin*, Lausanne, 1877; F. A. R. de la Bouillerie, *L'Homme, sa nature, son âme etc., d'après la doctrine de S. Thomas*, Paris, 1880; A. L. C. Bourquard, *Doctrine de la connaissance, d'après la doctrine de Thomas*, ib. 1880; A. Otten, *Allgemeine Erkenntnisslehre des heiligen Thomas*, Paderborn, 1882; J. Astromoff, *Introductio ad intelligendam doctrinam Angelici Doctoris*, Rome, 1884; A. Farges, *Études philosophiques pour vulgariser les théories d'Aristote et de S. Thomas*, 8 vols., Paris, 1887–1902; E. C. Lesserteur, *S. Thomas et la prédestination*, Mayenne, 1888; G. Feldner, *Die Lehre des heiligen Thomas über den Einfluss Gottes auf die Handlungen der vernünftigen Geschöpfe*, Graz, 1889; B. Antoniades, *Die Staatslehre des Thomas ab Aquino*, Leipsic, 1890; G. Feldner, *Die Lehre des heiligen Thomas v. Aquin uber die Willensfreiheit*, Graz, 1890; V. Lipperheide, *Thomas von Aquino und die platonische Ideenlehre*, Munich, 1890; P. E. Neumayer, *Theorie des Strebens nach Thomas von Aquin*, 2 parts, Leipsic, 1890; W. H. Nolens, *De leer van den h. Thomas von Aquin over het recht*, Utrecht, 1890; F. J. Van de Groot, *Summa apologetica de ecclesia catholica ad mentem S. Thomæ Aquinatis*, 2 vols., Regensburg, 1890; J. Gardier, *Philosophie de S. Thomas*, 4 vols., Paris, 1892–1896; J. J. Berthier, *De l'étude de la Somme théologique*, Freiburg, 1893; A. Portmann, *Das System der theologischen Summæ des heiligen Thomas von Aquin*, Lucerne, 1894; F. T. Esser, *Die Lehre des heiligen Thomas von Aquino über die Möglichkeit einer anfanglosen Schöpfung*, Münster, 1895; H. Gayraud, *S. Thomas et le prédéterminisme*, Paris, 1895; Guillemin, *S. Thomas et le prédéterminisme*, ib. 1895; A. Cappellazzi, *Persona nella dottrina di S. Tommaso d'Aquino*, Siena, 1900; C. Alibert, *La Psychologie thomiste et les théories modernes*, Lyons, 1902; J. Göttler, *Thomas von Aquin und die vortridentinischen Thomisten über die Wirkungen des Bussakraments*, Freiburg, 1904; F. Brommer, *Die Lehre vom sakramentalen Charakter in der Scholastik bis Thomas v. Aquin inklusive nach gedruckten und ungedruckten Quellen dargestellt*, Paderborn, 1908; A. Ott, *Thomas von Aquin und das Mendikantentum*, Freiburg, 1908; P. Rousselot, *L'Intellectualisme de Saint-Thomas*, Paris, 1908; W. Walker, *Greatest Men of the Christian Church*, Chicago, 1908; R. Eucken, *Die Philosophie des Thomas von Aquine und die Kultur der Neuzeit*, 2d ed., Bad Sachsa, 1910; A. D. Sertillanges, *St. Thomas d'Aquin*, 2 vols., Paris, 1910; P. Mandonnet, *Des écrits authentiques de S. Thomas d'Aquin*, Freiburg, 1910.

THOMAS OF CELANO: Franciscan author (thirteenth century). Of his life little is known; he is supposed to have lived last at the monastery of Tagliacozzo (44 m. e.n.e. of Rome). The one thing certain is that in 1221 he took part in the mission to Germany that was prompted by Francis of Assisi; and that in Germany he had charge of the stations at Mainz, Worms, and Cologne. He returned to Italy after 1223. He can hardly have been one of the most intimate disciples of Francis; it is accordingly remarkable that Gregory IX. detailed him to write the legend of the founder of that order, which was officially confirmed, Feb. 25, 1229. The value of this legend, *Vita I.*, has latterly become stoutly contested, and the upshot of the controversy may be summarized fairly as follows: (1) its main defect is its rhetoric, which clouds the portraiture of the saint. (2) As a writer under official commission, Thomas had to assume a certain politic reserve; hence he silently ignores the crisis of 1219–20, the friction within the order, and the warnings of the saint against privileges, while he lavishes exuberant praise on Gregory IX. and Elias of Cortona. (3) Nevertheless he meant to tell the truth, and so wrote without conscious opposition to the intimate disciples of Francis. For its contemporary proximity as well as for the author's conscientiousness, the *Vita I.* remains a source of the first rank. In 1230, Thomas was in a position to entrust some precious relics of St. Francis (hair and articles of clothing) to Jordanus de Giano; it is, therefore, not impossible that he wrote also the legend of St. Anthony of Padua (1232). This hypothesis was held to be probable by Ferdinand Marie d'Araules (*La Vie de St. Antoine par Jean Rigauld*, Paris, 1899); yet this probability may scarcely be maintained, because the style as a whole is distinctly different in the two legends (cf. Léon de Kerval, *S. Antonii de Padua vitæ duæ*, in *Collection d' études et des documents*, v. 7–8, Paris, 1904). Thomas himself made an extract from *Vita I.* for liturgical use, after 1230, *Legenda in usum chori;* but without new matter. The chapter general of 1244 commissioned the founder's associates to supplement the previous legends; and they then compiled their materials as directed by the letter, which, at all events, is surely genuine, and prefaces the so-called legend of the three associates (" not according to the usual manner of a legend, but, as if from a lovely meadow, have we culled some flowers "). There is no small dispute as to what this garland is; but the probability at least is, as a later source reports, that the General Crescentius delivered the material to Thomas, on which basis he produced the *Vita II.* This legend was composed in 1247, and purports to supplement *Vita I.* It takes account of the progressive development of the order, suppresses the name of the deposed General Elias, and combats the relaxing tendencies within the order. On the other hand, there is silence on the testament of the saint, his admonition concerning privileges, and the care of lepers. Yet here the author appears to be subjectively honest, and only a man of politic reserve. It is further supposed that by command of General Giovanni da Parma Thomas wrote a *tractatus de miraculis*. Such a document has been recently discovered and issued by F. d'Ortroy; but no compelling proof can be adduced that it was the work of Thomas. Whether the legend of St. Clara, composed between 1255 and 1261, was written by Thomas, as Paul Sabatier supposes, is doubtful. According to the *Liber conformitatum*, a work dating from the close of the fourteenth century, Thomas also composed the *Dies iræ, dies illa* (cf. Julian, *Hymnology*, pp. 1559, 1629).

[The *Dies iræ*, one of the most celebrated hymns of the Middle Ages, based on such passages as Zeph. i. 15; Ps. xcvi. 13, xcvii. 3, cii. 26, may have been suggested by similar judgment-hymns of an earlier date, like the *Libera me Domine*, a responsory in a manuscript in the British Museum. It was written in three-line stanzas and intended for private devotion. In its time it was remarkably impressive by its solemn grandeur and awful majesty. Cf. H. A. Daniel, *Thesaurus hymnologicus*, ii. 103–131, v. 110–116 (Leipsic, 1855); Abraham Cole, *Dies Iræ in Thirteen Original Versions* (4th ed., New York, 1866). The best English translations are by W. J. Irons, H. Alford, A. Cole, and R. C. French. There is a fivefold translation in verse of various meters, issued with the text, by President M. W. Stryker (privately printed, Clinton, N. Y., 1910)].

E. LEMPP.

BIBLIOGRAPHY: The best edition of the *Opera* so far as they relate to St. Francis is by Edward d'Alençon, Rome, 1906; and the best discussion is W. Götz, *Die Quellen zur Geschichte des heiligen Franz von Assisi*, Gotha, 1904. Consult also *KL*, xi. 1668–70.

THOMAS CHRISTIANS. See NESTORIANS, §§ 2, 8.

THOMAS, GOSPEL OF. See APOCRYPHA, B, I., 5.

THOMAS OF VILLANOVA: Spanish Roman Catholic; b. at Fuenlana, near Villanueva (40 m. n.w. of Valladolid), in the diocese of Leon, 1488; d. at Valencia Sept. 8, 1555. He studied at Alcala; lectured on moral science at the University of Salamanca, 1513–15; entered the order of the Augustinian hermits in 1517; became the provincial of his order for Andalusia and Castile; was confessor to Charles V., and bishop of Valencia, 1544–55. In 1658 he was canonized by Alexander VII. Fragments of the beginnings of his Commentaries on Canticles, Job, and Revelation were collected and published (best ed., with biography, Laurentius a Sancta Barbara, 2 vols., Milan, 1760). *Opera omnia* was edited and published (5 vols., Salamanca, 1761–64; another ed., Augsburg, 1757).

BIBLIOGRAPHY: *ASB*, Sept., v. 799 sqq.; F. Pösl, *Leben des heiligen Thomas von Villanova*, Münster, 1860; Bruder Bernards *Aphorismen über katholische Handlung der Bibel*, pp. 19 sqq., Freiburg, 1862; *Thomas von Villanova Büchlein von der göttlichen Liebe, übersetzt von F. Kaulen*, Freiburg, 1896; *KL*, xi. 1692–94.

THOMAS WALDENSIS. See NETTER (WALDENSIS), THOMAS.

THOMAS, ALLEN CLAPP: Friend; b. at Baltimore, Md., Dec. 26, 1846. He was educated at Haverford College, Haverford, Pa. (A.B., 1865), and after engaging in mercantile pursuits, 1869–78, became professor of history and librarian of Haverford College, which position he still holds. He has written *Edward Lawrence Scull, a Memoir* (privately printed, Cambridge, Mass., 1891); *A History of the United States for Schools and Academies* (Boston, 1894); *History of the Society of Friends in America* (in collaboration with R. H. Thomas; New York, 1894, 4th ed., 1905); and *Elementary History of the United States* (Boston, 1900).

THOMAS, DAVID: Congregationalist; b. at Hollybush-Vatson, near Tenby (10 m. e. of Pembroke), South Wales, Feb. 1, 1813; d. at Ramsgate (15 m. n.e. of Canterbury), England, Dec. 30, 1894.

After following a mercantile course for some years, he turned to theology, and studied at Newport Pagnel, now Cheshunt College, Buckingham, under T. B. and J. Bull; was minister of the Congregational Church at Chesham, 1841–44; of Stockwell Independent Church, London, 1844–77. He founded in 1855 the National Newspaper League Company, for cheapening and improving the daily press, which numbered ten thousand members; also the Working Men's Club and Institute, 1861, and was originator of the University of Wales, at Aberystwith, 1862. He was a man of broad ideas. In all his writings he recognized the fact that as Christ is the only revealer of absolute truth, he is not to be interpreted by the Old-Testament writers or by the apostles, but they are all to be interpreted by him. He conducted *The Homilist* (50 vols., London, 1852 sqq.); contributed to various volumes of *The Pulpit Commentary* (London and New York, 1880 sqq.); and was author of a homiletical commentary on Matthew (London, 1864), and on the Acts (1870); *The Crisis of Being. Six Lectures to young Men on religious Decision* (1849); *The Core of Creeds, or St. Peter's Keys* (1851); *The Progress of Being. Six Lectures on the true Progress of Man* (1854); *Problemata Mundi. The Book of Job exegetically considered* (1878); and his complete works appeared as the *Homilistic Library* (1882 sqq.).

BIBLIOGRAPHY: English *Congregational Year Book*, 1896, pp. 237–239; *DNB*, lvi. 177–178.

THOMAS, JESSE BURGESS: Baptist; b. at Edwardsville, Ill., July 29, 1832. He was educated at Kenyon College, O. (A.B., 1850). After practising law for a number of years, he held pastorates at Waukegan, Ill. (1862–64), First Baptist Church (now the Baptist Temple), Brooklyn, N. Y. (1864–1869), First Baptist Church, San Francisco, Cal. (1869–70), Michigan Avenue Baptist Church, Chicago, Ill. (1870–74), and was recalled to the First Baptist Church, Brooklyn, in 1874, serving until 1888. From 1888 to 1905 he was professor of church history in Newton Theological Institute, Newton Center, Mass., and in 1905 he was made professor emeritus. In theology he is a progressive conservative. He is the author of *The Old Bible and the New Science* (New York, 1877); and *The Mould of Doctrine* (Philadelphia, 1885).

THOMAS, NATHANIEL SEYMOUR: Protestant Episcopal missionary bishop of Wyoming; b. at Faribault, Minn., June 20, 1867. He was educated at the University of Minnesota (B.A., 1889), the University of Cambridge, and the Theological School of the diocese of Kansas, and was ordered deacon in 1891 and advanced to the priesthood in 1893. After being stationed at Ottawa, Kan. (1891–93), and Topeka, Kan. (1893–94), he was professor of New-Testament exegesis in the Theological School of the diocese of Kansas, dean of the Atchinson deanery in the same diocese, and priest-in-charge of St. John's and St. Paul's, Leavenworth, Kan., until 1897, when he became rector of St. Matthew's, Wheeling, W. Va. From 1900 until 1909 he was rector of the Church of the Holy Apostles, Philadelphia, and in 1909 was consecrated missionary bishop of Wyoming.

THOMASIUS (THOMAS), to-mä'sî-ūs, **CHRISTIAN:** German Lutheran; b. at Leipsic Jan. 1, 1655; d. at Halle Sept. 23, 1728. He studied philosophy at Leipsic (M. A., 1672), and jurisprudence at Frankfort, 1675–78; was lawyer and privat-docent at Leipsic, advocating with great boldness the natural law of Samuel Pufendorf (q.v.). In a disputation, *De crimine bigamiæ* (1685), he asserted that polygamy was not contrary to nature. In the footsteps of Pufendorf he published *Institutiones jurisprudentiæ divinæ* (1688), in which he advanced his views on natural right, disclaiming that it was derived from the primitive state of nature. His caricature of the pedantry of the scholars and the intolerance of the theologians, as well as personal attacks, led to many complaints and finally to an order, in 1690, from the superior consistory forbidding him to lecture or to publish. Cut off from all self-support, he went to Berlin, where Elector Frederick appointed him to the council and to lecture at Halle. Thomasius quickly gathered a large number of students, and laid the foundation for the University of Halle, which was dedicated in 1694, of which he became second professor of jurisprudence, and first professor in 1710.

Thomasius was not a creative spirit, but with a firm grasp he seized the progressive thoughts of his time and stood for them with intrepid courage. Endowed with a thorough, open, warm-hearted nature, he, too impulsively sometimes, combated and ridiculed the current prejudices, faith in authority, pedantry, and intolerance, thus becoming the first successful champion of the Enlightenment (q.v.) in Germany. His weapon was reason; but he was not a profound thinker going back to ultimate principles; his reasoning was that of common sense. He held the syllogism in contempt; and the mathematical method of Christian Wolff Thomasius regarded as merely a revised scholasticism. He was an empiricist, mentally related to Locke, by whom he was influenced in more than one respect. He was a typical representative of the practical tendency of the Enlightenment, the highest aim of which was common utility and happiness. Against speculation and logic in religion he defines faith as " trust of the heart in God," and is fond of lauding the influence of providence in the incidents of his life. He depreciates the Fathers, rejects the dictation of the creeds, regards the churches as sects, and scourges the heresy-hunting and domineering theologians. He was long regarded as a colleague of the Pietists at Halle. Agreeing with Pietism in his opposition to theological systems and the philosophy of the schools, the emphasis upon practical piety, recourse to Scripture, and liberality on the creeds, and choosing Francke as his confessor, and admiring Spener very highly, yet he was not in touch with the central points of Pietism, sin and grace.

His efforts in behalf of the Enlightenment were untiring. His services to learning were in the fields of jurisprudence and philosophy. His only basic philosophical activity was his psychological groundwork; the investigation of man's nature is to him the basis of all science. Otherwise his philosophy is popular, practical. Testimonies of his practical tendency are, *Einleitung zu der Vernunftlehre* (1691);

Ausübung der Vernunftlehre (1691); *Einleitung zur Sittenlehre* (1692); and *Ausübung der Sittenlehre* (1696). Between the spheres of revelation and philosophy Thomasius drew a sharp distinction. In his specialty, he further upheld the principle·of natural right in *Fundamenta juris naturæ* (1705). In a series of works on church law, he recognizes the State as purely secular and the Church as a society within its domain. The power of the sovereign is supreme over the theologians and the Church, limited only by revelation. He opposed certain forms of severity, such as those against Witchcraft (q.v.), which he denied (*De crimine magiæ*, 1701), and the rack (*De tortura ex foris*, 1705); and he favored the exercise of the right of pardon on the part of the sovereign, in cases of homicide.

(HEINRICH HOFFMAN.)

BIBLIOGRAPHY: J. G. Walch, *Religionsstreitigkeiten der evangelisch-lutherischen Kirche*, iii. 1–78, 10 vols., Jena, 1733–39; H. Luden, *Christian Thomasius nach seinen Schicksale und Schriften dargestellt*, Berlin, 1805; R. E. Prutz, *Geschichte des deutschen Journalismus*, Hanover, 1845; F. C. Biedermann, *Deutschland im 18. Jahrhundert*, Leipsic, 1854; A. Tholuck, *Das kirchliche Leben des 17. Jahrhunderts*, ii. 71–76, Hamburg, 1854; J. C. Bluntschli, *Geschichte des allgemeinen Staatsrechts*, Munich, 1864; H. Dernburg, *Thomasius und die Stiftung der Universität Halle*, Halle, 1865; B. A. Wagner, *Christian Thomasius: ein Beitrag zur Würdigung seiner Verdienste um die deutsche Litteratur*, Berlin, 1872; Klemperer, *Christian Thomasius, ein Vorkämpfer der Volksaufklärung*, Landsberg, 1877; A. Ritschl, *Geschichte des Pietismus*, ii. 545 sqq., Bonn, 1884; A. Nicoladoni, *Christian Thomasius: ein Beitrag zur Geschichte der Aufklärung*, Berlin, 1888; E. Landsberg, *Zur Lebensgeschichte des Chr. Thomasius*, Halle, 1894; idem, *ADB*, xxxviii. 93–103; A. Rauch, *Christian Thomasius und A. H. Francke*, Halle, 1898; R. Kayser, *Thomasius und der Pietismus*, Hamburg, 1900; idem, in *Monatshefte der Comenius-Gesellschaft*, 1900.

THOMASIUS, GOTTFRIED: Professor in Erlangen; b. at Egenhausen (circuit of Nagold, Württemberg, 16 m. w. of Tübingen), Bavarian Franconia, July 26, 1802; d. at Erlangen Jan. 24, 1875. He was a lineal descendant of Christian Thomasius (q.v.). He attended the gymnasium in Ansbach, entered the University of Erlangen in 1821, removed to Halle after a year and a half, and finished his academic studies in Berlin, where he was attracted by Schleiermacher, Hegel, Marheineke, and Tholuck. Leaving the university in 1825, Thomasius spent seventeen years in the active work of the pastorate, first in a village between Erlangen and Nuremberg, after 1829 in Nuremberg. Here his preaching attracted the intellectual men of the city and his success as religious instructor in the gymnasium led to his call to Erlangen as professor of dogmatics in Mar., 1842. He had previously published his *Grundlinien zum Religionsunterricht an den mittleren und oberen Klassen gelehrter Schulen* (Nuremberg, 1839), which met with wide approval (8th ed., 1901). Thomasius contributed his share to a development at Erlangen which combined strict adherence to the standards with the truly scientific spirit and genuine theological progress. The subjects on which he lectured were dogmatics and church history, and he excelled in the deep and lasting character of the impression he made. For almost thirty-three years he exerted an influence equalled by few teachers of his time.

His influence as writer was hardly less than that as teacher. An early work, *Origenes. Ein Beitrag zur Dogmengeschichte des dritten Jahrhunderts* (Nuremberg, 1837), helped to pave the way for his transition from the pulpit to the professor's chair. Three preliminary treatises (*Beiträge zur kirchlichen Christologie*, Nuremberg, 1845; *Dogmatis de obedientia Christi activa historia et progressiones inde a confessione Augustana ad formulam usque concordiæ*, 3 parts, Erlangen, 1845–46; *Das Bekenntnis der evangelisch-lutherischen Kirche in der Konsequenz seines Prinzips*, Nuremberg, 1848) preceded his greatest work—*Christi Person und Werk. Darstellung der evangelisch-lutherischen Dogmatik vom Mittelpunkte der Christologie aus* (3 parts, Erlangen, 1852–61), which treats the whole field of dogmatics in comprehensive expositions which are always based on the Scriptural proof and the consensus of the Church. For Thomasius's development of the doctrine of Kenosis (q.v.), see CHRISTOLOGY, X., 4, § 4. His exposition of the doctrine of the Trinity was criticized, but his teaching concerning the work of Christ is complete and satisfactory, combining the truth in the view of Anselm and in the old-Lutheran doctrine into the true conception of the atonement. The final treatment of the theme is to be sought in the third part of the *Dogmatik;* an earlier work, *Das Bekenntnis der lutherischen Kirche von der Versöhnung und die Versöhnungslehre D. von Hofmanns* (Erlangen, 1857), treats the same questions less conclusively. *Die christliche Dogmengeschichte als Entwickelungsgeschichte des kirchlichen Lehrbegriffs* (2 vols., Erlangen, 1874–76; 2nd ed., by N. Bonwetsch and R. Seeberg, Leipsic, 1886–88) was Thomasius's last publication. It combines the enthusiasm of youth and the maturity of age with learning, keen judgment, clearness of presentation, and thoroughness of investigation. The first volume treats of the ancient Church; the second, comprising the Middle Ages and the Reformation, was not fully completed at the author's death and was published posthumously by G. L. Plitt.

For thirty years from 1842 Thomasius was university preacher. A deep and conscientious dependence upon Scripture, a joyous and powerful faith, a clear and comprehensible form elevated by its content and even poetically inspired, are the characteristics which win attention in his published sermons (5 vols., Erlangen, 1852–60). His confessional point of view and inner development appear most clearly in *Wiedererwachen des evangelischen Lebens in der lutherischen Kirche Bayerns. Ein Stück süddeutscher Kirchengeschichte, 1800–1840* (Erlangen, 1867).

(A. VON STÄHLIN†.)

BIBLIOGRAPHY: A. von Stählin, *Löhe, Thomasius, Harless. Drei Lebens- und Geschichtsbilder*, Leipsic, 1887; F. Frank, *Geschichte und Kritik der neueren Theologie*, p. 244, Erlangen, 1894; G. Frank, *Die Theologie des 19. Jahrhunderts*, pp. 460 sqq., Leipsic, 1905; *ADB*, xxxviii. 102 sqq.

THOMASSIN, LOUIS: French cleric and canonist; b. at Aix (17 m. n. of Marseilles), Provence, Aug. 28, 1619; d. in Paris Dec. 24, 1697. He was educated in the Congregation of the Oratory, entered the congregation in 1632, and taught successively at Lyons, Saumur, and in the Seminary of St. Magloire at Paris. In 1668 he retired and devoted himself to study, supported by the French clergy. His chief work was the *Ancienne et nouvelle discipline de l'église touchant les bénéfices et les bénéficiers* (3 vols., Paris, 1678–79; Lat. transl., by himself, 1688), which is still one of the chief sources for the subject and made so great an impression on Pope Innocent XI. that he would have called the author to Rome and made him a cardinal had not Louis XIV. refused to allow so great a scholar to leave France. Besides many minor writings, Thomassin published *Dissertationes in concilia generalia et particularia* (Paris, 1667); *Mémoirs sur la grâce* (1668); *Dogmata theologica* (3 vols., 1680–89; ed. F. Ecalle, 6 vols., Paris, 1864–70); and a *Glossarium universale Hebraicum* (1697), in which he tried to prove that the Hebrew was the original language and the mother tongue.   (E. Friedberg†.)

Bibliography: L. E. Dupin, *Nouvelle bibliothèque*, xviii. 187–196, 35 vols., 1689–1711; C. Thomassin, *Louis de Thomassin, der grosse Theologe Frankreichs*, Munich, 1892.

THOMPSON, CHARLES LEMUEL: Presbyterian; b. at Allentown, Pa., Aug. 18, 1839. He was educated at Carroll College, Wis., (A.B., 1858), Princeton Theological Seminary (1858–60), and McCormick Theological Seminary, Chicago (1860–1861). He held pastorates in his denomination at Juneau, Wis. (1861–62), Janesville, Wis. (1862–67), First Presbyterian Church, Cincinnati, O. (1867–72), Fifth Presbyterian Church, Chicago (1872–78), Third Presbyterian Church, Pittsburg, Pa. (1878–1882), Second Presbyterian Church, Kansas City, Mo. (1882–88), and Madison Avenue Presbyterian Church, New York City (1888–98). Since 1898 he has been secretary of the Presbyterian Board of Home Missions. He was editor of *The Interior* (Chicago) in 1877–79, and has written: *Times of Refreshing: A History of American Revivals* (Chicago, 1877); *Etchings in Verse* (New York, 1890); and *The Presbyterians* (1903).

THOMPSON, JOSEPH PARRISH: Congregationalist and Egyptologist; b. in Philadelphia, Pa., Aug. 7, 1819; d. in Berlin, Germany, Sept. 20, 1879. He was graduated from Yale, 1838; studied theology at Andover Theological Seminary and at Yale, 1838–40, when he was ordained; was pastor of Chapel Street Church, New Haven, 1840–45; in 1843 was a founder of the *New Englander;* pastor of the Broadway Tabernacle, New York, 1845–71; in 1848 helped to establish *The Independent,* of which he was also an editor for many years. He visited Palestine and Egypt, 1852–53, and wrote much on that branch of study. During the whole period of the civil war he labored with assiduity for the maintenance of national unity on principles of universal freedom. Because he found in Germany a state of things which seemed to call for a defense of American institutions, and an exposition of American ideas, he took up that line of work, and became a link between the United States and Germany. During the " centennial " year, 1876, he vindicated his native land against European prejudices by a course of six philosophical lectures on American political history, which he delivered in Berlin, Florence, Dresden, Paris, and London, and published as *The United States as a Nation* (Boston, 1877). He resided in Germany, 1872–79, where he was active in oriental

studies, political, social, and scientific discussions, and in various foreign societies. In 1875 he went to England to explain publicly Germany's attitude in regard to Ultramontanism. His personal influence secured the insertion, in the Berlin Treaty of 1878, of a clause favoring religious liberty; and among his last works was the preparation, for the Evangelical Alliance at Basel (1879), of a memorial in behalf of religious liberty in Austria. He was the author of *Man in Genesis and Geology* (New York, 1869); *Theology of Christ, from his own Words* (1870); *Home Worship* (Boston, 1871); *Jesus of Nazareth: his Life for the Young* (1875); and *The Workman* (New York, 1879).

THOMPSON, RALPH WARDLAW: English Congregationalist; b. at Bellary (270 m. n.w. of Madras), South India, Aug. 28, 1842. He was educated at South African College, Cape Town, (B.A., University of the Cape of Good Hope) and at Cheshunt College, England (1861–65). He entered the Congregational ministry and was minister of the Ewing Place Congregational Church, Glasgow (1865–70), and of the Norwood Congregational Church, Liverpool (1871–80). Since 1881 he has been foreign secretary of the London Missionary Society. In 1908 he was chairman of the Congregational Union of England and Wales. He has at various times made official visits to the society's stations in India, China, South Africa, Madagascar, New Guinea, and the South Seas. His publications embrace, *My Trip in the John Williams* (London, 1900); and *Griffith John, Story of Fifty Years in China* (1906, new ed., 1908).

THOMPSON, ROBERT ELLIS: Presbyterian; b. near Lurgan (19 m. s.w. of Belfast), County Armagh, Ireland, Apr. 5, 1844. He left Ireland for the United States in early life, and was educated at the University of Pennsylvania (A.B., 1865) and the Reformed Presbyterian Theological Seminary, Philadelphia (1868). He was licensed to preach by the Reformed Presbytery of Philadelphia in 1867 and was ordained to the Presbyterian ministry in 1874. From 1868 to 1892 he was connected with the University of Pennsylvania, where he was professor successively of Latin and mathematics (1868–71), social science (1871–81), and history and English literature (1881–92). In 1894 he became president of the Central High School in Philadelphia. He was editor of *The Penn Monthly* (1870–81), and of *The American Weekly* (1881–92). Since 1892 he has been a member of the staff of *The Sunday-School Times.* His writings of theological interest are: *De civitate Dei: The Divine Order of Human Society* (Stone lectures; Philadelphia, 1891); *The National Hymn-Book of the American Churches* (1893); *History of the Presbyterian Churches of America* (New York, 1895); *The Hand of God in Human History* (1902); *Harvard University Lectures on Protection to Home Industry* (1908); *The Apostles as Everyday Men* (1910); and *The Historic Episcopate* (Philadelphia, 1910).

THOMSON, ANDREW MITCHELL: Presbyterian; b. at Sanquhar (50 m. s.w. of Edinburgh) July 11, 1779; d. at Edinburgh Feb. 9, 1831. He was educated at the University of Edinburgh; was schoolmaster at Markinch, Fife, 1800–02; became parish minister at Sprouston, Roxburghshire, in 1802; of East Church, Perth, in 1808; of Greyfriars, Edinburgh, in 1810, and of St. George's in the same city in 1814, where he remained till his death. Soon after he took up his work at Greyfriars he was recognized as one of the strongest preachers in the city, and his labors for the enrichment of the service were well recompensed, especially in the department of music, to which he was a contributor, composing several tunes for hymns. His influence continued to increase, and he became leader of the evangelical party in the Church of Scotland. He was also active in the work of education. The "Apocrypha controversy" was in part excited by him when, in 1827, he gave up his membership in the British and Foreign Bible Society and assailed that organization for binding the Apocrypha with the Bible. He edited *The Christian Instructor*, in which his attack upon the Bible Society appeared; wrote a *Catechism for the Instruction of Communicants* (Edinburgh, 1808); *Lectures Expository and Practical* (1816); *Lovers of Pleasure more than Lovers of God* (1818; ed. Dr. Candlish, 1867); *The Doctrine of Universal Pardon* (1830); and issued several volumes of sermons.

BIBLIOGRAPHY: A *Memoir* was prefixed to his *Sermons and Sacramental Exhortations*, Boston, 1832; cf. *DNB*, lvi. 234.

THOMSON, WILLIAM McCLURE: Presbyterian missionary; b. at Springfield (now Spring Dale), O., Dec. 31, 1806; d. in Denver, Col., Apr. 8, 1894. He was graduated from Miami University, Oxford, O., 1826; studied at Princeton Theological Seminary, N. J., 1826–27; was ordained an evangelist, 1831; was missionary in Syria and Palestine under the A. B. C. F. M. and the Presbyterian Board of Foreign Missions, 1833–49, 1850–57, and 1859–76. He then resided in New York City. He was an authority in the department of archeological Biblical research, and was the author of *The Land and the Book, or Biblical Illustrations Drawn from the Manners and Customs, the Scenes and Scenery, of the Holy Land* (2 vols., New York, 1859; new ed. revised and rewritten, with numerous illustrations, 3 vols., 1880–86, vol. i., *Southern Palestine and Jerusalem*, vol. ii., *Central Palestine and Phœnicia*, vol. iii., *Lebanon, Damascus, and Beyond Jordan*; reissue, 1 vol., 1911).

THORN, CONFERENCE OF: A Polish conference of 1645 held to prevent religious strife between Roman Catholics, Lutherans, and Reformed. About the middle of the seventeenth century in Poland party spirit was rife, and religion played an important part in the political struggles; the Roman Catholic party and in it especially the Jesuits possessed the greatest influence while the Protestants, Reformed, Lutherans, and Bohemian Brethren (q.v.) were not in harmony, and not a few were antitrinitarian Socinians. Officially, Protestantism had enjoyed political toleration since 1573, but the Roman Catholic party tried by every means to lead the Protestants back, after the Jesuits had gained ascendency over Sigismund III. (1587–1632) and his successor. This was the chief and final reason why King Ladislaus IV. issued a call to

the representatives of the three Christian confessions to a religious conference at Thorn on the Vistula, beginning Aug. 28, 1645. The dissidents were permitted to procure foreign speakers. The Polish Lutherans secured Johann Hülsemann (q.v.), orthodox professor of theology at Wittenberg, and Abraham Calovius (q.v.), rector of the gymnasium in Danzig. For the Königsberg Lutherans, the great elector of Brandenburg sent Georg Calixtus (q.v.), but the two former secured his rejection as a Lutheran representative (see SYNCRETISM, SYNCRETISTIC CONTROVERSIES). The king sent the grand chancellor of the crown, George of Teczyn, duke of Ossolin, as his deputy and conductor of the proceedings. The Roman Catholics chose twenty-six theologians for the conference, Professor Gregor Schönhof being their most prominent speaker. The Reformed party was represented by twenty-four theologians, among them Johannes Bythner, superintendent of the congregations of Greater Poland, who was joined by Amos Comenius (q.v.), Johann Berg, court preacher of the Elector Frederic William of Brandenburg-Prussia, and Professor Reichel of Frankfort-on-the-Oder. The Lutherans, numbering twenty-eight, were under the leadership of Hülsemann and Calovius. In an instruction issued by the king it was required that each of the three parties first give a statement of its doctrine; not till then should the correctness or incorrectness of the doctrines be (amicably) discussed; and, finally, a statement of customs and usages. The Roman Catholics evidently tried to prevent from the beginning every criticism of their official church doctrines. Each party deliberated in a special room of the town-hall, and conferred with the others only through the exchange of documents or through deputies. The conference consisted of thirty-six sessions, of which only four were public. After the formal preliminaries the Reformed on Sept. 1 drew up a general confession of faith; on the same day the Roman Catholics followed their example, and after these had presented their confession to the Lutherans on Sept. 7, the latter answered with a reply that essentially referred to the unchanged Augsburg Confession. After that there was to follow a detailed representation of the doctrine of the different parties. Such a document was issued first by the Roman Catholics, on Sept. 13, repeating only the teachings of the Council of Trent with plain ultramontane additions concerning the power of the pope. The Reformed presented their doctrine, a statement which later obtained great fame as the *Declaratio Thoruniensis*, more accurately *Specialior declaratio doctrinæ ecclesiarum Reformatorum Catholicæ de præcipuis fidei controversiis* (original printed in *Scripta partis Reformatæ*). The Lutherans presented *Kurzer Inbegriff der Lehre der augsburgischen Konfession*. The Roman Catholics were so embittered over the Lutheran document, as indeed they had been over the Reformed before, that they refused to receive it, much less to permit its reading, and the presiding grand chancellor Ossolinski had himself recalled. Count Johann Lesczinski, his successor, tightened the reins in behalf of his party, and stated, Sept. 25, that no progress had been made because of wandering from the king's instructions. To explain these he called upon the Jesuit Schönhof, who attempted intimidation of the Protestants. The third public session, Sept. 26, was passed in recriminatory debate. The fourth, on Oct. 3, continued the same way, the more energetically on the part of the Protestants, who regarded the presiding officer as the advocate of the Roman Catholic party. The many speeches that were delivered developed into personal abuses. Allusions to Charles V. and the elector of Saxony aroused the national pride of the Poles, and their lay representatives now refused to speak except in the Polish language. As the Protestants adhered firmly to their demands, Schönhof stole a march by a personal journey to the king, from whom he obtained a "declaration of his will in regard to the instruction for the conference of Thorn," containing about everything that the Roman Catholics had hitherto demanded. The king instructed that the declarations of the Lutherans and Reformed be received after being purged of the offensive and the superfluous; and that the conference was to be restricted to his representative, the presiding heads of the parties, and, respectively, two speakers and alternates, the scribe, and seven hearers of each. Consequently the Lutherans sent Güldenstern and the Reformed their confidant Rey to the king in order to present the situation from the standpoint of the Evangelicals. Two Roman Catholics, however, arrived a day ahead, Oct. 16, and were joined by Schönhof on the 18th. The king, aiming to show an attitude of fairness, had the two Protestant positions of doctrine submitted in writing, and, summoning all three representatives, Oct. 20, asked that his first instructions be carried out, and, in the written replies to the Lutherans and Reformed, they were directed to prove their obedience by expunging from their doctrinal position the disputed theses for later consideration. Upon the return of the deputies on Oct. 23, the Evangelicals rejoiced over the freedom of conscience guaranteed by the king in his domain, but declined to revise their doctrinal presentations, which the Roman Catholics now demanded. During November the Reformed entered into private conferences with the Roman Catholics, drawing on themselves the suspicion of the Lutherans, who were excluded. These conferences, though without result, proved that the Roman Catholics wished to create the impression that they would have been willing to confer upon material considerations on the rule of faith. The conference broke up unceremoniously. The Lutherans tarried a few days to draw up fifty grievances against their treatment and a revision of the protocol as it should have been from their point of view, both of which were officially filed. The conference was a failure. In Poland the lot of the Evangelicals became less favorable, and in Germany a result was the embitterment of the Lutherans against the Reformed, bearing fruit in the syncretistic controversies (see SYNCRETISM, SYNCRETISTIC CONTROVERSIES, I., § 2; II., 1, § 1).

(P. TSCHACKERT†.)

BIBLIOGRAPHY: The official Acta conventus Thorunsensis was published at Warsaw, 1646, and repeated in the Historia syncretistica of A. Calovius (q.v.), and in Scripta parta Reformatæ in colloquio Thoruniensi, Berlin, 1646. The Confessio fidei in Latin and German was printed at Danzig, 1735. The literature under CALIXTUS, GEORG, and CALOVIUS, ABRAHAM, is to be consulted, as well as the writings of those men. Consult further: C. Hartknoch, Preussische Kirchen-Historia, pp. 934 sqq., Frankfort, 1686; J. Lukaszewicz, Geschichte der reformierten Kirchen in Lithauen, i. 157 sqq., Leipsic, 1848; Ikier, Das Colloquium Charitativum, Halle, 1889; F. Jacobi, Das liebreiche Religionsgespräch zu Thorn 1645, Gotha, 1895; ZKG, vol. xv., parts 3–4 (best).

THORNDIKE, HERBERT: Church of England; b. probably in Lincolnshire in 1598; d. at Chiswick (6 m. s.w. of Charing Cross, London) July 11, 1672. In 1613 he became a pensioner at Trinity College, Cambridge (scholar, 1614; B.A., 1617; minor fellow, 1618; M.A., and major fellow, 1620). He was prebendary of Layton Ecclesia in Lincoln cathedral, 1636–40; held the crown living of Claybrook, Leicestershire, 1640–42; was Hebrew lecturer to Trinity College, Cambridge, 1640–44 (–46, officially); rector of Barley in Hertfordshire, 1642–44. Being a stanch churchman of the Anglo-Catholic type, he was ejected from his preferments during the civil wars, but, with the Restoration, he regained them as well as his fellowship at Trinity. He, however, resigned them on being appointed to a stall at Westminster Abbey in 1661. He assisted at the Savoy Conference (q.v.) in 1661, and had a share in the revision of the Prayer-Book the same year, being then a member of convocation. He resumed his residence at Cambridge, 1662, and afterward divided his time between the university and the abbey. The plague drove him from Cambridge in 1666; and in 1667 he vacated his fellowship, retiring to his canonry at Westminster. He was a most learned, systematic, and powerful advocate of Anglo-Catholic theology and High-church principles in the seventeenth century. The book which most succinctly unfolds his scheme is entitled An Epilogue to the Tragedy of the Church of England (1659), in which he treats of the principles of Christian truth, the covenant of grace, and the laws of the church. The covenant of grace is his central idea. He dwells upon the condition of the covenant as being baptism, the necessity of the covenant as arising out of original sin, the mediator of the covenant as the divine Christ, and the method of the covenant as an economy of grace. In the treatment of this branch, he brings out the Anglican doctrines of salvation as distinguished from those of Puritanism. His trains of thought were prolix and excursive, and his style was crabbed and unreadable; his works could never be popular, but they are of value to theological scholars. He was the author of a Hebrew, Syriac, and Arabic lexicon (London, 1635); The Due Way of Composing the Differences on Foot (1660); Just Weights and Measures (1662); and Theological Works (6 vols., Oxford, 1844–56). He also assisted Walton in the preparation of his Polyglot (see BIBLES, POLYGLOT, IV.).

BIBLIOGRAPHY: The Life by A. W. Haddan is in vol. vi. of the Theological Works, ut sup. Consult DNB, lvi. 290–292, where references to scattering notices are given; W. H. Hutton, The English Church (1625–1714), pp. 179, 329, 330, London, 1903.

THORNWELL, JAMES HENLEY: American Presbyterian, and educator; b. in Marlborough District, S. C., Dec. 9, 1812; d. at Charlotte, N. C., Aug. 1, 1862. He obtained the elements of a good education, and was graduated from South Carolina College, 1829; studied law for a while, but turned to theology; after teaching for two years he studied at Andover Theological Seminary, and at Harvard Divinity School. Returning to the South he was licensed to preach, 1834; ordained, 1835; was pastor of the Presbyterian church at Lancaster, 1835-1837; professor of logic and belles-lettres in South Carolina College, 1837-39; pastor at Columbia, 1839-41; professor of sacred literature and evidences of Christianity at South Carolina College, 1841-51; pastor of Glebe Street Church, Charleston, 1851; president of South Carolina College, 1852-55; professor of theology in the Presbyterian Theological Seminary, and pastor of the church at Columbia, 1855-62. He took a leading part in the organization of the Southern General Assembly in 1861. He had high logical and metaphysical faculties, and was a champion of the old school Presbyterian theology.

He was the author of *Romanists from the Infallibility of the Church and Testimony of the Fathers on Behalf of the Apocrypha, Discussed and Refuted* (New York, 1845); *Discourses on Truth* (1854); and his collected writings, ed. John B. Adger, appeared (4 vols., Richmond, 1871-73).

BIBLIOGRAPHY: B. M. Palmer, *Life and Letters of James Henley Thornwell*, New York, 1876.

THOROLD, ANTHONY WILSON: Church of England, bishop; b. at Hougham (17 m. s. of Lincoln), England, June 13, 1825; d. at Winchester July 25, 1895. He was educated at Queen's College, Oxford (B.A., 1847; M.A., 1850; D.D., 1877); ordained deacon, 1849; priest, 1850; was curate of Wittington, Lancashire, till 1854; at Holy Trinity, Marylebone, 1854-57; rector of St. Giles-in-the-Fields, London, 1857-67; minister of Curzon Chapel, Mayfair, 1868-69; vicar and rural dean of St. Pancras, London, 1869-74; resident canon of York, 1874-77; bishop of Rochester, 1877-90; and of Winchester, 1890-95. He was also examining chaplain to the archbishop of York for a number of years ranging about 1874; and select preacher at Oxford, 1878-80. He had a faculty for grasping detail and for organization. He was the author of *The Presence of Christ* (London, 1869); *The Gospel of Christ* (1881); *The Claim of Christ on the Young* (1882); *The Yoke of Christ in the Duties and Circumstances of Life* (1883); *Questions of Faith and Duty* (1892); *The Tenderness of Christ* (1894); and a volume of sermons, *The Gospel of Work*, included in *Preachers of the Age* (1891 sqq.). He had a rare spirituality and great felicity of expression, so that his practical writings are much-admired books of devotion.

BIBLIOGRAPHY: C. H. Simpkinson, *Life and Work of Bishop Thorold*, London, 1896; *DNB*, lvi. 312-313.

THREE-CHAPTER CONTROVERSY: One of the most important, though least edifying, episodes in the ecclesiastical policy of Justinian I. (q.v.), intimately connected with the Monophysite movement (see MONOPHYSITES). The conditions made it desirable to retain the powerful Monophysite party for the church by concessions, if it could be done without abandoning the position of the Council of Chalcedon. For this purpose it was thought advisable to take some action against the doctrines of

the school of Antioch, which was especially obnoxious to the Monophysites. Theodorus Ascidas, who had been bishop of Cæsarea in Cappadocia from 537, a zealous Origenist, hoped by thus advising the emperor at the same time to divert attention from the Origenistic controversy (see ORIGEN, ORIGENISTIC CONTROVERSIES). In 544 (according to F. Diekamp, in 543) Justinian issued an edict in which he condemned the so-called Three Chapters (the term *kephalaia*, or *capitula*, is used for formulated statements, then for special points mentioned in them, or even for persons or writings directly designated by them): namely, (1) the person and writings of Theodore of Mopsuestia (q.v.); (2) the writings of Theodoret of Cyrus (q.v.) in defense of Nestorius and against Cyril; and (3) the letter of Ibas of Edessa (q.v.) to the Persian Mares. As Theodore had died at peace with the Church, while Theodoret and Ibas had been expressly recognized as orthodox at Chalcedon, the concession to the Monophysites contained in the imperial edict appeared to undermine the authority of the council. There was, however, very little opposition to it in the Greek Church. In the West the controversy became the more violent, though the Roman Bishop Vigilius yielded to the wishes of the emperor in a way which aroused great scandal. In a synod held at Constantinople under Vigilius (548), the bishops were prevailed upon to give written verdicts for the condemnation of the Three Chapters, and Vigilius did the same in his *Judicatum* of Apr. 11, 548, at the same time insisting on the authority of the Council of Chalcedon. In the West the opposition found a leader in Bishop Facundus of Hermiane (q.v.), and an African synod excommunicated Vigilius. For a while he continued his uncertain policy; but when the emperor by a second edict (*homologia pisteōs*) pushed things to extremes, he arose in decisive opposition and had repeatedly to take sanctuary from the wrath of Justinian. He refused to be present at the fifth general council (Constantinople, May, 553), which considered the heresies of Theodore and the writings of Theodoret, and tried to prove that only individual members of the council of Chalcedon and not the council itself had approved of the epistle of Ibas. The *Constitutum de tribus capitulis* (May 14, 553) drawn up by Vigilius and signed by many Western bishops, which energetically opposed the condemnation of the Three Chapters, was not accepted by the emperor, who acquainted the synod with the terms in which Vigilius had formerly pledged himself in secret to the emperor's position. On June 2, 553, the council decided in accordance with the wishes of the emperor. The Greek Church yielded without succeeding in winning the Monophysites. The resistance of Vigilius was soon broken, and the opposition of the African Church was overcome by the endeavors of Primasius of Carthage after 559. But the churches of northern Italy, with Aquileia and Milan at their head, broke off communion with Rome, on account of the recognition of the fifth council by Vigilius and his successor, and this separation lasted, under the peculiar conditions caused by the Lombard conquest, till Gregory the Great succeeded in winning over Milan and Theodelinde, queen of the Lombards, who was under the archbishop's influence; though he attained this end by completely casting into the shade, or virtually repudiating, the fifth general council, of which the West had taken but little notice. The patriarchate of Aquileia, which as a result of the Lombard conquest had been transferred to Grado, resumed communion with Rome, under Greek rule, soon after the death of Gregory in 604; but the Roman Catholic bishops under the Lombard kings and the duke of Friali set up an opposition patriarchate, which remained separated from Rome till toward the end of the seventh century.   G. KRÜGER.

BIBLIOGRAPHY: The sources are easily accessible in *MPL*, lxvii. 521–878, 921–928, 1167–1254, lxviii. 956–960, 1049–1096; *MPG*, lxxxiv. 455–548. Consult: H. Noris, *Opera*, ed. Ballerini, i. 550–820, cf. iv. 985–1050, Verona, 1729 (highly necessary); J. G. Walch, *Historie der Ketzereien*, viii. 4–468, Leipsic, 1778; J. M. Schroeckh, *Christliche Kirchengeschichte*, xviii. 570–608, Leipsic, 1793; Schaff, *Christian Church*, iii. 768–772; J. Schwane, *Dogmengeschichte der patristischen Zeit*, pp. 374–378, Freiburg, 1895; A. Knecht, *Die Religionspolitik Kaiser Justinians I.*, pp. 125–140, Würzburg, 1896; H. Hutton, *The Church of the 6th Century*, pp. 162–179, London, 1897; F. Diekamp, *Die origenistischen Streitigkeiten im 6. Jahrhundert*, Münster, 1899; A. de Meissas, in *Annales de philosophie chrétienne*, July, 1904; Hefele, *Conciliengeschichte*, iii. 1 sqq., Eng. transl. iv. 258 sqq., Fr. transl., iii. 1, pp. 1 sqq. (valuable for the discussion of literature and notes); Harnack, *Dogma*, iv. 245 sqq., 346–349, v. 283; Mann, *Popes*, vol. i. passim.

THREE CHILDREN, SONG OF THE. See APOCRYPHA, A, IV., 3.

THUEMMEL, tüm'mel, **WILHELM:** Evangelical theologian; b. at Barmen (27 m. n.n.e. of Cologne) May 6, 1856. He received his education at the universities of Bonn and Leipsic; became assistant preacher at Geldern, and later at Lohne then near Soest; returned as pastor at Geldern in 1881, went in the same capacity to Remscheid, where, because of a harsh criticism of the Roman Catholic doctrine of transubstantiation, he was subjected to a three-weeks' term of imprisonment, on the termination of which he wrote the sharply worded tract in self-justification: *Rheinische Richter und römische Priester. Eine trostreiche Belehrung über die römische Messe* (Barmen, 1888); he later brought himself under police jurisdiction through a lecture on the pilgrimage to Aachen, and once again because of his *Antwort an der päpstlichen Priesterschaft in Breslau* (1894); he became privat-docent in church history at Berlin, 1900; extraordinary professor in 1901; and professor of practical theology at Jena in 1903, where he is also director of the homiletical and catechetical seminary. Besides the works already mentioned, he has issued: *Offener Brief an dem Herrn Erzbischof Krementz von Cöln* (1889); *Die Asche Clarenbach's, des Märtyrers der bergischen Kirche* (Berlin, 1890); *Zur Beurtheilung des Donatismus* (Halle, 1893); *Der Versagung der kirchlichen Bestattungsfeier, ihre geschichtliche Entwickelung und gegenwärtige Bedeutung* (Leipsic, 1902); and *Der Religionsschutz durch das Strafrecht* (1906); besides a considerable number of polemic tracts directed against the Roman Catholic Church or its doctrines.

THUMB BIBLE. See BIBLE VERSIONS, B, IV., § 9.

THUNDERING LEGION: Name of a Roman legion about which a celebrated legend arose. The story is that the Emperor Marcus Aurelius, when conducting a campaign against the Quadi in Hungary about 174 A.D., was surprised with his forces by a superior number of the enemy. At the same time his army was suffering so greatly from the lack of water that annihilation seemed imminent. The emperor prayed to the gods for rain, but no response was forthcoming. A legion, consisting wholly of Christians, was summoned to the emperor's aid, the soldiers of which prostrated themselves in prayer, and the response was a cold rain upon the Romans, which took the form of severe hail as it reached the Quadi, whom it discomfited. In consequence of this, the legion received the name "*Legio fulminatrix*."

The story has received the attention of many writers of church history, and its difficulties have been summarized as follows: A legion with this name was known before the time of Marcus Aurelius (Dio Cassius, lv. 23), though the exact form of the name was *Legio fulminata;* the proper station of this legion was in the East, not in Hungary. It is seen, however, that these data are not decisive against the story, since the legion might have been present owing to the emergency, such transfers not being unknown, and the slight change in the form of the name is not decisive. The principal incident is shown not to be improbable by the sculptures on the Antonine column at Rome, erected not long after, showing Jupiter Fluvius, from whose beard streams of water are caught in the soldiers' shields, while the enemy are overwhelmed by lightning. The least probable element in the story is that a whole legion was composed of Christians. In favor of a substantial basis of the legend is that it is first mentioned by Claudius Apollinaris (q.v.), who addressed his apology to Marcus Aurelius, while a contemporary of the assumed event who mentions it was Tertullian (*Apol.*, v.; *Ad Scapulam*, iv.). It is only miraculous through the interpretation, the event is not at all improbable.

BIBLIOGRAPHY: Besides the reference to Tertullian in the text (Eng. transl. in *ANF*, iii. 22, 107), and Dio Cassius, lxxi. 8–9, consult: Eusebius, *Hist. eccl.*, V., v., in *NPNF*, 2 ser., i. 219–220; W. Moyle, *De miraculo quod Legio Fulminatrix fecisse dicitur*, in Mosheim, *Dissertatio*, Görlitz, 1733; W. Whiston, *Of the Thundering Legion*, London, 1726; T. Woolston, *A Defence of the Miracle of the Thundering Legion against . . . W. Moyle*, ib. 1726; T. Hearne, *An Apology for the Writings of W. Moyle*, ib. 1727 (against Whiston and Woolston); B. Aubé, *Hist. des persecutions de l'église*, i., chap. viii., Paris, 1875; J. B. Lightfoot, *Apostolic Fathers*, II., i. 469–476, London, 1885; Schaff, *Christian Church*, ii. 56; Neander, *Christian Church*, i. 115–117; *DNB*, iv. 1023–24.

THURIBLE. See CENSER.

THURIFICATI. See LAPSED.

THURINGIA: A collective name applied to a group of small duchies and principalities situated between Prussian Saxony on the north and Bavaria on the south, and between the kingdom of Saxony on the east and Hesse-Nassau on the west. The duchies are Saxe-Weimar, Saxe-Meiningen, Saxe-Altenburg, and Saxe-Coburg-Gotha; the principalities are Reuss-Schleiz, Reuss-Greiz, Schwarzburg-Rudolstadt, and Schwarzburg-Sondershausen. The combined area is 4,744 square miles, and the population (1905) 1,503,125. Of these 1,455,949

(General Statistics.)

were Evangelical; 38,045 Roman Catholic; and 4,143 Jews. The church year-book of 1907 shows a Roman Catholic increase, by immigration, in Weimar of 27 per cent, and a Protestant increase of 6 per cent; in Rudolstadt, Roman Catholic increase 57 per cent, and Protestant, only 4 per cent. Thuringian Roman Catholics are distributed among five bishoprics; Weimar (with 9 parishes) belongs to Fulda, Meiningen (5) to Würzburg, Altenburg (1) and the two principalities of Reuss (3) belong to the apostolic vicariate of Saxony at Dresden, Gotha (1) and the two Schwarzburgs (3) to Paderborn, and Coburg (1) belongs to Bamberg. In the cities of Weimar church schools are maintained mostly through the " Society of Boniface," except in the Eisenach Highlands, where state schools prevail. The Unity of the Brethren have a settlement at Ebersdorf, Reuss-Schleiz, with female seminary and mission-school, and a location at Neudietendorf near Gotha. There is a small scattering of Mennonites, Baptists, Methodists, and Irvingites. At Blankenburg the Evangelical Alliance of Germany has a great hotel and auditorium where the radical wing of that society assembles the last week of August every year. The history of the church government in the various states is practically the same. There existed consistorial governments until **Govern-** the period of 1848–66, when they were **ment of the** abolished and their functions assigned **State** to a department of the territorial min-**Church.** istry of public worship and education. Under these departments there is a supervision of the churches by ephors or superintendents of respective districts. At the same time a local church government was instituted consisting in church meetings and church councils; in Meiningen the former have, besides the election of the church council, to decide upon the raising of funds, alterations in the liturgy, the use of catechisms and hymnals, the change of the parish, and the like. The local church councils, of which the pastor and local magistrate are generally *ex-officio* members, have to see after good morals and church order, the administration of property, legal representation, and local charity, in cooperation with civil boards, if such exist. In Altenburg and the two Schwarzburgs they exercised the *votum negativum*, or right of protest against the doctrine, conduct, or person of the pastor. In the Schwarzburgs (as also in Weimar) there are general church councils under the department of the ministry of public worship and education, which presides over them; its functions are examination of candidates, supervision of official conduct, and introduction of measures looking to the appointment and promotion of the clergy. To the local church councils belongs the prerogative of removing deficits by taxation. In Coburg the administration under the ministry of public worship and education is exercised through the division of the State Church into six ephories, each under the joint control of the local state councilor, or magistrate if in the city, and the magistrate's councilor, and the ephor; in Gotha each of the eight official church districts is under a board composed of the councilor or city magistrate, a senator, and the ephor. Exceptionally the old consistorial order yet exists in

Reuss-Greiz; to it was added in 1880 limited local church rule with governing council. Generally, the churches have no representative functions. Only in Weimar and Meiningen are there synods in which the local churches and the government have representatives. With the exception of four delegates out of thirty-five in Weimar and two out of twenty-two in Meiningen appointed by the dukes, and in the former one representative of Jena University, all are elected by the larger elective unions composed of the dioceses of the superintendents. These synods, however, have only advisory power; they have no voice in the levy of taxes or adoption of measures. The church government of Thuringia may be described, on the whole, as episcopal under strict control by the heads of the states, with a presbyterial appendage for local purposes. The official designation in Weimar and Meiningen is Evangelical State Church; in Altenburg, Evangelical Protestant; and in the Schwarzburgs and Reuss-Greiz, Evangelical Lutheran. The church governments of Thuringia are all represented at the Eisenach Conference (q.v.). All except Meiningen have assumed part in the Evangelical church union (see BUND, EVANGELISCHER). In common the Thuringian church governments have a loose affiliation and enter into mutual conference as occasion may require.

The grand-duchy of Weimar, with 21 dioceses, having each a superintendent and adjunct and a judge inspector of the circuit on the secular side, **Parochial** had (1905) 312 clerical positions with **Statistics.** c. 270 pastors and vicars. Many pastorates, in the cities chiefly, are filled by choice of the governing council, about one-fourth by the patron, usually by virtue of his patronage a member of the council, and the majority by the civil church government. Examination of candidates takes place before the council at Weimar and is participated in by a few Jena professors. Visitations take place at stated periods on the part of the general church council and members of the synodal committee. In Meiningen, where the order of appointment and visitation is the same as in Weimar, the State Church counts 14 ephories, 144 parishes, and about 130 clergy; in Altenburg 8 ephories, 116 parishes, and about 130 clergy; in Gotha 12 ephories, about 100 parishes, and about 120 clergy; in Coburg 4 ephories, 37 parishes, and about 35 clergy; in Sondershausen, 4 ephories, 58 parishes, and about 60 clergy; and in Rudolstadt, 5 ephories, 65 parishes, and about 60 clergy. There is throughout a graduated system of ground income with increment, of retiring allowances, and widows' pensions. In catechetics, liturgy, and use of hymnals there is much diversity; the system of pericopes is still firmly prevalent, limiting the minister in the use of Biblical material and in renewing interest. The church attendance is small, more so in the country and towns than in the cities. Charitable orders and institutions are semi-philanthropic and semi-ecclesiastical, owing to the close historical connection of Church and State. A network of women's associations overspreads Weimar, federated in the " Patriotic Institute of Women's Societies "; but, although possessing the Church as their main support, yet they do not constitute an ecclesiastical army of deaconesses. Orphanages have everywhere a firm footing; in Weimar this institution is an organic link of the State Church. Charity is in the hands of the local churches. The churches are devoting increasing attention to the Innere Mission (q.v.); and in all the states are juvenile asylums, hospices, houses for the fallen, and institutions for the feeble-minded and convalescent. Two institutions of deaconesses have been planted; one, the Sophia House in Weimar, with 146 sisters (1905), and the other the mother-house at Eisenach, with 115. The outer mission centers in the comprehensive annual Thuringian mission conference. Besides, there is a special Evangelical Lutheran missionary union. The University of Jena representing Thuringia as a whole reached its flourishing state in the nineteenth century, when K. A. Hase (q.v.) taught church history and R. A. Lipsius (q.v.) dogmatics. After their death, the general decline of theological study of the time specially affected the university. Recently there has occurred some increase in attendance, although the duchies are capable of furnishing but a small number of theological students, and the principalities prefer to send theirs elsewhere. For the promotion of the clergy, the Thuringian Church Conference assembles at Paulinzella in the autumn for addresses and discussions, and theologians take the autumn vacation course of three days at Jena conducted by the faculty, while in all state churches are conducted the diocesan and other monthly or quarterly free conferences.

(F. W. THÜMMEL.)

BIBLIOGRAPHY: L. Tümpel, *Die Gottesdienstordnung der thüringischen Kirchen*, Gotha, 1861; W. Rein, *Thuringia sacra*, 2 vols., Weimar, 1863–65; C. A. H. Burkhardt, *Geschichte der sächsischen Kirchen- und Schulvisitationen*, Leipsic, 1879; H. Gebhardt, *Pfarrer in Mohlschleben bei Gotha*, 33 vols., Gotha, 1881; O. Füsslein, *Amtshandbuch für Geistliche und Lehrer des Herzogtums Sachsen-Meiningen*, Hildburghausen, 1883; E. Friedberg, *Die geltenden Verfassungsgesetze der evangelischen deutschen Landeskirchen*, 2 vols., Freiburg, 1885; A. Gillwald, *Thüringen in Geschichte*, Eisenach, 1887; G. Einicke, *20 Jahre schwarzburgische Reformationsgeschichte, 1521–41*, part 1, Nordhausen, 1904; J. Freisen, *Staat und katholische Kirche in den deutschen Bundesstaaten*, Stuttgart, 1906; O. Holder-Egger, *Studien zu thüringischen Geschichtsquellen*, in *NA*, vol. xxi.; E. Sehling, *Die evangelischen Kirchenordnungen des 16. Jahrhunderts*, 2 parts, Leipsic, 1902–04; P. Glaue, *Das kirchliche Leben der evangelischen Kirchen in Thüringen*, Tübingen, 1910.

THWING, CHARLES FRANKLIN: Congregationalist; b. at New Sharon, Me., Nov. 9, 1853. He was graduated from Harvard (A.B., 1876) and Andover Theological Seminary (1879). He was then pastor of North Avenue Congregational Church, Cambridge, Mass. (1879–86), and Plymouth Church, Minneapolis, Minn. (1886–90), and since 1890 has been president of Western Reserve University and Adelbert College, Cleveland, O. He was editor of *The Chicago Advance* in 1888–91 and is now associate editor of the *Bibliotheca Sacra*, and has written *American Colleges: Their Students and Work* (New York, 1878); *The Reading of Books: Its Pleasures, Profits, and Perils* (Boston, 1883); *The Family: Historical and Social Study* (in collaboration with wife; 1887); *The Working Church* (New York, 1888); *Within College Walls* (1893); *The College Woman* (1894); *The American College in American Life* (1897); *The Best Life* (1898); *The Choice of a*

College for a Boy (1899); *College Administration* (1900); *The Youth's Dream of Life* (Boston, 1900); *God in His World* (1900); *If I were a College Student* (New York, 1902); *A Liberal Education and a Liberal Faith* (1903); *College Training and the Business Man* (1904); *History of Higher Education in America* (1906); and *History of Education in the U. S. Since the Civil War* (1910).

THYATIRA. See ASIA MINOR, IV.

TIARA. See VESTMENTS AND INSIGNIA, ECCLESIASTICAL.

TIBERIAS. See GALILEE, § 4.

TICHONIUS (TYCHONIUS), tik-ō'nî-ūs: African Donatist of the late fourth century. He is first mentioned by Gennadius, who places him between Rufinus (d. 410) and Sulpicius Severus (d. after 420), and states that he was learned in the Scriptures, history, and profane sciences, that he was full of zeal for the Church, and that he wrote *De bello intestino*, *Expositiones diversarum causarum*, and also a book containing seven rules for exegesis and a spiritual interpretation of the Apocalypse. He denied the future thousand-years' reign of the righteous on the earth after the resurrection, holding that the twofold resurrection described in the Apocalypse denoted, on the one hand, the growth of the Church, where those who were justified by faith were awakened by baptism from the deadness of their sins to the service of eternal life, and, on the other hand, the general resurrection of all flesh. Gennadius furthermore states that Tichonius was a contemporary of Rufinus, and that he flourished during the reign of Theodosius and his sons. The only later writer to add information concerning Tichonius is Johannes Trithemius (q.v.), who gives an extended list of the Donatist's writings, mentioning three books of the *De bello intestino* and also alluding to " numerous letters to divers persons, and many other things " (*De scriptoribus ecclesiasticis*, xcii.).

The exegetical rules of Tichonius (*MPL*, xviii. 15–66) were given in detail and exhaustively criticized by Augustine in *De doctrina Christiana* (iii. 30–37; *MPL*, xxxiv. 81–90; best by F. C. Burkitt, in *TS*, iii. 1, 1894, superseding entirely former editions; Eng. transl. of the chapters of Augustine in *NPNF*, 1 ser., ii. 568–573), and they thus received an approval which secured them long influence. The first rule, " on the Lord and his body," shows how, when the head and the body (or Christ and the Church) are set forth under one person, one may accurately determine what is said of each. Thus, the " stone that smote the image," according to Dan. ii. 35, is Christ, and the " great mountain " which it became is the Church. The second rule, " on the twofold body of the Lord," deals with the division into right and left, so that when the Church is described as " black, but comely " (Cant. i. 5), the first adjective refers to her left side and the second to her right. The third rule, " on the promises and the law," shows how, though no one is justified by the works of the law, some have fulfilled the law and have been justified. The fourth rule, " on species and genus," deals with those passages of Scripture in which there is a transfer from species to genus or *vice versa*. Thus, the words of Christ, " the dead . . .

that hear shall live " (John v. 25), refer to the first, or spiritual, resurrection, while " all that are in the tombs . . . shall come forth " (John v. 28) alludes to the second, or general, resurrection. The fifth rule, " on times," gives the mystic measure of time in the Bible either by synecdoche or by formulaic numbers. In the case of synecdoche, the three days between the death and resurrection of Christ (Matt. xii. 40) imply that the hour of his burial stands for the entire day and the preceding night, while the hour of the night at which he arose stands for the entire night and the following day, a whole day and a whole night intervening between the two parts. The "formulaic numbers" include seven, ten, and twelve, together with their squares and tenth powers. The sixth rule, " on recapitulation," affirms that what seems to be a continuation of a narrative in reality refers either to what has recently taken place or to what will occur in the future; and the seventh rule, " on the devil and his body," stresses the importance of determining in every case whether what is said concerning the devil refers to himself or to his body.

These rules were practically applied by Tichonius in his commentary on Revelation, which was preserved in manuscript in the library of the monastery of St. Gall as late as the ninth century. It has disappeared, however, and must be constructed from the extracts from it preserved by later exegetes of the Apocalypse. Here belong the five books of the commentary on Revelation by Primasius, bishop of Hadrumetum (*MPL*, lxviii. 793–936); and these are supplemented in part by the ten books of the commentary of Ambrosius Autpert (q.v.), who was followed by Alcuin (*MPL*, c. 1086–1156) and Haimo of Halberstadt (*MPL*, cxvii. 937–1120), the latter serving in his turn as the source of Walafried Strabo's *Glossa ordinaria* (*MPL*, cxiv. 710–752). Cassiodorus, in his *Complexiones in epistolas et Acta Apostolorum et Apocalypsin*, also cites briefly from Tichonius; and Bede, in his *Explanatio Apocalypsis* (*MPL*, xciii. 130–206), explicitly cites the commentary of Tichonius on a number of passages. Jerome likewise incorporated certain passages from Tichonius in his revision of the commentary of Victorinus of Petau. The pseudo-Augustinian homilies on the Apocalypse (*MPL*, xxxv. 2415–52) are de-Donatized extracts from Tichonius with additions from Victorinus; and all Donatism has likewise been expunged from the fragments on Rev. ii. 18–iv. 1 and vii. 10–xii. 6, preserved in a Turin manuscript and edited in *Spicilegium Casinense*, III., i. 261–331 (Monte Cassino, 1897). One of the most important sources for a reconstruction of Tichonius' commentary is the commentary of Beatus, a Spanish presbyter of Libana (ed. H. Florez, Madrid, 1770), who wrote in 776 and united in his work the most divergent tendencies of the earlier Latin exegesis of the Apocalypse. Finally, the heterogeneous production entitled *Etherii et Beatii adversus Elpandum* (*MPL*, xcvi. 894–1030) contains not only fragments from the commentary of Tichonius, but also, to all appearance, from his *De bello intestino*, a fact which is the more important since the latter work is otherwise unknown. The difficulty of the reconstruction of the commentary of Tichonius from the sources enumerated lies in the determination

which text represents in each instance not only the thoughts, but also the words, of Tichonius.
(J. Haussleiter.)

Bibliography: The " Introduction " to Burkitt's ed. of " The Rules," ut sup.; F. Ribbeck, *Donatus und Augustinus*, pp. 198–206, Elberfeld, 1858; J. Haussleiter, in *ZKW*, vii (1886), 239–257; idem, in T. Zahn, *Forschungen zur Geschichte des neutestamentlichen Kanons*, iv. 1–224, Leipsic, 1891; F. W. Farrar, *Hist. of Interpretation*, pp. 24–26, 276, 279, New York, 1886; T. Hahn, *Tyconius-Studien*, Leipsic, 1900; M. Schanz, *Geschichte der römischen Litteratur*, iv. 350–353, Munich, 1904; W. Bousset, in his commentary on Revelation, pp. 56–60, 65–72, 461, Göttingen, 1906; Ceillier, *Auteurs sacrés*, v. 100–105; *KL*, xii. 153–156; *DCB*, iv. 1025–26.

TIDEMANN, JOHANN. See Timann.

TIEFTRUNK, JOHANN HEINRICH: German theologian; b. at Stove near Rostock 1759; d. at Halle Oct. 7, 1837. He studied theology and philology at the University of Halle, became private tutor, and in 1781 rector of the town school and preacher in Joachimstal in Uckermark. In 1792 he was appointed professor of philosophy at Halle. His importance lies in his works on the philosophy of religion, through which he became one of the first and most effective mediators between Kant and the theology of his time. Tieftrunk energetically advocated the assertion of reason in the sphere of religion. Like Kant, he bases religion upon ethics. The religious objects can not be proved by theoretical reason, but by practical reason in advancing from the a priori law of morals to the conditions under which alone this can be thought possible. Tieftrunk is firmly convinced that the moral faith established in this way is a faith based on reason. Knowledge of God obtained in this way is symbolical. To make any assertions regarding the essential being of God in view of the limitations of reason is vain; hence all speculation is to be renounced. Tieftrunk's own contribution to this Kantian platform was to apply this rational faith to Christianity. The sole fundamental law of the religion of Jesus is love to God and neighbor; but this is identical with the religious principle of reason, "Act in accordance with the law of freedom as the supreme sanctity of the will." Prophecy, miracle, and revelation admit neither proof nor dogmatic denial. Revelation affords no new truths transcending reason, but only sensualizes the religious truths and hastens conscious apprehension. To interpret the rational moral content of the dogmas was the purpose of Tieftrunk's main work, *Zensur des christlichen protestantischen Lehrbegriffs* (3 vols., Berlin, 1791–95). In his *Religion der Mündigen* (1799–1800) he advances further to the liberation of all religion from the statutory and historical and to the pure religion of reason rising above all authority, even that of Jesus. It is a broad transcription of the Kantian philosophy of religion, without regard for Christian dogmas.   (Heinrich Hoffmann.)

Bibliography: G. Kertz, *Die Religionsphilosophie J. H. Tieftrunks*, Berlin, 1907; F. C. Baur, *Die christliche Lehre von der Versöhnung*, pp. 568 sqq., Tübingen, 1838; idem, *Dreieinigkeit und Menschwerdung*, iii. 782 sqq., ib. 1843; W. Gass, *Geschichte der protestantischen Dogmatik*, iv. 300 sqq., Berlin, 1867; G. Frank, *Geschichte der protestantischen Theologie*, iii. 189 sqq., Leipsic, 1875.

TIELE, tî'le, **CORNELIS PETRUS:** Dutch theologian; b. at Leyden Dec. 16, 1830; d. there

Jan. 11, 1902. He received his education at the Remonstrants' Seminary and the Athenæum Illustre at Amsterdam; became Remonstrant pastor at Moordrecht, 1853; and at Rotterdam, 1856; professor at the Remonstrants' Seminary, 1873, which was moved in that year to Leyden, dealing with practical theology, homiletics, and history of the Remonstrant Church. The classes were small and he had abundant leisure for study. From the beginning he displayed a remarkable literary activity. His pastoral work earned for him a reputation as a brilliant and eloquent preacher, and to this was added the impression made by his dignified but gracious personal bearing. But his type was rather intellectual than emotional; he avoided easily the ecclesiastical dissensions of his times. He was the venerated leader of the Remonstrants of his day, the number of whom was greatly increased by the ecclesiastical measures in the great Dutch Reformed Church.

His chosen field was the science of religions, in which he gained high repute at home and abroad, a repute deserved by the pioneer work which he did. Much of his work was path-breaking. The national " University Act " (1877) gave him an opportunity to express his belief as to the place in the curriculum of the science of theology, and while the results were only a partial embodiment of his ideas, the total effect was the establishment at Amsterdam and Leyden of chairs in this branch; that at Leyden naturally and rightly went to him. He had long before begun work in his *De Godsdienst van Zarathustra van haar onstaan in Baktrië tot den val van het Oud-Perzische Rijk* (Haarlem, 1864), continued in *Vergelijkende Geschiedenis van de Egyptische en Mesopotamische Godsdiensten* (Amsterdam, 1872; Eng. transl., *Comparative History of the Egyptian and Mesopotamian Religions*, London, 1882). This was intended as the first part of a work *Vergelijkende Geschiedenis der oude Godsdiensten*, of which the second part came out only in 1891–1902. In 1876 appeared *Geschiedenis van den Godsdienst tot aan de heerschappij der Wereldgodsdiensten*, in which he characterized the religions of antiquity. This was translated into most of the continental languages (Eng. transl., *Outlines of the History of Religion to the Spread of the Universal Religions*, London, 1877). In 1886 he issued a " History of Babylonia and Assyria " in two volumes. Between 1891 and 1902 appeared *Geschiedenis van den Godsdienst . . . tot op Alexander den Groote*, which treated the Asiatic religions, including those of the Aryan group, and was enriched by a bibliography. The crown of his work in this direction was his Gifford Lectures on *Elements of the Science of Religion*, published at the same time in English and Dutch. This publication reveals both Tiele's strength and his weakness —his talent for analyzing religious life and the lesser degree of aptitude for philosophy. In all his literary work he proved himself a master in methodical arrangement and clearness of style.

The aim which Tiele set himself at the outset was not the investigation of particular religions, but to learn the history of religion as a universal historical fact. To this purpose he held steadfast throughout his life. Underlying this was profound belief in the truth of evolution as applied to religion. The various processes of evolution he discovered in the growth of religion in general. Thus a unity is discovered in his life and accomplishments which is not diminished when the many contributions to periodical literature are examined. His life was a singularly happy one, to which his own cheerful disposition and continuous and conscious unity of direction made its own contributions. His worth and eminence were recognized in his own lifetime by suitable academic and other honors, and especially by the position which was accorded him in his own country.   S. CRAMER.

BIBLIOGRAPHY: P. D. Chantepie de la Saussaye, in *Jaarboek der Koninklijke Akademie van Wetenschappen*, Amsterdam, 1902; De Goeje, in *Eigen Haard*, 1898; W. B. Kristensen, in *Woord en Beeld*, 1899; *Mannen en Vrouwen van beteekenis*, pp. 358–364, Haarlem, 1902; M. Jastrow, in *The Independent* (New York), liv (1902), 510 sqq.; L. H. Jordan, *Comparative Religion, its Genesis and Growth*, passim (consult Index), New York, 1905; idem, in *Biblical World*, xxi (1903), 32 sqq., 124 sqq.

TIFFANY, CHARLES COMFORT: Protestant Episcopalian; b. at Baltimore, Md., Oct. 5, 1829; d. at Northeast Harbor, Mt. Desert, Me., Aug. 20, 1908. He was educated at Dickinson College, Carlisle, Pa. (A.B., 1850), at the universities of Halle, Heidelberg, and Berlin, and at Andover Theological Seminary (1854). He was a curate at Germantown, Pa. (1866–68), rector of St. James', Fordham, N. Y. (1868–71), curate on the Green Foundation, Trinity Church, Boston, Mass. (1871–74), rector of the Church of the Atonement, New York (1874–80), and of Zion Church, New York (1880–90); examining chaplain to Bishop Potter (1882–1902), and archdeacon of New York (1894–1902). During the last year of the Civil War he was chaplain of the Sixth Connecticut Volunteers, and at the taking of Fort Fisher he was aide to General Terry. He is the author of *Modern Atheism* (New York, 1874); *History of the Protestant Episcopal Church* (New York, 1895); and *The Prayer Book and the Christian Life* (1898).

TIGERT, JOHN JAMES: Methodist Episcopal Church, South; b. at Louisville, Ky., Nov. 25, 1856; d. at Tulsa, I. T., Nov. 21, 1906. He was educated at Vanderbilt University (A.B., 1877); was tutor and professor of moral philosophy there (1881–90); was a pastor in Kansas City, Mo. (1890–94), and book editor of the Methodist Episcopal Church, South, and editor of the *Methodist Quarterly Review* (1894–1906). In 1906, only six months before his death, he was elected bishop. He wrote *Handbook of Logic* (Nashville, Tenn., 1885); *Theology and Philosophy* (1888); *The Preacher Himself* (1889); *A Voice from the South* (1882); *Constitutional History of American Episcopal Methodism* (1894); *The Journal of Thomas Coke* (1894); *The Making of Methodism* (1898); *Theism—A Survey of the Paths that Lead to God* (1901); and *The Doctrines of the Methodist Episcopal Church in America* (2 vols., New York, 1902). He edited T. O. Sumner's *Systematic Theology* (2 vols., Nashville, 1886); H. N. McTyeire's *Passing through the Gates* (1889); and J. S. Banks' *Manual of Christian Doctrine* (1897).

TIGLATH-PILESER. See ASSYRIA, VI., 3, §§ 6, 9.

TIKHON. First Russian archbishop of America; b. in the Russian province of Pskov in 1865. He graduated from the St. Petersburg Theological Academy, and was immediately appointed professor in the seminary at Cholm. In 1897 he was consecrated bishop of Lublin, assistant to the bishop of Warsaw; was transferred to San Francisco · as bishop of Alaska and the Aleutian Islands, 1899; became the presiding bishop of the Russian church in America, 1904, when that year the number of bishops of the Russian church in America increased to three, and in 1905 was elevated to be archbishop of North America with his see at New York. His relations with the Episcopalians were friendly till the ordination to the priesthood of the Russian church of a deposed Episcopalian minister. In 1905 Archbishop Tikhon introduced a new departure, in holding at the New York cathedral the Sunday evening service in English. He was succeeded in 1907 by Dr. Platon as archbishop of North America.

A. A. Stamouli.

TIL, SALOMON VAN: Dutch preacher and professor; b. at Weesp (8 m. s.e. of Amsterdam) Dec. 26, 1643; d. in Leyden Oct. 31, 1713. He studied theology in Utrecht and under the influence of Frans Burman (q.v.) became a moderate adherent of Cocceianism. Later he studied at Leyden under Cocceius, who soon entertained great hopes of the promising disciple. In 1666 Van Til became preacher in Huisduinen, in 1676 in De Rijp, in 1682 in Medemblik, and in 1683 in Dort, where he more than fulfilled the high expectations caused by his faithful service in smaller places. In 1684 he was appointed professor of sacred history and languages, retaining his office as preacher, and in 1685 professor of theology. In 1702 he went to Leyden as professor of theology. Here his lectures on the prophets, on Cocceius' De fœdere, and on homiletics were heard by crowds of students, who welcomed him as a teacher and loved him as a personal friend.

In philosophy Til was a Cartesian and he recognized the right of reason even in the domain of theology. This led him to distinguish between natural and revealed theology (cf. his Theologiæ utriusque, cum naturalis tum revelatæ, compendium, Leyden, 1704). He had a good knowledge of oriental languages and used it especially in studies of the Old-Testament prophets, publishing a commentary on the song of Moses and the prophecy of Habakkuk (Leyden, 1700), Malachias illustratus (1701), and Commentaria analytica in varios libros propheticos (3 vols., 1744), in which he proved himself more than mere exegete or federal theologian. Other exegetical works treated of the Psalms (4 books in Dutch, Dort, 1693, 1696, 1699), the Gospel of Matthew (Dort, 1683), the Epistles to the Romans and Philippians (Haarlem, 1721), and I Corinthians, Ephesians, Philemon, and Colossians (Amsterdam, 1726). An archeological treatise on the tabernacle (Dort, 1714) belongs in the same class of works. A series of apologetic lectures delivered in Dort was published under the title Het Voorhof der Heidenen voor alle ongeloovigen geopent enz (Dort, 1694; continued 1696), and two collections of sermons (Dutch, Leyden, 1714; Latin, Utrecht, 1714) preserve specimens of his preaching, which was considered masterly in his time. A Methodus concionandi

(Franeker, 1712) contains some of the material of his homiletical lectures. Salems vreede in Liefde, Trouw en Waarheit behartigt (Dort, 1680) testifies to the author's hatred of dissension and desire to promote the peace of the Church. He was a man of moderate powers of thought but great learning, open-hearted, simple in his manner of life, and of upright piety.

(S. D. van Veen.)

Bibliography: A Vita by H. van de Wall is prefixed to Til's commentary on the Tabernacle, Amsterdam, 1714. Consult further: G. D. J. Schotel, Kerkelyk Dordrecht, ii. 15–60, Utrecht, 1845; B. Glasius, Godgeleerd Nederland, iii. 431–437, Bois-le-Duc, 1856; C. Sepp, Het godgeleerd Onderwijs in Nederland, vol. ii. passim, Leyden, 1874.

TILLEMONT, tîl′′mōn′, **LOUIS SÉBASTIEN LE NAIN DE:** French Roman Catholic church historian; b. of noble family in Paris Nov. 30, 1637; d. at his estate, Tillemont, near Paris (between Vincennes and Montreuil) Jan. 10, 1698. His family name was Le Nain, but he called himself Tillemont after his estate and is commonly so known. He was educated in the school of Port Royal and throughout his life shared the views and fortunes of the Port Royal Jansenists. He first took orders in 1676. Historical studies were always his chief delight and he furnished historical material, notes, and even entire chapters for historical works by his friends, including biographies for editions of several of the Church Fathers. Not until the fifty-third year of his life did he publish (anonymously) the first volume of his first great work, Histoire des empereurs et des autres princes qui ont régné durant les six premiers siècles de l'église, des persécutions qu'ils ont faites contre les Chrétiens, de leur guerres contre les Juifs, des écrivains profanes et des personnes illustres de leur temps (Paris, 1690). Three more volumes followed during the author's lifetime and the fifth and sixth after his death (1701, 1738), bringing the history down to Anastasius I. in the beginning of the sixth century. This work was intended as part of another which is Tillemont's greatest achievement, the Mémoires pour servir à l'histoire ecclésiastique des six premiers siècles justifiés par les citations des auteurs originaux; avec une chronologie et des notes. The first three volumes appeared (Paris, 1693 sqq.) during Tillemont's life; thirteen more were published from his manuscripts after his death (1698–1712; Eng. transl. by T. Deacon, Ecclesiastical Memoirs of the First Six Centuries, 2 vols., London, 1733–35; The History of the Arians and of the Council of Nice, translated from Tillemont's Memoirs, 2 vols., London, 1721), extending to the year 513. A Vie de Saint Louis, roi de France, was published from Tillemont's manuscript preserved in the Royal Library by J. de Gaulle in six volumes at Paris, 1847–51. Tillemont's church history was the first to be produced in France with faithful reference directly to the sources. It consists for the most part of a chronological arrangement of citations from ancient writers without critical examination. Tillemont's remarks are included in parentheses, and such investigations as he made into difficult questions are added in notes. The method of presentation is dry, but such a collection of the older sources was of great use in its time for the study of church history, and while Tillemont's criticism does not meet the requirements of modern standards, in no small number of cases he refuted error and opened the way to sound judgment. (C. Pfender.)

Bibliography: M. Tronchay, *Idée de la vie et de l'esprit de Le Nain de Tillemont*, Nancy, 1706; Fontaine, *Mémoires pour servir à l'hist. de Port-Royal*, vol. ii., Utrecht, 1736; B. Racine, *Abrégé de l'hist. ecclésiastique*, xii. 382–403, 13 vols., Paris, 1748–56; J. Bespigne, *Hist. de l'abbaye de Port Royal*, v. 75–101, Cologne, 1853; Lichtenberger, *ESR*, xii. 164–166.

TILLETT, WILBUR FISK: Methodist Episcopalian, South; b. at Henderson, N. C., Aug. 25, 1854. He was educated at Trinity College, Durham, N. C. (1871–73), Randolph-Macon College, Ashland, Va. (A.B., 1877), and Princeton Theological Seminary (1880); was pastor of the church of his denomination at Danville, Va. (1880–82). Since 1882 he has been connected with Vanderbilt University, Nashville, Tenn., where he has been chaplain and instructor in systematic theology in the Biblical department (1882–83), adjunct professor of the same subject (1883–84), and full professor of systematic theology (since 1884). Since 1886 he has also been dean of the theological faculty and *ex-officio* vice-chancellor of the university. In 1886–89 he was the secretary of the committee which prepared a new hymn-book for his denomination and was the editor of that publication, while in 1902–05 he was a member of the joint committee of the Methodist Episcopal Church, South, and the Methodist Episcopal Church which prepared a new hymnal for the two bodies, being again the editor. In theology he terms himself " a liberal and progressive conservative," and has written *Discussions in Theology* (Nashville, 1887); *Our Hymns and their Authors* (1889); *Personal Salvation: Studies in Christian Doctrine pertaining to the Spiritual Life* (1902); and *Doctrines and Polity of the Methodist Episcopal Church, South* (1903).

TILLOTSON, JOHN: Archbishop of Canterbury; b. at Sowerby, Halifax, England, 1630 (baptized Oct. 10, 1630); d. in London Nov. 22, 1694. He studied at Clare Hall, Cambridge (B.A., 1650; fellow, 1651; M.A., 1654; and D.D., 1666), where Puritan principles were inculcated, but he did not imbibe Puritan doctrines, leaning rather in a latitudinarian direction. Chillingworth, through his writings, is also said to have molded Tillotson's opinions. Early in 1657 he went, as private tutor, to London; he was ordained, and was preaching in 1661, apparently for the Presbyterian party, but in 1662 he submitted to the Act of Uniformity (q.v.), and in 1661 became curate to Thomas Hacket, who was vicar of Cheshunt, Hertfordshire. He was rector of Kedington, Suffolk, 1663–64; preacher at Lincoln's Inn, 1663–91; Tuesday lecturer at St. Lawrence Jewry, 1664–91; as chaplain to Charles II. he became second prebend at Canterbury, 1670, and dean 1672; was also prebend at St. Paul's, 1675–77; became clerk of the closet to the king, 1689; dean of St. Paul's, 1689; was appointed to exercise archiepiscopal jurisdiction, 1689; and became archbishop, 1691. He began as an author in 1664, by publishing a sermon on *The Wisdom of being Religious* (London, 1664), and *The Rule of Faith* (2 parts., 1666). It was as a preacher and as an author

of sermons that he became most distinguished; his plain, almost colloquial style, free from learned quotations, artificial arrangement, and endless subdivisions, made him popular with the middle classes, while his good sense and cultured mind made him acceptable also to the learned. He was a thorough Protestant, and at home in the Roman Catholic controversy, and appealed to reason as well as to revelation in support of his opinions. He was a Whig in politics, opposed to the despotism of the Stuarts, and an advocate of ecclesiastical comprehension. He welcomed the Revolution of 1688; and took part, in 1689, in the ecclesiastical commission for revising the Prayer Book. He showed moderation to nonjurors and non-conformists, though hearing their animosity, and exercised a liberal hospitality. T. Birch's edition of his works with his life appeared (3 vols., London, 1752; best ed., 12 vols., 1757).

Bibliography: Besides the *Life* by Birch, ut sup. consult: G. Burnet, *A Sermon . . . at the Funeral of John, Archbishop of Canterbury*, London, 1694; N. Tate, *An Elegy on . . John . . . Archbishop of Canterbury*, ib. 1695; L. Atterbury, *A Vindication of Archbishop Tillotson's Sermons*, ib. 1709; F. H., *The Life of . . . John Tillotson*, ib. 1717; G. Whitefield, *Three Letters from G. Whitefield*, ib. 1740; J. Hunt, *Religious Thought in England*, vols. ii.–iii., ib. 1871–73; W. G. Humphry, in J. E. Kempe, *The Classic Preachers of the English Church*, 2 ser., ib. 1878; W. H. Hutton, *The English Church . . . (1625–1714)*, ib. 1903; *DNB*, lvi. 392–398.

TIMANN, JOHANN (JOHANNES AMSTERDAMUS TIDEMANN): Lutheran Reformer; b. at Amsterdam before 1500; d. at Nienburg (30 m. n.w. of Hanover) Feb. 17, 1557. In 1522 he came to Wittenberg and the next year, accompanied by Jakob Propst (q.v.), he went to Bremen, and on the recommendation of Heinrich von Zütphen (q.v.) was called as pastor to the Church of St. Martin. After the departure of Zütphen, Nov., 1524, Timann and Propst led the Reformation in Bremen, and in 1525 German hymns and the administration of both elements of the Eucharist were introduced. With Johann Pelt, pastor of St. Ansgar, Timann was called to Emden in 1529 by Count Enno II. of East Friesland to counteract the influence of the Anabaptists. Having accomplished little, they returned to Bremen, 1529–30. On account of an uprising of the peasants in 1532, Timann and Propst removed for a month to Brinkum, after which they returned to their congregations. Timann had probably a prominent part in the drafting of the church order which, after submission to Luther and J. P. Bugenhagen, was adopted by the council. He represented Bremen at the convention at Hamburg which took measures against the Anabaptists, and also at the conference at Schmalkald, and at the Colloquy at Worms (1540–41), and he attended the Conference of Regensburg (q.v.) as ecclesiastical adviser of the councilors of Bremen. In the Hardenberg controversy on the Eucharist he wrote the pamphlet, *Farrago sententiarum consentientium* (Frankfort, 1555). For his part in that controversy see Hardenberg, Albert Rizaeus. (Carl Bertheau.)

Bibliography: Letters by Timann are in C. H. W. Sillem's *Briefsammlung des Joachim Westphal*, pp. 98, 172, 197, 239, Hamburg, 1903. Consult: *Altes und Neues aus den Herzogthümern Bremen und Verden*, iv (1771), 99–128; H. W. Rotermund, *Lexikon aller Gelehrten*, ii. 216 sqq., Bremen, 1818; *ADB*, xxxviii. 352 sqq.

TIME, BIBLICAL RECKONING OF.

I. Chronological System: There is doubtless a system of chronology in the Old Testament, indeed more than one, and these cross each other; the age and origin are unknown, though in the nature of things such systems are relatively late. It is a special and significant peculiarity of the Hebrew spirit that the Hebrews earlier than

1. Creation to the Flood. any other people conceived the idea of a common relationship of the nations and of a definite ordering of all events to a common purpose, leading them to orient their own history in universal history. The Hebrew chronological system comes out of this idea.

attached to the Babylonian system have long been known. The names of the patriarchs correspond to those of some of the Babylonian kings; the reigns of the latter covered long world-periods, corresponding to the lives of the patriarchs, except that the latter are systematically abbreviated. In the Babylonian system from the creation to Alexander the Great was 215 myriads of years; from the beginning to the end of creation 168 myriads, in the Bible 24 x 7 (= 168) hours; the Babylonians reckon from the first king Alorus to the flood 432,000 years (i.e., 72 x 6,000), in the Bible from Adam to Noah covers 1656 years (i.e., 72 x 23 years or 72 x 1,200 weeks).

	MASORETIC TEXT			SAMARITAN TEXT			SEPTUAGINT TEXT		
	Before the begetting	After	Total	Before the begetting	After	Total	Before the begetting	After	Total
1. Adam	130	800	930	130	800	930	230	700	930
2. Seth	105	807	912	105	807	912	205	707	912
3. Enos	90	815	905	90	815	905	190	715	905
4. Cainan	70	840	910	70	840	910	170	740	910
5. Mahalaleel	65	830	895	65	830	895	165	730	895
6. Jared	162	800	962	62	785	847	162	800	962
7. Enoch	65	300	365	65	300	365	165	200	365
8. Methuselah	187	782	969	67	653	720	167 (187)	802 (782)	969
9. Lamech	182	595	777	53	600	653	188	565	75%
10. Noah..................	500	...	...	500	...	...	500	....	...
To the flood	100	...	(950)	100	...	(950)	100	...	(950)
Total	1,656	...	...	1,307	...	...	2,242 (2,262)	...	...

For the period before the flood (Gen. v.) the system works out in the above table, each item containing the years of a patriarch's life before the begetting of his first son, the years after that till his death, and the sum. It is to be noticed, however, that the Masoretic text, the Samaritan text, and the Septuagint have each its own tradition.

Correspondences between this system and that

Other relationships might be discovered. The Biblical author has leaned upon the Babylonian exemplar, but has subordinated his material to his own idea.

For the period between the flood and Abraham the following table of the three chief types of text results (Gen. xi. 10 sqq.).

While one may question whether the figures in

	MASORETIC TEXT			SAMARITAN TEXT			SEPTUAGINT TEXT		
	Before the begetting	After	Total	Before the begetting	After	Total	Before the begetting	After	Total
1. Shem	100	500	600	100	500	600	100	500	600
2. Arphaxad................	35	403	438	135	303	438	135	430 (400)	565 (535)
3. Kainan.................	...	...	...	...	...	...	130	330	460
4. Salah	30	403	433	130	303	433	130	330	460
5. Eber	34	430	464	134	270	404	134	370 (270)	504 (404)
6. Peleg.................	30	209	239	130	109	239	130	209	339
7. Reu	32	207	239	132	107	239	132	207	339
8. Serug	30	200	230	130	100	230	130	200	330
9. Nahor	29	119	148	79	69	148	79 (179)	129 (125)	208 (304)
10. Terah	70	(135)	(205)	70	(75)	(145)	70	(135)	(205)
Total	390	...	...	1,040	...	...	1,170 (1,270)	...	...

the first table under Masoretic text represent the original tradition, those in the second table claim attention because of their modesty;

2. The Flood till the Exodus.

some, however, think those of the Samaritan text earlier, according to which Methuselah, Jared, and Lamech died in the year of the flood. It is to be remarked that 100 years of Shem may be deducted from the last table, and this results in the following:

	He-brew.	Sam-aritan.	Septu-agint.	[Eng. A. V.
From creation to the flood	1,656	1,307	2,262	1,656
From the flood to Abra-ham's birth	290	940	1,070	352
Total	1,946	2,247	3,332	2,008]

The figures from Abraham on are in Gen. xii. 4, xxi. 5, xxv. 26, xlvii. 9, xii. 40–41.

Age of Abraham at his call	75
Age of Abraham at Isaac's birth	100
Age of Isaac at Jacob's birth	60
Age of Jacob on entering Egypt	130
After Abraham's call	$\begin{cases} 25 \\ 60 \\ 130 \end{cases}$
	215

	He-brew.	Sam-aritan.	Septu-agint.
Length of the sojourn in Canaan	215	215	215
Length of the sojourn in Egypt	430	215	215
Earlier life of Abraham	75	75	75
From the creation to Abraham's birth	1,946	2,247	3,332
Total	2,666	2,752	3,837

These last figures give the lapse of time from creation till the exodus. What the second and third columns mean is doubtful, but it has long been seen that the number 4,000, a "world-number," representing 100 generations of 40 years each, is represented in the Masoretic column by two-thirds of that number, 2,666. This leaves the remainder of 1,333 years to be accounted for.

But first it must be noted that in I Kings vi. 1 the number 40 appears in the

3. The Exodus to Solomon.

number 480 (40 x 12), which last represents the period from the exodus to the building of the temple. The book of Judges does not easily work into this scheme, as the following tables show.

a. Major judges; times of peace.

Othniel, Judges iii. 11	40	years
Ehud, iii. 30	80	"
Deborah-Barak, v. 31	40	"
Gideon, viii. 28	40	"
(Jephthah, xii. 7	6	")
Samson, xv. 20	20	"
Total	220 or 226	

b. Times of oppression.

Under Mesopotamians, iii. 8	8	years
" Moab, iii. 14	18	"
" Canaan, iv. 3	20	"
" Midian, vi. 1	7	"
" Ammon, x. 8	18	"
" Philistines, xiii. 1	40	"
Total	111 years	

c. Minor judges

Tola, Judges x. 2	23	years
Jair, x. 3	22	"
Jephthah (ut sup.)	6	"
Ibzan, xii. 9	7	"
Elon, xii. 11	10	"
Abdon, xii. 14	8	"
Total	76 years	

d. Before and after the judges.

Moses in the wilderness	40	years
Joshua	x	"
Eli, I Samu. iv. 18 (LXX. 20)	40	"
Samuel	y	"
Saul	z	"
David, I Kings ii. 11	40	"
Solomon till building of Temple	4	"
Total	124 (104) + x + y + z	

The item concerning Elon is doubtful, since he is absent from the prehexaplaric Septuagint, in Eusebius, and perhaps also from Clement of Alexandria; this would leave 66 years for the minor judges. But the omission in the Septuagint may be accidental. The placing of Jephthah is a matter of judgment; his period, of course, is to be counted but once. To get the period between the exodus and the building of the temple the totals of the four tables above must be added, deducting the repeated item: 226+ 111+70+124=531 (or 534, in case Abimelech with 3 years is counted in; Judges ix. 22). But this is far beyond the 480 years of I Kings vi. 1. To relieve this it has been noted that it is usual to reckon the years of a usurper's reign in with the rightful kings, and the years of oppression constitute a sort of usurpation; then the reckoning would give 531− 111 = 420, and 60 years are left for x+y+z. But an objection to this is that in certain cases, those of Jephthah and Samson, the "usurpation" is longer than the reign. But this argument is deceptive, since in the case of Samson it is reasonable to suppose that the Philistine oppression is reckoned into the time of Eli. Similarly the reckoning with regard to Jephthah is doubtful (note the wording of Judges x. 8). At any rate, the foregoing shows that merely mechanical handling of the tables is not to be attempted. Another method of shortening the period seemingly indicated in the book of Judges is that of Nöldeke, who regards the tables *a* and *b* as so interlocked as to show the idea of the historian of the period of the judges; that would leave no room for the table *c*, dealing with the minor judges. In that case they were not in the original book and not in the chronological scheme, and that scheme calls for 441 years. But even this seems to allow too much time for x+y+z. Then it is helped by the fact that the oppression of the Philistines' rule included the period of Eli's government, so that Samson's 20 years and Eli's make up the 40 of Judges xiii. 1, leaving 79 (a round 80) for x+y+z, allotting 40 to Joshua, and 20 each to Samuel and Saul. That makes the scheme from the exodus as follows:

	Years		Years
Moses	40	Jephthah	6
Joshua	40 (20?)	Samson	20
Othniel	40	Eli (Septuagint, 20)	40
Ehud	80	Samuel	20
Deborah-Barak	40	Saul	20
Gideon	40	David	40

In this scheme there are two omissions; the minor judges are not taken into account. Then Jephthah has no place among the major judges, the 6 years being placed among the count of the minor judges (cf. Judges xii. 7 with x. 8). This leaves 76 years to account for, which vitiates the entire calculation. The sum of the twelve "reigns" noted, if either Jephthah or Eli receive only 20 years, gives 406 years, 74 short of the 480 called for. But the governance of the number forty appears especially in the first six periods of the last table. And this predominance of the number 40 (cf. the confirmation in I Chron. v. 29–34, = vi. 35–88) illustrates the Masoretic chronology. To the 2,666 years between creation and the exodus (66⅔ generations) 480 (12 generations) are now to be added.

For the next step assurance is not in our possession. Yet it seems significant that from the time of Solomon's ascent to the throne (c. 1015) to the return from exile (536 B.C.) almost exactly covers 480 years; and it is noteworthy that from Zadok's son Ahimaaz to the beginning of the exile are eleven generations (I Chron. vi. 8–15). This scheme may have arisen just before or just after the end of the exile. In that case, the chronologist had before him the 66⅔ generations + 12 + 12, leaving 9½ generations, if he was reckoning on the world era of 4,000 years; he must then have expected Messianic times about 157 B.C. The foregoing attempt at solving the scheme of Masoretic chronology, based upon the 2,666 years, is not the only one. Bousset starts from the data given in the Apocalypse of Ezra ix. 38 sqq. and Josephus, *Ant.*, VIII. §§ 61–62, and X. §§ 147–148 (Greek text), and reaches the conclusion that the beginning of the temple cult (twenty years after the beginning of the building of the temple) fell in the year 3000 from creation. Bousset holds that the Septuagint system is secondary to the Masoretic, arranged in the time when the Hebrews began to compare their chronology with that of Egypt and Babylon and so discovered that their own was too short. This system would work out thus:

4. Solomon till the Return.

upon the number 260, giving a total of 3,166, composed of 260×12+46, from creation to the consecration of the Temple. The first is a popular reckoning, the second is purely theoretical and under foreign influence.

II. The Historical Data: It has already been noted that the use of an artificial chronological system does not exclude the presence of historical data, which were probably taken from tradition and brought together and arranged or changed. How far this was the case may be seen by comparison of, e.g., the Book of Judges with other parts of Scripture. If such a combination appears in the Books of Kings, it would amount to proof that two systems were brought together, one systematically chronological and one based on traditionally transmitted numbers. In attempting to fix the dates of events the one essential thing lacking is a date of reckoning, an "era," in the earlier period; the attempt is not made to connect events with a recognized and fixed date. The reference to Adam or to the flood can not, in the nature of the case, give a definite starting point. More promising appears the reference in I Kings vi. 1 to the exodus; but, apart from the fact that the event itself has been called in question, a fixed date for that is not yet determined. Only in very late Biblical times did an era come into use, that of the Seleucidæ (I Macc. xiii. 41–42). The lack of a fixed date within Israelitic chronology forces a complete dependence upon foreign data, so far as contemporaneity can be established; and this comes first in comparatively late times—in the Assyrian period. Above all regrettable is the fact that no connection exists such that a starting point may be derived from Egypt. For there a calendar existed which carries one back to July 19, 4241, the oldest fixed date in history, depending upon the fact that the Egyptian new year's day (in a year of 365 days) theoretically began on the day when Sirius (Sothis) rose with the dawn at Memphis. The year being fixed for 365 days, every four years a day was lost, and 1,460 Julian years = 1,461 Sothic years. The coincidence of the Sothic and the Julian

1. Lack of a Basal Era.

	Year of the flood	Birth of Abraham	Leaving of Canaan	Exodus	Building of Temple
Original chronology; cf. Josephus, *Ant.*, VIII., §§ 61–62 (Greek text)	1656	1996	2071	2501	3001
Variation of 50 years (cf. Josephus, *Ant.*, X., 47–48)	1656	1946	2021	2451	2951
Basis for reckoning of Book of Jubilees	1307(1300)	1946	2021	2451	2951
Book of Jubilees	1307	1876	1951	2410	
Masora	1656	1946	2021	2666	3146
Septuagint	2242	3312	3387	3817	4257
Samaritan	1307	2367	2422	2852	.....

A new attempt by Bosse (*Die chronologischen Systeme im A. T. und bei Josephus*, in *Mittheilungen der vorderasiatischen Gesellschaft*, 1908) to unravel the chronological basis of reckoning results in Bosse's belief that he has discovered two systems worked together. The first uses the generation-number of forty years, reckoning from the birth of Shem to the end of the exile, giving 40×50+2,000 years (omitting Terah); the second is a great solar cycle based

new year's day occurred 2781 and 4241 B.C., and at the earliest of these the Egyptian calendar must have begun. In early Babylonia an early fixed date is lacking, and the dating of events depends upon data afforded by Nabonidus (see ASSYRIA, VI., 1, § 1; BABYLONIA VI., 1, §§ 1–2) which are seriously called in question. The dating of Sargon is, according to the shorter reckoning, brought down to about 2700 B.C. instead of c. 3750. But even were early Babylonian dates assured, they would be usable for Biblical chronology only were definite points of chronology (synchronisms) settled. Such synchronisms are practically entirely lacking. No stringently binding connection exists with a fixed date for the contacts of Abraham or Joseph with Egypt; even for the entrance into and exodus from Egypt the reigning Pharaoh is not known with absolute certainty—assuming the historicity of these events. Similarly with Babylonia; the wandering of the patriarchs in the East, the stay of Abraham in Babylonia or Haran, his stay in Canaan—once more granting the historicity of these events—none of these permit of connection with fixed early Babylonian history. Even Gen. xiv. with the kings there mentioned does not afford a relationship, since it is not certain that Amraphel is the Hammurabi (see HAMMURABI AND HIS CODE) whose date is approximately fixed. All of earlier Biblical chronology depends upon conclusions from later Biblical events so far as earlier and later events can be connected.

The first real synchronisms occur in the regal period, when certain settled events are related with Assyrian events. A supposed synchronism with the founding of Carthage and the list of Phenician

2. Synchro- (Tyrian) kings is only apparent.
nisms in Josephus (*Apion*, i. 18) gives from
I–II Kings. Menander a list of ten kings of Tyre, and also (*Ant.*, VIII., iii. 1) says that Solomon began the Temple in Hiram's eleventh year. But both sets of data are inconclusive. For the founding of Carthage Timæus assigns the year 814, but without corroboration and definite knowledge of the source this can not be accepted as basis for chronology. In the books of Kings there appears what looks like an extraordinarily exact system of reckoning, in which are two series of figures which seem to support and guarantee one another, though as a matter of fact they do not agree. The one series gives the lengths of the reigns of the rulers of both kingdoms, the other gives synchronisms, stating in what regnal years of the contemporary monarch of the other kingdom the kings of the one began their reigns. Were the system correct and the figures correctly transmitted, this would have high value. But the two systems are not by the same hand, the books having undergone a double redaction, the second at the earliest toward the end of the exile, probably after the exile. This second naturally used, at least for the later parts, traditional numbers, though it may have altered them to fit into the system. Benzinger in his commentary on Kings has sought to show that the period of 480 years (cf. I Kings vi. 1) rules for the time between Solomon and the end of the exile, that between the division of the kingdom and the fall of Samaria is half of this, 240 years (according to another reckoning 263 years). If between the fall of Samaria and of Jerusalem be reckoned 136 years, for the exile a duration of 50, and for Solomon's reign after beginning the Temple 36 years, the sum is 240 (263)+136+50+36=462 (485) years. Simple addition of the Biblical numbers to Hoshea gives in the Judean series 260 and in the Israelitic series 242 years, with a total to end of exile of 464 **and 482 years.** This suggests that Benzinger's at-

tempt has probability behind it, though nothing more. As to the manner of reckoning the length of reigns, it is assumed that the first full year was reckoned to a king, the preceding year being given to his predecessor, though it has been otherwise assumed that the last year of a king

3. Results should be given also to his successor,
from As- this leading to a doubling and re-
syrian quiring a subtraction of one year
Sources. from each except the first of the series. For assured reckoning points the Assyrian chronology furnishes a means, through the Eponym Canon and the eclipse of 763 B.C. (see ASSYRIA, VI., 1, § 1). Synchronisms rule as follows:

Shalmaneser II. ruled	859–825
Shalmaneser fought at Karkar	854
Shalmaneser fought with Damascus, Jehu's tribute	842
Tiglath-Pileser ruled	745–727
Tiglath-Pileser received Menahem's tribute	738
Tiglath-Pileser fought Aram and Israel	734
Tiglath-Pileser took Damascus	732
Shalmaneser IV. ruled	727–722
Sargon ruled	722–705
Sennacherib ruled	705–681
Sennacherib moved on Judah	701

In addition to these data there is the Canon of Ptolemy which gives a survey of Babylonian and Persian rulers of Babylon, and from Alexander of the Ptolemies in Egypt. Usable here are the data that

Nabopolassar ruled	625–605
Nebuchadrezzar ruled	604–562
Nebuchadrezzar took Jerusalem	587–586

From these numbers can be gained certain dates for Israel. From the last the dates of at least the latest kings can be obtained; in the battle of Karkar Ahab or Jehoram took part, while Jehu's tribute year was 842 when he must have been on the throne; 734 or 733 was Pekah's last regnal year and 722 Hoshea's last. There are several synchronisms between Israel and Judah: Jeroboam and Rehoboam, Jehu and Athaliah, respectively, entered upon their reigns in the same year. Mesha records (see MOABITE STONE) that Israel during forty years, i.e., during Omri's reign and half of the days of his sons (Ahab, Ahaziah, Joram), oppressed Moab. But Ahab, Ahaziah, and Joram reigned only 36 years, hence Omri's 12 + half of 36 = 18 are only 30 years, and the 40 of Mesha is a round number. It furnishes, however, an example of the reckoning by generations or forties. Remembering the inaptitude of modern orientals for exactness in figures, it is easy

4. General to see how in the absence of written
Result. records the exact numbers become lost and a system of round numbers grows up, illustrated also by the number in Judges.

A general but provisional scheme as the result of the foregoing investigation results as follows:

Exodus	c. 1350 (1400)
Judges' period	1250–1120
Philistine rule, Eli	c. 1120
Samuel	c. 1080
Saul	1037–1017
David	1017– 977
Solomon	977– 937

Rehoboam	937–920	Jeroboam I	937–915
Abijah	920–917	Nadab	915–914
Asa	917–876	Baasha	914–890
		Elah	890–889
		Zimri	889
		Omri	889–877
Jehoshaphat	876–851	Ahab	877–855
Jehoram	851–843	Ahaziah	855–854
Ahaziah	843–842	Joram	854–842
Athaliah	842–836	Jehu	842–814
Joash	836–796	Jehoahaz	814–797
Amaziah	796–78?	Joash	797–781
Uzziah	778?–740	Jeroboam II	781–740
		Zachariah	740
		Shallum	740
Jotham	740–735	Menahem	740–737
		Pekahiah	737–735
		Pekah	735–734–3
Ahaz	735–719	Hoshea	733–725
Hezekiah	719–686		
Manasseh	686–641		
Amon	641–639		
Josiah	639–608		
Jehoahaz	608		
Jehoiakim	608–597		
[Jehoiachin	597]		
Zedekiah	597–587–6		

For the time between the return from exile and Christ only one date is seriously in question, viz., the time of Ezra's visit to Jerusalem (see EZRA-NEHEMIAH). In spite of Kosters' attack on the Biblical reports, Ezra's visit must be placed 458 and the giving of the law 445 or 444.   (R. KITTEL.)

III. The Abrahamic Date: The determination of the date of Abraham is one of the most difficult problems which the chronology of the ancient orient has left. For its complete solution the chronological data of three oriental peoples must be brought into agreement,—the Hebrews, the Egyptians, and the Babylonians. Each of these systems affords difficulties of its own sufficiently complicated to tax the resources of the greatest experts, and no one of them is thoroughly scientific, though of the three the Babylonian presents more scientifically based data than either of the others. It will be well to take these in the order in which they have been named.

1. The Hebrew Chronology: The Book of Genesis contains in those portions of the book which were compiled and edited by the priestly historiographer (P) a most elaborate chronology in which families and individuals are knit up into a complete and self-contained system, every birth, marriage, and death receiving a proper note. Unhappily this system can not in some places be reconciled with the data given by the other chief authors whose works have found a place in Genesis, the Judaistic (J) and the Ephraimitic (E) sections of the book. For the present purpose the J and E portions may safely be left out of account as they do not materially affect the computation. Taking, then, P alone the dates down to Abraham from the creation may be summarized as follows:

	Maso-retic Text.	Sam-aritan.	Septu-agint.
From the creation of man to the flood (Gen. v., vii. 1)	1,656	1,307	2,262
From the flood to the call of Abraham (Gen. xi. 10–26, xii. 4)	365	1,015	1,145
From the creation of man to the call of Abraham	2,021	2,322	3,407

It seems to be perfectly clear that these figures are all artificial; they are the result of elaborate computations and theorizing carried on by the priests of Israel for centuries. But the most searching investigation of modern scholars has failed to find the ultimate basis on which they rest—the point from which they were calculated and the processes by which they were finally determined. The difficulty of dealing with them is enormously enhanced by the differences between the three recensions of the text. These can not be explained by the old device of accidental corruptions by copyists. Some of them must represent the labors of editors. Some of the older chronologists in modern times have taken freely and indifferently from either recension whatever figures might seem to them to be most agreeable to the system they were constructing. The more scrupulous investigations of recent times have unfortunately yielded no certain test for the determination of the relative value of these recensions. Several of the most eminent modern scholars have presented arguments to show that the Samaritan text has preserved the most probable list of figures, among them Budde, Dillmann, and Holzinger. But their reasoning has carried but little conviction and the majority of critical students content themselves with a general adherence to the Masoretic computations. If now these last be accepted, the conclusion is reached that Abraham's call fell in the year of the world 2021. But this is a most unsatisfying conclusion; it must be reduced to a known era, and one must ascertain to what year B.C. it corresponds. For the solution of this problem the book of Genesis affords no data of any kind. A fixed datum must be sought elsewhere by which a reckoning may be guided.

The greatest event in Israel's history was the exodus from Egypt; to it the poets and prophets continually hark back. Perhaps a point of departure may there be secured.

2. Chronology Based on the Exodus.

Years

From the call of Abraham to the birth of Isaac (cf. Gen. xii. 4 with Gen. xxi. 5)	25
Isaac's age at the birth of Jacob and Esau (Gen. xxv. 26)	60
Age of Jacob when he went down into Egypt (Gen. xlvii. 9)	130
The length of the sojourn in Egypt (Ex. xii. 40, 41)	430
From the call of Abraham to the Exodus	645

If now these figures could all be accepted as certain and if data could be discovered in the Bible itself for locating the exodus in terms of the Christian era, it would be possible at once to determine the date of Abraham; but unfortunately neither of these suppositions is true, as will appear upon a brief examination. In the first place the 430 years (Ex. xii. 40, 41), while in substantial agreement with the words of the promise: "thou shalt sojourn in a land that is not theirs, . . . and they shall afflict them 400 years" (Gen. xv. 13), is hopelessly at variance with the passages which assign only four generations from Jacob's children to Moses (Ex. vi. 16–20; Num. xxvi. 5–9, cf. Gen. xv. 16) or five to Joshua (Josh. vii. 1). This difficulty was evidently observed in antiquity, for an endeavor to meet it appears in the text of both the Samaritan and the Septuagint which read in Ex.

xii. 40, " The sojourning of the children of Israel in the land of Egypt, and in the land of Canaan was 430 years." This reduces the sojourn in Egypt from 430 to 215 years, which is exactly equal to the sojourn in Canaan, and this was, as shown above, 25 + 60 + 130 years. It is quite evident that this can not be genuine chronology based on ancient data, for it is highly improbable, to say the least, that the sojourns in Canaan and in Egypt should be of exactly the same duration. These figures are the result of computation and reckoning, not the result of exact records. But, in the second place, there are no data for locating the exodus chronologically in the book of Exodus or Numbers. To find its date according to the priestly compilers and computators it is necessary to come farther down in the Biblical books.

The passage used for this purpose by Archbishop Ussher is found in I Kings vi. 1 as follows: " And it came to pass in the four hundred and **3. Ussher's** eightieth year after the children of **Basis.** Israel were come out of the land of Egypt, in the fourth year of Solomon's reign over Israel, . . . that he began to build the house of Jehovah." This passage, far from easing the difficulties, simply increases them. In the first place the number 480 seems to be nothing else than a computation made by the writer of books of Kings who, about the beginning of the exile, compiled books with the object of presenting a complete chronology of Israel's historical life. There are a good many appearances of " forty " in the work of chronologists like him, for example in Judges, and it is probable that the number forty is either a round number or more likely the computed length of a generation. On this latter supposition 480 would mean twelve generations, a suggestion which finds support, if not confirmation, in the list of names with which he was operating, namely Moses (in the wilderness), Joshua, Othniel, Ehud, Deborah, Gideon, Jephthah, Samson, Eli, Samuel, Saul, and David. His method would seem to be plain. He computes twelve generations between the exodus and the Temple, and then simply translates these into 480 years. But even if it be assumed that the 480 was an exact number, the goal would still be no nearer, for the book of Kings gives no certain method of determining the fourth year of Solomon. To secure that it would be necessary to go on down through the book of Kings, hoping somewhere to find a king who could be located through his contemporaneity with some ruler or some event known from the outside world. This was Ussher's method, and it led him to date the fourth year of Solomon at 1012 B.C., and the exodus at 1491; if now to this be added the 645 years, the result would be 2136 B.C. as the date of Abraham's call, and this would give as the real Biblical date of Abraham's life 2211–2036 B.C.

This date must now be tested by the application to it of such comparisons and checks as Egypt and Babylonia may be able to furnish. It is best to begin with Egypt.

2. Egyptian Chronology: Prior to the beginning of the eighteenth dynasty Egyptian chronology provides many and complicated questions and few certainties, but from Ahmose I., the first king of this dynasty about 1580 B.C. [J. H. Breasted, *Hist. of the Ancient Egyptians*, p. 426, New York, 1908], there is substantial agreement among Egyptologists and the error is demonstrably small in any case. It was during this dynasty that the correspondence between the kings of Egypt and various rulers and governors of western Asia occurred. (See AMARNA TABLETS.) The two Egyptian kings Amenophis III. and Amenophis IV. are by Breasted located at 1411–1375 and 1375–1350, and other Egyptologists would but slightly change these figures. The correspondence shows quite clearly that during these reigns Egypt was completely master of Palestine, and only during the latter are there signs of a breaking of Egyptian supremacy through the attacks of small bodies of peoples seeking new homes. Among these the Ḥabiri find frequent mention, and efforts have been made by some scholars to identify them with the Hebrews under Joshua, but without success (see AMARNA TABLETS, IV., § 1). They are indeed probably of the same or of a closely related stock, but they are not the Hebrews of the Old Testament. Indeed the very allusions to these marauders, the Ḥabiri, show quite plainly that the conquest described in the summary in Judges i. was not taking place. The date of the exodus at 1491 is, therefore, shown to be impossible, for down to 1350 Egypt was still mistress of the whole territory of Canaan. If now this date be thus disposed of, one has next to ask whether any more suitable date may be discovered by the help of the Egyptians. For such a search Exodus i. 11 reports that the Israelites, before the exodus, built two store cities, Pithom and Rameses, for the Egyptians. Now the excavations of Edouard Naville have proved that Pithom was built by Rameses II. of the next, or the nineteenth, dynasty, and the very name of the city Rameses supports this deduction. Unless, therefore, the Hebrew historical recollections concerning these two cities are in hopeless error, it follows that Rameses II. was the Pharaoh of the oppression and his successor Merneptah the Pharaoh of the exodus (see EGYPT, I., 4, § 3). Breasted dates these two kings at 1292–1225 and 1225–1215 B.C., Petrie locates the former at 1300–1234, Maspero at 1320–1255, and Meyer 1310–1244. The differences between the experts are small, and according to these it is required to date the exodus at about 1230 instead of 1491.

If now this date be taken as a point of departure and the 645 years be added, it is necessary to locate the date of Abraham's call at 1875 B.C., and adding the seventy-five years of his life before that date, Abraham's date would be given as 1950–1775.

3. Babylonian Chronology: This date must now be tested by the data to be derived from Babylonia. Gen. xiv. 1 makes Abraham the contemporary of a certain Amraphel, king of Shinar. Schrader was the first to suggest that Amraphel was a corruption of the name of the well-known Babylonian king Hammurabi. The difficulties in this identification felt at first gradually vanished as other forms, more closely approximating the Hebrew form of the name, were found in Babylonian documents. There remained, however, a very great difficulty in bringing Hammurabi far enough down, or Abraham far enough back, in the chronologies of the two peoples to make an identification at all probable. Prior to 1907 Assyriologists generally dated Hammurabi to the twenty-third or twenty-fourth century, as will appear from the following figures as given by several writers: 2376–2333 (Sayce), 2342–2288 (Rogers), 2285–2242 (Johns). These dates can not, on any hypothesis, be brought into even approximate relationship with any of the calculated Biblical dates. But in 1907 Dr. L. W. King made a most happy discovery in the British Museum of new chronicles of early Babylonian kings which at once set the chronology of the first Babylonian dynasty in quite a new light. It had been supposed that the second dynasty followed upon the first and the third upon the second, but these new chronicles showed conclusively that the second dynasty was partly contemporaneous with the third, and that, therefore, the date of the first dynasty must be much reduced. The most probable date for Hammurabi, yielded by this reduction, is 2130–2088 B.C. (so Thureau-Dangin and Ungnad), though King would date the beginning of this dynasty not much earlier than 2000 or 2050, which would make Hammurabi's date 1938–1883 or 1888–1833 B.C. These dates are almost certainly too low and the dates 2130–2088 B.C. may safely be regarded as a much closer approximation. If King's date were correct there would result a most striking correspondence between it and the date of Abraham's call 1875 B.C. as reckoned above from the exodus date at 1230 B.C. King is himself so much struck by this that he remarks: " We may conclude that the chronology of the Pentateuch, with regard to the length of time separating Abraham from Moses, exhibits far greater accuracy than we have hitherto had reason to believe " (*Chronicles concerning Early Babylonian Kings*, i. 25). Considered in the light of all that is said above, this statement should probably be regarded as stronger than is warranted. If the date circa 2100 be the date of Hammurabi and 1875 the date of Abraham's call, the discrepancy between them is two centuries and a quarter, and there appears to be no means of bringing them closer together. This, of course, does not prove that Hammurabi is not Amraphel; it also does not prove that Gen. xiv. 1 is in error in making Amraphel and Abraham contemporaries. It merely proves that the chronological system of the Priest code is subject to the same errors as appear so abundantly in the chronological synchronisms which the books of Kings have worked out for the kings of Israel and Judah.   ROBERT W. ROGERS.

BIBLIOGRAPHY: Many of the commentaries on the books of Genesis, Samuel, Kings, Chronicles, and Ezra-Nehemiah contain important discussions concerning the chronology, and the same is true of the works on the history of Israel (under AHAB; and ISRAEL, HISTORY OF). Besides this literature, consult: M. Niebuhr, *Geschichte Assurs und Babels*, Berlin, 1857; W. B. Galloway, *Egypt's Record of Time to the Exodus . . . critically Investigated; with . . . Survey of the patriarchal Hist. and the Chronology of Scripture*, London, 1869; T. Nöldeke, *Untersuchung zur Kritik des A. Ts.*, pp. 173–198, Kiel, 1869; H. Brandes, *Abhandlung zur Geschichte des Orients im Altertum*, Halle, 1874; E. de Bunsen, *Chronology of the Bible, connected with Contemporaneous Events in the Hist. of Babylonians, Assyrians, and Egyptians*, London, 1874; B. Neteler, *Zusammenhang der alttestamenhang Zeitrechnungen mit der Profangeschichte*, 3 parts, Münster, 1879–86; A. Kamphausen,

Chronologie der hebräischen Könige, Bonn, 1883; V. A. Dumax, *Révision et reconstitution de la chronologie biblique et profane*, Paris, 1886–92; E. Mahler, *Biblische Chronologie und Zeitrechnung der Hebräer*, Vienna, 1887; C. Lederer, *Die biblische Zeitrechnung*, Erlangen, 1888; J. Orr, in *Presbyterian Review*, Jan., 1889; M. Macdonald, *Harmony of Ancient Hist. and Chronology of the Egyptians and Jews*, Philadelphia, 1891; A. A. van Hoonacker, *Zorobabel et le second temple*, Ghent, 1892; H. Winckler, *Alttestamentliche Untersuchungen*, pp. 77 sqq., Leipsic, 1892; W. H. Kosters, *Het Herstel van Israel*, Leyden, 1893; E. Kautzsch, *Die heilige Schrift des A. Ts.*, Beilagen, pp. 110–135, Freiburg, 1894; E. Meyer, *Entstehung des Judentums*, Halle, 1896; idem, in *SBA*, 1904 and 1907 (on Egyptian chronology); C. Niebuhr, *Die Chronologie der Geschichte Israels, Aegyptens, Babyloniens und Assyriens 2000–700 vor Christi*, Leipsic, 1896; C. C. Torrey, in *ZATW*, 1896; C. F. Lehmann, *Zwei Hauptprobleme der altorientalischen Chronologie*, ib. 1898; W. Bousset, in *ZATW*, 1900, pp. 136 sqq.; J. Urquhart, *How Old is Man? Some misunderstood Chapters in Scripture Chronology*, London, 1904; J. H. Breasted, *Hist. of Egypt from the Earliest Times*, New York, 1905; idem, *Short Hist. of the Egyptians*, ib. 1907; W. T. Lynn, *Bible Chronology*, London, 1905; L. W. King, *Chronicles concerning early Babylonian Kings*, 2 vols., ib. 1907; O. A. Toffteen, *Ancient Chronology*, Chicago, 1907, new ed., 1909 (comes down to 1050 B.C.); W. J. Beecher, *The Dated Events of the Old Testament: being a Presentation of Old Testament Chronology*, Philadelphia, 1908; D. R. Fotheringham, *The Chronology of the Old Testament*, Cambridge, 1908; R. Schram, *Kalendariographische und chronologische Tafeln*, Leipsic, 1908; S. Euringer, *Die Chronologie der biblischen Urgeschichte* (Gen. v., xi.), Münster, 1909; F. A. Herzog, *Die Chronologie der beiden Königsbücher*, Münster, 1909; F. A. Jones, *The Dates of Genesis. A Comparison of the Biblical Chronology with that of other Nations*, London, 1909; F. Westberg, *Die biblische Chronologie nach Josephus und das Todesjahr Jesu*, Leipsic, 1910; Smith, *Prophets*, pp. 145–151, 401–404, 413–419; Schrader, *KAT*; *DB*, i. 397–403; *EB*, i. 773–799; *JE*, iv. 64–70.

TIMOTHEUS ÆLURUS. See MONOPHYSITES, §§ 3 sqq.

TIMOTHY THE DISCIPLE OF PAUL.

In the Chief Pauline Epistles (§ 1).
In Acts (§ 2).
In the Pastoral Letters and Hebrews (§ 3).
Other Supposed or Apocryphal References (§ 4).

Timothy may be called Paul's disciple, companion, and fellow worker before all others. In six of the New-Testament epistles (II Cor., Phil., Col., I and II. Thess., Philemon) his name is joined with Paul's in the superscription. In the superscriptions to I and II Thess. (also in

1. In the II Cor. i. 19) Timothy is named after
Chief Silvanus, which implies that the latter
Pauline held a position of precedence and was
Epistles. probably the older; but too great stress
must not be laid on Timothy's youth. To be sure, the two epistles addressed to Timothy represent him as the type of a youthful bishop (I Tim. iv. 12; II Tim. ii. 22; cf. the Gk. *teknon* in I., i. 18; II., i. 2). But this is one reason among many for suspecting the genuineness of these epistles; the representation does not fit the man entrusted by Paul with difficult duties. The Timothy of the genuine epistles is by no means Paul's personal attendant or amanuensis, but his " workfellow " and helper like Aquila and Priscilla (Rom. xvi. 3, 21), a man competent to establish in the faith and strengthen the young congregation in Thessalonica (I Thess. iii. 2) and to repeat Paul's preaching for the Corinthians (I Cor. iv. 17; cf. Phil. ii. 19–23). Timothy seems to have hesitated to undertake

the mission to Corinth and Paul sent Titus to help him. But the Timothy of the genuine Pauline letters was clearly a fellow worker on equal terms with Paul—an apostle, in the language of the later Church—and, therefore, no doubt from the beginning old enough to undertake religious instruction according to current Jewish notions; furthermore he was devoted to Paul as a child to its father and in Paul's estimation was the most trustworthy interpreter of his gospel. Probably he studied in no other school than that of Paul; from Paul he learned Christianity, and he was free from all desire to develop a theology of his own.

The Acts adds but few details to this picture. From xvii. 14–15, xviii. 5, xix. 22, xx. 4, it appears that Silas and Timothy were with Paul on the second missionary journey in Macedonia and Achaia, afterward on the third journey in Ephesus, and still later Timothy and others accompanied

2. In the Acts. him in Macedonia. It is noteworthy that in all these passages Timothy is mentioned as member of a pair and in subordinate position; the Acts does not present Timothy as the trusted friend of the apostle. The most considerable notice of Timothy in the Acts is found in xvi. 1–3. He appears there as a Christian (Gk. *mathētēs;* cf. Acts xxi. 16) of either Derbe or Lystra, who was highly spoken of by the brethren in Lystra and Iconium, and on this recommendation Paul chose him as companion on the second missionary journey. Presumably he was converted on the first journey (Acts xiv.). Whether his home was in Derbe or Lystra has been much disputed, and the question seems hardly worth the controversy it has occasioned; the connection in Acts xvi. 1–2 favors Lystra (cf. Wohlenberg's commentary, p. 1, note 2; for Derbe, K. Schmidt, *Apostelgeschichte*, p. 42, note). It is learned further from Acts xvi. 1, that Timothy's father was a " Greek "—and doubtless not a Christian, as the fact is not mentioned—and his mother a believing Jewess. Verse 3 says that Paul circumcised Timothy " because of the Jews which were in those quarters; for they all knew that his father was a Greek." If Acts is entirely from the hand of Luke, this statement must be accepted, for it is incredible that Luke did not know the facts or that he misstated them. But if it be admitted that the text has been worked over by a redactor, there may be here a mistake or at least a clumsy statement of fact. The datum of verse 3 can not be reconciled with the epistle to the Galatians. It is not necessary to deny that Timothy was circumcised, or that he was circumcised after he became a Christian; but it must be denied that Paul, immediately after the Apostolic Council at Jerusalem (q.v.) and after his rebuke of Peter (Gal. ii. 11 sqq.), required a Christian to be circumcised before he would accept him as a companion in missionary labor.

The two epistles to Timothy, even if they be genuine, add nothing of importance to knowledge of the man to whom they were addressed—his mother was named Eunice, his grandmother Lois (II Tim. i. 5); from a child he had known the Scriptures (II Tim. iii. 15); he was Paul's faithful and trusted disciple, whom he wishes to be with

him in his Roman imprisonment (I Tim. i. 2, 18; II Tim. i. 2, 6, ii. 1, iii. 10–12, iv. 9–11, 13, 21); and various similar personal details (I Tim.

3. In the Pastoral Letters and Hebrews. i. 3, 18, iv. 14). But in these two epistles, as in the one to Titus, the personal notices are merely a framework for a catechism on the duties of a bishop. The three epistles are evidently by one hand, and weighty external as well as internal grounds are adduced to show that it was not Paul. The three epistles were not known to Marcion and have points of contact with the older " apostolic " fathers only in a coincidence of certain pastoral expressions. In content they lack all specifically Pauline ideas and present rather the post-Pauline Church. The style sometimes reminds of Paul's, it is true, for the author had doubtless read Paul's epistles; but more often a discrepancy is evident both in vocabulary and syntax. Even if fragments of genuine Pauline writings are incorporated in these letters, it can not be assumed that all the personal notices of those to whom the letters are addressed are such. Indeed it is in these personal notices that the address appears most clearly as purposed. The pastoral letters present the Timothy of the Acts only a little altered. From the Acts and the genuine epistles of Paul they draw their historical material (see Paul, II.). The last New-Testament passage in which Timothy is named is Heb. xiii. 23, where it is said that he " is set at liberty," and the writer adds " with him, if he come shortly, I will see you." Nothing is known from any other source of an imprisonment of Timothy.

Certain hypotheses by which it has been thought to increase knowledge of Timothy are mentioned here only for the sake of completeness; all are more or less fantastic and none of them can be accepted. Hengstenberg identified Timothy with the Pergamenian martyr Antipas of Rev. ii. 13; D. Völter with the " true yokefellow " of Phil.

4. Other Supposed or Apocryphal References. iv. 3; Spitta thinks he was responsible for the form of II Thess. and that ii. 1–12 is a fragment of the eschatological speculation of this half-Greek disciple; Sorof makes him the redactor of the Acts and assumes that he followed written sources, for the Pauline parts chiefly the journal of Luke. Others who distrust the tradition of Luke's authorship (e.g., De Wette and Bleek) ascribe the " we " portion of Acts (chaps. xvi. sqq.) to Timothy. The oldest church tradition concerning Timothy is an inference from the epistles addressed to him: he is named " the apostle," is counted as one of the seventy disciples, and appears in the lists as first bishop of Ephesus, consecrated by Paul. In 356 Constantius transferred Timothy's remains from Ephesus to Constantinople and placed them beneath the altar of the Church of the Apostles built by his father. In the next year the relics of Andrew and Luke were added. The Acts of Timothy contain no reference to these well-known events and say nothing concerning Timothy's doctrine and miracles. The author relates that Paul made his favorite disciple bishop of Ephesus under Nero and in the consulship of Maximus. In Ephesus he was associated with the Apostle John, who lived there after Nero's persecution. Domitian banished John to Patmos, and during John's absence Timothy openly rebuked the excesses of the Ephesians at a heathen feast, was stoned by the mob, died on the third day (Jan. 22, under Nerva, when Peregrinus was proconsul of Asia), and was buried on the hill " where now stands the holy church of his martyrdom." After his death John returned to Ephesus and filled the bishopric till the time of Trajan. Usener, the first editor of these Acts, dated them before 356 and, probably wrongly, thought that they were based on a veritable history of the Ephesian church. In the time when the traditions of both John and Timothy in Ephesus were current, an Ephesian may well have tried to utilize both traditions to exalt the greatness of his city. The definite data are suspicious because the proconsuls of Asia named are not known from any other source; the author of the Acts introduced them probably imitating Luke, as he did in his prologue. Actual knowledge of Timothy is not preserved except in the New Testament. (A. JÜLICHER.)

BIBLIOGRAPHY: The chief sources are of course the Pauline epistles. For the Acta Timothei consult: R. A. Lipsius, Die Apokryphen, Apostelgeschichten, und Apostellegenden, ii. 2, pp. 372–400, Brunswick, 1884; idem, Acta Apostolorum apocrypha, vol. i., Leipsic, 1891; and cf. the ed. by H. Usener, Bonn, 1877. The principal discussions are to be found in the commentaries on the Pauline epistles, particularly the pastoral epistles; in the works on the life of Paul; and those on the history of the Apostolic Age, e.g., A. C. McGiffert, 1897. Consult further: M. Sorof, Die Entstehung der Apostelgeschichte, Berlin, 1890; F. J. A. Hort, Judaistic Christianity, London, 1894; idem, The Christian Ecclesia, ib. 1897; E. Kautzsch, Die Apokryphen und Pseudepigraphen des N. Ts., pp. 46, 48, 102–103, 106–107, 110–111, Tübingen, 1900; W. Wrede, Das litterarische Rätsel des Hebräerbriefs, Göttingen, 1906; O. Pfleiderer, Das Urchristenthum, 2d ed., Berlin, 1902, Eng. transl., Primitive Christianity, 2 vols., New York, 1906–09; DB, iv. 767–768; EB, iv. 5074–79.

TIMOTHY, EPISTLES TO. See PAUL, II., 5; and TIMOTHY.

TINDAL, MATTHEW: English deist; b. at Beer Ferrers (5 m. n. of Plymouth), England, probably about 1653; d. in London Aug. 16, 1733. He studied at Lincoln and Exeter Colleges, Oxford (B.A., 1676; B.C.L., 1679; D.C.L., 1685; and law fellow at All Souls', 1678). Under James II. he joined the Roman Catholic Church, but returned to the Church of England, 1688. He was admitted as an advocate at Doctor's Commons, 1685. His principal work, Christianity as Old as the Creation, or the Gospel a Republication of the Law of Nature (vol. i., London, 1730), marks the culminating point of the deist controversy. The second volume of this work was withheld by Bishop Gibson, to whom the author had intrusted the manuscript. (For a discussion of the work see DEISM, I, § 6.) Conybeare, James Foster, Leland, and others attacked Tindal's work; and it was to it, more than to any other, that Bishop Butler's Analogy was meant to be a reply. Tindal's other works were The Rights of the Christian Church Asserted (2d ed., 1706), an attack upon High-church assumptions; A Defence of the Rights of the Christian Church, in Two Parts (1709); and some essays and pamphlets.

BIBLIOGRAPHY: E. C., Memoirs of the Life and Writings of Matthew Tindall, London, 1733; The Religious, Rational

and Moral Conduct of Matthew Tindal, ib. 1735; J. Hunt, Hist. of Religious Thought in England, ii. 431–462, ib. 1871; L. Stephen, Hist. of English Thought in the 18th Century, i. 134–163, New York, 1881; DNB, lvi. 403–405. The controversial literature called out by his works is well summarized in the British Museum Catalogue under his name.

TINGLEY, KATHERINE: Theosophist; b. at Newburyport, Mass., July 6, 1852. She was educated privately, and, becoming interested in theosophy, made in its interest two tours of the world in 1896–97 and 1904. In 1897 she established the International Brotherhood League, and among the many homes and educational institutions founded by her are the School of Antiquity and the Raja Yoga Academy at Point Loma and San Diego. Since 1898 she has been the official head of the Universal Brotherhood and Theosophical Society throughout the world, as well as the " outer head " of the Inner School of Theosophy (see THEOSOPHY). Besides editing the Century Path, the organ of her branch of the theosophical society, she has written Mysteries of the Heart Doctrine (2d ed., Point Loma, Cal., 1903) and Pith and Marrow of Some Sacred Writings (1905).

TIPHSAH, tif′sā: **1.** A proper name found in I Kings iv. 24 (Heb. text, v. 4), indicating with Gaza (A. V., " Azzah ") the boundaries of the district (properly the Persian province) called in certain Assyrian documents and in Persian times after Darius I. " Beyond the River " (Heb. 'ebher hannahar; Ezra viii. 36; Neh. ii. 7, 9, iii. 7; I Kings v. 4). As Gaza evidently marks the southwest limit, Tiphsah is to be sought in the northeast and (cf. I Kings iv. 21 [v. 1]; II Chron. ix. 26) on the Euphrates. It was doubtless the classical Thapsacus (Xenophon, Anabasis, I., iv. 11; Arrian, Anabasis, ii. 13, iii. 7; Strabo, ii. 79–80, xvi. 741; cf. C. Ritter, Erdkunde, x. 11 sqq., 1114–15, Berlin, 1843; M. Hartmann in ZDPV, xxii., 1899, p. 137), which was an important center of trade and intercourse in Persian times and has been identified with the village of Dibsah on the Euphrates two and one quarter hours below Balis (cf. Mordtmann in Petermanns Mittheilungen, 1865, pp. 54–55; B. Moritz in Abhandlungen der Berliner Akademie, 1880, Anhang, p. 31; J. P. Peters, Nippur, i. 96–99, New York, 1897). Extensive ruins of the ancient city lie about one quarter of an hour from the modern village. The common derivation from the Hebrew pasaḥ, giving the meaning " ferry " or " ford," does not fit well with the meaning of pasaḥ (" to leap "), and Lagarde's suggestion (Uebersicht über die im aramäischen, arabischen, und hebräischen übliche Bildung der Nomina, p. 131, Göttingen, 1889) of the Assyrian tapshahu, " resting-place," is better. The passage in I Kings iv. 24 (v. 4), which gives to Solomon's realm a fabulous extent, is late; the words " from Tiphsah even to Gaza " seem not to have been in the original Septuagint text.

2. A town named in II Kings xv. 16. From the reading of the Lucianic Septuagint-text (Taphōe), the " Tappuah " of Josh. xvii. 7–8 is probably meant, situated on the boundary between Ephraim and Manasseh; cf. the commentaries. (H. GUTHE.)

BIBLIOGRAPHY: J. P. Peters, in The Nation, May 23, 1889; idem, Nippur, i. 96 sqq., New York, 1897; B. Moritz, in the *Berichte* of the Berlin Academy, July 25, 1880; *DB*, iv. 778; *EB*, iv. 5097.

TIPPLE, EZRA SQUIER: Methodist Episcopalian; b. at Camden, N. Y., Jan. 23, 1861. He was educated at Syracuse University (A.B., 1884) and Drew Theological Seminary (1887). He then held pastorates in New York City at St. Luke's (1887–1892), Grace (1892–97), and St. James' (1897–1901), after which he was executive secretary of the Metropolitan Thank-Offering Commission until 1904. He was again pastor of St. Luke's (1904–05), and was appointed to his present position of professor of practical theology in Drew Theological Seminary in 1905. He has written *The Heart of Asbury's Journal* (New York, 1904); *The Minister of God* (1905); *Drew Sermons: First Series* (1906); *Drew Sermons on the Golden Texts for 1909* (1908); and *Freeborn Garrettson* (1910).

TISCHENDORF, tish'en-dŏrf, **LOBEGOTT (ÆNOTHEUS) FRIEDRICH CONSTANTIN VON:** German textual critic; b. at Langenfeld (53 m. s. of Leipsic), in the Saxon Voigtland, Jan. 18, 1815; d. at Leipsic Dec. 7, 1874. He studied theology at the University
            of Leipsic, 1834–38. To his theological
Early   professor at the university, Johann G.
Career.   B. Winer (q.v.), he owed the impetus to
            theological criticism of the fundamental
text of the New Testament, in which he was aided by his thorough philological training, the foundation of which was laid at the gymnasium of Plauen, 1829–34; and he dates his critical study of the Bible-text from 1837. He was instructor in a school at Grosstädeln near Leipsic, 1838–39; and then returned to Leipsic to qualify in the theological faculty. His essay *De recensionibus quas dicunt Ni. Ti. ratione potissimum habita Scholzii* appeared also as prolegomena to an edition of *Novum Testamentum Grœce* (Leipsic, 1841). In his work on the edition of the New Testament he came to realize the necessity for a new investigation of the Greek New-Testament manuscripts and other textual sources. Accordingly he went to Paris, Oct. 30, 1840, where, until 1843, he continued his original studies. He compared seven of the eight uncials, transcribing the greater part of their contents; and by means of the Giobertine tincture he was able to read not only almost the entire codex *Ephraemi Syri*, also the fragments of the Old Testament, but to distinguish the original characters from those made by two later correctors. He then published an edition, *Codex Ephraemi Syri rescriptus* (Leipsic, 1843–45). Three editions of the Greek New Testament were also published in Paris (1842). The so-called *editio catholica* always prefers the readings lying presumably at the basis of the Vulgate, and is printed parallel with the Vulgate. Another was the *editio non catholica*. The text of this was practically the same as that of the Leipsic edition of 1841, but in some places, especially the Gospels, other readings were preferred. The prolegomena were rewritten. In the mean time Tischendorf had visited Utrecht, Cambridge, Oxford, and London, where he examined the libraries. In Feb., 1842, he went to Rome, where he spent four months and thirteen in Italy; but in spite of his recommendations from the most eminent sources and the personal good-will of the pope, he was allowed only six hours in which to search the *Codex Vaticanus*, on account of the opposition of Angelo Mai, who had himself prepared an edition. Yet he was able, in this short time, to ascertain much for its correcter determination, and later obtained also certain renderings from Mai. However, he was well compensated for his disappointment at the Vatican by obtaining rich treasures in the Angelica at Rome, and in Naples, Florence, Venice, Modena, Milan, and Turin; and it is impossible to estimate the number of manuscripts that he examined, one of which was the Codex Amiatinus in Florence. His work now extended to the New-Testament Apocrypha and Pseudepigrapha; and he completed his collection for Philo. In Apr., 1844, he entered upon an extensive journey by way of Egypt, Sinai, Palestine, the Orient, Italy, Vienna, Munich, making researches in libraries, and discovering and gathering treasures from unknown manuscripts, in Greek, Arabic, Coptic, Hebrew, Ethiopian, and other languages, many of which he brought home with him. *Reise in den Orient* (2 vols., Leipsic, 1845) is an account of this journey, and in *Anecdota sacra et profana* (1855) he tells of the acquired manuscripts. Foremost among these were the forty-three leaves of an old Greek Bible on parchment (later called the *Codex Sinaiticus*), containing portions of the Old Testament, which were given to him in the Catherine Convent at the foot of Sinai. Eighty-six other leaves which he saw there, he could not obtain. He published a lithographic facsimile of the leaves which he had brought, named *Codex Friderico Augustanus* (1846), in honor of the king of Saxony. Soon after his return in Jan., 1845, Tischendorf was made associate professor of theology at Leipsic; and in 1859 regular professor of the same and of Biblical paleography. His literary labors are, however, of more value to theological science than his lectures. He furnished the treasures brought from European libraries, and the orient, in two lines of publications; first those works to which he afterward gave the collective name of "Library of Christian Monuments," and his editions (twenty) of the Greek New Testament. Among the former are the *Monumenta sacra inedita* (1846; *nova collectio*, vols. i.–vi., ix., 1855–70), containing fragments of New-Testament manuscripts; the *Evangelium Palatinum* (1847); the *Codex Amiatinus* (only the New Testament, 1850); and the *Codex Claramontanus* (1852). The *Anecdota sacra et profana* (1855) may be considered as a complement of these works.

At the same time Tischendorf prepared a new edition of the Greek New Testament, the *Editio Lipsiensis secunda* (1849). Among all his editions, this, although antiquated after the *octava*, was the
            epoch-making one, so far as the labor of
Editio   the author is concerned, and was so
Lipsiensis   considered by Tischendorf's contempo-
Secunda.   raries. The text derived from it, with
            a few changes, had the most extensive
circulation at the time, and of the twenty Greek New-Testament editions that appeared in Germany during his lifetime, under his name, thirteen, including this one, contain the text of the edition

of 1849, the Harmony not included. An octavo edition (1850) followed without commentary, with five changed readings, and with variations from the *textus receptus*. The *Triglottum Græce Latine Germanice* (1854) deviates, in the Greek text, from the edition of 1849 more frequently than that of 1850, especially in Matthew (sixteen times). Under the texts are variants of the *textus receptus* as well as noteworthy readings of other editors. The text of the Vulgate is critically revised according to the best manuscripts, in particular, *Codex Amiatinus* and *Codex Fuldensis*, the variations in the *editio Clementina* and in the above codices being given under the text. Special care is given to the edition of Luther's translation; the edition of 1545 is followed but earlier editions are also considered. A *Synopsis evangelica* (harmony) appeared (1851). Soon after completing the edition of 1849, Tischendorf undertook a version of the Septuagint, and the apocryphal New Testament. He went in the autumn of 1849 to Paris, London, and Oxford, and besides comparing anew the *Codex Claramontanus*, and making a transcript of the papyrus fragments of the Psalms in London, he devoted himself in particular to a comparison of the manuscripts of the New-Testament Apocrypha. He did not venture to give his own recension of the text of the Septuagint; but contented himself with appending to a much improved reprint of the text of the *Sixtine* the variants of the *Codex Alexandrinus*, the *Codex Ephraemi*, and the *Codex Friderico-Augustanus* (1850). The prolegomena contained valuable studies on the history of the text of the Septuagint. While waiting on the king of Saxony for the means to make a three-years' journey for the discovery and study of sources for the Septuagint, he published the *De evangelicorum apocryphorum origine et usu*, a prize essay for " The Hague Society for the Defence of the Christian Religion," published in *Verhandelingen*, part xii. (Leyden, 1851); *Acta apostolorum apocrypha* (Leipsic, 1851); and *Evangelia apocrypha* (1853). Tischendorf undertook a second oriental journey in Jan., 1853. He at once visited the Convent of St. Catherine on Sinai, but could not find the manuscript seen in 1844, and concluded that it had been taken to Europe, probably England. He found only a scrap of the codex, containing a few verses of Gen. xxiii. as a book-mark in a codex of a history of the saints. He brought back with him sixteen palimpsests, some of considerable extent, several Greek uncial manuscripts, and a series of papyrus fragments in various languages, all of which were noted in the *Anecdota* and most of them deposited later at St. Petersburg and published in *Monumenta, nova collectio*. In the introduction to vol. i., he announces the lost manuscript and claims, if found, the credit of its recovery. The vacations of 1854–57 were spent in researches in European libraries. A new edition of the Greek New Testament was under way. His aim was not only to construct consistently his critical apparatus which was more nearly perfected since 1849, but also a new critical elaboration of the Greek New Testament, the *editio septima major* (1859), accompanied by a *septima minor*. This recension deviates least from the *textus receptus*.

In Jan., 1859, Tischendorf entered upon his third oriental journey, under the auspices of the Russian government. After a fruitless search of the library of the Convent at Sinai he was about **Codex** to depart, when, on the evening of **Sinaiticus;** Feb. 4, the young econome produced **Editio** from a corner of his cell, wrapped in a **Octava** red cloth, not only the eighty-six leaves **Major.** but 112 in addition on the Old Testament, besides a complete New Testament, the Epistle of Barnabas, and fragments of Hermas. The *Codex Sinaiticus*, first loaned to make a copy at Cairo, then for publication, was finally (1869) presented by the monks to Czar Alexander II. Returning in 1859 to St. Petersburg with the Codex and a large number of other manuscripts, among which were twelve palimpsests, twenty Greek uncials, eight minuscules, and many oriental manuscripts, Tischendorf devoted himself for the next two and a half years to the preparations for the publication of the codex. He published *Notitia editionis codicis bibliorum Sinaitici* (Leipsic, 1860); and *Aus dem heiligen Lande* (1862), an account of his latest journey. The *Bibliorum codex Sinaiticus Petropolitanus* (4 vols., Leipsic, 1862), with prolegomena, commentary, and facsimile plates, now appeared; and the first edition was presented to the czar. The *Novum Testamentum Sinaiticum cum epistula Barnabæ et fragmentis Pastoris* (1863), with prolegomena and commentary, was also produced, as well as a *Novum Testamentum Græce. Ex Sinaitico codice* (1865), with later corrections and variations of the *Codex Vaticanus* and the *textus receptus*. The complete recension of the Greek New Testament based on the Codex Sinaiticus is the famous *editio octava major* (2 vols., 1864–72). On a journey to Rome, in 1866, he was permitted, by the grace of Pope Pius IX., to compare for forty-two hours the Codex Vaticanus with Mai's edition; but he was enabled to issue a new *Novum Testamentum Vaticanum* (1867). Meanwhile he published *Apocalypses apocryphæ* (1866); *Philonæ inedita altera* (1868); and *The New Testament* (1869), the authorized English version with the variants from the *Codex Sinaiticus*, the *Codex Vaticanus*, and the *Codex Alexandrinus*. The last three years of Tischendorf's activity, 1870–72, were devoted mainly to further work on the *octava*. Vol. ix. of the *Monumenta* (1870) contained the important *Codex Laudianus* of the Acts. A fourth edition of the *Synopsis* (1871) followed the text of the *Sinaiticus;* and a special reprint of the Epistles of Clement, based on the first edition in the *Appendix* (1867), was issued (1873). The prolegomena of the *octava*, which he expected but was unable to prepare as vol. i., were elaborated by Caspar René Gregory, *Prolegomena* (3 vols., 1884–94). S. P. Tregelles (q.v.; BIBLE TEXT, II., 2, § 7) had the use of the text of *Codex Sinaiticus* in the preparation of that part of the New Testament following the Gospels, and Ezra Abbot is of the opinion that " Tischendorf must have derived great advantage from the publication of the successive parts of Tregelles' elaborate edition." The opponents of his critical work have censured Tischendorf for departing so copiously from the *septima*. F. H. A. Scrivener notes that the text has been changed in 3,369 places "to the scandal of the science of comparative criticism"; but, after the issue of the *septima*, Tischendorf had become thoroughly familiar not only with the *Sinaiticus* and *Vaticanus*, but with manuscripts, translations, and the Fathers to such an extent that he could well undertake to determine the text alone according to the material results of the proofs of the witnesses, eliminating all personal prejudice. Though he may not infrequently have followed the *Codex Sinaiticus* more than was proper, yet the correspondence to the texts of Tregelles and Westcott and Hort (unknown to Tischendorf during the recension of the *octava*) is so great that the result may be taken as gratifying to New-Testament criticism. This is above all essentially advanced by the *octava* upon the way recognized since Carl Lachmann (see BIBLE TEXT, II., 2, § 5) as, on the whole, the correct one, because leading to relatively sure results. The enormous critical apparatus of the *octava* will continue to maintain its great value. An edition *octava minor* followed (1872–77) and three hand editions of the *major*. Two were reprints of the octavo edition (1850, 1862), of the *secunda* and of the *editio academica* (the Greek text of the *triglottum* separately; 1855, and often) as *editio stereotypa tertia* (1873) and *editio academica septima* (1873), both characterized as *ad editionem viii. criticam majorem conformata*. The last of the three and the last' directed by Tischendorf himself was the reprint of the text of the *octava* (1873) which with an edition of the Septuagint was to form the entire Greek Bible. He issued also the edition of the Vulgate (1873) begun by Theodore Heyse; and furnished the text of the translation of Jerome, *Liber Psalmorum* (1874), for the commentary on that book by S. Baer and Franz Delitzsch. See also BIBLE TEXT, II., 2, §§ 6–7. [The death of Tischendorf was caused by paralysis.]   (CARL BERTHEAU.)

BIBLIOGRAPHY: J. E. Volbeding, *Constantin Tischendorf in seiner 25-jährigen Wirksamkeit*, Leipsic, 1862; E. Abbott, in *Unitarian Review and Religious Magazine*, March, 1875; P. Schaff, *Companion to the Greek Testament*, passim, New York, 1883; C. R. Gregory, *Novum Testamentum Græce. . . . Prolegomena*, i. 3–22, Leipsic, 1884; idem, *Textkritik des N. Ts.*, i. 18–29, ii. 975–980, ib. 1900–02; idem, *Canon and Text of the N. T.*, pp. 329–340, 455–459 et passim, New York, 1907; G. Salmon, *Historical Introduction to the . . . Books of the N. T.*, 6th ed., London, 1892; F. H. A. Scrivener, *Plain Introduction to the Criticism of the N. T.*, 2 vols., passim, 4th ed., London, 1894; C. A. Briggs, *Study of Holy Scripture*, passim, New York, 1899; *ADB*, xxxviii. 371 sqq.

TITHES.

I. Hebrew: The tithe as a secular tax is mentioned in the Bible (Gen. xlvii. 24, a double tenth for Pharaoh; I Sam. viii. 15, 17, and Amos vii. 1 imply a tax on the first-fruits); but that it was levied originally for the king and only later for the deity is opposed by Gen. xxviii. 22. In late times

the Seleucidæ levied a secular tithe from the Jews, which was afterward remitted (I Macc. x. 31, xi. 35). The tithe imposed by the Maccabees was rather a sacred tax in virtue of their high priesthood. The sacred tithe was common to many Semitic peoples, and may have combined the ideas of tribute, gift, upkeep of the cultus, thank-offering, or consecration-offering (Lev. xxvii. 30; Num. xviii. 24). The history among the Hebrews is far from clear; two situations appear, that in Deuteronomy and that in P.

Deut. xiv. 22 sqq. requires a tithing of agricultural products and of the products of pastoral life, to be devoted to a communal meal at the central sanctuary. In case the home was too distant, the tithe might be commuted and material for the meal purchased at the sanctuary. The purpose of the tithe in this case was not the support of the services at the Temple, but a joyous meal of the agriculturist and his establishment with the Levites of his locality, the latter being included because they had no landed possessions. It did not go to the priests or temple officers. Purity of the participants was required. Deut. xiv. 28–29, xxvi. 12–15 require that in the third year the tithe shall be deposited at the home (not at the sanctuary) for the benefit of the Levite, stranger, fatherless, and widow; this is not a second tithing but a special employment of the tithe of the third year for charitable purposes. It may have been a sort of compensation for abolition of the early public offering and meal of which the needy partook. Of a second tithing expressly for the Levites Deuteronomy knows nothing. The relation of the tithe to the offering of first-fruits in Deuteronomy is not clear; possibly the two are identical, as it seems unlikely that each generation of the herd should be subjected to a double tax, and Deut. xxvi. 1–15 puts first-fruits and the tithe in close connection. In this case the basket of first-fruits brought to the priest is simply a part of the tithe which is devoted as a whole to the joyous meal. Against this Deut. xviii. 4 is no objection, even as a later insertion. And with this conception many difficulties vanish. "Tithe" becomes an expression for the entire offering of first-fruits, over which a sort of control is introduced (by supplementary provisions). The early law omits mention of the tithe, then, because it is identical with the offering of first-fruits. The treatment of the tithe in P must be considered an extension of the situation in Deuteronomy. Num. xviii. 26–28 gives the whole tithe to the Levites, and this was again tithed for the Aaronites (Neh. x. 38). Lev. xxvii. 31–33 requires the addition of a fifth of the tithe of the first-fruits when it is commuted, and aims to procure honesty in payment of tithes of cattle. This law is first mentioned in II Chron. xxxi. 5–6; it is not found in Neh. x. nor Mal. iii., hence it is deduced that it arose between the time of Nehemiah and that of the Chronicler.

In attempting to reconcile D and P William Robertson Smith supposes that the support of the sanctuaries was undertaken by the court while in connection with the sanctuaries, but when the former removed or fell, other arrangements were necessary. The one pre-Deuteronomic sanctuary, it is noticeable, was the royal one at Bethel (Gen. xxviii. 22; Amos vii. 13). Smith stresses the fact that the tithe of D is different from the tribute gifts to the northern sanctuaries; the feasts of Amos are not the joyous feasts of the Deuteronomic agriculturists, they are the luxurious banquets provided from the tribute wrung from the people, in which Smith sees the original character of the tithe. But there is no hint that in Judah the tithes were handed to the headmen, and that abuse arose from this which D attempts to correct. Smith seems to think the tithe for the poor is the only officially required tenth, while that for the other two years was a free-will offering, and this does not correspond with the presentation of D. The ordinary Semitic tenth for the cultus seems to have existed among the Hebrews with adaptations to their own religious genius. Some have thought that D had in view a second tenth, which came to light first after the tenth of the tithe had been deducted (ut sup.), though mention of such a thing seems to fail entirely. Even though in P earlier legislation than in D may be found, the law for the tithe is clearly a step in advance and later. The later practise (Tob. i. 6–8) seems to show the tithes of P and of D both claimed by the Levites. Theoretically there were three tithes, according to P for the Levites, according to D for the public meal, and that each third year for the poor. The first accrued wholly to the Levites and covered all that came from the earth (cf. Matt. xxiii. 23); the second was for the offerers' meal, though Philo gives it to the Levites, and so raises the question whether the twofold or threefold tithing was merely theoretical.

How the system worked out is not known. From II Chron. xxxi. 4 it has been inferred that till the time of Hezekiah the tithes were too small for the support of the personnel of the cultus, and from Deut. xii. 17 a misuse of the tithes is deduced. Evidently the people did not like the tithes (cf. Neh. xiii. 5 sqq.; Mal. iii. 8). But there is no report of the actual exaction of both the tithes of P and D, and Josephus mentions only the Levitical tenth which was converted into money on the spot (*Life*, xii. 15); so at the second temple a second tenth does not appear. But the Jews who were true to the law seem to have recognized loyally their duty in the matter of tithes (Ecclus. xxxv. 11; I Macc. iii. 49; cf. Matt. xxiii. 23). See PRIEST, PRIESTHOOD, I., § 6.   (R. ZEHNPFUND.)

II. Ecclesiastical: Tithes (" tenths ") are in general contributions of the tenth part or of some other defined portion of the yield of a piece of land or active property paid to the lawful claimant as ground rental. These are customary

1. Doctrine in connection with both spiritual and **and Practise** temporal domains, and are subject to **till 1517.** both public and private law. As a rule, however, the term tithes is confined to contributions payable to the Church, with which alone this article is concerned. The tithe customary with the Hebrews (see I., above) passed from the synagogue to the Church at a time when the latter's officiant came to be viewed as priest and the priesthood of the Church as the continuation and fulfilment of that in the Old Testament. Hence it was now required of all Christians to pay tithes as a religious obligation (cf. Apostolic Constitutions, II., xxv., xxxv., VII., xxix., VIII., xxx., *ANF*, vii. 408, 413, 471, 494; Apostolic Canons, IV., v., etc.; for the history of the introduction and extension of the tithes consult L. Thomassin, *Vetus ac nova ecclesiæ disciplina*, part III., book I., chaps. i.–x., cf. xii.–xiv., Paris, 1728). However, some time elapsed before this requirement was generally recognized. The tithes actually paid bore the appearance of a voluntary contribution, and so continued till the sixth century. On the other hand, the second Synod of Macon (585) commanded payment under threat of excommunication, and from that time forth payment was enjoined in various ways, especially through the confessional, where the omission to pay tithes was treated as a sin. Moreover, the liberality of princes had its effect, and when this fell short, recourse was had to legislation. The provision was made that of the goods of the Church which the State leased as benefices subject to reversion to the Church, the tithe, and, furthermore, a ninth of the remaining ninety per cent, or two tithes in all, were to be contributed. On this point, chap. xiii. of the *Capitulare Haristallense* (779 A.D.) reads as follows: " Of church property now under assessment, let the tithe and the ninth be paid conjointly with the rating itself." This ruling was afterward often repeated, and the obligation to pay tithes, as the Church affirmed it, was recognized on principle, even apart from these benefice arrangements, e.g., King Pepin's letter to Bishop Lul of Mainz: " You may provide and ordain by our mandate, that every man, willing or not, shall pay his tithe." And Charlemagne repeated this in chap. vii. of the *Capitulare* cited above. The bishops were thereby empowered to receive and to distribute tithes. The obligation was transferred to the newly converted Saxons, in the so-called *Capitulatio de partibus Saxoniæ*, chap. xvii. This position was thenceforward stoutly maintained, and the mandate was enforced under threat of severe penalties. From that time onward, the tithes were in continual use in Germany and France, also in other countries, coming in with the introduction of Christianity, though often fiercely opposed. Thus they were established in Portugal not until the close of the eleventh century, about the same time in Denmark and Iceland, and in Sweden not till the beginning of the thirteenth century. Moreover, the Church confirmed the tithe right by means of special provisos, many of which occur in the canonical collections. Some of these last aim to insure to the Church such tithes as had been withdrawn through alienation or otherwise. Possession of tithes by the laity was pronounced a sin. All attempts to contest the claims of the Church to tithes were opposed by the Council of Trent (session XXV., chap. xii., *De reformatione*).

In consequence of the Reformation, the Church of Rome suffered momentous losses in the tithes which she had hitherto drawn, which now were applied to Evangelical objects. For the point was hardly anywhere affirmed, that the exaction of the tithe is reprehensible. Only the Ana-

2. Change after the Reformation. baptists in Switzerland maintained that Christians owed neither interest nor tithes; even the turbulent [German] peasants, in their twelve articles of 1525 A.D., did not deny the obligation. Luther generally approved the payment of tithes and, in view of their practical convenience, regarded them as the most expedient form of taxing (*Werke*, ed. Walch, x. 1006, xvii. 46, 85). In Luther's opinion, tithes were to be paid to the temporal sovereignty; but in this he was not seconded. In the Evangelical State Churches, the tithes were retained, though with readjustments, and were more strictly defined. In the duchy of Prussia and in Saxony the church-inspectors were directed to devise the necessary measures for tithe payments (cf. the regulations of 1527 and 1528, in E. Sehling, *Die evangelischen Kirchenordnungen*, i. 144, 145, 172, Leipsic, 1902). Contributions in kind were frequently commuted, although the natural tithe continued legally in practise. But in the course of time, there grew up a dislike of tithes, partly on economic grounds, partly because of alienation from the Church; e.g., in France it provoked formal repeal of the tithes without indemnity (cf. art. 5 of the National Assembly's decrees, from Aug. 4 to Nov. 3, 1789). In other countries there was repeal with compensating indemnity, and only certain peculiar kinds of tithes were abolished. Even at present either the tithes direct, or some substitute ratings, are much in vogue, thus calling for a statement of the principles governing the application.

Originally viewed, the tithes are either temporal (for civil needs) or ecclesiastical (for the Church).

3. Classification. A further distinction is into lay and clerical tithes, which distinction turns on the question whether the recipient of the tithe is a layman or a cleric. Laymen may chance to be in possession of church tithes, and clerics in possession of temporal tithes, a change in ownership having been brought about through alienation or other circumstances. Theoretically this was forbidden, and the possession of ecclesiastical tithes by laymen was pronounced criminal. The distinction has continued to be of practical moment since certain obligations devolving upon the originally ecclesiastical tithes still rest upon the holder. The tithe is either paid from the proceeds of some industry and other personal profits, as a personal tithe (less frequently), or it is paid on the basis of other increments, as the "real tithe." But from time immemorial, the real tithe appears generally in practise, whether based on field, grain, sheaf or fruit, or on cattle. There also exist subdivisions into great and small tithes. Normally, the great natural tithe includes the so-called major fruits of the field, and the great live-stock tithe includes domestic and farm animals. Pope Alexander III. defines as articles under the small tithe fodder and garden products. The same category also includes the so-called small cattle—sheep, lambs, foals, calves, poultry, bees, etc. When the produce tithe is paid in kind from the soil itself, it becomes known as natural, sheaf, or almond tithe. Distinct from this is the sack, bushel, or village tithe, which is paid from grain already threshed and sacked, or is commuted, including therefore the money tithe as a cash equivalent.

Certain other frequently mentioned subdivisions of tithes belong more properly to the survey of the tithe law and obligation as follows: The tithe right

4. Tithe Law. is based either on canon or other law, or on tradition, contract, or custom. By legal definition, the tithes generally accrue to the Church, and modes of tithe payments were subject to the same principles as governed other ecclesiastical revenues. The bishop received the tithes for distribution to the several churches; but where the parish pastors drew the tithes, they were expected to transact the distribution in the presence of witnesses. The tithes paid to parish churches and baptisteries were to be employed for these alone, without any partial transfer to the cathedral or to the bishop. Subsequently, the traditional division of the church property into four portions, as observed at Rome, was also applied to the tithes, and the fourth part was assigned to the bishop, although this payment gradually lapsed and survived only locally. The bishop is therefore no longer entitled to the quarter of the tithes accruing to the parishes, though he may claim the tithes of such districts in his diocese as are not especially referred to some parish church. In all other cases the collection of tithes appertains to the parish churches by ordinary law. In this matter canon law proceeds from the premise that the parish pastors are entitled to demand tithes within the entire parish bounds, except as exemptions exist. Hence new tithes (those yielded by hitherto virgin soil) are also accredited to the parish church. The tithe right has its corresponding circumscriptions, and, within a given district, may cover either all or only certain particular fields, may embrace all fruits, or only stated kinds of produce, and the amount of the contribution itself may vary, except that there is a strong presumption to fix it as the actual tenth part. Concurrently with the tithe right goes the tithe obligation. While legislation once ruled that the duty to pay tithes was universal, this ruling fell short of unqualified expressness and eventually became a dead letter. Accordingly, the legal presumption in favor of the tithe obligation is not everywhere in force, and usually evidence is required of one who affirms that right. Another consideration qualifies the tithe obligation, viz., the distinction between real and personal tithes, as well as the religious belief of the persons obligated. Wherever the obligation attaches to real estate, the personal ownership is immaterial, since the real tithe is payable even by non-Christian owners. But the personal tithe is paid only by the actual parishioners. According to the maxim, "tithes are to be paid from the natural yield," tithes are due from the fruits produced, and from these directly. Hence the obligation attaches to the fruits, even when these are alienated, so that the tithe can be required of the third party who controls the produce. Where a release from the tithe obligation is affirmed, such release must be proved by exceptional ruling, as by appealing to laws, privileges, contract, or inveterate usage. Moreover, the clergy never tithe one another.

Methods of payment are controlled by legal provisos, custom, contracts, and the nature of the transaction. Personal tithes are paid, as a rule, at the close of the year. In case of ani-

5. Methods mals, usually the tenth head is taken, **of Payment.** just as it comes, nor is selection allowed. Of tithes in produce it is generally provided that so soon as the same is ready for division, the tithe-payer notifies the receiver, so that the division may be accomplished. The removal of the tithed portion devolves on the payer, although in practise the opposite custom has very generally grown up. The holders of tithes are canonically subject to various customary duties, such as that of contributing toward the building and maintenance of ecclesiastical edifices. Redemption of the tithes by means of fixed payments was usual even in medieval times; and the Curia sanctioned this custom in so far as it benefited the Church. On political and economic grounds the State promoted the repeal of tithes, though not always with due regard to the weal of the institutions which enjoyed the tithes and were partly founded thereon, as in France, some parts of Germany, and in Switzerland. Canon law views the tithes as objects collateral to things spiritual, and accordingly claims that any disputes in the matter must come before spiritual tribunals. This ruling, however, proved not to be permanently tenable against the State, and was modified at least in part. E. SEHLING.

BIBLIOGRAPHY: For the Biblical tithe the best discussions are to be found in the commentaries on the passages cited and in the works on O. T. theology and antiquities. Consult particularly: L. Saalschütz, *Das mosaische Recht*, Berlin, 1853; S. R. Driver, *Commentary on Deuteronomy*, pp. 166–173, New York, 1895; H. Lansdell, *The Sacred Tenth*, 2 vols., London, 1906; idem, *The Tithe in Scripture. Being Chapters from the Sacred Tenth. With a revised Bibliography on Tithe Paying and systematic and proportionate Giving*, ib. 1908; Smith, *Rel. of Sem*, 2d ed., pp. 245–253; Schürer, *Geschichte*, ii. 244–246, 251–252 et passim, Eng. transl., II., i. 233, 239 et passim; Nowack, *Archäologie*, ii. 257–259; Benzinger, *Archäologie*, pp. 384 sqq., 397; *DB*, iv. 780–781; *EB*, iv. 5102–05; *JE*, xii. 150–152.

For the ecclesiastical tithe consult: Bingham, *Origines*, V., v.–vi. (gives full and exact references to the earlier literature); J. Selden, *The Hist. of Tithes*, in *Works*, iii. 1069–1298, London, 1726; W. H. Hale, *The Antiquity of the Church-rate System*, London, 1837; R. Swan, *The Principle of Church-rates, from the Earliest Evidence of their Existence to the Present Time*, London, 1837; W. Goode, *A Brief Hist. of Church-rates*, 2d ed., London, 1838; E. Löning, *Geschichte des deutschen Kirchenrechts*, ii. 676 sqq., Strasburg, 1878; K. Lamprecht, *Deutsches Wirtschaftsleben im Mittelalter*, i. 113 sqq., 608 sqq., Leipsic, 1885; A. L. Richter, *Kirchenrecht*, 8th ed., by W. Kahl, pp. 1313 sqq., Leipsic, 1886; W. Easterby, *The Hist. of the Law of Tithes in England*, Cambridge, 1888; M. J. Fuller, *Our Title Deeds*, London, 1890; P. Fabre, *Recherches sur le dernier de S. Pierre en Angleterre*, in *Mélanges G. B. de Rossi*, pp. 159–182, Paris, 1892; Roundell Palmer, Earl of Selborne, *Ancient Facts and Fictions concerning Churches and Tithes*, 2d ed., London, 1892; H. W. Clark, *A Hist. of Tithes*, 2d ed., London, 1894; C. Meurer, *Zehnt und Bodenzinsrecht in Bayern*, Stuttgart, 1898; E. Perels, *Kirchliche Zehnten im karolingischen Reiche*, Berlin, 1904; E. Hennig, *Die päpstlichen Zehnten aus Deutschland im Zeitalter des avignonesischen Papsttums und während des grossen Schismas*, Halle, 1910; Hauck, *KD*, i. 137 sqq., ii. 222 sqq.; Pastor, *Popes*, iv. 83.

TITIUS, ti′tî-ūs or ti′tzî-ūs, **ARTHUR BENEDIKT WILHELM:** German Protestant; b. at Sensburg (67 m. s.e. of Königsberg) July 28, 1864. He was educated at the universities of Königsberg (1883–1885) and Berlin (1885–90; lic. theol., 1890), and in 1891 became privat-docent for systematic theology at Berlin. In 1895 he was appointed associate professor of systematic theology and New-Testament exegesis in the University of Kiel, and full professor five years later. Since 1906 he has been professor of systematic theology at Göttingen, and since 1910 one of the chief editors of the *Theologische Literaturzeitung*. He has written *Die neutestamentliche Lehre von der Seligkeit und ihre Bedeutung für die Gegenwart* (4 parts, Freiburg, 1895–1900); *Das Verhältnis der Herrnworte zu den Logia des Matthæus* (Göttingen, 1897); *Religion und Wissenschaft* (Tübingen, 1904); and *Der Bremer Radikalismus* (1908).

TITTMANN, tit′mån, **JOHANN AUGUST HEINRICH:** Professor in Leipsic; b. in Langensalza (10 m. n. of Gotha) Aug. 1, 1773; d. in Leipsic Dec. 30, 1831. He studied in Wittenberg (M.A., 1791), where his father was professor, and from 1792 in Leipsic, where he became bachelor of theology and morning preacher at the university in 1795, at the same time beginning to deliver lectures in theology. He was made professor extraordinary in philosophy in 1796 and in 1800 was transferred to a like position in the theological faculty, becoming professor primarius in 1818. A Ciceronian gift of oratory and marked ability in practical matters enabled him to render valuable services to his city and university in his various honorable and responsible positions in Church and State. His theological position was that of a rationalistic supernaturalism, which in his time passed for orthodoxy. Of his numerous publications the most noteworthy were a theological encyclopedia (Leipsic, 1798); a text-book of homiletics (1804); *Pragmatische Geschichte der Theologie und Religion in der protestantischen Kirche während der zweiten Hälfte des 18. Jahrhunderts* (Breslau, 1805); *Institutio symbolica ad sententiam ecclesiæ evangelicæ* (Leipsic, 1811); *Ueber Supranaturalismus, Rationalismus, und Atheismus* (1816); an edition of the symbolical books (1817); an edition of the New Testament (1820); and a series of programs on New-Testament synonyms (1820–29; collected into book i. 1829; book ii. ed. G. Beecher, 1832; Eng. transl., vols. iii. and xviii. of *The Biblical Cabinet*, Edinburgh, 1833–37). (E. SCHWARZ†.)

BIBLIOGRAPHY: *Allgemeine Kirchenzeitung*, 1832, no. 9; G. W. Frank, *Geschichte der protestantischen Theologie*, iii. 394, Leipsic, 1875; *ADB*, xxxviii. 385.

TITULAR BISHOP. See BISHOP, TITULAR.

TITUS: A prominent personage in the circle of Paul's disciples, known solely from the Pauline letters. From Gal. ii. 1–5, it appears that he was the son of heathen parents, that he was not circumcised on becoming a Christian, and that he remained uncircumcised after the Apostolic Council at Jerusalem (q.v.). It is not stated that he was converted by Paul, but such an assumption is natural; if it be true, Titus came from one of the provinces where Paul preached before the Apostolic Council, i.e., Syria or southeastern Asia Minor; most commentators think that his home was in Antioch. Paul's taking him to Jerusalem implies that he was competent to help in pleading the cause which called them thither and Titus can hardly have been new in the faith at that time; that he was a young man is pure imagination. In II Cor. (ii. 13, vii. 6–16, viii. 23, xii. 18) Titus appears as Paul's trusted friend and fellow-worker, who reconciled the Corinthian congregation to Paul when it was estranged from him; evidently Titus possessed both tact and energy. Paul sent him back to Corinth from Macedonia to collect the contributions for Jerusalem (II Cor. viii. 6, 16–17). To these data the epistle to Titus (i. 4–5, iii. 12), if it be genuine (see TIMOTHY, § 3), adds that Titus organized the churches in Crete founded by Paul. The Acts of Paul tell nothing that is not founded on II Tim. iv. 10, and the later Church has no independent tradition of Titus.

One can not help asking why Titus is not mentioned in the Acts and where he was between the Apostolic Council and his sudden appearance at Ephesus about six years later. Both questions are answered if he is the same as Silas or Silvanus, as assumed by some (e.g., by F. Zimmer; against the assumption, cf. JPT, 1882, 538 sqq.), and one at least if he completes the " we " of Acts xvi., xx., xxi., xxvii., xxviii. (so e.g., Krenkel). He can not be the redactor of the Acts because of Acts xv. Possibly Titus did not belong to the number of Paul's steady companions, but like Barnabas and Apollos went his own way and chose his own fields of labor. He is not mentioned in the Acts because interest there is concentrated on Paul. So far as is known Titus was the first purely Greek missionary. He may well have carried the Gospel to Crete and to Dalmatia, perhaps to other provinces in the neighborhood of Achaia and Macedonia, and have labored in these regions after the death of Paul. Herein may be the historical kernel of the pastoral letters; probably too, it was not pure invention which transferred Timothy to Ephesus (see TIMOTHY, § 5).

(A. JÜLICHER.)

BIBLIOGRAPHY: Besides the articles in the Bible dictionaries, the literature cited under Timothy is to be consulted.

TITUS OF BOSTRA: Bishop of Bostra in the Hauran; d. about 370. He had a severe conflict with Emperor Julian, apparently not of his seeking. At the Synod of Antioch (363) he signed a letter to Emperor Jovian which contained a new Nicene formula of faith. According to Jerome he died under Valens. His discourses against the Manicheans, which originated doubtlessly soon after the death of Julian, treat of the barbaric and illogical character of their writings, the problem of sin and providence, the Old and New Testament, and the relation of the Manicheans to the latter. These orations manifest a rich culture, and Titus furnished the best anti-Manichean polemic from a literary point of view. The extant fragments from his exegetical writings show that he followed the Antiochian traditions.

(J. LEIPOLDT.)

BIBLIOGRAPHY: The sources are Titus' own works—ed. from the Greek and the Syriac by P. de Lagarde, 2 vols., Berlin, 1859; Socrates, Hist. eccl., iii. 25, and Sozomen, Hist. eccl., iii. 14, vi. 4, both in NPNF, 2 ser., vol. ii.; Epiphanius, Hær., lxvi. 21; and Jerome, De vir. ill., cii., and

Epist., lxx., both in Eng. transl., in NPNF, 2 ser., iii., vi. Consult: J. Sickenberger, in TU, xxi. 1 (1901); Gallandi, Bibliotheca patrum magna, pp. 415–477, Leyden, 1677; Ceillier, Auteurs sacrés, iv. 339–345; DCB, iv. 1035–36.

TO REMAIN BIBLE. See BIBLE VERSIONS, B, IV., § 9.

TOBAGO. See WEST INDIES.

TOBIT: Apocryphal book. See APOCRYPHA, A, IV., 7.

TOBLER, TITUS: Authority on Palestinian geography; b. at Stein (26 m. n.e. of Zurich), Switzerland, June 25, 1806; d. in Munich Jan. 21, 1877. He studied medicine at Zurich and Vienna, and undertook for medical purposes a journey in Palestine, 1835–36; the result of which was Lustreise im Morgenland (2 pts., Zurich, 1839). Having become interested in the geographical and topographical investigations of the holy land, he made three more journeys to Palestine, the first in 1845, and as the literary results of this journey appeared, Bethlehem (St. Gall, 1849); Golgotha (1851); Die Siloahquelle und der Oelberg (1852); Denkblätter aus Jerusalem (1853); Topographie von Jerusalem und seinen Umgebungen (2 vols., Berlin, 1853–54); Beitrag zur medizinischen Topographie von Jerusalem (1855). After the second he published Planographie von Jerusalem (Gotha, 1858); and Dritte Wanderung nach Palæstina (1859). In 1865 he undertook his last journey to Palestine, and published Bibliographia geographica Palæstinæ (Leipsic, 1867); Nazareth in Palästina (Berlin, 1868); Palestinæ descriptiones ex sæculo iv., v., et vi. (St. Gall, 1869); and Descriptiones terræ sanctæ ex sæculo viii., ix., xii., et xv. (Leipsic, 1874). In 1871 he went to Munich, where he became active in the French society " Orient latin." He was the first authority of his day on the topography of Palestine, and although some of his results have been superseded by excavations, yet he remains unexcelled as a systematic investigator in archeology and topography from the sources.

BIBLIOGRAPHY; H. J. Heim, Dr. Titus Tobler, der Palästinafahrer, Zurich, 1879; R. Röhricht, Bibliotheca geographica Palæstinæ, no. 1824, Berlin, 1890.

TODD, HENRY JOHN: Church of England; b. about 1763 (baptized at Britford, 2 m. s.e. of Salisbury, Feb. 13, 1763); d. at Settrington (18 m. n.e. of York) Dec. 24, 1845. He studied at Magdalen College, Oxford (B.A., 1784); became fellow tutor and lecturer at Hertford College, M.A., 1786; in 1785 he was ordained deacon as curate at East Lockinge, Berkshire; took priest's orders, 1787; was curate of St. John and St. Bridget, Beckermet, 1787–1803; became a minor canon in Canterbury Cathedral; was sinecure rector of Orgarswick, 1791–92; vicar of Milton, near Canterbury, 1792–1801; rector of All Hallows, Lombard St., London, 1801–10; rector of Woolwich, 1803–05; vicar of Edlesbrough, Buckinghamshire, 1805–07; rector of Coulsdon, Surrey, 1807–12; vicar of Addington 1812–20; royal chaplain in ordinary 1812–45; rector of Settrington, 1820–45; prebendary of York, 1830–45; and archdeacon at Cleveland, 1832–45. He was also keeper of manuscripts at Lambeth Palace, 1803–07, and in

1824 became a member of the Royal Society of Literature. He edited the poetical works of Milton (London, 1801); and the works of Spenser (1805); wrote the life of Brian Walton (2 vols., 1821); and of Archbishop Cranmer (2 vols., 1831); also *Some Account of the Deans of Canterbury* (Canterbury, 1793); *Illustrations of the Lives and Writings of Gower and Chaucer* (London, 1810); *A Catalogue of the Archiepiscopal Manuscripts in the Library of Lambeth Palace* (1812); *Original Sin, Free-Will, Grace, Regeneration, Justification, Good Works, and Universal Redemption* (1818); *A Vindication of our Authorized Translation and Translators of the Bible* (1819); *An Account of Greek Manuscripts, chiefly Biblical, of the Late Professor Carlyle* (1823); *A History of the College of Bonhommes, at Ashridge* (1823); *Of Confession and Absolution* (1828); and *Repertorium Theologicum* (1838).

BIBLIOGRAPHY: J. Nichols, *Literary Anecdotes of the 18th Century*, ii. 672, iii. 192, 9 vols., London, 1812–15; idem, *Illustrations of the Literary Hist. of the 18th Century*, vi. 620, 681–686, vii. 54, 58–59, 8 vols., ib. 1817–58; *DNB*, lvi. 428–430.

TODD, JOHN: American Congregationalist; b. at Rutland, Vt., Oct. 9, 1800; d. at Pittsfield, Mass., Aug. 24, 1873. He was graduated from Yale College, 1822; taught for a year; studied four years at Andover Theological Seminary; was pastor in Groton, Mass., 1827–33; Northampton 1833–36; of the First Congregational Church, Philadelphia, 1836–42; and Pittsfield, 1842–72. He was a man of national reputation, and took an active interest in educational progress. He was the author of *Lectures to Children* (Northampton, 1834–58), translated into various languages, printed in raised letters for the blind, and used as a school-book for the liberated slaves in Sierra Leone; the *Student's Manual* (1835), which had a wide circulation and large influence; and numerous stories for the young. A collected edition of his books appeared (London, 1853, new ed., 6 vols., 1882).

BIBLIOGRAPHY: J. Todd, *The Story of his Life told mainly by himself*, New York, 1876.

TOELLNER, tŭl'ner, **JOHANN GOTTLIEB:** Professor in Frankfort-on-the-Oder; b. in Charlottenburg (a suburb of Berlin) Dec. 9, 1724; d. in Frankfort-on-the-Oder Jan. 26, 1774. He entered the University of Halle in 1741, living in the household of S. J. Baumgarten (q.v.) and having the care of his library. After being tutor in Pomerania and in Berlin, in 1748 he became chaplain of Count Schwerin's regiment at Frankfort; in 1756 professor of philosophy and theology in the university, where he endeared himself to the students by the warm personal interest he took in all their affairs. His health was never robust; and an extreme devotion to work brought on a complete breakdown and led to his death at the early age of forty-nine.

After Semler and J. D. Michaelis, Töllner was the most important representative of the semirationalistic tendency in Protestant theology of the eighteenth century, theoretically founded by Wolf but practically the outcome of Hallensian Pietism, which strove to retain the supernatural character of Christianity as a divine revelation, to hold fast to the divine mission of Jesus and above all to the "beautiful morality of Christianity," while it rejected the positive dogmas of the Church as untenable, indifferent, or morally worthless. He regarded creeds as a necessary evil; the Church or the papacy might set forth its system, but no one has the right to propound a system for all time and it is unreasonable and unchristian to reproach anyone for deviation from orthodoxy in merely theological matters. He makes inspiration assistance from God, but in no way extraordinary. The doctrine of the Trinity involves so much that is improbable and contradictory that one does best to disregard it. Original sin is opposed to both reason and Scripture. Of Töllner's many books, all dry and prolix, yet showing dogmatic acuteness and independence of judgment, the following are most noteworthy: *Predigten* (Frankfort, 1755); *Das Abendmahl des Herrn gegen alle Verächter desselben* (1756); *Leiden des Erlösers* (1757); *Ein Christ und Held oder Nachrichten von Feldmarschall Schwerin* (1758); *Gedanken von der wahren Lehrart in der dogmatischen Theologie* (1759), which best presents his views on the controversies of his time; a translation and continuation of Turretin's church history (1759); manuals of dogmatic theology (1760), moral theology (1762), hermeneutics (1765), and pastoral theology (1767); *Der thätige Gehorsam Jesu untersucht* (Breslau, 1768), and *Zusätze* (Berlin, 1770), which raised much controversy because of its departure from orthodox teaching; *Meine Ueberzeugungen* (1769); *Unterricht von symbolischen Büchern* (Züllichau, 1769); *Göttliche Eingebung der heiligen Schrift* (Mitau, 1772), important for his doctrine of inspiration (cf. also an earlier treatise, *Vom Unterschied der heiligen Schrift und des Wortes Gottes*, 1767); *Meine Vorsätze* (1772); *Versuch eines Beweises der christlichen Religion* (1772); *Theologische Untersuchungen* (2 vols., Riga, 1772–1774); *Commentatio de potestate Dei legislatoria non mere arbitraria* (Frankfort, 1775). A *System der dogmatischen Theologie* (2 vols., Nuremberg, 1775), claiming to have been published from a manuscript of Töllner's, is thought by many not to be his work or, if so, not to present his mature views (cf. Gass, 189 sqq.).   (J. A. WAGENMANN†.)

BIBLIOGRAPHY: F. C. G. Hirsching, *Historisch-litterarisches Handbuch berühmter . . . Personen*, xiv. 2, pp. 5 sqq., 17 vols., Leipsic, 1794–1815; C. W. F. Walch, *Neueste Religionsgeschichte*, iii. 309 sqq., 9 parts, Lemgo, 1771–83; W. Gass, *Geschichte der protestantischen Dogmatik*, iv. 188 sqq., 270 sqq., Berlin, 1867; M. A. von Landerer, *Neueste Dogmengeschichte*, Tübingen, 1881; *ADB*, xxxviii. 427.

TOFFTEEN, OLAF ALFRED: Protestant Episcopal, orientalist; b. in the parish of Sproge, Island of Gotland, Sweden, June 26, 1863. He received his education at the higher State College of Visby, Sweden (B.A., 1885), the University of Upsala, Johns Hopkins University, and Chicago University (fellow in Semitics, 1903–05; Ph.D., 1905); served as rector of St. Angarius' Church, Minneapolis, 1892–1901; was made priest, 1893; docent in Assyriology, University of Chicago, 1906; became professor of Semitic languages and Old-Testament literature in the Western Theological Seminary, Chicago, 1906; curator of the Oriental Society of the same institution in the same year; and librarian of the Hibbard Egyptian Library of that institution in 1907. He is the author of *Våra Fäders Kyrka* (Minneapolis, 1897); *Myths and the Bible* (1899); *Ancient Chronology*, part i. (Chicago, 1907); *Researches in Assyrian and Babylonian Geography*, part i. (1908); and *The Historic Exodus* (1909).

TOGARMAH. See TABLE OF THE NATIONS, § 4.

TOKEN, COMMUNION: A small plate of lead marked on one side with one initial or more or with some device, referring to the place or the minister or the date of the congregation, given to intending communicants and collected from them just prior to their receiving the communion. Such articles, differing very much in size, in workmanship, and in intrinsic worth, were at one time in general use in Presbyterian churches, but probably now they are not used at all. Their origin has been traced to the earliest times of the Christian Church and even before and beyond it. It is well known that the initiates in the Greek and Latin mysteries had marked stones or other articles as means of proving their membership in such brotherhoods, also that the primitive Christians had similar means of identification and that by showing these they were sure of reception and kind treatment from their fellow Christians. Such articles would be of particular value in times of persecution. It is probably not possible to write a consecutive history of the token but it can be shown that its use was known from time to time. At the present day printed cards with emblems on them are in use among the Roman Catholics of Italy, Bavaria, and other countries. So the use of similar means of evidence of membership in Protestant communions can be shown to have existed in England in Reformation times. They were once much used in France among the Huguenots. But the Scotch Presbyterians and their children in Ireland, Canada, and the United States were the first to adopt as a regular practise the use of tokens in connection with the Lord's Supper. The tokens for such use were part of the church outfit. Those who intended to commune and were entitled to do so applied for them on a specified day before the communion and brought them with them when communion-day came. It was the common practise for the communicants to sit at long tables and be served by the church officers, but before the elements were distributed the officers went along the tables and collected the tokens. It was a rare and thrilling experience to discover a person who had not the token. This offender was denied the sacrament. There are several large collections of these communion tokens in private hands and some on public exhibition.

BIBLIOGRAPHY: R. Shields, *The Story of the Token*, New York, 1891; 2d ed., Philadelphia, 1902; R. Dick, *Scottish Communion Tokens other than those of the Established Church*, Edinburgh, 1902.

TOLAND, JOHN: English deist; b. near Londonderry, Ireland, Nov. 30, 1670; d. at Putney (London, W.) Mar. 11, 1722. He was born of Roman-Catholic parentage, changed his original name, Junius Janus, at school, and became a Protestant at the age of sixteen. From 1687 he studied at the universities of Glasgow, Edinburgh (M.A., 1690), and Leyden, 1692–94. He spent several years at Oxford, and published his principal work, *Christianity not* *Mysterious* (1696; 2d. enlarged ed., London, 1696), which made a great sensation (see DEISM, § 5). The book was burned by the hangman at Dublin, Toland being in the city at the time. The rest of his career is obscure. He spent much of his time on the continent receiving favors. He engaged in miscellaneous literary work and in writing pamphlets, lapsing into distress. Other works were, *An Apology for Mr. Toland* (London, 1697); *Nazarenus, Containing the History of the Gospel of Barnabas, the Gospel of the Mahometans. Also the Original Plan of Christianity* (1718). *Pantheisticon* (1720); and *Tetradymus*, containing *Mangoneutes* (1720).

BIBLIOGRAPHY: To *A Collection of Several Pieces of Mr. John Toland*, 2 vols., London, 1726, there is prefixed a *Life* by Des Maizeaux. Consult further: *An Historical Account of the Life and Writings of . . . Mr. John Toland*, London, 1702; J. L. Mosheim, in *Vindiciæ antiquæ Christianorum disciplinæ*, 2d ed., Hamburg, 1722; V. Lechler, *Geschichte des englischen Deismus*, Stuttgart, 1841; J. Hunt, in *Contemporary Review*, viii (1868), 178–198; idem, *Religious Thought in England*, ii. 236–262, London, 1873; J. F. Nourrisson, *Philosophies de la nature*, Paris, 1887; *DNB*, lvi. 438–442; and literature under DEISM.

TOLEDO, CITY, BISHOPRIC, AND SYNODS OF.

    I. City and Bishopric.
        History and Remains (§ 1)..
        The Bishopric (§ 2).
    II. Synods.
        The Three Ecclesiastical Synods (§ 1).
        The Semi-Political Synods (§ 2).

I. City and Bishopric: Toledo, one of the most ancient and famous of the cities of Spain, is situated in the central part, 41 m. s.s.w. of Madrid. It rises on a bold promontory surrounded on three sides by a deep gorge of the river Tagus. Under the name *Toletum* it is mentioned by Livy in connection with
                the year 192 B.C. as a " small town but
1. History   strong in its situation." After the
and   Roman time it fell to the Visigoths,
Remains.   becoming their capital under King Leovigild (568–586)). Under the Moors (from 714) it was the center of Mohammedan power in Spain and enjoyed a long period of prosperity. On May 25, 1085, Alfonso VI. the Valiant, of Leon and Castile, wrested the city from the Mohammedans and gave the name of New Castile to the region. The city thenceforth was a favorite residence of the Castilian monarchs; it became the political and intellectual center of old Spain and no less important ecclesiastically. Its churches, convents, chapels, and hospitals occupied more than half of its area, while the archbishops of Toledo—with title of primate of all Spain—wielded a powerful influence. Their names are connected with the weightiest events in Spanish history; they commanded armies; with their immense wealth they built schools, hospitals, and public works; and, representing the best and highest civilization of their time, they fostered art and science. The cathedral of Toledo is an enormous structure occupying the site of a Christian church of the Visigothic period and dedicated to the Virgin by King Recared Apr. 12, 587. The Moors made this church their principal mosque. The foundation of the present structure was laid in 1227, and the work of building went on till 1492, when it was completed as at present: of the two projecting towers the southern is still unfinished. The style is

early Gothic with later features corresponding to the long period of building. The forty chapels, profusely decorated and rich in art treasures, are of later date than the main structure. In the chapel of the Holy Sacrament the Mozarabic Liturgy (q.v.) is still used, and the Capilla de la Virgen del Sagrario contains an ancient wooden statue of the Virgin overlaid with silver which is considered the palladium of the city. Many of the former churches and convents of Toledo are now in ruins; or, like the palace of the inquisition, have been converted to secular uses. The population, once estimated at 200,000, had fallen to 23,375 in 1900, but the city is rich in historical remains. Its surviving churches, not a few of them formerly Mohammedan mosques or Jewish synagogues, its hundred towers and lofty walls, its narrow tortuous streets with houses opening within on spacious courts and gardens, and the like, make it the most medieval city in modern Europe and the most Moorish city in present-day Spain. The provincial library of 70,000 volumes and numerous manuscripts is preserved in the archiepiscopal palace. The university, founded in 1490, was discontinued in 1845. The manufacture of ecclesiastical vestments is still, as formerly, one of the most important of the city's industries.

According to tradition the first bishop of Toledo was Eugenius, a disciple of Dionysius the Areopagite, by whom he was sent from Paris. The bishopric was certainly in existence in the early fourth century, since Bishop Melantius of Toledo was at the Synod of Elvira (300). Bishop Montanus (522–531) was proclaimed metropolitan at the synod **2. The** of 527 [or 531; see (3), below], not- **Bishopric.** withstanding the claim of the bishop of Carthagena to the dignity. Under Aurasius (603–615) the influence of Toledo began to increase owing to the residence of the Visigothic kings in the city. From 653 its archbishops presided at synods and were the first to sign their canons, and canon vi. of the synod of 681 [see (12), below] attests that the archbishop of Toledo had attained the primacy, triumphing over his rivals, the metropolitans of Seville and Tarragona. Ildephonsus (q.v.), archbishop 657–667, is honored in the Spanish church for his zeal for the veneration of Mary. Sindered (707–721) made little effort to check the corruption which found entrance among clergy as well as laity in the latter days of the Gothic rule and fled from his see to Rome before the Arabs. Elipandus (c. 783–808) became involved in the Adoptionist controversy (see ADOPTIONISM, §§ 2–4). King Alfonso, after he had regained the city, exerted himself to increase its Christian population, and was ably seconded in the restoration of the diocese by Bernard, a French monk whom he caused to be chosen archbishop in 1086. Bernard received the pallium from Pope Urban II., and was declared primate of all the Spanish realm at Rome in 1088. Rodrigo Ximenes de Rada (1209–47) was one of the most learned and zealous of the archbishops of Toledo. He fought against the Moslems, won the affection of the poor by his benevolence, helped to found and build the new cathedral, stoutly defended his right to the primacy against the other archbishops, and wrote several historical works (col-

lected by A. Schott in *Hispania illustrata*, vol. ii., Frankfórt, 1603–08). Cardinal Ximenes (see XIMENES DE CISNEROS, FRANCISCO; 1495–1517), as archbishop and statesman, exerted a mighty influence; he was chief inquisitor and a promoter of science and art. Bartolome Carranza (q.v.) is said to have expended more than 1,000,000 ducats in charitable foundations. Fernandez de Cordova (1755–71), whose philanthropy was inexhaustible, was expelled from court because of sympathies with the Jesuits. The revenues of the archdiocese have greatly declined and its influence has been weakened. The suffragan bishoprics at present are Coria, Cuenca, Madrid, Plasencia, and Siguenza. The chapter consists of sixty-four members, the number of priests is 600, of parishes 445, and of souls, 508,250.

II. Synods: The usual official reckoning of eighteen synods of Toledo is incorrect and arbitrary; since, on the one hand, not all were Spanish-Visigothic national synods; and, on the other hand, two which **1. The** met in the city on the Tagus are not **Three** included. Naturally the Arian synod **Ecclesias-** discussed in connection with that of **tical** 589 [see (3) below] would be passed by **Synods.** with silence. (1) Of a Spanish national synod, of the year 400, twenty canons and two documents concerning the reinstatement of Priscillianist bishops are preserved. Canons i., iii., iv., and viii. expressly contend for the celibacy of the priesthood. (2) The acts of the national synod of 447 contain eighteen anathemas against the Priscillianists and a symbol of faith (wrongly attributed to the first synod of Toledo), noteworthy since it first pronounces the orthodox doctrine of the Trinity, and thus early emphasizes the procession of the Holy Spirit from the Father and the Son (see FILIOQUE CONTROVERSY). (3) The third synod in 527 or 531 is not included in the official list, being a provincial, not a national, synod. Two letters of Archbishop Montanus concerning the consecration of the chrism are an appendix to this synod. The third official synod, May 8, 589, was the most important of the synods of Toledo, since the religious policy of Leander and Recared I. (586–601) here reached its highest point. The disciplinary decrees (capitula) degraded the State to the position of mere beadle of the Church, exalted the hierarchy above the crown, made the higher clergy princes, and transformed the national synods into diets of the realm in which the bishops had the decisive voice. The synod was preceded by a conference of Arian and Catholic prelates, in the course of which Recared went over to the Catholics and induced a considerable part of his people to abjure Arianism. The first thirteen canons are condemnatory of Arianism. The third is noteworthy as the first decided repudiation by a great western synod of the Greek view of the procession of the Holy Spirit. Canon xiv., at least indirectly, disapproves of the semi-Arian doxology, *gloria patri per filium in spiritu sancto*. Canon xv. condemns the Arian practise of rebaptizing converts. Canon xvi. condemns the semi-Arianism adopted by the Arian synod of 580, namely, of receiving proselytes from the Roman Church by the laying on of hands, the acceptance of the Lord's Supper (Arian), and the above-mentioned doxology. Canons xx.–xxiii. concern the acceptance of the first four ecumenical councils. Happily the decisions of the fifth ecumenical council (Second Constantinople, 553) were not submitted, and by tacitly rejecting them, the Spanish-Visigothic church was still in latent schism with Rome at the time of the Arab incursion in 711. The first of the twenty-three disciplinary chapters declares the old canons, the ordinances of the councils, and the synodal letters of the Roman bishops valid. Chapter v. enjoins the celibacy of the clergy. Chapter xiii. forbids clerics to bring suit against their fellows before a secular tribunal. Chapter xiv. excludes Jews from judicial positions and offices with power of inflicting punishment on Christians, and prohibits marriage or concubinage with a Christian woman, and possession of Christian slaves. Chapter xvi. reads: " Spiritual and secular judges shall work together to uproot the idolatry [i.e., old heathen practises retained by Christians] so wide-spread in Spain and Gaul [Septimania]." Chapter xvii. is directed against abortion, and shows the same tendency to make civil officials aid and serve the ecclesiastical. Chapter xviii. requires annual instead of semi-annual synods and makes judges and fiscal agents mere tools of the bishops. In like manner chapter xix., placing the care of all church property in the hands of the episcopal consecrator, and chapter. xxi. exalt the episcopal power.

(4) A national synod of Dec. 5, 633, was called by King Sisenand and presided over by Isidore of Seville. Seventy-five chapters were issued, the most noteworthy (lvii.–lxvi.) relating to the Jews. Chapter lvii. forbids the compulsory baptism of Israelites, but declares that the Jews already converted by force during the reign of

2. The Semi- Political Synods.
Sisebut (612–620; see SISEBUT) must remain Christians. Chapters lviii.– lxvi. imposed the harshest penalties upon Jews who returned to the faith of their fathers after baptism. (5) A national synod in 636, convened by the new King Chintila, and presided over by Archbishop Eugenius I., adopted in eight chapters what was merely a stronger repetition of chapter lxxv. of the preceding council in confirmation of the power of the throne. (6) Another national synod, 638, under King Chintila reviewed, in the nineteen chapters, all the anti-Jewish decrees of the fourth synod. Chapter iii. orders the expulsion of all Jews who refused baptism. Chapter xv., against the greed of the bishops, orders that the Church retain whatever the kings or others have donated. (7) A national synod, Oct. 18, 646. was called by King Chindasvinth, who by the deposition of Tulga had gained the throne. After suppressing a revolt he summoned the synod, and his purpose of drastic retaliation against the spiritual and temporal nobility appears in the Draconian measures and penalties of the first of the six chapters. (8) A national synod, Dec. 16, 653, called by Recesvinth, son of Chindasvinth, relaxed the harsh penalties provided by the preceding synod but reenacted the anti-Jewish laws of the fourth synod. (9) A provincial synod, Nov., 655, presided over by

the metropolitan Eugenius II., adopted seventeen canons mostly in favor of the bishops. Celibacy of the clergy is enforced, and the last canon requires the baptized Jews always to be present at divine service conducted by the bishop, under penalty of beating or fasting. (10) A national synod, Dec. 1, 656, decreed the deposition of clerics tainted with high treason, and forbade the clergy to sell Christian slaves to the Jews. (11) A provincial synod, Nov. 7, 675, called by King Wamba, revised the Apostles' Creed, and issued sixteen canons, which testify to the unexampled coarsening of the clergy, including the bishops. Canon i. forbids boisterous irreverent conduct at the synod. Canon ii. relates to the ignorance of the Scriptures on the part of the clergy. Canon v. is directed against bishops who commit murder and other acts of violence or seize the property of others. Canon vi. forbids the clergy to pronounce a sentence of death or impose a mutilation. (12) A national synod, Jan. 9–25, 681, presided over by Archbishop Julian, adopted thirteen chapters, the first of which shows that Julian knew of the perfidy of the reigning king, Ervig, against his predecessor and benefactor Wamba. Chapter vi., contrary to the existing canon law, invests the metropolitan with the primacy, doubtless in reward for Julian's support of the usurper. Chapter ix. approves of the twenty Antisemitic laws of Ervig, a codification of all legislation against the Jews since the time of Recared and Sisebut. Chapter xi. prescribes very severe measures against the remnants of heathenism. (13) A national synod, Nov. 4, 683, likewise presided over by Julian, aimed to protect the royal family against assassins. With an astonishing simulation of regard for continence the widow of Wamba is forbidden to marry. Chapter ix. reaffirms the primacy of Julian. (14) A synod, Nov. 9, 684, officially provincial but national by representation and validity, again presided over by Julian, was aimed to secure the ratification, by the Spanish church, of the acts of the sixth ecumenical council (Third Constantinople, 680–681), in particular the condemnation of the Monothelites (q.v.) and their doctrine. To secure this Pope Leo II. had sent four letters to Spain in 682. The chapters approved of the acts, including the teaching of the two wills and two energies in Christ, and accepted the council as ecumenical. (15) A national synod, May 11, 688, was called by King Egiza. Two years previously the Spanish bishops had sent to Rome a memorial, composed by Julian, expressing their agreement with the orthodox doctrines of the sixth ecumenical council. Pope Benedict II. asked for changes in certain dogmatic passages. The Spaniards, however, led by Julian, resented this interference of the Curia and now adopted a second apology drawn up by the militant primate and sent by him to Benedict's successor, Sergius, who seems to have been discreet enough to treat the matter with silence. (16) A national synod, called by King Egiza in 693, after a renewed condemnation of Monothelitism set up thirteen disciplinary chapters. Chapter i. reaffirms the old Antisemitic laws, but provides for Jewish converts exemption from the special taxes and almost equality with other subjects. Canon ii. enjoins bishops, priests, and judges to exterminate heathenism under penalty of a year's suspension and excommunication. Chapter iii. decrees for sodomy the penalties of deposition and banishment for life upon clericals; and the old law in general for that offense enforcing exclusion from all communion with Christians, scourging with rods, and banishment, is retained. Chapter ix. deposes, excommunicates, strips of all property, and banishes Archbishop Sisbert of Toledo, who plotted against the life of the king and his children. (17) On Nov. 9, 694, a national synod met under the same king, on account of a Jewish conspiracy. Of its eight chapters, the fifth imposes anathematization and excommunication on priests who said masses for the dead in behalf of the living that they might soon die. Chapter viii. ordains that Jews who had accepted baptism, as it proved by appearance only, and revolted should lose their property and become slaves forever; their children must be taken from them at the age of seven and later be married to Christians. (18) The acts of a general synod about 701 are lost; they are probably destroyed by clerical fanatics through hatred of Witiza, a king of the grossest licentiousness, who declared the law of celibacy abolished, and whose sons afterward brought in the Saracens, which terminates this period.   (Franz Görres.)

Bibliography: A. Helfferich, Entstehung und Geschichte des Westgothen-Rechts, Berlin, 1858; C. Perez Pastor, La Imprenta en Toledo, Madrid, 1887; Simonet, El Concilio III. de Toledo, ib. 1891; J. Moraleda y Esteban, Leyendas históricas de Toledo, Toledo, 1892; J. Jacobs, Sources of Spanish-Jewish Hist., London, 1895; H. Lynch, Toledo, London, 1898; J. López de Ayala, Toledo en el siglo xvi., Madrid, 1901; L. Williams, Toledo and Madrid, London, 1903; F. Görres, in ZWT, xl. 2, pp. 284–296, xli. 270–322, xlv. 41–72, xlvi. 524–553, xlviii. 1, pp. 96–111; Hefele, Conciliengeschichte, vols. ii.–iii. passim, and the Eng. and Fr. transls.; DCA, ii. 1966–72; JE, xii. 176–182; and the literature under Spain, particularly the works of Gams, Lembke, and Leclercq.

TOLEDOTH YESHU ("Generations [i.e., History] of Jesus"): A Jewish anti-Christian medieval apocryphal polemic made up of fragmentary Talmudic legends, which pretends to be a life of Jesus, but is in reality a clumsy and stupid fiction of unknown authorship. There are two widely different recensions. J. C. Wagenseil published a Latin translation of one in his Tela ignea Satanæ (Altdorf, 1681), and J. J. Huldrich of the other, in his Historia Jeschuæ Nazareni a Judæis blaspheme corrupta (Leyden, 1705). According to the first, Jesus was b. in the reign of Jannæus (106–179 b.c.); according to the second, 74–70 b.c.

Bibliography: R. Clemens, Die geheimgehaltenen oder sogenannten apokryphischen Evangelien, part v., Stuttgart, 1850; R. Alm, Die Urtheile heidnischer und jüdischer Schriftsteller der vier ersten christlichen Jahrhunderte über Jesus und die ersten Christen, Leipsic, 1864; G. Rosch, in TSK, 1877, pp. 77–115; S. Baring-Gould, The Lost and Hostile Gospels, pp. 76–115, London, 1874; JE, vii. 170–173.

TOLERATION. See Liberty, Religious.

TOLERATION, ACT OF: A statute passed by the English parliament in the first year of the reign of William and Mary (May 24, 1689) to relieve the legal disabilities of Protestant dissenters. The stated purpose of the act was to bring about union of English Protestants. It first restricted the application of laws against non-conformity passed in the reigns of Elizabeth, James I., Charles I., and Charles II. (see England, Church of, II., §§ 1–6; Uniformity, Acts of). Protestant dissenters, upon taking the oaths of allegiance and supremacy (which might be required by any justice of the peace), were not to be subject to legal action, either civil or ecclesiastical, under the laws noted above against attending "conventicles." But meetings behind locked doors were forbidden, and the payment of tithes and parochial duties was still obligatory. Even those who refused the oaths named might hold certain offices, but the duties were to be performed by deputies. Dissenting ministers who took the oath were exempt from jury duties and from holding parochial offices. Quakers might make affirmation of loyalty; but "Papists" and those who denied the doctrine of the Trinity were excepted from the benefits of the act. Protection to the worship of dissenters was furnished by providing penalties for those who should "disturb or disquiet" such worship. But the place of worship was to be certified to the bishop of the diocese, the archdeacon of the archdeaconry, or the justice of the peace having jurisdiction in the place. Thus a good beginning was made toward liberty of worship and conscience, though a long list of legislative acts was required to attain the present degree of liberty enjoyed by English subjects. The statute known as 53 George III., chap. 160, extended the benefits of the Act of Toleration to Unitarians; 18 George III., chap. 60, 31 George III., chap. 32, and 43 George III., chap. 30, removed the disabilities of Roman Catholics; the "Catholic Emancipation Act," 10 George IV., chap. 7, restored to Roman Catholics all civil rights; and 2–3 William IV., chap. 115, put Roman Catholics and Protestant dissenters on the same footing. Roman Catholics and Jews were admitted to full constitutional rights by 7–8 Victoria, chap. 102, and 9–10 Victoria, chap. 59. Still other statutes were required for various details, such as regulation of marriages performed by dissenting ministers (19–20 Victoria, chap. 119).

Bibliography: The text of the act is in Gee and Hardy, Documents, pp. 654–664. Consult J. H. Overton, The Church in England, ii. 178–179, London, 1897.

TOLET, FRANCIS: Jesuit writer; b. in Cordova Oct. 4, 1532; d. at Rome Sept. 14, 1596. After studying at Salamanca, he became, in 1555, doctor of theology, and teacher of philosophy there, and later at Rome. He entered the Jesuit order in 1558; became court preacher to Pius V., in 1569, and remained such till 1593. A succession of popes held him in the highest esteem, and employed him in diplomatic offices. Clement VIII. made him cardinal, 1593; he was the first Jesuit to receive this honor. Sixtus V. and Clement VIII. appointed him one of the laborers upon the new edition of the Vulgate. Among Tolet's numerous commentaries and philosophical works are Introductio in dialecticam Aristotelis (Rome, 1561); Instructio sacerdotum de septem peccatis mortalibus (1601), which was translated into French and Spanish, and has frequently appeared under the title Summa casuum conscientiæ. A collection of philosophical works appeared (Lyons, 1587).

BIBLIOGRAPHY: Besides the prefaces prefixed to various editions of Tolet's writings, consult: C. Vercellone, *Variæ lectiones Vulgatæ Latinæ bibliorum*, vol. i., prolegomena, Rome, 1860; *Der Katholik*, i (1864), 408 sqq.; F. Kaulen, *Geschichte der Vulgata*, Mainz, 1868; A. and A. De Backer, *Bibliothèque de la compagnie de Jésus*, viii. 64 sqq., Paris, 1898; *KL*, xi. 1870–72.

TOLLIN, HENRI GUILLAUME NATHANAEL: German Reformed pastor and church historian; b. in Berlin, where his father was pastor of a French colony, May 5, 1833; d. in Magdeburg May 11, 1902. He studied at the universities of Berlin and Bonn, and then taught in the French gymnasium in Berlin where he had received his early education. In 1862 he became pastor of the French congregation at Frankfort-on-the-Oder. Thence after several years he was transferred to a peasant congregation at Schulzendorf (circuit of Ruppin), a post little suited to his scholarly tastes and attainments. After a stormy pastorate of five years, in 1876 he went to the French Church in Magdeburg. The congregation there was small but wealthy, so that the new pastor found time and liberal support for the historical studies to which he devoted himself. He became preeminently the historian of the Huguenot refugees in Germany and a specialist on the life and time of Michael Servetus. In his many publications relating to Servetus he sought to apportion praise and blame with fairness, but recognizing that blame belongs often to the age rather than to individuals. His views concerning the story of Servetus are summarized in a preface which he wrote for the drama, *Servet*, by his friend, Professor Hamann of Potsdam (ed. Tollin). With all his devotion to study and science he was a faithful pastor. During the war between Prussia and Austria in 1866 he served the wounded in the hospitals of Frankfort with self-sacrificing faithfulness, undeterred by an epidemic of cholera which added to the horrors of war. He founded a society in Magdeburg for the education of poor children and was active in Sunday-school and home-mission work. He was first president and founder of the " German Huguenot Society " and wrote many of the articles in its yearly *Geschichts-blätter*. Other noteworthy publications were: *Biographische Beiträge zur Geschichte der Toleranz* (Frankfort, 1866); *Geschichte der französichen Kolonie in Frankfurt-an-der-Oder* (1868); *H. W. Beecher's geistliche Reden nebst Biographie* (Berlin, 1870); *Dr. Martin Luther und Servet* (1875); *Philipp Melanchthon und Servet* (1876); *Charakterbild Michael Servet's* (1876); *Die Entdeckung des Blut-kreislaufs durch Michael Servet* (1876), for which the author received the degree of doctor of medicine from Bern; *Das Lehrsystem Michael Servets* (3 vols., Gütersloh, 1876–78); *Servet und Martin Butzer* (Berlin, 1880); *Geschichte der französischen Kolonie von Magdeburg* (vols. i.–ii., Halle, 1886–87; vol. iii., part 2, Halle, 1889; vol. iii., parts 1, 3, Magdeburg, 1892–94).   (F. H. BRANDES.)

BIBLIOGRAPHY: Dr. Brandes gives an account of the life of Tollin, based on original and autographic sources, in *Geschichtsblätter des deutschen Hugenotten-Vereins*, vol. ii., Magdeburg, 1902.

TOLSTOY, tol-stoi', COUNT LEO: Novelist, dramatist, essayist, and religious reformer; b. on his mother's estate, Yásnaya Polyána, near Túla (130 m. s. of Moscow), Aug. 28 (O. S.; Sept. 9. N. S.), 1828; d. at Astápova, Russia, Nov. 20, 1910. He studied at Kazan University, but left without taking
a degree. In 1851 he entered the army in the Caucasus, became a lieutenant; in 1853–54 he served in Turkey and then in the Crimea. His " Sevastopol Sketches," written at the time, may be considered precursors of all that he subsequently wrote against war. After the end of hostilities he retired from the army. In 1861–62 he devoted himself to work in peasant schools which he established at and near Yásnaya Polyána. In 1862 he married Sophia Behrs, and during the next fifteen years managed his estates and wrote his great novels " War and Peace " (describing Napoleon's invasion of Russia) and " Anna Karénina," a story of contemporary life. A great change in his activities occurred from 1880 onward. He carefully examined, and ended by totally rejecting, the claims of the Russo-Greek Church, and incidentally those of the Roman Catholic and Protestant churches also. For some years he devoted himself to an ardent study of the Gospels, rejecting the miraculous elements as well as all that seemed unreasonable or incomprehensible in them. From what remained, he constructed a consecutive narrative, which his vivid insight into the great problems of life renders interesting and suggestive, though his rendering is not always justified by the text. His object was to rescue what he believed to be the real teaching of Christ, and to combat what he thought the Church's false interpretations—a process which he has compared to " depolarizing a magnetized watch."

Following this, he produced a series of works in which he elaborated his theory of non-resistance, inspired by abhorrence of physical violence, detestation of the legalized exploitation of the poor, and antipathy to the autocratic and bureaucratic government. The same theory is held in a fluid state by many Russian peasant sects, and traces of it can be found among the early Christians, the early Protestant Reformers (especially Peter of Chelcic—see Bohemian Brethren, I., § 1—and some of the Anabaptists), as well as among the Quakers, and more recently in the writings of Adin Ballou and William Lloyd Garrison. In the extreme form to which Tolstoy ultimately reduced it, it comes to this: all use of physical force employed by one man to restrain another, is a sign of malevolence and is immoral. Starting with this (which is his reading of the text " Resist not him that is evil; but whosoever smiteth thee on thy right cheek, turn to him the other also ") as an axiom, Tolstoy deduces the conclusion that all civil and criminal law, as well as the prison system and executions, are immoral. No man, he says, has any right to condemn another to suffer any penalty. More than that, all police force, as well as all armies and navies, are, on the same ground, immoral; as also are all war and all governments (imperial, federal, or local) which employ a policeman. To hold property which anyone wishes to take he also considers immoral.

Without defending the Tolstoyan theory of non-resistance, it may be pointed out how admirably it served to undermine the moral prestige of a brutal government and a persecuting church. Tolstoy practically said: " There are two kinds of people: the good, who rely on example, persuasion, exhortation; and the bad, who rely on physical force: police, gendarmes, and soldiers." Had the government banished him to Siberia, by so doing it would, apparently, have confirmed his indictment. Hesitating to crush him by brute force, it had to endure from him a continual stream of scathing criticism which the partizans of the Church and the autocracy were quite unable to meet. In another aspect Tolstoy's theory of non-resistance served a useful purpose. A curious superstition exists which causes people to assume that any amount of slaughter and destruction are justifiable provided they are undertaken for national aggrandizement. As a direct challenge to this came Tolstoy's proposition that to slay a man (or even to coerce a man) is always immoral and harmful. It served also as a challenge to what is brutal and vindictive in the criminal codes.

Tolstoy popularized his views in a series of short stories (" What Men Live By," " Ivan the Fool," etc.), which had an immense circulation among all classes, and carried the germs of his teaching far and wide. From about 1888 he commenced a series of interesting essays on a variety of questions: manual

Publication of his Views. labor, stimulants and narcotics, the famine, vegetarianism, war, the sex-problem, religion and morality, patriotism, corporal punishment, the agrarian question, etc. He gave his views of the connection between art and religion in " What is Art? " a work which at first met with a storm of hostile criticism, but the true value of which is gradually being recognized. In 1899 appeared his novel " Resurrection," in which he incidentally gave a scathing description of the head of the Holy Synod (M. Pobiedonostzeff; q.v.). After a preliminary threat, a decree of excommunication was launched at Tolstoy in 1901, to which he retorted with an outspoken " Reply to the Synod," and followed this up by a bold letter " To the Czar and his Assistants."

Concerning Tolstoy's simplification of his own life there has been much exaggeration. The plain facts are these. After some friction with his wife, whose views did not agree with those he adopted, he handed over to her, and to his children, the whole of his estates, as well as the copyrights in all his works published before 1880. His own position

Manner of Life. in the house became that of a guest who is very much at home. He declined to accept payment for his later works or to retain any rights in them. To this rule he made an exception when he accepted money for *Resurrection*, in order to assist the Dukhobors to migrate to Canada. Before this, in 1891–92, with several members of his family, he spent many months in the famine district to organize soup-kitchens and to administer the famine-relief funds which were sent to him with great liberality from all parts of Europe and America. Wishing to master a handicraft, he learned to make boots, but never devoted much time to this occupation. Even in early life he had been fond of plowing; and for about ten years (1880–90) he devoted a good part of each summer to manual labor out of doors, doing all the field work during one summer for a peasant woman who could not afford to hire a laborer.

Of no modern writer, probably, is it so difficult to compile a correct bibliography as of Tolstoy. Many of his works were forbidden in Russia and had to appear abroad (in Switzerland, Germany,

Writings. and England), and in addition to this, his rejection of copyrights led to many of his works being published with little attention to their proper sequence. With regard to the immense number of translations that have appeared in all languages, the case is even worse. Some of them have appeared with titles selected at the fancy of the publisher or translator. The following is a list of the chief of Tolstoy's works dealing with religion, with the year in which each work was completed: *A Criticism of Dogmatic Theology* (1881); *My Confession* (1882; written as an introduction to the preceding); *Four Gospels Harmonized and Translated* (1882); *Gospel in Brief* (1883); *What I Believe* (1884); *What Then Must We Do?* (1886); *On Life* (1887); *The Kingdom of God is Within You* (1893); *Patriotism and Christianity* (1895); *What is Art?* (1898); *The Christian Teaching* (1898); *The Slavery of Our Times* (1900); *Patriotism and Government* (1900); *A Reply to the Synod's Decree of Excommunication* (1901); *What is Religion, and Wherein lies its Essence?* (1902). Two collected editions of Tolstoy's works have appeared in the United States: an earlier one published by T. Y. Crowell & Co. (also by Chas. Scribner's Sons), and a later one (more nearly complete to 1902) by Dana Estes. Neither of these supplies a version which at all reproduces the mastery with which Tolstoy states his case in Russian. The booklets issued by the Free Age Press, Christchurch, Hampshire, England (though the versions of different works are by different hands and of unequal quality), are generally fairly reliable. In the *World's Classics Series*, the Oxford University Press has published excellent versions (specially commended by Tolstoy) of his tales for the people: *Twenty-three Tales*, and a selection, including the last three works in the above list, of his *Essays and Letters*. The latter volume is published in the United States by the Funk & Wagnalls Company, which has also an edition of an authorized translation of *What is Art?* Of his works of fiction, the best versions of *Sevastopol* and *Resurrection*, and also of his *Plays*, are by Louise Maude, and the best versions of *War and Peace* and *Anna Karénina* are by Constance Garnett.

AYLMER MAUDE.

BIBLIOGRAPHY: The literature on Tolstoy is voluminous, and the following is but a selection: A. Maude, *The Life of Tolstoy: first 50 Years*, London and New York, 1908, and *Later Years*, ib. 1910; idem, *Tolstoy and his Problems*, ib. 1901; C. A. Behrs, *Recollections of Count Tolstoi*, London, 1893; G. H. Perris, *Leo Tolstoy, the Grand Mujik*, London, 1898; Alice B. Stockham, *Tolstoi; a Man of Peace*, London and New York, 1900; J. C. Kenworthy, *Tolstoy, his Life and Works*, London, 1902; D. Merejkowski, *Tolstoi as Man and Artist*, London and New York, 1902; J. A. Hutton, *Pilgrims in the Region of Faith*, London and New York, 1907; E. A. Steiner, *Tolstoy, the Man, a biographical Interpretation*, New York, 1907; idem, *Tolstoy, the Man and his Message*, ib. 1909; J. A. T. Lloyd, *Two Russian Reformers: Ivan Turgenev, Leo Tolstoy*, London, 1910.

TOMBES, JOHN: Baptist; b. at Bewdley (13 m. n.n.w. of Worcester), England, 1603 (or 1602?); d. at Salisbury May 22, 1676. He studied at Magdalen Hall, Oxford (B.A., 1621; M.A., 1624; B.D., 1631); became catechism lecturer; gained a reputation as a tutor; took orders, 1624, and was a lecturer of St. Martin Carfax, 1624–30. He quickly came into note as a preacher, and was for a time, in 1630, preacher at Worcester, but from 1630 to the Restoration, except for the interval of 1643–54, he was vicar of Leominster, Herefordshire; of All Saints, Bristol, 1643; rector of St. Gabriel, London, 1643–45; master of the Temple, 1645–47; curate of Bewdley, 1647–50. While at Bewdley he was for awhile rector of Ross, Herefordshire, and later master of St. Catherine's Hospital, Ledbury. In 1654 he became one of Cromwell's triers. In 1660 he went to London and wrote in favor of the royal supremacy in both ecclesiastical and civil matters. He conformed in a lay capacity there, and had Clarendon for a friend. After 1661 he lived chiefly at Salisbury. He was a vigorous, learned, and unwearied opponent of infant baptism. He had public debates upon this topic with Baxter and others, and wrote numerous treatises upon it. Of his writings may be mentioned *Two Treatises and an Appendix to them Concerning Infant Baptism* (2 parts, London, 1645); *Apology for the Two Treatises* (1646); *Antipædobaptism* (3 parts, 1652–57); *A Public Dispute Touching Infant-Baptism* (1654); *Emmanuel, Concerning the Two Natures in Christ* (1669); *Animadversiones in librum G. Bulli, Harmonia apostolica* (1676).

BIBLIOGRAPHY: A. à Wood, *Athenæ Oxonienses*, ed. P. Bliss, iii. 1062–63, and *Fasti*, ii. 397, 415, 461, 4 vols., London, 1813–20; *DNB*, lvii. 2–4 (where references to scattering notices are given).

TONGUES, GIFT OF. See SPEAKING WITH TONGUES.

TONSURE: In Roman Catholic usage, a round-shaven spot on the top of the head which serves to distinguish clerics from laymen. It is regarded as a " preparation for receiving orders " (Roman catechism, *de ordinibus sacris*, iii.), hence is conferred previous to ordination, at present usually in connection with the lower grades. Bishops, cardinal priests (for their titular churches), and abbots (for regular members of their houses) have the right to confer it. No special time or place is prescribed for the ceremony. The recipient must be confirmed, must know the elements of the faith, and must be able to read and write; hence the tonsure can not be conferred before the completion of the seventh year. Some Roman Catholic liturgical writers conjecture without proof that it was introduced by Peter, and symbolizes the crown of thorns, the royal dignity of the priesthood, renunciation of the world and its vanities, and the like. It guarantees to the recipient the rights and privileges of a cleric, must always be retained, and is renewed monthly except for good reason, but clerics of lower grade without benefice may neglect renewal.

Tonsure is a heathen custom which entered the Church by way of monasticism. The priests of Isis and Serapis shaved the head, and Christian ascetics, both male and female, in Egypt and Syria imitated them as early as the middle of the fourth century. The practise spread rapidly and from the monastic discipline was transferred to both penitents and the clergy, leading in the latter case to the tonsure. Originally clerics were merely forbidden to let the hair grow long. The tonsure proper first appears in Christian monuments at the beginning of the fifth century. It was usual in Rome in the time of Gregory I. (d. 604) and was conferred there not only on clerics and monks but also on laymen who performed any sort of church service. The custom became general in the Frankish realm about the same time. The Fourth Synod of Toledo in 633, canon xii., attests it for Spain. Aldhelm (d. 709) and Ceolfrid (d. 716) are witnesses for England. For the East, cf. canon xxxiii. of the Trullan Synod of 692 (Mansi, *Concilia*, xi. 958–959).

There were three kinds of tonsure: (1) The Roman or coronal tonsure, that described above, which leaves a circle of hair around the head. Since Peter, according to legend, wore this tonsure, it is called also St. Peter's crown or tonsure. This was the prevalent form in Italy, the Frankish kingdom, England, and Spain. During the Middle Ages the size of the shorn spot tended to become smaller, not without opposition, which led to attempts to regulate the matter. Gradually it became customary for the size of the spot to increase by regular grades with the rank of the wearer from subdeacon to bishop. (2) The Iro-Scottish or British tonsure, called also tonsure of St. John or of St. James by its opponents, who regarded it as heretical (the tonsure of Simon Magus), differed from the Roman tonsure in that the ring of hair about the head was broken, the shaven spot being continued forward to the forehead. It was general in the old British Church until the seventh century and later, and was introduced here and there on the continent by British missionaries (see CELTIC CHURCH IN BRITAIN AND IRELAND). (3) The Greek tonsure or St. Paul's tonsure (cf. Acts xxi. 24, 26) consisted originally in shaving the entire front of the head. The Greek Church, in which entrance into clerical rank is signified by the tonsure, has now modified the custom into cutting the hair short over the whole head. The earliest mention of St. Paul's tonsure as distinguished from St. Peter's is in Bede (*Hist. eccl.*, IV., i.), who remarks of Theodore, archbishop of Canterbury, that he " wore the oriental or St. Paul's tonsure."

(A. HAUCK.)

BIBLIOGRAPHY: Bingham, *Origines*, VI., iv. 16–17, VII., iii. 6; G. Chamillard, *De corona, tonsura*, Paris, 1659; L. Thomassin, *Vetus et nova ecclesiæ disciplina*, I., ii. 34, Paris, 1728; E. Martene, *De antiquæ ecclesiæ ritibus*, ii. 14, Bassani, 1788; P. Hinschius, *Kirchenrecht*, i. 104 sqq., Berlin, 1869; E. Löning, *Geschichte des deutschen Kirchenrechts*, ii. 275 sqq., Strasburg, 1878; N. Milasch, *Kirchenrecht der morgenländischen Kirche*, p. 270, 2d ed., Mostar, 1905; *DCA*, ii. 1989–1990.

TOORENENBERGEN, tū'ren-en-bärh"en, JOHAN JUSTUS VAN: Dutch Reformed; b. at Utrecht Feb. 12, 1822; d. Dec. 12, 1903. He was educated at the university of his native city; was pastor at Elspeet (1844–48); and Flushing (1848–64); director of the missionary society at Utrecht (1864–1869) and gave instruction in dogmatics and other subjects; pastor at Rotterdam (1869–80); and professor of church history at Amsterdam (1880–92). Theologically he was Evangelical and confessional. In dogmas he emphasized the ethical side, being thus akin to A. R. Vinet (q.v.) whom he greatly admired. The historical creeds he regarded as historical memorials and as binding only in so far as they were in harmony with the Gospel. The main thing in the Gospel was what was essentially vital to salvation. His views on the creeds are presented in the introduction to his *Eene bladzijde uit de geschiedenis der nederlandsche geloofsbelijdenis* (The Hague, 1862), in which he published the original edition of such a confession. With it was connected his edition of *De symbolische schriften der nederlandsche Hervormde Kerk* (Utrecht, 1869). In criticism of J. H. Scholten (q.v.) on the doctrine of the Netherland church, he published his *Bijdragen tot de verklaring, toetsing en ontwikkeling van de leer der Hervormde Kerk* (1865), a storehouse of dogmatic and historical learning. His dogmatic point of view may be studied best in his *De christelijke geloofsleer* (Culemborg, 1876; 2d improved ed., 1893). Toorenenbergen was most important, however, as a church historian. In 1870 he was one of the founders of the Marnix-Vereeniging, and among his contributions to its publications of noteworthy documents for the history of the Reformed Church were: *Acten van colloquia der nederlandsche gemeenten in Engeland 1575–1609. 2de stuk 1612–24* (Utrecht, 1872), with appendix containing selected acts till 1706; *Gheschiedenissen ende handelingen die voornemelick aengaen de nederduytsche natie ende gemeynten woonende in Engelant ende int bysonder tot London* (1873); *Stukken betreffende de diaconie der vreemdelingen te Emden* (1876); *Handelingen van den kerkeraad der nederlandsche gemeente te Keulen 1571–91* (1881); and *Acten van classicale en synodale vergaderingen der verstrooide gemeenten in het land van Cleef, Sticht van Keulen en Aken, 1571–89* (1882; the latter two in collaboration with H. Q. Janssen). He specially devoted himself to the study of the works of Philips van Marnix (q.v.), and produced an admirable edition, *Philips van Marnix godstienstige en kerkelijke geschriften* (3 vols., The Hague, 1871–91), followed by his *Marnixiana anonyma* (1903). Toorenenbergen was also the editor of *Het oudste nederlandsche verboden boek 1523. Œconomica christiana. Summa der godliker schrifturen* (Leyden, 1882). (S. D. VAN VEEN.)

BIBLIOGRAPHY: A life by L. W. Bakhuizen van den Brink is in *Levensberichten der afgestorvene medeleden van de Maatschappij der Nederland. Letterkunde te Leiden*, pp. 133–159, Leyden, 1906.

TOPLADY, AUGUSTUS MONTAGUE: Calvinist and hymnist; b. at Farnham (20 m. s.w. of Windsor), England, Nov. 4, 1740; d. in London Aug. 11, 1778. He was for a while at Westminster school; removed to Ireland, 1755, and studied at Trinity College, Dublin (B.A., 1760; M. A., later); was converted, 1755; turned to extreme Calvinism, 1758; was ordained deacon, 1762; licensed to the curacy of Blagdon, 1762; ordained priest, 1764; was curate of Farleigh, Hungerford, 1764–66; held the benefice of Harpford with Venn-Ottery, 1766–1768; and that of Broad Hembury, 1768–78. In 1775, under leave of non-residence from his living

at Broad Hembury, he removed to London, where he ministered in the French Calvinist Reformed church in Orange Street. Toplady's talent and earnestness were great. He and Wesley clashed in Calvinism and Arminianism, and as a result his works, filled with the most advanced doctrine, also contained the most conscientiously acrimonious controversy. His poetry was better than his polemic. He was the author of the noted hymn "Rock of Ages," published in the *Gospel Magazine* (London, 1776); and *Poems on Sacred Subjects* (Dublin, 1759); *Historic Proof of the Doctrinal Calvinism of the Church of England* (London, 1774); collected *Psalms and Hymns* (1776); and wrote *A Course of Prayer* (1790?). A new edition of his works with a memoir appeared (6 vols., 1825); and his *Hymns and Sacred Poems* (reprint, 1860).

BIBLIOGRAPHY: Besides the *Memoir* in the *Works* and a sketch of the life in the *Hymns and Sacred Poems*, ut sup., consult: *Memoir of Some Principal Circumstances in the Life . . . of . . . A. M. Toplady*, London, 1778; *Memoirs of the Rev. Mr. Toplady*, ib. 1794, Boston, 1817; W. Winters, *Memoirs of the Life and Writings of the Rev. A. M. Toplady*, London, 1872; *DNB*, lvii. 57–59.

TO REMAIN BIBLE. See BIBLE VERSIONS, B, IV., § 9.

TORGAU ARTICLES. See AUGSBURG CONFESSION, § 1.

TORGAU, BOOK OF. See FORMULA OF CONCORD, § 3.

TORM, FREDERIK EMANUEL: Danish theologian; b. at Chefoo, China, Aug. 24, 1870. In 1874 his parents moved to Copenhagen, and he was graduated from the Metropolitan school there (1888), and from the University of Copenhagen (candidate in theology, 1894); and continued his studies in Italy, Germany, and England (1895–97). He published *En kritisk Fremstilling af Novatianus Liv og Forfattervirksomhed* (1901), and in the same year *Valentinianismens Historie og Lære*, for which he was granted the degree of Lic. theol. In 1899 he became a coeditor of *Theologisk Tidsskrift*, for which he has written many articles and reviews; and in 1903 was made professor of New-Testament exegesis in the University of Copenhagen. He is on the Danish Board of Missions which works among the Jews.   JOHN O. EVJEN.

BIBLIOGRAPHY: C. F. Bricka, *Dansk biografisk Lexikon*, xvii. 463, 19 vols., Copenhagen, 1887–1905.

TORQUEMADA, tōr″kê-mä′dā, **JUAN DE (JOHANNES DE TURRECREMATA):** Spanish theologian; b. at Valladolid 1388; d. at Rome Sept. 26, 1468. He entered the Dominican order, and, being distinguished for piety and learning, accompanied the Dominican superior, P. Luis, to the Council of Constance. He obtained the doctor's degree at Paris in 1423, and appeared next as prior of his cloister at Valladolid, later at Toledo. Eugenius IV. called him to Rome in 1431, appointed him *magister sacri palatii*, and sent him as theologian to the Council of Basel, where he appeared as indefatigable champion of the curialists. He was among those who left Basel to hold an opposing council at Ferrara. He became cardinal in 1439. Most of his writings are devoted to the vindication of curialism, though they include, as well, an exposition of the Psalms (Rome, 1476; Mainz, 1478), and *Questiones spirituales super evangelia totius anni* (Rome, 1477; Brixen, 1498; and often). K. BENRATH.

BIBLIOGRAPHY: For exact knowledge of Torquemada's writings use N. Antonio, *Bibliotheca Hispana vetus*, ii. 288–293, Rome, 1696. Consult further: S. Lederer, *Der spanische Kardinal Johann von Torquemada*, Freiburg, 1879; J. Quetif and J. Echard, *Scriptores ordinis prædicatorum*, i. 837–843, Paris, 1719; H. C. Lea, *Hist. of the Inquisition of Spain*, vols. i.–iii., New York, 1906–07; H. Gaultier de Saint-Amand, *Torquemada. Essai sur l'inquisition d'Espagne en 1483*, St. Denis, 1910; Pastor, *Popes*, vols. iii.–iv.; Creighton, *Papacy*, iii. 46–85; *KL*, xi. 1883–1885; Schaff, *Christian Church*, v. 2, passim; and literature under INQUISITION.

TORQUEMADA, TOMAS DE: Spanish inquisitor; b. at Valladolid 1420; d. in a monastery at Avila (53 m. n.w. of Madrid) Sept. 16, 1498. He belonged to the Dominican order, was prior of the cloister at Segovia for twenty-two years, and gave himself up wholly to the organization of the Spanish Inquisition, introduced in 1478 (see INQUISITION, II., § 5). In 1483 the pope appointed him general or grand inquisitor of Castile and Aragon. He set up four tribunals at Seville, Cordova, Jaen, and Villa Real (later removed to Toledo), and the laws and methods pursued there were his work. The laws were published under the title, *Copilacion de las instruciones del officio de la santa inquisicion, hechas par el muy reverendo senor Fray Thomas de Torquemada* (Madrid, 1576). At his instance Ferdinand and Isabella issued, Oct. 31, 1492, an edict by which all Jews who refused Christianity were to leave Spain. Many professed conversion but secretly practised their old religion, and the inquisition long directed its operations against these " Maranos." Equal sternness was manifested against all others who were mistrusted of lack of fidelity to the Church. Naturally Torquemada's name became a byword among opponents of the inquisition, and stood for fanatical persecution. Toward the end of his life Torquemada retired to the monastery near Avila, where he died.

TORREY, CHARLES CUTLER: Congregationalist; b. at East Hardwick, Vt., Dec. 20, 1863. He was educated at Bowdoin College (A.B., 1884), where he was tutor in Latin in 1885–86; he studied also at Andover Theological Seminary (1889), and for three years at the University of Strasburg (Ph.D., 1892). He was instructor in Semitic languages at Andover Theological Seminary (1892–1900), and since 1900 has been professor of the same subject in Yale University. He was director of the American School of Oriental Research in Palestine in 1900–01, and since 1900 has been associate editor of the *Journal of the American Oriental Society*. He has written *The Commercial-Theological Terms in the Koran* (Leyden, 1892); *The Composition and historical Value of Ezra-Nehemiah* (Giessen, 1896); a translation of Ibn 'Abd-al-Hakim's " Mohammedan Conquest of Egypt and North Africa in the Years 643 to 705 A.D." in *Biblical and Semitic Studies* (New York, 1901); and *Ezra Studies* (Chicago, 1910).

TORREY, JOSEPH: American Congregationalist; b. at Rowley, Mass., Feb. 2, 1797; d. at Burlington, Vt., Nov. 26, 1867. He was graduated from Dartmouth College, 1816, and from Andover Theological Seminary, 1819; preached for a time as a missionary; was pastor at Royalton, Vt., 1819–27; professor of Latin and Greek in the University of Vermont, 1827–42; of intellectual and moral philosophy, 1842–67; and president of the university, 1862–66. He edited with memoirs, the *Remains of President James Marsh* (1843); and the *Select Sermons of President Worthington Smith* (Andover, 1861); wrote *A Theory of Fine Art* (lectures, New York, 1874); and finished a masterly translation of Neander's *General History of the Christian Religion and Church* (9 vols., Edinburgh, 1847–55; 12th ed., 6 vols., Boston, 1881–82).

TORREY, REUBEN ARCHER: Congregationalist, evangelist; b. at Hoboken, N. J., Jan. 28, 1856. He was graduated from Yale University (B.A., 1875) and from the theological department there (B.D., 1878), and studied at the universities of Leipsic and Erlangen. He was pastor of the Congregational Church, Garretsville, O. (1878–82), Open Door Church, Minneapolis (1883–86); superintendent of the Minneapolis City Missionary Society (1886–89); pastor of People's Church, Minneapolis (1887–89); superintendent of Chicago Evangelization Society and Moody Bible Institute (1889–1908), having meanwhile been pastor of the Chicago Avenue Church, Chicago (1894–1905); and since Dec., 1901, has been engaged in evangelistic work, part of the time in a tour of the world, preaching in China, Japan, Australia, Tasmania, New Zealand, India, Germany, in the United Kingdom, and at home. He holds to the divine origin and absolute inerrancy of the Scriptures, to the virgin birth and bodily resurrection of Jesus Christ, to the doctrine that men are saved only through the atoning death of Christ and on condition of faith in him, to the resurrection of the body at the second coming of Christ, to the endless blessed consciousness of those who accept Christ in this life and the endless conscious misery of those who in this life reject Christ. He has written among other works *How I Bring Men to Christ* (New York, 1893); *Baptism with the Holy Spirit* (1895); *How to Study the Bible with Greatest Profit* (1896); *What the Bible Teaches* (1898); *Divine Origin of the Bible* (1899); *How to Promote and Conduct a Successful Revival* (1901); *How to Work for Christ* (1901); *Revival Addresses* (1903); *Talks to Men* (1904); *Anecdotes and Illustrations* (1907); *Studies in the Life and Teachings of our Lord* (1909); *The Person and Work of the Holy Spirit as Revealed in the Scriptures and Personal Experience* (1910); and commentaries and helps on the International Lessons Series.

BIBLIOGRAPHY: G. T. B. Davis, *Torrey and Alexander; the Story of a World-wide Revival*, New York, 1905; J. K. Maclean, *Triumphant Evangelism*, London, 1905.

TORTOSA. See PHENICIA, PHENICIANS, I., § 9.

TOSEPHTA. See TALMUD.

TOSSANUS. See TOUSSAIN.

TOTAL ABSTINENCE.

I. The Term and its Use.
　Meaning of the Term (§ 1).
II. History of the Total-Abstinence Idea.
　The Modern Problem Versus the Ancient (§ 1).
　Opinions Changed with the Problem (§ 2).
　Nineteenth-Century Movement (§ 3).
　Results of the Movement (§ 4).
III. Good and Bad Reasons for Total-Abstinence.
　Argument from the Evils of Drunkenness (§ 1).
　From the Evils of Moderate Use (§ 2).
　The Ethical Argument (§ 3).
　Arguments from the Scriptures (§ 4).
IV. Total Abstinence and Temperance Laws.

I. **The Term and Its Use:** Human society can not hold together, much less be prosperous and tolerable to live in, unless most persons voluntarily practise total abstinence from the grosser forms of crime, and an abstinence more or less stringent from many other possible acts and habits. Nothing is more essential to successful living, either individual or social, than the exercise of this form of the virtue of self-control. Opportunities for it occur in all regions of our experience; but the term is especially associated with the use of certain drugs which affect the nerves and the brain, and result in disastrous habits. Intoxicating alcoholic beverages are the best-known of these, and with them this article will mainly concern itself. But similar dangers arise, and the same principles apply in the case of opium, cocain, tobacco, hashish, and many other substances.

The term " total abstinence " has a history, and a historical meaning. There is an advantage in employing it in this historical mean-
1. Meaning ing, and guarding against the perver-
of the sions that have naturally crept in.
Term. The taking of the pledge was an important item in the temperance reform movements, and several different pledges were in use. They were alike in that they applied, with possible rare exceptions, only to liquids that might produce intoxication, and to these solely in their use as a " beverage " or " common drink." The substitution, in the pledges, of " alcoholic " for " intoxicating " came later; and whatever the reformers thought concerning alcoholic wine in the sacrament, for example, or the use of alcohol as medicine or in flavoring-extracts, they ordinarily left these uses outside the pledge. But there were other particulars in which the pledges differed, and sometimes two or three different pledges were offered at the same meeting, the people being invited to choose which pledge they would sign. One pledge was against the excessive use of intoxicants, as distinguished from the so-called moderate use. Another was against distilled liquors as distinguished from wine or beer or cider. Another was against all use as beverages of drinks that can intoxicate, whether distilled or fermented. This third was the total-abstinence pledge—total as including all intoxicants and not some only, and total as being against all use of intoxicants as a beverage, and not against excessive use only. There was a longer form of this pledge in which one promised not to sell or give away intoxicating drinks for beverage purposes, as well as not to drink them. Total abstinence, teetotalism, is therefore, historically, not abstinence from everything that contains alcohol, but from everything which so contains alcohol that one might get drunk upon it; not abstinence from such liquids for all purposes, but abstinence from them as a beverage. The historical total-abstinence position distinguishes the medicinal and other uses of alcohol from its use as a beverage, though it demands that it shall not be recklessly or needlessly used for these other purposes. It does not place the very light wines and beers on the same footing with those that will intoxicate, though it disapproves them as a matter of prudence, on account of their relations to the stronger beverages.

II. **History of the Total-Abstinence Idea:** Intoxicants, in the form of wine and beer at least, have been known from the earliest historical times;
　　　　　and the vice of drunkenness has also
1. The been known. This is evident from the
Modern familiar Biblical instances of Noah and
Problem Nabal and others, from the figures and
Versus the inscriptions on the Egyptian and Meso-
Ancient. potamian monuments, from the Greek
　　　　　myths concerning Dionysos, and from many other sources. But the conditions of the problem of drunkenness have been very materially changed within the last few centuries by the extent to which the art of distillation has developed. This art has long been known and practised; but it was not until a comparatively recent period that it came to be the powerful means it now is for increasing and cheapening the world's stock of intoxicating beverages. According to Theodore W. Dwight (*Independent*, Apr. 27, 1882) the earliest recognition of the existence of distilled liquors to be found in English legislation is in the year 1629; and it was not until much later in the seventeenth century that these came to be recognized as in general use. As might have been expected, their introduction greatly increased the evils of intemperance. Says the *Encyclopædia Britannica*, in its article on " Gin ":

"In the early part of the eighteenth century, gin-shops multiplied with great rapidity in London; and the use of the beverage increased to an extent so demoralizing that retailers actually exhibited placards in their windows, intimating that there people might get drunk for a penny, and that clean straw, in comfortable cellars, would be provided for customers."

Contemporaneously with these changes in the facilities for the practise of drunkenness occurred certain other changes in men's habits of living, which also greatly affected the question of the use of alcoholic drinks. Coffee was known as early as 875 A.D., but it was first brought from Abyssinia into Arabia early in the fifteenth century. Coffee houses were established in Constantinople about the middle of the sixteenth century, and in London in 1652; and, before the close of the seventeenth century, coffee was a customary beverage in Europe. Chocolate and tea came to be generally used, among Europeans, within a few years of the same time. In both these directions, throughout Europe and America and parts of Asia and Africa, the generation of men who were of middle age about the year 1700 witnessed a radical revolution in the conditions of human life. In their childhood, fermented alcoholic drinks were the one resource of men, not only for purposes of intoxication, but for all the purposes for which tea, cocoa, and coffee are now employed. They lived to see the fermented beverages largely superseded, in the one use of them by distilled liquors, and in the other use of them by the hot drinks which have ever since been on our tables. In their childhood, however relatively plentiful wine and ale may be said to have been, they were yet so scarce that habitual drunkenness was beyond the reach of any except those who had access to the cellars of the rich. Before they died anybody could get drunk for a penny. It should be added to this, that the use of tobacco became general during the seventeenth century. And as having a real, though less direct, connection with the temperance problem, account must be taken of all the marvelous discoveries and inventions which have rendered human life in these later centuries so much more complicated and strenuous than it was before.

These radical changes of condition naturally led to corresponding changes in the convictions of men in regard to the use of alcoholic drinks.

2. Opinions Changed with the Problem. To trace the development of these convictions would be to sketch the history of the modern temperance reform in America and the Old World. Until the nineteenth century, the general opinion of mankind certainly did not condemn the use of intoxicating drinks, nor even occasional drunkenness, provided the drinker kept himself prudently guarded from further bad results. Philo the Jew, just before the Christian era, wrote extensive treatises on " Drunkenness " and " Sobriety." These include a formal discussion of the question, " Whether the wise man will get drunk." Philo replies by citing the expressed opinions of men, as well as evidence of other sorts, on both sides of the question. He says that " the sons of physicians and philosophers of high repute . . . have left behind 10,000 commentaries entitled treatises on drunkenness," and censures these for the narrowness of their treatment of the subject. He insists on the difference between the drinking of " unmixed wine," which will produce intoxication, and that of lighter or diluted wines. He calls unmixed wine a poison and a medicine, and condemns the drinking-contests which were common in his day. But he none the less indorses what he represents to be the current opinion, namely, that a wise man may occasionally get drunk. His helplessness when drunk no more disproves his wisdom than if it resulted from a bilious attack, from sleep, or from death. Philo intimates that the opposite opinion is quite respectably defended, but proves, to his own complete satisfaction, that it is indefensible. His opinions concerning the drinking-habit are certainly those which have been commonly held until the last century. But, as far back as traces exist, there is found a highly reputable line of opinion in favor of total abstinence from intoxicating beverages. Of this, in the eighteenth century, the distinguished Samuel Johnson is an instance. Earlier in the century, Le Sage sarcastically admires " the patriotic forecast of those ancient politicians who established places of public resort, where water was dealt out gratis to all customers, and who confined wine to the shops of the apothecaries, that its use might be permitted but under the direction of physicians "; and the wisdom of those who frequented these resorts, not for " swilling themselves with wine, but . . . for the decent and economical amusement of drinking warm water " (*Adventures of Gil Blas*, book ii., chap. 4). This sarcasm must have been aimed at opinions held by respectable contemporaries of the author. In 1743 John Wesley, in his *General Rules*, mentions as sinful, " drunkenness, buying or selling spirituous liquors, or drinking them, unless in cases of extreme necessity." It is said that in 1733 the trustees of the colony of Georgia, who were living in London, enacted that " the drink of rum in Georgia be absolutely prohibited, and that all which shall be brought there be staved." In the colonies and in Great Britain, during that century, there were several instances of similar legislation. Samuel Pepys, in his *Diary*, 1659–69, figures as an inconsistent total abstainer. Going back with a bound to the times of Philo, he asserts (*Treatise on Drunkenness*, ii.) that " great numbers of persons, who, because they never touch unmixed wine, look upon themselves as sober," yet display the same foolishness, senselessness, lack of self-control, and the like, as are displayed by a drunken person. Still earlier familiar instances are those of the Rechabites and the Nazirites (q.v.), of Samuel, and Daniel. Nearly up to the present time, therefore, the world has been aware of the dangers and evils attendant upon the use of inebriating beverages, has been in possession of the idea of total abstinence from them, and has been compelled to look upon total abstainers with high respect, but has, on the whole, approved the use of such beverages, not merely in what is now sometimes called moderation, but up to the line of occasional and discreet drunkenness.

The revolution of opinion, at least as a great and controlling movement, began in America. A representative incident will indicate its nature. The incident is taken from **3. Nineteenth-Century Movement.** the *Collections* of the Cayuga County Historical Society, 1882. Joseph Tallcot was a member of the Society of Friends, living a few miles south of the town of Auburn, N. Y. In all that vicinity, in 1816, the crops were so short that poor people found it difficult to procure breadstuffs for food. At the same time, Tallcot noticed, the distilleries kept in operation. He says:

" The circumstances affected me not a little, and induced me to write an address to the sober and influential part of the community, inviting them to a serious consideration of the melancholy situation, and the evils and calamitous consequences of intemperance. I insisted that nothing short of the example of that part of society which gives habits to the world, of abstaining altogether from the use of ardent spirits, except for medical purposes, would correct this alarming evil."

It occurred to Joseph Tallcot to offer his views for the consideration of the members of the Presbyterian Synod of Geneva. In his narrative he says:

" I found my way to the house of Henry Axtell, the Presbyterian clergyman. . . . His brethren from the surrounding country soon began to come into the village, and call on him for instruction where they might find entertainment among their friends. The master of the house appeared very hospitable, inviting them to partake of his brandy; which they did, with what would be thought moderation.

He turned to me, and pleasantly said he 'supposed it would be useless to invite me to partake,' considering my business. I as pleasantly replied, that 'we had been in the same habit, but, seeing the evil of it, we had abandoned it,' and I hoped they would do the same."

Joseph Tallcot read his paper, first before a committee, and afterward before the synod, and went his way. The synod, after duly considering it, published it, with resolutions "fully approving it, and solemnly declaring, that from that time they would abandon the use of ardent spirits, except for medical purposes; that they would speak against its common use from the pulpit, . . . and use their influence to prevail with others to follow their example." Similar incidents were occurring in different parts of the country and among people of various religious persuasions. In 1789, 200 farmers of Litchfield, Conn., pledged themselves for that season not to use distilled liquors in their farm work. In 1794 Dr. Benjamin Rush of Philadelphia published his *Medical Inquiry*, in which he insisted that the use of distilled liquors as a beverage ought to be entirely abandoned. In 1812 the Presbyterian general assembly made a deliverance "not only against actual intemperance, but against all those habits and indulgences which may have a tendency to produce it." In the same year the General Association of Connecticut recommended entire abstinence from ardent spirits; while the Consociation of Fairfield County adopted the principle of total abstinence from all intoxicating drinks whatever, especially for "those whose appetite for drink is strong and increasing." The Temperate Society, formed at Moreau, N. Y., 1808, and the Boston Society for the Suppression of Intemperance, 1813, were not total-abstinence bodies. In 1818 the Presbyterian Assembly planted itself squarely on the principle that men ought to "abstain from 'even the common use' of ardent spirits." In 1823 President Nott of Union College published his *Sermons on the Evils of Intemperance.* In 1826 the American Temperance Society was organized, *The National Philanthropist* was started, and Lyman Beecher published his *Six Sermons on Intemperance.* In the same year Rev. Calvin Chapin, in *The Connecticut Observer*, advocated abstinence from all intoxicating drinks, and not from distilled spirits merely. From about 1836 this principle came to be generally accepted by the reformers.

The spread of the movement was very rapid in Great Britain, and marvelously rapid in the United States. Societies, local and general, were organized. Temperance books, pamphlets, and newspapers were published in great numbers. Public meetings were held. The pledge was circulated. Total abstainers came to be counted by millions. In 1840 six hard drinkers in Baltimore suddenly signed the pledge, and started the "Washingtonian" movement. In a few months, about 1838, the Irish Roman Catholic priest, Father Mathew (see MATHEW, THEOBALD) administered the pledge to nearly 150,000 persons in Cork alone. He was eminently successful in temperance-work in different parts of Great Britain, as well as in the United States.

In the United States the movement may be said to have culminated in the decade that began about 1846 A.D. Very seldom has a movement gained so complete control over public opinion. Among other forms of organization the temperance knightly orders appealed to the imagination of the young people; the order of the Sons of Temperance being founded in New York in 1842, that of the Rechabites being introduced from Great Britain about the same time, and that of the Good Templars originating in 1851. Temperance organization reached every hamlet, and the churches and Sunday-schools. Bands of Hope and the like were organized for the children. The habitual use of inebriating drinks became so rare among the members of the Protestant churches that those who used them attracted attention thereby, though this was more the case in the country than in the large cities. It was easy to pass prohibitory laws, and many were passed. They did not, however, prove as successful as their advocates had hoped. Most of them were either pronounced unconstitutional, or were repealed, or became a dead letter. Then the temperance interests were overshadowed by those that led to the Civil War. Since the war elaborate organizations have appeared, notably political prohibition parties, the Women's Christian Temperance Union, the Anti-Saloon League. Novel temperance movements have at times made great headway—blue-ribbon movements, white-ribbon movements, and praying "crusades" in the places where liquors are sold. There have been recurring waves of success and defeat in the matter of prohibitory and local-option laws. The total-abstinence tradition has been generally maintained by the descendants of those who originally accepted it. There have been sermons and addresses, the circulation of temperance literature, regular temperance lessons in the Sunday-schools, and compulsory temperance instruction in the public schools. A little has been done in the providing of substitutes for the saloon. Business interests have more or less rigidly insisted upon total abstinence as the condition of responsible employment. Athletic interests have powerfully influenced young men by requiring abstinence during the period of training; however, this may have been neutralized by the debauch that has too often followed the contest. In the navies of the world it is recognized that temperance is the condition of efficiency. Sociological and charitable interests are allies of temperance.

4. Results of the Movement.

III. Good and Bad Reasons for Total Abstinence: Nevertheless, present temperance convictions have less dynamic vitality than they ought to have. Intemperance is rife, and the public is apathetic. Unenforced temperance laws do harm by fostering disrespect for law. The dominance of the saloon is not checked except locally and temporarily. So far as this is due to weak elements in the temperance propaganda, the remedy is in the hands of the advocates of temperance; for it is in their power to search out and eliminate such elements.

The argument which experience has shown to be the most effective is that from the evils of drunkenness. These evils, moral and economical, individual and social, are monstrous, and total abstinence from the use of intoxicants as a beverage provides the only known adequate remedy. This argument is sound, and is by itself sufficient. It appeals to common experience. Its facts are facts which all intelligent persons know. But many advocates of temperance are not satisfied with this commonsense presentation. They are fascinated with the idea of making the argument scientific, and so they reinforce it with statistics, and with theories of social science. This is admirable provided they use sound theories and correct statistics; but when men advocate temperance on the basis of crude social theories and fake statistics, intelligent persons hear and disbelieve and become apathetic.

1. Argument from the Evils of Drunkenness.

The experience of some generations of total abstainers proves that alcohol is not necessary as food. Total abstainers live longer than moderate drinkers. It is an established fact that intoxicants injure one who uses them habitually, even if he never gets drunk. This is in itself a valid and sufficient argument for total abstinence; but the temperance advocate misuses it if, in his laudable ambition to be scientific, he deals in facts which he only half understands, and which he fails to state correctly. If one makes his fight against the chemical agent called alcohol rather than against intoxicants as such; if instead of using incontrovertible facts he insists mainly on propositions that are in dispute, for example, the proposition that alcohol has no food value, or the proposition that the character of alcohol as a poison is unaffected by dilution, he injures the cause which he is advocating. Such false reasonings are none the less weak for the fact that persons are sometimes convinced by them; when persons so convinced discover their error they become either lukewarm or hostile. Another misuse of this argument consists in putting it into the principal place. To do this is to treat the drink problem as if it were on the same footing as the question of a pork diet, or of ill-cooked food; and this involves a disastrous belittling of the moral and social issues.

2. From the Evils of Moderate Use.

The ethical principle in the case is that a person has no right to degrade himself, to injure others or the community, or to run undue risks of injuring himself or others. And there is always a double reply to the person who thinks that he is so strong that there are for him no risks in moderate drinking. First, no one knows beforehand what risks the drink-habit may have for him; second, even if he knew, he might still be under the obligation which rests upon the strong to deny themselves for the sake of the weak. Probably all advocates of total abstinence agree as to the existence of these obligations, and regard them as sufficient to cover the whole case. They should never be left in the background while weak though specious substitutes are pushed to the front.

3. The Ethical Argument.

From the beginning the total-abstinence movement has been deeply religious. This is true notwithstanding the fact that some of its advocates have been irreligious, and have even used temperance doctrines for venting their dislike to the Bible and the churches. Such instances attract attention mainly because they are exceptional. The movement being religious, both its advocates and its opposers appeal to the Scriptures. In relatively few passages the Scriptures speak of wine and strong drink as being good, and of their strength as being a good quality in them. They commend them for medicinal and for sacrificial uses. Very likely the writers of Scripture thought of them as being, in forms too diluted to be intoxicating, the natural drink of all who could afford them. Different from this is the question of the moderate drinking of liquids of intoxicating strength; whether the Scriptures for their own times approve this is a matter of uncertain inference, and is an academic question. In interpreting these utterances of the Scriptures the facts adduced in the earlier part of this article are important. One who approved the use of the light fermented beverages in the ancient world might now disapprove them, substituting such drinks as tea or coffee. Before intoxicants were made cheap by the art of distillation the evils and risks from them were immensely less than now. Most of the hundreds of passages in which the Scriptures mention or imply wine or strong drink are unsparing condemnations of the social drinking usages which then prevailed (e.g., Matt. xxiv. 49; Rom. xiii. 13; Gal. v. 21; I Cor. vi. 10; Isa. v. 11, 12, 22, xxviii. 7; Amos. iv. 1; Prov. xx. 1, xxiii. 30, 31). As a remedy they sometimes prescribe total abstinence, but never moderation in drinking. In their avoidance of any explicit approval of moderate drinking they are in significant contrast with such ancient literature as Ecclesiasticus or the writings of Philo. One should read these passages and observe that they contemplate habitual drunkenness as exclusively the vice of the rich and the aristocratic. They especially scathe the men and women who are the natural leaders of the people, and who through drink are ineffective in their public duties. In contrast with this the drunkenness of the twentieth century is especially prevalent among the poor. It is not now a question of relatively a few aristocrats drinking themselves to death, but of a drink curse affecting the millions of the common people, and bringing with it starvation and squalor and crime and wholesale race deterioration. The modern problem differs from the ancient. Supposably the teaching of the prophets and apostles may be that total abstinence is a duty for our time and environment, even though it could be proved not to be a universal duty for all times and environments. It can not be proved that Jesus drank beverages that would intoxicate, nor that the apostles and prophets approved even the limited common drinking of such beverages; but if this could be proved for the conditions then existent, the proof would not apply in the different conditions that now exist. The Scriptures either prescribe or commend total abstinence from intoxicants as a practise that should be followed in a good many cases (e.g., Num. vi.; Lev. x. 9; Jer. xxxv.; Dan. i.; Prov. xxiii. 31; Luke i. 15; I Tim. v. 23). They thus by implication prescribe total abstinence in all cases that are parallel to these. Are there now

4. Arguments from the Scriptures.

any cases that would not come under this prohibition? Finally, the Scriptures emphasize the principles on which the doctrine of total abstinence rests, particularly the principle of abstinence when indulging might result in harm to persons weaker than him who indulges (e.g., Rom. xiv.; I Cor. viii., x.). It is this that defines the position of the Scriptures on the subject. Particular statements may refer to local and temporary conditions, but these ethical principles are universal.

As the Scriptures, rightly understood, are thus the strongest bulwark of a true doctrine of total abstinence, so false exegesis of the Scriptures by temperance advocates, including false theories of unfermented wine, have done more than almost anything else to discredit the good cause. The full abandonment of these bad premises would strengthen the cause immeasurably.

IV. Total Abstinence and Temperance Laws: It is a mistake to think that the effort to secure the legal suppression of the liquor traffic is a later and more advanced stage of the temperance movement than the efforts for total abstinence. The leaders of the great movement attempted to restrict the use of liquors by moral suasion, but they accompanied this by demands for legislation. Lyman Beecher's *Six Sermons*, for example, emphatically declare that the remedy for intemperance includes " the banishment of ardent spirits from the list of lawful articles of commerce," and invoke the interference of legislation to this end, as well as that of public sentiment (ed. of 1828, p. 64). As noted above, that movement led to the general passing of prohibitory laws. But no conceivable legislation can do away with the need of voluntary self-control in this matter. The greatest thing that restrictive laws can possibly accomplish is to facilitate correct practise by individuals. To regard total abstinence as mainly a mere incident to prohibitory law is perhaps the most fatal mistake that can be made in the temperance propaganda.   W. J. BEECHER.

BIBLIOGRAPHY: The literature on total abstinence (and temperance reform) is very large and very uneven in quality, much of it in fiction. Some of the states have graded text-books for use in the schools. The reviews have many articles on the subject, e.g., *Presbyterian Quarterly*, vol. i., *Presbyterian Review*, vols. i.–iii., *North American Review*, vol. cxli., and *Forum*, vol. i. Consult further with reference to the Biblical side: E. Nott, *Lectures on Biblical Temperance. With an Introduction by T. Lewis*, London, 1863; G. Duffield, *The Bible Rule of Temperance; total Abstinence from all Intoxicating Drink*, New York, 1868; L. C. Field, *Oinos: a Discussion on the Bible Wine Question*, ib. 1883; G. W. Samson, *The Divine Law as to Wines, Established by the Testimony of Sages, Physicians and Legislators*, new ed., Philadelphia, 1884; G. G. Brown, *The Holy Bible Repudiates " Prohibition"; Compilation of all Verses containing the Words "Wine" or " Strong Drink" proving that the Scriptures commend and command the temperate Use of alcoholic Beverages*, Louisville, Ky., 1910.

On the history consult: S. Couling, *History of the Temperance Movement in Great Britain and Ireland, with biographical Notices of departed Worthies*, London, 1862; *Centennial Temperance Volume*, Philadelphia, 1876; W. H. Daniels, *The Temperance Reform and its Great Reformers*, New York, 1878; G. F. Clark, *History of the Temperance Reform in Massachusetts, 1813–83*, Boston, 1888; D. Burns, *Temperance History: a Consecutive Narrative of the Rise, Development and Extension of the Temperance Reform, with an Introductory Chapter*, London, 1889; *Cyclopedia of Temperance and Prohibition. A Reference Book of Facts, Statistics, and general Information in all Phases of the Drink Question, the Temperance Movement and the Prohibition Agitation*, New York; 1891; J. N. Stearns, *Temperance in all Nations. History of the Cause in all Countries of the Globe, together with the Papers, Essays, Addresses, and Discussions of the World's Temperance Society in Chicago, Ill., June, 1893*, ib. 1893; A. F. Fehlandt, *A Century of Drink Reform in the U. S.*, Cincinnati, 1904; Katherine L. Stevenson, *Brief Hist. of the Woman's Christian Temperance Union*, Evanston, Ill., 1907; W. F. Crafts and others, *Intoxicating Drinks and Drugs in All Lands and Times: a Twentieth Century Survey of Intemperance; based on a Symposium of Testimony from one hundred Missionaries and Travelers*, Washington, 1909.

For the legal aspects consult: F. A. McKenzie, *Sober by Act of Parliament*, New York, 1896 (compares the liquor laws of various countries); A. Shadwell, *Drink, Temperance and Legislation*, ib. 1902; E. A. Pratt, *Licensing and Temperance in Sweden, Norway and Denmark*, ib. 1907. The medical aspect is treated in: W. B. Carpenter, *On the Use and Abuse of Alcoholic Liquors in Health and Disease*, London, 1850; A. Gustafson, *The Foundation of Death: a Study of the Drink Question*, Boston, 1884; C. A. Story, *Alcohol: its Nature and Effects*, New York, 1874; J. S. Billings, *Physiological Aspects of the Liquor Problem*, Boston, 1903; T. N. Kelynack, *Drink Problem in its Medico-sociological Aspects, by Fourteen Medical Authorities*, New York, 1907.

On the moral and social sides consult: E. C. Delevan, *Consideration of the Temperance Argument and History*, New York, 1865; J. Parton, *Will the Coming Man Drink Wine?* in *Atlantic Monthly*, Aug., 1868; J. T. Crane, *Arts of Intoxication: the Aim and Results*, ib. 1870; W. Hargreaves, *Our Wasted Resources; the Missing Link in the Temperance Reform*, ib. 1881; R. B. Grindrod, *The Nation's Vice; the Claims of Temperance upon the Christian Church*, ed. by his son, London, 1884; H. W. Blair, *The Temperance Movement; or, the Conflict between Man and Alcohol*, 4th ed., Boston, 1888; E. J. Wheeler, *Prohibition: the Principle, the Policy, and the Party*, New York, 1889; J. C. Fernald, *The Economics of Prohibition*, ib. 1894; J. Rowntree and A. Sherwell, *Temperance Problem and Social Reform*, 4th ed., ib. 1899; H. C. Trumbull, *Border Lines in the Field of Doubtful Practices*, ib. 1899; R. Calkins, *Substitutes for the Saloon*, Boston, 1901; S. H. Maneval, *Prohibition of Intoxicating Liquors*, Canton, O., 1903; G. B. Culten, *Psychology of Alcoholism*, New York, 1907; A. A. Hopkins, *Profit and Loss in Man*, ib. 1909; H. S. Warner, *Social Welfare and the Liquor Problem; A Series of Studies in the Sources of the Problem and how they relate to its Solution*, Chicago, 1909. The various temperance societies are continually issuing tracts, pamphlets, and books, lists of which can be obtained on applications to the societies.

TOTEMISM. See COMPARATIVE RELIGION, VI., 1, b., §§ 2–5.

TOULMIN, JOSHUA: English Unitarian, and biographer; b. in London May 11, 1740; d. at Birmingham July 23, 1815. He studied at St. Paul's school, 1748–55 (or –56); prepared for the ministry at the independent academy supported by the Coward trust, 1756–61; was minister of the Presbyterian congregation of Colyton, Devonshire, 1761–64; of Mary Street General Baptist chapel, Taunton, 1765–1803; and colleague to John Kentish at the New Meeting, Birmingham, 1804–15. He was a founder of the Western Unitarian Society, 1792. He was a voluminous writer, and is of note for his biographical and historical work. He published *Sermons, principally addressed to Youth* (Honiton, 1770); *Dissertations on the Internal Evidences and Excellence of Christianity* (London, 1785); *The Practical Efficacy of 'he Unitarian Doctrine* (1796); *Sermons* (Bath, 1810); *Four Discourses on the Nature, Design, Uses, and History of the Ordinance of Baptism* (London, 1811); *An Historical View of the State of the Protestant Dissenters in England* (Bath, 1814); the lives of Faustus Socinus (London, 1777), J. Biddle (1789), S. M. Savage

(1796), Charles Bulkley (London? 1802), and S. Bourn (Birmingham, 1808); and edited with memoir a new edition of Neal's *History of the Puritans* (5 vols., Bath, 1793–97).

BIBLIOGRAPHY: The funeral sermons by J. Kentish and I. Worsley were published London, 1815–16. A *Memoir* by the former is in *Monthly Repository*, 1815, pp. 665 sqq. Consult further: J. R. Wreford, *Sketch of the Hist. of Presbyterian Nonconformity in Birmingham*, pp. 59, 89 sqq., Birmingham, 1832; *DNB*, lvii. 82–83.

TOULOUSE, tū″lūz′: Important town of southern France, and seat of a number of synods. The ancient Tolosa, it was the sacred capital of the Tectosages; was taken by the Romans 106 B.C.; was the capital of the Visigoths, 419–507; came under the power of the Franks, 507, but later regained its independence; was a county of hereditary princes, 778–1271, enjoying prosperity up to the Albigensian wars, after which it was united to France, 1271; it came under the influence of the Inquisition, and later became notorious for intolerance, in gross contrast to its earlier attitude. Its university, founded in 1229, is, after that of Paris, the oldest in France. It is also the seat of an archbishopric. At the suggestion of Louis, a synod was convened in Toulouse, 829, but the decrees are lost. One was held in 883 to adjust the complaint which Jews had made to Charles the Fat of being abused by clergy and laity. One in 1056, summoned by Pope Victor II., consisted of eighteen bishops, and passed thirteen canons forbidding simony, insisting upon the rule of celibacy, and placing the age of ordination to priests' orders at thirty, and to deacons' orders at twenty-five. The synod of 1118 was concerned with the inception of a crusade against the Moors in Spain. The synod of 1119, which Pope Calixtus II. presided over in person, reiterated the laws against simony, confirmed the right of the bishops to tithes, and in three of the ten canons teachers of false doctrine were anathematized. The synod of 1160, at which the kings of France and England, 100 bishops and abbots, and legates of Pope Alexander III. and his rival, Victor III., were present, declared Alexander pope, and pronounced excommunication upon Victor. The synod of 1219 forbade the conferment of offices upon the Cathari (see NEW MANICHEANS, II.), and forbade all work upon church-festival days which were mentioned by name.

The synod of 1229, in the pontificate of Gregory IX., is important. It obligated archbishops and bishops, or priests, and two or three laymen, to bind themselves by oath to search out heretics, and bring them to punishment. A heretic's house was to be destroyed. Penitent heretics were to be obliged to wear a cross on their right and left side, and might not receive an office until the pope or his legate should attest the purity of their faith. All men of fourteen years and over, and all women of twelve years and over, were to be required to deny all connection with heresy and heretics. This oath was to be repeated every two years. Laymen were also forbidden the possession of the Old and the New Testament; and the suppression of vernacular translations was especially commended. In 1590 a synod under Archbishop Francis II. of Joyeuse declared the Tridentine decrees binding, and took up various subjects, such as relics, the consecration of churches, oratories, and the administration of hospitals. As late as 1850 a provincial synod was held under the presidency of Archbishop d'Astros, which declared against the tendencies of modern thought, indifferentism, and socialism.

BIBLIOGRAPHY: M. R. Vincent, *In the Shadow of the Pyrenees*, pp. 211–232, New York, 1883; J. de Lahondès, *L'Église Saint Étienne*, Toulouse, 1890; L. Ariste and L. Braud, *Hist. populaire de Toulouse*, ib. 1898; L. V. Delisle, *La Prétendue Célébration d'un concile à Toulouse en 1160*, Paris, 1902; Hefele, *Conciliengeschichte*, vols., iv.– v. passim.

TOUSSAIN, tū″san′ **(TOSSANUS), DANIEL:** French Reformed; b. at Montbéliard (36 m. w. of Basel) July 15, 1541; d. at Heidelberg Jan. 10, 1602. His father was Pierre Toussain (q.v.), and the son was educated at Basel and Tübingen. Returning to France he preached for six months in his native town, and went to Orléans, 1560, where, after being a teacher of Hebrew, he was ordained minister of the local Reformed church in 1561. In 1568 he was forced to flee with other Protestants, but was soon discovered and imprisoned over two weeks. He then fled with his family to Montargis, where he was protected by the duchess of Ferrara until the king of France demanded the expulsion of all Huguenots. He now sought refuge in Sancèrre, and, after one year, returned to Montbéliard. Here he was charged with teaching Calvinistic and Zwinglian heresies, his reply being an affirmation of his Lutheran belief. In 1571 he was recalled to Orléans, and held services in the castle Isle, a few miles away, but at the news of the massacre of St. Bartholomew's Day, he fled just in time to escape the total massacre and pillage of Isle the next day; and he was concealed by a Roman Catholic nobleman at Montargis and later by the duchess in a tower of her castle. In Nov., 1572, he was able to return to his father at Montbéliard, but Lutheran intolerance again drove him out, and he accepted a call of the French refugees at Basel. In Mar., 1573, he was appointed chaplain to the Count Palatine Frederick III. at Heidelberg, but in 1576 the Calvinistic Frederick was succeeded by his son, the Lutheran Louis VI., and the Reformed were expelled. They found a Calvinistic patron, however, in John Casimir, the brother of the count, at Neustadt, where Toussain became inspector of churches and also helped found an academy in which he was one of the teachers. After the death of Zacharias Ursinus (q.v.) he was also preacher to the refugees' church of St. Lambert. In 1583 Louis VI. died, and John Casimir became regent. Calling Toussain into his council, he expelled the Lutherans from Heidelberg, and Toussain later became professor of theology, and, in 1584, rector. As an author he was prolific, being credited with no less than thirty-three works, for a list of which and his correspondence cf. F. W. Cuno, *Daniel Tossanus* (Amsterdam, 1898).

(JOHN VIÉNOT.)

BIBLIOGRAPHY: P. Tossanus, *Vitæ et obitus D. Tossani . . . narratio*, Heidelberg, 1603; A. Müller, *Daniel Tossanus, Leben und Wirken*, 2 vols., Flensburg, 1884; F. W. Cuno, *Daniel Tossanus*, Amsterdam, 1898; J. Viénot, *Hist. de la réforme dans le pays de Montbéliard*, Montbéliard, 1900.

TOUSSAIN (TOSSANUS), PIERRE: French Reformer of Montbéliard, and father of the preceding; b. at St. Laurent, near Marville (145 m. e.n.e. of

Paris), 1499; d. at Montbéliard (36 m. w. of Basel) Oct. 5, 1573. Educated at Metz, Basel, Cologne, Paris, and Rome, he became a canon of Metz in 1515, where he first heard of Protestant doctrines, and, being suspected of adherence to them, he was forced to flee to Basel. After a sojourn at Paris, he attempted to introduce the new doctrines into Metz, only to be imprisoned at Pont à Mousson. On Mar. 11, 1526, deprived of his benefice, he was expelled from Metz. He now returned to Paris, where he became an almoner of Margaret of Navarre, but in 1531 was again obliged to flee from France. After visiting Zwingli in Zurich, Gillaume Farel in Grandson, and Simon Sulzer in Basel, he went to Wittenberg. While in Tübingen on his return, he gladly accepted the invitation of Duke Ulrich of Württemberg to continue the Reformation begun by Johann Gayling and Farel in Montbéliard. Within four years (1535–39) Protestantism was definitely established, the mass was abolished, and the most of the canons retired to Besançon. Toussain became the head of the new ecclesiastical organization, which, being French and Swiss in character, became involved in serious controversies with the German chaplains of Count Christopher of Württemberg, who took up his residence at Montbéliard in 1542. As a result he retired to Basel, 1545–46, but returned to Montbéliard when the difficulty was finally adjusted. He was one of the few clergy undisturbed during the interim (1548–52), and on the second suppression of the Roman Catholics in Montbéliard in 1552 he resumed his position as superintendent at the head of the Protestant clergy. In 1559, under the guardians of the new count, Frederick, the Württemberg agenda were introduced, but the stubborn resistance of Toussain and his clergy forced the count's guardians to make concessions, especially to permit the use of Toussain's liturgy for the time being. In 1568, however, all pastors who refused to adopt the Württemberg agenda were deposed. When, in 1571, Jakob Andreä (q.v.) was sent by the Württemberg government to Montbéliard, the clergy were strictly examined, Daniel Toussain (q.v.), the reformer's son, was banished, and his father was pensioned and replaced by a Lutheran. All the clergy who professed either Zwinglianism or Calvinism were gradually removed, and the Tübingen dogmas were enforced. Strict in life, Evangelical in spirit, Toussain was a model pastor and wise organizer. His sole literary production was L'Ordre qu'on tient en l'église de Montbéliard en instruisant les enfans, et administrant les saints sacramens avec la forme du mariage et des prières (1559), of which only a single copy seems to exist.   (JOHN VIÉNOT.)

BIBLIOGRAPHY: J. Viénot, Hist. de la réforme dans le pays de Montbéliard, 2 vols., Montbéliard, 1903.

TOWNSEND, LUTHER TRACY: Methodist Episcopal; b. at Orono, Me., Sept. 27, 1838. He spent his early life in New Hampshire; studied at New Hampshire Conference Seminary; was graduated from Dartmouth College, Hanover, N. H., 1859; from Andover Theological Seminary, Mass., 1862; served as private and adjutant of the Sixteenth New Hampshire regiment, 1862–63; entered the Methodist Episcopal ministry, 1864; was professor of Hebrew, Chaldee, and New-Testament Greek at Boston University, 1868–70; of historical theology there, 1872; of practical theology and sacred rhetoric, 1872–93; and since then emeritus professor. Of his works may be mentioned Credo (Boston, 1869); The Sword and Garment (1871); God-Man (1872); Lost Forever (1874); Arena and Throne (1874); The Supernatural Factor in Religious Revivals (1877); The Intermediate World (1878); Bible Theology and Modern Thought (1883); Evolution or Creation (Chicago and New York, 1896); Story of Jonah in the Light of Higher Criticism (1897); Anastasis (1902); God's Goodness and Severity, or Endless Punishment (1903); Adam and Eve—History or Myth (1904); Collapse of Evolution (1905); God and the Nation (1905); The Deluge—History or Myth (1907); and Bible Inspiration (1909).

TOWNSEND, WILLIAM JOHN: English Methodist; b. at Newcastle-upon-Tyne Jan. 20, 1835. He was educated at Percy Street Academy in his native city, and was then engaged in business for several years, after which he studied for the ministry of the Methodist New Connection for a year (1859–60) under James Stacey, of Sheffield. He was minister of various churches of his denomination in Birmingham, Manchester, Leicester, Chester, Halifax, Stockport, and Newcastle until 1886, when he became president of the Methodist New Connection Conference, as well as general missionary secretary of the same body, a position which he held until 1891. In addition to the pastoral work which he then resumed in Birmingham and London, he was editor of the Methodist New Connexion in 1894–97 and was reappointed in 1902. In theology he " holds generally by Evangelical Christianity as expounded by leading modern Methodist theologians," and " has views on inspiration and the last things which differ from a hard and mechanical view of inspiration, or an arbitrary view of future retribution." He has written The Great Schoolmen of the Middle Ages (London, 1880); Robert Morrison, the Pioneer of Chinese Missions (1888); Alexander Kilham, the First Methodist Reformer (1890); Reminiscences and Memorials of Rev. James Stacey, D.D. (1891); Madagascar, its Missionaries and Martyrs (1892); Strength perfected in Weakness (1893); Handbook of Christian Doctrine (1897); Handbook to the Methodist New Connexion (1899); Life of Oliver Cromwell (1899); The Great Symbols (1901); History of Popular Education in England and Wales (1903); As a King ready to the Battle (1904); The Story of Methodist Union (1906); and A New History of Methodism (1909; in collaboration with others).

TOY, CRAWFORD HOWELL: Theist; b. at Norfolk, Va., Mar. 23, 1836. He was educated at the University of Virginia (A.M., 1856) after which he taught three years (1856–59), and studied for a year (1859–60) at the Southern Baptist Theological Seminary, Greenville, S. C. He was professor of Greek in Richmond College, Richmond, Va., in 1861, but left to enter the Confederate Army, in which he served until 1863. In 1864–65 he was professor in the University of Alabama, and after two years at the University of Berlin (1866–68), was professor of Greek in Furman University, Greenville, S. C., in 1868–69. From 1869 to 1879 he was professor of Hebrew in Southern Baptist Theological Seminary, which was located first at Greenville and after 1877 at Louisville, Ky., and since 1880 has been professor of Hebrew and oriental languages at Harvard University. Besides his work as editor of the Hellenistic department of the *Jewish Encyclopedia*, he has written *History of the Religion of Israel* (Boston, 1882); *Quotations in the New Testament* (New York, 1884); *Judaism and Christianity* (Boston, 1890); and *Commentary on Proverbs* (New York, 1899), and likewise prepared the Hebrew text and English translation of Ezekiel for the *Polychrome Bible* (New York, 1899).

TRACHONITIS, trac"o-nai'tis (**TRACHON**): A district of Palestine belonging to the Tetrarch Philip, son of Herod the Great (Luke iii. 1). The name, which is Greek and signifies " rough country," is sometimes used in the Targums and other Jewish writings to render the Argob of Deut. iii. 4, 13–14; I Kings iv. 13. Josephus, who repeatedly mentions Trachonitis, beside Auranitis (the Ḥauran) and Batanea (Bashan), describes it (*Ant.*, XV., x. 1) as a rocky inaccessible region, abounding in artificial reservoirs and caves and infested with robbers. It evidently lay to the east and northeast of Bashan, and an inscription found at al-Mismiyah, the site of the ancient Phæna, between twenty-five and twenty-eight miles south of Damascus, describes the place as " the chief village of Trachon." This point is situated on the northern edge of the Lejjah. The *Onomasticon* of Eusebius locates Trachonitis beyond Bostra in the desert south of Damascus, and Ptolemy (V., xv. 26) places the Arabs of Trachonitis east of Batanea. In 1858 J. G. Wetzstein studied the two Trachons, or rugged tracts, to the southeast and south of Damascus mentioned by Strabo (II., ii. 755–756). Of these only the latter has any connection with Bible history. It is now called al-Lejjah, or " place of refuge," and is a lava plateau, extending for twenty-eight miles northwest from the range of the Ḥauran. The upper surface, whose outer edge averages thirty-three feet above the surrounding region, is a sharply undulating plain of lava-stones, covered with heaps of basalt blocks. The jagged surface is rent by abrupt ravines. The intense humidity has made vegetation possible, while the winter rains are preserved in subterranean reservoirs easily concealed. The entire region corresponds closely to the description of Josephus, the name *Trachōn* itself being possibly an equivalent of the Arabic *wa'r*, " stony, inaccessible district," which is applied to the Ṣafah in the east and the Lejjah in the west.

After the death of Lysanias, king of Ituræa (36 B.C.), Zenodorus leased the southern parts of his domain from Cleopatra, and seems to have remained tributary ruler after her death in 30. They were located between Trachonitis and Galilee, and included Ulatha and Panias (*Ant.*, XV., x. 3). To increase his revenues Zenodorus had the inhabitants of Trachonitis make forays, especially against the people of Damascus. Augustus accordingly commanded that Trachonitis, Batanea, and Auranitis be assigned to the interests of Herod the Great (23 B.C.), to whom he also gave the domain of Zenodorus at his death (20 B.C.). Attempts to make the nomads of the country an agricultural people meeting with scant success, Herod settled 3,000 Idumæans there (10–9 B.C.). A few years later he likewise placed a colony of 600 Babylonian Jews in Trachonitis, and built for their leader Zamaris the fortress of Barthyra (probably the modern Bait Ari in the Jaulan). On the death of Herod (4 B.C.), Augustus made his son Philip ruler of Trachonitis, Batanea, Auranitis, and a part of the territory of Zenodorus (hence tetrarch of Trachonitis). At Philip's death (34 A.D.), his territory was incorporated with Syria, but in 37 was given by Caligula to King Agrippa, a grandson of Herod, who ruled it until his death in 44 A.D. (see HEROD AND HIS FAMILY). The district then came under the control of Roman procurators until, in 53 A.D., Claudius gave it to Agrippa II., who seems to have held it until his death (100 A.D.). Under Roman rule Trachonitis and the surrounding territory seems to have reached a ·high degree of prosperity, which was apparently destroyed by the Persian invasions about 615.

(H. GUTHE.)

BIBLIOGRAPHY: G. A. Smith, *Historical Geography of Palestine*, pp. 629 sqq., London and New York, 1896; J. L. Porter, *Five Years in Damascus*, 2 vols., London, 1855; idem, *Giant Cities of Bashan*, pp. 12 sqq., New York, 1871; J. G. Wetzstein, *Reisebericht über Hauran und die Trachonen*, Berlin, 1860; M. de Vogüé, *Syrie Centrale*, 2 vols., Paris, 1866–77; P. Le Bas and W. H. Waddington, *Inscriptions grecques et latines*, vol. iii., nos. 2524, 2396, Paris, 1870; S. Merrill, *East of the Jordan*, pp. 10 sqq., new ed., New York, 1883; H. Hildesheimer, *Beiträge zur Geographie Palästinas*, pp. 55–57, Berlin, 1886; A. Stubels, " *Journey to Tulul and Hauran, 1882*," ed. H. Guthe, in *ZDPV*, xii (1889), 225–302; Maj.-Gen. A. Heber-Percy. *A Visit to Bashan and Argob*, London, 1895; G. Rindfleisch, in *ZDPV*, xxi (1898), 1–46; Schürer, *Geschichte*, i. 425 sqq., Eng. transl., I., ii. 11 sqq.; *DB*, iv. 801; *EB*, iv. 5142–46.

TRACT: [In general literary use, a small work in which some subject of small range, or some aspect of a subject, is discussed (Lat. *tractare*, " to treat a subject "). It is distinguished from a treatise by being shorter, and by its persuasive as distinguished from its pedagogical aim. In its religious sense its Latin equivalent was much used in the Middle Ages, and continued to be used after the Reformation. In its modern use the word designates a brief exhortation to a religious life (see TRACT SOCIETIES)]. Liturgically it is an extension of the Gradual (q.v.) by a number of verses, especially from the Psalms, used from Septuagesima to Easter on Sundays and festivals, and also after Ash Wednesday on Mondays, Wednesdays, and Fridays, except in masses for the dead. The tract, like its name, seems to date back to the early Church. It essentially implies humility, and its designation is explained (as by the Pseudo-Alcuin, *De divinis officiis*, ix., in *MPL*, ci. 1186) as due to the fact " that it is sung slowly or sadly (*tractim*), and signifies the groaning of holy mother Church."

(A. HAUCK.)

TRACT AND COLPORTAGE SOCIETY OF SCOTLAND. See TRACT SOCIETIES, III., 3

TRACT SOCIETIES.

I. Origin and Character: Tract societies are associations for the dissemination of brief popular religious treatises, especially on present-day problems and questions of personal life, among wider circles than are immediately reached by the Church, thus seeking to counteract the circulation among the masses of tenets and principles either meager in faith or hostile to Christianity. The tract may be said to begin with the Reformation, as in Luther's ninety-five theses of 1517, which he followed with a long series of pamphlets, being imitated in this respect by other German, Swiss, and French Reformers. Later, English Puritans and Methodists, German pietists, and Moravians affected the circulation of tracts; but it was especially the Augsburg senior Johann Urlsperger and the English Hannah More, in the latter part of the eighteenth century, who were responsible for the formation of tract societies. In 1782 the former established at Basel the Deutsche Christentumsgesellschaft to unite Christians against the rationalism of the period; while the latter, after having combated French atheism by tracts which reached a circulation of 2,000,000, found her work carried on by the Edinburgh Tract Society (founded in 1796) and the London Religious Tract Society (established in 1799). On the model, and partly with the aid, of the latter organization, associations were soon formed in a number of places for the circulation of tracts, their work being carried on more or less in connection with home missions.

II. In Germany: The most important tract societies in Germany are as follows: Christlicher Verein im nördlichen Deutschland (Eisleben, 1811); Wupperthaler Traktatgesellschaft (Wupperthal, 1814); Hauptverein für christliche Erbauungsschriften in den preussischen Staaten (Berlin, 1814); Niedersächsische Gesellschaft zur Verbreitung christlicher Erbauungsschriften (Hamburg, 1820); Evangelische Gesellschaft (Stuttgart, 1832); Evangelische Bücherstiftung in Stuttgart, or Calwer Verein (Calw, 1833); Evangelische Gesellschaft in Strassburg (Strasburg, 1834); Verein zur Verbreitung christlicher Schriften (Basel, 1834); Agentur des Rauhen Hauses (Hamburg, 1842); Evangelischer Bücherverein (Berlin, 1845); Evangelische Gesellschaft für Deutschland (Elberfeld, 1848); Evangelischer Verein für die protestantische Pfalz (1848); Nürnberger evangelischer Verein für innere Mission (Nuremberg, 1850); Schriftenabteilung der Gesellschaft für innere Mission im Sinne der lutherischen Kirche (1850); Christlicher Kolportageverein in Baden (1867); Nassauischer Kolportageverein (Herborn, 1873); Deutsche evangelische Traktatgesellschaft (Berlin, 1879); and Christlicher Zeitschriftenverein (Berlin, 1880). The circulation of pfennig sermons begun by the Berlin city mission in 1881 serves a like purpose; the Verein für christliche Volksbildung für Rhein-

land und Westfalen (Cologne, 1882); and the Deutsche Zentralstelle zur Förderung der Volks- und Jugendlektüre (Hamburg, 1905), and the popularly scientific *Lehr und Wehr fürs deutsche Volk* (Hamburg, 1904 sqq.). The chief problems of German tract societies at the present time are, on the one hand, popular demonstration of the applicability of the Gospel to the problems of social and economic life to controvert the false glamour of Social Democracy, and, on the other hand, the defense of Christianity against rationalistic criticism and the theories of evolutionistic monism. The circulation of tracts is carried on chiefly by branch establishments of the societies and by colporteurs; and the desired results are best attained on the basis of personal acquaintance and with regard to the requirements of each case, inferior results being gained by promiscuous distribution of religious literature.   (H. RAHLENBECK.)

III. In Great Britain.—1. The Religious Tract Society: The great development of missionary interest which marked the last years of the eighteenth century led in 1799 to the formation by George

1. Origin and Development. Burder and others of the Religious Tract Society. Their act was the more fruitful in the case of Christian literature as, in 1804, its founders also originated the British and Foreign Bible Society. Starting with the production of simple tracts for home use, the society's work rapidly developed. The production of books and periodicals was added; work was undertaken for Roman Catholic countries on the continent of Europe; and, as early as the year 1814, assistance was given to Christian literature for China on the appeal of Drs. William Milne and Robert Morrison (qq.v.); while other parts of the heathen and Mohammedan world rapidly came under the society's influence. Its present operations extend to every quarter of the globe, the society continuing to be an agency for producing Christian literature in or for the mission fields of the world. So far it has used 272 languages and dialects in the course of this work, and every year sees some addition to this total.

Placing first its original work of producing English tracts, the society still provides literature of this type for all classes of the community. Its *Present Day Tracts* and its *Tracts for the*

2. Its Tracts. *Times*, written by men of learning and position in the churches, address themselves to the greater problems of theological criticism and social life. In its biographical series the lives of men and women eminent in the Christian Church of all ages are treated by writers of position. The necessity of producing special tracts for distribution among men originated its series of *Letters to My Brothers* and *The Men's Own*. Much of tract distribution being conducted upon a regular system, requiring a constant supply of new tracts, several series providing these at low prices are regularly issued. Special provision is made of tracts for women and children; and in the arrangement of the various series, regard is had to the particular needs of such classes as soldiers, sailors, and railway men. The work of providing tract literature happily has the sympathy of men distinguished both for scholarship and for position in the Christian Church. Thus modern authors of tracts published by the society include Bishop Handley Moule, the Earl of Northbrook, Sir William Muir, Alexander McLaren, Henry Wace, Griffith Thomas, Robert Forman Horton, Arthur Tappan Pierson, John Watson (Ian Maclaren), and Robert E. Speer. The method of the committee in choosing tracts is to-day what it was when the society began its work. Each tract is read by every member of the committee and a vote taken upon it. It is still required that the evangelical message be definite, and it is satisfactory to know that perhaps never in the history of the society have there been more frequent and more remarkable evidences of direct spiritual blessing through the reading of tracts than have been received during the last few years. It is clear that, although from time to time inexperienced observers allege that the day of the tract is past, the Evangelical and pastoral use of tracts has suffered no check.

In book publication the society has continued along the lines followed for many years. While primarily anxious to produce that which definitely conveys the Gospel message, or in some way illustrates or supports its claims, the society has felt increasingly the need of providing literature which, though not so definitely religious in its message, is decisively Christian in tone and character. The provision of such literature has again and again been pressed upon the society as a public duty in the face of the overwhelming development of literature, low or even debasing in moral tone, or, if otherwise beyond criticism, still anti-Christian in its influence. In recent years the more definitely theological part of the society's catalogue has been widely known for its series *By-Paths of Bible Knowledge*, to which authors of the standing of Professor Archibald Henry Sayce, Wallace Budge, Sir William Dawson, and others contributed; by such helps to Bible study as were furnished by Alfred Edersheim's volumes on *Bible History* and on *The Temple*, by Dr. Samuel Gosnell Green's *Handbook to Old Testament Hebrew*, and *Handbook to the Grammar of the Greek Testament;* and by devotional works from the pens of such authors as Newman Hall, John Angell James, and Canon Edward Hoare. Still more recent additions include the volumes of a *Devotional Commentary* by Bishop Handley Moule, Frederick Brotherton Meyer, Griffith Thomas, and other authors; an important series of works dealing with the controversy with Rome, including a translation with notes, of Karl August von Hase's *Protestantische Polemik* by Dr. Annesley William Streane; the *Handbook of the Bible,* of Dr. Joseph Angus, thoroughly revised by Dr. S. G. Green; together with practical and devotional works from the pens of such men as Bishop Welldon, Dr. Horton, William

3. Its Issues of Books.

L. Watkinson, John Henry Jowett, and Dr. Eugene Stock.

In general literature features in recent years have been the provision of full biographies of distinguished missionaries such as James Chalmers, Griffith John, and George Grenfell, and of finely illustrated works on natural history by Richard Kerr and others. No recent British artist engaged in illustration work is now more widely known than Harold Copping, whom the society sent to the East in order to provide Bible illustrations. The society has accordingly produced a Bible illustrated from Copping's sketches and in addition two finely illustrated works —*The Gospel in the Old Testament* and *Scenes in the Life of our Lord*, the letterpress of which was contributed by Bishop Handley Moule. In fiction the society has continued to produce books for adult readers as well as for the young, retaining old favorites and adding later authors of repute.

The periodicals of the society have always been a distinctive part of its work. *The Child's Companion,* begun in 1824, is still issued. The *Sunday at Home* has now more than fifty years of work behind it. *The Girl's own Paper,* started in 1880, has recently been entirely recast. *The Boy's own Paper* is still perhaps the most widely known publication of its kind. Other periodicals appealing to various classes continue the work originated nearly a century ago.

The aid of Foreign mission work has, from the earliest days of its existence, been an intimate concern of the society. As early as the year 1814, Morrison and Milne applied to it on behalf of China and promptly received aid. In the previous year, the first application for help in vernacular work came from India, and the first auxiliary tract society was formed at Bellary in 1817. Nearer home the society began to publish in Italian as early as 1806, and in Russian in 1814. The first effort on the part of France was made in 1819, and the work in Austria was begun ten years later. The society now maintains its own book and tract depot at Madrid for Spain; at Lisbon for Portugal; at Vienna for Austria; at Budapest for Hungary, and at Warsaw for Poland. In France it assists the Paris society, the McAll Mission (q.v.), and the Toulouse society; in Belgium, the work of the " Evangelical Mission " of Brussels; in Switzerland, the colportage work of the " Evangelical Society of Geneva "; in Italy, that of the " Evangelical Publication Society of Florence "; in Turkey and Bulgaria, the publication work of the American Board of Commissioners for Foreign Missions; in Greece, the " Evangelical Society's " work; and in Russia, Norway, Sweden, and Denmark, the publication and distribution of Christian literature through various societies and individual workers. The Religious Tract Society has thus for many years been a powerful supporter of those Protestant communities which, on the continent of Europe, are struggling against the power of Rome. It has continued this work in the face of many obstacles, but has gradually seen the liberty of the press and of the individual more and more freely conceded. By the aid and operations of the American Presbyterian press the society has pro-

4. Aids to Foreign Missions.

duced at, and distributed from, Beirut in Syria, a large and varied amount of Arabic literature, both definitely Christian in its message as well as some amount of general literature (see SYRIA, VI., 1, § 2). In Egypt it has lent important aid to the publication work of the Church Missionary Society, periodical and otherwise. Elsewhere in Africa, the mission of the Church Missionary Society in Uganda has received important help, while many other missions in different parts of that continent have been helped to produce Christian literature in various forms or have received grants of publications from home. In India the work is mainly carried on through subsidiary societies at Calcutta, Bombay, Madras, Lahore, Allahabad, Kottayam, and Nagercoil, while help has also been given to the Christian Literature and Religious Tract Society of Ceylon. Grants have been made, as in other fields, to individual workers among non-Christians as well as those working among the British soldiers and civilians. In China, as in India, the work is mainly done through the subsidiary tract societies organized at Shanghai, Hankow, Chungking, Peking, Foochow, Amoy, and Mukden. But here, too, individual grants are also made. The society has its own agent in China for the supervision of its work, more especially for that of the special China Fund started in the year 1908. In Japan, its chief agent is the Japan Book and Tract Society, Tokyo; and in Korea the Korean Tract Society. Scarcely a year passes in which one or more new languages is not added to the society's list, and it has already assisted to publish the *Pilgrim's Progress* in 112 languages and dialects.

The missionary operations at home consist in the supply of literature free, or at reduced prices, for pastoral and evangelistic work, for the help of ministers and students; for the encouragement of Evangelical missions, and for the instruction of inmates in hospitals and other institutions. In the ten years ending 1911, a special fund of £20,000 was also expended in the distribution of literature more especially directed against the claims of the Church of Rome.

2. Society for Promoting Christian Knowledge: This is not exclusively a tract society. Founded in 1698, it justly claims (*Report*, 1908) that its originators " were the first to care for settlers and colonists, the heathen in India and the Mohammedans in the Far East." But its grant operations have included help in founding bishoprics, in aid of church building and of education, as well as in providing Christian literature for the home and the mission fields. Its constitution confines its control and its operations to the Church of England and churches in communion with her. For these it has been a Bible society, a Christian literature society, and a tract society. It has been of great help to missionaries in its readiness to print works connected with the study of various languages used in their fields; in its generous provision for the printing of prayer-books and definite church literature; and in its aid of tract work. Its catalogue of English books is especially strong in works explaining and defending the faith and the position of the Anglican church. Great attention has been given to Christian evidence and to devotional literature, as well as to the

issue of popular fiction. Its tract catalogue is rich in tracts dealing with Anglican church doctrine, church seasons, and the defense of the church. The *Report* for 1908 gives the total number of works sold during the year (other than Bibles and prayer-books) as a little over 13,000,000. For the mission field, twenty-four works were produced in London and aid was given to thirty-two published abroad. Foreign publications were granted to the value of £1,360; and the total grants of publications (excluding half-price libraries) amounted to £5,815.

3. Other Societies: The Stirling Tract Enterprise was originated by Peter Drummond, of Stirling, in the year 1848, in order to meet a purely local need. The work met with so much local success that it was gradually extended. The *British Messenger* (formed on the model of the *American Messenger*) was started in 1853, the *Gospel Trumpet* in 1857, and *Good News* in 1862. On the death of Drummond in 1877, the Enterprise passed under the care of a body of trustees. It now produces books as well as magazines and tracts, and tracts are published in several continental languages as well as in English. The circulation amounts to about 10,000,000 publications per annum. The **Tract and Colportage Society of Scotland,** founded in 1793, and the oldest Bible, tract, and colportage agency, is rather an evangelistic and distributing society than a publishing house. Its colporteurs are mainly employed in Scotland, but a few work in England. They sell the Scriptures, evangelistic literature, and wholesome publications popular in type. There is also a depository in Edinburgh. About 700,000 tracts were distributed in the year last reported on. The **Children's Special Service Mission,** which began its work in 1867 as an agency for holding seaside services for children, while continuing its home work, now has an office and missioner in India, with native evangelists in India, Ceylon, and Japan. Its leaflets are now published in several continental languages, and are also issued for use in China, Japan, and other mission-fields.

Any survey of tract work done by British societies would be incomplete without reference to the **Christian Literature Society for China,** and the **Christian Literature Society for India.** These organizations confine their work exclusively to the fields stated in their titles, but, as missionary organizations, are large producers of tract and other literature. A fuller account of their work would more properly belong to a review of missionary enterprise in these two fields.   A. R. BUCKLAND.

IV. In America: Tract societies are voluntary associations of Christians to publish and circulate religious tracts, including volumes. The importance of adding to the influence of spoken truth and the permanent effectiveness of the printed page were early felt by Christians. What a good book can do and how its influence may germinate is shown in the history of Baxter's conversion aided by reading Dr. Gibbs's book entitled, *The Bruised Reed,* and Baxter's instrumentality in the conversion of Doddridge, by whose *Rise and Progress* Wilberforce was led to embrace the truth. It became evident that much good would be wrought by short, earnest, and strong tracts. Consequently efforts were early made by individuals to furnish these cheaply in such forms and quantities that they could be widely diffused.

One of the first American societies was the **Connecticut Religious Tract Society** at Hartford, founded as early as 1808; in 1812 the **New York Religious Tract Society** arose, and in 1814 the **New England Tract Society** of Andover, afterward transferred to Boston, which in 1823 changed its name to the American Tract Society. The friends of this form of Christian activity, however, were soon convinced that the needed work could be carried forward advantageously and effectively only by a national association, centrally located, and securing the confidence and support of all Evangelical Christians and denominations. Hence, there was organized in May, 1825, the **American Tract Society** at New York City. The movement received general approval and rapidly expanded, and took rank with the Bible Society among the chief interdenominational Christian charities of the nation. The society's first publications were tracts, and at the end of two years volumes were issued; hand-bills, leaflets, Christian tracts, illustrated cards, wall-rolls, etc., followed in quick succession. Publications have been issued in 174 languages, dialects, and characters.

Its publications are for all ages and classes, and treat all ordinary phases of truth and duty. As early as 1843 the publication of periodicals began. These have varied in number from time to time— *The American Messenger, Amerikanischer Botschafter, Apples of Gold,* and *Manzanas De Oro* being the periodicals now issued. The society furnishes large quantities of its publications either gratuitously or at reduced prices in order to aid missionaries and Christian workers in their efforts to reform and save. Its publications go to soldiers, sailors, to freedmen and immigrants, to hospitals, prisons and asylums, to needy mission-churches and Sunday-schools, to the destitute and neglected in cities, and throughout the entire country.

A large number of colporteurs have been employed to visit from house to house, supplying some of its publications to all, either by sale or grant, conversing with the household, holding meetings for prayer, and organizing Sunday-schools. The importance, necessity, and efficiency of this plan of evangelization has been only partially recognized. The time undoubtedly must come when it will be fully understood that the nation's greatest need is the need of the nation's homes, and that this need lies in the necessity of the moral and spiritual uplift of both parents and children unreached by saving influences. The one essential lesson yet to be learned is that national transformation can be effected only through the nation's homes. The Society, therefore, has never failed to prosecute this line of work to the fullest extent of its ability, and during seventy years of colportage has made 17,361,611 family visits and circulated 17,002,881 volumes. Its publications issued at the home office during eighty-four years are 456,-154,267 tracts, 34,206,914 volumes, and 285,634,668 periodicals, making a grand total of 775,995,849, not including the millions of tracts published at the mission stations abroad by aid of the society's appropriations. Its foreign work has been indispensable through the supplying of grants in money to create Christian literature in the vernacular at mission stations in the Orient. The total now reaches $779,267.43, not including many thousands of dollars in electrotypes. Special mention should be made of the publication of Christian literature in Benga, Bulu, Buluba-Lulua, Fan, Umbundu, and Mpongwe for missionary work in Africa, and the much-needed literature in the Portuguese language. The gratuitous distribution of literature has reached two and a half millions of dollars, more than $30,000 worth being sometimes distributed in a single year. The society has issued over 300 distinct publications in Spanish, which have been indispensable in successfully prosecuting missionary work in all Spanish-speaking countries. Its operations are directed by an executive committee, composed of constituent committees, known as publishing, distributing, and finance, six members each. The publishing committee represents six different denominations, which assures the interdenominational character of its publications, and the action of its committee must be unanimous. There is one general secretary with assistants and helpers to carry forward the work.

The society's work is wholly dependent upon donations and legacies. It makes an earnest appeal to all people for sufficient offerings to carry the Gospel truth into every non-Christian home throughout the land. The Western Tract Society of Cincinnati (1851) cooperates with the American Tract Society of New York.   Judson Swift.

Bibliography: The literature is to be sought in the *Reports,* etc., of the different societies.

TRACTARIANISM.

By Tractarianism is commonly understood the ecclesiastical-theological movement starting out from Oxford in 1833 and profoundly affecting the Church of England. It was an effort to overcome the religious decline of the beginning of the eighteenth century not by recourse to the deeper native resources, but to the older ecclesiastical traditions; such as the conversion of the creedal faith into devout mysticism, and an inner approximation to Roman Catholic principles. Following its course in the three forms of Tractarianism, Puseyism, and Ritualism, the new movement turned, on the basis of the Old Anglican theology, against the voiding of valuable religious assets, undertaken by the aggressive liberalism of the time, and against the encroachments of the State upon the rights of the Church. Theologically, it was an attempted answer to the inquiry concerning the nature of the Church and its attributes. Practically, it was an effort worthily to constitute the Christian life, and to elevate divine worship.

I. Preliminary Influences: The English Reformation of the sixteenth century had been political and ecclesiastical rather than religious. Deism two centuries later was sterile and depressing upon intellectual life in the Church. John Wesley and the Evangelical movement exerted a great redeeming power; however, their emotional one-sidedness forestalled the requisite influence upon the ecclesiastical theology. The undercurrent in the change of ideas which now set in was due to the idealism of Kant, Fichte, Coleridge, and Carlyle. A part of the wave of liberation which swept over Europe in the eighteenth century meant the annihilation of ecclesiastical despotism and the rising desire for the separation of Church and State, even a menace to the place of the Church itself. This was attended by a reaction on the soil of romanticism that rallied to the aid of the Church. Everywhere in Europe the order was the same; the hunger for freedom, which promised to make the individual absolutely self-dependent, turned into doubt and philosophic anguish, and resulted for many in the swallowing up of personality by the strongly authoritative spirit-life of the Roman Catholic Church. This gave rise in England to the new ecclesiastical devotion of the cultured. Following the tide back to nature which had borne along Wordsworth and Shelley, Walter Scott's revival of medieval romanticism included its picturesque piety and ecclesiastical enthusiasm. In Samuel Taylor Coleridge (q.v.), defender of the faith of the Church against rationalistic voidance, and advocate for the freer establishment of the traditional theology, the two tendencies which marked the English theology of the early nineteenth century were as yet combined. A new valuation came to be placed by the English national spirit, particularly at Cambridge, upon the heritage of the Church, that of faith exercised in love. Creed made way for personal faith; sacrament for preaching. The dividing-line between state church and dissent became dim, and the sole right of the state church as such came into question. With the beginning of the third decade, the ecclesiastical-political liberalism, following in the wake of the individualism of the French Revolution, endeavored to enforce its demands for freedom and equality. Leading the attacks on the historic rights of the Established Church by means of parliamentary measures was the ministry of John Russell, which represented the principle of freedom of conscience in the repeal of the Test Act (q.v.). This meant not only the admission of Non-conformists (q.v.) to parliament, but their participation in ecclesiastical measures and reforms. The following year (1829) Sir Robert Peel, to pacify Ireland, introduced the Roman Catholic relief bill despite High-church opposition. Reform of the Church or disestablishment was generally expected as a consequence of political reform. Still more perilous became the situation when the Whigs came in power and, in deference to a violent national demand, proceeded to press the parliamentary reforms against the house of lords and the bishops. They succeeded in transferring appeals in ecclesiastical cases from a spiritual court nominated by the king to a lay committee of the privy council, whereby the voice of the bishops was silenced also in parliament and in the higher instance of the privy council even on fundamental church questions. The doom of the Established Church was not only announced in parliament, but the passion of the populace vented itself in various acts of violence in London and elsewhere. The drift away from the church spread over all the land. The Reform Bill had placed the power in the hands of those most inimical to the church and most friendly toward dissent. The Church of England, it was said, was about to wrap itself in its shroud to die with dignity. The climax for a final rally to resistance was reached when the parliament of 1833 abolished one-half of the bishoprics of Ireland, professedly as an act of justice.

II. The Tractarian Development: This countermovement came forth from Oxford, the High-church citadel. The call proceeded from Oriel College, where, under the guidance of Richard Whately (q.v.), a group of young men, including Thomas Arnold, R. D. Hampden, J. H. Newman, R. H. Froude, John Keble, and E. B. Pusey (qq.v.), had become, as it were, the spiritual leaders of the university. The attacks of Whately on the orthodox doctrines of election and justification, and the theses of Arnold affirming the idea of a national church, in which the distinction between clericals and laity would be obliterated, and which relegated dogma, ritual, and organization to secondary importance, broke the group into two camps. The right wing of Keble, Froude, Newman, and Pusey forthwith espoused a church reform looking for relief beyond the sixteenth century. About this time Newman returned from a trip to the Mediterranean, Rome, and Paris in the ferment of altering views. Breaking with Whately and even with the High-church Edward Hawkins, to whom he owed his teachings of baptismal regeneration and Apostolic Succession (q.v.; see also SUCCESSION, APOSTOLIC), he reentered Oriel, now more congenial to him, and became more and more opposed to his old friends, the Evangelicals. Herein he was aided by his close association with Froude, from 1826, the fanatical protagonist of the new High-church ideas. The most gifted of the Oxford circle, intolerant and uncompromising, and possessing an ardent passion for truth and an ascetic purity of life, Froude had early seen the impossibility of reaching the truth by reason alone, and had consequently turned to the Church. Reverting to the past, he was repelled by the subjectivity of the advocates of the Reformation of the sixteenth century, kindling particularly in his *Remains* (London, 1838) his fevered animosity against it. Turning first to his own church of the period of Laud, he presently passed to the medieval Roman Church as the standard and type of all others, by its " always, everywhere, and by all " and doctrinal fulness. In

1. The Oxford Group.

England he hoped for a restoration of the Roman Church with a revival of medieval piety, fasting, good works, asceticism, celibacy, and the virgin cult. To this end he advocated the separation of Church and State. As late as the beginning of the fourth decade, Froude held reunion with Rome possible and desirable, but his journey to Rome changed his view and convinced him that the Roman Church likewise must be transformed to the model of the primitive Church. The spirit of a man who hated Protestantism and combated Rome, a Roman Catholic without a pope, and an Anglican without Protestantism, yet was the prophetic antecedent of the Tractarian system in all its phases. On their return from the south of Europe, Froude and Newman found Oriel in ferment. John Keble, then a member of Oriel and a man of deep piety and gentleness, had published his famous *Christian Year* (1827), a collection of poems which profoundly influenced Newman, who about this time broke with Whately. On the Sunday after Newman's return Keble preached before the university the Assize Sermon, published under the title *On the National Apostasy*, which became the alarm-cry for the assembling of the associates. A few days later Hugh James Rose, rector of Hadleigh, Suffolk, of his own accord, invited Froude, William Palmer, and A. P. Perceval to the famous Hadleigh Conference to consider the best means to avert the threatening liberalizing dangers. Keble and Newman, though invited, were unable to be present. The result of the conference was the formation of the Association of Friends of the Church, and Palmer was directed to frame two addresses to the primate, Archbishop Howley, one of which, within a few weeks, was signed by 7,000 clergy (more than half the total number in the country) and the other (drawn up by Joshua Watson) by 230,000 heads of households. The Scottish and American episcopates likewise subscribed, and the former requested archiepiscopal sanction, though in vain. The only point of difference was that of the separation of Church and State, which Keble and Froude strongly urged, while Newman wavered. In the interests of peace the point was not debated. Early in September Keble set forth the program of the new movement as follows: (1) the sole way to salvation is to eat the flesh and drink the blood of Christ; (2) the means ordained is the Holy Eucharist; (3) the right administration of the sacrament is guaranteed by the apostolic commission given to bishops and priests; (4) all possible means must be taken to impress and perpetuate the inestimable prerogative of communion with the Lord through the successors of the apostles, to strive for daily communion and worship in the churches, and oppose every alteration of the established liturgy. This was followed by *The Churchman's Manual* (Oxford, 1834) by Perceval, as the expression of the conservatives.

A new phase opened with the tracts undertaken by Newman, fixing a name upon the entire development. Newman was averse to organization and committees, preferring a wide popular movement stirred by personal sacrifice. The fitting points of dissemination were the universities, centers of intellectual and religious influence in England, such

as Oxford. The method must be by tracts or pamphlets, the favorite form of religious propaganda in that country. As history **2. The** proved, Newman was the one pecul- **Tracts.** iarly gifted to prepare the brief theological reviews. Of his own accord he issued *Tract* 1 (Sept. 9, 1833), followed by eighty-nine others (seventy before Nov., 1835) under the title of *Tracts for the Times* (6 vols., Oxford, 1833–1841). These, seldom over eight or ten pages in length, treated primarily of organization, discipline, and worship, of the nature of the Church and her relation to the primitive Church, on historic objections to the privileges, doctrines, and liturgy of the Anglican Church, her forms of prayer and her burial service, proposed changes in the liturgy, lax discipline, and the needs of the individual churches. The Roman Catholic problem, however, had not yet become prominent. Newman was the author of nos. 1, 2, 6–8, 10, 11, 19–21, 34, 38, 41, 45, 47, 71, 73, 75, 82, 83, 85, 88, and 90. Next to him was Keble, and then Pusey (no. 18, on fasting; nos. 40, 67–69, on baptism); Froude contributed but one (no. 63). The *Tracts* were supplemented, after 1833, by a series of extracts from such Church Fathers as Ignatius, Justin, and Irenæus, prepared by the other Oxford leaders under the title *Records of the Church;* while in 1838 Pusey, Keble, Newman, and Charles Marriott began a translation of all the Fathers, which appeared as the *Library of the Fathers of the Holy Catholic Church, Anterior to the Division of the East and West* (50 vols., 1838–85). All three works were polemical, and passed beyond the initiative of Keble and Rose, in demanding not only religious but ecclesiastical and ecclesiastico-political reform, the return development of the present Church to the Church of the first three centuries, before the rise of the cult of images, angels and saints, purgatory, transubstantiation, the restriction of the cup to the clergy, auricular confession, indulgences, and papal infallibility. By Newman's presentation of the doctrine of the visible Church as the source of all spiritual gifts and the channel of all grace, set forth in the teaching and usage of the early English Church, the *Tracts* at first gained a most cordial welcome, furnishing the bishops with the argument of divine right through apostolic succession, in their struggle with parliament, and the High-churchmen with a weapon against Evangelicals and Dissenters. Later *Tracts*, however, began to exceed the demand for the restoration of the system represented by the great Anglican divines of the sixteenth and seventeenth centuries, and were deemed suspiciously akin to Roman Catholic tenets, by their fogging of words and ideas and submerged sense becoming transparent (see below, High-church Doctrines). The Evangelical organ, *The Christian Observer*, clearly perceived the issue and began battle against the manifest tendency toward Rome. The old popular cry of the eighteenth century, " no popery," resounded again from press and thoroughfare.

In reply Newman, undisputed leader from 1834, came forward (*Tracts* 38, 41) with his doctrine of the *via media*. He maintained that it was the glory of the Anglican Church to have taken the middle course between the so-called Reformation and

Roman Catholicism. The later English Church had fallen from the faith of the sixteenth century, had disregarded the Prayer-Book, neglected the sacraments, and forsaken the church discipline. The teaching of the apostles and the early Church was the rule of faith, not the Thirty-nine Articles, which were no more than protests against gross errors. As the first Reformation retained the principles of the ancient Church shorn of their unsound accretions, so now the Thirty-nine Articles were not to be revolutionized, but interpreted, amended, and amplified, and the fundamental primitive ideas at their basis were to be revived and further unfolded, as an effective protest against the amalgamation of Church and State and the modern latitudinarianism. Alas, however, the *via media* was nothing else than the old road to Rome and proved repugnant specially to the religious sensibility of the nation. The first blow was dealt by Hampden in 1834, demanding that subscription to the Thirty-nine Articles by members of the university be dispensed with. Newman, supported by High-churchmen and Evangelicals alike, violently opposed the recommendation, which the university declined. When two years later Hampden was appointed regius professor of divinity, the Tractarians again assailed him, charging that he was a freethinker. He was, accordingly, condemned by the heads of the colleges with a vote of no confidence, but the two proctors of the university vetoed the condemnation. At the same time Thomas Arnold, the leader of the liberal theology at Oxford, sided with Hampden, and brought the menace to freedom of conscience to the attention of the lay public, with the result that in press and pamphlet the dissimulated aims of the " Malignants " and " Oxford Conspirators," were held up to public opprobrium. A tremendous gain was made when, in the latter part of 1834, Pusey, one of the most distinguished professors of the university, finally gave the weight and influence of his name to the party composed hitherto of young men. A power in high ecclesiastical circles, a scholar of renown, and descendant of a noble house with wide social connections, he was eminently fitted for leadership by character, services, and position. The effort became an organized movement and the adherents were from this time styled Puseyites. Moderated zeal, dignity, and discreetness in scientific presentation took the place of the extravagances and vagaries of the earlier tracts. His *Scriptural Views on Holy Baptism* (*Tracts* 67–69; 1835) was a solid doctrinal treatise instead of a series of flighty appeals; and the *Catenæ patrum* (nos. 71, 76, 78, 81) was designed to prove the historic continuity and the authority of the early Church. The Roman Catholic Church was not to be declined as such, since its doctrines were Scriptural and not contrary to the Thirty-nine Articles, but because it had violated the spirit of the Gospel, and had been materialized by the lust for power. On the other side the matter in hand was not Romanism, nor even reformulation, but simply the recognition and securing of the Anglican doctrine and cult, in their pristine purity, as repre-

3. John Henry Newman.

senting the native national faith. Meanwhile the *Tracts* pursued this tendency, leaving behind the *via media*. *Tract* 75 recommended the Roman Breviary as a book of devotion, and in *Tracts* 80, 87 Isaac Williams advocated the doctrine of reservation, holding that the holiest subjects should not be discussed before every one and on every occasion. Such reserve had been observed by Christ and the apostles; and the indiscriminating revelation of all truths of doctrine before the indifferent and unbelieving, like the general distribution of Bibles and tracts, was to be rejected as contrary to esoteric Christianity. Religious truth was revealed only to obedient faith, not to speculative investigation; and religious character was formed by the discipline of the Church, not by preaching, study, or piety of life. In *Tract* 89 Keble defended the mystical exegesis of Scripture employed by patristic allegory, and in *Tract* 90 Newman, with a subtle sophistication and legal dialectic, advanced the view that Roman Catholic convictions did not preclude subscription to the Thirty-nine Articles. The problem was not what the Articles teach, but what they do not reject. What the authors had in mind is immaterial, for they are no authorities. Thus the Articles were neither refuted, attacked, nor was their binding authority denied; but the meaning of their accessories was skilfully changed, and they were supplemented from what they did not state. The supplements were strained to prove that the Articles were directed purely against doctrinal opinions and not against the essential import, and under this view subscription was to be permissive. This tract marked Newman's inner break with his Church.

All Oxford was in commotion, the friends of the movement rejoicing that Roman tenets could find place in the Anglican Church, and its foes filled with indignation that the Thirty-nine Articles, the chief bulwark of the English Church against Rome, were broken down. The terror spread over the whole country, and the old cry of malignancy or moral depravity was again raised. Both sides urged that the matter be decided, and finally, in the middle of March, 1841, the vice-chancellor, heads of colleges, and proctors declared their condemnation of the *Tracts*. Bishop Bagot, of Oxford, hitherto well disposed toward the Tractarians, likewise wrote Newman that *Tract* 90 was offensive and perilous to the peace of the Church, and that the series could not be continued. To the authority of his bishop Newmann yielded. The unity of the Oxford school was broken by the stern consequences of *Tract* 90, and in the summer of 1841 Newman, feeling that the Tractarian cause was defeated, and convinced that he must seek peace and truth elsewhere, retired to Littlemore. The proposed Anglo-Prussian bishopric of Jerusalem brought the struggle within him to an end, and in 1845 he entered the Church of Rome. Individual conversions to the Roman Catholic Church had begun in 1840, and in 1842 the real exodus commenced. The more moderate drew back, others modified their views by excluding Romanizing ideas, and others still sought peace in labors in country parishes. W. G. Ward,

4. Repression.

"the fanatical advocate of private judgment," until he followed Newman in 1845, led the extreme right, Keble and Williams the right center, and Perceval the left. The leadership of the Oxford Movement; as a whole, however, devolved, after 1841, on Pusey, partly in consequence of the need of giving a scientific and historical basis to the concepts of the Tractarians to remedy the weakness resulting from their loss of unity.

III. Puseyism: The second period of the Oxford Movement was characterized, 1840–60, by the scientific foundation of the system, and, 1860–70, by the struggle for the recognition of Anglo-Catholic doctrine and liturgy in the Established Church. Under Pusey's guidance the movement assumed more moderate forms, and, gradually leaving dogmatics, zealously advocated the use of older rituals, closely akin to the Roman, and in the effect of which some rather precipitately with Carlyle foresaw the dissolution of the State Church. The rejection by Oxford of Ward's advocacy of the "non-natural sense" of the Articles upon individual conjecture was a decisive blow to the Tractarians; a result was that some retired, and others went over to the opposition, thus swelling the High-church nucleus. About 150 clerics, among them F. W. Faber (q.v.), and distinguished laymen followed into the Roman Catholic Church in 1845–46. On this turn of events followed energetic efforts to effect Romanizing consequences also in the matter of ritual; namely, to replace the wooden communion-table with the stone altar, and, against the spirit if not the letter of the English Prayer-Book, to introduce crucifixes, candles, the piscina, and the like; and as the Anglo-Catholic leaders stood by without protest, the old cry of "no popery" arose again. While on the one hand the Evangelicals were driven to closer union, the spread of this movement not only over England but into Wales and Scotland threatened the disorganization of the State Church. The doctrinal battles, beginning with 1847, turned upon the essential character of the Holy Church Catholic and its relation to the State, and whether the doctrines of the same are adequately reflected in creed and catechism to answer the necessity of the times. In Dec., 1847, the prime minister, Lord Russell, appointed Hampden to the diocese of Hereford. He was accused by his old opponents of holding unsound doctrines, was opposed by them and thirteen bishops, and rejected by the dean and the chapter, but was triumphantly sustained by the Court of Queen's Bench. The Gorham Case (q.v.), which, in contradiction of the Thirty-nine Articles, involved the denial of spiritual regeneration in connection with baptism, despite the remonstrance of Bishops Philpotts and Blomfield and of more than 1,500 distinguished clergy and laymen, representing the Tractarian trend, resulted in the assertion of the final authority of the crown (the lay instance of the privy council) in matters purely ecclesiastical. [Gorham and his Evangelical supporters maintained that his denial of baptismal regeneration was in accord with the letter and the spirit of the Thirty-nine Articles, and in this contention they were sustained by the courts. A. H. N.] Without the

1. Doctrinal Controversy.

approval of convocation, then in abeyance, an act of parliament in 1832 transferred the jurisdiction of the delegates to the privy council, and in the following year to a committee of the privy council, the judicial committee, a purely civil body whose members were not necessarily drawn from the clergy. Pusey, deeply incensed, threatened the separation of Church and State, and he and his followers, including Manning, Keble, and the bishops of Oxford, London, and Salisbury, showed their disapproval by the sensational dedication of the Church of St. Barnabas with the display of a considerable Roman pomp. Throughout the country associations were formed for the defense of the church, supported by Non-tractarians and Tractarians alike. A second exodus to Rome began, including H. E. Manning (q.v.), R. J. Wilberforce, H. Dodsworth (Pusey's assistant), and sixty members of a single London church (from 1833 to 1876, 385 clergy). In the latter part of August more than 600 High-churchmen, many of them belonging to distinguished families, migrated to New Zealand, that they might realize their ideal in the Canterbury Settlement.

A deep sense of fear and hope seized the nation, like the presentiment of an impending fate, threatening, perhaps, a transformation of the religious and moral conditions of life, when, suddenly, in Oct., 1850, the news came to England that Pius IX., in private consistory, had created the Vicar Apostolic Wiseman cardinal and archbishop of Westminster, and had provided England with a Roman Catholic hierarchy of twelve dioceses. The land echoed with agitation and protests, demanding national interference and forcing the Tractarians to declare against the hierarchy, while Lord Russell, who could not but regard the reestablishment of Roman Catholicism in England as a result of his Roman Catholic emancipation, attempted to meet the papal advance by the futile Ecclesiastical Titles Act of Feb., 1851. A series of High-church bishops, like Pusey himself, opposed the Roman presumption sharply. The restoration of convocation, at first declined by the government, was granted in 1852, at least so far as the permission to receive petitions was concerned, which served as a first step toward its complete reestablishment. This was the first triumph for the Oxford movement, which subsequently, by the pure separation of the powers of Church and State, proved a great benefit to both. In the Denison controversy, it did not fare so well. G. A. Denison (q.v.), archdeacon of Taunton, was accused of teaching the real presence by virtue of consecration. A decision against him by the archbishop's court was reversed by the Judicial Committee on a formal technicality. The verdict of the archbishop's commission, however, denied the Tractarian claim to read between the lines of the Thirty-nine Articles and appeal to the Fathers of the English Church. Thus, a second time, the contention nearest to the heart of Tractarianism, the independent jurisdiction of the Church over its own affairs, was set at naught by the interference of the highest temporal court, a blow from which, on the dogmatic side, the Oxford

2. Papal Interference.

movement never recovered. From about 1860, therefore, it turned into the channels of ritualism.

IV. Ritualism: See separate article, RITUALISM.

V. The Ecclesiastical Services of the Oxford Movement: So long as the Oxford School preserved its prime object in its original purity, the war upon a liberalism which sought to encroach upon the rights of the church to control its own affairs, it was a power in the national church; but Newman's

1. Practical Influence.

subtle dialectic proved fatal to further development, the Puseyites gained a futile triumph in the vain battle against a state power of splendid heritage, and the ritualists diverted their strength in their special aim. Though stirring the English Church profoundly, yet in theological science, dogmatic, historical, and exegetical, it proved lamentably fruitless. It, however, paved the way for patristics in Pusey's *Library of the Fathers* (ut sup.) followed by *Library of Anglo-Catholic Theology* (89 vols., Oxford, 1841 sqq.), consisting of the writings of fifty-six great Anglicans of the school of Laud. Both works being " tendency " productions, they can not be regarded as scientific contributions. Unquestioned results, however, stand to the credit of the Anglo-Catholics in the field of practical theology. They succeeded where the first Oxford movement of Wesley and Whitefield had failed, viz., in converting the torpid church into a vital national power. Methodism the church expelled; Anglicanism it could not shake off. To the Oxford movement is due largely the awakening in the Established Church of profound devotion to the Catholic Church of the Fathers, which was abundantly fruitful in modern labors of love. Its crowning merit is the revived church spirit in the Establishment. By fifty years of labor in the cure of souls, its representatives created a new epoch. Not only have they won many of the higher circles that had become estranged from the Church, but by their unselfish work among the poor, the sick, and the outcast, the lower levels of society, too, were induced to love the Church. They built hospitals, asylums, schools, and missions; to them are due nine new English dioceses; and the number of foreign sees under the archbishop of Canterbury rose from 23 in 1877 to 170 in 1900. In London and throughout England model parishes arose in which this new energy flourished, and developed a multiple variety of philanthropic organization and effort, flowing even beyond parish boundaries. All these agencies are the result of an organization which, rivaling in refinement that of the Roman Catholic Church, scarcely has its like in anything else in all practical England. The center of this organization, which embraces Great Britain and the colonies, is the priestly Society of the Holy Cross, founded in 1853, but known publicly only since 1873. Its work, which is carried on secretly, is to supervise home and foreign missions, questions of ritual, the distribution of tracts and books of devotion, the confessional, public assemblies, and gilds and societies. The Cowley Fathers (Society of St. John the Evangelist; see PROTESTANT EPISCOPALIANS, II., § 7), who work among the imperiled and Protestants, and are bound by the triple vow, seem to be allied to the former. In 1862 was founded the Confraternity of the Blessed Sacrament, with its thousands of members, including bishops, priests, and laity, leagued for the ritual adornment of the services and the churches, fasting, prayers for the dead, the exaltation of the Eucharist, and daily confession and mass. The Association for Promoting the Unity of Christendom, whose membership is not published, seeks the reunion of the Anglican, Roman, and Greek communions; and there are, besides, the Order of Corporate Reunion, which reordains the clergy of the State Church and holds the Roman pope to be the first bishop and visible head of the Church, the Gild of All Souls, the Alcuin Club, and the Church Extension Association. The English Church Union has *The Church Union Gazette*, *The Church Times*, and *The Church Review*, as organs for the public defense and promotion of the Anglo-Catholic cause. To these agencies must be added the network of gilds, orders, brotherhoods, and sisterhoods, among them the English Benedictines, the founder of whom, Father Ignatius (see LYNE, JOSEPH LEYCESTER) founded a monastery in Wales for the training of missioners; and the English Order of St. Augustine, preparing candidates for ordination in strict seclusion and discipline. The sisterhoods, of which the first· was established by Pusey, devote themselves to· the care of the sick and now control nearly all the great hospitals of London, aided by the money and the services of thousands of women of the upper and middle classes.

Absorbed in ecclesiastical antiquity, where of necessity it planted its main standard of apostolic succession, and proceeding no further than the

2. Doctrine; The Church.

revival and adaptation of the body of dogmas of the sixteenth and seventeenth centuries, the Oxford movement added no new thoughts and revealed no new facts or laws. Purely historical, it owed a great deal of its impetus to the contemporary rise of scientific historical method and, by its doting upon the past, contributed no little to the revival of romanticism. Without a creed or doctrinal writings of its own, except those of the Anglican Church, and having for its objects of contention far-reaching fundamentals affecting the right of ecclesiastical autonomy and outlying ritualistic adjustments rather than specific dogmas, it is difficult properly to present its teaching. To the private Tractarian literature, predominantly ascetic, belong, J. Purchas' *Directorium Anglicanum* (London, 1858; 4th enlarged ed., by F. G. Lee, 1879); T. T. Carter's *Treasury of Devotion* (London, 1869); William Gresley's *Ordinance of Confession* (London, 1851); *The People's Hymnal* (1867) by R. F. Littledale; besides a formidable array of breviaries, manuals, and ordinances, to be treated with precaution against their subjective, unwholesome modes of thought. A picture of the Tractarian teaching in outline therefore narrows itself to the deviations from the Thirty-nine Articles, and a consensus of the promulgations of the Oxford .school; namely, on the sources of religious knowledge, the means of grace, the Church, the apostolic succession, the real presence, and the derivative ideas from these subjects. The absolute truth is given objectively; the function of thought or spirit is not speculative inquiry but the interpretation of authoritative dogma given by the primitive Church. The Scriptures are held in a general sense only to be the rule of faith; but they require exegesis because of their manifold meaning, and supplementing because of their incompleteness. Valuable for right doctrine, they contain practically nothing concerning church discipline, liturgy, and government, and must be explained by tradition, which preceded the New Testament and formed the canon. They must be supplemented by the uniform consensus of the Fathers, the Roman Catholic bishops, and the ecumenical councils. For example, the witness of the entire Church at Nicæa determined the doctrine of the Trinity as true according to Scripture for the entire Church, whether understood or not. The Church is the sole divinely appointed authority for the interpretation of the Scriptures, the mediator of the doctrine and grace of the sacraments, and the total organic spring and norm of all its activities in liturgy, organization, and discipline. Presented as the original, generic, prophetic type, the Church is to be an object, like Word and sacrament, of reverent awe, the absolute foundation of all truth, even in the deeper mysteries and symbolic interpretations in which the entire teaching is not always revealed, thus leading, among the more advanced wing, to a distinction between exoteric and esoteric truth. Established on the apostolic foundation in faith and practise, the Church is the source of grace for all ages. This grace is communicated alone through the objective power of the sacraments. The only way to salvation is through the acceptance of the Eucharist, the efficacy of which depends on its ministration by the priest in virtue of his power derived by the succession of the bishops from the apostles, whereby the perpetuation and right dispensation of the sacrament are guaranteed.

This doctrine of the apostolic succession was central to all the factions of the movement in common, from its inception to its ultimate issues. Pronounced the arch-pillar of the priestly office, the defense against the encroachment of

3. **Apostolic Succession.** the power of the State upon the Church made it of necessity the ecclesiastical bulwark. Assumed to be implied in the ancient Anglican formula of ordination, it was brought to the front by the Tractarians in their resistance to the State. The gift depends on the laying on of hands and not on any formula attending the act, nor is it necessarily involved in the overseeing function of the episcopate, seeing that the apostles conferred it upon priests and deacons also. Therefore, to avoid, in consequence of this statement, the claim advanced by non-episcopal communions, the Oxford school maintained that history shows that from the apostolic age to the Reformation, and from that time in all true churches, ordination has been given by bishops. Nor is this succession merely a following in preaching, ministration of the sacraments, and the power of the keys, but a holy gift (Keble), preserved through time by the apostolic succession alone and its essen-

tial significance (Froude). Whoever is not a link in this chain has no right either to the office or to the administration of the sacrament. Inasmuch as the commission of Christ alone gives efficacy to Word and sacrament, this teaching leads further to the doctrine of the sole and necessary mediatorship of the priesthood between Christ and believers, and to the distinction between the clergy and the laity. The Oxford school sought to demonstrate also the historical continuity of the State Church from the apostles. The proof in individual detail being relinquished as impossible, it was replaced, historically, by the argument of probability found to be in the ratio of 8,000 to one, and dogmatically by Newman's theory of knowledge, that theoretical, inadequate probability becomes certainty by the supplement of the assumption of faith. Admitting that away from the proofs of reason and the facts of history and experience, the argument of emotional probability lends itself alike to faith and superstition, Newman finally converts it to one of positive authority, construing I Cor. xi. 23–24 in the sense that Christ conferred on the disciples as priests the gift of consecration. Linking this with the promotion of Titus and Timothy as bishops and the episcopate in the primitive Church, he thought that he had established the absolute necessity of episcopal consecration, falling back on the authority of the Church where Scripture was insufficient. To sum up, the sacrament is the material principle to which the Church is the correlate means or formal principle, representing the mediatorship of Christ. Fundamental and supreme is the principle of the sacrament as the sole means of saving grace. The visible Church assures participation in the invisible, and without the former there is no salvation; but, in turn, the essential mark of the true Church, inclusive of catholicity, apostolicity, and autonomy, is the apostolic succession. Hence the Anglican is the most perfect on earth. The Roman Catholic has the apostolic communion but has departed from the apostolic tradition (papal power and infallibility). The Greek Church has preserved this communion and doctrine more purely. Other episcopal churches, beside the Anglican, are healthy branches, while the non-episcopal churches, or sects, are amputated limbs, which may have retained the apostolic teaching or not, yet possess no apostolic office and no means of salvation.

The sacramental doctrine of the Oxford movement starting upon the basis of the Anglican Confession is an attempt to extend and deepen the Roman Catholic by strong emphasis upon regeneration. To the Calvinistic conception defined in the catechism, that the sacraments are effectual testimonies of divine grace, was opposed that they were the channels which conduct divine grace to the soul, closed by unbelief and opened by faith. Both sacraments are essentially one, natural man being regenerated through baptism, and this new

4. **The Sacraments; Baptism.** life being developed by the Eucharist, so that, as Pusey and Newman state, they form the sole means or rites of justification for atonement. Those who allege that the new spiritual life is due to the act of faith, not to the gift of God in the sacrament,

are met by the declaration of the objective reality of grace in the sacrament (*ex opere operato*). Penitent faith that justifies is a divine act in the subject, impotent without prevenient and cooperating grace. Man is justified before works, but potentially the future new obedience is contained through the grace of God in the justifying faith. God gives eternal life according to one's works and not as a free gift according to his good pleasure. The Anglican Confession had represented baptism as a testimony invariably associated with profession and regeneration, but prominent theologians of the State Church, under the influence of the Westminster Confession, had departed from this teaching, holding that the baptism of the Spirit was restricted to the elect, not in virtue of the sacramental act, but of the " absolute decree," while the non-elect were merely sprinkled with water. In the Gorham Case the judicial committee has declared this modification admissible, despite the Tractarian protests. Pusey opposed the new construction on the basis of John iii. 5; Titus iii. 5; I John iii. 9; I Pet. i. 23, as well as a strong array of patristic and creedal authority. Regeneration is instantaneous with baptism, by an act of God, contrary to the opinion of Evangelical parties that it takes place through the life of repentance, faith, prayer, and love. Several in the heat of emphasis, like Newman, Ward, and Carter, advanced to extremes with difficulty to be distinguished from the Roman Catholic; while admitting imputation in baptism, they laid main stress on the infusion of the Holy Spirit.

According to the Thirty-nine Articles, the Eucharist is not only a token of love among Christians, but a sacrament of redemption by Christ's death (xxviii.); the body of Christ is given and eaten in

5. The Real Presence. a heavenly and spiritual manner by faith. The Catechism, on the other hand, distinguishes between the " sign " (bread and wine) and the " thing signified " (the body and blood of Christ).

Tractarianism strongly emphasized the element of imparting and based its Eucharistic views on the Fathers and early Anglicanism. The consecrated elements become truly, though mystically, the body and blood of Christ; and Christ really present communicates himself to the believing unto salvation, but to the unbelieving unto damnation. This is the doctrine of the real presence, represented as the essential in the sacrament by all Tractarians in common, amid all the variants of opinion as to the manner or means. Perceval declares that he and his colleagues take the real presence as sacramental, spiritual, and mystical, while the Roman Catholics regard the same as substantial, corporeal, and miraculous. According to Wilberforce the sacrament is an objective fact, independent of the cooperation and assent of the recipient and carrying out the redemption begun in the incarnation of Christ. Pusey (*The Presence of Christ in the Holy Eucharist*, Oxford, 1853; *Doctrine of the Real Presence as Contained in the Fathers*, 1855; *The Real Presence*, 1857) sums up his view that the consecration elements become by virtue of the words of consecration of Christ (not the priests') truly and actually, though in a spiritual and inexpressible way, his body and blood.

To him all centers upon the consecration, committed by Christ to authorized persons, through the apostolic commission to the bishops and under them to the priests. Without the act of the right priest there is no consecration and no sacrament. It is the Roman conception and the sacrament is an *opus operatum*. As to the manner, most of the Tractarians represent a consubstantiation or conjunction of the elements with the body and blood of Christ objectively created by Christ's words of consecration. In view of the thorough adherence to the real objective presence in the elements, this consubstantiation can be regarded only in the sense of transubstantiation, though in a more refined and spiritual way, as also Newman would have it. The doctrine of the real presence develops into the further concept of the Eucharist as a sacrifice. This is not, however, a repetition of the sacrifice on the cross, for Christ was sacrificed once for all time, but by the sacrifice at the altar are appropriated the forgiveness of sins and the justification and reception of the sinner in the sight of God, rendered possible by the sacrifice on Calvary. This is involved in the larger thesis that not only is Christ offered as the subject of the sacrament, but the Church as the mystical body is included. The Eucharist, therefore, represents the offered collective Church and Christ, as well as the offering Christ and mystical body, the Church. Finally, from the doctrine of the real presence followed the conclusion, on the one hand, upon the objective real efficacy of the Eucharist, when it came to be generally held that not only the elements, but also the present Christ is received by worthy and unworthy alike, by the former to salvation and the latter to damnation. On the other hand, the doctrine led to the adoration of the body and blood of Christ, which were said to be really and truly present in the species of bread and wine; though to the elements themselves no adoration may be paid (Denison). Confession, in the Church of England, is left to the discretion of the individual. Tractarianism, however, made both confession and absolution sacraments and indispensable aids to salvation, ascribing to both the restoration of baptismal regeneration lost by sin, and the perfecting of the spiritual life. Absolution was not to be a declaratory act, but the judicial act of the priest. (The man who confesses to God may be forgiven, but who confesses to a priest must be forgiven.—*Tract for the Days*, 1.) Since, moreover, the priest, to give absolution, must have the confession not alone of the general sinful state of the penitent, but also of his individual sins, auricular confession, not required by the official Church, necessarily follows. It was also zealously promoted by the ritualists, calling forth a rich ascetic literature (cf. William Gresly, ut sup.; T. T. Carter's *Doctrine of Confession*, London, 1865; and the anonymous *The Priest in Absolution*, part i., 1866, and part ii., 1886, as guide for the clergy only).

In historical retrospect the Tractarian movement signifies the attempted logical conclusion of the uncompleted reaction on the part of the great Anglicans from Bishop Andrewes to Bishop Ken against the non-Catholic elements of the Reformation of the sixteenth century; or the restoration of the national Church according to the tendency of the reign of Edward VI. On the claim of histori-

6. Sacred Art.
cal, dogmatic, and organic continuity from the primitive Church and the repudiation of Roman medieval abuses, it insisted upon both names of reformed and Catholic. Dogmatically, the Oxford movement signified the transmutation of the ideal subjective life values into objective sensible facts; of inner experience into outer representation, of faith into works. Its aim was a church of outer realities, for which, as a final organism, it cherished the control of all activities, religious, educational, domestic, economic, and political. The wide and varied influence of the Oxford movement is in the highest degree apparent in a revival and deepening of the church spirit. It redeemed the Establishment from barren inactivity, spiritless superficiality, the ease of indulgence, and slavish formalism. It charged it with the priestly spirit, and spurred it to those heroic deeds that spring from the depths of the soul and lead to the heights of the passion for eternity. The truth and goodness that it contained worked on, while only its extreme Romanizing tendencies were lost behind. Undisputed results appear on the field of social effort and redemption. In its elevation of art Tractarianism created an ecclesiastical esthetic which served to reclaim many from the upper strata of society estranged from the Church. The danger of " perversion to Rome," so feared in the fifth and sixth decades of the last century, no longer exists, and it is now perceived that the Tractarians give to those of a mystical craving the satisfaction the lack of which would lead them to the faith of Rome. The results of the Roman propaganda have been brought to abeyance, and in the High-church party, into which it infused its cultus and cure of souls, ritualism has obtained a broad footing in the life of the Church. The Tractarian love for the early Catholic period has likewise influenced ecclesiastical architecture, painting, and music. Largely through its members, anticipated, as they were, by the Church Building Society in 1818–33, many ancient cathedrals and parish churches have been restored to their early beauty and stripped of hideous " improvements." New churches have been erected according to the best ancient models, and the interiors have been richly and tastefully decorated. In religious painting they have been pioneers, and it is no mere coincidence that the Pre-Raffaelites found their inspiration in the days of Tractarianism, seeking their ideal, like the Oxford movement, in the past, when all things visible confessed Christ, and when art, the handmaid of the Church, endeavored to express first truth, and then beauty. In music, by returning to the classics and by the formation of admirable choirs, the Tractarians checked the spreading dilettanteism, and, as in other instances, they transmitted their wholesome influence to all church circles.   (RUDOLPH BUDDENSIEG†.)

BIBLIOGRAPHY: Consult the articles in this work on the participants in the movement, the literature named in and under those articles, and further, the following: *Tracts for the Times, by Members of the University of Oxford,* 6 vols., and Index, London, 1833–42; J. B. Mozley, *Remains of Richard Hurrell Froude,* 4 vols., ib. 1838–39; J. Pridham, *The Church of England, as to her Excellencies and Defects,* ib. 1842; W. Palmer, *Narrative of Events Connected with the Publication of the Tracts for the Times,* ib. 1843; I. Taylor, *Ancient Christianity and the Doctrines of the Oxford Tracts for the Times,* ib. 1844; W. S. Bricknell, *The Judgment of the Bishops upon the Tractarian Theology,* ib. 1845; H. H. Beamish, *Truth Spoken in Love; or Romanism and Tractarianism refuted by the Word of God,* ib. 1853; J. C. Hare, *The Contest with Rome,* in *Charges to the Clergy,* vol. iii., Cambridge, 1856; E. G. Browne, *Annals of the Tractarian Movement, 1842–60,* London, 1861; C. H. Collette, *Dr. Newman and his Religious Opinions,* ib. 1866; J. J. Overbeck, *Catholic Orthodoxy and Anglo-Catholicism,* ib. 1866; Sir J. T. Coleridge, *A Memoir of the Rev. John Keble,* 2d ed., 2 vols., ib. 1874; J. Tulloch, *Movements of Religious Thought . . . during the 19th Century,* new ed., Edinburgh, 1874; T. Mozley, *Reminiscences chiefly of Oriel College and the Oxford Movement,* 2 vols., Boston, 1882; N. Pattison, *Memoirs,* London, 1885; E. A. Abbott, *The Anglican Career of Cardinal Newman,* 2 vols., ib. 1892; R. W. Church, *The Oxford Movement . . . 1843–55,* new ed., London and New York, 1892; W. Ward, *William George Ward and the Oxford Movement,* 2d ed., London, 1890; idem, *William George Ward and the Catholic Revival,* ib. 1893; G. Worley, *The Catholic Revival of the 19th Century,* ib. 1895; G. Wakeling, *Oxford Church Movement,* London and New York, 1895; J. Hunt, *Religious Thought in the 19th Century,* London, 1896; G. H. F. Nye, *Story of the Oxford Movement,* ib. 1899; J. H. Rigg, *Oxford High Anglicanism and its chief Leaders,* ib. 1899; W. Walsh, *Secret Hist. of the Oxford Movement,* ib. 1899; idem, *Hist. of the Romeward Movement in the Church of England,* ib. 1900; G. W. E. Russell, *The Household of Faith,* ib. 1903; W. S. Lilly, in his *Studies in Religion and Literature,* London and St. Louis, 1904; F. Meyrick, *Memories of Life at Oxford,* London, 1905; Sir S. Hall, *Short. Hist. of the Oxford Movement,* ib. 1906; A. B. Donaldson, *Five Great Oxford Leaders,* new ed., ib. 1908.

TRACY, CHARLES CHAPIN: Presbyterian; b. at Smithfield, Pa., Oct. 31, 1838. He was educated at Williams College (B.A., 1864) and Union Theological Seminary (1867). In 1867 he went to Marsovan, Turkey, as a missionary of the American Board of Commissioners for Foreign Missions. With the exception of three years (1870–73) spent in Constantinople, he has since remained at Marsovan, where, in 1884, he established a high school that developed into Anatolia College, of which he has been president since 1886. Of his English works the most important are *Myra: or, A Child's Story of Missionary Life* (Boston, 1876) and *Talks on the Veranda in a Far-Away Land* (1893).

TRADITION: In present-day Protestant usage, the body of faith and practise resting upon oral testimony in distinction from the written record of Holy Scripture. This limitation of the term was not known to the early Church. Primitive Christians received the apostolic message by word of mouth as well as by pen and passed it on orally from generation to generation by public preaching and catechetical instruction (cf. Irenæus, *Hær.*, III., iii., iv. 1–2; G. Thomasius, *Dogmengeschichte,* i. 37 sqq., Erlangen, 1874). Naturally, therefore, they considered and called the entire and complete message " tradition " (*traditio* from *tradere,* " to hand on ") regardless of the form in which it was delivered or preserved. The manner of transmission was rather that of free reproduction, yet the matter received early more or less of a fixed form; and a noteworthy agreement in essential content, which had its beginnings at least before the controversy with Gnosticism (cf. Irenæus, *Hær.*, I., x. 2), is attested almost contemporaneously and for widely separated sections of the Church by Irenæus, Tertullian, and Origen (cf. Thomasius, ut sup., p. 38). There is no express statement of the content of this current oral tradition; but beyond doubt it· is summed up in the baptismal confession (the so-called Apostles' Creed) and the "Rule of Faith" (see REGULA FIDEI). The third century also makes no distinction between oral and written tradition.

Church Fathers who defended the authenticity and validity of tradition nevertheless warned against setting too high a value upon it (Tertullian, *De virginibus velandis*, i.; Cyprian, *Epist.* lxxiv. [lxxv.]). They also acknowledged the adequacy of Scripture (Athanasius, *Oratio adv. gentes* (vol. i., part. i.; Augustine, *De doctrina Christiana*, ii. 9). Yet Augustine declared " I would not believe Scripture if the authority of the Church catholic did not impel me " (*Contra epist. Manichæi*, v.), meaning that the opinion of the Church catholic determined the books properly belonging to Scripture (cf. F. Loofs, *Dogmengeschichte*, § xliv. 1, Halle, 1906). The Church settled the New-Testament canon by means of tradition; and, being regarded as apostolic, tradition came to be the test of apostolicity, and this easily led to an overestimation of it. It became a source of Christian truth by the side of the Scriptures and was appealed to in support of propositions which are not found in the Bible or are found there only doubtfully. Chrysostom regarded the "unwritten deliverances" of the apostles as much matter of faith as their letters (on II Thess., *Homilia* iv., in *Opera*, xii. 385, cited in W. Münscher, *Handbuch der . . . Dogmengeschichte*, iii. 137, 4 vols., Marburg, 1809–18), and, before him, the orthodox Epiphanius expressly taught the validity of tradition by the side of the Scriptures (*Hær.*, lxi. 6). This became the doctrine of the Eastern Church (John of Damascus, *De fide orthodoxa*, iv. 12; Loofs, ut sup., § xliv.). Augustine, as already quoted, represents the same tendency in the West; and his opponent, Vincent of Lerins, declared that " the line of interpretation of prophets and apostles must follow the opinion of the Church catholic " (*Commonitorium*, ii.), and formulated the canon of catholicity (" that is catholic which has been believed always, everywhere, and by everybody," ib. iii.).

Throughout the Middle Ages it was orthodox doctrine that divine revelation flows in two streams— Bible and tradition. There was no advance in the teaching concerning revelation in general except that in the West, after Aristotle was made known by Mohammedan scholars, the natural reason was added as a third source of some knowledge of God (e.g., of his existence and unity; cf. Thomas Aquinas cited in Münscher, ut sup., ii. 1, p. 100). In the East the tendency was steadily to make the Bible secondary to oral tradition. It is true that individuals here and there in the West, influenced by widely different motives, raised a voice of protest against the supremacy of tradition; but they failed to produce any far-reaching or abiding effect. Abelard set contradictory utterances of the Fathers side by side in 157 rubrics in his *Sic et non*, and was condemned for it. The Waldenses fared still worse when they promoted Bible reading and so in a meas-

ure cut loose from tradition (cf. the edicts of the councils of Toulouse in 1229 and Tarragona in 1234; texts in Münscher, ut sup., ii. 1, p. 109). It was the so-called reformers before the Reformation who first challenged tradition clearly and boldly as a second source of Christian truth (cf. Wyclif, *Trial*, iv. 7, p. 199; Loofs, ut sup., § lxxii. 5); and it was in the Reformation that the doctrine of Scripture was thoroughly and earnestly developed.

The Reformation started with no special theory of Scripture. But as Luther developed his doctrine of justification by faith he found himself constantly compelled to appeal more and more to the written word of God and to discard all traditions of the Church. That sure testimony to the revelation of salvation is offered only in the Bible became the fundamental doctrine of the Reformation (cf. Thomasius, ut sup., ii. 197). Since Protestantism, however, believes that the Holy Spirit has always been present in the Church, it does not reject indiscriminately all tradition. It retains whatever of doctrine has the certain support of Scripture (cf. P. Tschackert, *Polemik*, pp. 3, 96, Gotha, 1885) and in matters of rite and ceremony it keeps what is not contradictory to Scripture. The Roman Church, on the other hand, decreed at Trent (session iv.) that divine truth is derived from two sources, Scripture and tradition, and that the latter is to be regarded with the same reverence as the former. It practically made tradition the first source by declaring that the Bible is to be interpreted by it (cf. Loofs, ut sup., § lxxiv. 2), the reason being that certain of its dogmas and rites—the mass and its ceremonies, the consecration of priests, the tonsure, the marriage sacrament, extreme unction, purgatory—have no Biblical ground and must be justified by extra-Biblical tradition. In promulgating the two latest Roman dogmas—the immaculate conception and the universal episcopate of the pope—the Roman Church has departed from Vincent of Lerins, and to cover the infallibility dogma, the jesuitical theology has made a new definition—" tradition is what has been taught as such in the Church of Rome." Further, the pope becomes the Church. Pius IX. declared " I am tradition," and wrote to the archbishop of Cologne (text in Tschackert, ut sup., p. 407, note 16) that the mere fact that a dogma is defined by the pope is sure and sufficient proof for all that it is founded in Scripture and tradition.

(P. TSCHACKERT†.)

BIBLIOGRAPHY: The subject is often treated in Protestant works on systematic theology (see DOGMA, DOGMATICS), and in all complete treatises of that subject by· Roman Catholics, since in the Roman Church it is so important a theme. The works on the history of doctrine also deal with it. Consult especially: E. van Ess, *Chrysostomus oder Stimmen der Kirchenväter über das nützliche und erbauliche Bibellesen*, Darmstadt, 1824 (Roman Catholic); J. L. Jacobi, *Die kirchliche Lehre von der Tradition und heiligen Schrift*, Berlin, 1847; J. H. Friedlieb, *Schrift, Tradition und Schriftauslegung*, Breslau, 1854 (Roman Catholic); A. Neander, *Christliche Dogmengeschichte*, ed. J. L. Jacobi, i. 75 sqq., 286–293, ii. 196 sqq., Berlin, 1857; idem, *Christian Church*, consult Index; H. J. Holtzmann, *Kanon und Tradition*, Ludwigsburg, 1859; J. Schwane, *Dogmengeschichte*, 2 vols., Münster, 1862–90 (Roman Catholic); F. Speil, *Die Lehren der katholischen Kirche gegenüber der protestantischen Polemik*, Freiburg, 1865 (Roman Catholic); F. Nitzsch, *Grundriss der christlichen Dogmengeschichte*, i. 243–268, Berlin, 1870; K. Hase,

Polemik, pp. 64–94, 3d ed., Leipsic, 1871; J. Bach, *Dogmengeschichte des Mittelalters*, 2 parts, Vienna, 1873–75 (Roman Catholic); C. Ullmann, *Reformers before the Reformation*, passim, 2 vols., Edinburgh, 1874–77; H. Reuter, *Geschichte der religiösen Aufklärung im Mittelalter*, 2 vols., Berlin, 1875–77; J. B. Heinrich, *Dogmatische Theologie*, vol. ii., Mainz, 1876 (Roman Catholic); P. Tschackert, *Evangelische Polemik gegen die römische Kirche*, pp. 91 sqq., Gotha, 1885; S. J. Hunter, *Outlines of Dogmatic Theology*, §§ 77–85, 93–109, 339, 795, 3 vols., New York, 1896; F. Kropatscheck, *Das Schriftprinzip der lutherischen Kirche*, vol. i., Leipsic, 1904; Harnack, *Dogma*, passim, consult Index (well worth noting); *KL*, xi. 1933–1971; Lichtenberger, *ESR*, xii. 191–199.

TRADUCIANISM. See SOUL AND SPIRIT.

TRAJAN, trê′jan, **MARCUS ULPIUS:** Roman emperor (98–117); b. at Italica (6 Roman m. n.w. of Seville), Spain, Sept. 18, 52; d. at Selinus on the west coast of Cilicia, Asia Minor, about Aug. 7, 117. His father was a high provincial officer of Latin origin; the son adopted his father's martial career, and was long posted at various points occupied by the Roman army both east and west. In the year 91 he obtained the consulate, but first came significantly into public notice in 97, when Nerva put him in command of Upper Germany, and adopted him in the same year. Trajan came to the throne Jan. 27, 98. He proved himself equal to the imminent military dangers that menaced the realm, and directed his energy to the task of girdling the Roman Empire with secure defenses. He was distinguished by sober judgment and maturely weighed action. While he veiled the strong sense of his imperial sovereignty under the semblance of freedom, his firmness and strength of will left ample room for personal affability and the practical exercise of contemporary modes of benevolence. The latter trait found particular expression in comprehensive provision for orphan children (cf. G. Uhlhorn, *Die christliche Liebestätigkeit in der alten Kirche*, i. 16 sqq., Stuttgart, 1882; Eng. transl., *Christian Charity in the Early Church*, p. 18, New York, 1883). His education was of average compass, and he highly cherished intercourse with poets and scholars. The weal of the realm in equity and good order was the unselfish goal of his policy. Under him the classic Roman Empire stands forth, for the last time, in the entire fulness of its political magnitude.

Trajan's religious views appear in thorough harmony with conventional popular piety. But formal piety was restricted within the general bounds of his personal and imperial ideals; hence not his religion but his political judgment was the root of that imperial decision which immediately connects his name with the Christian Church.

After Trajan had brought the province of Bithynia Pontus under control of the imperial government, he sent thither to restore order the Younger Pliny, a man stirred, like his chief, by the philanthropic ideas of that age. In the progress of a journey through the province, and dating down to the beginning of the year 113, he wrote sixty letters to Trajan, wherein he communicated his observations, and requested advice on all possible questions that crossed his path. These letters, together with Trajan's answers, are extant in chronological order (best edition with notes by Hardy, London, 1889). This province had a strong Jewish population. The Apos-

tle Paul once purposed to visit it, but was hindered by the Spirit (Acts xvi. 7 sqq.); Christians are included for Pontus and Bithynia among those addressed in I Pet. i. 1. Only in the eastern districts, perhaps at Amisus, was Pliny confronted with the Christian issue, and the situation is described in his famous letter no. 96. Trajan incisively adopted the policy of surveillance of corporate life as inaugurated by Julius Cæsar, especially in turbulent districts, and enforced a rigorous execution of the prohibition of *collegia*. It was in this sense that Pliny received a strict command with regard to the province in his charge.

Pliny perceived himself face to face with a wide extension of Christianity in town and country. Both sexes and all ages and ranks were implicated in the new faith; consequently, the worship of the gods was in neglect. Pliny felt that his responsibility embraced the right maintenance of the state religion, and interfered by virtue of his office. Capital sentence was executed upon persons confessing their charge when duly brought to trial and found guilty, save that Roman citizens were to be transported to the metropolis. But the situation grew more complex, and doubts possessed Pliny concerning the expediency or the justice of acts of repression. In view of the difficulties, from which Pliny saw no exit, an appeal was made to the emperor's decision. The imperial answer recognized the fundamental correctness of the course pursued by Pliny. Trajan regarded the Christian confession as an offense worthy of capital sentence. The matter of supplying standards of procedure for treating concrete forms and instances was declined on grounds of impossibility; but secret inquisition and attention to anonymous reports were forbidden. Lastly, those who renounced their adherence to Christianity by sacrificing to the gods were to go clear. Where such allegiance was judicially proved, the death sentence was to follow.

Two points are significant in this rescript—the preconceived culpability of the *nomen Christianum* and the offsetting legal alleviations. Opinions long diverged in respect to the import and bearings of this decision; but Theodore Mommsen's basic study, *Der Religionsfrevel nach römischem Recht* (*Historische Zeitschrift*, 1890), has cleared up the subject. The entire procedure rests in the so-called *coercitio* or official repression, not tied down to any defined forms of trial, but administered with reference to the maintenance of public order (see PERSECUTION OF THE CHRISTIANS IN THE ROMAN EMPIRE). Among eminent martyrs during Trajan's administration were Ignatius of Antioch and Simeon of Jerusalem (qq.v.).

Trajan came into conflict with the Jews, who started a furious insurrection in Egypt and Cyrene (115 A.D.), which soon spread to Cyprus. The emperor, just then detained in Mesopotamia, succeeded only after a severe campaign in mastering the situation through his field commander, Marcus Turbo (117).   VICTOR SCHULTZE.

BIBLIOGRAPHY: An extensive literature, much of which is pertinent, may be found under PERSECUTION OF CHRISTIANS. Consult further: H. Francke, *Zur Geschichte Trajans*, Leipsic, 1840; J. Dierauer, *Beiträge zu einer kritischen Geschichte Trajans*, ib. 1868; F. Overbeck, *Studien zur Geschichte der alten Kirche,* vol. i., Schloss Chemnitz, 1875; T. Keim, *Rom und das Christenthum,* Berlin, 1881; H. Schiller, *Geschichte der römischen Kaiserzeit,* vol. i., part 2, Gotha, 1883; V. Duruy, *Hist. of Rome and the Roman People,* 6 vols., London, 1883–86; T. Mommsen, *The Roman Provinces,* ib. 1887; F. Arnold, *Studien zur Geschichte der plinianischen Christenverfolgung,* Königsberg, 1887; P. Allard, *Hist. des persécutions pendant les deux premiers siècles,* chap. iii., Paris, 1892; W. E. Addis, *Christianity and the Roman Empire,* pp. 69–71, London, 1893; W. M. Ramsay, *The Church in the Roman Empire,* passim, New York, 1893; E. G. Hardy, *Christianity and the Roman Government,* pp. 102–124, London, 1894; Schaff, *Christian Church,* vol. ii., chap. ii., and in general works on the history of the Church and the history of the Empire of the period; Gibbon, *Decline and Fall,* chap. iii.

TRANSCENDENTALISM IN NEW ENGLAND.

Philosophical Background (§ 1).
Preparatory Movements (§ 2).
The " Transcendental Club " (§ 3).
The " Atmosphere of Reform " (§ 4).
Relation to Reforms and Religion (§ 5).
Influence of Transcendentalism (§ 6).

Toward the end of the eighteenth century and the beginning of the nineteenth, a strong reaction took place against materialism. As philosophy, it began in Germany. Voltaire brought from London to Paris the ideas of Hume. From Paris they

1. Philosophical Background. went with him to the court of Frederick, king of Prussia, and became ruling principles of thought. Kant subjected them to searching analysis in his famous *Critique of Pure Reason,* and became the leader in a great philosophical reform. Materialism took no deep root in the German mind. The great names in German idealism are Kant, Fichte, Schelling, and Hegel; and the sequence of their doctrine, so far as it can be conveyed in few words, is as follows: Kant sounded the depths of the human mind; Fichte imparted reality to the idea of the human person; Schelling combined the inward and the outward by supposing an Absolute, which he called reason; Hegel transformed what was to him the unsubstantial reason into a being, thus completing, as is claimed, the fundamental " categories " of Kant. The word " transcendentalism " is of Kantian origin. It means that which is valid beyond the experience of the senses, though present to the knowledge of the mind. It describes a form of idealism. In the judgment of James Hutchison Stirling, " The transcendental philosophy is a philosophy of the merely speculative pure reason; for all moral practise, so far as it involves motive, refers to feeling, and feeling is always of empirical origin." Again: " I call all cognition transcendental which is occupied not so much with objects as with the process by which we come to know them, in so far as that process has an a priori element. A system of such elements would be a transcendental philosophy." In France, materialism was represented by Condillac, Cabanis (author of the saying that " brain secretes thought, as the liver secretes bile "), and others; idealism, by Marie de Beràn, Destutt de Tracy, Cousin, Jouffroy, and others. In England, not to mention the poets who are always idealistic, Coleridge reflected Schelling, and Carlyle, Goethe and Richter. Coleridge's *Aids to Reflection* and *Friend* were early reprinted in America. The writings of Carlyle—articles, reviews, essays (produced from 1827 onward), *Signs of the Times, Characteristics,* later, *Sartor Resartus*— were eagerly read in American editions. So far as this goes, Transcendentalism was of foreign extraction, an invasion of the German intellect.

It would be a serious and unpardonable mistake, however, " to regard the transcendental movements as a simple importation from abroad, a servile imitation of English, French, or German

2. Preparatory Movements. ideas. It was," says a somewhat recent writer on the subject, " at the last remove from this, and was full of the sap of a spontaneity and freshness all its own. . . . Nine-tenths of the early transcendentalists rubbed but slightly against Kant, Fichte, Goethe, Schleiermacher, Schelling; but it was fructifying pollen they bore away from the contact, and by it their own minds were vitally impregnated." The whole movement was a spiritual outburst, a vital sense of newness, a local or New England renaissance, the roots of which reached far back into the past, but its flowers bloomed with a richness and a fresh luxuriance such as were possible nowhere else so well as on the shores of this new world. The soil for it had been carefully prepared. Materialism was abroad in New England, sometimes implicitly, sometimes by formal statement. Unitarianism, from which transcendentalism was an offshoot, if not indeed an outgrowth, was itself a protest, on the ground of common sense, against " Orthodoxy " and " Evangelicalism," and was infected with the metaphysics of John Locke. It was a system of rationalism—prosaic, critical, unimaginative. Its teaching, like most of the religious teaching of the day, was formal, and its worship at the time was becoming uninspiring. It was, in the main, a negative system, its forms mechanical, its beliefs traditional, its associations conventional. The elder men, like Channing and Lowell, retained the sentiments of piety which they had brought with them from the faith they had left, but the new movement had begun to lose something of its original enthusiasm. Meanwhile a spirit of individualism was in the air, running occasionally into deism and even atheism. In 1832 Abner Kneeland founded *The Investigator;* in 1836 he was prosecuted for blasphemy. There was a general interest in clairvoyance, mesmerism, and kindred doctrines. As early as 1824 F. H. Hedge, a Unitarian minister, raised the banner of revolt (in *The Christian Examiner* for November) against the materialism implied in phrenology, which even then was getting possession of the public mind. There was a rage for the expositions of Gall. The popular lectures of Spurzheim were attended by crowds. Later, Combe's book on the " Constitution of Man " was hailed as a gospel. Regeneration by bread was proclaimed in the name of Graham. Every kind of medicament was called in to do the work of the Holy Spirit.

At this juncture, idealism appeared in the shape of a protest against the drift of the time toward animalism and externalism. The soil was prepared by orthodox mystics, who proclaimed " the life of God in the soul of man "; by the spiritualism taught by Jonathan Edwards; by the Reformed Quakers, with their doctrine of an all-sufficing " inner light ";

by the traditions of Abby Hutchinson, Mary Dwyer, and the apostles of soul-freedom. Not that the positions taken by these men and women were the same as those assumed by the transcendentalists. They were indeed quite different, in fact precisely opposite; for those all recognized some supernatural authority, whereas the transcendentalists as a class were pure " intuitionalists," believers in the inspiration of the individual soul; but they looked only at apparent results, disregarding adjacent beliefs. The leaders were young men, almost without exception, educated for the ministry, Unitarians, members of the best class in society, eloquent speakers and talkers, scholars, men of liberal culture, outspoken in the declaration of their opinions. Of these Ralph Waldo Emerson was chief, most seraphic and persuasive, most uncompromising, too, in his ecclesiastical action. He resigned his charge as a Unitarian minister in 1832, because of scruples in regard to the " communion service," which he regarded as a spiritual rite and was willing to continue as such, but not as an ordinance imposed by Church or Scripture. Later, he was unwilling to offer public prayer, except when so disposed, and retired from the pulpit altogether, making the secular platform his sole visible elevation above the multitude—an elevation not of authority, but of convenience. A few young men gathered around him. In September of 1836, at the celebration of the two-hundredth anniversary of the foundation of Harvard College, four persons—Emerson, Hedge, Ripley, and Putnam—met together in Cambridge, and, after discussing the theological and ecclesiastical situation, agreed to call a meeting of a few like-minded, with a view to strengthen each other in their opposition to the old way, and see what could be done to inaugurate a better. At a preliminary meeting at the house of George Ripley, in Boston, there were present Emerson, Hedge, Alcott, Bartol, Brownson, and Bartlett (a young tutor at Cambridge). Then and there it was resolved, on invitation of Emerson, to hold a convention at his house in Concord during the same month of September. Invitations were sent to as many as were known or supposed to be in sympathy with the objects of the meeting. From fifteen to twenty came, among them, William Henry Channing, John Sullivan Dwight, James Freeman Clarke, Ephraim Peabody, Chandler Robbins, George P. Bradford, Mrs. Samuel Ripley, Margaret Fuller, Elizabeth Peabody, perhaps Theodore Parker. Convers Francis and Caleb Stetson were the only men of the older generation who took a practical interest in the movement. Channing was in sympathy with its general aims, but took no active part at the time. His contemporaries either did not appear, or immediately withdrew. The public got intelligence of the Concord meeting, and gave to the little fellowship the name of the " Transcendental Club," why, it is not easy to discover; for a club it was not in any sense of the word. There was no organization, there were no officers, there was no stated time or place for assembling, there were no topics for discussion: in fact, there appears no good reason for calling it " transcendental," unless that term was

3. The "Transcendental Club."

supposed to carry with it ridicule or opprobrium. The meetings were fitful, and hastily prearranged. In ten years there were scarcely more than as many convocations. Some members remained in the Church, attempting to combine transcendental ideas with ecclesiastical forms: others left the Church for other vocations. Each followed the leading of the individual disposition. The short-lived *Dial* and the shorter-lived *Massachusetts Quarterly* were results of the " transcendental " spirit.

At the time when the transcendental movement was at its height, the atmosphere of New England was filled with projects of reform. Every kind of innovation on existing social arrangements had its advocate, its newspaper, its meetings, its convention. Temperance, non-resistance, woman's rights, anti-slavery, peace, claimed attention from those concerned for the progress of mankind. Some of these projects were wild, visionary, and, in the eyes of some observers, grotesque. It is not unlikely that they owed their origin to the same impulse which produced transcendentalism, though the historical and logical connection has not been discovered. That a large part of the ridicule which was vented on the transcendentalists was owing to their presumed affiliation with these summary iconoclasts is more than probable. Nor was such a presumption unreasonable; for the transcendentalists not merely took no pains to correct the impression, but rather gave it encouragement. Emerson's lecture on " Man the Reformer " was an eloquent arraignment of society. " One day all men will be lovers," he wrote, " and every calamity will be dissolved in the universal sunshine." In his lecture on " The Times," delivered the same year (1841), he says:

4. The "Atmosphere of Reform."

" These reformers are our contemporaries: they are ourselves, our own light and sight and conscience; they only name the relation which subsists between us and the vicious institutions which they go to rectify. . . . The reforms have their high origin in an ideal justice; but they do not retain the purity of an idea. . . . The reforming movement is sacred in its origin; in its management and details, timid and profane. These benefactors hope to raise a man by improving his circumstances: by combination of that which is dead, they hope to make something alive. In vain. By new infusions, alone, of the spirit by which he is made and directed, can he be remade and reenforced."

The transcendentalists by virtue of the very principles which underlay their philosophy, and as the foregoing quotations indicate, were interested in reforms of all kinds, some of which were none too sane or sober. Most of them were Abolitionists, many of them were Woman Suffragists, and all of them were free and radical thinkers in one direction or another. On the practical side the movement took interesting shape in the Brook Farm community, where a brave and self-sacrificing attempt was made to put into practise the principles of a social brotherhood. George Ripley, who had been settled over a Unitarian parish, was the leading spirit. Channing was deeply interested, and his hopes, though not extravagant, were very high. Nathaniel Hawthorne was a member of the community for a time. He found, however, that a man's soul may be " buried

5. Relation to Reforms and Religion.

under a dung-heap as well as under a pile of money."
He asked himself on leaving, " Is it a praiseworthy
matter that I have spent five golden months in providing fodder for cows and horses ?" In religion the
typical transcendentalist might be a sublimated
theist; he was always an idealist, and essentially a
mystic. He believed in no spiritual authority except that of his own soul. He was humanitarian
and optimistic. His faith had no backward look;
its essence was aspiration, not contrition. He had a
living and a glowing faith in the reality of spiritual
insight. " All are able to detect the supernatural,"
wrote Orestes Brownson, " because all have the supernatural in themselves." The divine was everywhere. The " Immanence of God " was not a doctrine; it became a reality.

> "Tell me, brothers, what are we?
> Spirits bathing in a Sea
> Of Deity."

So wrote a lesser, but a fervid poet of the faith.
It follows, therefore, that the transcendental believer was impressed with the glory of life, its privileges, its beauty. Very remarkable was his confidence in nature—in natural powers and capabilities,
in the results of obedience to natural law, in spontaneity, impulse, unfolding, growth. His love of
childhood, flowers, landscape, was proverbial. Emerson called transcendentalism " the Saturnalia, or
excess of faith." But the faith was in human nature
as a possible realization of the divine. It was a new
and joyous birth of the spirit. No strictly " rea-
soned doctrine " it was rather a " spiritual ferment,"
a wave of mysticism, which found expression in
social, intellectual, esthetic, and chiefly religious
channels.

The movement, according to T. W. Higginson,
provided an " ardent, effusive social atmosphere.
It was," he added, " a fresh, glowing, youthful,
hopeful, courageous period, and those
6. Influ- who were its children must always re-
ence of joice that they were born before it
Transcen- faded away. . . . To its immediate
dentalism. offspring it bequeathed a glow and a
joy that have been of life-long permanence. The material achievements, the utilitarian
philosophy of later years, may come or go, leaving
their ideal, their confidence, their immortal hope
unchanged. And now that much which transcendentalism sought is fulfilled, and that which was
ecstasy has—as Emerson predicted—become daily
bread, its reminiscences mingle with all youth's en-
chantment, and belong to a period when we too
' toiled, feasted, despaired, were happy.' " Except
for a few local and incidental extravagances, the influence of the movement was noble, inspiring, and
beautiful, and the idealism which was the essence
of it is the foundation of all spiritual belief. As one
form of the great intuitive school of philosophy, it
has, perhaps, seen its best days; but its elements
will render vital other faiths, which will endure
when it is forgotten.

O. B. FROTHINGHAM†. Rev. by P. R. FROTHINGHAM.

BIBLIOGRAPHY: O. B. Frothingham, *Transcendentalism in
New England, a History*, New York, 1876; F. Tiffany,
Transcendentalism: the New England Renaissance, in *Uni-
tarianism; its Origin and History*, Boston, 1890. J. Cook,
Transcendentalism, ib. 1877; H. C. Goddard, *Studies in
New England Transcendentalism*, New York, 1908.

TRANSFIGURATION, THE: The history of the
transfiguration of the Savior (Mark ix. 2–10 and
parallels) is under severe fire. Schmiedel's handling of it (*EB*, IV., 45–70) may be taken as representing a pronounced tendency in contemporary
criticism. The study of the sources ends in the dissolution of literary unity. Thus Schmiedel treats
the transfiguration as a part of the Petrine legend.
Along with this process of literary dissolution goes
the depreciation of the historical reality in the life
of Christ which is seen dimly, through the dust
raised by the study of the sources. The result
reached is that no considerable reality adheres to
the story of the transfiguration. " It can make no
claim to historicity."

But this critical method, apparently objective
and judicial, starts with a false bias. The Synoptic
Gospels are taken apart by themselves, dissected,
and reduced to separate sources. Then, to explain
the assembling of the sources into a so-called " Life
of Christ," the corporate messianic consciousness of
the Apostolic Age is summoned into court. Strauss
and the analytical literary critic join forces. The
transfiguration becomes a personification and ob-
jectification of the genius of the messianic community. But, before the analysis of the sources begins,
there is a fundamental fact that calls for explanation. It is, first, the existence of the messianic
consciousness in question; second, it is the peculiar quality of that consciousness. Without raising the question of the supernatural, students of
history may rightly insist that vast reality must be
assigned to the person and work of Jesus in order
to account for the corporate Christian messianism
which is supposed to account for the " Life of
Christ." The ultimate source of knowledge concerning Christ is the Christian consciousness which
he created. That consciousness drew upon Jewish
messianism for all its raw material. But an immense twofold revolution must have been carried
through in order to make Christian consciousness
possible. In the first place, it is the consciousness
of a triumphant messianic community, a thing
without real parallel in the history of Judaism. In
the second place, Christian messianism was completely freed from the appeal to force which was
inherent in all forms of Jewish messianism. Consequently, a sound historical method demands a pro-
digious spiritual and moral force and reality in the
life of the founder.

One can not, therefore, enter on the study of the
life of Christ with a predisposition to believe that
Christian messianism accounts for the main elements in the portrait. The truth in such a position
must be admitted. But, taken as a controlling principle, it invites history to stand on its head. The
ordinary predisposition of the Christian is in the
other direction. In approaching the account of the
transfiguration, the normal Christian bias is the
direct opposite of Schmiedel's. One is prepared to
believe that the story may be substantially historic.

The threefold report at this point presents the
same phenomena of agreement in the main joined

to incessant difference in detail that characterizes it in its whole course. Mark gives a simple, straightforward narrative. In describing the effects of the transfiguration on the Savior's person, he takes his illustration from the fuller's art. The disciples, speaking to Jesus, address him in the current Aramaic as " Rabbi." Luke (ix. 28–36) differs considerably. He changes the order of apostolic names, John taking precedence of James. The transfiguration comes upon Jesus while he is praying. The disciples address Jesus as *Epistata*, " Master "—possibly a deliberate avoidance of the Palestinian " Rabbi." He adds verses 31–32. In the voice from heaven " my chosen " takes the place of " my beloved." The solemn and detailed injunction of Jesus that the disciples should keep silent regarding the event is condensed into the simple statement, " they held their peace." Matthew (xvii. 1–13) abounds in his own sense. The Christology is more conscious and more advanced. The divine majesty of the Savior is brought out in every possible way. He is addressed as " Lord." His face and person shine " as the sun " and " like the light." In addressing him Peter says, " If thou wilt." The disciples fall on their faces in fear. The words from heaven are identical with the words used at the baptism. In brief, Matthew's molding of the event is deeply characteristic, in close keeping with the purpose and method of his Gospel.

In the light of the threefold narrative, the account of the transfiguration has quite as strong right to be considered historical as the happenings at Cæsarea Philippi, with which it is connected. Possibly its right is a shade better, for the variations are less substantial. The account may even be compared with the baptism and come off well. Unless, outside the Synoptists, some reason can be found for impugning the historicity of the narrative, it must be accepted as a solid part of the very earliest tradition regarding the Savior. By the test of position also, it shows up well. It is fixed near the end of the Galilean ministry. Contrasted with the Sermon on the Mount or with the materials which Luke groups under the so-called " Peræan ministry," it holds a position that does not vary. It is fixed as solidly as the baptism or the crucifixion. Tested, then, by such standards as an undogmatic criticism is able to provide, the account of the transfiguration is the report of a real event in the life of Jesus. Beyond doubt the facts have been interpreted and molded. The " Life of Christ," as the Gospels give it, is not a scientific history, but a religious history. It came into literature out of the life, the spiritual warfare, the unwritten memory and faith of Christians in the Apostolic Age. Unless God had worked an inconceivably immoral miracle, suspended all mental laws, then, under the conditions of Christianity in the first century, it could not but happen that the facts in the life of the Savior and the Church's interpretation of the facts should blend in the record. Therefore the fact of the transfiguration, like the other main facts in the Savior's life, has been interpreted, and the interpretation has fused itself with the fact reported. Matthew gives the most marked evidence of this process, particularly in the direction of developing the likeness between Jesus the su-

preme authority in spiritual matters and Moses the great lawgiver. But in Mark and Luke also the interpretative element appears.

None the less the threefold report makes the fact the necessary presupposition of the interpretation. The transfiguration was an event of vital moment in the experience of the Savior. In its importance for knowledge of his life and mind, it comes fairly near the level of the baptism. To find its meaning, the larger context, as sketched by Mark, will serve. The Galilean ministry lay behind him. Jerusalem is calling him to his passion and death. The tragedy inherent in every great life whose purpose both transcends its time and place and yet seeks intimacy with its time and place, is at its height in the life of Jesus. He had utterly failed to convert his own people. His deepening experience of his nation's incompetence and unbelief leads him to appropriate Isa. liii. as the word of Holy Scripture that makes his experience clear and intelligible to him. But the tragic strain of the situation can be relieved in only one way. In the intensity of communion with the Father, his will and nature are taken up into the will and being of God. On his mental side, the Savior must be described as the supreme prophetic mystic. So he realizes the divine being and purpose as every ancient mystic realized it, in terms of the " light " within the light. The experience of his soul shines out through his face and transfigures it. Science has nothing to say at this point which can justly interfere with the believer's rights.

The place where the transfiguration took place has been the subject of much learned discussion. A tradition as early as the fourth century fastened on Mt. Tabor. But modern investigation, beginning with Robinson, has made that site impossible. P. Schaff (*Dictionary of the Bible*, Philadelphia, 1880) with other scholars fixed on some high peak in the Anti-Lebanon range. If justification exists for searching for a definite mountain-peak, no other inference seems possible. The context in the Synoptists points in this direction. But it is to be remembered that the Synoptists, aside from vague suggestion, give no real help. Mark and Matthew say " a mountain." Luke writes " the mountain." All that the three make it safe to say is that the transfiguration took place in close connection with the events recorded in Mark viii. 27–33 (Cæsarea Philippi). The phrase " high mountain " does not justify thinking of some very high peak. The language is relative and mystical, not scientific and exact. The habit of climbing high mountain-peaks is distinctly modern. There is no reason to suppose that the Savior did what no other ancient ever did. The attempt at identification should be abandoned. The geography of the episode concerns the ways of the Spirit rather than the map made with hands.   HENRY S. NASH.

BIBLIOGRAPHY: D. F. Strauss, *Leben Jesu*, ii. 252 sqq., Tübingen, 1836. Eng. transl., iii. 1–21, London, 1846, and *Life of Jesus for the People*, ii. 281–285, ib. 1879; C. Weizsäcker, *Untersuchungen über die evangelische Geschichte*, pp. 480–484, Gotha, 1864; K. T. Keim, *Jesus o Nazara*, vol. iv., 6 vols., London, 1876–83; F. W. Farrar, *Life of Christ*, ii. 34–41, 13th ed., London and New York, n.d., S. J. Andrews, *Life of our Lord*, pp. 351–359, New York, 1891; A. Edersheim, *Jesus the Messiah*, ii. 94–101, ib. 1896; A. Réville, *Jesus de Nazareth*, vol. ii., Paris,

1897; A. Menzies, *Earliest Gospel*, London, 1901; W. J. Moulton, in *Biblical and Semitic Studies* (Yale University), pp. 157–210, New Haven, 1901; J. deQ. Donehoo, *The Apocryphal and Legendary Life of Christ*, New York, 1903; O. Holtzmann, *Life of Jesus*, London, 1904; W. Sanday, *Outlines of the Life of Christ*, 2d ed., Edinburgh, 1906; G. D. Barry, *The Transfiguration of our Lord*, London and New York; 1911; *DB*, iv. 807–808; *EB*, iv. 4570–71; *DCG*, ii. 742–745; B. W. Bacon, in *AJT*, 1902, pp. 236–265; and the commentaries on the passages in the Gospels. On the location consult Robinson, *Researches*, ii. 357–359.

TRANSMIGRATION: A phase of metempsychosis (see COMPARATIVE RELIGION, VI., 1, § 6) which assumes the rebirth of a soul into another body (reincorporation). Belief in transmigration is common among primitive peoples, has had a large part in the philosophy of India, and in the West has furnished the theme for a large body of folk-lore; in Greece it was advocated by Pythagoras and was held by the Orphics; it reappeared in the Cabala (q.v.), reminiscences of it are to be discovered in early obscure Christian sects, and even in the Middle Ages it was not altogether banished from thought. But nowhere else has the conception had so large and abiding influence as in India, where it is practically the key to almost all theological systems and furnishes the reason for the fundamental hope of the Indian of nearly every faith—escape from the *samsara* or cycle of births.

TRANSUBSTANTIATION.

I. Rise of the Concept: The doctrine of transubstantiation (namely, that in the Eucharist the substance in the elements of bread and wine is changed into the real substance of the body and blood of Christ, though retaining the accidents of the elements) was the result of four centuries of development. It was fixed as a dogma by the fourth Lateran Council in 1215, during the pontificate of Innocent III. The creed then adopted, a revision of the Apostolic, and promulgated against all heretics, forms the first chapter of the decrees, and is sometimes called the fourth symbol. It declares as follows: " There is verily one universal Church of the faithful, outside which no one at all is saved, in which the same priest is himself the **1. Earliest** sacrifice, Jesus Christ, whose body and **Evidences.** blood are truly contained in the sacrament of the altar under the species of bread and wine, the bread being transubstantiated into the body, and the wine into blood, by divine power." The term itself had already long been in use among theologians, and the concept longer still. The first authentic use of the term seems to have been in the *Tractatus de sacramento altaris*, xiii., xiv. (*MPL*, clxxii. 1291, 1293), a treatise assigned by Jean Mabillon to the first Stephen of Autun (d. 1139 or 1140), the former of the two bishops of Autun known as Peter in the twelfth century. The term, further employed by various theologians during the twelfth century, seems to have been freely current previous to the council of 1215. Innocent himself frequently used it as a current term in his *De sacramenti altaris mysterio;* and a citation from Alanus of Lille (*MPL*, ccx. 359) shows that it played a part specially in the controversy with the Cathari or Albigenses (see NEW MANICHEANS, II.), against whom the first chapter of the decree of the council was aimed. William of Auxerre (d. c. 1230) deals in his *Summa* with the special title *De transsubstantiatione*, followed by such scholars as William of Paris (or of Auvergne; d. 1249), Alexander of Hales, and Albert the Great. As to the concept it does not come to expression either in the " Sentences " of Peter Lombard, who represented the simple realistic idea of the Eucharist, or other text-books of that period. Apparently the term emerged unobserved, but may have been in circulation before the twelfth century. For indications discovered in a writer, Haimo, probably of Halberstadt (d. 853), or possibly of Hirschau (abbot, from 1091), shows the idea in its nascent stage. He employs the words: " Therefore we believe . . . that that substance, namely, of bread and wine, . . . that is, the nature of bread and wine, [is] substantially changed into another substance, that is, into flesh and blood "; and again: " The invisible priest changes his visible creatures into the substance of his flesh and blood " (*MPL*, cxviii. 815–816). Among twelfth-century authors, however, Peter of Poitiers (d. 1205) alone seems to consider or justify the use of the term *transsubstantio* for the change here indicated. Closely following Peter Lombard, he considers the process effected by consecration under the general category of " change " (*conversio*). The Lombard had already debated whether the " change " was formal or substantial, or of some other species. Totally denying the first, he, however, went no further as to the second than to cite the approval of previously named authorities and to reply to " others " who objected against it. He does not protest against the accepted statement that through the priest bread is made into flesh, but how this takes place is to him a mystery which is more wholesome to believe than to investigate. He classifies known views as follows: (1) not the substance of bread becomes the body, except as bread is made out of flour, when it may be said that flour is made, not is, bread; (2) what was bread and wine was afterward body and blood, so that the bread is no longer substance, and hence no longer bread; (3) " after consecration there is the substance of body and blood under those accidents under which there was formerly the substance of bread and wine "; (4) the substance of bread and wine remains, but in the same place, after the consecration, are the body and blood of Christ. The latter doctrine is evidently consubstantiation; the first, or theory of transformation, is the one widely held in the Greek Church; while the combination of the second and third (the annihilation doctrine), scarcely to be identified against the second, unmistakably represents, virtually, the doctrine of transubstantiation. Peter Lombard refrains from criticizing only the third, which doubtless holds the mystery forbidding investigation, but it is uncertain whether he accordingly does not dare to venture for conciseness upon the term transubstantiation, or that term had not yet appeared as available for the conception. Peter of Poitiers expressly introduces the term *transsubstantiatio* for the outlined conception, with the apology that no adequate term was previously afforded.

A new epoch in eucharistic doctrine had its inception with Paschasius Radbertus (q.v.), who, surpassing his predecessors in the earnestness and thrust by which he asserted the identity of the historic body of Christ with the Eucharist, without any intentional innovation on his part, furnished the impulse for a scientific theological treatment of the eucharistic problem by his *De corpore et sanguine Domini* (*MPL*, cxxi. 125 sqq.). His work was the first monograph in the West on the Eucharist, preceded only by the homily of Faustus of

2. Early Medieval Development.
Riez (q.v.), *De corpore et sanguine Christi* (*MPL*, xxx. 271 sqq.). At bottom the Christological and soteriological problem was at stake, which at the outset of the dogmatic development was thus afforded a symptomatic interest beyond mere formal speculation. The first real eucharistic controversy of the West was that conjured up against Berengar of Tours (q.v.) by his opponents, practically the authors of the doctrine of transubstantiation. Of these there were four: Hugo, bishop of Langres, *Tractatus de corpore et sanguine Christi* (c. 1048; *MPL*, cxlii. 1325 sqq.); Durand of Troarn (q.v.), *De corpore et sanguine Christi* (*MPL*, cxlix. 1375 sqq.); Lanfranc, *De corpore et sanguine Domini* (1069 or 1070; *MPL*, cl. 407 sqq.); and Guitmund, later archbishop of Aversa, *De corporis et sanguinis Domini veritate in Eucharistia* (between 1073 and 1078; *MPL*, cxlix. 1427 sqq.). Lanfranc was the first to teach that the body of Christ is received also by the unworthy, a view essentially implying the reality of the change of the bread. He apparently wavers, however, when he affirms that in the sacrament the flesh of Christ is daily sacrificed, distributed, and eaten, notwithstanding that according to another mode of speech the whole Christ is eaten, i.e., when he is longed for as eternal life by spiritual desire. Both kinds of communion he deems essential, the physical and the spiritual, though the latter is impossible without the former. Most important was the work of Guitmund, amended by Anselm and compiled and further developed by Alger of Liége (d. 1132) in his *De sacramentis corporis et sanguinis Dominici* (*MPL*, clxxx. 743 sqq.). The latter stated: "In the sacrament, the substance, not the form, being changed, the bread and wine do not become new flesh and new blood, but

the existing substance, both of bread and wine, is changed into the coexisting substance of the body of Christ." He holds that "the whole host is so the body of Christ that, nevertheless, each separate particle is the whole body of Christ." In this latter statement are contained four axioms of subsequent theologians: (1) not a part of the body of Christ (as the flesh), but the whole body, the whole Christ, is present in the Eucharist in virtue of the change; (2) the whole body, the whole Christ, is not only in the entire host, but no less entirely in each part; (3) even though a thousand masses are celebrated simultaneously at different places, the whole body of Christ is present in each individually and entirely in all; (4) by the breaking of the host and its crushing by the teeth the indivisible body of Christ is not divided. The views of Guitmund were further systematized by Peter Lombard (d. 1064 or 1060 ?), Anselm of Canterbury (d. 1109), Hugo of St. Victor (d. 1141), and Robert Pulleyn (d. about 1150); and by these pushed to their logical conclusions. Anselm, in *De corpore et sanguine Domini* (*MPL*, clix. 255), denied that with the blood only the soul of Christ is received and with the body only the body, but maintained that the entire Christ, both God and man, is received in each. Henceforth it was a standing formula that "the entire Christ exists and is received under either species," and though the conception of the Eucharist as spiritual sustenance prevailed later, yet the argument was repeatedly recalled. Guitmund also made an advance in a closer determination of the process in the sacrament. Of four alternative species of change (*mutatio*) the one in which one thing becomes another that already exists, like the sacramental bread changed into the body of Christ existing already in heaven, pertains exclusively to the Eucharist. Raising the question how this is possible, Alger of Liége, declining the view that this takes place by flight from heaven through space, affirmed that the human nature now exalted was capable by virtue of omnipotence to remain undivided and substantial where it is and at the same time to be at every other place where it will. Guitmund applied the logical categories of substance and accident to the Eucharist, in so far as he termed the surviving sense qualities of the changed substance accidents, and Alger further deduced the consequence that God made the accidents to continue without a subject. Both affirmed that as the substance of the bread was no longer present, any disturbance of the inherent substance (the body) was not only impossible but a disturbance of the accidents was merely illusory. The latter, however, seemed to their successors, Hugo, Robert, and Thomas, to impair the verity of the sacrament, and it was assumed that much could occur to the accidents not affecting the body in which they inhere, being not, according to Anselm and the rest, spatially circumscribed, gnawed by mice, or taken into the abdomen like the elements. A loose integration of the substance of the body and the accidents of the bread was thus postulated, yet it is to be taken as the first expression of a thought which was to remain an integrating factor in the Roman dogma. Radbertus had already represented the bread and wine as types or figures of the body and blood into which they are changed, but he restricted the body to a spiritual sustenance in which the unworthy and unbelieving had no part; this involved a self-contradiction, since a consequence of the reality of transformation is that these also partake, though without the blessing. This view promulgated by Lanfranc was further developed by Guitmund, teaching that the body present in the Eucharist is again a symbol of the regeneration of believers from the bosom of the Church, or of the Church itself, the mystical body; and that it is a sign by which the members testify to their spiritual birth. The unworthy, thus, do not partake of the spiritual communion in Christ, though partaking physically of the body and blood. Hugo of St. Victor formulated these views into the dogma that became permanent for scholasticism and the Church. To him, (1) the species are merely a type, not a fact; (2) the eucharistic body is at once fact, and in turn type of (3) the blessing of the sacrament, i.e., the spiritual content of being members in Christ, provided by faith in his body and blood; and this, finally, is objective fact, and type of nothing else. In this sense the unworthy receive the species and the body as born of man, in substance, but not in efficacy, i.e., participation in the mystical union.

II. Scholastic Development: Scholasticism gave the doctrine of transubstantiation the final form, as it appeared in the Roman Catholic catechism and the works of Cardinal Bellarmin. The matter on which the change is effected is unleavened wheat bread and wine somewhat diluted with water. The " form " of the sacrament consists of the words *Hoc est corpus meum, hic est calix sanguinis mei*. The effect of the form upon the matter is to

1. Nature of the Change. change it in the Aristotelian sense into the new, for which it possesses an inherent capability. But just as regards the operation of the sacrament one tendency was to consider the efficacy as immanent and the other as concomitant, so Albert and Thomas taught a created virtue residing in the words of consecration, while others like Bonaventura and Gabriel Biel held to a mere assistance by divine omnipotence to the words of consecration in virtue of the institution. The application of the form to the matter is effected by the consecration of the priest, with transubstantiation as the immediate result. The use of the word, with its philosophic substructure, was yet open to scholastic disputes. Alger represented that the substance of the bread ceases, but his contemporaries, Hugo of St. Victor, Robert Pulleyn, and Peter Lombard, insisted that the substance of the elements only ceases to be what it was and becomes something which it had not been previously. Duns Scotus brings the idea of transubstantiation under the third form of the Aristotelian category of " mutation." While the first form is from negative to positive (creation), and the second vice versa (annihilation), transubstantiation demands both positive termini, and its transition is from subject to subject or substance to substance. This transition is not to be conceived as though the substance of the " end to which " was first originated, but as beginning to exist in a new place (*adductiva*). The body does not succeed the bread according to the absolute existence of the body, but the bread is changed into the body according to the local existence of the same with refence to the preexisting bread. Here emerges to view the element broadly underlying the growth of the dogma from the beginning, namely, the presence in the Eucharist of the preexisting body of Christ. Inasmuch as the body gains the new presence without losing the old, while the bread undergoes a mutation of loss without gain, it would follow that the question at first hand would be only one of local presence or non-presence, and it would be concluded that the bread did not lose its substantial but only its local existence, and so far did not undergo destruction. If, however, the bread does not remain in its substantial existence and from the above would appear not destroyed, it must cease in some other way, and this is a change from simple existence to non-existence, which would virtually be annihilation, only this term must not apply beyond the " terminus from which," i.e., the bread. As further developed by the nominalists, the Scotist view appears in the Roman catechism as follows: " The substance of bread and wine is so changed into the very body of the Lord that the substance of bread and wine entirely ceases to be." Still more sharp is the definition of Bellarmin, who holds (*De eucharistia*, iii. 18) that the concept of true transubstantiation presupposes four things: that something ceases to be (*desitio*); that something takes the place of what has ceased to be (*successio*); that desistance and succession have a teleological causal nexus, one thing ceasing to be that another may take its place; and that both the " end from which " and the " end to which " are positive in nature. The body of Christ, besides its presence in heaven, obtains a new presence in the Eucharist; and transubstantiation depends not on a twofold but a single act of the divine will whereby the bread is made to cease and the body of Christ takes its place under the accidents.

The one effect of consecration is that the body and blood of Christ, and therefore their real presence under the accidents of the elements, have their inception in the sacraments. Thomas Aquinas contents himself with the fact of the real presence, to be grasped by neither senses nor reason, but only by faith depending on divine authority. Sometimes, however, he refers to the " true " body as it exists in heaven in contrast with its sacramental presence. Biel, following Occam, reasserts more strongly the absolute identity of the two as taught by Radbertus.

2. Concomitance. The body of Christ is thus said to be present in the Eucharist the same as enthroned at the right hand of the Father, a living, divine, immortal, and glorified body, with all celestial qualities and accidents. From this there issues a series of deductions, abroad since Anselm and now grounded by Thomas on his theory of " real concomitance." By virtue of the sacramental change not only the basic substance or the flesh, but the entire body is in the Eucharist; this must imply Christ as living in heaven, possessed of a soul, and joined with God. However, both soul and deity are not present by virtue of the sacramental change but of natural concomitance. And because living body and blood are inseparable the concept of real concomitance affords the conclusion that blood is under the bread and body under the wine as well, or the entire body of Christ is under each. This, too, became a fixed tenet of scholasticism, receiving very full elaboration at the hands of Biel. That the body of Christ may be present under the species of the host, the substance of the bread must cease to be and only its accidents remain. Scholasticism could not, therefore, avoid the problem whether these accidents could continue to exist without their subject. Thomas affirmed such possibility, proposing as analogous proof that the divine omnipotence as the first cause could sustain the effect of a terminated second cause, and assuming that after the substance of the bread had ceased the accidents continued inhering in the dimensive quantitativeness of the bread as a quasi-subject. The validity of this view was denied by Duns and specially by the nominalists, who answered Thomas that such quantitativeness, after the change, belonged to the accidents themselves; and they found less difficulty on their theory in presuming the accidents to be self-subsisting after the change. It may be said that accidents that may subsist without a subject can have but a very lax connection with the body after consecration. They do not inhere in or affect the body, and the latter may not be accessible to transactions affecting the accidents, such as the breaking of the bread, where the body as a whole or as entirely in each and every part is not affected.

The question of how long the body of Christ is present in the host was not answered conclusively by the older scholasticism. Thomas maintained that the presence continued in the species so long as they would not undergo such change **3. Duration of Presence.** as would alter the substance of the bread and wine were that substance existent. This view was repeated by Biel, who supplemented it by the conclusion of Occam, that when the body of Christ ceased to be present in the host, its place was taken either by the returning substance of bread or by some new substance, thus giving rise to the paradox that " from non-substances," the substanceless accidents, " substance may arise." When the process of digestion begins, the presence of the body of Christ in the accidents ceases, and its place is taken, by an absolute act of God, by a surrogate which has the nutritive power lacking to the accidents as such. The question likewise arose how the words, " this is my body," were to be interpreted. The followers of Berengar explained them, like Zwingli afterward, as representative; Richard of St. Victor substituted the future for the present; Bonaventura paraphrased the words into, " this which is as yet present under these species as bread will be transubstantiated into my body "; Alexander of Hales paraphrased the words as " this which is designated by the symbol is my body "; Thomas, followed by Biel and Bellarmin made *hoc* refer to a substance qualitatively undetermined, but considered present under the species, and then more closely defined by the predicate as the body of Christ. The proof of transub-

stantiation is drawn from the *hoc;* for if the substance of bread had remained, Christ would have said, " *Hic panis est corpus meum.*"

The most difficult question concerned the quantity of the eucharistic body and its relation to the host. Since the celestial body of Christ is in all points the same as it was on earth save its impassibility and immortality, it must quantitatively fill a certain amount of space in " dimensive " or " circumscriptive " fashion, so that the whole occupies its entire allotted room or space, and each part its specific exclusive space; and apparently this heavenly body as such can not be present in the host. This objection could be met only by the **4. Unity of Celestial and Sacramental Body.** doctrine that the sacramental body of Christ, though one and the same with his celestial body, has another mode of existence in the sacrament; namely, without quantitativeness. The earlier realistic scholasticism attributed to quantitativeness, like other absolute accidents, a real existence independent of substance and of qualities, holding that through the union of quantitativeness with unquantitative substance or quality the latter first become quantitative things gaining definite area and capacity. This quantitativeness was, according to realism, thus separable from material things without alteration to their real entity. Realists could therefore affirm, as some did, that the accident of quantitativeness existed only in the celestial body of Christ, not in the sacramental body. As to how this would be it was proposed that God can provide that one part of the body is entered by another, and this in turn by another (*subintrare*), so that each exists not under or beside but only in the other, and the whole has the smallest imaginable natural quantity. This was the subintration theory, and was objectionable; because if non-quantitative in the Eucharist, the body can not be living and organic and therefore not identical with the celestial body; or as Albert and Duns questioned, without collateral parts there was no form and consequently no real soul-possessing body in the Eucharist. The problem now assumed the shape of proving quantity without spatial extension not self-contradictory, as Bonaventura assumed. The first to attempt a dialectic solution along these lines was Thomas on the basis of transmutation and concomitance. The former has for its termini not dimensions, but substances, and accordingly only the substance of the bread is changed into the substance of the body of Christ. Since, however, the body of Christ is present in the sacrament as it exists in heaven, its dimensive quantity must also be present. But since this is in the sacrament only " concomitantly " and somewhat as an accident, it is present only according to the mode of substance, i.e., the body is present not as a dimensive quantity in dimensive space, but like a substance under its own dimensions. Accordingly, the nature of the substance is contained wholly in the entire body and wholly in each part, analogous to the air. To the objection that the spatial capacity of the species would thus be conceived as empty, he asserted that such was occupied only by the species of bread retaining, after the transmutation of its former substance, its former dimensions. The mediating thought of this theory is, that that which is in the sacrament by virtue of the change is there of necessity, although owing its presence merely to concomitance, thus assuring only an incidental existence, and liable to sacrifice its individuality, if the sacrament requires it. The dialectic fallacy is the confusion of substance with the abstract nature of substance in the course of the argument. As a consequence the idea of an organic body in the sacrament is emptied and reduced to a mathematical point. Thomas gets no further than the subintration theory; nevertheless, the Thomistic theory was adopted by the Roman catechism.

Duns Scotus, besides his objection to the organic disintegration of the body, insisted that bread and body must be present, each in all the attributes essential to its concept. Accordingly, he distinguishes in the quantitative existence of an object between a logical "intrinsic position" of the quantity considered absolutely, by which there is a differentiation and a correlation of distinct exclusive parts in the whole, and an "extrinsic position" with reference to space; which is again differentiated into the occupancy of space in general, and the coextensive collocation of the parts respectively with their spaces. The second distinction refers more specifically to the mere coexistence of two quantities, over against their coexistence together with the coextension of the parts. In application, the body is present in fact in its organic unity according to the intrinsic position, but, by a miracle, in the manner of coexistence without the coextension of parts. Hence, the presence is of "the whole in the whole and entirely in any part whatsoever." The fallacy lay in abstracting space from its integral relation, and in its realistic treatment as a quantity; nevertheless, the doctrine was thus assumed by Bellarmin.

Occam attacked the realistic conception of quantity. He rightly asserted that, since the conception of space is derived from the collocation of plural objects or spaces, the order of parts in the whole necessarily implies each part in its corresponding space. The fiction of the coexistence of quantities without coextension was thus exposed. In place he now denied that quantitativeness or extension was a thing, real and distinct, and intermediate between substance and quality, but he affirmed that it was one and the same with the substance or quality to which it belongs as accident, and denoted the thing itself so far as it was a quantity; or it was "the thing circumscriptively in place," whether this, more definitely, were substance or quality. If, then, a substance or quality coincided with space throughout, whole with whole and part with part, it was a quantum; and inversely, if a substance or quality coexists with space, whole with whole and the whole with every part, it must be a non-quantum. This he terms "definitive existence," which he asserts may also be applied to material, corporeal, divisible things, and necessarily thus to the body of Christ. As to the mode Occam points to concentration in digestion, holding that to divine omnipotence both are equally

feasible. This doctrine termed "condensation" takes the place of that of subintration, though the result is the same. The body exists in the sacrament without extension as a mathematical point. The contradiction of corporeity, or organic form, without dimension is also referred to divine omnipotence. Even in the bloom of ecclesiastical scholasticism it was felt that the doctrine of transubstantiation was not beyond question, and such men as Duns Scotus, Occam, and Pierre d'Ailly (q.v.) entertained alternative or modified views, though accepting and defending the orthodox doctrine because of the authority of the Church. The Council of Trent sanctioned it officially as did Pius VI. in his "Constitution," 1794.

III. Practical Results of the Dogmatization: With the establishment of the dogma of transubstantiation, 1215, it became more and more evident that the Eucharist was a sacrament utterly different in kind from all others. They were efficacious only in their administration to such a degree that (with the exception of marriage) their form came to consist only in the words of their exercise by the priest. In the Eucharist, on the contrary, the consecration itself was the sacramental act, and the object of this consecration was not communion, which remained a mere incident, but the transubstantiation of the elements, or the creation of the presence of Christ and of his body. The purpose of the consecration, moreover, is the sacrifice, the act of the priest, not of the congregation; this sacrifice was believed to be commanded in the words: "This do in remembrance of me." This development was of gradual growth, the original intention, as manifest from Radbert to Pulleyn, being to assure the faithful of the real presence for eucharistic communion; but when the perfection of the sacrament came to subsist in the consecration, the conclusion of the real identity of the sacrifice of the mass with the sacrifice on Calvary from the real presence proved inevitable. Berengar points out that the solemn celebration is not the passion of the Lord but its symbolic commemoration. Though Thomas holds to the fact and symbol, yet he not only identifies the real effects of the original act of atonement with the symbolic ceremony but explains that by the real presence, and not merely by symbol and significance, the sacrifice of the new law is to tower above the shadowed sacrifices of the old; and containing Christ in reality it is the culmination of all other sacraments, through which alone the power of Christ is imparted. If Christ be present from the moment that the sacrament is completed by consecration, and if he be present both in his humanity and his divinity, then veneration is due him, present in the host. Thomas emphasizes already that no bread substance must remain in the sacrament, lest anything created may hinder worship.

Veneration presupposes the reservation of the host. It is at least certain that in the ancient Church not only were the consecrated elements taken by the deacons to the houses of the sick, but that many took with them some of the consecrated bread; and it is also known that penitents, when

1. Sacrifice; Adoration; Reservation.

in sudden danger of death, received the consecrated bread as a viaticum, thus rendering probable the practise of reservation in the churches, and consequently the assignment of some place for preservation. In the sixth century the vessel for retaining the host was called *turris*. With the rise of the doctrine of transubstantiation, however, the consecrated host was reserved for the adoration of the worshipers, and to this end was placed in the monstrance (see VESSELS, SACRED). The Roman ritual requires that some consecrated particles must always be reserved for the communion of the sick and other believers prevented from attending mass, in a well-covered receptacle in the tabernacle, either on the high altar or some other altar suitable for the veneration and worship of so high a sacrament. Veneration at the elevation of the host in the mass, as well as when the host was borne through the streets to the sick, was first required at Cologne in 1203 by the papal legate Cardinal Guido; and in 1217 the elevation of the monstrance was required by canon law. Shortly afterward the feast of Corpus Christi (q.v.) was established, and the Council of Trent directed that latria, the worship due only to God and to Christ as God and man, be paid the blessed sacrament (*Sessio* xiii., *De eucharistia*, v.). A further consequence of the dogma of transubstantiation is the increased care taken of what remains over from the communion. Tertullian already states that the Christians took extreme pains to prevent any of the consecrated bread from falling on the ground. In Constantinople, on the other hand, the remaining particles of consecrated bread were given the small school-children, and in Gaul in 585 it is known by the Synod of Mâcon that the remnants were used in a children's communion (see LORD'S SUPPER, V.). Elsewhere it was the custom to burn what was left, fire being regarded as a pure element. The Roman Missal, in the chapter *De defectibus in celebratione missarum occurrentibus*, x., gives an entire series of rules in case a drop of consecrated wine falls from the chalice.

That the sacrament of the altar is the office of the priest, and of him alone, is a maxim of the Church, unalterable from the days of Cyprian. Even in the ancient Church "to consecrate" and "to produce the body of the Lord" were synonymous, though the latter phrase then implied merely that through consecration the elements received an importance and dignity for faith which they had not previously possessed. With the rise of transubstantiation, however, the expression came to mean the specific change wrought by the priest by means of the consecrating words and their divine efficacy, so that he, in a real sense, creates the body of Christ and produces his presence. This power, combined with the Power of the Keys (q.v.), forms the material significance of the priestly office, and at ordination is solemnly conferred on the candidate as inseparable from his person. The dogma of transubstantiation has thus led to an increased distinction between the clergy and the laity, so as to exalt the priest as a mediator between God and man. The doctrine of real concomitance served to promote the practise on the

2. Priestly Function; Communion in one Kind.

part of the laity of frequently refraining from the cup. This usage led finally to the canonical withdrawal of the cup from the laity (see MASS, II., § 5). The fear of spilling some of the contents of the chalice early led many communicants to refrain from the cup, though not only teachers of the Church but popes, such as Gelasius I. (cf. *MPL*, lix. 141), opposed the practise of refraining. When, however, Anselm of Canterbury declared that the eucharistic body was not without the blood, the practise was sustained by a new dogmatic basis. Nearly all the great church teachers of the twelfth century, as Bernard, Hugo, Peter Lombard, and Peter of Blois, speak of communion in both kinds as the right form, though their views were preceded by many exceptions; and Alexander of Hales demanded that the laity be free to receive only the bread, though he held that communion under both kinds is more perfect and efficacious than under one. The general chapter of the Cistercians of 1261 restricted the chalice to the priests, and the Lambeth Synod of 1281 allowed the laity only the chalice of ablution. Albert the Great declared communion in one kind imperfect, since the blood is not in the body in virtue of the sacrament but through "natural union." Thomas Aquinas, developing this "natural union" into the theory of concomitance, did not regard the cup as superfluous, because it represents the shedding of blood and its redeeming power; but as absolutely necessary only for the priest. Deeming that the laity should not receive the cup for reasons of expediency, he answered the charge that communion in one kind is imperfect by declaring that the perfection of the sacrament depends on the consecration by the priest, not on reception by the faithful. Bonaventura decided that communion in one kind was as efficacious as in both, only that the symbolism is less complete, a defect compensated by the communion of the priest representing the Church. After him Dominicans and Franciscans alike advocated the withdrawal of the cup from the laity, a practise finally sanctioned by the Council of Constance (1415) and the Council of Trent.

IV. Doctrine in the Greek Church: The Greek term corresponding to the Latin *transsubstantio* is *metousiōsis*, older (and less orthodox) appellations being *metabolē*, *metapoiēsis*, and occasionally *metarythmisis* (equaling the Latin *transformatio, mutatio, conversio,* and *transfiguratio*). The transit from a dynamistic to an essentially realistic interpretation of the effect of consecration on the relation between the elements and the body of Christ was accomplished, largely through the concept of *metabolē*, especially after Gregory of Nyssa. John of Damascus taught a real change of the elements of bread and wine, and through him this doctrine became the common property of the Greek Church. The teaching of earlier Greek theologians presupposes that the "substance" of the bread remains, and that only its "form" is changed; whereas in transubstantiation it is essential that the bread be replaced. The doctrine of *metousiōsis* (the idea is also expressed by *metastoicheiōsis*), as well as that of consubstantiation, never became an intense problem among the Greeks, because the idea of communion remained uppermost. That by this process the substance of the bread was affected was more or less self-evident to their realistic minds; but whether this was by " change " or " transubstantiation " was to them of comparative indifference. The latter has repeatedly been sanctioned by the authorities of the Greek Church, and is doubtless " official," though conveying an outer rather than inner view of the miracle. The earliest passage in which *metousiōsis* occurs is the letter, or confession of faith, sent by the Emperor Michael Palæologus to Gregory X. in 1247, and based on Roman dictation. True appreciation of the doctrine of transubstantiation was shown, about 1360, by the devoted Thomist Manuel Calecas, though he translates *substantia* not by *ousia*, but by *hypokeimenon* (" substratum "), thus not arriving at the term. Such important theologians as Nicolaus Cabasilas and Symeon of Thessalonica (qq.v.) do not use the term *metousiōsis*, but content themselves with *metabolē* and the like. Yet it was evidently prominent at the Council of Florence (1438–39), though it is not used by Marcos Eugenicos (q.v.). In the fifteenth century Johannes Plusiadenus, defending the Council of Florence, declares it proper to teach a *metabolē* from " out of substance into substance "; but in the next century the expression makes its frequent and pronounced appearance. The controversies roused by the " Calvinism " of Cyril Lucar (q.v.) after 1629 led to the official sanctioning of the term *metousiōsis*, which was dogmatized by the synods of Constantinople (1638, 1691), Jassy (1642), and Jerusalem (1672), which in a sense revised the entire doctrinal system of the Greek Church, especially the sacraments, and set forth the documents which the Greeks are wont to call their " symbolical books." However, the decrees of these synods do not occupy the eminence nor exercise the authority of the one symbol erected by the ancient Church, and deviation from those not embraced in that symbol is not necessarily a breach of orthodoxy. It seems that the doctrine of *metousiōsis* may to this day be declined, provided the concept of *metabolē*, the full and unconditioned reality of the real presence, be retained.

(F. KATTENBUSCH.)

V. Roman Catholic Arguments in Defense of the Doctrine, with their Refutation: (1) A literal interpretation (beginning with Paschasius Radbertus, q.v.) of the words of institution, " This is my body "; " this " (which, however, refers to the preceding " cup," the wine not being mentioned) " is my blood of the covenant " (Matt. xxvi. 26, 27).

1. Exegetical. The Lutheran symbols agree with this exegesis, but nevertheless reject transubstantiation. The Reformed symbols reject it for the following reasons: (a) the word " is " may indicate a figurative as well as a real relationship between the subject and the predicate, and often means " represents," or " sets forth," in the Septuagint and the Greek Testament (e.g., Gen. xli. 26, 27; Matt. xiii. 38, 39; Gal. iv. 24; Rev. i. 20). (b) The surrounding circumstances of the institution of the Holy Supper (the living Christ amidst his disciples, his body not yet broken, his blood not yet shed, etc.) forbid a strictly literal interpretation and application to the first celebration. (c) The literal interpretation can not be carried out, inasmuch as the Lord himself (Matt. xxvi. 27; Luke xxii. 19–20) and the Apostle Paul, in quoting the words of institution (I Cor. xi. 25, " this cup," etc.; x. 16, " the cup of blessing," etc.), substitute the " cup " which contains the wine, for the wine itself, i.e., they use the figure of synecdoche, the container for the contents, and yet no Roman Catholic assumes the transubstantiation of the vessel. (2) The mysterious discourse of our Lord in the synagogue of Capernaum, about eating his flesh, and drinking his blood (John vi. 52–59). To this may be objected, that this discourse serves theologians as basis for different theories of the Lord's Supper; that the reference of this section to the Lord's Supper is not certain; that in any case the words of John vi. 63, " It is the spirit that quickeneth; the flesh profiteth nothing: the words that I have spoken unto you are spirit and are life," point to a spiritual reference in the preceding figures (so Ratramnus as early as the ninth century); and that, finally, if any theory of the Lord's Supper is favored by that discourse, it is one which confines the fruition of the Lord's flesh and blood to the believer, since every one that eateth his flesh and drinketh his blood is said " to have eternal life," " to abide in Christ and Christ in him," and " to live forever " (vi. 54, 56, 58),—all of which can be said of believers only; while the Roman Church teaches that unworthy as well as worthy communicants partake of the literal body and blood of Christ, though with opposite effect.

The Roman Church appeals to the Fathers, especially Cyril of Jerusalem, Chrysostom, Cyril of Alexandria, and Ambrose. As has been already indicated, the conceptions of the real **2. Historical.** bodily presence of Christ and its materialistic fruition are easily drawn from the writings of Ignatius, Justin Martyr, and Irenæus. But it must be remembered that these writers had in mind chiefly, if not altogether, the gracious effect the Eucharist had, rather than the nature of the elements. On the other hand, it is equally true that the representations of the Fathers differ. The African divines, Tertullian, Cyprian, and Augustine, teach a symbolical and spiritual, rather than corporeal, presence; and the Alexandrian school of Clement and Origen put the whole design of the Eucharist in feeding the soul on the spiritual life and the divine word of Christ. Hence the Fathers have been appealed to for the Lutheran, Calvinistic, and Zwinglian theory, as well as for the Roman Catholic. Ratramnus already appeals to Augustine for the spiritual interpretation.

VI. Opposition to the Doctrine: This was begun by the forerunners of the Reformation, especially by Wyclif. He called transubstantiation a " doctrine of the moderns." In 1381 he issued twelve theses against the doctrine, which he followed up with an elaborate treatise on the Eucharist, *De eucharistia* (ed. J. Loserth for the Wyclif Society, London, 1892), and he returned to the subject again and again in his writings, pronouncing the doctrine idolatry and a lying fable. He taught the spiritual though real presence of Christ's body. In its dimensions it is in heaven. In the host it is present efficaciously but in a symbol; the "symbol represents" (*vicarius est*) the body. Christ is in the bread as a king is in all parts of his dominions and as the soul is in the body. The doctrine of transubstantiation is subversive of logic, grammar, and all natural science (*De eucharistia*, p. 11; *Trialogus*, ed. Lechler, pp. 248 261, Oxford, 1869). The words of institution are to be taken figuratively, just as are the words "'I am the vine." Transubstantiation would necessarily demand transaccidentation (a word Wyclif used before Luther); for if accidents can be separated from the thing itself, one can not tell what a thing is or even whether it exists. With reference to the discussion concerning the mouse which partakes of the host, he affirmed the first assumption to be false, because Christ is not in the host in a corporeal manner. The chief charge brought against Wyclif by Gregory XI. and at the Council of Constance (q.v.) was that he denied this doctrine. The Reformers were unanimous in rejecting transubstantiation as a fundamental error, contrary to Scripture, to reason, to the testimony of the senses, to the very nature of the sacrament, and leading to gross superstition. There was, however, a serious difference among the Reformers in the extent of opposition. Luther, adhering to the literal interpretation of the words of institution, taught "Consubstantiation" (q.v.); while Zwingli and Calvin gave up the literal interpretation, and the latter substituted for the idea of a corporeal presence the idea of a spiritual real presence, and for manducation by the mouth and the teeth a spiritual real fruition by faith alone. See Lord's Supper, II.

(P. Schaff†.) D. S. Schaff.

Bibliography: Pertinent literature will be found under Eucharist;[1] Lord's Supper; and Mass. For the Roman Catholic side consult: Paschasius Radbertus, *De corpore et sanguine Domini*, in *MPL*, cxx.; J. de Lugo, *De venerabili eucharistiæ sacramento*, in Migne's *Cursus theologiæ completus*, xxiii. 10 sqq. (" the profoundest and most thorough " on the scholastic side); N. P. S. Wiseman, *Lectures on the Real Presence of the Body and Blood of our Lord Jesus Christ in the Blessed Eucharist*, new ed., London, 1852; F. X. Wildt, *Explanatio mirabilium quæ divina potentia in eucharistiæ sacramento operatur*, pp. 29 sqq., Bonn, 1868; J. H. Oswald, *Die dogmatische Lehre von den heiligen Sakramenten der katholischen Kirche*, i. 375–427, Münster, 1870; G. Reinhold, *Die Lehre der örtlichen Gegenwart Christi in der Eucharistie bei Thomas von Aquin*, Vienna, 1893; F. Schmid, in *Zeitschrift für katholische Theologie*, 1894, pp. 108–128; J. Ernst, *Die Lehre des Paschasius Radbertus von der Eucharistie*, Freiburg, 1896; S. J. Hunter, *Outlines of Dogmatic Theology*, iii. 249–262, New York, 1896; P. H. Batiffol, *Études d'histoire*, Paris, 1906; F. W. D., *Elucidation of the Doctrine of Transubstantiation*, Littleborough, 1904; *KL*, xi. 1977–1996.

For the Protestant side consult: T. Cranmer, *Writings and Disputations Relative to the Sacrament of the Lord's Supper*, ed. J. E. Cox for Parker Society, pp. 239–343, Cambridge, 1844; J. Jewel, *Works*, ed. J. Ayre for Parker Society, i. 445 sqq., Cambridge, 1845; J. Cosin, *Hist. of Popish Transubstantiation*, London, 1679, new ed., 1850; P. K. Marheineke, *Christliche Symbolik*, 3 vols., Heidelberg, 1810–14; H. E. F. Guericke, *Allgemeine christliche Symbolik*, Leipsic, 1839; G. S. Faber, *Christ's Discourse at Capernaum Fatal to the Doctrine of Transubstantiation*, London, 1840; K. F. A. Kahnis, *Die Lehre vom Abendmahl*, Leipsic, 1851; T. B. Strong, *The Doctrine of the Real Presence*, London, 1899; Harnack, *Dogma*, passim (consult Index); the works on the history of doctrine by H. C. Sheldon, New York, 1886, R. Seeberg, 2d ed., Leipsic, 1907 sqq., F. A. Loofs, new ed., Halle, 1908; and the literature under Berengar; Radbertus, Paschasius; and Ratramnus.

For the Greek Church consult: I. R. Kiesling, *Hist. concertationis Græcorum Latinorumque de transsubstantione*, Leipsic, 1754; G. E. Steitz, in *Jahrbücher für deutsche Theologie*, xiii (1868), 649–700; M. Jugie, in *Echos d'orient*, x (1907), 5 sqq., 65 sqq.

TRAPP, JOHN: Church of England; b. at Croome d'Abetot (6 m. s.s.e. of Worcester), England, June 5, 1601; d. at Weston-on-Avon (30 m. n.e. of Gloucester) Oct. 16, 1669. He studied at Christ Church, Oxford (B.A., 1622; M.A., 1624); became usher of the free school of Stratford-upon-Avon, 1622, and headmaster, 1624; was made preacher at Luddington, near Stratford; became vicar of Weston-on-Avon. He sided with the parliament in the civil war, and took the covenant of 1643; acted as chaplain to the parliamentary soldiers in Stratford for two years; was rector of Welford in Gloucestershire and Warwickshire, 1646–1660; and again vicar of Weston, 1660–69. He was most industrious, and an excellent preacher. Besides *God's Love Tokens* (London, 1637), he issued a *Commentary* on the Old and New Testaments (5 vols., 1654 sqq.; reprinted and ed. H. Martin and W. Webster, with *Memoir* by A. B. Grosart, 5 vols., London, 1867–68). It is in some respects the best of the Puritan commentaries.

Bibliography: Besides the *Memoir* by Grosart, ut sup., consult: A. à Wood, *Athenæ Oxonienses*, ed. P. Bliss, iii. 843–844, 4 vols., London, 1813–20; *DNB*, lvii. 155.

TRAPPISTS (REFORMED CISTERCIANS): A Roman Catholic order distinguished by extreme severity and renunciation of learning. It was founded in the Cistercian abbey of Notre Dame de la Maison-Dieu (80 m. s.w. of Paris) established about 1140 in an unhealthy valley of Normandy

The Founder.　accessible by a narrow defile, hence called La Trappe ("The Trap"). The abbey, increasing in luxury, gradually declined in morality and popularity until, by the early part of the seventeenth century, it had but seven monks. In 1636 it came as a benefice to Armand Jean le Bouthillier de Rancé (b. at Paris Jan. 9, 1626; d. at La Trappe Oct. 27, 1700), who was to become its reformer. Before he was eleven years old he was canon of Notre Dame at Paris, abbot of La Trappe, and prior of other monasteries, and, distinguished no less for scholarship and ability as a preacher than for his lax mode of life, he was ordained priest in 1651. The sight of the severed head of a companion in 1660 and a narrow escape from death in 1662 exercised so profound an influence on him that in 1664 he entered upon a life of the most rigid asceticism. Surrendering all his other benefices or applying them to pious uses, he retired to La Trappe, restored the buildings, and began a reform of the discipline, but was driven away, and retired to Perseigne in 1663, but, becoming a professed in the following year, he assumed the abbacy of La Trappe (1664), and with a fanatical zeal enforced the original sterner rules. In 1664 and 1665 he visited Rome to secure the necessary papal concessions for his plans, which were sanctioned by Innocent XI. in 1678. The Trappist rule (*Constitutions et règlements de la Trappe*, 2 vols., Paris, 1701) binds the monks to arise at two o'clock in the morning from their beds, which consist of a sack of straw and a straw pillow laid on a plank and covered with a rug. Eleven hours daily are devoted to prayer and masses, the remainder of the day being given in silence to labor either on the field or within the monastery. All literary work is forbidden, since the monks are required to concentrate their thoughts on penance and death; and, except for prayers and hymns, and the greeting, " Remember that we must die," absolute silence is enjoined, wishes and needs being communicated by signs. The midday meal consists of roots, vegetables, fruit, bread, and water, though in special cases the sick may have meat and eggs. The order comprises lay brothers, professed (choir monks), and *frères donnés* (those connected with the monastery only temporarily for penance). The habit of the choir monks is a coarse, grayish, woolen cassock with wide sleeves, a cowl of black wool with two broad strips hanging to the knee, a black leathern girdle with a rosary and a knife (emblems of meditation and labor), and wooden shoes. The lay brothers have brown cassocks. Great philanthropy has been exercised; for instance, in one year of famine, 1,500 dependents were lodged, and 4,000 guests were entertained annually. The founder of the order was the object of many criticisms because of his severity and his disapproval of learning, as set forth in his *Traité de la sainteté et des devoirs de la vie monastique* (Paris, 1683), which led to a controversy that lasted until the second quarter of the eighteenth century. He resigned as abbot in 1695.

Trappist monasteries were founded near Florence (1705) and at Casamari (1777), and with the expulsion of the Trappists from France by the Revolution, they received a new home in Val-
History. sainte, Switzerland, which Pius VI. made the abbey in 1794, destroyed four years later by the French. Meanwhile the Trappists had founded monasteries at Poblat (Catalonia), near Antwerp, in the diocese of Münster, and in Piedmont. On the destruction of Valsainte, they found a refuge through Paul I. of Russia in Poland, only to be expelled in 1800. Wandering by way of Danzig to Altona, and by way of Paderborn and Driburg to Freiburg and Sion in the Swiss canton of Valais, they reestablished a monastery at Valsainte, as well as houses at Rieddray and Rapallo (near Naples). In 1804 a monastery was founded near Rome by Louis Henri de Lestrange (Dom Augustin), but it was destroyed in the French invasion. Germany, like France, expelled the Trappists, from the vicinity of Paderborn in 1802, from Freiburg in 1811, from Darfeld (near Münster) in 1812. On the restoration of the Bourbons in 1827, the Trappists were permitted to reenter France and again to possess their old home, La Trappe; and, by the time of the death of Dom Augustin (1827), they numbered there about 700. In 1829 all the Trappist monasteries were ordered closed by royal decree, but at the Revolution of July there were still nine houses. The order received new impetus in 1834 by a papal decree uniting the Trappists of all lands into the Congregation dés réligieux Cisterciens de Notre Dame de la Trappe. They then increased rapidly, especially in the archdiocese of

Le Mans, and in 1844 founded a house in Algiers, besides sending a number of monks to North America in 1848. In 1851 a branch of the Trappists was established at Pierrequi-Vire (near Avallon) by the " Trappist Preachers," which differs from the main order only in omitting the vow of silence with the permission of the superior, and of acting as missioners. In 1870 there were some eighteen Trappist monasteries, mostly in France; but ten years later 1,450 monks of the order were driven from France. Though they soon returned, the " Associations' Law " of 1901 compelled them again to retire, at least in part.

At present the Trappists have 56 monasteries (37 abbeys and 19 priories), with 3,700 members. Of these 44 monasteries with 2,500 monks
Statistics. are in Europe. The abbot general resides at Rome. In 1869 the Bosnian monastery of Mariastern was established, which now conducts Kafir missions in Natal with 20 principal stations, 50 substations, and 13,000 Roman Catholics. Trappists are likewise to be found in Asia Minor, Palestine, China, Japan, Algiers (suppressed in 1904), the Kongo State, German East Africa, Ireland, England, the United States, Canada, and Brazil. A branch of Trappist nuns was founded by Princess Louise de Condé in the nunnery of Les Clairets, near Chartres, receiving its rule from De Rancé. The nuns number about 900, with nine nunneries in France, and four elsewhere, with a priory in Japan. An order of Tertiary Trappists nuns was likewise founded for mission-work by Abbot Franz Pfanner in 1881. They are called " Missionary Sisters of the Precious Blood," and number some 400 in Natal, German East Africa, and Belgian Kongo. The union of the Trappists of all lands into a single Congrégation in 1834 was broken in 1847, and for many years there were five congregations, each with its own vicar general, who was subject to the general of the Cistercians. Since 1892, however, all the congregations have been reunited, and their abbot general has been made independent of the Cistercians. This new constitution was confirmed by Leo XIII. in 1894, and in 1902 a papal decree declared the monastery of Citeaux (acquired by the Trappists in 1898) the mother-house.

(EUGEN LACHENMANN.)

In the United States the Trappists have (1911) three houses: Gethsemane Abbey, in Nelson County, Ky., with 79 in the community; New Melleray Abbey, near Dubuque, Ia., with 35 members; and Monastery of our Lady of Jordan, Scio, Linn County, Ore., with 8 members. In Ireland they are at Mt. Melleray (30 m. n.e. of Cork) and number 70; also at Roscrea.

BIBLIOGRAPHY: The " Rule " was published Paris, 1671, 2 vols., 1701, and Graz, 1887. Consult: L. D[u] B[ois], *Hist. . . . de l'abbaye de la Trappe,* Paris, 1824; E. L. Ritfert, *Der Orden der Trappisten,* Darmstadt, 1833; C. Gaillardin, *Les Trappistes . . . au 19 siècle,* 2 vols., Paris, 1844; C. Tallon, *Notices . . . sur les monastères de l'ordre de la Trappe,* ib. 1855; *La Trappe, origine, esprit, organisation,* ib. 1870; E. Friedländer, *Geschichte der Trappisten im Münsterlande,* Paderborn, 1874; F. Pfannenschmidt, *Geschichte der Trappisten,* ib. 1874; Franz, *Die Trappisten-Mission in Südafrika,* Linz, 1889; F. Büttgenbach, *Mariawald, ein Bild des Trappistenordens,* Aachen, 1897; K. Ruff, *Die Trappistenabtei Oelen-*

berg, Freiburg, 1898; *De Lestrange et les Trappistes*, La Trappe, 1898; *Les Trappistes pendant la révolution*, ib. 1898; A. Hecker (Schneider), *Ein Besuch bei den Trappisten auf Oelenberg*, Mörishofen, 1904; Suchier, *Der Orden der Trappisten und die vegetarische Lebensweise*, 2d ed., Munich, 1906; Helyot, *Ordres monastiques*, vi. 1 sqq.; Heimbucher, *Orden und Kongregationen*, i. 460–473; Currier, *Religious Orders*, pp. 135–140; *KL*, xi. 1996–2008.

TREACLE BIBLE. See Bible Versions, B, IV., § 9.

TRECHSEL, trek′sel, **FRIEDRICH:** Swiss theologian; b. at Bern Nov. 30, 1805; d. there Jan. 30, 1885. He studied in the university of his native city, then in Paris, Göttingen, Halle, and Berlin. In 1829 he became chaplain of the city hospital at Bern, and privat-docent in the academy; pastor at Vechigen, 1837; of the Minster at Bern, 1859; retired on a pension, 1876. He was the author of *Ueber den Kanon, die Kritik und Exegese der Manichäer* (Bern, 1832); *Die protestantischen Antitrinitarier vor Faustus Socin, nach Quellen und Urkunden geschichtlich dargestellt* (2 vols., Heidelberg, 1839–1844); *Beiträge zur Geschichte der schweizerisch-reformirten Kirche, zunächst derjenigen des Kantons Bern* (Bern, 1841–42); and *Bilder aus der Geschichte der protestantischen Kirche* (1889), which included a sketch of the author.

Bibliography: Besides the sketch noted above, consult *Zeitschrift aus der Schweiz*, ii (1885), 312–314.

TREES. See Fruit-Trees in the Old Testament.

TREES, SACRED. See Groves and Trees, Sacred.

TREGELLES, tre-gel′es, **SAMUEL PRIDEAUX:** Textual critic of the New Testament; b. at Wodehouse Place, near Falmouth (44 m. s.w. of Plymouth), Jan. 30, 1813; d. at Plymouth Apr. 24, 1875. He attended the Falmouth classical school, 1825–28, when he was compelled to earn his living, and was engaged in the iron works at Neath Abbey, Glamorganshire, 1829–35; he then returned to Falmouth and taught privately. All this time he was zealous and intensely diligent in pursuing his own education, was earnest in his desire to contribute to knowledge of the Bible, and from his twenty-fifth year seems to have settled upon the New Testament as his sphere of labor. His first book was *Passages in the Old Testament Connected with the Revelation* (1836). The first well-known piece of work was an account of the English versions which served as introduction to *The English Hexapla* (London, 1841). He sought to further the study of Hebrew by a series of text-books: *Hebrew Reading Lessons* (1845); a translation of *Gesenius' Hebrew and Chaldee Lexicon to the Old Testament* (1847); *Heads of Hebrew Grammar* (1852); and *The Interlineary Hebrew and English Psalter* (1852). Meanwhile he had taken part in the publication of the *Englishman's Hebrew and Chaldee Concordance to the Old Testament* and the *Englishman's Greek Concordance to the New Testament* (1839–43), and had issued *Remarks on the Prophetic Visions in . . . Daniel* (1847), and *Defence of the Authenticity of . . . Daniel* (1852).

In his work on the New Testament in the study of Griesbach's New Testament he found the latter to agree too closely with the *textus receptus* to be in accord with what he regarded as the best authority, and proposed a plan for a new text, being in unconscious agreement with the principles of Lachmann, finally setting himself to prepare one. Accordingly in 1844 he edited critically in Greek the book of Revelation, with a new English version, the favorable reception of which confirmed him in his determination to carry out his project. He then began a systematic examination of the uncial manuscripts then available, both in England and on the continent, failing, however, to get permission to collate Codex Vaticanus, though his journeys in 1845–46, 1849–50, and 1852 resulted in correction of collations of important manuscripts, among them the noted Codex Colbertinus, a difficult manuscript the work upon which endangered his eyesight. At this period he made the acquaintance of Lachmann and Tischendorf. While Tregelles edited only Codex Zacynthius, and did not, like some others, discover numbers of manuscripts, he so carefully collated practically all of the uncials and important minuscules then known that his labors have lasting and permanent value. He also examined anew the citations of the Church Fathers down to Eusebius, as well as the ancient versions. Before issuing any portion of a new text, however, he prepared his *Account of the Printed Text of the New Testament* (1854), which served to expound his critical principles, and rewrote that part of Horne's *Introduction to the Study . . . of Holy Scriptures* which related to the textual criticism of the New Testament (1856). In 1857 the first part of his New-Testament text appeared, containing the Gospels of Matthew and Mark, which contained, beside also the text of Codex Amiatinus, a number of important variant readings and other critical apparatus, including the notation of the Eusebian Canons. The second part followed in 1861, and contained the Gospels of Luke and John. In that year an attack of paralysis compelled him to suspend his labors, and the third part did not appear till 1865, and contained the Acts and Catholic Epistles. The fourth part, making available his edition of the Pauline Epistles down to II Thessalonians, was issued in 1869. Early in 1870 a second stroke of paralysis fell while he was revising the final chapters of Revelation; the fifth part, containing the rest of the Pauline Epistles, was issued that year as he had prepared it, and Revelation in 1872, but without the prolegomena, this last being issued posthumously with addenda and corrigenda through the labors of Hort and Streane. His edition remains as a work of abiding merit and worth, being the fullest in critical apparatus after the eighth edition of Tischendorf's work, his exactness being extraordinary.

Tregelles regarded his labors upon the text, undertaken out of pure love for the Word of God, as a work of worship, and this was the spirit in which his entire labors were carried on. His life was simple, homely, and charitable. In his last years he received a pension on the civil service account of £200 a year. Tregelles was known also as a poet, and the *Lyra Britannica* and Schaff's *Christ in Song* contain poems by him.   (Carl Bertheau†.)

Bibliography: His own *Account of the Printed Text*, ut sup., is of high value for statement of his principles of work. Consult further: E. Abbot, in (New York) *Independent*, May 3, 1875; P. Schaff, *Companion to the Greek Testament*, pp. 262–266 et passim, New York, 1883; G. Salmon, *Historical Introduction to the Study of the Books of the N. T.*, pp. 43, 150, 283, London, 1892; F. H. A. Scrivener, *Introduction to the Criticism of the N. T.*, ii. 238–241 et passim, London, 1894; C. R. Gregory, *Textkritik des N. T.*, pp. 980–981, Leipsic, 1902; idem, *Canon and Text of N. T.*, pp. 346, 460, 461, New York, 1907; *DNB*, lvii. 170–174.

TREMELLIUS, tre-mel'î-us, **EMANUEL:** Hebrew scholar; b. at Ferrara, Italy, in 1510; d. at Sedan, France, Oct. 9, 1580. His parents being Jewish, Tremellius was thoroughly instructed in the Hebrew language; after 1530 he was in contact with Christians, and about 1540 was baptized in the house of Cardinal Reginald Pole (q.v.). In 1541 he became teacher of Hebrew in the cloister school newly instituted at Lucca by Pietro Martire Vermigli (q.v.), and published his first professional work, *Meditamenta* (Wittenberg, 1541). Compelled to flight by the introduction of the Inquisition, he found, in 1542, a new field of labor as teacher of Hebrew at the flourishing school in Strasburg, then directed by Johann Sturm. When driven away by the Schmalkald War, he accepted from Archbishop Cranmer an invitation to England, and received appointment to the Hebrew chair at Cambridge, in 1549. But in 1553, upon the accession of Mary Tudor, he and his family again had to flee. He then went, on invitation from Duke Wolfgang of the Bipontine Palatinate, as preceptor to the duke's three children. When Calvin, in 1558, sought to attract him to the Old-Testament professorship in Geneva, he would gladly have accepted that offer. But Wolfgang refused to let him go, and made him director of the new school in the former cloister of Hornbach, which was opened Jan. 16, 1559. Here he served till Mar. 7, 1561, when he took leave of Wolfgang in peace. Before his departure, Tremellius rendered a service to the oppressed Evangelical believers at Metz by taking part in a deputation to the royal court at Orléans, following the death of King Francis of France, in Jan., 1561, the result being that the Huguenots of Metz were permitted to use a house of prayer outside the city.

On Mar. 4, 1561, the Palatine Elector Frederick III. (see FREDERICK III., THE PIOUS) called him to the high school at Heidelberg. There, on June 22, 1561, Tremellius was graduated doctor in theology, and, in full accord with Boquin, Olevianus, and Ursinus, exhibited a fruitful academic industry, finding leisure also for larger literary works. He issued Butzer's lectures (Basel, 1562), which he had heard and copied at Cambridge; a Latin translation of Jonathan's Aramaic paraphrase of the twelve Minor Prophets (Heidelberg, 1567) and an edition of the Old Syriac translation of the New Testament which he supplemented with a Latin translation, as also with an Aramaic and Syriac grammar (1569). About 1570 he began his most important work, and continued it from 1575 to 1579 in company with his subsequent son-in-law, Francis Junius, a Latin translation of the Old Testament, issued in five volumes, and received with well-deserved favor (see BIBLE VERSIONS, A, II., 3). During his labors in Heidelberg, Tremellius remained in close correspondence with his friends in England, though he gratefully declined a professorship there that was offered him in 1565.

It was not permitted the aging Tremellius to end his days at Heidelberg. After the death of Frederick III., he was dismissed Dec. 5, 1577, and, after a short sojourn at Metz, was called by Henri de la Tour d'Auvergne as professor to the newly erected academy at Sedan, where he devoted his powers to the service of the French youth with the same ardor that he had shown toward those of Italy, Germany, and England. He was one of the most learned orientalists of his times. J. NEY.

BIBLIOGRAPHY: Biographies have been written by F. Butters, Zweibrücken, 1859; M. Becker, Breslau, 1887; and A. Neubauer, in *Westpfälzische Geschichtsblätter*, 1902, nos. 9 sqq.

END OF VOL. XI.